SPEECH INDEX

An Index to 259 Collections of World
Famous Orations and Speeches
For Various Occasions

by

Roberta Briggs Sutton

Fourth Edition

Revised and Enlarged

The Scarecrow Press, Inc.

New York 1966

L. C. Card No. 66-13749

To the memory of

Irvin and Caroline Briggs

Preface

The purpose of the Speech Index is to serve as a guide to speeches of famous orators from the earliest times to the present day, and to types of speeches. The amateur club, business, or civic speaker is ever seeking suggestions on how to prepare introductory speeches, how to respond when called upon to talk before an audience and therefore desires models he can adapt to his needs. The academic student seeks speeches by well known orators which exemplify the basic types of speeches, while the adult taking courses in public speaking seeks subject literature in speech form for class recitation. The need to fulfil these requests prompted the preparation of the Speech Index in hopes that reference librarians in high school, college, and public libraries might be saved repeated search through numerous volumes.

This fourth edition of the Speech Index incorporates all the materials in the three previous Speech Indexes: 1935, 1935-55, and 1956-1961, and augments it with widely held older titles inadvertently omitted, various editions of indexed titles, and new publications since 1961. It is limited to books published in English from 1900 through 1965 with a few exceptions.

Standard collections of speeches, single volumes of speeches by various authors, books and public speaking containing speeches and suggestions on how to prepare and deliver types of speeches, and a number of miscellaneous works giving valuable material in this field were included. Most of the volumes were used in their entirety, but some, especially ones on public speaking were indexed only for speeches or models of types of speeches. Short selections, extracts, documents, and other extraneous materials were omitted. Sources varied in their policy of denoting whether or not the speech quoted was a selection. Speeches which appeared to be given in their entirety have been found to have portions omitted. To locate the complete speech for comparison, sentence by sentence would

have been time-consuming, difficult, and often impossible. Therefore, to avoid misleading the user of the Speech Index, selections are not noted as such. The only exception is where the title of the speech as given in the source implies that it is not a complete speech.

Sometimes a speech appears with conflicting titles in more than one book. After checking carefully to make sure they are the same, the most popular title is used, with cross references to it from other titles dissimilar in wording or meaning. A speech appearing once, is entered as stated in the source. In many instances, too, the orator's name had to be verified and completed.

The material is arranged in dictionary form with entries by author, subject, type of speech, and cross references all in one alphabet. An Appendix contains a selected list of titles which the compiler thought would be difficult for the user to locate if the name of the orator is not known. and the title gives no clue as to the type of speech or subject entry under which the speech is indexed. Scanning this List of Selected Titles would quickly reveal the author or subject entry of such catchy or well known titles as "Acres of diamonds," "Rise and fall of the mustache," "Blood, sweat, and tears," or "Sun beams can be extracted from cucumbers but the process is tedious."

Sources are given by symbol, with page reference for quick location purpose. Inclusive paging is given only in instances where several examples of the same type of speech are cited.

Capital and lower case letters are used for author entries in contrast to all capital letters for subject entries. The name of a person in capital letters indicates that he is the subject of the material listed under his name. A subject entry for the name of a person being introduced is given if the introduction contains specific information about his personal life or achievements.

The eighth edition of Sears list of Subject Headings by Bertha M. Frick was used as the authority for subject headings. For those not in Sears, the following sources were consulted: Library of Congress - Subject Headings, Library of Congress Catalog: Books-Subjects, the Readers Guide to Periodical Literature, and the Essay

and General Literature Index.

The compiler wishes to express her appreciation to the following libraries for their courtesy in supplying volumes necessary to make this revised edition of the Speech Index as complete as possible: The Chicago Public Library, Northwestern University Library, The University of Chicago Library and the Library of Congress. She deeply appreciates the gracious and enthusiastic assistance of the many librarians who aided her in research, editorial advice, or in typing, especially Mr. Harold Teitelbaum, Miss Charity Mitchell, Miss Marjorie Feldman, Mr. George A. Schwegmann, Jr., Miss Mary Kinney, Mrs. Christine Longstreet, Miss Dorothy E. Simpson, and the reference librarians at Northwestern and the University of Chicago libraries.

List of Books Indexed

Key to Symbols

AB Abell, Marietta
High school banquets by Marietta Abell and Agnes J. Anderson. Minneapolis, Northwestern Press, 1935.

ACW Acker, Julius William, comp.
Wedding addresses. St. Louis Mo., Concordia Publishing House, 1955.

ADR Adams, Charles Kendall
Representative British orations with introduction and explanatory notes by Charles Kendall Adams. New York, G. P. Putnam's Sons, 1884-1900. 4 volumes

AMEO Ames, William Homer
One hundred master speeches by William Homer Ames and P. A. Miller. Harrisburg, Public Speakers Society, 1924. 2 volumes

AN Anderson, Evan Ernest, ed.
College orations of the war interim, edited by Evan Ernest Anderson and Egbert Ray Nichols. Redlands, California, Nichols Publishing House, 1947.

ANDS Andersch, Elizabeth
Speech for everyday use by Elizabeth Andersch and Loris C. Staats. New York, Rinehart and Company, 1950.
Indexed for speeches.

ANG Angle, Paul M., ed.
By these words; great documents of American liberty, selected and placed in their contemporary settings by Paul M. Angle. Chicago, Rand McNally and Company, 1954.

ANGC Angeles, Philip
Challenge to American youth.
Philadelphia, Macrae Smith Company, 1963.

ARNS Arnold, Carroll C.
The speaker's resource book; an anthology, handbook, and glossary, ed. by Douglas Ehninger, and John C. Gerber. Chicago, Scott Foresman and Company, 1961.

ASHF Ashley, Winston H., comp.
Fifty orations that have won prizes in speaking contests, including the orations that have won prizes in the Interstate Oratorical Association and other collegiate prize speaking contests. Compiled by Winston H. Ashley, with an introduction by William Norwood Brigance. New York, Noble and Noble, 1928.

BA Baird, Albert Craig, comp.
Representative American

speeches, 1937/38-1964/65. New York, H.W. Wilson Company. 28 volumes (Lester Thonssen, ed. 1959/60-1964/65).

BAAG Baird, A. Craig
General speech; an introduction. By A. Craig Baird and Franklin H. Knower. New York, McGraw-Hill Book Company, 1957.
Appendix indexed

BAAGA Baird, A. Craig
General speech; an introduction. By A. Craig Baird and Franklin H. Knower. 3d ed. New York, McGraw-Hill 1963.
Indexed for speeches and suggestions on preparation of types of speeches

BAAMP Baird, A. Craig, ed.
American public address, 1740-1952. New York, McGraw-Hill, 1956.

BAI Baicker, I. J.
Speak expertly in four weeks; a quick course in expert speech-making. New York, Exposition Press, 1955.

BAKF Baker, George Pierce, ed.
Forms of public address. New York, H. Holt and Company, 1904.
Speeches only are indexed

BAKS Baker, James Thompson
The short speech. New York, Prentice-Hall, 1928.

BARB Barber, Joseph
Barber's American book of ready made speeches with appropriate replies. New York, 1871.

BARR Barrett, Harold
Practical methods in speech. New York, Henry Holt and Company, 1959.
Indexed for suggestions for preparation of types of speeches, sample outlines of speeches, and model speeches.

BART Barrington Town-Warming; containing addresses delivered at Barrington Town-warming meetings. Barrington, Illinois, 1939-1942. 4 volumes
v. 1 Jan. 22-Feb. 2, 1939
v. 2 Jan. 7-16, 1940
v. 3 Jan. 26-Feb. 9, 1941
v. 4 Jan. 25-Feb. 5, 1942

BEA Beable, William Henry, comp. and ed.
Celebrated and historical speeches: an anthology of ancient and modern oratory, compiled by William Henry Beable with a foreword by the Rt. Hon. Lord Comrose. London, Heath Cranton, Ltd., 1933.

BEB Belson, David
Tributes and forms for public occasions. New York, The author, 1951.

BEC Belson, David
What to say and how to say it. New York, Citadel Press, 1955.

BED Belson, David
Chairman and speaker's role made easy. Examples of testimonials, installations, fund raising drives, memorial services, dedications, presentations, patriotic observances, and other public ceremonies for organizations, civic groups, churches, schools and oth-

er group activities. New York, The author, 1957. Printed by Futuro Press, 476 Broadway, New York

BEDA Belson, David and Ruth Belson
Chairman and speaker's role made easy. New York, Citadel Press, 1964.
Notes: Many speeches are exactly the same as in his 1957 edition, others vary slightly

BERS Berquist, Goodwin F., Jr.
Speeches for illustration and example. Chicago, Scott, Foresman and Company, 1965.

BIR Birley, Robert, ed.
Speeches and documents in American history. London, Oxford University Press, 1951. 4 volumes
Indexed for speeches

BL Blau, Joseph L., ed.
American philosophical addresses, 1700-1900. New York, Columbia University Press, 1946.

BLAA Blackstone, Harriet, comp.
The best American orations of today. New York, Hinds, Noble and Eldredge, 1903

BLAB Blackstone, Harriet, comp.
Best American orations of today, enl. ed. New York, Hinds and Noble, 1926.

BLUE Blue ribbon orations; a collection of prize-winning orations written by students of American colleges and universities. Franklin, Ohio, Eldridge Entertainment House, 1931.

BO Bolding, Amy
Words of welcome and other helps for speakers. Grand Rapids, Michigan, Baker Book House, 1965.
Indexed for examples of types of speeches

BOA Boone, Lester, ed.
New declamations; modern short speeches on current subjects for class study and speaking contests. New York, Noble and Noble, 1943.

BOAM Boardman, Lester Wells, ed.
Modern American speeches, edited with notes and introduction by Lester W. Boardman. New York, Longmans, Green and Company, 1923.

BOB Boone, Lester, comp.
One hundred new declamations; modern short speeches on current subjects for use in high school and college contests in public speaking. rev. ed. New York, Noble and Noble, 1932.

BOU Boutwell, William D., ed.
Great speeches from Pericles to Kennedy, edited by William D. Boutwell, Wesley P. Callender, Jr., and Robert E. Gerber. New York, Sholastic Book Services, 1965.

BRA Brigance, William Norwood
Speech; its techniques and disciplines in a free society. New York, Apple-

ton-Century-Crofts, 1952. Indexed for speeches only.

BRAB Brigance, William Norwood.
Speech; its techniques and disciplines in a free society. 2d ed. New York, Appleton-Century-Crofts, 1961.
Indexed for speeches and suggestions for preparation of types of speeches.

BRAC Brigance, William Norwood, comp.
Classified speech models of eighteen forms of public address. New York, F. S. Crofts and Company, 1928.

BRAO Bradley, Cornelius Beach, ed.
Orations and arguments by English and American statesmen, edited with notes, explanatory and critical by Cornelius Beach Bradley. Boston, Allyn and Bacon, 1894.

BRAP Braden, Waldo W.
Speech practices; a resource book for the student of public speaking, by Waldo W. Braden and Mary Louise Gehring. New York, Harper and Brothers, 1958.
Indexed for speeches.

BRAR Brainerd, Cephas, ed.
New England Society orations; addresses, sermons, and poems delivered before the New England Society in the City of New York, 1820-1885. Edited by Cephas Brainerd and Eveline Warner Brainerd. Published for the society by Century Company, 1901. 2 volumes

BRAS Brandt, Carl G., ed.
Selected American speeches on basic issues (1850-1950). Ed. by Carl G. Brandt and Edward D. Shafter, Jr. Boston, Houghton Mifflin Company, 1960.

BRC Brings, Lawrence Martin, ed.
Clever introductions for chairmen; a compilation of practical speeches and stories. Minneapolis, T. S. Denison, 1954.
Indexed for speeches only.

BRE Brown, Stuart Gerry, ed.
We hold these truths; documents of American democracy, selected and edited with an introductory essay by Stuart Gerry Brown. 2d ed. New York, Harper and Brothers, 1948.
Indexed for speeches only

BREA Brown, Stuart Gerry, ed.
We hold these truths; documents of American democracy, selected and edited with an introductory essay be Stuart Gerry Brown. 1st ed. New York, Harper and Brothers, 1941.
Indexed for speeches only.

BREW Brewer, David Josiah, ed.
World best orations, representing the development of civilization from the earliest times to the present. Chicago, F.P. Kaiser Publishing Company, 1923. 10 volumes

BRH Brings, Lawrence Martin, comp.
Humorous introductions

for emcees; a compilation of practical speeches and stories to be used in introducing talent of all types. Minneapolis, T. S. Denison, 1955.
Indexed for speeches only

BRIM Brink, Clark Mills
Making of an oration. Chicago, A. C. McClurg, 1913.
p. 209-243 indexed

BRM Brings, Lawrence M.
Master guide for speakers; a compilation of practical material to aid speakers in responding to introductions, using repartee, telling stories, styling their speech openings, and in using effective conclusions. Minneapolis, T. S. Denison and Company, 1956.
Indexed only for suggestions on how to begin and end speeches. Short extracts given as examples of parts of speeches not indexed individually

BRP Brings, Lawrence Martin, comp.
Prize winning orations for high school contests. Minneapolis, Northwestern Press, 1931-1940. 10 volumes

BRTH British historical and political orations from the 12th to the 20th century. London, J. M. Dent and Sons, 1945.

BRTHA British orations from Ethelbert to Churchill. London, J. M. Dent, 1960.

BRY Bryant, Donald Cross
Fundamentals of public speaking by Donald C. Bryant and Karl R. Wallace. 2d ed. New York, Appleton-Century-Crofts, 1953.
Indexed for speeches and suggestions for preparation of types of speeches

BRYA Bryant, Donald C.
Fundamentals of public speaking by Donald C. Bryant and Karl R. Wallace. 3d ed. New York, Appleton-Century-Crofts, 1960.
Indexed for speeches and suggestions for preparation of types of speeches

BRYW Bryan, William Jennings, ed.
World's famous orations. New York, Funk and Wagnalls, 1906. 10 volumes

BU Buehler, Ezra Christian
Building the contest oration by E. C. Buehler, and Richard L. Johannesen. New York, The H. W. Wilson Company, 1965.
Indexed for speeches only

BURP Burton, Alexander
Public speaking made easy. New York, E. J. Clode, 1920.

BURS Burton, Alexander
Speeches; their preparation and delivery. New York, Edward J. Clode, 1922.
p. 166-252 indexed only

BUT Butler, Jessie Haver
Time to speak up; a speaker's handbook for women. rev. ed. New

York, Harper and Brothers, 1952.

BUTA Butler, Jessie Haver
Time to speak up; a speaker's handbook for women. New York, Harper and Brothers, 1946.

BUTB Butler, Jessie Haver
Time to speak up; a speaker's handbook for women. 2d rev. ed. New York, Harper and Brothers, 1957.

BYRA Bryon, Basil Gordon, ed.
America speaks; a library of the best spoken thought in business and the professions, edited by Basil Gordon Byron and Frederic René Coudert. New York, Modern eloquence Corporation, 1928.

CAP Capp, Glenn R.
Famous speeches in American history. Indianapolis, Bobbs-Merrill Company, 1963.

CARP Carr, Edwin Hamlin
Putnam's ready speech maker; what to say and how to say it. New York, G. P. Putnam's Sons, 1922. p. 18-13 indexed for procedure at various occasions and a few selections included

CATA Catholic orators
Addresses at patriotic and civic occasions. New York, J. F. Wagner, 1915. 2 volumes

CHAL Depew, Chauncey M., ed.
Library of oratory, ancient and modern, with critical studies of the world's great orators by eminent essayists. Chauncey M. Depew, editor in chief. New York, International Society, 1902. 15 volumes

CHEM Cheney, John Vance, comp.
Memorable American speeches, collected and edited by John Vance Cheney. Chicago, R. R. Donnelly and Sons, 1907-1910. 4 volumes

CHI Chief executive: inaugural addresses of the Presidents of the United States from George Washington to Lyndon B. Johnson with an introduction by Arthur Schlesinger, Jr., and commentary by Fred L. Israel. New York, Crown Pub. Inc., 1965.

CLAW Clark, Glenn, ed.
World's greatest debate. St. Paul, Macalester Park Publishing Company, 1940. Note: Speeches from three greatest debates in American history correlated and synthesized into one forensic battle. See Foreword of book for additional explanation.

CLAY Clark, S. H.
Practical public speaking; a text book for colleges and secondary schools by S. H. Clark and F. M. Blanchard. New York, Charles Scribner's Sons, 1907.
Indexed for speeches only.

CODS Cody, Sherwin
Selections from the world's great orations, illustrative of the history of oratory and the art of public speaking, chosen and

edited with a series of introductions by Sherwin Cody. Chicago, A. C. McClurg, 1904.

CODSA Cody, Sherwin
Selections from the world's great orations. Chicago, A. C. McClurg, 1931.

CON Connor, J. Hal
Clever speeches for all occasions; a useful book for public speakers. Franklin, Ohio, Eldridge Publishing Company, 1930?

COP Copeland, Lewis, ed.
The world's great speeches. Garden City, New York, Garden City Pub. Company, 1948.

COPA Copeland, Lewis, ed.
World's great speeches. New York, Book League of America, 1942.

COPB Copeland, Lewis, ed.
World's great speeches. 2d rev. ed. New York, Dover Publications, 1958.

CORP Cortez, Edmund Arthur
Project speaking for secondary schools and colleges. Boston, Expression Company, 1929.

COUW Coursey, Oscar William, comp.
Winning orations: Inter-Collegiate contests, South Dakota. Mitchell, South Dakota, Educator Supply Company, 1917.

CRAI Craig, Asa H.
Pros and cons; complete debates. Important questions fully discussed in the affirmative and the negative. New York, Noble and Noble, 1926. p. 401-449 indexed

CROC Crosscup, Richard, ed.
Classic speeches: words that shook the world. New York, Philosophical Library, 1965.

DAVC Davis, Harry Cassell, comp.
Commencement parts: valedictories, salutatories, orations, essays, class poems, ivy orations, toasts; also original speeches and addresses for the national holidays and other occasions compiled by H. C. Davis. New York, Noble and Noble, 1925.

DICD Dickson, Henry
Dickson's How to speak in public. Chicago, Dickson School of Memory, 1911.
Speeches in parts 3 & 4 only are indexed.

DICE Dickson, Henry
Dickson's How to speak in public. Chicago, Dickson School of Memory, 1913.
Speeches in parts 3 & 4 only were indexed.

DO Dodd, M. R., ed.
Young America speaks: orations on American ideals and institutions. Boston, Allyn and Bacon, 1944.

DOA Doxsee, Herald M., ed.
Practical study of American speeches. Milwaukee, Bruce Publishing Company, 1935.

DR Droke, Maxwell, ed.
Speech outlines for all occasions, edited by Maxwell Droke and Dorothy Rayle. Indianapolis, Droke House, 1951.

DU DuTeau, Elsworth Francis
How to succeed through speech. Boston, Christopher House, 1938.
Indexed for speeches only.

DUNM Dunbar, Alice Moore
Masterpieces of Negro eloquence. New York, Bookery Publishing Company, 1914.

ED Edgerton, Mrs. Alice (Craig)
More speeches and stories for every occasion, new speeches. New York, Noble and Noble, 1936.

EDGS Edgerton, Mrs. Alice (Craig)
A speech for every occasion. New York, Noble and Noble, 1931.

EDW Edwards, Lewis
Guide to Masonic speechmaking. Hackensack, New Jersey, Wehman Brothers, 1957.

EMS Emden, Cecil S.
Selected speeches on the Constitution. London, Oxford University Press, 1939. 2 volumes

ESEH Esenwein, Joseph Berg
How to attract and hold an audience; a practical treatise on the nature, preparation, and delivery of public addresses, with a course of exercise lessons in public speaking. New York, Noble and Noble, 1928.
p. 186-239 indexed

EXEE Executive Club of Chicago
Executive speeches; selected addresses given before the Executive Club of Chicago from September 1924 to June 1928. Chicago, Executive Club, 1928.

FIP Filler, Louis
The President speaks; from William McKinley to Lyndon B. Johnson. New York, G. P. Putnma, 1964.

FKA Foerster, Norman, ed.
American ideals, edited by Norman Foerster and W. W. Pierson, Jr. Boston, Houghton Mifflin Company, 1917.
Indexed for speeches only

FO Foundation of America. New York, The Sun Dial Press, 1938.

FOS Foster, William Trufant, ed.
Washington's Farewell address to the people of the United States, bound with Webster's First Bunker Hill oration and Lincoln's Address at Gettysburg. Cambridge, Mass., Houghton Mifflin Company, 1937.

FRE Freeman, Kathleen
Murder of Herodes and other trials from the Athenian law courts. London, Macdonald and Company, 1946.

FRIE Friedman, Edward L.
The speechmaker's complete handbook: a storehouse of colorful point-making material and complete planning guide for public speakers. New York, Harper and Brothers, 1955.
Indexed for complete

speeches and talks only.

FRIT Friedman, Edward L.
Toastmaster's treasury, a complete guide for the toastmaster, master of ceremonies, and program chairman. New York, Harper and Brothers, 1960.
Indexed for speeches and types of speeches

FRY Fryer, Irving, ed.
Famous orators and their orations: a series of momentous speeches of all time that affected the course of many peoples. Cincinnati, Ridpath Historical Society, 1938.

FUL Fulton, Robert I.
Patriotic eloquence relating to the Spanish American War and its issues, compiled by Robert I. Fulton and Thomas Clarkson Trueblood. New York, Charles Scribner's Sons, 1900.

FULB Fulton, Robert Irving
British and American eloquence edited by Robert Irving Fulton and Thomas Clarkson Trueblood. New York, Ginn and Company, 1912.

GA Garland, Jasper Vanderbilt
Public speaking for women. New York, Harper and Brothers, 1938.

GLAD Glasgow, George M.
Dynamic public speaking. New York, Harper and Brothers, 1950.
Indexed for speeches and types of speeches only

GOOD Goodrich, Chauncey A.
Select British eloquence embracing the best speeches entire of the most eminent orators of Great Britain for the last two centuries. Indianapolis, Bobbs-Merrill, 1963. (Reprint of 1878 edition).
Extracts omitted

GRAC Graebner, Norman A.
Cold war diplomacy: American foreign policy, 1945-1960. Princeton, New Jersey, D. Van Nostrand, 1962.
Indexed for speeches only

GRIS Grisso, Walker Dixon, ed.
From where the sun now stands; addresses by a Posse of famous Western speakers. Sante Fe, Stagecoach Press, 1963.

Haber, Charlotte, pseud.
See
Morath, Dale H.

HAN Hansen, Harold A., ed.
Fighting for freedom; historic documents selected and edited with interpretive comments by Harold A. Hansen, John G. Herndon, and William B. Langsdorf. Philadelphia, John C. Winston, 1947.

HAPR Hapgood, George
Ready-made speeches. Philadelphia, Penn Publishing Company, 1922.

HAR Harding, Harold Friend, ed.
Age of danger; major speeches on American problems. New York, Random House, 1952.

HARS Harding, Samuel Ban-

nister, ed.
Select orations illustrating American political history, with an introduction on oratorical style and structure. New York, Macmillan Company, 1928.

HARSO Harris, Albert Mason
Select orations: a collection of one hundred choice speeches and selections. Nashville, Tenn. Cokesbury Press, 1924. Only speeches are indexed, other selections omitted

HAY Hayward, John, comp. and ed.
Silver tongues; famous speeches from Burke to Baldwin. London, Michael Joseph, 1937.

HAZO Hazeltine, Mayo W., ed.
Orations from Homer to William McKinley. New York, P. F. Collier and Son, 1902. 25 volumes

HE Henry W. H. F.
How to organize and conduct a meeting by W. H. F. Henry and Levi Seeley. rev. ed. New York, Noble and Noble, 1938.

HELE Heller, Louie Regina, ed.
Early American orations, 1760-1824, edited with an introduction and notes by Louie Regina Heller. New York, Macmillan Company, 1902.

HIB Hibbitt, George W., ed.
Dolphin book of speeches. New York, Dolphin Books, Doubleday and Company, 1965.

HIBS Hibbs, Paul
Speech for today by Paul Hibbs, Seth A. Fessenden, P. Marville Larson, and Joseph A. Wagner. St. Louis, Webster Division, McGraw-Hill Book Company, 1965. Indexed for speeches and suggestions for preparation of types of speeches

HICF Hicks, Frederick C., ed.
Famous speeches by eminent American statesmen, collected and edited by Frederick C. Hicks. St. Paul, West Publishing Company, 1929.

HICJ Hicks, Frederick C., ed.
Famous American jury speeches; addresses before juries and fact-finding tribunals, collected and edited by Frederick C. Hicks. St. Paul, West Publishing Company, 1925.

HILK Hill, Roy L.
Rhetoric of racial revolt. Denver, Colorado, Golden Bell Press, 1964.

HILL Hill, Thomas Edie
Hill's manual of business and social information. New and improved Twentieth century edition, rev. and enl. by Prof. C. M. Stevens. Chicago, W. B. Conkey, 1921. p. 460-471 indexed for speeches

HNWS Hobbs, Herschel H.
Welcome speeches and emergency addresses for all occasions. Grand Rapids, Michigan, Zondervan Publishing House, 1960.

HOA Hoffman, William George

Public speaking for businessmen, 3d ed. New York, McGraw-Hill Book Company, 1949.
Indexed for speeches only

HOAP Hoffman, William George
Public speaking for businessmen. New York, McGraw-Hill Book Company, 1923.

HOB Hoffman, William George
Public speaking today. New York, McGraw-Hill Book Company, 1940.

HOC Hoffman, William George
Speaker's notebook. New York, McGraw-Hill Book Company, 1943.
Indexed for speeches only

HOD Holley, Donald L.
Extempore speaking; a handbook for the student, the coach, and the judge. New York, H.W. Wilson, 1947.
Indexed for speeches only

HURG Hurd, Charles
Treasury of great American speeches: our country's life and history in the words of its great men. New York, Hawthorn Books, 1959.

HUS Huston, Alfred D.
Everyday business speech by Alfred D. Huston and Robert A. Sandberg. New York, Prentice-Hall, 1943.
Indexed for speeches only

IMMD Immel, Ray Keeslar
Delivery of a speech; a manual for course I in public speaking. Ann Arbor, Michigan, George Wahr Publishing Company, 1921.
Indexed for speeches only

INTW Interstate Oratorical Association
Winning orations of the Interstate Oratorical Association, 1933. New York, Noble and Noble, 1933.

IOCP Iowa State College
Commemorative papers from the Iowa State College Centennial; Founders' Day Convocation; Founders' Day Luncheon Academic Symposia. Ames, Iowa, Iowa State College Press, 1958.

JA Jacobs, James Vernon
81 short speeches for 44 occasions. Cincinnati, Standard Publishing Company, 1954.

JAI Jacobs, James Vernon
Inspiring talks for superintendents, youth leaders, teachers, speakers. Cincinnati, Standard Publishing Company, 1962.

JAS Jacobs, James Vernon
60 short talks for superintendents and youth leaders. Cincinnati, Standard Publishing Company, 1957.

JEYO Jessel, George
You too can make a speech. New York, Grayson Publishing Company, 1956.

JOHA Johnston, Alexander
American orations; studies in American political history, edited with introduction by Alexander Johnston, edited with historical and textual notes by James Albert Wood-

burn. 5th ed. New York, G. P. Putnam's Sons, 1927. 2 volumes

JON Jones, Louis Thomas
Aboriginal American oratory; the tradition of eloquence among the Indians of the United States. Los Angeles Southwest Museum, 1965.
Indexed for speeches

JUD Judson, Lyman Spicer, ed.
Intercollegiate after-dinner speaking, edited by Lyman Spicer Judson and Floyd W. Lambertson. New York, Noble and Noble, 1937.

KES Keith, Arthur Berriedale, ed.
Selected speeches and documents in British colonial policy, 1763-1917. London, Oxford University Press, 1918. 2 volumes
Indexed for speeches only

KESB Keith, Arthur Berriedale, ed.
Speeches and documents on the British Dominions, 1918-1931. London, Oxford University Press, 1932.
Indexed for speeches only

KESI Keith, Arthur Berriedale, ed.
Speeches and documents on Indian policy, 1750-1921. London, Oxford University Press, 1922. 2 volumes
Indexed for speeches only

KESK Keith, Arthur Berriedale, ed.
Speeches and documents on international affairs, 1918-1937. London, Oxford University Press, 1938. 2 volumes
Indexed for speeches only

KET Kettle, Thomas Michael, ed.
Irish orators and oratory, with introduction by Professor T. M. Kettle. Dublin, Talbot Press, Ltd. 1916?
Short extracts omitted

KLEB Kleiser, Grenville
Best speeches by eminent speakers. 1st series. New York, Funk and Wagnalls Company, 1935.

KLEG Kleiser, Grenville
Great speeches and how to make them. New York, Funk and Wagnalls, 1911.

KLEM Kleiser, Grenville
Model speeches for practice. New York, Funk and Wagnalls, 1920.

KNAS Knapp, Ella Adelaide, ed.
The speech for special occasions, edited by Ella Adelaide Knapp and John C. French. New York, Macmillan Company, 1921.

KNASA Knapp, Ella Adelaide, ed.
The speech for special occasions, edited by Ella Adelaide Knapp and John C. French. New York, Macmillan Company, 1929.

LA Lawrence, Edwin Gordon
How to talk to people and make an impression. New York, Fleming H. Revell, 1938.

LAD Lawrence, Edwin Gordon
Speech-making, explicit instructions for the build-

ing and delivery of speeches. New York, A. S. Barnes, 1911.
Short extracts omitted

LARW Larson, Orvin Prentiss
When its your turn to speak. New York, Harper and Brothers, 1962.
Chapter 9 indexed for model speeches.

LEEW Lee, Guy Carleton, Ed.
World's orators, comprising the great orations of the world's history with introductory essays, biographical sketches and critical notes. New York, G. P. Putnam's Sons, 1900. 10 volumes

LEHS Lehman, Louis Paul
Short talks for banquets. Grand Rapids, Zondervan Publishing House, 1958.
Indexed for speeches

LEIO Leigh, Randolph
Oratory; a handbook for participants in the National Oratorical Contest, containing the winning orations of each year. New York, G. P. Putnam's Sons, 1927.
Short extracts omitted

LEW Lewis, William Mather, comp.
Voices of our leaders; a collection of addresses delivered by statesmen of the United States and her Allies in the Great War. New York, Hinds, Hayden and Eldredge, 1917.

LINM Lindgren, Homer D., comp.
Modern speeches. New York, F. S. Crofts and Company, 1930.

LINP Linkugel, Wil A.
Contemporary American speeches: a sourcebook of speech forms and principles, by Wil A. Linkugel, R. R. Allen, and Richard L. Johannesen. Belmont, California, Wadsworth Publishing Company, 1965.

LOMS Lomas, Charles Wyatt
Speech: idea and delivery, by Charles W. Lomas and Ralph Richardson. Boston, Houghton Mifflin Company, 1956.
Indexed for speeches only

LOMSA Lomas, Charles Wyatt
Speech: idea and delivery. 2d ed. By Charles W. Lomas and Ralph Richardson. Boston, Houghton Mifflin Company, 1963.
Indexed for speeches only

LOTI Lott, Davis Newton, ed.
Inaugural addresses of the American Presidents from Washington to Kennedy, annotated by Davis Newton Lott. New York, Holt, Rinehard and Winston, 1961.

LU Lupton, Martha, ed.
Encyclopedia of creative thought, edited by Martha Lupton, Alta Gwinn Saunders, and Maxwell Droke. Indianapolis, Maxwell Droke, 1941.
p. 1113-1357 indexed for speeches

LY Lyle, Guy Redvers, comp.
I am happy to present; a book of introductions, compiled by Guy R. Lyle and Kevin Guinagh. New York, H. W. Wilson Company, 1953.

MAS Masterpieces of eloquence; famous orations of great leaders from early Greece to the present time, edited by Mayo W. Hazeltine and others. New York, P. F. Collier and Son, 19--. 25 volumes

MCK McKeldin, Theodore Roosevelt
Art of eloquence; a guide to effective speech with selected addresses by the authors; a governor and a scientist look at public speaking. By Theodore R. McKeldin and John C. Krantz, Jr. Foreword by Lowell Thomas. Baltimore, Williams and Wilkins Company, 1952.

MEAR Mears, A. G.
Right way to speak in public. New York, Emerson Books, Inc., 1953.
Indexed for speeches

MIA Mills, Glen Earl
Composing the speech. New York, Prentice-Hall, 1952.
Appendices indexed

MICS Micken, Ralph A.
Speaking for results; a guide for business and professional speakers. Boston, Houghton Mifflin Company, 1958.
Indexed for speeches

MINA Minor Attic Orators with an English translation by K. J. Maidment. Cambridge, Mass., Harvard University Press, 1941. 2 volumes (Loeb Classical Library nos. 308, 395)

MO Monroe, Alan Houston
Principles and types of speech. 3d ed. New York, Scott, Foresman, 1949.
Short extracts omitted

MOA Monroe, Alan H.
Principles and types of speech. 4th ed. Chicago, Scott, Foresman and Company, 1955.
Indexed for speeches; short extracts omitted

MORA Morath, Dale H.
Officers' speech book, by Charlotte Haber, pseud. New York, Creative Studio, 1954.
Indexed for speeches only

MOUG Mouat, Lawrence Henry
Guide to effective public speaking. Boston, Heath, 1953.
Indexed for speeches and suggestions for preparation of types of speeches

MOUGA Mouat, Lawrence Henry
Guide to effective public speaking. Boston, D. C. Heath, 1959.
Indexed for speeches and suggestions for preparation of types of speeches

NAT National Reference Library
Friendly speeches. Cleveland, National Reference Library, 1955.
Indexed by paging rather than number of speech, as given in Table of Contents

NATM National Reference Library
Speech manuscript book. Cleveland, National Reference Library n. d.
Indexed for speeches only

NATS National Reference Library
Speeches for every occasion. Cleveland, National Reference Library n. d.

Indexed for speeches only.

NATT National Reference Library
Town and club talks. Cleveland, National Reference Library, n. d.
Indexed for speeches only

NESA Nesbit, Wilbur D.
After-dinner speeches and how to make them. Chicago, Reilly and Lee Company, 1927.

NI Nizer, Louis
Thinking on your feet; adventures in speaking, with an introduction by Bruce Barton. New York, Liveright Publishing Corporation, 1940.
Indexed for speeches

NIA Nizer, Louis
Thinking on your feet. New York, Liveright, 1963.
Indexed for speeches

NOR Northern Oratorical League
Winning orations of the Northern Oratorical League contest, 1934-1950. Minneapolis, Northwestern Press, 1934-1950. 9 volumes
Speeches are paged by volume, but indexed by year of contest

NORR Northup, Clark Sutherland, ed.
Representative Phi Beta Kappa orations.
1st ser. Edited for the United chapters of Phi Beta Kappa by Clark Sutherland Northrup, William C. Lane, and John C. Schwab. Boston, Houghton Mifflin, 1915.
2d ser. With introduction by Charles F. Thwing. New York, Elisha Press, 1927.
3d ser. edited by William T. Hastings. Title-Man thinking. New York, Cornell University Press, 1962.

ON O'Neill, James Milton
Extemporaneous speaking. New York, Harper and Brothers, 1946.

ONEC O'Neill, James Milton, comp.
Contemporary speeches compiled by James Milton O'Neill and Floyd K. Riley. New York, Century Company, 1930.

ONEM O'Neill, James Milton, comp.
Classified models of speech composition; 95 complete speeches. New York, Century Company, 1921.

ONES O'Neill, James Milton
Modern short speeches. New York, Century Company, 1923.

ORAMA Orations of American orators, including biographical and critical sketches with a special introduction by Chauncey C. Starkweather. rev. ed. New York, The Colonial Press, 1900. 2 volumes

ORBR Orations of British orators, including biographical and critical sketches. rev. ed. London, New York, Colonial Press, 1900.
2 volumes

PAIC Painton, Edith F. A. U. (Palmer)
Commencement manual; salutatories, valedictories,

addresses and responses, class poems, songs, histories, baccalaureate sermons, prophecies, wills, yells, mottoes, flowers, colors, class plays, novel programs. Chicago, T.S. Denison Company, 1915. Indexed for speeches

PAR Parrish, Wayland Maxfield, ed.
American speeches, edited by Wayland Maxfield Parrish and Marie Hochmuth. New York, Longmans, Green and Company, 1954.

PAUF Paul, Herbert
Famous speeches, selected and edited with introductory notes by Herbert Paul. London, Isaac Pitman and Sons. 1st series, 1911; 2d series, 1912.

PE Peterson, Houston, ed.
A treasury of the world's great speeches, each speech prefaced with its dramatic and biographical setting and placed in its full historical perspective. New York, Simon and Shuster, 1954.

PEA Peterson, Houston, ed.
A treasury of the world's great speeches, each speech prefaced with its dramatic and biographical setting and placed in its full historical perspective. rev. and enl. ed. New York, Simon and Shuster, 1965.

PEAE Pearson, Paul M.
Extemporaneous speaking by Paul M. Pearson and Philip M. Hicks. New York, Hinds, Noble and Eldredge, 1912.

PITT Pittenger, William
Toasts and forms of public address for those who wish to say the right thing in the right way. Philadelphia, Penn Publishing Company, 1906. Indexed for speeches

PL Platz, Mabel, ed.
Anthology of public speeches. New York, The H.W. Wilson Company, 1940.

PO Pomfret, John Edwin, ed.
12 Americans speak; facsimilies original editions, selected and annotated by John E. Pomfret. San Marino, Huntington Library, 1954.

PR Prochnow, Herbert Victor
Toastmaster's handbook. New York, Prentice-Hall, 1949.
Indexed for speeches only

PRC Prochnow, Herbert Victor
Complete toastmaster; a new treasury for speakers. Englewood Cliffs, Prentice-Hall, 1960.
Chapter 2 indexed

PRNE Prochnow, Herbert Victor, comp.
New guide for toastmasters and speakers. Englewood Cliffs, Prentice-Hall, 1956.
Chapters 2 and 3 indexed

PROS Procter, Leslie C., comp.
Selections for public speaking, compiled and adapted by Leslie C. Procter and Gladys T. Stroop. New York, C. Scribner's

Sons, 1930.

RE Reager, Richard Cranston
Speech is easy by Richard C. Reager and Ernest E. McMahon. New Brunswick, Rutgers University Press, 1938.
Indexed for suggestions on how to make various types of speeches

REAB Reager, Richard C.
You can talk well, revised by Norman P. Crawford and Edwin L. Stevens. 1st rev. ed. New Brunswick, Rutgers University Press, 1960.
Indexed for preparation of types of speeches

REAC Reade, Charles, comp.
Commencement essays and orations, salutatories, valedictories, class songs, essays, addresses, etc. for commencement and other occasions, arranged by Charles Reade. Chicago, A. Flanagan Company, 1924.
Essays and anonymous selections omitted

REEM Reed, Thomas B.
Modern eloquence. New York, Modern eloquence Corporation, 1923. 12 volumes 3 sup. volumes, 1927.

REEMA Reed, Thomas B.
Modern eloquence. Philadelphia, John D. Morris Company, 1901-1903. 15 volumes

REEMB Modern eloquence. New York, Lincoln Scholarship Fund, 1928. 15 volumes

RID Ridpath, John Clark
Memorable addresses by American patriots. Chicago, DeBower-Elliott Company; Cincinnati, Jones Brothers Publishing Company, n. d.

RINM Ringwalt, Ralph Curtis, ed.
Modern American oratory; seven representative orations, edited with notes and an essay on the theory of oratory by Ralph Curtis Ringwalt. New York, H. Holt and Company, 1898.

RUS Communist Party of the Soviet Union
Russia enters the 1960s: a documentary report on the 22nd Congress of the Communist Party of the Soviet Union, edited with commentary by Harry Schwartz. Philadelphia, J. B. Lippincott, 1962.
Indexed for speeches

SAA St. John, Robert Porter, ed.
Landmarks of liberty; the growth of American political ideals as recorded in speeches from Otis to Hughes, ed. with introduction and notes by Robert P. St. John and Raymond L. Noonan. New York, Harcourt Brace and Company, 1941.

SAB Sandford, William Phillips
Practical business speaking by William Phillips Sandford and Willard Hayes Yeager. 3d ed. New York, McGraw-Hill Book Company, 1952.

SABA Sandford, William Phillips
Effective busines speech. 4th ed. of Practical business speaking, by William Phillips Sandford and Wil-

lard H. Yeager. New York, McGraw-Hill Book Company 1960.
Indexed for speeches and preparation of types of speeches.

SAC Sandford, William Phillips
Speak well-and win! A short cut to results. New York, McGraw-Hill Book Company, 1944.
Indexed for speeches only.

SAR Sarett, Lew
Modern speeches on basic issues, compiled and edited by Lew Sarett and William Trufant Foster. Boston, Houghton Mifflin Company, 1939.

Schell, Stanley
Commencement week recitations. New York, Wehman.
Same as Werner's readings and recitations. v. 54

SCHS Schermerhorn, James
Schermerhorn's speeches for all occasions. New York, G. Sully and Company, 1930.

SHAH Shaw, Warren Choate
History of American oratory. Indianapolis, Bobbs-Merrill Company, 1928.

SHE Shoemaker, Ann Green (Mrs. Harry J.)
The Red man speaks. Doylestown, Pa., Doylestown Printing Shop, 1947.

SHU Shurter, Edwin DuBois, ed.
Winning declamations and how to speak them. Rev. ed. New York, Noble and Noble, 1929.

SHUC Shurter, Edwin Dubois, ed.
Representative college orations. New York, Macmillan Company, 1909.

SHUM Shurter, Edwin DuBois, ed.
Masterpieces of modern oratory. Boston, Ginn and Company, 1906.

SHUO Shurter, Edwin DuBois, ed.
Oratory of the South; from the Civil War to the present time. New York and Washington, The Neale Publishing Company, 1908.

SHUP Shurter, Edwin DuBois
Practical speech making; the extempore method by Edwin DuBois Shurter and Charles Almer Marsh. New York, Houghton Mifflin Company, 1929.
p. 4, 155-231 indexed.

SMI Smithey, William Royall, ed.
Virginia oratory, containing selections from native Virginians, arranged in chronological grouping to illustrate outstanding epochs in Virginia history. Designed for special use in high schools and colleges. By William Royall Smithey and Calvin Hull Phippins. Charlottesville, Historical Publishing Company, 1934.

SOBP Soper, Paul L.
Basic public speaking. 3d ed. New York, Oxford University Press, 1963.
Indexed for types of speeches and speeches.

SOES Sothman, Alma
Everyday speeches; what to say and how to say it. New York, The William

Frederick Press, 1949.

SOU The South in the building of the nation. A history of the southern states designed to record the south's part in the making of the American nation, to portray the character and genius, to chronicle the achievements and progress and to illustrate the life and traditions of the southern people. Richmond, Southern Historical Publication Society, 1909-1913. 13 volumes
Only vol. 9 indexed: History of southern oratory

SPIM Spillman, Harry Collins
Making the business speech effective; a manual of practical suggestions for speech making with outlines and analyses of speech materials. New York, Gregg Publishing Company, 1925.
p. 117-260 indexed

STOC Stern, Renée Bernd
Clubs, making and management. Chicago, Rand McNally and Company, 1925.

STON Stern, Renée Bernd
101 ideas for clubs. New York, Sterling Publishing Company, 1956. (Same as her Clubs, making and management)

SUM Sumner, Guy Lynn
'We have with us tonight:" secrets of success at the speaker's table. New York, Harper and Brothers, 1941.

THOS Thomas, Benjamin F.
A speech and a story for every occasion. Omaha, The Odyx Company, 1926.

THOT Thorn, W. E.
A bit of honey; after-dinner addresses of inspiration, wit, and humor. Grand Rapids, Zondervan Publishing House, 1964.

THOU Thoughts for the occasion Series 1, 2, 3 New York, E. B. Treat and Co., 1894 (Same 1905 ed.)
Ser. 1 Thoughts for the occasion, patriotic and secular, ed. by Joseph Sanderson.
Ser. 2 Thoughts for the occasion, anniversary and religious, ed. by Franklin Noble.
Ser. 3 Thoughts for the occasion, fraternal and benevolent ed. by Franklin Noble.

TIN Southern Historical Association
Pursuit of Southern history; Presidential addresses of the Southern Historical Association, 1935-1963, edited by George Brown Tindall. Baton Rouge, Louisiana State University Press, 1964.

TRUW Trueblood, Thomas C., ed.
Winning speeches in the contests of the Northern Oratorical League, edited for the league by Thomas C. Trueblood, William G. Caskey, and Henry E. Gordon. New York, American Book Company, 1909.

TWJ Two hundred and fiftieth anniversary of the settlement of the Jews in the

United States; addresses delivered at Carnegie Hall, New York on Thanksgiving Day, 1905, together with other selected addresses and proceedings. New York Cooperative Society, 1906. Indexed for speeches only

UAR United Arab Republic (Egyptian Region)
The Conference on the Problems of Economic Development. Cairo, General Organization for Government Printing Office, 1962. Indexed for speeches only

USIN United States. 87th Congress, 1st Session, House Document 218.
Inaugural addresses of the Presidents of the United States from George Washington 1789 to John F. Kennedy, 1961. Washington, D. C. United States Government Printing Office, 1961.

USINA United States. 89th Congress 1st Session, House Document 51
Inaugural addresses of the Presidents of the United States from George Washington, 1789 to Lyndon Baines Johnson, 1965. Washington, D. C. United States Government Printing Office, 1965.

University Oratorical Annual
See
Year book of college oratory

VO Voices of history; great speeches and papers of the years, 1941, 1942/43-1945/46 New York, Gramercy Publishing Company, 1942-1946. 5 volumes
Sub title varies.
1941 ed. by Franklin Watts
1942/43 ed. by Franklin Watts and Barbara Leighton
1943/44 ed. by Franklin Watts and Nathan Ausubel
1944/45 and 1945/46 ed. by Nathan Ausubel
Extraneous type of material omitted

WAGN Wagner, Harr, ed.
Notable speeches by notable speakers. San Francisco, Whitaker, Ray and Company, 1902.

WE Weaver, David Andrew, ed.
Builders of American universities; inaugural addresses. Alton, Shurtleff College Press, 1949-1952. 2 volumes

Werner, E. S.
Famous modern speeches. New York, Wehman

Same as
Werner's readings and recitations v. 42

WERN Werner's readings and recitations. vols. 42, 54. New York, E. S. Werner and Company, 1908.
v. 42 Famous modern orations.
v. 54 Commencement week recitations ed. by Stanley Schell

WHIP White, William Allen
Politics: the citizen's business. New York, Macmillan Company, 1924.
p. 155-321 indexed for Republican and Democratic Convention speeches

WOON Woodson, Carter Goodwin, ed.

Negro orators and their orations. Washington, The Associated Publishers, 1925.

WPRA Wrage, Ernest J., ed.
American forum: speeches on historic issues, 1788-1900, edited by Ernest J. Wrage and Barnett Baskerville. New York, Harper and Brothers 1960.

WPRC Wrage, Ernest J., ed.
Contemporary forum: American speeches on 20th century issues, edited by Ernest J. Wrage and Barnett Baskerville. New York, Harper and Brothers 1962.

WRA Wright, C.W.
Better speeches for all occasions. New York, Crown Publishers, 1948.

WRB Wright, C.W.
How to speak in public. New York, Crown Publishers, 1943.
Indexed for speeches only

YE Yeager, Willard Hayes
Effective speaking for every occasion. 2d ed. New York, Prentice-Hall, 1951.
Indexed for speeches only

YR Year book of oratory. New York, Noble and Noble, 1929-1938. 10 volumes. v. 1-3, 1929-31 entitled: University oratorical annual; v. 4-8, 1932-36 entitled: The year book of college oratory. Vols. 8-10 have also additional titles: v. 8 The college youth speaks. - v. 9-10 Prize-winning orations. v. 1-3, 1929-31 ed. by B. E. Youngdahl and E.E. Anderson; V. 4-9, 1932-37 comp. and ed. by E. E. Anderson; v. 10, 1938 comp. and ed. by J.K. Noble.

ZEL Zelikowitch, G., comp. and ed.
Bar-Mitzva speeches; a collection of various Bar-Mitzva speeches in English, Hebrew, and Yiddish, compiled by famous Jewish scholars and orators. New York, Hebrew Publishing Company, 1908.

ZU Zutshi, C.N., ed.
Inspiring speeches: great thoughts of great people for college students, edited and annotated by C. N. Zutshi and J.J. Sebastian. Delhi, S. Garg and Company, 1954.

SPEECHES

Abbatt, William
History of trees. THOU 1:43
Abbot, Francis Ellingwood
Genius of Christianity and religion. BL:680
Abbott, Hershell
It might happen to you. BRP 9:24; YR 10:201
Abbott, Lyman
Cure for anarchism. BLAB: 158; BLAA:158
Faith and duty. REEM 1:1; REEMB 1:1
International brotherhood. FUL: 1, 4; REEMA 7:1
Law of service. BOB:60
Nation's greatness. BOB:121
Resurrection. THOU 2:104
Abbott, William L.
Functions of the governing board in the administration of a university. ONES:273
Abbott, William R.
University of Virginia (before Alumni Association). SHUO: 102
Abelard, Pierre
Divine tragedy. PL:208; BREW 1:27; BRYW 7:17
Last entry into Jerusalem. BREW 1:26
Resurrection of Lazarus. BREW 1:24
Sermon on Marcellinus, Pope and martyr. MAS 3:1250; HAZO 3:1250
Abernathy, Thomas Perkins
Democracy and the Southern frontier. TIN:42

ABOLITION MOVEMENT See Slavery in the United States
Abrams, Mason M.
Guardians of the light. NOR 1940:21

ABSENT SPEAKER See Extemporaneous speeches

ACADEMIC DEGREES See Acceptance speeches-Degrees, academic; Presentation speeches-Degrees, academic

ACADEMIC FREEDOM See Teaching, Freedom of

ACCEPTANCE SPEECHES
Suggestions for preparation of speechs of acceptance. BRA:509; LARW:112. With examples of. BRY:374; GA: 42; HIBS:279; MCK:191

See also Presentation speeches; Responses; Thanks

---- ALTAR CLOTHS
Acceptance of an altar cloth by the head of a church or lodge. EDGS:376

---- ARMORIES
Mayor's address of acceptance of new armory. AMEO 2:191

---- AWARDS See Acceptance speeches-Rewards (Prizes)

---- BADGES
Temple, R. A.
Responsive address on being presented a badge. THOU 3:486

---- BOOKS
Acceptance of a set of Dickens' novels by best scholar in school. HAPR:44

Gildersleeve, B. L.
Accepting a book. ONES:54
Response of the teacher on being presented with a book. HILL:465

---- BUILDINGS
Champ, F. P.
Address of acceptance. SAR:110

---- CANTEEN
Churchill, W. L. S.
Acceptance of a trailer canteen presented by Austrians in Britain to the WVS (Women's Volunteer Service). VO 1942-43:156

---- CHAIRS
Gladstone, W. E.
Accepting a chair from the Liberals of the Borough of Greenwich. KNAS:163; KNASA:163; ONEM:714

---- CHARTERS
Accepting a charter. BEB:13

---- CITATIONS
Acceptance speech by woman civic leader. BEDA:44
Accepting a citation. BEB:13
Ford, B.
Moral basis for our leadership. MIA:388
Guest-of-honor acknowledges praise and citation (at testimonial to philanthropist). BED:25; BEDA:47
Thanking speaker (at Camera Club). BEDA:20

---- CUPS
Response by guest-of-honor (at testimonial on retirement of public official). BED:30; BEDA:51
Wilson, G. T.
On receiving a loving cup. REEM 3:412; REEMB 3: 419

---- DEGREES, ACADEMIC
Address on receiving the degree of Doctor of laws. DAVC:593
Churchill, W. L. S.
Sinews of peace (speech at Fulton, Missouri), BA 1945-46:20; COPB:614; GRAC: 144; HIB:298; PE:803; PEA:803
Lynch, G. J.
Pursuit of security (accepting an honorary degree by University of Dayton at graduation exercise). LINP: 186
Root, E.
On receiving his degree of LL.D., 1907. KNAS:180; KNASA:180
Washington, B. T.
Address delivered at the Harvard Alumni dinner in 1896. BAKF:420; BOU:154; CHAL 14:318; COP:331; COPA:331; COPB:331; HAZO 25:10859; HILK:43; HURG:144; MAS 25:10859; REEM 7:421; REEMA 9: 1140; REEMB 8:437; WOON:584
Whitney, J. H.
Challenges and excellences (accepting degree). BA 1964-65:120

---- DIPLOMAS
Response of a class president on presentation of diploma PAIC:228

---- DONATIONS
Minister's reply to donation presentation speech. BARI 203

---- EMBLEMS
Response by retiring officer of the lodge on being presented an emblem. EDGS: 372
Response by a retiring office of the lodge on receiving emblem. HE:119

---- FLAGS
Acceptance of a flag by a commanding officer. EDGS:55
Acceptance of a flag by the presiding officer. EDGS: 374
Accepting flag presented to a military organization. HAPR:13
Andrew, J. A.
Accepting the battle flags. CHAL 9:311; HAZO 19: 7896; MAS 19:7896; ONEM: 712
Reply of Captain to flag presentation speech. BARB:12
Reply of Colonel to a presentation speech of a stand of colors. BARB:15
Reply to a banner presentation speech. BARB:29
Response of a Scout master to presentation of flag. EDGS: 248
Response of the Captain on being presented with a flag. HILL:464

---- GATEWAYS
Hadley, A. T.
Acceptance of the Cheney-Ives gateway. KNAS:161; KNASA:161; ONEM:713; ONES:48

---- GAVELS
Appreciation and thanks (at induction of a Judge) BEDA: 120
Ballou, F.W.
Acceptance of a gavel. BRAC:268

---- GIFTS
Acceptance by teacher of farewell gift. HAPR:32
Acceptance of a gift from an institution or organization. DR:25; LU:1130
Acceptance of gift by manager of a baseball club. HAPR: 69
Acceptance speech by a retiring executive. SOES:20
Accepting a gift. BEC:31
Accepting a gift at office staff meeting. WRA:97
Accepting a travelling bag by officer leaving to accept promotion. WRA:96
Bryant, W. C.
Accepting a portfolio on his seventieth birthday. KNAS: 165; KNASA:165; ONEM: 715
Farewell address (by retiring secretary of labor union) BED:81; BEDA:154
Gift acceptance (of lodge matron) - examples of. MORA: 35-36
Hughes, C. E.
Accepting a gift from the Washington correspondents. ONEC:53
McLain, H. O.
Accepting gift on retirement as club president. PR:103
Marshall, T. R.
Thanking the French ambassador for vases presented to the Senate. REEM 2:389; REEMB 2:406
Model and outline of an acceptance speech. BAKS:128, 136
Outline of a response to a presentation speech. CARP: 11
Reply by a public officer on being presented with a souvenir. BARB:40
Reply of a principal on being presented with a souvenir by pupils. BARB:37
Reply of teacher on being presented with a remembrance by her pupils. BARB:35
Reply to ring or pin presentation speech. BARB:25
Response by a retiring officer to presentation speech. EDGS:129
Response of a public official to presentation speech. EDGS:79

Roosevelt, T.
Accepting a horse and saddle. ONES:56
Seven model speeches for accepting a gift. BEB:14-15
Suggestions for preparation of speech accepting a gift BARR:232; BRAB:497; BRY:374; BRYA:405; BUT:98; BUTA:98; BUTB:98; MOUG:151; RE:165; REAB:155. With examples of. SOES:19; WRA:93; WRB:198; YE:156
Thanks for a gift - six examples of. STOC:154; STON:160-162
Two speeches of response to presentation speeches. THOS:111-12

---- JUDICIAL ROBES
Appreciation and thanks (at induction of a Judge) BEDA:120

---- KEYS
Accepting building key (at dedication of home for aged) BED:34; BEDA:75
Lowell, A. L.
Accepting the keys of the George F. Baker Foundation. ONEC:53
Response by distinguished guest on being presented the key to the city. EDGS:90

---- LETTER OF CREDENCE
Roosevelt, F.D.
Reply to Ambassador Escobar. VO 1944-45:93

---- MEDALS
Acceptance of medal by victorious baseball club. HAPR:37
Accepting a medal. BEB:15
Accepting a medallion at fifth anniversary of founding of Big Brother Athletic Association. BEDA:113
Hampden, W.
On receiving a gold medal. REEM sup 1:418; REEMB 6:160
Hand, L.
Fanfare for Prometheus (accepting American Liberties medallion) BA 1955-56:39
Hoover, H.C.
Benjamin Franklin - accepting the gold medal of the International Benjamin Franklin Society. BA 1953-54:81
Hull, C.
Economic barriers to peace. SAR:276
Mackay, C.H.
In response to the award of the Gold Medal of the National Institute of Social Sciences. KLEB:169
McCrae, A.
Acceptance of Saunders medal. GA:46
Responding to tribute (by labor union official) BED:84; BEDA:157
Vaughan, E.R.
Accepting the Florence Nightingale medal. GA:45

---- MEMBERSHIP
Accepting honor and acknowledging tributes (at physician-of-the-year award) BED:53; BEDA:56
Eisenhower, D.D.
Acceptance of honorary membership in Chamber of Commerce of State of New York. MO:506; MOA:510

---- MEMORIAL HALLS
Bryan, J.S.
Acceptance of the Phi Beta Kappa Memorial Hall. BRAC:268

---- MEMORIALS
Commander's speech of thanks on presentation of a mem-

orial. Hill:474
Irwin, I. H.
Acceptance of Amelia Earhart collection. GA:47
Suggestions for accepting a gift, an award, or a memorial. BRY:374

---- MILITARY COMMISSIONS
Washington, G.
Acceptance of military commission. BRAC:267; BRYW 8:77

---- MONEY
Acceptance of purse by captain of a fishing schooner for heroic rescue. HAPR: 122

---- MONUMENTS
Roosevelt, T.
Accepting a soldiers' and sailors' monument. ONES: 49

---- NOMINATIONS
Bryan, W. J.
Imperialism (accepting Democratic nomination for Presidency, 1900) WPRA: 358
Creasy, W. T.
Accepting a nomination. ONES:51
Curtis, C. L.
Accepting the Republican nomination to the Vice-Presidency. ONEC:56
Dewey, T. E.
Acceptance speech. BA 1943-44:259; ON:377; VO 1944-45:280
Goldwater, B. M.
Extremism in defense of liberty (accepting nomination for Presidency) HIB: 291
Hoover, H. C.
Accepting the nomination for Presidency. SHU:114; CORP:231
Kennedy, J. F.
New frontier. BA 1960-61: 7
Model and outline for an acceptance speech of a nomination. BAKS:154
Nixon, R. M.
It is time to speak up for America. BA 1960-61:15
Preparation of a nomination acceptance speech. CORP: 230
Reply by nominee to an announcement of his nomination. BARB:124-5
Roosevelt, F. D.
Acceptance of renomination for the Presidency, June 27, 1936. BIR 4:193
Acceptance speech on renomination, July 20, 1944. VO 1944-45:309
Speech accepting a nomination. PITT:96
Stevenson, A. E.
Agrees to run for President. BA 1952-53:66; BAAMP: 289; CAP:220; COPB:597; HURG:302; PE:821; PEA: 821
Suggestions for preparation of speech accepting nomination. With examples of. BRAB:497; GLAD:166
Taft, W. H.
Strikes, boycotts, and injunctions (acceptance speech, July 28, 1908) BREW 9:340
Thomas, N.
Acceptance speech. BA 1943-44:277
Willkie, W. L.
Acceptance speech. BA 1940-41:93
Wilson, W.
First political address (accepting the nomination for governor of New Jersey) PE:684; PEA:684

---- OFFICES See Offices-acceptance

---- PARTIES
Acknowledgments to a surprise party, by the party surprised. BARB:203

---- PICTURES
Acceptance of author's picture by publisher. HAPR:183

---- PINS
Acceptance of pin by popular political leader. HAPR:56
Acceptance of pin on resigning as foreman. HAPR:21

---- PLAQUES
Acceptance (of plaque for Labor Temple). BED:87; BEDA:160
Accepting a plaque. BEC:32

---- PLATE
McAdams, T.B.
Accepting a silver service. HOA:382; HOAP:272
Maddox, R.F.
Response to presentation of token of esteem. ONES:97
Public official's acceptance of a silver service upon his retirement. HAPR:50
Reply to presentation speech at a silver wedding. HILL: 465
Response to a silver presentation speech. BARB:20

---- PORTRAITS
Acceptance and thanks (by past president of labor union at unveiling of portrait). BED:91; BEDA:164
Carter, J.C. On the presentation of his portrait. KNAS:177; KNASA:177

---- RESIGNATIONS See Resignations

---- REWARDS (PRIZES)
Acceptance of a prize for target shooting by an officer. EDGS:62
Acceptance of science award. BEDA:61
Accepting an award. BEC:31
Accepting prize for marksmanship. HAPR:28
Faulkner, W.
On accepting the Nobel prize, exhorts the young writers of the world. BOU:9; COPB: 637; HAR:397; HIBS:508; HURG:291; PE:814; PEA: 814
Hoffman, P.G.
Accepting the Robert Dollar award. SAB:221
Response on receiving Freedom House award. BA 1951-52:77
Jessel, G.
Accepting the Humanitarian award at Friars' Club dinner, 1954. JEYO:118
Kettering, C.F.
Accepting award of American Alumni Council. YE: 159
Luthuli, A.J.
Africa and freedom (accepting 1960 Nobel Peace Prize). CROC:306
MacArthur, D.
Farewell to the cadets (accepting Sylvanus Thayer award for service to his nation). HIB:58; LINP:150
Murrow, E.R.
Accepting the Peabody award. YE:157
Phelps, W.L.
Acceptance of American Education award. BA 1939-40:364
Reply of captain on the distribution of a collection of prizes among the successful marksmen of a target company. BARB:27
Reply of the winner of a rowing match to presentation prize speech. BARB:32

---- REWARDS (PRIZES) (cont.)
Reply to a prize presentation speech by the winner of a sailing match. BARB:39
Response to presentation of life membership award. MORA:121
Sabin, F.R.
Acceptance of the M. Carey Thomas award. GA:48
Seaborg, G.T.
Scientist as a human being (accepting Charles Lathrop Parsons award) BA 1964-65:129
Stanton, F.
Remarks on government regulation of broadcasting (accepting Printers' Ink gold medal). ARNS:116
Stein, L.
Accepting 1959 National Brotherhood award. SABA:301
Suggestions for accepting a gift, an award, or a memorial. BRY:374
Thanks and appreciation (by guest of honor at testimonial dinner to journalist). BED:22; BEDA:37
Two model speeches for accepting an award. BEB:12
Waterman, A.T.
Science in the Sixties (accepting the William Proctor Prize of the Scientific Society of America) BA 1960-61:189
See also Acceptance speeches-Medals; Acceptance speeches-Trophies

---- RESIGNATIONS
See Resignations

---- SCHOLARSHIP
Brick, A.W., Jr.
After dinner speech on the occasion of accepting a scholarship. JUD:301

---- SCROLLS
Appreciation and acceptance (at presentation of Brotherhood award). BED:57; BEDA:66
Thanks and appreciation (at testimonial to a musician). BEDA:40

---- SILVERWARE
See Acceptance Speeches-Plate

---- SOUVENIRS
See Acceptance speeches-Gifts

---- STATUES
Phelan, J.D.
Goethe-Schiller memorial address. WAGN:356
Rowland, D.
Influence of the poet (accepting bust of Irwin Russell). SHUO:83
Stone, H.F.
Accepting bust of Brandeis. ON:327
Wallace, R.M.
Stephen F. Austin and Sam Houston (at acceptance of their statues in Capitol). SHUO:211

---- SWORDS
Acceptance of a sword and memorial. HAPR:18
Acceptance of a sword by an army officer. EDGS:58
Lee, R.E.
Acceptance of the sword. SMI:173
Two replies for sword presentation speeches. BARB:17, 19

---- TABLETS
Schwab, C.M
On being awarded a bronze tablet. REEM 4:387; REEMB 5:274

---- TESTIMONIALS
Reply of a retiring president

or superintendent to a testimonial presentation. BARB:33
Reply to a testimonial of esteem. HILL:467

---- TRIBUTES
Crabtree, J.W.
Response to presentation of a volume of tributes. YE: 157
See also Responses to tributes

---- TROPHIES
Acceptance of a trophy. BURS: 231
Acceptance of trophy by winner of a golf tournament. EDGS:396
Reply by winner in a baseball match to presentation speech. BARB:44
Reply by winner of cue in a billiard tournament. BARB: 42
Response by the winner in a swimming contest on being given a trophy. EDGS:399
Response in accepting a trophy by the captain of a crew. EDGS:403
Response in accepting a trophy in a sailing race. EDGS: 400

---- WATCHES
Acceptance of a watch by a young man. HAPR:115
Accepting a gold watch at a club meeting. WRA:95
Accepting a watch. BEC:32
Reply to a watch presentation speech. BARB:22
Response of a clergyman on being presented with a watch. HILL:466

ACCORDIAN PLAYERS See Music and musicians

ACCOUNTANTS
Atkinson, J.
Welcome to the Society of Certified Public Accountants. LINM:382
Day, E.E.
Accountancy as a profession. LINM:475
Roberts, R.
Introducing an accountant. BRC:138
Williams, H.
Introducing a certified public accountant. BRC:62

ACCUSATION SPEECHES See Blame, speeches of
Acheson, Dean G.
Basis for Russian-American peace. BA 1949-50:38; HAR:85
Deterring the aggressor. MIA: 350
Ethics in international relations today, BA 1964-65:53
North Atlantic Pact. BA 1948-49:15
North Atlantic Treaty Organization. BA 1951-52:47
Speech in Washington, April 22, 1950. GRAC:155
Speech in Washington, January 12, 1950. GRAC:159
Statement on liberation, January 15, 1953. GRAC:164
Tensions between the United States and the Soviet Union. -Same as his Basis for Russian-American peace
United Nations and Soviet aggression. BA 1950-51:25
United States policy toward Asia. HAR:154

ACHILLES
Homer. Achilles to the envoys. BRYW 1:3; HAZO 1: 4; LEEW 1:27; MAS 1:4; PL:23

ACHIEVEMENT See Success
Ackerman, Carl W.
Role of the press as a factor in public opinion and economic changes. BA 1937-38:198

Ackerman, Edward A. See Chang, J. M., jt. auth.

ACKNOWLEDGMENTS See Acceptance speeches; Thanks

ACROBATS See Circus

ACTORS AND ACTING
Branen, J.
Introducing an entertainer
" an old time entertainer. BRH: 106, 67
Clifford, V.
Introducing a French comedian
Introducing a ventriloquist. BRH:153, 55
Collins, A.
Introducing a comedian. BRC:295
Dickens, C.
Actor's art. REEMA 1:401
Drummond, R.
Introducing an impersonator. BRH:108
Gilbert E. J.
Introducing a comedian
" a juggler
" a magician. BRH:58, 90, 69
Gilbert, J.
Playing "old men" parts. REEM 2:87; REEMA 2:522; REEMB 2:79
Halle, R.
Guilty until proven innocent. SOBP:348
Huber, L. J.
Introducing an actor. BRC: 55
Introducing an actor
" an animal imitator
" an " trainer
" a comedian
" a hypnotist
" an impersonator
" a juggler
" a magician
" a mind reader
" a novelty act
" an old time entertainer
Introducing a sharpshooter
" a strong man
" a swimming or diving act
Introducing a tumbling act
" a variety revue
" a ventriloquist.
BRH See Table of contents, section II for paging
Kaser, A. L.
Introducing an actor
" a comedian
" an English comedian
" a gay nineties revue or act
" a German comedian
" an Irish comedian
" a lady monologuist
" a magician
" a mind reader
" a Scotch comedian
" a Swedish comedian
" variety revue

BRH See Table of contents, section II for paging
Phelps, F.
Introducing an animal trainer. BRH:62
Posner, G. A.
Introducing an animal trainer or animal act
Introducing a children's act or child entertainer
Introducing a magician. BRH:98, 164, 78
Royce, B.
Absent entertainer (to be used when an entertainer fails to appear). BRH:331
Steele, S.
Introducing an impersonator. BRH:51
Visk, A. G.
Introducing a comedian
" a juggler. BRH:124, 120
See also Art and artists; Circus; Dancing; Drama; Humorists; Moving pictures; Music and musicians; Opera; Radio broadcasting; Television broadcasting; Theater.

Also names of actors, e.g. Booth, Edwin

ACTUATE, SPEECHES TO
Carmichael, C.W.
One man in his time. BU: 146; SOBP:352
Pinkstaff, K.
We are not ashamed. SOBP:355
Adams, Brooks
Beginning of government. THOU 1:207
Adams, Charles Francis, 1807-86
The States and the Union. BREW 1:29; CHAL 7:275; HAZO 15:6191; MAS 15:6191
Adams, Charles Francis, Jr., 1835-1915
Battle of Gettysburg. BREW 1:33
College fetish. CHAL 12:415; HAZO 23:9829; MAS 23: 9829; REEM 6:1; REEMA 7:10; REEMB 7:1
Lessons of life. REEM 1:10; REEMB 1:10; REEMA 1:1
Adams, Charles Kendall
Relations of higher education to national prosperity. NORR 1st ser:152
Adams, Elmer B.
Introducing H.C. Caldwell to New England Society of St. Louis, December 21, 1895. REEM 1:201; REEMB 1: 202
Adams, Frances Louise
Present significance of the Constitution. BOA:85; BOB: 73
Adams, John
Inaugural address. BREW:1: 41; CHI:6; HAZO 6:2561; LOTI:9; MAS 6:2561; ORAMA 1:49; REEMA 11:1; USIN:7; USINA:7
On the Boston Massacre. BREW 1:47; CHAL 3:2; HARS:12; HAZO 6:2569; MAS 6:2569
On the Constitutional war over slavery. REEMA 11:17
Stamp Act, 1765. HELE:11
(Supposed speech of John Adams) Part of Webster, D. Eulogy on Adams and Jefferson

ADAMS, JOHN
Everett, E.
Adams and Jefferson. COP: 269; COPA:269; COPB: 269; HURG:64; KLEG:259; REEM 5:146; REEMA 8: 439; REEMB 9:181
Tyler, J.
Adams and Jefferson. SMI: 104
Webster, D.
Eulogy on Adams and Jefferson. BREW 10:186; CHAL 5:296; CLAY:10; FKA:9; HARSO:348; HAZO 11:4447; KLEG:135; MAS 11:4447; PE:327; PEA: 327; PROS:139; REEMA 15:2082; SHAH:134, 138
Wirt, W.
Death of Jefferson and Adams. BREW 10:259
Adams, John P.
Webster's defense of the Constitution. TRUW:7
Adams, John Quincy
Inaugural address. CHI:51; LOTI:51; USIN:47; USINA: 47
Jubilee of the Constitution (50th). BREW 1:74; HAZO 9:3698; MAS 9:3698; REEM 10:68; REEMA 11:8; REEMB 11:69
Life and character of Lafayette. BREW 1:72; HAZO 9:3691; MAS 9:3691; PL: 641
On American independence. July 4, 1793. LEEW 9:23
On the Constitutional war power over slavery. JOHA 1 pt 2:115
Oration at Plymouth (commemoration of the landing of the Pilgrims) BREW 1:58; CHAL 4:273; HAZO 9:3671

HURG:51; MAS 9:3671; ORAMA 1:327

ADAMS, JOHN QUINCY
Seward, W. H.
Address to John Quincy Adams. KNAS:211; KNASA: 211
Tribute to John Quincy Adams. KNAS:85; KNASA: 85

Adams, L. C.
Higher soldiery. BOB:179
Adams, M. Dell
Our class colors. WERN 54: 84
Adams, Samuel
American independence. BREW 1:83; BRYW 8:110; CHAL 2:312; CHEM 1:69; COP: 234; COPA:234; COPB:234; HAZO 5:2010; HELE:67; HURG:31; JOHA 1 pt 1:24; LEEW 8:239; MAS 5:2010; ORAMA 1:3; PL:583; REEM 10:5; REEMA 11:21; REEMB 11:5

ADAMS, SAMUEL
Everett, E.
Adams and Jefferson. KLEG:259; REEM 5:146
Adams, William
Address, 1852. BRAR 2:163
Home gathering (Thanksgiving address). THOU 2:264
Thanksgiving: its memories and habits. THOU 2:286
Adamson, William
Speech in House of Commons, December 5, 1919 (on India). KESI 2:263
Addams, Jane
Closing the International Congress of Women. GA:175
Governmental efforts toward world peace. DOA:162
In memory of Henry Lloyd. REEM 5:1; REEMB 9:1
Opening fourth International Congress. GA:168
Seconding the nomination of Roosevelt for President, 1912. REEMB 8:1
Washington's birthday. COP: 346; COPA:346; COPB: 346; GA:73; HURG:163; REEM 1:16; REEMB 1:16
Women and war. HICF:439

ADDAMS, JANE
Douglas, P. H.
Five great Americans. BA 1951-52: 85
Hunt, F.
Story of Jane Addams. DOA:112
Sampson, E.
Jane Addams's unfinished business (at Jane Addams centennial observance, Springfield, Ill.). HILK:294
Shoeler, M.
America's mother of men. YR 9:285
Ade, George
Cincinnatus from Indiana. REEM 1:20; REEMB 1:20
Tribute to Lipton. NESA:180
Adelman, Albert
Merely players. BRP 8:86; NOR 1937:29
Adenauer, Konrad
Integration of Europe. HAR: 237
Responds to introduction by C. W. D. Hanson. PRC:27

ADENAUER, KONRAD
Hanson, C. W. D. Introduces His Excellency Dr. Konrad Adenauer, Chancellor, Federal Republic of Germany. PRC:26
Adler, Felix
Marcus Aurelius. REEM 6:14; REEMA 7:23; REEMB 7:14
Nature and the religious mood. REEM 6:30; REEMB 7:30
Adolfson, Lorentz H.
Ultimation of youth. YR 5:143

ADULT EDUCATION See Education, adult

ADVERTISING
Advertising. DU:161
Advertising by a display artist. EDGS:187
Advertising goes early to the colors. SCHS:1
Barton, B.
Advertising a force for greater civilization. HOA: 243
Which know not Joseph. BRAC:24; BRY:461; BRYA: 500; HUS:279; LINM:358; SABA:243
Beam, G.
Let's advertise. HUS:276
Burnham, H. L. W. L.
Welcome to the Associated Advertising Clubs of the World. LINM:28
Chevalier, W.
Advertising in war and postwar. SAC:108
Coolidge, C.
Advertising profession. REEM sup 1:199; REEMB 4:130
Financial advertisers. SCHS: 129
Fox, A. N.
Advertising, the dynamo of civic and commercial life. EXEE:597
Frisbie, M. T.
Unknown quantities. PEAE: 81
Gideonse, H. D.
Reply to Nadine Miller's address "Is advertising responsible for our high standard of living?" MOA:463
Jordan, E. S.
Advertising automobiles. REEM sup 2:126; REEMB 5:32
Kaser, A. L.
Introducing an advertising manager. BRC:109
McClure-Patterson, E.
How women regard advertising. REEM sup 2:194; REEMB 5:144
Marvin, C.
Introducing an advertising executive. BRC:211
Miller, N.
Is advertising responsible for our high standard of living? MOA:463
Mr. Noad on adless day. SCHS:197
Myers, N. J.
Moppet manipulation. ARNS: 113
O'Donnell, H. A.
Comparative advertising methods-east and west. PEAE:93
Opydyke, J. B.
Relation of literature to advertising. REEM sup 2:261; REEMB 5:207
Signology. SCHS:245
Woodbridge, C. K.
Salesmanship and advertising. BYRA:469; REEM sup 3:183; REEMB 5:396
See also Sponsors
Adzhubei, Aleksei I.
Speech of October 26. RUS:103
Aelred, Saint
Farewell. BREW 1:99
Funeral sermon. HAZO 3:1268; MAS 3:1268
On manliness. BREW 1:102
Sermon after absence. BREW 1:100

AERONAUTICS
Airplanes, by a well-known aviator. EDGS:162
Airports. SCHS:10
Aviation. SCHS:23
Aviation (civilization must be served). ED:156
Aviation vs. articulation. SCHS:26
Bremen flyers. SCHS:45
Farnsworth, D.
Introducing an airline executive. BRC:220
Henderson, P.
Aircraft for industry. BYRA: 200; REEM sup 2:40; REEMB 4:389
Jouett, J. H.

AERONAUTICS (cont.)
The air. HUS:269
Kaser, A. L.
Introducing an airline stewardess. BRC:113
Luce, C.B.
America in the post-war air world. BA 1943-44: 143; BOA:37
Maxim, H.
Airships and high explosives in war (1909). BREW 8:126
Tribute to our air mail pilots. ED:160
Warren, L. C.
Dedicating national shrine at Kitty Hawk. CORP: 189
See also Balloons; International Civil Aviation Conference; Space flight

---- COMMERCIAL
Air age. FRIE:166
Carmichael, J.H.
Air transportation-our second line of defense. SAB:180
Lentz, H.J.
Air-borne traveling man. SAB:29; SABA:31

---- MILITARY
Baden-Powell, B. F. S.
Explosives from balloons. BREW 9:298
Capper, J.E.
Dropping down explosives. BREW 9:297
Lindbergh, C. A.
Our air defense. BA 1940-41:75
Nye, G. P., Jr.
For an adequate defense. BA 1938-39:65
Seversky, A. P. de
Aviation vs. isolationalism. ON:121
Will air power win this war? BA 1941-42:186
Spencer, P.
Bombarding London. BREW 9:299
Stone, F. G.
Limiting bombardment by law. BREW 9:295
See also World war 1939-1945 -Aerial operations

AERONAUTICS AS A CAREER
Omilie, P. F.
Youth and aviation. GA:130
Aeschines.
Against crowning Demosthenes. CHAL 1:144; HAZO 1:226; MAS 1:226
Against Ctesiphon. BREW 1: 104; BRYW 1:186; LEEW 1: 301; PL:60; REEM 9:14; REEMB 10:15
First oration on the crown. - Same as his Against Ctesiphon

AESCHINES.
Demosthenes. Oration on the embassy. HAZO 1:338; MAS 1:338

AFRICA
Blyden, E.W.
Political outlook for Africa. DUNM:263
Coppin, L.J.
Negro's part in the redemption of Africa. DUNM:243
Luthuli, A.J.
Africa and freedom (accepting 1960 Nobel Prize). CROC:306
Pitt, W., 1759-1806
Indicts the slave trade and foresees a liberated Africa. FULB:53; GOOD:579; HAY: 80; HAZO 8:3369; MAS 8: 3369; PAUF 1:125; PE:220; PEA:220; REEMA 14:1613
Smuts, J. C.
Basis of trusteeship in African policy. CROC:400
Stanley, H.M.
Through the dark continent. COP:627; COPB:664; REEMA 3:1077; REEMB 3: 280
Through the great forest.

AFRICA (cont.)
REEM 8:372; REEMA 6: 1029; REEMB 13:377
See also World War, 1939-1945-Africa; World War, 1939-1945-Campaigns-African front

AFRICA, NORTH
DeGaulle, C.
Political problem of North Africa. VO 1943-44:37

AFRICA, SOUTH
Churchill, W. L. S.
On the Transvaal Constitution. KES 2:3
Crewe, R. O. A.
On South African Bill. KES 2:25
Milner, A. M
"Never again." REEMA 14:1474
Rhodes, C.
Crisis in South Africa. CHAL 14:292; HAZO 25: 10833; MAS 25:10833; REEMA 14:1730
See also Labor and laboring classes-Africa; South African War, 1899-1902

AFTER-DINNER SPEECHES
Address at a banquet of a volunteer fire department. AMEO 2:149
Address at a girls' high "Y" banquet. AMEO 2:157
Address of the principal or superintendent at a Junior-Senior banquet. AMEO 1:16
Ade, G.
Cincinnatus from Indiana. REEM 1:20; REEMB 1:20
After-dinner address at a Masonic banquet. AMEO 2:42
After-dinner address at insurance banquet. AMEO 2:133
After dinner beginner. SCHS:3
After-dinner humor. NATM: 31
After-dinner remarks. FRIE: 315
After dinner remarks. NAT:1
After dinner speaking program of the 1936 Rocky Mountain Speech Conference. Speeches by the toastmaster and representatives from various colleges. JUD:313-36
After-dinner speech. NATM:4
After dinner speech by an extra speaker. FRIT:30
After dinner speech on everything in general and nothing in particular. DR:237; LU: 1248
After-dinner speeches-ancient and modern. PITT:13-20
After dinner talk. NATS:2
Arnold, E.
Ties of kinship and common speech. REEMA 1:7
Allen, J. M.
Appropriation for a fish hatchery. CHAL 14:126; YE:320
Bald truth. NAT:22
Banquet remarks. NATM:32
Barrett, M.
Music goes 'round and 'round. JUD:117
Barrie, J. M.
Inoffensive gentleman on a magic island. REEM 1:75; REEMB 1:68
Bartlett, W. F.
Speech at Harvard commencement dinner. BAKF: 428
Bassett, L. E.
From dog house to doctorate. MOUG:244; MOUGA: 244
Bede, J. A.
Problems. NESA:112
Brick, A. W., Jr.
After dinner speech on the occasion of accepting a scholarship. JUD:301
Brigance, S.
Landladies. YE:332
Burdette, R. J.
Rise and fall of the mus-

tache. IMMD:273; REEM 8:102; REEMA 4:145; REEMB 13:104

Byrd, M.E.
Hobo hobbies. JUD:301

Candland, H.
Toast to our school. JUD: 227

Chester, C.M.
How liberal is business? SAR:349

Child, R.
Speech of the American Ambassador at a banquet offered by the Associazione Italo-Americana at Rome, June 28, 1923. LINM:386

Choate, J.H.
British Lion and the American Eagle. REEM 1:267; REEMB 1:268
Sons and guests of Harvard. ONEM:631; REEMA 1:187

Clemens, S.L.
Babies. BRAC:311; COP: 669; COPB:696; MO:383; MOA:383; NESA:108; REEM 1:297; REEMA 1: 221; REEMB 1:298
"Littery" episode. ONEM: 645; REEM 1:292; REEMA 1:214; REEMB 1:293
Mistaken identity. REEM 1:302; REEMA 1:223; REEMB 1:303
New England weather. BOU:193; CHAL 12:447; COP:666; COPB:693; DOA:296; HAZO 23:9871; HIB:94; HURG:128; LOMSA:295; MAS 23:9871; REEM 1:288; REEMA 1: 210; REEMB 1:290
Saint Andrew and Saint Mark. REEM 1:286; REEMB 1:287
Woman, God bless her! COP:671; COPB:698; REEM 1:304; REEMA 1: 225; REEMB 1:305

Confessions of a side-line athlete. CON:18

Cox, S.S.
Smith and so forth. REEM 1:351; REEMA 1:286; REEMB 1:352

Crosby, J.
How to get along in a free world without being subpoenaed. BA 1951-52:71; BAAG:381

Curtis, G.W.
Puritan principle: liberty under law. BAKF:430; BRY: 468; BYRA:554; ONEM:573; PAR:359; REEM 1:355; REEMA 1:290

Cynic critic. THOT:97

Dalton, T.
Radio's raucous rattle. JUD: 139

Darlington, T.
Our association: American Climatological and Clinical Association. REEM sup 1: 221; REEMB 6:67

Daugherty, L.A.
Royal road. JUD:209

Davis, R.H.
Recalls when Job Hedges unearthed a speech for all occasions. LINM:65

Depew, C.M.
Mutations of time. REEMA 1:373
Pilgrims in Holland. YE: 324

Dickens, C.
As a literary guest of America. BRYW 4:150; ONEM: 694
Friends across the sea. KNAS:169; KNASA:169; REEM 1:402; REEMA 1:389; REEMB 1:408

Dinner in a foreign land. EDGS:347

Dodds, H.W.
Education and mother government. SAR:103

Dooling, M.T.
On the firing line. WAGN: 267

Drooping wings. THOT:60
Elliott, A.R.
Sandwich-grabber. WERN 54:146
Elliott, E.C.
Qualifications of a college president. BRAC:305
Examples of toastmaster's comment after speeches. FRIT:19, 24, 29, 31
Executive addresses employees at party. DR:26
Fairfield, W.
Whom should the Republicans nominate for the president? JUD:185
A few words by a humorist (the funniest speech on the program). EDGS:344
First after dinner speech. FRIT:17
Fisher, Mrs. J.W.
Praying mantis. BUT:186; BUTB:186
Fisher, M.
Telomaniacs. JUD:147
For a ball supper. BARB:171
For a boat club dinner. BARB:158
For a cotton planters' banquet. BARB:194
For a cricket club dinner. BARB:159
For a grocers' entertainment. BARB:190
For a jockey club dinner. BARB:169
For a lawyer's dinner. BARB:172
For a leather merchant's dinner. BARB:181
For a mercantile banquet. BARB:175
For a printers' banquet. BARB:191
For a railroad directors' dinner. BARB:176
For a shoe trade entertainment. BARB:192
For a telegraphic banquet. BARB:178
For a tobacco trade banquet. BARB:198
For a whist club supper. BARB:165
For today. THOS:116
Fuller, C.D.
Debate judges. JUD:61
Functions of an alumni organization: for the alumni banquet. CON:45
Gannon, R.I.
Abraham Lincoln. ON:356
Gaw, J.G.
Ye olde time forensics. JUD:91
Geren, P.
Secrets of debating. JUD:65
Gildersleeve, B.L.
Teacher to his pupils. REEM sup 1:368; REEMB 6:157
Gillilian, S.W.
After dinner speech before Ohio Society. PEAE:251
Gilmer, Mrs. E.M.
Experiences of a woman columnist. YE:327
Grady, H.W.
New South. BAAMP:180; BOAM:41; BOU:80; BRAC:287; BRIM:301; BRYA:558; BRYW 10:141; CAP:96; CHAL 14:215; CLAW:159; CLAY:248; ESEH:226; FULB:385; HARS:490; HAZO 25:10724; IMMD:263; MAS 25:10724; ONEM:577; ORAMA 2:427; PAR:450; PE:628; PEA:628; PL:686; PROS:64; REEM 2:105; REEMA 8:579; REEMB 2:97; RINM:278; SAA:207; SAC:45; SHAH:496; SHU:45; SHUM:177: SOU 9:374; THOU 1:270, 273
Grant, U.S.
Characteristics of newspaper men. HOA:374; HOAP:261; REEMA 2:559
Grosvenor, E.B.
Memories of my father. YE:329
Hardin, B.L.
Mother Eve. SOU 9:480
Hardin, M.

Truth about lies. JUD:307
Harlan, R.E.
Tragedies of this tournament. JUD:83
Haroldson, W.
Adult education. JUD:177
Harrison, H.T.
Whither midst falling due. HOC:27; ON:156; SAR: 141
Have you tried to live your own life lately? NAT:22
Hay, J.
Omar Khayyam. COP:679; COPB:706; HAZO 24: 10211; MAS 24:10211; REEM 2:179; REEMA 2: 598; REEMB 2:181
Hays, W.H., Jr.
Behind the scenes in Hollywood. JUD:263
Hazlit, W.
On wit and humor. BREW 6:412
Helburn, T.
Theater versus pictures. GA:109
Here comes the bull. NAT:21
Higdon, H.
Desirability of war. JUD: 281
Hole, S.R.
With brains, Sir! REEMA 2:622
Holmes, O.W., Jr.
Speech at a Bar dinner. ONEM:624; ONES:218
How to make a hole in one. CON:24
Howie, R.
This tournament. JUD:77
Howland, H.E.
Our ancestors and ourselves. REEM 2:247; REEMA 2:661; REEMB 2:251
Hull, C.
Happy mean. SAR:154
Hunt, L.B.
Maiden speeches. JUD:43
Huxley, T.H.
Science and art. COP:655; COPB:682; REEM 2:262; REEMA 2:670; REEMB 2: 266
Imrie, N.A.
Give and take. EXEE:377
Jackson, J.
In behalf of the Kaghlir pledges. JUD:223
Kildee, R.
Speech for honors day banquet. JUD:199
Kooker, E.M.
Response to welcome of honor students. JUD:203
Landis, F.
Witty after-dinner speech on Will Hays. BRAC:302; LY: 213; NESA:185
Last speaker. SCHS:256
Lawrence, E.G.
Our country. LA:176
Longden, Mrs. J.
New steel world. BUT:187; BUTB:187
Lowell, J.R.
After-dinner speaking. BOU: 189; COP:619; COPB:659; KLEM:29; REEM 2:359; REEMA 2:750; REEMB 2: 372
Ludlum, M.E.
My experiences as a teacher. YE:334
Luther, Mrs. L.
Political implications of Mother Goose. BUT:182; BUTB:182
Luxuries a Christian cannot afford. THOT:68
Lytton, H.B.
After dinner speech. KLEG: 150
McCormick, A.H.
Crime prevention through probation. HOC:29; SAR:316
McKelway, St. C.
Smashed crockery. ONEM: 649; ONES:227; REEMA 2: 807
Makar, J.
Bald head and a mustache. JUD:53
Marx, K.

Gives an after dinner speech. PE:475; PEA:475
Matthews, B.
Mark Twain as speechmaker and storyteller. DOA:295
Maxwell, K. L.
What college has done for me. JUD:215
Million dollars worth of assets. THOT:24
Morley of Blackburn. J. M.
Testifying. REEM 2:426; REEMB 2:442
Morris, M. H.
Conquering West. BUT: 180; BUTB:180
Morrow, E. P.
Cost of heritage. BRAC: 279
Observations on our times. FRIE:321
Outline on after dinner speaking. BAKS:180
Phillips, C. R.
On berth control. JUD:133
Phillips, L. M.
Today's challenge to women. GA:102
Platt, H. G.
Speech at banquet for Chauncey Depew. WAGN: 216
Poetic effusion. THOS:118
Porter, A. J., Jr.
Southern chivalry enemy number one. JUD:153
Porter, H.
Woman. ANDS:208; COP: 651; COPB:678; KLEM: 100; ONEM:653; REEM 3:84; REEMA 3:913; REEMB 3:85
Purcell, J. E. and others.
Greetings from Mexico. JUD:107
Raether, H. C.
Speech of tomorrow. JUD: 99
Raish, D. R.
Once in a lifetime. JUD: 191
Reid, W.
At the dinner in his honor. REEM 3:139; REEMB 3:140
Relief worker. SCHS:218
Restful occasion. THOS:116
Retort instant. SCHS:224
Ritchie, A. C.
Which way America? SAR: 139
Rogers, W.
Settling the corset problem of this country. NESA:197
Roosa, D. B. St. J.
Salt of the earth. REEM 3: 146; REEMA 3:992; REEMB 3:149
Roosevelt, E. A.
Banquet address. GA:105
Root, E.
At a luncheon given by General Brusiloff. REEM 3:162; REEMB 3:165
Rose, G. B.
Home brew. NESA:126
Rowe, M. J.
Youth and the depression. JUD:241
Sample form for speech outline -informative, persuasive, or entertaining speeches. BUT: 49; BUTA:49; BUTB:49
Sayre, F. B.
Challenge of international law. SAR:273
Schurz, C.
Old world and the new. COP: 656; COPB:683; HURG:135; REEM 3:192; REEMA 3:1036; REEMB 3:199
Second after dinner speech. FRIT:21
Simpson, H.
Decline of the writer. GA: 116
Smith, A. E.
Fashions in love. JUD:159
Smith, C. E.
President's prelude. REEM 3:227; REEMA 3:1062; REEMB 3:244
Smuts, J. C.
British Commonwealth of Nations. ONEM:603; REEM 3: 237; REEMB 3:254

Snake bites. THOT:81
Some A B C directions for making speeches, toasts and responses. PITT:32-36
Soul of America - God. THOT:114
Speech at a base-ball dinner. HILL:479
Speech at a printer's dinner. HILL:484
Speech at the annual dinner of a militia company. BARB:155
Speech for a bachelor's dinner. BARB:160
Speech for a baseball dinner. BARB:156
Speech for a workingmen's banquet. BARB:174
Speech for an oyster and champagne supper. BARB:166
Stag party, by one of the guests. EDGS:335
Sportsmanship. CON:14
Steele, S.
Emcee at a banquet. BRH:320
Stegall, F.
Sport broadcast of a contest debate. JUD:73
Stepp, J. M.
If I were a candidate for the presidency. JUD:171
Stewardship fantasy. THOT:49
Studebaker, J. M.
Greetings to the Association of Land-Grant Colleges and Universities. YE:311
Sudow, M.
Masters of men. JUD:165
Suggestions for preparation of after-dinner speeches or speeches after dinner. BRAB:505; MICS:198; MOUG:153; MOUGA:153-6
Suggestions for preparation of the after dinner speech or speeches of entertainment. BRA:517; BRY:379, 381; LARW:114; REAB:149; With examples of: BRYA:410,412; BUT:74,176; BUTA:74; BUTB:74,176; CON:13; GA:98; GLAD:176; HIBS:282; HOC:86; MO:372,540; YE:316
Sumner, C.
Qualities that win. KLEG:153; KLEM:71; REEM 3:292; REEMA 3:1115; REEMB 3:309
Take along a bit of honey. THOT:15
Talmadge, T. D.
Behold the American. COP:646; KLEG:160; REEM 3:307; REEMA 3:1122; REEMB 3:324; THOU 1:339
Tarkington, B.
Where we come from. YE:318
Taylor, L.
Shrimps (short people). JUD:117
Thackeray, W. M.
On charity and humor. BRYW:4:201; CHAL 8:325; MAS:17; 7136; HAZO 17:7136
That odd creater, the preacher. THOT:90
Third after dinner speech. FRIT:25
To the doctors. CON:38
To the gentlemen: for a ladies' banquet. CON:41
To the ladies: for a man's banquet. CON:35
Tribute to the boss at the annual office banquet. DR:19; LU:1124
Tucker, H. E.
Depression versus youth. JUD:235
Typical luncheon timetable with examples of opening remarks, introductions, tributes and closing remarks. SUM:167-175
Van Dyke, H.
Typical Dutchman. DOA:301;

AFTER DINNER SPEECHES(cont.)
ONEM:641; ONES:232; REEM 3:347; REEMA 1: 418; REEMB 3:363
Warning, flying rocks. THOT:74
Waters, R.
After dinner speaking. WERN:54:145
Watterson, H.
Puritan and the Cavalier. BRAC:297; COP:675; COPB:702; ONEM:627; ONES:222; REEM 3:359; REEMA 3:1191; REEMB 3:375; SHUM:237
Whalen, R. S.
Give us a break. JUD: 255
What do you want for Christmas? THOT:31
What I believe about people. THOT:106
Wieferich, R.
Youth and the depression. JUD:247
Willis, E. E.
Colleges for cabbage. JUD:111
Wilson, M. E.
Stage fright. JUD:49
Wilson, W.
At Lotus Club dinner, 1906. NESA:169
World today. NATT:29
World's greatest things. THOT:39
"You pay too damn much." NAT:12
Young, O. D.
Courage for the future. HOC:29; SAR:9
See also Debates and debating; Dinners and dining; Emcees; Introductions; Public speaking; Toastmasters; Toasts. Also types of banquets, i. e. Employees; Showers; Surprise parties; etc.

Agar, Herbert
Program for the citizens of a democracy. NORR 3d ser:71

Agassiz, Louis Jean Rodolphe
Man and monkeys. REEMA 4:1

AGASSIZ, LOUIS
Wager, R.
Agassiz, a great teacher. WERN 54:59

Age See Age and employment; Aged-Medical care; Old age; Youth

AGE AND EMPLOYMENT
After 40-the best years. NAT: 2
Mead, J. M.
Older worker. ON:247
Annis, E. R.
Medical care through social security: why it should not be supported. HIB:312
Kennedy, J. F.
Medical care through social security: why it should be supported. HIB:305

Aggert, Otis, Jr.
Shadows. YR10:227

Agricola.
To his army in Scotland. BRYW 2:253; LEEW 2:260

AGRICOLA.
Tacitus. On the death of Agricola. LEEW 2:263

AGRICULTURAL ADMINISTRATION-UNITED STATES
Benson, E. T.
Farm surpluses and the soil bank. BA 1955-56:90

AGRICULTURE
Brannon, C. F.
Farm plan for the future. BA 1949-50:203
Cardon, P. V.
Some American agricultural policies and their impact on foreign relations. IOCP:115
Clifford, J.
Farmer's song. THOU 2:227
Cobden, R.
Effects of protection in ag-

riculture. ADR 3:109; BEA:129; BRYW 4:156; COP:179; COPA:179; COPB:179; HAY:186; ORBR 2:187; PAUF 1:312; PL:465

Coolidge, C.
Vetoing the farmer: Non-planning as a way of life. FIP:160

Everett, E.
Vegetable and mineral gold. REEMA 8:456; LAD:137

Farm relief (suitable for Grange and other community occasions). EDGS:150

Farming (solution of the farm problem). ED:162

Grady, H. W.
Farmer and the cities. SHAH:517

Gunning, J.
First in agriculture. YR 10:159

Hensrud, R.
Introducing a commissioner of agriculture or county agent. BRC:314

Hillman, S.
Agriculture, industry, and labor. BA 1938-39:142

Huber, A. L.
Introducing a cattle raiser. BRC:247

Huntington, H.
Introducing a farm bureau or farmer's union man. BRC:320

Inciong, D.
Necessity for trained farmers. YR 10:169

Jefferson, J.
My farm in Jersey. REEM 2:275; REEMA 2:688; REEMB 2:279

Kaser, A. L.
Introducing a farmer or agricultural expert
Introducing a speaker on animal husbandry.
BRC:95, 107

Kline, A. B.
Long range farm program. BA 1949-50:196

Lacey, J. J.
Farmers need public understanding. SAB:143; SABA:236

Lowden, F. O.
Plea for the farmer. REEM sup 2:178; REEMB 2:351

Mast, C. L., Jr.
Will a million members be enough? SAC:93

Miller, M. G.
Introduces Charles F. Brannon, Secretary of Agriculture. PRNE:25

Modern farming for modern living. NAT:30

Morgan, N.
When men decay. YR 10:175

Mowrer, J. M.
Great future. BU:170

Parson, E.
Future of the American farmers. DOA:95

Pedrick, W.
Tantalus. YR 8:113

Posner, G. A.
Introducing a farmer. BRC:296

Roosevelt, F. D.
Broadcast on the 9th anniversary of the National Farm Program. VO 1942-43:194
Fireside chat: AAA and NRA: July 24, 1933. FIP:206

Sevareid, E.
Vanishing family farm. BRAP:140

Speech at a county agriculture fair. HILL:487

Truman, H. S.
Message to Congress September 6, 1945. VO1945-46:546

Vail, T. N.
Lifc on the farm. REEM 6:401; REEMB 7:403

Wallace, H. A.
Community of interest between labor, capital, and agriculture. BA 1937-38:146

AGRICULTURE (cont.)
Tenant farming and its evils. SAR:332
Webster, D.
To the Royal Agriculture Society. KNAS:290; KNASA:290
What a Farm Bureau can do for farmers. AMEO 2:166
See also Dairying; Food
Ahrend, Herbert G. See Young, B., jt. auth.
Ahrendts, Harold
Illinois disease. YR 9:145
Aiken, D.D.
Certified conditions. THOU 3:422
Aiken, Frederick A.
Defense of Mrs. Mary E. Surratt. BREW 1:109
Aiken, George D.
Off-shore oil Bill. BA 1953-54:60
Ainslie, George
Welcome to Richmond. ONES:22

AIR - POLLUTION
Commoner, B.
Scientific statesmanship. BA 1962-63:68

AIRPORTS See Aeronautics

AIRSHIPS See Aeronautics
Akaka, Abraham Kahikina
Aloha Ke Akua. BA 1959-60: 46

ALAMO
Lawrence E. G.
Fall of the Alamo. LA: 163

ALASKA
Gruening, E.
Independence Day address. BA 1959-60:31
LaFollette, R.M.
Alaska; the nation's storehouse. PEAE:129
Stuck, H.
Alaska, fish and Indians. REEM 3:284; REEMB 3:301
Williams, C.C.
Blazing an international trail by motorcycle. BART 2:231

ALBANIA See Communism-Albania
Albert I, King of the Belgians
Belgium ready. REEM 11:36; REEMB 12:39
Albert Honoré Charles Grimaldi, Prince of Monaco
Two months in the United States. REEM 2:418; REEMB 2:434
Albertson, Charles Carrol
Gather inspirations from the past. WERN 42:93
Albertus Magnus, bp. of Ratisbon
Blessed dead. BREW 1:138
Meaning of the Crucifixion. BREW 1:136
Alcibiades.
In support of the Athenian expedition to Sicily. BRYW 1: 41; HAZO 1:137; MAS 1:137
To the Spartans. BRYW 1:47

ALCIDIADES
Andocides. Against Alcidiades. MINA 1:542

ALCOHOLISM
Dailey, B.
Den of youth. BRP 10:82
Karos, P.A.
Haven of the defeated. ARNS:160; NOR 1950:187
Lindquist, C.
Liquor problem and youth. BRP 10:68
Simmons, G.
Cocktail hour. YR8:39
Tyler, F.
Sovereign alchemist. NOR 1948:139
Alderman, Edwin Anderson
Farewell to the class of 1920. ONEM:687; ONES:33; SHU: 20
Greetings to John Hopkins. ONES:82
Leaders of public spirit.-Same as his Farewell to the class

Alderman, E. A. (cont.)
of 1920
Making of a national spirit. REEM 1:32; REEMB 1:35
New England and the South. - Same as his Sectionalism and nationality.
Sectionalism and nationality. REEM 1:40
University of Virginia in the life of the nation: inaugural address as president of University of Virginia. WE 2:73
Virginia. REEM 1:23; REEMB 1:26
Woodrow Wilson. HICF:702; LINM:186; REEM sup 1:21; REEMB 9:6
Aldrich, Winthrop W.
Free enterprise and "planned economy." COP:434; COPA: 434
Alessandroni, Venan
Curbing the Supreme Court. YR 8:153
Alexander, Charlton H.
Majesty of law. SHUO:54
Alexander, Sir Harold Rupert Leofric George
Broadcast to the people of Rome. VO 1944-45: 256
Alexander, Magus Washington
Citizenship. REEM 7:3; REEMB 8:3
Alexander, Ruth
Religion as a force in government. BART 1:173
Which way America? BA 1948-49:145

ALEXANDRA, QUEEN CONSORT OF EDWARD VII OF ENGLAND
MacDonald, J. R.
Tribute to Queen Alexandra. YE:103
Alfaro, Rucardo
What will Latin America do? BART 4:281

ALIEN AND SEDITION LAWS, 1798
Dickerson, M.
Alien and Sedition Acts of the Adams administration. BREW 5:212
Livingston, E.
On the Alien Bill. HAZO 9:3552; MAS 9:3552
Nicholas, J.
On the proposed repeal of the Sedition law. JOHA 1 pt 1:131

ALIENS
Fields, H.
Alien in our midst. SAR: 320
See also Japanese in the United States
Allen, Ethan
Call to arms (1861). BREW 1: 139
Allen, Florence E.
Challenge to the citizen. BA 1960-61:100
Women and world peace. REEM sup 1:50; REEMB 6:1
Allen, George T.
Washington and Lincoln's part in the Emancipation. THOU 1:261
Allen, Gracie
Response to tributes at Friars' Club dinner. JEYO:111
See also Burns, G.
Allen, Henry Justin
Are European isms taking root in Western democracy? BART 1:353
Kansas Industrial Court. REEM 7:9; REEMB 8:9

ALLEN, HENRY JUSTIN
Price, C. E.
Kansas and its governor. REEM 3:112; REEMB 3:113
Allen, John G., Jr.
Shall we make a rendezvous with death? YR 7:281
Allen, John M.
Appropriation for a fish hatchery. CHAL 14:126; YE:320
Great Mississippi Valley. SHUO:183

Allen, Shirley W.
Conservation of our natural resources. SHUC:207
Allen, William Philip
Speech from dock. KET:365
Allenby, Edmund
Opening the Hebrew University at Jerusalem. REEM 9:281; REEMB 7:33

ALLIED MILITARY GOVERNMENT
Eden, A.
Address in the House of Commons, September 22, 1943. VO 1943-44:405
Eisenhower, D. D.
Announces establishment of Allied Military Government (AMG) to rule occupied Germany. VO 1944-45:420
Statement covering activities of the Allied Military Government in Germany. VO 1944-45:430
Havighurst, R. J. and others.
What should America do now in Bizonia? MO:621
See also Berlin Conference, 1945; Council of Foreign Ministers; Moscow Conference of Foreign Ministers, 1945

ALSACE
Gambetta, L.
Address to the Delegation from Alsace. COP:109; COPA:109; COPB:109; LEEW 5:259; REEM 9:281; REEMA 13:1037; REEMB 10:289
Alseth, C. A.
Lions of the North. COUW:195

ALTAR CLOTHS See Acceptance speeches-Altar cloths; Presentation speeches-Altar cloths
Altgeld, John Peter
Children of toil. HICF:156
On municipal and governmental ownership. BRYW 10:208; REEM 10:344; REEMB 11:358

ALTGELD, JOHN PETER
Douglas, P. H.
Five great Americans. BA 1951-52:85
John Peter Altgeld and the Bill of Rights. BA 1947-48:207
Alton, Baxter
Introducing an insurance salesman. BRC:199
Alton, Horace
Introducing a shoe salesman (traveling). BRC:228

ALUMNI See Reunions, class
Aly, Bower
Remarks on Jefferson Day. BA 1955-56:59
See also McBurney, J. H., jt. auth.

AMATEURS
Perry, B
Amateur spirit. NORR 1st ser:263

AMBASSADORS
Child, R. W.
Speech of the American Ambassador at a banquet offered by the Associazione Italo-Americana at Rome, June 28, 1923. LINM:386
Collins, A.
Introducing an ambassador (British) or diplomat. BRC:277
Harvey, G.
Confirming an ambassador. REEM 2:170; REEMB 2:172
Leverone, N.
Introduces Billy B. Van, "Ambassador of good-will from New England." PR:74

AMBITION
Jerome, J. K.
Ambition. SHU:221
Ambrose, Saint
Funeral oration on his brother.

Ambrose, Saint (cont.)
HAZO 3:1154; MAS 3:1154
Sermon against Auxentius. LEEW 3:249
Sermon on belief in the resurrection. PL:176

AMERICA See United States

AMERICAN EDUCATION AWARD
Campbell, J. A.
American Education award. BA1939-40:364
Graham, B.
Presenting the American Education award to W. L. Phelps. BA 1939-40:364
Phelps, W. L.
Acceptance of American Education award. BA 1939-40:364

AMERICAN FEDERATION OF LABOR
Gompers, S.
American Federation of Labor. REEM 4:156; REEMB 4:299

Green, W.
Acceptance of the presidency of the American Federation of Labor. LINM:61
Labor, freedom and democracy. BA 1940-41:243
See also Labor unions

AMERICAN FORUM OF THE AIR
Reynolds, R. B.
Origin and character of the American forum of the air. BA 1939-40:86

AMERICAN LEGION
American Legion. NATS:29
Coolidge, C.
American Legion. BLAB: 309
Hergenroeder, P. J.
In the service of our country. NOR 1935:130
Local American Legion post reaffirms its pledge of service. DR:202; LU:1233
Owsley, A.
American Legion and the nation. REEM 7:303; REEMB 8:323
Stevenson, A. E.
Speech to the American Legion. BRY:471
Truman, H. S.
Slandermongers and the Bill of Rights. BA 1951-52:65
See also Service men's posts.

AMERICAN MEDICAL ASSOCIATION
Henderson, E. L.
American Medical Association presidential inaugural address. HAR:337

AMERICAN PHARMACEUTICAL ASSOCIATION
Gregg, H. H.
Accepting the presidency of the American Pharmaceutical Association. SAB:217; SABA:299

AMERICAN WAR MOTHERS See Club speeches

AMERICAN WAY See United States-Economic policy

AMERICANISM See Citizenship; National characteristics, American; Nationalism-United States

Amery, Leopold Stennett
Broadcast, August 9, 1942. VO 1942-43:434
Famine conditions in India. VO 1943-44:439
Speech in Parliament for India. VO 1943-44:132

Ames, Bayard H.
Castelar. TRUW:82

Ames, Fisher
Biennial election. CHEM 1:279
Eulogy on Washington, 1800. HELE:113; LEEW 9:41; THOU 1:161
Jay Treaty. BREW 1:145; BRYW 8:155; CHAL 4:12;

Ames, Fisher (cont.)
HARS:128; HAZO 8:3268; JOHA 1 pt. 1:112; LAD:128; MAS 8:3264; ORAMA 1:269; PL:593; REEMA 11:43; SHAH:55
Ames, Kenneth
America beware. BRP 8:50; YR 9:79
Ames, Oliver
Address of greeting. THOU 3:493
Amidon, Jeanette
Tragedy of incomplete thinking. BRP 6:95; YR 7:223
Ammoun, Fuad
Inaugural speech at Conference on the Problems of Economic Development. UAR: 25
Speech at final session of Conference on the Problems of Economic Development. UAR:403

AMNESTY
Amory, Heathcote
Addresses the American Chamber of Commerce in London. PRNE:55
Schurz, C.
General amnesty. BAKF: 353; BRYW 10:27; HARS: 469; ONEM:272; PAR:381; RINM:93
Amos, Milbourne B.
Crash (1929). BLUE:39
October. YR 3:29

AMUNDSEN, ROALD
Hauge, G.
Roald Amundsen. YR 4:273

ANALOGY
Wayland, F.
Philosophy of analogy. BL: 344

ANARCHISM AND ANARCHISTS
Abbott, L.
Cure for anarchism. BLAA:158; BLAB:158
Goldman, E.
Anarchy vs. patriotism. HURG:166
Seelye, L. C.
State versus anarchy. BLAA: 250; BLAB:250

ANCIENT ORDER OF FORESTERS
See Foresters, Ancient Order of

ANCIENT ORDER OF HIBERNIANS See Hibernians, Ancient Order of

ANCIENT ORDER OF UNITED WORKMEN See United Workmen, Ancient Order of
Anderson, Archer
Lee's statue in Richmond. SMI:175
Anderson, Charles W.
Limitless possibilities of the Negro race. DUNM:211
Anderson, Eugenie
July fourth address (1951). BUT:248
Anderson, Frances
I discover America. AN:45
Anderson, Joseph G.
Church, the greatest conservative force. CATA 2:120
Anderson, Louis R.
Prisoner at the bar. YR 1:113
Anderson, Marian
Committee IV, on the report of the Trustee Council. HILK: 222
Anderson, Martin Brewer
Genius and achievement of Morse. REEMA 7:40
Anderson, Mary
Peculiar problems of women workers. GA:133
Anderson, Paul E.
Press despotism. YR 2:163
Anderson, Stuart
Technocracy passes. BRP 4:59; INTW 1933:19; YR 5:231
Andocides.
Against Alcidiades. MINA 1:542
Fragments. MINA 1:580
On his return. MINA 1:462
On the mysteries. CHAL 1:65; HAZO 1:103; LEEW 1:71

Andocides (cont.)
MAS 1:103; MINA 1:338
On the peace with Sparta.
MINA 1:498
Andrew, John Albion
Accepting the battle flags.
CHAL 9:311; HAZO 19:
7896; MAS 19:7896; ONEM:
712
Eve of war. CHAL 9:295;
HAZO19:7879; MAS 19:7879
In honor of patriot heroes.
CHAL 9:304; HAZO 19:7888;
MAS 19:7888
Valedictory to two branches of
the legislature on retiring
from office. CHAL 9:313;
HAZO 19:7897; MAS 19:
7897
Andrews, Charles McLean
Present-day thoughts on the
American Revolution. NORR
2d ser: 320
Andrews, E. G.
Dedication of Embury Chapel,
Brooklyn. THOU 2:460
Andrews, Elisha Benjamin
Inaugural address as president
of Nebraska University.
WE 2:301
Social plaint. NORR 1st ser:
216
Andrews, Mary R. S.
Perfect tribute. PROS:80

ANESTHESIA
Krantz, J., Jr.
Anesthesia-man's redemption from pain. MCK:150
Angell, James Burrill
Inaugural address as president
of University of Michigan.
WE 2:47
New era in higher education.
BLAA:98; BLAB:98;
REAC:110
War and arbitration. FUL:7, 9
Angell, James Rowland
National morality.
REEM 1:52; REEMB 1:43
Angell, James W.
Presents Harry J. Carman.
LY:116

ANGLO-AMERICAN UNION (Proposed)
Thompson, D. and others.
Should the English-speaking
democracies unite now? BA
1940-41: 209

ANIMAL HUSBANDRY See Agriculture

ANIMAL IMITATOR OR ANIMAL
TRAINER See Actors and
acting.

ANIMALS
Huber, L. J.
Animal-loving emcee. BRH:
346
See also Hunters and hunting
Annis, Edward Roland
Medical care through social
security: why it should not
be supported. HIB:312

ANNIVERSARIES
Adams, J. Q.
Jubilee of the Constitution
(50th) BREW 1:74; HAZO 9:
3698; MAS 9:3698; REEM 10:
68; REEMA 11:8; REEMB
11:69
Address for Odd Fellows anniversary. AMEO 2:25
Albertson, C. C.
Gather inspiration from the
past. WERN 42:93
Alumni day-alumnus of ten
years greets his class. DR:
71; LU:1149
Anniversaries (for a wedding or
birthday anniversary). ED:
345
Anniversary of a magazine
(25th) BEC:150
Anniversary of an organization.
BEC:150
Austin, A.
Chaucer (at 500th anniversary of his death). REEMA
7:45
Baldwin, S. B.
Kellogg Pact (10th anniversary of League of Nations)

BEA:17
Barnett, A. E.
Masonry triumphant (anniversary sermon). THOU 3: 70
Baruch, B.
Woodrow Wilson (commemorating centennial anniversary of birth of Wilson). BA 1956-57:141
Beck, R. J.
Salute to General Motors-50th anniversary. SABA: 292
Beecher, H.W.
Religious freedom (68th anniversary of New England Society). BEA:31; REEM 1:92; REEMA 1:41; REEMB 1:87
Belasco, D.
Forty years a theatrical producer. GLAD:168; REEM 1:110; REEMB 1:105
Browder, E.
Soviet Union (21st anniversary). SAR:163
Brown, H. A.
Dangers of the present: delivered at the centennial of the First Colonial Congress. BREW 2:285
One century's achievement (Valley Forge centennial). BREW 2:283
Bryant, W. C.
Fiftieth anniversary of the Mercantile Library Association. HAZO 12:5211; MAS 12:5211
Business anniversary by a popular employee. EDGS: 125
Butler, N. M.
New critics of democracy (at 184th birthday of T. Jefferson). ONEC:103
Will to peace (7th anniversary of the League of Nations). BRAC:325
Cable, C.
Sovereign Grand Lodge (I. O. O. F. annual address). THOU 3:97
Carty, J.J.
Twenty-five years of research. ONEC:114
Celebrating an anniversary of Women's clubs. SOES:41
Chiang Kai Shek
Message on the thirtieth anniversary of the founding of the Chinese Republic. VO 1941:459
Message to nation on the tenth anniversary of the Monkden incident. VO 1941: 407
Statement on the occasion of the sixth anniversary of the outbreak of war with Japan. VO 1943-44:263
Thirty-second national anniversary message. VO 1943-44:432
Choate, R.
On American nationality (82nd anniversary of American independence). CHAL 6: 318; HAZO 13:5493; MAS 13: 5493
Clapp, E. H.
Annual address to the Sons of Temperance. THOU 3:500
Clark, F. G.
Founder's Day address (Southern University). HILK: 73
Cleveland, G.
Address at 250th anniversary of the settlement of the Jews in the United States. TWJ: 11
Influence of universities (Sesquicentennial anniversary of signing of charter of College of New Jersey). BAKF: 187; BOB:185; REEMA 7: 249
Clifford, V.
Emcee at a school centennial. BRH:236
Cohen, S.S.
Way in the sea and a path in the mighty waters. TWJ:106

ANNIVERSARIES (cont.)
Compton, K. T.
Electron, its intellectual and social significance (30th anniversary of discovery of electron) SAR:363
Conant, J. B.
Address of welcome; tercentenary conference at Harvard University. ON:39; SAR:111
Skeptical chemist looks into the crystal ball (diamond jubilee of American Chemical Society) BA 1951-52:137
Coolidge, C.
150th anniversary of Philips Academy. CORP:111
Curtis, G. W.
At Concord centennial celebration. BRYW 10:65; CHAL 10:333; CLAY:135; HAZO 20:8668; MAS 20: 8668; SHU:198
Curtis, J. L.
Abraham Lincoln (at centenary of his birth). DUNM: 321
De Gaulle, C.
Address in Tunis on the anniversary of the liberation of Tunisia. VO 1944-45: 201
Depew, C. M.
Example of Washington: centennial of his death. THOU 3:302
Half century with a railroad. REEM 4:86; REEMB 4:171
One hundredth anniversary of Washington's inauguration. HAZO 23:9713; KLEG: 169; MAS 23:9713; RINM: 220
Outline of address at the centennial of capture of André. PITT:87
Diamond jubilee of a church. SCHS:104
Dirksen, E.
At 44th anniversary of Congressional service of Speaker Sam Rayburn. BRAP:137
Douglas, W. O.
John Peter Altgeld and the Bill of Rights (100th anniversary of his birth) BA 1947-48:207
Dunbar, A. M.
Life of social service as exemplified in David Livingstone (at centennary of his birth). DUNM:425
Edison, T. A.
Looking back over forty years. REEM sup 1:276; REEMB 4:209
Emerson, R. W.
Minute-man (at centennial celebration at Concord). HAZO 14:6000; MAS 14: 6000
Oration and response (250th anniversary of the landing of the Pilgrims). BRAR 2: 371
Emrich, R. S.
Greatness of Lincoln (sesquicentennial of Lincoln's birth). BA 1958-59:169
Everett, E.
Patriotic oration (50th anniversary of the independence of the United States of America). CHAL 6:92; HAZO 12: 5148; MAS 12:5148
Fiske, H.
Fifty years of life insurance. BYRA:165; REEM sup 1:320; REEMB 4:266
Franklin, J. H.
Booker T. Washington, the man and the education (Tuskegee Institute Founder's Day Speech). HILK:212
Friedman, L. M.
Address delivered at Faneuil Hall on 250th anniversary of the settlement of the Jews in the United States. TWJ:61
Fullen, J. B.
Many happy returns of the day (75th anniversary of Ohio State University). YE: 303

Gallagher, B.G.
Preface to the study of Utopias (Founders Day lecture on the anniversary of Antioch College). BA 1960-61:201
Gore, A.
At 44th anniversary of Congressional service for Speaker Sam Rayburn. BRAP:136
Granik, T.
Introductory remarks as radio moderator at celebration of 150th anniversary of Bill of Rights. BA 1941-42: 96
Green, W.
Science of labor relations (88th birthday of University of Wisconsin). SAR:353
Greer, D.H.
Address at 250th anniversary of the settlement of the Jews in the United States. TWJ:49
Greetings to individuals and organizations on various anniversaries-seventeen examples. BEB:83-89
Growth and condition of I.O.O.F.: an annual address. THOU 3:94
Guild, C., Jr.
Address delivered at Faneuil Hall on 250th anniversary of the settlement of the Jews in the United States. TWJ:65
Hadley, A.T.
Opening the ceremonies held in observance of a university centennial (Yale Medical School). ONES:67
Hagemann, H.H.
Remarks at Iowa State College centennial. IOCP:17
Hancher, V.M.
Higher education in Iowa (at Founders' Day luncheon-Iowa State College centennial). IOCP:37
Harper, F.E.W.
Address at the centennial anniversary of the Pennsylvania Society for promoting the abolition of slavery. DUNM: 101
Harrison, B.
Plea for patriotism (100th anniversary of Washington's inauguration). ESEH:199
Heller, M.
Address delivered at New Orleans on 250th anniversary of the settlement of the Jews in the United States. TWJ:164
Higgins, F.W.
Address at 250th anniversary of the settlement of the Jews in the United States. TWJ: 23
Hilton, J.H.
Closing remarks at Iowa State College centennial luncheon. IOCP:43
Concluding remarks at Academic symposia-Iowa State College centennial. IOCP: 163
Hitler, A.
Address on eleventh anniversary of the National Socialist regime. VO 1944-45:73
Broadcast on 12th anniversary of National Socialist regime. VO 1945-46:46
Message on the occasion of the 25th anniversary of the announcement of the National Socialist party's program. VO 1945-46:68
Proclamation on the tenth anniversary of his accession to power. VO 1943-44:27
Speech commemorating the twentieth birthday of the Nazi party. CROC:238; VO 1943-44:520
Speech on the 19th anniversary of the 'Beer Hall Putsch." VO 1942-43:610
Hoover, H.C.
Franklin, a characteristic American (100th anniversary of Franklin Institute) HOB:169

ANNIVERSARIES (cont.)
Hoover, H.C.
South, national problem, and the American home (158th anniversary of battle of King's Mountain). HICF: 852
Huber, L. J.
Emcee at an anniversary party. BRH:254
Hughes, C. E.
150th anniversary of the First Congress. BA 1938-39: 161; COP:431; COPA: 431; COPB:424; HURG:237
150th anniversary of the United States Supreme Court. ON:345
Hugo, V. M.
On the centennial of Voltaire's death. BREW 7:98; CHAL 7:1; COP:91; COPA: 91; COPB:91; HAZO 14: 5776; MAS 14:5776; REEM 5:277; REEMA 8:710; REEMB 9:265
Humorous Yankee speech for the anniversary of the landing of the Pilgrims. BARB: 102
Introducing program chairman (at United Nations anniversary ceremony). BEDA: 124
Introduction of Congressman Fess of Ohio (at anniversary of Boston Club) HOA: 369
Johnson, L. B.
At 44th anniversary of Congressional service of Speaker Sam Rayburn. BRAP:136
Jones, L. W.
Spirit of '76 and the barbarian culture (175th anniversary of Phi Beta Kappa) NORR 3d ser:203
Keating, J. T.
Progress of the Order (Hibernian's address at 42nd biennial convention). THOU 3:544
Kirk, G.
Responsibilities of the educated man (at centennial of University of Denver). LINP: 165
Krantz, J., Jr.
Anesthesia-man's redemption from pain (100th anniversary of its discovery). MCK:150
Krauskoff, J.
Jewish Pilgrim fathers. TWJ: 121
Langfitt, J. A.
Twenty-fifth anniversary greeting. THOU 3:350
Langston, J. M.
Address at the centennial of the Pennsylvania Society for promoting the abolition of slavery. DUNM:97
Equality before the law (anniversary of adoption of the Fifteenth Amendment). WOON: 436
Laurier, W.
Queen's diamond jubilee. CHAL 13:379; HAZO 24: 10444; MAS 24:10444
Lawrence, E. G.
Fall of the Alamo (centennial) LA:163
Lively little speech for the 8th of January: anniversary of the battle of New Orleans. BARB:105
Loveless, H. C.
Welcome address at Iowa State College centennial. IOCP:13
Lowell, J. R.
National growth of a century. REEM 2:254; REEMA 2:741; REEMB 2:367
Oration at 250th anniversary of the founding of Harvard College. CHAL 9:354; HAZO 19:7929; MAS 19:7929
Our literature (100th anniversary of Washington's inauguration). BAKF:423; REEMA 2:758
McClellan, G. B.
Address at 250th anniversary

of the settlement of the Jews in the United States. TWJ:26
MacLeish, A.
This cause is our cause (25th anniversary of F. Kirchwey as editor of Nation magazine). BA 1943-44: 243
McGindley, H. A.
Centennial address (Druids) THOU 3:205
Mansfield, M.
At 44th anniversary of Congressional service of Speaker Sam Rayburn. BRAP: 136
Marshall, L.
Address delivered in Albany on 250th anniversary of the settlement of the Jews in the United States. TWJ:93
Mayhew, J.
Discourse on the anniversary of the death of Charles I. HAZO 5:1989; MAS 5: 1989
Memorial speech on the anniversary of the death of a well-known public figure by civic official. WRA:146
Mendes, H. P.
Address at 250th anniversary of the settlement of the Jews in the United States. TWJ:58
Millerand, A.
Semi-centennial of the French Revolution. BREW 8:148; REEM 11:423; REEMB 12:447
Models and outline of an anniversary speech. BAKS:161
Molotov, V. M.
28th anniversary speech. VO 1945-46:676
Moore, C. W.
Universal fraternity of Masonry (at centennial anniversary of Lodge of St. Andrew). REEMA 9:880
Morinère, C. E. de la.
Centennial of the battle of New Orleans. CATA 1:146
Morrill, J. L.
Unchanging challenge-lest we forget (at Iowa State College centennial) IOCP:19
Müller, F. M.
Frankfort to Stratford-on-Avon (Shakespeare tercentenary). KNAS:261; KNASA: 261
Mussolini, B.
Speech to the Chamber of Fasci and Corporations, December 2, 1942 (20th anniversary). VO 1942-43:705
On the anniversary of a Young Men's Christian Association. BARB:143
Opening speech at fifth anniversary of founding of Big Brother Athletic Association. BEDA:110
Opening speech at United Nations anniversary ceremony. BEDA:122
Oppenheimer, J. R.
Prospect in the arts and sciences (at Columbia University bicentennial anniversary celebration). COPB:642; HURG:319
Pardee, G. C.
Address delivered in San Francisco at 250th anniversary of the settlement of the Jews in the United States. TWJ:172
Park, M. E.
Welcome to Bryn Mawr's fiftieth anniversary. GA:22
Phelps, E. J.
Supreme Court and popular sovereignty (at centennial anniversary of organization of Supreme Court of the United States). REEMA 9:955
Phelps, F.
Emcee at a bachelors' club anniversary. BRH:309
Potter, H. C.
Washington and American aristocracy (100th anniversary of Washington's first

ANNIVERSARIES (cont.)
inauguration). BREW 8:365
Preparation of an anniversary speech. CORP:109
Presenting a gift in appreciation of twenty-five years of service. BEB:9
Quincy, J., Jr.
At the second centennial of Boston. BREW 8:402
Rahskoff, H. G.
Speech at mid-century (36th anniversary of Speech Association of America) BA 1950-51:141
Ranson, R. C.
William Lloyd Garrison: a centennial oration: DUNM: 305; WOON:531
Reed, G. S. T. M.
Fifty years of Washington Masonry (semi-centennial address). THOU 3:66
Reed, T. B.
Immortality and good deeds (semi-centennial of Girard College). BLAA:33; BLAB: 33; BREW 9:44; REAC: 103; SHUM:266
Reply of the Worshipful Master (Masonic) to the toast of a Lodge on its twenty-fifth anniversary meeting. EDW: 65
Rice, F. H.
Washington (memorial address at 100th anniversary of his death). THOU 3:298
Roosevelt, F. D.
Address on the seventh anniversary of the government of the Commonwealth of the Philippines. VO 1942-43:670
Bill of Rights address (150th anniversary). VO 1941:622
Broadcast on the 9th anniversary of the National Farm Program. VO 1942-43:194
Statement on the anniversary of the signing of the Declaration by the United Nations. VO 1944-45:4
Root, E.
Seventy-fifth anniversary of the Century Club. REEM 6: 374; REEMB 7:365
Rosebery, A. P. P.
At the Free Trade Hall, at the centenary of the Manchester Chamber of Commerce. BEA:369; PAUF 2: 367
Oration on Robert Burns (delivered before tomb at Dumfries, Scotland). ORBR 2: 409
Sampson, E.
Jane Addams's unfinished business (at Jane Addams centennial observance, Springfield, Illinois). HILK: 294
Sandburg, C.
On Lincoln (at 150th anniversary of Lincoln's birth). HURG:347
Schiff, J. H.
Introduction at the 250th anniversary of the settlement of the Jews in the United States. TWJ:8
Schmitt, W. A.
Centennial oration (Druids). THOU 3:200
Schurman, J. G.
Welcome to Cornell's 25th anniversary. ONES:23
Semmes, T. J.
Personal characteristics of the Chief Justices (at centennial celebration of Supreme Court). REEMA 9:1029
Silver anniversary (of membership in a club). MORA:14
Smith, G.
Lamps of fiction (at centenary of Sir Walter Scott). BREW 9:233; ONEM:541; REEMA 9:1068
Smith, W. B.
Opening of Colonial magazine and guardhouse (250th anniversary of Williamsburg, Va.) YE:201
Social club anniversary (mem-

ber tells a few tales) ED: 383
Stafford, W. P.
College a training school for public service (college sesquicentennial) ONEM: 547; ONES: 120
Stalin, I.
Order of the day, November 7, 1942 (25th anniversary of the Russian revolution) VO 1942-43: 593
Order of the day on the twenty-fifth anniversary of the Red Army. VO 1943-44: 85
Order of the day on the 24th anniversary of the Red Army. VO 1942-43: 170
Order of the day on the 26th anniversary of the October revolution. VO 1943-44: 518
Order of the day on the 26th anniversary of the Red Army. VO 1944-45: 122
Order of the day on the 27th anniversary of the Red Army and Navy. VO 1945-46: 65
Position of Russia, November 6, 1941. HAN: 164
Report on international relations, November 6, 1942 (25th anniversary of Soviet State) VO 1942-43: 582
Report on the 27th anniversary of the Revolution. VO 1944-45: 546
Report on the 26th anniversary of the October revolution. HAN: 232; VO 1943-44: 509
Speech on Red Square on anniversary celebration, November 7, 1941. VO 1941: 480
27th anniversary order of the day. HAN: 288; VO 1944-45: 554
Stevenson, A. E.
There are no Gibraltors. WPRC: 277
Stone, H. F.
Fifty years' work of the United States Supreme Court. HICF: 803
Storrs, R. S.
Rise of constitutional liberty (centennial oration at the Academy of Music, New York). CHAL 10: 101; HAZO 19: 8257; MAS 19: 8257
Straus, O. S.
Address delivered at Faneuil Hall on 250th anniversary of the settlement of the Jews in the United States. REEM 7: 374; REEMB 8: 395; TWJ: 69
Suggestions for preparation of anniversary speech. BRA: 513; LARW: 112. With examples of. CON: 92; GA: 70; GLAD: 167
Suggestions for preparation of speeches commemorating an event or action of the past. BRAB: 500
Suggestions for preparation of speeches to praise the achievements of organizations. With examples of. SABA: 283
Sulzberger, M.
Oration at the 250th anniversary of the settlement of the Jews in the United States. TWJ: 30
Tojo, H.
Radio address on the second anniversary of the Greater East Asia war. VO 1943-44: 573
Tonsor, C.A.
Masonic retrospect. THOU 3: 64
Tribute by contrast (34th anniversary of a sanitarium). NIA: 208
Tribute to the boss at the annual office banquet. LU: 1124
Twenty-five years an employee congratulatory speech by president of company at 25 year club. WRA: 159

ANNIVERSARIES (cont.)
Urey, H. C.
Science and society (at 100th anniversary Academic convocation of Cooper Union for the advancement of science and art) ARNS:79
Valkenberg, J. van
Biennial address of Knights of Pythias. THOU 1:133
Van Dyke, H.
Democratic aristocracy (sesquicentennial of Phi Beta Kappa). BRAC:315; NORR 2d ser:528
Village centenary. SCHS:63
Walters, A.
Abraham Lincoln and fifty years of freedom. DUNM: 325; WOON:554
Warren, E.
Free investigation and faithful experiment (200th anniversary of Columbia University). BA 1953-54:87
Webster, D.
Character of Washington (at centennial anniversary of Washington's birthday). HAZO 10:4400; MAS 10: 4400
Welles, S.
America's foreign policy (25th anniversary of Foreign Policy Assoc.). BA 1943-44:53
Wheeler, B.
United Mine Worker's convention (50th anniversary) BA 1939-40:316
Williams, G.
Fifty years old (Y. M. C. A. talk). THOU 2:493
Willkie, W.
Function of a political party (90th anniversary of the Republican Party). BA 1943-44:267
Winthrop, R. C.
Centennial at Yorktown. HAZO 16:6646; MAS 16:6646
Woodford, S. L.
Greeting from the founders (Cornell University 25th anniversary). ONES:81
Young, O. D.
How we meet ourselves (semi-centennial of Hendrix College). COP:706; COPB: 733; HURG:227
See also Birthdays; Commemorative addresses; Officers, retiring; Retirement. Also names of special days, e. g. Fourth of July

---- WEDDING
Anniversaries (for a wedding or birthday anniversary) ED: 345
Brustat, A. W.
Help in times past (10th wedding anniversary) ACW:152
For a wedding anniversary, and husband's reply. BARB:68-69
Outline of a speech for a wedding anniversary. CARP:13
Toast to wife on wedding anniversary. FRIT:88
Tribute to the celebrating pair on their wedding anniversary. DR:189; LU:1215
Two wedding anniversary speeches by the husband and a guest. BURS:225
Wedding anniversary, by a guest, and response by husband. EDGS:264, 266
See also Responses to congratulations
---- ---- CRYSTAL
Congratulatory remarks for a crystal wedding and response. BARB:75, 78
Crystal wedding, by a guest, and response by husband. EDGS:274, 276
Toasts for a crystal wedding. BARB:208
---- ---- GOLDEN
Gilbert, E. J.
Emcee at a golden wedding anniversary. BRH:214
Golden wedding anniversary. CON:99

Golden wedding anniversary. DR:191
Golden wedding, by a guest, and response by husband. EDGS:280, 281
Hecht, H. L.
Days which the Lord hath made (50th wedding anniversary). ACW:160
Huber, L. J.
Emcee at a golden wedding anniversary. BRH:262
Jessel, G.
Suggestions for preparation of golden wedding anniversary speech, with example of. JEYO:29
Presentation of a bouquet of yellow roses to a bride of fifty years ago. EDGS:282
Ramsey, H.
Introducing a speaker at a golden wedding anniversary party. BRC:127
Riess, O.
Delightful marriage (50th wedding anniversary) ACW: 157
Rossnagel, W. T.
Abide with us (50th wedding anniversary). ACW:165
Royce, B.
Emcee at a golden wedding celebration. BRH:306
Speech for a golden wedding and reply by "happy man." BARB:79-80
Toasts for a golden wedding. BARB:209

---- ---- SILVER
Anniversary celebration remarks. NAT:6
Gilbert, E. J.
Emcee at a silver wedding anniversary. BRH:280
Golden wedding anniversary (with slight variations, this outline may be used to mark a silver anniversary). DR: 191
Huber, L. J.
Emcee at a silver wedding anniversary party. BRH:208
Jessel, G.
Suggestions for preparation of silver wedding anniversary speech, with example of. JEYO:26
Moeller, T. C.
Worthy wedding anniversary observance (25th). ACW:147
Presentation speech at a silver wedding and reply. HILL: 464-465
Reply to presentation speech at a silver wedding. HILL:465
Silver wedding, by a guest and response by husband. EDGS: 277,279
Toasts for a silver wedding. BARB:208
Visk, A. G.
Emcee at a silver wedding anniversary. BRH:313

---- ---- TIN
Address for a tin wedding and bridegroom's acknowledgments. BARB:72, 74
Tin wedding, by a guest, and response by husband. EDGS: 271, 273

---- ---- WOODEN
Bridegroom's response to wooden wedding anniversary speech. PITT:69
Speech at a wooden wedding. HILL:467
Speech at a wooden wedding. THOS:161
Speech for a wooden wedding and bridegroom's reply. BARB:70-71
Suggestions for preparation of wedding anniversary speeches. With example of. PITT:67 (for wooden wedding)
Toasts for a wooden wedding. BARB:207
Wooden anniversary, by a guest and response by husband. EDGS:268, 270

ANNOUNCEMENTS
Announcing a special speaker. WRA:26
Announcing bazaar. NATT:26
Announcing entertainment. WRA:27
Announcing entertainment for father and son night. WRA: 28
Announcing extemporaneous speakers. FRIT:36
Announcing forthcoming convention. WRA:29
Announcing funeral arrangements. WRA:27
Announcing membership drive. WRA:29
Announcing person (to read resolution of sympathy). BED:45; BEDA:86
Announcing program. FRIT:16
Announcing question period. BEDA:69
Examples for announcing the offering. BO:43-46
Examples of announcements for a testimonial dinner:
Testimonial dinner announcement
Request for reservation
Ad for journal
Greeting for journal
Appreciation for good wishes
From guest of honor
Dinner schedule
Reservation acknowledgment
Reservation reminder
Serve on reception committee
Serve as sponsor.
BEC:62-67
Examples of opening and closing announcements. SUM:24
Examples of various types of announcements. BEC:59
Forms of oral announcements. HILL:461
Model and outline for an announcement. BAKS:87, 95
Moran, E. B.
Announcements at time of death of club members-examples of. PR:108
Announcement of birthdays of club members-examples of. PR:107
Notices and announcements of death. BEC:164
Question and answer period. BEDA:71
Speech announcing change of program. HILL:461
Suggestions for preparation of announcements. With examples of: BARR:227; BUT: 43; BUTA:43; BUTB:43; GLAD:164; WRA:22; YE: 349
Trumbull, L.
Announcing the death of Douglas. BREW 9:436
See also Introductions

ANNOUNCERS See Emcees; Radio broadcasting; Television broadcasting

ANNUAL ADDRESSES See Anniversaries
Annunzio, Gabriele d'
To the officers of the Piave. REEM 11:148; REEMB 12: 160
War cry to America. BREW 4: 391
Anselm, Saint
Invocation to the Saviour. HAZO 3:1247; MAS 3:1247
Our Lord walking on the sea. Same as his Sea of Life
Sea of life. BREW 1:154; LEEW 3:335

ANTARCTIC
Byrd, R. E.
Conquering the Antarctic by air. DOA:76
Anthony, Katy V.
Response to address of welcome. YE:169
Anthony, Susan B.
Are women persons? HIBS: 451

Enfranchisement of women. BOU:136; BRYW 10:58; COP:321; COPA:321; COPB:321; HICF:104; HURG:123; PL:691
For the Woman Suffrage Amendment. WPRA:318

ANTHONY, SUSAN B.
Salmon, L. M.
Susan B. Anthony. KNAS: 100; KNASA:100

ANTI-CORN LAW
Rosebery, A. P. P.
At the Free Trade Hall, at the centenary of the Manchester Chamber of Commerce. BEA 369; PAUF 2: 367

ANTIOCH COLLEGE
Gallagher, B. G.
Preface to the study of Utopias (Founders Day lecture at the anniversary of Antioch College). BA 1960-61:201

ANTI-TRUST LAWS See Trusts, Industrial

Antiphon.
Against a step-mother, on a charge of poisoning. FRE: 86; MINA 1:14
First tetralogy; first and second speeches for the defence. MINA 1:58, 76
First tetralogy: anonymous prosecution for murder (first and second speeches). MINA 1:52, 68
Fragments. MINA 1:290
On the choreutes. MINA 1:246
On the murder of Herodes. CHAL 1:18; FRE:63; HAZO 1:55; MAS 1:55; MINA 1: 160; PL:36
Preoration on the murder of Herodes. LEEW 1:61
Second tetralogy: first and second replies to a charge of accidental homicide. MINA 1:90, 108
Second tetralogy; prosecution for accidental homicide (first and second speeches). MINA 1:88, 98
Third tetralogy: first and second replies to a charge of murder, arguing that the accused killed in self-defence. MINA 1:124, 136
Third tetralogy: prosecution for murder of one who pleads that he was acting in self-defence (first and second speeches) MINA 1:120, 130

Antony, Mark
Funeral oration for Julius Caesar: from Shakespeare. COP:58; COPA:58; COPB: 58; HIB:10; LAD:27; REEM 9:43; REEMB 10:44
Funeral oration over the dead body of Caesar. BRYW 2:200

ANTONY, MARK
Cicero, M. T.
First oration against Mark Antony. BRYW 2:148; HAZO 3:911; MAS 3:911; PL:129
Second oration against Mark Antony. BRYW 2:169
Mark Antony. DAVC:43

Apeland, Casper
Welcome to new citizens. PRNE:219

APHORISMS See Proverbs

APOLOGIES
Apology for being unable to sing. BARB:134
Apology for delayed start. NAT:7
Examples of. FRIE: See index

APPALACHIAN FOREST RESERVE See Forests and forestry

APPEASEMENT See Czechoslovakia; International relations; War; World war 1939-1945

Appleby, Paul H. and others (Morton Grodzins and Charner M. Perry)

Complexity of America (Round Table discussion). MOA:627
Applegate, A. Ward
Target practice. YR 1:45
Appleton, Daniel F.
Presenting the Pilgrim statue to the New England Society. KNAS:153; KNASA:153

APPLIANCE DEALERS See Business men

APPOMATOX See United States - History-Civil War
Apponyi, Albert
On the death of Louis Kossuth. BRYW 7:262

APPRECIATION See Thanks
Arabi, Shamsuldin
Inaugural speech at Conference on the Problems of Economic Development. UAR: 231
Speech at final session of Conference on the Problems of Economic Development. UAR:377
Aranha, Oswaldo
New order through the United Nations. COPB:621

ARBITRATION
Butler, N. M.
International conciliation. PEAE:179
Evarts, W. M.
Geneva Tribunal of Arbitration. KNAS:339; KNASA: 339; REEMA 2:448
Faulkinberry, F. A.
International arbitration. SHUC:56
Field, D. D.
On an international code of arbitration. CHAL:7:234; HAZO 15:6121; MAS 15: 6121
Palmerston, H. J. T.
Arbitration. ORBR 2:119
Schurz, C.
International arbitration. SHUM:296

ARBOR DAY
Abbatt, W.
History of trees. THOU 1: 43
Arbor Day a necessity. THOU 1:32
Arbor Day address. AMEO 2: 11
Arbor Day for the Sunday School. THOU 1:40
Arbor Day lessons. THOU 1: 22
Arbor Day (plea for conservation). EDGS:15
Arbor Day proclamation. THOU: 1:21
Arbor Day-the object to be attained. THOU 1:45
Arbor Day-when and how to observe. THOU 1:25
At the tree-planting ceremony on Arbor Day. DR:158; LU: 1084
Beauty and benefits of Arbor Day. THOU 1:30
Cuyler, T. L.
Trees of the Lord. THOU 1: 33
Destruction of forests. THOU 1:31
Higley, W.
Warnings of history (Arbor day address). THOU 1:37
Northrop, B. G.
Arbor Day in schools. THOU 1:18
Observation of tree growth. THOU 1:48
Old custom revived. THOU 1: 39
Skinner, C. R.
Age and growth of trees. THOU 1:46
Value of rural beauty. THOU 1: 29
What trees to plant Arbor Day. THOU 1:27
Wilson, J. L.
Arbor Day, the children's holiday. THOU 1:41
Arch, Joseph
Debate on the question of allotments, January 26, 1886.

PAUF 2:325

ARCHIAS.
Cicero, M. T.
For the poet Archias. BREW 3:363; BRYW 2:131; CHAL 1:343; HAZO 3:875; MAS 3:875

ARCHITECTURE
Gropius, W.
Creative education: key to good architecture and design. BA 1963-64:182
Heckscher, A.
Challenge of ugliness. BA 1961-62:124
McGovern, S.
Introducing an architect. BRC:106
Jeffries, P.
Introducing an architect. BRC:208
Wright, F. L.
On architecture. COPB:633; HURG:241

ARCTIC REGIONS
Stéfansson, V.
Northward course of Empire. EXEE:518

ARGENTINA
Braden, S.
Farewell speech to the Argentine people. ON:323
Escobar, D. A. C.
Speech upon presentation of letters of credence as Ambassador of Argentina to the United States. VO 1944-45:91
Molotov, V. M.
Speech opposing admission of Argentina to the San Francisco conference. VO 1945-46:185
Roosevelt, F. D.
Reply to Ambassador Escobar. VO 1944-45:93

ARGUMENTATIVE SPEAKING
See Debates and debating

Argyll, George Douglas Campbell, 8th Duke of
Eastern question: address in answer to the Queen's speech in 1877. PAUF 2:198
Welcome to Garrison. HAZO 20:8423; MAS 20:8423

ARISTOGITON.
Deinarchus. Against Aristogiton. CHAL 1:250; HAZO 2:649; MAS 2:649; MINA 2:264

ARKANSAS
Change the name of Arkansas! Hell, No! GRIS:27

ARKANSAS, UNIVERSITY OF
Jones, L. W.
Inaugural address as president of Arkansas. We 2:327

Arkwright, Preston S.
Don't hate your customers. SABA:267; SAC:29; YE:305

Arliss, George
Curtain speech.
REEM sup 1:62; REEMB 6:12

Arlt, Carl Tristan
Plea for action. YR 5:115

ARMAMENTS See Conference on Limitations of Armaments, Washington, November 21, 1921; Disarmament; Munitions

ARMIJO, MANUEL
Kearny, S. W. and others.
Armijo is no longer your governor. GRIS:48

ARMISTICE DAY See Unknown soldier; Veterans' Day

Armitage, Thomas
Our national influence. THOU 1 212

ARMORIES, ACCEPTANCE OF
See Acceptance speeches - Armories

Armstrong, Richard H.
Opens his address after he has

Armstrong, R. H. (cont.)
received a flowery introduction. PRNE:60
Response where toastmaster or chairman not only was flowery in his introduction, but gave him titles or offices to which he was not entitled. PRNE:61

ARMY
Army, by an army officer. EDGS:47
Army (soldier defends armed protection). ED:71
Army's all right (by an officer) ED:76
Cockran, W. B.
Evils of a standing army. FUL:61, 64, 68, 71
Collins, A.
Introducing an army officer. BRC:278
Drummond, R.
Emcee at a G. I. homecoming. BRH:299
Huber, L. J.
Soldier emcee. BRH:345
Introducing an officer (prominent citizen presents the colonel) ED:75
Kaser, A. L.
Emcee at an army buddies' reunion. BRH:176
Kirk, L.
Introducing a General. BRC:322
Posner, G. A.
For the emcee at an office party or ceremony honoring a member leaving for army service. BRH:180
Pulteney, W.
Against standing armies (1738). BREW 8:380
Reserve officers. SCHS:222
Response to the toast "The Army." HILL:482
Toast at a military dinner by a soldier. EDGS:53
Wolfe, J.
To his army before Quebec. BRYW 3:191
See also Conscription; Recruiting. Also Names of countries, subhead Army, e. g. United States - Army

ARMY-NAVY MERGER See United States-Army; United States-Navy
Arnall, Ellis
Response to introduction. PR:120

ARNOLD, BENEDICT
Lippard, G.
Black horse and his rider. HARSO:305
Death bed of Benedict Arnold. HARSO:311
Marble, S.
From fame to infamy. COUW:227
Treason of Benedict Arnold. DAVC:105
Arnold, Carroll C.
Speech as a liberal study. ARNS:2
Arnold, Sir Edwin
Ties of kinship and common speech. REEMA 1:7
Arnold, Henry Harley
Our air power. HAN:245
Arnold, Matthew
Numbers; or the majority and the remnant. HAZO 20:8347; REEM 7:23; REEMA 4:27; REEMB 8:23; MAS 20:8347
On Emerson. CHAL 10:126; HAZO 20:8321; MAS 20:8321
Realm of literature. REEMA 1:14
To the Wordsworth Society. KNAS:43; KNASA:43

ARNOLD, MATTHEW
Holmes, O. W.
Introduces Matthew Arnold. REEM 7:23; REEMA 4:27; REEMB 8:23
Shairp, J. C.
Literary theory of culture. REEMA 9:1052
Arnold, Ruby
By rote control. BRP 10:78

Arnold, Thomas
Alive in God. - Same as his Realities of life and death
Realities of life and death. BREW 1:159; CHAL 6:140; HAZO 12:5250; MAS 12:5250
Arnold, Thurman W.
Full production after the war. HOC:166
Arpaia, Anthony
Matter of necessity. LINP:240

ART AND ARTISTS
Appreciation of art. DR:53
Artists, by a fellow artist. EDGS:198
Artists' reunion. Response to the toast "Our Art and Artists." HILL:484
Ball, R.
Kinship of art and science. REEMA 1:16
Bancroft, G.
People in art, government, and religion. BL:94; BRYW 8:230; HAZO 13:5630; LAD:96; MAS 13:5630; REEM sup. 1:88; REEMA 7:69; REEMB 7:55; WPRA:65
Barnard, F. A. P.
Art culture: its relation to national morality. NORR 2d ser:111
Bond, A. D.
Review of "The Arts." GA:220
Bryant, W. C.
Address at the founding of the Metropolitan Art Museum. CHAL 6:134; HAZO 12:5205; MAS 12:5205
Bryson, L. and others.
Opportunities for success in the creative arts. SAR:403
Cousin, V.
Eloquence and the fine arts. BREW 4:186; CHAL 6:1; HAZO 12:5000; MAS 12:5000
Drummond, R.
Introducing a chalk talk artist. BRH:82
Engineers of art. NI:253; NIA:191
Farrar, F. W.
Poet and painter. REEMA 2:479
Fine arts (for a poet, musician, or artist). ED:273
For a reunion of artists. BARB:196
Gladstone, W. E.
Commercial value of artistic excellence. BREW 6:258; CODS:408; CODSA:408
Hart, R.
Introducing an art dealer. BRC:294
Huxley, T. H.
Science and art. COP:655; COPB:682; REEM 2:262; REEMA 2:670; REEMB 2:266
Jebb, R. C.
Literature and art. REEMA 2:686
Jusserand, J. J.
Truth and beauty in books and art. BREW 7:184
Kahn, O. H.
Value of art to the people. LINM:227
Kaser, A. L.
Introducing an artist. BRC:253
Leighton of Stretton, F. L.
Variety in British art. REEMA 2:713
McGovern, S.
Introducing an artist. BRC:189
Morris, W.
Art and beauty of the earth. REEM 6:329; REEMA 9:891; REEMB 7:279
Oppenheimer, J. R.
Prospect in the arts and sciences (at Columbia University bicentennial celebration) COPB:642; HURG:319
Pach, W.
Stake of the arts in the democratic way of life. HAR:398

ART AND ARTISTS (cont.)
Palmerston, H. J. T.
Illusions created by art. REEM 3:39; REEMA 3:876; REEMB 3:39
Phillips, W.
Los arts. CHAL 8:200; HAZO 16:6931; MAS 16: 6931; REEM 8:276; REEMA 6:831; REEMB 13:281
Posner, G. A.
Introducing an artist. BRC: 240
Raffaelli, J. F.
Universality of art. REEMA 9:980
Read, H.
In defense of abstract art. ARNS:57
Rosebery, A. P. P.
Portrait and landscape painting. REEM 3:176; REEMA 3:1008; REEMB 3: 182
Schliemann, H.
Beginnings of art. REEMA 3:1034
Taft, L.
Art and modern life. SAR: 377
Tribute to the fine arts. ED: 276
Two pictures. PROS:56
Tyndall, J.
Art and science. REEM 3: 345; REEMA 3:1160; REEMB 3:361
Value of fine arts. AMEO 2: 173

ARTHRITIS See Medicine

ARTISTS See Art and artists
Ascoli, Max
Scarcity of ideas. ARNS:226
Ashburton, John Dunning, 1st Baron
Right to commit. EMS 1:215
Ashfield, Albert Henry Stanley, 1st Baron
Man and machine in industry. REEM sup 1:64; REEMB 4:1
Ashmore, Harry Scott
Education in a time of testing. BA 1958-59:117
Ashmore, Henry L.
Pursuit of truth. ANGC:44
Ashton, DeWitt C.
Citadel of freedom. BLUE:115

ASIA
Koiso, K.
Speech asking greater East Asia collaboration. VO 1944-45:594
Nehru, J.
Asia finds herself again (inaugurating Asian Conference at New Delhi) COPB:617
Wallace, H. A.
Broadcast from Seattle, Washington. VO 1944-45:300
Werner, J.
Sleeping giant. MIA:333

ASPLEY, J. C.
Moran, E. B.
Introduces J. C. Aspley, chairman of day. PR:101
Asquith, Herbert Henry See Oxford and Asquith, Herbert Henry, 1st Earl of
Asquith, Margot (Tennant) Countess of Oxford and Asquith. See Oxford and Asquith, Margot (Tennant) Countess of

ASSETS See Success

ASSOCIATIONS See also Club speeches; Mutual benefit associations; Trade and professional associations; Also names of associations, e. g. National Education Association
Astor, Nancy Witcher (Langhorne) Viscountess
Reform of the franchise (Women's suffrage) EMS 2:199
Women in politics. COP:207; COPA:207; COPB:207; REEM 7:36; REEMB 6:14

ASTRONAUTICS AND CIVILIZATION
Seaborg, G. T.
United States in the space age. ANGC:124

ASTRONOMY
Payne-Gaposchkin, C.
New light on cosmic history. IOCP:85
Athanasius, Saint
Christ the eternal God. -Same as his Divinity of Christ
Divinity of Christ. BREW 1:181; LEEW 3:73
Third discourse against the Arians. HAZO 3:1121; MAS 3:1121

ATHENOGENES.
Hypereides.
Against Athenogenes. CHAL 1:132; HAZO 1:214; MAS 1:214; MINA 2:430

ATHENS
Andocides.
On the peace with Sparta. MINA 1:498

ATHLETES
Adelman, A.
Merely players. BRP 8:86; NOR 1937:29

ATHLETICS
Address at fifth anniversary of founding of Big Brother Athletic Association. BEDA:111
Athletic club, by a member. EDGS:386
Confessions of a side-line athlete. CON:18
Little, L.
Function of national associations in intercollegiate athletics. GLAD:295
Opening speech at fifth anniversary of founding of Big Brother Athletics Association. BEDA:110
Phelps, F.
Emcee at an athletic banquet. BRH:315
Rockne, K.
Athletics and leadership. EXEE:107
Value of athletics. DR:284

See also Physical education; sports; Toasts
Atkins, Gaius Glenn
Our university. YE:299
Atkinson, John
Welcome to the Society of Certified Public Accountants. LINM:382
Atkinson, Marjorie Louise
Queen takes a king. YR 9:1
Atkinson, Maurice E.
From klansman's robe to justice's gown. YR 10:193
Rivers did not forget. YR 9:61

ATLANTIC (PERIODICAL)
Warner, C. D.
Rice of the "Atlantic." REEMA 3:1186

ATLANTIC CABLE
Field, C.W.
Story of the Atlantic cable. REEM 4:99; REEMA 8:473; REEMB 4:221

ATLANTIC CHARTER See Atlantic Declaration, August 14, 1941
ATLANTIC DECLARATION, AUGUST 14, 1941
Attlee, C.R.
Atlantic Charter. COP:487; COPA:487; COPB:457
Roosevelt, F.D.
Eight common principles for a better world. BA 1941-42:247; FIP:244; VO 1941:379

ATOMIC AGE
Einstein, A.
Peace in the atomic era. BA 1949-50:63; COPB:635; HAR:58
Hutchins, R.M. and others.
America and the atomic

ATOMIC AGE (cont.)
age. HAR:19
Warren, S.
Biology in the atomic age. IOCP:71

ATOMIC BOMB
Attlee, C.R.
Speech in Commons on atomic bomb. VO 1945-46: 743
Byrnes, J.F.
Speech in Charleston on atomic bomb policy. VO 1945-46:719
Churchill, W.L.S. and others.
Statement by Prime Minister Attlee and former Prime Minister Churchill on the atomic bomb. VO 1945-46:413
Gustavson, R.G.
Story behind the atomic bomb. BRA:563
Kaufman, I.J.
Sentencing the atomic bomb spies. BA 1951-52:55
Rutherford, E.
Electrons and atomic explosions. BREW 9:135
Stimson, H.L.
Statement on the atomic bomb. VO 1945-46:407
Truman, H.S.
Announcement of the first use of the atomic bomb. FIP:269; VO 1945-46:405
Message to Congress on the atomic bomb. VO 1945-46: 613
Urey, H.C.
Atom bomb and war. BA 1945-46:95
See also Hydrogen bombs

ATOMIC ENERGY
Baruch, B.M.
International control of atomic energy (June 14, 1946). BA 1945-46:120; BOU:124; COPB:587; HURG:279
Toward effective international atomic energy control (December 5, 1946) GLAD: 235
Cisler, W.L.
Introducing Leland I. Doan, speaker on atomic energy. MOA:500
Compton, A.H.
Social implications of atomic energy. BA 1945-46:109; MO:400; MOA:400
Eisenhower, D.D.
International control of atomic power for peaceful purposes. BA 1953-54:22; COPB:607; FIP:335
Lilienthal, D.E.
Atomic energy. BA 1946-47: 134
Atomic energy-where do we stand today? BA 1947-48: 69
Osborn, F.
United States, Russia, and the atomic bomb. HAR:211
Steele, R.
Introducing an atomic scientist. BRC:316
Taft, R.A.
Against the appointment of Lilienthal. BA 1946-47:113
Vandenberg, A.H.
For the appointment of Lilienthal. BA 1946-47:122
Waymack, W.W.
King of energies. BA 1947-48:80
Weinberg, A.M.
Nuclear energy development and military technology. HAR:321

ATOMIC POWER See Atomic energy

ATOMIC WARFARE
Humphrey, H.H., Jr.
Disarmament in the nuclear age. BA 1959-60:81
Johnson, L.B.
Address to Nation, October 18, 1964. BA 1964-65:45
Kennedy, J.F.

Step toward peace. BA 1963-64:20
McGovern, G.
New perspectives on American security. BA 1963-64:132
Murray, T. E.
Dismantling of the era of terror. BA 1959-60:69

ATOMIC WEAPONS
Lippmann, W.
Frustration of our time. BA 1961-62:162

---- TESTING
Humphrey, H. H., Jr.
Banning nuclear tests. BA 1958-59:48

ATOMS
Millikan, R. A.
Atom. REEM sup 2:230; REEMB 7:272
See also Electrons
Atterbury, William Wallace
Public can secure the railroad service it wants. REEM 4:1; REEMB 4:12
Attlee, Clement R.
Address before Congress. VO 1945-46:705
Address on British demobilization plans. VO 1945-46:536
Atlantic Charter. COP:487; COPA:487; COPB:457
Broadcast on Japan's surrender. VO 1945-46:437
On Bilbao blockade (speech in House of Commons, April 14, 1937) KESK 2:214
Speech in Commons on atomic bomb. VO 1945-46:743
Speech in Commons on the United Nations charter. VO 1945-46:479
Speech on the King's address. VO 1945-46:448
Statement in Commons on termination of lend lease. VO 1945-46:489
See Churchill, W. L. S., jt. auth.

ATTUCKS, CRISPUS
Ruffin, G. L.
Crispus Attucks (commemorative speech on Boston Massacre) DUNM:125

AUCTIONS
Huber, L. J.
Emcee at an auction. BRH:204
Selling goods at auction (the words of the auctioneer) HILL:470
Augus, Tuscarora Nation chief
At a council, Lancaster, 1762. SHE:31
August, Elizabeth P.
Publicity programs and professional consciousness. GA:125
Augustine, Saint
On our Lord's prayer. BREW 1:187; BRYW 7:7; CHAL 1:368; HAZO 3:1187; MAS 3:1187; PL:180; REEM 9:51; REEMB 10:53
Sermon on the remission of sins. LEEW 3:231
Sermon on the transfiguration. LEEW 3:238
Aulish, Felix J.
Welcome to new citizens. SABA:290
AURELIUS, MARCUS
Adler, F.
Marcus Aurelius. REEM 6:14; REEMA 7:23; REEMB 7:14
Auriol, Vincent
Report from the President of France. HAR:230

Aurner, Robert R.
Message of Flanders Fields. ONES:326
Austin, Alfred
Chaucer (at 500th anniversary of his death). REEMA 7:45

AUSTIN, STEPHEN F.
Wallace, R. M.
Stephen F. Austin and Sam Houston (at acceptance of

AUSTIN, STEPHEN F. (cont.)
their statues in Capitol). SHUO:211

Austin, Warren R.
Accusing Chinese communists of intervention in Korea. YE:140
Policies of the United Nations. BA 1946-47:13
United Nations and Korea. BA 1950-51:13

AUSTRALIA
Chamberlain, J.
Speech on the introduction of the Constitution Bill in the House of Commons, May 14, 1900. KES 1:337
See also World War 1939-1945 - Australia

AUSTRIA
Carter, B.
Germany takes Austria. BA 1937-38:97

AUSTRIAN SUCCESSION, WAR OF THE, 1740-1748
Pitt, W., 1708-1778
On motion for an address of thanks after the battle of Dettingen. GOOD:95

AUTHORS AND AUTHORSHIP
See Literature; Negro literature; Poets and poetry

AUTOMATION
McDonald, D.J.
Plan for prosperity. BA 1960-61:156
Outline of speech: Should we endorse the trend toward automation in American industry? BAAGA:307
Snyder, J.I., Jr.
Total challenge of automation. BA 1963-64:154

AUTOMOBILE ACCIDENTS See Automobile drivers; Safety; Traffic accidents

AUTOMOBILE CLUBS
How can an automobile club best serve the state? AMEO 2:50

AUTOMOBILE DRIVERS
Automobiles (back-seat driver). ED:148
Clifford, V.
Emcee at a bus drivers' party. BRH:316
Motoring madness. NAT:32
Safety, a city-wide plea for careful drivers and cautious pedestrians. DR:42

AUTOMOBILE INDUSTRY AND TRADE
Bolden, J.
Introducing an automobile dealer. BRC:254
Collins, A.
Introducing an automobile salesman. BRC:280
Curtice, H.
Administered prices (before U.S. Senate). ARNS:208
Holler, W.E.
Automobile dealer. SAC:88
Jordan, E.S.
Advertising automobiles. REEM sup 2:126; REEMB 5:32
Reuther, W.
Administered prices (before U.S. Senate). ARNS:199

AUTOMOBILES
Automobile manufacturers. SCHS:20
Automobiles: suitable for meetings of automobile clubs or automobile dealers. EDGS:165
Hoffman, P.G.
Prices of things which farmers buy, including so-called management of prices by industry. HUS:255
Outline for a speech "Grand wagon" (station wagon). BARR:65

AUXILIARIES See Club speeches

Avebury, John Lubbock, 1st Baron
Blessing of friends. CHAL 12: 377; HAZO 23:9773; MAS 23:9773
Choice of books. CHAL 12: 365; HAZO 23:9761; MAS 23:9761
Duty of happiness. CHAL 12: 351; HAZO 23:9747; MAS 23:9747
Free libraries (opening a free library at Rotherhithe, England) REEMA 8:808
Hundred best books. BREW 7: 397
Avery, Charles H.
Growth of fraternity. THOU 3: 357

AVIATION See Aeronautics

AWARDS
Material for use in composing awards. BEC:46
See also Acceptance speeches -Rewards (Prizes); American Education Award; Presentation speeches-Rewards (Prizes); Rewards (Prizes)
Axson, Stockton
World and the new generation. REEM 6:33; REEMB 7:34
Ayers, Albert D.
In memory of a pal. NESA: 212
Ayers, J.H. See Lloyd, W. P. jt. auth.
Azeglio, Massimo Yaparelli, Marquis d'
On presenting the estimates for the Ministry of Foreign Affairs. CHAL 6:274; HAZO 13:5420; MAS 13: 5420

AZORES See World War, 1939-1945 - Portugal

BABIES See Children; Showers, baby

BACCALAUREATE ADDRESSES
Baccalaureate sermons: God of the living; Think on these things; Children of God; End of the course. PAIC:343-368
Beecher, H.W.
Perfect manhood; sermon to graduating class of West Point Military Academy. BOU:12; ONEM:741
Brown, C.R.
Life complete. WAGN:270
Compton, K.T.
Stuff of life; our talents and their care. SAR:13
Conant, J.B.
National philosophy. BA 1948-49:165
Statement of faith. HOC:182
Unique idea of American life. BA 1939-40:337
Conwell, R.H.
Men of low estate. WERN 54:23
Cutten, G.B.
Arise, let us go hence. BA 1938-39:210
Dodds, H.W.
Importance of being an individual. BA 1955-56:142
Gilkey, C.W.
Bridges into a better world. BA 1938-39:234
Gunn, J.E.
Riddle of modern unrest. CATA 2:141
Hadley, A.T.
Faith in mankind. KLEM: 177
Spirit of devotion. KLEG:372
Hale, E.E.
"What will he do with it?" REEMA 8:601
Howard, F.W.
Progress true and false. CATA 2:155
Jordan, T.W.
Penalties of progress (baccalaureate address) SHUO: 86
Life university. NIA:155
McArthur, H.K.
Truth and freedom. BA 1950-51:182

BACCALUAREATE ADDRESSES (cont.)
Newton, J. F.
What to do with life today. BA 1945-46:214
Nurses: a baccalaureate address. NI:265; NIA:199
Seeking the abundant life. JA:17
Sense of destiny. JA:14
Taylor, J. M.
First and great commandment (baccalaureate sermon) WERN 54:25
Van Dyke, H.
Salt. BRYA:505; ONEM:732; REEMA 7:380; SHUM:326
Vincent, J. H.
Perfect life. WERN 54:21
Wilson, W.
Be not conformed to this world (baccalaureate sermon). WERN 54:18
See also Commencement addresses
Bacheller, Irving
Sense, common and preferred. REEM 1:64; REEMB 1:55
Yankee. REEM 1:59; REEMB 1:50

BACHELORS
Bachelor's dinner. EDGS:337
Gannett, J.
Emcee at a bachelors' club meeting. BRH:308
Huber, L. J.
Introducing a bachelor. BRH:161
Jessel, G.
Suggestions for preparation of speeches at a bachelor dinner, with examples of. JEYO:23
Phelps, F.
Emcee at a bachelors' club anniversary. BRH:309
Posner, G. A.
For the emcee at a bachelor dinner. BRH:264
Speech for a bachelor's dinner. BARB:160
Speeding the would-be groom to his matrimonial doom at the bachelor dinner. DR:185; LU:1211
Visk, A. G.
Twisted news (to be delivered by an emcee at bachelor parties, bridal parties, or wedding receptions) BRH:328
Bacon, Augustus Octavius
Case of Senator Reed Smoot. SHUO:129
Character and capacity of the Filipinos. REEMA 11:77
Bacon, Francis, Viscount of St. Albans
Against dueling. BREW 1:198
Charge to Justice Hutton. REEM 9:61; REEMB 10:63
On the undertakers. LEEW 6:23
Speech of the three subsidies. BRTH:16; BRTHA:16
Bacon, Leonard
Address, 1838. BRAR 1:165
Grand mission of America. THOU 1:201
Our heritage, how gained-our duty. THOU 1:223
Bacon, Walter S.
Introducing a Catholic priest. BRC:49
Baden-Powell, B. F.S.
Explosives from balloons. BREW 9:298
BADGES See Acceptance speeches-Badges; Presentation speeches-Badges
Baekeland, Leo Hendrick
Engineer. REEM 4:9; REEMB 4:20
Baez, Antonio M.
Constitutional government. LEIO:126
Bagstad, Anna
Goethe. COUW:125
Bagwell, Paul D.
American Swastika. BRP 7:100
Bailey, Isaac H.
Introducing and toasting Charles Sumner at New England Society of N. Y., December

22, 1873. REEM 3:292
Introducing Roscoe Conkling to New England Society of N.Y., December 22, 1874. REEM 1:332; REEMB 1:333
Bailey, Joseph Weldon
Competition (Oleomargarine Bill) HICF:252
Constitutional convention. SHU: 32
Division of Texas. PROS:26; SHUO:221
Porto Rico tariff. REEMA 11: 84
Republic of our fathers. SHU: 146
Bailey, Louise
Case of Mr. James Crow. YR 10:185
Bain, George W.
Life lessons (commencement address at Pierce Business College) SHU:204; SHUO: 237
Platform experience. LINM: 494
Bain, Mary Elizabeth
Possibilities. BOA:167; BOB: 196
Baird, A. Craig
Academic critic's view of General MacArthur's speech to Congress. BRAP:155
Propaganda. ON:244
Responsibilities of free communication. BRAP:150
Baird, Charles Washington
Scholar's duty and opportunities. NORR 2d ser:246
Baker, E.D.
American theatre speech. WAGN:15
Baker, E.E.
Public opinion: its genesis, growth, and value, with an incidental discussion of fashion. WAGN:305
Religion and the nation. WAGN:318
Baker, Edward D.
On suppression of insurrection. BRYW 10:3; CHEM 4:161; JOHA 2 pt. 3:51; SAA:173
Baker, George F.
Presenting the keys of the George F. Baker Foundation to President Lowell. ONEC: 50

BAKER, GEORGE F.
Young, O.D.
Dedication of the George F. Baker Foundation. ONEC:79
Baker, James H.
Phillips Brooks. BLAA:277; BLAB:277
Baker, Newton Diehl
Challenge of America. HICF: 529
League of Nations. WHIP:266
March toward liberty. REEM 11:249; REEMB 12:264
Baker, Smith
Meaning of the Lord's Supper. THOU 2:424

BAKERS AND BAKING
Collins, A.
Introducing a baker. BRC: 304
Bakhmetieff, Boris
New Russia. LEW:145
Bakke, W. Wight
Creative citizenship. ASHF:112
Balch, Durward
Real criminal. BRP 2:45; YR 3:119

BALDNESS See Hair
Baldwin, James and others (Ossie Davis, and John O. Killens)
Negro writer in American society (panel discussion). HILK:357
Baldwin, Reverdy E.
Presenting a chair to a president of a normal college. WERN 54:72
Baldwin, Roger N.
Individual and the state. ONES: 350
Rough road ahead. HAR:437
Baldwin, Stanley Baldwin, 1st Earl of Bewdley
British defence policy (Novem-

Baldwin, Stanley B. (cont.)
ber 18, 1936 speech). KESK 2:175
Collective responsibility of the Ministry. EMS 1:96
Goodwill in industry. REEM sup 1:75; REEMB 4:33
Kellogg Pact (10th anniversary of League of Nations). BEA:17
Protect the democracies. PL: 804
Reform of the franchise (Women's suffrage). EMS 2:202
Romance of the West. HAY: 376

Balfour, Arthur James Balfour, 1st Earl of
Control over foreign policy. EMS 1:255
Cooperation of English-speaking peoples. FKA:322; ONES:317; SHUP:158
Dreadnoughts and dukes. BREW 1:218
Dry humor in Latin. BREW 1:215
Empire and alien domination. BREW 1:216
Fourth of July in London. COP:204; COPA:204; COPB:204; REEM 11:233; REEMBA 12:248
House of Lords and financial measures. EMS 1:174
Imperial relations, December 8, 1926. EMS 2:279
Imperial relations, Jan. 27, 1927 speech. EMS 2:285
Introducing Chief Justice Taft. REEM 1:69; REEMB 1:60
Lords as upholders of government "of, by and for the people." BREW 1:217
Lust of Empire as the cause of catastrophe. BREW 1:207
Oldest free assemblies. LEW: 85
On the Boer War. REEMA 11: 99
Parliament Bill, 1911. EMS 1: 192
Pleasures of reading. BRYW 5:161; CHAL 14:134; HAZO 25:10643; MAS 25:10643; REEM 6:40; REEMA 7:49; REEMB 7:41
Speech at the Washington Conference on the Limitation of Armaments (November 15, 1921) BREW 1:210; REEM 11:390; REEMB 12:409
Speech at the Washington Conference, November 21, 1921 (Resisting domination at any cost) BREW 1:213
Speech at the Washington Conference February 4, 1922 (America's moral power for peace) BREW 1:214

Balghiti, Mostapha El
Inaugural speech at Conference on the Problems of Economic Development. UAR:207
Speech at final session of Conference on the Problems of Economic Development. UAR: 411

Balk, S.
For an orphan to his Bar Mitzva. ZEL:32

Ball, George W.
Reallocation of world responsibilities. BA 1963-64:77

Ball, John
Bondmen and freemen: address to the rebels at Blackheath. BRTH:3; BRTHA:3
We have the pain and travail. CROC:1

Ball, Sir Robert
Kinship of art and science. REEMA 1:16

BALLET See Dancing

BALLINGER-PINCHOT INVESTIGATION
Taft, W. H.
Castastrophe: The Ballinger affair. FIP:77

BALLOONS
International balloon contests. SCHS:158

BALLOT See Elections; Woman-

suffrage
Ballou, Frank W.
Acceptance of a gavel. BRAC: 268
Balmuth, Saul
Man with a hat over his face. YR:6:45

BALZAC, HONORÉ de
Hugo, V.
Oration on Honoré de Balzac. BREW 7:94; CHAL 7:5; HAZO 14:5780; MAS 14:5780
Bancroft, E. A.
Loneliness of genius. HARSO: 98; SHU:139
Bancroft, George
People in art, government, and religion. BL:94; BRYW 8:230; HAZO 13:5630; LAD:96; MAS 13:5630; REEM sup 1:88; REEMA 7:69; REEMB 7:55; WPRA:65
Political career of Andrew Jackson. CHAL 6:416; HAZO 13:5652; MAS 13:5652; REEMA 11:110
William Cullen Bryant. DOA: 265; KNAS:96; KNASA:96; REEMA:18
Bancroft, Wilder D.
Future of chemistry (at dedication of the Chemistry Building of the College of New York City). PEAE:187
Banks, Evald C.
Farewell to a district manager. BRC:325
Introducing a chairman of the day-2 examples of. BRC: 36, 38

BANKS AND BANKING
Address at County Federation Bankers' meeting. AMEO 2:94
Bankers' club. SCHS:30
Benton, T. H.
Against the United States Bank. BREW 2:30
Bones: short and over can mean short of publicity and overlooking a patron (a speech to bank personnel, changeable for many occasions-business meeting or convention of sales personnel, at a graduation of nurses' group, for fund raising drives, to a telephone group, or by a political or labor speaker). BAI:94
Creations: a place, a plan, a pledge (a bank publicity speech for any business group, for a P. T. A. meeting, or for a student body). BAI: 72
Ford, S.
Bank-notes. NESA:131
Run on the banker. REEM 2: 55; REEMA 2:507; REEMB 2:55
Gilbert, E. J.
Introducing a banker-2 examples of. BRC:80, 92
Glass, C.
Banking act. SMI:282
Headley, W. C.
Bank of England. REEM 4: 62; REEMB 4:144
Henderson, T. S.
Banker as a citizen. SHUO: 204
Huber, L. J.
Introducing a financier. BRC: 153
Jackson, A.
Veto message, July 10, 1832. BIR 2:84
Kaser, A. L.
Introducing a banker. BRC: 171
Lamont, T. W.
American bankers' responsibility. BYRA:265; HOA:271; HOAP:257; REEM 4:272; REEMB 5:93
Lindquist, R.
Beyond the dollar sign. MIA: 375
Loasby, A. W.
Opportunities for the American bank clerk. LINM:450
Marlow, F.

BANKS AND BANKING (cont.)
Introducing a bank cashier or teller. BRC:59
Opening address of The American Bankers' Association. HOAP:256
Roberts, R.
Introducing a banker. BRC: 112
Roosevelt, F.D.
Address to the American Bankers' Association. KLEB: 3
First "fireside chat" on banking. DOA:146; MO: 564; MOA:569; PE:751; PEA:751
Sifter: know your dough and you will grow (Pep talk for bank personnel and business groups-adaptable for club members, a war-veteran post member, or any auxiliary member). BAI: 31
See also Independent treasury; Money

Banning, Margaret Culkin
Test of an education. ANGC: 50

BANQUETS See After-dinner speeches; Announcements; Club speeches; Dinners and dining; Emcees; Toastmasters. Also types of speeches e.g. Introductions; Toasts; Welcoming addresses. Also types of banquets e.g. Employees; Fathers and sons; Mothers and daughters; Showers, baby; Showers, bridal; Stag dinners; Surprise parties; Thanksgiving Day

BAPTISMS See Christenings

BAR See Law and lawyers

BAR MITZVAH SPEECHES
Address for a Bar Mitzvah - 2 speeches. ZEL:72, 85
Balk, S.
For an orphan to his Bar Mitzwa. ZEL:32
Broidy, H.
For a Bar Mitzvah. ZEL:40
Buchhalter, J.
For a Bar Mitzvah. ZEL:76
Cathpah, M.
For a Bar Mitzvah of an orphan. ZEL:34
Cohen, J.
For a Bar Mitzvah-3 speeches. ZEL:42, 45, 27
Dolitzky, M.M.
For a Bar-Mitzwa. ZEL:13
Doyne, A.
For a Bar-Mitzwa - 2 speeches. ZEL:11, 74
Father's speech at home. ZEL: 18
For a Bar Mitzvah-by the Lithuanian philosopher. ZEL:9
Leavitt, E.
To a Bar-Mitzvah. ZEL:55
Leberman, H.
For a Bar Mitzvah. ZEL:21
Malachovsky, H.
For a Bar Mitzvah-3 speeches. ZEL:15, 66, 68
Thankfulness: address of a poor boy speaking in the name of all pupils and expressing his thanks in public. ZEL:90
Pailey.
For a Bar Mitzvah. ZEL:81
Pearlman, Rev.
Address to a Bar Mitzvah. ZEL:58
Philips, J.
For a Bar Mitzvah. ZEL:70
Rabinowitz, H.
For a Bar Mitzvah. ZEL:80
Radack, Rev.
For a Bar Mitzvah. ZEL:38
Reicherson.
For a Bar Mitzwa. ZEL:19
Rosen, A.
For a Bar-Mitzwa. ZEL:27
To a Bar Mitzvah. ZEL:60
Rosenberg, A.H.
Address for a Bar Mitzvah. ZEL:83

S. B.
Address for a Bar Mitzvah. ZEL:94
S. P.
For a Bar Mitzvah. ZEL: 87
Scribe, M.
For a bar Mitzvah. ZEL: 23
Selikowitz, G.
Speech for a Bar Mitzvah: address of a Jewish boy when he becomes 13 years of age. ZEL:64
Speech for a Bar Mitzvah-3 examples. ZEL:3, 5, 7
Silbert, A.
To a Bar Mitzvah. ZEL:62
Tashrak.
For a Bar Mitzvah. ZEL:52
Ter, J.
To a Bar Mitzvah: speech delivered by a pupil of a Talmud Torah. ZEL:29
Zeff, J.
Our children: address at a Bar Mitzvah. ZEL:49
Baradi, Mauro
That America may know. BRP 2:49
Barber, Paul
Wake up, America. DO:23

BARBERS
Kaser, A. L.
Emcee at a barbers' convention. BRH:246
Wilford, H. C.
Introducing a barber. BRC: 148
Barbour, James
Treaties as supreme laws. BREW 1:220
Barère de Vieuzac, Bertrand
On the necessity for teaching the French language. CHAL 3:453; HAZO 8:3210; MAS 8:3210
Report on the 'Vengeur.'' BRYW 7:161; LEEW 5:153

BARGAIN SALES
You can't get something for nothing. NAT:5
Buying a bargain. NATS:9
Bariko, Laurent Jean Pierre
Inaugural speech at Conference on the Problems of Economic Development. UAR:237
Barker, Lewellys Franklin
Wider influence of the physician. REEM 6:53; REEMB 6:19
Barkley, Alben William
Against Roosevelt's Tax Bill veto. BA 1943-44:188
Foreign policies of Roosevelt. BA 1938-39:53
People's crusade. BA 1952-53:55
Preserving the Constitution. BOA:99
Response to an introduction. PR:128
Response to tribute by A. H. Vandenberg. BA 1948-49:98
Tribute to President Roosevelt. BA 1944-45:156
BARKLEY, ALBEN WILLIAM
Vandenberg, A. H.
Tribute to Senator Barkley. BA 1948-49:96
Barksdale, L. S.
Meaning of America. BOA:318

BARN-RAISING
Speech after a barn-raising by the party obliged. BARB: 153
Barnard, Frederick A. P.
Art culture: its relation to national refinement and national morality. NORR 2d ser: 111
Barnave, Antoine Pierre Joseph Marie
Commercial politics. BREW 1: 232; CHAL 4:163; HAZO 9: 3515; MAS 9:3515
Oration for the crown. CHAL 4:165; HAZO 9:3517; MAS 9:3517
Representative democracy against majority absolutism. BREW 1:229; BRYW 7:112; CHAL 4:159; HAZO 9:3511; MAS 9:3511

Barnes, G. O.
Everlasting pyramids. BOA: 172; BOB:199
Barnes, George N.
Speech at Peace Conference (Session of February 15, 1919). REEM 11:343; REEMB 12:360
Barnes, Julius Howland
Problems of modern business. LINM:411
Team play between government and industry. BYRA:25; REEM sup 1:106; REEMB 4:46
Barnes, W. H. L.
Redwoods. WAGN:50
Speech at music-stand dedication. WAGN:46
Spirit of the phonograph. WAGN:52

BARNES, W. H. L.
Shortridge, S. M.
Eulogy on General Barnes. WAGN:84
Barnett, A. E.
Masonry triumphant (anniversary sermon). THOU 3:70
Barnhart, Barbara
Wherever diamonds. BRP10: 73
Barr, Stringfellow
How can our schools meet the war emergency? BA 1941-42:231
Barré, Isaac
America's obligation to England. CHAL 2:341; HAZO 5:2039; MAS 5:2039
Right to commit. EMS 1:221
Barrett, Mary
"Music goes 'round and 'round." JUD:125
Barrie, Sir James Matthew, Bart
Barrie bumps Stevenson. REEMB 1:73
Inoffensive gentleman on a magic island. REEM 1:75; REEMB 1:68
Literature and the press. COP:692; COPB:719; GLAD:181

BARRIE, SIR JAMES MATTHEW, BART
Walkley, A. B.
Toast to "Drama and Barrie." REEM 1:75; REEMB 1:66

BARRIERS
Jones, L.
Breaking down of barriers. YR 8:177
Barrington, J. W.
National problem. COUW:37
Barrington, James
Responds to an introduction at an International Conference on Asian Problems. PRNE: 52
Barrow, Isaac
Slander. BREW 1:235
Barrows, John Henry
Immortality. THOU 2:143
National Peace Jubilee. FUL: 11, 14
Barry, Thomas Henry
Introduces George Washington Goethals to Class of 1912 at United States Military Academy. REEM 7:160; REEMB 8:181
Barsness, John
Our last chance. NOR 1946:41
Barss, Richard
Great stampede. BOA:200; YR: 6:55
Bartlett, E. O.
Installation of Rev. J. M. Dickson as pastor of the Pilgrim Congregational Church, Providence, R.I. THOU 2:465
Bartlett, W. F.
Speech at Harvard commencement dinner. BAKF:428

BARTLETT, WASHINGTON
Irish, J. P.
Memorial address on Governor Bartlett. WAGN:281
Bartlett, Willard
Introduces William Bourke Cockran to New England Society of Brooklyn. REEMA 1:232

Barton, A.
Introducing James Bryce to New York Chamber of Commerce. REEM 1:172
Barton, Bruce
Advertising a force for greater civilization. HOA:243
Faith of Lincoln. BA 1939-40: 161
How long should a wife live? ONEC:255
One great issue. HOB:137; ON:253; SAR:132
Unknown. BRP 2:7; BOB:38; PROS:1; SHU:111
What to do in a revolution. SAC:68
Which knew not Joseph. BRAC: 24; BRY:461; BRYA:500; HUS:279; LINM:358; SABA: 243

BARTON, BRUCE
Introducing Bruce Barton-2 different examples. NI:86; NIA:68; SUM:97
Barton, George
Ideal man. BOA:175
Baruch, Bernard M.
Full economic mobilization. BA 1950-51:83
Government and the individual. ONEC:189
International control of atomic energy. (June 14, 1946.) BA 1945-46:120; BOU:124; COPB:587; HURG:279
Patriotism in industry. REEM 4:22; REEMB 4:62
Toward effective international atomic energy control (December 5, 1946). GLAD:235
Tribute to General George C. Marshall. SAB:203
Woodrow Wilson (commemorating centennial anniversary of birth of Wilson). BA 1956-57:141
Barzun, Jacques
Place and the price of excellence. ARNS:26

BASEBALL
Baseball dinner, by one of the club. EDGS:392
Baseball (fan toasts the umpire). ED:421
Cameron, W.J.
Don't die on third. SAR:43; SHU:42
Frick, F.
Responds to introduction by Wilfrid Smith. PRC:18
Kaser, A. L.
Introducing a baseball player. BRC:157
My ode to the "Orioles." SPIM:253
Presentation and acceptance of medal to victorious baseball club. HAPR:34, 37
Presentation by players to the manager of a baseball club and his response. HAPR:66, 69
Reception of a baseball club (speech of welcome and reply by the president of the club) BARB:114-115
Speech at a baseball dinner. HILL:479
Speech for a baseball dinner. BARB:156
Togo, H.
Baseball. WERN 54:170
Welcome to a visiting baseball team and response by a member of the team. EDGS: 390, 391
Royce, B.
Emcee at a baseball fan club. BRH:199
Wilford, H.C.
Introducing a baseball player. BRC:110
Bashford, James W.
Crisis. FUL:20
Philippines. FUL:18
Basil the Great, Saint
Admonition to a fallen virgin. - Same as his On a recrean nun
Hexaemeron. PL:167; LEEW 3 89
Homily of Caesarea. HAZO 3: 1128; MAS 3:1128

Basil the Great, Saint (cont.)
On a recreant nun. BREW 1: 243; LEEW 3:107

BASIL THE GREAT, SAINT
Gregory of Nazianzus.
Eulogy on Basil of Caesarea. BREW 6:300; LEEW 3:151; PL:160
Bassett, Lee Emerson
From dog house to doctorate. MOUG:244; MOUGA:244
Batchelder, Nathaniel Horton
Purpose of Loomis Institute (Founder's Hall of Loomis). ONES:107

BATE, WILLIAM B.
Carmack, E.W.
Eulogy of William B. Bate. SHUO:323
Bates, Harry
Presenting gavel to George Mean, President of AFL-CIO. BA 1955-56:79
Bates, Katherine Lee
Response-America the beautiful. DOA:83
Bates, Lewis B.
Lincoln. HARSO:210; WERN 42:39

BATHING BEAUTY CONTESTS
See Beauty contests
Battle, George Gordon
Propaganda in America. ON: 44
Battle, Kemp Davis
Democracy and the trust. SHUC:254
Baukhage, Hilmar R.
Tribute to Roosevelt. BA 1944-45:167
Baumer, Franklin L.
Religion and the sceptical tradition. NORR 3d ser:312
Baxter, Richard
Sermon on making light of Christ. HAZO 4:1548; MAS 4:1548
Unwillingness to improve. BREW 1:250
Bayar, Celel
Begins an address before the American-Turkish Society. PRNE:73
Bayard, James Asheton
Commerce and naval power. BREW 1:267
Federal judiciary. BREW 1: 257; HAZO 9:3612; MAS 9: 3612
Bayard, Thomas F.
On the United States Army. CHAL 11:182; HAZO 21:9037; MAS 21:9037; REEMA 11: 134
Plea for conciliation in 1876. BREW 1:270

BAYLOR UNIVERSITY
Brooks, S. P.
Inaugural address as president of Baylor University. WE 1:199

BAZAARS See Fairs
Beaconsfield, Benjamin Disraeli, 1st Earl of
Against democracy for England. BREW 1:301; HAZO 14:6003; MAS 14:6003; PL:482
Assassination of Lincoln. BREW 1:300
Berlin Treaty, House of Lords, July 18, 1878. CHAL 7:179; PAUF 1:340
Civil rights of the people. EMS 2:46
Franchise and reform, 1867. BRTH:284; BRTHA:284
Meaning of Conservatism. ADR 3:216; BREW 1:314; BRYW 5:38; CHAL 7:140; CROC: 169; EMS 1:30; HAY:245; HAZO 14:6022; MAS 14: 6022; PE:554; PEA:554; REEMA 11:143
Occasions for appeal to the people. EMS 1:81
On the Berlin Congress, July 27, 1878. - Same as his Peace with honor
On the evacuation of Candahar. LEEW 7:271
On the political situation.

ORBR 2:213
Peace with honor. BEA:25; COP:185; COPA:185; COPB:185; HAZO 14:6063; MAS 14:6063; REEM 9:303; REEMA 1:21; REEMB 10:312
Reform of the franchise. EMS 2:159
Reply in defence of his budget. PAUF 2:96
Sovereign and the Constitution. -Same as Meaning of Conservatism
To the King of the Belgians. KNAS:208; KNASA:208; REEMA 1:30
Tory principles. -Same as his Meaning of Conservatism

BEACONSFIELD, BENJAMIN DISRAELI, 1st Earl of
Gladstone, W. E.
On Lord Beaconsfield. BREW 6:266
On the Beaconsfield ministry. CHAL 7:458; HAZO 15:6377; MAS 15:6377
Scott, W. F.
Introduces Lord Beaconsfield. REEM 9:303; REEMB 10:312
Beadle, George W.
Education and bio-cultural evolution. IOCP:139
Beam, George
Let's advertise. HUS:276
Bean, F. Atherton
Master or victim? YR 2:21
Beard, Charles A.
Written history as an act of faith. LINP:73
Yes, we are ready. SAR:101
Beard, Geoffrey G.
United Engineering and Foundry Company. SABA:192
Beard, Mary R.
Status of woman and the modern state. GA:282
Beard, Raymond S.
This trash must go. NOR 1940:3
Beard, S. C., Jr.
Soul aflame. YR 10:9
Bearman, Anita
Gilded curtain. BRP 7:37; YR 2:48
Bearman, G. F.
Lincoln and the Constitution. LEIO:90

BEATNIKS
Brown, J. M.
"Beat" generation. HURG:341
Beatty, David
Comrades of the mist. REEM 11:415; REEMB 12:437
Beaubien, Charles Philippe
Canada and peace. REEM sup 1:106; REEMB 8:36

BEAUTY, PERSONAL
Beauty. CON:83
Drummond, R.
Introducing a beauty expert. BRC:287
Flaxman, J.
Physical and intellectual beauty. BREW 6:139
Handsome. NATM:33
Huber, L. J.
Handsome emcee. BRH:340
Kaser, A. L.
Introducing a beauty expert. BRC:69
Lincoln, H.
Introducing a beautician. BRC:150

BEAUTY CONTESTS
Posner, G. A.
Introducing a bathing beauty contest. BRH:187
Steele, S.
Emcee at a beauty contest. BRH:318
Beaver, Howard T.
Real problem of world peace. ASHF:294
Beaverbrook, William Maxwell Aiken, Lord
Russia must be sustained. COP:482; COPA:482
Bebel, August
Socialism and assassination.

Bebel, August (cont.)
REEM 9:349; REEMA 11: 159; REEMB 10:360
Beck, James M.
America and the Allies. REEM 11:117; REEMB 12: 127
Democracy of the 'Mayflower.'' REEMA 1:33
Fourth of July. REEM 1:83; REEMB 1:78
Future of democratic institutions. HICF:742
Future of the Supreme Court. LINM:435
John Marshall, jurist and statesman. SAR:206
Laurels of a mother. HARSO: 206; PROS:101
Successful life. SHU:23
Uncrowned queen. BOA:264; BOB:136
Beck, Robert J.
Salute to General Motors-50th anniversary. SABA:292
Becker, Mrs. William A.
Introducing honorary president general Mrs. Russell Magna. GA:15
Beckwith, David E.
Weapons for a cold war. NOR 1949:169
Bede (The Venerable)
Meeting of mercy and justice. BREW 1:345
On the nativity of St. Peter and St. Paul. CHAL 1:380; HAZO 3:1230; MAS 3:1230
Sermon for any day. BREW 1: 348
Sermon on all Saints. BRYW 3:3; PL:198
Torments of hell. BREW 1:349
Bede, J. Adam
Problems. NESA:112
Bedford, Alfred Cotton
France in the reconstruction period. REEM 4:32; REEMB 4:72
Beebe, Howard F.
Introducing W. E. Creed. MO: 497; ONES:12
Beecher, Henry Ward
Abolition of slavery. THOU 1: 268
Abraham Lincoln: memorial sermon. SHAH:437; THOU 1:471
American flag. PROS:17
Books. REAC:132
Difficulties of Union. (Edinburgh, October 14, 1863). FULB:350
Effect of the death of Lincoln. BREW 1:370; CHAL 8:390; CLAY:64; HAZO 17:7274; MAS 17:7274
Freedom and prosperity. -Same as his Liverpool speech, October 16, 1863
Glory of New England. REEM 1:97; REEMA 1:46; REEMB 1:92
Home Rule for Ireland. REEM 1:108; REEMA 1:60; REEMB 1:103
Liverpool speech, October 16, 1863. BRAC:40; BRIM:250; BRYW 10:9; BURS:88; CHEM 4:201; CODS:429; CODSA: 429; COP:317; COPA:317; COPB:317; FULB:354; HARS 395; HAZO 17:7254; JOHA 2 pt. 2:93; LEEW 10:259; MAS 17:7254; SAA:188; SHAH: 427
Merchants and ministers. COP: 631; COPB:668; REEM 1:102; REEMA 1:54; REEMB 1:97
Moral conflict (London, October 20, 1863). FULB:357
Nation's duty to slavery. CROC: 3
Nature of Christ. CLAY:284
On fellowship. HURG:118
Our national emblem. SHU:173; THOU 1:289
On man and his institutions. HAZO 17:7280; MAS 17:7280
Perfect manhood: sermon to graduating class of West Point Military Academy. BOU: 12; ONEM:741
Principles of self-government (at Manchester, England, October 9, 1863). FULB:341

Progress of the Franchise. THOU 1:259
Raising the flag over Fort Sumter. BREW 1:352; CHAL 8:395; HAZO 17: MAS 17: 7306; ORAMA 2:295 PL:672; REEM 10:239; REEMA 11: 180; REEMB 11:251; THOU 1:305
Regulated Christian liberty (at Glasgow, October 13, 1863). FULB:345
Reign of the common people. REEM 8:1; REEMA 4:51; REEMB 13:1
Religious freedom (68th anniversary of New England Society). BEA:31; REEM 1:92; REEMA 1:41; REEMB 1:87
Sepulcher in the garden. RINM:292
Squandering the voice. SHU: 245
System of slavery. -Same as his Liverpool speech
Tribute to Harriet Beecher Stowe. REEMA 1:51
Tribute to Munkacsy. REEMA 1:62
Tribute to our honored dead. LA:173; REAC:78
Two revelations. BAAMP:160

BEECHER, HENRY WARD
Storey, C. L.
Minister plenipotentiary. TRUW:137

Beecher, Lyman
Faith once delivered to the Saints. WPRA:99

Begg, James T.
Our foreign relations and their effect on business. EXEE:449

BEHAVIOR
Better life. FRIE:260
Big things of life. NATS:13
Bonnell, J. S.
Making life worth living. BA 1952-53:169
Boosting. NATM:3
Business is life. NATT:28
Can every man be bought? JAI: 82
Can you keep a secret? JAI:75
Cynic critic. THOT:97
DeBeer, R.
Privilegitis Americanus. BRP 8:18
Drooping wings. THOT:60
Eliot, C.W.
Durable satisfactions of life. REEM 6:169; REEMB 7:151
Face the future unafraid. NAT: 47
Fellowship. DU:140
Follow the rules of the game. NAT:40
Foolish promises. JAI:38
Get off the ball. NATT:41
Getting what you want out of life. NATT:1
Give just credit. NATT:8
Grains of sand. FRIE:223
Grunwald, E.
Toward saner values. BRP 4:64; INTW 1933:46; YR 5: 311
Hocking, W. E.
Crisis of our time. BA 1944 45:194
Hold that tiger! JAI:58
Holmes, O.W.
Mechanism in thought and morals. BL:415
How brave are you? JAI:62
How shall we behave in church? JAS:102
How to face temptation. JAI:66
How to keep out of trouble. JAI:69
Hutchins, R. M.
Crisis of our time. BA 1944 45:199
Its the human thing to do. NAT 18
Jordan, D. S.
Strength of being clean. WAGN:423
Living a useful life. FRIE:254
Look for the good things. NAT 7
Luxuries a Christian cannot afford. THOT:68
Maury, M. F.

BEHAVIOR (cont.)
Rules of conduct-attributes of success. SMI:144
Moral rearmament. FRIE:228
Morreim, P. E.
Price of integrity. BRP 7:65
Nichols, E. R., Jr.
Everyman. BRP 7:112; YR 8:103
Niebuhr, R.
Christin life and an economy of abundance. BA1956-57:191
Crisis of our time. BA 1944-45:191
Our task. NATS:16
Outline for a speech "Love thyself in order to love thy neighbor." BARR:64
Personal code of ethics. NAT:8
Rebuilding one's life. NATS:17
Redfield, R.
Crisis of our time. BA 1944-45:197
Right or wrong? JAI:84
Roosevelt, T.
Strenuous life. CHAL 14:341; COP:345; COPA:345; COPB:345; HAZO 25:10870; HURG:150; KLEG:351; MAS 25:10870; PE:655; PEA:655; PL:710; REEM 7:334; REEMA 9:995; REEMB 8:362; SAA:216
Rush, B.
Influence of physical causes on the moral faculty. BL:312
Schmitz, H. E.
Old crank next door. BRY:437; BRYA:488
Smith, W. H.
Other fellow. SHU:218
Snake bites. THOT:81
Talk to young people. NATT:31
Thy speech betrayeth thee. JAI:12
Waiting for heaven. NATS:15
Warning, flying rocks. THOT:74
Wasted efforts. NATT:39
We are all human. FRIE:284
Werner, E. M.
Others. BRP 8:7
What I believe about people. THOT:106
Wycliffe, J.
Rule for decent living. BREW 10:272; BRYW 3:8
"You pay too damn much." NAT:12
Your brother's keeper. JAI:90
See also Business ethics; Children; Courage; Courtesy; Culture; Ethics; Etiquette; Fear; Friendship; Hypocrisy; Justice; Patriotism; Pessimism; Solitude; Success; Truthfulness and falsehood; Youth

Behrends, A. J. F.
Dedication sermon for Bethesda People's Church, Brooklyn. THOU 2:462

Belasco, David
Forty years a theatrical producer. GLAD:168; REEM 1:110; REEMB 1:105

Belford, Samuel W.
Influence of Abraham Lincoln. SHU:118

BELGIUM
Kaltenborn, H. V.
Germany invades Holland and Belgium. BA 1939-40:68
Marshall, T. R.
To the Belgian War Mission. REEM 2:391; REEMB 2:408

Belhaven, John Hamilton, 2d Baron
On the union of England and Scotland. -Same as his Plea for the national life of Scotland.
Plea for the national life of Scotland. BREW 1:376; BRTH:53; BRTHA:53; CHAL 2:127; GOOD:21; HAZO 4:1664; MAS 4:1664; ORBR 1:129

BELIEF AND DOUBT See Religion
Belin, David W.
Party plight. NOR 1950:212

BELL, ALEXANDER GRAHAM
Grosvenor, E. B.
Memories of my father. YE:329
Bell, Bernard Iddings
Not taps but reveille. BA 1944-45:307
Bell, Charles Henry
Worship of success. NORR 1st ser:174
Bell, Chauncey Frederick
Statesman and nation. SHUC: 96
Bell, Clark
Introducing D. D. Field to the Saturday Night Club, April 5, 1890. REEM 2:45
Bell, John
Against extremists, North and South. BREW 1:389
On non-intervention. CHAL 6: 248; HAZO 13:5394; MAS 13:5394
Trans-continental railroads. BREW 1:395
Bell, Landon C.
Thomas Jefferson. SMI:294
Bell Telephone Companies, Volunteers speakers of
Telstar. LINP:45
Bellows, Henry Whitney
At the funeral of William Cullen Bryant. CHAL 8:454; HAZO 18:7435; MAS 18: 7435
Belmont, Mrs. August See Belmont, Eleanor Robson
Belmont, Eleanor Robson
Tribute to Katherine Cornell. GA:94

BELMONT, ELEANOR ROBSON
Lamont, T. R.
Presents Eleanor Robson Belmont. LY:49
Benchley, Robert C.
Treasurer's report. BOU:198; HIBS:505; HURG:211

BENCHLEY, ROBERT C.
Introducing Robert Benchley. NI:97; NIA:76
Benedict, Kirby
José Maria Martinez! Stand up (pronouncing death sentence) GRIS:13
Benes, Eduard
Appeal to the American people on the seizure of his nation. HAN:72
What are we fighting for? BA 1942-43:56

BENES, EDUARD
Lucas, S. W.
Welcoming President Eduard Benes. BA 1942-43:56

BENEVOLENT AND PROTECTIVE ORDER OF ELKS. See Elks, Benevolent and Protective Order of
Ben-Gurion, David
Road to valor. CROC:17
Benjamin, Judah Philip
Education, the foundation stone of republican government. REEMA 11:200
Farewell to the Union. BREW 1:401; HICF:94
On the property doctrine. -Same as his Slavery as established by law
Right of secession. HICF:57
Slavery as established by law. BREW 1:408; CHAL 8:245; HAZO 16:6976; JOHA 2 pt 1: 129; MAS 16:6976
Virtue the cornerstone of Republican government. LEEW 10:99
Bennet, Lily L.
America's biggest business. YR 8:225
Bennett, John C.
Christian ethics and foreign policy. BA 1961-62:132
Bennett, R. B.
Statue of Westminster (June 30, 1931 speech) KESB:255
Bennett, William Rainey
Man who can. EXEE:48

Benny, Jack
Remarks at Friars' Club dinner to Burns and Allen. JEYO:66, 68, 105, 108
Speech as toastmaster at Friars' Club dinner honoring George Jessel. JEYO:136

BENNY, JACK
Jessel, G.
Introducing Jack Benny. JEYO:48
Toastmaster's speech at dinner honoring Jack Benny. JEYO:131
Mirken, B.
Introduces Jack Benny at Friars' Club dinner to Burns and Allen. JEYO:65
Benschoten, William Henry
Opening address for the defendant in the Barnes-Roosevelt libel case. HICJ: 742
Benson, Ezra Taft
Farm surpluses and the soil bank. BA 1955-56:90
Responds to introduction by Howard D. Murphy. PRC: 31
See also Eisenhower, D.D., jt. auth.

BENSON, EZRA TAFT
Murphy, H.D.
Introduces Ezra Taft Benson, Secretary of Agriculture. PRC:31
Benson, Sydney
Soviet Russia. ONES:344
Bentinck, Lord William
On the suppression of Sati, November 8, 1829. KESI 1:208
Bentley, Ann
Warriors of the broken sword. BOA:163
Bentley, William
Sermon preached at the stone chapel in Boston. BL:537
Benton, Thomas Hart
Against the United States bank. BREW 2:30
On Foote's resolution. LEEW 9: 143
On the Expunging Resolution. BRYW 8:240; CHAL 5:152; HAZO 10:4232; JOHA 1 pt. 1:320; MAS 10:4232; ORAMA 2:79
Political career of Andrew Jackson. BREW 2:16; REEMA 11:208
"There is East; there is India." BREW 2:34

BENTON, THOMAS HART
Blair, F.P.
Character and work of Benton. BREW 2:114
Deathbed of Benton. BREW 2:119
Benz, Lucile L.
Shadow of the Swastika. BRP 6:71; NOR 1934:79
Bergen, Tunis Garrett
First settlers of New Netherlands. ONES:242; REEMA 1:64
Bergerot, P.A.
Funeral of President Sadi Marie Carnot. WAGN:366
Personal and political interference with the administration of school affairs. WAGN: 359
Bergquist, Greta
Held in bondage. BRP:84; YR 4:343
Berle Adolf A., Jr.
Civil Aviation Conference. HAN: 395
Irrepressible issues of the 60s. ARNS:165
Relations between the two Americas. SAR:292
Warfare of free souls. BA 1941-42:57

BERLIN CONFERENCE, 1945
Shigemitsu, M.
Statement on Japan's observance of Potsdam Declaration. VO 1945-46:464
Truman, H.S.
Report to the nation on the

Potsdam Conference. VO 1945-46:424
See also Council of Foreign Ministers, 1954 (Berlin)

BERLIN, CONGRESS AND TREATY OF
Beaconsfield, B. D.
Berlin Treaty, House of Lords, July 18, 1878. CHAL 7:179; PAUF 1:340
Peace with honor. BEA:25; COP:185; COPA:185; COPB:185; HAZO 14:6063; MAS 14:6063; REEM 9:303; REEMA 1:21; REEMB 10: 312

BERLIN QUESTION 1945-
Kennedy, J. F.
Berlin crisis. BA 1951-62: 7
"Let us call a truce to terror." BA 1961-62:41
Smith, M. C.
Address to the United States Senate, September 21, 1961. BA 1961-62:27

Bernard, Saint
Advice to young men. BREW 2:38
Against luxury in the Church. BREW 2:39
Deliverance of the Holy Land. -Same as his Why another Crusade?
On the Canticles. BREW 2:40
On the death of his brother. LEEW 3:351
Second crusade. -Same as his Why another crusade?
Sermon on the passion of our Lord. HAZO 3:1254; MAS 3:1254
Shows that the name of Jesus is a salutary medicine. PE:71; PEA:71
Why another Crusade? BREW 2:37; BRYW 7:20; COP:63; COPA:63; COPB:63; PL: 206; REEM 9:55; REEMB 10:56
Bernard, Worth
Crumbling pillars. YR 5:129
Bernhardt, J. J.
Relation of the child to the kingdom of God and the Church. THOU 2:171
Bernstein, Leonard
World of Jazz. ARNS:62
Berolsheimer, Howard
Clean hands. BLUE:27
Berrien, John M.
Conquest and territorial organization. BREW 2:41
Effect of the Mexican conquest. BREW 2:44
Berryer, Pierre Antoine
Censorship of the press. BREW 2:48; HAZO 12:4943; MAS 12:4943
Bestor, Arthur E.
Essentials of leadership. EXEE: 542
Wendell Phillips the agitator. TRUW:117
Bethman-Hollweg, Theobold von
Germany begins the war. COP: 124; COPA:124; COPB:124; FRY:64; REEM 11:31; REEMB 12:33

BERTHS
Phillips, C. R.
On berth control. JUD:133
Bethune, Mary MacLean See Hughes, L., jt. auth.

BETTER BUSINESS BUREAU
Huntington, H.
Introducing a secretary of the Better Business Bureau. BRC:308
Beveridge, Albert J.
America only: opening the 1916 Republican campaign. BRAC: 77; ONEM:372
American people. NESA:114
Decalogue of Americanism. SHU:96
For the greater Republic not for imperialism. -Same as his Republic that never retreats
March of the flag. CHAL 14: 426; FUL:27; HAZO 25:

Beveridge, Albert J. (cont.)
10979; HIB:43; HICF:188; LA:125; MAS 25:10979; PROS:58; REEM 10:358; REEMA 11:224; REEMB 11:372; WERN 42:89; WPRA:352
Meaning of the times. WERN 42:13
Mission of America. -Same as his Philippine question
Our duty in the East. -Same as his Philippine question
Partisanship and patriotism. - Same as his Takes up the white man's burden
Philippine question. BAAMP: 201; FUL:34; HARSO:219; SHAH:573; WERN 42; 99
Public speaking. BYRA:13; REEM 1 xxxvii
Puritan spirit. BLAA:4; BLAB:4
Republic's task. -Same as his Republic that never retreats
Republic that never retreats. CHAL 14:449; COP:336; COPA:336; COPB:336; FUL 31; HAZO 25:11002; MAS 25:11002; REEM 1:116; REEMA 1:70; REEMB 1:111
Star of empire. BRAS:221
Takes up the white man's burden (speech commemorating birth of General Grant). FUL:24; PE:650; PEA: 650
Tribute to Marcus A. Hanna. SHUM:274
Work and habits. KLEG:187

evin, Ernest
Labor and the war against Nazism. COP:481; COPA: 481
Report to Commons on Foreign Ministers' Council. VO 1945-46:627
Speech in Commons on foreign policy. VO 1945-46: 468
Statement on Palestine. VO 1945-46:710

eyer, Lynn
'Release us unto us Barabbas." BLUE:11

BIBLE
Adventures of the Book. JA: 229
Bible for the people. JAS:118
Bible found in a wastebasket (Codex Sinaitius) JAS:120
Boy who changed his name. JAS:12
Damiani, P.
New Testament history as allegory. BREW 4:381
Gillis, J. A. M.
Bible and the Catholic Church. CATA 2:273
Gregory, I.
On Job. LEEW 3:201; PL: 191
Ingersoll, R. G.
Victory of man. WPRA:301
Is the Bible true? JAI:88
Lost books of the Bible. JA: 232
Poetic Bible. AMEO 2:90
Roosevelt, T.
On reading the Bible. REEMA 15:1770
Shall we simplify the Bible? NATT:35
Spurgeon, C. H.
Bible. BEA:391
Three important books. JAS: 110
Value of the Bible as literature. AMEO 2:204
Wilson, W.
Bible and progress. PEAE: 163

BIBLE CLASS
Address to Bible Class. AMEO 2:77

Biddle, Francis
Columbus day address. HOC: 191
Democracy and racial minorities. BA 1943-44:172

Biddle, Francis and others (R. K. Carr; A. Simpson; A. E. Stevenson, and H. C. Urey)
National security and individu-

al freedom. HAR:440
Biel, Kurt W.
Jesus-the savior of the home. ACW:84
Big Elk, Teton Sioux Chief
Funeral speech for dead chief. JON:89
Big Mouth, Chief of Brulé Sioux
Speech at Council. JON:105

BILBAO BLOCKADE See Spain

BILL OF RIGHTS (UNITED STATES) See Bill of Rights Day; United States-Constitution

BILL OF RIGHTS DAY
Closing speech at Bill of Rights Day program. BEDA:175
Address at Bill of Rights Day program. BEDA:174
Opening speech at Bill of Rights Day program. BEDA:172
Prayer (for Bill of Rights program). BEDA:172
Billings (District Judge)
United States v. Workingmen's Amalgamated Council of New Orleans, 1893. BIR 3:174
Billings, Josh, pseud. See Shaw, Henry Wheeler

BIMETALISM See Currency question
Binder, Carroll
World in the news. BART 4:103
Bingham, Hiram
American way. BOA:324
Bingham, John A.
Against assassins of President Lincoln. BREW 2:50
Sectional party. CHAL 9:77; HAZO 18:7567; MAS 18:7567
Bingham, Jonathan B.
Enlightened materialism. YR 6:151
Binkley, William C.
South and the West. TIN:255

BIOLOGY
Warren, S.
Biology in the atomic age. IOCP:71

BIRD HOUSES
Lloyd, L.
Wanted: 10,000 new martin homes. BRAP:48

BIRDS
Francis of Assisi, Saint. Sermon on birds. COP:64; COPA:64; COPB:64; REEM 9:56; REEMB 10:58
Birdsall, William W.
What Quakerism stands for. WERN 42:75
Birge, Edward A.
In Lucem gentium. NORR 2d ser:392
Birkenhead, Frederick Edwin Smith, 1st Earl of
Lawyers who really count. LINM:350
Marriage and divorce. HAY:356
Reform of the franchise (Women's suffrage) EMS 2:209
Reform of the House of Lords. EMS 1:123
Welsh disestablishment. BEA:35
Welcome to the American Ambassador. REEMB 1:114

BIRKETT, SIR NORMAN
Daniels, J.
Presents Sir Norman Birket[t]. LY:147
Lusty, R.
Presents Sir Norman Birket[t]. LY:68
Mulroy, T. R.
Introduces Sir Norman Birkett. PR:112
Birkins, H. H.
Our flag. THOU 1:292
Birrell, Augustine
Edmund Burke. BEA:43; BRY 5:131; CHAL 14:151; HAZO

Birrell, Augustine (cont.)
25:10660; MAS 25:10660; REEM 5:10; REEMA 4:71; REEMB 9:39
Transmission of Dr. Johnson's personality. REEM 1:119; REEMA 7:87; REEMB 1:116

BIRTH CONTROL
Durant, W.
Crisis in American civilization. BA 1939-40:208
Forsythe, C.
For those yet to be. ASHF: 221
Norton, M. T.
Upholding the American standards of motherhood. GA:161
Nye, L. E.
Title 28, number 426. YR: 4:67
Oberg, W.
Lifestream of the nation. NOR 1941:29
Sanger, M.
Is birth control legal? GA: 273
Plea for birth control legislation. GA:157
Webster, P.
From behind closed doors. YR 5:209

BIRTHDAYS
Anniversaries (for a wedding or birthday anniversary). ED:345
Birthday anniversary of an elderly man. EDGS:289
Birthday greetings. BEG:151
Birthday greetings. SOES:44
Birthday greetings to a young person. SOES:45
Birthday of a great person-Franklin Delano Roosevelt. BEC:156
Birthday speech. BURS:249
Birthday tribute. BEDA:31
Birthday tribute and presentation of award. BEDA:29
Bryant, W. C.
Accepting a portfolio on his 70th birthday. KNAS:165; KNASA:165; ONEM:715
Birthday address. KNAS: 188; KNASA:188; REEM 1: 167; REEMA 1:103; REEMB 1:164
Bullis, H. A.
White light: introducing Dr. Alfred P. Haake at sales-managers' conference on his birthday. BRC:324
Byrd, H. F.
80th anniversary of the birth of Senator Glass. YE:102
Celebration of Queen Victoria's birthday in America. HILL: 489
Closing speech at birthday testimonial. BEDA:32
Congratulating a young man on reaching his majority, and reply. BARB:86-87
Davis, J.W.
Shakespeare's birthday memorial. REEM 1:369; REEMB 1:370
Depew, C. M.
Eighty-seventh birthday. DOA: 308; REEM 1:371; REEMB 1:372
Outline of address at dinner on the 70th birthday of John Jay. PITT:89
World at 91: address at banquet given in his honor on his 91st birthday. LINM:154
Dostoevsky, F.
Celebrates the centenary of Pushkin's birth. PE:569; PEA:569
Eliot, C. W.
On his ninetieth birthday. REEM sup 1:278; REEMB 7: 154
Elizabeth II. Twenty-first birthday speech. BUT:240; BUTB:233
Father to his son, just twenty-one. DU:167
For a birthday celebration. DR: 230
For a birthday party, and re-

ply. BARB:84, 85
Hedges, J.E.
Birthday of Dr. Kane. REEM 2:185; REEMB 2:187
Holmes, O.W., Jr.
"Live-I am coming:" response to a birthday greeting. COP:377; COPA:377; COPB:377; HURG:215; YE:148
Hoover, H.C.
Begins an address on the occasion of the State of Iowa's celebration of his eightieth birthday at his birthplace, West Branch, Iowa. PRNE:65
Meaning of America (at homecoming in West Branch, Iowa) BA 1948-49:89; YE: 286
Howe, J.W.
Tribute to Oliver Wendell Holmes. COP:618; COPB: 658; REEMA 2:645; REEMB 2:240
Howells, W.D.
"Atlantic" and its contributors: Whittier's 70th birthday and 20th year of the Atlantic. REEM 2:244; REEMA 2:653; REEMB 2: 248
Huber, L.J.
Emcee at a birthday celebration. BRH:284
Hughes, C.E.
Speech of introduction at the celebration of the eightieth birthday of Elihu Root. KLEB:127; LINM:253
Introducing Anna Reese Richardson on her 75th birthday. SUM:80
Jessel, G.
Sweet sixteen (suggestions for a girl's sixteenth birthday party). JEYO:18
Leo I.
Sermon on his birthday. LEEW 3:267
Lowell, A.L.
90th birthday of C.W. Eliot. REEM sup 2:188; REEMB 7: 260
MacArthur, D.
Seventy-fifth birthday address. BA 1954-55:34
Macdonald, C.
Lady of the lamp (anniversary of Florence Nightingale's birthday). GA:78
Milliken, F.
Emcee at a birthday celebration. BRH:228
Moran, E.R.
Announcement of birthdays of club members-examples of. PR:107
Opening speech at birthday testimonial. BEDA:28
Posner, G.A.
For an emcee at a birthday party. BRH:258
Roosevelt, F.D.
Address on his 60th birthday. VO 1942-43:128
Root, E.
American ideals during the past half century (birthday speech). ONEC:209; REEM sup 2:363; REEMB 8:373
Response on eightieth birthday. KLEB:139; LINM:259
Shaw, G.B.
On his 70th birthday. COP: 208; COPA:208; COPB:208; REEM sup 2:387; REEMB:3: 212
Speech of congratulation to a seventy year old guest. WRA:166
Stubbs, C.W.
Thanksgiving for William Shakespeare (birthday sermon). MAS 25:10559; HAZO 25:10559
Thanks and appreciation (at birthday testimonial) BEDA: 32
Twenty-first birthday, by a guest, and response to congratulations. EDGS:282, 284
Two birthday anniversary speeches and response by host. EDGS:285, 286, 288

BIRTHDAYS (cont.)
See also Anniversaries; Bar Mitzvah speeches; Responses to congratulations; Responses to tributes. Also names of famous men, e.g. Lincoln, A., Washington, G.
Bisel, Dorothy
For what do we fight? DO:93
Bishop, Dorothy Ann Cresap
Bryan's use of ethical proof in the "Cross of gold" speech. BRAP:157
Bishop, Morris
Faith in literature. NORR 3d ser:167
Bismarck, Otto von
Against liberalism: a Prussian royalist confession of faith. CHAL 9:57; HAZO 18:7543; MAS 18:7543
Canossa speech. BRYW 7:243; LEEW 5:323
German solidarity. HAZO 18:7550; MAS 18:7550
Ideal of a Christian state. HAZO 18:7547; MAS 18:7547
Mount the guards at the Warthe and the Vistula! CROC:21
Plea for Imperial armament. BREW 2:61; CHAL 9:38; HAZO 18:7524; MAS 18:7524; PE:586; PEA:586
Recommends the values of blood and iron. PE:529; PEA:527
Responsibility of the Imperial Chancellor. LEEW 5:331
War and armaments in Europe. COP:121; COPA:121; COPB:121; PL:733; REEM 9:336; REEMA 11:244; REEMB 10:346
Björnson, Björnstjerne
Address at the grave of Ole Bull. CHAL 12:96; HAZO 22:9503; MAS 22:9503
Black, Hugh
Religion and commerce. REEM 1:129; REEMB 1:126
Black, Hugh L.
Bill of Rights. LINP:126
Wages and Hours Bill. ON:173

BLACK, HUGO L.
Atkinson, M. E.
From klansman's robe to justice's gown. YR 10:193
Black, Jeremiah Sullivan
Corporations under eminent domain. BREW 2:76
Right to trial by jury. BRAC:100; ONEM:83; RINM:131
Black, John C.
Mother of Lincoln. HARSO:229

BLACK, NELLIE PETERS
Lamar, Mrs. W.D.
Eulogy on Nellie Peters Black. GA:90
Black Hawk, Sac chief
Fourth of July speech near Fort Madison. JON:93
To General Street. 1832 (on surrendering himself) BRYW 8:22; SHE:50
Blackburn, Joseph C.S.
John C. Breckenridge (unveiling statue at Lexington, Kentucky) REEMA 7:97
Retort to Inglass. HICF:132
Blacktooth, Cecilio, Captain of the Cupeños
To the government commissioners, as interpreted by Celsa Apapas. JON:115
Blackwelder, Oscar F.
Contribution of the Christian faith. BA 1940-41:255
Blaine, James B.
Introduces Clare Boothe Luce
" Claude Pepper
" James E. Gheen, humorous lecturer. PR:91, 49, 59
Blaine, James Gillespie
Century of protection. REEM 10:293; REEMA 11:259; REEMB 11:307
Irish question. HICF:111
Life and character of J.A. Garfield. BAKF:130; BAKS:177; BREW 2:87; BRYW 10:111; CHAL 11:282; CLAY:141; COP:325; COPA:325; COPB:325; HARSO:178; HAZO 21:

9147; HURG:137; LA:139; MAS 21:9147; ONEM:408; ORAMA 2:321; PROS:124; REEM 5:14; REEMA 7:113; REEMB 9:43; SHU:176; WERN 42:72
On the remonetization of silver. CHAL 11:312; HAZO 21:9177; JOHA 2 pt 2:312; MAS 21:9177
Our Merchant Marine. REEMA 1:73
Response to the Chicago Board of Trade's welcome. HILL: 479

BLAINE, JAMES GILLESPIE
Ingersoll, R. G.
Nominating Blaine. BIR 3: 113; BRAC:404; BREW 7: 126; BRYW 10:77; CHAL 12:184; COP:322; COPA 322; COPB:322; HAZO 22: 9580; HIBS:292; HICF:108; HILL:463; HURG:154; MAS 22:9580; ONEM: 470; ORAMA 2:377; PE:616; PEA:616; REEM 10:279; REEMA 13:1252; REEMB 11:292; SHAH:458
Blair, Austin
Military government. BREW 2:109
Blair, Francis G.
Response to election as president of the National Education Association. BRAC:247
Blair, Francis Preston
Character and work of Benton. BREW 2:114
Deathbed of Benton. BREW 2: 119
On the 15th Amendment. BREW 2:121

BLAIR, FRANK P.
Clark, C.
Frank P. Blair. SHUO:208
Blair, Henry William
On free schools. CHAL 12: 406; HAZO 23:9802; MAS 23:9802
Blake, Edward
Suffrage for women. CHAL 12: 230; HAZO 22:9611; MAS 22:9611
Blake, Eugene Carson
Good faith. BA 1957-58:168
Proposal toward the reunion of Christ's Church. BA 1960-61:141
Blake, Eugene H.
Flood-gate flung wide. SHUC: 291
Blakely, Robert
Modern primitivists. BRP 7:94; NOR 1936:34
Blakely, Robert J.
Constant crusades. BA 1951-52: 152
Education for multiple leadership (American and Russian education). BA 1958-59:147
Greatest lack. BA 1945-46:241
What is a free society? BA 1955-56:46
Blakesley, Raphael H.
Mastery of mind. SHUC:131

BLAME, SPEECHES OF
Austin, W. R.
Accusing Chinese communists of intervention in Korea. YE:140
Stennis, J. C.
For censure of Senator McCarthy. BA 1954-55:109
Suggestions for preparation of speeches of blame, with examples of. YE:139
See also Prosecution
Blanchard, Newton C.
Lincoln and the South. SHUO: 164
Blanche, August Theodor
On the dethronement of Gustav IV. CHAL 8:242; HAZO 16: 6973; MAS 16:6973
Bland, Richard P.
Free silver. REEMA 11:273
Parting of ways. BREW 2:132; BRYW 10:165
Blankenburg, Rudolph
Philadelphia. REEM 1:133; REEMB 1:130

Blencowe, E.
Star of the Wise Men. THOU 2:366

BLIND
Do you have "eyes that see not?" JAI:48
Keller, H.
Appeal for the blind. DOA: 190
Williams, V.
Inner light. YR 9:275
Bliven, Bruce
Mid-century pessimists. NORR 3rd ser:303
Bloch, Charles J.
Lawyer's duty to the courts or to his country and to his people. BRAB:551
Blomfield, Leila M.
Democracy rampant. BART 2: 133

BLOOD-DISEASES
Zimmerman, R.
Mingled blood. ARNS:99; LINP:197

BLOOD DONORS
Appeal for blood donation. BEB:25; BEC:40
Bloom, Sol
At the home of Mary Ball Washington. DOA:15
Bloomstein, Max
Fords with balloon tires. SHU:142
Blouet, Paul (Max O'Rell)
Monsieur and Madame. REEMA 1:79
Blough, Roger M.
Great expectations. MICS:144
Price and the public interest. BA 1958-59:65
Blough, Roy See Taft, R.A., jt. auth.
Blume, Clarence E.
Introducing Harold E. Stassen. YE:127

BLUNDERS
Talmage, T.D.
Big blunders. BEA:397; ONEM:828; REEMA 6:1071
We all make mistakes. NAT: 24
Blunt, Katharine
Dedication of Windham House. GA:64
Blyden, Edward Wilmot
Political outlook for Africa. DUNM:263
Boardman, Mabel T.
Dedication of Delano memorial. GA:65

BOARDS OF TRADE See Chambers of Commerce

BOAT CLUB
For a boat club dinner. BARB: 158
Presentation of trophy to the winner of a rowing match, and response by captain. EDGS:401, 403
Presentation of trophy to the winner of a sailing race, and response by winner. EDGS: 399, 400
Visit of a boat club-reception address and reply. BARB: 119-120
Yacht club, by an officer. EDGS:404
Boddy, William Henry
Life: a mirage or a fountain. SAR:436

BOER WAR See South African War, 1899-1902

BOHEMIANISM See Beatniks
Bohn, Frank
Changes in the business map of America. EXEE:300

BOILER MANUFACTURING
Boiler manufacturers. SCHS: 39
Bok, Edward W.
Keys to success. BLAA:172; BLAB:172; REEM 8:19; REEMA 4:95; REEMB 13:21
Bolden, James
Introducing an automobile

dealer.
Introducing a credit man
" a salesmanager. BRC 254, 142, 264
Bolingbroke, Henry Saint-John, 1st Viscount
Misfortune and exile. BREW 2:138
Patriotism. BREW 2:147
Bolivar, Simon
At the Congress of Angostura. COP:386; COPA:386; COPB:386; PL:349
I will act as trustee of the Supreme Authority. CROC: 29

BOLIVAR, SIMON
Muñoz-Cota, J.
Bolivar and the Latin-American peoples. LEIO:72
Bolton, H.W.
Abraham Lincoln. THOU 1:470
None but himself can be his parallel. (U.S. Grant) THOU 1:373
True patriotism. THOU 1:200

BOMBINGS See also Aeronautics, military; World War 1939-1945-Aerial operations
Bonacker, Ralph
Mandate to the college bred. BRP 4:39; INTW 1933:29; YR 5:67
Bonaparte, Charles J.
Chief Justice Marshall. SHUO: 327
Introducing Ambassador Bryce at Harvard Commencement exercises, 1907. KNAS:264
Our national dangers, real and unreal. HICF:196
Bonar, Andrew
Resurrection miracle. THOU 2:120
Bonaventura, Saint
Life of service. BREW 2:149
Bond, Alice Dixon
Review of "The Arts." GA:220
Bond, Niles See Chang, J.M., jt. auth.
Bondfield, Margaret
Science and the human factor. REEM sup 1:127; REEMB 4:74

BONDS, GOVERNMENT
Roosevelt, F.D.
Broadcast in connection with the opening of the Third War Loan Drive. VO 1943-44:336
Opening the Fifth war loan drive. VO 1944-45:68
United States savings bonds. DR:211
See also Stocks and bonds

BONDS: SCHOOL See Education-Finance

BONIFACE, SAINT
Damiani, P.
Sermon on Saint Boniface. HAZO 3:1242; MAS 3:1242
Bonilla, Raoul Cepero
Inaugural speech at Conference on the Problems of Economic Development. UAR:259
Bonnell, John Sutherland
Glory and tragedy of man. BA 1946-47:239
Making life worth living. BA 1952-53:169
Bonnin, Gertrude S.
Pleads the cause of the American Indian home. JON:119
Bonsal, Philip W.
Inter-American relationship. HOC:144
Bontemps, Arna
Negro's contribution reconsidered. HILK:185

BONUS See Pensions, military

BONUS EXPEDITIONARY FORCE See Pensions, military
Booher, Edward E.
What makes a good editor? HIBS:473

BOOK REVIEWS
Bond, A.D.
Review of "The Arts." GA: 220

BOOK REVIEWS (cont.)
Discussion and examples of book reviews. GA:207
Kyburg, E. E.
The rains came-a review. GA:212
Booker, Ivan A.
American school board. DOA: 184

BOOKS See Acceptance speeches -Books; Libraries and librarians; Presentation speeches-Books

BOOKS AND READING
Gallup, G.
Mass information or mass entertainment. MOA:400
Powell, L. C.
Value of reading. ANGC:26
Three important books. JAS: 110
Which book is an authority? JAS:96
See also Literature

BOOMS See Business cycles
Boone, Lester
Constitution - wherein lies its greatness. BOB:72

BOOSTER SPEECHES
A druggist-speech before a service club meeting. WRA: 240
The grocer-speech before a club. WRA:238
Suggestions for preparation of booster speeches with examples of. WRA:235

BOOTH, EDWIN
Collyer, R.
Tribute to Edwin Booth. REEM 1:329; REEMA 1: 266; REEMB 1:330
Jefferson, J.
Memory of Edwin Booth. REEM 2:277; REEMA 2: 691; REEMB 2:281
Matthews, B.
Edwin Booth. REEM 5:311; REEMB 9:351
Booth, Newton
Debit and credit of the war. WAGN:38
Michigan Bluff oration. WAGN: 36
On labor. WAGN:40
Borah, William E.
Against the repeal of Embargo. BA 1939-40:38
Americanism. -Same as his League of Nations
Anti-lynching Bill. BA 1937-38:17
Being true to ourselves. BOA: 316; BOB:92
Broadcast address, Feb. 22, 1936. BIR 4:172
Consumer and small business. KLEB:245
Curse of liquor. BOB:45
Hideous doctrine of Prussianism. BREW 2:152
How to end war. LINM:74
League of nations. BAAMP:255; BLAB:359; BRAS:391; COP: 368; COPA:368; COPB 368; HICF:642; HURG:190; REEM 11:365; REEMB 12:383
Liquor problem. HICF:914
Munitions manufacturers must be curbed. DOA:198
Nominating Charles Curtis for the Vice-Presidency. ONEC: 496
Old faith. BOA:277; BOB:24
Our imperative task: to mind our own business. SAR:279
Possible results of a European war. BA 1938-39:29
Summation for the people in the Coeur D'Alene riot murder trial. HICJ:354
Borden, Sir Robert Laird
Address to the graduating class of Acadia University. KLEB:97
Canadian navy. BREW 2:156
Canadians at the front. REEM 1:141; REEMB 1:138
Cost of prosperity. BREW 2:156
Growing confidence. REEM 1: 149; REEMB 1:146
Hope for liberty and democracy. BREW 2:154

Imperial relations. EMS 2:266
Naval policy of Canada. KES 2:308
Speech at Imperial War Conference, 1917. KES 2:376
Voice of the Empire. COP: 384; COPA:384; COPB:384; REEM 11:92; REEMB 12: 101
Walk, and not faint. REEM 7: 41; REEMB 8:39
Young Canada, and the years to come. BREW 2:156

Borden, William
Introducing C.W. Eliot to New England Society of New York, Dec. 22, 1877. REEM 2:4
Introducing Horace Porter to New England Society of New York, Dec. 22, 1877. REEM 3:72

Borders, William Holmes
Some Negro contributors to American civilization. HILK:79

BORGLUM, GUTZON
Raish, D.R.
Once in a lifetime. JUD: 191

Bose, Sir Jagdish Chandra
Greater India to be. ZU:35

Bosley, Harold
If anywhere, then everywhere. BA 1943-44:337

Boss, Edwin A.
How to modernize and manage a hotel. HUS:242

BOSS RULE See Corruption (in politics)

Bossuet, Jacques Bénigne, bp.
Funeral oration of the Prince Conde. BREW 2:161; BRYW 7:63; CHAL 2:92; HAZO 4: 1558; LEEW 4:219; MAS 4: 1558; PL:263; REEM 9:76; REEMB 10:78
Funeral oration on Henriette of England, Duchess of Orleans. CODS:63; CODSA:63

BOSTON
Hale, E.E.
Boston. COP:663; COPB:690; REEM 2:149; REEMA 2:149; REEMB 2:141
Boston's place in history. BREW 6:319
Quincy, J., Jr.
At the second centennial of Boston. BREW 8:402
Spring, G.
Remarks against the religion and morals of the people of Boston and its vicinity. BRAR 1:57

BOSTON MASSACRE, 1770
Adams, J.
On the Boston Massacre. BREW 1:47; CHAL 3:2; HARS:12; HAZO 6:2569; MAS 6:2569
Hancock, J.
Boston Massacre. BREW 6: 357; CHAL 3:59; COP:229; COPA:229; COPB:229; HAZO 7:2627; HELE:36; HURG:24; LEEW 8:71; MAS 7:2627; ORAMA 1:127; REEMA 13:1125
Quincy, J.
Lenity of the law to human infirmity (Weem et al: British soldiers arraigned for the Boston Massacre) BREW 8:399
Ruffin, G.L.
Crispus Attucks (commemorative speech on Boston Massacre). DUNM:125
Warren, J.
Boston Massacre. CHEN 1: 43; CHAL 3:107; HAZO 7: 2675; LEEW 8:93; MAS 7: 2675

BOSTON-OLD SOUTH CHURCH
Phillips, W.
Plea for the Old South Church-Boston. CLAY:198

Botha, Louis
Critical speech at Imperial Conference of 1911. KES:2:297

Bottome, Margaret
International Order of the King's Daughters and Sons. THOU 2:509
Boudinot, Elias
Mission of America. BREW 2:181; CHAL 3:90; HAZO 7:2658; MAS 7:2658
Oration before the Cincinnati. -Same as his Mission of America
Boughter, James G.
Opinion on Knights of Malta. THOU 3:151
Bourdaloue, Louis
Passion of Christ. BREW 2:190; BRYW 7:67; CHAL 2:106; HAZO 4:1611; LEEW 4:285; MAS 4:1611; PL:250
Bourgeois, Leon
Peace Conference at Paris, Session Jan. 25, 1919. REEM 11:324; REEMB 12:342
Peace Conference at Paris, Session Feb. 15, 1919. REEM 11:333; REEMB 12:351
Bourinot, Sir John George
Early Canadian literature. CHAL 13:132; HAZO 23:10068; MAS 23:10068
Boutwell, George Sewall
On the progress of American independence. CHAL 9:223; HAZO 18:7769; MAS 18:7769
President Johnson's 'High crimes and misdemeanors." BREW 2:204
Bowen, C.W.
Introducing J.R. Angell to New England Society of New York., Dec. 22, 1921. REEM 1:52
Bower, Herbert Francis de
Price of success. BYRA:136; REEM 4:34; REEMB 4:170
Bowers, Claude G.
Keynote speech of Democratic National Convention. HICF:781; ONEC:507
Sword bearer of democracy. BOA:243; BOB:150
Bowers, Eaton J.
Negro problem. SHUO:258
Bowers, John M.
Summation for the defendant in the Barnes-Roosevelt libel case. HICJ:762
Bowers, Russell E.
Disciples of determinism. NOR 1941:17

BOWES, EDMUND
Fairfield, W.
Whom should the Republicans nominate for President? JUD:185
Bowles, Chester
Give one day. HOA:400
New directions for foreign aid. BA 1959-60:93
Price control and inflation. BA 1945-46:144
BOWLES, CHESTER
Brorby, M.
Introduces Chester Bowles, former United States Ambassador to India. PRNE:33
Bowles, George E.
Caesar's friends. YR 7:301
BOWLING
Bowling. SCHS:42
Bowling (player makes a suggestion). ED:426
Bowlus, Nettie
Moral wealth of Uncle Sam. REAC:198
Bowman, Geline Macdonald
Address of the president. GA:179
Bowman, J. Beatrice
Welcome to American nurses. GA:18
Bowman, James
Gold in the clay jars (Dead Sea Scrolls) SOBP:344

BOY SCOUTS
Appeal for funds (annual Boy Scout drive). BEDA:108
Closing speech at annual Boy Scout drive. BEDA:109
Curtis, D.W.

Introducing a Boy Scout executive. BRC:288
Idea and ideals of the Boy Scouts. AMEO 1:91
Kaser, A. L.
Introducing a Boy Scout executive. BRC:58
Master and his troops. JA:23
Ramsey, H.
Introducing a speaker on Boy Scouts. BRC:221
These would have made good scouts. JA:20
Welcome to a delegation of boy or girl scouts (or other youth groups). HNWS:50
Welcome to annual Boy Scout drive. BEDA:107

BOYCOTTING
Parnell, C. S.
At Ennis (boycotting defined and defended). KET:405
Russell of Killowen, C. R.
Boycotting. KET:394
Boyd, Julian P.
Thomas Jefferson survives. NORR 3d ser: 178
Boyd, Rufin W.
Introduces his former pastor. PRNE:11
Boyd, William R., Jr.
Presentation of API gold medal to Charles F. Kettering. SAB:209; SABA:289
Boyle, James Patrick
Democracy and foreign immigration. SHUC:298

BOYLE, ROBERT, JR.
Krantz, J.
Architect designed a needle (hypodermic) MCK:237
Boynton, Nehemiah
Homeland. PROS:73; SHU:209

BOYS
Boy and his gang. AMEO 2:195
Boy who never grew up. JAI:43
Huber, L. J.
Schoolboy emcee. BRH:341
Hamaishi, G.
Story of a boy. NOR 1943:5
McKeldin, T.
Training boys for responsible citizenship. MCK:225
Mott, J. R.
Boyhood the greatest asset of any nation. LINM:3
See also Boy Scouts; Children; Youth

BOYS TOWN
Flanagan, E. J.
Boys Town. BART 3:55
Braasch, William K.
Essentials of a pleasing personality. EXEE:356
Bracken, Herbert
Economic color line. BRP 10:62
Brackett, Edgar Truman
Summation for the managers in the Sulzer impeachment trial. HICJ:692
Braden, Spruille
Farewell speech to the Argentine people. ON:323
Bradford, Louis
Vanadium steels. PEAE:103
Bradlaugh, Charles
At the bar of the House of Commons. CHAL 12:205; HAZO 22:9586; MAS 22:9586
His plea at the bar of the House BRYW 5:91
Right of public meeting. EMS 2:64
Bradley, F. M.
Loyal crusaders. THOU 3:515
Work among the young. THOU 3:509
Welcome to Washington. THOU 3:481
Bradley, Omar N.
Four courses of action in Korea. BA 1952-53:21
Long range military policy. BA 1949-50:66
Tribute to Ernie Pyle. SABA:285
Bradley, Preston
Business of religion and the religion of business. ONE

479
Response to an introduction. PR:125
Romance of life. BART 1:63
Bradley, William O.
Blue and the Gray (dedication of Kentucky monument in Chickamauga National Park) SHUO:302
Brady, Thomas Pickens
Segregation and the South. WPRC:333
Bragstad, Robert
Child shall lead them. BRP 9:113
BRAIN See Intellect; Thought and thinking
Branch, William B.
Strange fruit. NOR 1946:65
Brandeis, Louis Dembitz
Business-a profession. LINM:101; REEM 4:35; REEMB 4:79
True Americanism. REEM 7:47; REEMB 8:44
Branen, Jeff
Emcee at a Christmas party for employees;
Emcee at a 'Do it yourself' club
Emcee at a plumbers' convention. BRH:229, 210, 179
Introducing an entertainer
" a girl trio
" an old time entertainer
" a speaker on dogs. BRH:106, 146, 67, 44
Brannon, Charles F.
Farm plan for the future. BA 1949-50:203

BRANNON, CHARLES F.
Miller, M. G.
Introduces Charles F. Brannon, Secretary of Agriculture. PRNE:25
Brant, Joseph, Mohawk chief
Request to the Court of St. James for extensive land grant for his people north of Lake Erie. JON:47
To Lord Germaine. BRYW 8:5
Braunstein, Baruch
Italy, vs. Great Britain. SAR:286
Braxton, Allen Caperton
Fifteenth Amendment (response to toast) SHUO:266
Brayman, Harold
Formula for reform. MOUG:196; MOUGA:196
Brebner, J. Bartlett
Common ground of humility. BA 1954-55:123
Breckenridge, John C.
Address preceding removal from Senate. CHAL 10:93; HAZO 19:8239; MAS 19:8239; REEMA 11:296
Buford case. SOU 9:396
Dred Scott decision, December 1859. BREW 2:215
Extracts from the speeches of Senator Breckenridge. BURP:135-47
On suppression of insurrection. CHEM 4:161; JOHA 2 pt 2:51; SAA:170
Proto-martyrs of liberty. THOU 1:496

BRECKENRIDGE, JOHN C.
Blackburn, J. C. S.
John C. Breckenridge (unveiling statue at Lexington, Ky.) REEMA 7:97
Breckenridge, William C. P.
Jeffersonian democracy. SHUO:194
Who were the Confederate dead? SOU 9:418
Breeden, H. O.
Supremacy of love. THOU 3:112
Brenner, Sidney M.
Propaganda in a democracy. DO:48
Brent, Charles Henry
Call to the church-to develop a Christian international life. REEM 7:54; REEMB 6:25
Finding God among the Tommies. REEM 1:154; REEMB 1:151

BRETTON WOODS See United Nations Monetary and Financial Conference

Brewer, David J.
Combination of capital and consolidation of labor. BLAA:189; BLAB:189; THOU 1:444
Does the individual count for nothing? BOB:57
Political and personal liberty. THOU 1:210
Brewster, Benjamin Harris
Bench and Bar of Pennsylvania. REEMA 1:82
Briand, Aristide
German peace proposal. REEM 11:136; REEMB 12:147
Imperialism, democracy, and peace. BREW 2:218
On compelling Germany to pay. BREW 2:220
On the anti-war treaty. PL:770
Speech at the Washington Conference on the Limitations of Armaments. COP:145; COPA:145; COPB:145; REEM 11:396; REEMB 12:416

BRIAND, ARISTIDE
Butler, N. M.
Welcoming Briand. REEM 1:187; REEMB 1:188
Depew, C. M.
To Premier Briand. REEM 1:396; REEMB 1:397

BRIAND KELLOGG PACT, AUGUST 27, 1928 See Kellogg Briand Pact, August 27, 1928; Leage of Nations
Brick, Anthony W., Jr.
After-dinner speech on the occasion of accepting a scholarship. JUD:301

BRICK MANUFACTURERS AND MANUFACTURING
Brickmen. SCHS:48
Bricker, John W.
Against censure of Senator McCarthy. BA 1954-55:113
Robert A. Taft. BA 1953-54:75

BRICKER AMENDMENT See Treaties

BRIDES See Engagements; Marriage; Showers, bridal; Wedding speeches

BRIDGES
Gilkey, C. W.
Bridges into a better world. BA 1938-39:234
Brigance, Shirley
Landladies. YE:332
Brigance, W. Norwood
Backwash of war. BA 1945-46:75
Demogogues, "good" people, and teachers of speech. ARNS:13
1946; year of decision. BA 1946-47:225
Briggs, George Waverley
Service the genius of progress. REEM sup 1:132; REEMB 4:87

BRIGHT, JESSE DAVID
Johnson, A.
Proposed expulsion of Mr. Bright from the Senate of the United States. SOU 9:345
Bright, John
Against Mr. Roebuck's motion for recognition of the Southern Confederacy, HAZO 16:6846; MAS 16:6846
Angel of death. -Same as his Russia: negotiations at Vienna, House of Commons, Feb. 23d, 1855
At the opening of the new room of the Junior Liberal Association of Birmingham. KNAS:148, KNASA:148
Canadian fortifications. HAZO 16:6864; MAS 16:6864
Educates English public opinion in the cause of the North. -Same as his Trent affair
Foreign policy (1858). -Same as his Morality and military

Bright, John (cont.)
greatness
Free trade. FULB:132
Misery of war. -Same as his Russia; negotiations at Vienna, House of Commons, Feb. 23, 1855
Morality and military greatness. BREW 2:237; HAZO 16:6872; MAS 16:6872
On slavery in America. CHAL 8:188; HAZO 16:6901; LAD 184: MAS 16:6901
On the Eastern crisis and the danger of war, 1878. BRTH:273; BRTHA:273
On the English foreign policy. ADR 3:159; BRYW 4:222
Peace. KLEG:357; LEEW 7: 291; PL:473
Peace and war. ORBR 2:335
Right of public meeting. EMS 2:57
Russia: negotiations at Vienna, House of Commons, Feb. 23, 1855. BEA:59; HAY: 234; PAUF 1:364
Suspension of the Habeas Corpus Act. CLAY:290
Tax Bills: power of the House of Lords, House of Commons, July 6, 1860. PAUF 1:370
Trent affair. BRYW 4:243; CHAL 8:156; COP:182; COPA:182; COPB:182; HAZO 16:6814; MAS 16: 6814; PE:512; PEA:512; REEM 9:239; REEMA 11: 303; REEMB 10:246; SAA: 179
Will the United States subjugate Canada? BREW 2:223

BRIGHT, JOHN
Morley, J. M.
Unveiling the statue of John Bright. BEA:315; PAUF:2: 356
Brightman, Edgar Sheffield
Three conceptions of culture. NORR 3d ser:55
Bristol, F. M.
Lincoln's choice and destiny. THOU 1:474
Bristol, George Digby, 2d Earl of
Army in domestic politics. BREW 5:240; CHAL 2:63; GOOD:16; HAZO 4:1503; MAS 4:1503; ORBR 1:107
Grievances and oppressions under Charles I. BREW 5:236
Speech on the Bill of Attainder against Lord Strafford. - Same as his Army in domestic politics
Broadhurst, W. A.
True fraternity. THOU 3:368
Brockett, Joshua A.
Emancipation Proclamation. THOU 1:246
Brodsky, John C.
Student activities in undergraduate life. SHUC:359
Broidy, H.
For a Bar Mitzvah. ZEL:40
Bromfield, Edward T.
Rallying day and after. THOU 2:217
Rallying day for the church. THOU 2:219
Some telling facts and figures. THOU 2:169
Bromley, George T.
Sloat monument address. WAGN:339
Uncle George's school speech. WAGN:335
Bromley, Isaac Hill
Connecticut's part in the business. REEMA 1:86
Bronk, M.
Modern spirit of brotherhood. THOU 3:381
Brooks, Phillips, Bp.
Address at a meeting in behalf of the Children's Aid Society. BAKF:319
Beauty of a life of service. CHAL 13:19; HAZO 23:9886; MAS 23:9886
Character of Abraham Lincoln. BREW 2:244; CHAL 13:38; HAZO 23:9905; MAS 23:9905; REEM 5:37; REEMA 7:137; REEMB 9:67

Christ in whom Christians believe. HAZO 23:9923; MAS 23:9923
First Good Friday. THOU 2:65
Fourth of July. BAKF:185
Is it I? ONEM:757
Lincoln as a typical American. -Same as his Character of Abraham Lincoln
Power over the lives of others. BREW 2:251
Sermon of greeting. FULB:369
True liberty. HAZO 23:9945; MAS 23:9945

BROOKS, PHILLIPS, Bp.
Baker, J.H.
Phillips Brooks. BLAA:277; BLAB:277
Farrar, F.W.
Phillips Brooks. KNAS:70; KNASA:70
Potter, H.C.
Eulogy on Phillips Brooks. CHAL 13:1; HAZO 23:9811; MAS 23:9811
Brooks, Preston S.
Assault on Sumner. BREW 2:254; BRYW 9:174; CHAL 9:453; HAZO 19:8085; JOHA 2 pt. 1:121; MAS 19:8085; REEMA 11:328
Brooks, Samuel Palmer
Inaugural address as president of Baylor University. WE 1:199
Brooks, Stratton Duluth
Inaugural address as president of University of Oklahoma. WE 2:407
Brorby, Melvin
Introduces Arnold J. Toynbee, professor, author and historian of Great Britain. PRNE:39
Introduces Chester Bowles, former United States Ambassador in India. PRNE:33
Brosseau, A.J.
Highways and the tax payer. BYRA:49; REEM sup 1:135; REEMB 4:90

BROTHERLINESS
Appreciation and acceptance (at presentation of Brotherhood award) BED:57; BEDA:66
Barriers to racial brotherhood. JA:184
Bronk, M.
Modern spirit of brotherhood. THOU 3:381
Brotherhood. THOS:59
Brotherhood-the spirit of fraternal organization. DR:101; LU:1168
Closing remarks (at presentation of Brotherhood award). BED:58; BEDA:67
Fraternal brotherhood. NATS:14
Fraternity, the brotherhood of man. DICD:106
Goodfellowship. NATS:13
Greeting and welcome (at presentation of Brotherhood award). BED:55; BEDA:63
Introducing civil liberties champion (at presentation of Brotherhood award). BED:55; BEDA:64
Johnston, E.A.
High cost of bigotry. BA 1950-51:112
Presenting scroll (at presentation of Brotherhood award). BED:56; BEDA:64
Response to welcome of a guest speaker in men's Brotherhood. HNWS:59
Stein, L.
Accepting 1959 National Brotherhood award. SABA:301
Stevenson, A.E.
World brotherhood in a space age. BA 1957-58:59
Warren, E.
Charles Evans Hughes and the spirit of tolerance (dedication of hall in memory of Hughes) BA 1956-57:135
Welcome to visitors in Men's

BROTHERLINESS (cont.)
Brotherhood. HNWS:25
Winston, A.
There lies our frontier. BA 1952-53:175
See also Human Rights Day and Week; International co-operation; Secret societies; Youth
Brougham and Vaux, Henry Peter Brougham, 1st Baron
Against Pitt and war with America. BREW 2:261; BRTH:214; BRTHA:214; HAZO 10:4142; MAS 10:4142; REEMA 11:333
Closing argument for Queen Caroline. BREW 2:265; HAZO 10:4148; KLEG:134; MAS 10:4148
Immortal statesman: election speech at Liverpool, October 8, 1812. -Same as his Against Pitt and war with America.
In behalf of Williams when prosecuted for a libel on the Clergy of Durham. GOOD:896
Inaugural discourse. GOOD:937; KLEG:294
On emancipation for the Negro. BRYW 4:138; CHAL 5:88; HAZO 10:4160; MAS 10:4160; PL:457; REEMA 11:338
On the army estimates. GOOD:891; LEEW 7:237
On the invasion of Spain by France. GOOD:904
Supports the Reform Bill. FULB:118; GOOD:915; HAY:164; PE:429; PEA:429
True conquerors. CODS:466; CODSA:466

BROUN, HAYWOOD
Introducing Heywood Broun. NI:80; NIA:64
Brousseau, Grace H.
Defense of home and country. HICF:943
Browder, Earl
Soviet Union. SAR:163
Browder, Wilbur F.
Happy is the nation whose kings are philosophers, and whose philosophers are kings. SOU 9:441
Brown, Alfred
Children's hour. BRP 9:36
Brown, Benjamin Gratz
On slavery in its national aspect as related to peace and war. CHAL 10:460; HAZO 21:8867; MAS 21:8867
Prophecy. BREW 2:278
Brown, Charles Reynolds
Life complete. WAGN:270
Brown, Charlotte Hawkins
Bennett College (memorial service for Dr. Dett) HILK:84
Place of nursing profession in America (at capping exercise). HILK:89
Brown, Edwin K.
March of the Constitution. TRUW:150
Brown, Frank
Patriotism of Stephen A. Douglas. SHUC:14
Brown, Gilbert Patten
First Grand Master of Virginia. THOU 3:59
Brown, Harrison S.
Science, technology, and world development. ARNS:84
Social responsibility of science. BA 1948-49:139
Brown, Henry Armitt
Dangers of the present. BREW 2:285
One century's achievement (Valley Forge centennial) BREW 2:283
Plea of the future. BREW 2:286
Brown, Howard
Filtering our industrial waste (outline) MO:450; MOA:454
Brown, Inez B.
Electric service in the American home. BLUE:68
Brown, J. Douglas

Education for leadership. ANDS:155
Brown, James
Introducing Julius H. Barnes at the Bankers Club, New York, LINM:411

BROWN, JAMES
Brown, M. V.
Confessional. YE:99
Brown, John
Last speech at Charleston, West Virginia. ANG:277; BAKF:247; BIR 2:231; BRYW 9:187; CHAL 6:406; COP:298; COPA:298; COPB 298; CROC:35; HAZO 13: 5612; HURG:103; MAS 13: 5612; PE:499: PEA:499
Words to Governor Wise at Harper's Ferry. CHAL 6: 405; HAZO 13:5611; MAS 13:5611

BROWN, JOHN
Finley, J. H.
John Brown. HARSO:202; WERN 42:150
Garrison, W. L.
On the death of John Brown. BREW 6:210; BRYW 9:189; COP:299; COPA:299; COPB:299; ORAMA 2:209; REEM 10:179; REEMA 13: 1065; REEMB 11:183
Phillips, W.
John Brown and the spirit of "59." BREW 8:318; FULB:326; HAZO 16:6913; MAS 16:6913; REEM 10: 182; REEMA 14:1588; REEMB 11:186
Puritan principle and John Brown. LEEW 10:179
Roosevelt, T.
New nationalism (at dedication of John Brown Memorial Park (Osawatomic, Kansas) WPRC:27
Simons, C. C.
John Brown. TRUW:96
Brown, John Mason
'Beat" generation. HURG:341
Brown, Joseph Emerson
Against the Woman Suffrage Amendment. WPRA:333
Brown, Kenneth I.
Men and women with antennae. BRAP:132
Brown, Lewis H.
Change is the essence of progress. -Same as his Private agencies and public goals in the postwar world
Freedom or planned economy: there is no middle road. BA 1945-46:133
Private agencies and public goals in the postwar world. BA 1942-43:202; ON:76
Brown, Mary Virginia
Confessional. YE:99
Brown, Rollo Walter
Crime against youth. SAR:81
Brown, W. R.
Flag. PROS:28
Brown, William
Tomorrow's extra. YR 2:63
Browne, Charles Farrar
Mormons. REEM 8:47; REEMA 4:123; REEMB 13:47
Browne, Lewis and others (G. V. Denny Jr.; Lin Yu Tang; H. Shapley; J. H. Smith)
Has twentieth century civilization improved mankind? BA 1947-48:188
Brownell, Herbert, Jr. See Eisenhower, D. D., jt. auth.
Brownlow, William Gannaway
Grape shot and hemp. BREW 2:290
Value of the American Union. BREW 2:290
Brownson, Orestes Augustus
Laboring classes. BL:171
Oration on liberal studies. HAZO 14:5884; MAS 14:5884

BROWNSVILLE (TEXAS) RIOT, 1906
Carmack, E. W.
Brownsville affair. HARSO: 18
Roosevelt, T.
Brownsville incident. FIP:54

Bru, Frederico Laredo
United hemisphere defense. COP:567; COPB:471
Brubacher, R. R.
Speech on election as president of Iowa Bankers Association. PR:127
Bruce, Blanche K.
Address delivered to the United States Senate in behalf of admitting P. B. S. Pinchback as Senator from the State of Louisiana. WOON:267
Speech delivered in March, 1876, when it became necessary for the Senate to introduce a resolution appointing a committee to investigate election practices in Mississippi. WOON:270
Bruce, Roscoe Conkling
Freedom through education. WOON:585
Bruce, Wallace
Flag. BLAA:191; BLAB:191
Bruce, William Cabell
General Robert E. Lee. DOA: 33
Brueggemann, G. R.
Keep yourselves in the love of God. ACW:140
Bruehl, Charles P.
Conditions of labor. CATA 1: 63
Bruening, William F.
Dual obligation of marriage. ACW:127
Bruisloff, Alexis
Welcoming Elihu Root, June 27, 1917. REEM 3:162
Bruntz, George G.
Men to match our mountains (installation speech). MOUG:147; MOUGA:147

BRUSSELS EXPOSITION, 1959
See Exhibitions
Brustat, August W.
Help in times past (10th wedding anniversary). ACW:152
Bryan, John Stewart
Acceptance of Phi Beta Kappa Memorial Hall. BRAC:268
Bryan, William Jennings
Against militarism. SHU:164
America's mission. BOB:209; FUL:48; ONEM:598; ONES; 196; REEM 1:161; REEMA 1:94; REEMB 1:158; SHUP: 193
Annexation. FUL:39
Campaign speech of 1900. CORP:285
Cross of gold. BAAMP:193; BIR 3:214; BOU:171; BRAS: 182; BREW 2:294; BRIM: 314; CAP:119; CHAL 14: 415; COP:333; COPA:333; COPB:333; CORP:284; CROC:37; FO:225; FRY:45; HARS:169; HAZO 22:10935; HIB:155; HIBS:461; HICF: 179; HURG:147; MAS 25: 10935; PAR:492; PE:637; PEA:637; PO:103; REEM 10:326; REEMB 11:340; RID: 75; SHAH:551; WERN 42:44
Essence of patriotism. BOA:80; BOB:112
Future of the Philippines. FUL: 44
Imperialism. FUL:42
Imperialism (accepting Democratic nomination for Presidency, 1900). WPRA:358
Lincoln as an orator. LINM: 221
Moses vs. Darwin. WPRC:107
Naboth's vineyard. BRAC:5
On the income tax. REEMA 11: 350
Opposing Parker for the temporary chairman of Baltimore Convention. CORP:287
Presentation of Gray's Elegy. BRAC:258
Prince of peace. BLAB:367; IMMD:165; PL:697; REEM 8:68; REEMB 13:70
Religious liberty and the Ku Klux Klan. WHIP:290
Response to a welcome address. HOAP:34
Spoken word. REEM 9:89; REEMB 13:91

Tariff. CORP:284
Stampedes the Democratic national convention.—Same as his Cross of gold
Thanksgiving address in London. CORP:286
Valedictory at Illinois College. CORP:283
Thou shalt not steal. BOA: 333; BOB:56

BRYAN, WILLIAM JENNINGS
Bishop, D.A.C.
Bryan's use of ethical proof in the "Cross of gold" speech. BRAP:157
Daniels, J.
Eulogy on W.J. Bryan. CORP:272
Depew, C.M.
Presents William Jennings Bryan. LY:217
Jones, E.D.
Adventures among great Americans. BART 1:115

Bryant, William Cullem
Accepting a portfolio on the seventieth birthday. KNAS: 165; KNASA:165; ONEM: 715
Address at the founding of the Metropolitan Art Museum. CHAL 6:134; HAZO 12: 5205; MAS 12:5205
Birthday address. KNAS:188; KNASA:188; REEM 1:167; REEMA 1:103; REEMB 1: 164
Fiftieth anniversary of the Mercantile Library Association. HAZO 12:5211; MAS 12:5211
Greatness of Burns. -Same as his To the Burns Club
Introduces Lord Houghton. REEMA 2:635
Introducing a foreign patriot - Louis Kossuth. BRYW 9: 144; CHAL 6:130; HAZO 12:5201; MAS 12:5201; ONEM:664; REEM 5:45; REEMA 1:100; REEMB 9: 75
Poetry. REEMA 7:145
Press. REEMA 1:107
Sir Walter Scott (unveiling statue in Central Park, New York) REEMA 7:155
To the Burns Club. BREW 2: 302; KNAS:48; KNASA:48

BRYANT, WILLIAM CULLEN
Bancroft, G.
William Cullen Bryant. DOA: 265; KNAS:96; KNASA:96; REEM 1:72; REEMA 1:18; REEMB 1:63
Bellows, H.W.
At the funeral of William Cullen Bryant. CHAL 8:454; HAZO 18:7435; MAS 18:7435

Bryce, James Bryce, Viscount
Ass, laden with gold. BREW 2:311
At a Harvard commencement. KNAS:265; KNASA:265
Changes of forty years in America. REEM 1:172; REEMB 1:168
Justice to Ireland. -Same as his On the government of Ireland Bill
On the government of Ireland Bill. BRYW 5:145; LAD:220
Peace. REEM 1:180; REEMB 1:176
Political destinies of the globe. BREW 2:306
Reform of the House of Lords. EMS 1:116
War and despotism. BREW 2: 307
War spirit and the God of battles. BREW 2:309
World's future. BREW 2:310

BRYCE, JAMES BRYCE, VISCOUNT
Choate, J.H.
Farewell to Ambassador Bryce. REEM 1:273; REEMB 1:274
Presents James Bryce. LY: 231

BRYN MAWR
Park, M. E.
Welcome to Bryn Mawr's fiftieth anniversary. GA:22
Sabin, F. R.
Acceptance of the M. Carey Thomas award. GA:48
Thomas, M. C.
Farewell to Bryn Mawr. GA:57

Bryson, Lyman
What should we do with the radio? BART 4:133

Bryson, Lyman and others (H. Hansen; R. Kent; D. Taylor; O. Welles)
Opportunities for success in the creative arts. SAR:403

Bryson, Thomas Hugh
Catholic Total Abstinence Movement. CATA 2:89

Buchan, Alastair
Argument for graduated deterrence, Dec. 1, 1955. GRAC: 171

Buchanan, James
Inaugural address. BREW 2: 134; CHAL 5:448; CHI:119; HAZO 12:4958; LOTI:111; MAS 12:4958; USIN:111; USINA:111

BUCHANAN, JAMES
Cannon, J. G.
Buchanan and Secession. BREW 3:111

Buchanan, John G.
Presents Augustus N. Hand. LY:145

Buchanan, Lloyd
Army and Navy football. WERN 54:164

Buchhalter, J.
For a Bar Mitzvah. ZEL:76

Buck, Charles F.
Oration of Druids. THOU 3: 209

BUCK, FRANK
Introducing Frank Buck. NI: 125; NIA:95

BUCK, GENE
Introducing Gene Buck. NI:146; NIA:109

Buck, Pearl
Women's place in a democracy. BUTA:212

Buckhorn, Elmer A.
Wolves of industry. YR 2:75

Buckingham, George T.
Power and civilization. NESA: 157

Buckley, J. M.
Demands of the hour. THOU 1: 224

Buckmaster, Stanley Owen
Statue of Westminster, 1931. EMS 2:293

Buckner, Emory R.
Securing justice. ONEC:410

Budd, Ralph
Introduces Charles F. Kettering. PR:48

BUDGET MESSAGES See United States - Congress

Buffington, Joseph
John Marshall, the foundation builder. BOA:245; BOB:153

Buhler, Irene
Modern Shylocks. BRP 5:81

BUILDING
Building officials. SCHS:51
Dickson, P.
Introducing a general contractor. BRC:306

BUILDING AND LOAN ASSOCIATIONS
Jacobi, H.
Introducing a building and loan executive. BRC:290

BUILDINGS, DEDICATION OF
See Dedication addresses, subheads Auditoriums; Churches; Cornerstones; Dormitories; Hospitals; Schools

Bulganin, Nikolai Alexandrovich
Lessening of international tension. COPB:631

Bullinger, Heinrich
Sermon on faith. LEEW 4:109

Bullis, Harry A.
White light: introducing Dr. Alfred P. Haake at sales managers conference. BRC: 324
Bullitt, William C.
America is in danger. COP: 570
Bullock, Alexander H.
Intellectual leadership in American history. NORR 1st ser: 128

BULWER-LYTTON, EDWARD GEORGE EARLE LYTTON
See Lytton, E. G. L. B. -L.
Bumby, J. H.
Sacrifice that failed (failure of our war-time ideals). ASHF:382
Bunce, Arthur C., Jr. See Chang, J. M., jt. auth.
Bunche, Ralph J.
Barriers of race can be surmounted. YE:282
Challenge of human relations: Lincoln birthday dinner. BA 1949-50:142; HAR:452
Dreams and realities (installation of Gamma chapter of Phi Beta Kappa). NORR 3d ser:264
See also Hughes, L., jt. auth.
Bungay, George W.
Grandeur of Grant's character. THOU 1:375
Bunyan, John
Heavenly footman. BREW 2: 323; BRYW 3:149; HAZO 4:1572; MAS 4:1572; ORBR 1:115
Burdette, Robert Jones
Advice to a young man. REAC: 220
Rise and fall of the mustache. IMMD:273; REEM 8:102; REEMA 4:145; REEMB 13: 104
Burges, Tritram
Rebuke to John Randolph. CHAL 4:392; HAZO 9:3820; MAS 9:3820
Supreme Court. BREW 2:329
Burgess, W. Randolph
Presents Paul H. Douglas. LY:223
Burgh, Walter Hussey
Free trade debate, 1783. KET: 110
Burke, Edmund
Against coercing America. BREW 2:406
Age of chivalry. BREW 2:417; CODS:182; CODSA:182; GOOD:365; REEM 9:131; REEMB 10:137
Attempts to vindicate himself before his estranged constituents. -Same as his Principle in politics: speech at Bristol, previous to the election, 1780.
Conciliation with America. ADR 1:182; BEA:65; BERS:41; BOU:33; BRAO:3; BRYW 6: 3; CHAL 2:344; COP:157; COPA:157; COPB:157; FULB:23; GOOD:266; HAZO 5:2114; HIB:124; KET:43; KLEG:130; MAS 5:2114; ONEM:139; ORBR 1:229; PAUF 1:62; PE:131; PEA: 131; PL:410; REEM 9:109; REEMA 11:368; REEMB 10: 114; SAA:26; SHUM:11
East India Bill of Mr. Fox. GOOD:312; PE:175; PEA: 175
Frequency of elections. EMS 2: 113
Impeachment of Warren Hastings. BREW 2:337, 343; BRYW 6:50; CLAY:55; CODS: 168; CODSA:180; COP:163; COPA:163; COPB:163; CROC:46; GOOD:362; HAZO 6:2193; KESI 1:114; MAS 6:2193; MEAR:118; PE:178; PEA:178; REEM 9:126; REEMB 10:131
Marie Antoinette. -Same as his Age of chivalry
On American taxation, April, 1774. CLAY:182; CODS:120; CODSA:120; EMS 2:221; GOOD:241; HARSO:353; KET:

Burke, Edmund (cont.)
On declining the election at Bristol, September 9, 1780. GOOD:310
On the Nabob of Arcot's debts. GOOD:330; KET:65; LEEW 6:169
Plea for domestic reform. HAY:31
Principle in politics: speech at Bristol, previous to the election, 1780 (defends his Parliamentary conduct) BRAO:89; BREW 2:412; BYRW 6:40; GOOD:292; HIB:143; PE:160; PEA:160
Speech at his arrival at Bristol before the election in that city, 1774. BRTH:65; BRTHA:65
Speech to the electors of Bristol, November 3, 1774 (on being elected to Parliament). BRTH:67; BRTHA:67

BURKE, EDMUND
Birrell, A.
Edmund Burke. BEA:43; BRYW 5:131; CHAL 14:151; HAZO 25:10660; MAS 25:10660; REEM 5:10; REEMA 4:71; REEMB 9:39
Burke, Edward R.
How long will the American Republic last? HOC:28; SAR:200
Burke, Thomas F.
"Righteousness of revolt" (from dock at Dublin). HAZO 24:10324; MAS 24:10324
Burkhard, Charles
Indian's problem faces the white man. YR 4:197
Burlingame, Anson
Massachusetts and the Sumner assault. BREW 2:420; CHAL 10:52; HAZO 19:8180; MAS 19:8180; REEMA 11:429
Burnett, Albert G.
Young men in politics. WAGN:256
Burnett, H. E.
Americans rallying 'round the national flag. THOU 1:301
Burnett, Henry L.
Summation for the defendant in the Page case. HICJ:63
Burnham, Harry Lawson Webster, 1st Viscount
Journalism. BEA:77
Welcome to the Associated Advertising Clubs of the world. LINM:28
Burns, Charles Wesley
Good will to men. ONEC:471
Burns, George
Response to tributes at Friars' Club dinner. JEYO:111, 113, 114

BURNS, GEORGE
Benny, J.
Remarks at Friars' Club dinner to Burns and Allen. JEYO:66, 68, 105, 108
Cagney, J.
Speech at Friars' Club dinner to Burns and Allen. JEYO:81
Cantor, E.
Remarks at Friars' Club dinner to Burns and Allen. JEYO:77, 78
Goetz, W. E.
Speech at Friars' Club dinner to Burns and Allen. JEYO:75
Goldwyn, S.
Speech at Friars' Club dinner to Burns and Allen. JEYO:99
Jessel, G.
Introduces George Burns and Gracie Allen at Friars' Club dinner in their honor. JEYO:109
Kaye, D.
Speech at Friars' Club dinner to Burns and Allen. JEYO:102
Mirken, B.
Introduces Jack Benny at Friars' Club dinner to Burns and Allen. JEYO:65
Paley, W. S.

Speech at Friars' Club dinner to Burns and Allen. JEYO:90
Reagan, R.
Speech at Friars' Club dinner to Burns and Allen. JEYO:88
Schary, D.O.
Speech at Friars' Club dinner to Burns and Allen. JEYO:72
Thomas, D.
Speech at Friars' Club dinner to Burns and Allen. JEYO:93
Burns, James A.
Making of character. EXEE:176

BURNS, ROBERT
Bryant, W.C.
To the Burns Club. BREW 2:302; KNAS:48; KNASA:48
Curtis, G.W.
Robert Burns. LA:137
Emerson, R.W.
Memory of Burns. BEA:179; COP:613; COPB:653; HAZO 14:5994; HURG:106; KNAS:104; KNASA:104; MAS 14:5994; ONEM:467; REEM 2:24; REEMA 2:439; REEMB 2:24
Rosebery, A.P.P.
Oration on Robert Burns (delivered before tomb at Dumfries, Scotland). ORBR 2:409
Robert Burns (delivered in St. Andrews Hall, Glasgow, at Burns centennary). BRYW 5:174; LAD:212; REEM 5:333; REEMA 9:1007; REEMB 9:375
Rowell, A.B.
Robert Burns. COUW:57
Tanner, B.F.
Robert Burns. COUW:141
Burns, Robert W.
Freedom and war. ANGC:108
Burnstein, Jack
Operation crossroad. NOR 1947:101

BURR, AARON
Clark, C.
Aaron Burr. REEMA 7:230
Green, J.E., Jr.
Aaron Burr: a splendid failure. SHUC:325
Hardy, C.D.
From fame to infamy. COUW:117
Randolph, E.
In defence of Aaron Burr, 1807. BREW 9:23; HELE:146
Wirt, W.
Burr and Blennerhasset (at trial of Burr) BREW 10:262; CHAL 4:457; HAZO 10:3955; LEEW 9:83; MAS 10:3955; REEMA 15:2135; SOU 9:386
Burrell, David James
Belief of an unbeliever. LAD:168
Christian endeavors and the dramshops. THOU 1:566
Forefather's day. THOU 1:328
Incentives to patriotism. SHU:160
Sursum Corda: Thanksgiving address. THOU 2:289
Taxing under Cyrenius. THOU 2:343
Burroughs, Jack
Integrity of youth. YR 7:115
Burroughs, John
Let there be light. YR 2:103
BURROUGHS, JOHN
Osburn, H.F.
John Burroughs. REEM 5:325; REEMB 9:366
Burrowes, Peter
King v. Edward Sheridan, M.D. KET:247
King v. Robinson for bigamy. KET:263
Burrows, A.S.
Royal Arcanum and the Royal law. THOU 3:382
Burton, Ernest D.
Business and scholarship-what have they to do with one

Burton, E.D.(cont.)
another? EXEE:73
Burton, H.C.
What price freedom. DO:7
Burton, Harold H.
America's road to lasting peace. BA 1943-44:106
Burton, Laurence J.
Rights we fight for. DO:145
Burton, Marion L.
Nominating speech for Calvin Coolidge. WHIP:185
Burton, Miriam
Military occupation of Japan. HOD:104
Burton, Theodore E.
Republican keynote speech, 1924. WHIP:155

BUS DRIVERS See Automobile drivers
Busch, Francis X.
Introducing Emory R. Buckner. ONEC:67
Bush, Douglas
On being one's self. NORR 3d ser:229
Bush, Frank E.
New liberty. BOB:89
Bush, Irving T.
In honor of Secretary Hughes. REEM sup 1:145; REEMB 1:183

Introducing Charles Evans Hughes. YE:131
Bush, Vannevar
Defense of the free world. HAR:54

BUSH, VANNEVAR
Trippe, J.T.
Presents Vannevar Bush. LY:175
Bushnell, Horace
Dignity of human nature. BREW 3:11
Founders, great in their unconsciousness, 1849. BRAR 2:81
I, Christian nurture. BL:605
Sermon on the outside saints. HAZO 14:5763; MAS 14:5763
True wealth or weal of nations. NORR 1st ser:1

BUSINESS
Adjusting ourselves to a new era in business. SPIM:157
"All wool and a yard wide" (business man praises American standards) ED:135
Arkwright, P.S.
Don't hate your customers. SABA:267; SAC:29; YE:305
Barnes, J.
Problems of modern business. LINM:411
Beard, G.G.
United Engineering and Foundry Company. SABA:192
Begg, J.T.
Our foreign relations and their effect on business. EXEE:449
Blough, R.M.
Great expectations. MICS:144
Bohn, F.
Changes in the business map of America. EXEE:300
Bones: short and over can mean short of publicity and overlooking a patron (a speech to bank personnel, changeable for many occasions-business meeting or convention of sales personnel, at a graduation of nurses' group, for fund raising drives, to a telephone group, or by a political or labor speaker) BAI:94
Borah, W.E.
Consumer and small business. KLEB:245
Bradley, P.
Business of religion and the religion of business. ONEC:479
Brandeis, L.D.
Business-a profession. LINM:101; REEM 4:35; REEMB 4:79
Burton, E.D.

Business and scholarship-what do they have to do with one another? EXEE:73
Business. NATT:32
Business courtesy. FRIE:168
Business enterprise (for a convention of business men) ED:131
Business in wartime. DR:34
Business is business. SCHS:53
Business is life. NATT:28
Cadman, P.
Imagination in business. EXEE:86
Cameron, W. J.
Business mind. SAC:77
Shovel-leaners. HOB:285
Canham, E. D.
Value of self-criticism for business and labor. ARNS:187
Carver, T. N.
Employee and customer ownership. BYRA:72; REEM sup 1:163; REEMB 4:114
Catching the customer. FRIE:161
Cattell, E. J.
Bigger men, broader views and better business. EXEE:610
Chalmers, H.
Principles of business success. PEAE:75
Chester, C. M.
How liberal is business? SAR:349
Management's new responsibility in our changing social economy. BA 1939-40:293
Clark, H. N.
Management and the laws of human relations. EXEE:473
Coolidge, C.
Government and business. FRY:100
Cooperation between labor and management. DR:28
Cortelyou, G. B.
Efficiency. REEM 4:56; REEMB 4:139
Creations; a place, a plan, a pledge (a bank publicity speech for any business group, for a P. T. A. meeting, or for a student body) BAI:72
Eliot, C. W.
Ethics of corporate management. PEAE:59
Uses of education for business. BLAA:163; BLAB:163; ONES:256; REAC:128; REEM 4:94; REEMA 8:413; REEMB 4:211; SHUP:231
Executive ability. AMEO 2:103
Farley, J. A.
Politics as a profession for businessmen. BA 1939-40:266
Firestone, H. S.
Prosperity and better business methods. ONEC:274
Ford, H.
Free world can't trade on a one-way street. BA 1952-53:131
Frank, G.
Statesmanship of business and the business of statesmanship. EXEE:553
Fraternity and business. THOU:3:370
Gannon, R. I.
Peace through business. GLAD:263
Garret, P.
If I had your chance. HOA:36
Gary, E. H.
Ethics in business. REEM 1:145; REEMB 4:288
Science of business. BLAB:333; LINM:112
George, H.
Business depression. WERN 42:68
Gifford, W. S.
To Chicago Association of Commerce. SAC:101
Golden rule. AMEO 2:105
Greenlinger, L.
Business budgets. REEM 4:170

BUSINESS (cont.)
Hart, C. S.
Imagination in business. REEM sup 2:33; REEMB 4:370
Hendricks, T. V.
Coming through the wry. EXEE:166
Hoffman, P. G.
Business, government and education. HAR:429
Insull, S.
Just as one friend to another. REEM sup 2:114; REEMB 5:20
Kahn, O. H.
Talk to young business men. REEM sup 2:136; REEMB 5:55
Kappel, F. R.
Business needs basic research. SABA:230
Larger significance of the invention of the typewriter. SPIM:239
Marshall, J.
Trustees of Dartmouth College v. Woodward: opinion for the Supreme Court. BIR 2:19; BRE:140
Meany, G.
New horizons for labor and management. BA 1956-57:126
Mellon, A. W.
Nation's business. BYRA:299; NESA:99; REEM sup 2:227; REEMB 5:175
Metzger, G. E.
Proposed grain marketing program. SAB:118
No man is worth his salt without pepper. NAT:3
Our business world. FRIE:156
Plan outline for speech: American business enterprise is not a malefactor but a benefactor to mankind. MOUGA:204
Progress and prosperity. FRIE:170
Purchasing agents. SCHS:213
Randall, C. B.
Explaining what to whom. BA 1951-52:112
Redfield, W. C.
Facts and ideals. LINM:244; REEM 4:349; REEMB 5:229
First get the facts. REEM 6:362; REEMB 7:340
Reynolds, G. M.
Unleashing business for war. REEM 4:357; REEMB 5:237
Rockefeller, J. D., Jr.
Character, the foundation of successful business. BYRA:379; LINM:69; ONEC:220; REEM 4:364; REEMB 5:250
Root, E.
Business and politics. REEM 3:164; REEMB 3:167; WPRC:44
Service in business. NATS:8
Sherman, S. P.
To business men only. REEM sup 2:398; REEMB 5:284
Shoup, P.
Necessity of moving on. ONEC:263
Sifter: know your dough and you will grow (pep talk for bank personnel and business groups-adaptable for club members, a war-veteran post member, or any auxiliary member) BAI:31
Smith, A. E.
Business administration. REEM sup 2:408; REEMB 5:294
Smith, H.
How backward is the front office? YE:51
Speech at a manufacturer's convention giving the causes of depression in business. HILL:485
Spillman, H. C.
Adjusting ourselves to a new era in business. BYRA:407; REEM 7:359; REEMB 5:309
Under the red seal; speech delivered before Remington typewriter managers. SPIM:

127
Wiers, C.R.
Swarm of bees (business advice) REEM sup 3:171; REEMB 5:386
Wilson, W.
Education and trade. SHU: 153
Yeager, W.H.
Art of speaking effectively to employees. SAB:150; SABA:248
You and your job. DR:32
You can't get something for nothing. NAT:5
Young, R.R.
Marriage of business and education. BA 1952-53:135
See also Advertising; Capitalism; Chambers of Commerce; Corporations; Employees; Executives; Industrial relations; Industry; Industry and state; Laissez faire; Stores, retail-Location; Success; United States-Economic conditions; Women in business

BUSINESS CYCLES
George, H.
Business depression. WERN 42:68
Hoover, H.C.
Combatting the depression. FRY:106
Lawrence, D.
Booms and depressions. DOA:154
Rowe, M.J.
Youth and the depression. JUD:241
Taft, W.H.
Panic of 1907. FRY:51
Tough times. FRIE:256
Tucker, H.E.
Depression versus youth. JUD:235
Wieferich, R.
Youth and the depression. JUD:247

BUSINESS DEPRESSION See Business cycles; United States-Economic conditions

BUSINESS EDUCATION
Farrand, L.
Educating for business. EXEE:211
Hepburn, A.B.
Business education. BYRA: 208; REEM 2:204; REEMB 2:209

BUSINESS ETHICS
Business ethics. NATS:8
Norris, L.W.
On mixing ethics with business. BRAB:539
Schenck, N.H.
Truth and trade. REEMA 3: 1026

BUSINESS FORECASTING
McCracken, P.W.
Begins an address on economic outlook. PRC:7

BUSINESS MEN
Beecher, H.W.
Merchants and ministers. COP:631; COPB:668; REEM 1:102; REEMA 1:54; REEMB 1:97
Colton, F.
Introducing a French wine merchant. BRC:312
Crawford, W.
Introducing a moving and storage executive. BRC: 310
Gilbert, E.J.
Introducing a businessman (merchant) BRC:166
Gregory, A.C.
Introducing a floor covering dealer
Introducing a grocer (supermarket manager)
Introducing a shoe merchant BRC:102, 258, 71
Grocer-speech before a club. WRA:238
Hargrave, M.
Introducing a millinery buyer

or proprietor of a ladies hat store. BRC:195
Hart, R.
Introducing a hardware dealer. BRC:56
Hintz, A.
Introducing an implement dealer. BRC:209
Huber, L. J.
Introducing a businessman. BRC:35
Humphrey, G. M.
Businessmen must be active in politics. SABA:223
Hurley, J., Jr.
Introducing a tire distributor or dealer. BRC:276
Jacobi, H.
Introducing a building and loan executive. BRC:290
Kaser, A. L.
Introducing a businessman.
" a telephone executive BRC:152, 154
Emcee at a businessmen's get-together. BRH:235
Lincoln, H.
Introducing an appliance dealer. BRC:144
McGovern, S.
Introducing a clothing merchant. BRC:224
Marvin, C.
Introducing a German industrialist. BRC:291
Merchants (plea for the neighborhood store) ED:197
Milliken, F.
Emcee at a merchants' banquet. BRH:178
Pearson, C.
Introducing a packing house executive. BRC:282
Self-made man needs working parts. NAT:4
Strauss, G.
Introducing a furrier. BRC:275
Wade, A. C.
Introducing a filling station manager
Introducing a restaurant or cafe manager. BRC:99, 100
Walker, B.
Introducing a department store buyer. BRC:235
Winthrop, P. C.
Introducing a business man (head of the firm) BRC:98
See also Success
Butler, Benjamin Franklin
"Article Ten;" (Impeaching A. Johnson) BREW 3:18
Character and results of the war. CHAL 9:264; HAZO 18:7848; MAS 18:7848; REEMA 12:445
Humorous response to the toast "Our forefathers." PITT:50
Our debt to England. REEMA 1:110
Butler, Edith Kinkaid
Service the final test. WERN 54:77
Butler, Hugh
For the Bricker Amendment. BA 1953-54:122
Butler, Joseph
Government of the tongue. BREW 3:21
Butler, Nicholas Murray
Abdication of democracy. ON:252; SAR:181
American plan to prevent war. BA 1941-42:259
De Juventute. ON:33
Events are temporal, principles eternal. SHU:74
Five evidence of an education. BRYA:513; REEM 6:59; REEMB 7:73; HIB:49
Growth; an evidence of education. BLAA:182; BLAB:182
How long must the war go on? BOB:30
Imponderable move the world. COP:443; COPA:443
Individual liberty. -Same as his Abdication of democracy
International conciliation. PEAE:179
Introduces Andrew W. Mellon to Lotus Club. REEM sup 2:27; REEMB 5:175
Nationality and beyond. BOAM:147

Butler, N. M. (cont.)
New critics of democracy (at 184th birthday of T. Jefferson) ONEC:103
Presents Wilbur L. Cross. LY:115
Progress in medicine. REEM 1:193; REEMB 1:194
Responsibility of youth. BA 1944-45:241
Scholarship and service: inaugural address as president of Columbia. WE 1:83
Search for excellence. KLEB: 13
Spirit of Locarno. HICF:420
True and false democracy. REEM 7:63; REEMB 8:51
University is a democracy. PEAE:193
Welcoming Briand. REEM 1: 187; REEMB 1:188
Which way is progress? BA 1937-38:138
Why war? BA 1938-39:13
Will to peace (7th anniversary of the League of Nations) BRAC:325
See also Young, B., jt. auth.

Butt, Isaac
At the bar of the House of Lords. BRYW 6:18; PL:533
Speech on Home Rule. KET: 341

BUYING AND MARKETING See Business; Sales talks and salesmanship

Bwa, Sain
Inaugural speech at Conference on the Problems of Economic Development. UAR:203

Byars, William Vincent
English spelling since Wycliffe. BREW 2:11

Bylund, Helen
Lincoln and the Constitution. LEIO:87

Byrd, Harry Flood
80th anniversary of the birth of Senator Glass. YE:102
Jefferson day. SMI:276

Byrd, Mary E.
Hobo hobbies. JUD:293

Byrd, Richard Evelyn
Conquering the Antarctic by air. DOA:76
Response to introduction. PR: 121

BYRD, RICHARD EVELYN
Admiral Byrd. SCHS:56
Grosvenor, G.
Byrd: the explorer and the man. DOA:72

Byrne, Andrew
Address at end of law lecture course. WERN 54:36

Byrnes, James Francis
Broadcast on Foreign Ministers' meeting. VO 1945-46:616
Common interests of the United Nations. BA 1945-46:39
General Assembly a great forum. GLAD:173
Radio address on Moscow big-three agreement. VO 1945-46:790
South respects the written Constitution. ARNS:144
Speech in Charleston on atomic bomb policy. VO 1945-46:719
Statement on meetings of Council of Foreign Ministers. VO 1945-46:612
Statement on the Soviet declaration of war on Japan. VO 1945-46: 416
War against inflation. BA 1942-43:189

BYRNES, JAMES FRANCIS
Fraser, L.
Presents James F. Byrnes. LY:206

Byron, George Gordon Byron, Baron
Strikes an early blow for the rights of labor. PE:318; PEA:318

C. I. O See Labor unions

Cabaniss, George W.
United States forest ranger. BRAP:28

Cable, C.
Sovereign Grand Lodge (I. O. O. F.

Cable, C. (cont.)
annual address) THOU 3:97

CADETS OF TEMPERANCE
Bradley, F. M.
Loyal crusaders. THOU 3: 515
Work among the young. THOU 3:509
Cadman, S. Parkes
Imagination in business. EXEE:86
Is prohibition a failure? BLAB:300
Lure of Paris. LINM:233
Stonewall Jackson. REEM 5: 49; REEMB 9:79
Cadogan, Sir Alexander
Remarks at opening of second phase of the Dumbarton Oaks conversations. VO 1944-45: 458
Remarks at the conclusion of the first phase of the Dumbarton Oaks conversations. VO 1944-45:456
Statement at opening of Dumbarton Oaks Conference. VO 1944-45:384
Caesar, Caius Julius
On punishing the conspirators. BOU:165; BRYW 2:222; CHAL 1:332; COP:51; COPA:51; COPB:51; HAZO 2:728; HIB:33; LEEW 2: 39; MAS 2:728; PE:39; PEA:39; PL:95
On the conspiracy of Catiline. BREW 3:25

CAESAR, CAIUS JULIUS
Antony, M.
Funeral oration for Julius Caesar: from Shakespeare. COP:58; COPA:58; COPB: 58; HIB:10; LAD:27; REEM 9:43; REEMB 10:44
Funeral oration over the dead body of Caesar. BRYW 2:200
Caffery, Donelson
Acquisition of foreign territory. FUL:54, 57
Cagney, James
Speech at Friars' Club dinner to Burns and Allen. JEYO: 81
Cahill, Daniel W.
Last judgment. BREW 3:30
Cahill, M.
Down with the Pope. KET:363
Cain, R. L.
Unknown mother. BOA:260
Cain, Richard H.
Civil Rights Bill. WOON:328
Caird, John
Art of eloquence. BREW 3:34; HOB:18
Caldwell, Henry C.
Blend of Cavalier and Puritan. REEM 1:201; REEMA 1:112
Caldwell, John Tyler
New birth. BA 1948-49:196
Caldwell, Joshua W.
Appalachian Forest Reserve. SHUO:280
Calhoun, John C.
Champions States' rights. - Same as his Force Bill
Compact theory of the Constitution. -Same as his Force Bill
Denouncing Andrew Johnson. BREW 3:72
Force Bill. BREW 3:45; HAZO 10:4265; MAS 10:4265; PE:350; PEA:350; REEMA 12:485; SHAH:183; WPRA: 120
In support of State Rights. SHAH:184
Increase of the army. ORAMA 1:443
Individual liberty. BREW 3:78
On internal improvement, 1817. HELE:162
On nullification. JOHA 1 pt 1: 303; LEEW 9:357
On the Clay compromise measures. -Same as his On the slavery question
On the Expunging Resolution. BRYW 9:104

On the slavery question. BAAMP:176; BIR 2:163; BOU:57; BRAO:271; BRAS: 44; BRE:164; BREA:148; BRYW 9:108; CHAL 5:310; CODS:472; CODSA:472; COP:286; COPA:286; COPB:286; FULB:246; HAZO 10:4276; HURG:77; JOHA 1 pt. 2:123; MAS 10: 4276; PE:397; PEA:397; PL:613; REEM 10:103; REEMA 12:457; REEMB 11: 105
Oregon question. SOU 9:303
Reply to Webster, Feb. 26, 1833 (inserted in speech by Patrick Henry) CLAW:136; (See note in list of books indexed) FKA:27
Replying to Henry Clay (from 'Independent treasury debate') BREW 3:74
Self-government and civilization. BREW 3:77
Slavery a positive good. HARSO:249
Speech on Abolitionis petitions. 1838. BIR 2:139
Treasury notes. SOU 9:308

CALHOUN, JOHN C.
Kennedy, J. F.
Portraits of five senators in the Senate reception room. BA 1957-58:84
Winthrop, R. C.
Death of John C. Calhoun. REEMA 9:1219
Calhoun, John C. (Col.)
Introducing J. R. Fellows to Southern Society of New York, Feb. 22, 1889. REEM 2:37
Calhoun, Robert L.
Christ-the hope of the world. BA 1954-55:161

CALIFORNIA
Davis, J. F.
Discovery of gold in California. WAGN:115
Platt, H. G.
California. WAGN:212
Roosevelt, J.
Welfare state. BA 1949-50: 127
Seward, W. H.
On the admission of California to the Union. HICF:1
Tracy, F. P.
Pioneer celebration speech. WAGN:29
Turrill, C. B.
Foundations of California. CATA 1:163

CALIFORNIA, UNIVERSITY OF
Sproul, R. G.
Inaugural address as president of University of California. WE 2:251
Calvin, Bartholomew
Letter of thanks to New Jersey legislature - read to the two houses of the legislature. SHE:64
Speech in behalf of the Delaware tribe of Indians to New Jersey legislature. SHE:63
Calvin, John
Necessity for courage. BREW 3:81; BRYW 7:50; CHAL 1: 446; COP:67; COPA:67; COPB:67; HAZO 4:1363; MAS 4:1363; PL:243
On suffering persecution.-Same as his Necessity for courage
Privileges of being in the Church of God. LEEW 4:123
Camacho, Manuel Avila
Address to President Roosevelt in Monterrey. VO 1943-44: 169
War message to the extraordina session of the Mexican Congress, May 28, 1942. VO 1942-43:314
Cambon, Pierre Joseph
Crisis of 1793. BREW 3:84; BRYW 7:152; CHAL 3:447; HAZO 8:3194; MAS 8:3194

CAMBRIDGE UNIVERSITY
D'Ewes, S.
Antiquity of Cambridge. BREW

CAMBRIDGE UNIVERSITY (cont.)
5:194
Camden, Charles Pratt, 1st Earl of
Taxation of colonies. EMS 2:218

CAMERAS See Photography
Cameron, William J.
Business mind. SAC:77
Christmas, 1940. BA 1940-41:232
Don't die on third. SAR:43; SHU:42
Liberal youth. SAR:46
Rock and flood. BA 1940-41:235
Shovel-leaners. HOB:285
Too soon to quit. SAR:41
What shall we tell the young men of to-day? SAR:41

CAMPAIGN FUNDS
Dewey, T.E.
Calendar of unpunished crimes. BA 1939-40:257
Nixon, R.M.
Apologia. BA 1952-53:72; BERS:196

CAMPAIGN SPEECHES
Beveridge, A.J.
America only: opening the 1916 Republican campaign. BRAC:77; ONEM:372
March of the flag. CHAL 14:426; FUL:27; HAZO 25:10979; HIB:43; HICF:188; LA:125; MAS 25:10979; PROS:58; REEM 10:358; REEMA 11:224; REEMB 11:372; WERN 42:89; WPRA:352
Booster club campaigns to "improve our city." DR:37
Brougham and Vaux, H.P.B.
Against Pitt and the war with America. BREW 2:261; BRTH:214; BRTHA:214; HAZO 10:4142; MAS 10:4142; REEMA 11:333
Bryan, W.J.
Campaign speech of 1900. CORP:285
Naboth's vineyard. BRAC:5
Burke, E.
Speech at his arrival at Bristol before the election in that city, 1774. BRTH:65; BRTHA:65
Burton, T.E.
Republican keynote speech, 1924. WHIP:155
Chandler, Z.
Campaign speech. CHAL 8:447; HAZO 17:7428; MAS 17:7428
Cockran, W.B.
An answer to William J. Bryan. BREW 4:116; CHAL 14:329; HAZO 25:10967; MAS 25:10967; PE:642; PEA:642; REEM 10:335; REEMA 12:710; REEMB 11:349
Conkling, R.
Issues of the campaign (1880) CHAL 11:262; HAZO 21:9127; MAS 21:9127
Dawes, C.G.
Speech in support of Hoover. ONEC:551
Dewey, T.E.
Boston campaign speech. VO 1944-45:533
Calendar of unpunished crimes. BA 1939-40:257
Campaign speech in Buffalo. VO 1944-45:524
Madison Square Garden address. BA 1948-49:101
Minneapolis campaign speech. VO 1944-45:498
Oklahoma City campaign speech. BA 1944-45:143; VO 1944-45:432
Rendezvous with despair. COP:436; COPA:436; COPB:419
Opening campaign speech in Philadelphia. VO 1944-45:407
St. Louis campaign speech. VO 1944-45:485
Dewey, T.E. and others
(Shall the Communist Party

in the United States be outlawed?) BA 1947-48:144
DeYoung, R.
Women in the headlines. GA:149
Ditzen, L.
Sweet meats on gilded trays. BRP 3:12; YR 4:39
Douglas, H. G.
Address before the New York Herald Tribune Forum. BUTA:236
Douglas, P. H.
Vote Democratic. BA 1954-55:81
Douglas, S. A.
Fifth joint debate at Galesburg, October 7, 1858. CLAW:83
Lincoln-Douglas joint debate at Alton, October 15, 1858. BAAMP:93
Opening speech of Lincoln-Douglas debate (Ottawa, August 21, 1858) BRYW 9:259; CHAL 8:421; CLAW:55; HARSO:310; HAZO 17:7401; MAS 17:7401; SHUM:142
Reply to Lincoln at Chicago, July 9, 1858. SHAH:387; WPRA:188
Earhart, A.
Speech for Roosevelt. GA:154
Eisenhower, D. D.
Crusade for peace. BA 1952-53:92
Madison Square Garden address, October 25, 1956. BA 1956-57:53
Republican precinct day rally. BA 1954-55:71; LOMS 235; LOMSA:299
Speech to Detroit supporters. BERS:193
Example for conciliatory speech on new plan for districting. MICS:176
Ford, T. L.
National issues. WAGN:374
Gladstone, W. E.
Equality of all nations. LAD:205
Responsibilities of Empire. BRTH:298; BRTHA:298; HAY:275
Goldwater, B.
Campaign speech at Madison Square Garden, October 26, 1964. BA 1964-65:35
Greeley, H.
During his campaign for President. BRYW 10:54
Harrison, P.
Democratic keynote speech, 1924. WHIP:235
Hayes, R. B.
Campaign speech, August 5, 1867. CHAL 10:191; HAZO 20:8412; MAS 20:8412
Hoar, G. F.
Favoring McKinley's re-election. CHAL 11:18; HAZO 21:8904; MAS 21:8904
Hoover, H. C.
Final campaign speech (Palo Alto, Calif.) ONEC:238
Government ownership. ONEC:521
Hoover stands on the record, November 5, 1932 speech (St. Paul, Minnesota) FIP:194
Speech at New York City, October 22, 1928. BIR 4:84
Ingersoll, R. G.
Chicago and New York Gold speech. BRAS:193
Speech at Indianapolis, September, 1876. BIR 3:115
Just before the election, by the party leader. EDGS:68
Kefauver, E.
Speech at National Corn Picking Contest in Nebraska. BRAP:47
Vote Democratic. BA 1956-57:85
Kennedy, J. F.
Religion in government (to Greater Houston Ministerial Association) HIB:178
Kennedy, J. F. and others.
Kennedy-Humphrey television debate. BERS:156

CAMPAIGN SPEECHES (cont.)
LaFollette, R. M.
Official statement as Progressive candidate. WHIP: 306
Lane, F. K.
Campaign speech. WAGN: 401
Lewis, J. L.
In support of Willkie. BA 1940-41:113
Lincoln, A.
Closes campaign against Douglas, October 30, 1858. PE:497; PEA:497
First joint debate at Ottawa, August 21, 1858. BRYW 9:227; CLAW:63; FULB:291; HARS:323; HAZO 16:6586; MAS 16: 6586
Lincoln-Douglas joint debate at Alton, October 15, 1858. BAAMP:101; BIR 2:226; CLAW:90
Morse, W. L.
Constitutional liberalism and the Democratic Party. BA 1956-57:93
Morton, O. P.
On the issues of 1868. HAZO 20:8486; MAS 20: 8486
Nixon, R. M.
Prosperity and the economic health of the nation. BA 1956-57:74
Republican cause in 1956. BA 1955-56:108
Vote Republican (1954) BA 1954-55:89
Vote Republican (1958) BA 1958-59:101
Norton, M. T.
Upholding the American standards of motherhood. GA:161
On being called on for a political speech just before election. BARB:131
Pardee, G. C.
Campaign speech. WAGN: 414
Pinchback, P. B. S.
Address during Presidential campaign of 1880. DUNM: 151
Planning a campaign. FRIE:87
Reed, J. A.
Red line of corruption. BRAC:66
Reynolds, Q.
Campaign and men in uniform. BA 1944-45:123
Roosevelt, F. D.
Address to the Commonwealth Club, September 23, 1932. WPRC:146
Boston campaign speech, November 4, 1944. VO 1944-45:541
Campaign address before the Foreign policy association in New York. VO 1944-45:492
Campaign broadcast from the White House, October 5, 1944. VO 1944-45:466
Campaign broadcast from the White House, November 2, 1944. VO 1944-45:538
Campaign for re-election, October 30, 1936. FIP:217
Campaign speech in Soldiers Field, Chicago. VO 1944-45: 514
Navy day campaign speech in Shibe Park, Philadelphia. VO 1944-45:509
Opening speech at dinner of International Brotherhood of Teamsters. BA 1944-45: BAAMP:267; MIA:356; ON: 383; PAR:510; VO 1944-45: 425
Philosophy of social justice through social action (campaign speech in Detroit, October 2, 1932) ARNS:129
Republican leadership and national defense. BA 1940-41: 124
Welfare state. BA 1949-50: 127
Roosevelt T.
Right of the people to rule HICF:396; REEM 10:408;

REEMB 11:426
Speech before the Ohio Constitutional Convention, 1912. BIR 3:298; FKA:114
Sanger, M.
Plea for birth-control legislation. GA:157
Schurz, C.
Hill and Hillism: campaign speech for E. P. Wheeler. HICF:165
Shepard, J.
Anvil chorus. YR 8:81
Smith, A. E.
Cooing dove. BRYA:528
Government ownership. ONEC:536
Religion and politics. COP:408; COPA:408; COPB:408; HICF:837; HURG:209
Stanton, E. C.
Keynotes the first Woman's Rights Convention. PE:388
Stevenson, A. E.
America's role. BA 1952-53:83
Cooper Union address. BA 1954-55:99
Madison Square Garden address, October 23, 1956. BA 1956-57:62
Reply to Eisenhower's speech of October 8th, 1954. LOMS:244; LOMSA:309
Scoring the Republican record. BA 1955-56:120
Speech at Yale University, October 5, 1956. BRAP:59
Speech to the American Legion. BRY:471
Suggestions for preparation of campaign speeches, with examples of. GA:139
Suggestions for women campaign speakers. BUT:110; BUTA:110; BUTB:110
Taft, R. A.
Failures of the Truman administration. BA 1951-52:100
Vote Republican. BA 1950-51:117
Thanking a speaker at a campaign canvassers' meeting. WRA:44
Thanking campaign workers. FRIE:85
Thompson, D.
Address, October 29, 1944. BUTA:239; ON:365
Government by propaganda. GA:142
Thurman, A. G.
Tilden-Hayes election. BREW 9:403; REEMA 15:1986
Truman, H. S.
"Doctor" Dewey and the Republican record. FIP:291
Madison Square Garden address. BA 1948-49:110
Wallace, H. A.
"I shall run in 1948." BA 1947-48:137
Progressive party commitments. BA 1948-49:122
Willkie, W.
We cannot win with quick dramatics or momentary heroics. HAN:107
Why are you unemployed? BA 1939-40:306
Wilson, W.
New call to duty. BRAC:3
Yancey, W. L.
South does not seek to aggrandize herself. SOU 9:337
See also Acceptance speeches-Nominations; Candidates; Democratic Party; Political conventions; Republican Party; Socialist Party
Campbell, Alexander
Mind the master force. BREW 3:88
Campbell, Glen R.
For a mess of pottage. NOR 1948:121
Campbell, Jack
Pseudo patriotism. YR 7:339
Campbell, James A.
American Education award. BA 1939-40:364
Campbell, William Wallace
Universities and the truth (Presiden's inaugural address) ONEC:145

CAMPBELL, WILLIAM WALLACE
Merriam, J.C.
Presents William W. Campbell. LY:187
Campbell-Bannerman, Sir Henry
"Duma is dead: long live the Duma." BRYW 5:239
House of Lords as a check on legislation, December 20, 1906 speech. EMS 1:149
House of Lords as a check on legislation, June 24, 1907 speech. -Same as his Supremacy of the people
On the policy of the Liberal Party. BRYW 5:226
Supremacy of the people. BREW 3:97; EMS 1:151

CAMPING
Garland, H.
Joys of the trail. REEM 2:67; REEMB 2:67
Campoamor Y Campoosorio, Ramon de
Against the Press Law. CHAL 9:205; HAZO 8:7751; MAS 18:7751

CANADA
Baldwin, S.
Romance of the West. HAY:376
Beaubien, C. P.
Canada and peace. REEM sup 1:106; REEMB 8:36
Borden, R. L.
Canadian navy. BREW 2:156
Naval policy of Canada. KES:2:308
Young Canada and the years to come. BREW 2:156
Bright, J.
Canadian fortifications. HAZO 16:6864; MAS:16:6864
Will the United States subjugate Canada? BREW 2:223
Cartwright, R. J.
What the Liberal Party has done for Canada. CHAL 12:459; HAZO 23:9883; MAS 23:9883
Dawson, S. E.
On the progress of science in Canada. HAZO 19:8166; MAS 19:8166
Prose writers of Canada. CHAL 12:142; HAZO 22:9538; MAS 22:9538
Denison, G. T.
United Empire loyalists. CHAL 13:283; HAZO 24:10264; MAS 24:10264
Falconer, R. A.
United States as a neighbor. REEM sup 1:285; REEMB 8:153
Foster, G. E.
Foods for the homeland. CHAL 14:120; HAZO 25:10637; MAS 25:10637
Grant, G. M.
Our national objects and aims. CHAL 12:462; HAZO 23:9962; MAS 23:9962
Hailsham, D. M. H.
Ottawa Conference. BEA:251
King, W. L. M.
British Constitution in the dominions (speech of July 23, 1926) KESB:149
France and Canada. REEM 7:198; REEMB 8:225
Laurier, W.
Canada. REEM 2:310; REEMA 2:702; REEMB 2:314
Canada, England and the United States in 1899. BREW 7:301; COP:381; COPA:381; COPB:381; FUL:181, 183; PL:542; REEMA 13:1297
Canada's participation in the war with Germany. KES 2:357; REEM 11:63; REEMB 12:70
Macdonald, J. A.
On Canadian Federation. BRYW 5:3; CHAL9:1; COP:378; COPA:378; COPB:378; HAZO 18:7487; KES 1:269; LAD:225; MAS 18:7487; REEMA 14:1387

On the treaty of Washington. BREW 8:29; PL:539
McGee, T.D.
"Land we live in." CHAL 10:427; HAZO 21:8782; MAS 21:8782
Policy of conciliation. CHAL 10:432; HAZO 21: 8787; MAS 21:8787
Mackintosh, J.
Canada and the autonomy of British colonies. BREW 8: 48
Meighen, A.
Canada's problems and outlook. REEM 2:399; REEMB 2:416
Montague, S.R.
North to adventure. BART 3:169
Moran, H.
Canada's part in the new world. LEIO:75
Riddell, W.R.
Canada. REEM sup 2:325; REEMB 8:345
Roosevelt, F.D.
Address in Ottawa, August 25, 1943. VO 1943-44:309
Broadcast to Canadians. VO 1942-43:149
Canadian position of the United States. BA 1938-39: 25; BIR 4:259
Thompson, D.
Hitler's plans for Canada and the United States. COP: 601; COPB:577; HURG:257
Tilley, S.L.
On national policy. CHAL 9:251; HAZO 18:7835; MAS 18:7835
Tupper, C.
National measure (in granting land to Canadian Pacific Railway) HAZO 19:8232; MAS 19:8232
White, T.
Twenty years of Liberal-Conservative administration in Canada. CHAL 11:324; HAZO 22:9207; MAS 22: 9207
See also Quebec (Province); World War, 1939-1945-Canada

CANADA-DEFENSES
Foster, G.E.
Defense and protection. CHAL 14:117; HAZO 25: 10634; MAS 25:10634
Canassatego, Onondaga chief
At a council held at the Proprietors, Philadelphia, 1742. SHE:10
Speech at Treaty in courthouse at Lancaster, June 26, 1774. SHE:37

CANCER See Medicine

CANDIDATES
Address of candidate for State Senatorial Committee. AMEO 2:128
Address to a successful candidate and his reply. BARB: 126-127
Burke, E.
On declining the election at Bristol, September 9, 1780. GOOD:310
Congratulating a candidate on his election and reply by candidate. BARB:89-90
Congratulating a candidate on his nomination and his reply BARB:87-88
Congratulating a candidate on his nomination, by a member of his political party and his response. EDGS:65-66
Congratulating a successful candidate, by the party leader, and his response. EDGS 69, 71
Congratulations to the successful candidate on his election to public office. DR:215; LU:1238
Eisenhower, D.D.
I am a candidate. BA 1955-56:101
Installation speech of a successful candidate-with a very

CANDIDATES (cont.)
small majority at a public meeting. WRA:122
Installation speech of the successful candidate. WRA: 123
Introducing a candidate for office. DR:213; LU:1236
Just before the election, by the party leader. EDGS:68
Nixon, R.
Apologia. BA 1952-53:72; BERS:196
Resolution endorsing political candidate-two examples of. BEB:33
Speech of a candidate when serenaded. HILL:467
Speech of congratulation to a candidate. HILL:468
Speech of Congressional candidate from hotel balcony. HILL:465
Speech upon being nominated as a candidate for office. HILL:465
Stating the qualifications of a candidate: examples of. BEC:94
Stepp, J. M.
If I were a candidate for the Presidency. JUD:171
Toast to a successful candidate. FRIT:90
Webster, D.
On being defeated for the candidacy of the Presidency, 1852. HILL:468
See also Campaign speeches; Nominations; Political conventions

Candland, Helen
Toast to our school. JUD:227

Candler, Ezekiel S.
Development of the South. SHUO:276

Candler, Warren A.
Tribute to Lucius Q. C. Lamar. SHUO:234

CANES, PRESENTATION OF
See Presentation speeches-Canes

Canham, Erwin D.
Authentic revolution. HAR:517
Darkness into dawn. BA 1951-52:161
Responds to an introduction. PRNE:66
Value of self-criticism for business and labor. ARNS:187
---- and others (G. V. Denny Jr.; M. Ernst; R. McCrary and M. Straight)
Is the American press really free? BA 1946-47:159

Canning, George
Christianity and oppression. BREW 3:106
England in repose. BREW 3: 103; CODS:464; CODSA:464; GOOD:873
Fall of Napoleon, 1814. BRTH: 190; BRTHA:190; COP:176; COPA:176; COPB:176; GOOD:859; REEM 9:177; REEMA 12:494; REEMB 10: 184
Honour vindicated. HAY:125
On radical reform, March 18, 1820. EMS 2:36; GOOD:865
On the policy of granting aid to Portugal. ADR 3:13; BRYW 4:115; CHAL 4:368; GOOD:875; HAZO 9:3837; LEEW 7:75; MAS 9:3837; ORBR 2:57; PL:447
Recognition of the South American republics. BEA:81; PAUF 1:257
Right of public meeting. -Same as his On radical reform, March 18, 1820
Sees the world at peace in the shadow of the British Navy. PE:418; PEA:418
Speech at Plymouth. -Same as his England in repose

Cannon, Joseph Gurney
Buchanan and secession. BREW 3:111
Mark Twain. REEM 5:64; REEMB 9:94
Patriotism and partisanship. BREW 3:109
Response to tributes. HOA:361

CANNON, JOSEPH GURNY
Clark, C.
Tribute to Uncle Joe Cannon. HOA:358
Sherwood, I. R.
Tribute to Uncle Joe Cannon. HOA:359
Tributes to "Uncle Joe and his response. HOAP:273
Cantor, Eddie
Remarks at Friars' Club dinner to Burns and Allen. JEYO:77, 78

CANTOR, EDDIE
Introducing Eddie Cantor. NI: 56; NIA:47
Jessel, G.
Introduces Eddie Cantor at Friars' Club dinner to Burns and Allen. JEYO:76

CANVASSING
Two examples of speeches thanking a speaker at canvassers' meetings. WRA: 44-45
Capen, J. S.
Installation address. THOU 3: 394

CAPITAL AND LABOR See Industrial relations

CAPITAL PUNISHMENT
Capital punishment. FRIE:100
Hugo, V. M
On capital punishment (defence of Charles Hugo) CHAL 7:8; HAZO 14:5783; MAS 14:5783
Moore, G.
Death penalty. BRP 3:76
Robespierre, M.
Against capital punishment. BREW 9:63; HAZO 8:3279; MAS 8:3279; REEM 9:202; REEMA 14:1746; REEMB 10:209

CAPITALISM
Alexander, R.
Which way America? BA 1948-49:145
Bryce, J. B.
Ass, laden with gold. BREW 2:311
Capitalist system. DR:30
Communism vs. capitalism. FRIE:98
Debs, E.
The issue. WPRC:13
Gordon, S.
Is war inevitable under capitalism? YR 7:327
Green, W.
Preservation of free enterprise the common objective of capital and labor. GLAD: 300
Houser, T. V.
Today's challenge to people's capitalism. IOCP:95
Johnston, E.
Competition-lifeblood of American capitalism. BA 1953-54:162
Kirby, J. H.
Re-Americanize America. BOA:397
Nearing, S.
Capitalism vs. Socialism. REEM sup 3:51, 63, 71
O'Brien, Q.
New revolution. BOA:389
O'Mahoney, J. C.
Industrial democracy. BOA: 343
Plan outline of speech: Modern capitalism cannot meet needs of modern man. MOUGA:137
Reuther, W. P.
Capital-labor problems (March 9, 1948) GLAD:287
Seligman, E. R. A.
Capitalism vs. Socialism. REEM sup 3:42, 58, 69
Straight, M.
Can modern capitalism meet the needs of modern man? MOUG:141
Thomas, N.
Can modern capitalism meet

CAPITALISM (cont.)
the needs of modern man? MOUG:138
Villard, O. G.
Capitalism vs. Socialism (chairman's remarks) REEM sup 3:39
Capper, John Edward
Dropping down explosives. BREW 9:297
Cappon, Lester J.
Provincial South. TIN:239
Caprivi de Caprera de Montecuccoli, George Leon von
On colonial possessions. CHAL 11:483; HAZO 22:9394; MAS 22:9394
Cardon, Philip V.
Some American agricultural policies and their impact on foreign relations. IOCP:115
Cardozo, Benjamin N.
Helvering et al. v. Davis: opinion for the Supreme Court. BRE:353; BIR 4:249
Modern trends in the study and treatment of the law. BYRA:59; REEM sup 1:150; REEMB 6:34
Steward Machine Company v. Davis, 1937; opinion for the Supreme Court. BIR 4:238

CARDS
Card club supper by a member of the club. EDGS:340
For a whist club supper. BARB:165

CAREERS See Vocational guidance
Carey, James B.
Enemies within the house of labor. BA 1957-58:98
This I believe. BA 1951-52:92
Carhart, Raymond T.
Crime wears a star. BRP 3:101; YR 4:261
Carleton, William G.
Effective speech in a democracy. ARNS:5; BRAP:153
New Conservatism and the mass society. NORR 3d ser:332
Take your college in stride. BA 1946-47:222; BAAG:368
What of free enterprise? BA 1943-44:209
Carlisle, Von Allan
Mankind's quarrel with war. YR 3:139
Carlson, Dorothy
What the Constitution should mean to an American citizen. PROS:22
Carlyle, Thomas
Heroic in history. BREW 3:124
Inaugural address at Edinburgh. BREW 3:113; BRYW 5:17; CHAL 6:178; HAZO 13:5289; HOB:35; MAS 13:5289; REEM 6:69; REEMB 7:83
Mahomet. REEMA 4:181
Carmack, Edward W.
Brownsville affair. HARSO:18
Builders of men. BOA:262; BOB:134
Character, or the making of a man. HARSO:28
Eulogy of William B. Bate. SHUO:323
On the contest over his seat in Congress. HARSO:116

CARMAN, HARRY J.
Angell, J. W.
Presents Harry J. Carman. LY:116
Carmichael, Carl W.
One man in his time. BU:146; SOBP:352
Carmichael, Sir Charles, 1st Baron Monro See Monro, Sir Charles Carmichael, 1st Bart.
Carmichael, J. H.
Air transportation-our second line of defense. SAB:180
Carnegie, Andrew
Common interest of labor and capital. REEM 4:42; REEMB 4:100
Congratulating General Goethals. COP:688; COPB:715; REEM 1:208; REEMB 1:209

New century greeting. BLAA: 261; BLAB:261
Scotch-American. REEM 1: 215; REEMA 1:119; REEMB 1:216
Scotland and Holland. REEM 1:210; REEMB 1:211

CARNEGIE, ANDREW
Clemens, S. L.
Saint Andrew and Saint Mark. REEM 1:286; REEMB 1:287
Schwab, C. M.
Andrew Carnegie-his methods with men. REEM 5: 247; REEMB 9:389
Carneiro, Octavio Augusto Dias
Inaugural speech at Conference on the Problems of Economic Development. UAR:43
Speech at final session of Conference on the Problems of Economic Development. UAR:415
Carnot, Lazare N. M.
Against imperialism in France. BREW 3:129; BRYW 7:179; CHAL 3:420; COP:87; COPA:87; COPB:87; HAZO 8:3157; MAS 8:3157; PE:312; PEA:312; REEMA 12:510

CARNOT, SADI MARIE
Bergerot, P. A.
Funeral of President Sadi Marie Carnot. WAGN:366
Carnovan, Henry Howard Molyneux Herbert, 4th Earl of
Freemasonry (at installation of Albert Edward, Prince of Wales as Grand Master) REEM 7:82; REEMA 7:159

CAROLINE AMELIA ELIZABETH, CONSORT OF GEORGE IV, KING OF GREAT BRITAIN
Brougham and Vaux, H. P. B.
Closing argument for Queen Caroline. BREW 2: 265; HAZO 10:4148; KLEG:134; MAS 10:4148
Carothers, Neil
Response to introduction. PR: 130
Carpenter, Matthew Hale
In favor of universal suffrage. BREW 3:140
Louisiana Returning Board. BREW 3:138
On the mission and future policy of the United States (dedication of Memorial Hall, Beloit College) CHAL 10:414; HAZO 21:8767; MAS 21:8767
Replying to the Grand Duke Alexis. BREW 3:136
Carpenter, Rhys
Learning and living. NORR 3d ser:284
Carr, Clark E.
Genius and character of Grant. BLAA:225; BLAB:225
Carr, Lewis E.
Lawyer and the hod carrier. REEM 1:223; REEMA 1:127; REEMB 1:224
Carr, Robert K. See Biddle, F., jt. auth.
Carrock, Thelma
Democracy will survive the war. DO:152
Carroll, John P.
Catholic higher education. CATA 2:17
Labor day. CATA 1:52
Carruth, William Herbert
Heroisms of peace. NORR 2d ser:343
Carson, Alexander
Glories of immortality. BREW 3:143
Carson, Hampton L.
American liberty. BREW 3:147; RID:67
Our Navy. REEMA 1:133
Carson, Ralph M.
Scholar and the socialist. ONES:388
Carter, Boake
Free speech on the news. BART 1:81
Germany takes Austria. BA 1937-38:97

Carter, James C.
Introduction of U.S. Grant to New England Society of N.Y., December 22, 1880. REEM 2:137
On the presentation of his portrait. KNAS:177; KNASA:177
Carter, Randall Albert
Whence and whither (commencement address) WOON: 626
Carter, W. Justin
Duty and responsibility of the Anglo-Saxon idea of citizenship. DUNM:265
Cartwright, Sir Richard John
Services of a patriotic militia. CHAL 12:452; HAZO 23: 9876; MAS 23:9876
What the Liberal Party has done for Canada. CHAL 12: 459; HAZO 23:9883; MAS 23:9883
Carty, John J.
Twenty-five years of research. ONEC:114
Wireless telephone. REEM 1: 229; REEMB 1:230

CARTY, JOHN J.
Lawrence, F.R.
Introduction of a club guest (at dinner in honor of John J. Carty) REEM 2: 313; REEMB 2:317
Carty, Wesley
Big parade. BRP 5:11; YR 6: 235
Cartzafner, John P.
Puppets of propaganda. BRP 3:95; YR:295
Carver, Thomas Nixon
Employee and customer ownership. BYRA:72; REEM sup 1:163; REEMB 4:114
Cary, Archibald J.
Address to the Republican National Convention. HILK: 149
Cary, Lucius, 2d Viscount Falkland See Falkland, L.C.

CASABLANCA CONFERENCE, 1943
Churchill, W.L.S.
Report to Parliament on the war situation, February 11, 1943. VO 1943-44:40
Case, Alma J.
Student's ups and downs. WERN 54:61
Case, Francis
Modern paradox. COUW:257
Casement, Roger David
Patriotism is not enough. HAY: 332
Caserio, Martin J.
Responds to an introduction. PRC:10
Casey, James P.
Impending disaster. BRP 2:92
Casey, Virginia
America - a leader or a hermit. YR 10:123
Cass, Lewis
American progress and foreign oppression. BREW 3:151
On the spirit of the age. CHAL 5:336; HAZO 10:4249; MAS 10:4249
Cassidy, Charles See Purcell, J.E., jt. auth.
Castelar, Emilio
Abolition of slavery. REEMA 12:523
Candidature of Amadeus. LEEW 5:267
In the Camp Santo of Pisa. BREW 3:165; HAZO 22: 9477; MAS 22:9477
On the political oath. CHAL 12: 73; HAZO 22:9480; MAS 22: 9480
Plea for Republican institutions. BREW 3:160; BRYW 7:255; CHAL 12:65; FRY:40; HAZO 22:9469; MAS 22:9469; PL:345; REEM 9:275; REEMA 12:517; REEMB 10: 283

CASTELAR, EMILIO
Ames, B.H.
Castelar. TRUW:82
Castillo, A. Canovas del

On Constitutional reform. CHAL 10:451; HAZO 21: 8806; MAS 21:8806
Cathpah, Michael
For a Bar Mitzvah of an orphan. ZEL:34

CATHOLIC CHURCH See Roman Catholic church

CATHOLIC EDUCATION
Carroll, J. P.
Catholic higher education. CATA 2:17
Catholic education. AMEO 2: 88
Ireland, J.
Catholic schools for Catholic youth. CATA 2:1
Catiline.
To his soldiers. BRYW 2:219; CHAL 1:274; COP:50; COPB:50; HAZO 2:671; LEEW 2:36; MAS 2:671; PE:46; PEA:46
To the conspirators. BRYW 2: 216; CHAL 1:272; COP:49; COPB:49; HAZO 2:669; LEEW 2:33; MAS 2:669

CATILINE.
Cicero, M. T.
First oration against Catiline. BREW 3:333; BRYW 2:293; CHAL 1:278; COP: 36; COPA:36; COPB:36; HAZO 2:675; HIB:66; HIBS: 437; LEEW 2:174; MAS 2: 675; PE:27; PEA:27; PL:119; REEM 9:30; REEMB 10:31
Fourth oration against Catiline. HAZO 2:740; MAS 2: 740
Second oration against Catiline. BRYW 2:113; CHAL 1: 297; HAZO 2:694; MAS 2: 694
Third oration against Catiline. CHAL 1:313; HAZO 2:710; MAS 2:710
Cato, Marcus Porcius, known as Uticensis
Against the accomplices of Catiline. BREW 3:169; BRYW 2:230; CHAL 1:338; COP:55; COPA:55; COPB:55; LA: 130; PE:43; PEA:43
Against the conspirators. HAZO 2:735; LEEW 2:47; MAS 2: 735; PL:99
Cato, Marcus Porcius, known as The Censor
Exordium of the speech for the Rhodians. CHAL 1:259; HAZO 2:656; LEEW 2:133; MAS 2: 656
In support of the Oppian law. BRYW 2:14; CHAL 1:261; COP:30; COPA:30; COPB: 30; HAZO 2:659; MAS 2:659
Catt, Carrie Chapman,
Call to action. REEM 7:91; REEMB 8:77
Political parties and women voters. REEM 7:84; REEMB 8:70
World movement for woman suffrage. HICF:368
Cattell, Edward James
Bigger men, broader views and better business. EXEE:610

CATTLE See Agriculture

CAVALIERS
Caldwell, H. C.
Blend of Cavalier and Puritan. REEM 1:201; REEMA 1 112; REEMB 1:202
Grady, H. W.
Lincoln as Cavalier and Puritan. THOU 1:477
Watterson, H.
Puritan and the Cavalier. BRAC:297; COP:675; COPB 702; ONEM:627; ONES:222; REEM 3:359; REEMA 3:119 REEMB 3:375; SHUM:237
Cavanaugh, John
Our flag. CATA 1:36
Cavendish, Spencer Compton, 8th Duke of See Devonshire, Spencer Compton Cavendish, 8th Duke of

Cavour, Camillo Benso, Conte di
Rome and Italy.
BREW 3:174; BRYW 7:232; CHAL 8:62; COP:103; COPA:103; COPB:103; HAZO 16:6678; MAS 16:6678; REEM 9:269; REEMA 12:530; REEMB 10:277

Cawley, Norman
Worth of the Jew. ASHF:142

Cecil of Chelwood, Edgar Algernon Robert Gascoyne Cecil, 1st Viscount
Englishmen and Americans.-Same as his Speech in response to introduction by C. Depew at a Pilgrim dinner
Great example (Taft) LINM:240
International relations.-Same as his Speech of response to introduction by C. Depew at Pilgrim dinner
Speech at Peace Conference (Session of February 15, 1919) REEM 11:388; REEMB 12:355
Speech in response to introduction by C. Depew at a Pilgrim dinner. COP:690; COPB:717; LINM:398; REEM sup 1:179; REEMB 8:81

CECIL OF CHELWOOD, EDGAR ALGERNON ROBERT GASCOYNE CECIL, 1st VISCOUNT
Depew, C.M.
Introducing Lord Cecil. REEMB 1:402

Cecil of Salisbury, Robert Arthur Talbot Gascoyne-Cecil, 3d Marquis See Salisbury, R.A.T.G.-C.

CELEBRATIONS See Anniversaries

CENSORSHIP
Berryer, P.A.
Censorship of the press. BREW 2:48; HAZO 12:4943; MAS 12:4943
See also Moving pictures-Censorship

CENTENNIAL CELEBRATIONS
See Anniversaries

Centner, William A.
True liberty. BRP 7:88; NOR 1936:28

CENTURY CLUB
Root, E.
Seventy-fifth anniversary of the Century Club. REEM 6:374; REEMB 7:365

CERTIFICATE OF MERIT
Certificate of merit. BEB:32

CEYLON
Maharoof, M.M.
Inaugural speech at Conference on the Problems of Economic Development. UAR:73

Chafee, Zrvhariah, Jr.
Deluge is after Us. NORR 3d ser:28

CHAIRMEN See Emcees; Officers, presiding; Toastmasters, Toasts

CHAIRS. See Acceptance speeches-Chairs; Presentation speeches-Chairs

Challemel-Lacour, Paul Amand
Humboldt and the Teutonic intellect. BREW 3:183

Chalmers, Hugh
Principles of business success. PEAE:75

Chalmers, Thomas
Fury not in God! HAZO 10:4196; MAS 10:4196
God's sympathy for men. ORBR 2:103
Use of living. BREW 3:190
War and truth. BOU:117; BREW 3:189; PI:498
When old things pass away. BREW 3:188; BRYW 4:112

Chamberlain, Austen
Anglo-American friendship. BEA:87
Speech in House of Commons,

November 18, 1925 (on Locarno Pacts) KESB:357

Chamberlain, Joseph
- At the first meeting of the Colonial Conference of 1897. KES 2:208
- Conception of the British Empire (March 31, 1897) ADR 4:303; EMS 2:258
- Empire and home rule. BREW 3:192
- Future of the British Empire (November 6, 1895 speech) BRTH:325; BRTHA:325; COP:194; COPA:194; COPB:194; ORBR 2:401; REEM 1:236; REEMA 1:141
- Home rule for Ireland. BEA: 91; PAUF 2:331
- Imperial Federation (November 6, 1895 speech)-Same as his Future of the British Empire
- Imperial Federation (June 24, 1897 speech) EMS 2:263
- Megaphone and manhood suffrage. BREW 3:196
- On Liberal aims. CHAL 13: 57; HAZO 23:9993; MAS 23:9993
- Patriotism. REEM 7:95; REEMA 7:161; REEMB 8:93
- Speech on the introduction of the Constitution Bill in the House of Commons, May 14, 1900. KES 1:337
- Splendid isolation. ADR 4:292; REEMA 12:541
- True conception of the Empire (June 31, 1887) BRYW 5: 184; REEMA 12:536

Chamberlain, Mellen
- Notable day (Liberty day) THOU 1:489

Chamberlain, Neville
- Britain must go to war. PL: 826
- England's defense of her position. -Same as his Munich Agreement
- Munich Agreement. COP:457; COPA:457; COPB:457; ON:90
- Renunciation of appeasement. HAN:88
- Returns in triumph from Munich. PE:765; PEA:765
- Speech in House of Commons, December 14, 1932 (on war debts) KESK 1:234
- Churchill

CHAMBERLAIN, NEVILLE
- Churchill, W. L. S.
  - Tribute to Neville Chamberlain. HIBS:290

CHAMBERS OF COMMERCE
- Chamber of Commerce. NATS: 24
- Chamber of Commerce. SCHS: 65
- Chamber of Commerce by a local businessman. EDGS:119
- Low, S.
  - Chamber of commerce. REEM 4:298; REEMA 2:731; REEMB 5:138
- Nagel, C.
  - Chambers of Commerce. BYRA:302; REEM sup 2: 244; REEMB 5:188
- Rosebery, A. P. P.
  - At the Free Trade hall, at the centenary of the Manchester Chamber of Commerce. BEA:369; PAUF 2: 367
- Smith, H.
  - Introducing a Chamber of Commerce official. BRC:50

Champ, Frederick P.
- Address of acceptance. SAR: 110

Chandler, Julian Calvin Carroll
- Inaugural address as president of William and Mary College. SMI:261

Chandler, Zachariah
- Campaign speech. CHAL 8:447; HAZO 17:7428; MAS 17:7428
- On Jefferson Davis. BREW 3: 198

Chang, John M. and others (Ackerman, E. A.; Bond, N; and Bunce, A. C. Jr.)
- Background of Korea. HAR:109

Channing, William Ellery
Character of Christ. CHAL 5: 130; HAZO 10:4210; MAS 10:4210
Likeness to God. BL:563
Man above the state. BREW 3:200
Present age. CODS:478; CODSA:478
Self-culture. REEMA 7:182
Unitarian Christianity. PAR: 230; WPRA:82
Chapin, Edwin Hubbel
Ballot box. BOA:366; BOB: 53
District school house. BOB: 182
Eulogy on Horace Greeley. CHAL 8:475; HAZO 18: 7477; MAS 18:7477
Modern chivalry. BOA:165; BOB:194; REEMA 4:215
Nicodemus: the seeker after religion. HAZO 18:7460; MAS 18:7460
Peaceful industry. BREW 3: 205
Rectitude higher than morality. BREW 3:208
Scientia Liberatrix. BREW 3: 207
Source of modern progress. BREW 3:206
Sovereignty of ideas. BREW 3:204
Chapleau, Sir Joseph Adolphe
On the execution of Louis Riel. CHAL 13:365; HAZO 24:10346; MAS 24:10346
Chaplin, Ralph
Our responsibility to America. ON:51
Chapman, Mrs. Charles C.
Introducing Mrs. Mabel W. Hughes. YE:130
Chapman, John Jay
Unity of human nature. LOMS: 221; LOMSA:279; NORR 1st ser:254; REEM 6:89; REEMA 7:206; REEMB 7: 102
Chapman Leonard F.
Next step in our economic development. SHUC:228
Chapman, Virgil
On the war resolution against Japan. BA 1941-42:40
Saviors of civilization. BOB: 65

CHARACTER
Burns, J.A.
Making of character. EXEE: 176
Cap: a testimonial speech. BAI:113
Carmack, E.W.
Character, or the making of a man. HARSO:28
Character the basis of credit-address to a graduating class by a financier. DAVC:556
Compton, G.B.
Character and politics. SHUC:159
Discipline of life and character. DAVC:71
Do you have a weak spot? JAS:126
Environment necessary for character building. AMEO 2: 137
Gibbons, J.
Truth and sincerity of character. SHUO:123
Influence of manual training on character. AMEO 2:163
Hatlen, T.
National recovery of character. BRP 5:96; YR 6:141
Ludlow, L.
Department of good works. BOA:180
Missing part. JAS:48
Moody, D.L.
On Daniel and the value of character. BREW 8:188
Petty, C.W.
Anatomy of character. EXEE:255
Rockefeller, J.D., Jr.
Character: the foundation of successful business. BYRA: 379; LINM:69; ONEC:220; REEM 4:364; REEMB 5:250
Roosevelt, T.

Character and courage. WERN 42:190
Short address on character. THOS:133
Trine, R.W.
Man's true self. WERN 42: 190
Warriors of the broken sword. BOB:193
See also Behavior; Temperament

CHARITIES
Charity bazaar. EDGS:241
Charity the keynote of fraternalism. THOU 3:191
Glennon, J.J.
Charity. CATA 2:116
Hayes, P.J.
Christian charity. LINM:125
Heart's statistics. NI:244; NIA: 185
Joy of giving. FRIE:281
Lend a hand and lend a heart, or the healthy heart vs. the heavy heart (a speech for a heart drive) BAI:103
Olmsted, W.C.
Virtue, mercy and charity. THOU 3:377
Opening speech (at testimonial to philanthropist) BED:24; BEDA:45
Presenting the citation (at testimonial to philanthropist) BED:24; BEDA:46
Suggestions for proposing a toast of Masonic Charities. With example of. EDW:39
Thackeray, W.M.
On charity and humor. BRYW 4:201; CHAL 8:325; HAZO 17:7136; MAS 17: 7136
See also Fund raising
Charles I, King of England
From the scaffold. CROC:72
Liberty and discipline: address to his troops at Wellington. BRTH:31; BRTHA: 31

CHARLES I, KING OF ENGLAND
Mayhew, J.
Discourse on the anniversary of the death of Charles I. HAZO 5:1989; MAS 5:1989

CHARM
Charm talk-teen-agers. DR:303

CHARTERS
Accepting a charter. BEB:13
Petition for charter. BEB:36
Presenting a charter. BEB:7
See Presentation speeches-Charters
Chase, E.A.
Pursuit of wealth. COUW:15
Chase, Harry Woodburn
Spirit of Washington, February 22, 1929. HICF:935
State university and the new South: inaugural address as president of University of North Carolina. WE 2:31

CHASE, HARRY WOODBURN
Nizer, L.
Presents Harry Woodburn Chase. LY:102; NI:101; NIA:79
Chase, Ilka
Responds to Clinton Youle's introduction. PRC:7

CHASE, ILKA
Mulroy, T.S.
Presents Ilka Chase. LY:35; PR:51
Youle, C.
Introduces Ilka Chase. PRC: 6
Chase, Jack
Supreme court of the ether. BRP 9:84; NOR 1938:15
Chase, Salmon P.
Mississippi v. Johnson, 1867; opinion for the Supreme Court. BIR 3:58
On the Kansas-Nebraska Bill. CHAL 7:307; HAZO 15:6226; JOHA 2 pt 1:3; MAS 15: 6226; REEMA 12:547
Texas v. White, 1869: opinion for the Supreme Court.

Chase, Salmon P. (cont.)
BIR 3:84
Thomas Jefferson and the Colonial view of manhood rights. BREW 3:212
Three great eras. BREW 3:224

CHASE, SALMON P.
Taft, W.H.
Address at the unveiling of a monument to Chief Justice Salmon P. Chase. LINM:144

CHASE, SAMUEL
Harper, R.G.
Defending Judge Chase. BREW 6:389

Chateaubriand, François Auguste René, Viscomte de
Against the monarcy of July. LEEW 5:215
Has one government the right to intervene in the internal affairs of another? BREW 3:228; CHAL 4:311; HAZO 9:3729; MAS 9:3729

Chatham, William Pitt, 1st Earl of See Pitt, W.-1708-1778

CHAUCER, GEOFFREY
Austin, A.
Chaucer (at 500th anniversary of his death) REEMA 7:45

Chauncy, Charles
Good news from a far country (repeal of Stamp Act) BREW 3:258; HAZO 5:1814; MAS 5:1814
Thanksgiving sermon on the repeal of the Stamp Act.-Same as his Good news from a far country

CHEERFULNESS See Happiness

Cheever, George B.
Avalanches of the Jungfrau. CLAY:100
Elements of national greatness, 1842. BRAR 1:287

Chelmsford, Frederick John Napier Thesiger, 1st Baron
House of Lords and financial measures. EMS 1:137

Chelwood, Edgar Algernon Robert Gascoyne-Cecil, 1st Viscount Cecil of See Cecil of Chelwood, E.A.R.G.-C.

CHEMICAL WARFARE
Garvan, F.P.
Chemical warfare. HICF: 656
Roosevelt, F.D.
Statement on the use of poison gas. VO 1942-43:337

CHEMISTRY AND CHEMISTS
Bancroft, W.D.
Future in chemistry. PEAE: 187
Coleman, W.
Introducing a chemist. BRC: 200
Conant, J.B.
Skeptical chemist looks into the crystal ball. BA 1951-52: 137
Crookes, W.
Realization of a dream. BREW 4:260
Elder, A.L.
Chemist looks at the world population explosion. BA 1960-61:165
Nichols, W.H.
Chemist and reconstruction. REEM 4:334; REEMB 5:198
Slosson, E.E.
Creative chemistry. EXEE: 187

Chenery, E.
Battle against alcohol. THOU 1:556

Cheney, William A.
America. WAGN:107

Chess, T. Louis
Concise introduction of a naval officer. PR:79

CHESS CLUB
For a chess club festival. BARB:162

Chester, C.M.
How liberal is business? SAR:349

Management's new responsibilities in our changing social economy. BA 1939-40: 293
Chesterfield, Philip Dormer Stanhope, 4th Earl of
Against revenues from drunkeness and vice (1743) BREW 3:263; CHAL 2:194; GOOD:46; HAZO 5:1763; MAS 5:1763
Against the Gin Bill of the Ministry (1741) BRYW 3: 165; ORBR 1:161; PL:390
Chesterton, Gilbert Keith
For the leisured woman. REEM sup 3:83
Chevalier, Willard
Advertising in war and postwar. SAC:108
See also Douglas, P.H., jt. auth.
Cheves, Langdon
In favor of a stronger navy. BREW 3:269

CHEVRILLON, ANDRE
Phelps, W.L.
Presents Andre Chevrillon. LY:63
Chiang Kai-Shek
Address at the inaugural meeting of the Committee for the Establishment of Constitutional Government. VO 1943-44:540
Address at the inaugural meeting of the People's Council. VO 1941:114
Before the Preparatory Commission for Constitutional Government in Chungking. VO 1945-46:113
Closing address of the People's Political Council. VO 1941: 523
Excerpts from victory message, September 3, 1945. VO 1945-46:533
First speech as President of the Republic of China at the inaugural session of the second convention of the third People's Political Council in Chungking. VO 1943-44:374
Message following the Sian coup. PL:797
Message on the thirtieth anniversary of the founding of the Chinese Republic. VO 1941: 459
Message to friendly nations, July 7, 1941. VO 1941:337
Message to friendly powers, July 7, 1939. HAN:67
Message to nation on the tenth anniversary of the Monkden incident. VO 1941:407
Message to the fourth session of the New York Herald Tribune Forum on current problems. VO 1942-43:673
Message to the Indian people, February 21, 1942. VO 1942-43:158
New Year's message to the Chinese people, 1944. HAN: 336; VO 1944-45:7
Speech before Kuomintang executive on China's aims. VO 1945-46:491
Statement on the occasion of the sixth anniversary of the outbreak of war with Japan. VO 1943-44:263
Thirty-second national anniversary message. VO 1943-44: 432
Victory message, August 15, 1945. VO 1945-46:446
War between justice and force. COP:523; COPA:523; COPB: 501
Chiang, Mei-Ling (Sung) Mme. Chiang Kai Shek
Address at the citizen's mass meeting at Hollywood Bowl. VO 1943-44:147
Address at Congress.-Same as her Japan is first U.S. foe
Fighting for the common cause. BA 1942-43:81; ON:83
Japan is first U.S. foe. BA 1942-43:85; HAN:201; VO

Chiang, Mei-Ling (Sung) Mme Chiang Kai-Shek (cont.)
1943-44:60

CHICAGO-CENTURY OF PROGRESS
Kaplan, A.
How many centuries of progress? BRP 6:31; YR 7:47

CHICAGO-WORLD'S COLUMBIAN EXPOSITION, 1893
Depew, C. M.
Colombian oration. BREW 5:149; CHAL 12:332; COP: 330; COPA:330; COPB: 330; REEM 7:116; REEMA 13:893; REEMB 8:129
Child, Richard Washburn
Speech of the American Ambassador at a banquet offered by the Associazone Italo-Americana at Rome, June 28, 1923. LINM:386

CHILD LABOR
Flouton, A. B.
System of child labor-the modern minotaur. SHUC: 332
Lovejoy, O. R.
Twentieth Amendment (affirmative) ONEC:311, 341
Powderly, T. V.
New slavery. BOB:58
Thomas, C. S.
Twentieth Amendment (negative) ONEC:321
Wagner, R. F.
Emancipation of childhood. BOA:379

CHILDREN
Address at a meeting of the Children's Aid Society. BAKF:319
Bergquist, G.
Held in bondage. BRP 3: 84; YR 4:343
Bowles, C.
Give one day. HOA:400
Brooks, P.
Address at a meeting in behalf of the Children's Aid Society. BAKF:319
Child health day. DR:151
Child welfare. AMEO 2:69
Clemens, S. L.
Babies. BRAC:311; COP: 669; COPB:696; MO:383; MOA:383; NESA:108; REEM 1:297; REEMA 1:221; REEMB 1:298
Dickens, C.
For the hospital for sick children. KNAS:21; KNASA: 21
Field, D. D.
Child and the state. BAKF: 310
Geiman, C. K.
Are they really unteachable? LINP:122
Grandchildren. SCHS:141
Hoover, H. C.
Opening address at the White House Conference on Child Health and Protection. DOA: 173
International president's speech dedicating a home for underprivileged children-sponsored by the civic service club. WRA:141
Jessel, G.
To welcome a newly born-a model speech. JEYO:13
Kaser, A. L.
Introducing a speaker to discuss the problem child. BRC:146
Kingsley, C.
Human soot: address at Liverpool in behalf of the Kirkdale Ragged Schools. BREW 7:196
Myers, N. J.
Moppet manipulation. ARNS: 113
Oberg, W.
Lifestream of the nation. NOR 1941: 29
Outline of a speech to children. BAKS:231
Parker, T.

Children of the poor. ESEH:189
Posner, G. A.
Introducing a children's act or a child entertainer. BRH:164
Recreation and the child. AMEO 2:71
Shahan, L.
Through a child's eyes. AN:42
Stone, H. L.
Introduces club members to compete with Quiz Kids. PR:79
Third after dinner speech. FRIT:25
Thomas, C.
"Children of the gloom." COUW:235
Worden, J. A.
United movement for gathering in the neglected children. THOU 2:206
See also Bar Mitzvah speeches Boys; Child labor; Fathers and daughters; Fathers and sons; Girls; Mothers and daughters; Parent and child; Showers, baby; Youth

CHILDREN'S DAY
Beginning of Children's Day. JAS:64
Bernhardt, J.
Relation of the child to the kingdom of God and church. THOU 2:171
Bromfield, E. T.
Some telling facts and figures. THOU 2:169
Children's day. DR:147
Children's day, by a visitor. EDGS:232
Donnell, A.
Children's sermon. THOU 2:168
Judson, E.
Child conversion. THOU 2:177
Parkhurst, C. H.
Sermon to children. THOU 2:164
Perry, S. T.
Children's day. THOU 2:182
Prime, S. I.
Children and the church. THOU 2:174
Spurgeon, C. H.
Jesus and the children. THOU 2:156
Wishard, S. E.
Unconverted children. THOU 2:179

Childs, Marquis W.
Responds to an introduction. PRNE:63

CHILE
McAdoo, W. G.
Republic of Chile. ONEM:71

Chillingworth, William
False pretenses. BREW 3:274
Sermon on making friends with the mammon of uprighteousness. HAZO 4:1493; MAS 4:1493

CHINA
Buck, P.
Women's place in a democracy. BUTA:212
Chiang-Kai-Shek.
Address at the inaugural meeting of the Committee for the establishment of constitutional government. VO 1943-44:540
Address at the inaugural meeting of the People's Council. VO 1941:114
Before the Preparatory Commission for Constitutional Government in Chungking. VO 1945-46:113
Closing address of the People's Political Council. VO 1941:523
Excerpts from victory message, September 3, 1945. VO 1945-46:533

First speech as President of the Republic of China at the inaugural session of the second convention of the third People's Political Council in Chungking. VO 1943-44:374
Message following the Sian coup. PL:797
Message on the thirtieth anniversary of the founding of the Chinese Republic. VO 1941:459
Message to friendly nations, July 7, 1941. VO 1941:337
Message to friendly powers, July 7, 1939. HAN:67
Message to nation on the tenth anniversary of the Monkden incident. VO 1941: 407
Message to the fourth session of the New York Herald Tribune Forum on current problems. VO 1942-43: 673
Speech before Kuomintang executive on China's aims. VO 1945-46:491
Thirty-second national anniversary message. VO 1943-44:432

Cushing, C.
England and America in China. BREW 4:358

Davis, C.K.
"Open door" policy in China. BLAA:108; BLAB:108

Dulles, J.F.
Our policies toward Communism in China. BA 1957-58:48; GRAC:176
Policy for the Far East. BA 1958-59:36

Emerson, R.W.
Wisdom of China. REEMA 2:445

Hsieh, T.
Inside lights on Chinese situations. EXEE:338

King-Chau Mui
China and the international situation. HAN:327

Lindberg, A.M.
Experiences in the Chinese flood. DOA:128

Mao Tse-tung
On the people's democratic dictatorship. CROC:319

Quo, T-C. F.
Restoration of the surplus Boxer indemnity to China by the United States. SHUC:305

Sumner, C.
Intercourse with China. REEMA 3:1110

Sun, Yat Sen
National morale and world tranquility. COP:399; COPA: 399; COPB:399; CROC:436
Takes up the yellow man's burden. PE:664; PEA:664

Tang, C.Y.
Cycle of civilization: China's need of western civilization and a spirit of nationalism. ASHF:74

Wallace, H.A.
Broadcast from Seattle, Washington. VO 1944-45:300

Whipple, E.P.
China emerging from her isolation. REEMA 3:1225

See also World War, 1939-1945 - China

CHINA (PORCELAIN) See Presentation speeches - Pottery

CHIVALRY

Burke, E.
Age of chivalry. BREW 2: 417; CODS:182; CODSA:182; GOOD:365; REEM 9:131; REEMB 10:137

Chapin, E.H.
Modern chivalry. BOA:165; BOB:194; REEMA 4:215

Porter, A.J., Jr.
Southern chivalry enemy number one. JUD:153

Choate, Joseph Hodges
America's golden age. REEMA 1:167
Argument in Admiralty for the "Republic" (steamship) HICJ:

Choate, J.H. (cont.)
183
Argument in equity for the plaintiff in the Union Club case. HICJ:1
At a dinner in his honor in N.Y., January 17, 1917. REEM 2:436
Bench and bar. COP:641; COPB:675; HURG:133; REEM 1:250; REEMA 1:156; REEMB 1:251
British evacuation of New York. REEMA 1:179
British Lion and the American Eagle. REEM 1:267; REEMB 1:268
Farewell to Ambassador Bryce. REEM 1:273; REEMB 1:274
Farragut. BREW 3:277; ORAMA 2:363
Harvard University. REEM 1:262; REEMA 1:173; REEMB 1:263
Impressions of Abraham Lincoln. LAD:78
Introducing and toasting Sir Ernest Shackelton to Pilgrim Society, February 4, 1913. REEM 3:201
Peace between nations. REEM 1:256; REEMA 1:195; REEMB 1:257
Pilgrim mothers. COP:643; REEM 1:253; REEMA 1:164; REEMB 1:254
Presenting a loving cup to George T. Wilson. REEM 3:412
Presents James Bryce. LY:231
Sons and guests of Harvard. ONEM:631; REEMA 1:187
Sorcerer's responses. REEMA 1:159
Test examination. REEM 1:245; REEMA 1: 147; REEMB 1:246
Tribute to General Miles. REEMA 1:193
Tribute to Lord Houghton. REEMA 1:152
Unveiling the statue of Rufus Choate. BLAA:262; BLAB:262; CHAL 12:56; HAZO 22:9461; KLEG:172; MAS 22:9461
War for freedom. REEM 1:242; REEMB 1:243

CHOATE, JOSEPH HODGES
Murphy, P. F.
In honor of Joseph Hodges. REEM 2:436; REEMB 2:452
Reed, T. B.
At the dinner to Joseph J. Choate. REEM 3:136; REEMB 3:137
Stetson, F. L.
Joseph Hodges Choate. REEM 5:355; REEMB 9:398

Choate, Rufus
Age of the Pilgrims the heroic period of our history, 1843. -Same as his Puritan and Spartan heroism
Birthday of Washington. REAC:70
Books and civilization in America. BREW 3:288; HAZO 13:5448; MAS 13:5448
Death of Webster (October 28, 1852 speech) HAY:218; LEEW 10:73; REEM 5:69; REEMA 7:216; REEMB 9:99
Necessity of compromises in American politics. BREW 3:295; HAZO 13:5458; MAS 13:5458
On American nationality (82nd anniversary of American independence) CHAL 6:318; HAZO 13:5493; MAS 13:5493
On the death of Daniel Webster (Speech at Dartmouth, July 27, 1853) BRYW 9:149; CHAL 6:294; HAZO 13:5469; KLEG:236; MAS 13:5469; PL:633; SHAH:258
Preservation of the Union. COP:284; COPA:284; COPB:284; HURG:80; ORAMA 2:175; REEM 10:139; REEMA 12:575; REEMB 11:143
Puritan and Spartan heroism.

BREW 3:303; BRAR 1:321; CODS:484; CODSA:484; FULB:259

CHOATE, RUFUS
Choate, J.H.
Unveiling statue of Rufus Choate. BLAA:262; BLAB:262; CHAL 12:56; HAZO 22:9461; KLEG:172; MAS 22:9461

CHORUS See Music and musicians
Chou En-lai, Premier
Speech of October 19. RUS:29

CHRISTENINGS
Christening of a daughter by a guest and response by father. EDGS:293, 294
Christening of a son by a guest and response by father. EDGS:290, 292
For a girl's christening and father's reply. BARB:83
Speech for a boy's christening and father's response. BARB:81-82
Christensen, Darrell E.
Slavery of man. AN:25
Christensen, Gordon
Darkness and the dawn. NOR 1945:5
Christensen, Roland
Ellis Island and Plymouth Rock. NOR 1941:23

CHRISTIAN ENDEAVOR, YOUNG PEOPLE'S SOCIETY OF
See Young People's Society of Christian Endeavor

CHRISTIAN ETHICS
Bennett, J.C.
Christian ethics and foreign policy. BA 1961-62:132

CHRISTIAN SCIENCE
Ewing, W.G.
On Christian Science. CHAL 13:355
Kimball, E.A.
On Christian Science. CHAL 13:491

CHRISTIANITY
Abbot, F.E.
Genius of Christianity and religion. BL:680
Blackwelder, O.F.
Contribution of the Christian faith. BA 1940-41:255
Bosley, H.
If anywhere, then everywhere. BA 1943-44:337
Canning, G.
Christianity and oppression. BREW 3:106
Channing, W.E.
Unitarian Christianity. PAR:230; WPRA:82
Dix, J.A.
Christianity and politics. BREW 5:261
Doyle, D.C.
Will this war end Christianity? BART 4:83
Ethelbert.
Coming of Christianity. BRTH:1; BRTHA:1
Fraternity and Christianity. THOU 3:187
Niebuhr, R.
Christian life and an economy of abundance. BA 1956-57:191
O'Brien, J.A.
Communism and Christianity. BA 1947-48:235
Rockefeller, J.D., Jr.
Christian church-what of its future? BA 1944-45:291
Royce, J.
What is vital in Christianity. NORR 1st ser:404
Savage, M.J.
What is Christianity? CHAL 13:408
Spirit that should animate. DAVC:94
Stanley, A.P.
Our common Christianity. HAZO 18:7609; MAS 18:7609

CHRISTIANITY (cont.)
Stanley, F. V.
Optimism of Christianity. SHUC:5
Talmage, T. D.
Victory for God. WPRA: 289
Wheeler, B. I.
Christianity and life. SHU: 249
Christianson, Theodore
Our Constitution. BOA:96
Patrick Henry, the agitator. TRUW:197

CHRISTMAS
Address by a teacher or principal at Christmas exercise. AMEO 1:70
Address to a party of youngsters on Christmas Eve. BARB:151
Appropriate toasts and speech thoughts for Christmas. PITT:51-52
Art of Christmas. AMEO 2:23
Blencowe, E.
Star of the Wise Men. THOU 2:366
Blessed fact. THOU 2:369
Branen, J.
Emcee at a Christmas party for employees. BRH: 229
Burrell, D. J.
Taxing under Cyrenius. THOU 2:343
Cameron, W. J.
Christmas, 1940. BA 1940-41:232
Christmas. FRIE:233
Christmas. NATM:17
Christmas. NATS:22
Christmas fantasy. LEHS:22
Christmas (for any Christmas Day celebration) EDGS:28
Christmas (word in defense of Christmas giving) ED:44
Christmas Eve (for a Sunday-school Christmas tree party) EDGS:25
Christmas Eve address. CRAI: 440
Christmas greetings: 2 examples of. BEC:151
Christmas speech. BURS:206
Christmas speech for Knights Templars. THOS:56
Christmas sympathy. THOU 2: 371
Christmas traditions. DR:178
Christmas usages in Europe. THOU 2:330
Clifford, J.
Christmas in December. THOU 2:334
Curtis, G. W.
Christmas. THOU 2:362
Denison, H. G.
Christmas. THOU 2:370
Eternal spirit of the Christmas season. DR:175; LU:1207
Forgotten birthday. JA:47
George VI Christmas message of peace, 1939. SAA:288
Gifts for the King. LEHS:19
Henson, P. S.
Angel's song. THOU 2:356
Hocking, W. E.
Crisis of our time. BA 1944-45:194
How to trim a tree. LEHS:16
Huber, L. J.
Emcee at a Christmas party for employees. BRH:275
Hughes, H. P.
Lesson of Christmas Day. THOU 2:350
Huss, J.
Christmas meditation. PL: 224
Krantz, J. C., Jr.
Star-a Christmas message. MCK:147
Liddon, H. P.
What Christmas brought. THOU 2:364
Lost star. JAS:122
Meaning of Christmas. THOU 2:332
Moody, D. L.
Holiday sermon (Christmas) THOU 2:338
Niebuhr, R.
Crisis of our time. BA 1944-45:191

Pius XII.
Christmas broadcast, December 24, 1944. VO 1944-45:625
Christmas broadcast to the world, 1943. VO 1943-44: 585
Christmas message to the world, 1942. VO 1942-43: 730
Posner, G. A.
Emcee at a Christmas party. BRH:268
Quest of the Wise Men. JA: 44
Rogers, W.
Ah, them was the days, lad! GRIS:59
Roosevelt, F. D.
Christmas eve broadcast to the nation, 1943. VO 1943-44:579
Christmas message, December 24, 1942. VO 1942-43:729
Christmas message to the American people, December 24, 1944. VO 1944-45: 624
Santa Claus. SCHS:234
Selected outline of an effective little Christmas speech. PITT:52
Speech at a Christmas festival. HILL:469
Speech for a Christmas party. BARB:100
Three notes in one song. LEHS:25
Truman, H. S.
Spirit of peace. GLAD:233
What do you want for Christmas? THOT:31
What was your happiest Christmas? DR:181

Chrysostom, John, Saint, patriarch of Constantinople
Avarice and usury. BREW 3: 309
Blessing of death. BREW 3: 306; BRYW 7:3
Heroes of the faith. BREW 3: 307
On the statues. LEEW 3: 179; PL:169
Preaches on the fall of Eutropius, Minister of State. PE:58; PEA:58
Sermon on foolishness of the cross conquering. HAZO 3: 1168; MAS 3:1168

CHURCH
Anderson, J. G.
Church, the greatest conservative force. CATA 2:120
Bernard, St.
Against luxury in the Church. BREW 2:39
Birkenhead, F. E. S.
Welsh disestablishment. BEA:35
Blake, E. C.
Proposal toward the reunion of Christ's Church. BA 1960-61:141
Breaking away from the church. AMEO 2:92
Brent, C. H.
Call to the Church-to develop a Christian international life. REEM 7:54; REEMB 6: 25
Calvin, J.
Privileges of being in the Church of God. LEEW 4:123
Can the churches unite? JAS: 66
Collyer, R.
Church and the stage. REEM 1:330; REEMA 1:267; REEMB 1:331
Cuyler, T. L.
Knock at the door of Christ's church. THOU 3:474
Davis, E.
Annual church service. THOU 3:272
Doctrine of good fellowship. DR:224
Dulles, J. F.
Church and international disorder. BA 1948-49:207
Emerson, R. W.
Divinity school address. BL:586

CHURCH (cont.)
Four speeches of welcome to visitors in midweek prayer service. HNWS:25-26
Fox, C.J.
Relief of Protestant dissenters. BEA:191
How shall we behave in church? JAS:102
Hulbert, H.B.
Samson and the pillars. BRP 1:12
Ireland, J.
Church and the age. ONEM: 719
Kenngott, G.E.
Church and fraternity. THOU 3:372
Krantz, J.C., Jr.
Every member canvass appeals-two speeches requesting church pledges. MCK: 127, 128
Ladies' auxiliary of the church begins a new season. DR:222
Link or a barrier? JAS:48
Manning, W.T.
Vision of unity. BLAB:388; REEM sup 2:212; REEMB 6: 269
Raising money at the business meeting of the church. DR: 219; LU:1241
Reverence toward God and the Church. AMEO 2:83
Rockefeller, J.D., Jr.
Christian church-what of its future? BA 1944-45:291
Savonarola, G.
On the degeneration of the Church. CHAL 1:393; HAZO 3:1280; MAS 3:1280; PL: 221
Scherer, P.
Until he comes. BA 1955-56:175
Slattery, F.E.
Church and liberty. CATA: 2:243
Source of strength. JAS:116
Stewardship fantasy. THOT:49
Tertullian, Q.S.F.
Prescription against heretics. LEEW 3:217
"Theses" that shook the world. JAI:78
Two speeches welcoming visitors in a worship service. HNWS:21
Two welcome speeches to new Christians. HNWS:31-32
Welcome to a delegation of laymen. HNWS:52
Welcome to a denominational leader. HNWS:45
Welcome to a district or state church convention. HNWS:47
Welcome to a new Sunday school superintendent (or other church official) HNWS:18
Welcome to new church members (transfers from another church) HNWS::30
Welcome to visitors at general church dinner. HNWS:27
Welcome to visitors in Men's Brotherhood. HNWS:25
Welcome to visitors in midweek church dinner. HNWS: 26
Welcome to visitors in revival service. HNWS:29
Welcome to visitors in the Baptist Training Union. HNWS: 23
What is the Church? JAS:54
See also Clergy; Religion; Tithes

CHURCH AND STATE
Dowling, A.
Relations of Catholics to civil government. CATA 1:129
Mansfield, F.W.
Relations of labor to church and state. CATA 1:83
Wilkinson, H.C.
How separate should government and God be? LINP:112
See also Religious liberty; Rome

CHURCH OF IRELAND
Gladstone, W.E.
Established church of Ireland. ORBR 2:283

Russell, J. R.
Church of Ireland. ORBR 2:133
See also Ireland
Churchill, Lord Randolph Henry Spencer
Administration of Chips. HAY: 293
Age of action. BREW 3:312
Desertion of General Gordon (February 16, 1884 speech) REEMA 12:592
Desertion of General Gordon (May 13, 1884 speech) ORBR 2:419
Gladstone's Egyptian inconsistencies. BREW 3:316
On the Egyptian crisis. CHAL 14:144; HAZO 25:10653; MAS 25:10653
Policy of Lord Salisbury's second Ministry, Dartford, October 2, 1886. PAUF 2: 226
Political life and thought in England. REEMA 1:201
"Trust the people" speech. BRYW 5:99
Churchill, Sir Winston Leonard Spencer
Acceptance of a trailer canteen presented by Austrians in Britain to the WVS (Women's Volunteer Service) VO 1942-43:156
Address at the Lord Mayor's luncheon, November 9, 1943. VO 1943-44:532
Address at the Lord Mayor of London's luncheon, November 9, 1944. VO 1944-45: 556
Address in Commons on relations among Britain, the U.S., and the U.S.S.R. VO 1945-46:19
Address in Commons on the Crimea Conference. VO 1945-46:75
Address in House of Commons on U.S. troops in Iceland. VO 1941:345
Address in the House of Commons, September 21, 1943. VO 1943-44:380
Address on receiving the freedom of the city of London. VO 1943-44:251
Address to Commons on the occasion of the fall of France. -Same as his "Their finest hour"
Address to Congress, December 26, 1941. BA 1941-42: 20; BERS:91; COP:720; COPB:451; HAN:183; HOC: 31; VO 1941:630; YE:167, 350
Address to Congress, May 19, 1943. BA 1942-43:30; VO 1943-44:205
Address to Congress, January 17, 1952. BA 1951-52:30; MOUG:220; MOUGA:220
Address to the Pilgrims, January 9, 1941. VO 1941:27
Address to the Pilgrims, March 18, 1941. ON:313; VO 1941:137
Addressed the House of Commons in a review of the war, September 8, 1942. VO 1942-43:187
Allied war gains. -Same as his Speech in Commons on the war situation, August 2, 1945
American independence day. REEM 7:105
Announcement to the House of Commons of Sir Stafford Cripps' mission to India, March 11, 1942. VO 1942-43:196
Anticipates the battle of Britain. -Same as his "Their finest hour"
"Blood, sweat and tears." BOA: 3; BOU:102; BRTHA:350; COP:459; COPA:459; COPB: 431; CROC:76; HAN:132; HIB:280; PE:772; PEA:772
Britain stands alone in the breach. HAN:140
British-American cooperation. BA 1943-44:27; VO 1943-44:

CHURCHILL, W. L. S. (cont.)
331
Churchill, Sir Winston Leonard Spencer
Broadcast, February 15, 1942. VO 1942-43:142
Broadcast, November 29, 1942. VO 1942-43:695
Broadcast, March 21, 1943 on the post war world. VO 1943-44:118
Broadcast from Quebec, August 31, 1943. HAN:226; SAC:42; VO 1943-44:316
Broadcast on "five years of war." VO 1945-46:203
Broadcast on the war overseas and reconstruction at home. VO 1944-45:139
Broadcast on war with Japan. VO 1941:555
Broadcast report on war, May 10, 1942. VO 1942-43:280
Broadcast to the Polish people, May 3, 1941. VO 1941:190
Broadcast to the world about the meeting with President Roosevelt, August 24, 1941. VO 1941:380
Causes of war. KLEB:43
Debate in House of Commons, June 10, 1941 (Defense of Crete) VO 1941:255
Debate in the House of Commons, January 27, 1942. VO 1942-43:66
Debate in the House of Commons, February 24, 1942. VO 1942-43:179
Debate in the House of Commons, July 2, 1942. VO 1942-43:364
Debate in the House of Commons, November 11, 1942. VO 1942-43:651
Debate in the House of Commons on Libyan operations and bombing of Germany. VO 1942-43:332
Debate with Anthony Eden on withdrawal of Forces from Greece, April 30, 1941. VO 1941:184
Defiance of Hitler. -Same as his "Blood, sweat and tears"
Dunkirk. BRTHA:351; COP:461; COPA:461; COPB:433; HAN:133; PE:774; PEA:774
Eulogy in Commons for the late President Roosevelt.- Same as his Humanity's loss
Excerpts from address before the annual Conference of the Conservative Party. VO 1945-46:121
False security. HAN:83
Fiscal retaliation. BEA:117
Free trade and the "unearned increment." BREW 3:325
Freeman of Edinburgh. HOC:202
Fulton, Missouri speech. -Same as his Sinews of peace
Germany surrenders. BA 1944-45:40; VO 1945-46:193
"Give us the tools, and we'll finish the job." ON:88; VO 1941:77
Humanity's loss. BA 1944-45:170; VO 1945-46:154
Iron curtain has descended. -Same as his Sinews of peace
Lights are going out. SAR:289
Message from Rome to the people of Italy. VO 1944-45:391
Message to the Yugoslav people April 13, 1941. VO 1941:16
Never in the field of human conflict. BRTHA:364
North African campaign. HAN:218
On Soviet-German war. -Same as his War on Russia
On the creation of an Imperial squadron. KES 2:343
On the Transvaal Constitution. KES:2:3
Perceives an iron curtain. -Same as his Sinews of peace
Presents his program, May 13, 1940. -Same as his "Blood, sweat and tears"
Promise of aid to Russia. -Same as his War on Russia

Reply in Commons to allegations made by Marshal Petain. VO 1945-46:287
Report on the war, April 27, 1941. VO 1941:175
Report to Parliament on the war situation, February 11, 1943. VO 1943-44:40
Report to the House of Commons on the policy of the British government in India. VO 1942-43:503
Report to the House of Commons on the war, February 17, 1942. VO 1942-43:150
Review of the war in the House of Commons, November 12, 1941. VO 1941:506
Review of the war to the House of Commons, September 30, 1941. VO 1941: 416
Review of the war to the House of Commons, December 11, 1941. VO 1941:600
Review of war before the House of Commons, April 9, 1941. VO 1941:155
Save Europe by uniting Europe. (May 14, 1947) HIBS:452
Shall we commit suicide? REEM sup 1:191; REEMB 8:103
Sinews of peace (speech at Fulton, Missouri) BA 1945-46:20; COPB:614; GRAC: 144; HIB:298; PE:803; PEA:803
Speech at Bradford town hall. VO 1942-43:723
Speech at Edinburgh, Scotland, October 12, 1942. VO 1942-43:553
Speech at the Mansion House, November 10, 1941. VO 1941:498
Speech at the Mansion House, November 10, 1942. VO 1942-43:640
Speech following the King's speech from the throne, November 29, 1944. VO 1944-45:575
Speech in Commons asking for the prolongation of Parliament. VO 1944-45:521
Speech in Commons on British policy in liberated countries. VO 1944-45:602
Speech in Commons on Commonwealth and Empire unity. VO 1944-45:175
Speech in Commons on foreign affairs, May 24, 1944. VO 1944-45:219
Speech in Commons on robot bomb attacks. VO 1944-45: 294
Speech in Commons on Syria and Lebanon. VO 1945-46:257
Speech in Commons on the military and political scene. VO 1944-45:108
Speech in Commons on the Soviet-Polish frontier. VO 1944-45:611
Speech in Commons on the war, September 28, 1944. HAN: 282; VO 1944-45:438
Speech in Commons on the war, October 27, 1944. VO 1944-45:503
Speech in Commons on the war situation, August 2, 1945. HAN:278; HIB:232; VO 1944-45:351
Speech in the House of Commons, January 29, 1942. VO 1942-43:90
Speech in the House of Commons, July 27, 1943. VO 1943-44:285
Speech in the House of Commons on the war situation, June 8, 1943. VO 1943-44: 234
Speech to the Allied delegates, June 12, 1941. VO 1941:278
Speech to the Canadian Parliament, December 30, 1941. VO 1941:642
Speech to VE crowds in London. VO 1945-46:195
Statement in Commons on lend-lease. VO 1944-45:584
Statement in Commons on the

Churchill, Sir W. L. S. (cont.)
German use of V-2 long range rockets. VO 1944-45:559
Statement in Commons on the liberation of Rome and the landings in France. VO 1944-45:264
Statement in Commons on the situation in Greece. VO 1944-45:595
Statement in the House of Commons on the British occupation of the Azores. VO 1943-44:435
Statute of Westminster, November 20, 1931 speech. KESB:274
Taking stock. -Same as his "Give us the tools and we'll finish the job"
"Their finest hour" BRTHA: 359; COP:467; COPA:467; COPB:439; CROC:78; HAN:138; PE:781; PEA: 781
To the British public on the bombings. HAN:146
To the Central Council of the Conservative party. VO 1942-43:204
To the French people (October 21, 1940) BRAP:65
Tribute to Neville Chamberlain. HIBS:290
Tribute to the late Duke of Kent. VO 1942-43:502
Troops will cross the channel. -Same as his broadcast from Quebec, August 31, 1943
Twentieth century-its promise and its realization. -Same as his United we stand secure
United we stand secure. BA 1948-49:35; HAR:3
Voice of Europe (May 7, 1948) GLAD:239
War on Russia. COP:475; COPA:475; COPB:439; HAN:156; VO 1941:320
Welcome to Ambassador Winant. -Same as his Address to the Pilgrims, March 18, 1941
and others (C. R. Attlee)
Statement by Prime Minister Attlee and former Prime Minister Churchill on the atomic bomb. VO 1945-46: 413

CHURCHILL, SIR WINSTON LEONARD SPENCER
Stevenson, A. E.
Address at the memorial service for Sir Winston Churchill. BA 1964-65:103
Thompson, D.
Let's face the facts. BA 1940-41:137
Truman, H. S.
Presents Winston Churchill. LY:195

Cicero, Marcus Tullius
Catiline's departure. BREW 3: 345; KLEG:127
Cato and the Stoics. BREW 3: 356
Crucifixion of Cavius. BREW 3:348
Fifth Philippic. HAZO 3:1028; MAS 3:1028
First oration against Catiline. BREW 3:333; BRYW 2:293; CHAL 1:278; COP:36; COPA:36; COPB:36; HAZO 2:675; HIB:66; HIBS:437; LEEW 2:174; MAS 2:675; PE:27; PEA:27; PL:119; REEM 9:30; REEMB 10:31
First oration against Mark Antony. BRYW 2:148; HAZO 3:911; MAS 3:911; PL:129
First oration against Verres. BRYW 2:51; HAZO 2:755; LA:129; MAS 2:755; PL:108
First Philippic. -Same as his First oration against Mark Antony
For the poet Archias. BREW 3:363; BRYW 2:131; CHAL 1:343; HAZO 3:875; MAS 3: 875
Fourteenth Philippic. HAZO 3:

1084; MAS 3:1084
Fourth book of the second pleading in the prosecution of Verres about the statutes. HAZO 2:781; MAS 2:781
Fourth oration against Catiline. HAZO 2:740; MAS 2:740
Fourth Philippic. BREW 3:375; COP:45; COPA:45; COPB:45; HAZO 3:1020; MAS 3:1020; REEMA 12:598
Great orators and their training. BEA:125
"I am a Roman citizen" (from 6th oration against Verres) CODS:42; CODSA:42
In opposition to a new Agrarian Law. BREW 2:71
On the Agrarian Law. REEMA 12:604
On the punishments. LEEW 2:143
Second oration against Catiline. BRYW 2:113; CHAL 1:297; HAZO 2:694; MAS 2:694
Second oration against Mark Antony. BRYW 2:169
Second Philippic. CROC:57; HAZO 3:933; LEEW 2:196; MAS 3:933
Sixth Philippic. HAZO 3:1058; MAS 3:1058
Speech in defence of Quintus Ligarius. HAZO 3:892; MAS 3:892
Supernatural justice. BREW 3:352
Tenth Philippic. HAZO 3:1068; MAS 3:1068
Third oration against Catiline. CHAL 1:313; HAZO 2:710; MAS 2:710
Third Philippic. HAZO 3:998; MAS 3:998

CICERO, MARCUS TULLIUS
Declamation against Cicero (speech attributed to Sallust, to Vibius Crispus, and to Porcius Latro) LEEW 2:76

CIRCUS
Cobb, I. S.
Acrobat. HURG:251
Drummond, R.
Introducing an acrobat-clown act. BRH:47
Gilbert, E. J.
Introducing an acrobatic group. BRH:115
Huber, L. J.
Introducing clowns. BRH:75
Ringmaster emcee. BRH:348

Cisler, Walker L.
Introducing Leland I. Doan, speaker on atomic energy. MOA:500

CITATIONS
Citation given to Edward R. Murrow with an honorary degree, Dr. of Human Letters. BA 1954-55:128
Material for use in composing citations. BEC:46

CITIES AND TOWNS
All soul city. SCHS:71
Best place to live. NATM:1
Booster club campaigns to 'Improve our city." DR:37; LU:1132
Civic pride. NATS:7
Cities - their slogans, slanders, songs. SCHS:68
Cook, O.W.E.
City and the state. SHUC:319
Dinwoodie, S.D.
Inner city-our shame. ARNS:246
Dykstra, C. A.
American city. YE:383
Fosdick, R. B.
'Middletown"-and the way out. SAR:22
Jones, G. P.
American cities. TRUW:177
Lazaron, M. S.
American city. SHUC:313
Opening address at Town Hall

CITIES AND TOWNS (cont.)
meeting. BEDA:70
Our city. NATS:5
Razz neighboring town. NATT:26
Schermerhorn, J.
Soul of a city. NESA:149; SCHS:252
Stevenson, A. E.
City-a cause for statesmanship. ARNS:250
What makes a good city? FRIE:85
What makes a good city? NATS:6
See also Community life; Municipal government

CITIZENSHIP
Abbott, I.
Law of service. BOB:60
Address to Woman's Club on civic duty. EDGS:101
Alexander, M.W.
Citizenship. REEM 7:3; REEMB 8:3
Allen, F.E.
Challenge to the citizen. BA 1960-61:100
Apeland, C.
Welcome to new citizens. PRNE:219
Aulish, F.J.
Welcome to new citizens. SABA:290
Bakke, E.W.
Creative citizenship. ASHF: 112
Barsness, J.
Our last chance. NOR 1946: 41
Briggs, G.W.
Service the genius of progress. REEM sup 1:132; REEMB 4:87
Businessmen's civic obligation. EDGS:99
Butler, N.M.
Scholarship and service; inaugural address as president of Columbia University. WE 1:83
Carter, W.J.
Duty and responsibility of the Anglo-Saxon idea of citizenship. DUNM:265
Citizenship. FRIE:102
Citizenship. NATS:14
Citizenship. THOS:147
Citizenship responsibility. NATM:13
Civic pride (address to a local club) ED:117
Colton, E.T.
Decline of citizenship. COUW:77
Community service. FRIE:82
Cropsey, J.C.
Responsibilities of citizenship. LINM:310
Culture and service. DAVC:18
Curtis, G.W.
Public duty of educated men. BOU:15; BRIM:281; PAR: 365; SHU:194; SHUM:192
Davis, T.A.
Vocation and citizenship. CATA 2:213
Dwyer, J.F.
Dream come true. SHU:47
Dykstra, C.A.
Individual and the democratic adventure. BA 1939-40:141
Exchange. SCHS:121
Eyrich, G.F., Jr.
Thrift and citizenship. BYRA: 148; REEM sup 1:282; REEMB 4:216
Farber, W.O.
Changing concepts of public service. ARNS:233
Finley, J.H.
Thirtieth man. SHU:178; PROS:67
Frye, W.P.
Citizenship. BLAA:89; BLAB:89
Protection of American citizens. SHU:162
Gibbons, J.
Necessity of a moral or religious sense in the formation of good citizens. CATA 2:100
Giving service. FRIE:238
Goff, N.

Slackers in peace. BOA: 190; BOB:176
Good citizenship. DR:207
Hand, L.
Preparation of citizens for their political duties. BA 1952-53:121
Harding, W. G.
Citizenship. REEM 2:161; REEMB 2:163
Harrison, L.
American citizenship and the American Jew. SHUO: 119
Hart, W. S.
American Indian and American citizenship. SHU:130
Hobby, O. C.
Citizen responsibilities. BRAP:56
Hoover, H. C.
Weaving of our destiny. BOA:208; BOB:177
Humphrey, G. M.
Businessmen must be active in politics. SABA:223
Introducing speaker (at testimonial to a woman civic leader) BEDA:42
Kahn, O. H.
Prussianized Germany. SAA:274
Kaser, A. L.
Introducing a public-spirited citizen. BRC:128
Kenworthy, R. J.
Freemasonry and citizenship. REEM 2:292; REEMB 2:296
Local American Legion post reaffirms its pledge of service. LU:1233
McDonnell, G.
American citizen. BRP 9: 109
McKeldin, T.
Training boys for responsible citizenship. MCK:225
Meaning of service. NAT:28
Melone, G. H. V.
American ideal (civilization rests not upon force but upon service to humanity) ASHF:213
Mintz, S.
Editorial. BRP 8:74; NOR 1937:17
Opening speech at testimonial to a woman civic leader. BEDA:41
Padget, F., Jr.
Citizen's appreciation. BRP 10:7
Parkhurst, C. H.
Piety and civic virtue. BLAA:131; BLAB:131
Romney, G.
Citizenship responsibility in education. BA 1959-60:159
Roosevelt, T.
Elemental citizenship virtues. SHU:14
Greatness in citizenship (dedication of Law School of University of Chicago) ONES: 114
Rosebery, A. P. P.
Duty of public service. ADR 4:318
Service. MORA:105
Smith, R. L.
Born rich. BRP 3:62
Snavely, G. E.
Inaugural address as president of Birmingham-Southern College. WE 1:229
Stafford, W. P.
College a training school for public service (college sesquicentennial) ONEM:547; ONES:120
Tributes at a testimonial to a woman civic leader. BEDA: 42
Useful life. FRIE:56
Van Dyke, H.
Aristocracy of service. BOA: 193; BOB:206
Webster, D.
American citizenship. PROS: 126
Wesley, C. H.
Education for citizenship in a democracy. HILK:55
Willard, F. E.
Work done for humanity

CITIZENSHIP (cont.)
(1890) BRYW 10:162; PL: 694; REEM 7:424; REEMB 7:414; WERN 42:162
Wilson, W.
Equipment for service: inaugural address as president of Princeton University. BLAA:177; BLAB: 177; BOA:159; BOB:168; WE 1:63
"Too proud to fight" speech. BRAS:298; FIP:106; FKA: 178
Ziffren, P.
Creative citizen. BRP 6: 65; NOR 1935:118
See also Suffrage

CIVIL LIBERTY See Democracy; Human Rights Day and Week; Liberty; United States-Economic policy

CIVIL RIGHTS
Ashmore, H. S.
Education in a time of testing. BA 1958-59:117
Beaconsfield, B. D.
Civil rights of the people. EMS 2:46
Bradlaugh, C.
Right of public meeting. EMS 2:64
Bright, J.
Right of public meeting. EMS 2:57
Canning, G.
On radical reform. EMS 2: 36; GOOD:865
Cushing, C.
Primordial rights of the universal people. BREW 4: 356
Douglas, P. H.
For the Civil Rights Bill. BA 1957-58:112
Eisenhower, D. D.
Federal Court orders must be upheld. BA 1957-58:130; FIP:357
Ervin, S. J., Jr.
Against the Rights Bill. BA 1957-58:117
Fox, C. J.
Right to public meeting (November 10, 1795 speech) EMS 2:19
Right to public meeting (May 22, 1797 speech) EMS 2:22
Grimke, F. J.
Equality of rights for all citizens, black and white, alike. DUNM:347
Haldane, R. B.
Right of association (February 5, 1913 speech) EMS: 2:75
Right of association (June 30, 1927 speech) EMS 2:93
Halisbury, H. S. G.
Right of association. EMS 2: 72
King, M. L., Jr.
"I have a dream." BA 1963-64:43; BOU:157; HIB:173; HILK:371; LINP; 156; PEA: 835
Hughes, C. E.
Rights of manhood. BREW 7: 85
Kennedy, J. F.
Birmingham. FIP:399
Loreburn, R. T.
Right of association. EMS 2: 66
Right of public meeting. EMS 2:61
McDonald, D. J.
Labor's responsibility for human rights. BA 1958-59:92
Macdonald, J. A.
Prerogative and public right. BREW 8:33
Morse, W. L.
Civil rights and trial by jury BA 1957-58:123
Muhammad, E.
We must have justice. HILK 292
Palmerston, H. J. T.
Protection of British subjects abroad. EMS 2:51
Romilly, S.
Security against unlawful imprisonment. EMS 2:31

Roosevelt, T.
Property rights and predatory wealth (H.W. Lawrence monument) BREW 9:94
Simon, J.A.
Right of association. EMS 2:82
Taylor, W.L.
Civil rights and Federal responsibility. BA 1964-65: 21
Truman, H.S.
Civil Rights, February 2, 1948. FIP:285
Weaver, R.C.
Negro as an American. BA 1963-64:58
Wheatley, J.
Right of association. EMS 2:87
See also Free speech; Liberty of the press; Religious liberty; Segregation in education

CIVIL RIGHTS ACT (1866)
Cain, R.H.
Civil Rights Bill. WOON: 328
Elliot, R.B.
Civil Rights Bill. DUNM: 67; WOON:309
Lynch, J.R.
Civil Rights and social equality. DUNM:89; WOON: 356
Rapier, J.T.
Civil Rights Bill. WOON: 338

CIVIL SERVICE
Schurz, C.
Necessity and progress of civil service reform. JOHA 2 pt 2:400
See also Corruption (in politics)

CIVILIZATION
Bain, M.E.
Possibilities. BOA:167; BOB:196
Beecher, H.W.
Reign of the common people. REEM 8:1; REEMA 4:51; REEMB 13:1
Browne, L. and others
Has twentieth century civilization improved mankind? BA 1947-48:188
Buckingham, G.T.
Power and civilization. NESA:157
Butler, N.M.
Imponderable move the world. COP:443; COPA:443
Responsibility of youth. BA 1944-45:241
Calhoun, J.C.
Self-government and civilization. BREW 3:77
Cass, L.
On the spirit of the age. CHAL 5:336; HAZO 10:4249; MAS 10:4249
Choate, R.
Books and civilization in America. BREW 3:288; HAZO 13:5448; MAS 13:5448
Curzon of Ledleston, G.N.C.
All civilization as the work of aristocracies. BREW 4:348
Cutten, G.B.
Fifth column of civilization. HOC:158
Davis, E.
Are we worth saving: and if so, why? BA 1953-54:96; NORR 3d ser:246
Dickinson, H.
Man's development and attainment. WERN 42:118
Durant, W.
Crisis in American civilization. BA 1939-40:208
Edgerton, J.E.
Candles of understanding (20th century life) REEM sup 1:257; REEMB 4:190
Fellowship. DU:140
Fosdick, H.E.
Being civilized to death. BA 1937-38:210
Grunwald, E.
Toward saner values. BRP 4:64; INTW 1933:46; YR 5:311

CIVILIZATION (cont.)
Guizot, F. P. G.
Civilization and the individual man. BREW 6:309; CHAL 5:390; HAZO 12:4867; MAS 12:4867
Hocking, W. E.
Crisis of our time. BA 1944-45:194
Holmes, J. H.
One supreme issue of this hour. BA 1939-40:391
Horn, F. H.
Prospect for civilization. BA 1962-63:82
Hull, C.
We shall not fail. COP:566
Hutchins, R. M.
Crisis of our time. BA 1944-45:199
John, V. S.
Civilized interiors. HILK: 70
Kennedy, J. B.
'What's wrong with the world?" BART 2:209
Kiefer, A. F.
Trumpets of the dawn. INTW 1933:24; YR 5:175
King, T. S.
Substance and show. REEMA 5:669
Lloyd, A. H.
Time of day. NORR 2d ser: 446
Lloyd George, D.
Civilization disorganized by hate. BREW 7:373
Lovald, S. D.
Unless they act. BRP 10: 106
McKeldin, T.
Five nations. MCK:240
Influence of ancient Greece on modern life. MCK:212
McKinley, W. G.
World's work in civilization. BREW 8:41
McKissick, J. R.
Common people. SHUC:28
McLaughlin, C.
Conquerors. BLAA:234; BLAB:234
McVay, W.
Civilization and the prophet. COUW:69
Niebuhr, R.
Crisis of our time. BA 1944-45:191
Page, T. N.
Torch of civilization. REEM 3:28; REEMA 3:861; REEMB 3:28
Redfield, R.
Crisis of our time. BA 1944-45:197
Rowan, C. T.
Address delivered at Simpson College. HILK:108
Sampson, M. W.
Problem of American civilization. NORR 2d ser:278
Sarnoff, D.
Six thousand years. COP: 429; COPA:429
Stoddard, G. D.
Science and civilization. BA 1947-48:179
Tang, C. Y.
Cycle of civilization: China's need of western civilization and a spirit of nationalism. ASHF:74
Wade, M. J.
Highest achievement of civilization. SHU:93
Watson, T. J.
Essence of civilization. COP: 451; COPA:451
Young, O. D.
World of today. SHUP:200
See also Astronautics and civilization; Culture; Education; Ethics; Learning and scholarship

Claflin, John
Introducing Alton B. Parker to Chamber of Commerce of New York, November 20, 1913. REEM 3:42

CLAFLIN UNIVERSITY
Richardson, H. V.
Claflin yesterday, today and tomorrow (inaugural address as sixth President of Claflin University) HILK:193

Clapp, E.H.
Annual address to the Sons of Temperance. THOU 3:500
Installation of officers; retiring speech. THOU 3:485
Claretie, Jules Arsène Arnaud
Shakespeare and Moliere. REEMA 4:229
Clark, B. Preston
Opening Conference on Immigrant Education. ONES:61
Clark, Champ
Aaron Burr. REEMA 7:230
Courage of leadership. BREW 3:381
Frank P. Blair. SHUO:208
National growth. REEM 1:279; REEMB 1:280
On the annexation of Hawaii. REEM 10:352; REEMA 12:615; REEMB 11:366
Rearmament. BA 1938-39:71
Tribute to Uncle Joe Cannon. HOA:358
Clark, Felton G.
Founder's Day address (Southern University) HILK:73
Clark, Fred H.
Problem of the century. COUW:21
Clark, Grenville
Conservatism and civil liberty. SAR:151
Clark, Harry N.
Management and the laws of human relations. EXEE:473
Clark, Mark W.
Mobilizing and training a citizen army. HAR:265

CLARK, THOMAS C.
Lewe, J.C.
Presents Thomas C. Clark. LY:149; PR:73
Clark, Thomas D.
Country newspapers: a factor in Southern opinion, 1865-1930. TIN:211

CLARK UNIVERSITY
Hall, G.S.
Inaugural address as president of Clark University. WE 1:361
Clarke, James Freeman
Why am I a Unitarian? CHAL 8:70; HAZO 16:6686; MAS 16:6686
Clarke, Lydia
Day after V-day. NOR 1945:29

CLASS DAY ADDRESSES See Commencement addresses; Farewell addresses; Salutatory addresses; Valedictory addresses; Welcoming addresses

CLASS PROPHECIES See Commencement addresses-Class prophecies

CLASS RESOLUTIONS See Resolutions

CLASS REUNIONS See Reunions, class

CLASSICAL EDUCATION
Deutsch, M.E.
Foes of the humanities. BA 1952-53:158
Evarts, W.M.
Classics in education. REEM 2:32; REEMA 2:465; REEMB 2:32
Klausner, N.W.
Humanities; mirrors of genius. BRAP:96
Schelling, F.E.
Humanities, gone and to come. NORR 1st ser:286
Claudius, Appius
Against the Tribunes. LEEW 2:87
Claxton, Philander P.
Democracy in education. BOB:189: FKA:156
Clay, Cassius Marcellus
Address at Yale College (centennial birthday of Washington) CHAL 8:134; HAZO 16:6792; MAS 16:6792
America as a moral force. BREW 3:387

Clay, C.M. (cont.)
Aspirations for the Union. BREW 3:386
Rhapsody. BREW 3:385
Clay, Clement C., Sr.
Subtreasury Bill of 1837. BREW 3:390
Clay, Henry
American industry, 1824. HELE:174
American system. BREW 4: 39; BURP:151; CHAL 5:59; HAZO 10:4068; JOHA 2 pt. 2:202; MAS 10:4068; REEMA 12:642
Attack on Jackson. -Same as his Dictators in American politics
Compromise of 1850 (February 5&6, 1850 speech) BAAMP: 88; BRAO:271; BRAS:7; BRE:162; BREA:146; BREW 4:44; BRYW 9:95; CODS:468; CODSA:468; COP:288; COPA:288; COPB:288; FULB:214; HARS:270; HAZO 10:4101; HURG:82; MAS 10:4101; PE:392; PEA:392; SMI:162
Dictators in American politics. BREW 4:14; BRYW 9: 87; CHAL 5:28; HAZO 10: 4033; MAS 10:4033; REEMA 12:632
Disunion and war inseparable. Same as his Compromise of 1850
Emancipation of South American Republics. BREW 4:30; BRYW 9:76; CHAL 5:46; FKA:194; HAZO 10:4055; MAS 10:4055; PL:606; REEM 10:133; REEMA 12: 676; REEMB 11:137
Expunging Resolution. BREW 4:23; CODS:470; CODSA: 470; HAZO 10:4046; MAS 10:4046
Farewell address on leaving Senate. KLEG:368
Final speech. BIR 2:188
Free trade and seamen's rights. CHAL 5:74; HAZO 10:4089; MAS 10:4089
Greek revolution. CLAY:29; FULB:211; HAZO 10:4095; MAS 10:4095; SHAH:111
In favor of a paternal policy of internal improvements. BREW 4:43; HAZO 10:4083; MAS 10:4083
Makes his last effort to preserve the Union. -Same as his Compromise of 1850
New Army Bill. -Same as his On the War of 1812
Noblest public virtue. HAZO 10: 4099; MAS 10:4099
On the Compromise of 1850 (May 21, 1850 speech) CROC: 88
On the Compromise of 1850 (July 22, 1850) JOHA 1 pt 2: 202; REEM 10:125; REEMA 12:663; REEMB 11:128
On the increase of the Navy. LEEW 9:95
On the Seminole War. BREW 4 26; CHAL 5:41; HAZO 10: 4050; MAS 10:4050; REEMA 12:672; SOU 9:193
On the War of 1812. CHEM 2: 67; CLAY:47; FRY:15; JOHA 1 pt. 1:205; ORAMA 1:415; SHAH:100
Reply to John Randolph. CHAL 5:867; HAZO 10:4116; MAS 10:4116
Sixty years of sectionalism. - Same as his Compromise of 1850
Subtreasury Bill of 1837. BREW 3:390
To Lafayette. CHAL 5:84; HAZO 10:4114; HELE:180; KNAS:216; KNASA:216; MAS 10:4114; REEM 5:83; REEMA 7:247; REEMB 9:11

CLAY, HENRY
Crittenden, J.J.
Henry Clay and the 19th century spirit. BREW 4:239
Jones, E.D.
Adventures among great Americans. BART 1:115

Kennedy, J. F.
Portraits of five senators in the Senate reception room. BA 1957-58:84

CLAY COMPROMISE See Slavery in the United States
Clayton, John M.
Clayton-Bulwer treaty and expansion. BREW 4:54
Justice the supreme law of nations. BREW 4:61

CLEANING AND DYERS See Laundry and dry cleaning
Cleary, J. M.
Saloon the giant curse. THOU 1:559
Cleary, Thomas P.
Constitution. LEIO:97
Clemenceau, Georges
Debates with Jean Jaures on question of capital and labor. -Same as his Democracy vs socialism
Democracy vs socialism (debate with J. Jaures) BRYW 7:214; PE:671; PEA:671; REEM 9:375; REEMB 10:386
Future seen "Through the blood red mists." BREW 4:72
Logic of blood and iron. BREW 4:63
One aim: victory. COP:136; COPA:136; COPB:136; FRY:89; HIB:215; PL:748; REEM 11:169; REEMB 12:182
Opening address at Peace Conference, January 18, 1919. BREW 4:71; REEM 11:315; REEMB 12:332
Winning the right to peace. BREW 4:70
Clemens, Jeremiah
Cuba and "manifest destiny." BREW 4:75
Clemens, Samuel Langhorne
Babies. BRAC:311; COP:669; COPB:696; MO:383; MOA:383; NESA:108; REEM 1:297; REEMA 1:221; REEMB 1:298
Coyote. SHU:202
Introducing Charles Kingsley. ANDS:197; ONEM:668; REEMA 5:691
"The Ladies." NESA:105
"Littery" episode. ONEM:645; REEM 1:292; REEMA 1:214; REEMB 1:293
Mistaken identity. REEM 1:302; REEMA 1:223; REEMB 1:303
New England weather. BOU:193; CHAL 12:447; COP:666; COPB:693; DOA:296; HAZO 23:9871; HIB:94; HURG:128; LOMSA:295; MAS 23:9871; REEM 1:288; REEMA 1:210; REEMB 1:290
Presents Henry M. Stanley
" James Whitcomb Riley and Edgar Wilson Nye
" Joseph B. Hawley. LY:252, 75, 156
Saint Andrew and Saint Mark. REEM 1:286; REEMB 1:287
Sandwich Islands. REEM 8:131; REEMA 4:253; REEMB 13:133
Unconscious plagiarism. REEM 1:300; REEMA 1:221; REEMB 1:301
Woman, God bless her! COP:671; COPB:698; REEM 1:304; REEMA 1:225; REEMB 1:305

CLEMENS, SAMUEL LANGHORNE
Cannon, J. G.
Mark Twain. REEM 5:64; REEMB 9:94
Howells, W. D.
In memory of Mark Twain. REEM 5:224; REEMB 9:262
McKelway, St. C.
Tribute to Mark Twain. REEMA 2:811
Matthews, B.
Mark Twain as speechmaker

Clemens, S. L. (cont.)
and story teller. DOA:288
Clement, George Clinton
Boards for life's building (at dedication of new auditorium, Livingstone College) WOON:637
Clement, M.W.
Whither the railroads. YE:260
Clement, Rufus E.
"How would you have us?" BA 1959-60:181
Clemes, William
Sold! The temple of humanity. YR 10:77
Cleon.
Democracies and subject colonies. -Same as his On the punishment of the Mytileneans
On the punishment of the Mytileneans. BREW 4:79; BRYW 1:34; HAZO 1:43; MAS 1:43

CLERGY
Bacon, W.S.
Introducing a Catholic priest. BRC:49
Beecher, H.W.
Merchants and ministers. COP:631; COPB:668; REEM 1:102; REEMA 1:54; REEMB 1:97
Boyd, R.W.
Introduces his former pastor. PRNE:11
Brougham and Vaux, H.P.B.
In behalf of Williams when persecuted for a libel on the Clergy of Durham. GOOD:896
Called or commanded? JAS:56
Gilbert, E.J.
Introducing a Catholic priest " a Protestant minister. BRC:70, 130
Howard, J.M.
Call of the ministry. SHUC:385
Introducing a clergyman-six examples of. BEB:51-53
Introducing clergyman (at memorial services) BED:99; BEDA:177
Kaser, A.L.
Introducing a minister. BRC: 48
McGovern, S.
Introducing a minister - 2 examples of. BRC:122, 131
Posner, G.A.
Introducing a minister. BRC 248
Response to welcome by a former pastor. HNWS:55
Response to welcome by a gue evangelist. HNWS:57
Response to welcome by a new pastor. HNWS:54
Response to welcome speech by a minister as a civic club speaker. HNWS:56
That odd creature, the preach THOT:90
Welcome to a delegation of pastors. HNWS:51
Welcome to a former pastor b present pastor. HNWS:13
Welcome to a guest evangelist HNWS:34
Welcome to a guest minister. HNWS:34
Welcome to a minister as civi club speaker. HNWS:17
Welcome to a minister of another denomination. HNWS: 43
Welcome to a minister of another nationality. HNWS:44
Welcome to a minister of another race. HNWS:44
Welcome to a new associate pastor and family. HNWS:1
Welcome to a new minister of music and family. HNWS:1
Welcome to a new minister of religious education and family. HNWS:15
Welcome to a new pastor and family. HNWS:11
Welcome to a newly-ordained minister. HNWS:20
See also Missions and missionaries

Cleveland, Grover
Address at 250th anniversary of the settlement of the Jews in the United States. TWJ:11
Education and the self-made man. BLAA:66; BLAB:66
Eulogy of McKinley. BRYW 10:137; CHAL 13:155; KLEM:164
First inaugural address. BREW 4:82; BRYW 10:130; CHAL 13:149; CHI:164; COP:327; COPA:327; COPB:327; HAZO 24:10117; KNAS:35; KNASA:35; LOTI:151; MAS 24:10117; ORAMA 2:405; USIN:149; USINA:149
Influence of universities (Sesquicentennial anniversary of signing of charter of College of New Jersey) BAKF:187; BOB:185; REEMA 7:249
On tariff revision. REEMA 12:687
Second inaugural address. CHI:180; LOTI:165; USIN:163; USINA:163
True democracy. REEM 10:308; REEMA 1:229; REEMB 11:322

CLEVELAND, GROVER
Jones, E.D.
Adventures among great Americans. BART 1:115
Clifford, John
Christmas in December. THOU 2:334
Farmer's song. THOU 2:227
Clifford, Vance
Emcee at a bus drivers' party
" at a housewarming
" at a neighborhood meeting
" at a St. Patrick's day party
" at a school centennial celebration. BRH:316, 218, 310, 231, 236
Introducing a basso
" a chorus
" a French comedian
" a ventriloquist
Introducing a vocal soloist. BRH: See Table of contents, section II for paging

CLIMATE See Weather
Cline, E.W.
Spirit of the past. BOA:213
Clinton, DeWitt
Achievements and responsibilities of the age. NORR 2d ser:9
Against the military spirit. BREW 4:90
Federal power and local rights. BREW 4:87
Phi Beta Kappa address, July 22, 1823. CHAL 4:318; HAZO 9:3736; MAS 9:3736
Clinton, Stanford
Ropes (heredity and environment in relation to crime) ASHF:95; BLUE:51; BRP 3:23

CLOSING SPEECHES
Addams, J.
Closing the International Congress of Women. GA:175
Closing speech and benediction at a convention. BEDA:143
Closing speech and prayer (at cornerstone dedication of youth center.) BED:42; BEDA:83, 84
Closing speech and prayer (at physician-of-the-year award) BED:54; BEDA:57
Closing speech at a Garden Club meeting. BEDA:70
Closing speech at annual Boy Scout drive. BEDA:109
Closing speech at Bill of Rights Day program. BEDA:175
Closing speech at birthday testimonial. BEDA:32
Closing speech (at ceremony honoring retiring secretary of labor union) BED:82; BEDA:155
Closing speech (at conclusion of installation ceremony at Speakers' Club) BED:19; BEDA:28

CLOSING SPEECHES (cont.)
Closing speech (at dedication of home for aged) BED:36; BEDA:77
Closing speech (at dedication of recreation center) BED:39; BEDA:80
Closing speech at Flag Day ceremonies. BEDA:97
Closing speech (at hospital fund drive and testimonial) BED:66; BEDA:103
Closing speech (at induction of members to labor union) BED:76; BEDA:148
Closing speech (at installation of officers at labor union) BED:79; BEDA:152
Closing speech (at Labor Day observance) BED:98; BEDA:171
Closing speech (at memorial service) BED:45; BEDA:87
Closing speech (at mental health fund drive) BED:61; BEDA:106
Closing speech (at newly formed Speakers' Club) BED:12; BEDA:17
Closing speech at organization of a Camera Club. BEDA:21
Closing speech (at political rally urging citizens to vote) BED:95; BEDA:132, 167
Closing remarks (at presentation of Brotherhood award) BED:58; BEDA:67
Closing speech at presentation of scientific award. BEDA:62
Closing speech (at testimonial dinner to journalist) BED:23; BEDA:38
Closing speech at testimonial for woman civic leader. BEDA:44
Closing speech (at testimonial on retirement of public official) BED:31; BEDA:52
Closing speech at testimonial to a musician. BEDA:40
Closing speech (at testimonial to labor union official) BED:84; BEDA:157
Closing speech (at testimonial to philanthropist) BED:26
Closing speech at Town Hall meeting. BEDA:72
Closing speech (at United Nations anniversary ceremony) BEDA:126
Closing speech (at unveiling of plaque for Labor Temple) BED:88; BEDA:161
Closing speech (at unveiling of portrait presented to labor union) BED:92; BEDA:165
Closing speech (at Veterans' Day observance) BED:49; BEDA:94
Closing speech (on Human Rights Day) BED:70; BEDA:130
Examples of remarks for closing a meeting. BO:47-50
Examples of toastmaster's closing remarks. FRIT:32, 45
Hilton, J.H.
Closing remarks at Iowa State College centennial luncheon. IOCP:43
Concluding remarks at Academic symposia-Iowa State College centennial. IOCP:163
Page, W.H.
Closing educational conference. ONES:59
Seven examples of closing remarks. BEB:48
Speech at conclusion of a club program. STOC:128
Speech at conclusion of a club program-two examples of. STON:134
Suggestions on how to make dramatic conclusions. With examples of. BRM:315-320
Suggestions on how to make general conclusions. With examples of. BRM:271-286
Suggestions on how to make humorous conclusions. With examples of. BRM:293-306

Suggestions on how to make inspirational conclusions. With examples of. BRM: 307-314
Suggestions on how to make narrative conclusions. With examples of. BRM:287-293
Suggestions on how to make successful conclusions of speeches. With examples of. BRM:267-270
Symington, W. S.
Truth makes us free (speech at closing session of Seventh Annual Philadelphia Bulletin Forum) BA 1952-53: 42
Temple, R. A.
The conclusion. THOU 3:506
Three examples of closing speeches making doers out of believers: Voting for school bond issue; Join campaign against segregation; Taking out insurance policy. MICS:174
Toast "The ladies"-annual meeting of mixed club (final meeting of any organization to mark close of season) WRA:50
Toastmaster's closing remarks. NAT:45

CLOSING YEAR ADDRESSES
Closing days of the year. THOU 2:400
Departing year. THOU 2:390
Dying year. THOU 2:387
Harris, J. L.
What have we gained in the year? THOU 2:405
Hubbert, J. M.
Dying year. THOU 2:379
Noble, F.
God's faithfulness vindicated by our experience. THOU 2:393
Old year review. THOU 2:399
The record. THOU 2:389
Clothier, Robert Clarkson
Inaugural address as president of University of New Jersey (Rutgers) WE:2:15

CLOTHING AND DRESS
Wesley, J.
On dressing for display. BREW 10:218

CLOTHING MERCHANT See Business men

CLOWNS See Circus

CLUB SPEECHES
Address of a new president of a Womans club. AMEO 2:34
Address to a club of working boys. HAPR:146
Announcing membership drive. WRA:29
Apology for delayed start. NAT:7
Arnold, M.
To the Wordsworth Society. KNAS:43; KNASA:43
Assumptive techniques. NATT: 15
Attendance. NATM:27
Attendance. NATT:4
Booster club campaigns to 'Improve our city." LU:1132
'Booster" club dinner, by an enthusiastic member. EDGS: 83
Bryant, W. C.
To the Burns Club. BREW 2:302; KNAS:48; KNASA:48
Building club strength. FRIE: 54
Building membership. NATM:9
Building our club for the future. NAT:7
Card club supper, by one of the members of the club. EDGS:340
Celebrating an anniversary of Women's clubs. SOES:41
Classification. FRIE:72
Closing remarks; various models of. BEC:137
Club classification. NATM:24
Club ideals. AMEO 2:142
Club ideals. FRIE:57
Club managers. SCHS:77

CLUB SPEECHES (cont.)
Club officer's refrain. NAT: 39
Club (or lodge) membership. NATT:23
Club responsibility. NATM:29
Club speeches, such as Nominations-Resignations-Presidents Resolutions-Introductions, etc. STOC:102-120; STON:108-126
Community club dinner, by an official of the club. EDGS: 91
Convention report at a club meeting. WRA:189
Corlett, B. C.
Presents a past president's pin to the retiring president, Anderson Borthwick. PRC:8
Cut out the gossip. FRIE:61
Dedication of a new club house. LU:1222
Ending an argument. FRIE:64
Examples of speech openings. BEC:69
Farewell address to a club member moving to another territory. WRA:175
Farewell speech at complimentary dinner to retiring member of school board after twenty-five years' service. WRA:177
Flowers and auxiliaries; an inspirational speech for auxiliary members or chapter members, changeable for a membership speech or a testimonial speech. BAI: 131
Get out and work. FRIE:60
Gift presentation-examples of (in appreciation for good work as club officer) MORA:31-33
Good of the order-five examples of. MORA:37-40
Honoring past matrons and past patrons-five examples of. MORA:50-51
Humorous club speech for Banker's Current Review, Golf, Traffic, Twentieth Century, and Izaak Walton clubs. SCHS:30, 92, 139, 265, 269, 275
In memoriam (on death of club member)-examples of. MORA:53-59
Inaugural address (as president of a club) SOES:22
Indifferent members. NATM:36
Informal chat with members of a youth organization about their and other similar groups. DR:117; LU:1220
Introducing an honorary member. STOC:119; STON:125
Jackson, J.
In behalf of the Kaghlir pledges. JUD:223
Kindred societies, by a membe of the entertaining society. Response by visitor. EDGS: 365, 366
Kiwanis Club (suitable for any civic club) EDGS:85
Know the other fellow better. FRIE:77
Ladies' auxiliary of the churc begins a new season. DR: 222; LU:1218
Ladies' night. FRIE:52
Ladies' night address. NAT:2
Limiting projects. NATM:27
Lodges (visitor is asked to speak) ED:402
Lowly nickel: don't pickle the nickel (a membership spee for auxiliaries) BAI:39
Making our club go. NATT:1
Male and female. FRIE:75
New officers. NATM:5
On being elected president of club. BARB:146
On being elected president of a club. EDGS:355
Opening address by the presi dent of a Ladies' social club. HAPR:160
Opening address for Woman's literary club. AMEO 2:140
Opening speech by temporary chairman at civic associa-

tion. BED:14; BEDA:22
Organization and attendance. DICD:109
Organizing a Camera Club (opening speech by presiding officer) BEDA:17
Organizing a club (welcoming new chapter to Speakers' Club at opening meeting) BED:11; BEDA:15
Our club. FRIE:51
Our club's place in the community. NATM:26
Outside interests. FRIE:53
Passing the buck. NATT:27
Past presidents' day. FRIE: 73
Plans for the next season. STON:151
Plans for the next year. STOC:145
Posner, G. A.
Emcee at a ladies' day meeting (at the lodge, athletic club, social club, or other meetings) BRH:302
Presenting a gift to a club leader. SOES:18
Presenting honorary membership card (at physician-of-the-year award) BED:52; BEDA:55
Proposing an honorary member. STON:125
Proposing for membership-two examples of. STON:113
Proposing, introducing, and speech of an honorary member. STOC:119-120
Reaching the inner man. FRIE: 56
Recreational club-speech to establish a recreational club at an inner office meeting. WRA:201
Response to invitation to speak by a club member at an annual meeting. WRA: 249
Response to presentation of life membership award. MORA:121
Response to the invitation, "A few words" at a club meeting. WRA:247
Review of club's history. STOC: 146; STON:152
Roll call of departed members. BEB:73
Speech appointing committee to draft constitution. BED:15; BEDA:24
Sandford, W. P.
Membership meetings that click. SAB:66; SABA:88
Service. NATM:22
Short talk by a new member on admission to Ladies Rotary club. AMEO 2:67
Show-your-self (speech for the war veteran or auxiliary) BAI:144
Sifter: know your dough and you will grow (pep talk for bank personnel and business groups-adaptable for club members, a war-veteran post member or any auxiliary member) BAI:31
Silver anniversary (of membership in a club) MORA:14
Smith, G.
English women's institutes receive official recognition. BUT:144; BUTA:144; BUTB: 144
Social club anniversary (member tells a few tales) ED: 383
Society (speech for a social club dinner) ED:381
Speech announcing a change of program. HILL:461
Speech at conclusion of a club program-two examples of. STON:134
Speech of a newly elected honorary member. STON:126
Speeches calling attention to the illness or misfortune of a member. STOC:114-117; STON:120
Speeches explaining object of meeting. HILL:460
Strikes: the striker and the strike-breaker (a changeable

CLUB SPEECHES (cont.)
speech adaptable for Servicemen's posts, American War Mothers' or Gold Star Mothers' chapters, for a membership drive or a pep talk for co-operation) BAI: 47
Suggestions for the presentation of secretary's and treasurer's reports. REAB:160
Tale of a treasurer. SOES:42
Toast "Our visitors"-at regular meeting of almost any club. WRA:53
Toast to charter member. FRIT:91
Toasts to oldest member and new member of any club or group. WRA:52, 53
Tribute to guest of honor. NAT:46
Two model speeches expressing appreciation for support. BEB:20, 21
Two speeches proposing club membership. STOC:107
Typical luncheon timetable with examples of opening remarks, introductions, tributes, and closing remarks. SUM:167-175
Useful life. FRIE:56
Voltage: the jolt of a volt (a changeable speech for many occasions, for a sales speech, a membership drive, or a pep talk) BAI: 85
Welcome to a minister as civic club speaker. HNWS: 17
Welcome to visiting club members. FRIT:34
Welcoming new member. NATM:31
What our club means. FRIE: 65
What you can do. FRIE:62
Women's auxiliaries (visiting sister has a word to say) ED:407
Word to the wives. NAT:19
See also Announcements; Charters; Emcees; Fund raising; Officers; Offices; Resignations; Resolutions. Also types of speeches, e.g. Acceptance speeches; Closing speeches; Congratulations; Inaugural addresses; Installation speeches; Introductions; Memorial speeches; Nominations; Oaths; Reports; Responses; Retirement; Roll call; Thanks; Toasts; Welcoming addresses. Also names or types of clubs, e.g. Kiwanis Club; Lions Club; Service clubs

COAL
Dennis, R. E.
King coal is still on the throne. SAB:174
Goldsborough, T. A.
Lewis contempt case. BA 1947-48:93
Lewis, J. L.
Declaration to coal mine operators, March 19, 1946. BA 1945-46:180
United Mine Workers demands. BA 1945-46:180

COAL MINES
Roosevelt, F. D.
Broadcast address to the coal miners. VO 1943-44:191

COAST DEFENSES
Coast defenses. CRAI:450

--- See Names of countries or hemispheres with subdivision Defenses, e.g. United States-Defenses; Western hemisphere-Defenses
Cobb, Howell
"Fifty-four forty or fight." BREW 4:94
Cobb, Irvin Shrewsbury
Acrobat. HURG:251
Lost tribes of the Irish in the South. COP:695; COPB:722;

NESA:144; REEM 1:308; REEMB 1:309
Our country. REEM 1:318; REEMB 1:319
Cobbett, William
God's vengeance against public robbers. HAZO 9:3521; MAS 9:3521
Man on the tower (defending himself against a charge of libel) BREW 4:98
Cobbs, John A.
My problem and yours. YR 5:53
Three score and ten. BRP 7:25; NOR 1934:97
Cobden, Richard
Effects of protection in agriculture. ADR 3:109; BEA:129; BRYW 4:156; COP:179; COPA:179; COPB:179; HAY:186; ORBR 2:187; PAUF 1:312; PL:465
Free trade. -Same as his Effects of protection in agriculture.
Free trade with all nations. BREW 4:103; PE:450; PEA:450; REEM 9:227; REEMA 12:698; REEMB 10;234
On the Corn laws (February 24, 1842) CHAL 7:190; HAZO 14:6074; MAS 14:6074
Reform of the franchise. EMS 2:162
Repeal of the corn laws. -Same as his Effects of protection in agriculture
Small states and great achievements. BREW 4:113
War with Russia. BRTH:258; BRTHA:258

COBDEN, RICHARD
Palmerston, H.J.T.
On the death of Cobden. BREW 8:268
Cockburn, Sir Alexander
On the Greek difficulty. CHAL 7:53; HAZO 14:5865; MAS 14:5865
Cockran, William Bourke
An answer to William J. Bryan. BREW 4:116; CHAL 14:329; HAZO 25:10967; MAS 25:10967; PE:642; PEA:642; REEM 10:335; REEMA 12:710; REEMB 11:349
Decoration day. BLAA:102; BLAB:102
Evils of a standing army. FUL:61,64,68,71
Marshall and the Constitution. SHUM:280
Our Constitutional system. REEMA 1:232
Porto Rican tariff. FUL:74, 77
Coffee, John M.
What does freedom of speech mean to us today? BA 1941-42:97
Coffin, Henry Sloane
God's mysterious educator. BA 1941-42:236
Coffman, Lotus Delta
Inaugural address as president of University of Minnesota. WE 2:187
Coghlan, Joseph Bullock
Battle of Manila. REEM 1:323; REEMA 1:239; REEMB 1:324
Cohen, Joseph
For a Bar Mitzvah-3 speeches. ZEL:42, 45, 47
Cohen, Solomon Solis
Way in the sea and a path in the mighty waters. TWJ:106
Coke, Edward
Prosecuting Sir Walter Raleigh. BREW 4:120; PL:377
Speech on the gunpowder plot. HAZO 4:1401; MAS 4:1401
Coker, Tracy
United States and the Monroe Doctrine. ASHF:189

COLBERT, LESTER L.
McDonough, J.J.
Introduces Lester J. Colbert, President, Chrysler Corporation. PRNE:27
Colby, Bainbridge
Religious liberty and the Ku Klux Klan. WHIP:298

COLBY, BAINBRIDGE
Mulroy, T.R.
Introduces Bainbridge, Colby. PR:60
Colden, Cadwallder
Introduction to the study of philosophy in America for the use of a young gentleman. BL:287
Coleman, Geneva
Golden age lies onward. YR 5:81
Coleman, Henry F.
Philosophy of the race problem. ASHF:158
Coleman, Walter
Introducing a chemist
" a forester
" a sporting goods manager. BRC:200, 217, 207
Colenso, John William
Example of our Lord. HAZO 18:7451; MAS 18:7451
Colepeper, John, 1st Baron
Against monopolies. BREW 4:265
On the grievances of church and commonwealth. CHAL 2:140; HAZO 4:1677; MAS 4:1677
Coleridge, John Duke Coleridge, 1st Baron
Henry Irving's versatility. REEMA 1:246
In golden chains. REEMA 1:253
On the value of clear views as to the laws regulating the enjoyment of property. CHAL 9:478; HAZO 19:8202; MAS 19:8202
Sacredness of matrimony. BREW 4:127
Colfax, Schuyler
Confiscation of rebel property. BREW 4:133

COLLEGE EDUCATION See Colleges and universities; Education, higher; Knowledge, theory of; Learning and scholarship

COLLEGE PRESIDENTS See Educators; Inaugural addresses

COLLEGE STUDENTS See Students

COLLEGES AND UNIVERSITIES
Abbott, W. L.
Functions of the governing board in the administration of a university. ONES:273
Allenby, E.
Opening of the Hebrew University at Jerusalem. REEM sup 1:61; REEMB 7:33
Atkins, G. G.
Our university. YE:299
Butler, N. M.
University is a democracy. PEAE:193
Campbell, W.W.
Universities and the truth (President's inaugural address) ONEC:145
Cleveland, G.
Influence of universities (sesquicentennial anniversary of signing of charter of College of New Jersey) BAKF:187; BOB:185; REEMA 7:249
Foreign influence upon American universities. DAVC:562
Gilman, D. C.
Characteristics of a university. REEM 6:212; REEMA 8:515; REEMB 7:193
Era of universities. REEMA 2:528
Inaugural address as president of Johns Hopkins University. WE 1:293
Hill, B. H.
Work of universities in the South. REEMA 8:624
Hutchins, R. M.
What is a university? SAR:51
Lewis, W. S.
Trustees of the privately endowed university. NORR 3d ser:217

McCabe, W.G.
First university in America, 1619-1622. SMI:20
McCracken, H.M.
Relation of metropolis and university: inaugural address as president of New York University. WE 1:185
McVey, F. LeR.
University and its relations: inaugural address as president of University of North Dakota. WE 2:369
Morrill, J.L.
Unchanging challenge-lest we forget (at Iowa State College centennial) IOCP: 19
Prather, W.L.
National unity and the state university. BLAA:214; BLAB:214
Sterling, J.E.W.
Lofty purpose shared. BA 1950-51:150
Stoke, H.W.
University assembly. BA 1949-50:245
Thornton, W.M.
Liberty and slavery in universities. NORR 2d ser:480
University and true patriotism. DAVC:67
Wert, R.J.
Restless generation and undergraduate education. BA 1964-65:145
Wheeler, B.I.
Introductory address to students of the University of California. WAGN:428
Willis, E.E.
Colleges for cabbages. JUD:111
See also Education, higher; Educators. Also names of colleges and universities, e.g. Harvard University; Iowa State University; Yale University
Collier, William Miller
Presenting Doctor of Laws degree to Sir Auckland Campbell Geddes. REEM 6:205; REEMB 7:176
Colling, Hal
Reply to Mr. Post on Taft-Ellender-Wagner Housing Bill. MO:462
Collins, Alexander
Introducing an ambassador (British) or diplomat
Introducing an army officer
" an automobile salesman
" a baker
" comedian
" small manufacturer. BRC: See Table of contents for paging
Collins, D. Edward
Government. WAGN:147
Collins, Fred C., Jr.
Bell tolls for thee. NOR 1946: 53
Collins, LeRoy
Speech to the directors of the National Association of Broadcasters. BA 1960-61:178
Collins, Michael
Independence for Ireland. REEM 7:111; REEMB 8:111
Collins, Patrick A.
Ireland's dream of nationality. REEMA 1:257
Collins, Tom
Response to an introduction. PR:118
Response to an introduction which included only his name and his title. PR:126
Collins, Wilkie
American hospitality. REEMA 1:261
Collyer, Robert
Church and the stage. REEM 1:330; REEMA 1:267; REEMB 1:331
Clear grit. REEMA 4:261
Saxon grit. REEMA 1:263
Tribute to Edwin Booth. REEM 1:329; REEMA 1:266; REEMB 1:330
Colton, E.T.
Decline of citizenship. COUW: 77

Colton, Frank
Introducing a French wine merchant. BRC:312

COLUMBUS, CHRISTOPHER
Corrigan, M. A.
Character of Columbus. WERN 42:71
Depew, C. M.
Columbus and Hendrik Hudson. THOU 1:70
Dowling, V. J.
Christopher Columbus: at unveiling of monument to Columbus. CATA 1:100
Fiske, J.
Columbus, the navigator (400th anniversary of discovery of America by Christopher Columbus) CHAL 13:442; REEM 5:171; REEMA 8:490; REEMB 9:206
Mott, F. L.
Christopher Columbus. TRUW:223

COLUMBUS DAY
Biddle, F.
Columbus day address. HOC:191
Christopher Columbus' faith. THOU 1:63
Christopher Columbus in America today. THOU 1:67
Columbus and his treatment of the Indians. THOU 1:73
Columbus Day address. BURS: 199
Columbus Day-America after 450 years. DR:167; LU: 1202
Columbus Day (commemorating the great adventure) EDGS:20
Columbus Day (tribute to our first hero) ED:34
Columbus in history. THOU 1:59
Date of the Columbus dedication. THOU 1:63
Depew, C. M.
Columbus and Hendrick Hudson. THOU 1:70
Harrison, B.
National holiday proclamation (Columbus Day) THOU 1:61
Harvest time holiday. THOU 1:62
Haygood, S. G.
America-its national and individual ideals. THOU 1:76
Man for the time. THOU 1:72
O'Meara, T. B.
Great adventure of Christopher Columbus. DU:150
Roosevelt, F. D.
Broadcast to the nation, October 12, 1942. VO 1942-43: 545
Wilson, W.
Discovery and conquest of America. THOU 1:65
Winthrop, R. C.
Pioneer of American independence. THOU 1:69

COMEDIANS See Actors and acting

COMER, HUGH
Given, W.
Introduces Hugh Comer. PR: 97

COMIC MAGAZINES See Literature

COMMANDMENTS, TEN See Ten commandments

COMMEMORATIVE ADDRESSES
Adams, J. Q.
Oration at Plymouth (commemoration of the landing of the Pilgrims) BREW 1:58; CHAL 4:273; HAZO 9:3671; HURG:51; MAS 9:3671; ORAMA 1:327
Andrew, J. A.
In honor of patriotic heroes. CHAL 9:304; HAZO 19:7888; MAS 19:7888
Bancroft, G.
Political career of Andrew

Jackson. CHAL 6:416; HAZO 13:5652; MAS 13: 5652; REEMA 11:110
Baruch, B.
Woodrow Wilson (commemorating centennial anniversary of birth of Wilson) BA 1956-57:141
Beck, J. M.
John Marshall, jurist and statesman. SAR:206
Beveridge, A. J.
Takes up the white man's burden (speech commemorating birth of General Grant) FUL:24; PE:650; PEA:650
Burke, E. R.
How long will the American Republic last? HOC: 28; SAR:200
Conant, J. B.
Civil courage. BA 1945-46: 223
Devens, C.
Sons of Harvard. CHAL 10:7; HAZO 19:8121; KLEM:199; MAS 19:8121
Emerson, R. W.
War (commemoration of patriot heroes of Harvard College in Civil War) HAZO 14:5997; MAS 14:5997; REEMA 2:442
Evarts, W. M.
What the age owes to America. REEMA 13:962; REEMB 8:144; THOU 1:225
Farley, J. A.
Lincoln, the politician. ON: 348
Field, C. W.
Story of the Atlantic cable. REEM 4:99; REEMA 8:473; REEMB 4:221
Grigsby, H. B.
American revolution (commemorating birth of American independence) SMI:69
Hadley, A. T.
Commemorative address. REEM 11:418; REEMB 12: 440
Hitler, A.
Speech commemorating the twentieth birthday of the Nazi party. CROC:238; VO 1943-44:520
I. O. O. F. in memoriam. THOS: 183
Kelvin, W. T.
Inspiration and the highest education (commemoration of J. P. Nichol) BREW 7:189
Lewis, W. H.
Address before the Massachusetts House of Representatives, February 12, 1913. DUNM:409; WOON:562
Madden, M. B.
Abraham Lincoln. HARSO:3
Mitchell, D. G.
Irving as author and man (commemoration of 100th anniversary of birth of Washington Irving) REEMA 9:872
Opening of commemorative services (at Veterans Day observance) BED:47; BEDA: 92
Paget, J.
Scientific mind (commemorating John Hunter) HAY:261
Porter, H.
In commemoration of William Tecumseh Sherman. CHAL 13:104; HAZO 23:10040; MAS 23:10040
Ruffin, G. L.
Crispus Attucks (commemorative speech on Boston Massacre) DUNM:125
Stryker, H. M.
Introducing Lt. Gen. Walter Bedell Smith at 250th anniversary of Williamsburg. YE:128
Suggestions for preparation of speeches of commemoration. BRA:511. With examples of. HIBS:288
Taft, L.
Art and modern life. SAR: 377
Tyler, J.
American liberty. SMI:129

COMMEMORATIVE ADDRESSES (cont.)
Watterson, H.
Heroes in homespun. PROS: 75; SHU:39
Wertenbaker, T. J.
James Watt, inventor and pioneer. SAR:369
Williams, J. S.
Southern gentleman (commemorating Edward C. Walthall) SHUO:45
Young, O. D.
Courage for the future. HOC:29: SAR:9
See also Anniversaries; Dedication addresses; Eulogies; Memorial day; Memorial speeches; Tributes

COMMENCEMENT ADDRESSES
Address at commencement of state graded school. AMEO 1:85
Address at rural high school commencement. AMEO 1: 65
Address for class day by class president. AMEO 1: 134
Address of a superintendent to graduating class. AMEO 1: 60
Address of county superintendent of schools. AMEO 1: 191
Address of the principal or superintendent, presenting the graduation class to the board of education. AMEO 1:18
Address of welcome to graduates of Hamilton High School by association president. WRA:71
Address to a college graduating class. AMEO 1:30
Address to a college graduating class. DAVC:579
Address to a graduate class of nurses. DAVC:547
Address to a graduating class. THOS:127
Address to graduating class (School of Commerce) AMEO 1:52
Address to a graduating class by a teacher. AMEO 1:37
Address to a graduating class by a teacher. DAVC:545
Address to a graduating class of trained nurses, by head of the hospital staff. EDGS: 184
Address to a school graduating class by a clergyman. DAVC: 551
Address to graduating class of trained nurses. HAPR:175
Address to the Junior-Senior classes. AMEO 1:40
Alexander, M. W.
Citizenship. REEM 7:3; REEMB 8:3
Allen, F. E.
Challenge to the citizen. BA 1960-61:100
Ashmore, H. L.
Pursuit of truth. ANGC:44
Bain, G. W.
Life lessons (commencement address at Pierce Business College) SHU:204; SHUO: 237
Banning, M. C.
Test of an education. ANGC: 50
Bartlett, W. F.
Speech at Harvard commencement dinner. BAKF:428
Baruch, B. M.
Government and the individual. ONEC:189
Beck, J. M.
Successful life. SHU:23
Blakesley, R. H.
Mastery of mind. SHUC:131
Bones: short and over can mean short of publicity and overlooking a patron (a speech to bank personnel, changeable for many occasions, business meeting or convention of sales personnel, at a graduation of nurses' group, for fund rais-

ing drives, to a telephone group, or by a political or labor speaker) BAI:94
Borden, R. L.
Address to the graduating class of Acadia University. KLEB:97
Bose, J. C.
Greater India to be. ZU:35
Brandeis, L. D.
Business-a profession. LINM:101; REEM 4:35; REEMB 4:79
Brief remarks to a class of young ladies on graduation day by a visitor. DAVC: 546
Brown, J. M.
"Beat" generation. HURG: 341
Brown, K. I.
Men and women with antennae. BRAP:132
Bryce, J. B.
At a Harvard commencement. KNAS:265; KNASA: 265
Bunche, R. J.
Barriers of race can be surmounted. YE:282
Burns, R. W.
Freedom and war. ANGC: 108
Butler, N. M.
Abdication of democracy. (184th Columbia Univ. commencement) ON:252; SAR: 181
American plan to prevent war. BA 1941-42:250
Responsibility of youth. BA 1944-45:241
Byrne, A.
Address at end of law lecture course. WERN 54:46
Candland, H.
Toast to our school. JUD: 227
Canham, E. D.
Authentic revolution. HAR: 517
Darkness into dawn. BA 1951-52:161
Carter, R. A.
Whence and whither (commencement address) WOON: 626
Chapman, J. J.
Unity of human nature. LOMS:221; LOMSA:279; NORR 1st ser:254; REEM 6: 89; REEMA 7:206; REEMB 7:102
Character the basis of credit-address to a graduating class by a financier. DAVC:556
Class calendar. AMEO 1:160
Class colors. PAIC:167
Class colors. WERN 54:84
Class day toasts; philosophy, religion, music, art, literature, history, language and science. WERN 54:91-96
Class eulogy. PAIC:334
Class flowers. PAIC:180
Class greeting. WERN 54:35
Class growler. WERN 54:71
Class grumbler. AMEO 1:182
Class grumbler. PAIC:215
Class mottoes. PAIC:253-283
Class scrap bag. AMEO 1:179
Class voyage. PAIC:125
Class yells. PAIC:201, 205
Commencement. FRIE:217
Commencement. SCHS:81
Commencement address. BEC: 156
Commencement address. BURS: 246
Commencement address. FRIE: 203
Commencement address. NATM:14
Commencement day. THOS:157
Commencement farewell address. REAC:55
Conzelman, J. G.
Young man's physical and mental approach to war. SAC:60
Craven, L.
College graduate's debt to society and the state. SHUC: 355
Cutten, G. B.
Fifth column of civilization.

COMMENCEMENT ADDRESSES (cont.)
HOC:158
Day, E. E.
What really threatens American democracy? BA 1938-39:79
Dean, V. M.
United States and the Communist threat. ANGC:139
Do it now-an address by a faculty member. AB:65
Donnelly, W. P.
Our responsibility to Latin America. ANGC:177
Dux's speech delivered at the Class Tree exercises, Emory College, March 1898. DAVC:201
Eckels, J. H.
Address to graduates. REAC:58
Education and life. AMEO 1:60
Education (short talk on graduation) ED:285
Eisenhower, D. D.
"Don't join the book burners." FIP:324
Elvehjem, C. A.
Education and democracy. ANGC:83
Emerson, R. W.
Divinity school address. BL:586
Fosdick, R. B.
"Middletown"-and the way out. SAR:22
Frankfurter, F.
Worth of our past. HOC:111
Funston, G. K.
Memo to the Class of 1957: our economic world and you. BA 1957-58:136
Garret, P.
If I had your chance. HOA:36
Gary, E. H.
Ethics in business. REEM 4:145; REEMB 4:288
Labor. BYRA:178; REEM 4:136; REEMB 4:279
Geddes, A. C.
Commencement address. REEM 6:205; REEMB 7:176
Getting a job-speech by well-known business man at closing exercises of a school. WRA:224
Goldwater, B. M.
Freedom: heritage and responsibility. ANGC:198
Graduation exercises address. NATS:10
Greenewalt, C. H.
To reach high places. ANGC:18
Guerard, A. L.
Land where hatred expires. HARSO:93
Hammarskjold, D.
Values of nationalism and internationalism (Stanford University commencement address) COPB:628
Hancher, V. M.
Art of contemplation. BA 1948-49:174; BAAGA:401
Postwar planning-for what? BA 1943-44:319
Harris, R. C.
Free society. ANGC:87
Heater, L. A.
Ivy oration. WERN 54:48
Senior charge. WERN 54:76
Heilbrin, L. H.
Look at academic freedom. ANGC:95
High school commencement. EDGS:209
Holmes, O. W.
Practical ethics of a physician. REEM 6:262; REEMA 8:677; REEMB 6:175
Horton, M. M.
Predictions for the unpredictable future. BRA:551
Hull, C.
We shall not fail. COP:566
Hutchins, R. M.
Philosophy of life. BA 1937-38:184
Ivy oration. DAVC:209, 215, 225

Jha, A.
Educational problems. ZU: 52
Johnson, M.
Cry baby! YR 5:357
Johnson, M.W.
Faith of the American Negro (at Harvard commencement) WOON:658
Jones, R.E.
Few remarks on making a life (commencement address) DUNM:455
Kahn, B.M.
Marks of an educated man. ANGC:34
Kaltenborn, H.V.
College and the press. SHUC:10
Kennedy, J.F.
Intellectual and the politician. BA 1956 57:165; BARR: 285; LINP:279
Toward a strategy of peace. BA 1963-64:9
Kirk, G.
Historic perspective and current issues. BA 1952-53: 151
United States and the world. ANGC:218
Knowledge is power-speech by president of successful business enterprise to a graduating class. WRA:219
Krantz, J.C., Jr.
On being a scientifically-minded physician. MCK:169
Lane, F.K.
American spirit incarnate. SHU:166
Lang, W.C.
"The gold go toward their time." BA 1960-61:71
Lehman, F.W.
Third house (commencement address) SHUO:312
Littleton, M.W.
Commencement address. KLEB:57
Lord, Mrs. O.B.
World around us (commencement address at Temple University, Philadelphia) BUTB:236
Lynch, G.J.
Pursuit of security (accepting an honorary degree by University of Dayton at graduation exercise) LINP:186
MacArthur, D.
Our national goals. ANGC: 208
MacCracken, H.N.
Idologies, their dynamics and their excesses. HOB:184
McGhee, G.C.
American women and the goal of world community. ANGC:159
McKeldin, T.
This is a good place to start. MCK:162
Martin, W.B.
United States in Pan-American trade. SHUC:123
Massey, V.
Our problem and yours. NORR 3d ser:14
Michaels, M.G.
Builders of empire. SHUC: 74
Millikan, R.A.
Science and spiritual values. ONEC:177
Morrill, J.L.
Begins commencement address to a School of Banking at the University of Wisconsin. PRC:19
Foreign aid and education. ANGC:168
Mollenhoff, C.R.
Need for balanced thinking. ANGC:68
Munshi, K.M.
Our greatest need; freedom from fear. ZU:18
Murrow, E.R.
Commencement address. BA 1954-55:128
Not evening but dawn. AMEO 1: 96
"The old and new." DAVC:234
O'Neal, B.
Democracy is on trial.

COMMENCEMENT ADDRESSES (cont.)
MOUGA:238
Outline of a commencement address. BAKS:265
Pecker, E.
Consecration to humanity man's mission. WERN 54: 54
Phelps, W. L.
Commencement address. LINM:325
Powell, L. C.
Value of reading. ANGC: 26
President's address. REAC:52
President's address delivered at the commencement of the Woman's College, Baltimore, June, 1897. DAVC: 190
Price, B.
We must recapture valour. BA 1946-47:213
Ramsey, H.
Introducing a parent at a graduation banquet. BRC: 103
Ribicoff, A.
To tomorrow's doctors. ANGC:114
Roosevelt, F. D.
Italy enters the war. BA 1939-40:76
Modern education and the government. ONEC:183
Sastri, V. S. S.
Advice to students. ZU:9
Seaborg, G. T.
United States in the space age. ANGC:124
Shank, C. D.
Class day address. WERN 54:45
Sheldon, V.
Boots for paving stones. WERN 54:56
Should auld acquaintance be forgot? SOES:48
Sizoo, J. R.
Call to self-discipline. BA 1958-59:161
Spaulding, A. T.
Wanted! More George Leigh-Mallorys. There are so many Mount Everests. HILK: 231
Stanley, F. V.
Optimism of Christianity. SHUC:5
Stevenson, A. E.
Commencement address. BA 1951-52:172
Educated ciritizen (commencement address at Princeton) BOU:18; BRYA:520
To the graduating class at Smith College. COPB:647
United States and the U. S. S. R. ANGC:184
Stoddard, G. D.
Fallacies and roadblocks. ANGC:150
Frontiers of youth. BA 1941-42:219
Stricker, M.
Intellectual: his journey and his home (talk to secondary-school graduates who have won college scholarships) BRAB:533
Suggestions for preparation of a commencement address. BRA:516; BRAB:504. With examples of. MCK:161
Suggestions for junior-senior banquet-theme: "Gypsy camp." AB:55-60
Suggestions for a junior-senior banquet-theme: "Last round up." AB:73-77
Suggestions for a junior-senior banquet-theme: 'Theatre." AB:91-94
Suggestions for toasts and speeches for a junior-senior banquet-theme. 'Ireland." AB:64-69
Suggestions for toasts for a junior-senior banquet-theme. "Colonial." AB:34
Suggestions for toasts for a junior-senior banquet-theme. 'Dutch." AB:40
Suggestions for toasts for a junior-senior banquet-theme.

"French." AB:49
Suggestions for toasts and speeches for a junior-senior banquet-theme. "Robin Hood." AB:80-84
Symington, W. S.
Freedom and military security. BA 1949-50:75
Our air force policy. YE: 228
Talk to graduates. FRIE:213
Talk to graduates. KLEG:199
Talk to students. NAT:43
Taylor, H.
Younger generation. BA 1947-48:179
Thomas, E. J.
High school commencement address. HAR:386
Thompson, D.
Freedom's back is against the wall. SAR:185
Thonssen, L.
Unrecorded legacy. BA 1958-59:133
Thrall, H. M.
Dignity and potency of language. WERN 54:57
Tittle, E. T.
Learning to speak. HUS: 284; MO:424; MOA:428
To the graduating class of a boys' academy. HAPR:134
To the graduating class of a young ladies' seminary. HAPR:81
Toast to the graduating class. STON:136
Toastmaster's welcome to the seniors. SOES:49
Tojo, H.
Graduation address at Imperial University, Manchukuo. VO 1942-43:506
Udall, S. L.
Conservation: physical and spiritual. ANGC:59
Vail, T. N.
Life and the farm. REEM 6:401; REEMB 7:403
Verplanck, G. C.
Advantages and dangers of the American scholar. BL: 115
Voss, L. C.
Success by overcoming obstacles. WERN 54:58
Wager, R.
Agassiz, a great teacher. WERN 54:59
Walker, H. J.
Intensive and extensive development. SHUC:118
Watson, T. E.
Truth, in its relation to individuals, professions, laws and institutions. SOU 9:454
Watson, T. J., Jr.
Self protection: individualism (commencement address at Brown University) HIB: 331
Waymack, W. W.
King of energies. BA 1947-48:80
Weiss, J.
Task of religion. REEMA 9: 1162
Wheeler, B. I.
Effective living. SHU:86
Where brook and river meet: commencement triolet. PAIC: 95
Whipple, F. L.
Personal goals. ANGC:11
White, W. A.
Education of a democracy. SHU:128
Your young men shall see visions. SAR:1
Willis, H. P.
Changing status of American scholarship. ONEC:194
Wilson, H. A.
Challenge and the broad view. ANGC:130
Wilson, O. M.
United States and the changing world. ANGC:145
Windolph, F. L.
Religio advocati. NORR 3d ser:101
Young, O. D.
St. Lawrence University summer school commencement address. GLAD:255

COMMENCEMENT ADDRESSES (cont.)
See also Acceptance speeches-Degrees, academic; Acceptance speeches-Diplomas; Baccalaureate addresses; Farewell addresses; Presentation speeches-Diplomas; Salutatory addresses; Valedictory addresses; Welcoming addresses

---- CLASS HISTORIES
Class chronicles. PAIC:107
Class chronicles. WERN 54:67
Class history (model) AMEO 1:148
Class history: student's ups and downs. WERN 54:61
Class history: sunshine and moonshine. WERN 54:64
Class pedigree. AMEO 1:158
Class pedigree. PAIC:121
Class picture. PAIC:118
Reith, E. A.
Sunshine and moonshine (class history) WERN 54:64

---- CLASS PROPHECIES
Class prophecies: advertiser, fortune, horoscope, revelations, scrap bag. PAIC:141-166
Class prophecy. STOC:183
Class prophecy (model) AMEO 1:150, 186
Class prophecy: magic mirror revelations. WERN 54:80
Class prophecy: service the final test. WERN 54:77
Class prophecy-two examples of. STON:187-190
Class will. DAVC:219
Class will. PAIC:208
Class will and testament (outline) AMEO 1:189
Class will and testament. WERN 54:53

COMMERCE
Barnave, A. P. J. M.
Commercial politics. BREW 1:232; CHAL 4:163; HAZO 9:3515; MAS 9:3515
Bayard, J. A.
Commerce and naval power. BREW 1:267
Black, H.
Religion and commerce. REEM 1:129; REEMB 1:126
Blaine, J. G.
Our Merchant Marine. REEMA 1:73
Coolidge, C.
Age of commercial criticism. REEM 1:339; REEMB 1:340
Cullom, S.
Our commercial relations. BLAA:244; BLAB:244; FUL:95, 97, 99
Curtis, G. W.
Commerce and literature. REEMA 1:307
Hanna, M. A.
Promotion of commerce and increase of trade. CHAL 13:110; HAZO 23:10046; MAS 23:10046
Hull, C.
Radio address on National Foreign Trade week. VO 1941:213
Johnston, E.
Steps toward a good world. HAN:374
Knox, P. C.
Commerce clause of the Constitution and trusts. BLAA:270; BLAB:270
Livernash, E. J.
Spirit of commercialism. WAGN:417
Lowell, J. R.
Commerce. REEM 2:358; REEMA 2:748; REEMB 2:371
Martin, W. B.
United States in Pan-American trade. SHUC:123
Mead, S. C.
Fundamentals of commercial organization. REEM sup 2:218; REEMB 5:166
Newman, J. P.
Commerce. REEM 3:1; REEMA 2:845; REEMB 3:1

Olney, R.
Commerce and its relations to the law. BYRA:307; REEM 3:9; REEMB 3:9
Peabody, F. G.
Commercialism and idealism. SHU:257
Van Dyke, H.
Commerce. BLAA:140; BLAB:140
Webster, H.
Commerce and the world peace. ASHF:278
White, A. D.
Commerce and diplomacy. REEMA 3:1232
See also Banks and banking; Chambers of commerce; Free trade and protection; Monopolies; Price regulation; Tariff; Trusts, industrial

COMMISSION MERCHANTS
Commission merchants. SCHS:83

COMMITTEE FOR INDUSTRIAL ORGANIZATION See Labor unions

COMMITTEE REPORTS See Club speeches; Congresses and conventions; Reports

COMMITTEES
Safety first on our highways-speech to establish a "safety first" committee at a convention. WRA:196

COMMON SENSE
Bacheller, I.
Sense, common and preferred. REEM 1:64; REEMB 1:55
Commoner, Barry
Scientific statesmanship. BA 1962-63:68

COMMUNICATION
Baird, A. C.
Responsibilities of free communications. BRAP:150
Carmichael, C. W.
One man in his time. BU:146; SOBP:352
Mackay, C. H.
History of communications. LINM:268
Oliver, R. T.
Culture and communication. LINP:201
Wallace, K. R.
Ethical basis of communication. BERS:181
Weaver, A. T.
Toward understanding through speech. BERS:2
Ziebarth, E. W.
Introducing a first class man. BRC:39
See also Aeronautics; Commerce; Radio broadcasting; Railroads; Telegraph; Telephone; Television broadcasting

COMMUNICATION SATELLITES
Bell Telephone Companies, Volunteer speakers of
Telstar. LINP:45

COMMUNION
Baker, S.
Meaning of the Lord's Supper. THOU 2:424
Crosby, H.
True meaning of the Lord's Supper. THOU 2:433
Deems, C. F.
Eating and drinking unworthily. THOU 2:429
Lord's supper. JAI:28
MacLeod, N.
Why not 'Do this in remembrance of Christ?" THOU 2:431
Patterson, R. M.
Communion sermon. THOU 2:421

COMMUNISM
Ames, K.
America beware. BRP 8:50; YR 9:79

COMMUNISM (cont.)
Canham, E. D.
Authentic revolution. HAR: 517
Communism vs. capitalism. FRIE: 98
Dean, V. M.
United States and the Communist threat. ANGC: 139
Dewey, T. E.
Boston campaign speech. VO 1944-45: 533
Douglas, P. H.
Internal security. BA 1950-51: 103
Dulles, J. F.
Freedom or despotism? BA 1956-57: 25
Our policies toward Communism in China. BA 1957-58: 48; GRAC: 176
United front against red aggression. BA 1950-51: 54
Fischer, L. and others.
What are the real issues in our fight against Communism? HAR: 196
Gitlow, B.
How Communists make converts. HAR: 202
Halle, R.
Guilty until proven innocent. SOBP: 348
Hurley, P. J.
Americanism or Communism? BOA: 301
Kaser, A. L.
Introducing a speaker on Communism. BRC: 279
Malik, C. H.
Challenge to Communism. BA 1950-51: 169
Mao Tse-tung
On the people's democratic dictatorship. CROC: 319
Menace of Communism. DR: 241
O'Boyle, P. A.
Vision of faith. BA 1955-56: 151
O'Brien, J. A.
Communism and Christianity. BA 1947-48: 235
Russell, W. F.
How to beat Communism. HOB: 204
Swabb, J.
Irresponsibles. BU: 137
Thomas, N.
Communism and fascism: resemblances and differences. BART 2: 93
Toynbee, A. J.
Russian catfish and western herring. GLAD: 279
Truman, H. S.
"Red herrings." FIP: 303
We fear Communism. NATM: 3

COMMUNISM-ALBANIA
Hoxha, E.
Reply to Khrushchev (November 7) RUS: 147
Kozlov, F. R.
Speech of October 28. RUS: 138
Mikoyan, A. I.
Speech of October 20. RUS: 45
Suslov, M. A.
Speech of October 21. RUS: 57
---- CHINA
Chou En-lai
Speech of October 19. RUS: 29

---- UKRAINE
Podgorny, N. V.
Speech of October 18. RUS: 36

COMMUNIST PARTY OF AMERICA
Dewey, T. E. and others
Shall the Communist Party in the United States be outlawed? BA 1947-48: 144
Dies, M.
Trojan horse in America. BART 3: 305

COMMUNIST PARTY-RUSSIA (22nd CONGRESS)
Adzhubei, A. I.
Speech of October 26.

RUS:103
Chou En-lai
Speech of October 19. RUS: 29
Golikov, F.I.
Speech of October 28. RUS: 135
Hoxha, E.
Reply to Khrushchev (November 7) RUS:147
Ignatov, N. G.
Speech of October 23. RUS: 65
Ilyichev, L. F.
Speech of October 24. RUS: 70
Khrushchev, N.S.
Basic indictment (speech of October 17) RUS:17
Future of the Soviet economy (from his report on the Third Program of the Soviet Communist Party-delivered October 18) RUS: 234
Rejoinder to debate (October 27) RUS:118
State of the Soviet economy (from his report for the Central Committee-delivered October 17) RUS:184
Kosygin, A.N.
Speech of October 21. RUS: 216
Kozlov, F.R.
Speech of October 28. RUS: 138
Kuusinen, O.V.
Speech of October 26. RUS: 93
Malinevsky, R.Y.
Speech of October 23. RUS: 59
Mao Tse-tung
C C P greetings. RUS:34
Mazurov, K.T.
Speech of October 19. RUS: 39
Mikoyan, A.I.
Speech of October 20. RUS: 45
Podgorny, N.V.
Speech of October 19. RUS: 36
Polyansky, D.S.
Speech of October 23. RUS: 62
Ponomarev, B.N.
Speech of October 24. RUS: 83
Pospelov, P.N.
Speech of October 26. RUS: 110
Satyulov, P.A.
Speech of October 25. RUS: 85
Shelepin, A.N.
Speech of October 26. RUS: 96
Shvernik, N.M.
Speech of October 24. RUS: 78
Suslov, M.A.
Speech of October 21, RUS: 57
Voronov, G.I.
Speech of October 19. RUS: 227
Voroshilov, K.Y.
Statement to the Congress (October 26) RUS:116

COMMUNITY CHEST See Fund raising

COMMUNITY LIFE
Buy at home. NATS:5
Clifford, V.
Emcee at a neighborhood meeting. BRH:310
Community leadership. FRIE: 80
Community club dinner, by an official of the club. EDGS: 91
Community fund. SCHS:86
Community service. FRIE:82
Extract from a discussion on a community issue. MICS:185
High schools as a community asset. AMEO 1:50
Local pride. NAT:23
Merchants (plea for the neighborhood store) ED:197
Our club's place in the community. NATM:26

COMMUNITY LIFE (cont.)
Patronize home industry. FRIE:84
Roosevelt, F.D.
Mobilization of community needs. VO 1942-43:543
Successful mothers and their relationship to the community. AMEO 2:152
Sunday school and the community. AMEO 2:179
See also Cities and towns

COMPETITION
Johnston, E.
Competition-lifeblood of American capitalism. BA 1953-54:162
Loomis, D. P.
Why not let competition go to work in transportation? LINP:269
Schurman, J. G.
Competition. BLAA:206; BLAB:206

COMPROMISE OF 1850 See Slavery in the United States
Compton, Arthur H.
Own method of speech training. BA 1945-46:109
Science and religion. BA 1939-40:421
Social implications of atomic energy. BA 1945-46:109; MO:400; MOA:400
Truth makes us free. BART 1:327
Compton, George B.
Character and politics. SHUC: 159
Compton, Karl T.
Electron, its intellectual and social significance. SAR: 363
Introducing James Bryant Conant. YE:129
Presents Harold Edward Stassen. LY:104
State of science. HAR:294
Stuff of life; our talents and their care. SAR:13
Comstock, Ada Louise
Dedication of the gates. GA:68
Conant, James Bryant
Address of welcome: tercentenary conference at Harvard University. ON:39; SAR:111
Aid to Allies. HAN:150
America's fitness to survive. YE:253
Civil courage. BA 1945-46:223
National philosophy. BA 1948-49:165
Present danger. HAR:256
Response to toast "Forefathers Day." HOC:30
Science and spiritual values. ARNS:89
Skeptical chemist looks into the crystal ball. BA 1951-52:137
Social dynamite in our large cities: unemployed, out-of-school youth. HIB:324
Statement of faith. HOC:182
Unique ideal of American life. BA 1939-40:337
Valedictory service address. BA 1942-43:257
What are we arming to defend? COP:573; COPB:558

CONANT, JAMES BRYANT
Compton, K.T.
Introducing James Bryant Conant. YE:129
Conboy, Martin
Summation for the Judiciary Committee in the investigation of the New York Socialists by the Assembly, Albany. HICJ:891

CONCLUDING SPEECHES See Closing speeches

CONDEMNATION SPEECHES See Blame, speeches of

CONDOLENCES
Messages of sympathy and condolence. BEC:164
Speeches calling attention to the illness or misfortune of a member. STOC:114-117; STON:120

See also Resolutions, memorial
Condon, Randall J.
Heroes in time of peace. PROS:60
Presentation of a gavel. BRAC: 260

CONDUCT OF LIFE See Behavior; Character; Charities; Conscience; Courage; Duty; Ethics; Golden rule; Habit; Honesty; Human relations; Justice; Life; Love; Loyalty; Man; Patience; Patriotism; Success; Temperance; Truthfulness and falsehood

CONFECTIONERY
Irwin, D.
Introducing a confectioner. BRC:219

CONFEDERATE STATES OF AMERICA
Breckenridge, W. C. P.
Who were the Confederate dead? SOU:9:418
Davis, J.
Inaugural address of 1861. ANG:344; BREW 5:41; CHAL 7:294; HAZO 15:6213; JOHA 2 pt 2:32; MAS 15: 6213
Gordon, J. B.
Last days of the Confederacy. REEM 8:169; REEMA 5:471; REEMB 13:171; SHUO:39
Harris, N. E.
Visions of the Civil War (at Confederate Veterans reunion, 1905) SHUO:26
Scott, C.
Women of the Confederacy. SHUO:34
Speer, E.
Last stand of Lee's veterans. SHUO:332
Stephens, A. H.
On the Confederate Constitution. BIR 2:234; BREW 9:283; CHAL 8:368; HARS: 383; HAZO 17:7213; JOHA 2 pt 2:39; MAS 17:7213; REEMA 15:1936
Taylor, R. L.
Address to ex-Confederates. HARSO:8; PROS:92
Whitfield, A. H.
Tribute to the women of the South (at dedication of Mississippi's new Capitol) SHUO:36
See also United States-History-Civil War

CONFERENCE OF THE LIMITATIONS OF ARMAMENTS, WASHINGTON, NOVEMBER, 1921
Balfour, A. J. B.
Speech at the Washington Conference on the Limitations of Armaments (November 15, 1921. BREW 1:210; REEM 11:390; REEMB 12: 409
Speech at the Washington Conference, November 21, 1921 (Resisting domination at any cost) BREW 1:213
Briand, A.
Imperialism, democracy and peace. BREW 2:218
Speech at the Washington Conference on the Limitations of Armaments. COP: 145; COPA:145; COPB:145; REEM 11:396; REEMB 12: 416
Harding, W. G.
Speech at Washington Conference on the Limitations of Armaments, November 12, 1921. REEM 11:379; REEMB 12:398
Hughes, C. E.
Speech at Washington Conference on Limitations of Armaments. BIR 4:62; BOAM: 127; BYRA:237; PL:765; REEM 11:383; REEMB 12: 402
Ten years naval holiday.

CONFERENCE ON THE LIMITATIONS OF ARMAMENTS, WASHINGTON, NOVEMBER, 1921 (cont.)
BREW 7:82
Kato, K.
Speech at the Washington Conference on the Limitations of Armaments (November 15, 1921) REEM 11: 396; REEMB 12:416
Viviani, R. R.
Peace made possible by justice. BREW 10:55

CONFERENCE ON THE LIMITATIONS OF ARMAMENTS, WASHINGTON, FEBRUARY, 1922
Balfour, A. J. B.
Speech at the Washington Conference, February 4, 1922 (America's moral power for peace) BREW 1: 214
Harding, W. G.
Washington Naval Conference. February 6, 1922. FIP:147

CONFERENCE ON THE LIMITATIONS OF NAVAL ARMAMENTS, LONDON, 1930
MacDonald, J. R.
Speech at Naval Conference, April 23, 1930. KESB:418
Stimson, H. L.
London Naval Arms Conference. ONEC:233

CONFERENCE ON THE PROBLEMS OF ECONOMIC DEVELOPMENT, CAIRO, JULY 9-18, 1962
Ammoun, F.
Inaugural speech at Conference on the Problems of Economic Development. UAR:25
Speech at final session of Conference on the Problems of Economic Development. UAR:403
Arabi, S.
Inaugural speech at Conference on the Problems of Economic Development. UAR:231
Speech at final session of Conference on the Problems of Economic Development. UAR:377
Balghiti, M.
Inaugural speech at Conference on the Problems of Economic Development. UAR: 207
Speech at final session of Conference on the Problems of Economic Development. UAR:411
Bariko, L. J. P.
Inaugural speech at Conference on the Problems of Economic Development. UAR:237
Bonilla, R. C.
Inaugural speech at Conference on the Problems of Economic Development. UAR:259
Bwa, S.
Inaugural speech at Conference on the Problems of Economic Development. UAR:203
Carneiro, O. A. D.
Inaugural speech at Conference on Problems of Economic Development. UAR:43
Speech at final session of Conference on the Problems of Economic Development. UAR:415
Gauhar, A.
Inaugural speech at Conference on the Problems of Economic Development. UAR:153
Speech at final session of Conference on the Problems of Economic Development. UAR:409
Ghani, H.
Inaugural speech at Conference on the Problems of

Economic Development.
UAR:83
Speech at final session of Conference on the Problems of Economic Development.
UAR:417

Ghazali, I. M.
Speech at final session of Conference on the Problems of Economic Development.
UAR:419

Goka, F. K. D.
Inaugural speech at Conference on the Problems of Economic Development.
UAR:89
Speech at final session of Conference on the Problems of Economic Development.
UAR:383

Guerrero, M. P.
Inaugural speech at Conference on the Problems of Economic Development.
UAR:313

Gurra, A. H.
Inaugural speech at Conference on the Problems of Economic Development.
UAR:163
Speech at final session of Conference on the Problems of Economic Development.
UAR:425

Hakimi, A. K.
Inaugural speech at Conference on the Problems of Economic Development.
UAR:131
Speech at final session of Conference on the Problems of Economic Development.
UAR:389

Ibrahim, H. B.
Inaugural speech at Conference on the Problems of Economic Development.
UAR:137
Speech at final session of Conference on the Problems of Economic Development.
UAR:393

Kaissouni, A. M.
Inaugural speech at Conference on the Problems of Economic Development.
UAR:321
Speech at final session of Conference on the Problems of Economic Development.
UAR:427

Maharoof, M. M.
Inaugural speech at Conference on the Problems of Economic Development.
UAR:73
Speech at final session of Conference on the Problems of Economic Development.
UAR:405

Maulina, R.
Inaugural speech at Conference on the Problems of Economic Development.
UAR:307

Maurice, G.
Inaugural speech at Conference on the Problems of Economic Development.
UAR:251
Speech at final session of Conference on the Problems of Economic Development
UAR:413

Mazidi, F.
Inaugural speech at Conference on the Problems of Economic Development.
UAR:279
Speech at final session of Conference on the Problems of Economic Development.
UAR:407

Mekonnen, L. E.
Inaugural speech at Conference on the Problems of Economic Development.
UAR:31
Speech at final session of Conference on the Problems of Economic Development.
UAR:375

Mestiri, A.
Inaugural speech at Conference on the Problems of Economic Development.

CONFERENCE ON THE PROBLEMS OF ECONOMIC DEVELOPMENT, CAIRO, JULY 9-18, 1962 (cont.)
UAR:169
Speech at final session of Conference on the Problems of Economic Development. UAR:387
Mukhtar, A.
Inaugural speech at Conference on the Problems of Economic Development. UAR:217
Speech at final session of Conference on the Problems of Economic Development. UAR:381
Nasser, G. A.
Speech at the inaugural session of the Conference on Problems of Economic Development. UAR:19
N'Doure, H.
Speech at final session of Conference on the Problems of Economic Development. UAR:373
Njotowijono, O.
Inaugural speech at Conference on the Problems of Economic Development. UAR:57
Speech at final session of Conference on the Problems of Economic Development. UAR:397
Patsalidis, A.
Inaugural speech at Conference on the Problems of Economic Development. UAR:177
Speech at final session of Conference on the Problems of Economic Development. UAR:421
Popović, V.
Inaugural speech at Conference on the Problems of Economic Development. UAR:101
Speech at final session of Conference on the Problems of Economic Development. UAR:399
Radwan, T.
Speech at final session of Conference on the Problems of Economic Development. UAR:385
Salas, O. C.
Inaugural speech at Conference on the Problems of Economic Development. UAR:285
Shah, M.
Inaugural speech at Conference on the Problems of Economic Development. UAR:187
Speech at final session of Conference on the Problems of Economic Development. UAR:369
Shhong, S.
Inaugural speech at Conference on the Problems of Economic Development. UAR:243
Sijaona, L. N.
Inaugural speech at Conference on the Problems of Economic Development. UAR:295
Speech at final session of Conference on the Problems of Economic Development. UAR:423
Sylla, A.
Inaugural speech at Conference on the Problems of Economic Development. UAR:143
Vargas, A. S.
Inaugural speech at Conference on the Problems of Economic Development. UAR:303
Speech at final session of Conference on the Problems of Economic Development. UAR:391

CONFERENCE SPEECHES See Congresses and conventions; Debates and debating.

CONFIDENCE
Confidence plus optimism total success. NAT:9
No man is worth his salt without pepper. NAT:3
Jessel, G.
Confirmation speech (model for a Jewish boy) JEYO:16

CONFIRMATION See also Bar Mitzvah speeches

CONFUCIUS
Wu Ting-Fang
Teachings of Confucius. REEM 8:429; REEMA 6: 1225; REEMB 13:437

CONGO
Davidson, R. T.
"Hideous outrages" of subjugation. BREW 5:16; MEAR:115
Eisenhower, D. D.
Address at the United Nations, September 22, 1960. BA 1960-61:55

CONGRATULATIONS
Address of congratulation at the opening of a new political club. HAPR:125
Address of congratulation by mayor or high civic official at opening of a memorial library. WRA:164
Address to the captain at the end of an ocean voyage, by a passenger. EDGS:349
Address to the captain of a steamer at the conclusion of a voyage. BARB:148
Best wishes to the host and hostess at their housewarming. LU:1244
Carnegie, A.
Congratulating General Goethals. COP:688; COPB: 715; REEM 1:208; REEMB 1:209
Congratulating owner on the opening of a new restaurant by a guest. EDGS:159
Congratulations to a newly-appointed company official. DR:21; LU:1126
Congratulations to the successful candidate on his election to public office. DR:215; LU:1238
Congratulatory address by international president of Acme Service Club at special meeting. WRA:161
Congratulatory letter to a club member who has received honors. EDGS:412
Congratulatory messages-various models of. BEC:141
Congratulatory speech by mayor at opening of a new school. WRA:156
Congratulatory speech to a friend on his return from Europe. BARB:93
Felicitating a bridegroom. Also his response to the congratulatory speech. BARB: 66, 67
Greetings to individuals and organizations on various anniversaries-seventeen examples of. BEB:83-89
Lamartine, A. M. L.
Congratulatory speech. CHAL 5:430; HAZO 12:4930; MAS 12:4930
Speech congratulating a young man on reaching his majority. BARB:86
Speech of congratulation to a seventy year old guest. WRA:166
Suggestions for making, and examples of various types of congratulatory speeches. WRA:153
Twenty-five years an employee-congratulatory speech by president of company at 25

CONGRATULATIONS (cont.)
year club. WRA:159
See also Candidates; Responses to congratulations

CONGRESS OF INDUSTRIAL ORGANIZATIONS See Labor unions

CONGRESSES AND CONVENTIONS
Acceptance of office (at a convention) BEDA:141
Address before an educational convention. AMEO 1:32
Address of welcome at a convention. BEDA:135
Address of welcome at a sales convention by the president of the company. WRA:82
After dinner address at insurance convention. AMEO 2:133
Announcing forthcoming convention. WRA:29
Bones: short and over can mean short of publicity and overlooking a patron (a speech to bank personnel, changeable for many occasions, business meeting or convention of sales personnel, at a graduation of nurses' group, for fund raising drives, to a telephone group, or by a political or labor speaker) BAI:94
Branen, J.
Emcee at a plumbers' convention. BRH:179
Business enterprise (for a convention of businessmen). ED:131
Closing speech and benediction at a convention. BEDA:143
Convention remarks. FRIE:63
Convention report at a club meeting. WRA:189
Huber, L. J.
Emcee at a convention. BRH:278
Invocation at a convention. BEDA:134
Kaser, A. L.
Emcee at a barbers' convention.
Emcee at a salesmen's convention (2) BRH:246, 230, 295
Mayor's address of welcome at a business convention. WRA:68
Mayor's address of welcome to convention of Knights Templar. AMEO 2:58
Most important letter in a salesman's alphabet-speech by president or salesmanager at a sales convention. WRA:213
Nomination of president at a convention, call for nomination, nomination, closing nominations and balloting. BEDA:139-140
Opening address at a sales convention by the president of the company. WRA:80
Opening address at a sales convention by the salesmanager. WRA:81
Opening address of The American Bankers' Association. HOAP:256
Opening speech at a convention. BEDA:134
Presenting newly-elected president (to a convention) BEDA:140
President's annual report. BEDA:137
Publicity committee report. BEDA:138
Resolution of appreciation for hospitality (at a convention) BEDA:142
Reuther, W. P.
Labor's principles and program. BA 1951-52:123
Safety first on our highways-speech to establish a "safety first" committee at a convention. WRA:196
Sales convention report at company sales meeting. WRA:18

Suggestions for speaking in conferences and discussions. With examples of. BAAG: 287; SAB:275; SABA:372
Temporary chairman's remarks. BECA:138
To a convention. THOS:101
Wagner, R. F., Jr.
Welcomes the convention of Lions International. PRNE: 71
Welcome to a district or state church convention. HNWS: 47
Welcome to a national convention. HNWS:48
Wheeler, B.
United Mine Workers' Convention. BA 1939-40:316
See also Types of speeches, e.g. Closing speeches; Introductions; Opening addresses; Political conventions; Responses; Welcoming addresses
Conick, H. C.
Begins an address on the occasion of the 88th annual meeting of National Board of Fire Underwriters. PRNE:53
Conklin, Edwin G.
Education for democracy. BA 1939-40:346
Conkling, Roscoe
Against Senator Sumner. BREW 4:146
Nomination of U.S. Grant for a third term. BAKF:125; BREW 4:138; BRYW 10:94; CHAL 11:257; HAZO 21: 9122; MAS 21:9122; ONEM: 472; ORAMA 2:315; REEM 10:256; REEMA 12:719; REEMB 11:268
Stalwart standpoint. BREW 4: 141
Issues of the campaign (1880) CHAL 11:262; HAZO 21: 9127; MAS 21:9127
State of New York. REEM 1: 332; REEMA 1:269; REEMB 1:333
Summing up in the Haddock court-martial. CHAL 11:251; HAZO 21:9116; MAS 21:9116
Conn, Jerome and others (Dorfman, A. and Seyle, H.)
Stress and disease. HAR:328
Conn, R. Hugh
Tariff and the debenture clause. DOA:90
Connally, Thomas T.
America and post-war international cooperation. BA 1943-44:96
Report to the Senate on the San Francisco conference. VO 1945-46:348
Connaught, Arthur William Patrick Albert, Duke of
To the Indian Assembly on its inauguration, February 9, 1921. KESI 2:335

CONNECTICUT
Bromley, I. H.
Connecticut's part in the business. REEMA 1:86
Field, D. D.
Early Connecticut. REEM 2: 45; REEMA 2:493; REEMB 2:45

CONSCIENCE
Dolly, W. L.
Era of conscience. SHUC:173
Fonville, D. R.
Public conscience. SHUC: 166
Morgan, C., Jr.
Time to speak. BERS:87
Schmitz, H. E.
Old crank next door. BRY: 437; BRYA:488
Williams, J. F.
Evolution of conscience. SHUC:182; TRUW:230

CONSCRIPTION
Borah, W. E.
Hideous doctrine of Prussianism. BREW 2:152
Fosdick, H. R.
Military conscription. ON: 168

CONSCRIPTION (cont.)
Lazar, W. T.
Reveille of the dead. NOR 1941:35
Roosevelt, F. D.
Message to Congress on extension of selective service men. VO 1941:348
Truman, H. S.
Message to Congress, September 6, 1945. VO 1945-46:546
Wilson, W.
Conscription Proclamation. FKA:175

CONSERVATION OF NATURAL RESOURCES
Allen, S. W.
Conservation of our natural resources. SHUC:207
Atkinson, M. E.
Rivers did not forget. YR 9:61
Chapman, L. F.
Next step in our economic development. SHUC:228
Hill, J. J.
Canadian lesson for the United States. BREW 7:57
Natural wealth of the land and its conservation. REEM 4:198; REEMB 4:198
Sanderson, J. K.
Plan or perish. BRP 8:108; YR 9:69
Udall, S. L.
Conservation: physical and spiritual. ANGC:59

CONSERVATISM
Carleton, W. G.
New Conservatism and the mass society. NORR 3d ser:332
Clark, G.
Conservatism and civil liberty. SAR:151
Emerson, R. W.
Conservative. HAZO 14:5973; MAS 14:5973; REEMA 4:377
McBurney, J. H.
Plight of the conservative in public discussion. BA 1949-50:212

CONSERVATIVE PARTY See Great Britain-Politics and government
Constant, Benjamin
Free speech necessary for good government. BREW 4:148; CHAL 4:250; HAZO 9:3642; MAS 9:3642; PL:325
On the discussion of the Chamber of Deputies. CHAL 4:255; HAZO 9:3647; MAS 9:3647
Constantine I, the Great, Emperor of Rome
On the coming of our Lord in the flesh. LEEW 3:61

CONSTITUTION See Names of countries with the subhead Constitution e. g. United States-Constitution

CONSUMPTION (ECONOMICS)
Haas, C. G.
I was a jockey. YR 9:249

CONTESTS See Debates and debating

CONTRACTORS See Building

CONVENTIONS See Congresses and conventions; Political conventions

CONVERSATION
Griswold, A. W.
On conversation-chiefly academic. BRAP:109

CONVINCE, SPEECHES TO
Bowman, J.
Gold in clay jars (Dead Sea Scrolls) SOBP:344

CONVOCATION ADDRESSES
Bose, J. C.
Greater India to be. ZU:35
Cowley, W. H.

Fire always makes room for itself. HOC:25; WPRC: 226
Jha, A.
Educational problems. ZU: 52
Munshi, K. M.
Our greatest need, freedom from fear. ZU:18
Sastri, V. S. S.
Advice to students. ZU:9
Stevenson, A. E.
There are no Gibraltors. WPRC:277
Conway, Moncure Daniel
Demonology and English folk-lore. REEMA 4:287
Conwell, Russell Herman
Acres of diamonds. BRAP:70; HURG:202; IMMD:73; REEM 8:138; REEMA 4:307; REEMB 13:140; WPRA:263
Men of low estate. WERN 54: 23
Conwill, Allan
Hitler wins. NOR 1943:17
Conzelman, James G.
Young man's physical and mental approach to war. SAC:60

CONZELMAN, James G.
Stone, H. L.
Introduces James Conzelman, football coach. PR:38
Cook, George William
Two seals. DUNM:379

COOK, JOHN E.
Voorhees, D.W.
In defence of John E. Cook. CHAL 11:125; HAZO 21: 8982; MAS 21:8982
Cook, Joseph
Certainties in religion. CHAL 13:173; HAZO 24:10125; MAS 24:10125
New England scepticism. HAZO 24:10156; MAS 24: 10156
Temperance. THOU 1:541
Ultimate America. BREW 4: 153
Watchwords of the 20th century. THOU 2:502
Cook, Orwyn W. E.
City and the state. SHUC:319
Cook, Patrick F.
Robert Emmet, the ideal patriot of Ireland's Age. CATA 1:271
Cooke, Dwight See Taft, R. A., jt. auth.
Cooke, John Esten
Dead, he was immortal (Stonewall Jackson) HARSO:43

COOKERY
Caterers. SCHS:60
Cooley, Thomas M.
To the Harvard Law school. KNAS:245; KNASA:245
Coolidge, Calvin
Address at International oratorical contest of 1925. LEIO:61
Address at the finals of the International oratorical contest. LEIO:56
Advertising profession. REEM sup 1:199; REEMB 4:130
Age of commercial criticism. REEM 1:339; REEMB 1:340
American Legion. BLAB:309
Armistice day. BEA:145
Education in a republic. SHU: 229
Government and business. FRY: 100
Inaugural address. CHI:239; LOTI:215; USIN:215; USINA: 215
Introducing Henry Cabot Lodge and A. Lawrence Lowell. HOA:368; HOAP:250; ONEM: 667; ONES:3; YE:125
Laying the cornerstone of the Jewish Community Center building. ONEC:92
Limitations of Armaments, February 10, 1927. FIP:172
Neighbors and strangers: ways to peace. FIP:166
150th anniversary of Phillips Academy. CORP:111
Statesmanship of peace (Liberty

Coolidge, Calvin (cont.)
Memorial, Kansas City, November 11, 1926) HICF: 762
To the Senate on being elected its President. LINM:318
Toleration. REEM sup 1:208; REEMB 8:116
Vetoing the farmer: Non-planning as a way of life. FIP:160
Welcome to Charles A. Lindbergh. BRAC:240; SHU:7; SHUP:163

COOLIDGE, CALVIN
Burton, M. L.
Nominating speech for Calvin Coolidge. WHIP:185
Magidson, A. B.
Mediocrity triumphant. YR 5:3
Cooper, R. Conrad
"Let us look at the doughnut." BA 1961-62:148

COOPERATION
Balfour, A. J. B.
Cooperation of English-speaking peoples. FKA:322; ONES:317; SHUP:158
Eisenhower, D. D.
Unity won the war. HAN: 309; ON:330; PE:798; PEA:798
Everett, E.
Universal and uncoerced co-operation. BREW 6:87
Intelligent co-operation. THOU 3:459
Strikes: the striker and the strike-breaker (a changeable speech adaptable for Service men's posts, American War Mothers' or Gold Star Mothers' chapters, for a membership drive or a pep talk for co-operation) BAI:47
Washington, B. T.
Teamwork. HILK:45
You've got to be on the team. JAS:100
See also International cooperation; Labor unions
Cope, Norma Grace
They tip their hats. BRP 9:48
Copley, John Singleton, 1st Baron Lyndhurst See Lyndhurst, J. S. C.
Coppin, Fanny Jackson
Plea for industrial opportunity. DUNM:251
Coppin, Levi J.
Negro's part in the redemption of Africa. DUNM:243
COPYRIGHT
Lowell, J. R.
International copyright. REEMA 2:761
Macaulay, T. B.
Copyright. ONEM:294
Corbett, Alvin
Achievement of peace. BLUE: 34
Corbett, Frank E.
Weighted scales. BRP 2:10; YR 2:81
Corbin, Francis
Answering Patrick Henry. BREW 4:166
Corlett, Ben C.
Presents a past president's pin to the retiring president, Anderson Borthwick. PROC:8
Corley, Pauline
In defense of fiction. GA:226

CORN
Oglesby, R.
Royal corn. REEM 3:6; REEMA 2:853; REEMB 3:6

CORN-LAWS
Bright, J.
Free trade. FULB:132
Cobden, R.
Effects of protection in agriculture. ADR:3:109; BEA: 129; BRYW 4:156; COP:179 COPA:179; COPB:179; HAY 186; ORBR 2:187; PAUF 1: 312; PL:465
On the Corn laws (Feb. 24, 1842) CHAL 7:190; HAZO

14:6074; MAS 14:6074
Derby, E. G. V. S.
Second reading of the Corn Importation Bill. PAUF 2: 47
Peel, R.
On the repeal of the Corn Laws. BREW 8:285; BRTH: 233; BRTHA:233; BRYW 4: 180; CHAL 5:409; HAZO 12: 4886; MAS 12:4886; REEMA 14:1539

CORNELL, KATHARINE
Belmont, Mrs. A.
Tribute to Katharine Cornell. GA:94

CORNELL UNIVERSITY
Schurman, J. G.
Welcome to Cornell's 25th anniversary. ONES:23
White, A. D.
Inaugural address as president of Cornell University. WE 1:245
Woodford, S. L.
Greeting from the founders (Cornell University's 25th anniversary) ONES:81

CORNERSTONE LAYING See Dedication addresses-Cornerstones

Cornplanter, Seneca chief
To the great counsellors of the 13 fires-1790. SHE:15

CORONATION See Monarchy

CORONERS
Walker, B.
Introducing a coroner. BRC:205

CORPORATIONS
Black, J. S.
Corporations under eminent domain. BREW 2:76
Eliot, C. W.
Ethics of corporate management. PEAE:59
Ripley, W. Z.
Control of corporations. BYRA:374; REEM sup 2:342; REEMB 5:244

CORREGIDOR
Sayre, F. B.
Corregidor. BA 1941-42:179

Corrigan, Joseph M.
Memorial Day at League Island navy yard. CATA 1:24

Corrigan, Michael Augustine, abp.
Character of Columbus. WERN 42:71

CORRUPTION See Civil service; Corruption (in politics); Crime and criminals; Elections-Corrupt practices

CORRUPTION (IN POLITICS)
Brackett, E. T.
Summation for the managers in the Sulzer impeachment trial. HICJ:692
Curtis, G. W.
On the spoils system. HAZO 20:8627; JOHA 2 pt 2:367; MAS 20:8627; REEM 10:287; REEMA 12:782; REEMB 11: 300
Dewey, T. E.
Calendar of unpunished crimes. BA 1939-40:257
Hines policy-number case. BA 1938-39:181
Inside story of a racket. BA 1937-38:163
Ditzen, L.
Sweetmeats on gilded trays. BRP 2:12; YR 4:39
Fergen, G.
Blazing bulwarks. YR 7:289
Field, L.
One conspicuous failure of our government. YR 6:105
Hibbs, H. L.
Mirage. YR 2:95
Hinman, W. D.
Opening address for the respondent in the Sulzer impeachment trial. HICJ:660
Howells, P. K.
Simple fools. BRP 6:59; YR 5:197

CORRUPTION (IN POLITICS) (cont.)
Langdon, W.H.
Treason to democracy. BOA:361; BOB:150
Pitt, W., 1708-1778
Reply when attacked by Horatio Walpole, March 6, 1741. BEA:109; CHAL 2:263; GOOD:81; HAZO 5:1870; MAS 5:1870; PAUF 1:43
Prentiss, S.S.
Defalcations of the government. REEMA 14:1646
Reed, J.A.
Red line of corruption. BRAC:66
Rogness, B.M.
Minute men of a new era. BRP 5:60; YR 6:223
Root, E.
Boss rule. REEM 10:392; REEMB 11:408
Russell, J.R.
Rotten boroughs of England. PL:463
Shepard, E.
Dishonor in American public life. NORR 2d ser:207
Stanley, A.O.
New despotism. BOA:358; BOB:49
Van Dyke, H.
Sign of the muck-rake. BOA:363; BOB:51
Wood, R.
Feet of clay. BRP 4:96
Cortelyou, George Bruce
Efficiency. REEM 4:56; REEMB 4:139
Men of vision with their feet on the ground. REEM 1:342; REEMB 1:343
Corwin, Thomas
Against the Compromise Bill. LEEW 9:371
In reply to General Crary. SHAH:195
War with Mexico
BREW 4:172; BRYW 9:123; CHAL 6:113; HAZO 12:5184; MAS 12:5184; PE:378; PEA:378; PL:637; REEMA 12:724; SHAH:205

COST AND STANDARD OF LIVING
Gideonse, H.D.
Reply to Nadine Miller's address 'Is advertising responsible for our high standard of living?" MOA:463
Miller, N.
Is advertising responsible for our high standard of living? MOA:463
See also Price regulation
Cotterill, Robert S.
Old South and the new. TIN:234
Cotton, John
God's promise to his plantations. CHAL 2:1; HAZO 4:1422; MAS 4:1422

COTTON
Cotton planters, by a member of the Cotton Growers Association. EDGS:146
For a cotton planters' banquet. BARB:194
Couch, Darius Nash
Return of the flags. ONEM:708
Coudert, Frederick R.
City of New York. REEMA 1:277
Greetings from the alumni. ONES:76
Our clients. BYRA:88; REEM 1:347; REEMA 1:282; REEMB 1:348
Coughlin, Charles E.
Spirit of the Reorganization Bill. BA 1937-38:111
Coultas, Thomas I.
Culture, a basis for brotherhood. HARSO:173
Coulter, E. Merton
What the South has done about its history. TIN:3
Coulter, Thomas H.
Introduces Dr. Will Durant, author and philosopher on Ladies' day at Executive Club of Chicago. PRNE:43
Introduces W. Alton Jones,

President, Cities Service Company. PRNE:38
Introducing Marguerite (Maggie) Higgins to the Executives' Club of Chicago. LARW:107; LY:129
Presents Lee Wulff. LY:255

COUNCIL OF FOREIGN MINISTERS, 1945
Bevin, E.
Report to Commons on Foreign Ministers' Council. VO 1945-46:627
Byrnes, J. F.
Broadcast on Foreign Ministers' meeting. VO 1945-46:616
Statement on meetings of Council of Foreign Ministers. VO 1945-46:612
See also Berlin Conference, 1945; Moscow Conference of Foreign Ministers, 1945

COUNCIL OF FOREIGN MINISTERS, 1947 (LONDON)
Dulles, J. F.
"Not war, not peace." BA 1947-48:58
Marshall, G. C.
Collapse of the London Big Four Conference. BA 1947-48:15

COUNCIL OF FOREIGN MINISTERS, 1947 (MOSCOW)
Marshall, G. C.
Moscow Peace Conference. BA 1946-47:89

COUNCIL OF FOREIGN MINISTERS, 1954 (BERLIN)
Dulles, J. F.
Berlin Conference. BA 1953-54:33

COURAGE
Bruntz, G. G.
Men to match our mountains (installation speech) MOUG:147; MOUGA:147
Calvin, J.
Necessity for courage. BREW 3:81; BRYW 7:50; CHAL 1:446; COP:67; COPA:67; COPB:67; HAZO 4:1363; MAS 4:1363; PL:243
Collyer, R.
Clear grit. REEMA 4:261
Saxon grit. REEMA 1:263
Conant, J. B.
Civil courage. BA 1945-46:223
Courage in adversity. CON:62
Hoar, S.
American courage. HARSO:158
Roosevelt, T.
Character and courage. WERN 54:137

COURTESY
Arkwright, P. S.
Don't hate your customers. SABA:267; SAC:29; YE:305
Business courtesy. FRIE:168
Courtney, Leonard Henry Courtney, 1st Baron
Speech in House of Lords, February 24, 1909 (on India) KESI 2:98

COURTS See Judges; Jury; Law and lawyers
Cousin, Victor
Eloquence and the fine arts. BREW 4:186; CHAL 6:1; HAZO 12:5000; MAS 12:5000
Foundation of law. BREW 4:195; HAZO 12:5013; MAS 12:5013
Liberty an inalienable right. BREW 4:193; CHAL 6:11; HAZO 12:5010; MAS 12:5010
True politics. BREW 4:198; HAZO 12:5018; MAS 12:5018
Cousins, Robert G.
Causes and issues of the Spanish War. FUL:86
Heroes of the "Maine disaster." DAVC:495; FUL:84; REEMA 12:738
Regular army. FUL:90
Cove, W. G.
New education. ONES:280

Covell, W.E.R.
Welcome to educational group. BRAC:243
Cowen, Joseph
British Empire. BEA:153
Cowles, Gardner
Responds to an introduction. PRNE:62
Cowley, William Harold
Fire always makes room for itself. HOC:25; WPRC: 226
What should a college president be? BA 1949-50:230
Cox, Garfield V.
Challenge of war. ASHF:339
My brother's keeper (plea for common ideals and world fellowship) ASHF:134
Cox, Robert
Humpty dumpty. YR 9:9
Cox, Samuel Sullivan
Against the ironclad oaths. BREW 4:203
On secession. CHEM 4:103; JOHA 2 pt 1:312
On the beauties of diplomacy. CHAL 10:368; HAZO 20: 8721; MAS 20:8721
On the revival of American shipping. CHAL 10:377; HAZO 20:8730; MAS 20: 8730
Sermon on the mount. BREW 4:213
Smith and so forth. REEM 1: 351; REEMA 1:286; REEMB 1:352
Stephen A. Douglas and his place in history. BREW 4: 216
Cox, T.E.
Single tax. REAC:116
Coyle, John G.
Army of democracy. ONEM: 570; ONES:137
Catholic American and anti-Catholic crusade. CATA 1: 202
Fredericksburg. CATA 1:181
Socialism from a Catholic viewpoint. CATA 2:77

COYOTES
Clemens, Samuel L.
Coyote. SHU:202
Crabtree, James William
Response to the presentation of a volume of tributes. YE: 157

CRABTREE, JAMES WILLIAM
Givens, W.E.
Tribute to James William Crabtree. YE:98
Craig, Asa H.
Toast to the printing press. EDGS:192
Cram (Moravian missionary)
Expounds his religious precepts to Red Jacket. JON:54
Cram, Harold
Men or machines. BRP 3:106; YR 4:205
Cranmer, Thomas
Against the fear of death. BREW 4:225
Forgiveness of injuries. BREW 4:226
Good works annexed unto faith. CHAL 1:422; HAZO 4:1319; MAS 4:1319
Speech at the stake. BREW 4: 222; BRYW 3:18; ORBR 1: 23
Crary, Daniel R.
Plague of people. LINP:211
Crassus, L. L.
In defence of Cneius Plancus. CHAL 1:270; HAZO 2:667; MAS 2:667
Craven, Arthur J.
Cause of the Gracchi. HARSO: 165; WERN 42:115
Craven, Avery
Price of union. TIN:269
Craven, Leslie
College graduate's debt to society and the state. SHUC: 355
Crawford, Francis Marion
Pope Leo XIII. REEM 5:85; REEMA 4:339; REEMB 9:11

CRAWFORD, FREDERICK C.
Pratt, P.A.

Introduces Frederick C. Crawford. PR:35
Crawford, William
Introducing a moving and storing executive. BRC:310
Crawford, William Harris
Issue and control of money under the Constitution. BREW 4:229

CRAWLEY, SIR FRANCIS
Waller, E.
Tyrant's plea, necessity (impeaching Justic Crawley) BREW 10:63
Creasy, William T.
Accepting a nomination. ONES: 51

CREATION
Creations; a place, a plan, a pledge (a bank publicity speech for any business group, for a P.T.A. meeting, or for a student body) BAI:72
Helmholtz, H. L. F.
Mystery of creation. BREW 6:428; HAZO 19:8211; MAS 19:8211
Munger, T. T.
Man the final form in creation. BL:709
See also Universe

CREDIT
Bolden, J.
Introducing a credit man. BRC:142
Character the basis of credit-address to a graduating class by a financier. DAVC:556
Credit men's association. SCHS:90
Hamilton, A.
First report on public credit. BIR 1:150
Harrison, H.T.
Whither midst falling due. HOC:27; ON:156; SAR:141
Keller, S.
Introducing a collection manager. BRC:180

CREEDS
Rockefeller, J.D., Jr.
Our family creed. COP:708; COPB:735
Wigmore, J.H.
My creed for the nation. REEM 3:394; REEMB 3:401

CRETE See World war 1939-1945 - Greece
Crewe, Robert Offley Ashburton Crewe-Milnes, 1st Marquis of
On South African Bill. KES 2:25

CRICKET CLUB
For a cricket club dinner. BARB:159
Visit of a cricket club-reception address and reply by president of the club. BARB: 119-120

CRIME AND CRIMINALS
Balch, D.
Real criminal. BRP 2:45; YR 3:119
Benedict, K.
Jose Maria Martinez! Stand up (pronouncing death sentence) GRIS:13
Bennet, L. L.
America's biggest business. YR 8:225
Beyer, L.
'Release unto us Barabbas." BLUE:11
Bingham, J.A.
Against assassins of President Lincoln. BREW 2:50
Blakeley, R.J.
Constant crusades. BA 1951-52:152
Blasting the romance of crime. DR:245; LU:1142
Caesar, C.J.
On punishing the conspirators. BOU:165; BRYW 2:222; CHAL 1:332; COP:51; COPA: 51; COPB:51; HAZO 2:728;

CRIME AND CRIMINALS (cont.)
HIB:33; LEEW 2:39; MAS 2:728; PE:39; PEA:39; PL:95
Carhart, R.T.
Crime wears a star. BRP 3:101; YR 4:261
Child criminals. NI:281; NIA: 211
Clinton, S.
Ropes (heredity and environment in relation to crime) ASHF: 95; BLUE:51; BRP 3:23
Cobbett, W.
God's vengeance against public robbers. HAZO 9: 3521; MAS 9:3521
Cunningham, A.B.
Challenge of crime. ASHF: 103
Darrow, C.
Crime and criminals. ARNS:136
Dewey, T.E.
A B C of racketeering. SAR: 311
Inside story of a racket. BA 1937-38:163
Fiske, A.W.
Underworld on top. BRP 7: 49
Fossey, L.
Shoot to kill. YR 8:207
Gardiner, C.H.
By the power invested. YR 8:249
Gerry, M.B.
In the shadows of the mountain (pronouncing sentence on Alfred Packer, tried for murder) GRIS:16
Goldman, D.
Sinister shadows. BRP 3: 56; YR 4:17
Gray, W.H., Jr.
Broaden our horizons for correctional service. HILK: 140
Griffin, R.S.
Strange drama. ASHF:120
Hartger, H.V.
Skeleton of the press. YR 8:237
Hatfield, M.
Children in court. BART 3: 193
Hedberg, R.E.
American high standard of living as a cause of crime. SHUP:168
Jones, H.W.
Triumvirate of crime. BRP 3:80; YR 4:141
Judson, L.S.
Crime and the criminal court. ASHF:126
Juvenile delinquency. DR:248
Kaufman, I.J.
Sentencing the atomic bomb spies. BA 1951-52:55
Kefauver, E.
Menace of organized crime. BA 1951-52:51
Lawes, L.E.
Crime and the home. BART 4:53
McCormick, A.H.
Crime prevention through probation. HOC:29; SAR:316
Macon, A.R.
Problem of the age. YR 4: 369
Morse, J.
"But for the grace of God." YR 10:141
Pickell, C.S.
Last line of defense. YR 2: 119
Pleasants, A.W.
Reign of technicality. SHUC: 398
Plummer, J.M.
America's medieval empire. BRP 2:30; YR 3:65
Poverty and crime. AMEO 2:38
Pratt, A.
Rivers of crime. YR 9:259
Prisoners. SCHS:210
Reynolds, R.R.
Suppression of crime. BOA: 281
Robinson, M.G.
Eleventh commandment. BLUE:19; BRAC:18
Sackett, S.

Justice and little boys. AN:50
Said, J.
'Don't give up the ship." BRP 4:17
Smart, L.J.
Vindication of a faith. BOA: 284; BRP 5:66
Tessman, A.
Tomorrow, what? YR 4:217
Willis, E.E.
Colleges for crooks. BRP 6:13; YR 7:189
Wines, F.H.
Indeterminate sentence, the parole and the new criminology. PEAE:219
See also Capital punishment; Defense, speeches of; Prosecution; Third degree

CRIMEA CONFERENCE, 1945
Churchill, W.L.S.
Address in Commons on the Crimea Conference. VO 1945-46:75
Roosevelt, F.D.
Yalta Conference. BA 1944-45:19; VO 1945-46: 103; FIP:260
Thorneycroft, C.M.
Speech in British House of Commons, February 28, 1945. GRAC:139

CRIMEAN WAR, 1853-1856
Bright, J.
Russia: negotiations at Vienna, House of Commons, February 23, 1855. BEA: 59; HAY:234; PAUF 1:364
Cobden, R.
War with Russia. BRTH: 258; BRTHA:258
Lyndhurst, J.S.C.
Russia and the Crimean War. BREW 7:419; HAZO 9:3901; MAS 9:3901
Lytton, E.G.E.L B.-L.
On the Crimean war. CHAL 7:72; HAZO 14:5906; MAS 14:5906

CRIPPLES See Handicaps; Medicine
Cripps, Sir Stafford
Review of negotiations with the All-India Congress. VO 1942-43:407
Statement on India, August 5, 1942. VO 1942-43:423
Statue of Westminster, November 20, 1931 speech. KESB: 297
Crisp, Charles Frederick
Closing the Wilson Tariff Bill debate.-Same as his Tariff reform
Tariff reform. BRYW 10:186; REEM 10:318; REEMB 11: 332
Crisp, Charles R.
Here's to peace. BOB:27
Crispi, Francesco
Address to the Italian electors. CHAL 9:458; HAZO 19:8094; MAS 19:8094
At the unveiling of Garibaldi's statue. BREW 4:234; HAZO 19:8090; MAS 19:8090
Socialism and discontent. BREW 4:236
CRITICISMS
Stephen, L.
The critic. REEM 3:271; REEMA 3:1091; REEMB 3: 288
Crittenden, John Jordan
Against warring on the weak. BREW 4:244
Henry Clay and the 19th century spirit. BREW 4:239
On the Crittenden Compromise. CHAL 5:376; HAZO 12:4853; JOHA 2 pt 1:275; MAS 12: 4853
Raccoon in the bag. BREW 4: 249
Crocker, Lionel
Leadership and the spoken word. BA 1941-42:100
On seas of ink. MOUG:189; MOUGA:189
Croessmann, Dwight
Whatsoever things are true. NOR 1940:9

Cromwell, Oliver
Address to Parliament, September 4, 1654. CHAL 2:45; HAZO 4:1475; MAS 4:1475
At the opening of Parliament under the Protectorate. BRYW 3:117; PL:379
Debating whether or not to become King of England. BRTH:33; BRTHA:33; BREW 4:252
On dissolving Parliament (Second Protectorate Parliament) LEEW 6:67; REEMA 12:741
On the dissolution of Parliament (First Protectorate Parliament) COP:147; COPA:147; COPB:147; ORBR 1:65; REEM 9:170; REEMB 10:73
Protector and Parliament. - Same as his Debating whether or not to become King of England.
Speech delivered September 17, 1656. PAUF 1:3
Speech to the nominated Parliament. CROC:103

CROMWELL, OLIVER
Crowther, J.E.
Oliver Cromwell. COUW:133
Lord, J.
Oliver Cromwell. REEMA 5:787

CROMWELL, RICHARD
Vane, H.
Against Richard Cromwell. BREW 10:38; BRYW 3:137; LEEW 6:87
Crookes, Sir William
Realization of a dream. BREW 4:260
Cropsey, James C.
Responsibilities of citizenship. LINM:310
Crosby, Howard
True meaning of the Lord's supper. THOU 2:433
Crosby, John
How to get along in a free world without being subpoenaed. BA 1951-52:71; BAAG:381
Cross, Milton
Radio and opera. GLAD:291

CROSS, WILBUR L.
Butler, N.M.
Presenting Wilbur L. Cross. LY:115

CROSS EXAMINATION See Law and lawyers

CROTHERS, RACHEL
Watkins, A.
Introducing Rachel Crothers. ON:339

CROW, CARL
Introducing Carl Crow, author and authority on China. SUM:78
Crowder, Enoch Herbert
Begin now! REEM 11:303; REEMB 12:320

CROWDS
Ward, A.
Faces in the crowds. EXEE:118
Crowe, Robert E.
Closing argument for the prosecution in the Leopold-Loeb murder trial. HICJ:1090
Crowley, Karl A.
States rights. BOA:120
Crowley, Leo F.
Statement on termination of lend lease. VO 1945-46:490
Crowther, James E.
Oliver Cromwell. COUW:133
Crozier, Lowell
Spirit of Texas. BOB:104

CRUCIFIXION
Albertus Magnis.
Meaning of the crucifixion. BREW 1:136

CRUSADES

Bernard, Saint
Why another crusade?
BREW 2:37; BRYW 7:20; COP:63; COPA:63; COPB:63; PL:206; REEM 9:55; REEMB 10:56

CRUDUP, Josiah C.
House, R. B.
Presents Josiah C. Grudup. LY:110
Crummell, Alexander
Black woman of the South: her neglects and her needs. DUNM:159

CTESIPHON.
Aechines.
Against Ctesiphon. BREW 1:104; BRYW 1:186; LEEW 1:301; PL:60; REEM 9:14; REEMB 10:15

CUBA
Bonilla, R. C.
Inaugural speech at Conference on the Problems of Economic Development. UAR:259
Clemens, J.
Cuba and "manifest destiny." BREW 4:75
Giddings, J. R.
Slavery and the annexation of Cuba. BREW 6:234; CHAL 6:148
Logan, J. A.
On the independence of Cuba. CHAL 11:56; HAZO 21:8815; MAS 21:8815
Nesmith, G. T.
Antonio Maceo. TRUW:103
Proctor, R.
Condition of Cuba. FUL:250, 253
Thurston, J. M.
Affairs in Cuba. BRIM:324; CHAL 14:98; CLAY:35; ESEH:221; HARS:244; HAZO 25:10615; LA:152; MAS 25:10516; SHUP:219
Spain's heartless cruelty. FUL:304, 307
See also United States-Foreign Relations-Cuba
Culberson, Charles A.
Tribute to Ireland (St. Patrick's Day address) SHUO:219
Cullom, Shelby
Our commercial relations. BLAA:244; BLAB:244; FUL:95, 97, 99
Right of possession. -Same as his Our commercial relations
Culpeper, John. See Colepeper, John

CULTURE
Brightman, E. S.
Three conceptions of culture. NORR 3d ser:55
Coultas, T. I.
Culture, a basis of brotherhood. HARSO:173
Culture and service. DAVC:18
Derby, E. H. S.
Life and culture. ORBR 2:159
Hale, E. E.
Mission of culture. CHAL 10:153; HAZO 20:8374; MAS 20:8374; REEM 2:142; REEMA 2:570; REEMB 2:134
Hebraism and culture. DAVC:37
Ise, J.
Values in a crazy world: a plea for more culture. HOB:149
Lippmann, W.
Education without culture. BA 1940-41:292; NORR 3d ser:132
Mines, F. J.
Exponent of culture for common humanity. TRUW:164
Morize, A.
Foreign cultures and the world crisis. NORR 3d ser:153
Oliver, R. T.
Culture and communication. LINP:201
Oxford & Asquith, H. H.

CULTURE (cont.)
Culture. BEA:331
Prentice, W.K.
Hellenic standards for the modern world. NORR 2d ser:296
Pritchett, H.S.
Modern culture and the human spirit. NORR 2d ser: 372
Rhees, R.
Modernizing of liberal culture: inaugural address as president of University of Rochester. WE 1:215
Shairp, J.C.
Literary theory of culture. REEMA 9:1052
Shelby, J.
New frontiers for smart people. BART 3:277
Smith, H.L.
Culture afforded by scientific training (at Alumni reunion) SHUO:98
Thomas, I.
Culture and service. SHUC: 380
Young, O.D.
How we meet ourselves (semi centennial of Hendrix College) COP:706; COPB: 733; HURG:227
See also Civilization; Education; Humanism; Intellect; Learning and scholarship

Cummings, Amos J.
On the Naval Appropriation Bill. CHAL 13:419; HAZO 24:10431; MAS 24:10431

Cummings, Homer S.
Keynote 1920 Democratic convention. ONEM:390
Modern tendencies and the law. KLEB:79

Cunliffe, Walter, 1st Baron Headley See Headly, W.C.

Cunningham, A.B.
Challenge of crime. ASHF:103

CUPS See Acceptance speeches-Cups; Presentation speeches -Cups

CURIE, MARIE S.
Harding, W.G.
Presents Marie S. Curie. LY:178

Curran, John Philpot
Against pension. BREW 4:314; KET:145
Defense of Rowan.-Same as his England and English liberties-in the case of Rowan
Diversions of a Marquis. BREW 4:310
Election at Newry. KET:192
England and English liberties-in the case of Rowan. BREW 4:317; BRYW 6:99; CHAL 3:320; ESEH:201; GOOD:790; HAZO 7:2974; KET:147; MAS 7:2974; PL: 516; REEMA 12:764
Farewell to the Irish Parliament. BREW 4:323; REEMA 12:769
For Peter Finnerty and free speech. BREW 4:308; CODS: 221; CODSA:221; GOOD:805; KET:175; ORBR 1:337
In the case of Justice Johnson-Civil liberty and arbitrary arrests. BREW 4:270; BRYW 6:127
Liberties of the indolent. BREW 4:321
Massey v. Headfort. GOOD: 814; KET:178
On government by attachment. BREW 4:328; REEMA 12:774
On the liberty of the press.-Same as his For Peter Finnerty and free speech
Press.-Same as his For Peter Finnerty and free speech
Second speech for Archibald Hamilton Rowan, February 4, 1795) KET:170

CURRENCY See Money

CURRENCY QUESTION
Hill, D.B.
For bimetalism. REEMA 13: 1182
See also Gold, Silver

Curtain, Andrew G.
Introducing Fitzhugh Lee to Friendly Sons of St. Patrick, September 17, 1887. REEM 2:318
Curtice, Harlow
Administered prices (before U.S. Senate) ARNS:208
Curtin, Andrew Gregg
People's heritage squandered. CHAL 9:62; HAZO 18: 7552; MAS 18:7552
Curtin, John
Broadcast to Britain, May 7, 1944. VO 1944-45:204
Speech from the Melbourne Herald. VO 1941:638
Curtis, Benjamin R.
Defense of President Johnson. BREW 4:334; HARSO:444
Instruction to the jury. ONEM: 112
Curtis, Charles L.
Accepting the Republican nomination to the Vice-Presidency. ONEC:56
Dedication of the auditorium at Atlantic City. DOA:44
Response to the nomination for Vice-Presidency. ONEC. 22
~~Borah~~,
CURTIS, CHARLES L.
Borah, W.E.
Nominating Charles Curtis for the Vice-Presidency. ONEC:496
Curtis, D.W.
Introducing a Boy Scout executive. BRC:288
Curtis, Dale
Introducing a laundry and dry cleaning executive. BRC: 318
Curtis, George William
American doctrine of liberty, July 17, 1862. NORR 1st ser:94
At Concord centennial celebration. BRYW 10:65; CHAL 10:333; CLAY:135; HAZO 20:8668; MAS 20: 8668; SHU:198
Christmas. THOU 2:362
Commerce and literature. REEMA 1:307
Duty of the American scholar. CHAL 10:326; HAZO 20: 8651; MAS 20:8651
English-speaking race. KLEM: 88; REEMA 1:303
Eulogy on Wendell Phillips. BREW 4:342; CHAL 10:346; HAZO 20:8699; KLEG:218; MAS 20:8699; SHU:169
Greeting the autocrat (Oliver Wendell Holmes) REEMA 1: 299
His sovereignty under his hat (1884) BREW 4:341; HAZO 20:8649; MAS 20:8649; REEMA 12:780
James Russell Lowell. REEM 5:93; REEMA 7:255; REEMB 9:124
Leadership of educated men. BAKF:282; ONEM:816; RINM:256
Liberty under the law. COP:624; REEMB 1:356
Lowell's Americanism. REEMA 1:312
Minute man of the Revolution. - Same as his At Concord
Noblesse oblige (at Harvard Alumni dinner) REEMA 1: 295
On the Spoils system. HAZO 20:8627; JOHA 2 pt 2:367; MAS 20:8627; REEM 10:287; REEMA 12:782; REEMB 11: 300
Oration, 1885 (unveiling of statue "The Puritan" in Central Park) BRAR 2:397
Paul Revere's ride. -Same as his At Concord centennial
Public duty of educated men. BOU:15; BRIM:281; PAR: 365; SHU:194; SHUM:192
Puritan principle: liberty under law. BAKF:430; BRY:468; BRYA:554; ONEM:573; PAR: 359; REEM 1:355; REEMA 1:290
Robert Burns. LA:137

Curtis, G.W. (cont.)
Sir Philip Sidney. REEMA 4: 357
'We are Americans."-Same as his Liberty under law HOC:158

CURTIS, GEORGE WILLIAM
Warner, C.D.
George William Curtis, litterateur. REEMA 9:1130
Curtis, James F.
Plea for liberalism. YR 7:103
Curtis, James L.
Abraham Lincoln (at centenary of his birth) DUNM:321
Curzon of Kedleston, George Nathaniel Curzon, 1st Marquis
All civilization as the work of aristocracies. BREW 4: 348
House of Lords and financial measures. EMS 1:159
Ministry's request to the Sovereign for the creation of peers. EMS 1:38
Most valuable British asset. BREW 4:352
'Native gentlemen" at home and abroad. BREW 4:348
Speech in House of Commons, March 28, 1892 (on India) KESI 2:46
Woman's work. BEA:161
Cushing, Caleb
England and America in China. BREW 4:358
Extermination of the Indians. BREW 4:359
On Negro colonization. CHAL 6:392; HAZO 13:5598; MAS 13:5598
Primordial rights of the universal people. BREW 4:356
Cushman, Robert E.
How to use civil liberty in wartime. BA 1941-42:91

CUSTOMERS See Business
Cutten, George Barton
Arise, let us go hence. BA 1938-39:210
Fifth column of civilization. HOC:158
Cuyler, Theodore L.
Bad example a stumbling block. THOU 1:574
Knock at the door of Christ's church. THOU 3:474
Risen with Christ. THOU 2:144
Shot at the decanter. THOU 1: 573
Soul's Easter. THOU 2:138
To the workingmen of Scotland. THOU 1:575
Trees of our Lord. THOU 1:33

CYPRESS
Patsalides, A.
Inaugural speech at Conference on the Problems of Economic Development. UAR: 177
Cyprian, Saint, bp. of Carthage
On the benefit of patience. HAZO 3:1114; MAS 3:1114
Unshackled living. BREW 4:363
Cyril, Saint, bp. of Jerusalem
Infinite artifices of nature. BREW 4:369
On the maker of heaven and earth. HAZO 3:1199; MAS 3: 1199

CZECHOSLOVAKIA
Benes, E.
Appeal to the American people on the seizure of his nation. HAN:72
Kaltenborn, H.V.
Czechoslovakia capitulates. BA 1938-39:18
See also World war 1939-1945-Czechoslovakia

CZECHOSLOVAKIA-FOREIGN RELATIONS-POLAND
Fierlinger, Z.
Broadcast on Czech-Polish discussions in Moscow. VO 1945-46:373

D-DAY See World War, 1939-1945-Campaigns-Western front
Daggett, David

Sun-beams may be extracted from cucumbers, but the process is tedious. WPRA: 37
Dailey, Barbara
Den of youth. BRP 10:82
Dailey, Marion
Influence of the movies on marriage and divorce. SHUP:172

DAIRYING
Bailey, J.W.
Competition (Oleomargarine Bill) HICF:252
Dairymen. SCHS:95
Depew, C.M.
Cow and honest competition (Oleomargarine Bill) HICF:285
Dolliver, J.P.
Cow (Oleomargarine Bill) HICF:223
Daladier, Edouard
Broadcast on declaration of war on Germany. HAN:121
France cannot stand by. PL: 832
Nazis' aim is slavery. COP: 491; COPA:491; COPB:461

DALE, SIR DAVID
Grey, E.G.
Industry. BEA:243
Daley, Thomas A.
Introduction of a speech upon poetry of business, and vice versa. HOAP:35
Dalhousie, James Andrew Broun Ramsey, 1st Marques
Speech of February 28, 1856 (on India) KESI 1:284
Dallam, John M., III
Constitution. LEIO:122
Dallas, George M.
Eulogy on Andrew Jackson. CHAL 6:25; HAZO 12:5035; MAS 12:5035
Pennsylvania idea. BREW 4: 374
Dallinger, Carl
They that take the sword. BRP 5:36; YR 6:191
Dalton, Crate
Crisis in American economics. SHUC:220
Dalton, Terry
Radio's raucous rattle. JUD: 139
Daly, W.J.B.
Memorial Day. CATA 1:17
Damiani, Peter, Saint
Glory of the Cross of Christ. LEEW 3:314
New Testament history as allegory. BREW 4:381
Secret of true greatness. BREW 4:380
Sermon on Saint Boniface. HAZO 3:1242; MAS 3:1242
Speech at Milan. LEEW 3:309

DAMS
Truman, H.S.
At dedication of Gilbertsville dam. VO 1945-46:631
Dana, Charles Anderson
Diplomacy and the Press. REEMA 1:318
Journalism. REEM 6:97; REEMA 7:278; REEMB 6:47
New England in journalism. REEMA 1:321

DANA, CHARLES ANDERSON
Smith, C.E.
Introduces Charles A. Dana to New England Society. REEMA 1:321
Dana, John Cotton
Mere words. REEM 6:108; REEMB 6:59
Dana, Olive
Historic Thanksgiving. THOU 2: 305
Dana, Richard Henry, Jr.
Russia and the United States. REEMA 1:323
Danaher, John A. See Thompson, D., jt. auth.

DANCING
Gilbert, E.J.
Introducing a dancer or dancing act. BRH:68

DANCING (cont.)
Huber, L.J.
Introducing a dancing act
" a square dance caller
BRH:125, 156
Kaser, A.L.
Introducing a ballet
" a dancing team. BRH: 142, 61
Porter, A.J., Jr.
Southern chivalry enemy number one. JUD:153
Dancy, John C.
Future of the Negro church. DUNM:475
Danforth, Elliott
Mind cultivation man's noblest object (new Scholastic Academy) WERN 54:118
Daniel, John Warwick
Dedication of the Washington monument. BREW 4:383; PROS:107; REEM 5:112; REEMA 7:295; SMI:215
Eulogy of Robert E. Lee (at unveiling of figure of General Lee) HARSO:277; PROS: 105; SHU:150; SHUM:244; SHUO:149; SMI:169
Under the Southern flag. -Same as his Eulogy of Robert E. Lee
Under which flag? -Same as his Eulogy of Robert E. Lee
Was Jefferson Davis a traitor? SMI:193
Daniels, Bernard
Peace. BRP 4:91
Daniels, Josephus
Eulogy on W.J. Bryan. CORP: 272
Invention. REEM 1:360; REEMB 1:361
Presents Sir Norman Birkett. LY:147
D'Annunzio, Gabriele See Annunzio, Gabriele d'
Danton, George Jacques
Against imprisonment for debt. BREW 4:399; CHAL 4:110; HAZO 8:3345; MAS 8:3345
Assassination of LePeletier. CHAL 4:117; HAZO 8:3352; MAS 8:3352
Disasters on the frontier. -Same as his Let France be free
Education, free and compulsory. CHAL 4:111; HAZO 8: 3346; MAS 8:3346
Establishment of a Revolutionary tribunal. LEEW 5:145; PE:264; PEA:264
Freedom of worship. BREW 4: 402; BRYW 7:132; CHAL 4: 114; HAZO 8:3349; MAS 8: 3349; PL:302
Let France be free. BREW 4: 397; COP:78; COPA:78; COBP:78; HAZO 8:3342; KLEM:193; LEEW 5:141; MAS 8:3342; REEM 9:198; REEMA 12:800; REEMB 10: 205
On the abolition of slavery. CHAL 4:123; HAZO 8:3358; MAS 8:3358
Reinvigorates his countrymen. -Same as his Establishment of a Revolutionary tribunal
Reply to the accusation that he aspired to the dictatorship. HAZO 8:3340; MAS 8:3340
Squeezing the sponge. BREW 4: 402; BRYW 7:134; CHAL 4: 115; HAZO 8:3350; MAS 8: 3350; REEM 9:200; REEMA 12:802; REEMB 10:207
Thunders for unity. -Same as his To dare again, ever to dare
To dare again, ever to dare. BREW 4:396; BRYW 7:130; CHAL 4:108; COP:77; COPA: 77; COPB:77; HAZO 8:3338; HIB:39; MAS 8:3338; PE:253; PEA:253; PL:300; REEM 9: 197; REEMA 12:799; REEMB 10:204
To the tribunals. CROC:122
Dar, Bishan Narain
Tendencies and movements of Indian national life. ZU:31
Darlan, Jean François
Address to all French at home and abroad. VO 1942-43:680

Broadcast to the French people, May 23, 1941. VO 1941:217
Speech to the French people, June 10, 1941. VO 1941: 253
Darlington, Thomas
Our association: American Climatological and Clinical Association. REEM sup 1: 221; REEMB 6:67
Darrow, Clarence
Crime and criminals. ARNS: 136
Defense of Richard Loeb and Nathan Leopold. BOU:178; BRAC:136; BYRA:92; COP: 413; COPA:413; COPB: 412; HIB:88; HICJ:992; HURG:196; REEM sup 1: 234; REEMB 6:80
Evolution. EXEE:200
Haywood trial; plea for the defense. SHU:255
Plea for mercy. -Same as his Defense of Richard Loeb and Nathan Leopold
Pleads for justice for the Negro. CROC:129; PE:737; PEA:737
Race prejudice and self defense: argument in the Sweet case. -Same as his Pleads for justice for the Negro

DARWIN, CHARLES
Huxley, T.H.
Examines Darwin's "Origin of species." PE:533; PEA: 533

DAUGHTERS See Fathers and daughters; Mothers and daughters

DAUGHTERS OF THE AMERICAN REVOLUTION
Harding, W.G.
Welcome to the Daughters of the American Revolution. LINM:140
Nominating vice-presidents general of the Daughters of the American Revolution. GA:190
Daugherty, Lola A.
Royal road. JUD:209
Davenport, Daniel
Summation for the plaintiffs in the Danbury Hatters case. HICJ:527

DAVENPORT, RUSSELL
Introducing Russell Davenport, editor of Fortune. SUM:90
Davidson, Carter
Common confusions. BRA:556; BRAP:100
Davidson, Randall Thomas
"Hideous outrages" of subjugation. BREW 5:16; MEAR: 115
Davis, Albert
Challenge of the war to American youth. DO:87
Davis, Cushman K.
"Open door" policy in China. BLAA:108; BLAB:108
Our relations with Spain. FUL:101
Treaty of Paris. FUL:104, 108
United States in Hawaii. REEMA 12:804
Davis, D. Webster
Sunday-school and church as a solution of the Negro problem. DUNM:291
Davis, David
Ex parte Milligan, 1866: opinion for the Supreme Court. ANG:374; BIR 3:29
On appeal from the caucas. BREW 5:20

Davis, Dwight F.
Altar to an ideal. BOB:118
Davis, E.
Annual church service. THOU 3:272
Davis, Elmer
Are we worth saving: and if so, why? BA 1953-54:96; NORR 3d ser:246

Davis, Elmer (cont.)
Finland surrenders. BA 1939-40:63
If we're good enough, we can take it. BA 1941-42:111
Davis, Francis B., Jr.
Response to introduction. PR: 43

DAVIS, FRANCIS B., Jr.
McLain, H.O.
Introduces Francis B. Davis, Jr. PR:40
Davis, Henry Winter
Constitutional difficulties of reconstruction. BREW 5: 32; CHAL 9:175; JOHA 2 pt 2:129
On reconstruction. HAZO 18: 7721; MAS 18:7721
Reasons for refusing to part company with the South. BREW 5:27
Davis, James J.
Fraternalism. NESA:115
Davis, Jefferson
Against Clay and compromise. BREW 5:45
Inaugural address in 1861. ANG:344; BREW 5:41; CHAL 7:294; HAZO 15:6213; JOHA 2 pt 2:32; MAS 15: 6213
Message to Congress, April 29, 1861. BIR 2:260
No divided flag. CHAL 7:298; HAZO 15:6217; MAS 15: 6217
On withdrawing from the Senate. -Same as his On withdrawing from the Union
On withdrawing from the Union. BREW 5:36; BRYW 8:203; CHAL 7:287; COP:305; COPA:305; COPB:305; HARS:364; HAZO 15:6206; HURG:109; JOHA 2 pt. 1: 333; LEEW 10:225; MAS 15: 6206; PE:503; PEA:503 PEAE:139; PL:664; REEM 10:186; REEMA 12: 815; REEMB 11:190; SOU 9:412

DAVIS, JEFFERSON
Chandler, Z.
On Jefferson Davis. BREW 3:198
Daniel, J.W.
Was Jefferson Davis a traitor? SMI:193
Fenner, C.E.
Justice to Jefferson Davis. SHUO:139
Williams, J.S.
Jefferson Davis: a giant among men. BOA:234; HICF:431; PROS:49
Davis, John F.
Discovery of gold in California. WAGN:115
Tribute to the American flag. WAGN:122
Davis, John William
For segregation in the schools. BA 1953-54:113
George Washington, REEM 1: 363; REEMB 1:364
Old order. COP:410; COPA: 410
Our brethren overseas. BYRA: 98; REEM 6:116; REEMB 6:86
Presents Lester B. Pearson. LY:208
Shakespeare's birthday memorial. REEM 1:369; REEMB 1:370

DAVIS, JOHN WILLIAM
Holt, J.H.
Nominating speech for John W. Davis. WHIP:262
Simon, J.A.
Toast to 'His Excellency, the American Ambassador.' REEM 3:216; REEMB 3:233
Davis, Marcellus L.
Upon the death of William McKinley. SHUO:72

DAVIS, NORMAN H.
Price, J.
Presents Norman H. Davis. LY:250
Davis, Ossie See Baldwin, J., jt. auth.

Davis, Robert
Youth and the Constitution. DO:224
Davis, Robert H.
Recalls when Job Hedges unearthed a speech of all occasions. LINM:65

DAVIS, SAMUEL
Patterson, M.R.
Sam Davis. HARSO:124
Davis, Thomas
Washington and the cause of '76. THOU 1:156
Davis, Thomas A.
Vocation and citizenship. CATA 2:213
Davis, Watson
Creative and defensive science. ON:76
Davis, William R.
All's well. WAGN:155
Torch or shadow-which? WAGN:165

DAVIS, WINNIE
Young, B.H.
Tribute to Winnie Davis. SHUO:145
Davison, Henry P.
American Red Cross. REEM 11:296; REEMB 12:313
Davitt, Michael
Against the South African War. KET:422
Ireland a nation, self-chartered and self-ruled. BREW 5:47
On the Irish Land League. BRYW 6:244; HAZO 25:10586; MAS 25:10586
Dawes, Charles Gates
Address at the finals of the International Oratorical contest. LEIO:60
Business organization of the government. REEM 4:68; REEMB 4:150
Reparation. BLAB:329
Speech in support of Hoover. ONEC:551
Welcoming the Jewish Welfare Board. ONEC:13
Dawes, Henry Laurens
On the Indian policy. CHAL 9:124; HAZO 18:7656; MAS 18:7656
Tariff Commission of 1880. BREW 5:52

DAWES PLAN See European War, 1914-1918 - Reparations

DAWN
Everett, E.
Glories of the dawn. CLAY:98; ESEH:216
Dawson, George
Ill-used men. REEMA 7:322
Dawson, Sir J. William
On the higher education of women. CHAL 10:40; HAZO 19:8154; MAS 19:8154
Dawson, John
Adoption of the Constitution. SMI:65
Dawson, Samuel Edward
On the progress of science in Canada. HAZO 19:8166; MAS 19:8166
Prose writers of Canada. CHAL 12:142; HAZO 22:9538; MAS 22:9538
Dawson, William L.
Segregation in the armed forces. HAR:469
Day, Edmund E.
Accountancy as a profession. LINM:475
What really threatens American democracy? BA 1938-39:79
Day, James E.
Introduces Gardner Cowles, publisher. PRNE:15
Introduces John L. Lewis, American labor leader. PRNE:19
Introduces Lee Wulff who presented fishing and hunting films. PRNE:12
Introduces Robert H. Jackson, Associate Justice of Supreme Court of the United States. PRNE:4

Day, James E. (cont.)
Introduces United States Senator, Alexander Wiley. PRNE:36

DAY, JAMES R.
Milburn, J. G.
Presents James R. Day. LY:101
Dayton, William L.
Arraigning President Polk. BREW 5:56
Issues against slavery forced by the Mexican War. BREW 5:59

DEAD SEA SCROLLS
Bowman, J.
Gold in clay jars (Dead Sea Scrolls) SOBP:344

DEAFNESS
Huber, L. J.
Deaf emcee. BRH:323
Dean, James J.
Things that are Caesar's. ONEM:768
Dean, Vera Micheles
Anti-Westernism: cause and cure. BA 1959-60:116; LINP:234
United States and the Communist threat. ANGC:139
Dearing, W. P.
Uplift and the undertow. SHU: 103
DeArmond, David A.
For a Constitutional Convention. SHUO:254

DEATH
Albertus Magnus. Blessed dead. BREW 1:138
Arnold, T.
Realities of life and death. BREW 1:159; CHAL 6:140; HAZO 12:5250; MAS 12: 5250
Bernard, Saint
On the death of his brother. LEEW 3:351
Chrysostom, J.
Blessing of death. BREW 3:306; BRYW 7:3
Cranmer, T.
Against the fear of death. BREW 4:225
Franzen, F. M.
"Sword shall pierce they heart." CHAL 4:408; HAZO 9:3876; MAS 9:3876
House which never was finished. JAS:74
Page, E. C.
Arrangements on this side. BERS:116
Short address on death. THOS: 132
Trumbull, L.
Announcing the death of Douglas. BREW 9:436
What happens when we die? JAI:36
See also Announcements; Condolences; Eulogies; Funeral sermons; Obituaries

DEATH PENALTY See Capital punishment

DEBATES AND DEBATING
Debate (address by the chairman) EDGS:222
Ending an argument. FRIE:64
Extract from a discussion on a community issue. MICS: 185
Fuller, C. D.
Debate judges. JUD:61
Gaw, J. G.
Ye olde time forensics. JUD:91
Geren, P.
Secrets of debating. JUD:65
Harlan, R. E., Jr.
Tragedies of this tournament. JUD:83
Howie, R.
This tournament. JUD:77
McBurney, J. H.
Plight of the conservative in public discussion. BA 1949-50:212
Maker, J.
Bald head and a moustache. JUD:53

Mulroy, T. R.
Introducing two debaters, Sylvia Porter and Leon Henderson. PR:78
Presiding officer's address at a public debate. DAVC:596
Pulteney, W.
Secrecy of debates. EMS 1:208
Stegall, F.
Sport broadcast of a contest debate. JUD:71
Suggestion for argumentative speaking. BAAG:253. With examples of. BAAGA:256
Suggestions for discussional speaking. With examples of. BAAGA:206
Suggestions for round table discussion groups, forums (lecture, panel, symposum) and conference groups. BUT:154; BUTA:154; BUTB:154; BRYA:416. With examples of. MOUGA:159
Suggestions for speaking in conferences and discussions. With examples of. SAB:275; SABA:372
Suggestions for taking part in a discussion or conference, with outline for discussion on "What should be the role of the United States in the Middle East?" MICS:183
Suggestions on how to handle a question period, and value of discussion period to lecture. BUT:88, 89; BUTA:88, 89; BUTB:88
Wyndham, Sir W.
Secrecy of debates. EMS 1:205

DeBoer, Ray
Nature's ice-pack. YR 7:245
Privilegitis Americanus. BRP:8:18

Debs, Eugene
The issue. WPRC:13
On receiving sentence. COP:372; COPA:372; COPB:372; HURG:183; PE:721; PEA:721; REEM sup 1:240; REEMB 7:110

DEBTS
Danton, G. J.
Against imprisonment for debt. BREW 4:399; CHAL 4:110; HAZO 8:3345; MAS 8:3345

DEBTS, PUBLIC
Forgan, D. R.
America and the Allied debts. EXEE:510
Hoover, H. C.
Message to Congress, December 10, 1931 (on public debts) KESK 1:232
Moratorium. FIP:180
Lawson, R.
If we cancel. BRP 4:70; INTW 1933:62
M'Kenna, R.
Economic aspects of world debts. REEM 4:304; REEMB 5:147
Roosevelt, F. D.
Message to Congress, June 1, 1934 (on public debts) KESK 1:247
Vanderlip, F. A.
Allied debt to United States. REEM 4:396; REEMB 5:348

Dechanal, Paul
Harvest of justice. LEW:97

Decker, Clarence R.
Automatons or men? ASHF:205

DECLARATION OF INDEPENDENCE See United States-Declaration of Independence

DECLINING AN OFFICE See Offices-Refusal

DECORATION DAY See Memorial Day

DECORATIONS OF HONOR
Commander's speech on decoration. HILL:474

DEDICATION ADDRESSES
Abstract of an address at the dedication of a Hall of Science and Art. DAVC:623
Barnes, W. H. L.
Speech at music-stand dedication. WAGN:46
Bright, J.
At opening of the new rooms of the Junior Liberal Association of Birmingham. KNAS:148; KNASA:148
Dedication address. THOS:85
Depew, C. M.
American Hall of Fame. WERN 42:20
Eisenhower, D. D.
Dedication of the St. Lawrence Seaway. SABA:292
General dedication speech. HNWS:64
Lodge, H. C.
Webster as an orator. SHU:76
Model and outline of a dedication speech. BAKS:156
Preparation of a dedicatory speech. CORP:188
Suggestions for preparation of a dedication address. BRA:514; BRAB:501. With examples of. GA:61; HIBS:286; MCK:119; MOA:532; SOES:28; WRA:133; YE:180
See also Opening addresses

---- AUDITORIUMS
Clement, G. C.
Boards for life's building (at dedication of new auditorium, Livingstone College) WOON:637
Curtis, C.
Dedication of the auditorium at Atlantic City. DOA:44
---- BANNERS
Consecration of a (Masonic) Lodge banner. EDW:73

---- BRIDGES
Roosevelt, F. D.
Canadian position of the United States. BA 1938-39:25; BIR 4:259
Quarantining the aggressors. ANG:477; BRE:357; BRYA:539; FIP:233; HAN:91

---- BUILDINGS
Bancroft, W. D.
Future in chemistry (at dedication of the Chemistry Building of the College of New York City) PEAE:187
Carpenter, M. H.
On the mission and future of the United States (dedication of Memorial Hall, Beloit College) CHAL 10:414; HAZO 21:8767; MAS 21:876
Champ, F. P.
Address of acceptance. SAR 110
Church of the living stones. JA:26
Closing speech (at dedication of home for aged) BED:36; BEDA:77
Closing speech (at dedication of recreation center) BED:39; BEDA:80
Consecration prayer (at dedication of home for aged) BED:35; BEDA:76
Dedicating a new building at a public meeting. WRA:137
Dedicating a parsonage. HNWS 62
Dedicating an educational building. HNWS:63
Dedication of a new club house DR:105; LU:1222
Dedication of home for aged. BEC:158
Dedication of new building. NATS:7
Dedicatory address (at dedication of home for aged) BEI 33; BEDA:74
Dedicatory address (at dedication of recreation center) BED:38; BEDA:79
Dewey, T. E.
Dedication of the Corning Glass Center. SAB:195

Galloway, C.B.
Reconstruction in the South; past and present (at dedication of Mississippi's new Capitol) SHUO:294
Grant, R.F.
Dedication of the Chamber of Commerce of the United States. REEM sup 1:371; REEMB 4:314
Greeting and welcome (at dedication of home for aged) BED:32; BEDA:73
Greeting and welcome (at dedication of recreation center) BED:37; BEDA:78
Guest speaker at the dedication of the new Chamber of Commerce building. DR:49; LU:1147
Gymnasium dedication. SCHS:102
Harrison, C.C.
Opening the ceremonies at the dedication of a new law building. ONES:64
Hotel dedication. SCHS:147
International president's speech dedicating a home for underprivileged children-sponsored by the civic service club. WRA:141
Invocation (at dedication of recreation center) BED:37; BEDA:78
Kellogg, F.B.
Thomas Jefferson: champion of the common people (dedicating Jefferson's home) BRAC:347
Kennan, G.F.
Liberal arts in contemporary American society. BA 1953-54:171
Krantz, J., Jr.
Dedication address (Bressler Research Laboratory-University of Maryland) MCK:121
Montague, A.J.
Dedication of Elks national home. THOU 3:156
Opening and divine blessing (at dedication of home for aged) BED:32; BEDA:72
Presenting key (at dedication of home for aged) BED:34; BEDA:75
Scanlon, R.
Public address as a social force (dedicating new quarters for Speech Department at Queens College) BA 1961-62:159
Shrine address at dedication of new Masonic Temple. AMEO 2:62
Truman, H.S.
Slandermongers and the Bill of Rights (dedication of American Legion headquarters in Washington, D.C.) BA 1951-52:65
Two speeches dedicating a new church or building unit. HNWS:61
Warren, E.
Charles Evans Hughes and the spirit of tolerance (dedication of hall in memory of Hughes) BA 1956-57:135
Home for American jurisprudence (dedication of American Bar Center in Chicago) COPB:611
Whitfield, A.H.
Tribute to the women of the South (at dedication of Mississippi's new Capitol) SHUO:36
Young, O.D.
Dedicating the George F. Baker Foundation. ONEC:79
See also Open house; Also this subject, subheads Churches, Cornerstones; Dormitories; Hospitals; Libraries; Schools

---- BUSTS
Hay, J.
Sir Walter Scott (at unveiling of bust of Sir Walter Scott in Westminster Abbey) REEMA 8:614

DEDICATION ADDRESSES - CEMETERIES
Everett, E.
Dedicating the national cemetery at Gettysburg. PE:519; PEA:519
Gittelsohn, R. B.
That men might be free. BA 1945-46:16
Lincoln, A.
Gettysburg address. See Lincoln, Abraham Gettysburg address

---- CHURCHES
Andrews, E. G.
Dedication of Embury Chapel, Brooklyn. THOU 2:460
Behrends, A. J. F.
Dedication sermon for Bethesda People's Church of Brooklyn. THOU 2:462
Hildebert of Lavardin.
Rebecca at the well. BREW 7:42
Reed, G. E.
Dedication of Embury Chapel, Brooklyn. THOU 2:461
Stevens, W. B.
Divine strength and beauty of holy worship (dedication sermon at St. Thomas's Church, New York) THOU 2:449

---- CORNERSTONES
Address at laying of cornerstone of World War memorial. AMEO 2:115
Bromley, G. T.
Sloat monument address. WAGN:339
Closing speech and prayer (at cornerstone dedication of youth center) BED:42; BEDA:83, 84
Coolidge, C.
Laying the cornerstone of the Jewish Community Center building. ONEC:92
Cornerstone laying address (at cornerstone dedication of youth center) BED:41; BEDA:82
Danforth, E.
Mind cultivation man's noblest object (new Scholastic Academy) WERN 54:118
Dedication prayer and proclamation (at cornerstone dedication of youth center) BED:40; BEDA:82
Depew, C. M.
At laying of the cornerstone of the New York 'World' building. BRAC:354
Edsall, S. C.
Remarks at the laying of the cornerstone of the St. Peter's Church, Chicago. THOU 2:445
MacArthur, R. S.
Christ a living stone. THOU 2:440
Myers, C.
Remarks on the laying of the cornerstone of the First Baptist Church of Brooklyn. THOU 2:447
Opening speech (at cornerstone dedication of youth center) BED:40; BEDA:81
Preliminary remarks at the laying of a cornerstone. EDGS:94
Presenting trowel (at cornerstone dedication of youth center) BED:42; BEDA:83
Randolph, E. H.
City of Shreveport (at laying of cornerstone of new City Hall) SHUO:226
Roosevelt, T.
Greatness in citizenship (dedication of Law School of University of Chicago) ONES:114
Man with the muck-rake (at dedication of Office Building of the House of Representatives) ARNS:102; BAAMP:211; BRAS:278; CAP:134; DOA:275; FIP:49; KNAS:133; KNASA:133;

ONEM:530; PAR:482;
SHAH:603; WERN 42:55
Scott, I. M.
Development of science (Academy of Science of San Francisco) WAGN:234
Smith, C. E.
Republic's higher glory (at laying of cornerstone of new Federal Building at Chicago) FUL:294
Stewart, M. B.
Priest and soldier. NESA: 183
Webster, D.
At laying of the cornerstone of addition to Capitol. HAZO 11:4621; MAS 11: 4621
Wordsworth, W.
On laying the cornerstone of the new grammar school at Bowness. KNAS:121; KNASA:121

---- DAMS
Truman, H. S.
At dedication of Gilbertsville Dam. VO 1945-46:631

---- DOORS
Sarnoff, D.
Six thousand years. COP: 429

---- DORMITORIES
Blunt, K.
Dedication of Windham House. GA:64

---- EXHIBITIONS
Odell, B. B., Jr.
Westward Ho! (St. Louis World's Fair) WERN 42:121
Roosevelt, T.
Making of America: opening the Jamestown Exposition, April 26, 1907. BREW 9:85
National expansion (St. Louis World's Fair) WERN 42:9
Washington, B. T.
Address at the opening of the Atlanta Exposition. BAAMP:189; BAKF:210; BLAA:113; BLAB:113; BRAC:8; BRY:479; BRYA: 566; CAP:110; CHAL 14: 312; DOA:333; DUNM:181; HARS:503; HAZO 25: 10583; HILK:38; MAS 25: 10583; ONEM:509; ONES: 102; PAR:461; PE:633; PEA:633; PL:707; REEM 7:417; REEMA 9:1136; REEMB 8:433; SMI:206; WOON:580

---- FLAGPOLES
Dedicating flagpole (at Flag Day ceremonies) BEDA:96
Upon the dedication of a flag pole upon public school grounds. HAPR:92

---- GATES See Dedication addresses-memorials

---- HOSPITALS
Roosevelt, F. D.
Dedicatory address at the Naval Medical Center, Bethesda, Maryland. VO 1942-43:454

---- LIBRARIES
Avebury, J. L.
Free libraries (opening a free library at Rotherhithe, England) REEMA 8:808
Carnegie, A.
Common interest of labor and capital. REEM 4:42; REEMB 4:100
Dedication of a public library. DAVC:553
Dedication of a public library, by a city official. EDGS: 103
Munro, W. B.
Dedicating the Public Library of the City of Pasadena. ONEC:75
Smith, S. M.
Uses of a library (at dedi-

DEDICATION ADDRESSES - LIBRARIES (cont.)
cation of Carnegie Library, Winthrop College, Rock Hill, South Carolina) SHUO:80

---- LODGES
Suggestions for consecration of a (Masonic) Lodge. With example of. EDW:71

---- MEMORIALS
Comstock, A. L.
Dedication of the gates. GA:68
Coolidge, C.
Statesmanship of peace (Liberty, Memorial, Kansas City, November 11, 1926) HICF:762
Dedication services and speech at presentation of memorial shafts, statues, tablets, etc. HILL:474
Fraternal Woodmen memorial. THOS:70
Harrington, E.
Unveiling of a World War memorial. ONES:117
Minnigerode, L.
Dedication of Delano Memorial. GA:67
Roosevelt, F. D.
At the dedication of the Thomas Jefferson Memorial, Washington, D. C. VO 1943-44:163
Speech on the site of the Jefferson Memorial. YE: 204
Russell, W. T.
Unveiling of memorial in honor of the Spanish War heroes. CATA:1:142
Taft, W. H.
Lincoln Memorial. REEM 7:398; REEMB 8:419
Warren, L. C.
Dedicating national shrine at Kitty Hawk. CORP:189
Williams, J. S.
Jefferson Davis: a giant among men. BOA:234; HICF:431; PROS:49
Wilson, W.
Abraham Lincoln (dedicating Lincoln's birthplace) ONEM:537; ONES:98; SHU: 18
See also Dedication addresses -Tablets

---- MONUMENTS
Black, J. C.
Mother of Lincoln. HARSO: 229
Blair, F. P.
Deathbed of Benton. BREW 2:119
Bradley, W. O.
Blue and the Gray (dedication of Kentucky monument in Chickamagua National Park) SHUO:302
Breckenridge, W. C. P.
Who were the Confederate dead? SOU 9:418
Daniel, J. W.
Dedication of the Washington monument. BREW 4: 383; PROS:107; REEM 5: 112; REEMA 7:295; SMI:21
Davis, D. F.
Altar to an ideal. BOB: 118
Dedication of a monument or tablet for soldiers by a leading citizen. EDGS:59
Depew, C. M.
Our victorious General (Grant) THOU 1:370
Devens, C.
At the dedication of the soldiers' and sailors' monument in Boston Commons. CHAL 10:12; HAZO 19: 8126; MAS 19:8126
Douglass, F.
Oration in memory of Abraham Lincoln (at unveiling of Freedmen's monument, Washington, D. C.) CHAL 9 144; DUNM:133; HAZO 18: 7676; HIB:171; MAS 18: 7676; WOON:516

Dowling, V. J.
Christopher Columbus. CATA 1:100
Foraker, J. B.
Outline of speech at the dedication of Ohio's monument to the Andrews raiders at Chattanooga. PITT: 88
Historical address. THOS:75
Gordon, A. C.
John Tyler. SMI:134
Jonas, B. F.
Confederate dead (at laying of cornerstone to memory of Confederate dead) SHUO: 31
Joyner, J. Y.
Tribute to Calvin Henderson Wiley (at unveiling of monument) SHUO:284
McCabe, W. G.
First university in America, 1619-1622. SMI:20
McKinley, W.
American patriotism (at dedication of Cuyahoga County Soldiers' and Sailors' monument in Cleveland) BREW 8:35; CHAL 13:457; HAZO 24:10486; MAS 24: 10486; REEM 7:264; REEMA 9:847
Grant (at dedication of Grant monument in New York City) BREW 8:40; HAZO 24:10494; MAS 24: 10494; WERN 42:77
Matthews, B.
Edwin Booth. REEM 5:311; REEMB 9:351
Meighen, A.
Glorious dead. REEM 11: 431; REEMB 12:456
Modern Woodmen: at the unveiling of a monument. THOS:72
Moton, R. R.
Negro's debt to Lincoln (at dedication of Lincoln monument, Washington, D. C.) WOON:573
Roosevelt, T.
Property rights and predatory wealth (H. W. Lawrence monument) BREW 9:94
Sentimental address at the unveiling of a monument. THOS:76
Taft, W. H.
Address at the unveiling of a monument to Chief Justice Salmon P. Chase. LINM:144
Trinkle, E. L.
Custodians of glory. LINM: 344
Unveiling a monument in memoriam. THOS:68
Washington, B. T.
Address delivered at dedication of the Robert Gould Shaw monument in Boston, May 31, 1897. CHAL 14: 320; DUNM:205; HAZO 25: 10861; MAS 25:10861; WOON:527
Watterson, H.
Francis Scott Key (at dedication of monument) REEMA 9:1143
Webster, D.
Bunker Hill monument. BREW 10:166; BRYW 9:24; CHAL 5:268; CLAY:73; CODS:341; CODSA:341; CROC:463; DOA:239; ESEH:186; FOS:75; HAZO 11:4419; HURG:62; LEEW 9:303; MAS 11:4419; ONEM:492; PAR:102; PL: 621; REEM 10:101; REEMA 15:2090; REEMB 11:103; SAA:127; THOU 1:234
Wise, J. S.
Cadets at New Market. SMI:184

---- PARKS
Chamber of Commerce president's speech dedicating a recreational park. WRA: 139
Roosevelt, T.
New Nationalism (at dedication of John Brown Me-

---- PARKS (cont.)
morial Park, Osawatomic, Kansas. WPRC:27

---- PICTURES
Stephens, A. H.
At the unveiling of Carpenter's picture of Lincoln. LEEW 10:299

---- PLAQUES
Closing speech (at unveiling of plaque for Labor Temple) BED:88; BEDA:161
Dedication of a plaque. BEC: 159
Opening speech (at unveiling of plaque for Labor Temple) BED:86; BEDA:158

---- ROADS
Ben-Gurion, D.
Road to valor. CROC:17

---- SCHOOLS
At the dedication of a public schoolhouse. HAPR:88
Batchelder, N. H.
Purpose of Loomis Institute (Founder's Hall of Loomis) ONES:107
Dedication of a school building. DAVC:530
Dedication of a school building by a prominent citizen. EDGS:221
King, T. S.
High school dedication speech. WAGN:21
Spalding, J. L.
Opportunity (at opening of an educational institution) ONEM:512; REEM 6:379; REEMA 9:1076; REEMB 7: 383; SHUM:312

---- SHRINES
Roosevelt, F. D.
Democracy cannot survive in isolation. ON:146

---- STATUES
Anderson, A.
Lee's statue in Richmond. SMI:175
Blair, F. P.
Character and work of Benton. BREW 2:114
Blackburn, J. C. S.
John C. Breckenridge (unveiling statue at Lexington, Kentucky) REEMA 7:97
Bryant, W. C.
Sir Walter Scott (unveiling statue in Central Park, New York) REEMA 7:155
Choate, J. H.
Farragut (St. Gauden's statue) BREW 3:277; ORAMA 2:363
Unveiling the statue of Rufus Choate. BLAA:262; BLAB:262; CHAL 12:56; HAZO 22:9461; KLEG:172; MAS 22:9461
Crispi, F.
At the unveiling of Garibaldi's statue. BREW 4: 234; HAZO 19:8090; MAS 19:8090
Curtis, G. W.
Oration, 1885 (unveiling of statue "The Puritan" in Central Park) BRAR 2:397
Robert Burns. LA:137
Daniel, J. W.
Eulogy of Robert E. Lee (at unveiling of figure of General Lee) HARSO:277; PROS:105; SHU:150; SHUM 244; SHUO:149; SMI:169
Depew, C. M.
Unveiling the Statue of Liberty. BREW 5:162; CHAL 12:307; HAZO 23:9688; MAS 23:9688; PROS:70; WERN 42:106
Garnett, T. S.
Stuart, the Confederacy's Prince Rupert. SMI:190
Guizot, F. P. G.
At the unveiling of the statue of William the Conqueror. CHAL 5:404; HAZO 12:4881; MAS 12:4881
Hale, E. E.

Honor to the patriotic spy (at unveiling of statue to Nathan Hale) BLAA:241; BLAB:241
Hoge, M.D.
Stonewall Jackson. HARS: 273; PROS:116; SMI:181
Hunter, R.M.T.
Oration (dedication of equestrian statue of Washington) SMI:148
Hurley, P.J.
Pioneer woman (dedicating statue of the Pioneer woman in Ponca, Oklahoma) BOA:256; BOB:131; GRIS: 62
Ingersoll, R.G.
Oration on Humboldt (at unveiling of statue in Peoria, Illinois) CHAL 12:190
Jusserand, J.J.
Address at the unveiling of the bust of Abraham Lincoln in the Hall of Fame, New York University, May 1923. LINM:83
Littleton, M.W.
Robert E. Lee (Hall of Fame, N.Y. University) BLAB: BOA:222; BOB:151; LINM:80
Lloyd George, D.
Man of all peoples (Saint Gauden's statue of Lincoln in London) BREW 7:368; CARP:206; MO:534; MOA: 540
Lodge, H.C.
France and Rochambeau. WERN 42:129
On Daniel Webster (at unveiling of statue in Washington) CHAL 14:179; HAZO 25:10688; MAS 25:10688
Mabie, H.W.
Poe's place in American literature (unveiling of bust of Edgar Allan Poe) REEMA 9:815
McKinley, W.
Characteristics of Washington (at unveiling of Washington statue) KLEM:187; ONES:162; REEMA 9:845
Morley, J.M.
Unveiling the statue of John Bright. BEA:315; PAUF 2: 356
Morrow, W.W.
General Philip Kearny (Statuary Hall, House of Representatives) WAGN:226
Patterson, M.R.
Sam Davis. HARSO:124
Porter, H.
Eulogy on Ulysses S. Grant. REEM 3:98; REEMA 3:944; REEMB 3:99; SHU:81; SHUM:259
Root, E.
Unveiling the statue of Lincoln in London, July 28, 1920. BOAM:93
Teehee, H.B.
Dedicates marble statue of Sequoyah in Rotunda of Statuary Hall, Washington, D.C. JON:126
Unveiling of a statue. DR:68
Williams, R.G.
Robert E. Lee. SMI:299

---- TABLETS
Address at the dedication of a memorial tablet. AMEO 1: 124
Address at the dedication of a memorial tablet. DAVC: 517
Address at unveiling of class tablet. AMEO 1:153
Dedication of a memorial tablet for a benevolent citizen. EDGS:106

---- TREES
Dedicating United Nations tree (at United Nations anniversary ceremony) BEDA:125
Deems, Charles F.
Eating and drinking unworthily. THOU 2:429
Deever, Lawrence
Do you want to commit suicide? BRP 10:56

DEFEAT
Celebration of a political reverse by the party optimist. EDGS:73
Defeated candidate's reply to a serenade. HILL:468
Houston, S.
On his defeat as a Union candidate. BREW 7:74
Humorous address on the occasion of a political reverse. BARB:130
Speech after a political defeat (Selected) PITT:99
Speeches by the vanquished. STOC:143
Webster, D.
On being defeated for the candidacy of the Presidency, 1852. HILL:468
DEFECTIVE AND DELINQUENT CLASSES
Keesey, R.
Aristocracy of the unfit. BRP 8:44; YR 9:165

DEFENSE, SPEECHES OF
Aiken, F. A.
Defense of Mrs. Mary E. Surratt. BREW 1:109
Allen, W. P.
Speech from dock. KET: 365
Andocides.
On the mysteries. CHAL 1: 65; HAZO 1:103; LEEW 1: 71; MAS 1:103; MINA 1: 338
Antiphon.
First tetralogy; first and second speeches for the defence. MINA 1:58, 76
On the choreutes. MINA 1: 246
On the murder of Herodes. CHAL 1:18; FRE:63; HAZO 1:55; MAS 1:55; MINA 1: 160; PL:36
Preoration on the murder of Herodes. LEEW 1:61
Second tetralogy: first and second replies to a charge of accidental homicide. MINA 1:90, 108
Third tetralogy; first and second replies to a charge of murder, arguing that the accused killed in self-defence. MINA 1:124, 136
Benschoten, W. H.
Opening address for the defendant in the Barnes-Roosevelt libel case. HICJ: 742
Bowers, J. M.
Summation for the defendant in the Barnes-Roosevelt libel case. HICJ:762
Bradlaugh, C.
His plea at the bar of the House. BRYW 5:91
Breckenridge, J. C.
Buford case. SOU 9:396
Bricker, J. W.
Against censure of Senator McCarthy. BA 1954-55:113
Brougham and Vaux, H. P. B.
Closing argument for Queen Caroline. BREW 2:265; HAZO 10:4148; KLEG:134; MAS 10:4148
In behalf of Williams when prosecuted for a libel on the Clergy of Durham. GOOD:896
Brown, J.
Last speech, at Charleston, West Virginia. ANG:277; BAKF:247; BIR 2:231; BRYW 9:187; CHAL 6:406; COP:298; COPA:298; COPB:298; CROC:35; HAZO 13:5612; HURG:103; MAS 13:5612; PE:499; PEA:499
Bruce, B. K.
Address delivered to the United States Senate in behalf of admitting P. B. S. Pinchback as Senator from the State of Louisiana. WOON:267
Burke, E.
Attempts to vindicate himself before his estranged constituents. PE:160; PEA:

160
Principle in politics; speech at Bristol, previous to the election, 1780 (defends his Parliamentary conduct) BRAO:89; BREW 2:412 BRYW 6:40; GOOD:292; HIB:143; PE:160; PEA: 160
Burke, T. F.
'Righteousness of revolt'' (from dock at Dublin) HAZO 24:10324; MAS 24: 10324
Burnett, H. L.
Summation for the defendant in the Page case. HICJ:63
Burrowes, P.
King v. Edward Sheridan, M. D. KET:247
King v. Robinson for bigamy. KET:263
Canning, G.
Honour vindicated. HAY:125
Carmack, E.W.
On the contest over his seat in Congress. HARSO: 116
Casement, R.D.
Patriotism is not enough. HAY:332
Cato, M. P.
Exordium of the speech for the Rhodians. CHAL 1:259; HAZO 2:656; LEEW 2:133; MAS 2:656
Charles I.
From the scaffold. CROC: 72
Choate, J. H.
Argument in Admiralty for the 'Republic'' (steamship) HICJ:183
Argument in equity for the plaintiff in the Union Club case. HICJ:1
Cicero, M. T.
Speech in defence of Quintus Ligarius. HAZO 3:892; MAS 3:892
Cobbett, W.
Man on the tower (defending himself against a charge of libel) BREW 4:98
Cranmer, T.
Speech at the stake. BREW 4:222; BRYW 3:18; ORBR 1:23
Crassus, L. L.
In defence of Cneius Plancus. CHAL 1:270; HAZO 2:667; MAS 2:667
Curran, J. P.
England and English liberties-in the case of Rowan. BREW 4:317; BRYW 6:99; CHAL 3:320; ESEH: 201; GOOD:790; HAZO 7:2974; KET:147; MAS 7:2974; PL:516; REEMA 12:764
In the case of Justice Johnson-Civil liberty and arbitrary arrests. BREW 4:270; BRYW 6:127
Second speech for Archibald Hamilton Rowan (February 4, 1795) KET:170
Curtis, B.R.
Defense of President Johnson. BREW 4:334; HARS: 444
Curtis, G.W.
Lowell's Americanism. REEMA 1:312
Danton, G.J.
Reply to the accusation that he aspired to the dictatorship. HAZO 8:3340; MAS 8: 3340
Darrow, C.
Defense of Richard Loeb and Nathan Leopold. BOU: 178; BRAC:136; BYRA:92; COP:413; COPA:413; COPB:412; HIB:88; HICJ: 992; HURG:196; REEM sup 1:234; REEMB 6:80
Haywood trial: plea for the defense. SHU:255
Davenport, D.
Summation for the plaintiffs in the Danbury Hatters case. HICJ:527
Debs, E.V.
On receiving sentence.

DEFENSE, SPEECHES OF (cont.)
COP:372; COPA:372; COPB:372; HURG:183; PE: 721; PEA:721; REEM sup 1:240; REEMB 7:110
Delmas, D. M.
Argument for the petitioners in the Miller and Lux case. HICJ:300
Demades.
On the twelve years. MINA 2:336
Demosthenes.
Damage to a farm: defense against Callicles. FRE:140
Deseze, R.
Defending Louis XVI. BREW 5:187
Desmoulins, C.
Advocating the execution of Louis XVI. COP:70
Dexter, S.
Argument in Selfridge's trial. CHAL 4:154; HAZO 8:3492; MAS 8:3492
"Higher law" of self defense. BREW 5:201
Emmett, R.
Protest against sentence as a traitor. BEA:181; BOU: 144; BREW 5:400; BRYW 6:137; CHAL 5:105; COP: 214; COPA:214; COPB:214; CORP:90; CROC:195; HARSO:320; HAY:116; HAZO 10:4186; HIBS:442; KET:322; MAS 10:4186; ONEM:130; ORBR 2:93; PE:305; PEA:305; PL:522; REEM 9:169; REEMA 13: 941; REEMB 10:176
Erskine, T.
Defense of Lord Gordon, 1781. GOOD:638; ONEM: 49
Free speech and fundamental rights; defense of Tom Paine. BREW 6:43; BRTH: 121; BRTHA:121; BRYW 4: 71; PE:255; PEA:255
Homicidal insanity (J. Hadfield) BREW 6:32; LEEW 7:25; GOOD:766
In defense of Thomas Hardy. BREW 6:40; GOOD: 713
In behalf of John Frost, when indicted for uttering seditious words. GOOD:698
In behalf of Mr. Bingham on a trial for adultery. GOOD:708
In behalf of Rev. George Markham against John Fawcett for criminal conversation with his wife. GOOD: 778
Speech in behalf of John Stockdale. BRAO:141; BREW 6:24; CHAL 3:276; CODS:285; CODSA:285; FULB:69; GOOD:684; HAY: 73; HAZO 7:2918; MAS 7: 2918; PE:184; PEA:184
Evarts, W. M.
Weakest spot in the American system (at impeachment of A. Johnson) BREW 6:56
Gracchus, G.
In vindication of his political purity. LEEW 2:137
Grattan, H.
Invictive against Corry. BREW 6:294; BRYW 6:71; CODS:211; GOOD:396; HARS:327; HAZO 7:2806; MAS 7:2806; ONEM:330; PE:300; PEA:300
Hampden, J.
Patriot's duty defined: against own impeachment. BREW 6:349
Harper, R. G.
Defending Judge Chase. BREW 6:389
Harrison, T.
Speech on the scaffold. BREW 6:385; PE:95; PEA: 95
Hillquit, M.
Summation for the Socialists in the investigation of the New York Socialists by the Assembly, Albany. HICJ:819
Hinman, H. D.

Opening address for the respondent in the Sulzer impeachment trial. HICJ:660
Holborne, R.
In defense of John Hampden. BREW 7:66
Houston, D.
His defense at the Bar of the House. BREW 7:76
Houston, T.
Tell her to go in peace (defense of Minnie Stacey) GRIS:23
Hugo, V.M.
Guillotine. BRYW 7:193; ESEH:209; LEEW 5:253
On capital punishment (defense of Charles Hugo) CHAL 7:8; HAZO 14:5783; MAS 14:5783
Hypereides.
First and second speeches in defence of Lycophron. MINA 2:376; 400
In defence of Euxenippus. MINA 2:466
Ingersoll, R.G.
Summation for the contestants in the Davis will case. HICJ:214
Isaeus.
Estate of Ciro (claim to a legacy) FRE:147; LEEW 1:149
For Euphiletos. LEEW 1:168; PL:51
Langston, C.H.
Should colored men be subject to the pains and penalties of the Fugitive Slave law? DUNM:49
Larkin, M.
Speech from dock. KET:367
Lewis, D.
His speech on the scaffold. BREW 7:332
Lilienthal, D.E.
Credo. BA 1946-47:150; BAAG:370
Lindabury, R.V.
Argument for the complainants in the Prudential-Fidelity merger case. HICJ:408
Littleton, M.W.
Summation for the respondent in the investigation of Senator Jotham Allds. HICJ:557
Lodge, H.C., Jr.
Stop being afraid; reply to attack on United States by Andrei Vyshinski. BA 1950-51:37; YE:171
Logan, J.
On the murder of his family. BOU:115; BREW 7:117; BRYW 8:3; JON:49; LEIO:24; REEM 10:51; REEMB 11:52; SHE:36; SMI:11
Logan, J.A.
Vindication of President Grant. CHAL 11:62; HAZO 21:8821; MAS 21:8821
Lomasney, W.F.
Consciousness of innocence (from dock in Dublin) HAZO 24:10420; MAS 24:10420
Luther, M.
Before the Diet of Worms. BREW 7:406; BRYW 7:38; CHAL 1:406; COP:65; COPA:65; COPB:65; CROC:302; HAZO 3:1293; MAS 3:1293; PE:85; PEA:85; PL:226; REEM 9:58; REEMB 10:59
Lysias.
Defence of a farmer: on the sacred olive-tree. FRE:181
Defence of a state pension. FRE:163
To a gathering of friends. FRE:229
Wounding with intent to kill; quarrel over a boy. FRE:97
Wounding the intent to kill: quarrel over a slave-girl. FRE:107
MacArthur, D.
Defends his conduct of the war in Korea. ARNS:273;

DEFENSE, SPEECHES OF (cont.)
BA 1951-52:21; BOU:105; BRAP:61; CAP:206; COPB: 594; HAR:146; HIBS:465; HURG:293; MOUG:210; MOUGA:210 (outline p217); PE:816; PEA:816; YE: 371

McCarthy, J.
In defense of his colleagues. CHAL 11:448; HAZO 22: 9369; MAS 22:9369; REEMA 14:1365

Mackintosh, J.
In behalf of free speech: on trial of Jean Peltier accused of libelling Napoleon Bonaparte. ADR 2:185; BREW 8:54; BRYW 4:84; CHAL 4:208; GOOD:827; HAZO 9:3585; LEEW 7:111; MAS 9:3585; PL:453

Marat, C. P.
In his own defense. BRYW 7:148; CHAL 3:144; COP: 79; COPB:79; REEMA 14: 1433

Marshall, T.
Matt Ward case. SOU 9:398

Meagher, T. F.
Hope for Ireland (speech from the dock) HAZO 20: 8468; MAS 20:8468

Meany, S. J.
Legality of arrest (speech delivered from the dock) HAZO 21:9189; MAS 21: 9189

Menard, J. W.
Negro's first speech in Congress: in defense of his election to Congress when his seat was contested and won by his political opponent. WOON:263

Merritt, W. G.
Summation for the plaintiff in the Danbury Hatters case. HICJ:492

Mirabeau, H. G. R.
Against the charge of treason. BREW 8:170; BRYW 7: 97; CHAL 3:263; COP:74; COPA:74; COPB:74; HAZO 7:2904; LEEW 5:23; MAS 7:2904; REEM 9:184; REEMA 14:1477; REEMB 10:191

Mitchell, J.
Law in Ireland: delivered from dock. HAZO 18:7595; MAS 18:7595

More, T.
Speech when on trial for life. BREW 8:193; CROC: 327

Moreau, J. V.
In his own defence. CHAL 4:234; HAZO 9:3625; MAS 9:3625

Nixon, R. M.
Apologia. BA 1952-53:72; BERS:196

O'Brien, M.
Speech from dock. KET: 368

O'Connell, D.
In defence of John Magee. ADR 4:9

Pericles.
In defense of himself. BRYW 1:27; HAZO 1:30; MAS 1:30

Phillips, W.
Murder of Lovejoy. BAAMP:138; BOU:68; BRYW 8:222; CHAL 8:218; COP:281; COPA:281; COPB:281; FULB:323; HAZO 16:6949; HURG:74; JOHA 1 pt. 2:102; KNAS:8; KNASA:8; MAS 16:6949; PE:371; PEA:371; PL:648 SHAH:348

Prentiss, S. S.
Law of self-defense. LA: 141
Wilkinson trial. SOU 9:390

Quincy, J.
Defence of British soldier, 1770. CHAL 3:129; HAZO 7:2737; HELE:17; MAS 7: 2737
Lenity of the law to human infirmity (Weem et al: British soldiers arraigned for

the Boston Massacre) BREW 8:399
Raleigh, W.
Speech on the scaffold. BREW 9:19; BRYW 3:34
Randolph E.
In defense of Aaron Burr, 1807. BREW 9:23; HELE: 146
Rayner, I.
Hero of Santiago. SHUO: 252
Robespierre, M.
Defense from the charge of tyranny. BREW 9:78; BRYW 7:145; CODS:459; CODSA:459; ESEH:214; HAZO 8:3310; MAS 8:3310; PE:275; PEA:275
Rumbold, R.
Against booted and spurred privilege. BREW 9:119; BRYW 3:146; CHAL 2:89; HAZO 4:1555; MAS 4:1555
Sacco, N. & Vanzetti, B.
Proclaim their innocence. PE:741; PEA:741
Scipio Africanus Major, P.C.
In his own defence. CHAL 1:257; HAZO 2:654; MAS 2:654
Shapiro, H.
In defense of youth. BRY: 475
Sheares, J.
Address from dock. KET: 275
Sheil, R. L.
In defense of Irish Catholics. PL:536
Sidney, A.
Governments for the people, and not the people for governments (scaffold speech) BREW 9:222; BRYW 3:142
Socrates.
In his own defense. BRYW 1:65
On being declared guilty. BREW 9:261; BRYW 1:77
On his condemnation to death. BOU:211; BRYW 1: 82; COP:8; COPA:8; COPB:8; HIB:3; REEM 9: 10; REEMB 10:10
Strafford, T.W.
Defense before the House of Lords. BREW 9:309; BRTH:27; BRTHA:27; BRYW 3:38; CHAL 2:33; GOOD:11; HAZO 4:1454; LEEW 6:51; MAS 4:1454; ORBR 1:53; REEM 9:63; REEMB 10:65
Speech in the Tower. HAZO 4:1466; MAS 4:1466
Speech on the scaffold. HAZO 4:1472; MAS 4:1472
Sullivan, A. M.
"Disesteem of the law" (from the dock at Dublin, 1868) HAZO 22:9233; MAS 22:9233
Talfourd, T. N.
Queen against Moxon-Shelley as a blasphemer. BREW 9:345; HAZO 12:5216; MAS 12:5216
Tone, T.W.
On being found guilty. BRYW 6:132; KET:279
Tooke, J. H.
On the "Murders at Lexington and Concord" (at his trial for libel) BREW 9:415
Vane, H.
At his trial for high treason. BREW 10:39; BRYW 3:139; CHAL 2:71; HAZO 4:1511; MAS 4:1511
Voorhees, D.W.
In defence of John E. Cook. CHAL 11:125; HAZO 21: 8982; MAS 21:8982
Walpole, R.
On his proposed removal from office. BRYW 3:154; CHAL 2:171; GOOD:35; HAZO 4:1728; MAS 4:1728; ORBR 1:143; REEMA 15: 2025
On patriots (at motion to dismiss him from Council) BREW 10:78; COP:151; COPA:151; COPB:151; PL: 384

DEFENSE, SPEECHES OF (cont.)
Webster, D.
Defence of the Kennistons. CLAY:216
White, G.H.
Speech in defense of the Negro race. WOON:403
Xenophon.
Defence against false accusation. HAZO 1:180; MAS 1:180
Zola, E.
Appeal for Dreyfus. BREW 10:285; CHAL 13:355; COP: 112; COPA:112; COPB: 112; CROC:489; HAZO 24: 10330; HIB:80; MAS 24: 10330; PE:594; PEA:594; REEM 7:436; REEMA 9: 1126; REEMB 7:437
DeGaulle, Charles
Address before the French Consultative Assembly on the Levantine question. VO 1945-46:294
Address in Tunis on the anniversary of the liberation of Tunisia. VO 1944-45:201
Appeal to Frenchmen, June 18, 1940. CROC:153; HAN: 130; PE:782; PEA:782
At the opening session of the Provisional Consultative Assembly at Algiers. VO 1943-44:504
Before the French Consultative Assembly on the victory over Germany. VO 1945-46:208
Before the French Provisional Consultative Assembly on the future of France. VO 1944-45:322
Broadcast on French policy in war and peace. VO 1945-46:54
Broadcast to North Africa. HAN:222
Broadcast to the French people on liberation. VO 1944-45: 393
Declaration, January 2, 1943. VO 1943-44:5
Has the last word been said?-Same as his Appeal to Frenchmen, June 18, 1940
Invasion message to France. VO 1944-45:263
Political problem of North Africa. VO 1943-44:37
Press statement on Syria and Lebanon. VO 1945-46:247
Speech at the Brazzaville Conference. VO 1944-45:71
Speech on the liberation of Paris delivered at the Hotel de Ville in Paris. VO 1944-45:389
Statement after Giraud's address, March 15, 1943. VO 1943-44:118
V-E Day broadcast to the French people. VO 1945-46: 198
See also Giraud, H.H., jt. auth.

DEGREES, ACADEMIC See Acceptance speeches-Degrees, Academic
Deinarchus.
Against Aristogiton. CHAL 1: 250; HAZO 2:649; MAS 2: 649; MINA 2:264
Against Demosthenes. BRYW 1:233; LEEW 1:357; MINA 2:172
Against Philocles. MINA 2: 290
Fragments. MINA 2:310
Deiss, Jay
Undergraduate looks at war. YR 4:187
DeJean, Fannie L.
Rehabilitation and reassimilation of fighting men and nations. AN:66
Dekanisora, Onondaga chief
Refuses to support French interests. JON:38
Delmas, Delphin M.
Argument for petitioners in the Miller and Lux case. HICJ:300
Washington (response to toast 'The character of Washing-

ton'') WAGN:259
Delano, H. A.
Greatness of Lincoln's simplicity. THOU 1:476

DeLANO, JANE A.
Boardman, M. T.
Dedication of Delano Memorial. GA:65
Minnigerode, L.
Dedication of Delano Memorial. GA:67
DeLarge, R. C.
Speech on the enforcement of the Fourteenth Amendment. WOON:295
Demades.
On the twelve years. MINA 2:336

DEMOBILIZATION
Attlee, C. R.
Address on British demobilization plans. VO 1945-46: 536

DEMOCRACY
Abernathy, T. P.
Democracy and the southern frontier. TIN. 42
Agar, H.
Program for the citizen of a democracy. NORR 3d ser: 71
Allen, H. J.
Are European isms taking root in Western democracy? BART 1:353
Baldwin, S. B.
Protect the democracies. PL:804
Balfour, A. J. B.
Oldest free assemblies. LEW:85
Barnave, A. P. J. M.
Representative democracy against majority absolutism. BREW 1:229; BRYW 7:112; CHAL 4:159; HAZO 9:3511; MAS 9:3511
Battle, K. D.
Democracy and the trust. SHUC:254
Beaconsfield, B. D.
Against democracy for England. BREW 1:301; HAZO 14:6003; MAS 14:6003; PL:482
Beck, J. M.
Democracy of the ''Mayflower.'' REEMA 1:33
Future of democratic institutions. HICF:742
Biddle, F.
Democracy and racial minorities. BA 1943-44:172
Blomfield, L. M.
Democracy rampant. BART 2:133
Borden, R. L.
Hope for liberty and democracy. BREW 2:154
Bowers, R. E.
Disciples of determinism. NOR 1941:17
Boyle, J. P.
Democracy and foreign immigration. SHUC:298
Breckenridge, W. C. P.
Jeffersonian democracy. SHUO:194
Brenner, S. M.
Propaganda in a democracy. DO:48
Buck, P.
Women's place in a democracy. BUTA:212
Burnstein, J.
Operation crossroad. NOR 1947:101
Butler, N. M.
Abdication of democracy. ON:252; SAR:181
New critics of democracy. ONEC:103
True and false democracy. REEM 7:63; REEMB 8:51
Carrock, T.
Democracy will survive the war. DO:152
Clemenceau, G.
Democracy vs socialism (debate with J. Jaures) BRYW 7:214; PE:671; PEA: 671; REEM 9:375; REEMB 10:386

DEMOCRACY (cont.)
Cleon.
On the punishment of the Mytileneans. BREW 4:79; BRYW 1:34; HAZO 1:43; MAS 1:43
Cleveland, G.
True democracy. REEM 10:308; REEMA 1:229; REEMB 11:322
Conklin, E. G.
Education for democracy. BA 1939-40:346
Day, E. E.
What really threatens American democracy? BA 1938-39:79
Democracy for sale. FRIE:89
Democracy in the public schools. AMEO 1:101
Desmoulins, C.
Live free or die. BREW 5:191; BRYW 7:89; CHAL 4:125; HAZO 8:3463; MAS 8:3463
Dickson, W. B.
Democracy in industry. BOA:346
Dougherty, D.
On democracy. CHAL 11:92; HAZO 21:8935; MAS 21:8935
Douglas, W. C.
Function of democracy. BA 1940-41:225; BARR:275
Dykstra, C. A.
Individual and the democratic adventure. BA 1939-40:141
Elvehjem, C. A.
Education and democracy. ANGC:83
Equality and liberty. NAT:11
Estes, J. W., Jr.
Penny wise and pound foolish. YR 10:59
Evans, A. W.
What western democracy means to me. EXEE:408
Evatt, H. V.
What is democracy? MOA:484
Frankfurter, F.
Public opinion and democratic government. BA 1946-47:145
Green, F. M.
Democracy in the old South. TIN:177
Guizot, F. P. G.
Democracy in France. PL:318
Hand, L.
We seek liberty. BA 1943-44:254; HIB:183
Harris, R. C.
Free society. ANGC:87
Hart, A. B.
Hope of democracy. NORR 1st ser:362
Hoover, H. C.
Protection of democracy. BA 1937-38:80
Hough, L. H.
Genius of democracy. BA 1955-56:62
Howell, W. S.
Democratic issue. BA 1941 42:64
Hunter, W.
Disciplined democracy. YR 8:91
Jefferson, T.
First inaugural: democracy defined. ANG:220; BIR 1:251; BRE:111; BREA:109; BREW 7:160; BRYW 8:166; CHAL 3:122; CHI:13; COP 259; COPA:259; COPB:259; CROC:273; FKA:59; HARS:166; HAZO 7:2731; HELE:135; HIB:365; HURC 48; JOHA 1 pt. 1:155; KLEG:314; LEEW 9:73; LOTI:15; MAS 7:2731; ORAMA 1:141; PAR:95; P 49; REEM 10:46; REEMA 13:1255; REEMB 11:47; SMI:91; USIN:13; USINA:13; WPRA:50
Johnson, J. W.
Our democracy and the ballot. WOON:663
Kandt, W.
Prospects. YR 6:347
Kissling, W.

Living democracy. ASHF:9
Klein, A.
Tell me how to belong. BRP 10:17; NOR 1939:9
Leo XIII.
Christian democracy. COP: 117; COPA:117; COPB:117; REEMA 14:1323
Lilienthal, D. E.
My faith in democracy. HIBS:463; PE:808; PEA: 807
Spirit of democracy. BA 1948-49:65
Littleton, M. E.
Democracy, the hope of the world. BOB:35
Littleton, M. W.
Direct democracy. BYRA: 282; REEM 2:335; REEMB 2:339
Livingston, E. M.
Final test. ONES:361
Livingston, H.
Fool's gold. BOA:354; YR 6:213
Lowe, R.
Coming of democracy. ADR 4:232; HAY:240; PAUF 1: 393
Lowell, J. R.
Democracy: inaugural address on assuming Presidency of the Birmingham and Midland Institute, Birmingham, England, October 6, 1884. PAUF 2:205; REEM 7:234; REEMA 8:789; REEMB 8:254
Ludlow, L.
Objectives of democracy. BOA:328; BOB:86
McIlvenna, E. A.
Crisis of 1938. YR 10:115
MacLeish, A.
This cause is our cause. BA 1943-44:243
Melson, B.
Strength in democracy. YR 10:133
Monroe, J.
Federal experiments in history. BREW 8:172; CHAL 4:27; MAZO 8:3329; MAS 8:3329; SMI:62
Murphy, F.
Civil liberties. BA 1938-39:173
Murrow, E. R.
Nominating Presidential candidates. BA 1951-52:95
Oathut, J.
Individual in democracy. YR 5:275
O'Neal, B.
Democracy is on trial. MOUG:238; MOUGA:238
Parsons, E. L.
Democracy and prophetic idealism. NORR 1st ser: 377
Paulson, S.
Spectrum of democracy. NOR 1942:71
Pickens, W.
Kind of democracy the Negro race expects. WOON: 654
Pius XII.
Christmas broadcast, December 24, 1944. VO 1944-45:625
Pollock, C.
What can we do for democracy? BART 4:219
Radhakrishnan, S.
Real meaning of democracy. ZU:75
Robinson, E. E.
Can democracy survive the war? BA 1942-43:221
Rodiger, W.
Outward bound. NOR 1944: 41
Roosevelt, F. D.
Address to White House Correspondents' Association dinner, March 15, 1941. VO 1941:126
Democracy cannot survive in isolation. ON:146
Jackson day address from the U. S. S. Potomac in the harbor of Ft. Lauderdale, Florida. VO 1941:144
Third inaugural address.

DEMOCRACY (cont.)
CHI:271; LOTI:243; SAA: 292; USIN:244; USINA:244; VO 1941:37
Rudolph, W.C.
For democracy we fight. DO:125
Ryan, J.A.
Religion, the indispensible basis of democracy. BA 1939-40:408
Sarnoff, R.W.
Television's role in the American democracy. BA 1962-63:136
Schrader, D.
What will they believe? BRP 10:88
Smathers, G.
Put democracy on the offensive. MOA:461
Studebaker, J.W.
Democracy shall not be plowed under. BA 1939-40: 375
Thomas, N.
No democracy without civil liberty. BA 1937-38:45
Toynbee, A.J.
Continuing effect of the American Revolution. BA 1961-62:95
Turner, E.D.
Contributions of the West to American democracy. FKA:72; SHU:88
Tyndall, J.
Democracy and higher intellect. BREW 10:23
Wallace, H.A.
Address at Chicago, September 11, 1943. VO 1943-44:351
America's second chance. COP:609; COPB:580
Westcott, J.W.
Destiny of democracy. SHU: 238
What is democracy (outline of speech)? MOA:239
White, W.A.
Education of a democracy. BOB:188; SHU:128
Willkie, W.L.
Loyal opposition. COP:553; COPB:545; HURG:243
Wolfe, P.A.
Challenge to America. ASHF:17
Woll, M.
Labor's contribution to American democracy. BA 1939-40:327
See also Equality; Suffrage

DEMOCRATIC CONVENTIONS
See Political Conventions-Democratic

DEMOCRATIC PARTY
D.D.-Drafted Democrat. SCHS:107
Democratic Party (by an enthusiastic member) ED:100
Democratic speech. AMEO 2: 119
Dewey, T.E.
Calendar of unpunished crimes. BA 1939-40:257
Doolittle, J.R.
In favor of re-union. BREW 5:272
Douglas, P.H.
Vote Democratic. BA 1954-55:81
Harrison, P.
Democratic keynote speech-1924. WHIP:235
Jackson, R.H. and others.
Essential differences between the Republican and Democratic Parties. BA 1939-40:233
Kefauver, E.
Vote Democratic. BA 1956-57:85
Morse, W.L.
Constitutional liberalism and the Democratic Party. BA 1956-57:93
Roosevelt, E.A.
Before the Democratic National Convention. BA 1956-57:109
Roosevelt, F.D.
Victory dinner address.

BA 1937-38:101
Smith, A. E.
Come back to your father's house. WPRC:168
Smith, T. V.
Forward America. BA 1938-39:119
Stevenson, A. E.
Four fears. BA 1953-54:65
Reply to Eisenhower's speech of October 8th, 1954. LOMS:244; LOMSA: 309
Taft, R. A.
Forward America. BA 1938-39:130; BRYA:534
Thompson, D.
Address, October 29, 1944. BUTA:239; ON:365
Truman, H. S.
Democratic Party. BA 1949-50:117
Principles of the Democratic Party. BA 1958-59:105
Wallace, H. A.
Jackson day dinner address. VO 1944-45:53
Wilson, W.
Jackson day dinner (Washington, January 0, 1912) PEAE:227
Yancey, W. L.
Speech in protest in the Charleston Convention. BAAMP:118; BRYW 9:192; SOU 9:339
See also Acceptance speeches-Nominations; Campaign speeches; Political Conventions-Democratic

DeMOLAYS, ORDER OF
Foursquare lives. JA:50

DEMONOLOGY
Conway, M. D.
Demonology and English folklore. REEMA 4:287
DeMorgenstierne, W. M.
Tribute to America. BOA:309
Demosthenes.
Assault and battery; quarrel in camp (against Conon) FRE:114
Damage to a farm: defence against Callicles. FRE:140
Denounces the imperialistic ambition of Philip of Macedon. -Same as his Third Philippic
First Olynthiac oration. HAZO 2:439; LEEW 1:249; MAS 2:439
First Philippic. HAZO 2:466; LEEW 1:243; MAS 2:466; PL:72
Fourth Philippic. HAZO 2:549; MAS 2:549
Illegal union: against Neaera. FRE:191
On the Chersoneus. BRYW 1:120; HAZO 2:511; LEEW 1:289; MAS 2:511
On the crown. BREW 5:65; BRYW 1:143; CHAL 1:159; CODS:11; CODSA:11; COP:16; COPA:11; COPB:16; CROC:155; HAZO 1:245; HIB:105; KLEG:125; LA:128; LEEW 1:326; MAS 1:245; MEAR:106; PL:76; REEM 9:17; REEMA 12:821; REEMB 10:17
On the Navy Boards. HAZO 2:598; LEEW 1:227; MAS 2:598
Oration for the Megalopolitans. HAZO 2:624; MAS 2:624
Oration on Halonnesus. HAZO 2:501; MAS 2:501
Oration on the duties of the state. HAZO 2:587; MAS 2:587
Oration on the embassy. HAZO 1:338; MAS 1:338
Oration on the letter. HAZO 2:569; MAS 2:569
Oration on the liberty of the Rhodians. HAZO 2:611; MAS 2:611
Oration on the peace. BREW 5:136; HAZO 2:481; MAS 2:481
Oration on the treaty with

Demosthenes. (cont.)
Alexander. HAZO 2:637; MAS 2:637
Second Olynthiac. BREW 5: 131; HAZO 2:449; LEEW 1:253; MAS 2:449
Second Philippic. BREW 5: 140; BRYW 1:110; COP: 26; COPA:26; COPB:26; HAZO 2:489; LEEW 1:257; MAS 2:489
Third Olynthiac. HAZO 2:456; MAS 2:456
Third Philippic. BEA:165; HAZO 2:529; LEEW 1:263; MAS 2:529; PE:15; PEA: 15

DEMOSTHENES.
Aeschines.
Against crowning Demosthenes. CHAL 1:144; HAZO 1:226; MAS 1:226
Deinarchus.
Against Demosthenes. BRYW 1:233; LEEW 1:357; MINA 2:172
Dewey, O.
Genius of Demosthenes. BREW 5:198
Hypereides.
Against Demosthenes. MINA 2:500
Lytton, E. G. L. B. -L.
Demosthenes and the nobility of the classics. BREW 7:431

Denison, George Taylor
United Empire loyalists. CHAL 13:283; HAZO 24: 10264; MAS 24:10264

Denison, H. G.
Christmas. THOU 2:370

Denman, Thomas Denman, 1st Baron
"Poor Dukes" and "piratical tatterdemalions." BREW 5: 146

Denning, J. Edwin See Young, B., jt. auth.

Dennis, R. E.
King coal is still on the throne. SAB:174

Denny, George V., Jr. (moderator) See following jt. auths. Browne, L.; Canham, E. D.; DiSalle, M.; Donovan, W. J.; Douglas, P. H.; Fischer, L.; Kaltenborn, H. V.; Oursler, F.; Price, J. H.; Reuther, W. P.; Thompson, D.

DENTISTS See Physicians

Denton, Thomas G.
Student responsibility. AN:38

Depew, Chauncey M.
American Hall of Fame. WERN 42:20
America's new era. FUL:116
At laying the cornerstone of the New York "World" building. BRAC:354
Beggars of the sea. REEMA 1:366
Citizens of the world. REEMA 1:370
Columbian oration. BREW 5: 149; CHAL 12:332; COP: 330; COPA:330; COPB: 330; REEM 7:116; REEMA 13:893; REEMB 8:129
Columbus and Hendrick Hudson. THOU 1:70
Cow and honest competition. HICF:285
Eighty-seventh birthday. DOA: 308; REEM 1:371; REEMB 1:372
Empire state. KLEM:120; REEMA 1:333
England and America since the Spanish War. BREW 5: 170; FUL:118; ORAMA 2: 383
Example of Washington: centennial of his death. THOU 3:302
Forefathers were God's nobility. THOU 1:351
George Frisbie Hoar. ONES: 176
Half century with a railroad. REEM 4:86; REEMB 4:171
Ireland. ONEM:636; REEMA 1:343

Introducing Lord Cecil. REEMB 1:402
Military spirit in America. BREW 5:165
Mutations of time. REEMA 1: 373
New Netherlands. REEMA 1: 349
One hundredth anniversary of Washington's inauguration. HAZO 23:9713; KLEG:169; MAS 23:9713; RINM:220
Our English visitors (welcoming George Augustus Sala) REEMA 1:338
Our kin across the sea. -Same as his England and America since the Spanish War
Our National Guard. FUL:113
Our national safeguards. BLAA:143; BLAB:143
Our victorious General (Grant) THOU 1:370
Outline of address at dinner on the 70th birthday of John Jay. PITT:89
Outline of address at the centennial of capture of André. PITT:87
Outline of address at the reception to Henry M. Stanley by the Lotus Club. PITT: 90
Outline of speech on Decoration Day. PITT:47
Panama Canal. HICF:340
Pilgrims in Holland. YE:324
Presenting a loving cup to Admiral Dewey. ONES:42
Presents William Jennings Bryan. LY:217
Response to welcome. BRAC: 250
Senatorial forecast. REEMA 1:380
Speech as President of the Pilgrims, January 2, 1924. LINM:393
Speech at dinner to celebrate the anniversary of birth of General Grant. CHAL 12: 324; HAZO 23:9705; MAS 23:9705
To Premier Briand. REEM 1: 396; REEMB 1:397
Two responses to introductions. HOAP:34
Unsolved problems. REEMA 1:361
Unveiling the Statue of Liberty. BREW 5:162; CHAL 12: 307; HAZO 23:9688; MAS 23:9688; PROS:70; WERN 42:106
Washington and Lincoln. BOB: 148
Welcome to Mayor Cooper. REEMA 1:330
Woman. COP:639; COPB:673; HURG:125; KLEG:147; REEM 1:389; REEMA 1: 327; REEMB 1:389
World at 91: address at banquet given in his honor on his 91st birthday. LINM: 154
Yale University. REEM 1: 391; REEMA 1:356; REEMB 1:392

DEPEW, CHAUNCEY M.
Lawrence, F. R.
Introduces Chauncey M. Depew to Lotus Club, March 11, 1899. REEMA 1:380
Platt, H. G.
Speech at banquet for Chauncey M. Depew. WAGN: 216
Wayland, H. L.
Introduces Chauncey M. Depew to New England Society. REEMA 1:349

DEPRESSSIONS, BUSINESS See Business cycles; United States-Economic conditions
Derby, Edward George Villiers Stanley, 17th Earl of
Diplomatist. REEMA 1:387
Emancipation of British Negroes. BREW 5:176; CHAL 6:330; HAZO 13:5526; MAS 13:5526; REEMA 13: 908

Derby, E.G.V.S. 17th Earl of (cont.)
Second reading of the Corn Importation Bill. PAUF 2:47
Derby, Edward Henry Stanley, 15th Earl of
Life and culture. ORBR 2:159

DERELICTS
Karos, P.A.
Haven for the defeated. ARNS:160; NOR 1950:187
Dering, Sir Edward
For the encouragement of learning. BREW 5:181
Religious controversy in Parliament. BREW 5:184
Dern, George H.
How to fight the war peril. SAR:254
Deseze, Raymond
Defending Louis XVI. BREW 5:187
Desmoulins, Camille
Advocating the execution of Louis XVI. COP:70; COPA:70; COPB:70; REEMA 13:913
Appeal to the people (delivered during trial of Louis XVI) CHAL 4:128; HAZO 8:3466; MAS 8:3466
Live free or die. BREW 5:191; BRYW 7:89; CHAL 4:125; HAZO 8:3463; MAS 8:3463

DESPOTISM
Kossuth, L.
Present weakness of despotism. LEEW 5:221

DETECTIVES See Police

DETERMINISM
Bowers, R.E.
Disciples of determinism. NOR 1941:17

DETT, R. NATHANIEL
Brown, C.H.
Bennet College (memorial service for Dr. Dett) HILK:84
Deutsch, Monroe E.
Foes of the humanities. BA 1952-53:158
Preservation of the university. BA 1942-43:248
V emblem. HOC:34
De Valera, Eamon
Ireland among the nations. COP:446; COPA:446; COPB:466
League of Nations. BEA:173
Speech on Eire neutrality. VO 1941:607
Devan, S. Arthur
Growth of the United States as a world-power. SHUC:309
Devens, Charles
At the dedication of the soldiers' and sailors' monument in Boston Commons. CHAL 10:12; HAZO 19:8216; MAS 19:8126
Sons of Harvard. CHAL 10:7; HAZO 19:8121; KLEM:199; MAS 19:8121

DEVIL See Satan
Devonshire, Spencer Compton Cavendish, 8th Duke of
Home Rule Bill of 1886. PAUF 2:306
Occasions for appeal to the people. EMS 1:92
Dew, Thomas R.
Influence of republican government on literature and character. SMI:123
DeWater, Charles
Protests against withdrawal of sanctions against Italy. KESK 2:94
D'Ewes, Sir Simonds
Antiquity of Cambridge. BREW 5:194
Dewey, George
Navy. BLAA:125; BLAB:125

DEWEY, GEORGE
Depew, C.M.
Presenting a loving cup to

Admiral Dewey. ONES:42
Long, J.D.
Presentation of sword to Admiral Dewey. FUL:209; HAZO 24:10228; MAS 24:10228
Dewey, John
Apt introduction. BRC:37
Education and new social ideals. WPRC:216
Dewey, Orville
Evidence of genius. LA:120
Genius of Demosthenes. BREW 5:198
Homes of freedom. BOB:162
Lust of riches. BREW 5:199
Nobility of labor. REAC:127
Dewey, Thomas E.
A B C of racketeering. SAR:311
Acceptance speech. BA 1943-44:259; ON:377; VO 1944-45:280
Boston campaign speech. VO 1944-45:533
Calendar of unpunished crimes. BA 1939-40:257
Campaign speech in Buffalo. VO 1944-45:524
Dedication of the Corning Glass Center. SAB:195
Governmental integrity. -Same as his Oklahoma City campaign speech
Hines policy-numbers case. BA 1938-39:181
Inside story of a racket. BA 1937-38:163
Madison Square Garden address. BA 1948-49:101
Minneapolis campaign speech. VO 1944-45:498
Oklahoma City campaign speech. BA 1944-45:143; VO 1944-45:432
Opening campaign speech in Philadelphia. VO 1944-45:407
Party conflict and the modern dilemma. BA 1949-50:110
Rendezvous with despair. COP:436; COPA:436; COPB:419
St. Louis campaign speech. VO 1944-45:485
---- and others (H.E. Stassen)
Shall the Communist Party in the United States be outlawed? BA 1947-48:144

DEWEY, THOMAS E.
Grimm, P.
Introduces Thomas E. Dewey. PR:66
Introducing Thomas E. Dewey. NI:68; NIA:56
Thompson, D.
Address, October 29, 1944. BUTA:239; ON:365
Truman, H.S.
"Doctor" Dewey and the Republican record. FIP:291
Dexter, Samuel
Argument in Selfridge's trial. CHAL 4:154; HAZO 8:3492; MAS 8:3492
"Higher law" of self-defense. BREW 5:201
DeYoung, Ruth
Women in the headlines. GA:149
Diaz, Profirio
Mexican progress. BREW 5:208
Peace rooted in the hearts of all. CHAL 11:442; HAZO 22:9363; MAS 22:9363
Dibble, Henry C.
Loyalty to the nation. WAGN:295
Dickens, Charles
Actor's art. REEMA 1:401
As a literary guest of America. BRYW 4:150; ONEM:694
English friendliness for America. COP:615; COPB:655; REEMA 1:405
For the hospital for sick children. KNAS:21; KNASA:21
Friends across the sea. KNAS:169; KNASA:169; REEM 1:402; REEMA 1:389; REEMB 1:408
Macready and Bulwer-Lytton.

Dickens, Charles (cont.)
REEMA 1:398
Tribute to Washington Irving. REEMA 1:394
Volunteer student (on occasion of his inauguration as President of Birmingham and Midland Institute) REEMA 7:332

DICKENS, CHARLES
Lowry, H. F.
"A Christmas Carol" at Wooster. YE:96
Lytton, E. B.
Farewell to Charles Dickens. REEM 2:371; REEMA 2:774; REEMB 2:384
Quincy, J., Jr.
Welcome to Dickens. REEM 3:122; REEMA 3:964; REEMB 3:123
Dickerson, Mahlon
Alien and Sedition Acts of the Adams administration. BREW 5:212
Dickinson, Daniel S.
At War Ratification meeting. CHAL 6:408; HAZO 13:5622; MAS 13:5622
Rebuking Senator Clemens of Alabama. BREW 5:220
Dickinson, Herbert
Man's development and attainment. WERN 42:118

DICKINSON, JACOB M.
Lewis, H. H.
Introduction of Jacob M. Dickinson. BRAC:235; LY:205
Dickinson, John
Before the Pennsylvania Assembly, March 24, 1764. LEEW 8:31
Dickinson, John
Declaration of the Colonies on taking up arms. BREW 5:224; CHAL 2:435; HARS:31; HAZO 6:2533; MAS 6:2533

Dickinson, Mrs. LaFell
Citadels of peace, arsenals of power (inaugural address of President of General Federation of Women's Clubs) BUTA:229
Dickson, Paul
Introducing a general contractor. BRC:306
Dickson, William B.
Democracy in industry. BOA:346

DICTATORS AND DICTATORSHIP
Ames, K.
America beware. BRP 8:50; YR 9:79
Bolivar, S.
I will act as trustee of the Supreme Authority. CROC:29
Dulles, J. F.
Freedom or despotism? BA 1956-57:25
Grossman, H.
Scarlet letter. NOR 1940:15
Hitler, A.
Request for dictatorial powers. FRY:120
Lenin, N.
Dictatorship of the Proletariat. COP:141; COPA:141; COPB:141; FRY:93; PL:785; REEM 11:181; REEMB 12:196
McGahey, W.
Mad men in a world. BRP 10:47
McIlvenna, E. A.
Crisis of 1938. YR 10:115
Peterson, C. D.
Then Hitler came. BRP 10:41; NOR 1939:34
Roosevelt, F. D.
Message to Congress (January 4, 1939) SAR:119
Thompson, D.
Government by propaganda. GA:142
Didon, Henri
Christ and higher criticism. BREW 5:231; HAZO 24:10340; MAS 24:10340

Dies, Martin
Trojan horse in America. BART 3:305

DIET
Kaser, A. L.
Introducing an authority on diet. BRH:112
Digby, Lord See Bristol, G. D.
Dilke, Charles Wentworth
America. BREW 5:248
Omphalism. BREW 5:255
On the cost of the crown. CHAL 13:473; HAZO 24:10513; MAS 24:10513
Dill, C. C.
Mothers of men. BOA:253; BOB:129
Thomas Jefferson, the architect of Americanism. BOA:226; BOB:139
Dilley, James
Armament racket. BRP 6:105
Vanishing American. BRP 6:82; YR 6:33
Dillon, John
On the death of Gladstone. BRYW 6:252; REEM 5:138; REEMB 9:171
Tory Squires and servant girls' dollars. BREW 5:258

DINNERS AND DINING
Sherman, S. P.
Gaiety of Socrates. NORR 3d ser:1
Dinsmore, Hugh A.
South and the Constitution. SHUO:109
Dinwoodie, S. David
Inner city-our shame. ARNS:246

DIPLOMACY
Cox, S. S.
On the beauties of diplomacy. CHAL 10:368; HAZO 20:8721; MAS 20:8721
Dana, C. A.
Diplomacy and the Press. REEMA 1:318
Derby, E. G. V. S.
Diplomatist. REEMA 1:387
Hay, J.
American diplomacy. BLAA; 10; BLAB:10; REEM 2:173; REEMB 2:175
Johnson, H. N.
Diplomacy of good will. BRP 1:29; YR 1:65
Luce, C. B.
American morality and nuclear diplomacy. HIB:338
White, A. D.
Commerce and diplomacy. REEMA 3:1232

DIPLOMAS See Acceptance speeches-Diplomas; Presentation speeches - Diplomas

DIPLOMATS See Ambassadors
Dirksen, Everett
At 44th anniversary of Congressional service of Speaker Sam Rayburn. BRAP:137
DiSalle, Michael and others (G. V. Denny, Jr.; H. D. Newsom and W. P. Reuther)
How can we stop rising prices? HAR:285

DISARMAMENT
Applegate, A. W.
Target practice. YR 1:45
Coolidge, C.
Limitations of armaments, February 10, 1927. FIP:172
Eisenhower, D. D.
First steps in disarmament. BA 1955-56:19; FIP:342
Gibson, H. S.
Reduction of naval armaments. HICF:774
Graves, D.
Disarmament. YR 4:91
Harding, W. G.
Peace through disarmament. BREW 6:363
Humphrey, H. H., Jr.
Disarmament in the nuclear age. BA 1959-60:81
Miller, J.

DISARMAMENT (cont.)
Disarmament as the way to peace. HOD:108
Murray, T. E.
Dismantling of the era of terror. BA 1959-60:69
Rankin, J. E.
Naval supremacy or moral leadership. BRP 1:90
Roy, J. C.
Twenty thousand leagues under the sea. YR 1:55
Temple, W.
Members one of another. BEA:9
See also Conference on the Limitation of Armaments, Washington, 1921; Conference on the Limitation of Naval Armaments, 1930

DISARMAMENT CONFERENCE AT GENEVA, 1932 See Disarmament

DISASTERS
Wirick, R.
When disaster strikes. YR 2:149

DISCIPLINE
Sizoo, J. R.
Call to self-discipline. BA 1958-59:161
Sociological basis of school discipline. AMEO 2:135

---- MILITARY
Charles I.
Liberty and discipline: address to his troops at Wellington. BRTH:31; BRTHA: 31

DISCOVERY DAY See Columbus Day

DISCRIMINATION
Biddle, F.
Democracy and racial minorities. BA 1943-44:172
Bunche, R. J.
Dreams and realities (installation of Gamma chapter of Phi Beta Kappa) NORR 3d ser:264
Conwill, W.
Hitler wins. NOR 1943:17
Gossage, N.
Can minds be changed? NOR 1948:107
Johnston, E. A.
Intolerance. BA 1944-45: 175
Kennedy, J. F.
Addresses the General Assembly of the United Nations for the second and last time, September 22, 1963. PEA:840
McClain, W.
Our school of destiny. YR 6:81
Manak, J. F.
We sorely need tolerant minds. NOR 1942:47
Reed, J. A.
Toleration. BYRA:367; REEM sup 2:318; REEMB 8:338
Rifkin, H.
Racial intolerance. HOD: 106
Thurman, H.
Good news for the underprivileged. HILK:258
Webb, S.
On mousetraps. LINP:215
When color is forgotten. JAS: 22
Wright, T. S.
Prejudice against the colored man. WOON:92

DISCRIMINATION IN EMPLOYMENT See Labor Laws and legislation

DISCUSSIONS See Debates and debating

Disney, Lester
Napoléon Bonaparte: the saviour of France. SHUC: 78

DISNEY, WALT

Reid, Mrs. O.
Presents Walt Disney. LY: 42

DISPLACED PERSONS
Truman, H. S.
Statement and directive on displaced persons. VO 1945-46:777
See also Jews; Palestine; Refugees
Disraeli, Benjamin See Beaconsfield, Benjamin Disraeli, 1st Earl of

DISSENTERS
Crosby, J.
How to get along in a free world without being subpoenaed. BA 1951-52:71; BAAG:381
Ditzen, Lowell
Evasive politics and a third party. YR 3:51
Sweetmeats on gilded trays. BRP 3:12; YR 4:39

DIVINE RIGHT OF KINGS See Monarchy

DIVING See Swimming

DIVORCE
Birkenhead, F. E. S.
Marriage and divorce. HAY:356
Divorce problem. DR:251
See also Home; Marriage
Dix, Dorothy (pseud.) See Gilmer, Mrs. E. M.
Dix, John Adams
Christianity and politics. BREW 5:261
Flag-the old flag. REEM 1: 407; REEMA 1:410
Dixon, John Adams
On African colonization. CHAL 6:262; HAZO 13:5408; MAS 13:5408
Dixon, Sir Pierson
Against Soviet intervention in Hungary. BAAG:372
Dobeln, G. K. von
Address to the Finnish troops. CHAL 4:42; HAZO 8:3335; MAS 8:3335
Dobelstein, E. G.
God's order for a more abundant life. ACW:57
Dobert, Eitel Wolf
Convert to freedom. BART 3: 91
Dobson, James
Our Pacific outlook. COUW: 187
America's greatest problem. COUW:181; SHUC:103

DOCTORS See Physicians
Dod, Albert B.
Value of truth. BREW 5:263
Dodds, Harold W.
Education and mother government. SAR:103
Importance of being an individual. BA 1955-56:142
On the place of the intellectual in America. NORR 3d ser:356

DODGE, JOSEPH M.
McDonough, J. J.
Introduces Joseph M. Dodge, Director of the Bureau of the Budget of the United States. PRNE:13
Doe, Rilea W.
Response to an introduction. PR:121
Doenitz, Karl
Announcement of Hitler's death. VO 1945-46:182
Broadcast informing the German people of their unconditional surrender. VO 1945-46:190
Speech after attempt on Hitler's life. VO 1944-45:313

DOGS
Branen, J.
Introducing a speaker on dogs. BRH:44
Kaser, A. L.
Introducing a dog fancier. BRC:145

DOGS (cont.)
Vest, G. G.
Man's best friend-his dog. BOU:176; COP:650; COPB: 677; GRIS:21; HURG:161; SHU:201
Dolitzky, M. M.
For a Bar-Mitzwa. ZEL:13
Dollinger, John Joseph I
Founders of religions. REEMA 7:343
Dolliver, Jonathan Prentiss
American occupation of the Philippines. REEM 10:369; REEMA 13:919; REEMB 11: 384
Cow. HICF:223
On Porto Rico and the Philippines. CHAL 14:374
Robert Emmet (114th anniversary of the birth of Robert Emmet) ONES:142; REEM 5:140; REEMA 7:363; REEMB 9:174
Stand by the government. FUL: 128
Uphold the President. FUL: 122,125
Dolly, William L., Jr.
Era of conscience. SHUC:173

DONALDSON, JESSE M.
Miller, M. G.
Introduces Jesse M. Donaldson, Postmaster General of the United States. PRNE: 20

DONATIONS See Acceptance speeches - Donations; Fund raising; Presentation speeches-Donations
Donelan, Charles
Mental wealth of Uncle Sam. REAC:194
Donne, John
Delivers his own funeral sermon. PE:91; PEA:91
Man, immortal, body and soul. BREW 5:266
Donnell, Albert
Children's sermon. THOU 2: 168
Donnelly, Ignatius
On reconstruction. CHAL 12: 31; HAZO 22:9423; MAS 22:9423
Purpose of government. LA: 171
Donnelly, Mary Carroll
On scholastic despotism. BRP 9:118; YR 10:209
Donnelly, W. Patrick
Our responsibility to Latin America. ANGC:177
Donohue, Harold See Rayburn, S., jt. auth.
Donovan, Herman Lee
What I see from my window: inaugural address as President of University of Kentucky. WE 2:233
Donovan, William J. and others (G. V. Denny, Jr. and R. M. Hutchins)
Shall we do whatever is necessary to insure a British victory? BA 1940-41:33
D'Ooge, Martin Luther
Farewell to University of Michigan. ONES:36
Dooling, M. T.
On the firing line. WAGN:267
Our absent brothers. WAGN: 264
Doolittle, James H.
Response to an introduction. PR:134
Doolittle, James R.
Attitude of the West in the Civil War. BREW 5:269
In favor of re-union. BREW 5:272

DOPE See Drugs
Doran, Herbert J.
Eyes that see not. BRP 2:54; YR 3:45
Dorfman, Albert See Conn, J., jt. auth.
Dorset, Edward Sackville, 4th Earl of
In favor of slitting Prynne's nose. BREW 5:275
Dostoevsky, Feodor Mikhailovich
Celebrates the centenary of

Pushkin's birth. PE:569; PEA:569
Doub, George Cochran
Presidential inability: the Constitutional problem. BA 1959-60:131
Doudna, Edgar G.
Real business of the schools. BART 3:253
Dougherty, Daniel
"Hancock the superb." BREW 5:280
On democracy. CHAL 11:92; HAZO 21:8935; MAS 21: 8935
On the perils of the Republic. HAZO 21:8947; MAS 21: 8947
Douglas, Helen Gahagan
Address before the New York Herald Tribune Forum. BUTA:230
Cost of living and inflation. BA 1947-48:118
See also Rayburn, S., jt. auth.
Douglas, Lewis W.
Presents Lord Halifax. LY: 210
Douglas, Malcolm
Supremacy of ideas. SHUC:270
Douglas, Paul H.
Five great Americans. BA 1951-52:85
For the Civil Rights Bill. BA 1957-58:112
Foreign policy. BA 1950-51:72
Internal security. BA 1950-51: 103
Speech in Senate on United States foreign policy in the Middle East. BRAP:129
Vote Democratic. BA 1954-55: 81
---- and others (G.V. Denny, Jr. C. Fadiman; J.R. Killian Jr.; and G.D. Stoddard)
Are we educating for the needs of the modern man? BA 1948-49:179
---- and others (W. Chevalier and Roving reporter)
Is America's economic frontier closed? HOB:262
DOUGLAS, PAUL H.
Burgess, W.R.
Presents Paul H. Douglas, LY:223
Douglas, Stephen A.
Appeal of the Independent Democrats. ANG:267
"Expansion" and co-operation with England. BREW 5:294
Fifth joint debate at Galesburg, October 7, 1858. CLAW:83
Issues of 1861. BREW 5:302
John Brown raid. BREW 5:299
Kansas-Nebraska Bill. BRAS: 114; CHEM 3:147; HAZO 17: 7331; JOHA 2 pt. 1:50; LEEW 10:167; MAS 17:7331; PL:678; SHAH:287
Kansas and "Squatter sovereignty." BREW 5:297
Lincoln-Douglas debate at Alton, October 15, 1858. BAAMP:93
Opening speech of Lincoln-Douglas debate, Ottawa, August 21, 1858) BRYW 9: 259; CHAL 8:421; CLAW: 55; HARSO:310; HAZO 17: 7401, MAS 17.7401, SHUM. 142
Popular sovereignty.-Same as his Reply to Lincoln at Chicago, July 9, 1858
Reply to Lincoln at Chicago, July 9, 1858. SHAH:387; WPRA:188
Reply to Lincoln, Freeport, August 27, 1858. BIR 2:221; BREW 5:288; COP:301; COPA:301; COPB:301; HURG:94; JOHA 2 pt 1:184; ORAMA 2:285; REEM 10: 171; REEMA 13:933; REEMB 11:175
War with Mexico. HAZO 17: 7356; MAS 17:7356

DOUGLAS, STEPHEN A.
Brown, F.
Patriotism of Stephen A. Douglas. SHUC:14
Cox, S. S.

DOUGLAS, STEPHEN A. (cont.)
Stephen A. Douglas and his place in history. BREW 4:216
Long, W. L.
Lincoln's debates with Douglas. TRUW:110
Schurz, C.
Arraignment of Stephen A. Douglas. CHAL 11:193; HAZO 21:9048; MAS 21:9048
Trumbull, A.
Announcing the death of Douglas. BREW 9:436

Douglas, William O.
At the grave of Franklin D. Roosevelt. MO:533; MOA:539
Function of democracy. BA 1940-41:225; BARR:275
John Peter Altgeld and the Bill of Rights. BA 1947-48:207
World in revolution. HAR:169
---- and others (R. H. Jackson)
Freedom of speech: Terminiello vs. City of Chicago. BA 1948-49:78

Douglass, Frederick
'Men of color, to arms!" WOON:253
Nature of slavery (speech at Rochester, New York, December 1, 1850) CROC:182
Negro exodus from the gulf states. WOON:453
Negroes and the national war effort. -Same as his Union speech
Oration in memory of Abraham Lincoln (at unveiling of Freedmen's monument, Washington, D.C.) CHAL 9:144; DUNM:133; HAZO 18:7676; HIB:171; MAS 18:7676; WOON:516
Plea for free speech in Boston. BREW 5:282
Reception speech-at Finsbury Chapel, Moorsfield, England, May 12, 1846. WOON:158
Slavery (July 4, 1854) PE:477; PEA:477
Slavery: speech at Rochester, July 5, 1852. PE:477; WOON:197
Slavery Party. WOON:223
Speech at Glasgow, Scotland, May 29, 1846. WOON:170
Speech in Faneuil Hall, June 8, 1849. HILK:27; WOON:178
Union speech. HIB:165; WOON:247
What the black man wants. CHAL 9:133; HAZO 18:7665; MAS 18:7665
What to the slave is the Fourth of July? DUNM:41

Douglass, Joseph H.
Some significant results of the Emancipation, 1863-1963. HILK:327

Douglass, S. C. Howard
Acceptance of office in Knights of Pythias. THOU 3:137

Dow, E. E.
Danger of fraternity apathy. THOU 3:373

Dow, Lorenzo, Jr.
Hope and despair. BREW 5:307
Improvement in America. BREW 5:306

Dow, Neal
Beer, a harmless drink? THOU 1:553
Churches and the saloons. THOU 1:544
Effects of prohibition in Maine. THOU 1:571

Dowling, Austin
Church and the woman. CATA 1:281
Our critics. CATA 2:125
Relation of Catholics to civil government. CATA 1:129

Dowling, Victor J.
Christopher Columbus (at unveiling of monument to Columbus) CATA 1:100

DOWNIE, ROBERT C.
Peloubet, M. E.
Presents Robert C. Downie. LY:94

Doyle, Dennis Conan
Will this war end Christianity? BART 4:83
Doyle, Edmund D.
Constitution. YR 2:127
Sacred trust. BRP 2:82
Doyle, James
Price of liberty. YR 8:165
Doyle, James E.
Eagle comes to earth. NOR 1935:137
Doyne, Abraham
For a Bar Mitzwa - 2 speeches. ZRL:11,74

DRAFT See Conscription
Drake, Charles D.
Against "Copperheads." BREW 5:309

DRAMA
Arliss, G.
Curtain speech. REEM sup 1:62; REEMB 6:12
Bryson, L. and others.
Opportunities for success in the creative arts. SAR: 403
Claretie, J. A. A.
Shakespeare and Moliere. REEMA 4:229
Drama week. SCHS:111
Dramatic club. DR:66
Edlund, R.
Plea for American drama. SHUC:69
For a dramatic festival. BARB:170
Hampden, W.
On receiving a gold medal. REEM sup 1:418; REEMB 6:160
Hapgood, N.
Drama in America today. BAKF:303
Irving, H.
Drama. COP:681; COPB: 708; REEM 2:269; REEMA 2:678; REEMB 2:272
Nattkemper, L. G.
Appeal for dramatic art. SHUC:62
Pinero, A.W.
Drama. REEM 3:59; REEMA 3:892; REEMB 3:60
Suggestions for a junior-senior banquet-theme: "Theatre." AB:91-94
Thomas, A.
Gold medal for drama. REEM 6:387; REEMB 6:362
Walkley, A. B.
Toast to "Drama and Barrie." REEM 1:75; REEMB 1:66
See also Actors and acting; Opera; Theater
Draper, Andrew S.
Inaugural address as president of University of Illinois. WE 2:277
March of the Constitution. BLAA:61; BLAB:61
Draper, William Henry
Our medical advisers. REEM 1:412; REEMA 1:415; REEMB 1:418
Draper, William Henry, Jr. See Havighurst, R. J., jt. auth.
Drayton, William Henry
Charge to the Grand Jury. HAZO 7:2709; MAS 7:2709

DREAMS
Hunter, E.
Dream true. BRP 4:45; YR 5:155
Krantz, J. C., Jr.
New Years-what about your dreams? MCK:134
Morton, W.
Let us have our dreams. BRP 2:72; YR 3:37

DRED SCOTT DECISION
Breckenridge, J. C.
Dred Scott Decision. BREW 2:215
Lincoln, A.
Dred Scott Decision. FO: 150; JOHA 2 pt 1:154; REEMA 14:1356
Taney, R. B.
Dred Scott Case: opinion for the Supreme Court. BRE: 221; BREA: 205; BIR 2:206

Dreiling, Norbert R.
This is Kansas. AN:70
This paradox called war. AN: 62

DRESS See Clothing and dress

DREYFUS, ALFRED
Labori, F.
Conspiracy against Dreyfus. BREW 7:235; CHAL 14: 384; HAZO 25:10903; MAS 25:10903
Zola, E.
Appeal for Dreyfus. BREW 10:285; CHAL 13:355; COP:112; COPA:112; COPB: 112; CROC:489; HAZO 24: 10330; HIB:80; MAS 24: 10330; PE:594; PEA:594; REEM 7:436; REEMA 9: 1226; REEMB 7:437
Driftmier, Frederich
Molten gold. YR 8:283
Drown, Harold J.
Responds to an introduction before the Rotary Club. PRNE:68

DRUGGISTS See Pharmacy and Pharmacists

DRUGS
Conn, J. and others.
Stress and disease. HAR: 328
Deever, L.
Do you want to commit suicide? BRP 10:56
Fisher, L.
Marijuana peddlers. YR 8: 215
Gilbertson, A.
Assassin of youth. YR 10: 151
Locks, E. S.
Assassin of youth. BRP 9: 53
Pedley, E. A.
Hand of the living dead. BRP 3:89; YR 4:103
Resolution for the passage of an interstate narcotic law. HE:112
Rose, J.
Tomorrow should be the deadline. BRP 6:53
Sugarman, N. A.
Assassin of youth. BRP 9: 78; NOR 1938:9

DRUIDS, UNITED ANCIENT ORDER OF
Buck, C. F.
Oration on Druids. THOU 3:209
Centennial anniversary of the United Ancient Order of Druids. THOU 3:231
McGindley, H. A.
Centennial address (Druids) THOU 3:205
Malcolm, T. W.
Ancient Druidic history. THOU 3:215
Schmitt, W. A.
Centennial oration (Druids) THOU 3:200
Vaughan, W. R.
Druidism. THOU 3:237
Drum, Thomas Burns
Constitution. LEIO:140
Drummond, Henry
Alchemy of influence. HAZO 25:10805; MAS 25:10805
"First." (Speech to Boys' Brigade) REEM 6:134; REEMA 7:371; REEMB 7: 116
Greatest thing in the world. BREW 5:314; CHAL 14: 251; HAZO 25:10780; MAS 25:10780; ORBR 2:431; PI 505
Preparation for learning. BREW 5:232
Talk on books. BREW 5:337
Drummond, Richard
Emcee at a G. I. homecoming
" at an Izaak Walton conservation club meeting
" at a meeting of the old-timers
" at a writer's guild meetin
BRH:299, 233, 216, 243
Introducing a beauty expert

Introducing a golfer
" a humorist
" a hunter (wild animal)
" an instructor on conversation
" a movie star
" a "See America first" speaker. BRC: See Table of contents for paging
" an accordian player
" an acrobat-clown act
" an amateur theatrical
" a chalk talk artist
" an impersonator
" an instrumentalist
" a minstrel show
" a retiring teacher. BRH: See Table of contents, section II for paging

Drummond, Roscoe
Response to an introduction. PR:119

Drury, Samuel Smith
My country. PROS:133

DRY GOODS MERCHANTS
Dry-goods merchants, by a prominent member of the Dry Goods Association. EDGS:134
For a dry goods merchants' reunion. BARB:183
Speech at a dry-goods-merchants reunion. HILL:482

DuBois, W.E. Burghardt
Training of Negroes for social reform. DUNM:491

DUELING
Bacon, F.
Against dueling. BREW 1:198

Duesterbeck, Richard M.
Man's other society. LINP:264

DUFEK, GEORGE J.
Weyforth, B.S.
Introduces Rear Admiral George J. Dufek. PRC:16

DUFFIELD, EDWARD D.
Hedges, J.E.
Presents Edward D. Duffield. LY:89

Duffield, Howard
Faith and courage. SHU:30

Dulles, John Foster
Berlin Conference. BA 1953-54:33
Church and international disorder. BA 1948-49:207
Freedom or despotism? BA 1956-57:25
Goal of our foreign policy. BA 1954-55:19
Japanese Peace Treaty. BA 1951-52:41; HAR:175
Let us make peace. -Same as his Japanese Peace Treaty
Modern foreign policy. HURG:324
North Atlantic Pact. BA 1949-50:22
"Not war, not peace." BA 1947-48:58
Our policies toward Communism in China. BA 1957-58:48; GRAC:176
Policy for the Far East. BA 1958-59:36
Speech in New York, January 25, 1954. GRAC:167
United front against red aggression. BA 1950-51:54
Western European army. BA 1952-53:15

DULLES, JOHN FOSTER
Miller, M.G.
Excerpts from introduction of John Foster Dulles. PRNE:42

DULUTH
Knott, J.P.
Glories of Duluth. BREW 7:204; CHAL 11:425; HARSO:186; HAZO 22:9346; MAS 22:9346; ONEM:317; ORAMA 2:347; PE:604; PEA:604; REEM 7:204; REEMA 8:753; REEMB 8:231; SHUO:186

Dumas, Alexandre, Fils
Tribute to his father (on occa-

Dumas, A. F. (cont.)
sion of taking his seat in the French Academy) DUNM:95

DUMAS, ALEXANDRE
Dumas, A.
Tribute to his father (on occasion of taking his seat in the French Academy) DUNM:95
Dumas, George
Home. BOA:136

DUMBARTON OAKS CONFERENCE
Cadogan, A.
Remarks at opening of the second phase of the Dumbarton Oaks Conference. VO 1944-45:458
Remarks at the conclusion of the first phase of the Dumbarton Oaks Conference. VO 1944-45:456
Statement at opening of Dumbarton Oaks Conference. HAN:427; VO 1944-45:381
Gromyko, A. A.
Remarks at conclusion of the first phase of the Dumbarton Oaks Conference. VO 1944-45:456
Statement at opening of Dumbarton Oaks Conference. VO 1944-45:384
Halifax, E. F. L. W.
Statement at conclusion of the second phase of the Dumbarton Oaks conversations. VO 1944-45:472
Hull, C.
Remarks at opening of second phase of the Dumbarton Oaks Conference. VO 1944-45:457
Statement at opening of Dumbarton Oaks Conference. HAN:427; VO 1944-45:381
Koo, V. K. W.
Remarks at opening of the second phase of the Dumbarton Oaks Conference. VO 1944-45:459
Statement at conclusion of second phase of the Dumbarton Oaks conversations. VO 1944-45:471
Roosevelt, F. D.
Remarks to the delegates to the Dumbarton Oaks Conference. VO 1944-45:387
Stettinius, E. R., Jr.
Remarks at conclusion of the first phase of the Dumbarton Oaks Conference. VO 1944-45:456
Statement at conclusion of second phase of the Dumbarton Oaks conversations. VO 1944-45:470
Statement explaining policy of secrecy adopted for the Dumbarton Oaks Conference. VO 1944-45:395
Dunbar, Alice Moore
Life of social service as exemplified in David Livingstone (at centenary of his birth) DUNM:425
Dunbar, Earl M.
Supreme menace (denunciation of cause and effects of war) ASHF:256
Dunbar, Paul
Study in ghosts (broken homes) BLUE:58
Duncan, Paul
Planners. BRP 3:39; YR 4:3
Dunham, William H.
Materialistic idealism. YR: 4:53

DUNKIRK, FRANCE, BATTLE OF, 1940
Churchill, W. L. S.
Dunkirk. BRTHA:352; COP: 461; COPA:461; COPB:433; HAN:133; PE:774; PEA: 774
Dunn, Jack
49th State. BRP 10:51
Dunne, Peter F.
Summation for the Government in the San Francisco mint

case. HICJ:434
Dunning, John, 1st Baron Ashburton See Ashburton, J. D. 1st Earl of
Dupee, Gordon G.
Eyeless in Gaza. BRP 9:97; NOR 1938:28
Du Pont, Henry B.
Greatest invention of them all. ARNS:193
Durant, Will
World conflict. BART 3:221

DURANT, WILL
Coulter, T. H.
Introduces Dr. Will Durant, author and philosopher on Ladies' day at Executive Club of Chicago. PRNE:43
Miller, G. M.
Introduces Dr. Will Durant, author and philosopher. PRNE:48
Durant, William J.
Crisis in American civilization. BA 1939-40:208

DURANT, WILLIAM J.
Davis, C. R.
Presents William J. Durant. LY:73
Duranty, Walter See Gottschalk, L., jt. auth.
Durfee, Job
Influence of scientific discovery and invention on social and political progress. BL:381; NORR 1st ser:43

DUTCH IN THE UNITED STATES
Bergen, T. G.
First settlers of New Netherlands. ONES:242; REEMA 1:64
Depew, C. M.
Beggars of the sea. REEMA 1:366
New Netherlands. REEMA 1:349
Porter, H.
Assimilated Dutchman. REEMA 3:939
Roosevelt, T.
Hollander as an American. REEM 3:151; REEMA 3:998; REEMB 3:154
Stryker, W. S.
Dutch heroes in the new world. REEMA 3:1104
See also Forefathers' Day

DUTCHMEN
Puritan and the Dutchman. DAVC:392
Van Dyke, H.
Typical Dutchman. DOA:301; ONEM:641; ONES:232; REEM 3:347; REEMA 1:418; REEMB 3:363
See also National characteristics, Dutch
Dutter, Philip
Is the Constitution ours. DO:217

DUTY
Abbott, L.
Faith and duty. REEM 1:1; REEMB 1:1
O'Rourke, A. W.
Call of duty. SHUC:203
Shelley, D. N.
Devotion to duty. DOB:192
Dwight, Timothy
Pursuit of excellence. BREW 5:341
Sermon on sovereignty of God. HAZO 8:3147; MAS 8:3147
Dwyer, James Francis
Citizen. HARSO:32
Dream come true. SHU:47
Dyer, Gus W.
Constitution and the present day problems. EXEE:531
Dyke, Herbert Gordon
Negative America. YR 2:29
Dykstra, C. A.
American city. YE:383
Individual and the democratic adventure. BA 1939-40:141

EAGLES, FRATERNAL ORDER OF
Eagles eloquent. THOS:171
Earhart, Amelia
Speech for Roosevelt. GA:154

EARHART, AMELIA
Irwin, I. H.
Acceptance of Amelia Earhart collection. GA:47
Earle, George H.
New frontiers. BOA:415

EARTH
Morris, W.
Art and beauty of the earth. REEM 6:329; REEMA 9:891; REEMB 7:279

EAST HARLEM
Dinwoodie, S. D.
Inner city-our shame. ARNS:246

EAST INDIA BILL
Burke, E.
East India Bill of Mr. Fox. GOOD:312; PE:175; PEA:175
On the Nabob of Arcot's debts. GOOD:330; KET:65; LEEW 6:169
Fox, C. J.
On the East India Bill. BREW 6:164; BRYW 4:32; GOOD:462; PEA:171; PL:418
On the use of secret influence to defeat his East India Bill. GOOD:474; LEEW 6:317

EASTER
Abbott, L.
Resurrection. THOU 2:104
Ambrose, Saint
Sermon on belief in the resurrection. PL:176
Barrows, J. H.
Immortality. THOU 2:143
Bonar, A.
Resurrection miracle. THOU 2:120
Cuyler, T. L.
Risen with Christ. THOU 2:144
Soul's Easter. THOU 2:138
Easter. DR:135
Easter. MORA:43
Easter. NATS:20
Easter (glimpse of Macedonian customs) ED:37
Easter-its significance in a modern world. DR:137; LU:1182
Evans, L. H.
Alive. BA 1953-54:180
Fallows, S.
Resurrection of Christ. THOU 2:99
Goodwin, E. P.
Some Easter certainties. THOU 2:94
Haldeman, I. M.
Resurrection. THOU 2:114
Hendrix, E. R.
Living witness of the resurrection. THOU 2:101
If a man die, shall he live again? JA:56
If Christ had not died. JA:59
Judson, E.
Effect of the resurrection upon the character of Peter. THOU 2:128
Life that never ends. JA:53
Lorimer, G. C.
Logic of Easter. THOU 2:122
New bodies for a new world (Easter) JAS:44
Old Easter rites. THOS:144
Pius XII.
Appeal for peace. COP:525; COPA:525; COPB:503; VO 1941:167
Rabanus Magnentius Maurus.
On Palm Sunday. HAZO 3:1239; MAS 3:1239
Riggenbach, J. C.
Seven words of Jesus on the cross. THOU 2:141
Simpson, M.
On the resurrection of our Lord. CHAL 8:344; HAZO 17:7189; MAS 17:7189
Spurgeon, C. H.
First appearance of the risen Lord to the eleven. THOU 2:109
Talmage, T. D.

Sleepers awakened. THOU 2:132
Tomb with a broken seal. JAI: 30
See also Good Friday

EASTER ISLAND
Mystery Island. FRIE:119

EASTER SEALS See Medicine

EASTERN STAR, ORDER OF
Eastern Star. NATS:26
Eastern Star, by the officer of another chapter. EDGS: 359
Eastern Star address of welcome and response. THOS: 47, 57
Eastern Star work. AMEO 2: 48

Eastlake, Sir Charles Lock
Introducing Lord Palmerston to Royal Academy, May 2, 1863. REEM 3:39

Eastman, Joseph B.
How can we solve the railroad problem. BA 1938-39: 138

Easton, Thomas
Opinion on Knights of Malta. THOU 3:152

Eastvold, Donald
For seating Eisenhower delegates. BA 1952-53:49

Eaton, Charles A.
Thomas A. Edison. BOA:229; BOB:141

EATON, CHARLES A.
Wanacek, E. M.
Introduces Charles A. Eaton. PR:72

Eaton, Clement
Professor James Woodrow and the freedom of teaching in the South. TIN:438

Eaton, Cyrus
Professor talks to himself. ON:235

Eaton, Lewis, J., Jr.
Help today for health tomorrow. BRAP:33

Eberts, Harry W., Jr.
And there is no peace. AN:13

Eckels, James H.
Address to graduates. REAC: 58

Ecker, Frederick H.
Human factor in the balance sheet. BYRA:137; REEM sup 1:246; REEMB 4:179

Eckert, Robert A.
They are not mindreaders. AN:17

Ecklund, John Edwin, Jr.
Productive patriotism. YR 8: 297

ECONOMIC ASSISTANCE, AMERICAN
Bowles, C.
New directions for foreign aid. BA 1959-60:93
Morrill, J. L.
Foreign aid in education. ANGC:168
See also World War, 1939-1945-United States-Aid to Great Britain

ECONOMIC CONDITIONS
Good times for all. NATT:24
See also United States- Economic policy

ECONOMIC PLANNING See United States-Economic policy

ECONOMICS See Capitalism; Free trade and protection; Industry; Monopolies; Savings and thrift; Trusts, industrial; World's Economic Conference

ECONOMY
Holman, W. S.
Economy in public expenditures. REEMA 13:1220

Eddy, Edward D., Jr.
Our common denominator-the student. BA 1960-61:131

Eden, Anthony
Advocates abandonment of

Eden, Anthony (cont.)
Ethiopia. KESK 2:97
Address at first plenary session of San Francisco Conference. -Same as his Job to be done
Address in the House of Commons, September 22, 1943. VO 1943-44:405
America and Great Britain in the post war world. BA 1942-43:131
British war aims, May 29, 1941. VO 1941:232
Debate with Winston Churchill on withdrawal of Forces from Greece, April 30, 1941. VO 1941:185
Firm policy. COP:455; COPA: 455; COPB:427
International situation in 1937. KESK 2:198
Job to be done. BA 1944-45: 76; VO 1945-46:174
Response to welcome at United Nations Conference. MO:506; MOA:510
Speech in Commons on foreign affairs, May 25, 1944. VO 1944-45:234
Speech on power and responsibility. VO 1944-45:147
Statement on British policy in Greece. VO 1944-45:619
Statement on Hess. VO 1943-44:403
Statement on the Levant States. VO 1945-46:231

Edgar, Shoana
Strikes in public utilities. BRAP:78

Edgerton, John Emmett
Candles of understanding. REEM sup 1:257; REEMB 4:190

EDINBURGH UNIVERSITY
Elze, C.
To the University of Edinburgh. KNAS:249; KNASA: 249
Saffi, A.
To the University of Edinburgh. KNAS:251; KNASA: 251

Edison, Thomas Alva
Looking back over forty years. REEM sup 1:276; REEMB 4:209

EDISON, THOMAS ALVA
Eaton, C. A.
Thomas A. Edison. BOA: 229; BOB:141
Fish, F. P.
Edison and the electric light. REEM sup 1:313; REEMB 4:251
Mellon, A.W.
Presenting to Mr. Thomas A. Edison the medal bestowed upon him by Congress. ONEC:35
Slocum, W.
Wondersmith and the world. (Edison) BRP 4:27; INTW 1933:57; YR 5:333

EDITORS See Journalism and jouranlists

Edlund, Roscoe
Plea for American drama. SHUC:69

Edman, Irwin See Oursler, F., jt. auth.

Edmunds, George P.
Constitution and the Electoral Commission. BREW 5:344

EDMUNDS, GEORGE F.
Long, J.D.
Nominating George F. Edmunds for President. HOA: 288; KNAS:299; KNASA: 299

Edsall, Samuel C.
Remarks at the laying of the cornerstone of the St. Peter's Church, Chicago. THOU 2:445

EDUCATION
Address before an educational convention. AMEO 1:32
Address of a visitor to the children of a public school

BARB:201
Address of President of Board of Education. AMEO 1:198
Advantages of education. FRIE:211
Aim of a high school education. WERN 54:148
Ashmore, H. S.
Education in a time of testing. BA 1958-59:127
Beadle, G. W.
Education and bio-cultural evolution. IOCP:139
Beard, C. C.
Yes, we are ready. SAR: 101
Benjamin, J. P.
Education the foundation stone of republican government. REEMA 11:200
Blair, H. W.
On free schools. CHAL 12: 406; HAZO 23:9802; MAS 23:9802
Blakely, R. J.
Education for multiple leadership (American and Russian education) BA 1958-59; 147
Brebner, J. B.
Common ground of humility. BA 1954-55:123
Butler, N. M.
Five evidences of an education. BRYA:513; HIB:49; REEM 6:59; REEMB 7:73
Growth: an evidence of education. BLAA:182; BLAB: 182
Caldwell, J. T.
New birth. BA 1948-49:196
Chapin, E. H.
District school house. BOB: 182
Clark, B. P.
Opening the Conference on Immigrant Education. ONES: 61
Claxton, P. P.
Democracy in education. BOB:189; FKA:156
Cleveland, G.
Education and the self-made man. BLAA:66; BLAB:66
Conklin, E. G.
Education for democracy. BA 1939-40:346
Coolidge, C.
Education in a republic. SHU:229
Cove, W. G.
New education. ONES:280
Danton, G. J.
Education, free and compulsory. CHAL 4:111; HAZO 8:3346; MAS 8:3346
Dodds, H. W.
Education and mother government. SAR:103
Doudna, E. G.
Real business of the schools. BART 3:253
Douglas, P. H. and others.
Are we educating for the needs of the modern man? BA 1948-49:179
Education and life. AMEO 1: 20
Education as related to civic prosperity. DAVC:29
Education-past, present, and future. DR:80
Efficient education. AMEO 1: 110
Eliot, C. W.
Defects in American education revealed by the war. REEM 6:154; REEMB 7: 136
Uses of education for business. BLAA:163; BLAB: 163; ONES:256; REAC:128; REEM 4:94; REEMA 8:413; REEMB 4:211; SHUP:231
Everett, E.
Education favorable to liberty, morals, and knowledge. KLEG:137
Farrand, L.
Educating for business. EXEE:211
Fellow who wouldn't quit school. JA:82
Fergen, G.
Blazing bulwarks. YR 7:289

EDUCATION (cont.)
Fulbright, J.W.
Current crisis and need for education. BA 1957-58:158
Present-day American life: its order of values, and its sense of direction. BA 1958-59:127
Geiman, C.K.
Are they really unteachable? LINP:122
Hadley, A.T.
Modern changes in educational ideals. ONES:150; REEM 6:226; REEMA 8:594; REEMB 7:207
Hall, S.B.
Uncle Sam's responsibility for his children. SMI:303
Hand, L.
Preparation of citizens for their political duties. BA 1952-53:121
High school as a community asset. AMEO 1:50
Hildebrand, J.H.
Are we educating for national strength? BA 1940-41:271
Hill, B.H.
Education and progress. HARSO:48; SHUO:76
Hill, T.
Liberal education. NORR 2d ser:140
Hoffman, P.G.
Business, government, and education. HAR:429
Hootman, E.
Unfilled promise (possibilities of universal peace and ultimate attainment thru education) ASHF:347
Horn, F.H.
Education-for what? BA 1959-60:149
Horton, M.M.
American education and the world's needs. BA 1946-47:203
Houston, T.A.
Rise of the southern commons. SHUC:338
How parents hinder the school work of their children. AMEO 1:141
How the supervision should help the teacher. AMEO 1:13
Hutchins, R.M.
Where do we go from here in education? HAR:359
Huxley, T.H.
Education. REAC:90
Immigrant education. AMEO 1:227
Importance of education. DR:77
Kennedy, J.F.
Education of an American politician. BRAP:123
Lake, K.
Teaching and learning. NORR 2d ser:361
Lane, J.R.
What price speed: danger of sacrificing individual thought and appreciation to speed and efficiency in education. ASHF:362
Langdon, H.
Broken bulwark. ONEC:385
LeConte, J.
Effect of theory of evolution on education. WAGN:44
Lippmann, W.
Education without culture. BA 1940-41:292; NORR 3d ser:132
Educational deficit and national crisis. BA 1954-55:134
Macauley, T.B.
Popular education. BREW 8:21
McDowell, J.
Education-a state duty. SMI:136
McIntosh, M.C.
Goals of education are not sufficient today. HAR:382
McKeldin, T.
Relation of religion and morality to education. MCK:209
MacLeish, A.
Act of faith. BA 1950-51:131

Minor, L.
Education and republican institutions. SMI:119
Montalembert, C. F. R. de T.
For freedom of education. BREW 8:177; HAZO 16:6724; MAS 16:6724
Myers, N. J.
Moppet manipulation. ARNS:113
New chips off old blocks. NAT:10
No substitute for school. NATM:45
Page, W. H.
Closing educational conference. ONES:59
Parents are teachers. JA:41
Patterson, J. W.
Relations of education to public questions. NORR 2d ser:185
Purpose of education. NATS:10
Rahskopf, H. G.
Speech at mid-century. BA 1950-51:141
Rainey, J. H.
Speech on education. WOON:380
Rice, J. H.
Virginia's deficiencies. SMI:99
Ringe, T.
Streamlined student. YR 10:1
Rogers, W.
Education and wealth. COP:702; COPB:729; HURG:200; REEM sup 2:361; REEMB 3:147
Romney, G.
Citizenship responsibility in education. BA 1959-60:159
Rush, M.
Forays into education. NOR 1945:23
Savage, M. J.
Education for life. BLAA:26; BLAB:26
Schrader, D.
What will they believe? BRP 10:88
Schultz, A. L.
Creative education. ASHF:41
Studebaker, J. W.
Greetings to the Association of Land-grant Colleges and Universities. YE:331
Talk to school children by the principal or other school official. EDGS:212
Taylor, H.
Ideals of American youth. HAR:462
Thorndike, E. L.
Education for initiative and originality. REEM 6:389; REEMB 7:391
Tyler, J.
Educational needs of Virginia. SMI:95
Value of a high school education. AMEO 1:219
Visitor speaks to the pupils of a public school. HILL:478
Wendell, B.
Mystery of education. NORR 1st ser:442
What is real education and does it pay? AMEO 1:78
White, W. A.
Education of a democracy. BOB:188; SHU:128
Why an education? NATT:21
Wilson, W.
Education and trade. SHU:153
Wise, H. A.
Free schools for the farmer's children. SMI:139
Wriston, H. M.
Validity of the educational process. BA 1961-62:171
See also Business education; Catholic education; Colleges and universities; Commencement addresses; Educators; Learning and scholarship; Moral education; Parents and Teachers Associations; Religious education; Schools; Segregation in education; Students;

EDUCATION (cont.)
Teachers; Teaching, freedom of; Veterans-Education; Vocational education; War and education. Also this subject with subheads Education, adult; Education, higher; Education of women

EDUCATION, ADULT
Adult education. DR:83
Blakely, R.J.
Greatest lack. BA 1945-46: 241
Filene, E.A.
Adult education in this machine age. DOA:192
Haroldson, W.
Adult education. JUD:177

EDUCATION AND STATE
Elvehjem, C.A.
Education and democracy. ANGC:83
Fulbright, J.W.
Education and public policy. BA 1964-65:157
Lamar, L.Q.
On national aid to education. REEMA 13:1289
McDevitt, P.R.
State and education. CATA 2:26
Roosevelt, F.D.
Modern education and the government. ONEC:183
Washburne, E.
College as an element of the state. NORR 2d ser: 162

---- FINANCE
Example of a speech for a school bond. MICS:174
Wampler, W.N.
Why support the new bond issue? MICS:131
See also Schools-Financial conditions

EDUCATION, HIGHER
Adams, C.F., Jr., 1835-1915
College fetish. CHAL 12: 415; HAZO 23:9829; MAS 23:9829; REEM 6:1; REEMA 7:10; REEMB 7:1
Adams, C.K.
Relations of higher education to national prosperity. NORR 1st ser:152
Alderman, E.A.
University of Virginia in the life of the nation: inaugural address as president of University of Virginia. WE 2:73
Andrews, E.B.
Inaugural address as president of University of Nebraska. WE 2:301
Angell, J.B.
Inaugural address as president of University of Michigan. WE 2:47
New era in higher education. BLAA:98; BLAB:98; REAC: 110
Ashmore, H.L.
Pursuit of truth. ANGC: 44
Banning, M.C.
Test of an education. ANGC:50
Barzun, J.
Place and the price of excellence. ARNS:26
Bonacker, R.
Mandate to the college bred. BRP 4:39; INTW 1933:29; YR 5:67
Brigance, W.N.
1946:year of decision. BA 1946-47:225
Brooks, S.D.
Inaugural address as president of University of Oklahoma. WE 2:407
Brown, J.D.
Education for leadership. ANDS:155
Butler, N.M.
De Juventute. ON:33
Carleton, W.G.
Take your college in stride. BA 1946-47:222; BAAG: 368

Chandler, J. C. C.
Inaugural address as president of William and Mary College. SMI:261
Chase, H. W.
State university and the new South; inaugural address as president of University of North Carolina. WE 2:31
Clothier, R. C.
Inaugural address as president of University of New Jersey (Rutgers) WE 2:15
Coffman, L. D.
Inaugural address as president of University of Minnesota. WE 2:187
College education is a greater asset than a fifty acre farm. AMEO 1:155
Cowley, W. H.
Fire always makes room for itself. HOC:25; WPRC:226
What should a college president be? BA 1949-50:230
Craven, L.
College graduate's debt to society and the state. SHUC:355
Curtis, G. W.
Leadership of educated men. BAKF:282; ONEM:816; RINM:256
Public duty of educated men. BOU:15; BRIM:281; PAR:315; SHU:194; SHUM:192
Daugherty, L. A.
Royal road. JUD:209
Dewey, J.
Education and new social ideals. WPRC:216
Donovan, H. L.
What I see from my window: inaugural address as president of University of Kentucky. WE 2:233
Draper, A. S.
Inaugural address as president of University of Illinois. WE 2:277
Driftmier, F.
Molten gold. YR 8:283
Eddy, E. D., Jr.
Our common denominator-the student. BA 1960-61:131
Eliot, C. W.
Inaugural address as president of Harvard University. CHAL 12:270; CORP:135; HAZO 23:9651; MAS 23:9651; WE 1:13
Gebhart, D.
Why go to college? MOUG:206; MOUGA:206
Goheen, R. F.
Library and the chapel stand side by side (at opening exercises at Princeton University) BA 1964-65:113
Griswold, A. W.
Man thanking: inaugural address as president of Yale University. HAR:376
Gropius, W.
Creative education: key to good architecture and design. BA 1963-64:182
Hall, A. B.
Inaugural address as president of University of Oregon. WE 2:343
Halsey, J. H.
Education for freedom. BRY:433
Higher education's appalling responsibilities. MOUG:228; MOUGA:228
Hancher, V. M.
Higher education in Iowa (at Founders' day luncheon -Iowa State College centennial) IOCP:37
Inaugural address as president of Iowa State University. WE 2:149
Harding, H. F.
Can the liberal arts tradition survive? BA 1943-44:306
New directions for higher learning. BA 1945-46:229
Harrison, G. E.

EDUCATION, HIGHER (cont.)
Educated spectators. BRP 3:51; YR 4:129
Hazeltine, M.W.
Value of university study. WERN 54:138
Heckscher, A.
Paramount duty. YR 8:273
Hennesy, J.
Drama of life. YR 7:81
Higher education. DAVC:524
Hopkins, E.M.
Aristocracy of brains. REEM 6:286; REEMB 7:235
Hopkins, E.M.
College of the future; inaugural address as president of Dartmouth College. WE 1:119
Inaugural address as president of Williams College. WE 1:137
Huber, L.J.
Introducing a college graduate. BRH:63
Hutchins, R.M.
Education and social improvement. WPRC:220
Farewell for students. BA 1951-52:129
Issues in education: 1946. BA 1945-46:262
Organization and subject matter of general education. BA 1938-39:199
Jackson, R.H.
Why a college education? HOB:102; SAR:57
Jenkins, M.D.
Function of Morgan State College (inaugural address as President of Morgan State College) HILK:94
Jesse, R.H.
Inaugural address as president of University of Missouri. WE 2:129
Jha, A.
Education problems. ZU:52
Johnsrud, H.
Liberal college. ASHF:33
Jones, L.W.
Inaugural address as president of University of Arkansas. WE 2:327
Jordan, D.S.
Higher education of women. REEM 6:295; REEMA 8:745; REEMB 7:244
Kahn, B.M.
Marks of an educated man. ANGC:34
Keefe, D.F.
Our too liberal arts. YR 9:239
Kennan, G.F.
Liberal arts in contemporary American society. BA 1953-54:171
Kennedy, J.F.
Intellectual and the politician. BA 1956-57:165; BARR:285; LINP:279
Kiewiet, C.W. de
How different types of institutions are planning for the future. BA 1955-56:131
Killefer, F.
Challenge to college students. ASHF:50; BRAC:13
Kirk, G.
Responsibilities of the educated man (at centennial of University of Denver) LINP:165
Kooker, E.M.
Response to welcome of honor students. JUD:203
Lieberman, M.H.
Plea for democracy in higher education. YR 1:147
Lindley, E.H.
University and the vocations of man: inaugural address as president of University of Kansas. WE 2:217
Lloyd, W.P. and others.
Attitude of industry toward employment of college graduates. MOA:482
Lowell, A.L.
College factory. HOA:180
McVey, F.LeR.

University and its relations: inaugural address as president of University of North Dakota. WE 2:369
Maloney, M.J.
Call us dissenters. YR 8:21
Mason, M.
College woman and the 20th century home. ONES:383
Maxwell, K.L.
What college has done for me. JUD:215
Mezes, S.E.
Inaugural address as president of University of Texas. WE 2:387
Morgan, E.S.
What every Yale freshman should know. ARNS:33
Morrill, J.L.
Unchanging challenge-lest we forget (at Iowa State College centennial) IOCP:19
Morris, D.W.
Inaugural address as 8th president of Southern Illinois University. SAB:188
Morton, W.
Let us have our dreams. BRP 2:72; YR 3:37
Murray, P.
Labor's role in higher education. HAR:419
Newcomb, J.L.
Trends in higher education. SMI:289
Oppenheimer, J.R.
Talk to undergraduates. BA 1957-58:146
Osgood, C.G.
Proper study. NORR 3d ser:191
Outline of a talk to college students. BAKS:251
Oxford and Asquith, H.H.
Culture. BEA:331
Park, R.
Inaugural address (as President of Barnard College) BA 1963-64:173
Peel, R.
Plea for higher education (installation speech as Lord Rector of University of Glasgow) BREW 8:290
Rahl, J.A.
Died at twenty: buried at seventy. BRP 9:103; NOR 1938:34
Reid, L.D.
How to improve classroom lectures fifty percent. BRAP:127
Satterthwaite, J.B.
Learned dust. YR 9:231
Seelye, J.H.
Relation of learning and religion: inaugural address as president of Amherst College. WE 1:163
Shaft, H.D.
College man's creed. ASHF:25
Sockman, H.W.
Higher religion for higher education. BA 1948-49:216
Sproul, R.G.
Inaugural address as president of University of California. WE 2:251
Stafford, W.P.
College a training school for public service (college sesquicentennial) ONEM:547; ONES:120
Sterling, J.E.W.
Lofty purpose shared. BA 1950-51:150
Stoddard, G.D.
Fallacies and roadblocks. ANGC:150
Stricker, M.
Intellectual: his journey and his home (talk to secondary-school graduates who have won college scholarships) BRAB:533
Suzzallo, H.
Inaugural address as president of University of Washington. WE 2:207
Talk to graduates. FRIE:213
Thonssen, L.
Unrecorded legacy. BA

EDUCATION, HIGHER (cont.)
1958-59:133
Turner, J.
Tragedy of ninety-eight cents. BRP 9:14; YR 10:217
Tyler, C.
Industry and you; the field for college graduates. SAR:397
Van Hise, C.R.
Inaugural address as president of University of Wisconsin. WE 2:161
Venable, F. P.
Duty of the educated man to his country (at Lafayette College Alumni Association) SHUO:90
Warren, E.
Free investigation and faithful experiment. BA 1953-54:87
Whalen, R.S.
Give us a break. JUD:255
Why higher education? AMEO 1:42
Wilson, W.
American college. ONEM:612; ONES:202
Spirit of learning. NORR 1st ser:466
Wylie, A.
Inaugural address as president of Indiana University. WE 2:97
Young, R.R.
Marriage of business and education. BA 1952-53:135
Zacharias, M.
New freedom. YR 7:57
See also Catholic education; Colleges and universities; Knowledge, theory of; Students; War and education

EDUCATION OF WOMEN
Dawson, J.W.
On the higher education of women. CHAL 10:40; HAZO 19:8154; MAS 19:8154
M'Iver, C.D.
Education of women. SHUO:95

EDUCATORS
Cowley, W.H.
What should a college president be? BA 1949-50:230
Drummond, R.
Introducing an instructor on conversation. BRC:226
Elliott, E.C.
Qualifications of a college president. BRAC:305
Farnsworth, D.
Introducing a high school principal. BRC:182
Gilbert, E.J.
Introducing a professor. BRC:78
Kaser, A. L.
Introducing a college president
Introducing an educator
" a professor. BRC:53, 96, 43
Moore, H.E.
Welcome to secondary school principals. YE:135
Phelps, W.L.
Acceptance of American Education award. BA 1939-40:364
Posner, G.A.
Introducing a professor. BRC:84
See also Inaugural addresses; Teachers

Edward VII, King of England
Colonies. REEM 2:1; REEMA 3:1175; REEMB 2:1
Introducing Sir Wilfrid Laurier to Colonial Premiers, June 18, 1897. REEM 2:310; REEMA 2:702; REEMB 2:314

Edward VIII, King of England (abdicated)
Farewell of former King Edward VIII. COP:705; COPB:732; ON:37; PE:763; YE:177
Recollections of America. REEM sup 1:18; REEMB

1:23

EDWARD VIII, KING OF ENGLAND (ABDICATED)
Atkinson, M. L.
Queen takes a King. YR 9:1
Cox, R.
Humpty dumpty. YR 9:9
Edwards, Jonathan
Eternity of Hell torments. BREW 5:350
God glorified in man's dependence. BL:517
Sinners in the hands of an angry God. BAAMP:15; BREW 5:355; CHAL 2:236; COP:227; COPA:227; COPB:227; HAZO 5:1811; HURG:21; MAS 5:1811; PAR:73; PL:566; REEM 9:91; REEMB 10:94
Wrath upon the wicked to the uttermost. BREW 5:352; CHAL 2:222; HAZO 5:1797; MAS 5:1797

EFFICIENCY IN BUSINESS See Business
Egbert, Edward T.
Heart the source of power. HARSO:68; WERN 42:51
Eggleston, Edward
New history (Inaugural address as President of American History Association) REEM 6:142; REEMA 8:401; REEMB 7:124
Eggleston, George Cary
Southern literature. REEMA 2:423

EGYPT AND SUDAN CAMPAIGNS, 1882-1900
Churchill, R. H. S.
Desertion of General Gordon (February 16, 1884 speech) REEMA 12:592
Desertion of General Gordon (May 13, 1884 speech) ORBR 2:419
Gladstone's Egyptian inconsistencies. BREW 3:316
On the Egyptian crisis. CHAL 14:144; HAZO 25:10653; MAS 25:10653
Kitchener of Khartoum, H. H. K.
Relief of Khartoum. REEMA 2:694
Salisbury, R. A. T. G. -C.
Abandonment of General Gordon. BRYW 5:109; CHAL 11:362; HAZO 22:9283; MAS 22:9283; REEM 9:313; REEMA 15:1808; REEMB 10:322
Burning question. CHAL 11:360; HAZO 22:9281; MAS 22:9281
Egypt and the Soudan. BAKF:333; CHAL 11:355
Egyptian question. CHAL 11:355; HAZO 22:9276; MAS 22:9276
Ehninger, Douglas
Are we blind? BRP 7:82; NOR 1936:16
Ehrensperger, Ray
"King can do no wrong." BLUE:108
Eifert, William H.
Invitation to Jesus and his disciples. ACW:76
Einstein, Albert
Peace in the atomic era. BA 1949-50:63; COPB:635; HAR:58

EINSTEIN, ALBERT
Nizer, L.
Presents Albert Einstein. HIBS:496; LY:173; NI:53; NIA:45
Eiseley, Loren
Man: the lethal factor. BA 1962-63:39
Eisendrath, Maurice N.
Moral bankruptcy of television. ARNS:108
Eisenhower, Dwight D.
Acceptance of honorary membership in the Chamber of Commerce of the State of New York. MO:506; MOA:510
Address at the United Nations,

Eisenhower, D.D. (cont.)
September 22, 1960. BA 1960-65:55
Address before joint session of Congress. -Same as his Quality of America's fighting men
Agonized reappraisals: Hungary and Suez. FIP:346
American Red Cross. BA 1948-49:74
Announces establishment of Allied Military Government (AMG) to rule occupied Germany. VO 1944-45:420
Army hour broadcast from Paris on the need for ammunition. VO 1944-45:568
Atoms for peace. - Same as his International control of atomic power for peaceful purposes
Begins an address at the American Legion Convention. PRNE:73
Begins an address before the annual meeting of the Chamber of Commerce of the United States. PRNE:77
Broadcast to the Italian people, July 29, 1943. VO 1943-44: 295
Broadcast to the peoples of Western Europe. HAN:272; VO 1944-45:262
Campaign speech, Denver, October 8, 1954. -Same as his Republican precinct day rally
Challenge of our times. BA 1951-52:14; HAR:529; MIA:337
Conquers London. -Same as his Unity won the war
Crusade for peace. BA 1952-53:92
Dedication of the Saint Lawrence Seaway. SABA:292
"Don't join the book burners." FIP:324
Eisenhower Doctrine. FIP:351
European trip. BA 1959-60:7
Farewell address, January 17, 1961. FIP:365
Farewell address to the American soldier. GLAD: 175
Federal Court orders must be upheld. BA 1957-58:130; FIP:357
First inaugural address. ANG: 530; BA 1952-53:112; BAAMP:283; CHI:286; COPB:603; HURG:304; LOTI:257; USIN:257; USINA:257
First steps in disarmament. BA 1955-56:19; FIP:342
I am a candidate. BA 1955-56: 101
Instructions to German troops and to foreign workers, in preparation for defeat of Germany. VO 1945-46:130
Instructions to organized cells of foreign workers in Germany. VO 1944-45:432
Instructions to the underground resistance movements of Europe. VO 1944-45:219
International control of atomic power for peaceful purposes BA 1953-54:22; COPB:607; FIP:335
Korean armistice. BA 1953-54:19; FIP:331
Little Rock.- Same as his Federal Court orders must be upheld
Madison Square Garden address, October 25, 1956. BA 1956-57:53
Message to Allied invasion troops in France. VO 1944-45:267
Military defense of the North Atlantic Pact nations. BA 1950-51:75; HAR:220
New tax program (March 15, 1954 speech) MOA:573
On the Labor Bill-1959. BRYA:543
Open skies at the Summit - Same as his First steps in disarmament

Order of the day on the German counter-offensive in Belgium and Luxembourg. VO 1944-45:623
Order of the day to the Allied armies in France, August 13, 1944. VO 1944-45:380
Order of the day to the Allied troops invading France. HIB:54; VO 1944-45:260
Peace an absolute necessity. HIB:55
Peace and friendship, in freedom. BA 1959-60:25
Peace program. BA 1952-53: 31
Plan for peace in Lebanon. BA 1958-59:23
Plea to the French people upon the Allied invasion of Sicily. VO 1943-44:267
Price of peace: second inaugural address. BA 1956-57:19; BAAG:376; CHI: 294; LOTI:263; USIN:263; USINA:263; WPRC:313
Proclamation to the French, November 7, 1942. VO 1942-43:599
Quality of America's fighting men. BA 1944-45:114; HAN:312; VO 1945-46:288
Report to the nation (1951)- Same as his Military defense of the North Atlantic Pact nations
Republican precinct day rally. BA 1954-55:71; LOMS:235; LOMSA:299
Responds to an introduction by the Prime Minister of Canada. PRNE:51
Response on being made honorary citizen of the City of New York. ON:327
Response to home town welcome. ON:259
Review of the war. -Same as his Quality of America's fighting men
Science and national security. BA 1957-58:20
Second inaugural address. - Same as his Price of peace: second inaugural address
Speech to Detroit supporters. BERS:193
Spirit of Geneva. COPB:610
State of the Union (January 9, 1958) BA 1957-58:65
Statement covering activities of the Allied Military Government in Germany. VO 1944-45:430
Text of the proclamation broadcast on the surrender of Italy. VO 1943-44:335
U-2. FIP:362
Unity won the war. HAN:309; ON:330; PE:798; PEA:798
Victory order of the day, and his proclamation on Germany's defeat. VO 1945-46: 197
Warning to the people of Rhineland and the Ruhr. VO 1944-45:415
World peace: a balance sheet. BA 1949-50:51; YE:183
---- and others (E.T. Benson; H. Brownell, Jr.; O.C. Hobby; G.M. Humphrey)
Keeping the government house in order (television report to the nation) BA 1953-54: 45

EISENHOWER DOCTRINE See Middle East

Elder, Albert L.
Chemist looks at the world population explosion. BA 1960-61:165

Eldridge, G.D.
Future of fraternalism. THOU 3:362

ELECTION - ACCEPTANCE See Offices-acceptances

ELECTION LAWS
Johnson, L.B.
Address to a Joint Session of Congress, March 15, 1965. BA 1964-65:9

ELECTIONS
Address before League of Women Voters. AMEO 2:126
Ames, F.
Biennial election. CHEM 1: 279
Beaconsfield, B.D.
Franchise and reform, 1867. BRTH:284; BRTHA: 284
Reform of the franchise. EMS 2:159
Bruce, B.K.
Speech delivered in March, 1876, when it became necessary for the Senate to introduce a resolution appointing a committee to investigate election practices in Mississippi. WOON:270
Burke, E.
Frequency of elections. EMS 2:113
Catt, C.C.
Political parties and women voters. REEM 7:84; REEMB 8:70
Chapin, E.H.
Ballot box. BOA:366; BOB: 53
Closing speech (at political rally urging citizens to vote) BED:95; BEDA:132, 167
Cobden, R.
Reform of the franchise. EMS 2:162
Curran, J.P.
Election at Newry. KET: 192
Ely, E.S.
Duty of Christian freemen to elect Christian leaders. BL:548
Fox, C.J.
On the Westminster scrutiny. GOOD:481
Gladstone, W.E.
Reform of the franchise, May 11, 1864 speech. EMS 2:172
Reform of the franchise, April 12, 1866 speech. EMS 2:179
Reform of the franchise, February 28, 1884 speech. EMS 2:191
Grote, G.
Ballot. EMS 2:152
Harcourt, S.
Jurisdiction over Parliamentary elections. EMS 1: 203
Introducing a speaker on "The forthcoming election." WRA:38
Johnson, J.W.
Our democracy and the ballot. WOON:663
Kaser, A.L.
Introducing a speaker to junior voters. BRC:194
LaFollette, R.M.
Which shall rule, manhood or money? COP:343; COPA:343; COPB:343; HURG:158; REEM 7:217; REEMA 13:1281; REEMB 7:252
Lynch, J.R.
Speech in the case of his contested election. WOON: 273
Opening speech (urging labor union members to take active interest in politics) BED:93; BEDA:165
Peel, R.
Reform of the franchise. EMS 2:144
Pitt, W., 1708-1778
Reform of the franchise, January 22, 1770 speech. EMS 2:111
Pitt, W., 1759-1806
Reform of the franchise, May 7, 1782 speech. EMS 2:125
Reform of the franchise, May 7, 1783 speech. EMS 2:129
Root, E.
Invisible government: Short Ballot Amendment. BIR 4: 12; HICF:444; ONEM:306
Russell, J.R.
On the ballot. CHAL 6:36;

HAZO 12:5065; MAS 12: 5065
Reform of the franchise. EMS 2:137

Sumner, J. A. H.
Reform of the franchise. EMS 2:205
Thanking speaker (urging labor union members to vote) BED:94; BEDA:167
Thomas, L.
Election of Truman. BA 1948-49:134
Walpole, R.
Frequency of general elections. EMS 2:105
On the Septennial Bill. GOOD:32; LEEW 6:103
Wellington, A. W.
Reform of the franchise. EMS 2:148
What the woman voter should know and the responsibility of the ballot. AMEO 2:36
Yonge, W.
Constituents and members. EMS 2:108
Carpenter, M. H.
Louisiana Returning Board. BREW 3:138
See also Campaign speeches, Candidates; Defeat; United States-President-Election

ELECTIONS - CORRUPT PRACTICES

ELECTRIC APPLIANCE DEALERS See Business men

ELECTRIC RAILROADS
Harris, J. P.
Financing of electric railways. REEM sup 1:420; REEMB 4:360

ELECTRICITY
Brown, I. B.
Electric service in the American home. BLUE:68
Fish, F. P.
Edison and the electric light. REEM sup 1:313; REEMB 4:251

ELECTRONS
Compton, K. T.
Electron, its intellectual and social significance. SAR:363
Lodge, O. J.
Electrons and the infinity of the universe. BREW 7:382
Rutherford, E.
Electrons and atomic explosions. BREW 9:135
Eliot, Charles W.
Academic freedom. NORR 1st ser:344
Address delivered at Faneuil Hall on 250th anniversary of the settlement of the Jews in the United States. TWJ:78
Arming of the nations. REEM 2:8; REEMB 2:8
Defects in American education revealed by war. REEM 6:154; REEMB 7:136
Durable satisfactions of life. REEM 6:169; REEMB 7:151
Education is nonsectarian. - Same as his Harvard and Yale
Ethics of corporate management. PEAE:59
Fraternalism. THOU 3:20
Harvard and Yale. CHAL 12:302; COP:673; COPB:700; HAZO 23:9683; HURG:130; MAS 23:9683; REEM 2:4; REEMA 2:427; REEMB 2:4
Heroes of the Civil War. BAKF:183
Inaugural address as president of Harvard. CHAL 12:270; CORP:135; HAZO 23:9651; MAS 23:9651; WE 1:13
Julia Ward Howe. PEAE:155
On his ninetieth birthday. REEM sup 1:278; REEMB 7:154
Speech of welcome to Prince

Eliot, C.W. (cont.)
Henry of Prussia. BAKF: 211; ONEM:676; ONES:15
Truth and light. REEM 2:13; REEMB 2:13
Uses of education for business. BLAA:163; BLAB:163; ONES:256; REAC:128; REEM 4:94; REEMA 8: 413; REEMB 4:211; SHUP: 231

ELIOT, CHARLES W.
Lowell, A.L.
90th birthday of Charles W. Eliot. REEM sup 2:188; REEMB 7:260
Eliot, George Fielding
How safe are we from attack? BART 3:115
Eliot, Sir John
On the condition of England. - Same as his On the Petition of Right
On the Petition of Right. ADR 1:13; BRYW 5:358; BRTH: 21; BRTHA:21; BRYW 3: 39; CHAL 2:23; GOOD:3; HAZO 4:1444; LEEW 6:37; MAS 4:1444; PL:362
State of England, 1628. -Same as his On the Petition of Right
Eliot, Samuel A.
Source of song and story. REEMA 2:431
Eliot, T.S.
What is a classic? ARNS:47
Elizabeth I, Queen of England
Golden speech. CROC:192
Queen and the royal succession. BRTH:4; BRTHA:4
Rallies her army during the Armada peril. BUT:240; BUTB:233; HIBS:441; PE:89; PEA:89
To the House of Commons. KNAS:312; KNASA:312
Elizabeth II, Queen of England
Twenty-first birthday speech. BUT:240; BUTB:233
Elizabeth, Consort of George VI, King of England
Broadcast to the women of the Empire. BUTA:227

ELKS, BENEVOLENT AND PROTECTIVE ORDER OF
Brick, A.W., Jr.
After-dinner speech on the occasion of accepting a scholarship. JUD:301
Elks. NATS:23
Elks, by a prominent clubman. EDGS:364
Elks eulogy. THOS:172
Elks' memorial. SCHS:116
Elks' memorial. THOS:167
Elks' memorial address. THOS:176
Elks' university. THOS:169
Holland, R.L.
Order of the Elks. REEM sup 2:48; REEMB 7:230
Installation address; Order of Elks. AMEO 2:131
Jessel, G.
Tribute to the Elks. JEYO: 32
McFarland, J.G.
Memorial address at the tomb of President Harding, December 2, 1923 (speech as Past Exalted Grand Ruler of the Elks) LINM:34
Memory: an address before the Order of Elks. DAVC: 507
Montague, A.J.
Dedication address. THOU 3:156
Elliot, Daisy
Class day greeting. WERN 54: 35
Class growler. WERN 54:71
Elliott, A.R.
Sandwich-grabber. WERN 54: 146
Elliott, A. Randle
Modern harpies. BRP 5:101
Elliott, Edward C.
Qualifications of a college president. BRAC:305
Elliott, Eugene B.
Welcome to the National Education Association. ON:321

Elliot, Robert Browne
Civil Rights' Bill. DUNM:67; WOON:309
Eulogy of Charles Sumner. WOON:502
Ellis, Miriam
Our goal. DO:18
Ellsworth, Oliver
Power of Congress to levy taxes. HAZO 7:2760; MAS 7:2760
Union and coercion. BREW 5: 365
Elson, Edward L.R.
Nation under God. BA 1957-58:163
Elvehjem, Conrad A.
Education and democracy. ANGC:83
Edward, Rodney A.
Wandering Jew. TRUW:61

ELWELL, FAYETTE H.
Heymann, W.M.
Introduces Fayette H. Elwell then Dean of the School of Commerce of the University of Wisconsin. PRNE:37
Ely, Ezra Stiles
Duty of Christian freemen to elect Christian leaders. BL:548
Elyea, Charles Dwelle, Jr.
Plea of the unknown soldier. DO:44
Elze, Carl
To the University of Edinburgh. KNAS:249; KNASA: 249

EMANCIPATION DAY
Allen, G.T.
Washington and Lincoln's part in the Emancipation. THOU 1:261
Beecher, H.W.
Abolition of slavery. THOU 1:268
Progress of the franchise. THOU 1:259
Brockett, J.A.
Emancipation Proclamation. THOU 1:246
Evarts, W.M.
Emancipation Day. THOU 1:269
Future of the Negro. THOU 1: 256
Grady, H.
Negro and southern restoration. THOU 1:273
People emancipated by defeat. THOU 1:270
Hood, P.
Religion of the Negroes. THOU 1:266
Lawson, J.
Freedom's natal day. THOU 1:255
Swinton, J.
Rights of the Negro. THOU 1:265
Williamson, E.E.
Results achieved by the soldiers and sailors. THOU 1:264
See Slavery in the United States

EMANCIPATION PROCLAMATION
Lyon, E.
Emancipation and racial advancement (15th anniversary of Emancipation Proclamation) DUNM:461

EMBARGO
Borah, W.E.
Against repeal of Embargo. BA 1939-40:38
Nye, G.P., Jr.
Neutrality. BA 1939-40:53
Quincy, J.
Evils of the Embargo Act. PL:602
Roosevelt, F.D.
Message to Congress (on repeal of Embargo) BA 1939-40:26

EMBLEMS See Acceptance speeches - Emblems; Presentation speeches - Emblems

EMCEES
Branen, J.
Emcee at a Christmas party for employees
" at a "do it yourself" club
" " " plumbers' convention. BRH:229, 210, 179
Clifford, V.
Emcee at a bus drivers' party
" at a housewarming
" " a neighborhood meeting
" " a St. Patrick's day party
" at a school centennial celebration. BRH:316, 218, 310, 231, 236
Drummond, R.
Emcee at a G.I. homecoming
" at an Izaak Walton conservation club meeting
" at a meeting of old-timers
" " "writers' guild meeting. BRH:299, 233, 216, 243
Gannett, J.
Emcee at a bachelors' club meeting. BRH:308
Gilbert, E.J.
Emcee at a farewell bachelor party
" at a golden wedding anniversary
" at a housewarming
" at a silver wedding anniversary
" at a testimonial for a long-term employee. BRH:296, 214, 292, 280, 191
Huber, L.J.
Animal-loving emcee
Bridegroom "
Deaf "
Family man "
Forgetful "
Frightened "
Handsome "
Little girl "
Ringmaster "
Rural "
Schoolboy "
Soldier "
Tough "
Undertaker emcee. BRH: See Table of contents, section IV for paging
Emcee at an anniversary party
" at an auction
" at a birthday celebration
" " " bridal shower
" " " Christmas party for employees
" " " convention
" " " golden wedding anniversary celebration
" " " housewarming
" " an open house
" " a raffle
" " a retirement party
" " " silver wedding anniversary party
" " " stag dinner
" " " surprise party. BRH: See Table of contents, section III for paging
Emcee introducing himself. BRH:338
His honor, the emcee. BRH:324
Kaser, A. L.
Emcee at a army buddie's reunion
" at a barbers' convention
" at a business men's get-together
" at a camera fans' meeting
" at a family reunion
" " " foremen's banquet
" " " gardeners' club
" " " letter carriers' club meeting
" " " liars' club meeting
" " " newly-weds' party
" " " pre-game rally
" " " readers' and writers' club meeting
" " " salesmen's convention (2)
" " " stag dinner. BRH: See Table of contents, section III for paging
Time out for the sponsor (a fill-in for the emcee) BRH:

325
Milliken, F.
Emcee at a birthday celebration
" at a golfers' banquet
" " " merchants' banquet
" " " office workers' party
" " " writers' club. BRH: 228, 30, 178, 245, 234
Origin of emcee; duties, etc. of. BRH:19-40
Phelps, F.
Emcee at an athletic banquet
" at a bachelors' club anniversary. BRH:315, 309
Posner, G. A.
Emcee at a baby shower
" at a bachelor dinner
" " " birthday party
" " " bridal shower
" " " Christmas party
" " " Father's day party
" " " housewarming
" " " ladies' day meeting (at the lodge, athletic club, social club or other meeting)
Emcee at an office party or ceremony honoring a member leaving for army service
" at a retirement party (after thirty years of service in an office)
" at a surprise party. BRH: See Table of contents, section III for paging
Introductory remarks of an emcee to open a show. BRH:326
Royce, B.
Emcee at a baseball fan club
" at a golden wedding anniversary. BRH:199, 306
Steele, S.
Emcee at a banquet
" at a beauty contest
" at a book-of-the-month club meeting
" at a Lincoln day exercise
" " " policemen's ball. BRH:320, 318, 237, 312, 261
Visk, A. G.
Emcee at a silver wedding anniversary. BRH: 313
Twisted news (to be delivered by an emcee at bachelor parties, bridal parties, or wedding receptions) BRH:328
See also Introductions; Toastmasters; Toasts
Emerson, Charles Wesley
Oratory. WERN 42:131
Emerson, J. G.
America and peace in the Orient. ASHF:308
Emerson, Ralph Waldo
Abraham Lincoln.-Same as his Greatness of a plain American
American scholar. ARNS:36; BAAGA:410; BAAMP:122; BL:151; BREW 5:375; BRY:443; BRYW 8:253; CAP:64; CHAL 7:93; FKA:133; HAZO 14:5927; MAS 14: 5927; NORR 1st ser:24; PAR:265; PE:367; PEA: 367; REEM 6:172; REEMA 8:419; REEMB 6:104
Conservative. HAZO 14:5973; MAS 14:5973; REEMA 4: 377
Divinity school address. BL: 586
Eloquence. KLEG:380
England, Mother of nations. KLEM:37; REEM 2:22; REEMA 2:437; REEMB 2:22
Greatness of a plain American. BREW 5:371; FKA:66; MEAR:111
Literary ethics. CHAL 7:117; HAZO 14:5951; MAS 14: 5951
Man the reformer. BREW 5: 378
Memory of Burns. BEA:179; COP:613; COPB:653; HAZO 14:5994; HURG:106; KNAS:104; KNASA:104; MAS 14:5994; ONEM:467;

Emerson, R.W. (cont.)
REEM 2:24; REEMA 2: 439; REEMB 2:24
Minute-man (at centennial celebration at Concord) HAZO 14:6000; MAS 14: 6000
Oration and response (250th anniversary of the landing of the Pilgrims) BRAR:2: 371
Uses of great men. BREW 5: 382
War (commemoration of patriot heroes of Harvard College in Civil War) HAZO 14:5997; MAS 14:5997; REEMA 2:442
Wisdom of China. REEMA 2: 445
Young American. PL:644

EMERSON, RALPH WALDO
Arnold, M.
On Emerson. CHAL 10: 126; HAZO 20:8321; MAS 20:8321

EMIN PASHA
Stanley, H. M.
Rescue of Emin Pasha. REEMA 6:1047
Emmet, Robert
Protest against sentence as a traitor. BEA:181; BOU: 144; BREW 5:400; BRYW 6:137; CHAL 5:105; COP: 214; COPA:214; COPB: 214; CORP:90; CROC:195; HARSO:320; HAY:116; HAZO 10:4186; HIBS:442; KET:322; MAS 10:4186; ONEM:130; ORBR 2:93; PE:305; PEA:305; PL: 522; REEM 9:169; REEMA 13:941; REEMB 10:176

EMMET, ROBERT
Cook, P. F.
Robert Emmet, the ideal patriot of Ireland's heroic age. CATA 1:271
Dolliver, J. P.
Robert Emmet: 114th anniversary of birth of Emmet. ONES:142; REEM 5:140; REEMA 7:363; REEMB 9: 174
Plunket, W.
Prosecuting Robert Emmet. BREW 8:345; HAY:112

EMOTIONS
Park, E. A.
Theology of the intellect and that of the feelings. BL:624

EMPLOYEE OWNERSHIP See Business

EMPLOYEES
Branen, J.
Emcee at a Christmas party for employees. BRH: 229
Executive addresses employees at party. DR:26
Gilbert, E. J.
Emcee at a testimonial for a long-term employee. BRH:191
Huber, L. J.
Emcee at a Christmas party for employees. BRH: 275
Kaser, A. L.
Emcee at a foremens' banquet. BRH:283
Meditation of an employee. AMEO 2:189
Milliken, F.
Emcee at an office workers' party. BRH:245
Posner, G. A.
Emcee at a retirement party (after thirty years service in an office). BRH: 200
For the emcee at an office party or ceremony honoring a member leaving for army service. BRH:180
Trester, L. M.
Better employee relations are needed. SAB:132

Yeager, W.H.
Art of speaking effectively to employees. SAB:150; SABA:248
You and your job. DR:32

EMPLOYEES, TRAINING OF
Lloyd, W.P. and others
Attitude of industry toward employment of college graduates. MOA:482

EMPLOYERS
Toast to the "boss" by a faithful employee. EDGS:126

EMPLOYMENT
Coppin, F.J.
Plea for industrial opportunity. DUNM:251
Truman, H.S.
Message to Congress September 6, 1945. VO 1945-46: 546
See also Age and employment; Insurance, unemployment; Labor and laboring classes; Labor laws and legislation; Unemployed
Emrich, Richard S.
Greatness of Lincoln (sesquicentennial of Lincoln's birth) BA 1958-59:169

ENGAGEMENTS
Engagement. MORA:90
Engagement, by a guest and response by the fiance. EDGS:251-254
Engagement speech and response by fiance. BURS: 210, 212
Engagements (short speech at dinner to the bridegroom) ED:334
Engelbrecht, Harold H.
Follow after peace. ACW:91
Engels, Frederick
Says a few words at the burial of Karl Marx. PE:575; PEA:575

ENGINEERING AND ENGINEERS
Baekeland, L.H.
Engineer. REEM 4:9; REEMB 4:20
Engineers. SCHS:118
Haggard, H.W.
Physiology for the engineers. ON:19
Heald, H.T.
Aristocracy of the engineer. BA 1956-57:173
McGovern, S.
Introducing an engineer. BRC:74
Morgan, A.E.
Engineer and expanding government. SAR:390
Orrok, G.A.
Water-power costs versus steam-power costs. ONEC: 281
Reid, L.D.
Engineering of ideas (presenting Honor Awards to engineers) BRAB:545

ENGLAND
Canning, G.
England in repose. BREW 3:103; CODS:464; CODSA: 464; GOOD:873
Curran, J.P.
England and English liberties-in the case of Rowan. BREW 4:317; BRYW 6:99; CHAL 3:320; ESEH:201; GOOD:790; HAZO 7:2974; KET:147; MAS 7:2974; PL:516; REEMA 12:764
Emerson, R.W.
England, Mother of nations. KLEM:37; REEM 2:22; REEMA 2:437; REEMB 2: 22
George V.
Wake up, England! KLEM: 208
Kipling, R.
Strength of England. REEM 2:303; REEMB 2:307

ENGLAND-CONSTITUTION
King, W.L.M.
British Constitution in the

ENGLAND-CONSTITUTION (cont.)
dominions (speech of July 23, 1926) KESB:149
Oxford and Asquith, H.H.
Loaded dice-the Lords against the Constitution. BREW 1:170
Pitt, W., 1708-1778
English Constitution. BREW 3:245; FULB:15; GOOD: 108; LEEW 6:119
Salisbury, R.A.T.G.-C.
Tampering with the Constitution. CHAL 11:340; HAZO 22:9261; MAS 22:9261; REEMA 15:1821
See also Great Britain; World War, 1939-1945-Great Britain

ENGLISH LANGUAGE
Davidson, C.
Common confusions. BRA: 556; BRAP:100
Houghton, R.M.M.
Your speech and ours. REEMA 2:635
Swear off! NATM:38

---- WORDS
New chips off old blocks. NAT:10
Ensor, Wendell
Something lost. BRP 1:58
Enstrom, Ralph
Lag. BRP 1:79
"Lilliputians." BRP 2:25
More kindling. BRP 3:71

ENTERTAINMENT See Actors and acting; Introductions; Music; Theater

ENTERTAINMENT, SPEECHES OF See After-dinner speeches

ENTHUSIASM
How to get enthusiasm. FRIE: 261

ENVIRONMENT
Clinton, S.
Ropes (heredity and environment in relation to crime) ASHF:95; BLUE: 51; BRP 3:23
Environment necessary for character building. AMEO 1:137
Epes, Sydney P.
Tariff. SMI:225
Ephraem, Syrus, Saint
Pearl, or, seven rhythms on the faith. LEEW 3:195

EPIPHANY
Fénelon, F.
Festival of the Epiphany. CHAL 2:113; HAZO 4:1650; MAS 4:1650

EPWORTH LEAGUE
Stevens, E.P.
League prayer meeting. THOU 2:506

EQUALITY
Doran, H.J.
Eyes that see not. BRP 2: 54; YR 3:45
Gorton, G.F.
Delusion of equality. ASHF: 229
See also Democracy
Erdman, William
True greatness of the twentieth century. SHUC:373
Ernst, Morris See Canham, E.D., jt. auth.

ERRORS See Blunders
Erskine, Thomas
Against Thomas Williams for the publication of Paine's Age of reason. ADR 2:273; BREW 6:12; GOOD:761; ORBR 1:375; REEMA 13: 949
Defense of Lord Gordon, 1781. GOOD:638; ONEM:49
Free speech and fundamental rights: defense of Tom Paine. BREW 6:43; BRTH: 121; BRTHA:121; BRYW 4: 71; PE:255; PEA:255

Homicidal insanity (J. Hadfield) BREW 6:32; GOOD: 766; LEEW 7:25
In behalf of John Frost, when indicted for uttering seditious words. GOOD:698
In behalf of Mr. Bingham on a trial for adultery. GOOD: 708
In behalf of Rev. George Markham against John Fawcett for criminal conversation with his wife. GOOD: 778
In defense of Thomas Hardy. BREW 6:40; GOOD:713
Liberty of the press.-Same as his Speech in behalf of John Stockdale
On the rights of juries. GOOD: 655
Points out the inevitable consequences of Empire.-Same as his Speech in behalf of John Stockdale
Sovereign's intervention in politics. EMS 1:8
Speech in behalf of John Stockdale. BRAO:141; BREW 6: 24; CHAL 3:276; CODS: 285; CODSA:285; FULB: 69; GOOD:684; HAY:73; HAZO 7:2918; MAS 7:2918; PE:184; PEA:184

Ervin, Samuel J., Jr.
Against the Rights Bill. BA 1957-58:117

Erwin, Dale
Introducing a hunter or extensive traveler. BRC:266

ESCAPE See Crime and criminals

Escobar, Don Adrian C.
Speech upon presentation of letters of credence as Ambassador of Argentina to the United States. VO 1944-45:91

ESKIMOES
Eskimo life. FRIE:115
Montague, S.R.
North to adventure. BART 3:169

ESPIONAGE ACT
Holmes, O.W., Jr.
Schenck v. United States: opinion for the Supreme Court. BRE:320; BREA: 300

Essig, Erhardt H.
Give thanks to God. ACW:98

ESTATE PLANNING
Value of a co-pilot in estate planning. MICS:130

ESTEEM, SYMBOL OF See Presentation speeches-gifts

Estes, J.W., Jr.
Penny wise and pound foolish. YR 10:59

Estournelle de Constant, Paul H.B.
France and the United States. BRYW 7:200

Ethelbert.
Coming of Christianity. BRTH: 1; BRTHA:1

ETHICS
Acheson, D.G.
Ethics in international relations today. BA 1964-65: 53
Angell, J.R.
National morality. REEM 1: 52; REEMB 1:43
Chapin, E.H.
Rectitude higher than morality. BREW 3:208
Grunwald, E.
Toward saner values. BRP 4:64; INTW 1933:46; YR 5:311
Jones, J.L.
Who is tampering with the soul of America? LINP: 219
Lerner, D.
Comfort and fun: morality in a nice society. ARNS: 170
Lewis, C.S.

ETHICS (cont.)
Social morality. ARNS:179
Three parts of morality. ARNS:176
Mould, E.W.K.
Ethics in American public life. SHUC:154
Pinkstaff, K.
We are not ashamed. SOBP:355
See also Behavior; Business ethics; Character; Charities; Christian ethics; Courage; Courtesy; Crime and criminals; Duty; Friendship; Golden rule; Happiness; Honesty; Justice; Liberty; Love; Loyalty; Patience; Patriotism; Peace; Sin; Social problems; Success; Temperance; Truthfulness and falsehood

ETHIOPIA
DeWater, C.
Protests against withdrawal of sanctions against Italy. KESK 2:94
Eden, A.
Advocates abandonment of Ethiopia. KESK 2:97
Haile Selaisse I.
Appeal to the League Assembly. BOU:91; HAN:61; KESK 2:84
Position of Ethiopia. COP:450; COPA:450; COPB:470
Where are we to look for survival? BOU:97
Hoare, S.
Effects of conciliation (November 2, 1935) KESK 2:81
Laval, P.
Efforts on conciliation, November 2, 1935. KESK:2:81
Mussolini, B.
Call to arms. COP:510; COPA:510; COPB:488; FRY:126; PE:761; PEA:761
Potemkine, V.
Efforts of conciliation, November 2, 1935 (on Ethiopian situation) KESK 2:83
Swing, R. G.
Wheel of judgment. BA 1940-41:163

ETIQUETTE
Manners. NATT:17
Eubanks, Ralph T.
Leadership and the "sane society." LINP:178

EUGENICS
Aggert, O., Jr.
Shadows. YR 10:227

EULOGIES
Ames, F.
Eulogy on Washington. HELE:113; LEEW 9:41; THOU 1:161
Apponyi, A.
On the death of Louis Kossuth. BRYW 7:262
Austin, A.
Chaucer (at 500th anniversary of his death) REEMA 7:45
Beck, J. M.
John Marshall, jurist and statesman. SAR:206
Bellows, H. W.
At the funeral of William Cullen Bryant. CHAL 8:454; HAZO 18:7435; MAS 18:7435
Bjornson, B.
Address at the grave of Ole Bull. CHAL 12:96; HAZO 22:9503; MAS 22:9503
Blaine, J. G.
Life and character of J. A. Garfield. BAKF:130; BAKS 177; BREW 2:87; BRYW 10 111; CHAL 11:282; CLAY:141; COP:325; COPA:325; COPB:325; HARSO:178; HAZO 21:9147; HURG:137; LA:139; MAS 21:9147; ONEM:408; ORAMA 2:321; PROS:124; REEM 5:14;

REEMA 7:113; REEMB 9:43; SHU:176; WERN 42:72
Bricker, J.W.
Robert A. Taft. BA 1953-54:75
Carmack, E.W.
Eulogy of William B. Bate. SHUO:323
Chapin, E.H.
Eulogy on Horace Greeley. CHAL 8:475; HAZO 18:7477; MAS 18:7477
Choate, R.
Death of Webster (October 28, 1852 speech) HAY:218; LEEW 10:73; REEM 5:69; REEMA 7:216; REEMB 9:99
On the death of Daniel Webster (speech at Dartmouth, July 27, 1853) BRYW 9:149; CHAL 6:294; HAZO 13:5469; KLEG:236; MAS 13:5469; PL:633; SHAH:258
Cleveland, G.
Eulogy of McKinley. BRYW 10:137; CHAL 13:155; KLEM:164
Curtis, G.W.
Eulogy on Wendell Phillips. BREW 4:342; CHAL 10:340; HAZO 20:8699; KLEG:218; MAS 20:8699; SHU:169
Dallas, G.M.
Eulogy on Andrew Jackson. CHAL 6:25; HAZO 12:5035; MAS 12:5035
Daniel, J.W.
Eulogy of Robert E. Lee (at unveiling of figure of General Lee) HARSO:277; PROS:105; SHU:150; SHUM:244; SHUO:149; SMI:169
Daniels, J.
Eulogy on W.J. Bryan. CORP:272
Dillon, J.
On the death of Gladstone. BRYW 6:252; REEM 5:138; REEMB 9:171
Douglas, W.O.
John Peter Altgeld and the Bill of Rights. BA 1947-48:207
Eliot, C.W.
Julia Ward Howe. PEAE:155
Elks eulogy. THOS:172
Elliott, R.B.
Eulogy of Charles Sumner. WOON:502
Eulogy (at memorial service) BED:44; BEDA:85
Eulogy (at memorial services honoring deceased union member) BED:100; BEDA:178
Eulogy of a deceased member by a fellow member. EDGS:377
Eulogy of a deceased member by a fellow member. HE:122
Everett, E.
Adams and Jefferson. COP:269; COPA:269; COPB:269; HURG:64; KLEG:259; REEM 5:146; REEMA 8:439; REEMB 9:181
Farrar, F.W.
Funeral oration on Ulysses Simpson Grant. BREW 6:100; CHAL 12:12; HAZO 22:9404; MAS 22:9404; ORBR 2:283; REEM 5:163; REEMA 8:464; REEMB 9:198
Gannett, L.S.
Carl Sandburg. SAR:371
Garland, H.
In praise of Booth Tarkington. REEM 2:73; REEMB 2:74
Gladstone, W.E.
On Lord Beaconsfield. BREW 6:266
Graves, J.T.
Eulogy on Henry W. Grady. DOA:269; HARSO:193; PROS:128; REEMA 8:590; SOU 9:435
Green, W.
Samuel Gompers. YE:91
Gregory of Nazianzus.
Eulogy on Basil of Caesarea. BREW 6:300; LEEW 3:151; PL:160

EULOGIES (cont.)
Grigsby, H. B.
Littleton Waller Tazewell. SMI:152
Hoar, G. F.
Eulogy on William McKinley. CHAL 11:49
Holland, J. G.
Eulogy on Abraham Lincoln. CHAL 9:439; HAZO 19:8071; MAS 19:8071
Hudspeth, C. B.
Eulogy on Nestor Montoya. HOA:378; HOAP:266
Ingersoll, R. G.
Eulogy on Walt Whitman. HARSO:196; WERN 42:87
Napoleon. HOA:242
Ireland, J.
Joan of Arc. WERN 42:79
Isocrates.
Encomium on Evagoras. CHAL 1:87; HAZO 1:151; MAS 1:151; PL:54
Jessel, G.
Eulogy on Robert Riskin. JEYO:158
Eulogy to Sid Grauman. JEYO:162
Suggestions for eulogistic speeches. With examples. JEYO:157
Joseph M. Schenck-a eulogy. NIA:135
Kennedy, J. F.
Portraits of five senators in the Senate reception room. BA 1957-58:84
Knickerbocker, W. H.
He died in rawhide (eulogy on Riley Grannan, gambler) GRIS:29
Knights of Pythias eulogy. THOS:180
Lamar, L. Q. C.
Charles Sumner. BRYW 10:61; CHAL 10:441; HAZO 21:8796; LA:134; LAD:93; MAS 21:8796; REEM 5:260; REEMA 8:767; REEMB 9:299; SHUO:230
Lamar, Mrs. W. D.
Eulogy on Nellie Peters Black. GA:90
Lee, J.
Eulogy to Will Rogers. BOA:219
Lee, S. D.
Eulogy of General John B. Gordon. SHUO:43
Long, J. D.
Eulogy on Wendell Phillips. CHAL 13:247; HAZO 24:10216; MAS 24:10216
McConnell, F. J.
Eulogy on David D. Forsyth. BRAC:368
McCormack, J. W.
Eulogy on John F. Kennedy. HIB:19
McKinley, W.
Washington, a Masonic eulogy. THOU 3:80
Mansfield, M. J.
Eulogy on John F. Kennedy. HIB:20
Mason, J. M.
Eulogy on Washington. HAZO 9:3805; MAS 9:3805
Maxwell, W.
The chief (J. Marshall) SMI:126
Model and outline of eulogy. BAKS:170
Newman, J. P.
Eulogy of General Grant. THOU 1:380
Eulogy of Lincoln. ESEH:217
Nott, E.
On the death of Hamilton. BRYW 8:174; CHAL 5:1; HAZO 10:3990; MAS 10:3990
Parker, T.
Discourse on the death of Daniel Webster. BREW 8:274; PE:410; PEA:410; PL:669; SHAH:236
Parkhurst, C. H.
On Garfield. CHAL 13:430; HAZO 24:10474; MAS 24:10474
Phillips, W.
Eulogy on Daniel O'Connell. BRAC:373; ONEM:443;

RINM:182; SHAH:359; SHU: 252
Eulogy on Garrison. CHAL 8:228; HARS:260; HAZO 16:6959; KLEG:141; MAS 16:6959
Toussaint L'Ouverture. BAKF:156; CODS:490; CODSA:490; FULB:330; PAR:311; REEM 8:291; REEMA 6:846; REEMB 13: 296; SHAH:335

Poincare, R.
Eulogy on services of Marshall Foch to his country and the Allies. BEA:353

Porter, H.
Eulogy on Ulysses S. Grant. REEM 3:98; REEMA 3:944; REEMB 3:99; SHU:81; SHUM:259

Potter, H. C.
Eulogy on Phillips Brooks. CHAL 13:1; HAZO 23:9811; MAS 23:9811

Prentiss, S. S.
Lafayette. BRYW 8:218; KLEG:251; LAD:92; REEMA 9:971

Preparation of a eulogy. CORP:275

Ruthven, A. G.
Victor Clarence Vaughan and the University (Michigan) ONEC:127

Sheppard, M.
Eulogy on Washington. PROS:30; SHU:246

Short, F. H.
Our untimely dead: Lincoln, Garfield, and McKinley. WAGN:126

Shortridge, S. M.
Eulogy on General Barnes. WAGN:84

Silva, L. A. R.
Eulogy on Abraham Lincoln. CHAL 10:84; HAZO 19: 8248; MAS 19:8248

Speeches of tribute to deceased-examples of. BEC: 163, 166, 171

Stevens, E. R.
Dean Richards-his service to the state. ONEC:137

Stevenson, A. E.
Eulogy on Eleanor Roosevelt. BA 1962-63:178

Stewart, W. H.
Eulogy on General Lee. SHUO:157

Suggestions for preparation of eulogistic speeches. BRA: 512; BRAB:499. With examples of. GA:85; HIBS: 290; MO:526; RE:173; YE:87

Suggestions for preparation of the speech of praise. REAB:158

Taylor, D. S.
Something of a man (in praise of John L. Lewis) MICS:166

Taylor, H. J.
Integrity! mighty force (tribute to Otto Schnering, head of Curtiss Candy Company) LARW:110

Taylor, R. L.
Eulogy on Isham G. Harris. HARSO:84

Tyler, J.
Adams and Jefferson. SMI: 104

Valkenberg, J. V.
Knights of Pythias eulogy. THOU 3:142

Washington, B. T.
Abraham Lincoln. HICF: 359; KLEG:213

Weaver, A. T.
Charles Henry Woolbert. ONEC:129

Webster, D.
Eulogy on Adams and Jefferson. BREW 10:186; CHAL 5:296; CLAY:10; FKA:9; HARSO:348; HAZO 11:4447; KLEG:135; MAS 11:4447; PE:327; PEA: 327; PROS:139; REEMA 15:2082; SHAH:134, 138

White, S. M.
Eulogy on Senator Stanford. WAGN:41

EULOGIES (cont.)
Winthrop, R.C.
Death of John C. Calhoun. REEMA 9:1219
Death of President Taylor. REEMA 9:1222
Eulogy on Edward Everett. CHAL 8:41; HAZO 16:6637; MAS 16:6637
Wirt, W.
Death of Jefferson and Adams. BREW 10:259
Young, B.H.
Tribute to Winnie Davis. SHUO:145
See also Commemorative addresses; Memorial speeches; Obituaries; Tributes

EUROPE
Adenauer, K.
Integration of Europe. HAR:237
Churchill, W.L.S.
Save Europe by uniting Europe (May 14, 1947) HIBS:452
Voice of Europe (May 7, 1948) GLAD:239
Kaltenborn, H.V.
Looking at Europe from here. BART 1:143
Roberts, C.
What Europe is thinking. EXEE:324
Thompson, D. and others.
What does the European situation mean to us? BA 1937-38:52
United States of Europe. SCHS: 272

EUROPE-DEFENSES
Auriol, V.
Report from the President of France. HAR:230
See also North Atlantic Treaty Organization

EUROPE - DESCRIPTION AND TRAVEL
Porter, H.
Trip abroad with Depew. REEM 3:79; REEMA 3:908; REEMB 3:80

EUROPE-POLITICS AND GOVERNMENT
Bryce, J.B.
Political destinies of the globe. BREW 2:306

EUROPE-RECONSTRUCTION
See Reconstruction-European war, 1918-1939; Reconstruction-1939-1951

EUROPEAN WAR, 1914-1918
Albert I.
Belgium ready. REEM 11:36; REEMB 12:39
Annunzio, G.d'.
To the officers on the Piave. REEM 11:148; REEMB 12:160
War cry to America. BREW 4:391
Aurner, R.R.
Message of Flanders Fields. ONES:326
Baker, N.D.
Challenge to America. HICF:529
March toward liberty. REEM 11:249; REEMB 12:264
Bakhmetieff, B.
New Russia. LEW:145
Balfour, A.J.B.
Lust of Empire as the cause of catastrophe. BREW 1:207
Beatty, D.
Comrades of the mist. REEM 11:415; REEMB 12:437
Beck, J.M.
America and the Allies. REEM 11:117; REEMB 12:127
Bethman-Hollweg, T.
Germany begins the war. COP:124; COPA:124; COPB:124; FRY:64; REEM 11:31; REEMB 12:33

Borden, R. L.
Canadians at the front. REEM 1:141; REEMB 1:138
Growing confidence. REEM 1:149; REEMB 1:146
Voice of the Empire. COP: 384; COPA:384; COPB: 384; REEM 11:92; REEMB 12:101
Brent, C. H.
Finding God among the Tommies. REEM 1:154; REEMB 1:151
Briand, A.
German peace proposal. REEM 11:136; REEMB 12: 147
Bumby, J. H.
Sacrifice that failed: failure of our war-time ideals. ASHF:382
Choate, J. H.
War for freedom. REEM 1:242; REEMB 1:243
Clemenceau, G.
One aim: victory. COP: 136; COPA:136; COPB:136; FRY:89; HIB:215; PL:748; REEM 11:169; REEMB 12: 182
Crowder, E. H.
Begin now! REEM 11:303; REEMB 12:320
Dechanal, P.
Harvest of justice. LEW: 97
Foch, F.
To the French Academy (tribute to the French soldier) REEM 11:422; REEMB 12:445
French officer.
To the first Americans who fell in France. REEM 11: 414; REEMB 12:435
Ginisty, M. -A. C.
Verdun. REEM 11:413; REEMB 12:433
Gompers, S.
Labor's attitude. PL:754; REEM 11:271; REEMB 12: 287
Grey of Fallodon, E. G.
England's position. COP: 199; COPA:199; COPB: 199; HAY:318; REEM 11: 29; REEMB 12:13
Grimke, F. J.
Victory for the Allies and the United States a ground of rejoicing, of thanksgiving. WOON:690
Hoover, H. C.
Food control-a war measure. REEM 11:285; REEMB 12:302
Ishii, K.
Tribute to Washington. LEW:151
Jaures, J.
Last speech. COP:128; COPA:128; COPB:128; PL: 752; REEM 11:11; REEMB 12:11
Socialists and the war. REEM 11:6; REEMB 12:7
Jusserand, D. J.
American gratitude to France. BREW 7:183
"Der Tag." BREW 7:182
Kahn, O. H.
Prussianized Germany. SAA:274
Kerensky, A.
Declaration of the Labor Party. REEM 11:61; REEMB 12:68
Kipling, R.
American invasion of England. REEM 11:300; REEMB 12:317
Kitchener of Khartoum, H. H. K.
More men. REEM 11:86; REEMB 12:95
Korniloff, L. G.
Appeal to his soldiers. REEM 11:176; REEMB 12: 190
LaFollette, R. M.
Against war with Germany. BRAS:313
Lane, F. K.
Message of the West. REEM 11:254; REEMB 12: 270
Why do we fight Germany?

EUROPEAN WAR, 1914-1918
(cont.)
LEW:53
Lansing, R.
To Reserve Officers' Training Corps. LEW:63
Laurier, W.
Canada's participation in the war with Germany. KES:2:357; REEM 11:63; REEMB 12:70
Lenin, N.
Dictatorship of the Proletariat. COP:141; COPB: 141; FRY:93; PL:785; REEM 11:181; REEMB 12: 196
Peasants. REEM 11:187; REEMB 12:202
Lloyd George, D.
Appeal to the nation. BRTH: 341; BRTHA:341; COP: 201; COPA:201; COPB:201; CROC:299; FRY:69; PE: 692; PEA:692; PL:743; REEM 11:70; REEMB 12:78
British war aims. BREW 7: 374
Meaning of America's entrance into war. ONES:310; SAA:255
To American comrades in arms. REEM 11:200; REEMB 12:215
Victory or defeat: no halfway house. REEM 11:156; REEMB 12:169
Vision of the people. BEA: 203
Lodge, H. C.
Treaty of peace with Germany. HICF:592
Mercier, D. F. F. J.
Coronation day sermon. COP:132; COPA:132; COPB:132; FRY:75; PE: 702; PEA:702; REEM 11: 129; REEMB 12:140
Moncheur, L.
Greetings from Belgium. LEW:139
Nicholas II, Emperor of Russia.
REEM 11:60; REEMB 12: 67
Oxford and Asquith, H. H.
Call to arms. BRTH:334; BRTHA:334; SAA:228
England supports Belgium. HAY:328; REEM 11:51; REEMB 12:57
Tribute to America. LEW: 79
Owen, R. B.
Modern Arabian Knights. EXEE:484
Poincaré, R.
Call to arms. BREW 8:353
Declaration of war by France. PL:740; REEM 11: 38; REEMB 12:42
"Divine moment" of victory. BREW 8:356
Verdun-"On ne passe pas!" BREW 8:363
Powell, J., Jr.
War of righteousness. ONEM:378
Rankin, J.
War and world-control. BREW 9:39
Reading, R. D. I.
Across the flood. REEM 3: 127; REEMB 3:128
Redmond, J. E.
Ireland and the war. BRTH: 350; KET:443; REEM 11: 29; REEMB 12:30
Reynolds, G. M.
Unleashing business of war. REEM 4:357; REEMB 5: 237
Ribot, A. F. J.
Greetings to America. LEW:91
Roosevelt, T.
National duty and international ideals. REEM 11:99; REEMB 12:108
Our responsibilities. PROS: 103
Root, E.
War and discussion. REEM 11:241; REEMB 12:256
Royce, J.
Duties of Americans in the

present war. ONES:298
Spirit of '76 and '77 (77th Division U. S. Army) NI: 222; NIA:170
This side of Over there. SCHS:243
Trotsky, L.
To the Red Army. COP:140; COPA:140; COPB:140; PE:717; PEA:717; REEM 11:178; REEMB 12:192
Udine, Prince of.
To the House of Representatives. LEW:129
Underwood, O. W.
War Finance Corporation. BREW 10:27
Venizelos, S.
Greece enters the war. REEM 11:138; REEMB 12:150
Viviani, R. R.
Addresses in America (at Mount Vernon and Auditorium, Chicago) REEM 11: 208, 210; REEMB 12:223, 235
Declaration of war by France. REEM 11:40; REEMB 12:45
It has been sworn. BREW 10:53
Our heritage of liberty. LEW:103
Spirit of France. COP:129; COPA:129; COPB:129; REEM 11:82; REEMB 12: 91
Tribute to Lincoln. LEW: 121
Whitlock, B.
Lafayette, apostle of liberty. REEM 11:224; REEMB 12:239
William II.
Address to the German people. COP:127; COPA: 127; COPB:127; PL:738; REEM 11:6; REEMB 12:6
Wilson, W.
"Eyes of the people opened" (extract from address to Congress, December 4, 1917) BREW 10:258
Wilson, W.
Flag day address. LEW: 39; REEM 11:217; REEMB 12:232; SAA:263; SMI: 258
Force to the utmost. REEM 11:280; REEMB 12: 297
Fourteen points (January 8, 1918) BIR 4:38; BRE:316; BREA:296; BREW 10:243; CAP:161; COP:360; COPA: 360; COPB:360; CROC:477; FIP:126; FO:303; HICF: 541; HURG:180; KESK 1:1; PL:758; REEM 11:264; REEMB 12:280
Freedom of the seas: The "Sussex" affair. FIP:112
Issues against autocracy. BREW 10:251
Message to the Pope. LEW:155
Mount Vernon's message to mankind. SMI:255
Neutrality message to the Senate, August 19, 1914. BIR:4:1; FIP:105
Peace without victory. ANG: 428; BIR 4:20; COP:351; COPA:351; COPB:351; FIP:116; FKA:233; FO:287; HURG:173
War message to Congress, April 2, 1917. ANG:442; BAAMP:224; BIR 4:27; BRAS:301; BRE:302; BREA: 282; BREW 10:249, 250; CAP:147; COP:353; COPA: 353; COPB:353; FIP:122; FKA:242; FO:294; FRY:82; HAY:345; HICF:478; HURG: 177; LEW:13; PAR:472; PE:706; PEA:706; PROS: 122; REEM 11:190; REEMB 12:205; SAA:242; SHAH: 642; SMI:251
Wirth, F. A.
Four-minute man. ONES: 295; REEM 3:181; REEMB 6:400
See also Peace; Peace Conference, 1919; Peace Treaty,

EUROPEAN WAR, 1914-1918 (cont.)
1919

EUROPEAN WAR - RECONSTRUCTION See Reconstruction, 1918-1939

EUROPEAN WAR, 1914-1918 - REPARATIONS
Briand, A.
On compelling Germany to pay. BREW 2:220
Chamberlain, N.
Speech in House of Commons, December 14, 1932, (on war debts) KESK 1:234
Dawes, C.H.
Reparation. BLAB:329
Young, O.D.
Dawes plan. BYRA:478; REEM sup 3:192; REEMB 5:405
See also Debts, public

EUXENIPPUS.
Hypereides.
In defence of Euxenippus. MINA 2:466
EVAGORAS.
Isocrates.
Encomium on Evagoras. CHAL 1:87; HAZO 1:151; MAS 1:151; PL:54
EVANS, ALLAN
Mansfield, W.M.
Case of Allan Evans. ONEM:121
Evans, Arthur Walwyn
What Western democracy means to me. EXEE:408
Evans, Bert
Here stood an oak. YR 4:29
Evans, H.G.
Introduces and pays tribute to Eva Wirth, teacher, on her retirement. PR:86
Evans, Harry R.
House in order, to America lies the task of reconstruction. ASHF:377
Evans, Louis H.
Alive. BA 1953-54:180
Evans, Luther H.
Presents Lessing J. Rosenwald. LY:66
Evarts, William M.
Classics in education. REEM 2:32; REEMA 2:465; REEMB 2:32
Day we celebrate (at New England Society) HAZO 18:7798; MAS 18:7798
Emancipation day. THOU 1:269
English and French experiment. THOU 1:231
French alliance. REEMA 2:457
Geneva Tribunal of Arbitration. KNAS:339; KNASA:339; REEMA 2:448
Heritage of the Pilgrims, 1854. BRAR 2:235
Labor, the source of wealth. THOU 1:434
Liberty enlightening the world. COP:636; REEM 2:28; REEMA 2:469; REEMB 2:28
Progress of the divine ordinance of government. THOU 1:229
Republic and its outlook. REEMA 2:452
Tribute to Herbert Spencer. KLEM:113; REEMA 2:462
Weakest spot in the American system (defense at impeachment of A. Johnson) BREW 6:56
What the age owes to America. CHAL 9:238; HAZO 18:7784; MAS 18:7784; REEMA 13:962; REEMB 8:144; THOU 1:225
Evatt, Herbert Vere
What is democracy? MOA:484
Everett, Edward
Achievements of the Pilgrims. CODS:482; CODSA:482
Adams and Jefferson. COP:269; COPA:269; COPB:269; HURG:64; KLEG:259; REEM 5:146; REEMA 8:

439; REEMB 9:181
Character of Washington. FULB:275
Circumstances favorable to the progress of literature in America. BL:60
Dedicating the national cemetery at Gettysburg. PE:519; PEA:519
Education favorable to liberty, morals, and knowledge. KLEG:137
Glories of the dawn. CLAY: 98; ESEH:216
History of liberty. BREW 6: 64; HAZO 12:5080; LEEW 10:21; MAS 12:5080; ORAMA 2:151; PL:631; REEM 10:59; REEMA 13: 972; REEMB 11:60
Issue of the Revolution. BRYW 8:196
Mayflower. CODS:480; CODSA: 480
Moral forces which make American progress. BREW 6:84
On patriotism. CHAL 13:291; HAZO 24:10280; MAS 24: 10280
On the Kansas-Nebraska Bill. JOHA 2 pt. 1:32
Patriotic oration (50th anniversary of the independence of the United States of America) CHAL 6:92; HAZO 12: 5148; MAS 12:5148
Phi Beta Kappa oration. CHAL 6:52; HAZO 12:5108; MAS 12:5108
Universal and uncoerced cooperation. BREW 6:87
Vegetable and mineral gold. REEMA 8:456; LAD:137
Winthrop, R.C.
Eulogy on Edward Everett. CHAL 8:41; HAZO 16:6637; MAS 16:6637

EVERMANN, BARTON W.
Merriam, J.C.
Presents Barton W. Evermann. LY:191

EVOLUTION
Agassiz, L.J.R.
Man and monkeys. REEMA 4:1
Beadle, G.W.
Education and bio-cultural evolution. IOCP:139
Beecher, H.W.
Two revelations. BAAMP: 160
Bryan, W.J.
Moses vs. Darwin. WPRC: 107
Darrow, C.
Evolution. EXEE:200
Huxley, T.H.
Examines Darwin's "Origin of species." PE:533; PEA: 533
Kaser, A.L.
Introducing a speaker on evolution. BRC:234
LeConte, J.
Effect of the theory of evolution on education. WAGN: 44
Müller, F.M.
Impassable barrier between brutes and man. BREW 8: 223; HAZO 20:8580, MAS 20:8580
Munger, T.T.
Man the final form in creation. BL:709
Woodrow, J.
Evolution. BL:517
Ewald, Henry T.
Presents Virgil Pinkley. LY: 127
Ewert, W.F.
Individualism. COUW:63
Ewing, Oscar R.
What health insurance would mean to you. HAR:350
Ewing, Thomas C.
Ohio and the Northwest. REEMA 2:474
Ewing, William Gillespie
On Christian science. CHAL 13:335

EXAMINATIONS
Can you pass the exam? JAI:41

EXAMINATIONS (cont.)
Choate, J. H.
Test examination. REEM 1: 245; REEMA 1:147; REEMB 1:246
Lowell, A. L.
Art of the examination. ONES: 185; REEM sup 2:189; REEMB 7:261
Teaching (instructor gives his views on examinations) ED:290

EXCHANGE CLUB
Exchange Club. NATS:27

EXECUTIVES
Congratulations to a newly appointed company official. LU:1126
Executive ability-what is it? NAT:13
Executive addresses employees at party. DR:26
Frederick, J. G.
New type of executive. EXEE:587
Huber, L. J.
Introducing a boss. BRC:301
McGovern, S.
Introducing the president at a meeting of a manufacturing company. BRC:269
Tribute to the boss at the annual office banquet. DR:19; LU:1124
See also Business men; Officers; Retirement. Also executives in various fields, e.g. Advertising, Building and loan associations; Railroads, etc.

EXHIBITIONS
Depew, C. M.
Columbian oration. BREW 5:149; COP:330; COPA: 330; COPB:330; REEM 7: 116
Hoover, H. C.
At the Brussels Exposition. BA 1958-59:56
Lane, F. K.
American pioneer (at opening of Panama-Pacific Exposition), BRAP:106; REEM 7:226; REEMB 8: 246
McKinley, W.
At the Pan-American Exposition. BLAA:118; BLAB 118; BRYW 10:239; CHAL 13:465; COP:341; COPA: 341; COPB:341; FIP:27; HAZO 24:10505; KNAS:329; KNASA:329; MAS 24:10505; REEM 10:379; REEMA 14: 1397; REEMB 11:395; RID:88; WERN 42:138
Nixon, R. M.
Opening of the American National Exhibition in Moscow. SABA:209
Washington, B. T.
Address at the opening of the Atlanta Exposition. BAAMP:189; BAKF:210; BRAC:113; BLAB:113; BRAG:8; BRY:479; BRYA: 566; CAP:110; CHAL 14: 312; DOA:333; DUNM:181; HARS:503; HAZO 25: 10583; HILK:38; MAS 25: 10583; ONEM:509; ONES: 102; PAR:461; PE:633; PEA:633; PL:707; REEM 7:417; REEMA 9:1136; REEMB 8:433; SMI:206; WOON:580
See also Dedication addresses Exhibitions

EXPERIENCE
After 40-the best years. NAT 2
Experience pays but who collects? NAT:13

EXPLANATION AND INSTRUCTION, SPEECHES OF See Informative speeches
Expositions See Dedication addresses-Exhibitions; Exhibitions

EXPOSITORY SPEECHES See Informative speeches

EXPUNGING RESOLUTION

Benton, T. H.
On the Expunging Resolution. BRYW 8:240; CHAL 5:152; HAZO 10:4232; JOHA 1 pt. 1:320; MAS 10:4232; ORAMA 2:79
Calhoun, J. C.
On the Explunging Resolution. BRYW 9:104
Clay, H.
Expunging Resolution. BREW 4:23; CODS:470; CODSA: 470; HAZO 10:4066; MAS 10:4046

EXTEMPORANEOUS SPEECHES
After dinner speech by an extra speaker. FRIT:30
Announcing extemporaneous speakers. FRIT:36
Being suddenly asked to speak. DICD:111
Chiang, Mei-Ling
Fighting for the common cause. BA 1942-43:81
Cox, S. S.
Smith and so forth. REEM 1:351; REEMA 1:286; REEMB 1:352
For speaker called on unexpectedly. NAT:47
Humorous apology for inability to make a speech. BARB:56
Introduction for extemporaneous speech. FRIT:37
On being asked to make a speech or tell a humorous story. BARB:142
Outline for an impromptu speech. BAKF:195
Response to invitation to speak by a club member at an annual meeting. WRA: 249
Response to invitation to speak by a guest visiting an international service club for the first time. WRA:248
Response to invitation to speak by a visiting secretary of a trade association at regular meeting of a similar trade association. WRA: 250
Response to the invitation, "A few words" at a church gathering. WRA:246
Response to the invitation, "A few words" at a club meeting. WRA:247
Response to the invitation, "A few words" at a public meeting. WRA:246
Roberts, H. G.
Thinking on your feet. YE: 217
Royce, B.
Absent entertainer (to be used when an entertainer fails to appear) BRH:331
Speech of a speaker who had nothing to say. HILL:489
Speeches for the person unexpectedly called upon. STOC:148
Speeches for the person unexpectedly called upon-four examples of. STON: 154-156
Suggestions for making impromptu speeches. DARR: 226; BUT:105; BUTA:105; BUTB:226; MOUG:156; MOUGA:157. With examples of. WRA:243
Suggestions on how to respond when introduced without warning. With examples of. BRM:57-67
Thompson, D.
Responds to an introduction at Executive's Club, where she was substituting for Clare Booth Luce. PRNE: 74
See also After-dinner speeches

EYES
Haggard, H. W.
Physiology for the engineers. ON:19
Nature's gift of sight. FRIE: 183
O'Keefe, L.

EYES (cont.)
Introducing an optometrist. BRC:231
Eyrich, George F., Jr.
Thrift and citizenship. BYRA: 148; REEM sup 1:282; REEMB 4:216

FACES
Hubbard, E.
Masterpiece of God. SHU: 259
Ward, A.
Faces in the crowd. EXEE: 118

FACTORY AND TRADE WASTE
Brown, H.
Filtering our industrial waste (outline) MO:450; MOA:454
Fadiman, Clifton See Douglas, P.H., jt. auth.
Faigan, Zan
United States obligation for feeding Europe's millions. HOD:106

FAILURE See Success
Fairfield, William
Whom should the Republicans nominate for President? JUD:185
Fairless, Benjamin F.
BA 1949-50:164
What kind of America? BA 1953-54:131

FAIRS
Charity Bazaar. EDGS:241
Church fair (short speech for the program) ED:308
Huber, L.J.
Emcee at a raffle. BRH: 206
Introducing a kissing booth. BRH:74
Humorous speech for a state or county fair or festival. BARB:149
Speech at a county agriculture fair. HILL:487
Speech for the opening of a charity fair. BARB:110
See also Dedication addresses-Exhibitions; Exhibitions; Festivals

FAITH
Abbott, L.
Faith and duty. REM 1:1; REEMB 1:1
Beecher, L.
Faith once delivered to the Saints. WPRA:99
Bullinger, H.
Sermon on faith. LEEW 4: 109
Conant, J.B.
Statement of faith. HOC: 182
Cranmer, T.
Good works annexed unto faith. CHAL 1:422; HAZO 4:1319; MAS 4:1319
Ephraem Syrus, Saint.
Pearl, or, seven rhythms on the Faith. LEEW 3:195
Niebuhr, R.
Adequate faith for the world crisis. BA 1947-48:227
O'Boyle, P.A.
Vision of faith. BA 1955-56: 151
Oursler, F. and others.
How can modern man find faith? HAR:480; MOA:484
Poole, R.
Earth is the Lord's. AN:5
Redfield, W.C.
Three graces. REEM 3:134; REEMB 3:135
See also Religion
Falconer, Sir Robert A.
Modern medicine, a dispeller of fear. KLEB:211
United States as a neighbor. REEM sup 1:285; REEMB 8:153
Falkland, Lucius Cary, 2nd Viscount
Ship-money-impeaching Lord Keeper Finch. BREW 6:95
Fallows, Samuel
Resurrection of Christ. THOU 2:99

FAME
Barnes, G. O.
Everlasting pyramids. BOA: 172; BOB:199
Be a "somebody." JAI:19
Conwell, R. H.
Acres of diamonds. BRAP: 70; HURG:202; IMMD:73; REEM 8:138; REEMA 4: 307; REEMB 13:140; WPRA:263
Damiani, Peter, Saint.
Secret of true greatness. BREW 4:380
Dawson, G.
Ill-used men. REEMA 7: 322
Day, J. E.
Introduces Robert H. Jackson, Associate Justice of Supreme Court of the United States. PRNE:4
Emerson, R. W.
Uses of great men. BREW 5:382
How to tell a big shot. NAT: 3
Huber, L. J.
Introducing a celebrity. BRH:112
King, T. S.
True greatness. REAC:83
Milliken, F.
Introducing a celebrity. BRH:145
Mussen, M.
Men of destiny. SHUC:348
Rice, M. S.
Value of great men. EXEE: 567
Roosevelt, T.
Greatness through strife. BOB:211
Van Dyke, H.
Of fame. LINM:219

FAMILY
Durant, W.
Crisis in American civilization. BA 1939-40:208
Family life. DR:236
Family Service Association of America. DR:273
Havighurst, R. J.
American family. ARNS: 154; MO:258; MOA:258
Huber, L. J.
Family man emcee. BRH: 347
Kaser, A. L.
Emcee at a family reunion. BRH:216
Matthews, M. A.
Man's duty to his family. THOU 3:430
Parents are teachers. JA:41
Who is your family? JA:91
See also Fathers; Fathers and sons; Home; Mothers; Mothers and daughters

FAMILY REUNIONS See Reunions

FAMILY SERVICE ASSOCIATION OF AMERICA See Family

FAR EAST See Orient
Farber, William O.
Changing concepts of public service. ARNS:233

FAREWELL ADDRESSES
Address to a minister about to depart for Europe. HAPR:97
Aelred, Saint
Farewell. BREW 1:99
Alderman, E. A.
Farewell to the class of 1920. ONEM:687; ONES: 33; SHU:20
Banks, E. C.
Farewell to a district manager. BRC:325
Benjamin, J. P.
Farewell to the Union. BREW 1:401; HICF:94
Bolivar, S.
At the Congress of Angostura. COP:386; COPA:386; COPB:386; PL:349
Braden, S.
Farewell speech to the Argentine people. ON:323
Choate, J. H.

FAREWELL ADDRESSES (cont.)
Farewell to Ambassador Bryce. REEM 1:273; REEMB 1:274
Clay, H.
Farewell address on leaving the Senate. KLEG:368
Commencement farewell address. REAC:55
Curran, J. P.
Farewell to the Irish Parliament. BREW 4:323; REEMA 12:769
Dickens, C.
English friendship for America. COP:615; COPB: 655; REEMA 1:405
D'Ooge, M. L.
Farewell to the University of Michigan. ONES:36
Edward VIII.
Farewell of former King Edward VIII. COP:705; COPB:732; ON:37; PE: 763; YE:177
Eisenhower, D. D.
Farewell address, January 17, 1961. FIP:365
Farewell address to the American soldier. GLAD: 175
Examples for words of farewell. BO:55-59
Farewell address. THOS:82
Farewell address by a country school teacher. AMEO 1:23
Farewell address (by retiring secretary of labor union) BED:81
Farewell address to a club member moving to another territory. WRA:175
Farewell dinner speeding the traveler on his way. EDGS: 328
Farewell message of the class president. PAIC:91
Farewell remarks. DICD:112; DICE:112
Farewell remarks. FRIE:339
Farewell speech at complimentary dinner to retiring member of school board after twenty years' service. WRA:177
Farewell speech to club by graduate. STOC:180
Farewell to retiring worthy matron-examples of. MORA:19
Farrar, F. W.
Farewell thoughts on America. REEMA 5:395
Garmanicus.
To his friends when dying. BRYW 2:240
Gilbert, E. J.
Emcee at a farewell bachelor party. BRH:296
Gregory of Nazianzus, Saint.
Last farewell. LEEW 3: 165
Hilton, M. E.
Farewell to college. GA: 55
Hutchins, R. M.
Farewell for students. BA 1951-52:129
Jackson, A.
Farewell address, 1837. BRYW 8:209; CHAL 4:298; HAZO 9:3715; MAS 9:3715
Johnson, H. S.
Farewell address to the employees of the National Recovery Administration. DOA:63
Keokuk.
Farewell speech. JON:96
Lee, R. E.
To the Army of Northern Virginia. ANG:370; FO: 212; KNAS:230; KNASA: 230; SMI:174
Lincoln, A.
Speech to 166th Ohio Regiment. BAKF:245
Farewell to Springfield. BRYW 9:238; CHAL 8:2; COP:315; COPA:315; COPB:315; DOA:237; FO: 172; HAZO 16:6611; HIB: 271; HIBS:490; KNAS:229; KNASA:229; MAS 16:6611 ONEM:690; PAR:305; PE:

508; PEA:508; REEM 10: 235; REEMB 11:247; YE: 176
Lloyd George, D.
Our commission (speech made in New York in 1923 at a farewell dinner given in his honor) LINM:334
Lytton, E. G. E. L. -L.
Farewell to Charles Dickens. REEM 2:371; REEMA 2:774; REEMB 2:384
MacArthur, D.
Farewell to the cadets (accepting Sylvanus Thayer award for service to his nation) HIB:58; LINP:150
Macready, W. C.
Farewell to the stage. REEMA 2:791
Mantle oration. AMEO 1:202
Marshall, T. R.
Farewell to the United States Senate. BRAC:271; REEM 7:277; REEMB 8:290
Mechelynck, C.
Farewell to American nurses. GA:57
Morley of Blackburn, J. M.
Positively last appearance. REEM 2:431, REEMB 2:447
Murrow, E.
Farewell to England. BA 1945-46:33
Napoleon I.
Farewell to the Old Guard. BRYW 7:176; CHAL 4:350; COP:87; COPA:87; COPB: 87; HAZO 9:3788; HIB:245; HIBS:489; LEEW 5:171; MAS 9:3789; PE:324; PEA: 324; PL:317; REEM 9:218; REEMA 11:295; REEMB 10: 225
Osler, W.
To the medical profession of the United States and Canada. KNAS:231; KNASA: 231; ONEM:684; ONES:29; REEM sup 2:264; REEMB 6:285
Outline of a farewell speech. BAKS:202
Phelps, E. J.
Farewell to England: to his friends in a foreign country. CHAL 10:186; HAZO 20:8407; MAS 20: 8407; ONEM:681; ONES: 25; REEM 3:55; REEMA 3:887; REEMB 3:56
Plenty Coups.
Farewell address. JON:122
Posner, G. A.
For the emcee at an office party or ceremony honoring a member leaving for army service. BRH:180
Shepardson, F. W.
Farewell to members at Sesquicentennial to Phi Beta Kappa. BRAC:275
Speech on the departure of a friend for Europe and his reply. BARB:91-92
Stubbs, W.
On resigning the Regius Professorship of History. KNAS:237; KNASA:237
Suggestions for preparation of a farewell address. BRA: 510; HIBS:280; LARW:112; RE:170; REAB:157; SOES: 23. With examples of. GA: 53; GLAD:172; YE:176
Suggestions for preparation of the farewell or retirement speech. BRAB:497
Thomas, M. C.
Farewell to Bryn Mawr. GA:57
Toast by one leaving a city. THOS:159
Truman, H. S.
Farewell to the nation. BA 1952-53:101; WPRC:305
Washington, G.
Farewell address. ANG: 194; BIR 1:219; BRE:101; BREA:99; BREW 10:94; BRYW 8:85; CAP25; CARP: 151; CHAL 2:468; CHEM 2: 13; COP:248; COPA:248; COPB:248; CROC:447; DOA: 228; FKA:185; FO:108; FOS: 23; FRY:10; HARS:152;

FAREWELL ADDRESSES (cont.)
HAZO 6:2511; HIB:247; HURG:44; LEEW 8:293; MAS 6:2511; ORAMA 1:31; PO:29; REEM 10:29; REEMA 15: 2036; REEMB 11:30; RID: 12; SAA:103; SMI:79
Williams, J. S.
Farewell to his friends. BRAC:274
See also Closing year addresses; Good-night speeches; Officers, retiring; Response to farewell; Retirement; Valedictory addresses
Farish, Ellen
I knew Mary. YR 10:25
Farkas, Emil
How much land does a man need? BRP:4:76; YR 5:289
Farley, James A.
Lincoln, the politician. ON: 348
Politics as a profession for businessmen. BA 1939-40: 266
FARLEY, JAMES A.
Introducing James A. Farley. MIA:52; NI:63
Spencer, F.
Introduces James A. Farley. PR:77
Farley, James I.
Debt, not charity. BOA:417
Farley, John M.
George Washington. CATA 1: 10

FARM BUREAUS: FARM RELIEF; FARMERS; FARMING See Agriculture
Farnsworth, Dale
Introducing an airline executive " a high school principal. BRC:220, 182
Farr, Newton
Introductory remarks on proposed Federal chainstore tax. HOC:33

FARRAGUT, DAVID GLASGOW
Choate, J. H.
Farragut. BREW 3:277; ORAMA 2:363
Farrand, Livingston
Education for business. EXEE:211
Work of a great physician. REEM sup 1:285; REEMB 6:123
Farrar, Frederick William
Farewell thoughts on America. REEMA 5:395
Funeral oration on Ulysses Simpson Grant. BREW 6: 100; CHAL 12:12; HAZO 22:9404; MAS 22:9404; ORBR 2:283; REEM 5:163; REEMA 8:464; REEMB 9: 198
Phillips Brooks. KNAS:70; KNASA:70
Poet and painter. REEMA 2: 479
Farrier, E.
Law of protection-installation address. THOU 3:384

FASCISM
Ames, K.
America beware. BRP 8: 50; YR 9:79
Estes, J.W., Jr.
Penny wise and pound foolish. YR 10:59
Franco, F.
To Falangist party council praising German, Italian and Spanish fascism. VO 1942-43:725
Mussolini, B.
Aims of the Fascist Party of Italy. HIB:220
Stoner, N. A.
Conceived in liberty. YR: 8:49
Thomas, N.
Communism and fascism: resemblances and differences. BART 2:93

FATHERS
Fathers. AMEO 2:21
Father's speech at home. ZEL:18

Huber, L. J.
Introducing the father of a new baby. BRH:80
If I were the father I ought to be: for a Parent-Teacher banquet. CON:27

FATHERS AND DAUGHTERS
Toasts to daughters by fathers. LEHS:53-54

FATHERS AND SONS
Announcing entertainment for father and son night. WRA: 28
Does your son have faith in you? (Friend asks a few pertinent questions.) ED: 361
Father and son. SCHS:126
Father-son banquet. NAT:14
Father-son banquet. NATS:2
Father and son banquet, by a father. EDGS:315
Father and son banquet, by a son. EDGS:317
Father-son banquet remarks. FRIE:209
Father to his son, just twenty-one. DU:167
Fathers and sons. LEHS:43
Fathers' and sons' banquet. DR:107
Father's sacrifice. LEHS:38
Johnny ought to know. LEHS: 41
Mother and daughter - father and son (short speech by a father) ED:355
Porter, H.
Sires and sons. REEM 3: 94; REEMA 3:935; REEMB 3:95
Response to the toast "Our dads" at a father and son banquet. WRA:64
Response to welcome of a guest speaker at a father-son banquet. HNWS:58
Sons (father talks about them) ED:357
Suggestions for toasts and speeches for a father-son banquet-theme "Fishing." AB:27-29
Talk to sons. FRIE:74
Toast "Our dads" at father and son banquet. WRA:56
Toasts to fathers by sons. LEHS:54-57
Toasts to sons by fathers. LEHS:58-60
Welcome to a guest speaker at a father-son banquet. HNWS:38

FATHERS' DAY
Father-son banquet. FRIE:58
Fathers' Day. NATM:23
Fathers' Day. NATS:19
Fathers' Day. SCHS:124
Fathers who understand. JA: 62
For Father's day. CON:97
In honor of "Dear old Dad." SOES:38
My father (Fathers' day address of welcome by a son) EDGS:318
My son: response by a father. EDGS:321
Posner, G. A.
Emcee at a Father's day party. BRH:238
Ramsey, H.
Introducing a Father's day speaker. BRC:77
Remembering the "forgotten man" on Father's day. DR: 145; LU:1195
Which kind of father? JA:65
Faulkinberry, Frank A.
International arbitration. SHUC:56
Faulkner, William
On accepting the Nobel prize, exhorts the young writers of the world. BOU:9; COPB:637; HAR:397; HIBS:508; HURG:291; PE: 814; PEA:814

Faunce, William H. P.
George Washington. BLAB: 296

Favre, Jules
Before the Corps Législatif. CHAL 7:409; HAZO 15:6550; MAS 15:6550
Fay, Chauncey
Way of life. BRP 6:42; NOR 1934:113

FEAR
Bliven, B.
Mid-century pessimists. NORR 3d ser:303
Huber, L. J.
Frightened emcee. BRH:349
Munshi, K. M.
Our greatest need, freedom from fear. ZU:18
Pearlman, G.
Kingdom of fear. NOR 1950:205
Stevenson, A. E.
Four fears. BA 1953-54:65
What do you do when you're scared? JAI:56

FEDERAL AID FOR EDUCATION See Education and state

FEDERAL FAIR TRADE EMPLOYMENT PRACTICES ACT See Labor laws and legislation

FEDERAL GOVERNMENT
Marshall, J.
McCulloch v. Maryland: opinion for the Supreme Court. BIR 2:2; BRE:128; BREA:119
See also United States Politics and government

FEDERAL TRADE COMMISSION
Humphrey, W. E.
Federal Trade Commission. BYRA:241; REEM sup 2:92; REEMB 5:10
Feidler, Ernest
Intolerant still. YR 1:85
Fellows, John R.
North and south. REEM 2:37; REEMA 2:482; REEMB 2:37

FELLOWSHIP See Friendship
Fells, Samuel
Teacher, the hope of America. BOA:147; BOB:186
Felton, Cornelius Conway
Delivering the statue of Daniel Webster to the Mayor of Boston. KNAS:156; KNASA:156
Fénelon, François De Salognac de la Mothe
Festival of the Epiphany. CHAL 2:113; HAZO 4:1650; MAS 4:1650
Nature as a revelation. BREW 6:114; HAZO 4:1643; MAS 4:1643
Sermon on prayer. LEEW 4:267
True and false simplicity. BREW 6:109; BRYW 7:74; HAZO 4:1636; MAS 4:1636; PL:272; REEM 9:82; REEMB 10:85
Fennell, D. L.
Welcoming National Safety Congress. ON:320
Fenner, Charles E.
Justice to Jefferson Davis. SHUO:139

FENTON, WALTER S.
Simmons, D. A.
Presents Walter S. Fenton. LY:143
Fergen, Geraldine
Blazing bulwarks. YR 7:289
Ferguson, Donald F.
Upon this rock. DO:180
Ferguson, Miriam Amanda (Wallace)
Women in business. REEM sup 1:311; REEMB 4:219
Fergusson, E. M.
Use of Rallying day. THOU 2:211
Ferris, Elmer E.
Art of personal contact. LINM:456
Ferris, Woodbridge N.

Give American youths a chance. EXEE:459
Fess, Simeon D.
Putnam festival. CORP:266

FESTIVALS
For a chess club festival. BARB:162
For a dramatic festival. BARB:170
For a fireman's festival. BARB:157
For a hatters' festival. BARB:188
For an iron manufacturers' festival. BARB:185
Herbert, A.
Advocates a festival for Britain. PE:812; PEA:812
Speech at a Christmas festival. HILL:469
Speech at an iron manufacturer's festival. HILL:484
Speech for a sportsman's festival. BARB:168
Speech for a strawberry festival in aid of a church or charitable institution. BARB:108
See also Fairs; Harvest festivals

FEUDALISM
Peterson, S.H.
Modern feudalism. TRUW:252
Fichte, Johann Gottlieb
Addresses to the German nation. -Same as his People and the Fatherland
People and the Fatherland. CROC:202; LEEW 5:175

FICTION See Literature

FIELD DAY See Sports
Field, Cyrus West
Story of the Atlantic cable. REEM 4:99; REEMA 8:473; REEMB 4:221
Field, David Dudley
Child and the state. BAKF:310
Cost of 'Blood and iron." BREW 6:129
Early Connecticut. REEM 2:45; REEMA 2:493; REEMB 2:45
In re Milligan-martial law as lawlessness. BREW 6:119
In the case of McCardle-necessity as an excuse for tyranny. BREW 6:127
On an international code of arbitration. CHAL 7:234; HAZO 15:6121; MAS 15:6121
Telegraph. REEM 2:48; REEMA 2:490; REEMB 2:48
Field, Henry M.
Our feast of tabernacles. THOU 2:294
Field, Lyman
One conspicuous failure of our government. YR 6:105
Fields, Harold
Alien in our midst. SAR:320
Fields, James Thomas
Masters of the situation. REEMA 5:423
Fierlinger, Zdenek
Broadcast on Czech-Polish discussions in Moscow. VO 1945-46:373
Fieweger, William H.
Social security. YR 8:133

FIFTH COLUMN
Cutten, G.B.
Fifth column of civilization. HOC:158
See also Sixth column
"Fifty-four forty or fight" See Oregon
Filene, Edward A.
Adult education in this machine age. DOA:192
Way our for New England. LINM:52
Why men strike. BYRA:151; REEM 4:115; REEMB 4:237

FILLING STATION MANAGER

FILLING STATION MGR. (cont.)
See Business men

FINANCE
Holman, W.S.
Economy in public expenditures. REEMA 13:1220
Rosebery, A.P.P.
Steaks from the living ox. BREW 9:108
Sherman, J.
General financial policy of the government. BREW 9: 212

---- UNITED STATES
Sherman, J.
Financial situation. CHAL 10:202; HAZO 20:8441; MAS 20:8441; REEMA 15: 1904
See also Independent treasury; Inflation (finance); Tariff

FINANCIERS See Banks and banking
Finch, Charles A.
Failure of success. BRP 1: 90; YR 2:169
War prayer. BRP 1:49
Finch, Francis M.
Office of the law (assuming chair of Presidency of New York State Bar Association) REEMA 2:496
Finch, Sir Heneage See Nottingham, H.F.

FINCH OF FORDWICH, JOHN FINCH, 1st BARON
Falkland, L.C.
Ship-money-impeaching Lord Keeper Finch. BREW 6:95
Findlay, John V.L.
Lincoln at Gettysburg. SHUO: 167

FINE ARTS See Art and artists

FINLAND
Davis, E.
Finland surrenders. BA 1939-40:63
Dobeln, G.K.
Address to the Finnish troops. CHAL 4:42; HAZO 8:3335; MAS 8:3335
Vyshinsky, A.L.
On negotiations with Finland for an armistice. VO 1944-45:185

FINLEY, JOHN
Introducing John Finley. NI: 138; NIA:104
Finley, John Huston
City (New York) and the flag. REEM 7:139; REEMB 8: 176
John Brown. HARSO:202; WERN 42:150
Latitude and longitude. REEM 2:51; REEMB 2:51
Presenting a medal to Col. Lindbergh. ONEC:38
Thirtieth man. PROS:67; SHU: 178

FIRE PREVENTION
Fire prevention at home (outline of speech) MOA:315
Kaser, A.L.
Introducing a speaker on fire prevention. BRH:107, 118

FIREMEN
Address at a banquet of a volunteer fire department. AMEO 2:149
Firemen, by one of the fire-fighters. EDGS:113
For a firemen's festival. BARB:157
Reception of a visiting fire company and reply. HILL: 479
Smith, H.
Introducing a city fireman. BRC:64
Speech of mayor at a volunteer firemen's review. HILL:469
Visit of a fire company-recep tion speech addresses to the foreman, reply by fore

man. BARB:115, 116
Volunteer firemen, by the president of the village. EDGS:111
Firestone, Harvey S.
Prosperity and better business methods. ONEC:274
Fischer, John H.
Educational problems of segregation and desegregation of public schools. BA 1962-63:111
Fischer, Louis and others (G. V. Denny, Jr. and H. H. Velde)
What are the real issues in our fight against Communism? HAR:196
Fish, Frederick Perry
Edison and the electric light. REEM sup 1:313; REEMB 4:251
Fish, Hamilton
Have faith in America. BOB: 96
Fish, Stuyvesant
Economy. REEM 4:128; REEMB 4:258

FISH HATCHERIES
Allen, J. M.
Appropriation for a fish hatchery. CHAL 14:126; YE:320
Macdonald, J. A.
On Canadian fisheries. CHAL 9:26; HAZO 18:7512; MAS 18:7512

FISHBEIN, MORRIS
Introducing Morris Fishbein. NI:196
Fisher, Charles T., Jr.
Presents George C. Kenney. LY:159
Fisher, George J. B.
Demolition bombs. ON:233
Fisher, H. D.
Grace of thankfulness. THOU 2:291
Fisher, Henry Johnson
Presenting the Cheney-Ives gateway to Yale University. KNAS:160; KNASA:160; ONEM:710; ONES:41
Fisher, Herbert Albert Laurens
English heritage. BEA:187
Fisher, John
Jeopardy of daily life. BREW 6:136
Fisher, Mrs. John W.
Praying mantis. BUT:186; BUTB:186
Fisher, Lillian
Marijuana peddlers. YR 8:215
Fisher, Mildred
Telemaniacs. JUD:147

FISHING
Anglers' club, by an enthusiastic fisherman. EDGS:383
Day, J. E.
Introduces Lee Wulff who presented fishing and hunting films. PRNE:12
Drummond, R.
Emcee at an Izaak Walton conservation club meeting. BRH:233
Huber, L. J.
Introducing a fisherman. BRC:179
Izaak Walton Clubs. SCHS: 275
Kaser, A. L.
Introducing an expert fisherman. BRC:97
McGovern, S.
Introducing a fisherman. BRC:184
Presentation of prize to champion fisherman (humorous) HAPR:170
Suggestions for toasts and speeches for a father-son banquet-theme "Fishing." AB:27-29
Fiske, Arthur W.
Underworld on top. BRP 7:49
Fiske, Haley
Fifty years of life insurance. BYRA:165; REEM sup 1: 320; REEMB 4:266
Fiske, John
Columbus the navigator (400th anniversary of discovery of America by Christopher

Fiske, John (cont.)
Columbus) CHAL 13:442; REEM 5:171; REEMA 8: 490; REEMB 9:206
Fitz, Rachel K.
Five minute talk: Radcliffe as a matrimonial training school. BAKF:417
Fitzgerald, J. M.
Temperaments-the analysis of human talents. EXEE:421
Flack, Gene
Responds to an introduction. PRNE:59

FLACK, GENE
McDonough, J. J.
Introduces Gene Flack, Sales Counsel and Advertising Director, Sunshine Biscuit Company. PRNE:30

FLAG DAY
Address for Flag Day exercises. AMEO 2:208
American flag. DU:143
Beecher, H.W.
Raising the flag over Fort Sumter. BREW 1:352; CHAL 8:395; HAZO 17:7306; MAS 17:7306; ORAMA 2: 295; PL:672; REEM 10: 239; REEMA 11:180; REEMB 11:251; THOU 1: 305
Birkins, H. H.
Our flag. THOU 1:292
Burnett, H. E.
Americans rallying 'round the national flag. THOU 1: 301
Closing speech at Flag Day ceremonies. BEDA:97
Dedicating flagpole (at Flag Day ceremonies) BEDA:96
Flag day address. THOS:34
Flag day (address to a school) ED:57
Flag day-June 14. DR:156
For Flag Day. STOC:135; STON:141
Harrison, B.
Cultivating love for the flag. THOU 1:299
Headley, J. T.
Our flag in history. THOU 1:284
Lane, F. K.
Makers of the flag. CARP: 172; DOA:224; ONES:140; PROS:98; REEM 7:224; REEMB 8:244; SHU:157
Maxfield, W. R.
Notable flag-raising. THOU 1:295
No flag except "Old Glory." THOU 1:303
Old Glory. DAVC:431
Opening speech for Flag Day ceremonies. BEDA:95
Origin of national and patriotic songs. THOU 1:287
Our country. DAVC:429
Prosser, W. A.
Beautiful and glorious banner. THOU 1:304
Robertson, R. S.
Widespread influence of the flag. THOU 1:294
Roosevelt, F. D.
Flag day address, June 13, 1942. VO 1942-43:344
Stars and stripes. DAVC:430
Voice of the flag. DAVC:436
Voice of the flag (for Flag Day and other patriotic occasions) EDGS:37
Wilson, W.
Flag day address. LEW:39; REEM 11:217; REEMB 12: 232; SAA:263; SMI:258

FLAGS
Beecher, H.W.
American flag. PROS:17
Our national emblem. SHU: 173; THOU 1:289
Beveridge, A. J.
March of the flag. CHAL 14:426; FUL:27; HAZO 25: 10979; HIB:43; HICF:188; LA:125; MAS 25:10979; PROS:58; REEM 10:358; REEMA 11:224; REEMB 11: 372; WERN 42:89; WPRA: 352
Brown, W. R.

Flag. PROS:28
Bruce, W.
Flag. BLAA:191; BLAB:191
Business man's allegiance to the flag. AMEO 2:64
Cavanaugh, J.
Our flag. CATA 1:36
Couch, D.N.
Return to the flags. ONEM:708
Davis, J.F.
Tribute to the American Flag. WAGN:122
Dix, J.A.
Flag-the old flag. REEM 1:407; REEMA 1:410; REEMB 1:413
Finley, J.H.
City (New York) and the flag. REEM 7:139; REEMB 8:176
Fleming, W.H.
Flag of the Union. PROS:35
Graves, J.T.
Our country's flag. WERN 42:33
Hanz, J.E.
Cross and the flag. CATA 1:41
Hawley, J.R.
On the flag and the eagle. CHAL 11:104; HAZO 21:8955; MAS 21:8955
Hill, B.H.
Flag of our fathers. HARSO:53
Stars and stripes. SOU 9:354
Hughes, C.E.
What the flag means. BOA:293; BOB:79
Lee, F.
Flag of the Union forever. REEM 2:318; REEMA 2:710; REEMB 2:322; SHUO:241
Lodge, H.C.
American flag-not the dollar. BOA:294; BOB:79
Our flag. AMEO 1:217
Owsley, A.
Respect the flag. PROS:33; REEMB 8:331
Peck, G.R.
Sovereignty follows the flag. BLAA:231; BLAB:231; FUL:245,247
Porter, H.
Reverence for the flag. BLAA:92; BLAB:92
Presentation of flag. SOES:37
Presentation of a flag to a lodge or patriotic organization and response by the presiding officer. HE:120, 121
Putnam, R.B.
National emblem. BOA:289; BOB:77
Our flag. WERN 42:189
Staple, A.G.
Toast to the flag. PROS:43
Tribute to the flag. NESA:235
Truman, H.S.
Speech at American flag raising exercises in Berlin. VO 1945-46:388
Wallace, L.
Return to the flags (presenting battle flags to the state) ONEM:702; REEM 7:409; REEMA 9:1121; REEMB 8:424
Watterson, H.
Star-spangled banner. HARSO:269; PROS:24
Williams, J.S.
Who will haul down that flag? BRAC:206
Wilson, W.
Essence of the flag. BOA:297; BOB:81
See also Acceptance speeches-Flags; Fourth of July; Presentation speeches-Flags
Flanagan, E.J.
Boys Town. BART 3:55
Flanders, Ralph E.
Colossal innocence in the

Flanders, Ralph E. (cont.)
United States Senate. WPRC:301
Flannery, Edward A.
Is Socialism a home destroyer? CATA 2:57
Flavel, John
From a coronation sermon. HAZO 4:1598; MAS 4:1598
Flaxman, John
Physical and intellectual beauty. BREW 6:139
Fléchier, Esprit
Death of Turene. BREW 6:146; HAZO 4:1629; LEEW 4:245; MAS 4:1629; PL:255
Fleetwood, Christian A.
Negro as a soldier. DUNM:187
Fleischer, C.
Address delivered at Faneuil Hall on 250th anniversary of the settlement of the Jews in the United States. TWJ:89
Fleming, Denna Frank
Irrepressible issue. BA 1943-44:138
What is it that we fight? BA 1942-43:67
Who says it can't be done? BA 1941-42:265
Fleming, Dorothy
Reminiscence on starvation. AN:82
Fleming, William H.
Flag of the Union. PROS:35
Solution of the race problem. SHUO:269
Flood, Henry
Renunciation speech. CHAL 2:445; HAZO 6:2543; KET:96; MAS 6:2543
Vindication of the Volunteers. KET:96

FLOOD CONTROL
Atkinson, M.
Rivers did not forget. YR:9:61
Sanderson, J.K.
Plan or perish. BRP 8:108; YR 9:69

FLOODS
Lindbergh, A.M.
Experiences in the Chinese flood. DOA:128

FLOOR COVERING DEALERS
See Business men

FLORISTS
McGovern, S.
Introducing a florist. BRC:60
Florus.
Was Virgil an orator or a poet? LEEW 2:307
Flouton, Allen Brown
System of child labor-the modern minotaur. SHUC:332
Flowers, Montaville
Have faith in America. EXEE:621

FLOWERS
Thanksgiving bouquet. LEHS:7
See also Gardens and gardening; Presentation speeches-Flowers

---- LANGUAGE OF
Flowers and auxiliaries: an inspirational speech for auxiliary members or chapter members, changeable for a membership speech or a testimonial speech. BAI:131
Foch, Ferdinand
Napoleon. COP:144; COPA:144; COPB:144; REEM 5:183; REEMB 9:219
To the French Academy (tribute to the French soldier) REEM 11:422; REEMB 12:445

FOCH, FERDINAND
King, W.L.M.
To Marshall Foch. REEM 7:202; REEMB 8:229
Pepper, G.W.
Introducing Marshall Foch. LY:153; NESA:189

Poincare, R.
Eulogy on services of Marshall Foch to his country and the Allies. BEA:353
Fogel, Sam
We, You, and I. NOR 1945:11
Folk, Joseph W.
Americans for America. BOA: 204; BOB:173

FOLK-LORE
Conway, M.D.
Demonology and English folk-lore. REEMA 4:287
Fonville, DeRoy R.
Public conscience. SHUC:166

FOOD
Gregory, A.C.
Introducing a grocer (supermarket manager) BRC: 258
Grocer-speech before a club. WRA:238
Kaser, A. L.
Introducing a food specialist. BRC:111
McGovern, S.
Introducing a baby food executive. BRC:44
Olds, L.
Introducing a meat dealer. BRC:201
Roosevelt, F.D.
Message to Congress on the food program. VO 1943-44:482
Statement on continuance of the combined British-Canadian-American production, raw materials and food boards. VO 1945-46:38
Wallace, H.A.
Address at Cleveland, October 27, 1943. VO 1943-44:469
See also United Nations Conference on Food and Agriculture, 1943

FOOD SUPPLY
Elder, A.L.
Chemist looks at the world population explosion. BA 1960-61:165
Faigan, Z.
United States obligation for feeding Europe's millions. HOD:106
Foord, John
Land o' cakes. REEMA 2:500

FOOTBALL
Adelman, A.
Merely players. BRP 8:86; NOR 1937:29
Buchanan, L.
Army and Navy football. WERN 54:164
Football pep meeting. SCHS: 131
Football smoker. SCHS:133
Football (toast to the winning team) ED:428
Hall, E.K.
Football. REEM sup 1:385; REEMB 2:144
Kaser, A.L.
Introducing a football coach. BRC:94
McLain, H.O.
Introduces Alvin N. "Bo" McMillin, football coach. PR:114
Outline for a speech "Pigskin fans." BARR:99
Smith, R.L.
Greatest game in the world. BRP:20
Stone, H.L.
Introduces James Conzelman, football coach. PR: 38

FOOTE'S RESOLUTION See Foot's Resolution

FOOT'S RESOLUTION, 1829
Benton, T.
On Foot's resolution. LEEW 9:143
Hayne, R.Y.
On Foot's Resolution (January 19, 1830) CLAW:29
On Foot's Resolution (January 21, 1830) BREW 6:404;

FOOT'S RESOLUTION (cont.)
BRYW 9:3; CHAL 5:459; CLAW:104; CODS:475; CODSA:475; HAZO 12: 4969; JOHA 1 pt. 1:233; LEEW 9:151; MAS 12:4969; ORAMA 2:97; REEMA 13: 1170; SOU 9:342
Webster, D.
On Foot's Resolution (January 20, 1830) CLAW:41
Reply to Hayne. BAAMP: 54; BIR 2:66; BRAO:185; BRE:153; BREA:137; BREW 10:112; BRYW 9:38; CAP:45; CHAL 5:171; CHEM 2:107; CLAW:117; CLAY:87, 122; CODS:348; CODSA:349; COP:270; COPA:270; COPB:270; FKA:17; FRY:24; FULB: 228; HARS:212; HARSO: 330; HAY:152; HAZO 10: 4303; HIBS:447; JOHA 1 pt. 1:248; KLEG:102; LEEW 9:177; MAS 10:4303; ONEM:211; ORAMA:2:5; PAR:179; PE:340; PEA: 340; PL:627; REEM 10: 73; REEMA 15:2053; REEMB 11:74; SAA:144; SHAH:146
Foraker, J. B.
Trusts. BLAA:19; BLAB:19
Foraker, Joseph B.
Outline of speech at the dedication of Ohio's monument to the Andrews raiders, at Chattanooga. PITT:88
Ford, Benson
Moral basis for our leadership. MIA:388
Ford, Guy Stanton
Presents Christopher Morley. LY:70
Ford, Henry II
Challenge of human engineering. BRY:438
Free world can't trade on a one-way street. BA 1952-53:131
Presents Elmo Roper. LY:96
Ford, John J.
Catholicism and patriotism. CATA 1:187
Testimony of reason to the immortality of the soul. CATA 2:231
Ford, Kenny L.
Presentation of award to Charles F. Ketteri ng. YE: 121
Ford, Nick Aaron
What are you Negroes fighting for? ON:194
Ford, Simeon
Bank-notes. NESA:131
Me and Sir Henry. REEMA 2: 505
Palm Beach. REEM 2:58; REEMB 2:58
Run on the banker. REEM 2: 55; REEMA 2:507; REEMB 2:55
Ford, Tirey LaFayette
National issues. WAGN:374
Tribute to William McKinley. WAGN:371

FOREFATHERS' DAY
America's debt to Holland. THOU 1:324
Burrell, D. J.
Forefathers' Day. THOU 1: 328
Butler, B. F.
Humorous response to the toast "Our forefathers." PITT:50
Conant, J.B.
Response to toast "Forefather's day." HOC:30
Depew, C. M.
Forefathers were God's nobility. THOU 1:351
Duffield, H.
Faith and courage. SHU:30
Eliot, C.W.
Truth and light. REEM 2: 13; REEMB 2:13
Gregg, D.
Debt we owe to the Dutch. THOU 1:318
Hadley, A. T.
Forefathers' Day. BLAA: 83; BLAB:83
Hale, E. E.

Ruling sentiment of the Pilgrims. THOU 1:334
Kelman, J.
Puritanism today. REEM 2:286; REEMB 2:290
Lincoln, J.
Cape Cod folks. REEM 2:324; REEMB 2:328
Low, S.
Their ideal of education. THOU 1:353
Lowden, F. O.
Eternal vigilance. REEM 2:339; REEMB 2:343
Our debt to Puritan and Pilgrim. THOU 1:326
Plymouth and its surroundings. THOU 1:358
Prentiss, S. S.
On New England's Forefathers' Day. BREW 8:372
Raymond, A. V.
Dutch as neighbors. THOU 1:344
Robinson, D. C.
Their heritage to us (Pilgrims) THOU 1:354
Russell (ex-Judge) Benefits of its observance. THOU 1:316
Talmage, T. D.
Behold the American. COP:646; KLEG:160; REEM 3:307; REEMA 3:1122; REEMB 3:324; THOU 1:339
Van Dyke, H.
Advantages of a mixed ancestry. THOU 1:329
Wayland, H. L.
Our New England forefathers. THOU 1:321

FOREIGN AID IN EDUCATION
See Economic assistance, American

FOREIGN AID PROGRAM See Economic assistance, American; World War, 1939-1945-United States-Aid to Great Britain

FOREIGN MINISTERS CONFERENCES See Berlin Conference; Council of Foreign Ministers; Moscow Conference of Foreign Ministers

FOREIGN POPULATION See Immigration and emigration

FOREIGN VISITORS IN EUROPE
Smith, M.C.
Impatience and generosity. BRAP:55

FOREMEN See Employees

FORESTERS
Cabaniss, G. W.
United States forest ranger. BRAP:28

FORESTERS, ANCIENT ORDER OF
Davis, E.
Annual church service. THOU 3:272
Forester's Island. THOU 3:256
Loud, G. B.
Memorial address (Foresters) THOU 3:277
Montague, W. F.
"Our guest;" reply to the toast. THOU 3:265
Oronhytekha, W. F.
Foresters in Australia. THOU 3: 262
Regaining the loss. THOU 3:283

FORESTS AND FORESTRY
Caldwell, J. W.
Appalachian Forest Reserve. SHUO:280
Coleman, W.
Introducing a forester. BRC:217
See also Conservation of natural resources
Forgan, David R.
America and the allied debts. EXEE:510

FORGIVING
Magee, W. C.

FORGIVING (cont.)
Ethics of forgiveness. HAZO 19:8315; MAS 19: 8315

FORSYTH, DAVID D.
McConnell, F.J.
Eulogy on David D. Forsyth. BRAC:368
Forsythe, Carl
For those yet to be. ASHF: 221
Forten, James
Late bill before the Senate of Pennsylvania. WOON:42
---- and others (R. Perrott)
Address to the humane and benevolent inhabitants of the city and county of Philadelphia. WOON:52
Fortino, Alfred
Insidious germ. YR 9:185

FORTUNES See Wealth

FORUMS See American Forum of the Air
Fosdick, Harry Emerson
Being civilized to death. BA 1937-38:210
Christian conscience about war. BAAMP:274; BRAC: 222; HICF:731; PL:776; REEM sup 1:333; REEMB 6:126
Ethical problems of neutrality. BA 1939-40:427
Jesus' ethical message confronts the world. BA 1938-39:223
Military conscription. ON:168
Rough riders. SHUC:208
Shall Fundamentalists win? WPRC:97

FOSDICK, HARRY EMERSON
Gossett, W.T.
Presents Harry Emerson Fosdick. LY:167
Fosdick, Raymond B.
"Middletown" - and the way out. SAR:22
Fossey, Leighton
Shoot to kill. YR 8:207
Foster, E. (Mrs.)
License system. THOU 1:557
Foster, George Eulas
Defense and protection. CHAL 14:117; HAZO 25:10634; MAS 25:10634
Foods for the homeland. CHAL 14:120; HAZO 25: 10637; MAS 25:10637
Prudent compromise. CHAL 14:124; HAZO 25:10641; MAS 25:10641
Foster, John
Access to God. HAZO 9:3861; MAS 9:3861
Foster, William Trufant
Government cannot control prices. ON:114
Should students study? BRY: 465; SAR:64

FOUNDERS' DAY See Anniversaries

FOUR-H CLUBS
Four H clubs: what they are and why we should support them. DR:111

FOUR POWER PACT See Peace

FOURTH OF JULY
Adams, B.
Beginning of government. THOU 1:207
Adams, J.Q.
On American independence, July 4, 1793. LEEW 9:23
Anderson, E.
July fourth address (1951) BUT:248
Armitage, T.
Our national influence. THOU 1:212
Bacon, L.
Grand mission of America. THOU 1:201
Our heritage, how gained-our duty. THOU 1:223
Balfour, A.J.B.
Fourth of July in London. COP:204; COPA:204;

COPB:204; REEM 11:233; REEMB 12:248
Beck, J. M.
Fourth of July. REEM 1: 83; REEMB 1:78
Bolton, H.W.
True patriotism. THOU 1: 200
Booth, N.
Michigan Bluff oration. WAGN:36
Boudinot, E.
Mission of America. BREW 2:181; CHAL 3:90; HAZO 7:2658; MAS 7:2658
Brewer, D. J.
Political and personal liberty. THOU 1:210
Brief address for a Fourth of July dinner. BARB:97
Brooks, P.
Fourth of July. BAKF:185
Buckley, J. M.
Demands of the hour. THOU 1:224
Carson, H. L.
American liberty. BREW 3:147; RID:67
Cheney, W. A.
America. WAGN:107
Choate, R.
On American nationality (82nd anniversary of American independence) CHAL 6: 318; HAZO 13:5493; MAS 13:5493
Churchill, W. L. S.
American Independence Day. REEM 7:105
Cook, J.
Ultimate America. BREW 4: 153
Cost of the Revolution. THOU 1:235
Costly heritage. THOU 1:197
Daggett, D.
Sun-beams may be extracted from cucumbers, but the process is tedious. WPRA:37
Day we celebrate. THOU 1:188
Dougherty, D.
On democracy. CHAL 11:92; HAZO 21:8935; MAS 21: 8935
Douglas, F.
What to the slave is the Fourth of July? DUNM:41
Douglass, F.
Slavery: speech at Rochester, July 5, 1852. PE: 477; PEA:477; WOON:197
Ely, E. S.
Duty of Christian freemen to elect Christian leaders. BL:548
Evarts, W. M.
English and French experiment. THOU 1:231
Progress of divine ordinance of government. THOU 1:229
What the age owes to America. CHAL 9:238; HAZO 18: 7784; MAS 18:7784; REEMA 13:962; REEMB 8:144; THOU 1:225
Everett, E.
History of liberty. BREW 6:64; HAZO 12:5080; LEEW 10:21; MAS 12:5080; ORAMA 2:151; PL:631; REEM 10:59; REEMA 13: 972; REEMB 11:60
Fourth of July. HILL:470
Fourth of July. NATS 21
Fourth of July address. AMEO 2:9
Fourth of July address. BURS:188
Fourth of July address. CRAI: 426
Fourth of July address. THOS: 28
Fourth of July-birth of American independence. DR:161; LU:1197
Fourth of July celebration abroad. HILL:489
Fourth of July (for patriotic meetings) EDGS:35
Fourth of July salute. FRIE: 100
Fourth of July (speaker quotes from the Declaration of Independence) ED:61

FOURTH OF JULY (cont.)
Graves, J.T.
Our country's birthday. FUL:131, 134, 137
Great ideas that should be emphasized on Independence Day. THOU 1:190
Gruening, E.
Independence Day address. BA 1959-60:31
Hammond, J.H.
Fourth of July. REEM 2: 157; REEMB 2:159
Happy is the nation. JAS:72
Hecker, F.K.F.
Liberty in the New Atlantis. BREW 6:420
Hoover, H.C.
At the Brussels Exposition. BA 1958-59:56
Independence Day address. DAVC:445
James, H., Sr.
Social significance of our institutions. BL:231
Kazmark, L.A.
Honoring a great American day. PROS:10
Keeping alive our natural principles. THOU 1:194
Lee, J.
Religious repose and future of our country. THOU 1: 218
Lift up your hearts. DAVC: 447
Loose, J.W.
Liberty we need now. THOU 1:215
McKeldin, T.
Today is the Fourth of July. MCK:142
Mulligan, B.J.
Mission of the church: Fourth of July address. CATA 1:45
National holidays. THOU 1:184
Nation's birthday-past, present and future. THOU 1:185
O'Bryne, J.
Matchless story of American history. THOU 1:203
O'Donnell, T.J.
Honor the flag. SHU:69
Outline of a speech in response to the toast 'The day we celebrate." PITT: 39
Outline of a spread-eagle speech in a foreign land. PITT:40
Page, W.H.
Fourth of July in London. REEM 11:231; REEMB 12: 248
Parker, C.
Different motives of the settlers. THOU 1:222
Freedom of America the result of an open Bible. THOU 1:204
Parmele, L.
Independence Day. REAC: 79
Proper and improper modes of celebrating the day. THOU 1:198
Ramsey, D.
Advantages of American independence. CHEM 1:95
Reid, W.
Fourth of July. REEM 3: 144; REEMB 3:145
Riley, W.B.
Patriot's inheritance-its dangers. THOU 1:232
Roosevelt, F.D.
Broadcast on Independence day, 1941. ON:147; VO 1941:336

Independence day statement, 1942. VO 1942-43:388
Signers of the Declaration. THOU 1:226
Speech for a Fourth of July in a foreign land. BARB: 103
Suggestions for responding to Fourth of July speech. PITT:37
Sumner, C.
True grandeur of nations. BREW 9:317; CHAL 8:284; CODS:487; CODSA:487; HAZO 17:7017; LEEW 10:

113; MAS 17:7017; PL:652; RID:36
Toast to the United States on the Fourth of July. EDGS: 39
Whipple, E. P.
Patriotic oration. CHAL 9: 398; HAZO 19:8022; MAS 19:8022
Williams, P.
Slavery and colonization. WOON:77
Willkie, W. L.
American liberty. COP: 555; COPB:547
Wilson, W.
Meaning of the Declaration of Independence. BAKS:166; BOAM:109; ONEM:554; ONES:129
Mount Vernon's message to mankind. SMI:255
Patriotic speech. DOA:288
Winthrop, R. C.
Men of 1776. THOU 1:213
Our American age. THOU 1:205
Trust to succeeding generations. THOU 1:208
Wright, F.
Fourth of July oration. PE:359; PEA:359
See also Liberty; United States-DECLARATION OF INDEPENDENCE
Fowler, Charles H.
Impeachment of alcohol. THOU 1:574
Fox, Andrew N.
Advertising, the dynamo of civic and commercial life. EXEE:597
Fox, Charles James
Against Warren Hastings. BREW 6:164
Character of the Duke of Bedford. BREW 6:154
Constituents and members.-Same as his In favor of Mr. Grey's motion for Parliamentary reform
Foreign policy of Washington. BRYW 4:35
In favor of Mr. Grey's motion for Parliamentary reform. EMS 2:134; GOOD: 515
On peace with France.-Same as his On the rejection of Napoleon's overtures
On the British defeat in America. BRYW 4:29; FULB:39
On the East India Bill. BREW 6:164; BRYW 4:32; GOOD: 462; PEA:171; PL:418
On the rejection of Napoleon's overtures. ADR 2:108; BRTH:150; BRTHA:150; BRYW 4:37; CHAL 3:198; CODS:277; CODSA:277; COP:172; COPA:172; COPB:172; FULB:40; GOOD:529; HAY:95; HAZO 7:2827; MAS 7:2827; ORBR 1:291; PAUF 1:166; PE:288; PEA:288; REEM 9:162; REEMA 13:994; REEMB 10:169
On the Russian armament. GOOD:500
On the use of secret influence to defeat his East India Bill. GOOD:474; LEEW 6: 317
On the Westminster scrutiny. GOOD:481
Peace with France, House of Commons, February 23, 1800.-Same as his On the rejection of Napoleon's overtures
Relief of Protestant dissenters. BEA:191
Religious liberty, May 8, 1789 speech. EMS 2:6
Religious liberty, May 11, 1792 speech. EMS 2:12
Right to commit. EMS 1:219
Right to public meeting (November 10, 1795 speech) EMS 2:19
Right to public meeting (May 22, 1797 speech) EMS 2:22
War and peace.-Same as his On the rejection of Napole-

Fox, C.J. (cont.)
on's overtures
Washington as president. THOU 1:159
Foy, Fred C.
Responds to an introduction by B. Stuart Weyforth, Jr. PRC:29

FOY, FRED C.
Weyforth, B.S., Jr.
Introduces Fred C. Foy, Chairman of the Board and President of the Koppers Company. PRC:28
France, Anatole
Wanted-"Good Europeans." BREW 6:167

FRANCE
Bedford, A.C.
France in the reconstruction period. REEM 4:32; REEMB 4:72
Carnot, L.N.M.
Against imperialism in France. BREW 3:129; BRYW 7:179; CHAL 3:420; COP:87; COPA:87; COPB:87; HAZO 8:3157; MAS 8:3157; PE:312; PEA:312; REEMA 12:510
DeGaullle, C.
At the opening session of the Provisional Consultative Assembly at Algiers. VO 1943-44:504
Before the French Provisional Consultative Assembly on the future of France. VO 1944-45:322
Broadcast on French policy in war and peace. VO 1945-46:54
Declaration January 2, 1943. VO 1943-44:5
Favre, J.
Before the Corps Législatif. CHAL 7:409; HAZO 15:6550; MAS 15:6550
Giraud, H.
To the Alsace-Lorraine Society. VO 1943-44:114
----and others.
General Charles DeGaulle's and General Henri Giraud's appeal to France, June 4, 1943. VO 1943-44:226
Guizot, F.P.G.
Democracy in France. PL:318
Hugo, V.M.
Liberty tree in Paris. BREW 7:96; MEAR:117
King, W.L.M.
France and Canada. REEM 7:198; REEMB 8:225
Lamartine, A.M.L.
To a deputation of Poles, 1848. BRYW 7:187; CHAL 5:425; HAZO 12:4936; MAS 12:4936; PL:331
Millerand, A.
Semicentennial of the French Republic. BREW 8:148; REEM 11:423; REEMB 12:447
Petain, H.
Address November 19, 1943. VO 1943-44:553
Address to the French people, August 12, 1941. VO 1941:368
Broadcast, April 4, 1943. VO 1943-44:154
"I need your confidence." COP:494; COPA:494; COPB:464
Speech to French people, March 15, 1941. VO 1941:212
Pitt, W., 1759-1806
Against French Republicanism. BREW 8:339; BRTH:140; BRTHA:140; HAZO 8:3361; MAS 8:3361
Poincaré, R.
France and world-empire. BREW 8:360
Rouget de L'Isle and the Marseillaise. BREW 8:355
Reynaud, P.
France will live again. COP:493; COPA:493; COPB:463
Roosevelt, F.D.

Statement on United States recognition of the French Committee of National Liberation. VO 1943-44:311
Thiers, L. A.
On the wastefulness of imperial France. PL:322
See also European War, 1914-1918; Paris; World War, 1939-1945 - France

---- ARMY
Napoleon I.
Address to his army at the beginning of the Italian campaign. CHAL 4:344; COP:85; COPA:85; COPB: 85; HAZO 9:3782; MAS 9: 3782; REEM 9:215; REEMA 11:290; REEMB 10:222
Proclamation to his army. BRYW 7:168; CHAL 4:344; HAZO 9:3782; MAS 9:3782; PE:280; PEA:280; REEM 9:215; REEMA 11:290; REEMB 10:222
To his soldiers after the War of the Third Coalition. CHAL 4:348; HAZO 9:3786; MAS 9:3786; REEMA 11:293
To his soldiers during the siege of Mantua. CHAL 4: 347; HAZO 9:3785; MAS 9: 3784; REEMA 11:293
To his soldiers on the conclusion of the first Italian campaign. CHAL 4:347; HAZO 9:3785; MAS 9:3785; REEMA 11:292
To the soldiers on entering Milan. BRYW 7:169; CHAL 4:345; COP:86; COPA:86; COPB:86; CROC:333; ESEH:196; HAZO 9:3783; HIB:41; MAS 9:3783; LEEW 5:167; PL:315; REEM 9:216; REEMA 11: 291; REEMB 10:223

---- COLONIES
DeGaulle, C.
Political problem of North Africa. VO 1943-44:37
See Lebanon; Syria

---- CONSTITUTION, 1789-1799
Gambetta, L.
On the Constitutional laws 1878. REEMA 13:1043
Speech upon Constitutional laws 1875. CHAL 13:159; HAZO 24:10103; MAS 24: 10103
Guadet, M. E.
On maintaining the Constitution. LEEW 5:135
Puel, M. R.
French Constitution. LEIO: 83

---- FOREIGN RELATIONS-MEXICO
Hanna, K. A.
Roles of the South in the French intervention in Mexico. TIN:298
Theirs, L. A.
Mexico and Louis Napoleon's policies. BREW 9:389; HAZO 13:5369; MAS 13:5369; REEMA 15:1974

---- FOREIGN RELATIONS-UNITED STATES
Porter, H.
France and the United States. REEM 3:104; REEMB 3:105

---- HISTORY
Gambetta, L.
France after German conquest. BREW 6:189; BRYW 7:196; HAZO 24:10091; MAS 24:10091; PE:549; PEA:549; PL:335
Lamartine, A. M. L.
Congratulatory speech. CHAL 5:430; HAZO 12: 4930; MAS 12:4930
Manifesto to Europe. HAZO 12:4922; MAS 12:4922
Reply to club delegates. CHAL 5:432; HAZO 12: 4932; MAS 12:4932
Thiers, L. A.

FRANCE-HISTORY (cont.)
At Arcachon. CHAL 6:238; HAZO 13:5385; MAS 13:5385

---- ---- REVOLUTION, 1789-1799
Barnave, A. P. J. M.
Oration for the crown. CHAL 4:165; HAZO 9:3517; MAS 9:3517
Cambon, P. J.
Crisis of 1793. BREW 3:84; BRYW 7:152; CHAL 3:447; HAZO 8:3194; MAS 8:3194
Danton, G. J.
Establishment of a Revolutionary tribunal. LEEW 5:145; PE:264; PEA:264
Let France be free. BREW 4:397; COP:78; COPA:78; COPB:78; HAZO 8:3342; KLEM:193; LEEW 5:141; MAS 8:3342; REEM 9:198; REEMA 12:800; REEMB 10:205
To dare again, ever to dare. BREW 4:396; BRYW 7:130; CHAL 4:108; COP:77; COPA:77; COPB:77; HAZO 8:3338; HIB:39; MAS 8:3338; PE:253; PEA:253; PL:300; REEM 9:197; REEMA 12:799; REEMB 10:204
To the Tribunals. CROC:122
Gensonne, A.
Judgment of Louis XVI. LEEW 5:115
Guadet, M. E.
Reply to Robespierre. BREW 6:216
Lamartine, A. M. L. de
Revolution. LEEW 5:215
Mackintosh, J.
In behalf of free speech: on the trial of Jean Peltier accused of libelling Napoleon Bonaparte. ADR 2:185; BREW 8:54; BRYW 4:84; CHAL 4:208; GOOD:827; HAZO 9:3585; LEEW 7:111; MAS 9:3585; PL:453
Mirabeau, H. G. R. de
Address to the King. PL:297
Defying the French aristocracy. BREW 8:164; PE:231; PEA:231
Justifying Revolution. BREW 8:169
On Necker's project- "And yet you deliberate." BREW 8:158; BRYW 7:93; CHAL 3:259; HAZO 7:2900; MAS 7:2900; PE:233; PEA:233
On the removal of the troops around Paris. PL:296
Reason immutable and sovereign. BREW 8:167
Right of war and peace. CODS:75; CODSA:75; PE:241; PEA:241
Napoleon I.
Proclamation from Mantua. CROC:335
Price, R.
Hails the French Revolution. PE:236; PEA:236
Robespierre, M.
Against granting the King a trial. BRYW 7:136; CHAL 4:34; HAZO 8:3284; LEEW 5:99; MAS 8:3284; PL:310
Demanding the King's death. BREW 9:75; HAZO 8:3306; MAS 8:3306
His defense of terrorism. BREW 9:68; HAZO 8:3296; MAS 8:3296; PE:272; PEA:272
In defiance of assassins. CROC:378
Saint-Just, L. A. L. de
Invective against Danton. BRYW 7:156; CHAL 4:240; HAZO 9:3631; MAS 9:3631
Sheridan, R. B.
On the French Revolution. BREW 9:208
Patriotism and perquisites.

BREW 9:209
Vergniaud, P. M.
Reply to Robespierre. BREW 10:48; HAZO 8:3168; MAS 8:3168; PE:266; PEA: 266
Situation in France. BRYW 7:117; CHAL 3:428; HAZO 8:3174; LEEW 5:45; MAS 8:3174; PE:246; PEA: 246; PL:303
To the camp. BREW 10: 46; HAZO 8:3165; MAS 8: 3165
Windham, W.
On the peace of Amiens. HAZO 7:2963; MAS 7:2963
See also Napoleon I, Emperor of the French

---- ---- ---- 1848
Lamartine, A. M. L. de.
Revolution of 1848. BREW 7:253; HAZO 12:4912; MAS 12:4912
Tocqueville, A. de
Feels "A gale of revolution in the air." PE:454; PEA: 454

---- ---- SECOND EMPIRE
Napoleon III.
Address to the French Legislature, January 18, 1858. HAZO 15:6258; MAS 15:6258
Annual message to the Assembly, November, 1850. HAZO 15:6249; MAS 15: 6249
Famous speech at Dijon. HAZO 15:6256; MAS 15: 6256
Second annual message as President. HAZO 15:6251; MAS 15:6251
Speech in National Assembly. HAZO 15:6246; MAS 15: 6246

---- INVASION See World War, 1939-1945-Campaigns-Western front; World War, 1939-1945-France

---- POLITICS AND GOVERNMENT
Barnave, A. P. J. M.
Representative democracy against majority absolutism. BREW 1:229; BRYW 7:112; CHAL 4:159; HAZO 9:3511; MAS 9:3511
Constant, B.
On the dissolution of the Chamber of Deputies. CHAL 4:255; HAZO 9:3647; MAS 9:3647
Paine, T.
To the French National Convention. CHAL 3:74; HAZO 7:2642; MAS 7: 2642; REEMA 14:1532

FRANCHISE See Citizenship; Elections; Suffrage; Woman suffrage
Francis, Susan C.
Response to election as president of American Nurses' Association. GA:33
Francis De Sales, Saint, Bp.
Divine love in prayer. PL: 280
Sermon for the feast of Pentecost. LEEW 4:201
Sermon on meditation. HAZO 4:1412; MAS 4:1412
Sermon on perseverance in Holy Love. HAZO 4:1409; MAS 4:1409
Francis of Assisi, Saint, bp.
Sermon to the birds. COP:64; COPA:64; COPB:64; REEM 9:56; REEMB 10:58
Franco, Francisco
To Falangist Party council praising German, Italian and Spanish Fascism. VO 1942-43:725
Frank, Glenn
Jesus as a teacher. ONEC: 403
Statesmanship of business and the business of statesmanship. EXEE:553

Frank, G. (cont.)
Welcome to freshmen. REEM sup 1:344; REEMB 7:158
See also Jackson, R.H., jt. auth.
Frankfurter, Felix
Public opinion and democratic government. BA 1946-47: 145
Worth of our past. HOC:111
Franklin, Benjamin
Dangers of a salaried bureaucracy. BREW 6:171; BRYW 8:56; CHAL 2:256; HAZO 5:1849; MAS 5:1849
Disapproving and accepting the Constitution. BOU:44; BREW 6:169; BRYW 8:53; CHAL 2:254; COP:236; COPA:236; COPB:236; HAZO 5:1847; HURG:34; MAS 5:1847; PE:194; PEA: 194; PL:580
Examination before the House of Commons. BRYW 8:37
Freemasonry. THOU 3:85
Opening the assembly with prayer. REEM 10:8; REEMA 8:503; REEMB 11:8

FRANKLIN, BENJAMIN
Beck, J.M.
Successful life. SHU:23
Examination of Benjamin Franklin by the House of Commons, 1766. PO:1
Hoover, H.C.
Benjamin Franklin-accepting the gold medal of the International Benjamin Franklin Society. BA 1953-54:81
Franklin, a characteristic American. HOB:169
Little, A.D.
Fifth estate. REEM sup 2: 143; REEMB 6:244
Mirabeau, H.G.R.
Announcing the death of Franklin. BREW 8:166
Franklin, John Hope
America's window to the world: her race problem. HILK:201
Booker T. Washington, the man and the education (Tuskegee Institute Founder's Day speech) HILK:212
Franzen, Frans Michael
"Sword shall pierce they heart." CHAL 4:408; HAZO 9:3876; MAS 9:3876
Fraser, Leon
Presents James F. Byrnes. LY:206

FRATERNITY See Brotherliness; Greek letter societies; Secret societies. Also Names of secret societies, e.g. Eagles, Fraternal Order of; Elks, Benevolent and Protective Order of; Hibernians, Ancient Order of; Kiwanis Club; Lions Club; Oddfellows, Independent Order of; Royal Arcanum; Woodmen of the World
Frederick, J. George
New type of executive. EXEE: 587
Frederick II, The Great, King of Prussia
To his generals before invading Silesia. BRYW 7:239; COP:69; COPA:69; COPB: 69
To his generals before the battle of Leuthen. BRYW 7: 241; COP:69; COPA:69; COPB:69
Frederick William IV (of Prussia)
Opening of the Prussian Diet. CHAL 6:164; HAZO 13: 5275; MAS 13:5275

FREE ENTERPRISE See Industry and state; Laissez-faire

FREE SPEECH
Bagwell, P.D.
American Swastika. BRP 7: 100
Carter, B.

Free speech on the news. BART 1:81
Coffee, J.M.
What does freedom of speech mean to us today? BA 1941-42:97
Constant, B.
Free speech necessary for good government. CHAL 4:250; HAZO 9:3642; MAS 9:3642
Curran, J.P.
England and English liberties-in the case of Rowan. BREW 4:317; BRYW 6:99; CHAL 3:320; ESEH:201; GOOD:790; HAZO 7:2974; KET:147; MAS 7:2974; PL:516; REEMA 12:764
For Peter Finerty and free speech. BREW 4:308; CODS:221; CODSA:221; GOOD:805; KET:175; ORBR 1:337
Douglas, W.O. and others.
Freedom of speech: Terminiello vs. City of Chicago. BA 1948-49:78
Douglass, F.
Plea for free speech in Boston. BREW 5:282
Erskine, T.
Against Paine's "Age of reason. ADR 2:273; BREW 6:12; ORBR 1:375; REEMA 13:949
Against Thomas Williams for the publication of Paine's Age of reason. ADR 2:273; BREW 6:12; GOOD:761; ORBR 1:375; REEMA 13:949
Free speech and fundamental rights; defense of Tom Paine. BREW 6:43; BRTH:121; BRTHA:121; BRYW 4:71; PE:255; PEA:255
Speech in behalf of John Stockdale. BRAO:141; BREW 6:24; CHAL 3:276; CODS:285; CODSA:285; FULB:69; GOOD: 684; HAY:73; HAZO 7:2918; MAS 7:2918; PE:184; PEA:184
Hamilton, A.
In the case for Zenger-for free speech. ANG:53; BOU:131; BREW 6:336; PE:101; PEA:101
Holmes, O.W., Jr.
Dissenting opinion on Abrams vs. United States. ANG:458; FO:310
Schenck v. United States: opinion for the Supreme Court. BRE:320; BREA:300
Hughes, C.E.
Near v. Minnesota: opinion for the Supreme Court. BRE:323; BREA:303
LaFollette, R.M.
Free speech in wartime. BAAMP:244; BRE:311; BREA:291; BLAB:347; HICF:488
Mackintosh, J.
In behalf of free speech: on the trial of Jean Peltier accused of libelling Napoleon Bonaparte. ADR 2:105; BREW 8:54; BRYW 4:84; CHAL 4:208; GOOD:827; HAZO 9:3585; LEEW 7:111; MAS 9:3585; PL:453
Milton, J.
For the liberty of unlicensed printing. BREW 8:151; BRYW 3:79
Schneider, A.L.
Dilemma of democracy. BRP 10:35; NOR 1939:28
Phillips, W.
Murder of Lovejoy. BAAMP:138; BOU:68; BRYW 8:222; CHAL 8:218; COP:281; COPA:281; COPB:281; FULB:323; HAZO 16:6949; HURG:74; JOHA 1 pt 2:102; KNAS:8; KNASA:8; MAS 16:6949; PE:371; PEA:371; PL:648; SHAH:348

FREE SPEECH (cont.)
Wilber, L. A.
Without a word. BRAP:74

FREE TRADE AND PROTECTION
Blaine, J. G.
Century of protection. REEM 10:293; REEMA 11:259; REEMB 11:307
Bright, J.
Free trade. FULB:132
Burgh, W. H.
Free trade and protection. KET:110
Churchill, W. L. S.
Free trade and the 'Unearned increment." BREW 3:325
Clay, H.
Free trade and seamen's rights. CHAL 5:74; HAZO 10:4089; MAS 10:4089
Cobden, R.
Effects of protection in agriculture. ADR 3:109; BEA:129; BRYW 4:156; COP:179; COPA:179; COPB:179; HAY:186; ORBR 2:187; PAUF 1:312; PL:465
Free trade with all nations. BREW 4:103; PE:450; PEA:450; REEM 9:227; REEMA 12:698; REEMB 10:234
Reed, T. B.
Protection and prosperity. BRYW 10:175; REEM 10:311; REEMB 11:325
Rosebery, A. P. P.
At the Free Trade Hall, at the centenary of the Manchester Chamber of Commerce. BEA:369; PAUF 2:367
See also Corn laws; Tariff

FREEDOM See Intellectual freedom; Liberty; Religious liberty; Teaching, freedom of

FREEDOM OF SPEECH See Free speech

FREEDOM OF THE SEAS See Western hemisphere-Defenses
Freeman, Albert Thayer
Pleads for justice for the American Indian. JON:125
Freeman, James Edward
Bishop's charge. REEM sup 1:348; REEMB 6:137
Freeman, John
Solid South. SHUC:136
Freeman, Silas
Enemy of peace. BRP 4:49

FREEMASONS
Address of welcome. THOS:41
After dinner address at a Masonic banquet. AMEO 2:42
Barnett, A. E.
Masonry triumphant. THOU 3:70
Brown, G. P.
First Grand Master of Virginia. THOU 3:59
Carnovan, H. H. M. H.
Freemasonry (at installation of Albert Edward, Prince of Wales as Grand Master) REEM 7:82; REEMA 7:159
Consecration of a (Masonic) Lodge banner. EDW:73
Franklin, B.
Freemasonry. THOU 3:85
Freemasonry, a teacher of tolerance. AMEO 2:40
In memoriam (for a Masonic brother) EDW:69
Incident in Civil War. THOU 3:86
Irish Masonry. THOU 3:87
Jones, J. S.
Masonry and state. THOU 3:57
Kenny, M.
Freemasonry and Catholicism in American. CATA 2:194
Kenworthy, R. J.
Freemasonry and citizen-

ship. REEM 2:292; REEMB 2:296
McKinley, W.
Washington, a Masonic eulogy. THOU 3:80
Masonic address. THOS:88
Masonic ideals (their practical value in the community) ED:404
(Masonic) Master's reply to toast. EDW:43
Masonry. NATS:24
Masonic toast. THOS:42
Masons, by an officer of the lodge. EDGS:356
Master Mason's night-four examples of. MORA:73-76
Moore, C.W.
Universal fraternity of Masonry (at centennial anniversary of Lodge of St. Andrew) REEMA 9:880
Newton, J. F.
Ministry of Masonry. REEM sup 2:249; REEMB 7:304
Pound, D.
Renaissance of Masonry. THOU 3:41
Presentation of a jewel for any Masonic occasion. THOS: 106
Presentation of clothing to a (Masonic) brother who has been given office in Grand (or Provincial or District Grand) Lodge or has had London Grand Rank conferred upon him. EDW:67
Reality of the unseen. JA:130
Reed, G.
Fifty years of Washington Masonry (semi-centennial address) THOU 3:66
Reply for London Grand Rank (Freemason) EDW:37
Reply of the Worshipful Master (Masonic) to the toast of a lodge on its twenty-fifth anniversary meeting. EDW:65
Requirements of Masonry. THOU 3:62
Resolutions of respect and condolence on the death of a Freemason. HILL:417
Robbins, A. F.
Freemasonry in England and America. REEM sup 2: 348; REEMB 7:352
Shrine address at dedication of new Masonic Temple. AMEO 2:62
Suggestions for consecration of a (Masonic) Lodge. With example of: EDW:71
Suggestions for installing Master (Freemason). With example of toast of the initiate. EDW:45
Suggestions for proposing a toast for a Deputy of the Assistant Grand Master of a Provincial (Masonic Lodge) With example of. EDW:35
Suggestions for proposing a toast for a Provincial (or District Grand Master of a Masonic Lodge) With example of. EDW:33
Suggestions for proposing a toast of Masonic Charities. With example of. EDW:39
Suggestions for proposing a toast to a lecturer (at a Masonic meeting) With example of. EDW:73
Suggestions for proposing a toast to officers at a Masonic installation. With example of. EDW:57
Suggestions for proposing a toast to the Deputy Grand Master (of a Masonic Lodge) With example of. EDW:31
Suggestions for proposing a toast to "The Ladies" at a Masonic Ladies' Night. With examples of. EDW:61
Suggestions for proposing a toast to visitors (to Masonic Lodge) With example of. EDW:51
Suggestions for proposing the (Masonic) Master's toast. With example of. EDW:42
Thoughts about Masonry. NI:

FREEMASONS (cont.)
273; NIA:205
Tonsor, C.A.
Masonic retrospect. THOU: 3:64
Value of Masonry. THOS:126
White, J.H.
Odd Fellowship and Masonry. THOU 3:126
See also Eastern Star, Order of; Knights Templar; Mystic Shrine, Nobles of the Scottish Rite

Frelinghuysen, Frederick Theodore
In favor of universal suffrage. BREW 6:175

FREMONT, JOHN CHARLES
Wallace, H.C.
Southerner in the west. REEMA 3:1178

FRENCH ACADEMY
Foch, F.
To the French Academy (tribute to the French soldier) REEM 11:422; REEMB 12:445

FRENCH AFRICAN CONFERENCE OF BRAZZAVILLE, 1944
DeGaulle, C.
Speech at the Brazzaville Conference. VO 1944-45:71

FRENCH LANGUAGE
Barère de Vieuzac, B.
On the necessity for teaching the French language. CHAL 3:453; HAZO 8:3210; MAS 8:3210

Frick, Ford
Responds to introduction by Wilfrid Smith. PRC:18

FRICK, FORD
Smith, W.
Introduces Ford Frick, Commissioner of baseball. PRC:17

Friedman, Lee M.
Address delivered at Faneuil Hall on 250th anniversary of the settlement of the Jews in the United States. TWJ:61

Friedrich, C.J.
What America means to me. HOC:103

FRIENDS, SOCIETY OF
Birdsall, W.W.
What Quakerism stands for. WERN 42:75
Mirabeau, H.G.R.
To a Deputation of Quakers. CROC:325

FRIENDSHIP
Accepting favors. NATT:18
Address on friendship. BEC: 160
Avebury, J.L.
Blessing of friendship. CHAL 12:377; HAZO 23: 9773; MAS 23:9773
Ayers, A.D.
In memory of a pal. NESA:212
Beecher, H.W.
On fellowship. HURG:118
Collecting friends. FRIE:225
Doctrine of good fellowship. DR:224
Don't underrate your friends. JAS:80
Fellowship. DU:140
Fellowship. NATM:28
Five ways to make friends. JAI:59
Fraternal fellowship. FRIE: 66
Friends and neighbors. THOS: 99
Friendship. CON:65
Friendship. NATT:50
Friendship. THOS:134
Friendships. NATS:12
Joy of friendship. NATT:20
Know the other fellow better. FRIE:77
Lend a hand and lend a heart, or the healthy heart vs. the heavy heart (a speech for a

heart drive) BAI:103
Lysias.
To a gathering of friends. FRE:229
Modern Woodmen-friendship ties. THOS:78
Raish, D.R.
Once in a lifetime. JUD: 191
Ritter, C.R.
Friendship. BOA:177; BOB: 202
Should auld acquaintance be forgot? SOES:48
To a friend. THOS:94
Yeiser, N.E.
Fellowship. THOU 3:400
Frisbie, M.T.
Unknown quantities. PEAE: 81

FRONTIER AND PIONEER LIFE
Abernathy, T.P.
Democracy and the Southern frontier. TIN:42
Gunderson, R.G.
Davy Crockett's tongue-tied admirers. BRAP:83
King, J.L.
Pioneer blood. BLUE:81; BRP 3:33; YR 3:13
Lane, F.K.
American pioneer (at opening of Panama-Pacific Exposition) BRAP:106; REEM 7:226; REEMB 8:246
Philips, J.F.
Old settler's home (at reunion of Tri-State Old Settler's Association, Keokuk, Iowa) SHUO:201
Springer, J.W.
Pioneers. SHU:183
Tracy, F.P.
Pioneer celebration speech. WAGN:29

FROST, JOHN
Erskine, T.
In behalf of John Frost, when indicted for uttering seditious words. GOOD: 698

Froude, James Anthony
Influence of the Reformation on Scottish character. HAZO 18:7806; MAS 18: 7806
Men of letters. KLEM:133; REEMA 2:510
Science of history. REEMA 5: 443

FRUIT TRADE
Fruit growers (address for the Fruit Growers' Association) EDGS:148
Frye, William P.
Citizenship. BLAA:89; BLAB: 89
Protection of American citizens. SHU:162
Republican Party. REEMA 13: 1031

FUGITIVE SLAVE BILL See Slavery in the United States
Fulbright, James William
America and internationalism BA 1943-44:83
Current crisis and need for education. BA 1957-58:158
Education and public policy. BA 1964-65:157
Foreign policy-old myths and new realities. BA 1963-64: 91
Moral revival in government. BA 1951-52:60
Present-day American life: its order of values, and its sense of direction. BA 1958-59:127
Response to an introduction. PR:122
Fulkerson, Roe
Dollar chasing. LINM:374
Inheritance tax. BRAC:407
Fullen, John B.
Many happy returns of the day (75th anniversary of Ohio State University) YE: 303
Fuller, C. Dale
Debate judges. JUD:61

Fuller, Frederic L.
Our racial myopia. YR 2:55
Fuller, Melville Weston
Pollock v. Farmers' Loan and Trust Company, 1895: opinion for the Supreme Court. BIR 3:196
Supreme Court. REEMA 2:513
United States v. E. C. Knight Company, 1895: opinion for the Supreme Court. BIR 3: 191
Fuller, Thomas
How far examples are to be followed. ORBR 1:89
Ill match well broken off. ORBR 1:97

FUND RAISING
Address at fifth anniversary of founding of Big Brother Athletics Association. BEDA:111
Appeal for blood donation. BEB:25; BEC:40
Appeal for funds. EDGS:95
Appeal for funds (at annual Boy Scout drive) BEDA:108
Appeal for funds for blind. BEC:40
Appeal for funds for cancer patients. BEC:41
Appeal for funds for church. BEC:42
Appeal for funds for hospital. BEB:23, 24; BEC:42
Appeal for funds for needy. BEB:22; BEC:43
Appeal for funds for volunteer fire department. BEC:42
Appeal for funds-various models of. BEC:36
Appealing for funds and volunteers (at mental fund drive) BED:59; BEDA:105
Appealing for funds (for Camera Club) BEDA:18
Appealing for funds for the Red Cross. BEB:23; BEC: 43
Bones: short and over can mean short of publicity and overlooking a patron (a speech to bank personnel, changeable for many occasions; business meeting or convention of sales personnel, at a graduation of nurses' group, for fund raising drives, to a telephone group, or by a political or labor speaker) BAI: 94
Bowles, C.
Give one day. HOA:400
Bruce, W. C.
General Robert E. Lee (for restoration of Stratford, the home of the Lees) DOA 33
Closing speech at annual Boy Scout drive. BEDA:109
Closing speech (at hospital fund drive and testimonial) BED:66; BEDA:103
Closing speech (at mental health fund drive) BED:61; BEDA:106
Closing speech at organization of a Camera Club. BEDA: 21
Community fund drive. SCHS: 86, 113
Gilbert, E. J.
Introducing a fund raiser. BRC:270
Help the needy-speech to secure public support for a community chest canvasser WRA:199
In support of the community chest drive. DR:39; LU: 1134
Krantz, J., Jr.
Community fund. MCK:129
Every member canvass day appeals-two speeches requesting church pledges. MCK:127, 128
Lend a hand and lend a heart or the healthy heart vs. th heavy heart (a speech for a heart drive) BAI:103
McKeldin, T.
Hospital building fund. MCK:125

Opening address (at mental health fund drive) BED:59; BEDA:104
Opening speech at presentation of scientific award. BEDA: 58
Opening statement (at hospital fund drive and testimonial) BED:62; BEDA:98
Praise for raising funds-resolution of. BEB:36
Presenting a gift for successfully raising money. SOES: 18
Presenting check (at hospital fund drive and testimonial) BED:63; BEDA:100
Putting your project across (pep talk to be used at a sales meeting, to inspire a group of workers on a charity drive or any similar purpose. NAT:36
Raising funds. FRIE:333
Raising funds. NATM:23
Raising money at the business meeting of the church. DR: 219; LU:1241
Report of the building committee of the----church. MICS:155
Request for contribution or participation-various models of. BEC:38
Roosevelt, F.D.
Broadcast on the community mobilization of human needs. VO 1941:451
Mobilization of community needs. VO 1942-43:543
Sarnoff, D.
Appeal for popular support of the Metropolitan Opera Association. MOA:312
Speech soliciting funds for a park. HILL:477
Speech soliciting funds for a public fountain. HILL:478
Speech soliciting funds for church edifice. HILL:477
Spirit of sharing. FRIE:84
Thompson, D.
Community chest campaign. YE:377
Tribute to guest-of-honor and appeal for funds (at hospital fund drive and testimonial) BED:64; BEDA: 101
Welcome to annual Boy Scout drive. BEDA:107
See also Bonds, Government

FUNDAMENTALISM See Religion

FUNERAL SERMONS
Address at the funeral of an active, useful man who dies in middle-life. HILL: 475
Address delivered by a layman at a funeral in the absence of an ordained minister. HAPR:155
Address on the death of a young lady. HILL:476
Aelred, Saint.
Funeral sermon. HAZO 3: 1268; MAS 3:1268
Ambrose, Saint
Funeral oration on his brother. HAZO 3:1154; MAS 3:1154
Antony, M.
Funeral oration for Julius Caesar: from Shakespeare. COP:58; COPA:58; COPB: 58; HIB:10; LAD:27; REEM 9:43; REEMB 10:44
Funeral oration over the dead body of Caesar. BRYW 2:200
Bergerot, P.A.
Funeral of President Sadi Marie Carnot. WAGN:366
Big Elk.
Funeral speech for dead chief. JON:89
Boussuet, J.B.
Funeral oration of the Prince Condé. BREW 2:161; BRYW 7:63; CHAL 2:92; HAZO 4:1558; LEEW 4:219; MAS 4:1558; PL:263; REEM 9:76; REEMB 10:78

FUNERAL SERMONS (cont.)
Funeral oration on Henriette of England, Duchess of Orleans. CODS:63; CODSA:63
Brooks, P.
Character of Abraham Lincoln. BREW 2:244; CHAL 13:38; HAZO 23:9905; MAS 23:9905; REEM 5:37; REEMA 7:137; REEMB 9:67
Burial service, ode and ritual on death of a fellow lodge member. THOU 3:328-333
Candler, W. A.
Tribute to Lucious Q. C. Lamar. SHUO:234
Donne, J.
Delivers his own funeral sermon. PE:91; PEA:91
Emerson, R.W.
Greatness of a plain American. BREW 5:371; FKA:66; MEAR:111
Engels, F.
Says a few words at the burial of Karl Marx. PE:575; PEA:575
Fléchier, E.
Death of Turene. BREW 6:146; HAZO 4:1629; LEEW 4:245; MAS 4:1629; PL:255
Flower of the field. JA:71
G. A. R. burial service.
Ceremonies at the grave
Chaplain's address at the grave. HILL:474
Gorgias.
Funeral oration. LEEW 1:43
Gregory, Saint
Funeral oration of Meletius. LEEW 3:121
Hitler, A.
At the funeral of Reich Minister Dr. Fritz Todt. VO 1942-43:135
Honored dead. THOU 3:333
Hugo, V.
Oration on Honoré de Balzac. BREW 7:94; CHAL 7:5; HAZO 14:5780; MAS 14:5780
Hypereides.
Funeral oration. LEEW 1:204; MINA 2:536
I will see you again. JA:68
Ingalls, J. J.
Undiscovered country (death of B.H. Hill) BREW 7:122; REEM 5:237; REEMA 8:721; REEMB 9:276
Ingersoll, R.G.
At a child's grave. PAR:447
Keeping faith. JA:73
Lee, H.
Funeral oration on Washington. BREW 7:304; CHAL 3:474; HAZO 8:3242; HELE:103; LEEW 8:323; MAS 8:3242; ORAMA 1:243; REEM 5:274; REEMA 13:1304; REEMB 9:313; RID:26; SMI:86
Massillon, J. B.
Funeral oration on Louis XIV. PL:276
Melanchton, P.
On the death of Luther. BRYW 7:44; CHAL 1:427; HAZO 4:133; MAS 4:1333
Morris, G.
Oration over Hamilton. BREW 8:212; COP:263; COPA:263; COPB:263; HELE:142; HURG:54; KLEG:154; ORAMA 1:187; REEM 5:314; REEMA 9:887; REEMB 9:554
Pericles.
On those who died in the war. ARNS:216; BAAGA:404; BOU:205; BREW 8:306; BRYA:547; BRYW 1:16; COP:3; COPA:3; COPB:3; CROC:358; HAZO 1:15; HIBS:484; LEEW 1:47; MAS 1:15; MEAR:107; PE:7; PEA:7; PL:26; REEM 9:2; REEMA 14:1563; REEMB 10:2
Remarks on the death of a child. HILL:475

Stanley, A. P.
Palmerston and the duty of England (funeral oration) BREW 9:274; ORBR 2:349
Tillett, C.W.
On the death of Senator Vance. SHUO:180
Trueblood, D. E.
Herbert Clark Hoover. BA 1964-65:108
Untimely death. THOS:80

FUNERALS
Announcing funeral arrangements. WRA:27
Hartman, W.R.
Pomp and circumstance. NOR 1949:145
See also Undertakers
Funk, Bill
Constitution: a guide to the world of tomorrow. DO: 230
Funston, G. Keith
Memo to the Class of 1957: our economic world and you; BA 1957-58:136

FURRIERS See Business men
Furuseth, Andrew
Limitation of labor injunctions. ONEC:345, 376

FUTURE
Brown, H. A.
Plea for the future. BREW 2:286
Bryce, J.
World's future. BREW 2: 310
Butler, N. M.
Imponderable move the world. COP:443; COPA:443
Cline, E.W.
Spirit of the past. BOA:213
Face the future unafraid. NAT:47
Heyler, W. B.
Best is yet to be. ONES: 321
Hoover, H. C.
Future. BLAB:354
Horton, M. M.
Predictions for the unpredictable future. BRA:551
Maloney, M. J.
Call us dissenters. YR 8: 21
Mathews, S.
New opportunities in a new age. REAC:182
Petty, J. A.
New frontiers. BOA:336
Schaeffer, J.
Back to the future. AN:30
Speech on the future. THOS: 90
Stidger, W. L.
Look ahead. BART 4:1
Tobias, C.H.
Building for tomorrow's better living. HILK:159
Zekaria, H.
Flight from Bagdad. BRP 8:98; YR 9:119

GAIETY See Happiness
Gaines, William J.
Appeal to our brother in white. DUNM:257
Gale, Zona
Novel and the spirit. REEM 6:191; REEMB 7:162
Gallagher, Buell G.
Preface to the study of Utopias (Founders Day lecture on the anniversary of Antioch College) BA 1960-61:201
Gallagher, Hubert and others (H.W. Toll)
You and your government. SAR:174
Gallagher, Raymond M.
Century of isolation. ASHF: 197
Gallatin, Albert
Constitutional liberty and executive despotism. BREW 6:181
On the British treaty. JOHA 1 pt 1:84
Speech on the British Peace Treaty (terminating War of 1812-1814) CHAL 4:138; HAZO 8:3476; MAS 8:3476

Gallinger, Jacob H.
"Shell-shock" in the Senate. BREW 6:187
Galloway, Charles B.
Reconstruction in the South; past and present (at dedication of Mississippi's new Capitol) SHUO:294
Gallup, George
Judgment of the common people. ON:200
Mass information or mass entertainment? MOA:466

GALLUP, GEORGE
Grimm, P.
Introduces Dr. George Gallup. PR:65
Gambetta, Leon
Address to the Delegation from Alsace. COP:109; COPA: 109; COPB:109; LEEW 5: 259; REEM 9:281; REEMA 13:1037; REEMB 10:289
France after German conquest. BREW 6:189; BRYW 7:196; HAZO 24:10091; MAS 24: 10091; PE:549; PEA:549; PL:335
On the Constitutional laws, 1878. REEMA 13:1043
Speech upon Constitutional laws, 1875. CHAL 13:159; HAZO 24:10103; MAS 24: 10103
To the Alsatians.-Same as his Address to the Delegation from Alsace

GAMBLING
Harlan, J.M.
Lottery case (Champion v. Ames), 1903: opinion for the Supreme Court. BIR 3: 262

GAME WARDENS See Hunters and hunting
Gandhi, Mohandus Karamchand
Latest message to America, October 31, 1942. VO 1942-43:572
Non-cooperation. COP:395; COPA:395; COPB:395
Propounds his faith before an English judge. PE:727; PEA:727
Social service. ZU:71
Speech in London (1931) PL: 801
Strength of Satyagraha. CROC: 215
To All-Indian Congress, August 7, 1942. VO 1942-43: 430

GANDHI, MOHANDUS KARAMCHAND
Naidu, S.
My father, do not rest! ZU: 3
Nehru, J.
Glory has departed. BOU: 219; COPB:619
Speaks to mourning millions a few hours after the murder of Gandhi. HIBS:497; PE:809; PEA:809

GANGS
Boy and his gang. AMEO 2:195
Gannett, Jeff
Emcee at a bachelors' club meeting. BRH:308
Gannett, Lewis S.
Carl Sandburg. SAR:371
Gannon, Robert I.
Abraham Lincoln. ON:356
Peace through business. GLAD 263
Want of the world. BA 1948-49 229
Wisdom before information. BA 1941-42:192

GANTT, HENRY LAURENCE See Henry Laurence Gantt gold medal
Gantz, Gertrude
Doors without keys. YR 6:203
Ganz, John M.
Employes' mutual benefit association. ONES:288
Garden, Mary
Music in the United States. REEM 2:61; REEMB 2:61

GARDENS AND GARDENING
Address on subject of gardening. BEDA:68
Garden that had no weeds. JA: 79
Hole, S. R.
My garden. REEM 2:216; REEMA 8:673; REEMB 2: 221
How does your garden grow? NAT:15
Huber, L. J.
Introducing a gardener. BRH:119
Introducing a speaker on "rose culture." WRA:34
Introducing horticulturist (at Garden Club meeting) BEDA: 68
Kaser, A. L.
Emcee at a gardeners' club. BRH:232
Introducing a gardening expert. BRC:117
Mighty like a rose. JA:76
Your home grounds and the calendar (for the garden club) DR:314
See also Flowers, language of

Gardiner, C. Harvey
By the power invested. YR 8: 249

Garfield, James A.
Conflict of ideas in America. BREW 6:202
Death of Lincoln. PEAE:161
Inaugural address. CHAL 12: 1; CHI:156; HAZO 22: 9437; LOTI:143; MAS 22: 9437; USIN:141; USINA: 141
John Sherman for President. BRYW 10:99; KNAS:305; KNASA:305; LAD:104; REEM 10:261; REEMB 11: 273
On the restoration of the South. REEMA 13:1054
Revolution and the logic of coercion. BREW 6:198
Success in life. REAC:95

GARFIELD, JAMES A.
Blaine, J. G.
Life and character of J.A. Garfield. BAKF:130; BAKS: 177; BREW 2:87; BRYW 10:111; CHAL 11:282; CLAY:141; COP:325; COPA:325; COPB:325; HARSO:178; HAZO 21:9147; HURG:137; LA:139; MAS 21:9147; ONEM:408; ORAMA 2:321; PROS:124; REEM 5:14; REEMA 7:113; REEMB 9:43; SHU:176; WERN 42:72
Butler, N. M.
Events are temporal, principles eternal. SHU:74
James A. Garfield, a tribute from the Sons of Temperance. THOU 3:495
Parkhurst, C. H.
On Garfield. CHAL 13:430; HAZO 24:10474; MAS 24: 10474

Garibaldi, Guiseppe
Against the humiliation of the Southern Army. CROC:220
Last speech as a member of the Chamber. CHAL 7:270; HAZO 15:6186; MAS 15: 6186
To his soldiers. BRYW 7:229; CHAL 7:272; COP:102; COPA:102; COPB:102; HAZO 15:6188; MAS 15: 6188

GARIBALDI, GUISEPPE
Crispi, F.
At the unveiling of Garibaldi's statue. BREW 4: 234; HAZO 19:8090; MAS 19:8090

Garland, Hamlin
In praise of Booth Tarkington. REEM 2:73; REEMB 2:73
Joys of the trail. REEM 2: 67; REEMB 2:67
Realism versus romanticism. REEMA 2:518

Garnet, Henry Highland
Address to the slaves of the United States of America.

Garnet, H. H. (cont.)
WOON:150
Memorial discourse. DUNM: 107
Garnett, Theodore S.
Stuart, the Confederacy's Prince Rupert. SMI:190
Garrett, Charles
New Year's address. THOU 2:43
Garrett, Paul
If I had your chance. HOA:36
Garrison, William Lloyd
Address to the public, 1831. BIR 2:81
At Charleston, South Carolina, 1865. BREW 6:213; RID:56
Beginning a revolution. BREW 6:209
New day. -Same as his At Charleston, South Carolina, 1865
No compromise with slavery. WPRA:169
On the death of John Brown. BREW 6:210; BRYW 9:189; COP:299; COPA:299; COPB:299; ORAMA 2:209; REEM 10:179; REEMA 13:1065; REEMB 11:183
Speech in London, June 29, 1867. HAZO 15:6161; MAS 15:6161
Union and slavery. BREW 6:212; ORAMA 2:211
Words of encouragement to the oppressed. CHAL 7:250; HAZO 15:6150; MAS 15:6150

GARRISON, WILLIAM LLOYD
Argyll, G. D. C.
Welcome to Garrison. HAZO 20:8423; MAS 20:8423
Mill, J. S.
Tribute to Garrison. HAZO 15:6183; MAS 15:6183
Phillips, W.
Eulogy on Garrison. CHAL 8:228; HARS:260; HAZO 16:6959; KLEG:141; MAS 16:6959
Ranson, R. C.
William Lloyd Garrison: a centennial oration. DUNM: 305; WOON:531
Garvan, Francis P.
Chemical warfare. HICF:656
Opening address for the people in the Thaw murder trial. HICJ:488
Garvey, Marcus
Negro's place in world reorganization. HILK:50
Gary, Elbert Henry
Ethics in business. REEM 4:145; REEMB 4:288
Labor. BYRA:178; REEM 4:136; REEMB 4:279
Reconstruction and readjustment. HICF:622
Science of business. BLAB:333; LINM:112
Gascoyne-Cecil, Edgar Algernon Robert, 1st Viscount Cecil of Chelwood. See Cecil of Chelwood, E. A. R. G. -C.
Gascoyne-Cecil, Robert Arthur Talbot, 3d Marquis of Salisbury. See Salisbury, R. A. R. G. -C.

GASKILL, DAVID L.
Schultz, E.
David L. Gaskill. MO:536

GASPÉ
Longden, Mrs. J.
New steel world. BUT:187; BUTB:187

GASSES IN WARFARE See Chemical warfare
Gates, Edward D.
Time is running out. HAR:47

GATEWAYS See Acceptance speeches-Gateways Presentation speeches-Gateways
Gauhar, Altaf
Speech at final session of Conference on the Problems of Economic Development. UAR:409

Inaugural speech at Conference on the Problems of Economic Development. UAR:153
Gauss, Christian
Scholar and his country (installation of Alpha chapter of Phi Beta Kappa at Florida State College) NORR 3d ser: 43

GAVELS See Acceptance speeches-Gavels; Presentation speeches-Gavels
Gaw, J. G.
Ye olde time forensics. JUD: 91
Gayashuta, Seneca chief
To Friends in Philadelphia, 1790. SHE:41
Gaynor, William J.
Outlook. REEM 2:77
Gebhart, Donna
Why go to college? MOUG: 206; MOUGA:206
Geddes, Sir Auckland Campbell
Commencement address. REEM 6:205; REEMB 7: 176
Cooperation between Great Britain and America. REEM 2:85; REEMB 2:77

GEDDES, SIR AUCKLAND CAMPBELL
Collier, W. M.
Presenting Doctor of Laws degree to Sir Auckland Campbell Geddes. REEM 6: 205; REEMB 7:176
Geiman, Carolyn Kay
Are they really unteachable? LINP:122
Geiseman, O. A.
Blessings of a Christian marriage. ACW:48

GENERAL FEDERATION OF WOMEN'S CLUBS
Prout, Mrs. R. I. C.
Address (inaugural) as President of the General Federation of Women's Clubs. BUTB:243

GENERAL MOTORS CORPORATION
Beck, R. J.
Salute to General Motors-50th anniversary. SABA: 292

GENEVA CONFERENCE, 1955
Bulganin, N. A.
Lessening of international tension. COPB:631
Eisenhower, D. D.
Spirit of Geneva. COPB: 610

GENIUS
Bancroft, E. A.
Loneliness of genius. HARSO:98; SHU:139
Dewey, O.
Evidences of genius. LA: 120
Reynolds, J.
Genius and imitation. BREW 9:50
Silcox, L. L.
Loneliness of genius. YR 3:133
Gensonne, Armand
Judgment of Louis XVI. LEEW 5:115

GEORGE, GRACE
Taylor, D.
Presents Grace George. LY:38
George, Henry
Business depression. WERN 42:68
Crime of poverty. WPRA:244
Lectures on Moses, progress and poverty (June 1878) PE:620; PEA:620
Masses against classes (accepting the nomination as candidate for Mayor of New York City) HICF:121
Moses (December 28, 1884) REEM 5:191; REEMB 9:227
Tribute to liberty. DICD:151; DICE:151

GEORGE III, KING OF GREAT BRITAIN
Thackeray, W. M.
George III. HAZO 17:7155; MAS 17:7155
George V, King of Great Britain and Northern Ireland
Home rule for Ireland. BREW 6:220
Inauguration of the world's Economic Conference. BEA: 1
Message to the rulers of the Indian states on the inauguration of the Chamber of Princes, February, 1921. KESI 2:332
Priceless gift of printing. BREW 6:222
Wake up, England! KLEM: 208
George VI, King of Great Britain and Northern Ireland
Address at opening of Parliament, August 15, 1945. VO 1945-46:438
At the opening of the House of Lords and the House of Commons, November 12, 1941. VO 1941:505
Christmas message of peace, 1939. SAA:288
Empire called to prayer. HAN:266
King's broadcast on declaration of war on Germany. HAN:122
Speech delivered at the opening of Parliament, November 23, 1943. VO 1943-44: 553
Speech from the throne to both Houses of Parliament, January 29, 1944. VO 1944-45:573
Speech to Parliament, November 10, 1942. VO 1942-43: 635
To the British public, September 23, 1940. HAN:148
VE Day address. VO 1945-46: 195
George II, King of Greece
Address to U.S. Congress, June 15, 1942. VO 1942-43:347

GEORGE EDWARD ALEXANDER EDMUND, DUKE OF KENT
Churchill, W. L. S.
Tribute to the late Duke of Kent. VO 1942-43:502
Gerche, Daniel J.
Invocation before a convention of Arizona Bankers Association. PR:109
Geren, Paul
Secrets of debating. JUD:65
German, William M.
Speech in response delivered before the members of the Metropolitan Life Insurance Co. LINM:492
Germanicus.
To his mutinous troops. BRYW 2:237
To his friends when dying. BRYW 2:240

GERMANS IN THE UNITED STATES
Wenzel, R. E.
German-American. SHUC: 365

GERMANY
Benz, L. L.
Shadow of the Swastika. BRP 6:71; NOR 1934:79
Bismarck, O.
Against liberalism: a Prussian royalist confession of faith. CHAL 9:57; HAZO 18:7543; MAS 18:7543
German solidarity. HAZO 18:7550; MAS 18:7550
Recommends the values of blood and iron. PE:529; PEA:527
Caprivi de Caprera de Montecicoli, G. L.
On colonial possessions. CHAL 11:483; HAZO 22: 9394; MAS 22:9394
Carter, B.
Germany takes Austria.

BA 1937-38; 97
Dobert, E.W.
Convert to freedom. BART 3:91
Fichte, J.G.
People and the Fatherland. CROC:202; LEEW 5:175
Frederick William IV.
Opening of the Prussian Diet. CHAL 6:164; HAZO 13:5275; MAS 13:5275
Hitler, A.
Germany's aim. BEA:271
Proclamation on the tenth anniversary of his accession to power. VO 1943-44: 27
Proclamation to the German nation, October 14, 1933. KESK 1:283
Speech on the 19th anniversary of the 'Beer Hall Putsch." VO 1942-43:610
Speech to German Reichstag, May 21, 1935. KESK 2:33
I pity Germany. NI:228; NIA: 174
Kahn, O.H.
Prussianized Germany. SAA:274
Lassale, F.
Attacks the German Press. PE:529; PEA:529
Rivkin, D.H.
People incarnate. NOR 1943:29
William II.
German youth. WERN 42: 24
Is outraged and adamant; speeches on July 2, 27 and Aug. 2, 1900. PE:660-663; PEA:660-663
Mailed fist. BEA:431
Wyman, E.
Can these be the enemy? NOR 1944:47
See also Berlin Conference, 1945; European War, 1914-1918; Tripartite Pact; World War, 1939-1945-Campaigns-Western front; World War, 1939-1945-Germany

GERMANY--FOREIGN RELATIONS
Hitler, A.
Position of Germany today. SAR:297

---- ---- POLAND
Bismarck, O.
Mount the guards at the Warthe and the Vistula! CROC:21

---- ---- (UNITED STATES)
Hitler, A.
Announced to the Reichstag the declaration of war against the United States. VO 1941:572

---- NATIONAL SOCIALIST MOVEMENT See National socialism-Germany

---- OCCUPATION See Allied military government

---- REPARATIONS See European War, 1914-1918-Reparations

---- SURRENDER See Berlin Conference, 1945; World War 1939-1945-Germany-Surrender
Gerry, M.B.
In the shadows of the mountains (pronouncing sentence on Alfred Packer, tried for murder) GRIS:16

GERSHWIN, GEORGE
Introducing George Gershwin. NI:90; NIA:71
Getman, Anson
State and private rights to real property. ONEC:300

GETTYSBURG, BATTLE OF, 1863
Adams, C.F., Jr.

GETTYSBURG, BATTLE OF, 1863 (cont.)
Battle of Gettysburg. BREW 1:33
Ingraham, F. L.
Gettysburg. TRUW:68
Mason, A. S.
Battle of Gettysburg. TRUW: 13

GETTYSBURG NATIONAL CEMETERY See Dedication addresses-Cemeteries; Lincoln, A. -Gettysburg address

GETTYSBURG, PENNSYLVANIA
Wilson, W.
Address at Gettysburg. REEM 10:421; REEMB 11: 438

GHANA
Goka, F.K.D.
Inaugural speech at Conference on the Problems of Economic Development. UAR:89
Ghani, Hadi
Inaugural speech at Conference on the Problems of Economic Development. UAR: 83
Speech at final session of Conference on the Problems of Economic Development. UAR:417
Ghazali, Ieche Mohamed
Speech at final session of Conference on the Problems of Economic Development. UAR:419

GHEEN, JAMES E.
Blaine, J.B.
Introduces James E. Gheen, humorous lecturer. PR:59
Gibbons, Floyd
Mr. Pitkin is interviewed. SAR:37
Gibbons, James, Cardinal
Necessity of a moral religious sense in the formation of good citizens. CATA 2:100
Supremacy of the Catholic religion. REEM 7:144; REEMA 8:505; REEMB 7:183
To the Parliament of Religions. BREW 6:224; ORAMA 2:393
Truth and sincerity of character. SHUO:123
Gibson, Ernest W.
Patriotism, the soul of a nation. BOA:75; BOB:116
Gibson, Eustace
Reconstruction acts. SMI:196
Gibson, George M.
Invocation before national convention of Office Management Association. PR:109
Gibson, Hugh S.
Reduction of naval armaments. HICF:774
Giddings, Joshua Reed
Denunciation of slavery. HAZO 13:5259; MAS 13: 5259
Slavery and annexation of Cuba. BREW 6:234; CHAL 6: 148
Gideonse, Harry D.
Reply to Nadine Miller's address "Is advertising responsible for our high standard of living?" MOA: 463
When to prepare for peace. ON:299
Giffard, Hardinge Stanley, 1st Earl of Halisbury See Halisbury, H. S. G., 1st Earl of
Gifford, Walter S.
Address before the Bond Club. YE:275
Introducing General John J. Pershing. YE:126
To Chicago Association of Commerce. SAC:101

GIFTS See Acceptance speeches -Gifts; Presentation speeches-Gifts
Gilbert, Cass
Sir Christopher Wren. REEM sup 1:359; REEMB 6:148

Gilbert, Earl Jay
Emcee at a farewell bachelor party
" at a golden wedding anniversary
" at a housewarming
" at a silver wedding anniversary
" at a testimonial for a long-term employee. BRH:296; 214, 292, 280, 191
Introducing an acrobat group
" a comedian
" a dancer or dancing act
" a juggler
" a magician
" a minstrel show
" a orchestra
" a quartette. BRH: See Table of contents, section II for paging
Introducing an author
" a banker-2 examples of
" a businessman (merchant)
" a Catholic priest
" a dentist
" a doctor
" a fund raiser
" an inventor
" a governor
" a judge
" a lawyer
" a minister (Protestant)
" a politician
" a professor
" a psychologist
" a salesman (top)
" a tax consultant BRC: See Table of contents for paging
Gilbert, John
Playing "old men" parts. REEM 2:87; REEMA 2:522; REEMB 2:79

GILBERT, JOHN
Winter, W.
Tribute to John Gilbert. REEM 3:418; REEMA 3: 1257; REEMB 3:425
Gilbert, William Schwenk
"Pinafore." COP:659; COPB: 686; REEM 2:89; REEM 2: 524; REEMB 2:81

GILBERT, WILLIAM SCHWENK
Reid, W.
Presents William Gilbert. LY:41; REEM 2:89
Gilbertson, Al
Assassin of youth. YR 10:151

GILBERTSVILLE DAM See Dams
Gilder, Richard Watson
New patriotism. BLAA:40; BLAB:41; BOB:120
Gildersleeve, Basil L.
Accepting a book. ONES:54
Daniel Coit Gilman. KNAS: 86; KNASA:88
Teacher to his pupils. REEM sup 1:368; REEMB 6:157
Gilkey, Charles W.
Bridges into a better world. BA 1938-39:234
Gilkinson, Bryan A.
Old order changeth. ASHF: 324
Gillilan, Strickland W.
After dinner speech before Ohio Society. PEAE:251
Introducing Mrs. Asquith. REEM 2:95; REEMB 2:87
Me and the President. REEM 2:93; REEMB 2:85
Response to a long-winded toastmaster. HOA:367
GILLILAN, STRICKLAND W.
Introducing Strickland Gillilian-3 examples of; a humorous one, and 2nd and 3d return visits to same organization. SUM:82, 84, 86
Gillis, J. A. M.
Bible and the Catholic Church. CATA 2:273
Gilman, Daniel Coit
Characteristics of a university. REEM 6:212; REEMA 8:515; REEMB 7:193
Era of universities. REEMA 2:528
Inaugural address as president of Johns Hopkins University. WE 1:293
GILMAN, DANIEL COIT
Gildersleeve, B. L.
Daniel Coit Gilman. KNAS:

GILMAN, DANIEL COIT (cont.)
88; KNASA:88
Gilman, Ruth
Plea for my people. YR 6:327
Gilmer, Mrs. E. M. (Dorothy Dix)
Experiences of a woman columnist. YE:327
Gilmore, Ernest
Dignity of labor. THOU 1:417
Ginisty, Marie-André Charles
Verdun. REEM 11:413; REEMB 12:433
Ginn, Glenn
Yellow peril. ASHF:66

GIRARD COLLEGE
Reed, T. B.
Immortality and good deeds. (Semi-centennial of Girard College) BLAA:33; BLAB: 33; BREW 9:44; REAC:103; SHUM:266
Giraud, Henri Honore
Appeal to the French forces in North Africa, November 8, 1942. VO 1942-43:600
To the Alsace-Lorraine Society. VO 1943-44:114
---- and others (C. DeGaulle)
General Charles DeGaulle's and General Henri Giraud's appeal to France, June 4, 1943. VO 1943-44:226
Girdler, T. M.
Tomorrow's markets for steel. KLEB:181

GIRL SCOUTS
Welcome to a delegation of Boy or Girl Scouts (or other youth groups) HNWS: 50

GIRLS
Huber, L. J.
Little girl emcee. BRH:343
McBride, L.
Dancing daughters. BRP 5: 71
Talk to an organization of growing girls. DR:114
See also Fathers and daughters; Mothers and daughters; Rainbow girls, Order of
Gitlow, Benjamin
How Communists make converts. HAR:202
Gittelsohn, Roland B.
That men might be free. BA 1945-46:16
Given, William
Introduces Hugh Comer. PR: 97
Givens, Willard E.
Tribute to James William Crabtree. YE:98

GLADIATORS
Kellogg, E.
Spartacus to the gladiators. CLAY:114; DICD:139; DICE:139; HARSO:344; PROS:136
Gladstone, William Evart
Accepting a chair from the Liberals of the Borough of Greenwich. KNAS:163; KN KNASA:163; ONEM:714
Age of research. KLEM:44; REEM 2:96; REEMA 2:530; REEMB 2:88
Colonial policy. EMS 2:244
Commercial value of artistic excellence. BREW 6:258; CODS:408; CODSA:408
Destiny and individual aspirations. BREW 6:263
Eastern question. BEA:205; PAUF 1:421
Election speech in Midlothian. -Same as his Responsibilities of Empire
Equality of nations. LAD:205
Established church in Ireland. ORBR 2:283
Fundamental error of English Colonial aggrandizement. BREW 6:241; ONEM:785; PL:477
Government of Ireland Bill, April 8, 1886. HAZO 15: 6397; MAS 15:6397
Home Rule, April 13, 1886. HAZO 15:6460; MAS 15: 6460

Home Rule, June 7, 1886. HAZO 15:6518; KLEG:139; MAS 15:6518
Home Rule and autonomy, May 10, 1886. BREW 6,253; FULB:157; HAZO 15:6481; MAS 15:6481
Modern training for life. REEMA 8:534
Occasions for appeal to the people. EMS 1:87
On domestic and foreign affairs. ADR 3:287; BRYW 5: 66; CHAL 7:421; COP:188; COPA:188; COPB:188; FULB:149; HAZO 15:6339; MAS 15:6339; ORBR 2:253; REEM 9:288; REEMA 13: 1068; REEMB 10:296
On Lord Beaconsfield. BREW 6:266
On the Beaconsfield ministry. CHAL 7:458; HAZO 15: 6377; MAS 15:6377
On the Disestablishment of the Irish Church. LEEW 7:311
Power to make war. EMS 1: 242
Prospect of imperial disintegration. EMS 2:254
Reform of the franchise, May 11, 1864 speech. EMS 2: 172
Reform of the franchise, April 12, 1866 speech. EMS 2: 179
Reform of the franchise, February 28, 1884 speech. EMS 2:191
Reply on the second reading of the Irish Church Bill, 1869. PAUF 2:175
Responsibilities of Empire. BRTH:298; BRTHA:298; HAY:275
Speech in House of Commons, March 21, 1892 (on India) KESI 2:67
Supports the right of freethinkers to enter the House of Commons. PE:560; PEA: 560
Treaty-making power. EMS 1: 248
Use of books. BREW 6:264
Warfare and colonization. - Same as his Fundamental error of English Colonial aggrandizement

GLADSTONE, WILLIAM EVART
Churchill, R. H. S.
Gladstone's Egyptian inconsistencies. BREW 3:316
Dillon, J.
On the death of Gladstone. BRYW 6:252; REEM 5:138; REEMB 9:171
Laurier, W.
Character and work of Gladstone. BREW 7:296; ONES:167
Reid, W.
Gladstone England's greatest leader. REEMA 3:981

Glass, Carter
Banking act. SMI:282
Packing the Supreme Court. COP:422; COPA:422
Should Mr. Roosevelt's plan for enlarging the Supreme Court be adopted? (negative) SAR:224

GLASS, CARTER
Byrd, H. F.
80th anniversary of the birth of Senator Glass. YE: 102

Glatfelter, Philip
Abraham Lincoln and the Constitution. LEIO:114

Glenn, John H.
Address before the Joint Meeting of Congress. BA 1961-62:202; HIB:98

Glennon, John Joseph
Charity. CATA 2:110
Lincoln. CATA 1:1

GOALS See Success

GOD
Chalmers, T.
God's sympathy for man. ORBR 2:103

GOD (cont.)
Channing, W.E.
Likeness to God. BL:563
Cyril, Saint
On the maker of heaven and earth. HAZO 3:1199; MAS 3:1199
Drummond, H.
Greatest thing in the world. BREW 5:314; CHAL 14:251; HAZO 25:10780; MAS 25: 10780; ORBR 2:431; PL: 505
Dwight, T.
Sermon on sovereignty of God. HAZO 8:3147; MAS 8:3147
Edwards, J.
God glorified in man's dependence. BL:517
Foster, J.
Access to God. HAZO 9: 3861; MAS 9:3861
God. THOS:132
Goldstein, M.
Roar of the world and God. BRP 2:92; YR 3:167
How can we know God? JAS: 14
How can we love God? JAI:64
Martineau, J.
God of Revelation his own interpreter. HAZO 15:6139; MAS 15:6139
Parker, T.
Philosophical idea of God and its relation to the scientific and religious wants of mankind now. BL:659
Pusey, E.B.
Love of God for individual souls. HAZO 13:5614; MAS 13:5614
Reverence toward God and the Church. AMEO 2:83
Robespierre, M.
Festival of the Supreme Being. BREW 9:77; COP: 83; COPA:83; COPB:83; HAZO 8:3308; MAS 8:3308; REEM 9:211; REEMA 14: 1750; REEMB 10:218
"If God did not exist, it would be necessary to invent him." BREW 9:67; HAZO 8:3294; MAS 8:3294
Moral ideas and Republican principles. BREW 9:71; HAZO 8:3300; MAS 8:3300
Romeyn, J.B.
Duty and reward of honouring God, 1821. BRAR 1:73
Soul of America-God. THOT: 114
Tauler, J.
God alone. PL:202
Whitefield, G.
Kingdom of God. BREW 10: 223
Goddard, J. Leslie
Way to lasting peace. BRP 1: 71

GODFREY, ARTHUR
Haire, A. J.
Presents Arthur Godfrey. LY:44
GODWIN, PARKE
Stedman, E. C.
To Parke Godwin (speech proposing a vote of thanks) KNAS:199; KNASA:199

Goebbels, Paul Joseph
Broadcast, February 18, 1943. VO 1943-44:63
Broadcast describing plot to assassinate Hitler. VO 1944-45:337
New Year's speech, December 31, 1943. VO 1943-44: 599
Plea for clothing for troops on the Russian front. VO 1941: 624
Presenting Hitler's proclamation, January 30, 1943. VO 1943-44:19
Speech at harvest Thanksgiving festival in Berlin. VO 1943-44:421
Goering, Hermann
Broadcast, October 4, 1942. VO 1942-43:538
Order of the day, December 31, 1943. VO 1943-44:598

Speech (after attempt on Hitler's life) VO 1944-45:314
Speech, May 20, 1942. VO 1942-43:290
Goethals, George Washington
Panama Canal completed. REEM 2:100; REEMB 2:92
Serving your country. REEM 7:154; REEMB 8:181

GOETHALS, GEORGE WASHINGTON
Barry, T.H.
Introduces George Washington Goethals to Class of 1912 at United States Military Academy. REEM 7:160; REEMB 8:181
Carnegie, A.
Congratulating General Goethals. COP:688; COPB:715; REEM 1:208; REEMB 1:209
Willcox, W.R.
Presents George W. Goethals. LY:182

GOETHE, JOHANN WOLFGANG VON
Bagstad, A.
Goethe. COUW:125
Phelan, J.D.
Goethe-Schiller memorial address. WAGN:356
Taylor, B.
Tribute to Goethe. REEMA 3:1136
Goetz, William E.
Speech at Friars' Club dinner to Burns and Allen. JEYO:75

GOETZ, WILLIAM E.
Jessel, G.
Introduces William E. Goetz at Friars' Club dinner to Burns and Allen. JEYO:74
Goff, Charles Ray
Invocation before the convention of National Fraternal Congress of America. PR:110
Goff, Nathan
Lincoln - the man of God. BOA:237; BOB:145
Slackers in peace. BOA:190; BOB:176
Goheen, Robert F.
Library and the chapel stand side by side (at opening exercises at Princeton University) BA 1964-65:113
Goka, F.K.D.
Inaugural speech at Conference on the Problems of Economic Development. UAR:89
Speech at final session of Conference on the Problems of Economic Development. UAR:383
Gokhale, Gopal Krishna
Political testament (on India) KESI 2:111
Students and politics. ZU:12

GOLD
Everett, E.
Vegetable and mineral gold. LAD:137; REEMA 8:456
Ingersoll, R.G.
Chicago and New York Gold speech. BRAS:193

GOLD STAR MOTHERS See Club speeches

GOLDEN RULE
Golden rule. AMEO 2:105
Rule that works. JAS:88
Spillman, H.C.
Doing unto others. REEM 3:254; REEMB 3:271

GOLDEN WEDDING ANNIVERSARIES See Anniversaries, Wedding - Golden
Goldman, David
Sinister shadows. BRP 3:56; YR 4:17
Goldman, Emma
Anarchy vs. patriotism. HURG:166
Goldsborough, T. Alan
Lewis contempt case. BA

Goldsborough, T. Alan (cont.)
1947-48:93
Goldstein, Marvin W.
Builders of destiny. BRP 4:105; YR 6:93
Roar of the world and God. BRP 2:92; YR 3:167
Goldwater, Barry M.
Campaign speech at Madison Square Garden, October 26, 1964. BA 1964-65:35
Extremism in defense of liberty (accepting nomination for Presidency) HIB:291
Freedom: heritage and responsibility. ANGC:198
National objectives in American foreign policy. BA 1960-61:83
Goldwyn, Samuel
Speech at Friars' Club dinner to Burns and Allen. JEYO: 99

GOLDWYN, SAMUEL
Jessel, G.
Introducing Samuel Goldwyn at Friars' Club dinner to Burns and Allen. JEYO:98

GOLF
Day, J.E.
Introduces Gardner Cowles, publisher. PRNE:15
Drummond, R.
Introducing a golfer. BRC: 271
Golf (amateur offers a toast) ED:432
Golf club. SCHS:139
How to make a hole in one. CON:24
Huber, L.J.
Introducing a golfer. BRC: 274
McGovern, S.
Introducing a golfer. BRC: 174
Milliken, F.
Emcee at a golfers' banquet. BRH:301
Presentation of a golf trophy, by a member of the trophy committee and response. EDGS:394, 396
Toastmaster's before and after talk by man who plays golf. FRIT:42
Golikov, Filip I.
Speech of October 28. RUS: 135
Gompers, Samuel
American Federation of Labor. REEM 4:156; REEMB 4:299
Labor's attitude. PL:754; REEM 11:271; REEMB 12: 287
Shall a Labor Party be formed? BAAMP:249
Useful lessons of Labor Day. THOU 1:457
Voluntary nature of the Labor movement. LINM:120

GOMPERS, SAMUEL
Green, W.
Samuel Gompers. YE:91
Macy, V.E.
Samuel Gompers. REEM sup 2:209; REEMB 5:163

GOOD AND EVIL
Drama of the centuries. NIA: 216

GOOD FRIDAY
Brooks, P.
First Good Friday. THOU 2:65
Parkhurst, C.H.
Man of sorrows. THOU 2: 80
Potter, H.C.
Learn during Lent to say "No." THOU 2:86
Talmage, T.D.
Groups around the cross. THOU 2:72

GOOD-NIGHT SPEECHES
Good-night. THOS:96

GOOD TEMPLARS
Rapen, J.H.
Educating temperance

opinions. THOU 3:521

GOOD WILL SPEECHES
Blough, R.M.
Great expectations. MICS: 144
Clement, M.W.
Whither the railroads. YE: 260
Conant, J.B.
America's fitness to survive. YE:253
Eisenhower, D.
European trip. BA 1959-60: 7
Peace and friendship, in freedom. BA 1959-60:25
Gifford, W.S.
Address before the Bond Club. YE:275
To Chicago Association of Commerce. SAC:101
Good will. FRIE:158
Hoffman, P.G.
Price of things which farmers buy including so-called management of prices by industry. HUS:255
Ketcham, V.A.
Seven doors to the mind and how to open them. YE: 266
Nixon, R.M.
Opening of the American National Exhibition in Moscow. SABA:209
Radio-television address from Moscow. ARNS:240; BA 1959-60-14
Suggestions for preparation of speeches of good will. BUT: 47; BUTA:47
Suggestions for preparation of speeches of good will. With examples of. MO:508; SAB:178; YE:252
Suggestions for preparation of speeches to build good will. HIBS:282; With examples of. MICS:143; SABA:203
Walters, B.L.
Press-an unhidden persuader. SABA:205

GOODFELLOWS See Brotherliness
Goodwin, E.P.
Some Easter certainties. THOU 2:94
Gordon, Armstead C.
John Tyler. SMI:134

GORDON, CHARLES GEORGE
Churchill, R.H.S.
Desertion of General Gordon (February 16, 1884 speech) REEMA 12:592
Desertion of General Gordon (May 13, 1884 speech) ORBR 2:419
Salisbury, R.A.T.G.-C.
Abandonment of General Gordon. BRYW 5:109; CHAL 11:362; HAZO 22: 9283; MAS 22:9283; REEM 9:313; REEMA 15:1808; REEMB 10:322
Gordon, Donald
Responds to an introduction. PRC:9

GORDON, GEORGE
Erskine, T.
Defense of Lord Gordon, 1781. GOOD:638; ONEM: 49
Gordon, John Brown
Last days of the Confederacy. REEM 8:169; REEMA 5: 471; REEMB 13:171; SHUO:39
On silver coinage. CHAL 12: 100

GORDON, JOHN BROWN
Lee, S.D.
Eulogy of General John B. Gordon. SHUO:43
Meek, T.J.
John B. Gordon-the pacificator. TRUW:184
Gordon, Samuel
Is war inevitable under capitalism? YR 7:327
Gordon, Theodore H.
Watchdogs. ONEC:389; YR 1:15

Gore, Albert
At 44th anniversary of Congressional service of Speaker Sam Rayburn. BRAP:136
Gore, Victor M.
Induction address. ONES:57
Gorgias.
Encomium on Helen. CHAL 1:12; HAZO 1:49; MAS 1:49; PL:32
Funeral oration. LEEW 1:43
Gormley, Auston C.
Quo warranto? TRUW:1
Gorton, Guernsey F.
Delusion of equality. ASHF:229
Goschen, George Joachim
On the cultivation of the imagination. CHAL 12:21; HAZO 22:9413; MAS 22:9413
Uses of imagination (installation as Lord Rector of Edinburgh University) REEMA 8:557
Goss, Bert C.
Trial outside the courtroom. LINP:250
Gossage, Nancy
Can minds be changed? NOR 1948:107
Gossett, William T.
Presents Harry Emerson Fosdick. LY:167

GOSSIP
Barrow, I.
Slander. BREW 1:235
Butler, J.
Government of the tongue. BREW 3:21
Cut out the gossip. FRIE:61
Massillon, J.B.
Curse of a malignant tongue. BREW 8:114; BRYW 7:80; CHAL 2:163; HAZO 4:1700; MAS 4:1700
Smart, C.
Serpent in our midst. YR 7:37
Gottheil, Richard
Jews as a race and as a nation. BREW 6:269
Gottschalk, Louis and others (W. Duranty and S.N. Harper)
Soviet Russia at war (radio discussion) BA 1940-41:168
See also McBurney, J.J., jt. auth.
Gough, John Bartholomew
Social responsibilities. REEM 8:192; REEMA 5:495; REEMB 13:195
Temperance address, September 17, 1860. CHAL 9:184; HAZO 18:7730; MAS 18:7730
Use only the best liquor! THOU 1:572
What is minority? PROS:90

GOUGH, JOHN BARTHOLOMEW
Obituary reference for John B. Gough. THOU 3:498
Gould, Samuel B.
Flavor for our daily bread. BA 1962-63:122

GOVERNMENT See Democracy; Industry and state; Municipal government; Political science; State, The; State governments; State rights; Suffrage. Also Name of country or state with subdivision Politics and government, e.g. Great Britain-Politics and government; United States-Politics and government

GOVERNMENT BANKING See Banks and Banking; Independent treasury

GOVERNMENT OWNERSHIP
Altgeld, J.P.
On municipal and governmental ownership. BRYW 10:208; REEM 10:344; REEMB 11:358
Hoover, H.C.
Government ownership. ONEC:521

Smith, A.E.
Government ownership. ONEC:536

GOVERNMENT REGULATION OF INDUSTRY See Industry and state

GOVERNORS See Public officials
Gowacke, John C.
Hickory stumps. BRP 1:53
Gracchus, Gaius
Fragment by G. Gracchus. BRYW 2:35
In vindication of his political purity. LEEW 2:137
Men must be taken as they are. LEEW 2:135; PL:106
On the revenue. CHAL 1:268; HAZO 2:665; MAS 2:665
Peoples' rights above privilege. -Same as his Men must be taken as they are
Gracchus, Tiberius
Fragments by T. Gracchus. BRYW 2:31

GRADUATION EXERCISES See Commencement addresses
Grady, Henry W.
Against centralization. CLAY: 41
Democracy and the South. HARSO:182; SHUO:288
Effects of prohibition in Atlanta, Georgia. THOU 1: 568
Farmer and the cities. SHAH: 517
Home and the Republic. SHU: 155
Homes of the people. CLAY: 132; PROS:85
Lincoln as Cavalier and Puritan. THOU 1:477
Negro and southern restoration. THOU 1:273
New South. BAAMP:180; BOAM:41; BOU:80; BRAC: 287; BRYA:558; BRIM:301; BRYW 10:141; CAP:96; CHAL 14:215; CLAW:159; CLAY:248; ESEH:226; FULB:385; HARS:490; HAZO 25:10724; IMMD: 263; MAS 25:10724; ONEM: 577; ORAMA 2:427; PAR: 450; PE:628; PEA:628; PL:686; PROS:64; REEM 2:105; REEMA 8:579; REEMB 2:97; RINM:278; SAA:207; SAC:45; SHAH: 496; SHU:45; SHUM:177; SOU 9:374; THOU 1:270, 273
People emancipated by defeat. THOU 1:270
Race problem. BRAS:158; BREW 6:273; FULB:391; HARSO:258; HICF:139; IMMD:238; ONEM:585; REEM 2:115; REEMA 2: 534; REEMB 2:107; SHAH: 527; SHUM:214
Solid South. SHAH:511
South and her problems. SHAH:505
Typical American. -Same as his New South

GRADY, HENRY W.
Graves, J.T.
Eulogy on Henry W. Grady. DOA:269; HARSO:193; PROS:128; REEMA 8:590; SOU 9:435
Graff, Jans V.
Response to an introduction. PR:132

GRAFT (IN POLITICS) See Corruption (in politics) Elections-Corrupt practices
Graham, A. Vance
Constitution. LEIO:143
Graham, Ben
Presenting the American Education award to William Lyon Phelps. BA 1939-40: 364
Graham, Frank Porter
Presents Robert M. Hutchins. LY:114
Graham, William F. (Billy Graham)
National humility. HURG:339

Grand, Sarah
Mere man. REEM 2:132; REEMA 2:551; REEMB 2: 124

GRANDMOTHERS See Mothers and daughters
Grangula, chief of the Onondagas
Refuses to bow to French demands. JON:36
Granik, Theodore
Introductory remarks as radio moderator at celebration of 150th anniversary of Bill of Rights. BA 1941-42:96
---- and others (E. Lundeen; R.R. Reynolds, L.B. Schwellenbach; E.D. Thomas)
America's policy toward insular possessions of other countries. BA 1939-40:86
Grant, George Monro
Our national objects and aims. CHAL 12:462; HAZO 23: 9962; MAS 23:9962
Grant, Richard F.
Dedication of the Chamber of Commerce of the U.S. REEM sup 1:371; REEMB 4:314
Grant, Ulysses Simpson
Adopted citizen. REEM 2:139; REEMA 2:561; REEMB 2: 131
At Warren, Ohio. -Same as his Why I am a Republican
Characteristics of newspaper men. HOA:374; HOAP:261; REEMA 2:559
First inaugural address. CHI: 139; LOTI:129; USIN:129; USINA:129
New Englanders. -Same as his Remarkable climate
Remarkable climate. COP: 665; COPB:692; REEM 2: 137; REEMA 2:557; REEMB 2:129
Second inaugural address. CHAL 10:178; CHI:144; HAZO 20:8399; LOTI:133; MAS 20:8399; USIN:132; USINA:132
Why I am a Republican. BRYW 10:107; CHAL 10: 182; HAZO 20:8403; MAS 20:8403; REEM 10:284; REEMB 11:297; WERN 42: 170

GRANT, ULYSSES SIMPSON
Beveridge, A.J.
Takes up the white man's burden (speech commemorating birth of General Grant) FUL:24; PE:650; PEA:650
Bolton, H.W.
None but himself can be his parallel (U.S. Grant) THOU 1:373
Bungay, G.W.
Grandeur of Grant's character. THOU 1:375
Carr, C.E.
Genius and character of Grant. BLAA:225; BLAB: 225
Conkling, R.
Nomination of U.S. Grant for a third term. BAKF:125; BREW 4:138; BRYW 10:94; CHAL 11: 257; HAZO 21:9122; MAS 21:9122; ONEM:472; ORAMA 2:315; REEM 10: 256; REEMA 12:719; REEMB 11:268
Depew, C.M.
Our victorious General (Grant) THOU 1:370
Speech at dinner to celebrate the anniversary of birth of General Grant. CHAL 12:234; HAZO 23: 9705; MAS 23:9705
Farrar, F.W.
Funeral oration on Ulysses Simpson Grant. BREW 6: 100; CHAL 12:12; HAZO 22:9404; MAS 22:9404; ORBR 2:283; REEM 5:163; REEMA 8:464; REEMB 9: 198
Grant's place in history.

WERN 42:43
Headley, J. T.
Grant's character. THOU 1:376
Herbert, H. A.
Grant's magnanimity. THOU 1:385
Higginson, T. R.
Grant. CHAL 10:302; HAZO 20:8603; MAS 20:8603; WERN 42:68
Logan, J. A.
Vindication of President Grant. CHAL 11:62; HAZO 21:8821; MAS 21:8821
McKinley, W.
Grant (at dedication of Grant monument in New York City) BREW 8:40; HAZO 24:10494; MAS 24:10494; WERN 42:77
Newman, J. P.
Eulogy of General Grant. THOU 1:380
Porter, H.
Eulogy on Ulysses S. Grant. REEM 3:98; REEMA 3:944; REEMB 3:99; SHU:81; SHUM:259
Wu Ting-Fang
Grant. WERN 42:48
Grant, William
Uncle Sam-his character. REAC:202
Graper, Elmer E.
True defenders of liberty. BOA:125

GRASS
Ingalls, J. J.
Tribute to the universal beneficence of grass. SHUP:155
Grattan, Henry
Against English imperialism.-Same as his Declaration of Irish rights, April 19, 1780
Against the Union (January 15, 1800 speech) KET:136
Against the Union (March 19, 1800 speech) KET:138
Against the Union (May 26, 1800 speech).-Same as his Unsurrendering fidelity to country
Declaration of Irish rights, April 19, 1780. BREW 6:279; BRTH:91; BRTHA:91; BRYW 6:59; CHAL 3:165; CODS:189; CODSA:189; GOOD:386; HAY:48; HAZO 7:2784; KET:112; MAS 7:2784; ONEM:198; ORBR 1:361; PE:147; PEA:147; PL:509; REEMA 13:1100
Invictive against Corry. BREW 6:294; BRYW 6:71; CODS:211; GOOD:396; HARS:327; HAZO 7:2806; MAS 7:2806; ONEM:330; PE:300; PEA:300
Irish feeling. KET:133
Liberty as an inalienable right.-Same as his Declaration of Irish rights
Making his second motion for a Declaration of Irish rights, April 16, 1782. GOOD:391; KET:131
Plays a turncoat.-Same as his Invictive against Corry
Reply to Flood. CLAY:241; GOOD:394
Roman Catholic emancipation. BEA:225; PAUF 1:230
Tithes. KET:135
Triumph of Irish independence.-Same as his Making his second motion for a Declaration of Irish rights, April 16, 1782
Unsurrendering fidelity to country. BREW 6:297; HAZO 7:2811; KET:140; MAS 7:2811

GRAUMAN, SID
Jessel, G.
Eulogy to Sid Grauman. JEYO:162
Graves, Asenath L.
Constitution. LEIO:109
Graves, Don
Disarmament. YR 4:91
Graves, Eugene L.
Bible of democracy. SHU:57

Graves, John Temple
Eulogy on Henry W. Grady. DOA:269; HARSO 193; PROS:128; REEMA 8:590; SOU 9:435
Our country's birthday. FUL: 131, 134, 137
Our country's flag. WERN 42:33
Graves, John Temple, II
Second discovery of America. BART 2:191
Gray, Stanley E
Influence of the teaching of history on world peace. ASHF:286
Gray, William H., Jr.
Broaden our horizons for correctional service. HILK: 140

GREAT BRITAIN
Bristol, G.D.
Grievances and oppressions under Charles I. BREW 5: 236
Canning, G.
Sees the world at peace in the shadow of the British Navy. PE:418; PEA:418
Chamberlain, J.
Conception of the British Empire (March 21, 1897) ADR 4:303; EMS 2:258
Empire and home rule. BREW 3:192
Future of the British Empire (November 6, 1895 speech) BRTH:325; BRTHA: 325; COP:194; COPA:194; COPB:194; ORBR 2:401; REEM 1:236; REEMA 1:141; REEMB 1:237
True conception of Empire (Mar. 31, 1897) BRYW 5: 184; REEMA 12:536
Churchill, W.L.S.
Fiscal retaliation. BEA:117
Speech in Commons on Commonwealth and Empire unity. VO 1944-45:175
Cowen, J.
British Empire. BEA:153
Cromwell, O.
Debating whether or not to become King of England. BREW 4:252; BRTH:33; BRTHA:33
Elizabeth I.
Golden speech. CROC:192
Rallies her army during the Armada peril. BUT:20; BUTB:233; HIBS:441; PE: 89; PEA:89
Ethelbert.
Coming of Christianity. BRTH:1; BRTHA:1
Fisher, H.A.L.
English heritage. BEA:187
Flood, H.
Renunciation speech. CHAL 2:445; HAZO 6:2543; KET: 96; MAS 6:2543
Gladstone, W.E.
Fundamental error of English Colonial aggrandizement. BREW 6:241; ONEM: 785; PL:477
On domestic and foreign affairs. ADR 3:287; BRYW 5 66; CHAL 7:421; COP:188; COPA:188; COPB:188; FULB:149; HAZO 15:6339; MAS 15:6339; ORBR 2:253; REEM 9:288; REEMA 13: 1068; REEMB 10:296
Prospect of imperial disintegration. EMS 2:254
Responsibilities of Empire. BRTH:298; BRTHA:298; HAY:275
Grattan, H.
Tithes. KET:135
Hailsham, D.M.H.
Ottawa Conference. BEA: 251
Harcourt, W.V.
Our national position. CHA 11:157
Herbert, A.
Advocates a festival for Britain. PE:812; PEA:812
Howard of Penrith, E.W.H.
Sales representative for John Bull and Co. REEM

sup 2:69; REEMB 5:1
Laurier, W.
Canada, England and the United States in 1899. BREW 7:301; COP:381; COPA:381; COPB:381; FUL: 181,183; PL:542; REEMA 13:1297
Lloyd George, D.
The budget. HAY:305; PE: 680; PEA:680; REEM 9: 383; REEMB 10:395
MacDonald, J.R.
Empire Day. BEA:295
Murrow, E.R.
Farewell to England. BA 1945-46:33
Spring comes to England. BA 1940-41:157
Newton, W.M.
British Empire. LEIO:78
Oxford and Asquith, H.H.A.
Issues-true and false. CHAL 14:277
Pitt, W., 1708-1778
On a motion for an address on the marriage of the Prince of Wales. GOOD:76
On the state of the nation (January 22, 1770) GOOD: 114; HAZO 5:1915; MAS 5: 1915
Rosebery, A.P.P.
Questions of Empire. REEMA 15:1785
True leverage of Empire. CHAL 14:59; HAZO 25: 10600; MAS 25:10600
Smith, G.
English women's institutes receive official recognition. BUT:144; BUTA:144; BUTB:144
Evolution of the dominion. CHAL 10:249; HAZO 20: 8530; MAS 20:8530
Smuts, J.C.
British Commonwealth of Nations. ONEM:603; REEM 3:237; REEMB 3:254
See also England; Imperial Conferences; Ireland; Scotland; World War, 1939-1945-Great Britain

---- ARMY
Bristol, G.D.
Army in domestic politics. BREW 5:240; CHAL 2:63; GOOD:16; HAZO 4:1503; MAS 4:1503; ORBR 1:107
Brougham and Vaux, H.P.B.
On the army estimates. GOOD:891; LEEW 7:237
Cartwright, R.J.
Services of a patriotic militia. CHAL 12:452; HAZO 23:9876; MAS 23:9876
Pitt, W., 1708-1778
Speech on Sir W. Yonge's motion respecting the Hanoverian troops. GOOD:93; PAUF 1:53
Pulteney, W.
On a motion for reducing the army. CHAL 2:189; GOOD:43; HAZO 4:1758; MAS 4:1758

---- COLONIES
Balfour, A.J.B.
Imperial relations, December 8, 1926 speech. EMS 2:279
Imperial relations, January 27, 1927 speech. EMS 2: 285
Barre, I.
America's obligation to England. CHAL 2:341; HAZO 5:2039; MAS 5:2039
Borden, R.L.
Imperial relations. EMS 2: 266
Burke, E.
On American taxation, April, 1774. CLAY:182; CODS:120; CODSA:120; EMS 2:221; GOOD:242; HARSO:353; KET:3
Camden, C.P.
Taxation of colonies. EMS 2:218
Chamberlain, J.
At the first meeting of the Colonial Conference of

GREAT BRITAIN-COLONIES (cont.)
1897. KES 2:208
Splendid isolation. ADR 4:292; REEMA 12:541
Edward VII.
The Colonies. REEM 2:1; REEMA 3:1175; REEMB 2:1
Gladstone, W. E.
Colonial policy. EMS 2:244
Prospect of imperial disintegration. EMS 2:254
Grey of Fallodon, E. G.
Participation of the Dominions in future Hague conventions. KES 2:182
Mansfield, W. M.
Judgment in Campbell v. Hall, 1774. KES 1:35
Maseres, F.
Considerations on the expedience of procuring an act of Parliament for the settlement of the Province of Quebec. KES 1:12
Molesworth, W.
Colonial policy, June 26, 1849 speech. EMS 2:226
Colonial policy, February 8, 1850. EMS 2:233
Pitt, W., 1708-1778
Taxation of Colonies, December 17, 1765 speech. EMS 2:215
Smuts, J. C.
Imperial relations, April 16, 1917 speech. EMS 2:269
Imperial relations, May 15, 1917 speech. EMS 2:273
See also Africa; Australia; Canada; Imperial federation; United States-History-Revolution

---- COMMERCE
Oxford and Asquith, H. H. A.
Trade and the Empire. BRYW 5:201

---- CONSTITUTION See England-Constitution

---- DEFENSES
Baldwin, S. B.
British defence policy (November 18, 1936 speech) KESK 2:175

---- FOREIGN RELATIONS
Balfour, A. J. B.
Control over foreign policy. EMS 1:255
Cooperation of English-speaking peoples. FKA:322; ONES:317; SHUP:158
Bevin, E.
Speech in Commons on foreign policy. VO 1945-46:468
Bright, J.
Morality and military greatness. BREW 2:237; HAZO 16:6872; MAS 16:6872
On the Eastern crisis and the danger of war, 1878. BRTH:273; BRTHA:273
On the English foreign policy. ADR 3:159; BRYW 4:222
Churchill, W. L. S.
Address to Congress, January 17, 1952. BA 1951-52:30; MOUG:220; MOUGA:220
Broadcast to the world about the meeting with President Roosevelt, August 24, 1941. VO 1941:380
False security. HAN:83
Speech at the Mansion House, November 10, 1941. VO 1941:498
Speech in Commons on foreign affairs, May 24, 1944. VO 1944-45:219
Speech in Commons on Syria and Lebanon. VO 1945-46:257
Eden, A.
Address in the House of Commons, September 22, 1943. VO 1943-44:405
Speech in Commons on foreign affairs, May 25, 1944. VO 1944-45:234

Gladstone, W. E.
Power to make war. EMS 1:242
Treaty-making power. EMS 1:248
Grey of Fallodon, E. G.
Control over foreign policy. EMS 1:251
Houghton, A. B.
Open diplomacy. BEA:277
Lytton, H. B.
After dinner speech. KLEG: 150
Palmerston, H. J. T.
Power to make war. EMS 1:245
Pulteney, W.
Information on foreign policy. March 3, 1738 speech. EMS 1:231
Information on foreign policy. February 6, 1739 speech. EMS 1:236
Thurlow, E.
Treaty-making power. EMS 1:239
Toynbee, A. J.
Can we "live and let live?" MOA:457
Walpole, R.
Information on foreign policy. EMS 1:233

---- ---- FRANCE
Churchill, W. L. S.
Reply in Commons to allegations made by Marshall Petain. VO 1945-46:287
Fox, C. J.
On the rejection of Napoleon's overtures. ADR 2:108; BRTH:150; BRTHA:150; BRYW 4:37; CHAL 3:198; CODS:277; CODSA:277; COP:172; COPA:172; COPB:172; FULB:40; GOOD:529; HAY:95; HAZO 7:2827; MAS 7:2827; ORBR 1:291; PAUF 1:166; PE:288; PEA:288; REEM 9:162; REEMA 13:994; REEMB 10:169
Pitt, W., 1759-1806
On the refusal to negotiate with France, February 3, 1800. ADR 2:19; BRYW 4: 7; CHAL 4:46; COP:169; COPA:169; COPB:169; GOOD:604; HAZO 8:3375; MAS 8:3375; ORBR 2:3; PE:282; PEA:282; PL:426; REEM 9:149; REEMB 10: 156
On the rupture of negotiations with France. GOOD: 595; LEEW 6:279

---- ---- GREECE
Churchill, W. L. S.
Address in Commons on relations among Britain, the U. S., and the U. S. S. R. VO 1945-46:19
Eden, A.
Statement on British policy in Greece. VO 1944-45:619

---- ---- ITALY
Braunstein, B.
Italy vs. Great Britain. SAR:286

---- ---- JAPAN
Simon, J. A.
Address in House of Commons, April 30, 1934. KESK 2:10

---- ---- PORTUGAL
Canning, G.
On the policy of granting aid to Portugal. ADR 3:13; BRYW 4:115; CHAL 4:368; GOOD:875; HAZO 9:3837; LEEW 7:75; MAS 9:3837; ORBR 2:57; PL:447
Churchill, W. L.S.
Statement in the House of Commons on the British occupation of the Azores. VO 1943-44:435

---- ---- RUSSIA
Fox, C. J.
On the Russian armament. GOOD:500

GREAT BRITAIN-FOREIGN RELATIONS-SPAIN
Attlee, C.R.
On Bilbao blockade (speech in House of Commons, April 14, 1937) KESK 2:214
Eden, A.
International situation in 1937. KESK 2:198
Pitt, W , 1708-1778
On the Spanish Convention, March 8, 1739. GOOD:77
Speech in relation to the seizure of the Falkland Islands by Spain. GOOD:118; HAZO 5:1927; MAS 5:1927
Runciman, W.
On Merchant Shipping (conveyance of munitions to Spain) Bill. KESK 2:187
Sinclair, A.
On Bilbao blockade. KESK 2:221

---- ---- TURKEY
Argyll, G.D.C.
Eastern question: address in answer to the Queen's speech in 1877. PAUF 2:198
Gladstone, W.E.
Eastern question. BEA:205; PAUF 1:421

---- ---- UNITED STATES
Attlee, C.R.
Address before Congress. VO 1945-46:705
Bright, J.
Against Mr. Roebuck's motion for recognition of the Southern Confederacy. HAZO 16:6846; MAS 16:6846
Trent affair. BRYW 4:243; CHAL 8:156; COP:182; COPA:182; COPB:182; HAZO 16:6814; MAS 16:6814; PE:512; PEA:512; REEM 9:239; REEMA 11:303; REEMB 10:246; SAA:179
Chamberlain, J.
Anglo-American friendship. BEA:87
Churchill, W.L.S.
Address to the Pilgrims, January 9, 1941. VO 1941:27
British-American cooperation. BA 1943-44:27; VO 1943-44:331
United we stand secure. BA 1948-49:35; HAR:3
Depew, C.M.
England and America since the Spanish War. BREW 5:170; FUL:118; ORAMA 2:383
Dickens, C.
English friendliness for America. COP:615; COPB:655; REEMA 1:405
Geddes, A.C.
Cooperation between Great Britain and America. REEM 2:85; REEMB 2:77
Hanna, E.
What part should the United States play in the economic recovery of Britain? HOD:102
Herschell, F.
Great Britain and the United States. REEMA 2:609
Houghton, R.M.M.
Bonds of national sympathy. REEMA 2:639
Imrie, M.A.
America and Britain: some problems in common. NESA:154
Johnston, E.
Steps toward a good world. HAN:374
MacDonald, J.R.
Mystic kinship. REEM sup 2:205; REEMB 2:391
Taft, W.H.
America and England. REEM 3:299; REEMB 3:316
Tracy, S.H.
America and Britain for civilization. ONES:338
See also Anglo-American

Union (proposed); United States-History-Revolution; World War 1939-1945-United States-Aid to Great Britain

---- HISTORY
Eliot, J.
On the Petition of Right. ADR 1:13; BRYW 5:358; BRTH:21; BRTHA:21; BRYW 3:39; CHAL 2:23; GOOD:3; HAZO 4:1444; LEEW 6:37; MAS 4:1444; PL:362
Macaulay, T.B.
Survey of four centuries. REEMA 9:836
Pym, J.
On grievances in the reign of Charles I. ADR 1:37; BERS:18; BREW 8:388; BRYW 3:50; PL:368
See also Corn Laws; Reform Bills (1831, 1832). Also names of wars, e.g. Crimean War, 1853-1856; Egypt and Sudan Campaign, 1882-1900; European War, 1914-1918; South African War, 1899-1902; United States-History-Revolution; World War, 1939-1945-Great Britain; World War, 1939-1945-United States-Aid to Great Britain; Zulu War, 1879

---- NAVY
Churchill, W.L.S.
On the creation of an Imperial squadron. KES:2:343
Lloyd George, D.
Sea power and the British Empire. BREW 7:372
Pitt, W., 1708-1778
Against search-warrants for seamen. CLAY:261; GOOD:79
Debate in 1741 on wages of sailors. BREW 10:72,77; BRYW 3:193; KLEG:129
Walpole, H.
Debate in 1741 on wages of sailors. BREW 10:75
Debate in 1741 on wages of sailors. BREW 10:71,73

---- PARLIAMENT
Ashburton, J.D.
Right to commit. EMS 1:215
Balfour, A.J.B.
House of Lords and financial measures. EMS 1:174
Parliament Bill, 1911. EMS 1:192
Barré, I.
Right to commit. EMS 1:221
Birkenhead, F.E.S.
Reform of the House of Lords. EMS 1:123
Bradlaugh, C.
At the bar of the House of Commons. CHAL 12:205; HAZO 22:9586; MAS 22:9586
His plea at the bar of the House. BRYW 5:91
Bryce, J.B.
Reform of the House of Lords. EMS 1:116
Campbell-Bannerman, H.
House of Lords as a check on legislation, December 20, 1906 speech. EMS 1:149
Supremacy of the people. BREW 3:97; EMS 1:151
Chelmsford, F.J.N.T.
House of Lords and financial measures. EMS 1:137
Churchill, W.L.S.
Speech in Commons asking for the prolongation of Parliament. VO 1944-45:521
Cromwell, O.
Address to Parliament, September 4, 1654. CHAL 2:45; HAZO 4:1475; MAS 4:1475
At the opening of Parliament under the Protectorate.

---- PARLIAMENT (cont.)
BRYW 3:117; PL:379
On dissolving Parliament (Second Protectorate Parliament) LEEW 6:67; REEMA 12:741
On the dissolution of Parliament (First Protectorate Parliament) COP:147; COPA: 147; COPB:147; ORBR 1: 65; REEM 9:70; REEMB 10: 73
Speech to the nominated Parliament. CROC:103
Curzon of Kedleston, G. N. C.
House of Lords and financial measures. EMS 1:159
Dering, E.
Religious controversy in Parliament. BREW 5:184
Devonshire, S. C. C.
Occasions for appeal to the people. EMS 1:92
Elizabeth I.
To the House of Commons. KNAS:312; KNASA:312
Fox, C. J.
In favor of Mr. Grey's motion for Parliamentary reform. EMS 2:134; GOOD:515
Right to commit. EMS 1:219
George VI.
At the opening of the House of Lords and the House of Commons, Nov. 12, 1941. VO 1941:505
Gladstone, W. E.
Supports the right of freethinkers to enter the House of Commons. PE:560; PEA:560
Grimston, H.
Projecting canker worms and caterpillars. BREW 6: 305
Harcourt, S.
Jurisdiction over Parliamentary elections. EMS 1:203
Lenthall, W.
Opening the long Parliament under Charles I. BREW 7: 327
Lyndhurst, J. S. C.
House of Lords as a check on legislation. EMS 1:135
Mansfield, W. M.
On a Bill depriving Peers of certain privileges. GOOD:160; LEEW 6:159
Reply to the Earl of Chatham against Parliamentary exemption from arrest for debt. BREW 8:79
Macaulay, T. B.
Position of a Ministry not supported by the House of Commons. EMS 1:73
Morley of Blackburn, J. M.
Dummy Lords or dummy Commons? BREW 8:200
Oxford and Asquith, H. H. A.
House of Lords and financial measures, Dec. 2, 1909 speech. EMS 1:165
House of Lords and financial measures, April 7, 1910 speech. EMS 1:181
Parliament Bill, 1911. EMS 1:188
Sovereign and the Ministry's right to dissolution of Parliament. EMS 1:53
Palmerston, H. J. T.
House of Lords and financial measures. EMS 1:141
Peel, R.
Papers exempt from liability to libel. EMS 1:224
Position of a Ministry not supported by the House of Commons, April 8, 1835 speech. EMS 1:62
Position of a Ministry not supported by the House of Commons, May 27, 1841 speech. EMS 1:66
Pitt, W., 1708-1778
Against a motion for adjourning Parliament, Dec. 11, 1777. GOOD:139
Pitt, W., 1759-1806
Position of a Ministry not supported by the House of Commons. EMS 1:59
Pulteney, W.

Army and the Parliament, 1746. BRTH:62; BRTHA:62
Secrecy of debates. EMS 1:208
Rosebery, A. P. P.
Lord's veto. CHAL 14:73
Reform of the House of Lords. EMS 1:112
Russell, J. R.
Position of a Ministry not supported by the House of Commons. EMS 1:78
Salisbury, R. A. T. G.
House of Lords as a check on legislation. EMS 1:146
Thurlow, E.
Right to commit. EMS 1:211
Walpole, R.
House of Lords Bill, 1719. EMS 1:105
On the Septennial Bill. GOOD:32; LEEW 6:103
Peerage Bill. BEA:421; PAUF 1:33
Wentworth, P.
Liberty of the Commons. BRTH:6; BRTHA:6; CHAL 1:457; HAZO 4:1386; MAS 4:1386
Wilkes, J.
Commons and its rights, 1770. BRTH:81; BRTHA:81
Denies the right of the House of Commons to reject duly elected members. PE:126; PEA:126
Wyndham, W.
Royal prerogative delegated from the people (Army Bill, 1734) BREW 10:281
Secrecy of debates. EMS 1:205
Yonge, W.
Constituents and members. EMS 2:108
See also Reform Bills (1831, 1832)

---- POLITICS AND GOVERNMENT
Baldwin, S. B.
Collective responsibility of the Ministry. EMS 1:96
Balfour, A. J. B.
Lords as upholders of government-"Of, by and for the people." BREW 1:127
Beaconsfield, B. D.
Against democracy for England. BREW 1:301; HAZO 14:6003; MAS 14:6003; PL:482
Meaning of Conservatism. ADR 3:216; BREW 1:314; BRYW 5:38; CHAL 7:140; CROC:169; EMS 1:30; HAY:245; HAZO 14:6022; MAS 14:6022; PE:554; PEA:554; REEMA 11:143
Occasions for appeal to the people. EMS 1:81
On the political situation. ORBR 2:213
Bristol, G. D.
Army in domestic politics. BREW 5:240; CHAL 2:63; GOOD:16; HAZO 4:1503; MAS 4:1503; ORBR 1:107
Burke, E.
Plea for domestic reform. HAY:31
Principle in politics: speech at Bristol, previous to the election, 1780 (defends his Parliamentary conduct) BRAO:89; BREW 2:412; BRYW 6:40; GOOD:292; HIB:143; PE:160; PEA:160
Campbell-Bannerman, H.
On the policy of the Liberal Party. BRYW 5:226
Chamberlain, J.
On Liberal aims. CHAL 13:57; HAZO 23:9993; MAS 23:9993
Churchill, R. H. S.
Administration of Chips. HAY:293
Age of action. BREW 3:312
Policy of Lord Salisbury's second Ministry, Dartford, Oct. 2, 1886. PAUF 2:226
Political life and thought in England. REEMA 1:201
Churchill, W. L. S.
Excerpts from address before the annual Conference of the Conservative Party.

---- POLITICS AND GOVERNMENT (cont.)
VO 1945-46:121
Speech following the King's speech from the throne, November 29, 1944. VO 1944-45:575
To the Central Council of the Conservative Party. VO 1942-43:204
Curran, J.P.
On government by attachment. BREW 4:328; REEMA 12:774
Curzon of Kedleston, G.N.C.
Ministry's request to the Sovereign for the creation of peers. EMS 1:38
Erskine, T.
Sovereign's intervention in politics. EMS 1:8
Gladstone, W.E.
Occasions for appeal to the people. EMS 1:87
On the Beaconsfield ministry. CHAL 7:458; HAZO 15:6377; MAS 15:6377
Grey, C.
Ministry's request to Sovereign for creation of peers. EMS 1:11
Haldane, R.B.
Ministry's request to the Sovereign for the creation of peers. EMS 1:49
Lansdowne, W.P.F.
Sovereign's intervention in politics. EMS 1:2
Loreburn, R.
On the policy of the English Liberals. BRYW 5:247
Lowe, R.
Coming of democracy. ADR 4:232; HAY:240; PAUF 1:393
Macaulay, T.B.
Consent or force in government. BREW 8:26
Meighen, A.
British political tradition. REEM 2:402; REEMB 2:419
Morley of Blackburn, J.M.
Literature and politics. KLEM:139; REEMA 2:838
Nottingham, H.F.
Address to the throne. LEEW 6:93
Oxford and Asquith, H.H.A.
Government by competitive crime. BREW 1:169
Palmerston, H.J.T.
Sovereign advised to dismiss a Minister. EMS 1:26
Peel, R.
Occasions for appeal to the people. EMS 1:84; PAUF 1:295
Sovereign's responsibility for dismissal of Ministers. EMS 1:16
Pitt, W., 1708-1778
Speech in support of Lord Limerick's second motion. PAUF 1:52
Romily, S.
Sovereign's intervention in politics. EMS 1:5
Russell, J.R.
Sovereign advised to dismiss a Minister. EMS 1:20
Salisbury, R.A.T.G.-C.
Limehouse policy. BREW 3:180
One-man power. ORBR 2:316
Sheridan, R.B.
Reply to Lord Mornington, 1794. PAUF 1:225
Sidney, A.
Governments for the people and not the people for the government. Scaffold speech. BREW 9:222; BRYW 3:142
Smith, S.
"Wounds, shrieks, and tears" in government. BREW 9:258
Vane, H.
On the petition and advice. LEEW 6:75
See also Reform Bills (1831, 1832)

GREATNESS See fame

GREECE-ANCIENT
Isocrates.
On the union of Greece to resist Persia. BRYW 1:89; COP:11; COPA:11; COPB: 11
Primacy of Athens. CROC: 259
McKeldin, T.
Influence of ancient Greece on modern life. MCK:212
Xenophon.
In council of war. CHAL 1: 96; HAZO 1:172; MAS 1:172

---- MODERN
Clay, H.
Greek revolution. CLAY:29; FULB:211; HAZO 10:4095; MAS 10:4095; SHAH:111
Churchill, W. L. S.
Speech in Commons on British policy in liberated countries. VO 1944-45:602
Statement in Commons on the situation in Greece. VO 1944-45:595
Cockburn, A.
On the Greek difficulty. CHAL 7:53; HAZO 14:5865; MAS 14:5865
Eden, A.
Statement on British policy in Greece. VO 1944-45:619
Palmerston, H. J. T.
On affairs in Greece. BRYW 4:156; CHAL 5:348; HAZO 11:4819; MAS 12:4819
Pepper, C. D.
Against aid to Greece and Turkey. BA 1946-47:67
Truman, H. S.
Aid to Greece and Turkey. BA 1946-47:43; GRAC:149
Vandenberg, A. H.
For aid to Greece and Turkey. BA 1946-47:51
See also World War 1939-1945-Greece

GREED
Buhler, I.
Modern shylocks. BRP 5:81
Elliott, A. R.
Modern harpies. BRP 5:101

GREEK LETTER SOCIETIES
Bunche, R. J.
Dreams and realities (installation of Gamma chapter of Phi Beta Kappa) NORR 3d ser:264
Croessman, D.
Whatsoever things are true. NOR 1940:9
Gauss, C.
Scholar and his country (installation of Alpha chapter of Phi Beta Kappa at Florida State College) NORR 3d ser:43
Jones, L. W.
Spirit of '76 and the barbarian culture (175th anniversary of Phi Beta Kappa) NORR 3d ser:203
Larson, C.
Address of welcome (at Kappa Kappa Gamma initiation banquet) MOUG:242; MOUGA:242
Sororities (a sister sets forth the aims of the society) EDGS:370
Toast-"Our fraternity or sorority" -two examples of. STON.135-136
Van Dyke, H.
Democratic aristocracy (sesquicentennial of Phi Beta Kappa) BRAC:315; NORR 2d ser:528
Voorhees, O. M.
Presentation of a Phi Beta Kappa memorial hall. BRAC:262
Wilson, W.
Training the intellect. BAAGA:431; KLEG:203; ONEM:844; ONES:261
Greeley, Horace
During his campaign for president. BRYW 10:54
On the union of workers. CHAL 8:316; HAZO 17:7127; MAS 17:7127

GREELEY, HORACE
Chapin, E.H.
Eulogy on Horace Greeley. CHAL 8:475; HAZO 18: 7477; MAS 18:7477
Green, Fletcher M.
Democracy in the old South. TIN:177
Green, George E.
Patriotism of the order (Redmen) THOU 3:287
Green, John Edgar, Jr.
Aaron Burr: a splendid failure. SHUC:325
Green, William
Acceptance of the presidency of the American Federation of Labor. LINM:61
Do your part. BOB:15
Introducing James J. Davis. ONEC:70
Introducing Peter Heenan. ONEC:69
Labor, freedom, and democracy. BA 1940-41:243
Modern trade unionism. COP: 405; COPA:405; COPB: 405; HURG:205; REEM sup 1:374; REEMB 4:317
Preservation of free enterprise the common objective of capital and labor. GLAD: 300
Response to Toronto's welcome. ONEC:25
Samuel Gompers. YE:91
Science of labor relations. SAR:353
Greene, Theodore M.
In praise of reflective commitment. NORR 3d ser:142
Greener, Richard T.
Emigration of colored citizens from the southern states. WOON:473
Young men, to the front! DUNM:63
Greenewalt, Crawford H.
To reach high places. ANGC: 18

GREENFIELD, ALBERT M.
Stevenson, A.E.
World brotherhood in a space age. BA 1957-58:59
Greenhalge, F.T.
Beginning of constitutionality. THOU 1:494
Greenlinger, Leo
Business budgets. REEM 4: 170
Greenslade, John Wills
Our war in the Pacific. HAN: 331
Greenwell, Esther
Tramp! Tramp! Tramp! YR 9:41
Greer, David Hummell
Address at 250th anniversary of the settlement of the Jews in the United States. TWJ:49

GREETINGS See Salutatory addresses; Welcoming addresses

Gregg, David
Debt we owe to the Dutch. THOU 1:318
Way to honor our patriotic dead. THOU 1:102
Gregg, Henry H.
Accepting the presidency of the American Pharmaceutical Association. SAB:217; SABA:299
Gregory, Anthony C.
Introducing a floor covering dealer
" a grocer (super market manager)
" a shoe merchant
BRC:102, 258, 71
Gregory, James Francis
Social bearings of the fifth commandment. DUNM:397
Gregory, Joyce R.
We call them radicals. BRP 4:101
Gregory, Thomas Watt
Southern types. SHU:185
Gregory I, The Great
On Job. PL:191; LEEW 3: 281
Gregory, Saint, bp. of Nyssa

Funeral oration on Meletius. LEEW 3:121
On the baptism of Christ. LEEW 3:135
Gregory of Nazianzus, Saint
Eulogy on Basil of Caesarea. BREW 6:300; LEEW 3:151; PL:160
Last farewell. LEEW 3:165
Oration on the arrival of the Egyptians. HAZO 3:1144; MAS 3:1144
Gregory Thaumaturgus, Saint
Panegyric on Origen. LEEW 3:45; PL:154
Greiner, Fred H., Jr.
Call to politics. BRP 9:72; NOR 1938:3
Grew, Joseph Clark
Menace of Japan. BA 1942-43:72
Radio broadcast from Washington, August 30, 1942. VO 1942-43:447
Grey, Charles, 2nd Earl of (1764-1845)
Ministry's request to Sovereign for creation of peers. EMS 1:11
Grey of Fallodon, Edward Grey, 1st Viscount
Control over foreign policy. EMS 1:251
End of peace. -Same as his England's position
England's position. COP:199; COPA:199; COPB:199; HAY:318; REEM 11:12; REEMB 12:13
Industry. BEA:243
Participation of the Dominions in future Hague conventions. KES 2:182
Griffin, Clare E.
Presents James Palmer. LY: 83
Griffin, Lloyd
Walls of happiness. BRP 7:43
Griffin, R. S.
Strange drama. ASHF:120
Griffith, Arthur
Irish Free State (January 7, 1922) COP:223; COPA:223; COPB:223; REEM 7:160; REEMB 8:187
On establishment of Irish Free State (December 19, 1921) KESB:98
Griggs, Edward Howard
New social ideal. CHAL 14: 461; HAZO 25:11014; MAS 25:11014
Griggs, John W.
Ideal lawyer. KLEG:355
Social discontent. BLAA:146; BLAB:146; REEMA 2:564
Griggs, Robert F.
Our friend-the volcano. MOUG:184; MOUGA:184
Grigsby, Hugh Blair
American revolution. SMI:69
Littleton Waller Tazewell. SMI:152
Grimke, Archibald H.
On the occasions of the presentation of a loving cup to Hon. Joseph Benson Foraker, United States Senator. DUNM:337
Shame of America, or the Negro's case against the Republic. WOON:671
Grimke, Francis J.
Equality of rights for all citizens, black and white, alike. DUNM:347
Victory for the Allies and the United States a ground of rejoicing, of thanksgiving. WOON:690
Grimm, Peter
Introduces Dr. George Gallup
" Thomas E. Dewey (Governor of State of New York)
" V.K. Wellington Koo. PR: 65, 66, 62
Grimston, Sir Harbottle, Bart.
Projecting canker worms and caterpillars. BREW 6:305
Griswold, A. Whitney
Balancing moral responsibility and scientific progress. BA 1951-52:147
Man thinking: inaugural address as president of Yale University. HAR:376

Griswold, A. Whitney
On conversations-chiefly academic. BRAP:109
Grizzly (Medicine Bear), Indian chief
To the heads of department and members of legislature, in the House of Representatives. SHE:53

GROCERS
For a grocers' entertainment. BARB:190
Grocers, by a prominent tradesman. EDGS:143
See also Food
Grodzins, Morton See Appleby, P.E., jt. auth.
Gromyko, Andrei A.
Address at final plenary session of United Nations Conference on International Organization. VO 1945-46:307
Remarks at conclusion of the first phase of the Dumbarton Oaks conversations. VO 1944-45:456
Statement at opening of Dumbarton Oaks Conference. VO 1944-45:384
Gropius, Walter
Creative education: key to good architecture and design. BA 1963-64:182
Grossman, Howard
Scarlet letter. NOR 1940:15
Grossman, Mervin Hilf
Light that is darkness. YR 10:41
Grosvenor, Edwin Augustus
Attitude of the scholar. NORR 1st ser:395
Grosvenor, Elsie Bell
Memories of my father. YE: 329
Grosvenor, Gilbert
Byrd; the explorer and the man. DOA:72
Grosvenor, J.W.
Perseverance wins. THOU 3: 539
Grote, George
Ballot. EMS 2:152
Grow, Galusha Aaron
On Manila. CHAL 10:260; HAZO 20:8541; MAS 20: 8541
Gruell, E. F.
Put on charity. ACW:118
Gruening, Ernest
Independence Day address. BA 1959-60:31
Gruenther, Alfred M.
NATO. HURG:334
North Atlantic Treaty Organization and defense of Western Europe. BA 1955-56:25
Responds to an introduction before the English-speaking Union of the Commonwealth. PRNE:56
Grunwald, Ernest
Toward saner values. BRP 4: 64; INTW 1933:46; YR 5: 311
Guadet, Marguérite Elie
On maintaining the Constitution. LEEW 5:135
Reply to Robespierre. BREW 6:216
Guérard, Albert Léon
Land where hatred expires. HARSO:93

GUERILLAS
Hitler, A.
Order to his Western armies concerning guerilla warfare. VO 1945-46:160
Guernsey, S. Kendrick
Response to introduction. PR: 124
Guerrero, M. P.
Inaugural speech at Conference on the Problems of Economic Development. UAR:313

GUEST, EDGAR A.
Introducing Edgar A. Guest. NESA:192

GUESTS
Address by an honored guest at a Ladies Literary Society. AMEO 2:60
Cap: a testimonial speech.

BAI:113
Elmhurst club president's welcoming address to members of a visiting club. WRA:69
Guest gives thanks for courtesies extended-three examples of. STON:163-164
Introduction of special guests at banquet. FRIT:14
Reply to the toast to the visitors at club meeting. WRA:63
Speech in honor of a distinguished guest, and reply. BARB:53-54
Suggestions for proposing a toast to visitors (to Masonic Lodge) With examples of. EDW:51
Toast "Our visitors" -at regular meeting of almost any club. WRA:53
Toast to our guests-two examples of. FRIT:93
Tribute to guest of honor. NAT:46
Tribute to guest-of-honor and appeal for funds (at hospital fund drive and testimonial) BED:64; BEDA:101
See also Introductions; Welcoming addresses

Guggenheim, Charles
Heart disease. NOR 1948:115

Guild, Curtis, Jr.
Address delivered at Faneuil Hall on 250th anniversary of the settlement of the Jews in the United States. TWJ:65
Supremacy and its conditions. CHAL 14:394; HAZO 25:10914; MAS 25:10914

Guizot, François Pierre Guillaume
Address at the distribution of prizes at the University of Paris. CHAL 5:401; HAZO 12:4878; MAS 12:4878
At the unveiling of the statue of William the Conqueror. CHAL 5:404; HAZO 12:4881; MAS 12:4881
Civilization and the individual man. BREW 6:309; CHAL 5:390; HAZO 12:4867; MAS 12:4867
Democracy in France. PL:318

Gullion, Edmund
John Marshall and Federal supremacy. DOA:106

Gunderson, Robert G.
Davy Crockett's tongue-tied admirers. BRAP:83

Gunn, John E.
Riddle of modern unrest. CATA 2:141

Gunning, Jack
First in agriculture. YR 10:159

Gunnison, Ethel Mae
Bargains in sweat. BRP 5:92
Thumbs down. YR 7:257

GUNS
Huber, L. J.
Introducing a sharpshooter. BRH:130
See also Hunters and hunting; Munitions

Gunsaulus, Frank W.
Healthy heresies. BREW 6:317
Washington's genius. HARSO:292; WERN 42:142

Gurra, Ali Hussein
Inaugural speech at Conference on the Problems of Economic Development. UAR:163
Speech at final session of Conference on the Problems of Economic Development. UAR:425

Gustavson, Reuben G.
Story behind the atomic bomb. BRA:563
See also Hutchins, R. M., jt. auth.

GUSTAVUS II, KING OF SWEDEN
Alseth, C. A.
Lion of the North. COUW:195

GUSTAVUS IV, KING OF SWEDEN

GUSTAVUS IV, KING OF SWEDEN (cont.)
Blanche, A. T.
On the dethronement of Gustav IV. CHAL 8:242; HAZO 16:6973; MAS 16:6973

GUTENBERG, JOHANN
Boy who changed his name. JAS:12
Gwinn, Joseph M.
Presents Charles Lindbergh. LY:248
Introduction of Katherine Lee Bates. DOA:81

Haag, E. N.
Fraternity. THOU 3:17
Inherent strength of fraternalism. THOU 3:26
Haake, Alfred P.
Introduces Samuel B. Pettinger. PR:88

HAAKE, ALFRED P.
Bullis, H. A.
White light: introducing Dr. Alfred P. Haake at sales managers convention. BRC: 324
Snyder, F. B.
Introduces two debaters, Alfred P. Haake and Harold Laski. PR:84
Haas, C. Glen
I was a jockey. YR 9:249

HAAS, FRANCIS B.
Hill, H.
Presents Francis B. Haas. LY:106
HABIMAH See Theatre
HABIT
Beveridge, A. J.
Work and habit. KLEG:187
Can you quit? JAS:114
HADASSAH
Jessel, G.
To the Ladies of Hadassah. JEYO:146
Hadduck, Charles Brickett
Elements of national greatness, 1841. BRAR 1:261

HADFIELD, JAMES
Erskine, T.
Homicidal insanity (J. Hadfield) BREW 6:32; GOOD: 766; LEEW 7:25
Hadley, Arthur Twining
Acceptance of the Cheney-Ives gateway. KNAS:161; KNASA 161; ONEM:713; ONES:48
Commemoration address. REEM 11:418; REEMB 12: 440
Faith in mankind. KLEM:177
Forefathers' Day. BLAA:83; BLAB:83
Inaugural address as president of Yale. WE 1:43
Modern changes in educational ideals. ONES:150; REEM 6:226; REEMA 8: 594; REEMB 7:207
Opening the ceremonies held on observance of a university centennial (Yale Medical School) ONES:67
Spirit of devotion. KLEG:372
To the Brotherhood of Yale. KNAS:205; KNASA:205; ONEM:672; ONES:13
Hagemann, Harry H.
Remarks at Iowa State College centennial. IOCP:17
Haggard, Howard W.
Physiology for the engineers. ON:19
Hahn, Horace L.
Merchants of war. YR 7:201
Haile Selassie I, Emperor of Ethiopia
Appeal to the League Assembly. BOU:91; HAN:61; KESK 2:84
God and history will remember your judgment. -Same as his Appeal to the League Assembly
Position of Ethiopia. COP: 450; COPA:450; COPB: 450
Where are we to look for survival? BOU:97

HAILE SELASSIE I., EMPEROR OF ETHIOPIA
Swing, R. G.
Wheel of judgment. BA 1940-41:163
Hailsham, Douglas McGarel Hogg, 1st Viscount
Ottawa Conference. BEA:251

HAIR
Bald headed man. NATT:9
Haire, Andrew J.
Presents Arthur Godfrey. LY: 44
Hakimi, Abdel Karim
Inaugural speech at Conference on the Problems on Economic Development. UAR:131
Speech at final session of Conference on the Problems of Economic Development. UAR:389
Haldane, Richard Burdon, Viscount
Ministry's request to the Sovereign for the creation of peers. EMS 1:49
Right of association (Feb. 5, 1913 speech) EMS 2:75
Right of association (June 30, 1927 speech) EMS 2:93
Speech in House of Lords, June 16, 1926 (on Imperial Conference, 1926) KESB: 372
Haldeman, I. M.
Resurrection. THOU 2:114
Hale, Edward Everett
Boston. COP:663; COPB:690; REEM 2:149; REEMA 2: 577; REEMB 2:141
Boston's place in history. BREW 6:319
Honor to the patriotic spy (at unveiling of statue to Nathan Hale) BLAA:241; BLAB:241
Man without a country. PROS: 19
Mission of culture. CHAL 10: 153; HAZO 20:8374; MAS 20:8374; REEM 2:142; REEMA 2:570; REEMB 2: 134
Ruling sentiment of the Pilgrims. THOU 1:334
Sons of Massachusetts. CHAL 10:162; HAZO 20:8388; MAS 20:8388
What is the American people? NORR 2d ser:228
"What will he do with it?" REEMA 8:601
Hale, John Parker
On secession. CHAL 7:262; CHEM 4:13; HAZO 15:6175; JOHA 2 pt 1:230; MAS 15: 6175
Hale, Matthew
Introducing John S. Wise to New York Bar Association, Jan. 20, 1891. REEM 3: 421

HALE, NATHAN
Hale, E. E.
Honor to the patriotic spy (at unveiling of statue to Nathan Hale) BLAA:241; BLAB:241
Half King, Tanacharison, Oneida chief
Speech to the French, November, 1753. SHE:23
Halifax, Edward Frederick Lindley Wood, 3rd Viscount
Address at final plenary session of United Nations Conference on International Organization. VO 1945-46:306
Address to Association of Commerce, Baltimore, ON:196
All Britain is united. COP: 479; COPA:479
At annual dinner of American Society of International Law. VO 1944-45:189
Statement at conclusion of the second phase of the Dumbarton Oaks conversations. VO 1944-45:472

HALIFAX, EDWARD FREDERICK LINDLEY WOOD, 3rd VISCOUNT
Douglas, L.W.
Presents Lord Halifax. LY: 210
Halisbury, Hardinge Stanley Giffard, 1st Earl of
Right of association. EMS 2: 72
Hall, Arnold Bennett
Inaugural address as president of University of Oregon. WE 2:343
Hall, Christopher Newman
Christian victory. CHAL 9: 114; HAZO 18:7638; MAS 18:7638
Hall, E.K.
Football. REEM sup 1:385; REEMB 2:144
Plea for the man in the ranks. REEM sup 1:395; REEMB 4:328
Hall, Fitzhugh
Address of welcome to the Grand Council of New York Royal Arcanum. THOU 3: 398

HALL, G. STANLEY
Inaugural address as president of Clark University. WE 1: 361
William McKinley. BLAA:150; BLAB:150

Hall, John
Doctrines held by St. Patrick. THOU 1:525
Hall, Jonathan Prescott
Discourse, 1847. BRAR 2:1
Hall, Joseph B.
Begins an address before the Women's Advertising Club. PRNE:56
Hall, Sidney B.
Uncle Sam's responsibility for his children. SMI:303
Hall, William F.
Yarn of the manager bold. REEMA 2:581
Hall, Willis
Address before the Society of Phi Beta Kappa in Yale College. BL:205
Halle, Robert
Guilty until proven innocent. SOBP:348
Hallock, Gerard B. F.
Catch them young (Rallying day address) THOU 2:214

HALLOWEEN
Halloween fun. FRIE:112
Halsey, Don P.
Oratory is not a lost art. SHUO:15
Halsey, James H.
Education for freedom. BRY: 433
Higher education's appalling responsibilities. MOUG: 228; MOUGA:228
Halstead, Murat
Our new country. REEM 2: 152; REEMA 2:584; REEMB 2:154
Hamaishi, George
Story of a boy. NOR 1943:5
Hamer, Philip M.
Records of Southern history. TIN:50
Hamilton, Alexander
Coercion of delinquent states. BREW 6:325; FULB:189
First report on public credit. BIR 1:150
On section VIII of the Constitution. CHEM 1:261; CROC 225
On the Federal Constitution, June 20, 1788. CHEM 1: 235; HARS:104; SHAH:34
On the Federal Constitution, June 24, 1788. BRYW 8: 132; CHAL 4:2; CHEM 1: 249; COP:242; COPB:242; FULB:189; HAZO 8:3254; HELE:85; HURG:35; JOHA 1 pt. 1:39; LAD:81; LEEW 8:201; MAS 8:3254; ORAM 1:253; PE:201; PEA:201; PL:586; REEM 10:21; REEMA 13:1117; REEMB 11:22

Report on manufactures, 1791.
BIR 1:173

HAMILTON, ALEXANDER
Bell, C. F.
Statesman and nation.
SHUC:96
McBurney, J. H. and others.
Alexander Hamilton: his contribution to constitutional government. BA 1956-57: 149
Marshall, E.
Hamilton and the Constitution. TRUW:170
Morris, G.
Oration over Hamilton.
BREW 8:212; COP:263; COPA:263; COPB:263; HELE:142; HURG:54; KLEG: 154; ORAMA 1:187; REEM 5:314; REEMA 9:887; REEMB 9:354
Nott, E.
On the death of Hamilton.
BRYW 8:174; CHAL 5:1; HAZO 10:3990; MAS 10: 3990
Otis, H. G.
Hamilton's influence on American institutions. BREW 8:248; CHAL 4:189; HAZO 9:3567; MAS 9:3567
Hamilton, Andrew
In the case for Zenger-for free speech. ANG:53; BOU: 131; BREW 6:336; PE:101; PEA:101
Hamilton, J. G. De Roulhac
Three centuries of Southern records, 1607-1907. TIN: 129
Hamilton, John, 2d Baron Belhaven See Belhaven, J. H.
Hamlin, Hannibal
On the Slavery Compromise Bill. CHAL 8:51; HAZO 16: 6667; MAS 16:6667
Hamm, Huntington
At the sign of the dollar.
BOA:71; BOB:83
Hammarskjold, Dag
No right to resign. BOU:183
Values of nationalism and internationalism (Stanford University commencement address) COPB:628
Hammond, John Hays
Address at International Oratorical contest. LEIO:66
Enlightened self-interest in international relations. REEM 4:178; REEMB 4:351
Fourth of July. REEM 2:157; REEMB 2:159
Hampden, John
Patriot's duty defined: against own impeachment. BREW 6: 349

HAMPDEN, JOHN
Holborne, R.
In defense of John Hampden.
BREW 7:66
Hyde, E.
In John Hampden's case.
BREW 7:112
Hampden, Walter
On receiving a gold medal.
REEM sup 1:418; REEMB 6:160
Hancher, Virgil Melvin
Art of contemplation. BA 1948-49:174; BAAGA:401
Higher education in Iowa (at Founders' Day luncheon-Iowa State College centennial) IOCP:37
Inaugural address as president of Iowa State University.
WE 2:149
Introducing Joseph F. Newton at a combined honors convocation and baccalaureate service at the State University of Iowa. BA 1945-46: 214
Postwar planning-for what?
BA 1943-44:319
Presents Eleanor Roosevelt
" Franklyn Bliss Snyder.
LY:240, 119
Hancock, John
Boston Massacre. BREW 6: 357; CHAL 3:59; COP:229; COPA:229; COPB:229;

Hancock, John (cont.)
HAZO 7:2627; HELE:36; HURG:24; LEEW 8:71; MAS 7:2627; ORAMA 1:127; REEMA 13:1125
Moving the adoption of the Federal Constitution. BREW 6:353

HANCOCK, WINFIELD SCOTT
Dougherty, D.
"Hancock the superb." BREW 5:280

HAND, AUGUSTUS N.
Buchanan, J. G.
Presents Augustus N. Hand. LY:145
Hand, Learned
Fanfare for Prometheus (accepting American Liberties medallion) BA 1955-56:39
Preparation of citizens for their political duties. BA 1952-53:121
Presenting a portrait of Justice Holmes to the Harvard Law School. ONEC:43
We seek liberty. BA 1943-44: 254; HIB:183

HANDICAPS
Overcoming handicaps. DR: 293

HANDICRAFTS
Branen, J.
Emcee at a "do it yourself" club. BRH:210
Handlin, Irving
United we stand. DO:39

HANES, ROBERT M.
Houston, P. D.
Presents a gift of silver and a scroll of honor to retiring president of American Bankers Association, Robert M. Hanes. PR:106
Hanley, Joe R.
Response to introduction. PR: 119
Hanna, Elizabeth
What part should the United States play in the economic recovery of Britain? HOD: 102
Hanna, Kathryn Abbey
Roles of the South in the French intervention in Mexico. TIN:298
Hanna, Marcus A.
Labor and capital. BLAA:282; BLAB:282; REAC:97; WERN 42:147
Promotion of commerce and increase of trade. CHAL 13 110; HAZO 23:10046; MAS 23:10046

HANNA, MARCUS A.
Beveridge, A. J.
Tribute to Marcus A. Hanna SHUM:274
Hannibal.
Address to his soldiers. BRYW 2:9; COP:34; COPA 34; COPB:34; HIB:29; LEEW 2:107; REEM 9:48; REEMB 10:50
Hansen, Harry See Bryson, L., jt. auth.
Hanson, C. W. D.
Introduces Dr. Paul Dudley White, distinguished phsyician and cardiac specialist. PRC:29
Introduces His Excellency Dr. Konrad Adenauer, Chancellor, Federal Republic of Germany. PRC:26
Hanz, Joseph E.
Cross and the flag. CATA 1: 41
Hapgood, Norman
Drama in Ameria today. BAKF:303

HAPPINESS
Avebury, J. L.
Duty of happiness. CHAL 12:231; HAZO 23:9747; MAS 23:9747
Bloomstein, M.
Fords with balloon tires. SHU:142
Help yourself to happiness.

JAI:73
Measure of happiness. FRIE: 248
Measuring happiness. NATS: 17
Russell, B.
How to be free and happy. REEM sup 2:374; REEMB 7:370
Schindler, J. A.
How to live a hundred years happily. BERS:101; YE:236
Sherman, S. P.
Gaiety of Socrates. NORR 3d ser:1
Warner, C. D.
Pursuit of happiness. BLAA:187; BLAB:187; REAC:88; WERN 42:127
Where to find happiness. JAS: 30
Harcourt, Lewis Harcourt, 1st Viscount
Deportation of labour leaders from South Africa. KES 2: 109
Harcourt, Sir Simon
Jurisdiction over Parliamentary elections. EMS 1:203
Harcourt, Sir William George Granville Venables Vernon
Good will to America. HAZO 21:9034; KLEM:65; MAS 21:9034
Second reading of the Budget Bill, 1894. PAUF 2:286
Harcourt, Sir William Vernon
Our national position. CHAL 11:157
Hard, William
Medical care for all. SAR:309
Hardin, Ann
Jefferson and the Constitution. LEIO:91
Hardin, Ben Lee
Mother Eve. SOU 9:480
Hardin, Margaret
Truth about lies. JUD:307
Harding, Harold F.
Can the liberal arts tradition survive? BA 1943-44:306
College student as a critic. BRAP:152
New directions for higher learning. BA 1945-46:229
Harding, John
Temperance in New Zealand. THOU 3:527
Harding, Warren Gamaliel
At the grave of the unknown soldier. BLAB:321; BREW 6:368; PROS:7; SHU:36
Canadian-American relations. FIP:155
Citizenship. REEM 2:161; REEMB 2:163
Hallowed ground, May 30, 1921. PROS:114
Inaugural address. BREW 6: 366; CHI:230; LOTI:207; USIN:207; USINA:207
Introducing Charles G. Dawes. REEM 4:67; REEMB 4:150
"It is our purpose to prosper America first." FIP:143
On Lincoln's birthday. REEM 2:162; REEMB 2:164
Patriotic memorial speech, May 23, 1921. CARP:264
Peace through disarmament. BREW 6:363
Presents Marie S. Curie. LY:178
Speech at Boston, May 14, 1920. BIR 4:53
Speech at Washington Conference on the Limitations of Armaments, November 12, 1921. REEM 11:379; REEMB 12:398
United States-independent and sovereign. BREW 6:366
Washington Naval Conference, February 6, 1922. FIP: 147
Welcome to the Daughters of the American Revolution. LINM:140
World Court. FIP:149

HARDING, WARREN GAMALIEL
McFarland, J. G.
Memorial address at the tomb of President Harding, December 2, 1923 (speech as Past Exalted Grand

HARDING, WARREN GAMALIEL (cont.)
Ruler of the Elks) LINM: 34
Hardison, Elizabeth
Propaganda-a weapon of peace. YR 10:69

HARDWARE DEALERS See Business men
Hardwick, Philip Yorke, 1st Earl of
Liberty of the press. EMS 2:3
Hardy, Clarion D.
From fame to infamy. COUW: 117
Hargrave, Milton
Introducing a millinery buyer or proprietor of a ladies hat store. BRC:195
Harlan, John M.
Adair v. United States, 1908: opinion for the Supreme Court. BIR 3:292
Lottery case (Champion v. Ames) 1903: opinion for the Supreme Court. BIR 3:262
Northern Securities Company v. United States, 1904: opinion for the Supreme Court. BIR 3:275
Harlan, Roy Earle, Jr.
Tragedies of this tournament. JUD:83
Harlow, Harry F.
Nature of love. LINP:84
Harman, Carl H.
Promise of Christ's abiding presence. ACW:66
Haroldson, Wesley
Adult education. JUD:177
Tax racket. BRP 4:7; INTW 1933:40
Harper, Florence
Gethsemane. YR 6:169
Harper, Frances Ellen Watkins
Address at the centennial anniversary of the Pennsylvania Society for promoting the abolition of slavery. DUNM:101
Harper, Robert Goodloe
Defending Judge Chase. BREW 6:389
Harper, Samuel N. See Gottschalk, L., jt. auth.

HARPISTS See Music and musicians

HARRIMAN, EDWARD HENRY
Kahn, O. H.
Edward Henry Harriman. REEM 5:240; REEMB 9:279
Harriman, W. Averell
Mobilizing America's strength for world security. HAR:245

Speech at final meeting at the Conference of United States, Great Britain, and U. S. S. R. VO 1941:430
Harrington, Evelyn
Unveiling a World War memorial. ONES:117
Harris, Elaine
Thoughtlessness of American thought. AN:54
Harris, Harvey R.
Decoration of the graves-memorial address. THOU 3:415
Harris, Howard
America's peace responsibilities. DO:82

HARRIS, ISHAM G.
Taylor, R. L.
Eulogy on Isham G. Harris. HARSO:84
Harris, J. L.
What have we gained in the year? THOU 2:405
Harris, Joseph P.
Financing of electric railways. REEM sup 1:420; REEMB 4:360
Harris, Malcolm L.
Deontology, or the moral obligation of medicine. ONEC: 284
Harris, Nathaniel E.
Visions of the Civil War (at

Confederate Veterans reunion, 1905) SHUO:26
Harris, Rufus C.
Free society. ANGC:87
Harrison, Benjamin
Abraham Lincoln. BLAA:134; BLAB:134
Cultivating love for the flag. THOU 1:299
Inaugural address. BREW 6: 372; BRYW 10:155; CHAL 12:213; CHI:169; HAZO 22:9594; LOTI:155; MAS 22:9594; REEM 10:306; REEMA 13:1137; REEMB 11:320; USIN:153; USINA: 153
National holiday proclamation, (Columbus day) THOU 1:61
Plea for patriotism (100th anniversary of Washington's inauguration) ESEH:199
Union of states. REEM 2:167; REEMA 2:589; REEMB 2: 169
Views on capital and labor. THOU 1:429
Harrison, Charles Custis
Opening the ceremonies at the dedication of a law building. ONES:64
Harrison, Frederic
Choice of books. REEM 6: 232; REEMA 5:523; REEMB 7:213
Harrison, G. Ernest
Educated spectators. BRP 3: 51; YR 4:129
Harrison, Harvey T.
Whither midst falling due? HOC:27; ON:156; SAR:141
Harrison, Leon
American citizenship and the American Jew. SHUO:119
Harrison, Luther
Of the making of laws there is no end. GRIS:54
Harrison, Pat
Democratic keynote speech, 1924. WHIP:235
Harrison, Thomas
Speech on the scaffold. BREW 6:385; PE:95; PEA:95

HARRISON, THOMAS
Nottingham, H. F.
Opening the prosecution for regicide under Charles II (trial of T. Harrison) BREW 6:131
Harrison, William Henry
Inaugural address. CHI:76; LOTI:73; USIN:71; USINA: 71
To the Indiana legislature. SMI:93
Hart, Albert Bushnell
Hope of democracy. NORR 1st ser:362
Hart, Albert S.
Theodore Roosevelt. BOA: 231; BOB:142
Hart, Charles S.
Imagination in business. REEM sup 2:33; REEMB 4:370
Hart, John R.
Positive and negative personalities. NESA:124
Hart, Merwin K.
This American system: is it to be destroyed? SAR:203
Hart, Roger
Introducing an art dealer
" a hardware dealer
" a radio station or television station manager
BRC:294, 56, 293
Hart, William S.
American Indian and American citizenship. SHU:130
Hartger, H.V.
Skeleton of the press. YR 8: 237
Hartington, Marquis of See Devonshire, Spencer Compton Cavendish, 8th Duke of
Hartman, William R.
Pomp and circumstance. NOR 1949:145

HARVARD UNIVERSITY
Bartlett, W. F.
Speech at Harvard commencement dinner. BAKF: 428
Bryce, J.
At a Harvard commence-

HARVARD UNIVERSITY (cont.)
ment. KNAS:265; KNASA: 265
Choate, J.H.
Harvard University. REEM 1:262; REEMA 1:173; REEMB 1:263
Sons and guests of Harvard. ONEM:631; REEMA 1:187
Conant, J.B.
Unique idea of American life. BA 1939-40:337
Cook, G.W.
Two seals. DUNM:379
Cooley, T.M.
To the Harvard Law School. KNAS:245; KNASA:245
Curtis, G.W.
Noblesse oblige (at Harvard Alumni dinner) REEMA 1: 295
Devens, C.
Sons of Harvard. CHAL 10: 7; HAZO 19:8121; KLEM: 199: MAS 19:8121
Eliot, C.W.
Harvard and Yale. CHAL 12:302; COP:673; COPB: 700; HAZO 23:9683; HURG: 130; MAS 23:9683; REEM 2:4; REEMA 2:427; REEMB 2:4
Inaugural address as president of Harvard University. CHAL 12:270; CORP:135; HAZO 23:9651; MAS 23: 9651; WE 1:13
Lowell, J.R.
Harvard alumni. REEMA 2:737
Oration at 250th anniversary of the founding of Harvard College. CHAL 9:354; HAZO 19:7929; MAS 19:7929
Pusey, N.M.
Responds to an introduction. PRNE:59
Washington, B.T.
Address delivered at the Harvard alumni dinner in 1896. BAKF:420; BOU:154; CHAL 14:318; COP:331; COPA:331; COPB:331; HAZO 25:10859; HILK:43; HURG:144; MAS 25:10859; REEM 7:421; REEMA 9: 1140; REEMB 8:437; WOON: 584

HARVEST FESTIVALS
Goebbels, J.
Speech at harvest Thanksgiving festival in Berlin. VO 1943-44:421

HARVEST HOME DAY
At harvest time. THOU 2:235
Autumn days. THOU 2:256
Autumn homily. THOU 2:240
Autumn lesson. THOU 2:251
Clifford, J.
Farmer's song. THOU 2: 227
Glories of autumn. THOU 2: 237
Harvest tide. THOU 2:244
Joyous festival of the leaves. THOU 2:247
Paull, G.A.
Harvest thoughts. THOU 2: 249
Puddicombe, T.
Bread of life. THOU 2:254
Spurgeon, C.H.
Soul satisfying bread. THOU 2:252
Harvey, George
Confirming an ambassador. REEM 2:170; REEMB 2:172
Haskell, Henry J.
What of America? BOA:274; BOB:23
Hass, C. Glen
I was a jockey. YR 9:249

HASTINGS, WARREN
Burke, E.
Impeachment of Warren Hastings. BREW 2:337, 343; BRYW 6:50; CLAY:55; CODS:168; CODSA:180; COP:163; COPA:163; COPB: 163; CROC:46; GOOD:362; HAZO 6:2193; KESI 1:114; MAS 6:2193; MEAR:118; PE:178; PEA:178; REEM

9:126; REEMB 10:131
Fox, C. J.
Against Warren Hastings. BREW 6:164
Sheridan, R. B.
Against Warren Hastings. BREW 9:192; BRTH:106; BRTHA:106; BRYW 6:77; CHAL 3:393; CODS:265; COP:165; COPA:165; COPB:165; FULB:86; GOOD:407; HAY:53; HAZO 8:3069; LEEW 6:347; MAS 8:3069; ORBR 1:389; PAUF 1:212; PE:180; PEA 180; REEM 9:133; REEMA 15:1872; REEMB 10:139
Arraignment of Warren Hastings. PL:422
Desolation of Oude. CODSA: 265
Proceedings against Mr. Hastings in Westminster Hall: second or Begum charge (speeches of June 3, 6, 13, 1788) KET:217, 226, 236
Robbery of the Princesses at Oude. KET:202

HASTINGS, BATTLE OF, 1066
William, Duke of Normandy
Rage of battle: address to his army before the battle of Hastings, 1066. BRTH: 2; BRTHA:2
Hasty, Ed.
For the Eighteenth Amendment. BLUE:63

HAT TRADE
For a hatters' festival. BARB: 188
Hat manufacturers, by some well-known manufacturer. EDGS:141
Hatfield, Malcolm
Children in court. BART 3:193
Hatlen, Ted
National recovery of character. BRP 5:96; YR 6:141
Hauge, Gabriel
Roald Amundsen. YR 4:273
Havighurst, Robert J.
American family. ARNS:154; MO:258; MOA:258
---- and others (Draper, W. H., Jr.; Riddy, D. C.; and Taylor, J. W.)
What should America do now in Bizonia? MO:621

HAWAIIAN ISLANDS
Akaka, A. K.
Aloha Ke Akua. BA 1959-60:46
Clark, C.
On the annexation of Hawaii. REEM 10:352; REEMA 12:615; REEMB 11:366
Davis, C. K.
United States in Hawaii. REEMA 12:804
Dunn, J.
49th State. BRP 10:51
Hawes, Harry B.
Covered wagon. DOA:53
Hawkins, Eugenya
Bride of the State. BRP 10: 11; NOR 1939:3
Hawkins, W. Ashbie
Negro lawyer; his opportunity, his duty (at opening of Howard University Law School) DUNM:483

HAWKS, FRANK
Introducing Frank Hawks. NI: 161; NIA:120
Hawley, Joseph Roswell
On the flag and the eagle. CHAL 11:104; HAZO 21: 8955; MAS 21:8955
Press. HAZO 21:8964; MAS 21:8964; REEMA 2:593
Hawley, Paul R.
Prepayment plans. HAR:355
Hay, John
American diplomacy. BLAA: 10: BLAB:10; REEM 2: 173; REEMB 2:175
America's love of peace. BOAM:63
Omar Khayyam. COP:679; COPB:706; HAZO 24:10211;

Hay, John (cont.)
MAS 24:10211; REEM 2: 179; REEMA 2:598; REEMB 2:181
Power of the press. WERN 42:102
Sir Walter Scott (at unveiling of bust of Sir Walter Scott in Westminster Abbey) REEMA 8:614
Tribute to McKinley. BRYW 10:228; CHAL 13:223; ONEM:427; REEM 5:208; REEMA 13:1149; REEMB 9:244; WERN 42:164

HAY FEVER
Speech to the Hay Fever Association of America by the mayor of Duluth, Minnesota. LARW:113
Hayes, Carlton J. H.
American war aims. BA 1942-43:47
Hayes, Patrick Joseph, Cardinal
Christian charity. LINM:125
Faith and science. ONEC:463
Hayes, Rutherford B.
Campaign speech, August 5, 1867. CHAL 10:191; HAZO 20:8412; MAS 20:8412
Inaugural address. BREW 6: 397; CHI:148; LOTI:137; USIN:135; USINA:135
National sentiments. REEM 2: 183; REEMA 2:601; REEMB 2:185
Haygood, S. G.
Adjustments between labor and capital. THOU 1:448
America-its national and individual ideals. THOU 1:76
Hayne, Robert Young
Eulogium on South Carolina. - Same as his On Foot's Resolution (January 21, 1830)
On Foot's Resolution (January 19, 1830) CLAW:29
On Foot's Resolution (January 21, 1830) BREW 6:404; BRYW 9:3; CHAL 5:459; CLAW:104; CODS:475; CODSA:475; HAZO 12:4969; JOHA 1 pt. 1:233; LEEW 9: 151; MAS 12:4969; ORAMA 2:97; REEMA 13:1170; SOU 9:342
On the sale of public lands. - Same as his On Foot's Resolution (Jan. 21, 1830)
"South Carolina Doctrine."- Same as his On Foot's Resolution (Jan. 21, 1830)
Hays, Will H., Jr.
Behind the scenes in Hollywood. JUD:263
Teamwork. BYRA:188; REEM 4:187; REEMB 4:377

HAYS, WILLIAM H.
Landis, F.
Witty after-dinner speech on Will Hays. BRAC:302; LY:213; NESA:185

HAYTI
Saunders, P.
People of Hayti and a plan of emigration. DUNM:13
Smith, J. M.
Toussaint L'Ouverture and the Haytian revolution. DUNM:19
Hazeltine, M. W.
Value of university study. WERN 54:138
Hazlitt, William
Living poets. REEMA 5:541
On wit and humor. BREW 6: 142
Headley, J. T.
Grant's character. THOU 1: 376
Our flag in history. THOU 1: 284
Headley, Walter Cunliffe, 1st Baron
Bank of England. REEM 4:62; REEMB 4:144
Heald, Henry T.
Aristocracy of the engineer. BA 1956-57:173
Healey, Arthur D.
Control of industry. BOA:385

HEALTH

"Child health" day. DR:151
How to keep healthy and its value to success. AMEO 2:73
Kaser, A. L.
Introducing an authority on health
" a speaker on health and accident week. BRC:246, 132
Pacini, A. J.
Light and health. EXEE:578
See also Public health

HEALTH, DRINKING OF See Toasts

HEART
Egbert, T. E.
Heart the source of power. HARSO:68; WERN 42:51
Is your heart right? JAI:21
Klumpp, T. G.
New look at the old ticker. BRYA:489
Lend a hand and lend a heart, or the healthy heart vs. the heavy heart (a speech for a heart drive) BAI:103
Heater, Lo Amy
Ivy oration. WERN 54:48
Last will and testament of class. WERN 54:53
Senior charge. WERN 54:76

HEATING
Kaber, W. C.
Value of district heating to the community. MO:458

HEAVEN See Religion

HEBRAISM See Jews
Hecht, Harold L.
Days which the Lord hath made (50th wedding anniversary) ACW:160
Hecker, Frederick Karl Franz
Liberty in the New Atlantis. BREW 6:420
Heckscher, August
Challenge of ugliness. BA 1961-62:124
Paramount duty. YR 8:273
Yale's conservatism. YR 7:137
Hedburg, R. E.
American high standard of living as a cause for crime. SHUP:168
Hedges, Job Elmer
Birthday of Dr. Kane. REEM 2:185; REEMB 2:187
Last word. REEMB 2:205
Ohio, the Presidency and Americanism. REEM 2:195; REEMB 2:197
Presents Edward D. Duffield. LY:89
Hefferan, Joseph A.
Ireland's unfailing faith. CATA 1:239
Hegesippus.
On the Halonneus. LEEW 1:208
Heilbrin, Louis H.
Look at academic freedom. ANGC:95

HEISER, VICTOR
Introducing Dr. Victor Heiser. SUM:88
Helburn, Theresa
Theater versus pictures. GA:109

HELEN OF TROY
Gorgias.
Encomium on Helen. CHAL 1:12; HAZO 1:49; MAS 1:49; PL:32

HELL
Bede.
Torments of hell. BREW 1:349
Edwards, J.
Eternity of hell torments. BREW 5:350
Heller, M.
Address delivered at New Orleans on 250th anniversary of the settlement of the Jews in the United States. TWJ:164

HELLINISM See Culture
Helm, Wilbur
America I want to know. BART 1:295
Helman, Blair
Nationalism. AN:9
Helmholtz, Herman Ludwig Ferdinand von
Mystery of creation. BREW 6: 428; HAZO 19:8211; MAS 19:8211
Hemery, J. L.
Introduces Lynn Saylor, advertiser. PR:90

HEMOPHILIA See Blood-Diseases
Henderson, Elmer L.
American Medical Association presidential inaugural address. HAR:337
Henderson, Homer
New individualism. BOA:405; YR 6:159
Henderson, Leon
Equality of sacrifice. BA 1941-42:161
Henderson, Paul
Aircraft for industry. BYRA: 200; REEM sup 2:40; REEMB 4:389
Henderson, Thomas S.
Banker as a citizen. SHUO: 204
Henderson, Ward G.
What may man become? BRP 7:117
Henderson, Yandell
Physiology of Atelectasis. ONEC:295
Hendricks, Thomas V.
Coming through the Wry. EXEE:166
Hendrickson, Robert C.
Begins an address before the Secretary's Conference on Juvenile Delinquency. PRNE: 55
Hendrix, E. R.
Living witness of the resurrection. THOU 2:101
Hendrix, Joseph C.
Wampum of the Indian. ONES: 236; REEMA 2:603
Hennesy, Joe
Drama of life. YR 7:81
Henninger, L. L.
Man of steel. BLUE:74
Hennings, Thomas C., Jr.
Against the Bricker Amendment. BA 1953-54:128
Henry, Patrick
Adoption of the Constitution. - Same as his "We, the people" or "We, the States"
Against the Federal Constitution (June 5, 1788) BAAMP: 32; BIR 1:136; BREW 7:28; BRYW 8:67; CHAL 3:46; CLAW:7; HARS:67; HAZO 6:2613; MAS 6:2613; ORAMA 1:63; WPRA:7
At the Virginia Convention (from speeches of June 5th and 7th, 1788) CLAW:133
Before Convention of Delegates. -Same as his Liberty or death
Bill of Rights, June 14, 1788. BREW 7:24; CHAL 3:40; HAZO 6:2607; MAS 6:2607
Call to arms. -Same as his Liberty or death
Extract from speech on the Federal Constitution. -Same as his "We the people," or "We, the States"
Fears the strength of the proposed Constitution. PE: 197; PEA:197
June 4th, 1788 speech in the Virginia Ratifying Convention. BIR 1:133; CHEM 1: 123; LEEW 8:121; ORAMA 61
June 24th, 1788 speech in the Virginia Ratifying Convention. BIR 1:148
Liberty or death. BAAMP:29; BOU:39; BRE:23; BREA: 23; BREW 7:15; BRIM:209; BRYW 8:62; CAP:18; CHAL 3:28; CHEM 1:63; CLAY:5; CODS:321; CODSA:321; COP:232; COPA:232; COPB:232; CROC:234;

DICD:156; DICE:156; DOA: 327; ESEH:192; FKA:3; FRY:7; FULB:168; HARS: 26; HARSO:323; HAY:29; HAZO 6:2595; HELE:51; HIB:151; HIBS:443; HURG: 27; JOHA 1 pt. 1:18; LEEW: 8:115; MAS 6:2595; ONEM: 328; ORAMA 1:57; PAR: 91; PE:139; PEA:139; PL:569; PROS:130; REEM 10:1; REEMA 13:1178; REEMB 11:1; RID:8; SAA: 95; SHAH:14; SOU 9:171
Liberty or empire?- Same as his Against the Federal Constitution, June 5, 1788.
Nation-not a Federation, June 14, 1788 (on eighth section of Federal Constitution) BREW 7:20; CHAL 3:35; HAZO 6:2602; MAS 6:2602
Resistance to oppression. - Same as his Liberty or death
'We, the people" or 'We, the states." BREW 7:18; CHAL 3:32; HAZO 6:2599; KLEG: 132,344; MAS 6:2599; SMI: 41; SOU 9:175;

HENRY, PATRICK
Christianson, T.
Patrick Henry, the agitator. TRUW:197
Henry, Robert L.
Texas and the Panama Canal. SHUO:217
Henry, Robert S.
West by South. TIN:366
Henry, William Wirt
Settlement at Jamestown. SMI: 12
Henry-Haye, Gaston
Statement at Washington, June 6, 1941. VO 1941:247

HENRY LAURENCE GANTT GOLD MEDAL
Jones, T.R.
Presentation of Gannt gold to Fowler McCormick. YE: 114

Henson, Laurel
Protectors of freedom. DO: 172
Henson, P.S.
Angel's song. THOU 2:356
Hensrud, Ray
Introducing a commissioner of agriculture or county agent. BRC:314
Hepburn, A. Barton
Business education. BYRA: 208; REEM 2:204; REEMB 2:209
Introducing James Bryce. REEM 1:172; REEMB 1: 168
Herbert, Sir Allan Patrick
Advocates a festival for Britain. PE:812; PEA:812
Herbert, H.A.
Grant's magnanimity. THOU 1:385
Herbert, Henry Howard Molyneux
See Carnovan, H.H.M.H.
Herbon, Ellis, Jr.
America-upward and onward. DO:3
Herder, Johann Gottfried von
Meaning of inspiration. BREW 7:37

HEREDITY
Clinton, S.
Ropes (heredity and environment in relation to crime) ASHF:95; BLUE: 51; BRP 3:23
Ott, E.A.
Sour grapes. IMMD:196
Wilson, W.
Our ancestral responsibilities. REEMA 3:1248
See also Eugenics
Hergenroeder, Paul J.
In the service of our country. NOR 1935:130
Herman, George
See Kennedy, John F. and others
Hermocrates.
On the union of Sicily against invaders. BRYW 1:55

HERODES.
Antiphon.
On the murder of Herodes. CHAL 1:18; FRE:63; HAZO 1:55; MAS 1:55; MINA 1:160; PL:36

HEROES AND HEROISM
Bentley, A.
Warriors of the broken sword. BOA:163
Carlyle, T.
Heroic in history. BREW 3:124
Mahomet. REEMA 4:181
Choate, R.
Puritan and Spartan heroism. BREW 3:303; CODS:484; CODSA:484; FULB:259
Condon, R. J.
Heroes in time of peace. PROS:60
Saurin, J.
Christian heroism. HAZO 4:1746; MAS 4:1746
Warriors of the broken sword. PROS:13
Watterson, H.
Heroes in homespun. PROS:75; SHU:39
Herron, George Davis
Message of Jesus to men of wealth. WPRA:276
Herschell, Farrer, 1st Baron
Great Britain and the United States. REEMA 2:609

HERSHFIELD, HARRY
Introducing Harry Hershfield. NI:72; NIA:59
Herter, Christian A.
Peaceful change. BA 1959-60:51
Hertzog, J. B. M.
Imperial Conference, 1930. KESB:210
Hesburgh, Theodore M.
Science and man. BA 1962-63:56
Hess, Lloyd Franklin
Powers of the Speaker of the House of Representatives. SHUC:242

HESS, RUDOLF
Eden, A.
Statement on Hess. VO 1943-44:403
Hesseltine, William Best
Four American traditions. TIN:413
Hewart, Gordon H.
Modern oratory. BEA:265
Heyler, Walter B.
Best is yet to be. ONES:321
Heymann, Walter M.
Introduces Fayette H. Elwell, then Dean of the School of Commerce of the University of Wisconsin. PRNE:37
Hibben, John G.
Comrades in peace. BOB:28
Day's work. BLAB:343
Righteousness (address before Holland Society) REEM 2:208; REEMB 2:213
Hibbs, Howard Lee
Mirage. YR 2:95

HIBERNIANS, ANCIENT ORDER OF
Keating, J. T.
Progress of the order (Hibernian's address at the 42nd biennial convention) THOU 3:544
Hickerton, J. T. See Young, B., jt. auth.
Hickman, Addison
Case for the sit-down strike. BRP 8:68; NOR 1937:11
Hickman, Leon E.
Ideal American (Theodore Roosevelt) SHUP:225
Hicks, George
Invasion starts. HAN:268
Higashi-Kuni, Naruhito
Address before Diet on reasons for defeat. VO 1945-46:540
Speech to the Japanese people upon becoming Premier. VO 1945-46:462
Higdon, Hoke

Desirability of war. JUD:281
Higgins, Frank W.
Address at 250th anniversary of the settlement of the Jews in the United States. TWJ:23

HIGGINS, MARGUERITE (MAGGIE)
Coulter, T.H.
Introducing Marguerite (Maggie) Higgins to the Executives' Club of Chicago. LARW:107; LY:129
Higginson, Thomas Wentworth
Battle of the cowpens. REEMA 8:618
Dead upon the field of honor. - Same as his Decoration day, 1870
Decoration Day, 1870. BLAA: 246; BLAB:246; CHAL 10: 298; HAZO 20:8599; KLEM: 170; MAS 20:8599; REEM 7:166; REEMA 8:621; REEMB 8:193
For self-respect and self-protection. CHAL 10:309; HAZO 20:8610; MAS 20: 8610
Grant. CHAL 10:302; HAZO 20:8603; MAS 20:8603; WERN 42:66
Literature in a republic. REEMA 5:565

HIGH SCHOOL ORATIONS
America, twenty years hence. AMEO 1:205
American ideals: high school oration. AMEO 1:117
Burr of the wheel. AMEO 1: 73
Green but growing. AMEO 1: 214
High ideals. AMEO 1:99
Nation's temptation. AMEO 1: 212
Not evening but dawn. AMEO 1:96
Our flag. AMEO 1:217
University of patriotism. AMEO 1:120

HIGH SCHOOLS See Education

HIGHER EDUCATION See Education, higher
Highet, Gilbert
Historian's job. MOA:408
Highsaw, J.L., Jr.
Manufacture of consent. BOA: 351; YR 6:23

HIGHWAYS See Roads
Higley, Warren
Warnings of history (Arbor day address) THOU 1:37
Hilary, Saint
Homily on Psalm LIII. HAZO 3:1217; MAS 3:1217
Hildebert of Lavardin, abp. of Tours
Rebecca at the well. BREW 7:42
Hildebrand, Joel H.
Are we educating for national strength. BA 1940-41:271
Hill, Benjamin H.
Education and progress. HARSO:48; SHUO:76
Flag of our fathers. HARSO: 53
Hercules of the age. BOB: 212
Little personal history. BREW 7:47
On the perils of the nation. CHAL 10:276; HAZO 20: 8557; MAS 20:8557
Stars and stripes. SOU 9:354
Work of universities in the South. REEMA 8:624

HILL, BENJAMIN H.
Ingalls, J.J.
Undiscovered country (death of B.H. Hill) BREW 7:122; REEM 5:237; REEMA 8: 721; REEMB 9:276
Hill, David Bennett
For bimetalism. REEMA 13: 1182
Hill, Felix
They were exploitable. NOR 1947:71

Hill, Frank Pierce
Librarian of today. REEM 2: 214; REEMB 2:219
Hill, Henry
Presents Francis B. Haas. LY:106
Hill, James J.
Canadian lesson for the United States. BREW 7:57
Natural wealth of the land and its conservation. REEM 4: 198; REEMB 4:397
Hill, Oliver W.
Case against segregated schools. ARNS:150
Hill, Roy L.
I am somebody. HILK:333
Hill, Thomas
Liberal education. NORR 2nd ser:140
Hillard, George Stillman
Influence of men of genius. REEMA 2:616
Past and the future, 1851. BRAR 2:135
Hillis, Newell Dwight
John Ruskin. REEM 5:214; REEMA 5:579; REEMB 9: 251
Pulpit in modern life. REEM 6:249; REEMA 8:644; REEMB 6:162
Washington: the ideal American. HARSO:296; WERN 42:26
World a whispering gallery. BLAA:179; BLAB:179
Hillman, Sidney
Agriculture, industry, and labor. BA 1938-39:142
Hillquit, Morris
Summation for the Socialists in the investigation of the New York Socialists by the Asssmbly, Albany. HICJ: 819
Hills, Lee
Present Fred Sparks. LY:132
Hilton, James H.
Closing remarks at Iowa State College centennial luncheon. IOCP:43
Concluding remarks at Academic symposia-Iowa State College centennial. IOCP: 163
Hilton, M. Eunice
Farewell to a college. GA:55
Hinds, Charles G.
Fraternal greetings. THOU 3: 318

HINDUISM
Bentinck, W.
On the suppression of Sati, November 8, 1828. KESI 1:208
Hinman, Harvey D.
Opening address for the respondent in the Sulzer impeachment trial. HICJ:660
Hintz, Adolph
Introducing an implement dealer
" a plumber. BRC:209, 154
Hirohito, Emperor of Japan
Broadcast to the Japanese people on surrender. HAN: 357; VO 1945-46:436
Imperial rescript opening the 87th Diet. VO 1945-46:284
Japan accepts Potsdam declaration. -Same as his Broadcast to the Japanese people on surrender
Message at opening of 85th Diet, VO 1944-45:411
Rescript read before the Japanese Diet. VO 1945-46:540
Surrender rescript to Japanese troops. VO 1945-46: 460
Hirsch, Emil G.
Concordance of Judaism and Americanism. TWJ:148

HISTORIANS
Highet, G.
Historian's job. MOA:408

HISTORIC LANDMARKS
Phillips, W.
Plea for the Old South Church, Boston. CLAY:198

HISTORY
Beard, C. A.
Written history as an act of faith. LINP:73
Coulter, E. M.
What the South has done about its history. TIN:3
Eggleston, E.
New history. REEM 6:142; REEMA 8:401; REEMB 7:124
Froude, J. A.
Science of history. REEMA 5:443
Gordon, T. H.
Watchdogs. ONEC:389; YR 1:15
Gray, S. E.
Influence of the teaching of history on world peace. ASHF:286
Hamer, P. M.
Records of Southern history. TIN:50
Hamilton, J. G. de R.
Three centuries of Southern records, 1607-1907. TIN:129
Makers of history. BOB:214
Mossell, N. F.
Teachings of history considered in relation to race problems in America. DUNM:227
Müller, F. M.
On some lessons of antiquity. HAZO 20:8588; MAS 20:8588
Schlegel, K. W. F.
Philosophy of history. BREW 9:147; HAZO 10:3982; MAS 10:3982
Stephenson, W. H.
Half-century of Southern historical scholarship. TIN:155
White, A. D.
Field of historical study. REEMA 9:1177
Hithquoquean, Chief of Delaware Indians See Indians of North America
Hitler, Adolf
Address at Berlin Sports Palace, January 30, 1941. VO 1941:51
Address at opening of the winter relief campaign, September 30, 1942. VO 1942-43:507
Address on eleventh anniversary of the National Socialist regime. VO 1944-45:73
Address to Reichstag, May 4, 1941. -Same as his German conquests
Address to the Reichstag, April 26, 1942. VO 1942-43:217
Again we turned fate away. -Same as his New Year's broadcast to the German people, December 31, 1944.
Announced to the Reichstag the declaration of war against the United States. VO 1941:572
Appeal to the French on the entry of German troops into unoccupied France. VO 1942-43:644
At the funeral of Reich Minister Dr. Fritz Todt. VO 1942-43:135
Before the Old Guard of his party, November 8, 1941. VO 1941:482
Broadcast on 12th anniversary of National Socialist regime. VO 1945-46:46
Broadcast plea for winter aid, August 30, 1942. VO 1942-43:453
Broadcast to the German people, October 3, 1941. VO 1941:439
Broadcast to the world, March 21, 1943 (celebrating Heroes' Memorial day) VO 1943-44:129
German conquests. COP:506; COPA:506; COPB:484; VO 1941:192
Germany could no longer remain idle. PL:819
Germany will never capitu-

Hitler, Adolph (cont.)
late.-Same as his Speech commemorating the twentieth birthday of the Nazi Party
Germany's aim. BEA:271
Germany's claims. BERS:142; COP:496; COPA:496; COPB:474
Memorial address, 1941. VO 1941:133
Memorial day address, 1942. VO 1942-43:198
Message on the occasion of the 25th anniversary of the National Socialist Party's program. VO 1945-46:68
New Year proclamation, December 31, 1943. VO 1943-44:607
New Year's broadcast to the German people, December 31, 1944. HAN:291; VO 1944-45:637
New Year's order of the day to the German Armed Forces, December 31, 1940. VO 1941:4
No more territorial demands. COP:502; COPA:502; COPB:480
Order for a last stand in the East. VO 1945-46:152
Order of the day, December 31, 1943. VO 1943-44:604
Order of the day calling for invasion of Yugoslavia and Greece, April 6, 1941. VO 1941:152
Order of the day to the German troops on the Eastern front, October 2, 1941. VO 1941:437
Order to his Western armies concerning guerilla warfare. VO 1945-46:160
Position of Germany today. SAR:297
Proclamation on the tenth anniversary of his accession to power. VO 1943-44:27
Proclamation on war with Soviet Union, June 22, 1941. VO 1941:292
Proclamation to Nazi Party veterans. VO 1943-44:89
Proclamation to the German nation, October 14, 1933. KESK 1:283
Proclamation to the German people's army, broadcast by Heinrich Himmler. VO 1944-45:560
Radio speech after attempt on his life. VO 1944-45:312
Request for dictatorial powers. FRY:120
Speech at Berlin Sports Palace, January 30, 1942. VO 1942-43:101
Speech commemorating the twentieth birthday of the Nazi Party. CROC:238; VO 1943-44:520
Speech delivered at Munich, Germany February 24, 1941. VO 1941:95
Speech on the 19th anniversary of the "Beer Hall Putsch." VO 1942-43:610
Speech on the surrender of Italy. VO 1943-44:339
Speech to German Reichstag, May 21, 1935. KESK 2:33
Takes full responsibility for the blood purge. PE:755; PEA:755
Threat to destroy the British Empire. HAN:143
To Reichstag on the declaration of war against the United States. VO 1941: 572

HITLER, ADOLF
Benz, L.I.
Shadow of the Swastika. BRP 6:71; NOR 1934:79
Doenitz, K.
Announcement of Hitler's death. VO 1945-46:182
Speech after attempt on Hitler's life. VO 1944-45: 313
Goebbels, P.J.

Broadcast describing plot to assassinate Hitler. VO 1944-45:337
Goering, H.
Speech (after attempt on Hitler's life. VO 1944-45: 314
Kaltenborn, H.V.
Hitler's fifty-second birthday. BA 1940-41:149
Keane, S.
Son of Phaeton. BRP 5:31
Thompson, D.
Let's face the facts. BA 1940-41:137
Hoar, Ebenezer Rockwood
Appropriate name (for Liberty day) THOU 1:490
Hoar, George Frisbie
At the banquet of the New England Society.-Same as his South Carolina and Massachusetts
Daniel Webster. BLAA:75; BLAB:75; KNAS:109; KNASA:109
Delirium of conquest.-Same as his Philippine question
Eulogy on William McKinley. CHAL 11:49
Favoring McKinley's re-election. CHAL 11:18; HAZO 21: 8904; MAS 21:8904
Great men of Massachusetts. BREW 7:60
Lust of empire. FUL:139, 141, 144
Philippine question. BRIM: 339; FUL:148; LA:153; WERN 42:84
Question of Constitutional rights.-Same as his Philippine question
Subjugation of the Philippine in iniquitous. BRYW 10:220; HICF:291; REEM 10:373; REEMA 13:194; REEMB 11:388
South Carolina and Massachusetts. CHAL 11:2; HAZO 21: 8888; MAS 21:8888; REEM 7:169; REEMA 8:659; REEMB 8:196

HOAR, GEORGE FRISBIE
Depew, C.M.
George Frisbie Hoar. ONES:176
Hoar, Sherman
American courage. HARSO: 158
Hoare, Sir Samuel
Effects of conciliation (November 2, 1935) KESK 2:81

HOBBIES
Byrd, M.E.
Hobo hobbies. JUD:293
Hobbies-a few words in their favor before a mixed group. DR:92; LU:1153
Hobby, Oveta Culp
Citizen responsibilities. BRAP:56
See also Eisenhower, D.D., jt. auth.

HOBOES
Byrd, M.E.
Hobo hobbies. JUD:293
Hobson, Richard P.
For a larger Navy. SHUO: 245
Hock, Homer
Lincoln. YE:104
Hocking, William Ernest
Crisis of our time. BA 1944-45:194
Hodge, Frank S.
Is America safe? ASHF:58

HODGES, GILBERT T.
Introducing Col. Gilbert T. Hodges of the N.Y. Sun. SUM:93
Hodgkinson, H.D.
Welcome to the Conference on Distribution. YE:133
Hoeppner, Carl
Moral neutrality. NOR 1945:17
Hoey, Clyde R.
Response to introduction. PR: 133
Hoff, Myron C.
Jeepers creepers. BRP 10:29; NOR 1939:22

Hoffman, Arthur
Our Constitution and peace. DO:98
Hoffman, Harry G.
Introduces Morris Sayre. PR: 95
Hoffman, Paul G.
Accepting the Robert Dollar award. SAB:221
Business, government, and education. HAR:429
Prices of things which farmers buy, including so-called management of prices by industry. HUS:255
Response on receiving Freedom House award. BA 1951-52: 77

HOFFMAN, PAUL G.
Lamont, T. S.
Presents Paul G. Hoffman. LY:91
Stevens, E. T.
Introduces Paul G. Hoffman. PR:69
Hoge, Moses D.
Stonewall Jackson. HARS:273; PROS:116; SHU:79; SMI: 181
Hogg, Douglas
Speech in House of Commons, November 27, 1922 (on establishment of Irish Free State) KESB:128
Hogg, James Stephen
President (Theodore) Roosevelt. SHUO:65

HOGG, JAMES STEPHEN
Terrell, A.
Tribute to James S. Hogg. SHUO:67
Hogland, Gunnar E.
Time for greatness. NOR 1946:35
Holand, Don
Educational crisis. YR 6:277
Holborne, Sir Robert
In defense of John Hampden. BREW 7:66
Holden, Roberta
Progress toward peace. BRP: 3:29
Hole, Samuel R.
My garden. REEM 2:216; REEMA 8:673; REEMB 2: 221
With brains, Sir! REEMA 2: 622

HOLIDAYS
Holidays and festivals (their significance in our lives) ED:17
Our national holidays. REAC: 64
See also Names of holidays, e.g. Fourth of July; Labor Day; Thanksgiving Day
Holland, Josiah Gilbert
Eulogy on Abraham Lincoln. CHAL 9:439; HAZO 19: 8071; MAS 19:8071
Holland, Rush LaMotte
Order of the Elks. REEM sup 2:48; REEMB 7:230
Holland, Spessard L.
Tidelands oil. BA 1952-53:142

HOLLAND
Kaltenborn, H. V.
Germany invades Holland and Belgium. BA 1939-40: 68
Holler, William E.
Automobile dealer. SAC:88
Holly, Theodore
Auspicious dawn of Negro rule. WOON:242

HOLLYWOOD See Moving pictures
Holm, Warren
Introducing a track star. BRC: 227
Holman, William Steele
Economy in public expenditures. REEMA 13:1220
Holmes, George H.
Eleventh plague. BRP 8:80
Holmes, Jesse H.
Honor system. PEAE:225
Holmes, John Haynes
One supreme issue of this hour. BA 1939-40:391

Should Mr. Roosevelt's plan for enlarging the Supreme Court be adopted? (negative) SAR:219
Unknown soldier speaks. SAR: 425

HOLMES, JOHN HAYNES
Introducing John Haynes Holmes. NI:169; NIA:125
Holmes, Oliver Wendell
Dorothy Q. COP:622; COPB: 662; HURG:139; REEM 2: 220; REEMA 2:627; REEMB 2:225
Introduces Matthew Arnold. REEM 7:23; REEMA 4:27; REEMB 8:23
Leave no verbal message. CHAL 7:388; HAZO 15: 6285; MAS 15:6285
Lecture on religious poetry. CHAL 7:381; HAZO 15:6278; MAS 15:6278
Longfellow. KNAS:58; KNASA: 58
Mechanism in thought and morals. BL:415
Medical profession. LA:160
Oration, 1855. BRAR 2:267
Practical ethics of the physicians. REEM 6:262; REEMA 8:677; REEMB 6:175
Tribute to Paul Morphy. CHAL 7:394; HAZO 15:6291; MAS 15:6291
Welcome to alumni (1860) ONEM:674; REEMA 2:625; WERN 54:127
Welcome to alumni (1863) CHAL 7:403; KLEM:52; HAZO 15:6300; MAS 15:6300

HOLMES, OLIVER WENDELL
Clemens, S. L.
Unconscious plagiarism. REEM 1:300; REEMA 1:221; REEMB 1:301
Curtis, G.W.
Greeting the autocrat (Oliver Wendell Holmes) REEMA 1: 299
Howe, J.W.
Tribute to Oliver Wendell Holmes. COP:618; COPB: 658; REEMA 2:645; REEMB 2:240
Holmes, Oliver Wendell, Jr.
Class of '61. REEMB 2:232
Dissent in the case of the Russian aliens. -Same as his Dissenting opinion on Abrams vs. United States
Dissenting opinion on Abrams vs. United States. ANG: 458; FO:310
Education in the obvious. HICF:415
John Marshall. BLAA:110; BLAB:110
Joy of life. REEMA 2:631; REEMB 2:236
Law and the court. BRYA: 212; KLEB:33; REEMB 2:228
"Live-I am coming:" response to birthday greeting. COP: 377; COPA:377; COPB: 377; HURG:215; YE:148
Lochner v. New York, 1905; dissenting opinion for the Supreme Court. BIR 3:289
Memorial Day. BRAC:335; REEM 7:181; REEMA 8: 691; REEMB 8:208
Schenck v. United States: opinion for the Supreme Court. BRE:320; BREA: 300
Sons of Harvard who fell in battle. REEMA 2:630; REEMB 2:234
Speech at a Bar dinner. ONEM:624; ONES:218
Use of law schools. REEM 6: 276; REEMA 8:700; REEMB 6:189

HOLMES, OLIVER WENDELL, Jr.
Hunt, F.
Story of ex-Justice Holmes. DOA:120
Luce, H.R.
Reverse Mr. Justice Holmes. BRY:544

Holt, George N.
Address of welcome to Mystic Workers. THOU 3:463
Holt, John H.
Nominating speech for John W. Davis. WHIP:262
Holth, Irene
Youth aflame. YR 6:303

HOME
Adams, W.
Home gathering (Thanksgiving address) THOU 2:264
Biel, K.W.
Jesus-the savior of the home. ACW:84
Dewey, Orville
Homes of freedom. BOB: 162
Dumas, G.
Home. BOA:136
Duncan, P.
Study in ghosts (broken homes) BLUE:58
Grady, H.W.
Home and the Republic. SHU:155
Homes of the people. CLAY: 132; PROS:85
Home. BOB:159
Home and the wife (satisfied husband speaks) ED:323
Home, the seminary of the nation. BOB:160
Housewives (lauding the work of the homemaker.) EDGS: 193
Huber, L.J.
Introducing a housewife. BRH:105
Just a housewife (the homemaker's forum) DR:307
Kaser, A.L.
Introducing an interior decorator. BRC:108
Kramer, H.G.
Home blessed with peace. ACW:71
Lloyd, W.
Protected home. THOU 3: 198
Outline for a speech "A house and a home." BARR:77
Pickell, C.S.
Fireside and iron bars. BRP 2:63; YR:3:73
Probst, W.F., Jr.
Homeless America. BRP 5: 17; YR 6:291
Stevens, J.S.
More stately mansions. BRP 2:77; YR 3:97
Temple, G.
Beneath American roofs. BOA:133; BOB:158; BRP 1:25
Van Dyke, H.
Home as a nation builder. BOA:140; BOB:164
Wangerin, W.M.
King's prayer for your home. ACW:8
Wiggen, E.
American home. BUT:246
Wise, T.
Home, the seminary of the nation. BOA:138
See also Family; Housewarmings; Marriage; Parents and Teachers associations

HOME-COMING See Reunions

HOME FRONT See Inflation (finance); Labor and laboring classes; Price regulation; Rationing; United States-Defenses; World War, 1939-1945-Civilian activities

HOME RULE BILLS See Ireland
Homer.
Achilles to the envoys. BRYW 1:3; HAZO 1:4; LEEW 1: 27; MAS 1:4; PL:23
Speech of Odysseus. HAZO 1: 1; MAS 1:1
Speech of Phoinix. HAZO 1:8; MAS 1:8

HONESTY
Honesty (for any young people's meeting) EDGS:235
See also Truthfulness and falsehood
Honjo, Shigeru

Japan plans for world conquest. HAN:325

HONOR STUDENTS See Learning and scholarship
Hood, Clifford F.
Responds to an introduction. PRNE:69
Hood, P. Pastor
Religion of the Negroes. THOU 1:266
Hooker, Leroy
Lincoln the hero of his convictions. THOU 1:474
Hooker, Richard
Sermon on the nature of justice. LEEW 4:169
Hootman, Edith
Unfilled promise (possibilities of universal peace and ultimate attainment thru education) ASHF:347
Hoover, Herbert C.
Accepting the nomination for presidency. CORP:231; SHU:114
After war questions. REEM 4:212; REEMB 4:411
At the Brussels Exposition. BA 1958-59:56
Begins an address on the occasion of the State of Iowa's celebration of his eightieth birthday at his birthplace, West Branch, Iowa. PRNE:65
Benjamin Franklin-accepting the gold medal of the International Benjamin Franklin Society. BA 1953-54:81
Bill of Rights. COP:419; COPA:419; COPB:421; HURG:229
Bonus marchers: Press statement, March 29, 1932. FIP:189
Bonus marchers; Press statement, July 28, 1932. FIP:190
Bonus marchers; Press statement, September 14, 1932. FIP:191
Combating the depression. FRY:106
Final campaign speech (Palo Alto, Calif.) ONEC:238
Food control-a war measure. REEM 11:285; REEMB 12:302
Franklin, a characteristic American. HOB:169
Future. BLAB:354
Government by isms. BREW 7:72
Government ownership. ONEC:521
Governmental conduct of business. SHU:10
Holy crusade for liberty.- Same as his Road to freedom
Hoover stands on the record, November 5, 1932 speech (St. Paul, Minn.) FIP:194
Inaugural address. CHI:249; LOTI:223; USIN:225; USINA:225
Individual initiative. BOA:401
Leadership for a free world. MO:568
Meaning of America (at homecoming in West Branch, Iowa) BA 1948-49:89; YE:286
Message to Congress, December 10, 1931 (on public debts) KESK 1:232
Moratorium. FIP:180
National defense. BA 1939-40:126
New foreign policy is needed.- Same as his Our national policies in this crisis
Obedience to law and enforcement. HICF:957
Opening address at the White House Conference on Child Health and Protection. DOA:173
Our national policies in this crisis. BA 1950-51:45; YE:363
Principles and ideals of the United States government. PO:143
Protection of democracy. BA

Hoover, H. C. (cont.)
1937-38:80
Question of peace. BA 1940-41: 196
Recovering from destruction and inflation. BREW 7:71
Respect for law. BOA:271; BOB:22
RFC: Press statement, January 22, 1932. FIP:182
RFC: Press statement, July 6, 1932: The Garner Wagner Relief Bill. FIP:183
RFC: Report of activities, March 25, 1932. FIP:183
Road tc freedom. SAR:128; WPRC:198
South, national problem, and the American home (158th anniversary of battle of King's Mountain) HICF:852
Speech at New York City, October 22, 1928. BIR 4:84
United Nations. HURG:287
Waste-a problem of distribution. BYRA:217; REEM sup 2:53; REEMB 4:422
Weaving our destiny. BOA: 208; BOB:177
Youth and opportunity. -Same as his Accepting the nomination for presidency

HOOVER, HERBERT CLARK
Dawes, C. G.
Speech in support of Hoover. ONEC:551
McNab, J. L.
Nominating Herbert Hoover for Presidency. ONEC:489
Pratt, R.
Seconding the nomination of President Hoover. GA:202
Trueblood, D. E.
Herbert Clark Hoover. BA 1964-65:108

HOOVER REPORT See United States-Commission on Organization of the Executive Branch of the Government

HOPE
Dow, L., Jr.
Hope and despair. BREW 5: 307
Miller, H.
Pledge science give to hope. BREW 8:144

HOPPER, DEWOLF
DeWolf Hopper. NI:184

Hopkins, Ernest Martin
Aristocracy of brains. REEM 6:286; REEMB 7:235

Hopkins, Ernest Martin
College of the future: inaugural address as president of Dartmouth. WE 1:119
Orientation. ONEC:427

Hopkins, Mark
Central principle, 1853. BRAR 2:203
Inaugural address as president of Williams College. WE 1: 137

Hopkins, Woolsey Rogers
Beginnings of the New England Society of New York, 1884. BRAR 1:1

Horn, Francis H.
Education-for what? BA 1959-60:149
Prospect for civilization. BA 1962-63:82

HORSE RACING
Horse racing, by a sportsman. EDGS:405
Huber, L. J.
Introducing a horseman. BRC:298

Horton, Evelyn
International understanding. BRP 2:87; YR 3:89

Horton, Jim
American opportunities. DO: 13

Horton, Mildred McAfee
American education and the world's needs. BA 1946-47: 203
Predictions for the unpredictable future. BRA:551

HOSPITALS
Acknowledging appreciation (at

hospital fund drive and testimonial) BED:66; BEDA: 102
Appeal for funds for a hospital-two model speeches. BEB:23, 24
Closing speech (at hospital fund drive and testimonial) BED: 66; BEDA:103
Dickens, C.
For the hospital for sick children. KNAS:21; KNASA: 21
Doctor, the world is sick. NI:249; NIA:188
Eaton, L.H., Jr.
Help today for health tomorrow. BRAP:33
McKeldin, T.
Hospital building fund. MCK:125
Opening statement (at hospital fund drive and testimonial) BED:62; BEDA:98
Persecuted triumph. NI:257; NIA:194
Presentation speech (at hospital fund drive and testimonial) BED:62; BEDA:99
Presenting check (at hospital fund drive and testimonial) BED:63; BEDA:100
Roosevelt, F.D.
Dedicatory address at the Naval Medical Center, Bethesda, Maryland. VO 1942-43:454
Tribute by contrast (34th anniversary of a sanitarium) NIA:208
Tribute to guest-of-honor and appeal for funds (at hospital fund drive and testimonials) BED:64; BEDA:101
Vanderlip, Mrs. F.R.
Hospitals-yesterday and today. GA:276
Walsh, J.J.
Religious hospital as the need of our times. CATA 2:221
Hostettler, Gordon F.
Speech as a liberal art. BERS: 207

HOTELS
Boss, E.A.
How to modernize and manage a hotel. HUS:242
Hotels and restaurants (dining room a public benefactor) ED:179
Hotels, by the manager of a hotel. EDGS:157
Hough, Lynn Harold
Genius of democracy. BA 1955-56:62
Houghton, Alanson B.
Open diplomacy. BEA:277
Houghton, Mrs. Hiram Cole
Today's challenge. BUT:250
Houghton, Richard Monckton Milnes, 1st Baron
Bonds of national sympathy. REEMA 2:639
Your speech and ours. REEMA 2:635

HOUGHTON, RICHARD MONCKTON MILNES, 1st LORD
Bryant, W.C.
Introduces Lord Houghton. REEMA 2:635
Choate, J.H.
Tribute to Lord Houghton. REEMA 1:152

HOURS OF LABOR
Black, H.L.
Wages and Hours Bill. ON: 173
Holmes, O.W., Jr.
Lochner v. New York, 1905: dissenting opinion for the Supreme Court. BIR 3: 289
Macaulay, T.B.
Industrial worker. HAY: 197
Peckham, R.W.
Lochner v. New York, 1905: opinion for the Supreme Court. BIR 3:283
See also Labor and laboring classes

House, Robert B.
Presents Josiah C. Crudup. LY:110

HOUSE DECORATION See Interior decoration
Houser, Theodore V.
Today's challenge to people's capitalism. IOCP:95

HOUSEWARMINGS
Best wishes to the host and hostess at their housewarming. DR:229; LU:1244
Clifford, V.
Emcee at a housewarming. BRH:218
For a house warming: host's response. BARB:137
Gilbert, E. J.
Emcee at a housewarming. BRH:292
House-warming, by a guest, and response by husband. EDGS:259, 261
Huber, L. J.
Emcee at a housewarming. BRH:220
Posner, G. A.
Emcee at a housewarming. BRH:247

HOUSING
Colling, H.
Reply to Mr. Post on Taft-Ellender-Wagner Housing Bill. MO:462
Karos, P. A.
Haven of the defeated. ARNS:160
Post, L.
Taft-Ellender-Wagner Housing Bill. MO:460
Straus, N.
End the slums. ON:250; SAR:326
Truman, H. S.
Message to Congress, September 6, 1945. VO 1945-46:546
Houston, Daniel
His defense at the Bar of the House. BREW 7:76
On his defeat as a Union candidate. BREW 7:74
Houston, P. D.
Presents a gift of silver and a scroll of honor to retiring president of American Bankers Association, Robert M. Hanes. PR:106
Houston, Samuel
Closes ominous debate on the repeal of the Missouri Compromise. PE:482; PEA:482
On the Nebraska and Kansas Bill. CHAL 6:44; HAZO 12:5073; MAS 12:5073
HOUSTON, SAMUEL
Wallace, R. M.
Stephen F. Austin and Sam Houston (at acceptance of their statues in Capitol) SHUO:211
Houston, Temple
Tell her to go in peace (defense of Minnie Stacey) GRIS:23
Houston, Thomas Allen
Rose of the Southern commons. SHUC:338
Hoven, Ard
New lamps for old. BOA:420; YR 5:41
Howard, Sir Esme William See Howard of Penrith, E. W. H.
Howard, F. W.
Progress true and false. CATA 2:155
Howard, J. M.
Call of the ministry. SHUC:385
Howard of Penrith, Esme William Howard, 1st Baron
Sales representation of John Bull & Co. REEM sup 2:69; REEMB 5:1
HOWARD UNIVERSITY
Hawkins, W. A.
Negro lawyer: his opportunity, his duty (at opening of Howard University Law School) DUNM:483
Howe, Joseph
At International Commercial

Howe, J. (cont.)
Convention. CHAL 7:211; HAZO 14:6095; MAS 14: 6095
Howe, Julia Ward
Salon in America. REEMA 5: 591
Tribute to Oliver Wendell Holmes. COP:618; COPB: 658; REEMA 2:645; REEMB 2:240

HOWE, JULIA WARD
Eliot, C.W.
Julia Ward Howes. PEAE: 155
Howe, M. A. de Wolfe
New armor. BOB:31
Howe (Supreme Master)
Response. THOU 3:465
Howell, Clark
Man with his hat in his hand. BLAA:155; BLAB:155; SHUO:198
No need of pessimism. FUL: 160,164
Our reunited country. FUL: 153, 155, 157; ONES:190; REEMA 2:647; REEMB 2: 242; WERN 42:64
Howell, Wilbur S.
Democratic issue. BA 1941-42: 64
Howells, Paul Kenneth
Simple fools. BRP 6:59; YR 5:197
Howells, William Dean
"Atlantic" and its contributors: Whittier's 70th birthday and 20th year of the Atlantic. REEM 2:244; REEMA 2:653; REEMB 2: 248
In memory of Mark Twain. REEM 5:224; REEMB 9:262
Introduces Joseph Gurney Cannon. REEM 5:64; REEMB 9:94
Spanish prisoners of war. BLAA:78; BLAB:78

HOWELLS, WILLIAM DEAN
Van Dyke, H.
William Dean Howells. REEM 5:370; REEMB 9: 414
Howie, Roberta
This tournament. JUD:77
Howland, Henry E.
Our ancestors and ourselves. REEM 2:247; REEMA 2: 661; REEMB 2:251
Russia. REEMA 2:657
Hoxha, Enver
Reply to Khrushchev (November 7) RUS:147
Hrabanus Megnentius Maurus
See Rabanus Magnentius Maurus
Hsieh, Tehyi
Inside lights on Chinese situations. EXEE:338
Hubbard, Elbert
Masterpiece of God. SHU:259
Message to Garcia. HARSO: 216; PROS:15; SHU:171; WERN 42:152
Hubbard, Walter R.
Wendell Phillips. COUW:93
Hubbert, J.M.
Dying year. THOU 2:379
Huber, Louis J.
Animal-loving emcee
Bridegroom "
Deaf "
Family man "
Forgetful "
Frightened "
Handsome "
Little girl "
Ringmaster "
Rural "
Schoolboy "
Soldier "
Tough "
Undertaker " BRH: See Table of contents, section IV for paging
Emcee at an anniversary party
" at an auction
" " a birthday celebration
" " bridal shower
" " Christmas party for employees
" " convention
" " golden wedding anniver-

Huber, L. J. (cont.)
versary celebration
Emcee at a housewarming
" at an open house
" " a raffle
" " " retirement party
" " " silver wedding anniversary party
" at a stag dinner
" at a surprise party. BRH: see Table of contents, section III for paging
Emcee introducing himself. BRH:338
His honor, the emcee. BRH: 324
Introducing a timid soul. BRH: 330
" an actor
" " amateur show
" " animal imitator
" " " trainer
" a bachelor
" " celebrity
" " choir or chorus
" " clowns
" " college graduate
" " comedian
" " dancing act
" " father of new baby
" " gardener
" " housewife
" " humorist
" " hypnotist
" " impersonator
" an instrumental trio
" " instrumentalist
" " Irishman
" a juggler
" " kissing booth
" " magician
" " mind reader
" " minstrel show
" " newlywed
" " novelty act
" " old time entertainer
" " opera star
" " quartette
" " sharpshooter
" " square dance caller
" " strong man
" " swimming-diving act
" " tumbling act
Introducing a variety revue
" a ventriloquist
" " vocal soloist
" " woman driver. BRH: See Table of contents, section II for paging
Introducing an actor
" a boss
" " businessman
" " cattle raiser
" " doctor
" " financier
" " fisherman
" " golfer
" " horseman
" " hunter
" " musician
" " nurse
" " policeman
" " railroad executive
" " teacher
" " traveler
" " writer. BRC: See Table of contents for paging

Huckabee, Billy
Rights to peace. DO:128

HUDSON, HENDRIK
Depew, C. M.
Columbus and Hendrik Hudson. THOU 1:70
Hudspeth, C. B.
Eulogy on Nestor Montoya. HOA:378; HOAP:266
Hughes, Charles Evans
Accepting a gift from the Washington correspondents. ONEC:53
In honor of Lord Reading. REEM 2:256; REEMB 2:260
Judiciary. BA 1937-38:176
Latin-American relations. BLAB:293
Liberty and law. LINM:167
Maintaining the Declaration of Independence. SHU:120
National Labor Relations Board v. Jones and Laughlin Steel Corporation, 1937: opinion for the Supreme Court. BIR 4:218

Near v. Minnesota: opinion for the Supreme Court. BRE: 323; BREA:303
150th anniversary of the First Congress. BA 1938-39:161; COP:431; COPA:431; COPB:424; HURG:237
150th anniversary of the United States Supreme Court. ON:345
Opinion in the case of the Negro law student, Lloyd Gaines. ANG:486
Our government. -Same as his 150th anniversary of the First Congress
Pathway to peace. HICF:681
Response to a tribute. YE: 149
Rights of manhood. BREW 7: 85
Schechter Poultry Corporation v. United States, 1935: opinion for the Supreme Court. BIR 4:131
Speech at Washington Conference on Limitations of Armaments. BIR 4:62; BOAM:127; BYRA:237; PL: 765; REEM 11:383; REEMB 12:402
Speech of introduction at the celebration of eightieth birthday of Elihu Root. KLEB:127; LINM:253
Ten years naval holiday. BREW 7:82
To a Republican club. KNAS: 318; KNASA:318
United States Supreme Court building. ON:301
West Coast Hotel Co. v. Parrish: opinion for the Supreme Court. BIR 4:231; BRE:344
What the flag means. BOA: 293; BOB:79

HUGHES, CHARLES EVANS
Bush, I. T.
In honor of Secretary Hughes. REEM sup 1:145; REEMB 1:183
Introducing Charles Evans Hughes. YE:131
Pepper, G. W.
Presents Charles Evans Hughes. LY:137
Tighe, M. F.
Presenting a pair of golden shears to Secretary Hughes. ONEC:49
Warren, E.
Charles Evans Hughes and the spirit of tolerance (dedication of hall in memory of Hughes). BA 1956-57:135

Hughes, Hugh Price
Lesson of Christmas day. THOU 2:350
Hughes, Langston
Speech on selling writing. HILK:274
---- and others (Mary MacLean Bethune and Ralph Bunche)
Glory. HILK:266

HUGHES, MABLE W.
Chapman, Mrs. C. C.
Introducing Mrs. Mable W. Hughes. YE:130

Hughes, Thomas
Cause of freedom. CHAL 10: 287; HAZO 20:8568; MAS 20:8568
Highest manhood. BREW 7:87
Hugo, Victor Marie, Comte de
Against curtailing the right of suffrage. CLAY:149
Death penalty. -Same as his Guillotine
Guillotine. BRYW 7:193; ESEH: 209; LEEW 5:253
Liberty tree in Paris. BREW 7:96; MEAR:117
Moral force in world politics. BREW 7:101
On capital punishment (defense of Charles Hugo). CHAL 7:8; HAZO 14:5783; MAS 14: 5783
On the centennial of Voltaire's death. BREW 7:98; CHAL 7:1; COP:91; COPA:91; COPB:91; HAZO 14:5776; MAS 14:5776; REEM 5:277;

Hugo, V. M., Comte de (cont.)
REEMA 8:710; REEMB 9: 265
Oration on Honoré de Balzac. BREW 7:94; CHAL 7:5; HAZO 14:5780; MAS 14:5780
Hulbert, H. B.
Samson and the pillars. BRP 1:12
Hulbert, Murray
Inventions and inventors. REEM sup 2:78; REEMB 6: 199
Hull, Cordell
Address before the Pan American Union, April 14, 1943. VO 1943-44:164
Address before the Pan American Union, April 14, 1944. VO 1944-45:169
Address to a joint meeting of Congress, November 18, 1943. VO 1943-44:548
Broadcast on United States foreign policy. VO 1943-44: 357
Broadcast to the world, July 23, 1942. HAN:188; VO 1942-43:394
Economic barriers to peace. SAR:276
Foreign policy of the United States (April 9, 1944 speech). BA 1943-44:67; GRAC:133; VO 1944-45:161
Happy mean. SAR:154
Introducing Ricardo J. Alfaro. MO:498; MOA:502
On relation with the French Republic, June 5, 1941. VO 1941:245
Opening of the Pan American Conference. BA 1938-39:40
Pillars of enduring peace. COP:558; COPB:550
Radio address on National Foreign Trade week. VO 1941: 213
Remarks at opening of second phase of the Dumbarton Oaks conversations. VO 1944-45:457
Statement at opening of Dumbarton Oaks Conference. HAN:427; VO 1944-45:381
Statement on Franco-German collaboration, June 13, 1941. VO 1941:282
Statement on U.S. foreign policy. VO 1944-45:135
War and human freedom. - Same as his Broadcast to the world, July 23, 1942
We shall not fail. COP:566
Hull, William Jacob
Intellectual freedom in a managed state. YR 6:357
Philosophy reenthroned. YR 5: 165

HULL HOUSE
Shoeler, M.
America's mother of men. YR 9:285

HUMAN ENGINEERING
Ford, H., II
Challenge of human engineering. BRY:438

HUMAN NATURE
Bushnell, H.
Dignity of human nature. BREW 3:11
Chapman, J. J.
Unity of human nature. LOMS:221; LOMSA:279; NORR 1st ser:254; REEM 6:89; REEMA 7:206; REEMB 7:102
Jastrow, J.
Social traits and human nature. EXEE:97
Read, O.
Human nature and politics. EXEE:244
Shorey, P.
Unity of the human spirit. NORR 1st ser:481
Wheeler, B. I.
Things human. NORR 1st ser:276
See also Behavior; Man

HUMAN RELATIONS
Bunche, R. J.

Challenge of human relations: Lincoln birthday dinner. BA 1949-50:142; HAR:452
LaFarge, J.
Religious philosophy and intergroup progress. HAR: 506
Peale, N.V.
How to have good relations with other people. BA 1954-55:153
See also Behavior, Life; Religion

HUMAN RIGHTS DAY AND WEEK
Address (on Human Rights Day). BED:69; BEDA:128
Closing speech (on Human Rights Day) BED:70; BEDA: 130
Introducing speaker (On Human Rights Day). BED:68; BEDA:128
Opening statement (on Human Rights Day). BED:68; BEDA:127

HUMANISM
Birge, E.A.
In Lucem gentium. NORR 2nd ser; 392
Schelling, F.E.
Humanities, gone and to come. NORR 1st ser:286

HUMANITIES See Classical education

HUMBOLDT, ALEXANDER VON
Ingersoll, R.G.
Oration on Humboldt (at unveiling of statue in Peoria, Illinois). CHAL 12:190

HUMBOLDT, WILHELM FREIHERR VON
Challemel-Lacour, P.A.
Humboldt and the Teutonic intellect. BREW 3:183
Hume, F. Charles
Young lawyer. ONEM:658; ONES:248; REEM sup 2:85; REEMB 6:206; SHUO:50
Humes, B.A.
On trial. BRP 4:87

HUMILITY
Graham, W.F.
National humility. HURG: 339

HUMOR See After-dinner speeches; Humorists; Wit and humor

HUMORISTS
Blaine, J.B.
Introducing James Gheen, humorous lecturer. PR:59
Drummond, R.
Introducing a humorist. BRC:283
Huber, L.J.
Introducing a humorist. BRH:111
McGovern, S.
Introducing a humorist. BRC:124
Weston, P.
Introducing a humorist. BRC:309

HUMOROUS SPEECHES See After dinner speeches
Humphrey, C.J.
Believe it or not. YR 10:87
Crosspatch. BRP 8:23; YR 9: 213
Humphrey, George M.
Businessmen must be active in politics. SABA:223
See also Eisenhower, D.D., jt. auth.
Humphrey, Hubert H., Jr.
Banning nuclear tests. BA 1958-59:48
Disarmament in the nuclear age. BA 1959-60:81
See also Kennedy, J.F., jt. auth.
Humphrey, William E.
Federal Trade Commission. BYRA:241; REEM sup 2: 92; REEMB 5:10

Humphreys, Benjamin Grubb
Old traditions. REEM 7:190; REEMB 8:217
Traditions of the South. BOB: 100

HUMPHREYS, HARRY E., Jr.
Knight, J.R.
Introduces H.E. Humphries, Jr., Chairman of the U.S. Rubber Co. PRNE:18

HUNGARY
Dixon, P.
Against Soviet intervention in Hungary. BAAG:372
Eisenhower, D.D.
Agonized reappraisals: Hungary and Suez. FIP:346
Lodge, H.C., Jr.
Hungary's struggle for freedom. BA 1956-57:36
Soviet suppression of Hungarian liberty. BA 1957-58: 37
Hunt, Chester
Cotner College. BRP 5:42; YR 6:179
Hunt, Frazier
Story of ex-Justice Holmes. DOA:120
Story of Jane Addams. DOA: 112
Those incredible Russians. BA 1942-43:185
Hunt, L.B.
Maiden speeches. JUD:43
Hunt, Lester
Introducing a house to house salesman. BRC:178
Hunter, Evelyn
Dream true. BRP 4:45; YR 5: 155

HUNTER, JOHN
Paget, J.
Scientific mind. HAY:261
Hunter, R.M.T.
Oration (dedication of equestrian statue of Washington). SMI:148
Hunter, Willard
Disciplined democracy. YR 8: 91
New birth of freedom. BRP 6: 88

HUNTERS AND HUNTING
Drummond, R.
Introducing a wild animal hunter. BRC:268
Erwin, D.
Introducing a hunter or extensive traveler. BRC:266
Huber, L.J.
Introducing a hunter. BRC: 245
Hunters. SCHS:149
Smith, H.
Introducing a game warden. BRC:160
See also Guns
Huntington, Hal
Introducing a Better Business Bureau secretary
" a Farm Bureau or Farmers' Union man. BRC: 308, 320
Hurd, Frank H.
Tariff for revenue only. JOHA 2 pt 2:238
Hurlburt, Henry A.
Introduction of J.A. Dix to the New England Society of N.Y., December 22, 1863. REEM 1:407; REEMB 1:413
Hurley, Jack, Jr.
Introducing a tire distributor or dealer. BRC:276
Hurley, Patrick J.
Americanism or Communism? BOA:301
Pioneer woman (dedicating statue of the Pioneer woman in Ponce, Oklahoma). BOA:256; BOB:131; GRIS: 62

HURST, FANNIE
Introducing Fannie Hurst. NI: 83; NIA:66
Hurt, John
To the Virginia brigands. SMI:38
Huss, John

Christmas meditation. PL: 224
Husted, Harold R.
Ideals of the coming age. COUW:249
Huston, Bradley
Introducing a stock broker. BRC:303
Huston, H. Leo
Presents gavel to a retiring president. PR:110
Hutchings, Roxana
Toll of speed hysteria. BRP 2:59; YR 3:153
Hutchins, Harry B.
Introducing James B. Angell. ONES:6
Hutchins, Robert Maynard
Crisis of our time. BA 1944-45:199
Drifting into suicide. ON:300
Education and social improvement. WPRC:220
Farewell for students. BA 1951-52:129
Issues in education: 1946. BA 1945-46:262
Organization and subject matter of general education. BA 1938-39:199
Philosophy of life. BA 1937-38:184
Proposition is peace. COP: 592
University in war and peace. BA 1942-43:235
What is a university? SAR: 51
What price freedom? YE:367
Where do we go from here in education? HAR:359
---- and others (R. Gustavson; W. F. Ogburn; and R. Redfield)
America and the atomic age. HAR:19
See also Donovan, W. J., jt. auth.

HUTCHINS, ROBERT MAYNARD
Graham, F. P.
Presents Robert M. Hutchins. LY:114

Huxley, Thomas Henry
Education. REAC:90
Examines Darwin's "Origin of species" PE:533; PEA:533
Method of scientific investigation. ARNS:260; BRY:455; BRYA:482
On a piece of chalk. REEM 8:215; REEMA 5:603; REEMB 13:219
Science and art. COP:655; COPB:682; REEM 2:262; REEMA 2:670; REEMB 2:266
Threefold unity of life. BREW 7:105
Hyde, Arthur M.
Liberty. BART 1:187
Hyde, Edward
"Discretion" as despotism. BREW 7:110
In John Hampden's case. BREW 7:112
Hyde, William DeWitt
Art of optimism. BLAA:94; BLAB:94; WERN 42:104

HYDROGEN BOMB
Kaltenborn, H. V. and others
How can we secure peace in a hydrogen bomb world? BA 1949-50:101
Urey, H.
Hydrogen bomb and international government. BA 1949-50:95
Hypereides.
Against Athenogenes. CHAL 1:132; HAZO 1:214; MAS 1:214; MINA 2:430
Against Demosthenes. MINA 2:500
Against Philippides. LEEW 1:199; MINA 2:410
First and second speeches in defence of Lycophron. MINA 2:376, 400
Fragments. MINA 2:564
Funeral oration. LEEW 1:204; MINA 2:536
In defence of Euxenippus. MINA 2:466

HYPNOTISTS See Actors and acting

HYPOCRISY
False faces. JAS:104
Hypocrisy. NATT:18
Ibrahim, Hassan Ben Ali
Inaugural speech at Conference on the Problems of Economic Development. UAR:137
Speech at final session of Conference on the Problems of Economic Development. UAR:393

ICELAND
Churchill, W. L. S.
Address in House of Commons on U. S. troops in Iceland. VO 1941:345
Roosevelt, F. D.
In response to message from Prime Minister of Iceland. VO 1941:343
Message to Congress on U. S. occupation of Iceland. VO 1941:341
Ickes, Harold L.
Academic freedom. BOA:156
What constitutes an American? COP:588; COPB:567; HURG:260

IDEALS
American ideals. DAVC:13
American ideals: high school oration. AMEO 1:117
Bumby, J. H.
Sacrifice that failed (failure of our war-time ideals). ASHF:382
Carey, J. B.
This I believe. BA 1951-52:92
Club ideals. AMEO 2:142
Cox, G. V.
My brother's keeper (plea for common ideals and world fellowship). ASHF:134
Davis, D. F.
Altar to an ideal. BOB:118
Douglas, P. H.
Five great Americans. BA 1951-52:85
Griggs, E. H.
New social ideal. CHAL 14:461; HAZO 25:11014; MAS 25:11014
Handle with care. NAT:17
Haygood, S. G.
America-its national and individual ideals. THOU 1:76
High ideals: high school oration. AMEO 1:99
Hoffman, P. G.
Response on receiving Freedom House award. BA 1951-52:77
Husted, H. R.
Ideals of the coming age. COUW:249
Lehman, H. H.
This I believe. BA 1951-52:90
Loeb, M.
Idols and ideals. TRUW:191
McCartney, C. E.
National apostasy. BOA:61; BOB:88; HARSO:233; SHU:66; TRUW:130
Melone, G. H. V.
American ideal (civilization rests not upon force but upon service to humanity). ASHF:213
Miller, H. R.
American ideals. REEM 2:410; REEMB 2:426
Moore, J. B.
American ideals. REEM 2:422; REEMB 2:438
Murray, H. A.
Beyond yesterday's idealism. NORR 3d ser:379
Nation's soul. SHU:60
Peabody, F. G.
Commercialism and idealism. SHU:257
Reverence for ideals. CON:74
Roosevelt, T.
National duty and international ideals. REEM 11:99; REEMB 12:108

Root, E.
American ideals during the past half century (birthday speech). ONEC:208; REEM sup 2:363; REEMB 8:373
Swing, D.
Power of ideals. BOB:216
Taylor, H.
Ideals of American youth. HAR:462

IDEAS
Ascoli, M.
Scarcity of ideas. ARNS: 226
Chapin, E.H.
Sovereignty of ideas. BREW 3:204
Douglas, M.
Supremacy of ideas. SHUC: 276
Gallagher, B.G.
Preface to the study of Utopias (Founders Day lecture on the anniversary of Antioch College). BA 1960-61:201
Hill, B.H.
Hercules of the age. BOB: 212
Long, L.G.
Power of ideas. SHU:190
MacCracken, H.N.
Ideologies, their dynamics and excesses. HOB:184
Mitchell, D.
Power of an idea. NOR 1947:89
Reid, L.D.
Engineering of ideas (presenting Honor Awards to engineers). BRAB:545
Robertson, J.
One idea. MO:245; MOA: 245
See also Thought and thinking
Igleheart, Austin S.
Sale we've failed to make. SAB:169
Ignatov, Nikolai G.
Speech of October 23. RUS: 65
Ikeguchi, Joe
Promised land. AN:58
Iles, George
Trusteeship of literature. HAZO 25:10817; MAS 25: 10817

ILLINOIS, UNIVERSITY OF
Draper, A.S.
Inaugural address as president of University of Illinois. WE 2:277
Illness See Health; Medicine; Sick
Ilyichev, Leonard F.
Speech of October 24. RUS: 70

IMAGINATION
Goschen, G.J.
On the cultivation of the imagination. CHAL 12:21; HAZO 22:9413; MAS 22: 9413
Uses of imagination (installation as Lord Rector of Edinburgh University). REEMA 8:557
McLeod, G.
Imagination rules the world. YR 7:177

IMMIGRATION AND EMIGRATION
Barrington, J.W.
National problem. COUW: 37
Blake, E.H.
Flood-gate flung wide. SHUC:291
Boyle, J.P.
Democracy and foreign immigration. SHUC:298
Christensen, R.
Ellis Island and Plymouth Rock. NOR 1941:23
Dwyer, J.F.
Citizen. HARSO:32
Ginn, G.
Yellow peril. ASHF:66
Grant, U.S.
Adopted citizen. REEM 2: 139; REEMA 2:561; REEMB 2:131

IMMIGRATION AND EMIGRATION (cont.)
Halt! Who goes there? SCHS:144
Hodge, F.S.
Is America safe? ASHF:58
Johnnedes, M.
Immigrant in America. YR 1:131
Let them in. NI:238; NIA:181
Morrow, W.W.
Chinese immigration. WAGN:220
Parker, C.
Different motives of the settlers. THOU 1:222
Perkins, G.C.
Exclusion of the Chinese. REEMA 14:1572
Pool, F.
Restriction of immigration. COUW:219
Roosevelt, F.D.
Message to Congress calling for the repeal of the Chinese exclusion laws. VO 1943-44:434
Welcome to new Americans. SOES:36
Welday, W.J.
Danger signal of immigration. SHUC:281
See also Aliens

IMMORTALITY
Barrows, J.H.
Immortality. THOU 2:143
Best gift. JAS:62
Carson, A.
Glories of immortality. BREW 3:143
Castelar, E.
In the Campo Santo of Pisa. BREW 3:165; HAZO 22:9477; MAS 22:9477
Cooke, J.E.
Dead, he was immortal (Stonewall Jackson). HARSO:43
Donne, J.
Man immortal, body and soul. BREW 5:266
Ford, J.T.
Testimony of reason to the immortality of the soul. CATA 2:231
Hidden worlds. JAI:34
If a man die, shall he live again? JA:56
Leighton, R.
Immortality. BREW 7:231
Life that never ends. JA:53
Taylor, R.L.
Immortality. HARSO:72; SHU:63

IMPEACHMENTS See Names of individuals, e.g. Chase, S.; Crawley, F.; Finch, J.; Hampden, J.; Hastings, W.; Johnson, A.; Sacheverell, H.; Sulzer, W.

IMPERIAL CONFERENCE, 1911
Botha, L.
Critical speech at Imperial Conference of 1911. KES 2:297
Oxford and Asquith, H.H.A.
At the first meeting of the Imperial Conference of 1911. KES 2:240
Critical speech at Imperial Conference of 1911. KES 2:301
Ward, J.
Speech at the Imperial Conference of 1911. KES 2:247

---- 1921
Lloyd George, D.
Imperial Conference, 1921. KESB:43
Massey, W.F.
Imperial Conference, 1921. KESB:59
Sastri, V.S.
Imperial Conference, 1921. KESB:62
Smuts, J.C.
Imperial Conference, 1921. KESB:43

---- 1926
Haldane, R.B.
Speech in House of Lords,

June 16, 1926 (on Imperial Conference, 1926). KESB: 372

---- 1930
Hertzog, J. B. M.
Imperial Conference, 1930. KESB:210
MacDonald, J. R.
Imperial Conference, October 1, 1930 speech. KESB:206
Scullin, J. H.
Imperial Conference, 1930. KESB:208

IMPERIAL FEDERATION
Chamberlain, J.
Future of the British Empire (November 6, 1895 speech). BRTH:325; BRTHA: 325; COP:194; COPA:194; COPB:194; REEM 1:236
Imperial Federation (June 24, 1897 speech). EMS 2: 263

IMPERIAL WAR CONFERENCE, 1917
Borden, R. L.
Speech at Imperial War Conference, 1917. KES 2: 376
Massey, W. F.
Speech at Imperial War Conference, 1917. KES 2:381
Morris, E.
Speech at Imperial War Conference, 1917. KES 2:398
Sinha, S.
Speech at Imperial War Conference, 1917. KES 2:401
Smuts, J. C.
Speech at Imperial War Conference, 1917. KES 2:392

IMPERIALISM
Allen, F. E.
Challenge to the citizen. BA 1960-61:100
Bryan, W. J.
Imperialism. FUL:42
Imperialism (accepting Democratic nomination for Presidency, 1900). WPRA: 358
Cockran, W. B.
Porto Rican tariff. FUL: 74, 77
Jefferson, C. E.
Temptation from the mountain top. FUL:174, 178
Schurz, C.
Policy of imperialism. BRAS:242; CHAL 11:213; HAZO 21:9078; MAS 21: 9078; REEM 10:364; REEMA 15:1834; REEMB 11:378

IMPERSONATORS See Actors and acting

IMPLEMENT DEALERS See Business men

IMPROMPTU SPEECHES See After-dinner speeches; Extemporaneous speeches

IMPROVED ORDER OF RED MEN See Red men, Improved Order of

IMPROVEMENT MEETINGS
Speech at an improvement meeting. HILL:470
Imrie, Norman Allan
America and Britain: some problems in common. NESA: 154
Give and take. EXEE:377

INAUGURAL ADDRESSES
Adams, J.
Inaugural address. BREW 1:41; CHI:6; HAZO 6:2561; LOTI:9; MAS 6:2561; ORAMA 1:49; REEMA 11:1; USIN:7; USINA:7
Adams, J. Q.
Inaugural address. CHI:51; LOTI:51; USIN:47; USINA: 47
Alderman, E. A.
University of Virginia in

INAUGURAL ADDRESSES (cont.)
the life of the nation: inaugural address as president of University of Virginia. WE 2:73
Andrews, E.B.
Inaugural address as president of University of Nebraska. WE 2:301
Angell, J.B.
Inaugural address as president of University of Michigan. WE 2:47
Brief inaugural address of a mayor. HILL:462
Brooks, S.D.
Inaugural address as president of University of Oklahoma. WE 2:407
Brooks, S.P.
Inaugural address as president of Baylor University. WE 1:199
Brougham and Vaux, H.P.B.
Inaugural discourse. GOOD: 937; KLEG:294
Buchanan, J.
Inaugural address. BREW 2:134; CHAL 5:448; CHI: 119; HAZO 12:4958; LOTI: 111; MAS 12:4958; USIN: 111; USINA:111
Butler, N.M.
Scholarship and service: inaugural address as president of Columbia University. WE 1:83
Caldwell, J.T.
New birth (inaugural as president of Alabama College). BA 1948-49:196
Campbell, W.W.
Universities and the truth (President's inaugural address). ONEC:145
Carlyle, T.
Inaugural address at Edinburgh. BREW 3:113; BRYW 5:17; CHAL 6:178; HAZO 13:5289; HOB:35; MAS 13: 5289; REEM 6:69; REEMB 7:83
Chandler, J.C.C.
Inaugural address as president of William and Mary College. SMI:261
Chase, H.W.
State university and the new South: inaugural address as president of University of North Carolina. WE 2:31
Chiang Kai-Shek
First speech as President of the Republic of China at the inaugural session of the second convention of the third People's Political Council in Chungking. VO 1943-44:374
Cleveland, G.
First inaugural address. BREW 4:82; BRYW 10:130; CHAL 13:149; CHI:164; COP:327; COPA:327; COPB:327; HAZO 24:10117; KNAS:35; KNASA:35; LOTI: 151; MAS 24:10117; ORAMA 2:405; USIN:149; USINA: 149
Second inaugural address. CHI:180; LOTI:165; USIN: 163; USINA:163
Clothier, R.C.
Inaugural address as president of University of New Jersey (Rutgers). WE 2:15
Coffman, L.D.
Inaugural address as president of University of Minnesota. WE 2:187
Coolidge, C.
Inaugural address. CHI:239; LOTI:215; USIN:215; USINA:215
Cowley, W.H.
What should a college president be? BA 1949-50:230
Davis, J.
Inaugural address of 1861. ANG:344; BREW 5:41; CHAL 7:294; HAZO 15: 6213; JOHA 2 pt 2:32; MAS 15:6213
Dickens, C.
Volunteer student (on occa-

sion of his inauguration as President of Birmingham and Midland Institute). REEMA 7:332
Dickinson, Mrs. L.
Citadels of peace, arsenals of power (inaugural address as President of General Federation of Women's Clubs). BUTA:229
Donovan, H. L.
What I see from my window: inaugural address as president of University of Kentucky. WE 2:233
Draper, A. S.
Inaugural address as president of University of Illinois. WE 2:277
Eggleston, E.
New history (inaugural address as President of American Historical Association). REEM 6:142; REEMA 8:401; REEMB 7:124
Eisenhower, D. D.
First inaugural address. ANG:530; BA 1952-53:112; BAAMP:283; CHI:286; COPB:603; HURG:304; LOTI:257; USIN:257; USINA 257
Price of peace: second inaugural address. BA 1956-57:19; BAAG:376; CHI:294; LOTI:263; USIN:263; USINA:263; WPRC:313
Eliot, C. W.
Inaugural address as president of Yale University. CHAL 12:270; CORP:135; HAZO 23:9651; MAS 23:9651; WE 1:13
Form of a president's inaugural. HILL:462
Garfield, J. A.
Inaugural address. CHAL 12:1; CHI:156; HAZO 22:9437; USIN:141; USINA:141
Gilman, D. C.
Inaugural address as president of Johns Hopkins University. WE 1:293
Gore, V. M.
Induction address. ONES:57
Grant, U. S.
First inaugural address. CHI:139; LOTI:129; USIN:129; USINA:129
Second inaugural address. CHAL 10:178; CHI:144; HAZO 20:8399; LOTI:133; MAS 20:8399; USIN:132; USINA:132
Griswold, A. W.
Man thinking: inaugural address as president of Yale University. HAR:376
Hadley, A. T.
Inaugural address as president of Yale University. WE 1:43
Hall, A. B.
Inaugural address as president of University of Oregon. WE 2:343
Hall, G. S.
Inaugural address as president of Clark University. WE 1:361
Hancher, V. M.
Inaugural address as president of Iowa State University. WE 2:149
Harding, W. G.
Inaugural address. BREW 6:366; CHI:230; LOTI:207; USIN:207; USINA:207
Harrison, B.
Inaugural address. BREW 6:372; BRYW 10:155; CHAL 12:213; CHI:169; HAZO 22:9594; LOTI:155; MAS 22:9594; REEM 10:306; REEMA 13:1137; REEMB 11:320; USIN:153; USINA:153
Harrison, W. H.
Inaugural address. CHI:76; LOTI:73; USIN:71; USINA:71
Hayes, R. B.
Inaugural address. BREW 6:397; CHI:148; LOTI:137;

INAUGURAL ADDRESSES (cont.)
USIN:135; USINA:135
Henderson, E. L.
American Medical Association presidential inaugural address. HAR:337
Hoover, H. C.
Inaugural address. CHI:249; LOTI:223; USIN:225; USINA:225
Hopkins, E. M.
College of the future: inaugural address as president of Dartmouth College. WE 1:119
Hopkins, M.
Inaugural address as president of Williams College. WE 1:137
Inaugural address. DAVC:584
Inaugural address (as president of a club). SOES:22
Induction ceremonies for a judge. BEB:79
Induction ceremonies for an officer. BEB:79
Induction ceremonies for members of Union. BEB:78
Jackson, A.
First inaugural address. BIR 2:62; BRE:150; BREA:134; CHI:59; LOTI:57; USIN:55; USINA:55

Second inaugural address-"State rights and Federal sovereignty." BREW 7:145; BRYW 8:204; CHAL 4:294; CHI:63; COP:278; COPA:278; COPB:278; HAZO 9:3711; HURG:71; LOTI:61; MAS 9:3711; USIN:58; USINA:58
Jefferson, T.
First inaugural: democracy defined. ANG:220; BIR:1:251; BRE:111; BREA:109; BREW 7:160; BRYW 8:166; CHAL 3:122; CHI:13; COP:259; COPA:259; COPB:259; CROC:273; FKA:59; HARS:166; HAZO 7:2731; HELE:135; HIB:365; HURG:48; JOHA 1 pt. 1:155; KLEG:314; LEEW 9:73; LOTI:15; MAS 7:2731; ORAMA 1:141; PAR:95; PO:49; REEM 10:46; REEMA 13:1255; REEMB 11:47; SMI:91; USIN:13; USINA:13; WPRA:50
Second inaugural address. CHI:18; LOTI:19; USIN:17; USINA:17
Jenkins, M. D.
Function of Morgan State College (inaugural address as President of Morgan State College). HILK:94
Jesse, R. H.
Inaugural address as president of University of Missouri. WE 2:129
Johnson, A.
Inaugural address. BREW 7:169
Johnson, L. B.
Inaugural address. CHI:307; USINA:271
Jones, L. W.
Inaugural address as president of University of Arkansas. WE 2:327
Jordan, D. S.
Inaugural address as president of Stanford University. WE 1:351
Kennedy, J. F.
Inaugural address. ARNS:256; BA 1960-61:35; BAAGA:398; BOU:3; CAP:231; CHI:301; FIP:374; HIB:283; LINP:161; LOTI:269; PEA:831; SOBP:335; USIN:267; USINA:267; WPRC:317
Kirkland, J. H.
Inaugural address as chancellor of Vanderbilt University. WE 1:327
Lincoln, A.
First inaugural address. ANG:294; BAAMP:107; BAKF:227; BEA:287; BERS:133; BIR 2:240; BRE:255; BREA:220; BRIM:214; BRYW 9:

240; BURP:119; CARP:146; CHAL 8:27; CHI:127; FO: 172; HARS:371; HAZO 16: 6572; JOHA 2 pt. 2:16; LOTI:117; MAS 16:6572; ONEM:476; PAR:34; PAUF: 2:36; PE:510; PEA:510; PO:87; USIN:119; USINA: 119
Second inaugural address. ANG:365; BAAGA:409; BAAMP:116; BAKF:238; BIR 2:297; BOU:77; BRAC: 366; BRE:265; BREA:230; BREW 10:355; BRIM:227; BRYW 9:255; CAP:91; CARP:147; CHAL 8:38; CHI:137; CLAW:155; CLAY: 61; COP:315; COPA:315; COPB:315; FKA:45; FO: 210; HARS:418; HAZO 16: 6584; HIB:272; HIBS:491; HURG:114; JOHA 2 pt. 2: 125; LA:175; LEEW 10: 253; LOTI:125; MAS 16: 6584; ONEM:484; ORAMA 2:225; PAR:308; PAUF 1: 336; PE:523; PEA:523; PL:684; PO:98; REEM 10: 237; REEMA 8:775; REEMB 11:248; SAA:203; SHAH: 402; SHUP:209; USIN:127; USINA:127

Lindley, E H.
University and the vocations of man: inaugural address as president of University of Kansas. WE 2:217

Lowell, A. L.
Inaugural address. KLEG: 281

Lowell, J. R.
Democracy: inaugural address on assuming Presidency of the Birmingham and Midland Institute, Birmingham, England, October 6, 1884. PAUF 2:205; REEM 7:234; REEMA 8:789; REEMB 8:254

McAndrew, W.
Inauguration as president of the Department of Superintendence of National Education Association. BRAC: 359

MacCracken, H. M.
Relation of metropolis and university: inaugural address as president of New York University. WE 1:185

McKay, H. W.
Weighed in balance: inaugural address as president of the Southern Medical Association. HAR:343

McKeldin, T.
Inaugural address as Governor of Maryland. MCK:192

McKinley, W.
First inaugural address. CHI:186; LOTI:171; ORAMA 2:413; USIN:169; USINA:169
Second inaugural address. CHI:197; LOTI:179; USIN: 178; USINA:178

MacLeish, A.
Act of faith (inaugural of M. Clapp as President of Wellesley College). BA 1950-51:131

McVey, F. LeR.
University and its relations: inaugural address as president of University of North Dakota. WE 2:369

Madison, J.
First inaugural address. CHI:24; HAZO 7:3032; LOTI:25; MAS 7:3032; USIN:21; USINA:23
Second inaugural address. CHI:28; LOTI:29; USIN:26; USINA:26

Marshall, T. R.
Golden rule of government (inaugural address to the Senate, March 4, 1917). BREW 8:103

Mezes, S. E.
Inaugural address as president of University of Texas. WE 2:387

Monroe, J.
First inaugural address.

INAUGURAL ADDRESSES (cont.)
CHI:32; LOTI:33; USIN: 29; USINA:29
Second inaugural address. CHI:40; LOTI:41; USIN: 37; USINA:37
Morris, D.W.
Inaugural address as 8th president of Southern Illinois University. SAB:188
Nakai, R.
Inaugural address (as chairman of the Council of Navajos Indians). BA 1963-64:49; JON:129
Napoleon III.
First inaugural address as President. HAZO 15:6247; MAS 15:6247
Neilson, W. A.
Inaugural address as president of Smith College. WE 1:273
Park, R.
Inaugural address (as President of Barnard College). BA 1963-64:173
Pepper, W.
Inaugural address as president of University of Pennsylvania. WE 1:95
Perkins, G.
Inaugural address as Governor of California. WAGN: 348
Pierce, F.
Inaugural address. CHI:110; LOTI:103; USIN:103; USINA:103
Poincaré, R.
Inaugural speech (Peace Conference, 1919). REEM 11:306; REEMB 12:323
Polk, J.K.
Inaugural address. CHI:94; LOTI:89; USIN:89; USINA: 89
Preparation of an inaugural address. CORP:135
Prout, Mrs. R.I.C.
Address (inaugural) as President of the General Federation of Women's Clubs. BUTB:243
Rhees, R.
Modernizing of liberal culture: inaugural address as president of University of Rochester. WE 1:215
Richardson, H.V.
Claflin yesterday, today and tomorrow (inaugural address as sixth President of Claflin University). HILK:193
Rockefeller, N.A.
Inaugural address (as Governor of New York State). BA 1958-59:110
Roesch, C.E.
Inaugural address of the mayor of Buffalo. ONEC: 163
Roosevelt, F.D.
First inaugural address. BAAMP:260; BEA:365; BIR 4:95; BOA:210; BOB: 205; BRE:338; BREA:318; CAP:189; CHI:259; COP: 530; COPB:508; FO:363; FRY:114; HAY:370; HIB: 274; HURG:219; LOTI:231; PAR:501; PE:745; PEA: 745; PL:810; USIN:235; USINA:235; WPRC:157
Fourth inaugural address. BA 1944-45:153; CHI:275; LOTI:247; USIN:248; USINA:248; VO 1945-46: 40; WPRC:261
Second inaugural address. BA 1937-38:11; CHI:265; FIP:221; FO:370; LOTI: 237; USIN:240; USINA:240
Third inaugural address. CHI:271; LOTI:243; SAA: 292; USIN:244; USINA:244; VO 1941:37
Roosevelt, T.
Inaugural address (1905). BRYW 10:249; CHI:203; LA:122; LOTI:183; ONEM: 485; USIN:183; USINA:183
Scranton, W.W.
Inaugural address as Governor of Pennsylvania. BA

1962-63:173
Seelye, J.H.
Relation of learning and religion: inaugural address as president of Amherst College. WE 1:163
Short inaugural speeches. STOC:108
Short inaugural speeches (for club officers)-three examples of. STON:114
Snavely, G.E.
Inaugural address as president of Birmingham-Southern College. WE 1:229
Sproul, R.G.
Inaugural address as president of University of California. WE 2:251
Sterling, J.E.W.
Lofty purpose shared: inaugural address as fifth President of Stanford University. BA 1950-51:150
Stimson, H.L.
Inaugural address of the Governor-General of the Philippines. ONEC:157
Suggestions for preparation of an inaugural speech. BRA: 514; BRAB:501; MIA:61.
With examples of. SOES:20
Suzzallo, H.
Inaugural address as president of University of Washington. WE 2:207
Taft, W.H.
Inaugural address. BREW 9:332-40; CHI:207; LOTI: 189; USIN:187; USINA:187
Taylor, J.M.
Inaugural address as president of Vassar College. WE 1:241
Taylor, Z.
Inaugural address. CHI:106; LOTI:99; SMI:158; USIN: 99; USINA:99
Temple, R.A.
Inaugural address at his installation as M.W.P. of Sons of Temperance. THOU 3:505
Truman, H.S.
Inaugural address. BA 1948-49:27; CHI:277; COPB: 589; FIP:298; LOTI:251; USIN:251; USINA:251
Van Buren, M.
Inaugural address. CHI:67; LOTI:65; USIN:61; USINA: 61
Van Hise, C.R.
Inaugural address as president of University of Wisconsin. WE 2:161
Vincent, G.E.
Inaugural address as President of University of Minnesota. PEAE:197
Washington, G.
First inaugural address. ANG:184; BEA:427; BOU: 48; BRE:97; BREA:95; BREW 10:91; BRYW 8:79; CHAL 2:463; CHI:1; COP: 245; COPA:245; COPB: 245; HAZO 6:2506; HELE: 98; KLEG:195; LOTI:3; MAS 6:2506; ORAMA 1:27; PL:576; REEMA 15:2032; SMI:77; USIN:1; USINA:1
Second inaugural address. CHI:5; LOTI:7; USIN:5; USINA:5
White, A.D.
Inaugural address as president of Cornell University. WE 1:245
Whitehurst, Mrs. J.L.
Inaugural address (as President of General Federation of Women's Clubs). BUTA: 224
Wilson, W.
Equipment for service: inaugural address as president of Princeton University. BLAA:177; BLAB: 177; BOA:159; BOB:168; WE 1:63
First inaugural address. ANG:417; BAAMP:220; BIR 3:302; BRAC:361; BRIM: 398; CHI:220; FO:272; LOTI:199; ONEM:488;

INAUGURAL ADDRESSES (cont.)
PAR:466; USIN:199; USINA:199; WPRC:40
Second inaugural address. CHI:226; LEW:3; LOTI: 203; USIN:203; USINA:203
Wylie, A.
Inaugural address as president of Indiana University. WE 2:97
See also Conference on the Problems of Economic Development, Cairo, July 9-18, 1962; Installation speeches; Offices-Acceptance

Inciong, David
Necessity for trained farmers. YR 10:169

INCOME TAX See Taxation

INDEPENDENCE DAY See Fourth of July

INDEPENDENT ORDER OF ODD-FELLOWS See Odd-Fellows, Independent Order of

INDEPENDENT TREASURY
Calhoun, J. C.
Replying to Henry Clay (from the Independent Treasury debate). BREW 3:74
Clay, C. C.
Subtreasury Bill of 1837. BREW 3:390

INDIA
Adamson, W.
Speech in House of Commons, December 5, 1919 (on India). KESI 2:263
Amery, L. S.
Broadcast August 9, 1942. VO 1942-43:434
Famine conditions in India. VO 1943-44:439
Speech in Parliament for India. VO 1943-44:132
Bose, J. C.
Greater India to be. ZU:35
Churchill, W. L. S.
Announcement to the House of Commons of Sir Stafford Cripps' mission to India, March 11, 1942. VO 1942-43:196
Report to the House of Commons on the policy of the British government in India. VO 1942-43:503
Connaught, A. W. P. A.
To the Indian Assembly on its inauguration, February 9, 1921. KESI 2:335
Cripps, S.
Review of negotiations with the All-India Congress. VO 1942-43:407
Statement on India, August 5, 1942. VO 1942-43:423
Curzon of Kedleston, G. N. C.
Most valuable British asset. BREW 4:352
Speech in House of Commons, March 28, 1892 (on India). KESI 2:46
Courtney, L. H. C.
Speech in House of Lords, February 24, 1909 (on India). KESI 2:98
Dalhousie, J. A. B. R.
Speech of February 28, 1856 (on India). KESI 1:284
Dar, B. N.
Tendencies and movements of Indian national life. ZU:31
Gandhi, M. K.
Latest message to America, October 31, 1942. VO 1942-43:572

Non-cooperation. COP:395; COPA:395; COPB:395
Propounds his faith before an English judge. PE:727; PEA:727
Speech in London (1931). PL:801
Strength of Satyagraha. CROC:215
To all-Indian Congress, August 7, 1942. VO 1942-

43:430
George V.
Message to the rulers of the Indian states on the inauguration of the Chamber of Princes, February, 1921. KESI 2:332
Gladstone, W. E.
Speech in House of Commons, March 28, 1892 (on India). KESI 2:67
Gokhale, G. K.
Political testament (on India). KESI 2:111
Students and politics. ZU: 12
Kher, B. G.
Lokmanya Bal Gangadhar Tilak- a tribute. ZU:45
Lansdowne, H. C. K. -F.
Coercion and repression as imperial policies. BREW 7: 269
Lewis, G. C.
Speech in House of Commons, February 12, 1858 (on India). KESI 1:342
Lytton, E. R. B. -L.
Abandonment of Canahar, House of Lords, January 10, 1881. PAUF 2:245
Macaulay, T. B.
Government of India. KESI 1:226; PAUF 2:1
Monro, C. C.
Speech in House of Lords, December 12, 1919 (on India). KESI 2: 266
Montagu, E. S.
Speech in House of Commons, August 20, 1917 (on India). KESI 2:133
Speech in House of Commons, June 5, 1919 (on India). KESI 2:206
Morley of Blackburn, J. M.
Brutality as an imperial method. BREW 8:204
Speech in House of Lords, February 23, 1909 (on India). KESI 2:81
Munshi, K. M.
Our greatest need, freedom from fear. ZU:18
Napier, C.
On the occupation of Scinde, October 17, 1842. KESI 1: 274
Nehru, J.
Independence day. ZU:1
Palmerston, H. J. T.
Speech of February 12, 1858 (on India). KESI 1:319
Prasad, R.
Independence day message. ZU:26
Ray, P. C.
Social reform for India. ZU:61
Smith, R.V.
Speech in House of Commons, February 16, 1858 (on India). KESI 1:355
Tagore, R.
Nationalism in India. COP: 393; COPA:393; COPB: 393
Victoria.
Proclamation to the princes, chiefs and people of India, November 1, 1858. KESI 1: 382
Wavell, A. P.
At joint session of Legislative Assembly and Council of State of India. HAN: 340; VO 1944-45:94
Wood, C.
Speech in House of Commons, June 6, 1861 (on India). KESI 2:3
Youman, T.
Plea for India. YR 4:355
See also East India Bill; Hinduism

INDIA RUBBER See Rubber

INDIANA
Tarkington, B.
Indiana in literature and politics. REEM 3:314; REEMB 3:331
Where we come from. YE: 318

INDIANA, UNIVERSITY OF
Wylie, A.
Inaugural address as president of Indiana University. WE 2:97

INDIANS OF NORTH AMERICA
Bonnin, G. S.
Pleads the cause of the American Indian home. JON: 119
Brant, J.
Request to the Court of St. James for extensive land grant for his people north of Lake Erie. JON:47
Burkhard, C.
Indian's problem faces the white man. YR 4:197
Cushing, C.
Extermination of the Indians. BREW 4:359
Dawes, H. L.
On the Indian policy. CHAL 9:124; HAZO 18:7656; MAS 18:7656
Freeman, A. T.
Pleads for justice for the American Indian. JON:125
Harrison, W. H.
To the Indiana legislature. SMI:93
Hart, W. S.
American Indian and American citizenship. SHU:130
Hendrix, J. C.
Wampum of the Indian. ONES:236; REEMA 2:603
Hithquoquean and Tamanee.
Speech of at a Council held in Philadelphia, 1694. SHE: 9
Indian kings speak at a conference at Burlington. SHE: 69
Jefferson, T.
Speech to the chiefs of various Indian tribes. REEMA 13:1265
To Beaver, head-warrior of the Delawares. REEMA 13:1263
To the Wolf and people of the Mandan Indians. REEMA 13:1260
Joseph, Chief
From where the sun now stands. GRIS:47
Letter of Pennsylvania Indians to the King of England, 1701. SHE:5
Oconostota.
Pathetic prophecy. GRIS:37
Plume, C. E.
Indian's road to God. BART: 4:159
Pushmataha.
Attention, my good red warriors! GRIS:38
Shepherd, A. C.
Indian problem. COUW:29
Speech at a meeting with Indians where Ockanickon attended, 1677. SHE:2
Speech of a Cayuga chief before the New York Historical Society. SHE:58
Speech of a Seminole. SHE: 67
Speech of Delaware Nation of Indians at Fort Wayne, September 1, 1798. SHE: 46
Speech of the River Indians-Albany treaty, July 6, 1745. SHE:6
Sprague, C.
Passing of the Indian. BOB:124
Ten Bear.
Do not ask us to give up the buffalo for the sheep. GRIS:44
Warcaziwin.
Indian in American history. JON:116
Wheeler, B. K.
On Indian affairs. DOA: 211
Worth-while speech of an Indian chief. SHE:19
See also Names of Indians, e. g., Augus; Big Elk; Big Mouth; Blacktooth; Brant, J. Calvin, B.; Cornplanter; Dekanisora; Gayashuta;

INDIANS OF NORTH AMERICA (cont.)
Grangula; Grizzly; Half King; Keokuk; Little Carpenter; Little Turtle; Logan, J.; Nakai, R.; Ockanickon; Old Tassel; Plenty Coups; Pontiac; Pushmataha; Red Eagle; Red Jacket; Sassoonan; Satank; Scarrooyady; Seattle; Seneca George; Taiaeronk; Taminy Buck; Tarhe; Tecumseh; Teedyuscung; Teehe, H.B.; Tenskwatawa; Weatherford, W.; Webb, Col.; White Eyes; Wilson, P.

---- EDUCATION
Vest, G.G.
On Indian schools. CHAL 11:463; HAZO 22:9384; MAS 22:9384; REEMA 15:2013

---- WARS - See Seminole War, 1st, Florida, 1817-1818

INDIVIDUALISM
Dodds, H.W.
Importance of being an individual. BA 1955-56:142
Ewert, W.F.
Individualism. COUW:63
Henderson, H.
New individualism. BOA:405; YR 6:159
Hoover, H.C.
Individual initiative. BOA:401
Kehl, D.
Higher individualism. YR 3:111
Link, E.P.
Puppets. YR 1:139
Pearce, C.C.
Inglorious peace. TRUW:245
Purdy, C.O.
Triumph of the individual. SHUC:190
Watson, T.J., Jr.
Self protection: individualism (commencement address at Brown University). HIB:331
Wriston, H.M.
Introductory remarks on individualism. HOC:34
Young, T.
Triumph of individualism. SHUC:196

INDO-CHINA, FRENCH
Matsuoka, Y.
Address at opening of Thai-French Indo China Border Dispute Mediation Conference. VO 1941:76

INDONESIA
Njotowijono, O.
Inaugural speech at Conference on the Problems of Economic Development. UAR:57

INDUCTION See Inaugural addresses; Installation speeches

INDUSTRIAL ARTS
Webster, D.
Progress of mechanic arts. BREW 10:194
See also Engineering and Engineers; Inventions and inventors; Machinery; Manual training

INDUSTRIAL EDUCATION See Manual training

INDUSTRIAL RELATIONS
Brewer, D.J.
Combination of capital and consolidation of labor. BLAA:189; BLAB:189; THOU 1:444
Does the individual count for nothing? BOB:57
Bryan, W.J.
Thou shalt not steal. BOA:333; BOB:56
Carnegie, A.

INDUSTRIAL RELATIONS (cont.)
Common interest of labor and capital. REEM 4:42; REEMB 4:100
Hanna, M.
Labor and capital. BLAA: 282; BLAB:282; REAC:97; WERN 42:147
Harrison, B.
Views on capital and labor. THOU 1:429
Haygood, S. G.
Adjustments between capital and labor. THOU 1:448
Johnston, E.
Warning to labor-and to management. BA 1943-44: 200
Introducing members representing labor and management-five examples of. BEB:53-55
Poore, B. P.
Capital and labor. THOU 1: 427
Roberts, J.
House divided. BRP 9:59
Talmage, T. D.
Capital and labor. PL:718
Wallace, H.
Community of interest between labor, capital, and agriculture. BA 1937-38:146
White, W. A.
Speaking for the consumer. COP:427; COPA:427; COPB:417; HURG:234
See also Industry; Labor Unions

INDUSTRIAL REVOLUTION See Industry-History

INDUSTRIALISTS See Businessmen

INDUSTRY
Arnold, T. W.
Full production after the war. HOC:166
Ashfield, A. H. S.
Man and machine in industry. REEM sup 1:64; REEMB 4:1
Baldwin, S. B.
Goodwill in industry. REEM sup 1:75; REEMB 4:33
Baruch, B.
Patriotism in industry. REEM 4:22; REEMB 4:62
Blough, R. M.
Price and the public interest. BA 1958-59:65
Brayman, H.
Formula for reform. MOUG:196; MOUGA:196
Buckhorn, E. A.
Wolves of industry. YR 2: 75
Buhler, I.
Modern Shylocks. BRP 5: 81
Buy at home. NATS:5
Chapin, E. H.
Peaceful industry. BREW 3:205
Clay, H.
American industry, 1824. HELE:174
Dickson, W. B.
Democracy in industry. BOA:346
Fairless, B. F.
Detour ahead. BA 1949-50: 164
What kind of America? BA 1953-54:131
Girdler, T. M.
Tomorrow's markets for steel. KLEB:181
Ford, H., II.
Challenge of human engineering. BRY:438
Grey, E. G.
Industry. BEA:243
Hall, E. K.
Plea for the man in the ranks. REEM sup 1:395; REEMB 4:328
Henderson, P.
Aircraft for industry. BYRA 200; REEM sup 2:40; REEMB 4:389
Hillman, S.
Agriculture, industry, and labor. BA 1938-39:142

Hoffman, P. G.
Prices of things which farmers buy, including so-called management of prices by industry. HUS: 255
Hoover, H. C.
Waste-a problem of distribution. BYRA:217; REEM sup 2:53; REEMB 4:422
Kelley, G. V.
Fifth horseman: danger of antiquated state policies in industry. ASHF:87
Lewis, E. R.
Industrial conflict. ASHF: 150
Lloyd, W. P. and others.
Attitude of industry toward employment of college graduates. MOA:482
Murray, P.
Wages and prices in the steel industry. GLAD:305
Outline of speech: Should we endorse the trend toward automation in American industry? BAAGA:307
Patronize home industry. FRIE:84
Problems of the industrial worker. AMEO 2:206
Robinson, L. T.
Edict of industry (present impossibility of war due to the interdependence of nations, industry, and capital) ASHF:262
Root, E.
Profit of the laborer and consumer. BLAA:105; BLAB:105
Schwab, C. M.
Stability in industry. ONEC: 257
Shelby, J.
New frontiers for smart people. BART 3:277
Thornton, H. W.
Over-reaching. REEM sup 3:142; REEMB 5:339
Tibbetts, R. B.
America's industrial crisis. COUW:211
Tyler, C.
Industry and you: the field for college graduates. SAR: 397
White, F.E.
New ideas for an old industry (meat packing) REEM sup 3:160; REEMB 5:382
Wilson, C. E.
Five years of industrial peace. YE:221
See also Business; Industrial relations; Laissez-faire

---- HISTORY
Price some paid for progress (outline) SOBP:80

INDUSTRY AND STATE
Barnes, J. H.
Team play between government and industry. BRYA: 25; REEM sup 1:106; REEMB 4:46
Carleton, W. G.
What of free enterprise? BA 1943-44:209
Coolidge, C.
Government and business. FRY:100
Davis, J. W.
Old order. COP:410; COPA:410
Free enterprise. NATM:2
Green, W.
Preservation of free enterprise the common objective of capital and labor. GLAD: 300
Healey, A. D.
Control of industry. BOA: 385
Hoover, H. C.
Governmental conduct of business. SHU:10
Morgan, A. E.
Engineer and expanding government. SAR:390
Ritchie, A. C.
More business in government and less government

INDUSTRY AND STATE (cont.)
in business. LINM:14
Stanton, F.
Remarks on government regulation of broadcasting (accepting Printers' Ink Gold medal). ARNS:116
Van Hise, C.R.
Government regulation. REEM 7:403; REEMB 5:362
Waite, M.R.
Munn v. Illinois, 1876: opinion for the Supreme Court. BIR 3:117
Wriston, H.M.
Free enterprise. BA 1943-44:230
See also Price regulation; Public utilities

INFLATION (FINANCE)
Blough, R.M.
Price and the public interest. BA 1958-59:65
Bowles, C.
Price control and inflation. BA 1945-46:144
Byrnes, J.F.
War against inflation. BA 1942-43:189
Douglas, H.G.
Cost of living and inflation. BA 1947-48:118
Roosevelt, F.D.
Broadcast to the nation, April 28, 1942. VO 1942-43: 249
Message to Congress, April 27, 1942. VO 1942-43:242
Sloan, A.P., Jr.
Economic aspects of American defense. COP:438; COPA:438
Warburg, P.M.
Inflation as a world problem and our relations thereto. REEM 4:410; REEMB 5:368
Williams, B.J.
Inflation can be controlled without price ceilings. SAB: 140
See also Price regulation

INFORMATIVE SPEECHES
Beard, C.A.
Written history as an act of faith. LINP:73
Bell Telephone Companies, Volunteer speakers of.
Telstar. LINP:45
Carleton, W.G.
Take your college in stride. BA 1946-47:222; BAAG: 368
Compton, A.H.
Social implications of atomic energy. MOA:400
Crocker, L.
On seas of ink. MOUG:189; MOUGA:189
Douglas, P.H.
Speech in Senate on United States foreign policy in the Middle East. BRAP:129
Griggs, R.F.
Our friend-the volcano. MOUG:184; MOUGA:184
Highet, G.
Historian's job. MOA:408
How to sell a house. MICS: 138
Instruction course. FRIE:335
Kennedy, J.F.
Education of an American politician. BRAP:123
King, M.L.
Love, law, and civil disobedience. HILK:345; LINP: 52
Medina, H.R.
Equal justice for all. HIBS: 476
Menninger, K.
Healthier than healthy. LINP:26
Merrihue, W.V.
What a company looks for in seeking a new location. SABA:183
Murrow, E.R.
Orchestrated Hell. BA 1943-44:37; BAAG:361
Myers, F.J.
How a law is made. MOUG MOUGA:105
Nickerson, A.J.

Climbing the managerial ladder. BAAG:387
Peters, L.
What is totalitarianism? LINP:69
Petty, B.
Taking care of your roads (outline). MOA:398
Reid, L.D.
How to improve classroom lectures fifty percent. BRAP:127
Rogers, C.
What we know about psychotherapy-objectively and subjectively. LINP:36
'Row-throw-go" (outline of speech on how to rescue drowning persons). MOA:317
Suggestions for preparation of informative speeches. BAAGA:235; With examples of: ANDS:134; BAAG:231; BRAP:120; BRYA:97; MICS:137; MOUG:184; MOUGA:97; SABA:165; SOBP:178
Sumrall, H.D.
On reporting the weather. BRAP:121
Taylor, P.
Party games. BRAP:122
Thigpen, W.
Death among the dailies. SOBP:338
What is democracy (outline of speech)? MOA:239
Worsham, J.A.
Low pressure selling. SABA:172
Ingalls, John James
On the political situation (1891). CHAL 12:240; HAZO 22:9621; MAS 22:9621; REEMA 13:1229
Tribute to the universal beneficence of grass. SHUP:155
Undiscovered country (death of B.H. Hill). BREW 7:122; REEM 5:237; REEMA 8:721; REEMB 9:276
Inge, William Ralph
Causes of war. BEA:281
Faith and reason. REEM sup 2:102; REEMB 6:213
Ingersoll, Charles Jared
Influence of America on the mind. BL:17
Ingersoll, Robert Green
America's coming greatness. REAC:173
At a child's grave. PAR:447
At his brother's grave. BAAMP:177; BEA:285; BRAC:400; BREW 7:128; BRYW 10:81; CHAL 12:188; COP:324; COPA:324; COPB:324; HARSO:241; HAZO 22:9584; HOAP:269; HURG:156; IMMD:162; KLEG:384; LA:136; MAS 22:9584; ONEM:466; PE:619; PEA:619; PL:689; REEM 10:282; REEMB 11:294; SHAH:470
At the tomb of Napoleon. - Same as his Liberty of man, woman, and child
Chicago and New York Gold speech. BRAS:193
Decoration Day address. - Same as his Vision of war
Eulogy on Walt Whitman. HARSO:196; WERN 42:87
Liberty of man, woman and child. BREW 7:131; DICD:132; DICE:132; HARSO:199; IMMD:109; PAR:409; PROS:110; SHAH:465; SHU:71
Life. BREW 7:135
Music of Wagner. REEM 2:264; REEMA 2:672; REEMB 2:268
Napoleon. HOA:242
Nominating Blaine. BIR 3:113; BRAC:404; BREW 7:126; BRYW 10:77; CHAL 12:184; COP:322; COPA:322; COPB:322; HAZO 22:9580; HIBS:292; HICF:108; HILL:463; HURG:154; MAS 22:9580; ONEM:470; ORAMA 2:377; PE:616; PEA:616; REEM 10:279; REEMA 13:1252; REEMB 11:292;

Ingersoll, R. G. (cont.)
SHAH:458
Oration on Humboldt (at unveiling of statue in Peoria, Illinois). CHAL 12:190
Plumed knight. -Same as his Nominating Blaine
Reunion address. BRAP:104; REEM 10:269; REEMA 13:1241; REEMB 11:281
Shakespeare. BREW 7:133; HARSO:265; REEM 8:237; REEMA 5:627; REEMB 13:241; SHU:136
Speech at Indianapolis, September 1876. BIR 3:115
Summation for the contestants in the Davis will case. HICJ:214
Victory for man. WPRA:301
Vision of war, 1876 speech. BREW 7:130; DICD:136; DICE:136; REEM 10:266; REEMA 13:1238; REEMB 11:278; RID:59; SHAH:473
Vision of war (Decoration Day address, 1888). BAAMP:169; CODS:420; CODSA:420
Ingraham, Fred L.
Gettysburg, TRUW:68

INHERITANCE TAX See Taxation

INJUNCTIONS
Furuseth, A.
Limitation of labor injunction. ONEC:234, 376
Woll, M.
Limitation of labor injunctions (affirmative). ONEC:355
See also Strikes and lockouts

INSANE-CARE AND TREATMENT
Abbott, H.
It might happen to you. BRP 9:24; YR 10:201
Sikkind, D.
Dollars and sense. NOR 1949:175
See also Defective and delinquent classes

INSANITY
Erskine, T.
Homicidal insanity (J. Hadfield). BREW 6:32; GOOD:766; LEEW 7:25

INSCRIPTIONS
Materials for use in composing inscriptions. WRB:46
INSECTS
Fisher, Mrs. J.W.
Praying mantis. BUT:186; BUTB:186
Inskip, Sir Thomas
Statute of Westminster, November 20, 1931 speech. KESB:284

INSPIRATIONAL TALKS
Arkwright, P. S.
Don't hate your customers. SABA:267; SAC:29; YE:305
Atkins, G. G.
Our university. YE:299
Barton, B.
One great issue. HOB:137; ON:253; SAR:132
Beard, S. C., Jr.
Soul aflame. YR 10:9
Beauty. CON:83
Brown, K. I.
Men and women with antennae. BRAP:132
Bruntz, G. G.
Men to match our mountains (installation speech). MOUG:147; MOUGA:147
Bunche, R. J.
Barriers of race can be surmounted. YE:282
Buried gold. FRIE:253
Courage in adversity. CON:62
Dennis, R. E.
King coal is still on the throne. SAB:174
Eisenhower, D. D.
Price of peace: second inaugural address. BA 1956-57:19; BAAG:376; CHI:

294; LOTI:263; USIN:263; USINA:263; WPRC:313
Every salesman is a receptionist-speech by sales manager at retail sales meeting to encourage improved retail selling. WRA:216
Extracts from several inspirational talks. HOA:384-89; HOAP:283-288
Flowers and auxiliaries; an inspirational speech for auxiliary members or chapter members, changeable for a membership speech or a testimonial speech. BAI: 131
Friendship. CON:65
Fullen, J.B.
Many happy returns of the day. YE:303
Game of life or a top man is not a flop man (a changeable speech adaptable as an inspirational speech for sales people, student groups and for all workers, or for a sports dinner speaker). BAI:56
Getting a job-speech by well-known business man at closing exercises of a school. WRA:224
Gould, S.B.
Flavor for our daily bread. BA 1962-63:122
Halsey, J.H.
Higher education's appalling responsibilities. MOUG: 228; MOUGA:228
Hoover, H.C.
Meaning of America (at home-coming in West Branch, Iowa). BA 1948-49: 89; YE:286
Igleheart, A.S.
Sale we've failed to make. SAB:169
Kaiser, H.J., Jr.
Knowledge: our strongest weapon. SABA:271
Knowledge is power-speech by president of successful business enterprise to a graduating class. WRA:219
Krantz, J., Jr.
Architect designed a needle (hypodermic). MCK:237
Simplicity to wonder. MCK: 202
Liberty. CON:80
Loyalties. CON:86
McKeldin, T.
Five nations. MCK:240
Have faith in America. MCK:228
Influence of ancient Greece on modern life. MCK:212
Maryland. MCK:217
Relation of religion and morality to education. MCK: 209
Training boys for responsible citizenship. MCK:225
Most important letter in a salesman's alphabet-speech by president or the sales-manager at a sales convention. WRA:213
Myers, C.J.
Sources of our strength. MICS:158
O'Neal, B.
Democracy is on trial. MOUG:238; MOUGA:238
Reverence for ideals. CON: 74
Sherman, F.P.
Navy of the future. YE:291
Some thoughts on achieving success-speech of an older citizen at a young people's meeting. WRA:209
Spirit of achievement. CON:77
Suggestions for preparation of inspirational talks. With examples of. BRAP:131; CON: 59; MICS:157; MO:411; MOUG:144; MOUGA:144; SAB:162; SABA:260; WRA: 206; YE:281
Thanking a speaker for inspirational talk at a canvasser's dinner. WRA:45
Thinking. CON:69

INSTALLATION SPEECHES
Acceptance speech of Mayor at his installation. BEDA: 116
Adorning the cross (for women's class, council, etc.). JA:97
Bartlett, E.O.
Installation of Rev. J.M. Dickson as pastor of the Pilgrim Congregational Church, Providence, R.I. THOU 2:465
Benediction (at induction of a judge). BEDA:122
Bruntz, G.G.
Men to match our mountains (installation speech). MOUG:147; MOUGA:147
Bunche, R.J.
Dreams and realities (installation of Gamma chapter of Phi Beta Kappa). NORR 3d ser: 264
Capen, J.D.
Installation address. THOU 3:394
Carnovan, H.H.M.H.
Freemasonry (at installation of Albert Edward, Prince of Wales as Grand Master). REEM 7:82; REEMA 7:159
Charge to the Rev. H. Duffield at his installation as pastor of the First Presbyterian Church of New York. THOU 2:478
Clapp, E.H.
Installation of officers; retiring speech. THOU 3:485
Closing speech (at conclusion of installation ceremony at Speakers' Club). BED:19; BEDA:28
Closing speech (at induction of members to labor union). BED:76; BEDA:148
Closing speech (at installation of officers at labor union). BED:79; BEDA:152
Farrier, E.
Law of protection-installation address. THOU 3:384
Gauss, C.
Scholar and his country (installation of Alpha chapter of Phi Beta Kappa at Florida State College). NORR 3d ser:43
"Golden key" service (for any organization). JA:94
Good wishes to installed officers-various examples of. BEC:120
Goschen, G.J.
Uses of imagination (installation as Lord Rector of Edinburgh University). REEMA 8:557
Greeting at induction of a Judge. BEDA:117
Induction address (to newly inducted members of labor union). BED:75; BEDA:147
Induction of a president (fraternal). BEC:105
Induction of a president (union). BED:105
Induction of a secretary (fraternal). BEC:107
Induction of a secretary (union). BEC:107
Induction of a vice-president. BEC:106
Induction of an executive board. BEC:108
Induction of union members. BEC:109
Induction speech by chairman. BEC:104
Installation address-Order of Elks. AMEO 2:131
Installation of a president. BEB:74
Installation of a secretary. BEB:76
Installation of a union official. BEB:74
Installation of a vice-president. BEB:76
Installation of an executive board. BEB:77
Installation of the Rev. F.M. Ellis as pastor of the Washington Ave., Baptist Church of Brooklyn. THOU 2:489
Installation speech at annual

meeting of home and school club. WRA:117
Installation speech of a successful candidate with a very small majority at a public meeting. WRA:122
Installation speech of the successful candidate. WRA:123
Installing executive board. BED:18; BEDA:27
Installing executive board (at labor union). BED:79; BEDA: 152
Installing Mayor. BEDA:114
Installing president (at labor union). BED:77; BEDA:149
Installing president (of Speakers' Club). BED:16; BEDA: 25
Installing recording secretary. BED:18
Installing secretary. BED:18; BEDA:26
Installing secretary (at labor union). BED:79; BEDA:151
Installing treasurer. BED:17; BEDA:26
Installing treasurer (at labor union). BED:79; BEDA:152
Installing vice-president (at labor union). BED:78; BEDA: 151
Installing vice-president (of Speakers' Club). BED:17; BEDA:26
Introducing induction officer (at induction of members to labor union). BED:75; BEDA: 147
Introducing installing officer. BED:16; BEDA:25
Introducing installing officer (at induction of a Mayor). BEDA:114
Jones, J.S.
Masonry and the State, installation address. THOU 3: 57
Low, S.
Installation speech as President of Columbia. ONES:85
Messages and speeches of persons installed-four examples of. BEB:80-82
New president's installation speech at annual meeting. WRA:118
Newly elected presiding officer's installation speech at annual meeting of any service club. WRA:119
Newly elected union chairman's installation speech at annual meeting of shop union. WRA:121
Oath of installation. BEB:75
Official board installation. JA:103
Opening speech at induction of a Mayor. BEDA:114
Opening speech (at induction of members to labor union). BED:75; BEDA:147
Opening speech (at installation of officers of newly formed Speakers' Club). BED:16; BEDA:24
Opening speech (at installation of officials to labor union). BED:77; BEDA:149
Peel, R.
Plea for higher education (installation speech as Lord Rector of University of Glasgow). BREW 8:290
Presenting new Judge (at his induction). BEDA:119
President's installation-two typical speeches. WRA:114, 116
President's installation address at service club. WRA:115
Remarks of installing officer to club members. BUT: 203, 204; BUTB:203, 204
Remarks of installing officer to club officers. BUT:203; BUTB:203
"Shining lights" service (for youth). JA:100
Show-your-self (speech for the war veteran or auxiliary). BAI:144
Suggested installation service for officers. BUT:202; BUTB:202

INSTALLATION SPEECHES (cont.)
Suggestion for installing Master (Freemason). With example of toast of the initiate. EDW: 45
Suggestions for preparation of installation speeches. With examples of. WRA: 110; WRB: 177
Suggestions for proposing a toast to officers at a Masonic installation. With examples of. EDW: 57
Temple, R. A.
Inaugural address at his installation as M. W. P. of Sons of Temperance. THOU 3: 505
Tribute to a newly elected Mayor (at his installation) BEDA: 115
Tribute to installed official-six examples of. BEB: 62-64
Tributes to installed officers. BEC: 117
Words of appreciation by installed officers-various examples of. BEC: 110
See also Inaugural addresses; Oaths

INSTRUCTION, SPEECHES OF
See Informative speeches

Insull, Samuel
Just as one friend to another. REEM sup 2: 114; REEMB 5: 20
Training for leadership. REEM sup 2: 122; REEMB 5: 28

INSULL, SAMUEL
Balmuth, S.
Man with a hat over his face. YR 6: 45

INSURANCE
After dinner address at Insurance convention. AMEO 2: 133
Alton, B.
Introducing an insurance salesman. BRC: 199
Ecker, F. H.
Human factor in the balance sheet. BYRA: 137; REEM sup 1: 246; REEMB 4: 179
Example of a closing speech for taking out an insurance policy. MICS: 174
Insurance (advice to youthful agents by an expert). ED: 187
Insurance and law enforcement (appeal to fraternal insurance order). ED: 190
Insurance, by an agent or officer of the company. EDGS: 155
Kaser, A. L.
Introducing an insurance salesman. BRC: 82
Kunzmann, H. E., Jr.
Chance or a policy? BRAP: 85
Myers, C. J.
Sources of our strength. MICS: 158
Norton, C. D.
Enthusiasm. REEM 4: 340; REEMB 5: 204
Randall, J. W.
Insurance side of highway safety. MO: 518

---- ACCIDENT
Insurance-accident. SCHS: 152

---- HEALTH
Ewing, O. R.
What health insurance would mean to you. HAR: 350
See also Aged-Medical care; Medical care-Cost of

---- LIFE
Fiske, H.
Fifty years of life insurance. BYRA: 165; REEM sup 1: 320; REEMB 4: 266
Fraternal insurance. THOU 3: 189
Insurance-life. SCHS: 156
Life insurance a Christian duty. THOU 3: 347
Matthews, M. A.
Fraternal life insurance. THOU 3: 177

INSURANCE, SOCIAL
Biddle, F. and others.
National security and individual freedom. HAR:440
Campbell, G.R.
For a mess of pottage. NOR 1948:121
Cardoza, B.N.
Helvering et al. v. Davis: opinion for the Supreme Court. BIR 4:249; BRE:353
Steward Machine Company v. Davis, 1937: opinion for the Supreme Court. BIR 4:238
Eisenhower, D.D.
Science and national security. BA 1957-58:20
State of the Union (January 9, 1958). BA 1957-58:65
Fieweger, W.H.
Social security. YR 8:133
Lynch, G.J.
Pursuit of security (accepting an honorary degree by University of Dayton at graduation exercise). LINP:186
Nodel, J.J.
Freedom's holy light. BA 1960-61:213
Roosevelt, F.D.
Right to security. BOA:411; FIP:212
Security. FRIE:258
Siegenthaler, R.F.
New American tradition. YR 9:109
United savings bonds. DR:211
Winant, J.G.
Security for a people: a creative lift of the spirit. SAR:328

---- UNEMPLOYMENT
Truman, H.S.
Message to Congress asking emergency unemployment legislation. VO 1945-46:219
Message to Congress September 6, 1945. VO 1945-46:546

INTEGRATION
Kennedy, G.
Dedicated to a proposition. BA 1963-64:71
Lee, A.M.
New integration. YR 9:99

INTEGRETY
Morreim, P.E.
Price of integrity. BRP 7:65

INTELLECT
Blakesley, R.H.
Mastery of mind. SHUC:131
Campbell, A.
Mind the master force. BREW 3:88
Cowley, W.H.
Fire always makes room for itself. HOC:25; WPRC:226
Everett, E.
Cirumstances favorable to the progress of literature in America. BL:60
Huxley, T.H.
Method of scientific investigation. ARNS:260; BRY:455; BRYA:482
Ingersoll, C.J.
Influence of America on the mind. BL:17
Low-brows may be high-brows. FRIE:220
Park, E.A.
Theology of intellect and that of the feelings. BL:624
Wilson, W.
Training the intellect. BAAGA:431; KLEG:203; ONEM:844; ONES:261
See also Reason; Thought and thinking

INTELLECTUAL FREEDOM
Hildebrand, J.H.
Are we educating for national strength? BA 1940-41:271
Hull, W.J.
Intellectual freedom in a managed state. YR 6:357

INTELLECTUAL FREEDOM (cont.)
Randall, J. H., Jr.
Paradox of intellectual freedom. NORR 3d ser:86
Valentine, A.
Mobilizing the mind. BA 1940-41:263

INTELLIGENCE TESTS See Mental tests

INTER-AMERICAN CONFERENCE ON PROBLEMS OF WAR AND PEACE
Padilla, E.
At the Mexico City Conference. HAN:380
See also Western hemisphere-Defenses

INTERIOR DECORATION
Wilde, O.
Home decoration. ARNS:72
See also Home

INTERNATIONAL ARBITRATION See Arbitration

INTERNATIONAL BROTHERHOOD OF MAINTENANCE-OF-WAY EMPLOYEES
Intelligent cooperation. THOU 3:459
Mulkey, A. C.
Address by president of Auxiliary. THOU 3:444
Wagner, B. K.
Address. THOU 3:450
Wilson, J. T.
President's address. THOU 3:438

INTERNATIONAL BROTHERHOOD OF RAILWAY EMPLOYEES See International Brotherhood of Maintenance-of-way Employees

INTERNATIONAL CIVIL AVIATION CONFERENCE, 1944
Berle, A.
Civil Aviation Conference. HAN:395

INTERNATIONAL COOPERATION
Abbott, L.
International brotherhood. FUL:1, 4; REEMA 7:1
Brotherhood of man. DR:257
Burton, H. H.
America's road to lasting peace. BA 1943-44:106
Connally, T. T.
America and post-war cooperation. BA 1943-44:96
Cox, G. V.
My brother's keeper: plea for common world fellowship. ASHF:134
Elyea, C. D., Jr.
Plea of the unknown soldier. DO:44
Ford, H., II
Free world can't trade on a one-way street. BA 1952-53:131
Fulbright, J. W.
America and internationalism. BA 1943-44:83
Hammarskjold, D.
Values of nationalism and internationalism (Stanford University commencement address). COPB:628
Jones, L.
Breaking down barriers. YR 8:177
LeVander, H.
Date kernels. BRP 3:45; YR 4:151
McBurney, G. W.
Road back. NOR 1949:157
Mendès-France, P.
Search for international cooperation. COPB:623
Root, E.
Internationalism as tyranny. BREW 9:100
Stallings, J.
America and brotherhood. DO:139
Stassen, H. E.
Way to live as neighbors. ON:143
Truman, H. S.

Speech on world cooperation at Pemiscot county fair. VO 1945-46:625
Wheeler, B.K.
Against the resolution for collaboration for postwar peace. BA 1943-44:115

INTERNATIONAL LABOR CONFERENCE
Perkins, F.
Greetings from the United States. SAR:339

INTERNATIONAL LAW See Law and lawyers

INTERNATIONAL POLICE (PROPOSED)
Mundt, K.D.
Peace-if we want it. BA 1944-45:93

INTERNATIONAL RELATIONS
Acheson, D. G.
Ethics in international relations today. BA 1964-65:53
Ball, G.W.
Reallocation of world responsibilities. BA 1963-64:77
Cecil of Chelwood, E. A. R. G. - C.
Speech in response to introduction by C. Depew, at a Pilgrim dinner. COP:690; COPB:717; LINM:398; REEM sup 1:179; REEMB 8:81
Chateaubriand, F. A. R.
Has one government the right to intervene in the internal affairs of another? BREW 3:228; CHAL 4:311; HAZO 9:3729; MAS 9:3729
Doctor, the world is sick. NI:249; NIA:188
Eisenhower, D.D.
Address at the United Nations, September 22, 1960. BA 1960-61:55
Hammond, J.H.
Enlightened self-interest in international relations. REEM 4:178; REEMB 4:351
Hugo, V.
Moral force in world politics. BREW 7:101
Mays, J.H.
Internationalism. TRUW:54
Pfaf, R.A.
This diminishing world. BRP 2:67; YR 3:105
Schuman, F. L.
Peace without appeasement. HAR:40
Van Baarda, Mme. D.
Road toward international understanding. BUTB:245
See also Arbitration; Diplomacy; Disarmament; League of Nations; Monroe Doctrine; Nationalism; Peace; Permanent Court of International Justice; Treaties; War. Also Names of countries subhead Foreign relations, e.g. United States-Foreign relations

INTERNATIONALISM See International cooperation; Nationalism

INTERVIEWS AND INTERVIEWING
Gibbons, F.
Mr. Pitkin is interviewed. SAR:37
Suggestions for preparation of various types of business interviews (includes outlines, interview scripts, etc.). MICS:190; SABA: pt. III

INTOLERANCE See Religious liberty; Toleration

INTRODUCTIONS
Adams, E.B.
Introducing H.C. Caldwell to New England Society of St. Louis, December 21, 1895. REEM 1:201; REEMB 1:202
Address of the principal or superintendent, presenting the graduating class.

INTRODUCTIONS (cont.)
AMEO 1:18
Alton, B.
Introducing an insurance salesman. BRC:199
Introducing a shoe salesman (traveling). BRC:228
Angell, J.W.
Presents Harry J. Carman. LY:116
Bacon, W.S.
Introducing a Catholic priest. BRC:49
Bailey, I.H.
Introducing and toasting Charles Sumner at New England Society of New York, December 22, 1873. REEM 3:292
Introducing Roscoe Conkling to New England Society of New York, December 22, 1874. REEM 1:332; REEMB 1:333
Balfour, A.J.B.
Introducing Chief Justice Taft. REEM 1:69; REEMB 1:60
Banks, E.C.
Introducing a chairman of the day-2 examples of. BRC:36, 38
Barry, T.H.
Introduces George Washington Goethals to Class of 1912 at United States Military Academy. REEM 7:160; REEMB 8:181
Bartlett, W.
Introduces William Bourke Cockran to New England Society of Brooklyn. REEMA 1:232
Barton, A.
Introducing James Bryce to New York Chamber of Commerce. REEM :172
Becker, Mrs. W.A.
Introducing honorary president general, Mrs. Russell Magna. GA:15
Beebee, H.F.
Introducing W.E. Creed. MO:497; ONES:12
Bell, C.
Introducing D.D. Field to Saturday Night Club, April 5, 1890. REEM 2:45
Biographical outline for presenting a speaker to a meeting. BUT:96; BUTA: 96; BUTB:96
Blaine, J.B.
Introducing Clare Booth Luce
" Claude Pepper
" James Gheen, humorous lecturer. PR:91, 49, 59
Blume, C.E.
Introducing Harold E. Stassen. YE:127
Bolden, J.
Introducing an automobile dealer
" a credit man
" a salesmanager. BRC: 254, 142, 264
Bonaparte, C.J.
Introducing Ambassador Bryce at Harvard commencement exercises, 1907. KNAS:264
Borden, W.
Introducing C.W. Eliot to New England Society of New York, December 22, 1877. REEM 2:4
Introducing Horace Porter to New England Society of New York, December 22, 1877. REEM 3:172
Bowen, C.W.
Introducing J.R. Angell to New England Society of New York, December 22, 1921. REEM 1:52
Boyd, R.W.
Introduces his former pastor. PRNE:11
Branen, J.
Introducing an entertainer
" a girl trio
" an old time entertainer
" a speaker on dogs. BRH:106, 146, 67, 44
Brorby, M.
Introduces Arnold J. Toyn-

bee, professor, author, and historian of Great Britain. PRNE:39
Introduces Chester Bowles, former United States Ambassador to India. PRNE:33
Brown, J.
Introducing Julius H. Barnes at the Bankers' Club, New York. LINM:411
Bryant, W. C.
Introduces Lord Houghton. REEMA 2:635
Introducing a foreign patriot-Louis Kossuth. BRYW 9: 144; CHAL 6:130; HAZO 12: 5201; MAS 12:5201; ONEM: 664; REEM 5:45; REEMA 1:100; REEMB 9:75
Buchanan, J. G.
Presents Augustus N. Hand. LY:145
Budd, R.
Introduces Charles F. Kettering. PR:48
Bullis, H. A.
White light: introducing Dr. Alfred P. Haake at sales managers conference on his birthday. BRC:324
Burgess, W.R.
Presents Paul H. Douglas. LY:223
Busch, F.X.
Introducing Emory R. Buckner. ONEC:67
Bush, I.
Introducing Charles Evans Hughes. YE:131
Butler, N. M.
Introduces Andrew W. Mellon to Lotus Club. REEM sup 2:227; REEMB 5:175
Presents Wilbur L. Cross. LY:115
Calhoun, J. C. (Col.)
Introducing J.R. Fellows to Southern Society of New York, February 22, 1889. REEM 2:37
Carter, J.C.
Introducing U.S. Grant to New England Society of New York, December 22, 1880. REEM 2:137
Chairman's comments and his introduction of next speaker. HOA:370
Chairman's introduction of George Jessel at dinner in honor of Mannie Sack. JEYO:54
Chapman, Mrs. C.C.
Introducing Mrs. Mable W. Hughes. YE:130
Chess, T. L.
Concise introduction of a naval officer. PR:79
Choate, J. H.
Introducing and toasting Sir E. Schakleton to Pilgrim Society, February 4, 1913. REEM 3:201
Presents James Bryce. LY: 231
Cisler, W. L.
Introducing Leland I. Doan, speaker on atomic energy. MOA:500
Claflin, J.
Introducing Alton B. Parker to Chamber of Commerce of New York, November 20, 1913. REEM 3:42
Clemens, S. L.
Introducing Charles Kingsley. ANDS:197; ONEM:668; REEMA 5:691
Presents Henry M. Stanley
" James Whitcomb Riley and Edgar Wilson Nye
" Joseph B. Hawley.
LY:252, 75, 156
Clifford, V.
Introducing a basso
" a chorus
" a French comedian
" a ventriloquist
" a vocal soloist. BRH: See Table of contents section II for paging
Coleman, W.
Introducing a chemist
" a forester
" a sporting goods manager. BRC:200, 217, 207

INTRODUCTIONS (cont.)
Collins, A.
Introducing an ambassador (British)
" an army officer
" an automobile salesman
" a baker
" a comedian
" a manufacturer (small).
BRC: See Table of contents for paging
Colton, F.
Introducing a French wine merchant. BRC:312
Complimentary remarks-various examples of. BEC:80
Compton, K. T.
Introducing James Bryant Conant. YE:129
Presents Harold Edward Stassen. LY:104
Coolidge, C.
Introducing Henry Cabot Lodge and A. Lawrence Lowell. HOA:368; HOAP: 250; ONEM:667; ONES:3; YE:125
Coulter, T. H.
Introduces Dr. Will Durant, author and philospher on Ladies' day at Executive Club of Chicago. PRNE:43
Introduces W. Alton Jones, President, Cities Service Co. PRNE:38
Introducing Marguerite (Maggie) Higgins to the Executives' Club of Chicago. LARW:107; LY:129
Presents Lee Wulff. LY:255
Crawford, W.
Introducing a moving and storing executive. BRC:310
Curtain, A. G.
Introducing Fitzhugh Lee to Friendly Sons of St. Patrick, Sept. 17, 1887. REEM 2:318
Curtis, D.
Introducing a laundry and dry cleaning executive. BRC:318
Introducing a Boy Scout executive. BRC:288
Daniels, J.
Presents Sir Norman Birkett. LY:147
Davis, C. R.
Presents William J. Durant. LY:73
Davis, J. W.
Presents Lester B. Pearson. LY:208
Day, J. E.
Introduces Gardner Cowles, publisher. PRNE:15
Introduces John L. Lewis, American labor leader. PRNE:19
Introduces Lee Wulff who presented fishing and hunting films. PRNE:12
Introduces Robert H. Jackson, Associate Justice of Supreme Court of the United States. PRNE:4
Introduces United States Senator, Alexander Wiley. PRNE:36
Depew, C. M.
Introducing Lord Cecil. REEMB 1:402
Presents William Jennings Bryan. LY:217
Dewey, J.
Apt introduction. BRC:37
Dickson, P.
Introducing a general contractor. BRC:306
Douglas, L. W.
Presents Lord Halifax. LY: 210
Drummond, R.
Introducing an accordian player
" an acrobat-clown act
" an amateur theatrical
" a chalk talk artist
" an impersonator
" an instrumentalist
" a minstrel show
" a retiring teacher.
BRH: See Table of contents section II for paging
Introducing a beauty expert
" a golfer
" a humorist
" a hunter (wild animal

Introducing an instructor on conversation
" a movie star
" a "See America first" speaker. BRC: See Table of contents for paging
Eastlake, C. L.
Introducing Lord Palmerston to Royal Academy, May 2, 1863. REEM 3:39
Edward VII.
Introducing Sir W. Laurier to Colonial Premiers, June 18, 1897. REEM 2:310; REEMA 2:702; REEMB 2: 314
Erwin, B.
Introducing a hunter or extensive traveler. BRC: 266
Evans, H. G.
Introduces and pays tribute to Eva Wirth, teacher on her retirement. PR:86
Evans, L. H.
Presents Lessing J. Rosenwald. LY:66
Ewald, H. T.
Presents V. Pinkley. LY: 127
Examples of introduction speeches by experienced and capable men. HOAP:252
Examples of introductions for doctors. BO:16-19
Examples of introductions for men. BO:9-15
Examples of introductions for missionaries. BO:35-38
Examples of introductions for prize winners. BO:28-29
Examples of introductions for public officials. BO:24-27
Examples of introductions for speakers. FRIT:38-42
Examples of introductions for teachers. BO:20-23
Examples of introductions for women. BO:30-34
Examples of introductory remarks by toastmaster. FRIT:48-50
Farcical introduction of a well-known speaker. DR:10; LU: 1117
Farnsworth, D.
Introducing an airline executive
" a high school principal BRC:220, 182
Fisher, C. T., Jr.
Presents George C. Kenney. LY:159
Ford, C. S.
Presents Christopher Morley. LY:70
Ford, H., II
Presents Elmo Roper. LY: 96
Fraser, L.
Presents James F. Byrnes. LY:206
Gifford, W. S.
Introducing General John J. Pershing. YE:126
Gilbert, E. J.
Introducing an acrobat group
" a comedian
" a dancer or dancing act
" a juggler
" a magician
" a minstrel show
" an orchestra
" a quartette. DRII: See Table of contents, section II for paging
Introducing an author
" a banker-2 examples of
" a businessman (merchant)
" a Catholic priest
" a dentist
" a doctor
" a fund raiser
" an inventor
" a governor
" a judge
" a lawyer
" a minister (Protestant)
" a politician
" a professor
" a psychologist
" a salesman (top)
" a tax consultant. BRC: See Table of contents for paging

Gillilan, S.
Introducing Mrs. Asquith. REEM 2:95; REEMB 2:87
Given, W.
Introduces Hugh Comer. PR:97
Gossett, W. T.
Presents Harry Emerson Fosdick. LY:167
Graham, F. P.
Presents Robert M. Hutchins. LY:114
Granik, T.
Introductory remarks as radio moderator at celebration of 150th anniversary of Bill of Rights. BA 1941-42: 96
Green, W.
Introducing James J. Davis. ONEC:70
Introducing Peter Heenan. ONEC:69
Gregory, A. C.
Introducing a floor covering dealer
" a grocer (super market manager)
" a shoe merchant. BRC: 102, 258, 71
Griffin, C. E.
Presents James Palmer. LY:83
Grimm, P.
Introduces Dr. George Gallup
" Thomas E. Dewey
" V.K. Wellington Koo
PR:65, 66, 62
Grosvenor, G.
Byrd; the explorer and the man. DOA:72
Gwinn, J. M.
Introduction of Katherine Lee Bates. DOA:81
Presents Charles Lindbergh. LY:248
Haake, A. P.
Introduces Samuel B. Pettinger. PR:88
Haire, A. J.
Presents Arthur Godfrey. LY:44
Hale, M.
Introducing John S. Wise to Bar Association of New York, January 20, 1891. REEM 3:421
Hancher, V. M.
Introducing Joseph F. Newton at a combined honors convocation and baccalaureate service at the State University of Iowa. BA 1945-46:214

Presents Eleanor Roosevelt
" Franklyn Bliss Snyder.
LY:240, 119
Hanson, C. W. D.
Introduces Dr. Paul Dudley White, distinguished physician and cardiac specialist. PRC:29
Introduces His Excellency, Dr. Konrad Adenauer, Chancellor, Federal Republic of Germany. PRC:26
Harding, W. G.
Introducing Charles G. Dawes. REEM 4:67; REEMB 4:150
Presents Marie S. Curie. LY:178
Hargrave, M.
Introducing a millinery buyer or proprietor of a ladies hat store. BRC:195
Hart, R.
Introducing an art dealer
" a hardware dealer
" radio station manager
BRC:294, 56, 293
Hedges, J. E.
Presents Edward D. Duffield. LY:89
Hemery, J. L.
Introduces Lynn Saylor, advertiser. PR:90
Hensrud, R.
Introducing a commissioner of agriculture or county agent. BRC:314
Hepburn, A. B.
Introducing James Bryce. REEM 1:72; REEMB 1:168
Heymann, W. M.

Introduces Fayette H. Elwell, then Dean of the School of Commerce of the University of Wisconsin. PRNE:37

Hill, H.
Presents Francis B. Haas. LY:106

Hills, L.
Presents Fred Sparks. LY:132

Hintz, A.
Introducing an implement dealer
" a plumber. BRC:209, 154

Hoffman, H. G.
Introduces Morris Sayre. PR:95

Holm, W.
Introducing a track star. BRC:227

Holmes, O.W.
Introduces Matthew Arnold. REEM 7:23; REEMA 4:27; REEMB 8:23

House, R. B.
Presents Josiah C. Crudup. LY:110

Howells, W.D.
Introduces Joseph Gurney. Cannon. REEM 5:64; REEMB 9:94

Huber, L. J.
Emcee introducing himself. BRH:338
Introducing a timid soul. BRH:330
Introducing an actor
" an amateur show
" an animal imitator
" an animal trainer
" a bachelor
" a celebrity
" a choir or chorus
" a clown
" a college graduate
" a comedian
" a dancing act
" father of new baby
" gardener
" housewife
" humorist
Introducing a hypnotist
" an impersonator
" an instrumental trio
" an instrumentalist
" an Irishman
" a juggler
" a kissing booth
" a magician
" a mind reader
" minstrel show
" newlywed
" a novelty act
" an old time entertainer
" an opera star
" a quartette
" a sharpshooter
" a square dance caller
" a strong man
" a swimming-diving act
" a tumbling act
" a variety revue
" ventriloquist
" a vocal soloist
" a woman driver. BRH: See Table of Contents, section II for paging
Introducing an actor
" a boss
" a businessman
" a cattle raiser
" a doctor
" a financier
" a fisherman
" a golfer
" a horseman
" a hunter
" a musician
" a nurse
" a policeman
" a railroad executive
" a teacher
" traveler
" writer. BRC: See Table of contents for paging

Hughes, C. E.
Speech of introduction at the celebration of the eightieth birthday of Elihu Root. KLEB:127; LINM:253

Hull, C.
Introducing Ricardo J. Alfaro. MO:498; MOA:502

Humorous introduction. THOS:114

INTRODUCTIONS (cont.)
Hunt, L.
Introducing a house to house salesman. BRC:178
Huntington, H.
Introducing a Better Business Bureau secretary
" a Farm Bureau or Farmers' Union man
BRC:308, 320
Hurlburt, H. A.
Introduction of J. A. Dix to the New England Society of New York, December 22, 1863. REEM 1:407; REEMB 1:413
Hurley, J., Jr.
Introducing a tire distributor or dealer. BRC:276
Huston, B.
Introducing a stock broker. BRC:303
Hutchins, H. B.
Introducing James B. Angell. ONES:6
Introducing a candidate for office. DR:213; LU:1236
Introducing a clergyman-six examples. BEB:51-53
Introducing A. Harry Moore. NI:193
Introducing a lawyer-two examples. BEB:55
Introducing a past president at a convention. BEDA:136
Introducing a popular and frequent speaker at a man's club. DR:9; LU:1116
Introducing a relative. DR:12; LU:1119
Introducing a speaker. THOS: 98
Introducing a speaker on "planning a vacation." WRA:36
Introducing a speaker on "rose culture." WRA:34
Introducing a speaker on "The forthcoming election." WRA:38
Introducing a speaker on "The Thanksgiving holiday." WRA:37
Introducing a speaker on "vocational guidance." WRA:35
Introducing a speaker with a many-lettered and unpronounceable name. DR:9; LU:1116
Introducing after-dinner speaker. NATT:6
Introducing Alfred E. Smith. NI:154; NIA:114
Introducing Alfred J. McCosker. NI:120; NIA:92
Introducing an Attorney General at a political meeting. BEDA:130
Introducing an honorary member. STOC:119; STON:125
Introducing an officer (prominent citizen presents the Colonel). ED:75
Introducing Anna Steese Richardson on her 75th birthday. SUM:80
Introducing Bruce Barton-2 different examples. NI:86; NIA:68; SUM:97
Introducing Captain Norman Allan Imrie. NESA:202
Introducing Carl Crow, author and authority on China. SUM 78
Introducing Carl Laemmle. NI: 164; NIA:122
Introducing Charles S. Deneen. NESA:209
Introducing civic leader at fifth anniversary of founding of Big Brother Athletic Association. BEDA:112
Introducing civil liberties champion (at presentation of Brotherhood award). BED: 55; BEDA:64
Introducing clergyman at a convention. BEDA:134
Introducing clergyman (at memorial services). BED:99; BEDA:177
Introducing clergyman at Thanksgiving Day ceremoni[es] BEDA:88
Introducing colleague (at birthday testimonial). BEDA:30
Introducing colleague at pre-

sentation of scientific award. BEDA:58
Introducing Col. Gilbert T. Hodges of N.Y. Sun. SUM: 93
Introducing committee chairman (at dedication of home for aged). BED:33; BEDA:73
Introducing Dr. David Kinley. NESA:203
Introducing Dr. Ernest DeWitt Burton. NESA:205
Introducing Dr. Frederick F. Shannon. NESA:207
Introducing Dr. J.Y. Aitchison. NESA:208
Introducing Dr. Louis E. Bisch, psychiatrist. SUM: 68
Introducing Dr. Victor Heiser. SUM:88
Introducing donor of award (at hospital fund drive and testimonial). BED:62
Introducing donor of citation (at testimonial to philanthropist) BED:24; BEDA:46
Introducing donor of gift (at hospital fund drive and testimonial) BED:63; BEDA:100
Introducing donor of gift (at testimonial on retirement of public official). BED:27; BEDA:48
Introducing Dorothy Thompson. NI:45; NIA:39
Introducing Eddie Cantor. NI: 56; NIA:47
Introducing Edgar A. Guest. NESA:192
Introducing entertainment-examples of. FRIE:296
Introducing F. Hopkinson Smith to Holland Society, January 17, 1911. REEM 3:232
Introducing Fannie Hurst. NI: 83; NIA:66
Introducing Ferdinand Pecora. NI:118; NIA:91
Introducing Fiorello H. LaGuardia. NI:49; NIA:42
Introducing Frank Buck. NI: 125; NIA:95
Introducing Frank Hawks. NI: 161; NIA:120
Introducing Gene Buck. NI:146; NIA:109
Introducing Gene Tunney. SUM: 99
Introducing George Gershwin. NI: 90; NIA:71
Introducing Giovanni Martinelli. NI:150; NIA:112
Introducing Grover Whalen. SUM:72
Introducing guest-of-honor. BED:91; BEDA:164
Introducing guest of honor (at birthday testimonial). BEDA: 31
Introducing guest of honor (at Camera Club) BEDA:20
Introducing guest-of-honor (at ceremony honoring retiring secretary of labor union). BED:81; BEDA:154
Introducing guest-of-honor (at hospital fund drive and testimonial) BED:65; BEDA: 102
Introducing guest-of-honor (at presentation of Brotherhood award). BED:57; BEDA:65
Introducing guest of honor at presentation of scientific award. BEDA:61
Introducing guest of honor (at testimonial dinner to journalist). BED:22; BEDA:36
Introducing guest of honor at testimonial to a woman civic leader. BEDA:44
Introducing guest-of-honor (at testimonial on retirement of public official). BED:30; BEDA:51
Introducing Harry Hershfield. NI:72; NIA:59
Introducing Hendrik Van Loon-2 examples of; at 1st and 2nd visits to Advertising Club. SUM: 102, 104
Introducing Heywood Broun. NI:80; NIA:64
Introducing Honorable Robert Moses, Commissioner of

Parks of N. Y. City. SUM: 95
Introducing horticulturist (at Garden Club meeting). BEDA: 68
Introducing hospital official (at hospital fund drive and testimonial) BED:64; BEDA: 101
Introducing induction officer (at induction of members to labor union). BED:75; BEDA: 147
Introducing installing officer. BED:16; BEDA:25
Introducing installing officer (at induction of a Mayor). BEDA:114
Introducing James A. Farley. NI:63; NIA:52
Introducing James A. Johnson, Warden of Alcatraz Penitentiary. SUM:69
Introducing James G. McDonald. NI:172; NIA:127
Introducing James J. Walker. NI:142; NIA:107
Introducing John B. Kennedy, author and radio and newsreel commentator. SUM:76
Introducing John Finley. NI: 138; NIA:104
Introducing John Haynes Holmes. NI:169; NIA:125
Introducing journalist. BED: 20; BEDA:35
Introducing labor leader. BED: 93; BEDA:166
Introducing lawyer (at physician-of-the-year award). BED:50; BEDA:53
Introducing Lewis E. Lawes. NI:158; NIA:117
Introducing Louis Johnson. NI:108; NIA:84
Introducing Marian Chase Schaeffer. NESA:201
Introducing Mary Brian, motion picture star. SUM:69
Introducing Max Reinhardt. NI:129; NIA:97
Introducing Mayor (at induction of a Mayor). BEDA:116
Introducing Mayor at Town Hall meeting. BEDA:71
Introducing members representing labor and management-five examples. BEB: 53-55
Introducing military leader (at Flag Day ceremonies). BEDA:96
Introducing Mrs. Franklin Delano Roosevelt. SUM:74
Introducing modest speaker. FRIE:333
Introducing Morris Fishbein. NI:196
Introducing national representa tive (at charter presentatior to labor union). BED:73
Introducing Oscar S. Straus by toastmaster at Chamber of New York, November 17, 1910. REEM 3:279
Introducing out-of-town guests. FRIE:306
Introducing Paul Felix Warbur NI:189; NIA:140
Introducing presenter of awarc (at birthday testimonial). BEDA:29
Introducing presenter of gift (at Camera Club). BEDA:19
Introducing presenter of gift (at induction of a Judge). BEDA:118
Introducing program chairman BED:87; BEDA:160
Introducing program chairman (at United Nations anniversary ceremony). BEDA:124
Introducing program chairman (at unveiling of portrait presented to labor union). BED:89; BEDA:162
Introducing public official. BED:29; BEDA:49
Introducing public official at (B Scout fund drive). BEDA:10
Introducing public official (at memorial service). BED:44 BEDA:85
Introducing public official (at memorial services honorin deceased union member).

BED:100; BEDA:177
Introducing public official (at mental health fund drive). BED:59; BEDA:104
Introducing public official at Thanksgiving Day ceremony. BED:89
Introducing Rev. Carl Wallace Petty. NESA:206
Introducing Rev. Dr. Shailer Mathews. NESA:204
Introducing Rev. Ernest M. Stires to Southern Society of New York, December 13, 1905. REEM 3:274
Introducing Robert Benchley. NI:97; NIA:76
Introducing Robert F. Wagner. NI:134; NIA:101
Introducing Russell Davenport, editor of Fortune. SUM:90
Introducing Samuel Gompers to New York Editorial Conference. REEM 4:156; REEMB 4:299
Introducing Sara Delano Roosevelt. NI:152; NIA:113
Introducing second speaker at a banquet. FRIT:20
Introducing Shirley Wynne. NI:182; NIA:134
Introducing song leader. FRIT: 15
Introducing speaker-examples of. FRIE:303
Introducing speaker (Alice Foote McDougall on Recent impressions of Italy). SOES: 14
Introducing speaker at a convention. BEDA:135
Introducing speaker at Bill of Rights Day program. BEDA: 73
Introducing speaker (at ceremony honoring retiring secretary of labor union). BED:80; BEDA:153
Introducing speaker (at cornerstone dedication of youth center). BED:40; BEDA:82
Introducing speaker (at dedication of recreation center) BED:37; BEDA:78
Introducing speaker (at induction of a Judge). BEDA:117
Introducing speaker (at induction of a Mayor). BEDA:115
Introducing speaker (at Labor Day observance). BED:96; BEDA:169
Introducing speaker (at testimonial ceremony honoring union official). BED:83; BEDA:156
Introducing speaker (at testimonial to a woman civic leader) BEDA:42
Introducing speaker (at unveiling of plaque for Labor Temple). BED:86; BEDA: 159
Introducing speaker for presentation (at physician-of-the-year award). BED:51; BEDA:54
Introducing speaker for presentation (at testimonial to a musician). BEDA:39
Introducing speaker (George Morton on The highway beautiful). SOES:15
Introducing speaker (Harvey Meeker on Harmony between capital and labor). SOES:15
Introducing speaker (on Human Rights Day) BED:68; BEDA: 128
Introducing speaker (Stuart Taylor on Collecting antiques). SOES:15
Introducing Stephen S. Wise and Julian W. Mack. NI: 113; NIA:87
Introducing Strickland Gillilan-3 examples of; a humorous one, and 2nd and 3d return visit, to same organization. SUM:82, 84, 86
Introducing the after-dinner speaker-4 examples. DR: 11-12; LU:1118
Introducing the clergyman to give the invocation. FRIT: 13
Introducing the guest of honor-

three examples. BEB:53
Introducing the main speaker of the evening. DR:12; LU: 1119
Introducing the president at a convention. BEDA:136
Introducing the speaker at a Mothers and Daughter banquet. EDGS:301
Introducing Theodore Roosevelt, Jr. NI:186; NIA:138
Introducing Thomas E. Dewey. NI:68; NIA:56
Introducing Walter Winchell. NI:106; NIA:82
Introduction for distinguished speaker. FRIT:42
Introduction for extemporaneous speech. FRIT:37
Introduction for lady speaker. FRIE:272
Introduction of Champ Clark by toastmaster at Southern Society of New York. REEM 1:279
Introduction of Congressman Fess of Ohio. HOA:369
Introduction of George B. McClellan by toastmaster at Southern Society of New York, December 14, 1904. REEM 2:375
Introduction of head table guests at luncheon. SUM:169
Introduction of Lothrop Stoddard. HOA:370
Introduction of program chairman or toastmaster-five examples of. STOC:122; STON:128-131
Introduction of public officials-seven examples. BEB:50-51
Introduction of speaker. NATS: 3
Introduction of speaker by presiding officer-eight examples of. STOC:125; STON:131-134
Introduction of special guests at banquet. FRIT:14
Introduction of Thomas W. Lamont by 1922 President of American Bankers' Association. HOA:371
Introductions by toastmaster-6 examples of. MCK:100
Introductions of a more serious nature-examples of. DR:12-13; LU:1119

Irwin, D.
Introducing a confectioner. BRC:219

Jackson, S. D.
Introducing Quentin Reynolds. BA 1944-45:123

Jacobi, H.
Introducing a building and loan executive. BRC:290

Jeffries, P.
Introducing an architect. BRC:208

Jessel, G.
Introducing Danny Kaye at Friars' Club dinner to Burns and Allen. JEYO:101
Introducing Danny Thomas at Friars' Club dinner to Burns and Allen. JEYO:92
Introducing Eddie Cantor at Friars' Club dinner to Burns and Allen. JEYO:76
Introducing ex-Mayor Fletcher Bowron of Los Angeles. JEYO:49
Introducing George Burns. JEYO:47
Introducing George Burns and Gracie Allen at Friars' Club dinner in their honor. JEYO:109
Introducing Groucho Marx. JEYO:47
Introducing Jack Benny. JEYO:48
Introducing Jack Benny at Friars' Club dinner to Burns and Allen. JEYO:104
Introducing Jack Warner. JEYO:49
Introducing James Cagney at Friars' Club dinner to Burns and Allen. JEYO:80
Introducing Ronald Reagan at Friars' Club dinner to Burns and Allen. JEYO:82
Introducing Samuel Goldwyn

at Friars' Club dinner to Burns and Allen. JEYO:98
Introducing William E. Goetz at Friars' Club dinner to Burns and Allen. JEYO:74
Introducing William S. Paley at Friars' Club dinner to Burns and Allen. JEYO:89
Presenting Louella Parsons at dinner in her honor. JEYO:141
Remarks as toastmaster at Friars' Club dinner to Burns and Allen. JEYO:68
Response to introduction as Toastmaster General at dinner in honor of Mannie Sack, and introduction of principal speaker, David Sarnoff. JEYO:55
Toastmaster's speech at dinner honoring Jack Benny. JEYO:131

Kaser, A. L.
Introducing an actor
" an actress
" an authority on diet
" a ballet
" a comedian
" a dancing team
" an English comedian
" a gay nineties revue or act
" a German comedian
" a hillbilly pianist
" an Irish comedian
" a lady monologist
" a local orchestra
" a magician
" a mind reader
" a musician
" a quartette
" a retiring teacher (upper grades)
" a Scotch comedian
" a singing quartette
" a speaker on fire prevention (2)
" a Swedish comedian
" a television personality
" a variety revue. BRH: see Table of contents, section II for paging
Introducing an advertising man
" an airline stewardess
" an animal husbandry (speaker on)
" an artist
" a baby specialist
" a banker
" a baseball player
" a beauty expert
" a book publisher
" a Boy Scout executive
" a business man
" a college president
" a Communism (speaker on)
" a community singing expert
" a dentist
" a doctor
" a doctor speaking on obesity
" a dog fancier
" an educator
" an evolution (speaker on)
" a farmer or agriculturist
" a fisherman (expert)
" a food specialist
" a football coach
" a gardening expert
" a health (authority on)
" health and accident week (speaker on)
" an insurance man
" an interior decorator
" a Judge
" a Junior voters (speaker on)
" a labor leader
" a minister
" newspaper editor
" a nurse's training (speaker on)
" an optimist
" an orchestra leader
" a politician
" a poet
" a problem child (speaker to discuss)
" a P. T. A. president

Kaser, A. L. (cont.)
Introducing a professor
" a psychiatrist
" a public spirited citizen
" a radio actor
" a recruiting officer
" a salesman (top)
" a social reform (speaker on)
" a tax consultant
" a telephone executive
" town mayor
" a traffic officer
" a travel agent
" a world traveler. BRC: See Table of contents for paging

Keller, S.
Introducing a collection manager
" a detective or policeman
" a physician
BRC:180, 104, 68

Kidding introduction. FRIE:306

Kingsley, D. P.
Introducing M. Viviani, first War Premier of France. REEM 2:300; REEMB 2:303

Kirk, L.
Introducing a General. BRC: 322

Kirsten, K.
Introducing a Senator or Congressman. BRC:156

Knight, J.R.
Introduces H. E. Humphries, Jr., Chairman of the U.S. Rubber Company. PRNE:18

Lamont, T. S.
Presents Paul G. Hoffman. LY:91

Lamont, T.W.
Introducing General Hugh Johnson. HOC:17
Presents Eleanor Robson Belmont. LY:49
Presents W. L. Mackenzie King. LY:225

Landis, F.
Witty after-dinner speech on Will Hays. BRAC:302; LY: 213; NESA:185

Lane, G.W.
Introducing and toasting John P. Newman. REEM 3: 1

Lane, W. P., Jr.
Presents Walter Bedell Smith. LY:158

Lawrence, F.R.
Introduces Chauncey M. Depew to Lotus Club, February 22, 1896. REEMA 1: 373
Introduces Chauncey M. Depew to Lotus Club, March 11, 1899. REEMA 1: 380
Introduces Sir Edwin Arnold to Lotus Club. REEMA 1:7
Introducing Charles E. Hughes to the Lotus Club of New York, March 27, 1918. REEM 2:256
Introduction of a club guest (at dinner in honor of John J. Carty) REEM 2:313; REEMB 2:317

Leeson, J.
Introducing a railroad executive. BRC:299

Leighton of Stretton, F. L.
Introducing J. Tyndall to Royal Academy, May 5, 1888. REEM 3:345
Introducing Leslie Stephen to Royal Academy, April 29, 1893. REEM 3:271
Introducing Sir A. Sullivan to Royal Academy, May 2, 1891. REEM 3:298
Introducing Thomas H. Huxley to Royal Academy, May 2, 1891. REEM 3:262

Leverone, N.
Introduces Bill B. Van, "Ambassador of good-will from New England." PR:74

Lewe, J.C.
Presents Norman Vincent Peale. LY:165; PR:71
Presents Thomas C. Clark (Attorney General of the

United States) LY:149; PR: 73
Lewis, J.H.
Introduction of Jacob M. Dickinson. BRAC:235; LY: 205
Lincoln, H.
Introducing an appliance dealer
" a beautician
" a Red Cross worker. BRC:144,150,42
Livingston, J.J.
Introduces Clarence B. Randall, Chairman of the Inland Steel Company. PRNE: 8
Logan, W.S.
Introducing Lewis E. Carr to the New York State Bar Association, January 17, 1900. REEM 1:223; REEMB 1:224
Lord, C.S.
Introducing N.M. Butler. REEM 1:187; REEMB 1:188
Lovett, R.M.
Introducing Sam A. Lewisohn. ONEC:68
Low, S.
Introducing and toasting Robert E. Peary at New England Society of New York, December 22, 1909. REEM 3:47
Lowe, J.A.
Presents E.J. Pratt. LY: 58
Lusty, R.
Presents Sir Norman Birkett. LY:68
McAdoo, W.G.
Introducing W.J. Gaynor to Southern Society of New York, December 8, 1909. REEM 2:77
McCorkle, W.L.
Introduction of J.P. Mitchell to the New York Southern Society, December 10, 1913. REEM 2:414
McCutcheon, G.B.
Introducing Meredith Nicholson. BRAC:236
McCutcheon, J.T.
Introducing Booth Tarkington. YE:132
McDonough, J.J.
Introduces Allan Shivers, Governor of Texas. PRNE: 7
Introduces Clarence E. Manion, attorney, and formerly Dean of the Law School of Notre Dame University. PRNE:45
Introduces Dr. Will Durant, author and philosopher. PRNE:21
Introduces Edward T. McCormick, President of the American Stock Exchange. PRNE:26
Introduces Fulton Lewis, Jr., radio and TV commentator. PRNE:24
Introduces Gene Flack, Sales Counsel and Advertising Director, Sunshine Biscuit Company. PRNE:30
Introduces Heinz L. Krekeler, Ambassador of the Federal Republic of Germany to the United States. PRNE:46
Introduces Joseph M. Dodge, Director of the Bureau of the Budget of the United States. PRNE:13
Introduces Lester B. Pearson, Canadian statesman. PRNE:5
Introduces Lester L. Colbert, President, Chrysler Corporation. PRNE:27
Introduces United States Senator William F. Knowland. PRNE:41
McGovern, S.
Introducing an architect
" an artist
" a baby food executive
" a baby specialist-two speeches
" a band or orchestra leader

McGovern, S. (cont.)
Introducing a clothing merchant
" a druggist
" an engineer
" a fisherman
" a florist
" a golfer
" a humorist
" a labor leader
" a minister-2 speeches
" the president at a business meeting of a manufacturing company
" a salesman (successful)
" a salesman (top)
" a speaker small in stature
" a sportsman or where the speaker wants to use someone in the audience as the butt of his joke
" a world traveler. BRC: See Table of contents for paging

McLain, H. O.
Introduces Alvin N. "Bo" McMillin, football coach
" Francis B. Davis, Jr.
" Thomas R. Mulroy.
PR:114, 40, 55
Presents David Seabury. LY:117; PR:105

McSkimmons, M.
Introduction of Francis O. Blair. BRAC:239

Maddox, R. F.
Introducing Irving Fisher. ONES:11

Marlow, F.
Introducing a bank cashier or teller
" a state legislator. BRC: 59, 238

Marshall, T. R.
Introducing Ambassador Bakhmetieff. ONES:9
Introducing Baron Moncheur. ONES:8
Introduction of Henry Cabot Lodge. BRAC:239
Introduction of Prince Udine. ONES:7

Martin, J. W.
Introducing Speaker Sam Rayburn. SAB:208; SABA: 288

Martin, T. W.
Presents Charles F. Kettering. LY:180

Marvin, C.
Introducing an advertising executive.
Introducing a German industrialist. BRC:211, 291

Mason, W. C.
Presents George W. Pepper. LY:141

Mathews, S.
Introducing Woodrow Wilson. ONEM:671; ONES:6

Meloney, Mrs. W. B.
Introducing Dorothy Thompson. GA:13; LY:125

Merriam, J. C.
Presents Barton W. Evermann
" George H. Whipple
" Ray Lyman Wilbur
" William W. Campbell.
LY:191, 190, 189, 187

Milburn, J. G.
Presents James R. Day. LY:101

Miller, M. G.
Excerpts from introduction of John Foster Dulles. PRNE:42
Introduces Charles F. Brannon, Secretary of Agriculture. PRNE:25
Introduces Commander Irving Johnson. PRNE:40
Introduces Dr. Robert E. Wilson, Chairman Standard Oil Company of Indiana. PRNE:22
Introduces Dr. Will Durant, author and philosopher. PRNE:48
Introduces Henry J. Taylor, radio commentator. PRNE: 35
Introduces Jesse M. Donald

son, Postmaster General of the United States. PRNE:20
Introduces Lee Wulff, lecturer with films. PRNE:47
Introduces Mayor Edward J. Jeffries. PR:61
Presents Arthur H. Motley. LY:86; PR:44
Milliken, F.
Introducing a director of an amateur play
" a celebrity
" an opera star. BRH:72, 145, 109
Mirken, B.
Introduces Jack Benny at Friars' Club dinner to Burns and Allen. JEYO:65
Misner, P.J.
Introduces Dr. Arthur B. Moehlman, educator. PR:89
Model and outline for an introduction speech. BAKF:96, 104
Moran, E.B.
Introduces E.N. Ronnau
" Henry L. Porter
" J.C. Aspley, chairman of day
" Louis Ruthenberg. PR: 53, 99, 101, 96
Mulroy, T.R.
Introduces Bainbridge Colby
" Harold O. McLain
" secretary (club)
" Sir Norman Birkett
" two debaters, Sylvia Porter and Leon Henderson. PR:60, 81, 51, 112, 78
Presents Ilka Chase. LY: 35; PR:51
Murphy, H.D.
Introduces Basil Rathbone, distinguished actor. PRC:15
Introduces Ezra Taft Benson, Secretary of Agriculture. PRC:31
Introduces George Romney, President of American Motors Corporation. PRC:23
Introduces Willy Ley, distinguished rocket scientist. PRC:20
Nizer, L.
Presents Albert Einstein. HIBS:496; LY:173; NI:53; NIA:45
Presents Fulton John Sheen. LY:163; NI:111; NIA:85
Presents Grover A. Whalen. LY:81; NI:179; NIA:132
Presents Harry Woodburn Chase. LY:102; NI:101; NIA:79
Norton, C.E.
Introducing J.R. Lowell at Ashfield, Mass., August 27, 1885. REEM 2:363
Nuveen, J.
Introduces Dr. Walter H. Judd, Congressman from Minnesota. PRNE:14
O'Keefe, L.
Introducing a music dealer
" a newspaper reporter
" an optometrist
" a railroad executive
" a realtor BRC:218, 230, 231, 229, 206
Olds, L.
Introducing a meat dealer. BRC:201
Olney, R.
Presents Woodrow Wilson. LY:202
Opening announcement introducing Dr. Robert E. Cushman to radio audience. BA 1941-42:91
Orr, A.E.
Introducing M. Halstead to New York Chamber of Commerce, November 20, 1894. REEM 2:152
Outerbridge, E.H.
Introducing Lord Cunliffe to Chamber of Commerce of New York. REEM 4:61; REEMB 4:144
Park, M.E.
Introducing president Ada Louise Comstock. GA:14
Parker, J.
Introduction of Edwin P. Morrow. BRAC:236

Pearsons, C.
Introducing a packing house executive. BRC:282
Peloubet, M. E.
Presents Robert C. Downie. LY:94
Pepper, G. W.
Introducing Marshall Foch. LY:153; NESA:189
Presents Charles Evans Hughes. LY:137
Phelps, F.
Introducing an animal trainer
" a harpist. BRH:62, 77
Phelps, W. L.
Presents André Chevrillon
" Sir William Llewellyn. LY:63, 245
Plunkett, W. B.
Introducing President McKinley to the Home Market Club, Boston, February 12, 1899. ONES:11; REEM 2:382
Posner, G. A.
Introducing a bathing beauty contest. BRH:187
Introducing an animal trainer or animal act
" a children's act or child entertainer
" a judge (or member of legal profession)
" a magician
" a musical act
" a psychiatrist. BRH: See Table of contents, section II for paging
Introducing an artist
" a farmer
" a Hollywood actor
" a minister
" a politician-two examples
" a professor. BRC: See Table of contents for paging
Postle, A. S.
Introducing J. H. Ayres. MO:496
Pratt, P. A.
Introduces Frederick C. Crawford. PR:35
Preparation of an introductory speech. COUW:276
Presenting new Judge (at his induction). BEDA:119
Price, J.
Presents Norman H. Davis. LY:250
Prochnow, H. V.
Introduces Clarence B. Randall, Chairman of the Inland Steel Company. PRNE:9
Proposing, introducing, and speech of an honorary member. STOC:119-120
Ramsey, H.
Introducing a Boy Scout (speaker on)
" a Father's day speaker
" a golden wedding anniversary party (speaker at)
" a parent at a graduation banquet
" a P. T. A. meeting (speaker at)
" a public librarian
" a Sunday school banquet (speaker at)
" a Y. M. C. A. (speaker on)
" a Y. W. C. A. (speaker on). BRC: See Table of contents for paging
Razz introduction. NATM:33
Reed, P. D.
Introduces mayor of the convention city. PR:102
Reid, Mrs. O.
Introducing Matthew Woll to Ninth annual forum of the New York Herald Tribune. BA 1939-40:327
Presents Lillian Smith
" Walt Disney. LY:71, 42
Reid, W.
Introduces George Augustus Sala to Lotus Club. REEMA 3:1014
Introduces Wilkie Collins to Lotus Club. REEMA 1:261
Introduces William Gilbert and Sir Arthur Sullivan to Lotus Club. LY:41; REEM

2:89; REEMB 2:81
Roberts, R.
Introducing an accountant
" a banker
" a Congressman
" a small town newspaper publisher. BRC: 138, 112, 147, 73
Rogers, W.
Presents Franklin Delano Roosevelt. LY:197
Roosa, D.B. St.J.
Introducing Theodore Roosevelt to Holland Society of New York, January 15, 1896. REEM 3:151; REEMB 3:154
Root, E.
Introducing and toasting Joseph B. Coghlan at the Union League Club, April 21, 1899. REEM 1:323; REEMB 1:324
Introducing H. Watterson to New England Society of New York. ANDS:198; LY:123; ONEM:669; ONES:4; REEM 3:359
Russell, H.
Introduction of Edward O. Wolcott to New England Society of New York, December 22, 1887. REEM 3:431
Rydin, R. G.
Introduces Daniel P. Loomis, President of the Association of American Railroads. PRC:11
St. John, R.
Remarks preceding the reading over the radio of Chaplain Gittelsohn's address "That men might be free." BA 1945-46:16
Schiff, J.H.
Introduction at the 250th anniversary of the settlement of the Jews in the United States. TWJ:8
Schnadig, E.L.
Presents Gerald Wendt. LY:182; PR:93
Scott, G.
Introduces Heinrich Schliemann to Royal Academy, London. REEMA 3:1034
Introducing W.E. Gladstone to Royal Academy, May 5, 1877. REEM 2:96
Scott, W.F.
Introduces Lord Beaconsfield. REEM 9:303; REEMB 10:312
Seamon, Sir O.
Presents Stephen Leacock. LY:55
Shaw, G.B.
Presents Major Barbara. LY:60
Silliman, B.D.
Introducing and toasting Rev. E.E. Hale. REEM 2: 149
Introducing and toasting R. B. Hayes to New England Society of Brooklyn, December 21, 1880. REEM 2:183
Introducing General Sherman to New England Society of Brooklyn, December 21, 1880. REEM 3:206
Simmons, D. A.
Presents Walter S. Fenton. LY:143
Smith, C.E.
Introduces Charles A. Dana to New England Society. REEMA 1:321
Introducing and toasting Benjamin Harrison at New England Society of Pa., December 22, 1893. REEM 2: 167
Smith, C.S.
Introducing Horace Porter to Chamber of Commerce of New York, June 24, 1885. REEM 3:89
Introducing W.M. Evarts to Chamber of Commerce of New York, June 24, 1885. REEM 2:28
Smith, H.
Introducing a Chamber of Commerce official
" a doctor
" a fat man

Smith, H. (cont.)
Introducing a city fireman
" a game warden
" a Supreme Court justice. BRC:50, 161, 57, 64, 160, 302
Smith, W.
Introduces Ford Frick, Commissioner of baseball. PRC:17
Snyder, F.B.
Introduces two debaters, Alfred P. Haake and Harold Laski. PR:84
Speeches by the toastmaster at the 1936 Rocky Mountain Speech Conference. JUD: 318, 321-5; 329
Spencer, F.
Introduces James A. Farley. PR:77
Spencer, H.R.
Introducing Anne O'Hare McCormick. YE:127
Speyer, J.
Introducing Robert L. Owen to the Economic Club of New York, November 10, 1913. REEM 3:21
Presents Talcott Williams. LY:124
Steele, R.
Introducing an atomic scientist. BRC:316
Steele, S.
Introducing a contralto
" a high school symphony orchestra
" an impersonator
" a P.T.A. entertainment
" a pianist. BRH:87, 137, 51, 65, 89
Stevens, E.T.
Introduces Paul G. Hoffman. PR:69
Stevenson, A.E.
Presents Pandit Nehru. LY: 238
Stipp, J.E.
Introduces Dr. Will Durant, distinguished philosopher. PRNE:49
Introduces Edmund S. Muskie, Governor-elect of Maine. PRNE:31
Introduces Nathan M. Pusey, President, Harvard University. PRNE:29
Introduces Ralph D. Paine, Jr., Publisher of Fortune. PRNE:23
Introduces Warren Lee Pierson of Trans-World Airlines. PRNE:32
Stone, H.L.
Introduces club members to compete with Quiz Kids
" Gen. Carlos Romulo
" James Conzelman, football coach. PR:79, 54, 38
Introductory remarks for a ladies' day meeting. PR:99
Stratton, W.G.
Introduces Herbert Brownell, Jr., Attorney General of the United States. PRNE:17
Straus, G.
Introducing a furrier. BRC: 275
Streeter, F.S.
Introducing an educator (Frederick S. Jones). ONEM: 670; ONES:5
Stryker, H.M.
Introducing Lt. Gen. Walter Bedell Smith. YE:128
Suggestions for preparation of an introduction. BRY:369; BRYA:400; BUT:96; BUTA: 96; BUTB:96; MOUG:151; MOUGA:151; RE:110. With examples of. ANDS:193; BARR:228; BEB:55-59; BEC:82; BRA:504; BRAB: 492; CON:5; GA:10; GLAD: 161; HIBS:274; LARW:106; MCK:185; MO:491; MOA: 490; SABA:281; WRA:31; YE:122
Suitable forms for presiding officer when introducing speaker. HILL:461
Sumner, G.L.
Presents Gertrude Lawrence

LY:47; SUM:70
Talbot, P.
Introducing Sir Frederick James. MOA:501
Taylor, D.
Presents Grace George. LY:38
Three speeches presenting a guest speaker at men's fellowship dinner. HNWS:42
Toastmaster introduces extra speaker. FRIT:30
Toastmaster's introduction. THOS:113-114
Toastmaster's introductory speech. FRIT:33
Touchstone, W.W.
Introduces Dr. Francisco Villagran, Mexican Consul. PR:48
Trippe, J.T.
Presents Vannevar Bush. LY:175
Truman, H. S.
Presents Winston Churchill. LY:195
Van Dyke, H.
Introducing John Morley. NESA:162
Verdery, M.J.
Introducing August Thomas to Southern Society of New York, December 14, 1906. REEM 3:319
Visk, A. G.
Introducing a backwoods pianist
" a comedian
" a juggler. BRH:83, 124, 120
Wade, A. C.
Introducing a filling station manager
" a restaurant or cafe manager. BRC:99, 100
Wakefield, J. C.
Introduces Robert A. Walsh, pharmacist. PR:94
Walker, B.
Introducing a coroner
" a department store buyer
" a jeweler. BRC:205, 235, 222
Wallace, H. A.
Introducing Winston Churchill. ON:338
Waller, H.H.
Presents Bertrand Russell. LY:108
Presents Estes Kefauver. LY:221
Walsh, J.J.
Introducing the mayor-elect of Boston. HOAP:264
Wanacek, E. M.
Introduces Charles A. Eaton. PR:72
Ward, F. A.
Introducing Thomas N. Page to the New England Society of Brooklyn, December 21, 1899. REEM 3:28; REEMA 3:861; REEMB 3: 28
Watkins, A.
Introducing Rachel Crothers. ON:339
Watkins, F. C.
Introduces Robert A. Taft. PR:68
Wayland, H. L.
Introduces Chauncey M. Depew to New England Society. REEMA 1:349
Weaver, C.I.
Introduces Dr. Rees Edgar Tuloss. PR:64
Webb, W. P.
Speech that was never made (introduction of Harry S. Truman intended for Mississippi Valley Historical Association meeting), GRIS: 51
Weston, P.
Introducing a humorist
" a world traveler. BRC: 309, 284
Weyforth, B. S.
Introduces Fred C. Foy, Chairman of the Board and President of the Koppers Company. PRC:28
Introduces Rear Admiral

INTRODUCTIONS (cont.)
George J. Dufek. PRC:16
Wilcox, D.
Introducing a symphony orchestra conductor. BRC:286
Wilford, H.C.
Introducing a barber
" a baseball player
" a teacher. BRC:148, 110, 119

Willcox, W.R.
Presents George W. Goethals to the Economic Club of New York, March 5, 1914. LY:182; REEM 2:100

Williams, E.K.
Presents David A. Simmons. LY:139
Williams, H.
Introducing a certified public accountant
" a high government official BRC:62, 63
Williams, H.D.
Introducing George W. Pepper to the Citizens' Committee, University of Pittsburgh. LINM:481
Wilson, P.
Introduces Emil Schram, president N.Y. Stock Exchange. PR:46
Wilson, R.
Introduction of George White. BRAC:238
Winthrop, P.C.
Introducing a business man (head of firm)
" a dentist
" a highway patrolman. BRC:98, 66, 105
Woodford, S.L.
Introduces Frederick René Coudert to New England Society of New York. REEMA 1:277
Wooldridge, C.W.
Introducing Carl Bolte by stating qualities exactly opposite to his. PR:47
Woolley, M.E.
Introducing Mrs. Franklin D. Roosevelt. GA:12

Youle, C.
Introduces Ilka Chase. PRC:6
Introduces Maurice H. Stans, Director of the Bureau of Budget of the United States. PRC:14
Introduces Professor C. Northcote Parkinson. PRC:21
Introduces Robert F. Wagner, Mayor of New York City. PRC:12
Introduces William Veeck, President of the Chicago White Sox. PRC:25
Young, C.S.
Introduces William McChesney Martin, Chairman of the Board of Governors of the Federal Reserve System. PRNE:10
Yu, Tsune-Chi
Presents H.H. Kung. LY:200; ON:338
Ziebarth, Dr. E.W.
First class man: introducing Commissioner Robert E. Lee of Federal Communications Commission. BRC:39
See also Emcees; Responses to introductions; Welcoming addresses
Inui, Kiyo Sue
Mission of new Japan. TRUW:203

INVASION OF FRANCE See World War 1939-1945-France

INVENTIONS AND INVENTORS
Daniels, J.
Invention. REEM 1:360; REEMB 1:361
Du Pont, H.B.
Greatest invention of them

all. ARNS:193
Durfee, J.
Influence of scientific discovery and invention on social and political progress. BL:381; NORR 1st ser:43
Ensor, W.
Something lost. BRP 1:58
Gilbert, E. J.
Introducing an inventor. BRC:118
Hulbert, M.
Inventions and inventors. REEM sup 2:78; REEMB 6:199
Porter, H.
Men of many inventions. CHAL 13:96; HAZO 23:10032; MAS 23:10032; REEM 3:72; REEMA 3:897; REEMB 3:73
See also names of inventors, e.g. Bell, A. G., Edison, T. A.

INVESTIGATION See Research

INVESTMENTS
Harrison, H. T.
Whither midst falling due? HOC:27; ON:156; SAR:141

INVOCATIONS
Gerche, D. J.
Invocation before a convention of Arizona Bankers Association. PR:109
Gibson, G. M.
Invocation before national convention of Office Management Association. PR:109
Goff, C. R.
Invocation before the convention of National Congress of America. PR:110
Introducing the clergyman to give the invocation. FRIT:13
Invocation at a convention. BEDA:134
Invocation at banquet. FRIT:13
Invocation (at dedication of recreation center). BED:37; BEDA:78
Invocation (at induction of a Judge). BEDA:117
Invocation for a Thanksgiving Day ceremony. BEDA:92
Invocation for Thanksgiving Day ceremony. BEDA:89
Opening convocation by Rev. Snyder of the Mystic Workers. THOU 3:467
Palmer, Worthy Brother.
Invocation. THOU 3:468
Snyder, Rev.
Opening invocation of Rev. Snyder of the Mystic Workers. THOU 3:467

IOWA
Hancher, V. M.
Higher education in Iowa (at Founders' Day luncheon-Iowa State College centennial). IOCP:37
Hoover, H. C.
Begins an address on the occasion of the State of Iowa's celebration of his eightieth birthday at his birthplace, West Branch, Iowa. PRNE:65

IOWA STATE COLLEGE
Hagemann, H. H.
Remarks at Iowa State college centennial. IOCP:17
Hilton, J. H.
Closing remarks at Iowa State College centennial luncheon. IOCP:43
Concluding remarks at Academic symposia-Iowa State College centennial. IOCP:163
Loveless, H. C.
Welcome address at Iowa State College centennial. IOCP:13
Morrill, J. L.
Unchanging challenge-lest we forget (at Iowa State College centennial). IOCP:19

IOWA STATE UNIVERSITY
Hancher, V. M.
Inaugural address as president of Iowa State University. WE 2:149
Ireland, John
America a world power. BLAA: 202; BLAB:202; REAC:113
Catholic schools for Catholic youth. CATA 2:1
Catholicism and Americanism. CATA 1:109
Church and the age. ONEM: 719
Joan of Arc. WERN 42:79
On patriotism. CHAL 13:204; HAZO 24:10192; MAS 24: 10192
Peace in the wake of victory. ORAMA 2:445
Just war is holy. FUL:167, 170
Total abstinence. THOU 1:555

IRELAND
Beecher, H.W.
Home Rule for Ireland. REEM 1:108; REEMA 1:60; REEMB 1:103
Blaine, J. G.
Irish question. HICF:111
Bright, J.
Suspension of the Habeas Corpus Act. CLAY:290
Bryce, J.
On the government of Ireland Bill. BRYW 5:145; LAD:220
Burrowes, P.
King v. Edward Sheridan, M. D. KET:247
Butt, I.
At the bar of the House of Lords. BRYW 6:188; PL: 533
Speech on Home Rule. KET: 341
Cahill, M.
Down with the Pope. KET: 363
Chamberlain, J.
Home Rule for Ireland. BEA:91; PAUF 2:331
Collins, M.
Independence for Ireland. REEM 7:111; REEMB 8:111
Collins, P. A.
Ireland's dream of nationality. REEMA 1:257
Culberson, C. A.
Tribute to Ireland (St. Patrick's Day address). SHUO: 219
Davitt, M.
Ireland a nation, self-chartered and self-ruled. BREW 5:47
On the Irish Land League. BRYW 6:244; HAZO 25: 10586; MAS 25:10586
Depew, C. M.
Ireland. ONEM:636; REEMA 1:343
DeValera, E.
Ireland among the nations. COP:446; COPA:446; COPB:466
Devonshire, S. C. C.
Home Rule Bill of 1886. PAUF 2:306
George V.
Home Rule for Ireland. BREW 6:200
Gladstone, W. E.
Government of Ireland Bill, April 8, 1886. HAZO 15: 6397; MAS 15:6397
Home Rule, April 13, 1886. HAZO 15:6460; MAS 15: 6460
Home Rule, June 7, 1886. HAZO 15:6518; KLEG:139; MAS 15:6518
Home Rule and autonomy, May 10, 1886. BREW 6:253; FULB:157; HAZO 15:6481; MAS 15:6481
Grattan, H.
Against the Union (January 15, 1800 speech). KET:136
Against the Union (March 19, 1800 speech). KET:138
Declaration of Irish rights, April 19, 1780. BREW 6: 279; BRTH:91; BRTHA:91; BRYW 6:59; CHAL 3:165;

CODS:189; CODSA:189; GOOD:386; HAY:48; HAZO 7:2784; KET:112; MAS 7: 2784; ONEM:198; ORBR: 1:361; PE:147; PEA:147; PL:509; REEMA 13:1100
Irish feeling. KET:133
Making his second motion for a Declaration of Irish rights, April 16, 1782. GOOD:391; KET:131
Reply to Flood. CLAY:241; GOOD:394
Unsurrendering fidelity to country. BREW 6:297; HAZO 7:2811; KET:140; MAS 7:2811

Griffith, A.
Irish Free State (January 7, 1922). COP:223; COPA:223; COPB:223; REEM 7:160; REEMB 8:187
On establishment of Irish Free State (December 19, 1921). KESB:98

Hefferan, J. A.
Ireland's unfailing faith. CATA 1:239

Hogg, D.
Speech in House of Commons, November 27, 1922 (on establishment of Irish Free State). KESB:128

Lloyd George, D.
Speech in House of Commons, December 14, 1921 (on establishment of Irish Free State). KESB:83

Lomasney, W. F.
Consciousness of innocence (from dock in Dublin). HAZO 24:10420; MAS 24:10420

McCarthy, J.
Ireland's struggle. REEMA 2:795

Martin, J.
Indictment of millions. HAZO 17:7242; MAS 17: 7242
Irish martyrs: address at the cemetery in Dublin. HAZO 17:7238; MAS 17: 7238
National independence of Ireland. HAZO 17:7235; MAS 17:7235

Meagher, T. F.
Glory of Ireland (St. Patrick's Day speech). HAZO 20:8471; MAS 20:8471
Hope for Ireland (speech from the dock). HAZO 20: 8468; MAS 20:8468
Indictment of the Whigs. HAZO 20:8463; MAS 20: 8463
On abhorring the sword. BRYW 6:209; CHAL 10:214; HAZO 20:8453; KET:352; MAS 20:8453; PL:528
Orators of Ireland. HAZO 20:8477; MAS 20:8477

Mitchel, J.
Law in Ireland: delivered from dock. HAZO 18:7595; MAS 18:7595
On the Irish cause. HAZO 18:7597; MAS 18:7597

Morley of Blackburn, J. M.
Home Rule. CHAL 13:253; HAZO 24:10234; MAS 24: 10234; ONEM:357; REEM 9:324; REEMA 14:1497; REEMB 10:333

O'Connell, D.
Carries on the fight for Catholic emancipation. PE: 422; PEA:422
Demand for justice to Ireland. BREW 8:244; CODS: 461; CODSA:461; COP:211; COPA:211; COPB:211; FULB:109; HAZO 10:4028; MAS 10:4028; REEMA 14: 1522
On repeal of the Union. BAKF:387; BREW 8:236; BRYW 6:195; CLAY:204; CHAL 5:15; FRY:32; FULB: 101; HAZO 10:4015; LAD: 209; MAS 10:4015; ONEM: 334; PE:441; PEA:441; PL: 524; REEM 9:253; REEMB 10:260
On the Irish Disturbance Bill. CLAY:151

IRELAND (cont.)
Political outlook, 1814. KET:291
State of Ireland, House of Commons, February 5, 1833. PAUF 1:264
Palmerston, H. J. T.
Against war on Ireland. BREW 8:271
Parnell, C. S.
Against non-resident landlords. BREW 8:282; CHAL 14:31; HAZO 25:10572; MAS 25:10572
At Limerick-The land for the people. KET:402
Commission speech, 1888. KET:392
Meeting of Irish Parliamentary Party. KET:404
On a coercion bill in House of Commons. CHAL 14:35; HAZO 25:10576; KET:409; MAS 25:10576
On the Home Rule Bill. BRYW 6:230; COP:219; COPA:219; COPB:219; PAUF 2:159; PE:578; PEA:578
Peculiar spiritual and cultural ancestry of the Irish people. AMEO 2:187
Plunket, W. C. P.
Denunciation of the Union with England. CHAL 4:178; HAZO 9:3541; MAS 9:3541
Incompetence of Irish Parliament to pass the Union. KET:285
On the Irish Parliament and the Union. CHAL 4:174; HAZO 9:3538; MAS 9:3538
Redmond, J. E.
English government in Ireland. KET:440
Exclusion of the Irish members. KET:435
Home Rule as a dominant issue. BREW 9:41
Home Rule Resolution. KET:441
Ireland and the coronation. BRYW 6:255
Ireland and the war. BRTH:350; KET:443; REEM 11:29; REEMB 12:30
Irish freedom. BEA:359
Irish National Convention in Chicago, 1886. KET:427
Irish problem (1906). KET:437
Russell of Killowen, C. R.
American connection. KET:396
Parnell Commission October 1888 speech). KET:382
Two parties in Ireland. KET:400
Salisbury, R. A. T. G. -C.
Speech at Monmouthshire, October 8, 1885. PAUF 2:263
Sheil, R. L.
Ireland's part in English achievement. BREW 9:183; BRYW 6:173; REEMA 15:1865
Simon, J. A.
Speech in House of Commons, November 27, 1922 (on establishment of Irish Free State). KESB:119
Smith, C. E.
Ireland's struggle. REEMA 3:1059
Smith, S.
"Wounds, shrieks, and tears" in government. BREW 9:258
Sullivan, A. M.
"Disesteem of the law" (from the dock at Dublin, 1868). HAZO 22:9233; MAS 22:9233
On the Irish National demands. KET:372
Thomas, J. H.
Irish question. BEA:411

IRELAND-NEUTRALITY
De Valera, E.
Speech on Eire neutrality. VO 1941:607

---- RELIGION See Church of Ireland; Roman Catholics

in Ireland
Irish, John P.
Memorial address on Governor Bartlett. WAGN:281

IRISH
Depew, C. M.
Citizens of the world. REEMA 1:370
Huber, L. J.
Introducing an Irishman. BRH:152

IRISH IN THE UNITED STATES
Cobb, I. S.
Lost tribes of the Irish in the South. COP:695; COPB: 722; NESA:144; REEM 1: 308; REEMB 1:309
Taylor, R. L.
Address on Irish-American Day. HARSO:155

IRISH VOLUNTEERS
Flood, H.
Vindication of the Volunteers. KET:96

IRON MANUFACTURERS AND MANUFACTURING
For an iron manufacturers' festival. BARB:185
Iron manufacturers, by a well-known member of the iron industry. EDGS:132
Speech at an iron manufacturers' festival. HILL:484
Irving, Edward
Lord Jesus Christ. HAZO 12: 5047; MAS 12:5047
Irving, Henry
Character of Macbeth. REEMA 8:724
Drama. COP:681; COPB:708; REEM 2:269; REEMA 2:678; REEMB 2:272
Function of the newspaper. REEMA 2:681
Looking forward. REEMA 2:676

IRVING, HENRY
Coleridge, J. D.
Henry Irving's versatility. REEMA 1:246
Ford, S.
Me and Sir Henry. REEMA 2:505
Irving, Washington
Landing at New York. -Same as his My native land
My native land. KNAS:185; KNASA:185; REEM 2:272; REEMA 8:736; REEMB 2: 276

IRVING, WASHINGTON
Dickens, C.
As a literary guest of America. BRYW 4:150; ONEM:694
Tribute to Washington Irving. REEMA 1:394
Longfellow, H. W.
Washington Irving. KNAS: 55; KNASA:55; REEMA 8: 786
Mitchell, D. G.
Irving as author and man (commemoration of 100th anniversary of birth of Washington Irving). REEMA 9:872
Irwin, Dale
Introducing a confectioner. BRC:219
Irwin, Inez Haynes
Acceptance of Amelia Earhart collection. GA:47
Irwin, Ramon
Banners and bluebirds. BRP 7:70; NOR 1936:3
Irwin, William A.
American way. BA 1939-40:183
Isaeus.
Estate of Ciron (claim to a legacy). FRE:147; LEEW 1: 149
For Euphiletos. LEEW 1:168; PL:51
In the suit against Dicaegenes and Leochardes. BRYW 1: 101
Menexenus and others against Dicaeogenes and Leochares. CHAL 1:104; HAZO 1:187; MAS 1:187

Isaiah.
Come near, ye nations, to hear! CROC:256
Cries out for social justice. PE:5; PEA:5
Ise, John
Values in a crazy world: a plea for more culture. HOB:149
Ishii, Kikujiro, Viscount
To the United States Senate. REEM 11:239; REEMB 12:253
Tribute to Washington. LEW:151
Isle, Walter
Planting seeds of peace. BOB:33
Isocrates.
Areopagiticus-"A few wise laws wisely administered." BREW 7:137; HAZO 1:142; MAS 1:142
Economium on Evagoras. CHAL 1:87; HAZO 1:151; MAS 1:151; PL:54
On the union of Greece to resist Persia. BRYW 1:89; COP:11; COPA:11; COPB:11
Panegyric. HIB:25; LEEW 1:109
Primacy of Athens. CROC:259

ISOLATIONISM See United States-Neutrality

ITALIANS IN THE UNITED STATES
Biddle, F.
Columbus Day address. HOC:191

ITALY
Azeglio, M. T.
On presenting the estimates for the Ministry of Foreign Affairs. CHAL 6:274; HAZO 13:5420; MAS 13:5420
Cavour, C. B., di
Rome and Italy. BREW 3:174; BRYW 7:232; CHAL 8:62; COP:103; COPA:103; COPB:103; HAZO 16:6678; MAS 16:6678; REEM 9:269; REEMA 12:530; REEMB 10:277
Churchill, W. L. S.
Message from Rome to the people of Italy. VO 1944-45:391
Crispi, F.
Address to the Italian electors. CHAL 9:458; HAZO 19:8094; MAS 19:8094
Garibaldi, G.
Against the humiliation of the Southern Army. CROC:220
Mazzini, G.
To the young men of Italy. BAKF:406; BREW 8:130; BRYW 7:225; CHAL 7:226; COP:98; COPA:98; COPB:98; HAZO 14:6113; MAS 14:6113; PE:458; PEA:458; PL:342; REEM 9:262; REEMA 14:1467; REEMB 10:270
Mussolini, B.
Absurdity of eternal peace. PL:816; SAR:268
Call to arms. COP:510; COPA:510; COPB:488; FRY:126; PE:761; PEA:761
Fascist Italy. REEM sup 2:237; REEMB 8:316
Renders his first account to the Chamber of Deputies. PE:734; PEA:734
Roosevelt, F. D.
Italy enters the war. BA 1939-40:76
Sagasta, P. M.
In defence of the unity of Italy. CHAL 11:114; HAZO 21:8970; MAS 21:8970
Stettinius, E. R., Jr.
Statement on British policy in Italy. VO 1944-45:595
See also Fascism; Rome; Tripartite Pact; World War, 1939-1945-Campaigns-

Italian front; World War, 1939-1945-Italy

---- FOREIGN RELATIONS-GREAT BRITAIN
Braunstein, B.
Italy vs. Great Britain. SAR:286
Iverson, Alfred
On secession. CHAL 6:282; HAZO 13:5436; JOHA 2 pt 1:235; MAS 13:5436
Iverson, Samuel
Address of welcome. THOU 3: 323
Ivins, William Mills
Opening address for the plaintiff in the Barnes-Roosevelt libel case. HICJ:725

IVY ORATIONS See Commencement addresses

IZAAK WALTON CLUBS See Fishing
Jackson, Andrew
Farewell address, 1837. BRYW 8:209; CHAL 4:298; HAZO 9:3715; MAS 9:3715
First inaugural address. BIR 2:62; BRE:150; BREA:134; CHI:59; LOTI:57; USIN: 55; USINA:55
Protest to the Senate, April 15, 1833. BIR 2:90
Second inaugural address-"State rights and Federal sovereignty." BREW 7:145; BRYW 8:204; CHAL 4:294; CHI:63; COP:278; COPA: 278; COPB:278; HAZO 9: 3711; HURG:71; LOTI:61; MAS 9:3711; USIN:58; USINA:58
Veto message, July 10, 1832. BIR 2:84

JACKSON, ANDREW
Bancroft, G.
Political career of Andrew Jackson. CHAL 6:416; HAZO 13:5652; MAS 13: 5652; REEMA 11:110
Benton, T.H.
Political career of Andrew Jackson. BREW 2:16; REEMA 11:208
Bowers, C.G.
Sword of democracy. BOA: 243; BOB:150
Calhoun, J.C.
Denouncing Andrew Jackson. BREW 3:72
Clay, H.
Dictators in American politics. BREW 4:14; BRYW 9: 87; CHAL 5:28; HAZO 10: 4033; MAS 10:4033; REEMA 12:632
Dallas, G.M.
Eulogy on Andrew Jackson. CHAL 6:25; HAZO 12:5035; MAS 12:5035
Response to toast "General Jackson: a diamond in the rough, but a diamond." PITT:93
Roosevelt, F.D.
Jackson day address from the U.S.S. Potomac in the harbor of Ft. Lauderdale, Florida. VO 1941:144
Wallace, H.A.
Jackson Day dinner address. VO 1944-45:53
Wilson, W.
Jackson day dinner (Washington, January 8, 1912). PEAE:227
Jackson, Henry M.
United States in the United Nations: an independent audit. BA 1961-62:55
Jackson, Jerry
In behalf of the Kaghlir pledges. JUD:223
Jackson, Robert H.
Opening address before Nuremberg International Military Tribunal. BA 1945-46:60; VO 1945-46:734
Own method of speech training. BA 1945-46:60
Statement on War Trials Agreement. VO 1945-46:432
Why a college education?

Jackson, R. H. (cont.)
HOB:102; SAR:57
---- and others (G. Frank)
Essential differences between the Republican and Democratic parties. BA 1939-40: 233
See also Douglas, W. O., jt. auth.
Jackson, Samuel D.
Introducing Quentin Reynolds. BA 1944-45:123

JACKSON, THOMAS JONATHAN (STONEWALL JACKSON)
Cadman, S. P.
Stonewall Jackson. REEM 5:49; REEMB 9:79
Cooke, J. E.
Dead, he was immortal. HARSO:43
Hoge, M. D.
Stonewall Jackson. HARS: 273; PROS:116; SMI:181
Jacobi, Harold
Introducing a building and loan executive. BRC:290
Jacobi, Mary Putnam
Woman suffrage. WERN 42:17
Jacobs, Herbert H.
Patriotism. TRUW:33

JAMES, SIR FREDERICK
Talbot, P.
Introducing Sir Frederick James. MOA:501
James, Henry, Sr.
Social significance of our institutions. BL:231
James, Nevin S.
New frontier (distribution of wealth and labor conditions). ASHF:81
James I, King of England
State of monarchy and the divine right of kings. BRTH: 17; BRTHA:17
Jameson, John Franklin
Age of erudition. NORR 1st ser:326

JAMESTOWN, VIRGINIA
Henry, W.W.
Settlement of Jamestown. SMI:12

JAPAN
Dulles, J. F.
Japanese Peace Treaty. BA 1951-52:41; HAR:175
Higashi-Kuni, N.
Speech to the Japanese people upon becoming Premier. VO 1945-46:462
Hirohito.
Imperial rescript opening of the 87th Diet. VO 1945-46:284
Message at opening of 85th Diet. VO 1944-45:411
Inui, K. S.
Mission of new Japan. TRUW:203
Johnson, R. D.
White peril. BRP 6:112; NOR 1934:92
Kagawa, T.
New social order. PL:793
Koiso, K.
Address at opening of 85th Diet. VO 1944-45:413
Konoye, F.
Address before the 76th session of the Imperial Diet. VO 1941:40
Matsuoka, Y.
On the world state of emergency. VO 1941:330
Suzuki, U.
Speech before the Japanese Imperial Diet. VO 1945-46: 285
Togo, H.
Fallen heroes of Japan. WERN 42:50
Tojo, H.
Broadcast to the Japanese Empire. VO 1942-43:423
Remarks in cabinet meeting July 14, 1942. VO 1942-43:392
See also Tripartite Pact; World War 1939-1945-Japan; World War 1939-1945-Japan-Surrender

JAPAN-FOREIGN RELATIONS
Dallinger, C.
They that take the sword. BRP 5:36; YR 6:191
Matsuoka, Y.
Address delivered before the 76th session of the Imperial Diet. VO 1941:44
Statement on return to Tokyo from Europe, April 22, 1941. VO 1941:173
Togo, S.
To the Imperial Diet. VO 1941:515
Tojo, H.
At opening of Imperial Diet. VO 1942-43:308

---- ---- ASIA
Matsuoka, Y.
Address at opening of Thai-French Indo China Border Dispute Mediation Conference. VO 1941:76

JAPAN-HISTORY-ALLIED OCCUPATION, 1945-1952
Burton, M.
Military occupation of Japan. HOD:104
MacArthur, D.
Instructions to Japanese on occupation landings. VO 1945-46:486
Statement on policy in Japan. VO 1945-46:580
Statement on the occupation of Japan. VO 1945-46:581

JAPANESE IN THE UNITED STATES
Ikeguchi, J.
Promised land. AN:58
Kuroki, B.
War isn't over at home. BA 1945-46:208
Our greatest wartime blunder (by a Nisei student). LOMS: 228; LOMSA:287
Jason, William C.
Life's morn. DUNM:403
Jastrow, Joseph
Social traits and human nature. EXEE:97
Jaures, Jean
Debates with Clemenceau on question of capital and labor. -Same as his Program for socialism
Last speech. COP:128; COPA: 128; COPB:128; PL:752; REEM 11:11; REEMB 12: 11
Program of socialism (debate with G. Clemenceau). BRYW 7:208; PE:671; PEA:671; REEM 9:364; REEMB 10: 375
Socialists and the war. REEM 11:6; REEMB 12:7
Jay, John (1745-1829)
Address to the people of Great Britain. -Same as his Protest against colonial government
America free- or America slave. CHAL 9:159; HAZO 18:7691; MAS 18:7691
Protest against colonial government. BREW 7:149; CHAL 3:152; HAZO 7:2771; MAS 7:2771; ORAMA 1:149

JAY TREATY See Treaties

JAZZ MUSIC
Barrett, M.
"Music goes 'round and 'round." JUD:125
Bernstein, L.
World of jazz. ARNS:62
Pierson, L.
Jazz age. YR 4:285
Jeanne d'Arc See Joan of Arc
Jeans, Sir James
Why the sky looks blue. BRY: 432; BRYA:479
Jebb, Richard Claverhouse
Literature and art. REEMA 2: 686
Jefferson, Charles E.
Temptation from the mountain top. FUL:174, 178
Jefferson, Joseph
In memory of Edwin Booth. REEM 2:277; REEMA 2:

Jefferson, Joseph (cont.)
691; REEMB 2:281
My farm in Jersey. REEM 2:275; REEMA 2:688; REEMB 2:279
Jefferson, Thomas
First inaugural: democracy defined. ANG:220; BIR 1:251; BRE:111; BREA:109; BREW 7:160; BRYW 8:166; CHAL 3:122; CHI:13; COP:259; COPA:259; COPB:259; CROC:273; FKA:59; HARS:166; HAZO 7:2731; HELE:135; HIB:265; HURG:48; JOHA 1 pt. I:155; KLEG:314; LEEW 9:73; LOTI:15; MAS 7:2731; ORAMA 1:141; PAR:95; PO:49; REEM 10:46; REEMA 13:1255; REEMB 11:47; SMI:91; USIN:13; USINA:13; WPRA:50
Second inaugural address. CHI:18; LOTI:19; USIN:17; USINA:17
Speech to the chiefs of various Indian tribes. REEMA 13:1265
To Beaver, head-warrior of the Delawares. REEMA 13:1263
To the Wolf and people of the Mandan Indians. REEMA 13:1260

JEFFERSON, THOMAS
Aly, B.
Remarks on Jefferson Day. BA 1955-56:59
Bell, L. C.
Thomas Jefferson. SMI:294
Boyd, J. P.
Thomas Jefferson survives. NORR 3d ser:178
Breckenridge, W. C. P.
Jeffersonian democracy. SHUO:194
Byrd, H. F.
Jefferson day. SMI:276
Chase, S. P.
Thomas Jefferson and the Colonial view of manhood rights. BREW 3:212
Dill, C. C.
Thomas Jefferson, the architect of Americanism. BOA:226; BOB:139
Everett, E.
Adams and Jefferson. COP:269; COPA:269; COPB:269; HURG:64; KLEG:259; REEM 5:146; REEMA 8:439; REEMB 9:181
Hardin, A.
Jefferson and the Constitution. LEIO:91
Jones, E. D.
Adventures among great Americans. BART 1:115
Kellogg, F. B.
Thomas Jefferson: champion of common people (dedicating Jefferson's home). BRAC:347
King, S.
Americanism of Thomas Jefferson. YR 6:247
Roosevelt, F. D.
At the dedication of the Thomas Jefferson Memorial, Washington, D. C. VO 1943-44:163
Undelivered Jefferson Day address. CROC:392; VO 1945-46:147
Shaw, A.
Jefferson's doctrines under new tests. NORR 1st ser:298
Thomas Jefferson. DICD:134
Tyler, J.
Adams and Jefferson. SMI:104
Webster, D.
Eulogy on Adams and Jefferson. BREW 10:186; CHAL 5:296; CLAY:10; FKA:9; HARSO:348; HAZO 11:4447; KLEG:135; MAS 11:4447; PE:327; PEA:327; PROS:139; REEMA 15:2082; SHAH:134, 138
Williams, J. S.
Thomas Jefferson. REEM 5:405; REEMB 9:449

Wirt, W.
Death of Jefferson and Adams. BREW 10:259

JEFFRIES, EDWARD J.
Miller, M. G.
Introduces Mayor Edward J. Jeffries. PR:61
Jeffries, Henry A.
Salesman as a collector. LINM:47
Jeffries, Phil
Introducing an architect. BRC: 208
Jekyll, Sir Joseph
Resistance to unlawful authority (impeachment of H. Sacheverell). BREW 7:165
Jenkins, Martin D.
Function of Morgan State College (inaugural address as President of Morgan State College). HILK:94
Jenks, Almet F.
Observations of a jurist. REEM 2:281; REEMB 2:285
Jenks, Jeremiah Whipple
America's role in Europe. LINM:288
Jennings, H. C.
Outlook for the New Year. THOU 2:53
Jensen, Gordon
For this we fight. DO:103

JEPSON, R.W.
Potted thinking. HOB:69; SAR:26
Jepson, Stanley
Can our democracy survive our Congress? NOR 1943:23
Jeremiah.
Hear the word of the Lord, O King of Judah? (from the Bible). CROC:278
Jerome, Jerome K.
Ambition. SHU:221
Imaginary invalid. SHU:99
Jerrold, Douglas William
Whittington Club. REEMA 8: 739

JERUSALEM
Ben-Gurion, D.
Road to valor. CROC:17
Jesse, Richard Henry
Inaugural address as president of University of Missouri. WE 2:129
Jessel, George
Acceptance speech at Friars' Club dinner, 1948. JEYO: 125
Accepting the Humanitarian award at Friars' Club dinner, 1954. JEYO:118
Confirmation speech (model for a Jewish boy). JEYO:16
Eulogy on Robert Riskin. JEYO:158
Eulogy to Sid Grauman. JEYO: 162
"I am an American" Day. JEYO:153
Introducing Danny Kaye at Friars' Club dinner to Burns and Allen. JEYO:101
Introducing Danny Thomas at Friars' Club dinner to Burns and Allen. JEYO:92
Introducing Eddie Cantor at Friars' Club dinner to Burns and Allen. JEYO:76
Introducing ex-Mayor Fletcher Bowron of Los Angeles. JEYO:49
Introducing George Burns. JEYO:47
Introducing George Burns and Gracie Allen at Friars' Club dinner in their honor. JEYO:109
Introducing Groucho Marx. JEYO:47
Introducing Jack Benny. JEYO: 48
Introducing Jack Benny at Friars' Club dinner to Burns and Allen. JEYO:104
Introducing Jack Warner. JEYO:49
Introducing James Cagney at Friars' Club dinner to Burns and Allen. JEYO:80
Introducing Ronald Reagan at Friars' Club dinner to

Jessel, G. (cont.)
Burns and Allen. JEYO:82
Introducing Samuel Goldwyn at Friars' Club dinner to Burns and Allen. JEYO:98
Introducing William E. Goetz at Friars' Club dinner to Burns and Allen. JEYO:74
Introducing William S. Paley at Friars' Club dinner to Burns and Allen. JEYO:89
Presenting Louella Parsons at dinner in her honor. JEYO: 141
Remarks as toastmaster at Friars' Club dinner and introduction of David O. Schary. JEYO:71
Response to introduction as Toastmaster General at dinner in honor of Mannie Sack, and introduction of principal speaker, David Sarnoff. JEYO:55
Speech at Roastmaster dinner in honor of Dean Martin and Jerry Lewis. JEYO:45
Speech to a Kiwanis Club. JEYO:40
Speech to the Lions' Club. JEYO:35
Suggestions for eulogistic speeches. With examples of. JEYO:157
Suggestions for preparation of golden wedding anniversary speech. With example of. JEYO:29
Suggestions for preparation of silver wedding anniversary speech. With example of. JEYO:26
Suggestions for preparation of speeches at a bachelor dinner. With examples of. JEYO:23
Suggestions for preparation of valedictory address. With example of. JEYO:21
Suggestions for speeches to fraternal organizations. With examples of. JEYO:32
Sweet sixteen (suggestions for a girl's sixteenth birthday party). JEYO:18
To the Ladies of Hadassah. JEYO:146
To welcome a newly born-a model speech. JEYO:13
Toastmaster's speech at dinner honoring Jack Benny. JEYO:131
Tribute to the Elks. JEYO:32

JESSEL, GEORGE
Benny, J.
Speech as toastmaster at Friars' Club dinner honoring George Jessel. JEYO: 136

JESUITS
Thompson, J.S.
Question of simple justice. CHAL 14:3; HAZO 24:10533; MAS 24:10533

Jesus Christ
Delivers the Sermon on the Mount. PE:51; PEA:51
Jerusalem, Jerusalem (from the Bible). CROC:280

JESUS CHRIST
Aelred, Saint
On manliness. BREW 1:102
Anselm, Saint
Invocation to the Saviour. HAZO 3:1247; MAS 3:1247
Athanasius, Saint
Divinity of Christ. BREW 1:181; LEEW 3:73
Third discourse against the Arians. HAZO 3:1121; MAS 3:1121
Baxter, R.
Sermon on making light of Christ. HAZO 4:1548; MAS 4:1548
Beecher, H.W.
Nature of Christ. CLAY: 284
Bernard, Saint
Sermon on the passion of our Lord. HAZO 3:1254; MAS 3:1254

Shows that the name of Jesus Christ is a salutary medicine. PE:71; PEA:71
Bourdaloue, L.
Passion of Christ. BREW 2:190; BRYW 7:67; CHAL 2:106; HAZO 4:1611; LEEW 4:285; MAS 4:1611; PL: 250
Brooks, P.
Christ in whom Christians believe. HAZO 23:9923; MAS 23:9923
Bryan, W.J.
Prince of peace. BLAB: 367; IMMD:165; PL:697; REEM 8:68; REEMB 13:70
Calhoun, R.L.
Christ-the hope of the world. BA 1954-55:161
Channing, W.E.
Character of Christ. CHAL 5:130; HAZO 10:4210; MAS 10:4210
Colenso, J.M.
Example of our Lord. HAZO 18:7451; MAS 18:7451
Constantine I.
On the coming of our Lord in the flesh. LEEW 3:61
Cuyler, T.L.
Risen with Christ. THOU 2:144
Damiani, Peter, St.
Glory of the Cross of Christ. LEEW 3:314
Didon, H.
Christ and higher criticism. BREW 5:231; HAZO 24: 10340; MAS 24:10340
Drummond, H.
Alchemy of influence. HAZO 25:10805; MAS 25: 10805
Fallows, S.
Resurrection of Christ. THOU 2:99
Fosdick, Harry E.
Jesus' ethical message confronts the world. BA 1938-39:223
Fourth cross. JAS:40
Frank, G.
Jesus as a teacher. ONEC: 403
Gregory, Saint
On the baptism of Christ. LEEW 3:135
Herron, G.D.
Message of Jesus to men of wealth. WPRA:276
Irving, E.
Lord Jesus Christ. HAZO 12:5047; MAS 12:5047
Knox, J.
On the first temptation of Christ. BRYW 3:23; CHAL 1:436; HAZO 4:1341; MAS 4:1341
Latimer, H.
On Christian love. CHAL 1:396; HAZO 3:1283; MAS 3:1283
Luther, M.
Sermon on Peter's denial of Christ. HAZO 3:1298; MAS 3:1298
MacArthur, R.S.
Christ a living stone. THOU 2:440
Master and his troops. JA: 23
Mays, B.E.
Inescapable Christ. BA 1944-45:298
Moody, D.L.
What think ye of Christ? BRYW 10:74; CHAL 13:76; HAZO 23:10012; MAS 23: 10012; WERN 42:173
Nelson, B.G.
World's orator. TRUW:144
Parkhurst, C.H.
Man of sorrows. THOU 2: 80
Riggenbach, J.C.
Seven words of Jesus on the cross. THOU 2:141
Robertson, F.W.
Loneliness of Christ. CHAL 9:100; HAZO 18:7624; MAS 18:7624
Savonarola, G.
On the love of Jesus Christ. CHAL 1:389; HAZO 3:1276; MAS 3:1276

JESUS CHRIST (cont.)
Scherer, P.
Until he comes. BA 1955-56:175
Seabury, D.
How Jesus healed men's minds. BART 3:1
Spurgeon, C.H.
Condescension of Christ. CHAL 12:385; HAZO 23:9781; MAS 23:9781; PL:503
First appearance of the risen Lord to the eleven. THOU 2:109
Jesus and the children. THOU 2:156
Men made rich by the poverty of Christ. BRYW 5:119
Stanley, A. P.
Jesus of Nazareth. CHAL 9:94; HAZO 18:7604; MAS 18:7604
Star, the cross, and the cloud. JAS:58
Stephan, C. C.
Lord is your shepherd. ACW:17
Taylor, J.
Christ's advent to judgment. CHAL 2:83; HAZO 4:1533; MAS 4:1533
Tertullians, Q. S. F.
Shows. LEEW:3:225
Tittle, E. F.
Prince of Peace. BA 1943-44:329
Weinstock, H.
Jesus the Jew. WAGN:395
What does atonement mean? JAS:36
What manner of man is this? NATT:3
Whose child was Jesus? JAI:92
See also Good Friday

JEWELERS
Jewelers, by a fellow jeweler. EDGS:130
Walker, B.
Introducing a jeweler. BRC:222

Jewell, B.R.
Response to address of welcome. THOU 3:488

JEWELS, PRESENTATION OF
See Presentation speeches-Jewels

JEWS
Cawley, N.
Worth of the Jew. ASHF:142
Elward, R. A.
Wandering Jew. TRUW:61
Gilman, R.
Plea for my people. YR 6:327
Gottheil, R.
Jews as a race and as a nation. BREW 6:269
Harrison, L.
American citizenship and the American Jew. SHUO:119
Hebraism and culture. DAVC:37
Lehman, I.
Response of the President of the Jewish Welfare Board. ONEC:23
Macaulay, T. B.
Tribute to the Jews. BREW 8:24; CHAL 6:358; HAZO 13:5564; LEEW 7:215; MAS 13:5564; PE:431; PEA:431
Manning, H. E.
Persecution of the Jews. BEA:309; BOU:149; COP:191; COPA:191; COPB:191; REEM 7:270; REEMA 9:854; REEMB 7:266
Milner, S.
Jew. YR 7:231
Peel, Sir R.
On the disabilities of the Jews. LEEW 7:181; PL:443; REEMA 14:1544
Perlman, N. A.
Making a new start (sermon marking Jewish New Year). BA 1955-56:159
Rivkin, W.
Symbol of despotism.

BRP 10:23; NOR 1939:16
Samuels, M.
Where the fruit of freedom. LINM:365
Sheil, R. L.
On the disabilities of the Jews. BRTH:251; BRTHA: 251; BRYW 6:177; CHAL 5:438; HAZO 12:4948; MAS 12:4948
Sheppard, M.
Contributions of the Hebrew people to human advancement. SHUO:171
Sneed, L.
Wandering Jew. HARSO:288
Sunshine, M.
Procession. YR 6:339
Vance, Z. B.
Scattered nation. REEM 8: 390; REEMA 6:1115; REEMB 13:396; SHUO:175
Varney, G. R.
Jew. COUW:9
See also Bar Mitzvah speeches; Palestine

JEWS IN THE UNITED STATES
Cleveland, G.
Address at 250th anniversary of the settlement of the Jews in the United States. TWJ:11
Cohen, S. S.
Way in the sea and a path in the mighty waters. TWJ: 106
Eliot, C. W.
Address delivered at Faneuil Hall on 250th anniversary of the settlement of the Jews in the United States. TWJ:78
Fleischer, C.
Address delivered at Faneuil Hall on 250th anniversary of the settlement of the Jews in the United States. TWJ:89
Friedman, L. M.
Address delivered at Faneuil Hall on 250th anniversary of the settlement of the Jews in the United States. TWJ:61
Greer, D. H.
Address at 250th anniversary of the settlement of the Jews in the United States. TWJ:49
Guild, C., Jr.
Address delivered at Faneuil Hall on 250th anniversary of the settlement of the Jews in the United States. TWJ:65
Heller, M.
Address delivered at New Orleans on 250th anniversary of the settlement of the Jews in the United States. TWJ:164
Higgins, F. W.
Address at 250th anniversary of the settlement of the Jews in the United States. TWJ:23
Hirsch, E. G.
Concordance of Judaism and Americanism. TWJ:148
Kohler, K.
Room for all. TWJ:131
Krauskoff, J.
Jewish Pilgrim fathers. TWJ:121
Lawrence, W.
Address delivered at Faneuil Hall on 250th anniversary of the settlement of the Jews in the United States. TWJ:84
McClellan, G. B.
Address at 250th anniversary of the settlement of the Jews in the United States. TWJ:26
Mack, J. W.
Pledge of the American Jew. TWJ:142
Marshall, L.
Address delivered in Albany on 250th anniversary of the settlement of the Jews in the United States. TWJ:93

JEWS IN THE UNITED STATES (cont.)
Pardee, G. C.
Address delivered in San Francisco at 250th anniversary of the settlement of the Jews in the United States. TWJ:172
Philipson, D.
Jew as a liberal force. TWJ:136
Schiff, J. H.
Introduction at the 250th anniversary of the settlement of the Jews in the United States. TWJ:8
Straus, O. S.
Address delivered at Faneuil Hall on 250th anniversary of the settlement of the Jews in the United States. REEM 7:374; REEMB 8:395; TWJ:69
Sulzberger, M.
Oration at 250th anniversary of the settlement of the Jews in the United States. TWJ:30
Voorsanger, J.
Influence of Americanism upon the Jew. TWJ:183
Jha, Amarnath
Educational problems. ZU:52

JOAN OF ARC
Ireland, J.
Joan of Arc. WERN 42:79
Norvell, G.
Joan of Arc. COUW:165

JOBS See Business; Occupations, choice of; Vocational guidance; Work

JOB'S DAUGHTERS, INTERNATIONAL ORDER OF
Fairest in all the land. JA: 106

JOCKEY CLUB
For a jockey club dinner. BARB:169
John, Vernon S.
Civilized interiors. HILK: 70

JOHN, SAINT
Savonarola, G.
On the first epistle of St. John. CHAL 1:386; HAZO 3:1273; MAS 3:1273
Johnnedes, M.
Immigrant in America. YR 1: 131

JOHNS HOPKINS UNIVERSITY
Alderman, E. A.
Greetings to Johns Hopkins. ONES:82
Gilman, D. C.
Inaugural address as president of Johns Hopkins University. WE 1:293
Johnson, Andrew
Annual message to Congress, December 3, 1866. ANG: 387
At St. Louis. CHAL 7:364; HAZO 15:6321; MAS 15: 6321
Inaugural address. BREW 7: 169
Presidential plan of Reconstruction. HARSO:423
Proposed expulsion of Mr. Bright from the Senate of the United States. SOU 9: 345
Veto of the first Reconstruction Act, 1867. BIR 3:41

JOHNSON, ANDREW
Boutwell, G. S.
President Johnson's 'High crimes and misdemeanors.' BREW 2:204
Butler, B. F.
"Article Ten" (Impeaching A. Johnson). BREW 3:18
Chase, S. P.
Mississippi v. Johnson, 1867: opinion for the Supreme Court. BIR 3:58
Curtis, B. R.
Defense of President Johnson. BREW 4:334; HARS:

444
Evarts, W. M.
Weakest spot in the American system (defense at impeachment of Johnson). BREW 6:56
Johnson, Burges
Lost art of profanity. EXEE: 315
Johnson, Fred L.
Battleship bubble. BRP 7:13
Johnson, Gerald W.
Provincial scholar. NORR 3d ser:273
Johnson, Herbert N.
Diplomacy of good will. BRP 1:29; YR 1:65
Johnson, Hiram Warren
Against intimidating the Press. BREW 7:178
Johnson, Hugh S.
Depression and the President. COP:418; COPA:418
Farewell address to the employees of the National Recovery Administration. DOA:63
Follow the leader. BOB:13
Should Mr. Roosevelt's plan for enlarging the Supreme Court be adopted? (affirmative). SAR:221
Johnson, James Weldon
Our democracy and the ballot. WOON:663
Johnson, Louis A.
National defense. BA 1949-50: 85

JOHNSON, LOUIS A.
Introducing Louis Johnson. NI:108; NIA:84
Johnson, Lyndon Baines
Address to a Joint Session of Congress, March 15, 1965. BA 1964-65:9
Address to Nation, October 18, 1964. BA 1964-65:45
At 44th anniversary of Congressional service of Speaker Sam Rayburn. BRAP:136
First address to the nation, November 22, 1963. HIB: 18; PEA:843
Inaugural address. CHI:307; USINA:271
Remarks to a Joint Session of the Congress, November 27, 1963. BA 1963-64:37
State of the Union Message, January 8, 1964. FIP:409
Johnson, Marydee
Cry baby! YR 5:357
Johnson, Mordecai W.
Faith of the American Negro (at Harvard commencement). WOON:658
Speech to the Atlantic Congress. HILK:245
Johnson, R. D.
White peril. BRP 6:112; NOR 1934:92

JOHNSON, SAMUEL
Birrell, A.
Transmission of Dr. Johnson's personality. REEM 1:119; REEMA 7:87; REEMB 1:116
Johnsrud, Harold
Liberal college. ASHF:33
Johnston, Eric A
Competition: lifeblood of American capitalism. BA 1953-54:162
Crisis on the home front. SAC:114
High cost of bigotry. BA 1950-51:112; BAAGA:436
Intolerance. BA 1944-45:175
Mr. Perkins returns to the land of the Bolsheviks. BA 1956-57:40
Partners for peace (Marshall plan). HOA:145
Steps toward a good world. HAN:374
Warning to labor-and to management. BA 1943-44:200
Johnston, Howard A.
Sabbath school kite strings. THOU 2:212
Jonas, Benjamin F.
Confederate dead (at laying of corner-stone to memory of

Jonas, B. F. (cont.)
Confederate dead) SHUO:31
Jones, Cecil
International racketeer. BRP 6:36; YR 6:255
Jones, Edgar DeWitt
Abraham Lincoln. BART 2:7
Adventures among great Americans. BART 1:115
Faith of our fathers. BA 1942-43:287
Jones, George P.
American city. TRUW:177
Jones, Glenn
Telesis. YR 3:59
Jones, Harry W.
Triumvirate of crime. BRP 3:80; YR 4:141
Jones, Hilton Ira
Study in self management. EXEE:146
Jones, Jenkin Lloyd
Who is tampering with the soul of America? LINP:219

JONES, JENKIN LLOYD
Kent, W.
Jenkin Lloyd Jones. REEM 5:258; REEMB 9:297
Jones, Jesse S.
Masonry and the State. THOU 3:57
Jones, John George
Vision and progress. REEM 4:228
Jones, John P.
On treasury notes and silver. JOHA 2 pt 2:347
Jones, Leonard
Breaking down barriers. YR 8:177
Jones, Lewis Webster
Inaugural address as president of University of Arkansas. WE 2:327
Spirit of '76 and the barbarian culture (175th anniversary of Phi Beta Kappa). NORR 3d ser:203
Jones, Olive
'Watchman, tell us of the night'' (at 5th annual meeting of Dept. of Superintendence of N. E. A.) BRAC:30
Jones, Robert E.
Few remarks on making a life (commencement address). DUNM:455
Jones, Sam
Thunder and lightning on sinner's heads. SOU 9:500
Jones, Thomas Roy
Presentation of Gantt gold medal to Fowler McCormick. YE:114
Jones, W. Alton
Responds to an introduction. PRNE:76

JONES, W. ALTON
Coulter, T. H.
Introduces W. Alton Jones, President, Cities Service Company. PRNE:38
Jordan, David Starr
Higher education for women. REEM 6:295; REEMA 8:745; REEMB 7:244
Inaugural address as president of Stanford University. WE 1:351
Lest we forget. BLAA:127; BLAB:127
Nation's need of men. HARSO:238
Pyramids of skulls. BREW 7:180
Strength of being clean. WAGN:423
Jordan, Edward Stanlaw
Advertising automobiles. REEM sup 2:126; REEMB 5:32
Jordan, Thomas W.
Penalties of progress (baccalaureate address). SHUO:86

JORDAN
Eisenhower, D. D.
Plan for peace in Lebanon. BA 1958-59:23

Joseph, Chief, The Nez Perce
From where the sun now stands. GRIS:47
Jouett, John H.

Air. HUS:269
JOURNALISM AND JOURNALISTS
Amateur journalists. SCHS:16
Blakelev. R. J.
Constant crusade. BA 1951-52:152
Booher, E. E.
What makes a good editor? HIBS:473
Burnham, H. L. W.
Journalism. BEA:77
Clark, T. D.
Country newspaper: a factor in Southern opinion, 1865-1930. TIN:211
Country weekly. SCHS:87
Crocker, L.
On seas of ink. MOUG:189; MOUGA:189
Dana, C. A.
Journalism. REEM 6:97; REEMA 7:278; REEMB 6:47
New England in journalism. REEMA 1:321
Editors (country editor speaks). ED:250
Gilbert, E. J.
Introducing a newspaper editor. BRC:158
Gilmer, Mrs. E. M.
Experiences of a woman columnist. YE:327
Grant, U. S.
Characteristics of newspaper men. HOA:374; HOAP:261; REEMA 2:559
Introducing guest of honor (at testimonial dinner to journalist). BED:22; BEDA:36
Introducing journalist. BED:20; BEDA:35
Kaltenborn, H. V.
College and the press. SHUC:10
Kaser, A. L.
Introducing a newspaper editor. BRC:52
McClure, A. K.
Editorial retrospect. REEMA 2:799
Markel, L.
Future of the printed word. BRAP:143
O'Keefe, L.
Introducing a newspaper reporter. BRC:230
Opening speech (at testimonial dinner to journalist). BED:20; BEDA:34
Perry, J. H.
Newspaper law. BYRA:318; REEM sup 2:269; REEMB 6:290
Presenting award (to journalist at testimonial dinner). BED:20; BEDA:35
Thigpen, W.
Death among the dailies. SOBP:338
White, W. A.
Country newspaper. REEM 6:412; REEMB 6:381
Whitney, J. H.
Challenges and excellences (accepting degree). BA 1964-65:120
See also Press
Joyner, James Y.
Tribute to Calvin Henderson Wiley (at unveiling of monument). SHUO:284

JUBILEE CELEBRATIONS See Anniversaries
Judd, Walter H
Responds to an introduction. PRNE:51

JUDD, WALTER H.
Nuveen, J.
Introduces Dr. Walter H. Judd, Congressman from Minnesota. PRNE:14

JUDGES See Law and lawyers; United States-Supreme Court

JUDGMENT
Cynic critic. THOT:97
Gallup, G.
Judgment of the common people. ON:200

JUDGMENT (cont.)
Thwing, C. F.
Value of judgment. BLAA: 16; BLAB:16
Judson, Edward
Child conversion. THOU 2:177
Effect of the resurrection upon the character of Peter. THOU 2:128
Judson, Lyman S.
Crime and criminal court. ASHF:126

JUGGLERS See Actors and acting
Juliana, Queen of the Netherlands
Students of Paris. BUT:242; BUTB:235

JUNGFRAU See Switzerland
Junius, Marcus
On ransoming the prisoners. LEEW 2:112

JURY
Black, J.
Right to trial by jury. BRAC:100; ONEM:83; RINM:131
Curtis, B.R.
Instruction to the jury. ONEM:112
Erskine, T.
On the rights of juries. GOOD:655
Medina, H.R.
Charge to jury. BA 1949-50:136
Roberts, O.J.
Trial procedure-past, present, and future. ONEC:436
Taney, R.B.
Opinion in the Merryman Case. ANG:310
For speeches to the Jury See Defense, speeches of; Prosecution
Jusserand, Jean Jules
Address at the unveiling of the bust of Abraham Lincoln in the Hall of Fame, New York University, May 1923. LINM:83
American gratitude to France. BREW 7:183
"Der Tag." BREW 7:182
Tennis cabinet (on T. Roosevelt). BREW 7:187
Truth and beauty in books and art. BREW 7:184

JUSTICE
Buckner, E.R.
Securing justice. ONEC:410
Cicero, M.T.
Supernatural justice. BREW 3:352
Clayton, J.M.
Justice the supreme law of nations. BREW 4:61
Corbett, F.E.
Weighted scales. BRP 2:10; YR 2:81
Evolution of justice. FRIE:92
Example of conciliatory speech on new plan for districting. MICS:176
Hooker, R.
Sermon on the nature of justice. LEEW 4:169
Isaiah.
Cries out for social justice. PE:5; PEA:5
Mather, B.I.
Goal of delinquent justice. ONES:372
Medina, H.E.
Equal justice for all. HIBS:476
Mock justice. FRIE:103
Muhammad, E.
We must have justice. HILK:292
Nevin, A.P.
Speech for all occasions. MIA:416
Pleasants, A.W.
Reign of technicality. SHUC:398
Roosevelt, F.D.
Philosophy of social justice through social action (campaign speech in Detroit, October 2, 1932). ARNS:129
Roosevelt, T.
Social and industrial injus-

tice. SHU:214
Thompson, J. S.
Question of simple justice. CHAL 14:3; HAZO 24:10533; MAS 24:10533

JUSTIN MARTYR
Justin Martyr, courageous Christian. JAS:16

JUVENILE DELINQUENCY See Boys Town; Crime and criminals
Kaber, William C.
Value of district heating to the community. MO:458
Kabir, Humayun
Rabindranath Tagore. ZU:66
Kagawa, Toyohiko
New social order. PL:793
Kahn, Benjamin M.
Marks of an educated man. ANGC:34
Kahn, Julius
Civil government for the Philippine Islands. WAGN:405
Kahn, Otto Hermann
Edward Henry Harriman. REEM 5:240; REEMB 9:279
New York Stock Exchange and public opinion. BRYA:251; REEM 4:230; REEMB 5:42
Prussianized Germany. SAA: 274
Talk to young business men. REEM sup 2:136; REEMB 5:55
Value of art to the people. LINM:227
Kaiser, Henry J., Jr.
Knowledge: our strongest weapon. SABA:271
Kaissouni, Abdel Moneim El
Inaugural speech at Conference on the Problems of Economic Development. UAR:321
Speech at final session of Conference on the Problems of Economic Development. UAR:427
Kalas, J. Ellsworth
Call to spiritual greatness. NOR 1950:199
Kalinin, Mikhail
New Year's address. VO 1944-45:5
Kaltenborn, H. V.
College and the press. SHUC: 10
Czechoslovakia capitulates. BA 1938-39:18
Germany invades Holland and Belgium. BA 1939-40:68
Hitler's fifty-second birthday. BA 1940-41:149
Looking at Europe from here. BART 1:143
---- and others (G. V. Denny, Jr., and B. McMahon)
How can we secure peace in a hydrogen bomb world? BA 1949-50:101
Kandt, William
Prospects. YR 6:347
Kane, Frank G.
Michigan Union. KNAS:272; KNASA:272

KANE, ELISHA
Hedges, J. E.
Birthday of Dr. Kane. REEM 2:185; REEMB 2: 187

KANSAS
Douglas, S. A.
Kansas and "Squatter sovereignty." BREW 5:297
Dreiling, N. R.
This is Knasas. AN:70
Price, C. W.
Kansas and its governor. REEM 3:112; REEMB 3:113
Sumner, C.
Crime against Kansas. BREW 9:323; BRYW 9:160; CHAL 8:262; CHEM 3:225; COP:291; COPA:291; COPB: 291; HARS:294; HAZO 17: 6995; HURG:85; JOHA 2 pt. 1:88; MAS 17:6995; REEM 10:150; REEMA 15:1952; REEMB 11:154; SHAH:314

KANSAS INDUSTRIAL COURT
Allen, H. J.

KANSAS INDUSTRIAL COURT (cont.)
Kansas Industrial Court. REEM 7:9; REEMB 8:9

KANSAS-NEBRASKA BILL
Chase, S. P.
On the Kansas Nebraska Bill. CHAL 7:307; HAZO 15:6226; JOHA 2 pt 1:3; MAS 15:6226; REEMA 12: 547
Douglas, S. A.
Appeal of the Independent Democrats. ANG:267
Kansas-Nebraska Bill. BRAS:114; CHEM 3:147; HAZO 17:7331; JOHA 2 pt. 1:50; LEEW 10:167; MAS 17:7331; PL:678; SHAH:287
Everett, E.
On the Kansas-Nebraska Bill. JOHA 2 pt 1:32
Houston, S.
On the Kansas and Nebraska Bill. CHAL 6:44; HAZO 12:5073; MAS 12:5073
Kanzell, Herbert N.
And the patient began to die. NOR 1947:95
Kaplan, A.
Half slave, half free. YR 9: 195
Kaplan, Abraham
How many centuries of progress? BRP 6:31; YR 7:47

KAPPA KAPPA GAMMA See Greek letter societies
Kappel, Frederick R.
Business needs basic research. SABA:230
Karos, Peter A.
Haven for the defeated. ARNS: 160; NOR 1950:187
Kaser, Arthur L.
Emcee at an army buddies' reunion
" at a barbers' convention
" at a business men's get-together
" at a camera fans' meeting
Emcee at a family reunion
" at a foremen's banquet
" at a gardeners' club
" at a letter carriers' club meeting
" at a liars' club meeting
" at a newly-weds' party
" at a pre-game rally
" at a readers' and writers' club meeting
" at a salesmen's convention (2)
" at a stag dinner. BRH: See Table of contents, section III for paging
Introducing an actor
" an actress
" an authority on diet
" a ballet
" a comedian
" a dancing team
" an English comedian
" a gay nineties revue or act
" a German comedian
" a hillbilly pianist
" an Irish comedian
" a lady monologist
" a local orchestra
" a magician
" a mind reader
" a musician
" a quartette
" a retiring teacher (upper grades)
" a Scotch comedian
" a singing quartette
" a speaker on fire prevention (2)
" a Swedish comedian
" a television personality
" a variety revue. BRH: See Table of contents, section II for paging
Introducing an advertising man
" an airline stewardess
" an animal husbandry, speaker of
" an artist
" a baby specialist
" a banker
" a baseball player
" a beauty expert

Introducing a Boy Scout executive
" a book publisher
" a business man
" a college president
" a Communism, speaker on
" a community singing expert
" a Congressman
" a dentist
" a doctor
" a doctor speaking on obesity
" a dog fancier
" an educator
" an evolution, speaker on
" a farmer or agricultural expert
" a fisherman (expert)
" a food specialist
" a football coach
" a gardening expert
" a health, authority on
" a health and accident week, speaker on
" an insurance man
" an interior decorator
" a judge
" a junior voters, speaker on
" a labor leader
" a minister
" a newspaper editor
" a nurses' training, speaker on
" an optimist
" an orchestra leader
" a politician
" a poet
" a problem child, speaker on
" a P.T.A. president
" a professor
" a psychiatrist
" a public spirited citizen
" a radio actor
" a recruiting officer
" a salesman (top)
" a social reform, speaker on
" a tax consultant
" a telephone executive
" a town mayor
Introducing a traffic officer
" a travel agent
" a world traveler. BRC: See Table of contents for paging
Time out for the sponsor (a fill-in for the emcee). BRH: 325

Kato, K.
Speech at the Washington Conference on the Limitations of Armaments (November 15, 1921). REEM 11:396; REEMB 12:416

Kaufman, Irving J.
Sentencing atomic bomb spies. BA 1951-52:55

Kay-Schuttleworth, R.W.P. See Young, B., jt. auth.

Kaye, Danny
Speech at Friars' Club dinner to Burns and Allen. JEYO: 102

KAYE, DANNY
Jessel, G.
Introducing Danny Kaye at Friars' Club dinner to Burns and Allen. JEYO: 101

Kazmark, Leah Adkisson
Honoring a great American day. PROS:10

Keane, Steven
Son of Phaeton. BRP 5:31

KEARNY, PHILIP
Morrow, W.W.
General Philip Kerny (statuary Hall, House of Representatives). WAGN:226

Kearny, Stephen Watts and others (Bantista Vigil)
Armijo is no longer your governor. GRIS:48

Keating, Edward
Courage of Woodrow Wilson. HARSO:38

Keating, John T.
Progress of the Order (Hibernian's address at 42nd biennial convention). THOU 3:544

Keefe, Donald Foran
Our too liberal arts. YR 9: 239
Keesey, Ray
Aristocracy of the unfit. BRP 8:44; YR 9:165
Kefauver, Estes
Menace of organized crime. BA 1951-52:51
Our Presidential election system. MO:464
Speech at National Corn Picking Contest in Nebraska. BRAP:47
Vote Democratic. BA 1956-57: 85

KEFAUVER, ESTES
Waller, H. H.
Presents Estes Kefauver. LY:221
Kehl, Donald
Higher individualism. YR 3: 111
Keller, Helen
Appeal for the blind. DOA:190
Keller, Stephen
Introducing a collection manager
" a detective or policeman
" a physician. BRC:180, 104, 68
Kelley, G. V.
Fifth horseman: danger of antiquated state policies in industry. ASHF:87
Kellogg, Elijah (accredited to)
Regulus to the Carthagenians. CLAY:105; HARSO:333
Regulus to the Roman Senate. HARSO:337
Spartacus to the gladiators. CLAY:114; DICD:139; DICE:139; HARSO:344; PROS:136
Spartacus to the Roman envoys. HARSO:341
Kellogg, Frank Billings
Thomas Jefferson: champion of the common people (dedicating Jefferson's home). BRAC:347
To the American Society of international Law, April 28, 1928. KESB:398

KELLOGG BRIAND PACT, August 27, 1928
Briand, A.
On the anti-war treaty. PL:770
See also League of Nations
Kelly, Thomas F.
Lincoln and the Constitution. LEIO:137
Kelman, John
Puritanism today. REEM 2: 286; REEMB 2:290
Kelts, William P.
Spirit of Lincoln-the need of our time. SHUC:77
Kelvin, William Thompson, 1st Baron
Inspiration and the highest education (commemoration of J. P. Nichol). BREW 7: 189
Kemal Atatürk, Mustafa
Speech before the Republican Party. PL:788
Kendrick, B. B.
Colonial status of the South. TIN:90
Kennan, George F.
Liberal arts in contemporary American society. BA 1953-54:171
Kennan, George F.
National interest of the United States. HAR:80
Kennedy, Gerald
Awake the dawn. BA 1956-57: 181
Dedicated to a proposition. BA 1963-64:71
Kennedy, John B.
'What's wrong with the world?" BART 2:209

KENNEDY, JOHN B.
Introducing John B. Kennedy, author, radio and newsreel commentator. SUM:76
Kennedy, John Fitzgerald
Address to the nation October 22, 1962. BA 1962-63:7;

FIP:388
Addresses the General Assembly of the United Nations for the second and last time, September 22, 1963. PEA:840
Alliance for progress. FIP: 379
Berlin crisis. BA 1961-62:7
Birmingham. FIP:399
Cuba. I. FIP:385
Cuba II. - Same as his Address to the nation, October 22, 1962
Education of an American politician. BRAP:123
Inaugural address. ARNS:256; BA 1960-61:35; BAAGA: 398; BOU:3; CAP:231; CHI:301; FIP:374; HIB: 283; LINP:161; LOTI:269; PEA:831; SOBP:335; USIN: 267; USINA:267; WPRC:317
Intellectual and the politician. BA 1956-57:165; BARR: 285; LINP:279
Kennedy-Ives Bill. BA 1958-59:79
"Let us call a truce to terror." BA 1961-62:41
Medical care through social security: why it should be supported. HIB:305
New frontier. BA 1960-61:7
Peace Corps. FIP:378
Peace through the United Nations. HIB:344
Portraits of five senators in the Senate reception room. BA 1957-58:84
Religion in government (to Greater Houston Ministerial Association). HIB:178
Role of the President. BA 1959-60:123
Step toward peace. BA 1963-64:20
Tax cut. FIP:393
Toward a strategy of peace. BA 1963-64:9
Undelivered Dallas speech. FIP:402
---- and others (W. H. Lawrence; G. Herman and S. Vanocur). Conversations with the President. BA 1962-63:145
---- and others (Hubert H. Humphrey, Jr.) Kennedy-Humphrey television debate. BERS:156

KENNEDY, JOHN FITZGERALD
Johnson, L. B.
Remarks to a Joint Session of the Congress, November 27, 1963. BA 1963-64:37
McCormack, J. W.
Eulogy on John F. Kennedy. HIB:19
Mansfield, M. J.
Eulogy on John F. Kennedy. HIB:20
Stevenson, A. E.
Tribute to John Kennedy at the General Assembly of the United Nations. BA 1963-64:31
Warren, E.
Tribute to John F. Kennedy delivered in the Rotunda of the Capitol. BA 1963-64:33; HIB:21
Wilkins, R.
Tribute to John F. Kennedy delivered at City Hall Plaza in New York City. BA 1963-64:34

KENNEDY-IVES BILL See Kennedy, J. F.

KENNEY, GEORGE C.
Fisher, C. T., Jr.
Presents George C. Kenney. LY:159
Kenngott, George F.
Church and fraternity. THOU 3:372
Kenny, Michael
Freemasonry and Catholicism in America. CATA 2:194
Kent, Rockwell See Bryson, L., jt. auth.
Kent, William
Jenkin Lloyd Jones. REEM 5: 258; REEMB 9:297

KENTUCKY
Watterson, H.
Once a Kentuckian, always a Kentuckian. SOU 9:472

KENTUCKY, UNIVERSITY OF
Donovan, H. L.
What I see from my window: inaugural address as president of University of Kentucky. WE 2:233
Kenworthy, Robert Judson
Freemasonry and citizenship. REEM 2:292; REEMB 2:296
Keokuk, Sauk and Fox chief
Farewell speech. JON:96
Kerensky, Alexander
Declaration of the Labor Party. REEM 11:61; REEMB 12:68
Kerensky, Alexander
To working men and soldiers. COP:139; COPA:139; COPB:139; REEM 11:174; REEMB 12:187
Kernan, Thomas J.
Louisiana (response to toast). SHUO:224
Kerr, Deborah See Murrow, E.R., jt. auth.
Kerr, Robert S.
Congressional critic's view of General MacArthur's speech to Congress. BRAP:155
Ketcham, Victor Alvin
Passing of war. SHUC:269
Seven doors to the mind and how to open them. YE:266
Kettering, Charles F.
Accepting award of American Alumni council. YE:159
Muscles and machines. GLAD: 285

KETTERING CHARLES F.
Boyd, W.R., Jr.
Presentation of API gold medal to Charles F. Kettering. SAB:209; SABA: 289
Budd, R.
Introduces Charles F. Kettering. PR:48
Ford, K. L.
Presentation of award to Charles F. Kettering. YE: 121
Martin, T.W.
Presents Charles F. Kettering. LY:180

KEY, FRANCIS SCOTT
Watterson, H.
Francis Scott Key (at dedication of monument). REEMA 9:1143
Keyes, E.
Significance of this holiday (Liberty day). THOU 1:492
Keyes, Frances Parkinson
Current trends in literature. GA:237
Presenting a gift. GA:37

KEYNOTE SPEECHES See Campaign speeches

KEYS See Acceptance speeches-Keys; Presentation speeches-Keys
Kher, B. G.
Lokmanya Bal Gangadhar Tilak-a tribute. ZU:45
Khrushchev, Nikita S.
Basic indictment (speech of October 17). RUS:17
Future of the Soviet economy (from his report on the Third Program of the Soviet Communist Party-delivered October 18). RUS: 234
Rejoinder to debate (October 27) RUS:118
Reveals some of the crimes of Stalin. PEA:826
State of the Soviet economy (from his report for the Central Committee-delivered October 17). RUS:184
Kiefer, Alois F.
Trumpets of the dawn. INTW 1933:24; YR 5:175
Kiekhofer, William H.
Response to an introduction. PR:127

Kienzle, George J.
Report of a research study in public relations. SABA:197
Kiewiet, Cornelis W. de
How different types of institutions are planning for the future. BA 1955-56:131
Kildee, Regina
Speech for honors day banquet. JUD:199
Killefer, Frances
Challenge to college students. ASHF:50; BRAC:13
Killens, John O. See Baldwin, J., jt. auth.
Killian, James R., Jr. See Douglas, P.H., jt. auth.
Kiltz, Alfred A.
America goes abroad (attack upon America's foreign policy in East and South). ASHF:246
Kimball, Edward A.
On Christian science. CHAL 13:491
Kimball, Leonard L.
Case for American labor. YR 3:21
King, Ernest J.
American postwar seapower and control of Pacific bases. BA 1944-45:83
King, John Lewis
Long live the orator. BLUE: 88
Pioneer blood. BLUE:81; BRP:3:33; YR 3:13
King, Martin Luther, Jr.
"I have a dream." BA 1963-64:43; BOU:157; HIB:173; HILK:371; LINP:156; PEA:835
Love, law, and civil disobedience. HILK:345; LINP:52
King, Rufus
For federal government by the people. BREW 7:193
Navigation Act. HAZO 8:3200; MAS 8:3200; ORAMA 1:193
On the Missouri Bill. JOHA 1 pt. 2:33
King, Stephen
Americanism of Thomas Jefferson. YR 6:247
King, Thomas Starr
High school dedication speech. WAGN:21
On the privilege and duties of patriotism. CHAL 10:395; HAZO 20:8748; MAS 20: 8748
Substance and show. REEMA 5:669
True greatness. REAC:83
King, W. L. Mackenzie
Address to both Houses of Parliament at Westminster on Canada's war effort and the Commonwealth. VO 1944-45:207
British Constitution in the dominions, (speech of July 23, 1926). KESB:149
Canada and the war. COP:488; COPA:488; COPB:458
France and Canada. REEM 7: 198; REEMB 8:225
Speech in House of Commons, June 9, 1924 (on ratification of Treaty of Lausanne). KESB:322
To Marshall Foch. REEM 7: 202; REEMB 8:229

KING, W. L. MACKENZIE
Lamont, T.W.
Presents W. L. Mackenzie. LY:225
King-Chau Mui
China and the international situation. HAN:327

KINGS AND RULERS See Monarchy

KING'S DAUGHTERS AND SONS, ORDER OF
Bottome, M.
International Order of the King's Daughters and Sons. THOU 2:598
Kingsley, Charles
Human soot; address at Liverpool in behalf of the Kirkdale Ragged Schools. BREW 7:196

Kingsley, Charles (cont.)
Transfiguration. CHAL 9:428; HAZO 19:8060; MAS 19: 8060
Westminster Abbey. REEMA 5:691

KINGSLEY, CHARLES
Clemens, S. L.
Introducing Charles Kingsley. ANDS:197; ONEM:668; REEMA 5:691
Kingsley, Darwin Pearl
In honor of Charles M. Schwab. REEM 4:243; REEMB 5:62
Introducing M. Viviani, first War Premier of France. REEM 2:300; REEMB 2:303
Raise a standard. REEM 2: 294; REEMB 2:298
Kipling, Rudyard
American invasion of England. REEM 11:300; REEMB 12:317
Strength of England. REEM 2: 303; REEMB 2:307
Kirby, John, Jr.
Labor and legislation (valedictory as President of National Association of Manufacturers). REEM 4:248; REEMB 5:67
Kirby, John Henry
Patriotism. NESA:130
Re-Americanize America. BOA:397
Kirk, Grayson
Historical perspective and current issues. BA 1952-53: 151
Responds to an introduction. PRNE:70
Responsibilities of the educated man (at centennial of University of Denver). LINP:165
United States and the world. ANGC:218
Kirk, H. H.
Academic freedom: are we ready for it? SAR:93
Kirk, Leslie
Introducing a General. BRC: 322
Kirkland, James H.
Inaugural address as chancellor of Vanderbilt University. WE 1:327
Kirkpatrick, Russell
Hope of peace. ONES:333
Kirsten, Kirk
Introducing a Senator or Congressman. BRC:156

KISSING
Huber, L. J.
Introducing a kissing booth. BRH:74
Kissling, Albert
Living democracy. ASHF:9
Kitchen, John M.
Arm of the law. BRP 3:18
Kitchener of Khartoum, Horatio Herbert Kitchener, 1st Earl
More men. REEM 11:86; REEMB 12:95
Relief of Khartoum. REEMA 2: 694

KITCHENER OF KHARTOUM, HORATIO HERBERT KITCHENER, 1st EARL OF
Oxford and Asquith, H. H. A.
Lord Kitchener. REEM 5:7; REEMB 9:36
Salisbury, R. A. T. G.
Kitchener in Africa. REEM 3:184; REEMA 3:1018; REEMB 3:191

KIWANIS CLUB
Builder or wrecker. JA:112
Jessel, G.
Speech to a Kiwanis Club. JEYO:40
Kiwanis. NATS:23
Kiwanis. SCHS:160
Kiwanis Club. EDGS:85
Kiwanis Club (suitable for any civic club). EDGS:85
Message of appreciation before the local service club (Rotary, Kiwanis, Lions, etc.). DR:99; LU:1166

No figs from thistles. JA:109
Speech for retiring president of Kiwanis Club. AMEO 2:214
Klausner, Neal W.
Humanities: mirrors of genius. BRAP:96
Klein, Arthur
Tell me how to belong. BRP 10:17; NOR 1939:9
Kleiner, H. G.
Voice of God and the verdict of experience. ACW:52
Klemp, Oscar C.
Commit your way unto the Lord. ACW:25
Klepper, Raezella
Supreme jig saw puzzle of life. YR 5:253
Kline, Allan Blair
Long range farm program. BA 1949-50:196
Kline, B.J.
Fraternal societies, origin and history. THOU 3:185
Kline, R.E. Pattison
What do you think when you think? EXEE:218
Klumpp, Theodore G.
New look at the old ticker. BRYA:489
Knapp, Frank
America first. BOA:66
Knapp, Martin A.
Necessity for adequate railway revenues. PEAE:107
Knapp, Samuel L.
Address, 1829. BRAR 1:141
Knauth, Oswald W.
Fundamentals of merchandising. HOA:88
Knickerbocker, William H.
He died in rawhide (eulogy on Riley Grannan, gambler). GRIS:29
Knight, George A.
Speech at McKinley's nomination. WAGN:100
Knight, Harry W.
Challenge of the Hoover report. MIA:411
Knight, Joseph R.
Introduces H.E. Humphreys, Jr., Chairman of the U.S. Rubber Company. PRNE:18

KNIGHTHOOD
Modern knighthood. DAVC:50

KNIGHTS AND LADIES OF HONOR
Growth of fraternity. THOU 3:344
Life insurance a Christian duty. THOU 3:347
Twofold object of the order. THOU 3:341

KNIGHTS OF COLUMBUS
Address to Knights of Columbus. AMEO 2:46
Knights of Columbus. NATS:25
Knights of Columbus, by one of the Knights. EDGS:361

KNIGHTS OF MALTA
Boughter, J.G.
Opinion on Knights of Malta. THOU 3:151
Easton, T.
Opinion on Knights of Malta. THOU 3:152
Miller, O.R.
Opinion on Knights of Malta. THOU 3:152

KNIGHTS OF PYTHIAS
Address before the Knights of Pythias. AMEO 2:177
Address of welcome. THOS:39
Douglass, S.C.H.
Acceptance of office in Knights of Pythias. THOU 3:137
Fraternal loyalty. THOU 3:145
Knights of Pythias eulogy. THOS:180
Origin of Knights of Pythias. THOS:129
Valkenberg, J.V.
Biennial address of Knights of Pythias. THOU 3:133
Knights of Pythias eulogy. THOU 3:142

KNIGHTS TEMPLAR
Knights Templar: a Christmas address. THOS:56
Mayor's address of welcome to convention of Knights Templar. AMEO 2:58
Perkins, G. C.
Knights Templar address of welcome. WAGN:341
Knott, James Proctor
Glories of Duluth. BREW 7:204; CHAL 11:425; HARSO:186; HAZO 22:9346; MAS 22:9346; ONEM:317; ORAMA 2:347; PE:604; PEA:604; REEM 7:204; REEMA 8:753; REEMB 8:231; SHUO:186

KNOW NOTHING PARTY
Wise, H. A.
Know-Nothingism. REEMA 15:2141
Knowland, William F.
Coexistence and atomic stalemate. BA 1954-55:30
McDonough, J. J.
Introduces United States Senator, William F. Knowland. PRNE:41

KNOWLEDGE, THEORY OF
Bean, F. A.
Master or victim? YE 2:21
Burroughs, J.
Let there be light. YR 2:103
Chapin, E. H.
Sovereignty of ideas. BREW 3:204
Daughtery, L. A.
Royal road. JUD:209
Drummond, H.
Preparation for learning. BREW 5:332
Hall, W.
Address before the Society of Phi Beta Kappa in Yale College. BL:205
Kaiser, H. J., Jr.
Knowledge is our strongest weapon. SABA:271
Knowledge is power-speech by president of successful business enterprise to a graduating class. WRA:219
Knowledge of the ages. FRIE:214
Newman, J. H.
Knowledge viewed in relation to learning. REEM 6:347; REEMA 9:911; REEMB 7:297
Proper use of knowledge. NATS:12
Seek and find. FRIE:279
Value of knowledge. AMEO 1:113
Warren, E.
Free investigation and faithful experiment. BA 1953-54:87
Wayland, F.
Philosophy of analogy. BL:344
Young, O. D.
How we meet ourselves (semi centennial of Hendrix College). COP:706; COPB:733; HURG:227
See also Learning and scholarship
Knox, Frank
We must fight for our liberties. COP:606; COPB:571
Knox, John
Against tyrants. BREW 7:212; PL:235
God's power over that of kings. -Same as his Against tyrants
Homily on Isaiah XXVI, 13-21. LEEW 4:185
Prayer. ORBR 1:29
On the first temptation of Christ. BRYW 3:23; CHAL 1:436; HAZO 4:1341; MAS 4:1341

KNOX, JOHN
McClelland, C. B.
Life and work of John Knox and his influence on American ideals. ASHF:181
Knox, Philander Chase
Against the League of Nations.

BREW 7:220
Against the Treaty of Paris. BREW 7:219
Commerce clause of the Constitution and the trusts. BLAA:270; BLAB:270
Internationalism and American independence. BREW 7:221
Koch, Ruth
Between yesterday and tomorrow. NOR 1946:47
Kock, Kenneth H.
Whither, world? YR 4:175
Koehneke, M. L.
Two heirs of God on an adventure in faith. ACW:131
Kohler, Kaufmann
Room for all. TWJ:131
Koiso, Kuniaki
Address at opening of 85th Diet. VO 1944-45:413
Broadcast to Japanese people. HAN:346; VO 1944-45:368
New Year's address, 1945. VO 1945-46:4
Speech asking greater East Asia collaboration. VO 1944-45:594
Konoye, Fumimaro, Prince
Address before the 76th session of the Imperial Diet. VO 1941:40
Triple alliance. COP:522; COPA:522; COPB:500
Koo, V.K. Wellington
Address at final plenary session of United Nations Conference on International Organization. VO 1945-46:305
Remarks at opening of the second phase of the Dumbarton Oaks conversations. VO 1944-45:459
Speech at Peace Conference (session on February 15, 1919). REEM 11:346; REEMB 12:364
Statement at conclusion of second phase of the Dumbarton Oaks conversations. VO 1944-45:471
KOO, V. K. WELLINGTON
Grimm, P.
Introduces V.K. Wellington Koo. PR:62
Kooker, E. Merrill
Response to welcome of honor students. JUD:203
KOREA
Acheson, D.
United Nations and Soviet aggression. BA 1950-51:25
Austin, W.R.
Accusing Chinese Communists of intervention in Korea. YE:140
United Nations and Korea. BA 1950-51:13
Truman, H.S.
National emergency. BA 1950-51:94

KOREAN WAR, 1950-1953
Bradley, O.N.
Four courses of action in Korea. BA 1952-53:21
Chang, J.M. and others.
Background of Korea. HAR:109
Eisenhower, D.D.
Crusade for peace. BA 1952-53:92
Korean armistice. BA 1953-54:19; FIP:331
Limb, B.C.
Frank and candid light. HAR:118
Lodge, H.C., Jr.
Russian support of Korean War. BA 1952-53:25
MacArthur, D.
Defends his conduct of the war in Korea. ARNS:273; BA 1951-52:21; BOU:105; BRAP:61; CAP:206; COPB:594; HAR:146; HIBS:465; HURG:293; MOUG:210; MOUGA:210; PE:816; PEA:816; YE:371
Ridgway, M.B.
On assuming command of the 8th Army. HAR:138
Truman, H.S.

KOREAN WAR, 1950-1953 (cont.)
Korea, July 19, 1950. FIP:308
Preventing a new world war. BARR:291; FIP:311; HAR:140
Korniloff, L. G.
Appeal to his soldiers. REEM 11:176; REEMB 12:190
Kossuth, Louis
At Plymouth. CHAL 7:35; HAZO 14:5824; MAS 14:5824
Calls for aid to downtrodden Hungary. -Same as his On his welcome to New York
Local self-government. BREW 7:223; HAZO 14:5795; MAS 14:5795
On his welcome to New York. BRYW 7:249; CHAL 7:43; COP:106; COPA:106; COPB:106; HAZO 14:5832; MAS 14:5832; PE:465; PEA:465; PL:338
Present weakness of despotism. LEEW 5:221
Response to the Governor of Pennsylvania. KNAS:221; KNASA:221; ONEM:691
Speech in Faneuil Hall. CHAL 7:20; HAZO 14:5809; MAS 14:5809; REEMA 13:1269

KOSSUTH, LOUIS
Apponyi, A.
On the death of Louis Kossuth. BRYW 7:262
Bryant, W. C.
Introducing a foreign patriot-Louis Kossuth. BRYW 9:144; CHAL 6:130; HAZO 12:5201; MAS 12:5201; ONEM:664; REEM 5:45; REEMA 1:100; REEMB 9:75
Kosygin, Aleksei N.
Speech of October 21. RUS:216
Kottemann, Dorothy
Sleeping beauties. NOR 1944:35
Kovar, Lillian
All this, and for what? AN:78
Kozlov, Frol R.
Speech of October 28. RUS:138
Kramer, H. G.
Home blessed with peace. ACW:71
Krantz, John C., Jr.
Acceptance of club presidency. MCK:198
Anesthesia-man's redemption from pain. MCK:150
Architect designed a needle (hypodermic). MCK:237
Community fund. MCK:129
Dedication speech (Bressler Research Laboratory-University of Maryland.) MCK:121
Every member canvass day appeals-two speeches requesting church pledges). MCK:127-8
New Years-what about your dreams. MCK:134
On being a scientifically-minded physician. MCK:169
Presentation speech (watch). MCK:120
Simplicity to wonder. MCK:202
Star-A Christmas message. MCK:147
Welcome to Baltimore. MCK:178
Welcome to Maryland. MCK:179
Krasne, Philip N.
Cornerstone of American liberty. LEIO:145
Krause, Norman
We will not lay down arms. BA 1943-44:123
Krause, Norman L.
Man's reach. NOR 1940:34
Krauskopf, Joseph
Jewish Pilgrim fathers. TWJ:121

KREKELER, HEINZ L.
McDonough, J. J.

Introduces Heinz L. Krekeler, Ambassador of the Federal Republic of Germany to the United States. PRNE:46
Kroloff, Max N.
Constitution. LEIO:104
Krosigk, Lutz Scherwin, Von
Broadcast to the German people. VO 1945-46:188

KRUEGER, IVAR
Wright, W.B.
"Dr. Jekyll or Mr. Hyde?" YR 4:165
Krueger, Maynard See Miller, C.R., jt. auth.
Kruttschnitt, Julius
Railroad situation. REEM 4: 263; REEMB 5:83

KU KLUX KLAN
Bryan, W.J.
Religious liberty and the Ku Klux Klan. WHIP:290
Colby, B.
Religious liberty and the Ku Klux Klan. WHIP:298
Kuizenga, Henry Bernard
Significance of the insignificant. YR 7:269

KUNG, HSIANG HSI
Yu, Tsune-Chi
Presents H.H. Kung. LY: 200; ON:338
Kunzmann, Howard E., Jr.
Chance or a policy? BRAP: 85
Kuroki, Ben
War isn't over at home. BA 1945-46:208
Kurusu, Saburo
Broadcast, November 26, 1942. VO 1942-43:681
Kuusinen, Otto V.
Speech of October 26. RUS:93
Kyburg, Ellen Ely
Rains came -a review. GA: 212

LABOR AND LABORING CLASSES
Abbott, L.
Law of service. BOB:60
Booth, N.
On labor. WAGN:40
Brownson, C.A.
Laboring classes. BL:171
Bruehl, C.P.
Conditions of labor. CATA 1:63
Byron, G.
Strikes an early blow for the rights of labor. PE: 318; PEA:318
Canham, E.D.
Value of self-criticism for business and labor. ARNS: 187
Carr, L.E.
Lawyer and the hod carrier. REEM 1:223; REEMA 1:223; REEMB 1:224
Cooper, R.C.
"Let us look at the doughnut." BA 1961-62:148
Cooperation between labor and management. DR:28
Dewey, O.
Nobility of labor. REAC: 127
Dupee, G.G.
Eyeless in Gaza. BRP 9: 97; NOR 1938:28
Everett, E.
Universal and uncoerced co-operation. BREW 6:87
Experience pays but who collects? NAT:13
Gary, E.H.
Labor. BYRA:178; REEM 4:136; REEMB 4:279
Gompers, S.
Voluntary nature of the Labor movement. LINM:120
Green, W.
Preservation of free enterprise the common objective of capital and labor. GLAD: 300
Science of labor relations. SAR:353
Grey, E.G.
Industry. BEA:243
Gunnison, E.M.

LABOR AND LABORING CLASSES (cont.)
Bargains in sweat. BRP 5:92
Hall, E. K.
Plea for the man in the ranks. REEM sup 1:395; REEMB 4:328
Help! Help! FRIE:163
Hickman, A.
Case for the sit-down strike. BRP 8:68; NOR 1937:11
Hill, F.
They were exploitable. NOR 1947:71
Hillman, S
Agriculture, industry, and labor. BA 1938-39:142
James, N. S.
New frontier (distribution of wealth and labor conditions). ASHF:81
Johnston, E.
Warning to labor-and to management. BA 1943-44:200
Labor, the key of success. AMEO 1:56
Kimball, L.
Case for American labor. YR 3:21
Kirby, J., Jr.
Labor and legislation. REEM 4:248; REEMB 5:67
Larson, A.
Working people in the next twenty years. BA 1956-57:115
Lenin, N.
Dictatorship of the Proletariat. COP:141; COPA:141; COPB:141; FRY:93; PL:785; REEM 11:181; REEMB 12:196
Lewis, J. L.
United Mine Workers demands. BA 1945-46:180
Who are the Americans today? BA 1953-54:150
Luther, S.
Addresses workingmen of New England. PE:362; PEA:362
Lyda, H.
Human values. BRP 9:29; YR 10:95
Macaulay, T. B.
Industrial worker. HAY:197
McDonald, D. J.
Plan for prosperity. BA 1960-61:156
McGrady, E. F.
What does labor want? SAR:344
McNutt, P. V
Labor and the war. BA 1941-42:170
Meany, C.
New horizons for labor and management. BA 1956-57:126
Nobility of labor. THOS:137
O'Mahoney, J. C.
Industrial democracy. BOA:343
Randolph, A. P.
Labor and the struggle for a better tomorrow. HILK:175
Response to the toast "The working man: may he have plenty of it, with good wages promptly paid." PITT:94
Reuther, W. P.
Capital-labor problems (March 9, 1948). GLAD:287
---- and others.
Should industry grant labor's demands for a 30% wage increase? BA 1945-46:165
Roosevelt, F. D.
Expanding frontiers of social progress. SAR:305
Strahen, M.
Public waits. BRP 8:56
Sumner, W. G.
Forgotten man. WPRA:229
Tavenner, C. H.
Cause of labor. HARSO:23
Truman, H. S.
Railroad strike emergency. BA 1945-46:196

Statement on labor policy. VO 1945-56:458
Wilson, C. E.
Five years of industrial peace. YE:221
See also American Federation of Labor; Capitalism; Child labor; Industrial relations; Injunctions; International Labor Conference; Labor Unions; Strikes and lockouts; Work

---- AFRICA
Harcourt, L. H.
Deportation of labour leaders from South Africa. KES:2:109

---- ENGLAND
Arch, J.
Debate on the question of allotments, January 26, 1886. PAUF 2:325

---- GERMANY
Eisenhower, D.
Instructions to organized cells of foreign workers in Germany. VO 1944-45:432

LABOR DAY
Altgeld, J. P.
Children of toil. HICF:156
Bevin, E.
Labor and the war against Nazism. COP:481; COPA: 481
Brewer, D. J.
Combination of capital and consolidation of labor. BLAA:189; BLAB:189; THOU 1:444
Carroll, J. P.
Labor Day. CATA 1:52
Cause of much idleness and crime. THOU 1:458
Closing speech (at Labor Day observance). BED:98; BEDA:171
Courts and labor organization. THOU 1:413
Evarts, W. M.
Labor the source of wealth. THOU 1:434
Gilmore, E.
Dignity of labor. THOU 1: 417
Gompers, S.
Useful lessons of Labor Day. THOU 1:457
Green, W.
Labor, freedom and democracy. BA 1940-41:243
Harrison, B.
Views on capital and labor. THOU 1:429
Haygood, S. G.
Adjustments between labor and capital. THOU 1:448
Hays, W. H.
Teamwork. BYRA:188; REEM 4:187; REEMB 4:377
Labor and capital. THOU 1: 425
Labor Day. THOU 1:400
Labor Day. DR:163
Labor Day (a toast to the Union). EDGS:18
Labor Day address (by labor leader). BED:97; BEDA: 170
Labor Day addresss. BURS: 194
Labor Day and holidays. THOU 1:402
Labor Day-to the men who make the world go round. DR:165; LU:1199
Labor problem. THOU 1:409
Labor question-hobbies. THOU 1:406
Labor trouble. THOU 1:462
LaGuardia, F. H.
American labor. COP:416; COPA:416; COPB:410
Leach, C.
Land and labor. THOU 1: 431
McKeldin, T.
Labor Day. MCK:144
Meany, G.
Labor Day message. BA 1953-54:143
Northcott, W. A.
Rights of men. WERN 42:

LABOR DAY (cont.)
108
Opening speech (on Labor Day by union official). BED:96; BEDA:168
Poore, B. P.
Capital and labor. THOU 1:427
Profits of labor. JA:115
Prosser, W.
Free labor the basis of free America. THOU 1:421
Roche, J.
Labor day address. GA:81
Roosevelt, F. D.
Labor day address (1941). VO 1941:392
Labor day statement (1942). VO 1942-43:443
Storrs, R. S.
Discontent of the times. THOU 1:453
Talmage, T. D.
Labor question. THOU 1:436
Wheeler, A.
Labor question. THOU 1:404
Wishard, S. E.
Rights of laboring men. THOU 1:450
Worthy workman. JA:118
Zimmerman, C. H.
Labor organizations. THOU 1:411

LABOR INJUNCTIONS See Injunctions

LABOR LAWS AND LEGISLATION
Eisenhower, D. D.
On the Labor Bill-1959. BRYA:543
Goldsborough, T. A.
Lewis contempt case. BA 1947-48:93
Harlan, J. M.
Adair v. United States, 1908: opinion for the Supreme Court. BIR 3:292
Hughes, C. E.
National Labor Relations Board v. Jones and Laughlin Steel Corporation, 1937: opinion for the Supreme Court. BIR 4:218
Kennedy, J. F.
Kennedy-Ives Bill. BA 1958-59:79
Meany, G.
Labor's position on labor-management reform legislation. BA 1959-60:142
Powell, A. C.
For the Federal Fair Trade Employment Practices Act. BA 1949-50:154
Sims, H. S., Jr.
Against the Federal Fair Trade Employment Practices Act. BA 1949-50:159
Truman, H. S.
Message to Congress on labor legislation. VO 1945-46:756

---- TAFT HARTLEY LAW
Morse, W. L.
Independent in politics. BA 1946-47:153
Rayburn, S. and others.
Repeal of the Taft-Hartley law. BA 1948-49:155
Taft, R. A.
Should the Taft-Hartley Labor Bill become law? BA 1946-47:196
Truman, H. S.
Should the Taft-Hartley Labor Bill become law? BA 1946-47:190

LABOR PARTY
Gompers, S.
Shall a Labor Party be formed? BAAMP:249

LABOR UNIONS
Acceptance (of plaque for Labor Temple). BED:87; BEDA:160
Billings,
United States v. Workingmen's Amalgamated Council of New Orleans, 1893. BIR 3:174

Carey, J. B.
Enemies within the house of labor. BA 1957-58:98
Chaplin, R.
Our responsibility to America. ON:51
Closing benediction (at memorial services honoring deceased union member). BED: 101; BEDA:179
Closing speech (at induction of members to labor union). BED:76; BEDA:148
Closing speech (at installation of officers at labor union). BED:79; BEDA:152
Closing speech (at testimonial to labor union official). BED: 84; BEDA:157
Closing speech (at unveiling of portrait presented to labor union). BED:92; BEDA:165
Davenport, D.
Summation for the plaintiff in the Danbury Hatters case. HICJ:527
Eulogy (at memorial services honoring deceased union member). BED:100; BEDA: 178
Greeley, H.
On the union of workers. CHAL 8:316; HAZO 17: 7127; MAS 17:7127
Green, W.
Modern trade unionism. COP:405; COPA:405; COPB:405; HURG:205; REEM sup 1:374; REEMB 4:317
Greeting and welcome (at ceremony honoring retiring secretary of labor union). BED:80; BEDA:153
Greeting and welcome (at unveiling of portrait presented to Labor Temple). BED:89; BEDA:161
Huntington, H.
Introducing a farm bureau or farmers union man. BRC:320
Induction address (to newly inducted members of labor union). BED:75; BEDA:147
Installing executive board (at labor union). BED:79; BEDA:152
Installing president (at labor union). BED:77; BEDA:149
Installing secretary (at labor union). BED:79; BEDA:151
Installing treasurer (at labor union). BED:79; BEDA:152
Installing vice-president (at labor union). BED:78; BEDA: 151
Introducing induction officer (at induction of members to labor union) BED:75; BEDA:147
Introducing labor leader. BED:93; BEDA:166
Introducing national representative (at charter presentation to labor union). BED:73
Introducing public officials (at memorial services honoring deceased union member). BED:100; BEDA:177
Introducing speaker (at ceremony honoring retiring secretary of labor union). BED:80; BEDA:153
Introducing speaker (at testimonial ceremony honoring union official). BED:83; BEDA:156
Introducing speaker (at unveiling of plaque for Labor Temple). BED:86; BEDA: 159
Kaser, A. L.
Introducing a labor leader. BRC:158
Lewis, J. L.
Labor and the nation. COP: 425; COPA:425; COPB: 415; HURG:232; SAR:357
McCaffrey, J. L.
What road to labor peace? HAR:423
McDonald, D. J.
Labor's responsibility for human rights. BA 1958-59:

LABOR UNIONS (cont.)
92
McGovern, S.
Introducing a labor leader. BRC:46
Mansfield, F.W.
Relation of labor unions to church and state. CATA 1: 83
Meany, G.
Fallacies of labor criticism. BA 1958-59:84
Principles and program of AFL-CIO. BA 1955-56:78
Merritt, W.G.
Summation for the plaintiff in the Danbury Hatters case. HICJ:492
Murray, P.
CIO labor policies. BA 1949-50:178
Equality in sacrifice. BA 1950-51:109
Labor's role in higher education. HAR:419
Strikes, wages, and industrial profits. BA 1946-47: 177
Newly elected union chairman's installation speech at annual meeting of shop union. WRA:121
Opening speech (at induction of members to labor union). BED:75; BEDA:147
Opening speech (at installation of officials to labor union). BED:77; BEDA:149
Opening speech (at memorial service honoring deceased union member). BED:99; BEDA:176
Opening speech (at unveiling of plaque for Labor Temple). BED:86; BEDA:158
Opening speech by temporary chairman (at charter presentation to labor union). BED:73
Opening speech (urging labor union members to take active interest in politics). BED:93; BEDA:165
Presenting charter (at labor union ceremony). BED:73
Presenting plaque (at unveiling of plaque for Labor Temple). BED:86; BEDA: 159
Responding to tribute (by labor union official). BED:84; BEDA:157
Reuther, W.P.
Historical agreement. COPB:646
Labor's principles and programs. BA 1951-52:123
United Automobile Workers: aims and program. BA 1949-50:189
Richberg, D.R.
How shall we deal with labor union monopolies? BA 1955-56:67
Roll call (at memorial services honoring deceased union member). BED:101; BEDA:179
Romano, M.A.
Summation for the people in the O'Shea conspiracy case. HICJ:983
Roosevelt, F.D.
To the delegates of the International Labor Organization. VO 1941:475
Shaw, L.
Commonwealth v. Hunt. ANG:257
Sheil, B.J.
Industrial democracy. ON: 149
Stryker, M.W.
Recognize the unions. BLAA:197; BLAB:197
Tribute (to labor union official at testimonial ceremony). BED:83; BEDA:156
Tribute to retiring secretary of labor union). BED:80; BEDA:154
Unveiling portrait (of past president of labor union). BED:89; BEDA:162
Wheeler, B.
United Mine Worker's con-

vention. BA 1939-40:316
Woll, M.
Labor's contribution to American democracy. BA 1939-40:327
Organized labor and current international developments. HAR:410
See also American Federation of Labor; Labor Day; Labor laws and legislation; Strikes and lockouts
Labori, Fernand
Conspiracy against Dreyfus. BREW 7:235; CHAL 14:384; HAZO 25:10903; MAS 25: 10903
Lacey, John J.
Farmers need public understanding. SAB:143; SABA: 236
Lacordaire, Jean Baptiste Henri
Rationalism and miracles. BREW 7:246; HAZO 14: 5857; MAS 14:5857
Sacred cause of the human race (Panegyric of Daniel O'Connell) BREW 7:243; CHAL 6:478; HAZO 14: 5843; MAS 14:5843

LAEMMLE, CARL
Introducing Carl Laemmle. NI:164; NIA:122
LaFarge, John
Religious philosophy and intergroup progress. HAR: 506
Lafayette, Marie Joseph Paul Roch Yves Gilbert de Motier, Marquis de
Response to Henry Clay's address of welcome. KNAS: 218; KNASA:218

LAFAYETTE, MARIE JOSEPH PAUL ROCH YVES GILBERT DE MOTIER, MARQUIS DE
Adams, J.Q.
Life and character of Lafayette. BREW 1:72; HAZO 9:3691; MAS 9:3691; PL: 641
Clay, H.
To Lafayette. CHAL 5:84; HAZO 10:4114; HELE:180; KNAS:216; KNASA:216; MAS 10:4114; REEM 5:83; REEMA 7:247; REEMB 9: 113
Prentiss, S.S.
Lafayette. BRYW 8:218; KLEG:251; LAD:92; REEMA 9:971
Whitlock, B.
Lafayette, apostle of liberty. REEM 11:224; REEMB 12:239
LaFollette, Robert Marion, Sr.
Against war with Germany. BRAS:313
Alaska: the nation's storehouse. PEAE:129
Free speech in wartime. BAAMP:244; BLAB:347; BRE:311; BREA:291; HICF:488
Hours of service of railway employees. PEAE:111
Official statement as Progressive candidate. WHIP:306
Petition to the U.S. Senate as candidate for President on the Progressive ticket-1924. WHIP:305
Railway Rate Bill. PEAE:117
Which shall rule, manhood or money? COP:343; COPA: 343; COPB:343; HURG: 158; REEM 7:217; REEMA 13:1281; REEMB 7:252

LAFOLLETTE, ROBERT MARION, Sr.
Douglas, P.H.
Five great Americans. BA 1951-52:85
Kennedy, J.F.
Portraits of five senators in the Senate reception room. BA 1957-58:84
LaFollette, Robert Marion, Jr.
America's foreign policy. BA 1937-38:69

LaGuardia, Fiorello H.
American labor. COP:416; COPA:416; COPB:410
LaGUARDIA, FIORELLO H.
Introducing Fiorello H. LaGuardia. NI:49; NIA:42
LAISSEZ-FAIRE
Carleton, W.G.
What of free enterprise? BA 1943-44:209
Free enterprise vs. socialism. FRIE:245
Wriston, H.M.
Free enterprise. BA 1943-44:230
Lake, Kirsopp
Teaching and learning. NORR 2d ser:361
Lamar, Lucius Q.C.
Charles Sumner. BRYW 10:61; CHAL 10:441; HAZO 21:8796; LA:134; LAD:93; MAS 21:8796; REEM 5:260; REEMA 8:767; REEMB 9:299; SHUO:230
On national aid to education. REEMA 13:1289

LAMAR, LUCIUS Q.C.
Candler, W.A.
Tribute to Lucius Q.C. Lamar. SHUO:234
Lamar, Mrs. Walter D.
Eulogy on Nellie Peters Black. GA:90
Lamartine, Alphonse Marie Louis de
Congratulatory speech. CHAL 5:430; HAZO 12:4930; MAS 12:4930
Manifesto to Europe. HAZO 12:4922; MAS 12:4922
Reply to club delegates. CHAL 5:432; HAZO 12:4932; MAS 12:4932
Revolution. LEEW 5:215
Revolution of 1848. BREW 7:253; HAZO 12:4912; MAS 12:4912
To a deputation of Poles, 1848. BRYW 7:187; CHAL 5:425; HAZO 12:4936; MAS 12:4936; PL:331
LAMONT, THOMAS S.
Presents Paul G. Hoffman. LY:91
Lamont, Thomas William
American bankers' responsibility. BYRA:265; HOA:371; HOAP:257; REEM 4:272; REEMB 5:93
Introducing General Hugh Johnson. HOC:18
Presents Eleanor Robson Belmont. LY:49
Presents W.L. Mackenzie King. LY:225
Thanking General Hugh Johnson for speaking. HOC:19
Lampman, Robert J.
Morgen die ganze welt. NOR 1942:65

LAND GRANTS
Curtin, A.G.
People's heritage squandered. CHAL 9:62; HAZO 18:7552; MAS 18:7552
Landis, Frederick
Witty after-dinner speech on Will Hays. BRAC:302; LY:213; NESA:185
Landis, John C.
Foolish rich man. BRP 4:12

LANDLORDS
Brigance, S.
Landladies. YE:332
Lane, Franklin Knight
American pioneer (at opening of Panama-Pacific Exposition) BRAP:106; REEM 7:226; REEMB 8:246
American spirit incarnate. SHU:166
Campaign speech. WAGN:401
Makers of the flag. CARP:172; DOA:224; ONES:140; PROS:98; REEM 7:224; REEMB 8:244; SHU:157
Message of the West. REEM 11:254; REEMB 12:270
What is America? PROS:118
Why do we fight Germany? LEW:53
Unconquerable soul. PROS:37

Lane, George W.
Introducing and toasting J. P. Newman. REEM 3:1
Toast to the United States. REEM 2:139
Lane, J. Russell
What price speed: danger of sacrificing individual thought and appreciation to speed and efficiency in education. ASHF:362
Lane, William Preston, Jr.
Presents Walter Bedell Smith. LY:158
Lang, Andrew
How to fail in literature. REEM 6:303; REEMA 5:713; REEMB 6:225
Problem novels. REEMA 2:698
Lang, Cosmos Gordon
Socialism in England. BREW 7:260
Lest you forget. BEA:5
Lang, William C.
"The bold go toward their time." BA 1960-61:71
Langdon, Herschel
Broken bulwark. ONEC:385
Langdon, William H.
Treason to democracy. BOA: 361; BOB:150
Langfitt, Joseph A.
Fraternal system. THOU 3: 388
Twenty-fifth anniversary greeting. THOU 3:350
Langston, Charles H.
Should colored men be subject to the pains and penalties of the Fugitive Slave law? DUNM:49
Langston, John Mercer
Address at the centennial of the Pennsylvania Society for promoting the abolition of slavery. DUNM:97
Equality before the law (anniversary of adoption of Fifteenth Amendment).WOON: 436
Other phase of reconstruction. WOON:417
Speech laudatory of the Negro. WOON:387

LANGUAGE AND LANGUAGES
Lowell, J.R.
Plea for modern languages. CHAL 9:374; HAZO 19: 7998; MAS 19:7998
Outline for a speech "Lingual logic." BARR:47
Thrall, H.M.
Dignity and potency of language. WERN 54:57
See also Names of languages, e.g. English language
Lanham, Charles T.
Moral core of military strength. HAR:249
Lansdowne, Henry Charles Keith Petty Fitzmaurice, 5th Marquis
Coercion and repression as imperial policies. BREW 7: 269
Predatory taxation and nationalizing land. BREW 7:265
Sovereign's intervention in politics. EMS 1:2
Lansing, John
Answering Alexander Hamilton. BREW 7:271
Lansing, Robert
Pan-Americanism. FKA:200
To Reserve Officers' Training Corps. LEW:63
Lapointe, Ernest
Statute of Westminster (June 30, 1931 speech). KESD: 260
Lardner, Dionysius
Plurality of worlds. BREW 7: 277
Larkin, Michael
Speech from dock. KET:367
Larson, Arthur
Constitution and American youth. BRP 2:35; YR 2:69
Indian medicine. BRP 1:38
Timocracy-why not? (education of statesmen). YR 1:155
United States Information Service. BRAP:80
Working people in the next twenty years. BA 1956-57:

Larson, Arthur (cont.)
115
Larson, Carol
Address of welcome (at Kappa Kappa Gamma initiation banquet). MOUG:242; MOUGA:242
Larson, Don
Battle of baloney. BRP 5:22
Larson, L. A. See Young, B., jt. auth.
Lash, Joseph P.
We won't fight. SAR:261

LASKI, HAROLD
Snyder, F. B.
Introduces two debaters, Alfred P. Haake and Harold Laski. PR:84
Lassale, Ferdinand
Attacks the German Press. PE:529; PEA:529
Lasswell, Harold D. See MacLeish, A., jt. auth.
Latham, J. G.
Statute of Westminster (July 17, 1931 speech). KESB:263
Latimer, Hugh
Duties and respect of judges. BREW 7:282
On Christian love. CHAL 1:396; HAZO 3:1283; MAS 3:1283
On the pickings of office holders. BREW 7:290
Second sermon on the card. BRYW 3:11; LEEW 4:153
Sermon on the plow. BREW 7:285; ORBR 1:3; PL:231

LATIN AMERICA
Donnelly, W. P.
Our responsibility to Latin America. ANGC:177
Hughes, C. E.
Latin-American relations. BLAB:293
Muñoz-Cota, J.
Bolivar and the Latin-American peoples. LEIO:72
Wilson, W.
Address before the Southern Commercial Congress at Mobile on relations with Latin America. BIR 3:309; FO:276
See also Inter-American Conference on Problems of War and Peace; Pan American Day; South America; Western Hemisphere; World War, 1939-1945-Latin America

LATITUDE AND LONGITUDE
Finley, J. H.
Latitude and longitude. REEM 2:51; REEMB 2:51

LATTER-DAY SAINTS See Mormons

LAUBACH, FRANK C.
Smith, N.
Rushing to meet the sunrise. AN:1

LAUGHTER
Newcomb, C. M.
Psychology of laughter. EXEE:130

LAUNDRY AND DRY CLEANING
Curtis, D.
Introducing a laundry and dry cleaning executive. BRC:318
Laundry owners. SCHS:166
Laurier, Sir Wilfrid
British flag in Caesar's city. BREW 7:294
British policy in Africa. CHAL 13:394; HAZO 24:10459; MAS 24:10459
Canada. REEM 2:310; REEMA 2:702; REEMB 2:314
Canada, England and the United States in 1899. BREW 7:301; COP:381; COPA:381; COPB:381; FUL:181,183; PL:542; REEMA 13:1297
Canada's participation in the war with Germany. KES 2:357; REEM 11:63; REEMB 12:70

Character and work of Gladstone. BREW 7:296; ONES: 167
"Daughter nations," not satellites. BREW 7:293
On the death of Queen Victoria. BRYW 5:192; CHAL 13:381; HAZO 24:10446; LAD:197; MAS 24:10446; REEM 5:267; REEMB 9: 306
Queen's diamond jubilee. CHAL 13:379; HAZO 24: 10444; MAS 24:10444
Ready, aye, ready. -Same as his Canada's participation in the war with Germany
Unwritten alliance. -Same as his Canada, England, and the United States

LAURIER, SIR WILFRID
Edward VII.
Introducing Sir W. Laurier to Colonial Premiers, June 18, 1897. REEM 2:310; REEMA 2:702; REEMB 2: 314
Lemieux, R.
Tribute to Laurier. NESA: 160; REEM 5:276; REEMB 9:315
White, T.
Life and character of Sir Wilfrid Laurier. KLEB:21

LAUSANNE, TREATY OF
King, W. L. M.
Speech in House of Commons, June 9, 1924 (on ratification of Treaty of Lausanne). KESB:322
Laval, Pierre
Efforts on conciliation, November 2, 1935. KESK 2: 81
Lavelle, William
Spirit of peace. YR 2:157

LAW AND LAWYERS
Alexander, C. H.
Majesty of law. SHUO:54
Bacon, F.
Charge to Justice Hutton. REEM 9:61; REEMB 10:63
Bayard, J. A.
Federal judiciary. BREW 1:257; HAZO 9:3612; MAS 9:3612
Bench and bar. SCHS:36
Birkenhead, F. E. S.
Lawyers who really count. LINM:350
Bloch, C. J.
Lawyer's duty to the courts or to his country and to his people. BRAB: 551
Bowles, G. E.
Caesar's friends. YR 7: 301
Brewster, B. H.
Bench and Bar of Pennsylvania. REEMA 1:82
Bright, J.
Suspension of the Habeas Corpus Act. CLAY:290
Cardozo, B. N.
Modern trends in the study and treatment of the law. BYRA:59; REEM sup 1:150; REEMB 6:34
Carr, L. E.
Lawyer and the hod carrier. REEM 1:223; REEMA 1: 127; REEMB 1:224
Choate, J. H.
Bench and the bar. COP: 641; COPB:675; HURG: 133; REEM 1:250; REEMA 1:156; REEMB 1:251
Coudert, F. R.
Our clients. BYRA:88; REEM 1:347; REEMA 1:282; REEMB 1:348
Cousin, V.
Foundations of law. BREW 4:195; HAZO 12:5013; MAS 12:5013
Cummings, H. S.
Modern tendencies and the law. KLEB:79
Curtis, G. W.
Puritan principle: liberty under law. BAKF:430; BRY:468; BRYA:554;

LAW AND LAWYERS (cont.)
ONEM:573; REEM 1:355; REEMA 1:290
Davis, D.
Opinion in the Milligan Case. ANG:374; BIR 3:29
Davis, J.W.
Our brethren overseas. BYRA:98; REEM 6:116; REEMB 6:86
Ehrensperger, R.
"The King can do no wrong." BLUE:108
Field, D.D.
In re Milligan-martial law as lawlessness. BREW 6:119
Finch, F.M.
Office of the law (assuming chair of Presidency of New York State Bar Association). REEMA 2:496
For a lawyer's dinner. BARB:172
Gilbert, E.J.
Introducing a judge
" a lawyer. BRC:136, 67
Griggs, J.W.
Ideal lawyer. KLEG:355
Halifax, E.F.L.W.
At annual dinner of American Society of International Law. VO 1944-45:189
Halle, R.
Guilty until proven innocent. SOBP:348
Harrison, C.C.
Opening the ceremonies at the dedication of a new law building. ONES:64
Harrison, L.
Of the making of laws there is no end. GRIS:54
Hawkins, W.A.
Negro lawyer: his opportunity, his duty (at opening of Howard University Law School). DUNM:483
Holmes, O.W., Jr.
Education in the obvious. HICF:415
Law and the court. BYRA:212; KLEB:33; REEMB 2:228
Speech at a Bar dinner. ONEM:624; ONES:218
Use of law schools. REEM 6:276; REEMA 8:700; REEMB 6:189
Hughes, C.E.
Liberty and law. LINM:167
Hume, F.C.
Young lawyer. ONEM:658; ONES:248; REEM sup 2:85; REEMB 6:206; SHUO:50
Introducing a lawyer-two examples of. BEB:55
Introducing lawyer (at physician-of-the-year award). BED:50; BEDA:53
Invocation (at induction of a Judge). BEDA:117
Isocrates.
Arepagiticus-"a few wise laws wisely administered." BREW 7:137; HAZO 1:142; MAS 1:142
Jenks, A.F.
Observations of a jurist. REEM 2:281; REEMB 2:285
Jury is dismissed (outline of speech). MOA:338, 345
Kaser, A.L.
Introducing a judge. BRC:40
Latimer, H.
Duties and respect of judges. BREW 7:282
Lawyers, by a layman. EDGS:177
Lawyer's code of ethics. AMEO 2:175
Lawyers (one of them tells a few jokes on the profession). ED:260
Lee, R.
Raising potatoes. BRP 8:115
Lowell, J.
Humors of the Bench (retirement from Bench of United States Circuit Court). BYRA:292; REEM 2:368; REEMA 2:766; REEMB 2:381
Mansfield, W.M.

Case of Allan Evans. GOOD: 156; LAD:111; ONEM:121
In the case of John Wilkes. BREW 8:75; GOOD:154
In the case of the Dean of Asaph. BREW 8:77
Marshall, J.
Marbury v. Madison: opinion for the Supreme Court. BIR 1:259; BRE:116
Mayer, J.
Court and the law. BYRA: 295; ONES:358; REEM sup 2:214; REEMB 6:281
Medina, H. R.
Equal justice for all. HIBS: 476
Miller, S F.
Federal judges. REEMA 2: 834
Morris, G.
On the judiciary. CHAL 3: 410; HAZO 7:3051; MAS 7:3051
Myers, F. J.
How a law is made. MOUG: 105; MOUGA:105
Olney, R.
Commerce and its relation to law. BYRA:307; REEM 3:9; REEMB 3:9
Paciotti, A. F.
State! Keep your lawyers. YR 9:267
Palmer, G. M.
Lawyer in politics. REEMA 3:872
Perry, J. H.
Newspaper law. BYRA:318; REEM 2:269; REEMB 6:290
Posner, G.A.
Introducing a judge (or a member of the legal profession). BRH:48
Pound, R.
Frame of mind. LINM:109
Task of the American lawyer. BYRA:336; REEM sup 2:287; REEMB 6:308
Presenting gavel (at induction of a judge). BEDA:118
Presenting judicial robe (at induction of a judge). BEDA: 118
Pym, J.
Law as a safeguard of liberty. BREW 8:389
Robbins, W. L.
Pulpit and the Bar. REEMA 3:985
Root, E.
Public service by the Bar. HICF:458
Rocking chairs and respect for law. BREW 9:101; BYRA:391; REEM 3:172; REEMB 3:175
Royer-Collard, P. P.
Sacrilege in law. BREW 9: 112; CHAL 4:169; HAZO 9: 3532; MAS 9:3532
Sayre, F. B.
Challenge of international law. SAR:273
Southern court scene. SHU: 226
Spencer, S. P.
Lawyers and lawlessness. SHUO:61
Stafford, W. P.
Liberty under law. SHU: 240
Steuer, M. D.
Cross-examination, is it an art or an artifice? BYRA: 422; REEM sup 3:91; REEMB 6:326
Stinchfield, F. H.
Lawyer outside the court room. KLEB:201
Stone, H. F.
Training of lawyers. BYRA: 441; REEM sup 3:110; REEMB 6:345
Sydnor, C. S.
Southerner and the laws. TIN:62
Taft, W. H.
Wealth and poverty in the courts. BREW 9:343
Thurman, A. G.
Vested rights and the obligations of contracts. BREW 9:408
Tucker, J. R.
Virginia jurists. SMI:220

LAW AND LAWYERS (cont.)
Wade, M.J.
Highest achievement of civilization. SHU:93
Walton, C.
Our courts, a challenge. BRP 5:106
Warren, E.
Address at the Louis Marshall Award dinner. BA 1962-63:97
Home for American jurisprudence (dedication of American Bar Center in Chicago). COPB:611
Wickersham, G.W.
American Law Institute. BYRA:459; REEM sup 3:163; REEMB 6:390
Wise, J.S.
Legal profession. BYRA:467; REEM 3:421; REEMA 3:1271; REEMB 3:428
See also Defense, speeches of; Jury; Justice; Law enforcement; Real estate; United States - Supreme Court

LAW ENFORCEMENT
Borah, W.E.
Old faith. BOA:277; BOB:24
Carhart, R.T.
Crime wears a star. BRP 3:101; YR 4:261
DeLarge, R.C.
Speech on the enforcement of the Fourteenth Amendment. WOON:295
Enstrom, R.
More kindling. BRP 3:71
Haskell, H.J.
What of America? BOA:274; BOB:23
Hoover, H.C.
Obedience to law and enforcement. HICF:957
Respect for law. BOA:271; BOB:22
Insurance and law enforcement (appeal to fraternal insurance order). ED:190
Melson, B.
Strength in democracy. YR 10:133
Taft, W.H.
Delays and defects in the enforcement of laws in this country. PEAE:211
See also Third degree
Lawes, Lewis E.
Crime and the home. BART 4:53

LAWES, LEWIS E.
Introducing Lewis E. Lawes. NI:158; NIA:117
Lawrence, David
Booms and depressions. DOA:154
Lawrence, Edwin Gordon
Fall of the Alamo. LA:163
Ladies. LA:172
Our country. LA:176
Lawrence, Frank R.
Future of New York. REEMA 2:705
Introduces Chauncey M. Depew to Lotus Club, February 22, 1896. REEMA 1:373
Introduces Chauncey M. Depew to Lotus Club, March 11, 1899. REEMA 1:380
Introduces Sir Edwin Arnold to Lotus Club. REEMA 1:7
Introducing Charles E. Hughes to the Lotus Club, New York, March 27, 1918. REEM 2:256
Introduction of a club guest (at dinner in honor of John J. Carty). REEM 2:313; REEMB 2:317

LAWRENCE, GERTRUDE
Sumner, G.L.
Presents Gertrude Lawrence. LY:47; SUM:70
Lawrence, William
Address delivered at Faneuil Hall on 250th anniversary of the settlement of the Jews in the United States.

TWJ:84
Lawrence, William H.
See Kennedy, John F. and others
Lawson, Harry Lawson Webster, 1st Viscount. See Burnham, H. L. W. L.
Lawson, Jesse
Freedom's natal day-what has been done and what remains to be done. THOU 1:255
Lawson, Lucie
Must war be? BRP 7:19; NOR 1935:143
Lawson, Reginald
Furling the battle flags. YR 4:319
If we cancel. BRP 4:70; INTW 1933:62
Lawson, Roberta Campbell
Response to welcome. GA:28
Lawton, Peter I.
Nineteenth of April. SHUC: 150

LAWYERS See Law and lawyers
Lazar, William T.
Reveille of the dead. NOR 1941:35
Lazaron, Morris S.
American city. SHUC:313
Leach, Charles
Land and labor. THOU 1:431
Leacock, Stephen B.
Organization of prosperity. REEM 2:316; REEMB 2:320

LEACOCK, STEPHEN B.
Seamon, O.
Presents Stephen Leacock. LY:55

LEADERSHIP
American leadership. DR:197; LU:1228
Bestor, A. E.
Essentials of leadership. EXEE:542
Blakely, R. J.
Education for multiple leadership (American and Russian education). BA 1958-59: 147
Bramble king. JAS:92
Clark, C.
Courage of leadership. BREW 3:381
Community leadership. FRIE: 80
Crocker, L.
Leadership and the spoken word. BA 1941-42:100
Curtis, G. W.
Leadership of educated men. BAKF:282; ONEM: 816; RINM:256
Do you want to be a leader? JAI:14
Ely, E. S.
Duty of Christian freemen to elect Christian leaders. BL:548
Eubanks, R. T.
Leadership and the "sane society." LINP:178
Insull, S.
Training for leadership. REEM sup 2:122; REEMB 5:28
Jones, G.
Telesis. YR 3:59
Rankin, J. E.
Naval supremacy or moral leadership. BRP 1:95
Rockne, K.
Athletics and leadership. EXEE:107
Sheats, P. H.
Salvage. BRP 1:44
Smith, R. L.
Hardest thing in the world to be. BRP 5:27
Taylor, M. D.
Some reflextions on the subject of leadership. BRAP: 98
Williams, W.
Men wanted. YR 4:241

LEAGUE OF NATIONS
Baker, N. D.
League of Nations. WHIP: 266
Baldwin, S. B.
Kellogg Pact (10th anniversary of League of Nations).

LEAGUE OF NATIONS (cont.)
BEA:17
Borah, W.E.
League of nations. BAAMP: 255; BLAB:359; BRAS:391; COP:368; COPA:368; COPB:368; HICF:642; HURG:190; REEM 11:365; REEMB 12:383
Butler, N.M.
Spirit of Locarno. HICF: 420
Will to peace (7th anniversary of the League of Nations). BRAC:325
DeValera, E.
League of Nations. BEA: 173
Dunham, W.H.
Materialistic idealism. YR 4:53
Haile Selaisse I.
Appeal to the League Assembly. BOU:91; HAN:61; KESK 2:84
Inge, W.R.
Causes of war. BEA:281
Knox, P.H.
Against the League of Nations. BREW 7:220
Landis, J.C.
Foolish rich man. BRP 4: 12
Lewis, J.H.
League of Nations. HICF: 548
Litvinov, M.
League of Nations. COP: 448; COPA:448; COPB:468
Lloyd George, D.
Speech in House of Commons, July 3, 1919 (on League of Nations). KESB:31
Lodge, H.C.
Against the Constitution of the League of Nations. BRAS:357
In opposition to the Proposed League of Nations. WPRC:61
Lucking, A.
League of Nations. WHIP: 282
Root, E.
Plea for the League of Nations. COP:374; COPA:374; COPB:374; REEM sup 2: 369; REEMB 3:177
Taft, W.H.
League of Nations. BRAS: 338; REEM 11:348; REEMB 12:366
Venizelos, E.
On the League of Nations. BREW 10:43
Willkie, W.L.
Isolationism and the League of Nations. BA 1941-42:251
Wilson, W.
Constitution of the League of Nations (Paris, February 14, 1919). BREW 10:252
For the League of Nations (Des Moines, Iowa speech). BAAMP:232; CAP:171
Goes to the people in behalf of the League of Nations (Pueblo, Colorado speech). BOU:119; FIP:133; PE:724; PEA:724; WPRC: 76
League of Nations (Kansas City, September 6, 1919). SHAH:656

LEAGUE TO ENFORCE PEACE
Lowell, A.L.
League to Enforce Peace. FKA:207
Wilson, G.G.
Monroe Doctrine and the program of the League to Enforce peace. FKA:224

LEARNING AND SCHOLARSHIP
Baird, C.W.
Scholar's duty and opportunity. NORR 2d ser:246
Barzun, J.
Place and the price of excellence. ARNS:26
Browder, W.F.
Happy is the nation whose kings are philosophers, and whose philosophers are kings. SOU 9:441

Burton, E.D.
Business and scholarship-what have they to do with one another? EXEE:73
Bush, D.
On being one's self. NORR 3d ser: 229
Butler, N.M.
Scholarship and service; inaugural address as president of Columbia University. WE 1:83
Carpenter, R.
Learning and living. NORR 3d ser:284
Carson, R.M.
Scholar and the socialist. ONES:388
Curtis, G.W.
Duty of the American scholar. CHAL 10:326; HAZO 20:8651; MAS 20:8651
Dodds, H.W.
On the place of the intellectual in America. NORR 3d ser:356
Emerson, R.W.
American scholar. ARNS: 36; BAAGA:410; BAAMP: 122; BL:151; BREW 5:375; BRY:443; BRYW 8:253; CAP:64; CHAL 7:93; FKA: 133; HAZO 14:5927; MAS 14:5927; NORR 1st ser:24; PAR:265; PE:367; PEA: 367; REEM 6:172; REEMA 8:419; REEMB 6:104
Everett, E.
Circumstances favorable to the progress of literature in America. BL:80
Phi Beta Kappa oration. CHAL 6:52; HAZO 12:5108; MAS 12:5108
Foster, W.T.
Should students study? BRY:465; SAR:64
Gauss, C.
Scholar and his country (installation of Alpha chapter of Phi Beta Kappa at Florida State College). NORR 3d ser:43
Grosvenor, E.A.
Attitude of the scholar. NORR 1st ser:395
Jameson, J.F.
Age of erudition. NORR 1st ser:326
Johnson, G.W.
Provincial scholar. NORR 3d ser:273
Kennedy, J.F.
Intellectual and the politician. BA 1956-57:165; BARR:285; LINP:279
Kildee, R.
Speech for honors day banquet. JUD:199
Kirk, G.
Responsibilities of the educated man (at centennial of University of Denver), LINP:165
Lowell, A.L.
Scholarship. REEM sup 2: 187; REEMB 2:259
Lowther, J.B.
Man who walks alone. BRP:1:20; YR 1:75
March, F.A.
Scholar of today. NORR 1st ser:112
Morgan, E.S.
What every Yale freshman should know. ARNS:33
Nicholson, M.H.
Romance of scholarship. NORR 3d ser:118
Phillips, W.
Scholar in a Republic. BAAMP:144; BAKF:253; BL:257; BOB:183; NORR 1st ser:191; ONEM:795; PAR:333; SHUM:159
Rice, G.P.
Scholar and the twentieth century. BA 1949-50:220
Stephenson, W.H.
Half-century of Southern historical scholarship. TIN: 155
Stricker, M.
Intellectual: his journey and his home (talk to secondary-school graduates who have

LEARNING AND SCHOLARSHIP (cont.)
won college scholarships). BRAB:533
Tufts, J.H.
Present significance of scholarship. NORR 2d ser: 265
Verplanck, G.C.
Advantages and dangers of the American scholar. BL: 115
Willis, H.P.
Changing status of American scholarship. ONEC:194
See also Acceptance speeches-Scholarships; Education, higher; Humanism; Intellect; Knowledge, theory of; Research

Leary, Francis Woodburn
Shame of a nation. YR 7:167

LEATHER MERCHANTS
Leather (for a leather merchants' dinner). EDGS:136
Speech for a leather merchants' dinner. BARB:181
Leavitt, Ezekiel
To a Bar-Mitzvah. ZEL:55
Leavitt, Harvey L.
Men of vision. COUW:203

LEBANON
Churchill, W.L.S.
Speech in Commons on Syria and Lebanon. VO 1945-46:257
DeGaulle, C.
Address before the French Consultative Assembly on the Levantine question. VO 1945-46:294
Press statement on Syria and Lebanon. VO 1945-46: 247
Eden, A.
Statement on the Levant States. VO 1945-46:231
Eisenhower, D.D.
Plan for peace in Lebanon. BA 1958-59:23

Leberman, H.
For a Bar Mitzvah. ZEL:21
Lecky, William E.H.
Artistic side of literature. REEMA 2:708
LeConte, Joseph
Effect of the theory of evolution on education. WAGN: 44
Lee, Armistead Mason
New integration. YR 9:99
Lee, Duncan Chaplin
Function for patriotism during the period of change. YR 5:243
In defense of a perspective. YR 6:1
Lee, Elinor
Special tips to the amateur radio broadcaster. BUT: 127; BUTA:127
Lee, Fitzhugh
Flag of the Union forever. REEM 2:318; REEMA 2: 710; REEMB 2:322; SHUO: 241
Lee, Guy Carleton
Strength of the people. SHUO: 116
Lee, Henry
Funeral oration on Washington. BREW 7:304; CHAL 3: 474; HAZO 8:3242; HELE: 103; LEEW 8:323; MAS 8: 3242; ORAMA 1:243; REEM 5:274; REEMA 13: 1304; REEMB 9:313; RID: 26; SMI:86
Lee, Irving J.
Four ways of looking at a speech. ARNS:17
Lee, Ivy Ledbetter
Publicity for public service corporations. REEM 4:288; REEMB 5:110
Lee, John
Religious repose and future of our country. THOU 1:218
Lee, John A.
Fraternity. THOU 3:354
Lee, Josh
Lay the axe to the root of the evil. BLUE:94

Lee, Joshua Bryan
Drafting of wealth in time of war. BA 1938-39:60
Eulogy to Will Rogers. BOA: 219
Technological unemployment and relief. BA 1938-39: 108; ON:107, 200
Lee, Richard
Raising potatoes. BRP 8:115
Lee, Richard Henry
Address to the people of England. BREW 7:312; CHAL 2:423; HAZO 6:2493; HELE: 55; LEEW 8:221; MAS 6: 2493; REEMA 14:1313; SMI:32
Lee, Robert E.
Acceptance of the sword. SMI:173
To the Army of Northern Virginia. ANG:370; FO:212; KNAS:230; KNASA:230; SMI:174

LEE, ROBERT E.
Anderson, A.
Lee's statue in Richmond. SMI:175
Bruce, W. C.
General Robert E. Lee. DOA:33
Daniel, J.W.
Eulogy of Robert E. Lee (at unveiling of figure of General Lee). HARSO:277; PROS:105; SHU:150; SHUM: 244; SHUO:149; SMI:169
Last order Lee gave. THOS: 141
Littleton, M.W.
Robert E. Lee (Hall of Fame, New York University). BLAB:290; BOA:222; BOB:151; LINM:80
Moreland, T.W.
Robert E. Lee. SHUC:90
Stanley, A. O.
Lee and Appomatox. SHUO: 153
Stewart, W. H.
Eulogy on General Lee. SHUO:157
Walker, J. J.
Tribute to Robert E. Lee. SHU:107
Williams, R. G.
Robert E. Lee. SMI:299
Lee, Stephen D.
Eulogy of General John B. Gordon. SHUO:43
Leech, S. V.
Dying year. THOU 2:397
Leeson, James
Introducing a railroad executive. BRC:299
Legaré, Hugh S.
On submission. LEEW 9:339; SOU 9:271

Speech before the Union Party. -Same as his On submission

LEGISLATORS See Law and lawyers; Public officials; United States-Congress
Lehman, Frederick W.
Third house (commencement address). SHUO:312
Lehman, Herbert H.
Speech as director general of NNRRA. HAN:382
This I believe. BA 1951-52:90
Tidelands oil. BA 1952-53:146
Welcome to National Education Association of the United States. ON:316
Lehman, Irving
Response of the President of the Jewish Welfare Board. ONEC:23
Lehman, John H.
Introducing John Tyndall to Royal Academy, May 5, 1888. REEM 3:345
Introducing Leslie Stephen to Royal Academy, April 29, 1893. REEM 3:271
Power of propaganda. YR 1: 35
Leigh, Benjamin Watkins
Apportionment of representation. SMI:112

LEIGH, BENJAMIN WATKINS
McFarland, W.H.
Benjamin Watkins Leigh. SMI:141
Leighton, Robert
Immortality. BREW 7:321
Leighton of Stretton, Frederic Leighton, 1st Baron
Introducing J. Tyndall to Royal Academy, May 5, 1888. REEM 3:345
Introducing Leslie Stephen to Royal Academy April 29, 1893. REEM 3:271
Introducing Sir Arthur Sullivan to Royal Academy, May 2, 1891. REEM 3:298
Introducing Thomas H. Huxley to Royal Academy May 5, 1883. REEM 2:262
Toast "The health of her Majesty's Ministers." REEM 3:175
Variety in British art. REEMA 2:713
Leighty, G.E.
Responds to an introduction. PRC:9

LEISURE
Lindley, E.H.
University and the vocations of man: inaugural address as president of University of Kansas. WE 2:217
Lodge, H.C.
Uses and responsibilities of leisure. REEMA 8:777
Rockefeller, L.S.
Leisure: the new challenge. HIB:318
Leland, Charles Godfrey
Hans Breitman's return. REEMA 2:717
Lemass, S.
Statute of Westminster (July 19, 1931 speech). KESB:242
Lemieux, Rodolphe
Tribute to Laurier. NESA:160; REEM 5:276; REEMB 9:315
Lenarducci, David
Guarantee of freedom. DO:197

LEND LEASE LAW
Attlee, C.R.
Statement in Commons on termination of lend lease. VO 1945-46:489
Churchill, W.L.S.
Statement in Commons on lend-lease. VO 1944-45:584
Crowley, L.F.
Statement on termination of lend lease. VO 1945-46:490
Roosevelt, F.D.
Lend lease, March 12, 1941. FIP:242
Lenin, Nikolai
Dictatorship of the Proletariat. COP:141; COPA:141; COPB:141; FRY:93; PL:785; REEM 11:181; REEMB 12:196
Makes a world-shaking announcement, November 7, 1917. PEA:715
Peasants. REEM 11:187; REEMB 12:202
Speaks to a street crowd in Petrograd, Spring, 1917. PE:713; PEA:713
War, peace and revolutionary democracy. CROC:283
Lenroot, Irvine L.
Press and the government. LINM:39

LENT See Easter; Good Friday
Lenthall, William
Opening the long Parliament under Charles I. BREW 7:327
Lentulus, Lucius
On treating with the Samnites. LEEW 2:98
Lentz, Harold J.
Air-borne traveling man. SAB:29; SABA:31
Leo I, the Great, Saint, Pope
Blessedness of peace-making. PL:190
Homily on the Beatitudes. HAZO 3:1209; MAS 3:1209

On the feast of the Nativity. LEEW 3:274
Sermon on his birthday. LEEW 3:267
Sermon on the community of goods. PL:188
Leo XIII, Pope
Christian democracy. COP: 117; COPA:117; COPB: 117; REEMA 14:1323
LEO XIII, POPE
Crawford, F.M.
Pope Leo XIII. REEM 5:85; REEMA 4:339; REEMB 9:115

LEOCRATES.
Lycurgus.
Against Leocrates. CHAL 1:119; HAZO 1:201; LEEW 1:175; MAS 1:201; MINA 2:14

LEPELETIER DE SAINT-FARGEAU, LOUIS MICHAEL
Danton, G. J.
Assassination of LePeletier. CHAL 4:117; HAZO 8:3352; MAS 8:3352
Lepidus, Marcus A.
Against Sulla. LEEW 2:61
Lerner, Daniel
Comfort and fun: morality in a nice society. ARNS: 170
LeVander, Bernard
Meet your friends. BRP 6:19; YR 7:25
LeVander, Harold
Date kernels. BRP 3:45; YR 4:151
LeVander, Theodore
Curse of plenty. YR 3:145

LEVANT STATES See Lebanon; Syria
Leverone, Nathaniel
Introduces Billy B. Van, "Ambassador of goodwill from New England." PR:74
Levy, Nathan
America's domineering tradition. ONEC:395
Lewe, John C.
Presents Norman Vincent Peale. LY:165; PR:71
Presents Thomas C. Clark (Attorney General of the United States). LY:149; PR: 73
Lewis, C. S.
Social morality. ARNS:179
Three parts of morality. ARNS:176
Lewis, David
His speech on the scaffold. BREW 7:332
Lewis, E. R.
Industrial conflict. ASHF:150
Lewis, Fulton, Jr.
Responds to an introduction. PRNE:62

LEWIS, FULTON, Jr.
McDonough, J. J.
Introduces Fulton Lewis, Jr., radio and TV commentator. PRNE:24
Lewis, Sir George Cornewall Bart.
Speech in House of Commons, February 12, 1858 (on India). KESI 1:342
Lewis, Inez Johnson
Welcome to National Education Association. GA:20
Lewis, James Hamilton
Introduction of Jacob M. Dickinson. BRAC:235; LY:205
League of Nations. HICF:548
Response to presentation as toastmaster. BRAC:249

LEWIS, JERRY
Jessel, G.
Speech at Roastmaster dinner in honor of Dean Martin and Jerry Lewis. JEYO: 45
Lewis, John L.
Declaration to coal mine operators, March 19, 1945. BA 1945-46:180
In support of Willkie. BA 1940-41:113
Labor and the nation. COP: 425; COPA:425; COPB:

Lewis, John L. (cont.)
415; HURG:232; SAR:357
Responds to an introduction. PRNE:70
United Mine Workers demands. BA 1945-46:180
Who are the Americans today? BA 1953-54:150

LEWIS, JOHN L.
Day, J. E.
Introduces John L. Lewis, American labor leader. PRNE:19
Taylor, D. S.
Something of a man (in praise of John L. Lewis). MICS:166

Lewis, Lillian
Thanksgiving manna. THOU 2:300

Lewis, William H.
Address before the Massachusetts House of Representatives, February 12, 1913. DUNM:409; WOON:562
Booker T. Washington-a lover of his fellow-men. WOON:596

Lewis, Wilmarth S.
Trustees of the privately endowed university. NORR 3d ser:217

Ley, Willy
Conquest of space. BA 1960-61:115

LIABILITIES See Success

LIARS See Truthfulness and falsehood

LIBERAL ARTS See Education, higher

LIBERAL PARTY See Great Britain-Politics and government

LIBERALISM
Ascoli, M.
Scarcity of ideas. ARNS:226
Curtis, J. F.
Plea for liberalism. YR 7:103
Keefe, D.F.
Our too liberal arts. YR 9:239
Liberalistic temper. DAVC:76, 145
Machen, J. G.
Christianity vs. modern liberalism. WPRC:120
Schlesinger, A.M., Jr.
Challenge of abundance. ARNS:221
Sullivan, M.
What is liberalism? BART 1:209
Wallace, H. A.
Rebirth of liberalism. ON:201

LIBERIA
Teague, H.
Liberia: its struggles and its promises. DUNM:33

LIBERTY
Abrams, M. M.
Guardians of the light. NOR 1940:21
Aly, B.
Remarks on Jefferson Day. BA 1955-56:59
Baker, N. D.
March toward liberty. REEM 11:249; REEMB 12:264
Baldwin, R. N.
Rough road ahead. HAR:437
Baldwin, S. B.
Protect the democracies. PL:804
Ball, J.
Bondmen and freemen: address to the rebels at Blackheath. BRTH:3; BRTHA:3
Baruch, B.
Woodrow Wilson (commemorating centennial anniversary of birth of Wilson). BA 1956-57:141

Beecher, H.W.
Regulated liberty (at Glasgow October 13, 1863). FULB:345
Bell, E.I.
Not taps but reveille. BA 1944-45:307
Biddle, F. and others.
National security and individual freedom. HAR:440
Bisel, D.
For what do we fight? DO: 93
Blakely, R.J.
What is a free society? BA 1955-56:46
Borden, R.L.
Hope for liberty and democracy. BREW 2:154
Brewer, D.J.
Politics and personal liberty. THOU 1:210
Brooks, P.
True liberty. HAZO 23: 9945; MAS 23:9945
Burns, R.W.
Freedom and war. ANGC: 108
Burton, H.C.
What price freedom? DO:7
Burton, L.J.
Rights we fight for. DO: 145
Bush, F.E.
New liberty. BOB:89
Calhoun, J.C.
Individual liberty. BREW 3: 78
Carey, J.B.
This I believe. BA 1951-52:92
Carson, H.L.
American liberty. BREW 3: 147; RID:67
Centner, W.A.
True liberty. BRP 7:88; NOR 1936:28
Charles I.
Liberty and discipline: address to his troops at Wellington. BRTH:31; BRTHA: 31
Churchill, W.L.S.
Lights are going out. SAR: 289
Civil rights. DR:253
Clark, G.
Conservatism and civil liberty. SAR:151
Compton, A.H.
Truth makes us free. BART 1:327
Cousin, V.
Liberty, an inalienable right. BREW 4:193; CHAL 6:11; HAZO 12:5010; MAS 12:5010
Curran, J.P.
England and English liberties-in the case of Rowan. BREW 4:317; BRYW 6:99; CHAL 3:320; ESEH:201; GOOD:790; HAZO 7:2974; KET:147; MAS 7:2974; PL: 516; REEMA 12:764
In the case of Justice Johnson-Civil liberty and arbitrary arrests. BREW 4: 270; BRYW 6:127
Curtis, G.W.
American doctrine of liberty. July 17, 1862. NORR 1st ser:94
Liberty under law. COP: 624; REEMB 1:356
Puritan principle: liberty under law. BAKF:430; BRY:468; BRYA:554; ONEM:573; PAR:359; REEM 1:355; REEMA 1:290
Cushman, R.E.
How to use our civil liberty in wartime. BA 1941-42: 91
Depew, C.M.
Unveiling the Statue of Liberty. BREW 5:162; CHAL 12:307; HAZO 23:9688; MAS 23:9688; PROS:70; WERN 42:106
Dewey, O.
Homes of freedom. BOB: 162
Dobert, E.W.
Convert to freedom. BART 3:91

LIBERTY (cont.)
Douglas, P.H.
Internal security. BA 1950-51:103
Douglass, F.
Plea for free speech. BREW 5:282
Doyle, J.
Price of liberty. YR 8:165
Dulles, J.F.
Freedom or despotism? BA 1956-57:25
Dykstra, C.A.
Individual and the democratic adventure. BA 1939-40:141
Equality and liberty. NAT:11
Evarts, W.M.
Liberty enlightening the world. COP:636; REEM 2:28; REEMA 2:469; REEMB 2:28
Everett, E.
History of liberty. BREW 6:64; HAZO 12:5080; LEEW 10:21; MAS 12:5080; ORAMA 2:151; PL:631; REEM 10:59; REEMA 13:972; REEMB 11:60
George, H.
Tribute to liberty. DICD:151; DICE:151
Gittelsohn, R.B.
That men might be free. BA 1945-46:16
Goldwater, B.M.
Extremism in defense of liberty (accepting nomination for Presidency). HIB:291
Graper, E.E.
True defenders of liberty. BOA:125
Green, W.
Labor, freedom and democracy. BA 1940-41:243
Greetings to forum. BEC:161
Halle, R.
Guilty until proven innocent. SOBP:348
Halsey, J.H.
Education for freedom. BRY:433
Hand, L.
Fanfare for Prometheus (accepting American Liberties medallion). BA 1955-56:39
We seek liberty. BA 1943-44:254; HIB:183
Hart, M.K.
This American system: is it to be destroyed? SAR:203
Henry, P.
Liberty or death. BAAMP:29; BOU:39; BRE:23; BREA:23; BREW 7:15; BRIM:209; BRYW 8:62; CAP:18; CHAL 3:28; CHEM 1:63; CLAY:5; CODS:321; CODSA:321; COP:232; COPA:232; COPB:232; CROC:234; DICD:156; DICE:156; DOA:327; ESEH:192; FKA:3; FRY:7; FULB:168; HARS:26; HARSO:323; HAY:29; HAZO 6:2595; HELE:51; HIB:151; HIBS:443; HURG:27; JOHA 1 pt. 1:18; LEEW 8:115; MAS 6:2595; ONEM:328; ORAMA 1:57; PAR:91; PE:139; PEA:139; PL:569; PROS:130; REEM 10:1; REEMA:13:1178; REEMB 11:1; RID:8; SAA:95; SHAH:14; SOU 9:171
Henson, L.
Protectors of freedom. DO:172
Hoffman, P.G.
Response on receiving Freedom House award. BA 1951-52:77
Hoover, H.C.
Leadership for a free world. MO:568
Horton, J.
American opportunities. DO:13
Hughes, C.E.
Liberty and the law. LINM:167
Hugo, V.M.
Liberty tree in Paris.

BREW 7:96; MEAR:117
Hull, C.
Broadcast to the world, July 23, 1942. HAN:188; VO 1942-43:394
Hunter, W.
New birth of freedom. BRP 6:88
Hurley, P.J.
Americanism or Communism? BOA:301
Hutchins, R.M.
What price freedom? YE: 367
Hyde, A.M.
Liberty. BART 1:187
Ingersoll, R.G.
Liberty of man, woman and child. BREW 7:131; DICD: 132; DICE:132; HARSO: 199; IMMD:109; PAR:409; PROS:110; SHAH:465; SHU: 71
Johnston, E.A.
Intolerance. BA 1944-45: 175
Lang, W.C.
"The bold go toward their time." BA 1960-61:71
Lonarducci, D.
Guarantee of freedom. DO: 197
Liberty. CON:80
Lippmann, W.
In the service of freedom. BA 1943-44:248
Lowden, F.O.
Price of liberty. BOA:206; BOB:175
Lutz, R.H.
History of the concept of freedom. MIA:363
McArthur, H.K.
Truth and freedom. BA 1950-51:182
MacLeish, A.
This cause is our cause. BA 1943-44:243
Mangum, R.J.
Freedoms of the United States Constitution. DO:212
Montalembert, C.F.R. de T.
Devotion to freedom. BREW 8:179; HAZO 16: 6726; MAS 16:6726
Moore, J.O.
Common man. DO:67
Murphy, F.
Civil liberties. BA 1938-39: 173
Nodel, J.J.
Freedom's holy light. BA 1960-61:213
Oxman, S.A.
List. BU:154
Power of a free people. THOS:161
Power of liberty. BOB:119
Prentice, R.
Three jewels. BRP 9:7
Prentis, H.W., Jr.
Preserving the roots of liberty. BA 1941-42:201
Pym, J.
Law as a safeguard of liberty. BREW 8:389
Pyre, J.F.A.
Poetry and freedom. TRUW:19
Ripley, R.K.
Freedom's destiny. DO:60
Roosevelt, E.A.
Civil liberties-the individual and the community. BA 1939-40:173
Roosevelt, F.D.
Four human freedoms. ANG:495; BA 1940-41:185; BOA:7; BRE:362; CROC: 385; FIP:238; HAN:30; VO 1941:5
Truths that inspired Washington. BA 1942-43:217; VO 1943-44:83
Root, E.
Human freedom. REEM 3: 159; REEMB 3:162
Schurz, C.
True Americanism. BRE: 236; BOAM:11; REEMA 9: 1018
Sheen, F.J.
Liberty and the Republic. BA 1938-39:245
Slattery, F.E.
Church and liberty. CATA

LIBERTY (cont.)
2:243
Stafford, W. P.
Liberty under law. SHU:240
Stanley, A. O.
Perils of paternalism. HARSO:119
Stevenson, A. E.
Political relevance of moral principle (A. Powell Davies memorial address) WPRC: 355
Stoner, N. A.
Conceived in liberty. YR 8: 49
Storrs, R. S.
Rise of constitutional liberty (centennial oration at the Academy of Music, New York). CHAL 10:101; HAZO 19:8257; MAS 19:8257
Story, J.
Appeal for liberty. CLAY: 196
Swing, R.G.
Youth, war, and freedom. HAN:22
Symington, W. S.
Freedom and military security. BA 1949-50:75
Truth makes us free. BA 1952-53:42
Thomas, A.
Individual liberty. REEM 3:327; REEMB 3:344
Thomas, N.
No democracy without civil liberty. BA 1937-38:45
Thompson, D.
Freedom's back is against the wall. SAR:185
Trail, E.
Keep it America. DO:74
Turner, P. A.
Constitution-temple of liberty. BU:162
Tyler, J.
American liberty. SMI:129
Valentine, A.
Mobilizing the mind. BA 1940-41:263
Vanocur, S.
State of mind. NOR 1949: 163
Viviani, R. R.
Our heritage of liberty. LEW:103
Wallace, H. A.
Address at Chicago, September 11, 1943. VO 1943-44:351
Before the Free World Association. PE:792; PEA: 792; VO 1942-43:270
Welles, S.
Toward new horizons. HAN:370
Wentworth, P.
Liberty of the Commons. BRTH:6; BRTHA:6; CHAL 1:457; HAZO 4:1386; MAS 4:1386
Whitlock, B.
Lafayette, apostle of liberty. REEM 11:224
Willkie, W. L.
American liberty. COP: 555; COPB:547
Winant, J. G.
Response to welcome. ON: 94
Winthrop, J.
Little speech on liberty. CHAL 2:18; HAZO 4:1439; HURG:17; MAS 4:1439; PL:555
Woelfle, J.
What freedom means to me. BU:181
See also Bill of Rights Day; Civil rights; Democracy; Equality; Fourth of July; Free speech; Human Rights Day and Week; Liberty of the Press; Religious liberty; Teaching, Freedom of; United States-Constitution; United States-Economic policy

LIBERTY DAY
Breckenridge, J. C.
Proto-martyrs of liberty. THOU 1:496
Chamberlain, M.
Notable day (Liberty day).

THOU 1:489
Greenhalge, F.T.
Beginning of constitutionality. THOU 1:494
Hoar, E.R.
Appropriate name (for Liberty day). THOU 1:490
Keyes, E.
Significance of this holiday. THOU 1:492
Robinson, G.D.
Aim of the future. THOU 1:498
Warren, W.
Spirit of the Revolution. THOU 1:493
Spirit of true Americanism. THOU 1:500

LIBERTY LEAGUE
Robinson, J.T.
Jacob's voice but Esau's hands. WPRC:179

LIBERTY OF SPEECH See Free speech

LIBERTY OF THE PRESS
Canham, E.D. and others.
Is the American press really free? BA 1946-47: 159
Hardwick, P.Y.
Liberty of the press. EMS 2:3
Lytton, E.G.E.
Liberty of the press. EMS 2:43
Sheridan, R.B.
Liberty of the press. EMS 2:28

LIBRARIES AND LIBRARIANS
Address of congratulation by mayor or high civic official at opening of a memorial library. WRA:164
Bryant, W.C.
Fiftieth anniversary of the Mercantile Library Association. HAZO 12:5211; MAS 12:5211
Choate, R.
Books and civilization in America. BREW 3:288; HAZO 13:5448; MAS 13: 5448
Hill, F.P.
Librarian of today. REEM 2:214; REEMB 2:219
Iles, G.
Trusteeship of literature. HAZO 25:10817; MAS 25: 10817
Kaiser, H.J., Jr.
Knowledge is our strongest weapon. SABA:271
New libraries for old. SCHS: 194
Phelps, W.L.
Owning books. COP:704; COPB:731; HURG:225
Ramsey, H.
Introducing a public librarian. BRC:123
Smith, S.M.
Uses of a library (at dedication of Carnegie Library, Winthrop College, Rock Hill, South Carolina). SHUO: 80
See also Dedication addresses-Libraries

LIBRARIES, SCHOOL
High school library-why it should be and what it should be. AMEO 1:146
Liddon, Henry Parry
Adequacy of present opportunities. CHAL 11:232; HAZO 21:9097; MAS 21:9097
What Christmas brought. THOU 2:364

LIDICE (CZECHOSLOVAKIA)
See World War 1939-1945-Czechoslovakia

---- (ILLINOIS)
Lucas, S.W.
Address in honor of Eduard Benes. BA 1942-43:163
Lie, Trygve
Road to peace. HAR:61

Liebermann, Elias
"I am an American." PROS: 45; SHU:219
Lieberman, Myer H.
Plea for democracy in higher education. YR 1:147

LIES See Truthfulness and Falsehood

LIFE
Adams, C. F., Jr.
Lessons of life. REEM 1: 10; REEMA 1:1; REEMB 1:10
Adventures of life, by a mother. EDGS:306
Arnold, T.
Realities of life and death. BREW 1:159; CHAL 6:140; HAZO 12:5250; MAS 12: 5250
Bain, G.W.
Life lessons (commencemnt address at Pierce Business College). SHU:204; SHUO: 237
Beware of poison! JAS:86
Boddy, W.H.
Life: a mirage or a fountain. SAR:436
Bradley, P.
Romance of life. BART 1: 63
Brown, C.R.
Life complete. WAGN:270
Chalmers, T.
Use of living. BREW 3:190
Compton, K.T.
Stuff of life; our talents and their care. SAR:13
Davidson, C.
Common confusions. BRA: 556
Delayed obedience. JAS:34
Derby, E.H.S.
Life and culture. ORBR 2: 159
Diamonds in the rough. JAS: 68
Discipline of life and character. DAVC:71
Do you have "eyes that see not?" JAI:48
Don't be a dead bug! JAS:108
Don't be tricked. JAS:84
Dwight, T.
Pursuit of excellence. BREW 5:341
Ehninger, D.
Are we blind? BRP 7:82; NOR 1936:16
Fay, C.
Way of life. BRP 6:42; NOR 1934:113
Fisher, J.
Jeopardy of daily life. BREW 6:136
Game of life. JA:208
Game of life or a top man is not a flop man (a changeable speech adaptable as an inspirational speech for sales people, student groups and for all workers, or for a sports dinner speaker). BAI:56
Gantz, G.
Doors without keys. YR 6: 203
Getting started. FRIE:257
Gladstone, W.E.
Destiny and individual aspiration. BREW 6:263
Modern training for life. REEMA 8:534
Have you tried to live your own life lately? NAT:22
He who loves silver. JAI:72
Hennesy, J.
Drama of life. YR 7:81
Holmes, O.W., Jr.
Joy of life. REEMA 2:631; REEMB 2:236
Hutchins, R.M.
Philosophy of life. BA 1937-38:184
Huxley, T.H.
Threefold unity of life. BREW 7:105
In every today walks a tomorrow. AMEO 2:159
Ingersoll, R.
Life. BREW 7:135
Jason, W.G.
Life's morn. DUNM:403

Klepper, R.
Supreme jig-saw puzzle of life. YR 5:253
Let your light shine. JAS:26
Life can be fun. FRIE:241
Life, Neptune's cup. THOS: 149
Livermore, M.A.
Battle of life. REEMA 5: 739
Living a useful life. FRIE:254
Living or a life? JAS:20
Ludlow, L.
Department of good works. BOA:180
McEntegart, B.
Totality of outlook. LINP: 175
MacLeish, A.
Act of faith. BA 1950-51: 131
New generation meets the old. AMEO 2:200
Newton, J. F.
What to do with life today. BA 1945-46:214
Nicholson, M.
Sunny slopes of forty. REEM 6:354; REEMB 7:316
One year to live. JA:154
People are like apples. JAS: 94
Phelps, W. L.
Art of living. BART 4:23
Power of a song. JAS:28
Rainbows in the storm. JAI: 16
Salutatory- "Life." CRAI:420
Savage, M. J.
Education for life. BLAA: 26; BLAB:26
Schindler, J. A.
How to live a hundred years happily. BERS:101; YE:236
Shadows of tomorrow. JA:247
Sheats, P.H.
Salvage. BRP 1:44; YR 1: 121
Shulman, C.E.
Four philosophies of modern life. BA 1957-58:174
Smith, R. L.
Born rich. BRP 3:62
Greatest game in the world. BRP 2:20
Take along a bit of honey. THOT:15
This side of Heaven. JA:253
Tucker, W.J.
New movement in humanity. BLAA:23; BLAB:23
Tyndall, J.
Origin of life. BREW 10:19
Vandervoort, J.
No man is an island. BRAP:77
Vincent, J.H.
Perfect life. WERN 54:21
Warriors of the broken sword. BOB:193
Watch your patches. JAI:44
What are you worth? JAI:9
Wheeler, B.I.
Effective living. SHU:86
World's greatest things. THOT:39
Young, O.D.
Science of better living. BA 1937-38:190
You've got to be on the team. JAS:100
See also Behavior; Personality

LIFE INSURANCE See Insurance, life

LIFE ON OTHER PLANETS
Searle, G.M.
Are the planets habitable? REEMA 6:967

LIFESAVING
"Row-throw-go" (outline of speech on how to rescue drowning persons). MOA:317

LIGHT
Curtis, C.
Dedication of the auditorium at Atlantic City. DOA: 44
Haggard, H.W.
Physiology for the engineers. ON:19

LIGHT (cont.)
Pacini, A. J.
Light and health. EXEE: 578
Lilienthal, David E.
Atomic energy. BA 1946-47: 134
Atomic energy-where do we stand today? BA 1947-48:69
Bases of our nation's strength. HOA:159
Credo. BA 1946-47:150; BAAG:370
Offers a definition of democracy. -Same as his My faith in democracy
My faith in democracy. HIBS: 463; PE:808; PEA:807
Spirit of democracy. BA 1948-49:65

LILIENTHAL, DAVID E.
Taft, R. A.
Against the appointment of Lilienthal. BA 1946-47:113
Vandenberg, A. H.
For the appointment of Lilienthal. BA 1946-47:122
Lilio, Robert L.
American Constitution-for this we fight. DO:184
Lim-Yuen, Paul
Pacific charter. NOR 1942:59
Limb, Ben C.
Frank and candid light. HAR: 118

LIMITATION OF ARMAMENTS
See Disarmament
Lin Yu Tang See also Browne, L., jt. auth.
Lincoln, Abraham
Central ideas of the Republic. REEM 2:321; REEMA 2: 720; REEMB 2:325
Closes campaign against Douglas, October 30, 1858. PE: 497; PEA:497
Cooper Institute address. BRAS:137; BREW 7:351; CHAL 8:2; HAZO 16:6611; MAS 16:6611; ONEM:341; PAR:285; REEM 10:197; REEMA 14:1337; REEMB 11:208; SAA:156
Declaration of Independence. -Same as his Independence Hall speech
Delivers first great speech, October 4, 1854 at Springfield. PE:485; PEA:485
Dred Scott Decision. FO:150; JOHA 2 pt 1:154; REEMA 14:1356
Farewell to Springfield. BRYW 9:238; CHAL 8:2; COP:315; COPA:315; COPB:315; DOA:237; FO: 172; HAZO 16:6611; HIB: 271; HIBS:490; KNAS:229; KNASA:229; MAS 16:6611; ONEM:690; PAR:305; PE: 508; PEA:508; REEM 10: 235; REEMB 11:247; YE: 176
First inaugural address. ANG: 294; BAAMP:107; BAKF:227; BEA:287; BERS:133; BIR 2: 240; BRE:255; BREA:220 BRIM:214; BRYW 9:240; BURP:119; CARP:146; CHAL 8:27; CHI:127; FO: 172; HARS:371; HAZO 16: 6572; JOHA 2 pt. 2:16; LOTI:117; MAS 16:6572; ONEM:476; PAR:34; PAUF 2:36; PE:510; PEA:510; PO:87; USIN:119; USINA: 119
First joint debate at Ottawa, August 21, 1858. BRYW 9: 227; CLAW:63; FULB:291; HARS:323; HAZO 16:6586; MAS 16:6586
Gettysburg address. ANG: 361; BAAMP:114; BAKF: 207; BAKS:159; BEA:293; BIR 2:285; BOU:217; BRAO: 311; BRAP:44 (first draft); BRE:264; BREA:229; BREW 7:351; BRIM:226; BRYW 9:254; BURP:117; CAP:86; CARP:145; CHAL 8:26; CHEM 4:245; CLAY: 71; CODS:401; CODSA:401; COP:315; COPA:315;

COPB:314; CORP:193; CROC:295; ESEH:198; FKA:65; FO:205; FOS:124; FRY:38; HARS:416; HAY: 238; HAZO 16:6583; HIB: 16; HIBS:287; HICF:103; HURG:113; JOHA 2 pt 2: 123; LA:186; LEEW 10: 251; MAS 16:6583; MEAR: 109; ONEM:508; ORAMA 2:227; PAR:306; PAUF 1: 335; PE:522; PEA:522; PL:682; PO:97; REEM 10: 236; REEMA 8:774; REEMB 11:248; RID:54; SAA:200; SHAH:399; YE: 205

"A house divided against itself cannot stand." BIR 2:217; BRE:232; BREA:216; BREW 7:337; BRYW 9:222; COP: 309; COPA:309; COPB: 309; FO:156; HAZO 16: 6562; HICF:49; HURG:88; JOHA 2 pt. 1:168; KLEG: 323; LEEW 10:237; MAS 16:6562; ORAMA 2:217; PE:490; PEA:490; REEM 10:216; REEMB 11:227; SHAH:383; SHUM:133; WPRA:180

Independence Hall speech, February 2, 1861. CARP: 149; CHEM 4:157; SHUP: 156

Last public address, April 11, 1865. BIR 2:301; FO:213

Lincoln-Douglas joint debate at Alton, October 15, 1858. BAAMP:101; BIR 2:226; CLAW:90

Message to Congress, July 5, 1861. ANG:324

On his nomination to the United States Senate. -Same as his "A house divided against itself cannot stand."

Perpetuation of our political institutions (1837). HAY:184; SHU:90

Reply to Douglas at Chicago. SHAH:389

Reply to the working men of Manchester, England, January 19, 1863. FO:201

Second inaugural address. ANG:365; BAAGA:409; BAAMP:116; BAKF:238; BIR 2:297; BOU:77; BRAC: 366; BRE:265; BREA:230; BREW 10:355; BRIM:227; BRYW 9:255; CAP:91; CARP:147; CHAL 8:38; CHI:137; CLAW:155; CLAY:61; COP:315; COPA: 315; COPB:315; FKA:45; FO:210; HARS:418; HAZO 16:6584; HIB:272; HIBS: 491; HURG:114; JOHA 2 pt 2:125; LA:175; LEEW 10: 253; LOTI:125; MAS 16: 6584; ONEM:484; ORAMA 2:225; PAR:308; PAUF 1: 336; PE:523; PEA:523; PL:684; PO:98; REEM 10: 237; REEMA 8:775; REEMB 11:248; SAA:203; SHAH: 402; SHUP:209; USIN:127; USINA:127

Second joint debate at Freeport, August 27, 1858. BREW 7:345; REEM 10:224; REEMB 11:235

Speech at Peoria, October 16, 1854. BIR 2:196

Speech at Springfield, Ill., June 17, 1858. -Same as his "A house divided against itself cannot stand"

Speech before death. BREW 7: 356

Speech to 166th Ohio Regiment. BAKF:245

LINCOLN, ABRAHAM

Abraham Lincoln-a class oration. DAVC:251

Address for Lincoln's birthday. AMEO 2:17

Andrews, M.R.S.
Perfect tribute. PROS:80

Barton, B.
Faith of Lincoln. BA 1939-40:161

Bates, L.B.
Lincoln. HARSO:210;

LINCOLN, ABRAHAM (cont.)
WERN 42:39
Beaconsfield, B. D.
Assassination of Lincoln. BREW 1:300
Bearman, G. F.
Lincoln and the Constitution. LEIO:90
Beecher, H.W.
Effect of the death of Lincoln. BREW 1:370; CHAL 8:390; CLAY:64; HAZO 17:7274; MAS 17:7274
Belford, S. W.
Influence of Abraham Lincoln. SHU:118
Bingham, J. A.
Against the assassins of President Lincoln. BREW 2:50
Black, J. C.
Mother of Lincoln. HARSO: 229
Blanchard, N. C.
Lincoln and the South. SHUO:164
Bolton, H.W.
Abraham Lincoln. THOU 1: 470
Bristol, F. M.
Lincoln's choice and destiny. THOU 1:474
Brooks, P.
Character of Abraham Lincoln. BREW 2:244; CHAL 13:38; HAZO 23:9905; MAS 23:9905; REEM 5:37; REEMA 7:137; REEMB 9:67
Bryan, W. J.
Lincoln as an orator. LINM:221
Bunche, R. J.
Challenge of human relations: Lincoln birthday dinner. BA 1949-50:142; HAR: 452
Bylund, H.
Lincoln and the Constitution. LEIO:87
Choate, J. H.
Impressions of Lincoln. LAD:78
Curtis, J. L.
Abraham Lincoln (at centenary of his birth). DUNM: 321
Delano, H.
Greatness of Lincoln's simplicity. THOU 1:476
Depew, C. M.
Washington and Lincoln. BOB:148
Douglass, F.
Oration in memory of Abraham Lincoln (at unveiling of Freedmen's monument, Washington, D. C.). CHAL 9:144; DUNM:133; HAZO 18:7676; HIB:171; MAS 18: 7676; WOON:516
Emerson, R. W.
Greatness of a plain American. BREW 5:371; FKA: 66; MEAR:111
Emrich, R. S.
Greatness of Lincoln (sesquicentennial of Lincoln's birth). BA 1958-59:169
Farley, J. A.
Lincoln, the politician. ON: 348
Findlay, J. V. L.
Lincoln at Gettysburg. SHUO:167
Gannon, R. I.
Abraham Lincoln. ON:356
Garfield, J. A.
Death of Lincoln. PEAE: 161
Glennon, J. J.
Lincoln. CATA 1:1
Goff, N.
Lincoln-the man of God. BOA:237; BOB:145
Grady, H. W.
Lincoln as Cavalier and Puritan. THOU 1:477
Great emancipator. DU:158
Harding, W. G.
On Lincoln's birthday. REEM 2:162; REEMB 2: 164
Harrison, B.
Abraham Lincoln. BLAA: 134; BLAB:134
Hock, H.

Lincoln. YE:104
Holland, J. G.
Eulogy on Abraham Lincoln. CHAL 9:439; HAZO 19:8071; MAS 19:8071
Hooker, L.
Lincoln the hero of his convictions. THOU 1:474
In honor of Abraham on the day of his birth. DR:124; LU:1175
Jones, E.D.
Abraham Lincoln. BART 2:7
Adventures among great Americans. BART 1:115
Jusserand, J.J.
Address at the unveiling of the bust of Abraham Lincoln in the Hall of Fame, New York, May, 1923. LINM:83
Kelly, T.F.
Lincoln and the Constitution. LEIO:137
Kells, W.P.
Spirit of Lincoln-the need of our time. SHUC:77
Lewis, W.H.
Address before the Massachusetts House of Representatives, February 12, 1913. DUNM:409; WOON:562
Lincoln, SCHS:172
Lincoln the immortal. DAVC:452
Lincoln's birthday. BURS:172
Lincoln's birthday. CON:102
Lincoln's birthday. FRIE:110
Lincoln's birthday. NATS:19
Lincoln's birthday (in memory of the Great Commoner). EDGS:5
Lincoln's birthday (tribute to the nation's hero). ED:22
Littleton, M.W.
Washington and Lincoln. KLEM:181
Lloyd George, D.
Man of all peoples (dedication of Saint Gaudens' statue of Lincoln in London). BREW 7:368; CARP:206; MOA:540
Long, W.L.
Lincoln's debates with Douglas. TRUW:110
McKinlay, D.E.
Abraham Lincoln (birthday speech). WAGN:136
Madden, M.B.
Abraham Lincoln. HARSO:3
Mason, M.C.B.
Lincoln, the man of the hour. WOON:541
Moton, R.R.
Negro's debt to Lincoln (at dedication of Lincoln monument, Washington, D.C.). WOON:573
Newman, J.P.
Eulogy of Lincoln. ESEH:217
Tribute to Lincoln. THOU 1:476
Porter, H.
Abraham Lincoln. REEMA 3:931
Ramey, F.M.
Abraham Lincoln. BRP 1:16
Reynolds, L.G.
Abraham Lincoln. DOA:22
Rogers, E.E.
Lincoln's pluck and luck-what about ours? DICD:146; DICE:146
Root, E.
Unveiling the statue of Lincoln in London, July 28, 1920. BOAM:93
Ryan, O.
Abraham Lincoln. EXEE:347
Sandburg, C.
On Lincoln (at 150th anniversary of Lincoln's birth). HURG:347
Shortridge, S.M.
Abraham Lincoln. BOA:248; BOB:154
Silva, L.A.R.
Eulogy on Abraham Lincoln. CHAL 10:84; HAZO

LINCOLN, ABRAHAM (cont.)
19:8248; MAS 19:8248
Steele, S.
Emcee at Lincoln day exercises. BRH:312
Stephens, A.H.
At the unveiling of Carpenter's picture of Lincoln. LEEW 10:299
Swing, D.
Lincoln's birthday. THOU 1:470
Washington and Lincoln. CHAL 11:473
Taft, W.H.
Lincoln memorial. REEM 7:398; REEMB 8:419
Thurston, J.M.
Lincoln, a man called of God. HARSO:213; WERN 42:154
Viviani, R.R.
Tribute to Lincoln. LEW: 121
Wallace, H.A.
Lincoln's Day address. VO 1944-45:90
Walters, A.
Abraham Lincoln and fifty years of freedom. DUNM: 325; WOON:554
Washington, B.T.
Abraham Lincoln. HICF: 359; KLEG:213
Watterson, H.
Abraham Lincoln. HARSO: 262; PROS:262; REAC: 68; REEM 5:376; REEMA 6:1159; REEMB 9:420; SHUO:161
What Lincoln's Gettysburg address has meant to the world. AMEO 1:207
Wilson, W.
Abraham Lincoln (dedicating Lincoln's birthplace). ONEM: 537; ONES: 98; SHU:18
Wise, S.S.
Abraham Lincoln, man and American. COP:349; COPA: 349; COPB:349; HURG: 169; LINM:87; REEM 5:409; REEMB 9:454
Woodruff, T.L.
Lincoln and McKinley. WERN 42:95
Lincoln, Hugh
Introducing an appliance dealer
" a beautician
" a Red Cross worker. BRC:144, 150, 42
Lincoln, Joseph
Cape Cod folk. REEM 2:324; REEMB 2:328

LINCOLN, NANCY HANKS
Black, J.C.
Mother of Lincoln. HARSO: 229
Lindabury, Richard V.
Argument for the complainants in the Prudential-Fidelity merger case. HICJ: 408
Lindbergh, Anne Morrow
Experiences in the Chinese flood. DOA:128
Lindbergh, Charles Augustus
Independent policy. COP:576; COPB:561; HURG:254
Our air defense. BA 1940-41: 75
Response to New York's welcome. ONEC:21

LINDBERGH, CHARLES AUGUSTUS
Coolidge, C.
Welcome to Charles Lindbergh. BRAC:240; SHU:7; SHUP:163
Finley, J.H.
Presenting a medal to Col. Lindbergh. ONEC:38
Gwinn, J.M.
Presents Charles Lindbergh. LY:248
Ludlow, L.
Charles A. Lindbergh. BOA:224
Walker, J.J.
Welcoming Colonel Charles A. Lindbergh. ONEC:11; PROS:112
Lindemann, Herbert

Preservation for life's paths. ACW:45
Lindley, Ernest Hiram
University and the vocations of man: inaugural address as president of University of Kansas. WE 2:217
Lindquist, Carl
Liquor propaganda and youth. BRP 10:68
Lindquist, Robert
Beyond the dollar sign. MIA: 375
Lindsay, William
Law is with duty. FUL:187, 191
Link, Eugene Perry
Puppets. YR 1:139
Linner, Carol
Up from the balogney age. BRP 5:86

LIONS CLUB
Give the kids a break. JA:124
Jessel, G.
Speech to the Lions' Club. JEYO:35
Lions. NATS:31
Lions. SCHS:170
Man who had twelve eyes. JA: 127
Message of appreciation before the local service club (Rotary, Kiwanis, Lions, etc.). DR:99; LU:1166
Wagner, R.F., Jr.
Welcomes the convention of Lions International. PRNE: 71
Lippard, George
Black horse and his rider. HARSO:305
Death bed of Benedict Arnold. HARSO:311
Signing of the Declaration. PROS:62
Lippmann, Walter
Education vs. Western civilization. -Same as his Education without culture
Education without culture. BA 1940-41:292; NORR 3d ser: 132
Educational deficit and national crisis. BA 1954-55:134
Frustration of our time. BA 1961-62:162
In the service of freedom. BA 1943-44:248
Peace settlement with Russia. BA 1946-47:103
Philosophy and United States foreign policy. BA 1947-48: 48
Rise of personal government in the United States. BA 1937-38:122
Theatre Guild. REEM 2:331; REEMB 2:335

LIPTON, THOMAS
Ade, G.
Tribute to Lipton. NESA: 180

LIQUOR PROBLEM See Alcoholism; Prohibition; Temperance

LIQUORS
Colton, F.
Introducing a French wine merchant. BRC:312
This sir, is my stand. GRIS: 19

LITERARY PRIZES See Literature

LITERATURE
Arnold, M.
Realm of literature. REEMA 1:14
Avebury, J.L.
Choice of books. CHAL 12: 365; HAZO 23:9761; MAS 23:9761
Hundred best books. BREW 7:397
Balfour, A.J.
Pleasures of reading. BRYW 5:161; CHAL 14:134; HAZO 25:10643; MAS 25: 10643; REEM 6:40; REEMA 7:49; REEMB 7:41

LITERATURE (cont.)
Barrie, J.M.
Literature and the press. COP:692; COPB:719; GLAD:181
Beard, R.S.
This trash must go. NOR 1940:3
Beecher, H.W.
Books. REAC:132
Bishop, M.
Faith in literature. NORR 3d ser:167
Bourinto, J.G.
Early Canadian literature. CHAL 13:132; HAZO 23:10068; MAS 23:10068
Bryson, L. and others.
Opportunities for success in the creative arts. SAR:403
Business of writing. DR:63
Clemens, S.L.
"Littery" episode. ONEM:645; REEM 1:292; REEMA 1:214; REEMB 1:293
Corley, P.
In defense of fiction. GA:226
Current review club. SCHS:92
Curtis, G.W.
Commerce and literature. REEMA 1:307
Dana, J.C.
Mere words. REEM 6:108; REEMB 6:59
Dawson, S.E.
Prose writers of Canada. CHAL 12:142; HAZO 22:9538; MAS 22:9538
Dew, T.R.
Influence of republican government on literature and character. SMI:123
Drummond, H.
Talk on books. BREW 5:337
Drummond, R.
Emcee at a writers' guild meeting. BRH:243
Eggleston, G.C.
Southern literature. REEMA 2:423
Eliot, T.S.
What is a classic? ARNS:47
Emerson, R.W.
Literary ethics. CHAL 7:117; HAZO 14:5951; MAS 14:5951
Everett, E.
Circumstances favorable to the progress of literature in America. BL:60
Faulkner, W.
On accepting the Nobel prize, exhorts the young writers of the world. BOU:9; COPB:637; HAR:397; HIBS:508; HURG:291; PE:814; PEA:814
Froude, J.A.
Men of letters. KLEM:133; REEMA 2:510
Gale, Z.
The novel and the spirit. REEM 6:191; REEMB 7:162
Garland, H.
Realism versus romanticism. REEMA 2:518
Gilbert, E.J.
Introducing an author. BRC:272
Gladstone, W.E.
Use of books. BREW 6:264
Harrison, F.
Choice of books. REEM 6:232; REEMA 5:523; REEMB 7:213
Higginson, T.W.
Literature in a republic. REEMA 5:565
Hole, S.R.
With brains, Sir! REEMA 2:622
Huber, L.J.
Introducing a writer. BRC:89
Hughes, L.
Speech on selling writing. HILK:274
Jebb, R.C.
Literature and art. REEMA 2:686
Jusserand, J.J.

Truth and beauty in books and art. BREW 7:184
Kaser, A. L.
Emcee at a readers' and writers' club meeting. BRH:244
Keyes, F. P.
Current trends in literature. GA:237
Lang, A.
How to fail in literature. REEM 6:303; REEMA 5: 713; REEMB 6:225
Problem novels. REEMA 2: 698
Lecky, W.E.H.
Artistic side of literature. REEMA 2:708
Love of literature. DR:59
Lowell, J.R.
Our literature (100th anniversary of Washington's inauguration). BAKF:423; REEMA 2:758
Mabie, H.W.
Poe's place in American literature (unveiling of bust of Edgar Allan Poe). REEMA 9:815
Spirit of New England literature. REEMA 2:778
Macaulay, T.B.
Literature of England. BREW 8:14; HAZO 13:5535; MAS 13:5535
Matthews, B.
American literature. REEMA 9:861
Milliken, F.
Emcee at a writers' club. BRH:234
Montgomery, J.
Modern English literature. BREW 8:183
Morley of Blackburn, J.M.
Literature and politics. KLEM:139; REEMA 2:838
Opdycke, J.B.
Relation of literature to advertising. REEM sup 2:261; REEMB 5:207
Phelps, W. L.
Literature as a revelation of life. KLEB:225
Read, O.
Modern fiction. BLAA:194; BLAB:194; REAC:92; REEMA 3:976
Ruskin, J.
Reading for the thought. DICD:154; DICE:154
Russell, J.R.
Science and literature as modes of progress. BREW 9:126
Simpson, H.
Decline of the writer. GA: 116
Smith, C.A.
Literature and a lost cause. SHUO:19
Smith, G.
Lamps of fiction (at centenary of Sir Walter Scott). BREW 9:233; ONEM:541; REEMA 9:1068
Steele, S.
Emcee at a book-of-the-month club meeting. BRH: 237
Swing, D.
Novel in literature. REEMA 9:1114
Thackeray, W.M.
Authors and their patrons. BREW 9:383
Novelist's future labors. BREW 9:385
Reality of the novelist's creation. BREW 9:381
Van Dyke, H.
Books, literature, and the people. REEM 6:406; REEMA 7:391; REEMB 7: 408
Woolsey, J.M.
Opinion December 6, 1933 (Ulysses Case-freedom of reading). ANG:468
See also Book reviews; Books and reading; Criticism; Negro authors; Negro literature; Poetry and poets
Littell, J.S.
Address of welcome (Sons of Temperance). THOU 3:486

Littell, Norman
Path to peace. ASHF:355
Little, Arthur Dehon
Fifth estate. REEM sup 2:143; REEMB 6:244
Little, Lou
Function of national associations in intercollegiate athletics. GLAD:295
Little Carpenter (Cherokee Indian)
Speech before signing treaty to swear allegiance to King of England. JON:64
Little Turtle, Miami chief
Speech in Council. JON:77
Littlefield, Charles E.
Pearl of the Antilles. CHAL 14:227; HAZO 25:10755; MAS 25:10755
Littleton, Martin E.
Democracy, the hope of the world. BOB:35
Littleton, Martin Wilie
Armistice day 1921. REEM 7:230; REEMB 8:250
Commencement address. KLEB:57
Direct democracy. BYRA:282; REEM 2:335; REEMB 2:339
Robert E. Lee (Hall of Fame, New York University). BLAB:290; BOA:222; BOB:151; LINM:80
Summation for the respondent in the investigation of Senator Jotham Allds. HICJ:557
Washington and Lincoln. KLEM:181
Litvinov, Maxim
League of Nations. COP:448; COPA:448; COPB:468
Livermore, Mary Ashton
Battle of life. REEMA 5:739
Livernash, Edward J.
Spirit of commercialism. WAGN:417

LIVESTOCK See Agriculture
Livingston, E. M.
Final test. ONES:361
Livingston, Edward
On the Alien Bill. HAZO 9:3552; MAS 9:3552
Livingston, Harold
Fool's gold. BOA:354; YR 6:213
Livingston, Homer J.
Introduces Clarence B. Randall, Chairman of the Inland Steel Company. PRNE:8
Livingston, Robert R.
Oration before the Cincinnati. CHAL 3:187; HAZO 7:2815; MAS 7:2815
Wealth and poverty, aristocracy and Republicanism. BREW 7:361

LIVINGSTONE, DAVID
Dunbar, A. M.
Life of social service as exemplified in David Livingstone (at centenary of his birth). DUNM:425
Livius, (Patavinus) Titus
Appeal of Horatius. LEEW 2:85
LLEWELLYN, SIR WILLIAM
Phelps, W. L.
Presents Sir William Llewellyn. LY:245
Lloyd, Alfred Henry
Time of day. NORR 2nd ser:446

LLOYD, HENRY
Addams, J.
In memory of Henry Lloyd. REEM 5:1; REEMB 9:1
Lloyd, Leslie
Wanted: 10,000 new martin homes. BRAP:48
Lloyd, Wesley P. and others (J. H. Ayers, and Robert F. Lovett)
Attitude of industry toward employment of college graduates. MOA:482
Lloyd, William
Protected home. THOU 3:198
Lloyd George, David
Appeal to the nation. BRTH:341; BRTHA:341; COP:

201; COPA:201; COPB: 201; CROC:299; FRY:69; PE:692; PEA:692; PL: 743; REEM 11:70; REEMB 12:78
British war aims. BREW 7: 374
The budget. HAY:305; PE: 680; PEA:680; REEM 9: 383; REEMB 10:395
Bully will be torn from his seat. -Same as his Appeal to the nation
Calls for a steep increase in taxes. -Same as his The budget
Civilization disorganized by hate. BREW 7:373
Gives some advice to Prime Minister Chamberlain. PE: 768; PEA:768
Imperial Conference, 1921. KESB:43
In the name of ten million dead. BREW 7:370
Man of all peoples (dedication of Saint Gaudens' statue of Lincoln in London). BREW 7:368; CARP:206; MOA:540
Meaning of America's entrance into the war. ONES:310; SAA:255
Modern issues in ancient Welsh. BREW 7:379
Our commission (speech made in New York in 1923 at a farewell dinner in his honor). LINM:334
Scrap of paper. -Same as his Appeal to the nation
Sea power and the British Empire. BREW 7:272
Seconding the nomination of M. Georges Clemenceau for President of the Peace Conference. REEM 11:313; REEMB 12:331
Speech at January 25 Session, Peace Conference, 1919. REEM 11:322; REEMB 12: 340
Speech in House of Commons, July 3, 1919 (on League of Nations). KESB:31
Speech in House of Commons, December 14, 1921 (on establishment of Irish Free State). KESB:83
Speech in House of Commons, November 18, 1925 (on Locarno Pact). KESB:367
To American comrades in arms. REEM 11:200; REEMB 12:215
Victory or defeat: no halfway house. REEM 11:156; REEMB 12:169
Villany of landlords. -Same as his The Budget
Vision of the people. BEA: 203

LOANS See Lend Lease Law; Mortgages
Loasby, Arthur W.
Opportunities for the American bank clerk. LINM:450

LOCAL GOVERNMENT
Kossuth, L.
Local self-government. BREW 7:223; HAZO 14: 5795; MAS 14:5795
See also Municipal government

LOCARNO, PACT OF (1925)
Chamberlain, A.
Speech in House of Commons November 18, 1925 (on Locarno Pacts). KESB: 357
Lloyd George, D.
Speech in House of Commons, November 18, 1925 (on Locarno Pact). KESB: 367
Lochner, Louis P.
Inside Germany. BA 1942-43: 168
Locke, David Ross (Petroleum V. Nasby)
In search of the man of sin. REEMA 5:759

Locke, Richard F.
Preservative element in American society. COUW:51
Locks, Elizabeth S.
Assassin of youth. BRP 9:53
Lodge, Henry Cabot
Against the Constitution of the League of Nations. BRAS: 357
American flag-not the dollar. BOA:294; BOB:79
At Republican convention, June 21, 1900. CHAL 14: 200; HAZO 25:10709; MAS 25:10709
Battle of Santiago. BLAA:56; BLAB:56
Blue and the Gray. REEMA 2: 723
France and Rochambeau. WERN 42:129
In opposition to the Proposed League of Nations. WPRC: 61
On Daniel Webster (at unveiling of statue in Washington). CHAL 14:179; HAZO 25: 10688; MAS 25:10688
Our forefathers. HURG:141
Party harmony and political friendship. BYRA:286; REEM 10:386; REEMB 11: 402
Passing of "Valiant-for-truth." (Theodore Roosevelt). BREW 7:380; REEM 5:280; REEMB 9:319
Retain the Philippines (October 30, 1899) FUL:197, 201
Retention of the Philippines (March 7, 1900). COP:339; COPA:339; COPB:339
Treaty of peace. FUL:194
Treaty of peace with Germany. HICF:592
True Americanism. BOB:113
Uses and responsibilities of leisure. REEMA 8:777
Webster as an orator. SHU:76
Lodge, Henry Cabot, Jr.
Fruitful approach to a prolonged peace. BA 1942-43: 116
Hungary's struggle for freedom. BA 1956-57:36
Russian support of Korean aggression. BA 1952-53:25
Soviet suppression of Hungarian liberty. BA 1957-58:37
Stop being afraid: reply to attack on United States by Andrei Vyshinsky. BA 1950-51:37; YE:171
United Nations. HURG:344
United Nations and world opinion. BA 1954-55:43
What the United Nations means to the United States. MOA: 517
Lodge, Sir Oliver Joseph
Electrons and the infinity of the universe. BREW 7:382
Pure and applied science. REEM sup 2:160; REEMB 5:120

LODGE SPEECHES See Acceptance speeches-Emblems; Club speeches. Also Names of lodges, as Freemasons; Elks, Benevolent and Protective Order of; Knights of Malta
Loeb, Max
Idols and ideals. TRUW:191
Loeber, A. H. A.
Wilt thou go with this man? ACW:1
Logan, John, Chief of the Mingoes
On the murder of his family. BOU:115; BREW 7:117; BRYW 8:3; JON:49; LEIO: 24; REEM 10:51; REEMB 11:52; SHE:36; SMI:11
Logan, John A.
General orders inaugurating Decoration Day. THOU 1:98
On the independence of Cuba. CHAL 11:56; HAZO 21: 8815; MAS 21:8815
Response to Illinois Republican Association. HILL:485
Self-government in Louisiana. HAZO 21:8840; MAS 21: 8840

Vindication of President Grant. CHAL 11:62; HAZO 21: 8821; MAS 21:8821
Logan, Walter S.
Introducing Lewis E. Carr to the New York State Bar Association, January 17, 1900. REEM 1:223; REEMB 1:224
Lomasney, William Francis (Captain Mackay)
Consciousness of innocence (from dock in Dublin).HAZO 24:10420; MAS 24:10420
London, Meyer
International league to secure peace. HARSO:76

LONDON
Churchill, W. L. S.
Address on receiving the freedom of the city of London. VO 1943-44:251

LONDON NAVAL ARMS CONFERENCE See Conference on the Limitation of Naval Armaments, London, 1930

LONELINESS See Solitude

LONG, HUEY P.
Williams, T.H.
Gentleman from Louisiana: demagogue or Democrat? TIN:398
Long, Jefferson F.
Speech on disorders in the South. WOON:294
Long, John D.
American Navy. FUL:214; REEMA 2:727
Class of 1857. KNAS:278; KNASA:278
Eulogy on Wendell Phillips. CHAL 13:247; HAZO 24: 10216; MAS 24:10216
Nominating George F. Edmunds for President. HOAP:288; KNAS:299; KNASA:299
Our new problems. FUL:205; HAZO 24:10221; MAS 24: 10221
Our representatives in Congress. -Same as his Response to toast at National Druggists' Association
Presentation of sword to Admiral Dewey. FUL:209; HAZO 24:10228; MAS 24: 10228
Response to toast at National Druggists' Association. HOA:375; HOAP:262
Soldier boy (May 30, 1882). BAKF:193; BLAA:69; BLAB:69; KLEG:176; ONEM:561; REAC:75; WERN 42:58
Long, Lindley Grant
Power of ideas. SHU:190
Relation of modern-isms to progress. SHUC:42; TRUW:26
Long, Willard L.
Lincoln's debates with Douglas. TRUW:110
Longden, Mrs. John
New steel world. BUT:187; BUTB:187
Longenecker, Flora M.
Constitution. LEIO:106
Longfellow, Henry Wadsworth
Washington Irving. KNAS:55; KNASA:55; REEMA 8:786

LONGFELLOW, HENRY WADSWORTH
Holmes, O.W.
Longfellow. KNAS:58; KNASA:58

LONGITUDE See Latitude and longitude
Longworth, Nicholas
Legislating for a republic. REEM sup 2:168; REEMB 5:128
Lonn, Ella
Reconciliation between the North and the South. TIN: 193
Loomis, Daniel P.
Responds to introduction by Rudolph G. Rydin. PRC:12

Loomis, Daniel P. (cont.)
Why not let competition go to work in transportation? LINP:269

LOOMIS, DANIEL P.
Rydin, R. G.
Introduces Daniel P. Loomis, President of the Association of American Railroads. PRC:11
Loose, J.W.
Liberty we need now. THOU 1:215
Lord, Chester S.
Introducing N. M. Butler. REEM 1:187; REEMB 1:188
Welcoming Mary Garden to Lotus Club, New York, January 29, 1922. REEM 2:61
Lord, John
Oliver Cromwell. REEMA 5:787
Lord, Mrs. Oswald B.
World around us (commencement address at Temple University, Philadelphia) BUTB:236

LORD'S SUPPER See Communion
Loreburn, Robert Threshie, 1st Earl of
On the policy of the English Liberals. BRYW 5:247
Right of association. EMS 2:66
Right of public meeting. EMS 2:61
Lorimer, George C.
Logic of Easter. THOU 2:122

LOTTERIES See Gambling
Loud, George B.
Memorial address (Foresters). THOU 3:277
Loughran, John J.
Opposition to the church evidence of her divine origin and nature. CATA 2:185

LOUIS XIV, KING OF FRANCE
Massillon, J. B.
Funeral oration on Louis XIV. PL:276
LOUIS XVI, KING OF FRANCE
DeSeze, R.
Defending Louis XVI. BREW 5:187
Desmoulins, C.
Advocating the execution of Louis XVI. COP:70; COPA:70; COPB:70; REEMA 13:913
Appeal to the people (delivered during the trial of Louis XVI). CHAL 4:128; HAZO 8:3466; MAS 8:3466
Gensonne, A.
Judgment of Louis XVI. LEEW 5:115

LOUISIANA
Kernan, T. J.
Louisiana (response to toast). SHUO:224
Logan, J. A.
Self-government in Louisiana. HAZO 21:8840; MAS 21:8840
Quincy, J.
On the admission of Louisiana. CHAL 4:411; HAZO 9:3879; JOHA 1 pt 1:180; MAS 9:3879; REEMA 14:1663
L'Ouverture, Pierre Dominique Toussaint See Toussaint L'Ouverture, Pierre Dominique
Louvet, Jean Baptiste
Accusation of Robespierre. LEEW 5:75
Lovald, Scott D.
Unless they act. BRP 10:106
Love, George H.
Response to an introduction. PR:133

LOVE
Breeden, H. O.
Supremacy of love. THOU 3:112
Drummond, H.
Greatest thing in the world. BREW 5:314; CHAL 14:251;

HAZO 25:10780; MAS 25: 10780; ORBR 2:431; PL: 505
Harlow, H. F.
Nature of love. LINP:84
How do you know it's love? JA:250
Latimer, H.
On Christian love. CHAL 1: 396; HAZO 3:1283; MAS 3: 1283
Smith, A. E.
Fashions in love. JUD:159
Lovejoy, Owen R.
Twentieth Amendment (affirmative). ONEC:311, 341
Loveless, Herschel C.
Welcome address at Iowa State College centennial. IOCP:13
Lovett, Robert F. See Lloyd, W. P., jt. auth.
Lovett, Robert Morss
Introducing Sam A. Lewisohn. ONEC:68

LOVING CUPS See Acceptance speeches- Cups; Presentation speeches- Cups
Low, Seth
Chamber of Commerce. REEM 4:298; REEMA 2: 731; REEMB 5:138
Installation speech as President of Columbia. ONES:85
Introducing and toasting Robert E. Peary at New England Society, December 22, 1909. REEM 3:47
Response to welcome. ONES: 85
Their ideal of education. THOU 1:353

Lowden, Frank O.
Eternal vigilance. REEM 2: 339; REEMB 2:343
Plea for the farmer. REEM sup 2:178; REEMB 2:351
Price of liberty. BOA:206; BOB:175
Lowe, John Adams
Presents E. J. Pratt. LY:58
Lowe, Robert, 1st Viscount Sherbrooke
Coming of democracy. ADR 4:232; HAY:240; PAUF: 1:393
Representation of the People Bill, House of Commons, May 31, 1866. -Same as his Coming of democracy
Lowell, Abbott Lawrence
Accepting keys of the George F. Baker Foundation. ONEC:53
Art of examination. ONES: 185; REEM sup 2:189; REEMB 7:261
College factory. HOA:180
Inaugural address. KLEG:281
League to Enforce Peace. FKA:207
90th birthday of Charles W. Eliot. REEM sup 2:188; REEMB 7:260
Scholarship. REEM sup 2:187; REEMB 2:259
Lowell, Amy
Poetry and criticism. REEM 2:347; REEMB 2:360
Lowell, James Russell
After-dinner speaking. BOU: 189; COP:619; COPB:659; KLEM:29; REEM 2:359; REEMA 2:750; REEMB 2: 372
Commerce. REEM 2:358; REEMA 2:748; REEMB 2: 371
Democracy: inaugural address on assuming the Presidency of the Birmingham and Midland Institute, Birmingham, England, October 6, 1884. PAUF 2:205; REEM 7:234; REEMA 8:789; REEMB 8: 254
For the Old South Meeting-house. KNAS:1; KNASA:1
Harvard alumni. REEMA 2:737
International copyright. REEMA 2:761
National growth of a century. REEM 2:354; REEMA 2: 741; REEMB 2:367

Lowell, J.R. (cont.)
Oration at 250th anniversary of the founding of Harvard College. CHAL 9:354; HAZO 19:7979; MAS 19:7979
Our literature (100th anniversary of Washington's inauguration). BAKF:423; REEMA 2:758
Plea for modern languages. CHAL 9:374; HAZO 19:7998; MAS 19:7998
Poetical and the practical in America. BREW 7:385
Pope and his times. BREW 7:392
Return of the native (response to a welcome home). ONEM:697; REEM 2:362; REEMA 2:753; REEMB 2:376
Stage. REEMA 2:745

LOWELL, JAMES RUSSELL
Curtis, G.W.
James Russell Lowell. REEM 5:93; REEMA 7:255; REEMB 9:124
Lowell's Americanism. REEMA 1:312
Matthews, B.
James Russell Lowell. REEM 2:394; REEMB 2:411
Lowell, John
Humors of the Bench (retirement from Bench of United States Circuit Court). BYRA:292; REEM 2:368; REEMA 2:766; REEMB 2:381
Lowry, Howard F.
"A Christmas Carol" at Wooster. YE:96
Lowther, James B.
Man who walks alone. BRP 1:20; YR 1:75

LOYALTY
Goethals, G.W.
Serving your country. REEM 7:154; REEMB 8:181
Loyalties. CON:86
Rickey, B.
Greatest single thing a man can have. EXEE:268
Lubbock, Sir John See Avebury, J. L.
Lucas, Scott W.
Address in honor of Eduard Benes. BA 1942-43:163
Welcoming President Eduard Benes. BA 1942-43:56
Luce, Clare Boothe
Address to the Republican National Convention. BUTA:231
America in the post-war air world. BA 1943-44:143; BOA:37
American morality and nuclear diplomacy. HIB:338

LUCE, CLARE BOOTHE
Blaine, J.B.
Introduces Clare Boothe Luce. PR:91
Luce, Henry R.
Reverse Mr. Justice Holmes. BRA:544
Lucking, Alfred
League of Nations. WHIP:282
Ludlow, Louis
Charles A. Lindbergh. BOA:224
Department of good works. BOA:180
Mother's love. BOA:258; BOB:132
Objectives of democracy. BOA:328; BOB:86
Ludlum, Mary Ellen
Buy Reynolds' wrap. SAB:160; SABA:258
My experiences as a teacher. YE:334

LUMBER AND LUMBERING
Lumbermen. SCHS:175
Lumpkin, J. Howard
Where to, America? YR 5:323
Lundeen, Ernest See Granik, T., jt. auth.
Lusty, Robert
Presents Sir Norman Birkett. LY:68
Luther, Mrs. Lloyd

Political implications of Mother Goose. BUT:182; BUTB:182
Luther, Martin
Before the Diet of Worms. BREW 7:406; BRYW 7:38; CHAL 1:406; COP:65; COPA:65; COPB:65; CROC: 302; HAZO 3:1293; MAS 3: 1293; PE:85; PEA:85; PL: 226; REEM 9:58; REEMB 10:59
Pith of Paul's chief doctrine. BREW 7:410
Sermon on Peter's denial of Christ. HAZO 3:1298; MAS 3:1298
Sermon on the Good Shepherd. LEEW 4:69

LUTHER MARTIN
Martin Luther, bonfire builder. JAS:106
Melanchton, P.
On the death of Luther. BRYW 7:44; CHAL 1:427; HAZO 4:1333; MAS 4:1333
"Theses" that shook the world. JAI:78
Luther, Seth
Addresses workingmen of New England. PE:362; PEA:362
Luthuli, Albert John
Africa and freedom (accepting 1960 Nobel Prize). CROC: 306
Lutz, Ralph H.
History of the concept of freedom. MIA:363

LYCEUM
Pond, J.B.
Memories of the lyceum. REEM 8:313; REEMA 6: 893; REEMB 13:318

LYCOPHRON.
Hypereides.
First and second speeches in defence of Lycophron. MINA 2:376, 400
Lycurgus.
Against Leocrates. CHAL 1: 119; HAZO 1:201; LEEW 1:175; MAS 1:201; MINA 2:14
Fragments. MINA 2:138
Lyda, Harold
Human values. BRP 9:29; YR 10:95
Lynch, Gerald J.
Pursuit of security (accepting an honorary degree by University of Dayton at graduation exercise). LINP:186
Lynch, John R.
Civil Rights and social equality. DUNM:89; WOON:356
Speech in the case of his contested election. WOON:273
Lynch, Rebecca
Wanted: a Marshall Plan for the arts in America. ARNS: 76

LYNCHING
Borah, W.E.
Anti-lynching Bill. BA 1937-38:17
Leary, F.W.
Shame of a nation. YR 7: 167
Mob violence. FRIE:104
Thomas, P.E.
American infamy. TRUW: 124
Lyndhurst, John Singleton Copley, 1st Baron
House of Lords as a check on legislation. EMS 1:135
Russia and the Crimean War. BREW 7:419; HAZO 9: 3901; MAS 9:3901
Lyon, Ernest
Emancipation and racial advancement (15th anniversary of Emancipation Proclamation). DUNM:461
Lyon, J.H.
Right hand of fellowship (welcoming one into the Pilgrim Church of Providence, R.I.). THOU 2:471
Lysias.
Against Eratosthenes for mur-

Lysias. (cont.)
der (on the execution without trial of Polemarchus). BREW 7:428; BRYW 1:61; CHAL 1:78; FRE:54; HAZO 1:115; LEEW 1:81; MAS 1:115; PL:43
Against Pancleon (a claim to citizen's rights). FRE:173
Defence of a farmer: on the sacred olive-tree. FRE:181
Defence of a state pension (on behalf of a disabled person). FRE:163
Embezzlement of trust funds: against a guardian (Diogeiton). FRE:131
For Mantitheus. LEEW 1:99
Olympiac oration. LEEW 1:96
On the murder of Eratosthenes. FRE:43
To a gathering of friends (accusation of slander). FRE:229
Wounding with intent to kill: quarrel over a boy (against Simon). FRE:97
Wounding with intent to kill: quarrel over a slave-girl. FRE:107

LYTTELTON, ALFRED
Oxford and Asquith, H.H.A. Alfred Lyttelton. REEM 5:6; REEMB 9:35

Lytton, Edward George Earle Lytton Bulwer-Lytton, 1st Baron
Demosthenes and the nobility of the classics. BREW 7:431
Farewell to Charles Dickens. REEM 2:371; REEMA 2:774; REEMB 2:384
Liberty of the press. EMS 2:43
Macready and the English stage. REEMA 2:769
On the Crimean war. CHAL 7:72; HAZO 14:5906; MAS 14:5906
On the Reform Bill. LEEW 7:261

Lytton, Edward Robert Bulwer-Lytton, 1st Earl of
Abandonment of Candahar, House of Lords, January 10, 1881. PAUF 2:245

Lytton, Henry Bulwer
After dinner speech. KLEG:150

Mabie, Hamilton Wright
Poe's place in American literature (unveiling of bust of Edgar Allan Poe). REEMA 9:815
Spirit of New England literature. REEMA 2:778
Work and play. BLAA:58; BLAB:58

McAdams, Thomas B.
Accepting a silver service. HOA:381; HOAP:272

McAdoo, William Gibbs
Introducing W.J. Gaynor to Southern Society of New York, December 8, 1909. REEM 2:77
Republic of Chile. ONES:71
Soldiers' bonus. REEM 7:253; REEMB 8:273

McAndrew, William
Inauguration as president of the Department of Superintendence, National Education Association. BRAC:359

MacArthur, Douglas
Address to Congress. -Same as his Defends his conduct of the war in Korea
American policy in the Pacific. -Same as his Defends his conduct of the war in Korea
Defends his conduct of the war in Korea. ARNS:273; BA 1951-52:21; BOU:105; BRAP:61; CAP:206; COPB:594; HAR:146; HIBS:465; HURG:293; MOUG:210; MOUGA:210 (outline p. 217); PE:816; PEA:816; YE:371
Farewell to the cadets (accepting Sylvanus Thayer

award for service to his nation. HIB:58; LINP:150
Instructions to Japanese on occupation landings. VO 1945-46:486
Old soldiers never die. -Same as his Defends his conduct of the war in Korea
On the re-establishment of the Philippine government. HAN:349; VO 1945-46:92
Our national goals. ANGC:208
Remarks and final speech at Japanese surrender. BA 1945-46:13; HAN:360; VO 1945-46:528, 529
Seventy-fifth birthday address. BA 1954-55:34
Speech delivered to the Massachusetts legislature. MIA:342
Statement at the conclusion of Manila conference with Japanese surrender envoys. VO 1945-46:467
Statement on policy in Japan. VO 1945-46:580
Statement on the occupation of Japan. VO 1945-46:581

MACARTHUR, DOUGLAS
Baird, A. C.
Academic critic's view of General MacArthur's speech to Congress. BRAP:155
Kerr, R. S.
Congressional critic's view of General MacArthur's speech to Congress. BRAP:155
Nelson, D. M.
MacArthur Day celebration speech. BA 1941-42:152
Rovere, R. H.
Journalist critic's view of General MacArthur's speech to Congress. BRAP:155

McArthur, Harvey K.
Truth and freedom. BA 1950-51:182

MacArthur, Robert Stuart
Christ a living stone. THOU 2:440
Present heroic era in American history. HARSO:254; WERN 42:124
Real cause of the war. THOU 1:99

Macaulay, Thomas B.
Consent or force in government. BREW 8:26
Copyright. ONEM:294
Government of India. KESI:1 226; PAUF 2:1
Industrial worker. HAY:197
Literature of England. BREW 8:14; HAZO 13:5535; MAS 13:5535
On Parliamentary reform. - Same as his Reform Bill.
On the disabilities of the Jews. -Same as his Tribute to the Jews
People's charter. REEMA 14:1377
Popular education. BREW 8:21
Position of a Ministry not supported by the House of Commons. EMS 1:73
Reform Bill. ADR 3:62; BRAO:252; BRTH:219; BRTHA:219; BRYW 4:126; CHAL 6:339; COP:177; COPA:177; COPB:177; HAZO 13:5545; MAS 13:5545; PE:426; PE:426; REEM 9:219; REEMB 10:226
Survey of four centuries. REEMA 9:836
Tribute to the Jews. BREW 8:24; CHAL 6:358; HAZO 13:5564; LEEW 7:215; MAS 13:5564; PE:431; PEA:431

MacBride, Dexter
Brass checks. YR 10:49

McBride, Louise
Dancing daughters. BRP 5:71

McBurney, George W.
Road back. NOR 1949:157

McBurney, James H.
Plight of the conservative in public discussion. BA 1949-50:212

McBurney, James H. and others. (B. Aly; L. Gottschalk; C. Ver Steeg; and J.H. Williams)
Alexander Hamilton: his contribution to constitutional government (TV panel). BA 1956-57:149
McCabe, F.X.
Can a Catholic be a citizen of the United States? CATA 1:231
McCabe, William Gordon
First university in America, 1619-1622. SMI:20
Puritan and Cavalier. SHUO:21; SMI:229

MACCABEES
Aiken, D.D.
Certified conditions. THOU 3:422
McCaffrey, John L.
Begins an address before the National Industrial Conference Board. PRNE:75
What road to labor peace? HAR:423
McCall, Samuel Walker
Porto Rico tariff. HAZO 25:10736; MAS 25:10736
McCann, William Robert
New Russia. YR 2:133
McCarthy, Eugene J.
Nomination of Adlai E. Stevenson. BA 1960-61:30
McCarthy, Joseph Raymond
Great betrayal. WPRC:294

McCARTHY, JOSEPH RAYMOND
Bricker, J.W.
Against censure of Senator McCarthy. BA 1954-55:113
Flanders, R.E.
Colossal innocence in the United States Senate. WPRC:301
Stennis, J.C.
For censure of Senator McCarthy. BA 1954-55:109
Truman, H.S.
McCarthyism, November 1, 1952. FIP:315
McCarthy, Justin
In defense of his colleagues. CHAL 11:448; HAZO 22:9369; MAS 22:9369; REEMA 14:1365
Ireland's struggle. REEMA 2:795
McCartney, Clarence E.
National apostasy. BOA:61; BOB:88; HARSO:233; SHU:66; TRUW:130
McClafferty, John J. See Murrow, E.R., jt. auth.
McClain, William
Our school of destiny. YR 6:81
Scroll of destiny. BRP 5:54
McClellan, George B.
Address at 250th anniversary of the settlement of the Jews in the United States. TWJ:26
New York and the South. REEM 2:375; REEMB 2:388
McClelland, C. Bruce
Life and work of John Knox and his influence on American ideals. ASHF:181
McClure, Alexander Kelly
Editorial retrospect. REEMA 2:799
McClure, Herbert
People of the South. BOB:99
McClure-Patterson, Edith
How women regard advertising. REEM sup 2:194; REEMB 5:144
M'Clurg, Monroe
Tribute to President McKinley. SHUO:70
McConnell, Francis John
Eulogy on David D. Forsyth. BRAC:368
Giants and grasshoppers. REEM sup 2:197; REEMB 6:261
McCorkle, Walter L.
Introduction of John P. Mitchell to Southern Society of New York, December 10, 1913. REEM 2:414
McCormack, John W.
Eulogy on John F. Kennedy.

HIB:19
McCormick, A. H.
Crime prevention through probation. HOC:29; SAR:316

McCORMICK, ANNE O'HARE
Spencer, H. R.
Introducing Anne O'Hare McCormick. YE:127

McCORMICK, EDWARD T.
McDonough, J. J.
Introduces Edward T. McCormick, President of the American Stock Exchange. PRNE:26

McCORMICK, FOWLER
Jones, T. R.
Presentation of Gantt gold medal to Fowler McCormick. YE:114
McCormick, John
Human wreckage. YR 9:21

McCOSKER, ALFRED J.
Introducing Alfred J. McCosker. NI:120; NIA:92
McCoy, Ford
Shadow slaves. YR 1:105
MacCracken, Henry Mitchell
Relation of metropolis and university: inaugural address as president of New York University. WE 1:185
MacCracken, Henry Noble
Ideologies, their dynamics and their excesses. HOB:184
Student's share in college government. SAR:76
McCracken, Paul W.
Begins an address on economic outlook. PRC:7
McCracken, Robert J.
To have and not to hold. BA 1959-60:173
When you pray, "Thy Kingdom come," what do you mean? BA 1955-56:167
McCrae, Annabella
Acceptance of Saunders medal. GA:46
McCrary, Reagan See Canham, E. D., jt. auth.
McCreight, W. Edward
Through the eyes of youth. YR 7:67
M'Cullough, Joseph A.
South Carolina and Civil War. SHUO:306
McCutcheon, George Barr
Introducing Meredith Nicholson. BRAC:236
McCutheon, John T.
Introducing Booth Tarkington. YE:132
McDevitt, P. R.
State and education. CATA 2:26
Macdonald, Claudine
Lady of the lamp. GA:78
McDonald, David J.
Labor's responsibility for human rights. BA 1958-59:92
Plan for prosperity. BA 1960-61:156

McDONALD, JAMES G.
Introducing James G. McDonald. NI:172; NIA:127
MacDonald, James Ramsay
Address to the House of Representatives. ONEC:10
Address to the Senate. LINM:431; ONEC:7
Empire Day. BEA:205
Imperial Conference, October 1, 1930 speech. KESB:206
Mystic kinship. REEM sup 2:205; REEMB 2:391
Peace. COP:206; COPA:206; COPB:206
Response to the Honorable James J. Walker. LINM:427
Speech at Naval Conference, April 23, 1930. KESB:418
Tribute to Queen Alexandra. YE:103

MACDONALD, JAMES RAMSAY
Snowden, P.
Attack on the Prime Minister Ramsay Macdonald. BEA:387

Macdonald, Sir John Alexander
On Canadian Federation. BRYW 5:3; CHAL 9:1; COP:378; COPA:378; COPB:378; HAZO 18:7487; KES 1:269; LAD:225; MAS 18:7487; REEMA 14:1387
On Canadian fisheries. CHAL 9:26; HAZO 18:7512; MAS 18:7512
On the treaty of Washington. BREW 8:29; PL:539
Prerogative and public right. BREW 8:33
Speech in Canadian Parliament, February 6, 1865. -Same as his On Canadian Federation
MacDonald, Tyler
Eagle of Golgotha. AN:21
McDonnell, Gene
American citizen. BRP 9:109
McDonough, John J.
Introduces Allan Shivers, Governor of Texas. PRNE:7
Introduces Clarence E. Manion, attorney, and formerly Dean of the Law School of Notre Dame University. PRNE:45
Introduces Dr. Will Durant, author and philosopher. PRNE:21
Introduces Edward T. McCormick, President of the American Stock Exchange. PRNE:26
Introduces Fulton Lewis, Jr., radio and TV commentator. PRNE:24
Introduces Gene Flack, Sales Counsel and Advertising Director, Sunshine Biscuit Company. PRNE:30
Introduces Heinz L. Krekeler, Ambassador of the Federal Republic of Germany to the United States. PRNE:46
Introduces Joseph M. Dodge, Director of the Bureau of the Budget of the United States. PRNE:13
Introduces Lester B. Pearson, Canadian statesman. PRNE: 5
Introduces Lester L. Colbert, President, Chrysler Corporation. PRNE:27
Introduces United States Senator William F. Knowland. PRNE:41
McDowell, James
Education-a state duty. SMI: 136
McDuffie, George
Tariff. SOU 9:287
McElmeel, Eugene F.
John Marshall and the Constitution. LEIO:101
McEntegart, Bryan
Totality of outlook. LINP:175

MACEO, ANTONIO
Nesmith, G. T.
Antonio Maceo. TRUW:103
McFarland, James G.
Memorial address at the tomb of President Harding, December 2, 1923 (speech as Past Exalted Grand Ruler of the Elks). LINM:34
McFarland, William H.
Benjamin Watkins Leigh. SMI:141
McGahey, William
Mad men in a world. BRP 10: 47
McGee, Gale
Academic looks at Vietnam. BA 1964-65:73
McGee, Thomas D'Arcy
"Land we live in." CHAL 10: 427; HAZO 21:8782; MAS 21:8782
Policy of conciliation. CHAL 10:432; HAZO 21:8787; MAS 21:8787
McGenty, Denis
Where peace abides. YR 2:13
McGhee, George C.
American women and the goal of world community. ANGC 159
McGilligan, P.
Statute of Westminster (Speeches of July 16, 17, 23, 1931)

KESB:231, 245, 251
McGindley, Henry A.
Centennial address (Druids) THOU 3:205
M'Glynn, Edward
Lessons from St. Patrick's character and work. THOU 1:520
McGovern, George
New perspectives on American security. BA 1963-64: 132
McGovern, Sylvester
Introducing an architect
" an artist
" a baby food executive
" " " " specialist-2 examples
" a band or orchestra leader
" a clothing merchant
" a druggist
" an engineer
" a fisherman
" a florist
" a golfer
" a humorist
" a labor leader
" a minister-2 examples of
" the president at a business meeting of manufacturing company
" a salesman (successful)
" " " (top)
" a speaker small in stature
" a sportsman or where the speaker wants to use someone in the audience as the butt of his joke
" a world traveler. BRC: See Table of contents for paging
McGrady, Edward F.
What does labor want? SAR: 344
McGregor, Alexander
Charge to the people. THOU 2:473
Macgregor, Rob Roy
Allegiance dominant! PROS: 95
Machen, John Gresham
Christianity vs. modern liberalism. WPRC:120

MACHINE AGE See Machinery

MACHINERY
Ashfield, A. H. S.
Man and machine in industry. REEM sup 1:64; REEMB 4:1
Cram, H.
Men or machines. BRP 3: 106; YR 4:205
Decker, C.R.
Automatons or men? ASHF:205
Filene, E. A.
Adult education in this machine age. DOA:192
Kettering, C.F.
Muscles and machines. GLAD:285
Mancke, D. B.
Challenge of the machine age. YR 3:125
Marx, K.
Give an after dinner speech. PE:475; PEA:475
Salton, M. E.
Machine age. BOA:392
See also Inventions and inventors
McIlvenna, Elizabeth Ann
Crisis of 1938. YR 10:115
McIntosh, Gertrude
Keep the home fires burning. YR 10:33
McIntosh, Millicent Carey
Goals of education are not sufficiant today. HAR:382
M'Iver, Charles D.
Education of women. SHUO:95
Mack, Julian W.
Pledge of the American Jew. TWJ:142

MACK, JULIAN W.
Introducing Stephen S. Wise and Julian W. Mack. NI: 113; NIA:87
Mackay, Captain See Lomasney, William Francis

Mackay, Clarence H.
History of communications. LINM:268
In response to the award of the Gold Medal of the National Institute of Social Sciences. KLEB:169
Mackay, Donald Sage
Dutch Domine. REEMA 2:782
McKay, Hamilton W.
Weighed in balance: inaugural address as president of the Southern Medical Association. HAR:343
McKeldin, Theodore R.
Five nations. MCK:240
Have faith in America. MCK: 228
Hospital building fund. MCK: 125
Inaugural address as Governor of Maryland. MCK:192
Influence of ancient Greece on modern life. MCK:212
Labor Day. MCK:144
Maryland. MCK:217
Memorial Day. MCK:139
Relation of religion and morality to education. MCK:209
St. Patrick's Day. MCK:136
This is a good place to start. MCK:162
Today is the Fourth of July. MCK:142
Training boys for responsible citizenship. MCK:225
McKelway, Benjamin M.
Welcoming the members of Congress to Washington. SAB:210
McKelway, St. Clair
Prayer and politics. REEM 2:378; REEMB 2:395
Smashed crockery. ONEM: 649; ONES:227; REEMA 2: 807
Tribute to Mark Twain. REEMA 2:811
M'Kenna, Reginald
Economic aspects of world debts. REEM 4:304; REEMB 5:147
MACKENZIE, ALEXANDER
Thompson, J.S.
On the death of Alexander Mackenzie. CHAL 14:1; HAZO 24:10531; MAS 24: 10531
McKeon, Richard P. See also MacLeish, A., jt. auth.
McKinlay, Duncan E.
Abraham Lincoln (birthday speech). WAGN:136
McKinley, William
American patriotism (at dedication of Cuyahoga County Soldiers' and Sailors' monument in Cleveland). BREW 8:35; CHAL 13:457; HAZO 24:10486; MAS 24:10486; REEM 7:264; REEMA 9:847
At the Pan-American Exposition. BLAA:118; BLAB: 118; BRYW 10:239; CHAL 13:465; COP:341; COPA: 341; COPB:341; FIP:27; HAZO 24:10505; KNAS:329; KNASA:329; MAS 24:10505; REEM 10:379; REEMA 14: 1397; REEMB 11:395; RID: 88; WERN 42:138
Characteristics of Washington (at unveiling of Washington statue). KLEM:187; ONES: 162; REEMA 9:845
Country reunited. WERN 42: 133
Duty determines destiny. FUL: 218
First inaugural address. CHI: 186; LOTI:171; ORAMA 2: 413; USIN:169; USINA:169
Future of the Philippines. FUL:224, 226, 229; REEM 2:382; REEMA 2:818; REEMB 2:399
Grant (at dedication of Grant monument in New York City). BREW 8:40; HAZO 24:10494; MAS 24:10494; WERN 42:77
High obligations. -Same as his Future of the Philippines
Instructions to the Philippine Commission. ANG:407

Last address.-Same as his At the Pan-American Exposition
Nation indivisible forever. FUL:220, 222
Nation's duties and opportunities. HAZO 24:10497; MAS 24:10497
Our country. REEMA 2:815
Period of exclusiveness is past.-Same as his At the Pan American Exposition
Second inaugural address. CHI:197; LOTI:179; USIN: 178; USINA:178
To the soldiers. WERN 42:37
War message, April 11, 1898. BIR 3:230; FO:245
Washington, a Masonic eulogy. THOU 3:80
World's work in civilization. BREW 8:41

MCKINLEY, WILLIAM
Cleveland, G.
Eulogy of McKinley. BRYW 10:137; CHAL 13:155; KLEM:164
Davis, M. L.
Upon the death of William McKinley. SHUO:72
Ford, T. L.
Tribute to William McKinley. WAGN:371
Hall, G. S.
William McKinley. BLAA: 150; BLAB:150
Hay, J.
Tribute to McKinley. BRYW 10:228; CHAL 13:223; ONEM:427; REEM 5:208; REEMA 13:1149; REEMB 9: 244; WERN 42:164
Hoar, G. F.
Eulogy on William McKinley. CHAL 11:49
Favoring McKinley's reelection. CHAL 11:18; HAZO 21:8904; MAS 21: 8904
Knight, C.A.
Speech at McKinley's nomination. WAGN:100
M'Clurg, M.
Tribute to President McKinley. SHUO:70
Roosevelt, T.
Seconding McKinley's nomination. CHAL 14:354; HAZO 25:10883; MAS 25: 10883
William McKinley (tribute). ONES:173
Smith, C. E.
McKinley. WERN 42:135
Woodruff, T. L.
Lincoln and McKinley. WERN 42:95
Mackintosh, Sir James
Canada and the autonomy of British colonies. BREW 8: 48
In behalf of free speech: on the trial of Jean Peltier accused of libelling Napoleon Bonaparte. ADR 2:185; BREW 8:54; BRYW 4:84; CHAL 4:208; GOOD:827; HAZO 9:3585; LEEW 7:111; MAS 9:3585; PL:453
McKissick, James Rion
Common people. SHUC:28
McLain, Harold O.
Accepting gift on retirement as club president. PR:103
Introduces Alvin N. 'Bo'' McMillin, football coach
" Francis B. Davis, Jr.
" Thomas R. Mulroy. PR: 114, 40, 55
Presents David Seabury. LY: 117; PR:105
Two responses to introductions. PR:83, 131

McLAIN, HAROLD O.
Mulroy, T.R.
Introduces Harold O. McLain. PR:81
Maclaren, Alexander
Ahab and Micaiah. BRIN:388
MacLaren, Ian (pseud.). See Watson, J.
MacLaughlin, Creswell
Conquerors. BLAA:234; BLAB:234

McLaughlin, John J.
Peace in tomorrow's world. DO:119
MacLean, Angus W.
Welcoming aviators to Kitty Hawk. CORP:260
McLean, Charles Mossman
Poet Shelley. SHUC:144
MacLean, Donald A.
Americas in the world crisis. HOC:121
MacLeish, Archibald
Act of faith. BA 1950-51:131
Psychological front. HOC:127
This cause is our cause. BA 1943-44:243
Tribute to Wendell Willkie. BA 1944-45:186
---- and others (H. D. Lasswell and R. P. McKeon)
Propaganda, good and bad. BA 1941-42:75
McLeod, George
Imagination rules the world. YR 7:177
MacLeod, Norman
Why not 'Do this in remembrance of Christ?" THOU 2:431
McMahon, Brien See Kaltenborn, H. V., jt. auth.
McMaster, S. J.
Welcoming the American Federation of Labor. ONEC:15
McMillin, Alvin N.
Response to an introduction. PR:115

McMILLIN, ALVIN N.
McLain, H. O.
Introduces Alvin N. 'Bo" McMillin, football coach. PR:114
McNab, John L.
Nominating Herbert Hoover for the Presidency. ONEC:489
M'Nall, Webb
Response to address of welcome by mayor to the United Workmen. THOU 3:325
McNamee, Graham
Announcing the Republican National Convention. ONEC:229
McNutt, Paul V.
Labor and the war. BA 1941-42:170
Macomber, William H.
News deal. BRP 4:82
Macon, Arthur R.
Problem of the age. YR 4:369
Macready, William Charles
Farewell to the stage. REEMA 2:791

MACREADY, WILLIAM CHARLES
Dickens, C.
Macready and Bulwer-Lytton. REEMA 1:398
Lytton, E. G. E. L. -B.
Macready and the English stage. REEMA 2:769
McSkimmon, Mary
Introduction of Francis G. Blair. BRAC:239
M'Teer, James P.
My Country! My Mother! My God! HARSO:223
McVay, Winifred
Civilization and the prophet. COUW:69
MacVeagh, Franklin
Anti-expansion bugbear. FUL:234, 237, 240
MacVeagh, Franklin
Nation's heroism. FUL:232
Our relations with the world. BLAA:218; BLAB:218
MacVeagh, Wayne
Ideals in American politics. CHAL 12:111; HAZO 22:9507; MAS 22:9507
McVey, Frank LeRand
University and its relations: inaugural address as president of University of North Dakota. WE 2:369
Macy, V. Everit
Samuel Gompers. REEM sup 2:209; REEMB 5:163
Madden, Martin B.
Abraham Lincoln. HARSO:3
Maddox, Robert F.
Introducing Irving Fisher. ONES:11

Presenting a silver service to the retiring president of the Bankers' Association. HOA: 381; HOAP:271
Response to presentation of token of esteem. ONES:97
Madison, James
British treaty. ORAMA 1:161; REEMA 14:1404
Federalist No. X. BRE:68; BREA:66
First inaugural address. CHI: 24; HAZO 7:3032; LOTI: 25; MAS 7:3032; USIN:21; USINA:23
For adoption of the Federal Constitution. -Same as his State sovereignty and Federal supremacy
On the expediency of adopting the Federal Constitution. CHEM 1:199; HARS:89; JOHA 1 pt 1:53
Power to lay taxes. -Same as his State sovereignty and federal supremacy
Second inaugural address. CHI:28; LOTI:29; USIN: 26; USINA:26
Shall the states take precedence over the central government? CLAW:75
State sovereignty and federal supremacy. BAAMP:37; BREW 8:61; CHAL 3:366; CHEM 1:219; CLAW:19; COP:237; COPA:237; COPB:237; HAZO 7:3020; HURG:40; MAS 7:3020; SMI:55; WPRA:23
War message, 1812. BIR 1: 273; PO:65
Magee, William Connor
Disestablishment of the Irish Church. PAUF 2:134
Ethics of forgiveness. HAZO 19:8315; MAS 19:8315

MAGICIANS See Actors and acting
Magidson, Arthur B.
Mediocrity triumphant. YR 5:3
MAGNA CARTA
Rose, U.M.
Magna Carta. SHUO:318
Magnussen, J. Woodrow
Enough of this. BRP 7:7; YR 8:261
Maharoof, M.M.
Inaugural speech at Conference on the Problems of Economic Development. UAR:73
Speech at final session of Conference on the Problems of Economic Development. UAR:405
Makar, John
Bald head and a moustache. JUD:53
Makino, Nobuaki, Baron
Speech at Peace Conference (Session of February 15, 1919). REEM 11:342; REEMB 12:360
Malachovsky, H.
For a Bar Mitzvah-3 speeches. ZEL:15, 66, 68
Malachowsky, Hilel
Thankfulness: address of a poor boy speaking in the name of all pupils and expressing his thanks in public. ZEL:90
Malcolm, T.W.
Ancient Druidic history. THOU 3:215
Malcolm X.
Proclaims Muhammad as the man of the hour. HILK:304
Malik, Charles H.
Challenge to Communism. BA 1950-51:169
Developing leadership in new countries. BA 1963-64:115
Malinovsky, Rodion Y.
Speech of October 23. RUS: 59
Malone, Ted
Lady of the lamp. YE:395
Out of the storm. YE:390
Maloney, Hugh S.
"Prospects good." BRP 2:40; YR 3:81

Maloney, Martin J.
Call us dissenters! YR 8:21
Maloney, Mary
Speech at Rocky Mountain Conference-original speech and dictaphone recording of the speech as actually presented. JUD:330
Maloney, Patricia Ryan
Hard way. NOR 1944:53
Malott, Deane W.
Response to introduction. PR:120

MAN
Aelred, Saint.
On manliness. BREW 1:102
Barton, G.
Ideal man. BOA:175
Beecher, H.W.
On man and his institutions. HAZO 17:7280; MAS 17:7280
Blouet, P.
Monsieur and Madame. REEMA 1:79
Channing, W.E.
Man above the state. BREW 3:200
Eiseley, L.
Man: the lethal factor. BA 1962-63:39
Grand, S.
Mere man. REEM 2:132; REEMA 2:551; REEMB 2:124
Hughes, T.
Highest manhood. BREW 7:87
Ideal man. BOB:200
Ingersoll, R.G.
Victory of man. WPRA:301
It's the human thing to do. NAT:18
Manhood-its standard. THOS:143
Mars, G.C.
Dignity of man. WERN 42:92
Moore, J.O.
Common man. DO:67
Munger, T.T.
Man the final form in creation. BL:709
Neal, J.
Man. BL:364
Northrop, C.
Manly fellow. BLAA:73; BLAB:73; WERN 42:123
Osgood, C.G.
Proper study. NORR 3d ser:191
People are funny. FRIE:277
Porter, N.
Sciences of nature versus the science of man. BL:455
To the gentlemen: speech for the Ladies' banquet. CON:41
Vandervoort, J.
No man is an island. BRAP:77
We are all human. FRIE:284

---- STATURE
McGovern, S.
Introducing a speaker small in stature. BRC:223
Taylor, L.
Shrimps. JUD:117

MANAGEMENT See Business
Manak, Joseph F.
We sorely need tolerant minds. NOR 1942:47

MANCHURIA
Johnson, R.D.
White peril. BRP 6:112; NOR 1934:92
Mancke, Donald Bell
Challenge of the machine age. YR 3:125
Mangum, R. Jennings
Freedoms of the United States Constitution. DO:212

MANILA BAY, BATTLE OF, 1898 See United States-History-War of 1898

MANION, CLARENCE E.
McDonough, J.J.
Introduces Clarence E.

Manion, Attorney, and formerly Dean of the Law School of Notre Dame University. PRNE:45
Mann, Horace
Institution of slavery. CHAL 6:223; HAZO 13:5334; MAS 13:5334
On the threatened dissolution of the Union. CHAL 6:215; HAZO 13:5326; MAS 13:5326
Orient yourself. DICD:158; DICE:158
Mann, Louis L.
Converting liabilities into assets. BA 1953-54:185; HIBS:499
Manning, Henry Edward, Cardinal
On progress. ORBR 2:231
Perseuction of the Jews. BEA:309; BOU:149; COP:191; COPA:191; COPB:191; REEM 7:270; REEMA 9:854; REEMB 7:266
Rome the eternal. BREW 8:69; PL:500
Triumph of the Church. CHAL 7:332; HAZO 15:6260; MAS 15:6260
Manning, William T.
Vision of unity. BLAB:338; REEM sup 2:212; REEMB 6:269
Mansfield, Frederick W.
Relations of labor union to church and state. CATA 1:83
Religious bigotry. CATA 2:175
Mansfield, Michael J.
At 44th anniversary of Congressional service of Speaker Sam Rayburn. BRAP:136
Eulogy on John F. Kennedy. HIB:20
Mansfield, William Murray, 1st Earl of
Case of Allan Evans. GOOD:156; LAD:111; ONEM:121
In the case of John Wilkes. BREW 8:75; GOOD:154
In the case of the Dean of St. Asaph. BREW 8:77
Judgement in Campbell v. Hall, 1774. KES 1:35
On a Bill depriving Peers of certain privileges. GOOD:160; LEEW 6:159
On the right to tax America. ADR 1:150; BRYW 3:230; CHAL 2:239; GOOD:148; HAZO 5:1832; MAS 5:1832; ORBR 1:199; PL:403; REEMA 14:1422
Reply to the Earl of Chatham against Parliamentary exemption from arrest for debt. BREW 8:79

MANUAL TRAINING
Influence of manual training on character. AMEO 2:163

MANUFACTURERS AND MANUFACTURING
Collins, A.
Introducing a small manufacturer. BRC:292
Edgerton, J. E.
Candles of understanding. REEM sup 1:257; REEMB 4:190
Hamilton, A.
Report on manufactures, 1791. BIR 1:173
McGovern, S.
Introducing the president at a meeting of a manufacturing company. BRC:269
Mao Tse-tung
C C P greetings. RUS:34
On the people's democratic dictatorship. CROC:319
Mara, Evelyn
If we break faith. BRP 1:84
Marat, Jean Paul
In his own defense. BRYW 7:148; CHAL 3:144; COP:79; COPB:79; REEMA 14:1433
Speech before National Convention, September 25, 1792. HAZO 7:2752; MAS 7:2752

Marble, Samuel
From fame to infamy. COUW: 227

MARCELLINUS, SAINT
Abelard, P.
Sermon on Marcellinus, Pope and martyr. HAZO 3: 1250; MAS 3:1250
March, Francis Andrew
Scholar of to-day. NORR 1st ser:112
Marconi, Guglielmo
Conquest of the Atlantic. BREW 8:81
Progress of wireless telegraphy. REEM 6:321; REEMB 6:274

MARCONI, GUGLIELMO
Pupin, M.
In honor of Marconi. REEM 3:116; REEMB 3:117
Margulies, Harold
No pot-luck peace. BRP 9:91; NOR 1938:22
Margulies, Newton
Age of anxiety. MO:453
Modern "medicine men." BRP 8:92; NOR 1937:35

MARIE ANTOINETTE, CONSORT OF LOUIS XVI, KING OF FRANCE
Burke, E.
Age of chivalry. BREW 2: 417; CODS:182; CODSA: 182; GOOD:365; REEM 9: 131; REEMB 10:137

MARIJUANA See Drugs
Marius, Caisus
On being accused of low origin. BRYW 2:43
Markel, Lester
Future of the printed word. BRAP:143

MARKHAM, GEORGE
Erskine, T.
In behalf of Rev. George Markham against John Fawcett for criminal conversation with his wife. GOOD: 778
Marlow, Fuller
Introducing a bank cashier or teller
" a state legislator. BRC: 59, 238

MARRIAGE
Coleridge, J.D.
Sacredness of matrimony. BREW 4:127
Dailey, M.
Influence of the movies on marriage and divorce. SHUP:172
Fitz, R.K.
Five minute talk: Radcliffe as a matrimonial training school. BAKF:417
Huber, L.J.
Introducing a newlywed. BRH:163
Kaser, A.L.
Emcee at a newly-weds' party. BRH:311
McIntosh, G.
Keep the home fires burning. YR 10:33
Man and wife. NATM:35
Married life. FRIE:268
Meaning of the wedding vows. JA:235
Seeking happiness in marriage. JA:38
See also Anniversaries, wedding; Divorce; Family; Home; Wedding speeches
Mars, Gerhardt C.
Dignity of man. WERN 42:92
Marsh, George Perkins
Address, 1844. BRAR 1:371
Marshall, Eugene
Hamilton and the Constitution. TRUW:170
Marshall, George C.
Address at Harvard University. ANG:525; GLAD:251; GRAC:152; HURG:283
Collapse of the London Big Four Conference. BA 1947-48:15
Moscow Peace Conference.

BA 1946-47:89
National military strength. BA 1945-46:85
Statement before the Senate Armed Forces Committee and the Senate Foreign Relations Committee. HAR: 225
We are ready to carry the war to the enemy. HAN:258

MARSHALL, GEORGE C.
Baruch, B.M.
Tribute to Gen. George C. Marshall. SAB:203
Marshall, John
Barron v. Baltimore: opinion for the Supreme Court. BRE:158; BREA:142
Cohens v. Virginia, 1821: opinion for the Supreme Court. BIR 2:34
Gibbons v. Ogden, 1824: opinion for the Supreme Court. BIR 2:253
Justice and the Federal Constitution. BREW 8:86; BRYW 8:143; CHAL 3:463; COP: 240; COPA:240; COPB: 240; HAZO 8:3222; MAS 8:3222; ORAMA 1:215; REEM 10:10; REEMA 14: 1440; REEMB 11:10; SMI: 58
McCulloch v. Maryland: opinion for the Supreme Court. BIR 2:2; BRE:128; BREA: 119
Marbury v. Madison: opinion for the Supreme Court. BIR 1:259; BRE:116
Trustees of Dartmouth College v. Woodward: opinion for the Supreme Court. BIR 2: 19; BRE:140

MARSHALL, JOHN
Beck, J.M.
John Marshall, jurist and statesman. SAR:206
Bonaparte, C.J.
Chief Justice Marshall. SHUO:327
Buffington, J.
John Marshall, the foundation builder. BOA:245; BOB:153
Cockran, W.B.
Marshall and the Constitution. SHUM:280
Gullion, E.
John Marshall and the Federal supremacy. DOA:106
Holmes, O.W., Jr.
John Marshall. BLAA:110; BLAB:110
McElmeel, E.F.
John Marshall and the Constitution. LEIO:101
Maxwell, W.
The chief. SMI:126
Olney, R.
John Marshall. REEM 5: 318; REEMA 9:932; REEMB 9:358
Platt, H.G.
John Marshall. WAGN:190
Tarrant, J.G.
John Marshall and the Constitution. LEIO:147
Marshall, Louis
Address delivered in Albany on 250th anniversary of the settlement of the Jews in the United States. TWJ:93
Marshall, Thomas R.
Farewell to the United States Senate. BRAC:271; REEM 7:277; REEMB 8:290
Golden rule of government (inaugural address to the Senate, March 4, 1917). BREW 8:103
Introducing Ambassador Bakhmetieff. ONES:9
Introducing Baron Moncheur. ONES:8
Introducing Prince Udine. ONES:7
Introduction of Henry Cabot Lodge. BRAC:239
National power and the national peace policy (on public land sales, 1841). BREW 8: 100
Representative government.

Marshall, T.R. (cont.)
NESA:103
Russian War Mission. REEM 2:392; REEMB 2:409
Thanking the French ambassador for vases presented to the Senate. REEM 2:389; REEMB 2:406
To the Belgian War Mission. REEM 2:391; REEMB 2:408
Welcome to the Italian Commission. BRAC:245
Marshall, Thurgood
Against segregation in the schools. BA 1953-54:118
Cry for freedom. HILK:318
Marshall, Tom
Matt Ward case. SOU 9:398

MARSHALL PLAN See Reconstruction, 1939-1951

MARTIN, DEAN
Jessel, G.
Speech at Roastmaster dinner in honor of Dean Martin and Jerry Lewis. JEYO: 45
Martin, J. Sella
Speech before the Paris Antislavery Conference, August 27, 1867. WOON:256
Martin, John
Indictment of millions. HAZO 17:7242; MAS 17:7242
Irish martyrs: address at the cemetery in Dublin. HAZO 17:7238; MAS 17:7238
National independence of Ireland. HAZO 17:7235; MAS 17:7235
Martin, Joseph W.
Begins an address at the Lions International Convention. PRNE:54
Introducing Speaker Sam Rayburn. SAB:208; SABA:288
See also Rayburn, S., jt. auth.
Martin, Luther
Is the government federal or national? BREW 8:105
Portion of the report of the proceedings of the General Convention held at Philadelphia in 1787. SOU 9:179
Martin, Maryfern
Character in the shadow. YR 7:93
Martin, Thomas W.
Presents Charles F. Kettering. LY:180

MARTIN, WILLIAM McCHESNEY
Young, C.S.
Introduces William McChesney Martin, Chairman of the Board of Governors of the Federal Reserve System. PRNE:10
Martin, Wyatt B.
United States in Pan-American trade. SHUC:123
Martineau, James
God of Revelation of his own interpreter. HAZO 15:6139; MAS 15:6139
Marvel, Ike See Mitchell, Donald Grant (Ike Marvel)
Marvin, Charles
Introducing an advertising executive
" a German industrialist. BRC:211, 291
Marx, Karl
Gives an after dinner speech. PE:475; PEA:475

MARX, KARL
Engels, F.
Says a few words at the burial of Karl Marx. PE: 575; PEA:575

MARY, VIRGIN
Zwingli, H.
Sermon on Mary, the pure mother of God. LEEW 4:93

MARYLAND
McKeldin, T.
Maryland. MCK:217

MASARYK, JAN
Murrow, E.R.
Jan Masaryk. BA 1947-48: 220

Maseres, Francis
Considerations on the expediency of procuring an act of Parliament for the settlement of the Province of Quebec. KES 1:12
Mason, Albert S.
Battle of Gettysburg. TRUW: 13
Mason, George
Adoption of the Constitution. SMI:44
Natural propensity of rulers to oppress. BREW 8:110
Mason, John Mitchell
Eulogy on Washington. HAZO 9:3805; MAS 9:3805
Mason, M. C. B.
Lincoln, the man of the hour. WOON:541
Mason, Mabel
College woman and the 20th century. ONES:383
Mason, William Clarke
Presents George Wharton Pepper. LY:141

MASONRY (SECRET ORDER) See Freemasons

MASSACHUSETTS
Hale, E. E.
Sons of Massachusetts. CHAL 10:162; HAZO 20: 8388; MAS 20:8388
Hoar, G. F.
Great men of Massachusetts. BREW 7:60
South Carolina and Massachusetts. CHAL 11:2; HAZO 21:8888; MAS 21:8888; REEM 7:169; REEMA 8: 659; REEMB 8:196
Kossuth, L.
Speech in Faneuil Hall. CHAL 7:20; HAZO 14:5809; MAS 14:5809; REEMA 13: 1269
Massey, John E.
Barbour Bill. SMI:201
Massey, Vincent
Our problem and yours. NORR 3d ser:14
Massey, W. F.
Imperial Conference, 1921. KESB:59
Speech at Imperial War Conference, 1917. KES 2:381
Massillon, Jean Baptiste
Curse of a malignant tongue. BREW 8:114; BRYW 7:80; CHAL 2:163; HAZO 4:1700; MAS 4:1700
Funeral oration on Louis XIV. PL:276
Sermon on spirit of the Ministry. HAZO 4:1707; MAS 4:1707
Small number of the Elect. LEEW 4:301
Mast, C. L., Jr.
Will a million members be enough? SAC:93

MATERIALISM
Bingham, J. B.
Enlightened materialism. YR 6:151
Humphrey, C. J.
Belive it or not. YR 10:87
Shuler, B., Jr.
Nation out of balance. YR 9:89
Mather, Benjamin I.
Goal of delinquent justice. ONES:372
Mather, Cotton
At the sound of the trumpet. BREW 8:120; PL:561
"Bostonian Ebenezer." CHAL 2:144; HAZO 4:1681; MAS 4:1681
Joyful sound of salvation. HIB:195
Mathews, Shailer
Introducing Woodrow Wilson. ONEM:671; ONES:6
New opportunities in a new age. REAC:182
Matsuoka, Yosuke
Address at opening of Thai-French Indo China Border Dispute Mediation Conference. VO 1941:76
Address delivered before the 76th session of the Imperi-

Matsuoka, Yosuke (cont.)
al Diet. VO 1941:44
On the world state of emergency. VO 1941:330
Reply to Ribbentrop. VO 1941:144
Statement on return to Tokyo from Europe, April 22, 1941. VO 1941:173
Matthews, Brander
American character. REEM 7:280; REEMB 8:293
American literature. REEMA 9:861
Edwin Booth. REEM 5:311; REEMB 9:351
James Russell Lowell. REEM 2:394; REEMB 2:411
Mark Twain as speechmaker and story-teller. DOA:295
Matthews, M. A.
Fraternal life insurance. THOU 3:177
Man's duty to his family. THOU 3:430
Maulina, R.
Inaugural speech at Conference on the Problems of Economic Development. UAR:307
Maurice, Gamara
Inaugural speech at Conference on the Problems of Economic Development. UAR:251
Speech at final session of Conference on the Problems of Economic Development. UAR:413
Maury, Matthew Fontaine
Rules of conduct-attributes of success. SMI:144
Maxfield, W.R.
Notable flag-raising. THOU 1:295
Maxim, Hudson
Airships and high explosives in war (1909). BREW 8:126
Maxted, Stanley
Are you a little bored with war? HAN:273
Maxwell, Kenneth L.
What college has done for me. JUD:215
Maxwell, William
The chief. SMI:126

MAY DAY
Stalin, I.
Order of the day, May 1, 1943. VO 1943-44:187
Order of the day, May 1, 1944. VO 1944-45:198
Order of the day on "May Day," May 1, 1942. VO 1942-43:262
Mayer, Julius M.
Court and the law. BYRA:295; ONES:358; REEM sup 2:214; REEMB 6:281

MAYFLOWER (SHIP)
Beck, J. M.
Democracy of the "Mayflower." REEMA 1:33
Everett, E.
The Mayflower. CODS:480; CODSA:480
See Pilgrim Fathers
Mayhew, Jonathan
Discourse on the anniversary of the death of Charles I. HAZO 5:1989; MAS 5:1989

MAYORS See Public officials
Mays, Benjamin E.
Christian in race relations. HILK:120
Inescapable Christ. BA 1944-45:298
Mays, James H.
Internationalism. TRUW:54
Mazidi, Feisal
Inaugural speech at Conference on the Problems of Economic Development. UAR:279
Speech at final session of Conference on the Problems of Economic Development. UAR:407
Mazurov, Kirill T.
Speech of October 19. RUS:39
Mazzini, Guiseppe
Martyrs of Cosenza. LEEW 5:239

To the young men of Italy. BAKF:406; BREW 8:130; BRYW 7:225; CHAL 7:226; COP:98; COPA:98; COPB: 98; HAZO 14:6113; MAS 14:6113; PE:458; PEA: 458; PL:342; REEM 9:262; REEMA 14:1467; REEMB 10:270

Mead, James M.
Older worker. ON:347

Mead, S. C.
Fundamentals of commercial organization. REEM sup 2: 218; REEMB 5:166

Meagher, Thomas Francis
Glory of Ireland (St. Patrick's Day speech). HAZO 20:8471; MAS 20:8471
Hope for Ireland (speech from the dock). HAZO 20:8468; MAS 20:8468
Indictment of the Whigs. HAZO 20:8463; MAS 20:8463
On abhorring the sword. BRYW 6:209; CHAL 10:214; HAZO 20:8453; KET:352; MAS 20:8453; PL:528
Orators of Ireland. HAZO 20: 8477; MAS 20:8477
Withering influence of provincial subjection. BREW 8: 136

Meany, George
Fallacies of labor criticism. BA 1958-59:84
Labor Day message. BA 1953-54:143
Labor's position on labor-management reform legislation. BA 1959-60:142
New horizons for labor and management. BA 1956-57: 126
Principles and program of AFL-CIO. BA 1955-56:78

Meany, Stephen Joseph
Legality of arrest (speech delivered from the dock). HAZO 21:9189; MAS 21: 9189

MEAT DEALERS See Food

MECHANIC ARTS. See Industrial arts

Mechelynck, Cecile
Farewell to American nurses. GA:57

MEDALS See Acceptance speeches- Medals; Presentation speeches- Medals

MEDICAL CARE-COST OF
Hawley, P. R.
Prepayment plans. HAR: 355
Readinger, C.
Dollars, doctors, and disease. BRP 6:78
See also Insurance, health

MEDICARE See Aged-Medical care

MEDICINE
Acceptance of science award. BEDA:61
Arthritis and rheumatism. DR:266
At the opening of a meeting of physicians. HAPR:77
Butler, N. M.
Progress in medicine. REEM 1:193; REEMB 1:194
Cancer program. DR:271
Closing speech at presentation of scientific award. BEDA: 62
Conn, J. and others.
Stress and disease. HAR: 328
Falconer, R. A.
Modern medicine, a dispeller of fear. KLEB:211
Harris, M. L.
Deontology, or the moral obligation of medicine. ONEC:284
Henderson, Y.
Physiology of Atelectasis. ONEC:295
Holmes, O. W.
Medical profession. LA:160
Infantile paralysis or poliomyelitis. DR:263

MEDICINE (cont.)
Jerome, J.K.
Imaginary invalid. SHU:99
Krantz, J., Jr.
Anesthesia-man's redemption from pain. MCK:150
Architect designed a needle (hypodermic). MCK:237
On being a scientifically-minded physician. MCK:169
McKay, H.W.
Weighed in balance: inaugural address as president of the Southern Medical Association. HAR:343
Medical association. SCHS:177
Osler, W.
To the medical profession of the United States and Canada. KNAS:231; KNASA 231; ONEM:684; ONES:29; REEM sup 2:264; REEMB 6:285
Paget, J.
Scientific mind. HAY:261
Physicians (after-dinner speech for medical association meetings). EDGS:179
Rush, B.
Influence of the physical causes on the moral faculty. BL:312
Sarbin, H.
Let medicine wash its hands. NOR 1946:59
Schindler, J.A.
How to live a hundred years happily. BERS:101; YE:236
Smith, R.
Professor anonymous. BRP 4:33; INTW 1933:35; YR 5:93
Vincent, G.E.
The doctor and the changing order. REEM sup 3:151; REEMB 6:364
Your Easter seal agency (National Society for Crippled Children and Adults). DR:269
Zinsser, H.
Scientist's view of the Medical Center. REEM sup 3:204; REEMB 6:402
See also Aged-Medical care; American Medical Association; Drugs; Hospitals; Insurance, health; Medical care-cost of; Mental health; Physicians; Physiology

---- STATE
Hard, W.
Medical care for all. SAR:309
Peril of socialized medicine. DR:243
Medina, Harold R.
Charge to jury. BA 1949-50:136
Equal justice for all. HIBS:476
Meek, Thomas J.
John B. Gordon-the pacificator. TRUW:184
Meighen, Arthur
British political tradition. REEM 2:402; REEMB 2:419
Canada's problems and outlook. REEM 2:399; REEMB 2:416
Glorious dead. REEM 11:431; REEMB 12:456
Meisel, George I.
Wanted: spunk, sense, and stamina. NOR 1941:11
Mekonnen, Lija Endalkachew
Inaugural speech at Conference on the Problems of Economic Development. UAR:31
Speech at final session of Conference on the Problems of Economic Development. UAR:375
Melanchthon, Philip
On the death of Luther. BRYW 7:44; CHAL 1:427; HAZO 4:1333; MAS 4:1333
Safety of the virtuous. BREW 8:140; HAZO 4:1324; MAS 4:1324
Meldrum, A.B.
Power and aim. REAC:186

Melish, William B.
Ladies. REEM 2:404; REEMA 2:825; REEMB 2:421

MELLETT, DON R.
Blakeley, R.J.
Constant crusade. BA 1951-52:152
Mellon, Andrew William
Nation's business. BYRA:299; NESA:99; REEM sup 2: 227; REEMB 5:175
Presenting to Mr. Thomas A. Edison the medal bestowed upon him by Congress. ONEC:35

MELLON, ANDREW W.
Butler, N.M.
Introduces Andrew W. Mellon to Lotus Club. REEM sup 2:227; REEMB 5:175
Thomas, A.
Honoring Secretary Mellon. NESA:176
Melone, Gerald H.V.
American ideal (civilization rests not upon force but upon service to humanity). ASHF:213
Meloney, Mrs. William Brown
Introducing Dorothy Thompson. GA:13; LY:125
Melson, Barbara
Strength in democracy. YR 10: 133

MEMBERSHIP DRIVES See Club speeches; Fund raising

MEMBERSHIPS See Acceptance speeches-Memberships; Club speeches; Presentation speeches-Memberships
Memmius, Caisus
Against the power of the nobility. BRYW 2:37; LEEW 2:54

MEMORIAL DAY
Abstract of a Grand Army speech. DAVC:625
At the graves of the nation's dead. THOU 1:104
Bell, E.I.
Not taps but reveille. BA 1944-45:307
Bruce, R.C.
Freedom through education. WOON:585
Ceremonies at the grave. HILL:474
Chaplain's address at the grave. HILL:475
Chaplain's prayer. HILL:473
Cockran, W.B.
Decoration Day. BLAA: 102; BLAB:102
Commander's dedication speech. HILL:474
Commander's speech of thanks. HILL:474
Commander's speech on decoration. HILL:474
Corrigan, J.M.
Memorial Day at League Island Navy Yard. CATA 1: 24
Daly, W.J.B.
Memorial Day. CATA 1:17
Davis, W.R.
All's well. WAGN:155
Day of memorial. FRIE:104
Decoration Day. BURS:184
Decoration Day address. CRAI:401
Decoration Day address. DAVC:461
Decoration of unknown graves and address at cemetery. HILL:473
Dedication services. HILL:474
Dibble, H.C.
Loyalty to the nation. WAGN:295
Depew, C.M.
Outline of speech on Decoratio Day. PITT:47
Destruction of war. THOU 1: 108
Eliot, C.W.
Heroes of the Civil War. BAKF:183
G.A.R. burial service. HILL: 474
G.A.R. public exercises in a

MEMORIAL DAY (cont.)
hall. HILL:474
Gregg, D.
Way to honor our patriotic dead. THOU 1:102
Harding, W. G.
Hallowed ground, May 30, 1921. PROS:114
Higginson, T.W.
Decoration Day, 1870. BLAA:246; BLAB:246; CHAL 10:298; HAZO 20: 8599; KLEM:170; MAS 20: 8599; REEM 7:166; REEMA 8:621; REEMB 8:193
Holmes, O.W., Jr.
Memorial Day. BRAC:335; REEM 7:181; REEMA 8: 691; REEMB 8:208
Honor to our patriotic dead. MORA:62
Humphreys, B. G.
Old traditions. REEM 7: 190; REEMB 8:217
In remembrance. JAS:60
Ingersoll, R. G.
Vision of war (Decoration Day address, 1888). BAAMP: 169; CODS:420; CODSA: 420
Lest we forget. JA:136
Logan, J. A.
General orders inaugurating Decoration Day. THOU 1:98
Long, J.D.
Soldier boy (May 30, 1882). BAKF:193; BLAA:69; BLAB:69; KLEG:176; ONEM:561; REAC:75; WERN 42:58
Lyon, E.
Emancipation and racial advancement (15th anniversary of Emancipation Proclamation). DUNM:461
MacArthur, R. S.
Real cause of the war. THOU 1:99
McKeldin, T.
Memorial Day. MCK:139
Map: a thought for changing a speech (for a patriotic speech, for Memorial Day, or a speech for peace). BAI:123
Margulies, N.
Age of anxiety. MO:453
Memorial Day. CON:104
Memorial Day. FRIE:107
Memorial Day. MORA:64
Memorial Day. NATM:19
Memorial Day. NATS:21
Memorial Day. SCHS:179
Memorial Day-a tribute to those who offered their lives for their country. DR:154; LU:1193
Memorial Day: in memory of those who gave their lives for their country. EDGS: 33
Memorial Day address. THOS: 23
Memorial Day addresses. AMEO 1:88; AMEO 2:13
Memorial of a preserved nation. THOU 1:102
Morize, A.
"1918-1925"--a Memorial Day address. LINM:464
Nation remembers. JA:133
Shortridge, S. M.
Memorial Day address. WAGN:53
Sketch of a speech in response to the toast "Our honored dead." PITT:43
Taft, W.H.
Our national dead. BLAB: 305
Thoughts pertinent to Decoration Day. THOU 1:109
Turrill, C.B.
Memorial Day address at Calvary Cemetery, San Francisco. CATA 1:32
Vandenberg, A. H.
Memorial Day address. BA 1937-38:39
Watterson, H.
Memorial Day. FUL:337; WERN 42:82
Welles, S.
Memorial Day address at the Arlington amphitheater. VO 1942-43:321

What the war settled. THOU 1:101
Wilson, W.
Memorial Day address, 1917. LEW:33
Words of the officer and chaplain. HILL:474
Words of welcome. HILL:474

MEMORIAL HALLS See Acceptance speeches-Memorial Halls; Presentation speeches-Memorials

MEMORIAL SPEECHES
Alderman, E. A.
Woodrow Wilson. HICF: 702; LINM:186; REEM sup 1:21; REEMB 9:6
Anderson, M. B.
Genius and achievement of Morse. REEMA 7:40
Beatty, D.
Comrades of the mist. REEM 11:415; REEMB 12: 437
Beautiful memorial. JAS:42
Beecher, H. W.
Abraham Lincoln--memorial sermon. SHAH:437; THOU 1:471
Benediction (at memorial services honoring deceased union member). BED:99; BEDA:177
Brown, C. H.
Bennet College (memorial service for Dr. Dett) HILK: 84
Closing benediction (at memorial services honoring deceased union member). BED: 101; BEDA:179
Closing speech (at memorial service). BED:45; BEDA:87
Closing speech (at unveiling of plaque for Labor Temple). BED:88; BEDA:161
Davis, J. W.
Shakespeare's birthday memorial. REEM 1:369; REEMB 1:370
Davis, M. L.
Upon the death of William McKinley. SHUO:72
Dooling, M. T.
Our absent brothers. WAGN: 264
Douglas, W. O.
At the grave of Franklin Delano Roosevelt. MO:533; MOA:539
Elks memorial. SCHS:116
Elks memorial. THOS:167
Elks memorial address. THOS:176
Eulogy (at memorial service). BED:44; BEDA:85
Eulogy (at memorial services honoring deceased union member). BED:100; BEDA: 178
Everlasting memorial. JAS: 98
Fenner, C. E.
Justice to Jefferson Davis. SHUO:139
Fiske, J.
Columbus the navigator (400th anniversary of discovery of America by Christopher Columbus). CHAL 13:442; REEM 5:171; REEMA 8:490; REEMB 9: 206
Foch, F.
Napoleon. COP:144; COPA: 144; COPB:144; REEM 5: 183; REEMB 9:219
French officer, A.
To the first Americans who fell in France. REEM 11: 414
Garnet, H. H.
Memorial discourse. DUNM: 107
Ginisty, M-A. C.
Verdun. REEM 11:413; REEMB 12:433
Gittelsohn, R. B.
That men might be free. BA 1945-46:16
Harding, W. G.
Patriotic memorial speech, May 23, 1921. CARP:264
Harris, H. R.

MEMORIAL SPEECHES (cont.)
Deocration of graves--memorial address. THOU 3:415
Higginson, T.W.
Grant. CHAL 10:302; HAZO 20:8603; MAS 20:8603; WERN 42:66
Hitler, A.
Broadcast to the world, March 21, 1943 (celebrating Heroes' Memorial day). VO 1943-44:129
Memorial address, 1941. VO 1941:133
Memorial day address, 1942. VO 1942-43:198
Holmes, O.W., Jr.
Sons of Harvard who fell in battle. REEMA 2:630; REEMB 2:234
Howells, W.D.
In memory of Mark Twain. REEM 5:224; REEMB 9:262
Hugo, V.M.
On the centennial of Voltaire's death. BREW 7:98; CHAL 7:1; COP:91; COPA:91; COPB:91; HAZO 14:5776; MAS 14:5776; REEM 5:277; REEMA 8:710; REEMB 9:265
In memoriam (for a fellow brother in the Sons of Temperance). THOU 3:499
In memoriam (for a Masonic brother). EDW:69
In memoriam (on death of club member)-examples of. MORA:53-59
Irish, J. P.
Memorial address on Governor Bartlett. WAGN:281
Jefferson, J.
In memory of Edwin Booth. REEM 2:277; REEMA 2:691; REEMB 2:281
Kent, W.
Jenkins Lloyd Jones. REEM 5:258; REEMB 9:297
Lewis, W.H.
Booker T. Washington - a lover of his fellow-men. WOON:596
Lodge, H.C.
Passing of "Valiant-for-truth" (Theodore Roosevelt). BREW 7:380; REEM 5:280; REEMB 9:319
Loud, G.B.
Memorial address (Foresters). THOU 3:277
McFarland, J.G.
Memorial address at the tomb of President Harding, December 2, 1923 (speech as Past Exalted Grand Ruler of the Elks). LINM:34
Macy, V.E.
Samuel Gompers. REEM sup 2:209; REEMB 5:163
Matthews, B.
James Russell Lowell. REEM 2:394; REEMB 2:411
Memorial address at meeting to honor the founder of James Gray Home for Underprivileged Children. WRA:150
Memorial address (at Veterans' Day observance). BED:47; BEDA:93
Memorial address shortly after the death of a well-known citizen by civic official at a public meeting. WRA:148
Memorial ceremonies. BED:157
Memorial speech. THOS:164
Memorial speech by club president shortly after death of a member. WRA:145
Memorial speech on the anniversary of the death of a well-known public figure by civic official. WRA:146
Miller, D.H.
Woodrow Wilson. HICF:696
Morrow, E.P.
Theodore Rooselvet--American. NESA:193
Moton, R.R.

Life of achievement (at memorial meeting in honor of Booker T. Washington). WOON:602
Murrow, E.R.
Jan Masaryk. BA 1947-48: 220
Naidu, S.
My father, do not rest! ZU:3
Nehru, J.
Glory has departed. BOU: 219; COPB:619
Speaks to mourning millions a few hours after the murder of Gandhi. HIBS:497; PE:809; PEA:809
Nimitz, C.W.
Remarks at Japanese surrender. VO 1945-46:531
O'Leary, J.
Military mass of Spanish American war veterans in Boston. CATA 1:28
Olney, R.
John Marshall. REEM 5: 318; REEMA 9:932; REEMB 9:358
Opening address (at memorial service). BED:43; BEDA: 84
Opening speech (at memorial service honoring deceased union member). BED:99; BEDA:176
O'Reilly, J.B.
Moore, the Bard of Erin. REEM 3:13; REEMA 2:856; REEMB 3:13
Osburn, H.F.
John Burroughs. REEM 5: 325; REEMB 9:366
Outline for memorial speeches. CARP:8
Palmerston, H.J.T.
On the death of Cobden. BREW 8:268
Paraphrase of Lincoln's Gettysburg address as a fitting memorial address. BAKS:165
Phelan, J.D.
Verdi memorial exercises address. WAGN:351
Prayer (at memorial service). BED:43; BEDA:84
Rice, F.H.
Washington (memorial address on 100th anniversary of his death). THOU 3:298
Roll call (at memorial services honoring deceased union member). BED:101; BEDA:179
Rosebery, A.P.P.
Robert Burns (delivered in St. Andrews Hall, Glasgow, at Burns centenary). BRYW 5:174; LAD:212; REEM 5:333; REEMA 9: 1007; REEMB 9:375
Savage, H.P.
Address to the Legion dead. SHUP:216
Scott, E.J.
Memorial address (on Booker T. Washington). WOON:607
Smith, C.E.
McKinley. WERN 42:135
Stedman, E.C.
Work of Robert Louis Stevenson. REEMA 9:1098
Stetson, F.J.
Joseph Hodges Choate. REEM 5:355
Stevenson, A.E.
Address at the memorial service for Sir Winston Churchill. BA 1964-65:103
Political relevance of moral principle (A. Powell Davies memorial address). WPRC:355
Straus, O.S.
Roosevelt pilgrimage. REEM 7:380; REEMB 8:401
Suggestions for preparation of memorial speeches-with examples of. BEB:71; WRA:143
Tributes to deceased officer of a local union-ten examples of. BEB:67-71
Truman, H.S.
Broadcast to the armed

MEMORIAL SPEECHES (cont.)
forces of the United States upon his assumption of office. VO 1945-46:152
Van Dyke, H.
William Dean Howells. REEM 5:370; REEMB 9:414
Warner, C.D.
George William Curtis, litterateur. REEMA 9:1130
Wilson, W.
Address at Gettysburg. REEM 10:421; REEMB 11:438
Heroes of Vera Cruz. BRAC:343
Woodmen of the world- in memoriam. THOS:185
See also Acceptance speeches-Memorials; Commemorative addresses; Dedication addresses-Memorials; Eulogies; Presentation speeches-Memorials; Resolutions, memorial; Tributes

MEMORY
Huber, L.J.
Forgetful emcee. BRH:342
Things I can't remember. NAT:29
Menard, John Willis
Negro's first speech in Congress: in defense of his election to Congress when his seat was contested and won by his political opponent. WOON:263
Mendes, Henry Pereira
Address at 250th anniversary of the settlement of the Jews in the United States. TWJ:58
Mendès-France, Pierre
Search for international cooperation. COPB:623
Menninger, Karl
Healthier and healthy. LINP:26

MENTAL HEALTH
Appealing for funds and volunteers (at mental health fund drive). BED:69; BEDA:105
Closing speech (at mental health fund drive). BED:61; BEDA:106
Introducing public official (at mental health fund drive). BED:59; BEDA:104
Menninger, K.
Healthier than healthy. LINP:26
Opening address (at mental health fund drive). BED:59; BEDA:104
Seabury, D.
How Jesus healed men's minds. BART 3:1

MENTAL TESTS
Intelligence tests. AMEO 1:200

MERCHANTS See Business men
Mercier, Desire Felicien Francois Joseph, Cardinal
Coronation day sermon. COP:132; COPA:132; COPB:132; FRY:75; PE:702; PEA:702; REEM 11:129; REEMB 12:140

MERCY
Bede.
Meeting of mercy and justice. BREW 1:345
Olmsted, W.C.
Virtue, mercy and charity. THOU 3:377
Prescott, R.W.
"Mercy that condemns." SHUC:392
Wycliffe, J.
Mercy to damned men in Hell. BREW 10:276
Merriam, John Campbell
Presents Barton W. Evermann
" George H. Whipple
" Ray Lyman Wilbur
" William W. Campbell. LY:191, 190, 189, 187
Merrihue, Willard V.
What a company looks for in seeking a new location.

SABA: 183
Merritt, Walter G.
Summation for the plaintiff in the Danbury Hatters case. HICJ: 492
Mertz, Paul A.
Opens a discussion meeting. PR: 100

MESSAGE TO GARCIA
A message to Garcia. AMEO 2: 165
See also Hubbard, E.
Mestiri, Ahmed El
Inaugural speech at Conference on the Problems of Economic Development. UAR: 169
Speech at final session of Conference on the Problems of Economic Development. UAR: 387

METROPOLITAN OPERA ASSOCIATION
Sarnoff, D.
Appeal for popular support of the Metropolitan Opera Association. MOA: 312
Metzger, George E.
Proposed grain marketing program. SAB: 118

MEXICO
Camacho, A.
Address to President Roosevelt in Monterrey. VO 1943-44: 169
Diaz, P.
Mexican progress. BREW 5: 208
Hanna, K. A.
Roles of the South in the French intervention in Mexico. TIN: 298
Reed, J. A.
Toleration (trouble of 1927). BYRA: 367; REEM sup 2: 318; REEMB 8: 338
Roosevelt, F. D.
Reply to President Camacho at Monterrey. VO 1943-44: 171
See also United States-Foreign Relations-Mexico; World War, 1939-1945-Mexico
Meyer, Agnes E.
Address to the Regional Conference of the American Red Cross. BUTA: 246
Meyer, Ellsworth
Constitution. LEIO: 135
Mezes, Sidney Edward
Inaugural address as president of University of Texas. WE 2: 387
Michaels, Morris Gabriel
Builders of empire. SHUC: 74

MICHELANGELO BUONARROTI
Miles, L. E.
Michael Angelo. COUW: 149

MICHIGAN (STATE)
Michigan. SCHS: 182

MICHIGAN, UNIVERSITY OF
Angell, J. B.
Inaugural address as president of University of Michigan. WE 2: 47
D'Ooge, M. L.
Farewell to University of Michigan. ONES: 36
Kane, F. G.
The Michigan Union. KNAS: 272; KNASA: 272
Ruthven, A. G.
Victor Clarence Vaughan and the University (Michigan). ONEC: 127

MICROPHONE SPEAKING
Suggestions for speaking over public-address systems. SOBP: 287

MIDDLE CLASSES
Dilley, J.
Vanishing American. BRP 6: 82; YR 6: 33

MIDDLE EAST See United States-Foreign Relations-Middle East

Mikolajczyk, Stanislaw
Broadcast to Poland. VO 1944-45:19
Mikoyan, Anastas I.
Speech of October 20. RUS:45
Milburn, John G.
Presents James R. Day. LY: 101
Miles, Lou E.
Michael Angelo. COUW:149
Miles, Nelson Appleton
Spanish-American war. REEMA 2:831

MILES, NELSON APPLETON
Choate, J.H.
Tribute to General Miles. REEMA 1:193

MILITARY COMMISSIONS, ACCEPTANCE OF See Acceptance speeches-Military commissions
MILITARY TRAINING See United States-Army

MILITIA BILL See United States History-War of 1812

MILK
Milk dealers. SCHS:185
Shaw, H.W.
Milk. REEM 8:358; REEMA 6:1011; REEMB 13:363
Mill, John Stuart
Reform of the franchise (Women's suffrage). EMS 2:182
Tribute to Garrison. HAZO 15:6183; MAS 15:6183
Miller, Clarence A.
Man out of employment. WERN 42:42
Miller, Clyde R. and others (M. Krueger; H.C. Peterson)
Propaganda. BA 1939-40:191
Miller, David Hunter
Woodrow Wilson. HICF:696
Miller, Emma Guffey
Seconding nomination of President Roosevelt. GA:203
Miller, Henry Russell
American ideal. REEM 2:410; REEMB 2:426
Second birth. REEM 7:298; REEMB 8:311
Miller, Hugh
Pledge science gives to hope. BREW 8:144
Miller, J.R.
Thanksgiving thoughts. THOU 2:282
Miller, Janice
Disarmament as the way to peace. HOD:108
Miller, Kelly
Education for manhood. DUNM:445
Miller, M. Glen
Excerpts from introduction of John Foster Dulles. PRNE: 42
Introduces Charles F. Brannan, Secretary of Agriculture. PRNE:25
Introduces Commander Irving Johnson. PRNE:40
Introduces Dr. Robert E. Wilson, Chairman, Standard Oil Company of Indiana. PRNE:22
Introduces Dr. Will Durant, author and philosopher. PRNE:48
Introduces Henry J. Taylor, radio commentator. PRNE: 35
Introduces Jesse M. Donaldson, Postmaster General of the United States. PRNE: 20
Introduces Lee Wulff, lecturer with films. PRNE:47
Introduces Mayor Edward J. Jeffries. PR:61
Presents Arthur H. Motley. LY:86; PR:44
Miller, Mildred E.
Rights we defend. DO:114
Miller, Monroe V.
Higher patriotism. BOA:63; BOB:109
Miller, Nadine
Is advertising responsible for our high standard of living?

MOA: 463
Miller, O.R.
Opinion on Knights of Malta. THOU 3:152
Miller, Samuel F.
Federal judges. REEMA 2:834
Slaughter house cases, 1875: opinion for the Supreme Court. BIR 3:102
Wabash, St. Lous and Pacific Railroad Company v. Illinois, 1886: opinion for the Supreme Court. BIR 3:150
Miller, Samuel H.
Gospel of insecurity. BA 1964-65:138
Millerand, Alexandre
Semicentennial of the French Republic. BREW 8:148; REEM 11:423; REEMB 12:447
Millikan, Robert Andrews
Atom. REEM sup 2:230; REEMB 7:272
Isolationist fallacies. COP:604
Science and spiritual values. ONEC:177
Science and the world tomorrow. BA 1938-39:187
Science leads us forward. BOA:145
Milliken, Forbes
Emcee at a birthday celebration
" at a golfers' banquet
" at a merchants' banquet
" at an office workers' party
" at a writers' club. BRH: 228, 301, 178, 245, 234
Introducing a director of an amateur play
" a celebrity
" an opera star. BRH:72, 145, 109

MILLINERY TRADE See Business men
Mills, Charles
Instituting a new council. THOU 3:536
Mills, Thornton Anthony
Fiddles and fortunes. EXEE: 11
Milner, Alfred Milner, Viscount
"Never again." REEMA 14: 1474
Milner, Sam
Jew. YR 7:231
Milnes, Frank J.
Exponent of culture for common humanity. TRUW:164
Milton, John
For the liberty of unlicensed printing. BREW 8:151; BRYW 3:79

MIND See Intellect; Thought and thinking

MIND READERS See Actors and acting

MINISTERS See Church; Clergy; Religion

MINNESOTA, UNIVERSITY OF
Coffman, L.D.
Inaugural address as president of University of Minnesota. WE 2:187
Minnigerode, Lucy
Dedication of Delano Memorial. CA:67
Minor, Lucian
Education and republican institutions. SMI:119

MINORITIES
Gough, J.B.
What is minority? PROS: 90
Newman, J.E.
Case for minorities. NOR 1947:77
Minow, Newton N.
Television and the public interest. BA 1961-62:64

MINSTREL SHOWS
Drummond, R.
Introducing a minstrel show. BRH:92
Gilbert, E.J.
Introducing a minstrel show. BRH:171

MINSTREL SHOWS (cont.)
Huber, L. J.
Introducing a minstrel show. BRH:108
Mintz, Samuel
Editorial. BRP 8:74; NOR 1937:17
Mirabeau, Honore Gabriel Riqueti, Comte de
Address to the King. PL:297
Against the charge of treason. BREW 8:170; BRYW 7:97; CHAL 3:263; COP:74; COPA:74; COPB:74; HAZO 7:2904; LEEW 5:23; MAS 7:2904; REEM 9:184; REEMA 14:1477; REEMB 10:191
Against the establishment of religion. BREW 8:165
Announcing the death of Franklin. BREW 8:168
Argues for the King's right to make war and peace. -Same as his Right of war and peace
Defends desperate financial measures. -Same as his On Necker's project-"And yet you are deliberate"
Defying the French aristocracy. BREW 8:164; PE:231; PEA:231
Insurrection of October 5th. -Same as his Against the charge of treason
Justifying Revolution. BREW 8:169
On Necker's project-"And yet you deliberate." BREW 8:158; BRYW 7:93; CHAL 3:259; HAZO 7:2900; MAS 7:2900; PE:233; PEA:233
On the abolition of the slave trade in the French colonies. HAZO 7:2887; MAS 7:2887
On the removal of the troops around Paris. PL:296
Reason immutable and sovereign. BREW 8:167
Right of war and peace. CODS:75; CODSA:75; PE:241; PEA:241
To a Deputation of Quakers. CROC:325
Warns the nobility and clergy of Provence of the impending storm. -Same as his Defying the French aristocracy

MIRABEAU, HONORE GABRIEL RIQUETI, COMTE DE
Sadler, F. P.
Mirabeau. TRUW:40

MIRACLES
Lacordaire, J. B. H.
Rationalism and miracles. BREW 7:246; HAZO 14:5857; MAS 14:5857
Mirken, Barry
Introduces Jack Benny at Friars' Club dinner to Burns and Allen. JEYO:65
Misner, Paul J.
Introduces Dr. Arthur B. Moehlman, educator. PR:89

MISSIONS AND MISSIONARIES
Christian mission. AMEO 2:75
Examples of introductions for missionaries. BO:35-38
Needs and benefits of missions. AMEO 2:81
Tales from distant lands. JAI:46
Welcome to a guest missionary. HNWS:37
Welcome to a guest speaker in Woman's Missionary Society. HNWS:41
Welcome to visitors in the Woman's Missionary Society. HNWS:24

MISSISSIPPI
Silver, J. W.
Mississippi: the closed society. TIN:466

MISSISSIPPI VALLEY
Allen, J. M.
Great Mississippi Valley.

SHUO:183

MISSOURI
Stone, W. J.
Reconstruction in Missouri. SHUO:131

---- UNIVERSITY OF
Jesse, R. H.
Inaugural address as president of University of Missouri. WE 2:129

MISSOURI COMPROMISE See Slavery in the United States

MISTAKES See Blunders
Mitchel, John
Law in Ireland: delivered from dock. HAZO 18:7595; MAS 18:7595
On the Irish cause. HAZO 18: 7597; MAS 18:7597
Mitchell, Donald
Power of an idea. NOR 1947: 89
Mitchell Donald Grant (Ike Marvel)
Irving as author and man (commemoration of 100th anniversary of birth of Washington Irving). REEMA 9:872
Mitchell, John Purroy
Mayor of New York. REEM 2: 414; REEMB 2:430
Mitchell, O. M.
First view of the heavens. CLAY:103
Mitchell, S. L.
Tamina traditions. THOU 3: 311

MITCHELL, WILLIAM
MacDonald, T.
Eagle of Golgotha. AN:21

MOEHLMAN, ARTHUR B.
Misner, P. J.
Introduces Dr. Arthur B. Moehlman, educator. PR:89
Moeller, Theodore C.
Worthy wedding anniversary observance (25th). ACW:147

MOHAMMED
Carlyle, T.
Mahomet. REEMA 4:181
Molesworth, Sir William
Colonial policy, June 26, 1849 speech. EMS 2:226
Colonial policy, February 8, 1850. EMS 2:233
Moley, Raymond
Minding America's own business. BART 3:37

MOLIERE, JEAN BAPTISTE POQUELIN
Claretie, J. A. A.
Shakespeare and Moliere. REEMA 4:229
Mollenhoff, Clark R.
Need for balanced thinking. ANGC:60
Molotov, Viacheslav Mikhailovich
Address at first plenary session of San Francisco Conference. HAN:437; VO 1945-46:170
Nazi war on Russia. COP: 515; COPA:515; COPB: 493; VO 1941:318
Report on ratification of the Anglo-Soviet treaty to the Supreme Soviet of the Union of Soviet Socialist Republics. VO 1942-43:349
Report to the Supreme Soviet of the U. S. S. R. VO 1944-45:82
Speech opposing admission of Argentina to the San Francisco Conference. VO 1945-46:185
28th anniversary speech. VO 1945-46:676

MOLOTOV, VIACHESLAV MIKHAILOVICH
Polyansky, D. S.
Speech of October 23. RUS: 62
Monaco, Prince of. See Albert Honoré Charles Grimaldi, Prince of Monaco

MONARCHY
Dilke, C.W.
On the cost of the crown. CHAL 13:473; HAZO 24: 10513; MAS 24:10513
Elizabeth I.
Queen and the royal succession. BRTH:4; BRTHA: 4
Flavel, J.
From a coronation sermon. HAZO 4:1598; MAS 4:1598
James I.
State of monarchy and the divine right of kings. BRTH: 17; BRTHA:17
Seat of power. FRIE:97
Sheridan, R.B.
Example of kings. BREW 9:210
Moncheur, Baron Ludovic
Greetings from Belgium. LEW:139

MONEY
Calhoun, J.C.
Treasury notes. SOU 9:308
Crawford, W.H.
Issue and control of money under the Constitution. BREW 4:229
Finance (real value of money). ED:171
Golden text. NAT:31
Hamm, H.
At the sign of the dollar. BOA:71; BOB:83
Hendrix, J.C.
Wampum of the Indians. ONES:236; REEMA 2:603
Lowly nickel: don't pickle the nickel (a membership speech for auxiliaries). BAI:39
McCracken, R.J.
To have and not to hold. BA 1959-60:173
Money and wealth. NATT:7
Money makes the world go. NAT:27
Owen, R.L.
Currency Bill. BYRA:311; REEM 3:21; REEMB 3:21
Phelps, W.W.
On sound currency. CHAL 13:276; HAZO 24:10257; MAS 24:10257
Power of the penny; serious talk on the value of money. ED:294
Relationship of money to the Evangelization of the whole world. AMEO 2:98
Ruskin, J.
Iscariot in modern England. BREW 9:121
Sinclair, J.F.
Money--its uses and abuses. EXEE:436
"You pay too damn much." NAT:12
See also Acceptance speeches-Money; Banks and banking; Credit; Currency question; Fund raising; Gold; Inflation (finance); Presentation speeches-Money; Silver; Wealth

MONEY RAISING See Fund raising

MONKEYS
Harlow, H.F.
Nature of love. LINP:84

MONOLOGIST See Actors and acting

MONOPOLIES
Colepeper, J.
Against monopolies. BREW 4:265
Fairless, B.F.
Detour ahead. BA 1949-50: 164
Fuller, M.W.
United States v. E.C. Knight Company, 1895: opinion for the Supreme Court. BIR 3:191
Marshall, J.
Gibbons v. Ogden, 1824: opinion for the Supreme Court. BIR 2:53
Pedrick, W.

Tantalus. YR 8:113
Richberg, D.R.
How shall we deal with labor union monopolies? BA 1955-56:67
See also Trusts, industrial
Monro, Sir Charles Carmichael, 1st Bart.
Speech in House of Lords, December 12, 1919 (on India). KESI 2:266
Monroe, James
Adoption of the Constitution. - Same as his Federal experiments in history
Federal experiments in history. BREW 8:172; CHAL 4:27; HAZO 8:3329; MAS 8:3329; SMI:62
First inaugural address. CHI: 32; LOTI:33; USIN:29; USINA:29
Monroe Doctrine. ANG:229; BIR 2:48; BRE:147; BREA: 130; FKA:190; FRY:21; HURG:59; PO:79; RID:34
Second inaugural address. CHI:40; LOTI:41; USIN: 37; USINA:37

MONROE DOCTRINE
Coker, T.
United States and the Monroe Doctrine. ASHF:189
Gallagher, R.M.
Century of isolation. ASHF: 197
Monroe, J.
Monroe Doctrine. ANG: 229; BIR 2:48; BRE:147; BREA:130; FKA:190; FRY: 21; HURG:59; PO:79; RID: 34
Polk, J.K.
First annual message. BIR 2:146
Roosevelt, T.
Annual message, December 6, 1904. BIR 3:256
Corollary to the Monroe Doctrine (from message to Congress, December 5, 1905) BRE:300; BREA:280; FIP:45
On foreign affairs (from message to Congress, December 6, 1904). BRE:299: BREA:279; PO:117
Smith, G.
Liberty destroyed by national pride (Mexican Treaty and Monroe Doctrine). BREW 9:227
Wilson, G.G.
Monroe Doctrine and the program of the League to Enforce Peace. FKA:224
Montagu, Edwin S.
Speech in House of Commons, August 20, 1917 (on India). KESI 2:133
Speech in House of Commons, June 5, 1919 (on India). KESI 2:206
Montague, Andrew J.
Dedication of Elks national home. THOU 3:156
George Washington. SMI:269
Montague, Sydney R.
North to adventure. BART 3: 169
Montague, W.F.
"Our guest;" reply to the toast. THOU 3:265
Montalembert, Charles Forbes René de Tryon, Comte de
Deo et Caesari fidelis. BREW 8:181; HAZO 16:6729; MAS 16:6729
Devotion to freedom. BREW 8:179; HAZO 16:6726; MAS 16:6726
For freedom of education. BREW 8:177; HAZO 16: 6724; MAS 16:6724
Montgomery, Sir Bernard Law
Message to his invasion troops. VO 1944-45:260
Montgomery, James
Modern English literature. BREW 8:183

MONTOYA, NESTOR
Hudspeth, C.B.
Eulogy on Nestor Montoya. HOA:368; HOAP:266

MONUMENTS See Acceptance speeches- Monuments; Dedication addresses- Monuments
Moody, Dwight Lyman
Holiday sermon (Christmas). THOU 2:338
On Daniel and the value of character. BREW 8:188
What think ye of Christ? BRYW 10:74; CHAL 13:76; HAZO 23:10012; MAS 23: 10012; WERN 42:173
Moore, A. B.
One hundred years of reconstruction of the South. TIN:106

MOORE, A. HARRY
Introducing A. Harry Moore. NI:193
Moore, Charles E.
Profit in loss. BRP 6:7; YR 7:155
Moore, Charles Whitlock
Universal fraternity of Masonry (at centennial anniversary of Lodge of St. Andrew). REEMA 9:880
Moore, Don
Depose king selfishness. BRP 3:66; YR 4:307
Moore, Glenn
Death penalty. BRP 3:76
Moore, Harold E.
Welcome to secondary school principals. YE:135
Moore, James R.
Washington, nation builder. YR 4:117
Moore, Jean Oliver
Common man. DO:67
Moore, John Bassett
American ideals. REEM 2: 422; REEMB 2:438
Permanent Court of International Justice. ONEC:241
Moore, John M.
Crisis. CORP:103

MOORE, THOMAS
O'Reilly, J. B.
Moore, the Bard of Erin. REEM 3:13; REEMA 2:856; REEMB 3:13

MORAL EDUCATION
Is the moral side of the school receiving proper attention? AMEO 2:193

See also Behavior

MORALE
Davis, E.
If we're good enough, we can take it. BA 1941-42: 111
Snyder, F. B.
Another "shot heard round the world." BA 1941-42: 142; HOC:35; ON:249; SAC:46
Studebaker, J. W.
Morale building in our schools and colleges. BA 1941-42:120

MORALS See Behavior; Ethics
Moran, Edwin B.
Announcements at time of death of club members-examples of. PR:108
Announcement of birthdays of club members-examples of. PR:107
Chairman's remarks before introducing guests at speakers table. PR:90
Introduces E.N. Ronnau
" Henry L. Porter
" J. C. Aspley, chairman of day
" Louis Ruthenberg. PR: 53, 99, 101, 96
Moran, Herbert
Canada's part in the new world. LEIO:75
More, Sir Thomas
Speech when on trial for life. BREW 8:193; CROC:327
Moreau, Jean Victor
In his own defence. CHAL 4: 234; HAZO 9:3625; MAS 9: 3625

Moreland, Thomas W.
Robert E. Lee. SHUC:90
Morgan, Arthur E.
Engineer and expanding government. SAR:390
Morgan, Charles, Jr.
Time to speak. BERS:87
Morgan, Edmund S.
What every Yale freshman should know. ARNS:33
Morgan, Fred E.
True socialism. REAC:177
Morgan, John Tyler
On the Nicaragua Canal. REEMA 14:1490
Morgan, Nora
When men decay. YR 10:175
Morgan, W. L.
Don't forget those who gave us fraternity. THOU 3:181

MORGAN STATE COLLEGE
Jenkins, M. D.
Function of Morgan State College (inaugural address as President of Morgan State College). HILK:94
Morgenthau, Henry
Final address at the United Nations Monetary and Financial Conference at Bretton Woods. VO 1944-45:316
Opening the United Nations monetary and financial conference at Bretton Woods, N.H. VO 1944-45:291
Morinère, E. C., de la
Centennial of the battle of New Orleans. CATA 1:146
Morize, Andre
Foreign cultures and the world crisis. NORR 3d ser: 153
"1918-1925"-a Memorial Day address. LINM:464

MORLEY, CHRISTOPHER
Ford, G. S.
Presents Christopher Morley. LY:70
Morley of Blackburn, John Morley, 1st Viscount
Address at Pittsburgh. BRYW 5:211
Aphorisms. REEMA 5:809
Brutality as an imperial method. BREW 8:204
Dummy Lords or dummy Commons? BREW 8:200
Golden art of truth telling. BREW 8:206
Home Rule. CHAL 13:253; HAZO 24:10234; MAS 24: 10234; ONEM:357; REEM 9:324; REEMA 14:1497; REEMB 10:333
Literature and politics. KLEM: 139; REEMA 2:838
"Millennium," "Pandemonium," and "Pons Asinorium." BREW 8:202
Positively last appearance. REEM 2:431; REEMB 2:447
Speech in House of Lords, February 23, 1909 (on India). KESI 2:81
Testifying. REEM 2:426; REEMB 2:442
Unveiling the statue of John Bright. BEA:315; PAUF 2: 356

MORLEY OF BLACKBURN, JOHN MORLEY, 1st VISCOUNT
Van Dyke, H.
Introducing John Morley. NESA:162

MORMONS AND MORMONISM
Bacon, A. O.
Case of Senator Reed Smoot. SHUO:129
Browne, C. F.
The Mormons. REEM 8:47; REEMA 4:123; REEMB 13: 47

MORPHY, PAUL
Holmes, O. W.
Tribute to Paul Morphy. CHAL 7:394; HAZO 15: 6291; MAS 15:6291
Morreim, Paul E.
Price of integrity. BRP 7:65

Morrill, James L.
Begins an address at the University of Minnesota. PRNE:78
Begins commencement address to a School of Banking at the University of Wisconsin. PRC:19
Foreign aid and education. ANGC:168
Unchanging challenge-lest we forget (at Iowa State College centennial). IOCP:19
Morrill, Justin Smith
On the remonetization of silver. JOHA 2 pt. 2:296
Tariff and the public debt. CHAL 8:92; HAZO 16:6708; MAS 16:6708
Morris, Delyte W.
Inaugural address as 8th president of Southern Illinois university. SAB:188
Morris, Sir Edward
Speech at Imperial War Conference, 1917. KES 2:398
Morris, George Maurice
Presenting the bust of Brandeis. ON:326
Morris, Gouverneur
On the judiciary. CHAL 3:410; HAZO 7:3051; MAS 7:3051
Oration over Hamilton. BREW 8:212; COP:263; COPA:263; COPB:263; HELE:142; HURG:54; KLEG:154; ORAMA 1:187; REEM 5:314; REEMA 9:887; REEMB 9:354

MORRIS, MIRIAM HUBBARD
Conquering West. BUT:180; BUTB:180
Morris, William
Art and beauty of the earth. REEM 6:329; REEMA 9:891; REEMB 7:279
Morrow, Edwin P.
Cost of heritage. BRAC:279
Theodore Roosevelt-American. NESA:193
Morrow, W.W.
Chinese immigration. WAGN:220
Foreign policy of the United States. WAGN:229
General Philip Kearny (Statuary Hall, House of Representatives). WAGN:226
Morse, June
"But for the grace of God." YR 10:141

MORSE, SAMUEL BREESE
Anderson, M.B.
Genius and achievement of Morse. REEMA 7:40
Morse, Wayne L.
Civil rights and trial by jury. BA 1957-58:123
Constitutional liberalism and the Democratic Party. BA 1956-57:93
Independent in politics. BA 1946-47:153
To what purpose war in Asia? BA 1964-65:62

MORTGAGES
Dilley, J.
Vanishing American. BRP 6:82; YR 6:33
Harrison, H.T.
Whither midst falling due? HOC:27; ON:156; SAR:141
Morton, Oliver Perry
On reconstruction. CHAL 10:224; HAZO 20:8501; MAS 20:8501
On the issues of 1868. HAZO 20:8486; MAS 20:8486
Reasons for Negro suffrage. BREW 8:216
Morton, T.B.
Emancipation and its obligation. WAGN:330
Improvement of the colored race. WAGN:323
Morton, Wanda
Let us have our dreams. BRP 2:72; YR 3:37

MOSCOW CONFERENCE, 1943
Hull, C.
Address to a joint meeting

of Congress, November 18, 1943. VO 1943-44:548

MOSCOW CONFERENCE OF FOREIGN MINISTERS, 1945
Byrnes, J. F.
Radio address on Moscow Big-three Agreement. VO 1945-46:790
Moses.
Ten commandments. PE:2; PEA:2

MOSES.
George, H.
Lectures on Moses, progress and poverty (June 1878) PE:620; PEA:620
Moses (December 28, 1884). REEM 5:191; REEMB 9:227
Moses, George H.
Presenting silver tray to Vice-President Dawes. CORP: 270

MOSES, ROBERT
Introducing Honorable Robert Moses, Commissioner of Parks of New York City. SUM:95
Mossell, Nathan F.
Teachings of history considered in relation to race problems in America. DUNM:227

MOTHER GOOSE
Luther, Mrs. L.
Political implications of Mother Goose. BUT:182; BUTB:182

MOTHERS
Adventures of life, by a mother. EDGS:306
Beck, J. M.
Laurels of a mother. HARSO:206; PROS:101
Uncrowned queen. BOA: 264; BOB:136
Black, J. C.
Mother of Lincoln. HARSO: 229
Bloom, S.
At the home of Mary Ball Washington. DOA:15
Cain, R. L.
Unknown mothers. BOA: 260
Choate, J. H.
Pilgrim mothers. COP: 643; REEM 1:253; REEMA 1:164; REEMB 1:254
Dill, C. C.
Mothers of men. BOA:253; BOB:129
Ludlow, L.
Mother's love. BOA:258; BOB:132
Mother. AMEO 2:19
Roosevelt, T.
American motherhood. BRYW 10:253; WERN 42: 157
Smart, L. J.
Vindication of a faith. BOA: 284; BRP 5:66
Successful mothers and their relationship to the community. AMEO 2:152
Unknown mother. BOB:133
Wilson, H. T.
America's uncrowned queen. HARSO:162; REEMA 6: 1213
For American War Mothers and Gold Star Mothers See Club speeches

MOTHERS AND DAUGHTERS
Daughters (mother classifies them). ED:363
For Mother's and daughter's banquet. SOES:40
Grandmothers' club. DR:119
Great woman. LEHS:33
Mother and daughter - father and son (short speech by a father). ED:355
Mothers' and daughters' banquet. DR:109
Mother's throne. LEHS:36
My daughter, by a mother. EDGS:304
My granddaughter, by a grandmother. EDGS:308

MOTHERS AND DAUGHTERS (cont.)
Reconstructed world, by a guest at a Mother and daughter banquet. EDGS: 309
Response to a toast to "Our mothers" (at mother and daughter banquet). WRA:64
Response to welcome of a guest speaker at a mother-daughter banquet. HNWS:58
Suggestions for toasts and speeches for a mother-daughter banquet-theme "Alice in wonderland." AB: 99-103
Suggestions for toasts and speeches for a mother-daughter banquet-theme "Spring." AB:106-109
Toast "Our mothers"-Girl guide company entertaining mothers at a mothers and daughter banquet. WRA:55
Toasts and introductions at a Mother and daughter banquet. EDGS:301
Toasts to daughters by mothers. LEHS:51
Toasts to mothers by daughters. LEHS:45-48

MOTHERS AND SONS
Toasts to sons by mothers. LEHS:60

MOTHERS' DAY
Commemoration of Mothers' Day. DR:138; LU:1186
Faith of a mother. JA:145
For Mother's Day. CON:93
For Mothers' Day. SOES:39
Four Bible mothers. JAS:50
Good mothers of great men. JAS:52
Mother's Day. FRIE:265
Mother's Day. MORA:95
Mothers' Day. NATM:21
Mothers' Day. NATS:18
Mother's Day. SCHS:187
My mother, by a daughter. EDGS:305
Understanding your mother. JAI:40
Waste, W.H.
Mother's influence. ONEC: 119
Worthy of honor. JA:148

MOTLEY, ARTHUR H.
Miller, M.G.
Presents Arthur H. Motley. LY:86; PR:44
Moton, Robert Russa
Cooperation between races. SMI:273
Life of achievement (at memorial meeting in honor of Booker T. Washington). WOON:602
Negro's debt to Lincoln (at dedication of Lincoln monument, Washington, D.C.) WOON:573
Some elements necessary to race development. DUNM: 367
Mott, Frank L.
Christopher Columbus. TRUW:223
Mott, John R.
Boyhood, the greatest asset of any nation. LINM:3
Meditation. REEM 6:339; REEMB 7:289
Mottley, John Lothrop
Poet's corner. REEMA 2:842
Mould, Elmer W.K.
Ethics in American public life. SHUC:154
Moulton, Harold G.
Wartime price control. BA 1940-41:82

MOVING AND STORAGE BUSINESS See Business men

MOVING PICTURES
Dailey, M.
Influence of the movies on marriage and divorce. SHUP:172
Drummond, R.
Introducing a movie star. BRC:141

Educational value of moving pictures. AMEO 1:68
Engineers of art. NI:253; NIA:191
Hays, W.H., Jr.
Behind the scenes in Hollywod. JUD:263
Helburn, T.
Theater versus pictures. GA:109
Introducing Mary Brian, motion picture star. SUM:69
Posner, G. A.
Introducing a Hollywood actor. BRC:212
Scherer, R. M.
Blundering giant. BRP 7:31; YR 1:25
Wilson, D. J.
Eighty million suckers. BRP 8:28

---- CENSORSHIP
Murrow, E. R. and others.
Movies and censorship. ARNS:121
Mowrer, John M.
Great future. BU:170
Mucklestone, Mrs. Melville
Armistice Day address. GA:77
Response to election as president of the American Legion Auxiliary. GA:31
Muehl, E. Wm.
Empires within. NOR 1940:27
Müller, Friedrich Max
Frankfort to Stratford-on-Avon (Shakespeare tercentenary). KNAS:261; KNASA:261
Impassable barrier between brutes and man. BREW 8:223; HAZO 20:8580; MAS 20:8580
On some lessons of antiquity. HAZO 20:8588; MAS 20:8588
Muhammad, Elijah
We must have justice. HILK:292

MUHAMMAD, ELIJAH
Malcolm X.
Proclaims Muhammad as the man of the hour. HILK:304
Mukhtar, Ahmed
Inaugural speech at Conference on the Problems of Economic Development. UAR:217
Speech at final session of Conference on the Problems of Economic Development. UAR:381
Mulkey, A. C.
Address by president of Auxiliary. THOU 3:444
Mullarky, Joseph A.
Constitution. LEIO:94
Mullens, Charles J., Jr.
Living Constitution. DO:202
Mulligan, J. B.
Mission of the church: Fourth of July address. CATA 1:45
Mullins, E. Y.
Christ's law of service. SOU 9:492
Mulroy, Thomas R.
Introduces Bainbridge Colby
" Harold O. McLain
" club secretary
" Sir Norman Birkett
" two debaters, Sylvia Porter and Leon Henderson. PR:60, 81, 51, 112, 78
Presents Ilka Chase. LY:35; PR:51

MULROY, THOMAS R.
McLain, H. O.
Introduces Thomas R. Mulroy. PR:55
Mundt, Karl E.
Peace-if we want it. BA 1944-45:93
What's right with America? MIA:394
Munger, Theodore T.
Man the final form in creation. BL:709

MUNICH FOUR POWER AGREEMENT, 1938
Chamberlain, N.

MUNICH FOUR POWER AGREEMENT, 1938 (cont.)
Munich Agreement. COP: 457; COPA:457; COPB: 429; ON:90

MUNICIPAL GOVERNMENT
Field, L.
On conspicuous failure of our government. YR 6:103
Munro, W.B.
Bossism in municipal government. ONEC:215
MUNICIPAL OWNERSHIP See Government ownership
MUNITIONS
Bismarck, O.
Plea for Imperial armament. BREW 2:61; CHAL 9:38; HAZO 18:7524; MAS 18:7524; PE:586; PEA: 586
Borah, W.E.
Munitions manufacturers must be curbed. DOA:198
Dilley, J.
Armament racket. BRP 6: 105
Eisenhower, D.D.
Army hour broadcast from Paris on the need for ammunition. VO 1944-45:568
Hahn, H.L.
Merchants of war. YR 7: 201
Jones, C.
International racketeer. BRP 6:36; YR 6:255
Schlicten, E. von
International racketeers. BRP 8:11; YR 6:67
Young, B. and others.
Shall we have government monopoly on armaments? SAR:246

MUNKACSY, MIHALY
Beecher, H.W.
Tribute to Munkacsy. REEMA 1:62
Munoz, Joseph
Optimism. BU:177
Muñoz-Cota, José
Bolivar and the Latin-American peoples. LEIO:72
Munro, William Bennett
Bossism in municipal government. ONEC:215
Dedicating the Public Library of the City of Pasadena. ONEC:75
Munsey, Frank Andrew
Problems of the hour (1922). REEM 4:320; REEMB 5: 178
Munshi, Kanaialal Maneklal
Our greatest need, freedom from fear. ZU:18
Murphy, Charles T.
Constitution. LEIO:131
Murphy, Frank
Civil liberties. BA 1938-39: 173
Murphy, Howard D.
Introduces Basil Rathbone, distinguished actor. PRC: 15
Introduces Ezra Taft Benson, Secretary of Agriculture. PRC:31
Introduces George Romney, President of American Motors Corporation. PRC: 23
Introduces Willy Ley, distinguished rocket scientist. PRC:20
Murphy, Patrick Francis
In honor of Joseph Choate. REEM 2:436; REEMB 2: 452
Murphy, T.
Gospel temperance reform. THOU 1:546
Murray, George
On public speaking. CHAL 11: 380; HAZO 22:9301; MAS 22:9301
Murray, Henry A.
Beyond yesterday's idealisms. NORR 3d ser:379
Murray, M. Jean
America is worth fighting for. DO:133
Murray, Philip
CIO labor policies. BA 1949-

50:178
Equality in sacrifice. BA 1950-51:109
Labor's role in higher education. HAR:419
Strikes, wages and industrial profits. BA 1946-47:177
Wages and prices in the steel industry. GLAD:305
Murray, Thomas E.
Dismantling of the era of terror. BA 1959-60:69
Murray, William, 1st Earl of Mansfield. See Mansfield, William Murray, 1st Earl of
Murrow, Edward R.
Accepting the Peabody award. YE:157
Commencement address. BA 1954-55:128
Farewell to England. BA 1945-46:33
Jan Masaryk. BA 1947-48:220
Nominating Presidential candidates. BA 1951-52:95
Orchestrated Hell. BA 1943-44:37; BAAG:361
Spring comes to England. BA 1940-41:157
---- and others (D. Kell, O. Preminger and J. J. McClafferty)
Movies and censorship. ARNS:121

MURROW, EDWARD R.
Citation given to Edward R. Murrow with an honorary degree, Dr. of Humane Letters. BA 1954-55:128

MUSIC AND MUSICIANS
Appreciation of music. DR:55
Bates, K. L.
Response-America the beautiful. DOA:83
Branen, J.
Introducing a girl trio. BRH:146
Bryson, L. and others.
Opportunities for success in the creative arts. SAR:403
Clifford, V.
Introducing a basso
" a chorus
" a vocal soloist. BRH: 142, 123, 71
Closing speech at testimonial to a musician. BEDA:40
Drummond, R.
Introducing an accordian player
" an instrumentalist. BRH:151, 57
Garden, M.
Music in the United States. REEM 2:61; REEMB 2:61
Gilbert, E. J.
Introducing an orchestra
" a quartette. BRH:148, 60
Huber, L. J.
Introducing a choir or chorus
" an instrumental trio
" an instrumentalist
" a quartette
" a vocal soloist. BRH: 124, 76, 143, 154, 46
Introducing a musician. BRC:311
Introducing an opera star. BRH:45
Ingersoll, R. G.
Music of Wagner. REEM 2:264; REEMA 2:672; REEMB 2:268
Introducing song leader. FRIT:15
Kaser, A. L.
Introducing a community singing expert
" an orchestra leader. BRC:97, 115
Introducing a hillbilly musician
" a local orchestra
" a musician
" a quartette
" a singing quartette. BRH:147, 162, 144, 105, 150
Lynch, R.
Wanted: A Marshall Plan for the arts in America. ARNS:76

MUSIC AND MUSICIANS (cont.)
McGovern, S.
Introducing a band or orchestra leader. BRC:72
Majesty of music. DR:57
Milliken, F.
Introducing an opera star. BRH:109
Music supervisors. SCHS:188
Musicians (for any musical occasion). EDGS:200
O'Keefe, L.
Introducing a music dealer. BRC:218
Phelps, F.
Introducing a harpist. BRH:77
Posner, G. A.
Introducing a musical act. BRH:134
Presentation of scroll (at testimonial to a musician). BEDA:39
Song of the Lord. JA:35
Songs we sing. JAI:52
Steele, S.
Introducing a contralto
" a high school symphony orchestra
" a pianist. BRH:87, 137, 89
Sullivan, A. S.
Music. COP:662; COPB: 689; REEM 3:290; REEMA 3:1108; REEMB 3:307
Taylor, D.
University of music. BA 1940-41:238
Two speeches welcoming a guest soloist. HNWS:35-36
Visk, A. G.
Introducing a backwoods pianist. BRH:83
Welcome to a new minister of music and family. HNWS:16
Welcome to an evangelist singer. HNWS:36
Welcoming address at testimonial to a musician. BEDA:38
Wilcox, D.
Introducing a symphony orchestra conductor. BRC: 286
See also Art and artists; Jazz music; Metropolitan Opera Association; Opera
Muskie, Edmund S.
Responds to an introduction. PRNE:58

MUSKIE, EDMUND S.
Stipp, J. E.
Introduces Edmund S. Muskie, Governor-elect of Maine. PRNE:31
Mussen, Martin
Men of destiny. SHUC:348
Mussolini, Benito
Absurdity of eternal peace. PL:816; SAR:268
Address delivered at Rome, Italy February 23, 1941. VO 1941:87
Aims of the Fascist Party of Italy. HIB:220
Anniversary of Italy's entry in the war. COP:511; COPA:511; COPB:489
Applies the torch of civilization to Ethiopia. -Same as his Call to arms
Call to arms. COP:510; COPA:510; COPB:488; FRY:126; PE:761; PEA: 761
Calling to Italians to resume fighting against the Allies. VO 1943-44:377
Fascist Italy. REEM sup 2: 237; REEMB 8:316
Four-Power Pact. BEA:323
Hour of irrevocable decision has come! CROC:331; HIB:225
Italy enters the war. -Same as his Hour of irrevocable decision has come
Renders his first account to the Chamber of Deputies. PE:734; PEA:734
Response to Ambassador Child's speech. LINM:390
Speech before Chamber of Fasces and Corporations,

June 10, 1941. VO 1941: 249
Speech of the Prime Minister of Italy at a banquet offered by the Associazione-Americana at Rome, June 28, 1923. LINM:390
Speech to the Chamber of Fasci and Corporations, December 2, 1942. VO 1942-43:705
War statement, December 11, 1941. VO 1941:597

MUSSOLINI, BENITO
Skeyhill, T.
Mussolini. EXEE:497

MUTUAL BENEFIT ASSOCIATIONS
Ganz, J. M.
Employes' mutual benefit association. ONES:288
Myer, C. Robert
Remember Pearl Harbor. DO: 34
Myers, Clarence J.
Sources of our strength. MICS:158
Myers, Cortland
Remarks on the laying of the cornerstone of the First Baptist Church of Brooklyn. THOU 2:447
Myers, Francis J.
How a law is made. MOUG: 105; MOUGA:105
Myers, Nancy Jeanne
Moppet manipulation. ARNS: 113

MYSTIC SHRINE, NOBLES OF THE
Nobles of the Mystic shrine: an address of welcome. THOS:39

MYSTIC WORKERS OF THE WORLD
Holt, G. N.
Address of welcome. THOU 3:463
Howe, Supreme master.
Response. THOU 3:465
Palmer, Worthy Brother.
Invocation. THOU 3:468
Snyder, Rev.
Opening invocation of Rev. Snyder of the Mystic Workers. THOU 3:467

MYTHOLOGY
Ruskin, J.
On the Greek myths. CHAL 9:345; HAZO 19: 7929; MAS 19:7929
N R A See National Recovery Administration

NATO See North Atlantic Treaty Organization
Nagel, Charles
Chambers of Commerce. BYRA:302; REEM sup 2: 244; REEMB 5:188
Naidu, (Mrs.) Sarojini
My father, do not rest! ZU:3
Nakai, Raymond
Inaugural address (as chairman of the Council of Navajos Indians). BA 1963-64: 49; JON:129
Napier, Sir Charles
On the occupation of Scinde, October 17, 1842. KESI 1: 274
Napoleon I, Emperor of the French
Address after Austerlitz. LEEW 5:169
Address to his army at the beginning of the Italian campaign. CHAL 4:344; COP:85; COPA:85; COPB: 85; HAZO 9:3782; MAS 9: 3782; REEM 9:215; REEMA 11:290; REEMB 10:222
Addresses his triumphant army of Italy. -Same as his Proclamation to his army
After the return from Elba, 1815. BRYW 7:177
During the Egyptian campaign, 1789. BRYW 7:173
Farewell to the Old Guard. BRYW 7:176; CHAL 4:350;

Napoléon I, Emperor of the French (cont.)
COP:87; COPA:87; COPB: 87; HAZO 9:3788; HIB: 245; HIBS:489; LEEW 5:171; MAS 9:3789; PE:324; PEA: 324; PL:317; REEM 9:218; REEMA 11:295; REEMB 10: 225
On beginning the Russian campaign. CHAL 4:350; COP: 86; COPB:86; HAZO 9: 3788; MAS 9:3788; REEMA 11:294
On the anniversary of Austerlitz, 1806. BRYW 7:175
Proclamation from Mantua. CROC:335
Proclamation of his army. BRYW 7:168; CHAL 4:344; HAZO 9:3782; MAS 9:3782; PE:280; PEA:280; REEM 9:215; REEMA 11:290; REEMB 10:222
Speech to the Directory. BRYW 7:172; REEM 9:217; REEMB 10:224
To his soldiers after the War of the Third Coalition. CHAL 4:348; HAZO 9:3786; MAS 9:3786; REEMA 11: 293
To his soldiers during the siege of Mantua. CHAL 4: 347; HAZO 9:3785; MAS 9: 3785; REEMA 11:293
To his soldiers on the conclusion of the first Italian campaign. CHAL 4:347; HAZO 9:3785; MAS 9:3785; REEMA 11:292
To the soldiers on entering Milan. BRYW 7:169; CHAL 4:345; COP:86; COPA:86; COPB:86; CROC:333; ESEH:196; HAZO 9:3783; HIB:41; MAS 9:3783; LEEW 5:167; PL:315; REEM 9: 216; REEMA 11:291; REEMB 10:223

NAPOLÉON I., EMPEROR OF THE FRENCH
Canning, G.
Fall of Napoléon, 1814. BRTH:190; BRTHA:190; COP:176; COPA:176; COPB: 176; GOOD:859; REEM 9: 177; REEMA 12:494; REEMB 10:184
Disney, L.
Napoléon Bonaparte: the saviour of France. SHUC:78
Foch, F.
Napoléon. COP:144; COPA: 144; COPB:144; REEM 5: 183; REEMB 9:219
Ingersoll, R.
Napoléon. HOA:242
Phillips, C.
Character of Napoleon. BRYW 6:157
Serviss, G. P.
Napoléon Bonaparte. REEMA 6:983
Seward, W.H.
Death of Napoleon. CODS: 488; CODSA:488
Sheehan, P. A.
Napoléon and O'Connell. WERN 42:38
Victor of Marengo. SHU:223

Napoléon III (Louis Napoléon)
Address to the French Legislature, January 18, 1858. HAZO 15:6258; MAS 15:6258
Annual message to the Assembly, November 1850. HAZO 15:6249; MAS 15:6249
Famous speech at Dijon. HAZO 15:6256; MAS 15:6256
First inaugural address as President. HAZO 15:6247; MAS 15:6247
Second annual message as President. HAZO 15:6251; MAS 15:6251
Speech in National Assembly. HAZO 15:6246; MAS 15:6246

NARCOTICS See DRUGS
Narot, Joseph
Dare we discuss it? BRP 7:76; NOR 1936:10
Nasby, Petroleum V. See Locke,

David Ross (Petroleum V. Nasby)
Nason, J.T.
Some people learn the hard way. BRAP:31
Nasser, Gamal Abdel
Speech at the inaugural session of the Conference on Problems of Economic Development. UAR:19

NATIONAL CHARACTERISTICS, AMERICAN
Alderman, E.A.
Making of a national spirit. REEM 1:32; REEMB 1:35
Sectionalism and nationality. REEM 1:40; SHUO:104
American ideals. DAVC:13
American ideals. AMEO 1:117
American ideals: high school oration. AMEO 1:117
Bachellor, I.
Yankee. REEM 1:59; REEMB 1:50
Beveridge, A.J.
American people. NESA:114
Bowlus, N.
Moral wealth of Uncle Sam. REAC:198
Depew, C.M.
Military spirit in America. BREW 5:165
Collins, W.
American hospitality. REEMA 1:261
Donelan, C.
Mental wealth of Uncle Sam. REAC:194
Everett, E.
Moral forces which make American progress. BREW 6:84
Garfield, J.A.
Conflict of ideas in America. BREW 6:202
Grant, W.
Uncle Sam-his character. REAC:202
Hale, E.E.
What is the American people? NORR 2nd ser:228
I am an American. PROS:120
Ickes, H.L.
What constitutes an American? COP:588; COPB:567; HURG:260
Levy, N.
America's domineering tradition. ONEC:395
Lieberman, E.
"I am an American." PROS:45; SHU:219
Lodge, H.C.
Our forefathers. HURG:141
Lowell, J.R.
Poetical and the practical in America. BREW 7:385
Matthews, B.
American character. REEM 7:280; REEMB 8:293
Root, E.
American ideals during the past half century (birthday speech). ONEC:209; REEM sup 2:363; REEMB 8:373
Shorey, P.
Can an American be an optimist? NORR 2d ser:496
Story, J.
Intellectual achievement in America. BREW 9:300; CHAL 5:115; HAZO 10:4117; MAS 10:4117; NORR 2:37; ORAMA 1:378
Twichell, J.H.
Yankee notions. REEM 3:339; REEMA 3:1147; REEMB 3:355
Uncle Sam. BOB:125
Wingate, H.S.
Beyond the ranges: conflict between tradition and progressive spirit and its application to America. ASHF:237

---- DUTCH
Mackay, D.S.
Dutch Dimine. REEMA 2:782
Raymond, A.V.V.
Dutch as enemies. REEMA 3:970
Talmage, T.D.
What I know about the

NATIONAL CHARACTERISTICS, DUTCH (cont.)
Dutch. REEMA 3:1128
Van de Water, G.R.
Dutch traits. REEMA 3:1162
See also Dutch in the United States; Dutchmen

---- ENGLISH
Collyer, R.
Saxon grit. REEMA 1:263
Curtis, G.W.
English-speaking race. KLEM:88; REEMA 1:303

---- FILOPINO
Bacon, A.O.
Character and capacity of the Filopinos. REEMA 11:77

---- FRENCH
Porter, H.
Friendliness of the French. REEM 3:89; REEMA 3:919; REEMB 3:90

---- GERMAN
Challemel-Lacour, P.A.
Humboldt and the German intellect. BREW 3:183

---- SCOTTISH
Watson, J.
Scottish traits. BEA:299; REEM 8:416; REEMA 6:1143; REEMB 13:423

NATIONAL DEFENSES See Aeronautics, military North Atlantic Treaty Organization; Price regulation; World War, 1939-1945-Civilian activities. Also Names of countries or hemispheres with subdivision Defenses, e.g. United States-Defenses; Western hemisphere-Defenses

NATIONAL EDUCATION ASSOCIATION
Elliott, E.B.
Welcome to the National Education Association. ON:321
Jones, O.
"Watchman, tell us of the night" (at 5th annual meeting of Dept. of Superintendence of N.E.A.). BRAC:30
Lehman, H.
Welcome to the National Education Association of the United States. ON:316

NATIONAL INDUSTRIAL RECOVERY ACT
Green, W.
Do your part. BOB:15
Hughes, C.E.
Schechter Poultry Corporation v. United States, 1935: Opinion for the Supreme Court. BIR 4:131
Johnson, H.S.
Follow the leader. BOB:13
Richberg, D.R.
Freedom and security under the N.R.A. BOB:17
Rockefeller, J.D., Jr.
Sign of the Blue Eagle. BOB:12
Wilson, E.B.
New war. BOB:18

NATIONAL LABOR RELATIONS BOARD See Labor laws and legislation

NATIONAL PARKS AND RESERVES
Our national park system (outline of speech). MOA: 278, 280, 343

NATIONAL RECOVERY ADMINISTRATION
Doyle, J.E.
Eagle comes to earth. NOR 1935:137
Johnson, H.S.
Farewell address to the employees of the National Recovery Administration. DOA:63

Roosevelt, F.D.
Fireside chat: AAA and NRA, July 24, 1933. FIP: 206

NATIONAL RESOURCES PLANNING BOARD
Roosevelt, F.D.
Message to Congress submitting two reports of the National Resources Planning Board. VO 1943-44:103

NATIONAL SAFETY CONGRESS
Fennell, D. L.
Welcoming National Safety Congress. ON:320

NATIONAL SOCIALISM- GERMANY
Daladier, E.
Nazis' aim is slavery. COP: 491; COPA:491; COPB:461
Goebbels, J.
Broadcast, February 18, 1943. VO 1943-44:63
Presenting Hitler's proclamation, January 30, 1943. VO 1943-44:19
Hitler, A.
Address at Berlin Sports Palace, January 30, 1941. VO 1941:51
Address on eleventh anniversary of the National Socialist regime. VO 1944-45: 73
At the funeral of Reich Minister Dr. Fritz Todt. VO 1942-43:135
Broadcast on 12th anniversary of National Socialist regime. VO 1945-46:46
Broadcast to the world March 21, 1943 (celebrating Heroes' Memorial day). VO 1943-44:129
Message on the occasion of the 25th anniversary of the announcement of the National Socialist Party's program. VO 1945-46:68
Proclamation to Nazi Party veterans. VO 1943-44:89
Proclamation to the German people's army, broadcast by Heinrich Himmler. VO 1944-45:560
Request for dictatorial powers. FRY:120
Speech at Berlin Sports Palace, January 30, 1942. VO 1942-43:101
Speech commemorating the twentieth birthday of the Nazi Party. CROC:238; VO 1943-44:520
Takes full responsibility for the blood purge. PE:755; PEA:755
Keane, S.
Son of Phaeton. BRP 5:31
Lochner, L.
Inside Germany. BA 1942-43:168

NATIONAL SOCIETY FOR CRIPPLED CHILDREN AND ADULTS See Medicine

NATIONAL UNION
Matthews, M. A.
Man's duty to his family. THOU 3:430

NATIONALISM
Butler, N. M.
Nationality and beyond. BOAM:147
Hammarskjold, D.
Values of nationalism and internationalism (Stanford University commencement address). COPB:628
Helman, B.
Nationalism. AN:9
Sun, Yat Sen
National morale and world tranquility. COP:399; COPA: 399; COPB:399; CROC:436
Woodburn, J. A.
Nationalism and humanity. NORR 2d ser:423
See also Citizenship

---- UNITED STATES
Americanism. AMEO 2:15
Beveridge, A. J.
Decalogue of Americanism. SHU:96
Brandeis, L. D.
True Americanism. REEM 7:47; REEMB 8:44
Curtis, G. W.
Lowell's Americanism. REEMA 1:312
Hedges, J. E.
Ohio, the presidency and Americanism. REEM 2:195; REEMB 2:197
Hull, C.
Happy mean. SAR:154
Hurley, P. J.
Americanism or Communism? BOA:301
Lodge, H. C.
True Americanism. BOB:113
Phillips, N.
True American. SHU:83
Roosevelt, T.
Americanism. BLAA:1; BLAB:1; PROS:88; REAC:84
True Americanism and expansion. REEMA 3:1002
Schurz, C.
True Americanism. BOAM:11; BRE:236; REEMA 9:1018
Sweet, B. S.
Americanism. PROS:47
Taylor, L.
Americans for America. BOA:313; BOB:91; PROS:83
Verhage, W.
Meaning of Americanism. ASHF:1
Watterson, H.
New Americanism. ESEH:207
Wilson, W. H.
Americanism. BOA:305
See also National characteristics, American
Nattkemper, Leonard G.
Appeal for dramatic art. SHUC:62

NATURAL RESOURCES
Our plenty is not so plentiful (outline of speech). MOA:337, 338, 345
Roosevelt, T.
Public domain: the people's heritage. FIP:62
Truman, H. S.
Message to Congress, September 6, 1945. VO 1945-46:546
See also Ballinger-Pinchot Investigation

---- CONSERVATION OF See Conservation of natural resources

NATURE
Adler, F.
Nature and the religious mood. REEM 6:30; REEMB 7:30
Cyril, Saint.
Infinite artifices of nature. BREW 4:369
Fénelon, F.
Nature as a revelation. BREW 6:114; HAZO 4:1643; MAS 4:1643
Hillis, N. D.
World a whispering gallery. BLAA:179; BLAB:179
Porter, N.
Sciences of nature versus the science of man. BL:455

NAVAJO INDIANS
Nakai, R.
Inaugural address (as chairman of Navajos Indians). BA 1963-64:49; JON:129

NAVAL BASES
King, E. J.
American postwar seapower and control of Pacific bases. BA 1944-45:83

NAVIGATION ACT, 1817

King, R.
Navigation Act. HAZO 8:3200; MAS 8:3200; ORAMA 1:193

NAVY
Dewey, G.
The navy. BLAA:125; BLAB:125
It's a gay life in the navy (by one who knows). ED:79
Landsman's response to the toast of "The Navy." HILL:482
Tribute to the Navy (by a naval officer). EDGS:50
See also Conscription; Recruiting. Also Names of countries, subhead Navy, e.g. United States-Navy

NAVY DAY See United States-Navy
Naylor, Emmett Hay
Trade association. REEM 4:330; REEMB 5:193

NAZI PARTY See National socialism-Germany; World War, 1939-1945-Germany
N'Doure, Hamacire
Speech at final session of Conference on the Problems of Economic Development. UAR:373
Neal, John
Man. BL:364

NEAR EAST See Lebanon; Syria
Nearing, Scott
Capitalism vs. Socialism. REEM 3:51, 63, 71

NEBRASKA, UNIVERSITY OF
Andrews, E. B.
Inaugural address as president of University of Nebraska. WE 2:301
Neff, Pat M.
Battles of peace. BOA:185; BOB:167

NEGRO AUTHORS
Baldwin, J. and others.
Negro writer in American society (panel discussion). HILK:357

NEGRO LITERATURE
Hughes, L.
Speech on selling writing. HILK:274
Redding, J. S.
Sanctions of the American Negro's literary art. HILK:279
Negro soldiers See United States-Army

NEGRO SUFFRAGE See Negroes-Politics and suffrage

NEGROES
Anderson, C. W.
Limitless possibilities of the Negro race. DUNM:211
Bailey, L.
Case of Mr. James Crow. YR 10:185
Bontemps, A.
Negro's contribution reconsidered. HILK:185
Borders, W. H.
Some Negro contributors to American civilization. HILK:79
Bruce, R. C.
Freedom through education. WOON:585
Carter, R. A.
Whence and whither (commencement address). WOON:626
Cobbs, J. A.
My problem and yours. YR 5:53
Coppin, F. J.
Plea for industrial opportunity. DUNM:251
Coppin, L. J.
Negro's part in the redemption of Africa. DUNM:243
Crummel, A.
Black woman of the South: her neglects and her needs.

NEGROES (cont.)
DUNM:159
Dancy, J. C.
Future of the Negro church. DUNM:475
Darrow, C.
Pleads for justice for the Negro. CROC:129; PE: 737; PEA:737
Douglass, F.
"Men of color, to arms!" WOON:253
Negro exodus from the gulf states. WOON:453
What the black man wants. CHAL 9:133; HAZO 18:7665; MAS 18:7665
Douglass, J. H.
Some significant results of the Emancipation, 1863-1963. HILK:327
DuBois, W. E. B.
Training of Negroes for social reform. DUNM:491
Ford, N. A.
What are you Negroes fighting for? ON:194
Forten, J.
Late bill before the Senate of Pennsylvania. WOON:42
Future of the Negro. THOU 1: 256
Gaines, W. J.
Appeal to our brother in white. DUNM:257
Garrison, W. L.
Words of encouragement to the oppressed. CHAL 7:259; HAZO 15:6150; MAS 15: 6150
Garvey, M.
Negro's place in world organization. HILK:50
Gray, W. H., Jr.
Broaden our horizons for correctional service. HILK: 140
Greener, R. T.
Emigration of colored citizens from the southern states. WOON:473
Young men, to the front. DUNM:63
Grimke, A.
Shame of America, or the Negro's case against the Republic. WOON:671
Hill, R. L.
I am somebody. HILK:333
Holly, T.
Auspicious dawn of Negro rule. WOON:242
Hood, P. P.
Religion of the Negroes. THOU 1:266
Hughes, L. and others.
Glory. HILK:266
Johnson, M. W.
Faith of the American Negro (at Harvard commencement). WOON:658
King, M. L., Jr.
"I have a dream." BA 1963-64:43; BOU:157; HIB:173; HILK:371; LINP:156; PEA: 835
Langston, J. M.
Speech laudatory of the Negro. WOON:387
McClain, W.
Our school of destiny. YR 6:81
Morton, O. P.
Reasons for Negro suffrage. BREW 8:216
Morton, T. B.
Improvement of the colored race. WAGN:323
Negro and the south. DAVC: 57
Pickens, W.
Kind of democracy the Negro race expects. WOON: 654
Purvis, R.
Appeal of forty thousand citizens threatened with disfranchisement to the people of Pennsylvania. WOON:96
Ranney, R. L.
Justice and the Negro. YR 1:95
Remond, C. L.
Rights of colored citizens in traveling. WOON:144
Roman, C. V.

Knowledge of history conducive to racial solidarity. WOON:643
Saunders, P.
People of Hayti and a plan of emigration. DUNM:13
Scarborough, W.S.
Party of freedom and the freedman. DUNM:219
Swinton, J.
Rights of the Negro. THOU 1:265
Vance, J.M.
In the wake of the coming ages. DUNM:177
Vernon, W.T.
"Plea for a suspension of judgment." WOON:618
Walters, A.
Abraham Lincoln and fifty years of freedom. DUNM: 325; WOON:554
Washington, B.T.
Address at the opening of the Atlanta Exposition. BAAMP:189; BAKF:210; BLAA:113; BLAB:113; BRAC:8; BRY:479; BRYA: 566; CAP:110; CHAL 14: 312; DOA:333; DUNM:181; HARS:503; HAZO 25:10583; HILK:38; MAS 25:10583; ONEM:509; ONES:102; PAR: 461; PE:633; PEA:633; PL:707; REEM 7:417; REEMA 9:1136; REEMB 8: 433; SMI:206; WOON:580
Negro in the late war. CHAL 14:325; FUL:333
Test of the American Negro. FUL:330; WERN 42:34
Watterson, H.
Negro question. WERN 42: 97
Weaver, R.C.
Negro as an American. BA 1963-64:58
White, G.H.
Speech in defense of the Negro race. WOON:403
See also Brownsville (Texas) Riot 1906; Civil Rights; Civil Rights Act (1866); Discrimination; Emancipation Day; Integration; Race problems; Segregation; Segragation-Resistance to; Segregation in education; Slavery in the United States. Also subheads under this subject

---- EDUCATION
Clark, F.G.
Founder's Day address (Southern University). HILK: 73
Jenkins, M.D.
Function of Morgan State College (inaugural address as President of Morgan State College). HILK:94
Miller, K.
Education for manhood. DUNM:445
Proctor, S.D.
Address (before United Negro College convocation). HILK:225
Richardson, H.V.
Claflin yesterday today and tomorrow (inaugural address as sixth President of Claflin University). HILK:193
Ruffin, J.S.
Open letter to the Educational League of Georgia. DUNM:173
Troup, C.V.
Two kinds of vision. HILK: 155
Wesley, C.H.
Education for citizenship in a democracy. HILK:55
Wright, S.J.
Price of excellence. HILK: 321

---- POLITICS AND SUFFRAGE
Bruce, B.K.
Address before the United States Senate in behalf of admitting P.B.S. Pinchback as Senator from Louisiana. WOON:267
Speech on election practices

NEGROES-POLITICS AND SUFFRAGE (cont.)
in Mississippi. WOON:270
DeLarge, R. C.
Speech on the enforcement of the Fourteenth Amendment. WOON:295
Langston, J. M.
Equality before the law. WOON:436
Lynch, J. R.
Speech in the case of a contested election. WOON: 273
Menard, J. W.
Negro's first speech in Congress: in defense of his election to Congress when his seat was contested and won by his opponent. WOON:263
Morton, O. P.
Reasons for Negro suffrage. BREW 8:216
Ransier, A. J.
Speech delivered at Charleston, South Carolina, March 9, 1871. WOON:411
Revels, H. R.
Speech on the Georgia Bill. WOON:286
Tilden, S. J.
Negro suffrage. REEM 10: 246; REEMA 15:1992; REEMB 11:258
See also Civil Rights Act (1866)

NEGROES IN AFRICA
Cushing, C.
On Negro colonization. CHAL 6:392; HAZO 13:5598; MAS 13:5598
Dixon, J. A.
On African colonization. CHAL 6:262; HAZO 13: 5408; MAS 13:5408

Nehru, Jawaharlal
Asia finds herself again (inaugurating Asian Conference at New Delhi). COPB:617
Glory has departed. BOU:219; COPB:619
Independence day. ZU:1
Speaks to mourning millions a few hours after the murder of Gandhi. HIBS:497; PE:809; PEA:809

NEHRU, PANDIT See Pandit, Vijaya Lakshmi (Nehru)

NEIGHBORS
Friends and neighbors. THOS: 99
Welcome to new neighbors. DR:234
See also Community life; Housewarmings

Neilson, William Allan
Inaugural address as president of Smith College. WE 1:273
Nelson, Bertram G.
World's orator. TRUW:144
Nelson, Culver H.
Youth and lasting peace. AN: 74
Nelson, Donald M.
MacArthur Day celebration speech. BA 1941-42:152
Nelson, Simon P.
"Knight among the nations." COUW:241
Nerger, Edwin A.
To remain in perfect love. ACW:87
Nesmith, George T.
Antonio Maceo. TRUW:103

NETHERLANDS
Carnegie, A.
Scotland and Holland. REEM 1:210; REEMB 1:211
Hibben, J. G.
Righteousness (address before Holland Society). REEM 2:208; REEMB 2:213
Smith, F. H.
Holland today. REEM 3:232; REEMB 3:249
See also Dutchmen; National characteristics, Dutch

NEUTRALITY See Ireland-Neutrality; United States-Neutrality

Nevin, A. Parker
Speech for all occasions. MIA: 416
Trick speech. LINM:65; SHUP:4

NEW DEAL See Democratic Party; United States-Economic conditions

NEW ENGLAND
Bacon, L.
Address, 1838. BRAR 1: 165
Beecher, H.W.
Glory of New England. REEM 1:97; REEMA 1:46; REEMB 1:92
Religious freedom (68th anniversary of New England Society). BEA:31; REEM 1: 92; REEMA 1:41; REEMB 1:87
Clemens, S. L.
New England weather. BOU: 193; CHAL 12:447; COP: 666; COPB:693; DOA:296; HAZO 23:9871; HIB:94; HURG:128; LOMSA:295; MAS 23:9871; REEM 1:288; REEMA 1:210; REEMB 1: 290
Cook, J.
New England scepticism. HAZO 24:10156; MAS 24: 10156
Curtis, G.W.
Liberty under law. COP: 624; REEMB 1:356
Evarts, W.M.
Day we celebrate (at New England Society). HAZO 18: 7798; MAS 18:7798
Filene, E.A.
Way out for New England. LINM:52
Grant, U.S.
Remarkable climate. COP: 665; COPB:692; REEM 2: 137; REEMA 2:557; REEMB 2:129
Hadduck, C.B.
Elements of national greatness, 1841. BRAR 1:261
Hayes, R.B.
National sentiments. REEM 2:183; REEMA 2:601; REEMB 2:185
Knapp, S.L.
Address, 1829. BRAR 1:141
Marsh, G.P.
Address, 1844. BRAR 1:371
Porter, H.
How to avoid the subject. REEMA 3:904
Sires and sons. REEM 3: 94; REEMA 3:935; REEMB 3:95
Shurter, E.D.
Influence of New England upon American institutions. SHU:27
Spring, G.
Tribute to New England, 1820. BRAR 1:9
Thomas, M.
Man and the soil. SHU:181
Upham, C.W.
Spirit of the day and its lessons, 1846. BRAR 1:417
Wayland, H.L.
Causes of unpopularity. REEMA 3:1201
Force of ideas. REEMA 3: 1197
Winthrop, R.C.
Address, 1839. BRAR 1:211

NEW ENGLAND SOCIETY
Choate, J.H.
Sorcerer's responses. REEMA 1:159
Hopkins, W.R.
Beginnings of the New England Society of New York. BRAR 1:1

NEW ORLEANS, BATTLE OF
Lively little speech for the 8th of January (anniversary of the battle of New Orleans). BARB:105
Morinère, C.E. de la
Centennial of the battle of New Orleans. CATA 1:146

NEW YEAR
Approach of New Year. AMEO 2:29
Chiang Kai-Shek
New Year's message to the Chinese people, 1944. HAN: 336; VO 1944-45:7
Clean out the attic. JAI:7
Closing year. FRIE:114
Garrett, C.
New Year's address. THOU 2:43
Goebbels, P. J.
New Year's speech, December 31, 1943. VO 1943-44: 599
Hitler, A.
New Year proclamation, December 31, 1943. VO 1943-44:607
New Year's broadcast to the German people, December 31, 1944. HAN:291; VO 1944-45:637
Jennings, H. C.
Outlook for the New Year. THOU 2:53
Kalinin, M.
New Year's address. VO 1944-45:5
Koiso, K.
New Year's address, 1945. VO 1945-46:4
Krantz, J., Jr.
New Years-what about your dreams? MCK:134
Make the New Year a happy one. THOU 2:52
Milestones of life. THOU 2: 51
New Year. FRIE:109
New Year. MORA:41
New Year greetings. BEC:152
New Year longings. THOU 2: 48
New Year's Day. BURS:166
New Year's Day. (Why we celebrate January first). EDGS:3
New Year's thoughts. NATM: 18
One year to live. JA:154
Perlman, N. A.
Making a new start (sermon marking Jewish New Year). BA 1955-56:159
Progress of years. THOU 2: 26
Simpson, M.
Reflections on the New Year. THOU 2:41
Starting the New Year right. DR:121; LU:1172
Stoddard, C. A.
Another year of time. THOU 2:37
Tailored just for you. LEHS: 31
Talmage, T. D.
God among the centuries. THOU 2:30
Tholuck, A.
New Year's meditation. THOU 2:46
Thomas, J. B.
Anno Domini (New Year sermon). THOU 2:20
Tojo, H.
New Year's address, 1944. VO 1944-45:11
Value of vows. JA:151
What will the New Year bring? JAS:8
What will the New Year bring? THOU 2:47
You can take it with you. LEHS:28
See also CLOSING YEAR ADDRESSES

NEW YORK (CITY)
Coudert, F. R.
City of New York. REEMA 1:277
Finley, J. H.
City and the flag. REEM 7: 139; REEMB 8:176
Gaynor, W. J.
Outlook. REEM 2:77
Lawrence, F. R.
Future of New York. REEMA 2:705
McClellan, G. B.
New York and the South. REEM 2:375; REEMB 2:388
Outerbridge, E. H.

Port of New York. December 13, 1921. REEM 3:16; REEMB 3:16
Port of New York. April 25, 1922. REEM 4:343; REEMB 5:210
See also East Harlem

---- METROPOLITAN MUSEUM OF ART
Bryant, W.C.
Address at the founding of the Metropolitan Art Museum. CHAL 6:134; HAZO 12:5205; MAS 12:5205

---- WALL STREET
Verdery, M.J.
South in Wall Street. REEMA 3:1168

NEW YORK (STATE)
Choate, J.H.
British evacuation of New York. REEMA 1:179
Conkling, R.
State of New York. REEM 1:332; REEMA 1:269; REEMB 1:333
Depew, C.M.
Empire state. KLEM:120; REEMA 1:333
Smith, A.E.
Governorship of New York. REEM 3:220; REEMB 3:237
Wilson, P.
On the Empire state. BRYW 8:25

NEW YORK LIFE INSURANCE COMPANY
Myers, C.J.
Sources of our strength. MICS:158

NEW YORK UNIVERSITY
MacCracken, H.M.
Relation of metropolis and university: inaugural address as president of New York University. WE 1:185

NEW ZEALAND
Blomfield, L.M.
Democracy rampant. BART 2:133

Newburn, Ruth
Constitution of the United States. LEIO:119
Newcomb, Charles Limton
Psychology of laughter. EXEE:130
Newcomb, John Lloyd
Trends in higher education. SMI:289
Newman, James E.
Case for minorities. NOR 1947:77
Newman, John Henry, Cardinal
Catholicism and the religions of the world. BRYW 4:216
Communion with God. CHAL 6:446; HAZO 14:5682; MAS 14:5682
Evils of money-getting. -Same as his Property as a disadvantage
Immortality of the soul. ORBR 2:177
Knowledge viewed in relation to learning. REEM 6:347; REEMA 9:911; REEMB 7:297
Lecture on the use of private judgment. HAZO 14:5693; MAS 14:5693
Property as a disadvantage. DREW 8:230; PL:496

Newman, John Philip
Commerce. REEM 3:1; REEMA 2:845; REEMB 3:1
Eulogy of General Grant. THOU 1:380
Eulogy of Lincoln. ESEH:217
Tribute to Lincoln. THOU 1:476
Newsom, Herschel D. See Di-Salle, M., jt. auth.

NEWSPAPERS See Free speech; Journalism and Journalists; Liberty of the Press; Publishers and publishing

Newton, Joseph Fort
Ministry of Masonry. REEM sup 2:249; REEMB 7:304
What to do with life today. BA 1945-46:214

NEWTON, JOSEPH FORT
Hancher, V.
Introducing Joseph F. Newton at a combined honors convocation and baccalaureate service at the State University of Iowa. BA 1945-46:214
Newton, William M.
British Empire. LEIO:78

NICARAGUA See United States-Foreign Relations-Nicaragua

NICHOL, JOHN PRINGLE
Kelvin, W.T.
Inspiration and the highest education (commemoration of J.P. Nichol). BREW 7:189
NICARAGUA CANAL
Morgan, J.T.
On the Nicaragua Canal. REEMA 14:1490
Nicholas, John
On the proposed repeal of the Sedition law. JOHA 1 pt. 1:131
Nicholas II, Emperor of Russia
Russia enters the war. REEM 11:60; REEMB 12:67
Nichols, Egbert Ray, Jr.
Everyman. BRP 7:112; YR 8:103
Nichols, William Henry
Chemist and reconstruction. REEM 4:334; REEMB 5:198
Nicholson, Marjorie Hope
Romance of scholarship. NORR 3d ser:118
Nicholson, Meredith
Sunny slopes of forty. REEM 6:354; REEMB 7:316
Nicias.
Address to troops. HAZO 1:40; MAS 1:40
Against the Sicilian expedition. BRYW 1:49; HAZO 1:35; MAS 1:35
To the Athenian Assembly.-Same as his Against the Sicilian expedition
Nickerson, Albert J.
Climbing the managerial ladder. BAAG:387

NICODEMUS.
Chapin, E.H.
Nicodemus: the seeker after religion. HAZO 18:7460; MAS 18:7460
Niebler, Chester J.
Wanted-patriotism for American youth. YR 8:31
Niebuhr, Reinhold
Adequate faith for the world crisis. BA 1947-48:227
Christian life and an enemy of abundance. BA 1956-57:191
Crisis of our time. BA 1944-45:191

NIGHTINGALE, FLORENCE
Macdonald, C.
Lady of the lamp. GA:78
Malone, T.
Lady of the lamp. YE:395
Nikhilananda, Swami
Need for a spiritual revival. HAR:495
Nimitz, Chester W.
Remarks at Japanese surrender. VO 1945-46:531

NINETEENTH CENTURY
Cass, L.
On the spirit of the age. CHAL 5:336; HAZO 10:4249; MAS 10:4249
Nixon, Richard M.
Apologia. BA 1952-53:72; BERS:196
Checker speech.-Same as his Apologia
Expense fund speech.-Same as his Apologia
It is time to speak up for America. BA 1960-61:15
Opening of the American Na-

tional Exhibition in Moscow. SABA:209
Prosperity and the economic health of the nation. BA 1956-57:74
Radio-television address from Moscow. ARNS:240; BA 1959-60:14
Republican cause in 1956. BA 1955-56:108
Vote Republican (1954). BA 1954-55:89
Vote Republican (1958). BA 1958-59:101

Nizer, Louis
Presents Albert Einstein. HIBS:496; LY:173; NI:53; NIA:45
Presents Fulton John Sheen. LY:163; NI:111; NIA:85
Presents Grover A. Whalen. LY:81; NI:179; NIA:132
Presents Harry Woodburn Chase. LY:102; NI:101; NIA:79

Njotowijono, Oemarjadi
Inaugural speech at Conference on the Problems of Economic Development. UAR:57
Speech at final session of Conference on the Problems of Economic Development. UAR:397

NOBEL PRIZES
Faulkner, W.
On accepting the Nobel prize, exhorts the young writers of the world. BOU:9; COPB:637; HAR:397; HIBS:508; HURG:291; PE:814; PEA:814

Noble, Edith
Tito Melema. COUW:109

Noble, Franklin
God's faithfulness vindicated by our experience. THOU 2:393

NOBLES OF THE MYSTIC SHRINE. See MYSTIC SHRINE, NOBLES OF THE

NOBLES OF THE SCOTTISH RITE
Scottish Rite: short welcome address. THOS:43

Nodel, Julius J.
Freedom's holy light. BA 1960-61:213

NOMINATIONS
Addams, J.
Seconding the nomination of Roosevelt for President, 1912. REEMB 8:1
Announcement of a nomination and reply by the nominee. BARB:124-5
Borah, W.E.
Nominating Charles Curtis for the Vice Presidency. ONEC:496
Burton, M.L.
Nominating speech for Calvin Coolidge. WHIP:185
Conkling, R.
Nomination of U.S. Grant for a third term. BAKF:125; BREW 4:138; BRYW 10:94; CHAL 11:257; HAZO 21:9122; MAS 21:9122; ONEM:472; ORAMA 2:315; REEM 10:256; REEMA 12:719; REEMB 11:268
Dougherty, D.
"Hancock the superb" (nominating W.S. Hancock, Dem., 1880). BREW 5:280
Fairfield, W.
Whom should the Republicans nominate for President? JUD:185
Garfield, J.A.
John Sherman for President. BRYW 10:99; KNAS:305; KNASA:305; LAD:104; REEM 10:261; REEMB 11:273
George, H.
Masses against the classes (accepting the nomination as candidate for Mayor of New York City). HICF:121
Holt, J.H.
Nominating speech for John

NOMINATIONS (cont.)
W. Davis. WHIP:262
Ingersoll, R. G.
Nominating Blaine. BIR 3: 113; BRAC:404; BREW 7: 126; BRYW 10:77; CHAL 12:184; COP:322; COPA: 322; COPB:322; HAZO 22: 9580; HIBS:292; HICF: 108; HILL:463; HURG:154; MAS 22:9580; ONEM:470; ORAMA 2:377; PE:616; PEA:616; REEM 10:279; REEMA 13:1252; REEMB 11:292; SHAH:458
Knight, G. A.
Speech at McKinley's nomination. WAGN:100
Lincoln, A.
'House divided against itself cannot stand." BIR 2: 217; BRE:232; BREA:216; BREW 7:337; BRYW 9:222; COP:309; COPA:309; COPB:309; FO:156; HAZO 16:6562; HICF:49; HURG: 88; JOHA 2 pt 1:168; KLEG: 323; LEEW 10:237; MAS 16:6562; ORAMA 2:217; PE:490; PEA:490; REEM 10:216; REEMB 11:227; SHAH:383; SHUM:133; WPRA:180
Lloyd George, D.
Seconding the nomination of M. G. Clemenceau for President of the Peace Conference. REEM 11:313; REEMB 12:331
Long, J.D.
Nominating George F. Edmunds for President. HOAP: 288; KNAS:299; KNASA: 299
McCarthy, E.J.
Nomination of Adlai E. Stevenson. BA 1960-61:30
McNab, J. L.
Nominating Herbert Hoover for the Presidency. ONEC: 489
Miller, E. G.
Seconding the nomination of President Roosevelt. GA: 203
Model and outline for a nomination speech. BAKS:138, 146
Murrow, E.R.
Nominating Presidential candidates. BA 1951-52:95
Nominating a candidate for president at annual club meeting-two typical speeches. WRA:102
Nominating a candidate for president of a ladies' organization. WRA:108
Nominating a vice president at annual meeting of any club. WRA:106
Nominating a candidate for political office at a convention. WRA:103
Nominating for office-four examples of. STON:113
Nominating of president at a convention, call for nomination, nomination, closing nominations and balloting. BEDA:139-140
Nominating speech. PITT:94
Nominating vice-presidents general of the Daughers of the American Revolution. GA:190
Nomination and election of officers of newly formed civic association. BED:14; BEDA:22
Nomination and election of secondary officers (at newly formed civic association). BED:15; BEDA:23
Nomination speeches. STOC: 107
Nominations at Town Hall meeting. BEDA:71
Placing the nomination: various examples of. BEC:97
Pratt, R.
Seconding the nomination of President Hoover. GA:202
Preparation of a nomination speech. CORP:217
Rogers, W.
Nominating Calvin Coolidge.

BARR:298
Roosevelt, F.D.
Nomination of Alfred E. Smith. CORP:217; HICF: 796; LINM:131; ONEC: 497; YE:107
Roosevelt, T.
Seconding McKinley's nomination. CHAL 14:354; HAZO 25:10883; MAS 25:10883
Sonnino, S.C.
Seconding the nomination of M.G. Clémenceau for President of the Peace Conference. REEM 11:314; REEMB 12:332
Speech declining a nomination for office. HILL:463
Speech upon being nominated as a candidate for office. HILL:465
Speeches nominating a candidate for office. HILL:463
Suggestions for nomination or speech of praise. BARR: 231; BRAB:502; MOUG:152; REAB:160
Suggestions for preparation of nominating speeches. MO: 532; MOUGA:152; RE:176. With examples of: BEB: 107; BEC:97; BRA:515; GA:188; GLAD:165; HIBS: 291; WRA:99; WRB:173; YE:105
Towner, J.H. and Rucker, W.W.
Nomination of opposing candidates for Speaker of the House of Representatives. BRAC:402
Westcott, J.W.
Destiny of democracy (Wilson, 2nd term). SHU:238
Wilson, W.
Nomination of M. Georges Clémenceau as President of the Peace Conference. REEM 11:312; REEMB 12: 329
See also Acceptance speeches-Nominations; Candidates
Norris, George Bowling
Constructive patriotism. YR 9:205

NORRIS, GEORGE W.
Douglas, P.H.
Five great Americans. BA 1951-52:85
Norris, Louis W.
On mixing ethics with business. BRAB:539
Norstad, Lauris
France-American Society speech. BA 1962-63:129

NORTH AMERICA See Western Hemisphere

NORTH ATLANTIC PACT See North Atlantic Treaty Organization

NORTH ATLANTIC TREATY ORGANIZATION
Acheson, D.
North Atlantic Pact. BA 1948-49:15
North Atlantic Treaty Organization. BA 1951-52:47
Buchan, A.
Argument for graduated deterrence, December 1, 1955. GRAC:171
Dulles, J.F.
North Atlantic Pact. BA 1949-50:22
Eisenhower, D.D.
Military defense of the North Atlantic Pact nations. BA 1950-51:75; HAR:220
Gruenther, A.M.
NATO. HURG:334
North Atlantic Treaty Organization and defense of Western Europe. BA 1955-56:25
Johnson, M.W.
Speech to the Atlantic Congress. HILK:245
Marshall, G.C.
Statement before the Senate Armed Forces Committee and the Senate Foreign Relations Committee. HAR:225

NORTH ATLANTIC TREATY ORGANIZATION (cont.)
Norstad, L.
France-American Society speech. BA 1962-63:129
Taft, R. A.
North Atlantic Pact. BA 1949-50:15

NORTH CAROLINA, UNIVERSITY OF
Chase, H.W.
State university and the new South: inaugural address as president of University of North Carolina. WE 2:31

NORTH DAKOTA, UNIVERSITY OF
McVey, F. LeR.
University and its relations: inaugural address as president of University of North Dakota. WE 2:369

NORTH POLE
Peary, R. E.
Farthest north. COP:683; COPB:710; REEM 3:48; REEMB 3:49
North Pole. REEM 3:47; REEMB 3:48
Northcott, W. A.
Rights of men. WERN 42:108

NORTHERN STATES
Fellows, J. R.
North and South. REEM 2:37; REEMA 2:482; REEMB 2:37
Northrop, B. G.
Arbor day in schools. THOU 1:18
Northrop, Cyrus
Manly fellow. BLAA:73; BLAB:73; WERN 42:123

NORTHWESTERN UNIVERSITY
Stevenson, A. E.
There are no Gibraltors. WPRC:277
Norton, Charles Dyer
Enthusiasm. REEM 4:340; REEMB 5:204
Norton, Charles Eliot
Castles in Spain. REEMA 2:850
Introducing James Russell Lowell at Ashfield, Mass., August 27, 1885. REEM 2:363
Norton, Mary T.
Upholding the American standards of motherhood. GA:161
Norvell, George
Joan of Arc. COUW:165
Nott, Eliphalet
"How are the mighty fallen."- Same as his On the death of Hamilton
On the death of Hamilton. BRYW 8:174; CHAL 5:1; HAZO 10:3990; MAS 10:3990
Nottingham, Heneage Finch, 1st Earl of
Address to the throne. LEEW 6:93
Opening the prosecution for regicide under Charles II (trial of T. Harrison). BREW 6:131
Novar, Lillian F.
Price for pity. AN:34

NUCLEAR WARFARE See Atomic warfare
Nuesse, Celestine
Bourne of youth. YR 4:251
Nuetzman, Delmar
Steel spike. BRP 9:66

NULLIFICATION See United States-History-Civil War-Causes

NURSES AND NURSING
August, E. P.
Publicity programs and professional consciousness. GA:125
Brown, C. H.
Place of nursing profession in America (at capping exercise). HILK:89

Huber, L. J.
Introducing a nurse. BRC: 307
Kaser, A. L.
Introducing a speaker on nurse's training. BRC:83
Nurses: a baccalaureate address. NI:265; NIA:199
Nursing as a profession. DR: 298
See also Red Cross
Nuveen, John
Introduces Dr. Walter H. Judd, Congressman from Minnesota. PRNE:14

NYE, EDGAR WILSON
Clemens, S. L.
Presents James Whitcomb Riley and Edgar Wilson Nye. LY:75
Nye, Gerald P., Jr.
For an adequate defense. BA 1938-39:65
Neutrality. BA 1939-40:53
See also Thompson, D., jt. auth.
Nye, Laurence E.
Title 28, number 426. YR 4: 67
Oathout, John
Individual in democracy. YR 5:275

OATHS
Castelar, E.
On the political oath. CHAL 12:73; HAZO 22:9480; MAS 22:9480
Cox, S. S.
Against the iron-clad oath. BREW 4:203
Oath (member). BEB:41
Oath (officer). BEB:41
Oath of installation. BEB:75
Pledge for faithful performance. BEB:41
Pledge of loyalty, confidence, and support-two examples of. BEB:40
Pledge to faithfully perform the duties of office: various examples of. BEC:112
See also Inaugural addresses; Installation speeches; Offices-Acceptance
Oberg, Winston
Lifestream of the nation. NOR 1941:29
Oberholzer, H. J.
American road. BLUE:4

OBESITY
Smith, H.
Introducing a fat man. BRC: 57

OBITUARIES
DeWolf Hopper. NI:184
Obituary reference for John B. Gough. THOU 3:498
Roxy-an obituary. NI:175; NIA:130
See also Eulogies
O'Boyle, Patrick A.
Vision of faith. BA 1955-56: 151

O'Brien, Frank M.
Armistrice Day. SHU:207
O'Brien, John A.
Communism and Christianity. BA 1947-48:235
O'Brien, Michael
Speech from dock. KET:368
O'Brien, Quin
New revolution. BOA:389
O'Byrne, James
Matchless story of American history. THOU 1:203
O'Callaghan, P. J.
Temperance. CATA 2:84

OCCUPATIONS, CHOICE OF
Meisel, G. I.
Wanted: spunk, sense, and stamina. NOR 1941:11
Modern careers for men. DR: 295
Modern careers for women. DR:297
Vocational guidance. LU:1155
See also Vocational guidance; Vocations
Ockanickon, Indian chief
Last speech. SHE:3

Ockerlander, Doris
Building stairways. DO:29
O'Connell, Daniel
Carries on the fight for Catholic emancipation. PE:422; PEA:422
Catholic Association (June 16, 1815 speech). KET:302
Catholic rights in Ireland. BRTH:203; BRTHA:203; ORBR 2:79; REEMA 14: 1510
Charms of Kildare. -Same as his On repeal of the Union
Demand for justice to Ireland. BREW 8:244; CODS:461; CODSA:461; COP:211; COPA:211; COPB:211; FULB:109; HAZO 10:4028; MAS 10:4028; REEMA 14: 1522
In defence of John Magee. ADR 4:9
Ireland is worth dying for. - Same as his On repeal of the Union
On repeal of the Union. BAKF: 387; BREW 8:236; BRYW 6:195; CLAY:204; CHAL 5: 15; FRY:32; FULB:101; HAZO 10:4015; LAD:209; MAS 10:4015; ONEM:334; PE:441; PEA:441; PL:524; REEM 9:253; REEMB 10: 260
On the Irish Disturbance Bill. CLAY:151
Political outlook, 1814. KET: 291
Speech at Tara. -Same as his On repeal of the Union
State of Ireland, House of Commons, February 5, 1833. PAUF 1:264
Struggle for Catholic emancipation. BEA:327

O'CONNELL, DANIEL
Lacordaire, J.B.H.
Sacred cause of the human race (Panegyric of Daniel O'Connell). BREW 7:243; CHAL 6:478; HAZO 14:5843; MAS 14:5843
Phillips, W.
Eulogy on Daniel O'Connell. BRAC:373; ONEM:443; RINM:182; SHAH:359; SHU:252
O'Connell, William, Cardinal
Position of Catholics. CATA 2:113
Oconostota, The Cherokee
Pathetic prophecy. GRIS:37

ODD-FELLOWS, INDEPENDENT ORDER OF
Address for Odd Fellow's anniversary. AMEO 2:25
Breeden, H. O.
Supremacy of love. THOU 3:112
Cable, C.
Sovereign grand lodge. THOU 3:97
Fraternity. THOU 3:127
Friendship, love and truth. THOU 3:125
I. O. O. F. in memoriam. THOS: 183
Members that read Odd Fellows register. THOU 3:128
Odd Fellows by a loyal member. EDGS:360
Odd Fellows anniversary speech. AMEO 2:25
Pinkerton, A. S.
Growth and conditions of I. O. O. F. THOU 3:94
Spirit of Odd-Fellowship. REEM 7:327; REEMA 9:964; REEMB 7:333
Prettyman, J.
Odd Fellowship exemplified in Jesus only. THOU 3:124
Teves, V.W.
Three links of I. O. O. F. THOU 3:102
Thou shalt love. JA:157
White, J.H.
Odd Fellowship and Masonry THOU 3:126
Odell, Benjamin Barker, Jr.
Westward, ho! (St. Louis World's Fair). WERN 42: 121

O'Donnell, Hugh A.
Comparative advertising methods-east and west. PEAE: 93
O'Donnell, Thomas J.
Honor the flag. SHU:69

ODYSSEUS.
Homer.
Speech of Odysseus. HAZO 1:1; MAS 1:1
Off-Shore Oil Bill See Territorial waters

OFFICE OF PRICE ADMINISTRATION See Price regulation

OFFICE WORKERS AND OFFICE WORKERS' PARTIES See Employees

OFFICERS
Bowman, G. M.
Address of the president. GA:179
McGovern, S.
Introducing the president at a business meeting of a manufacturing company. BRC:269
Past presidents' day. FRIE:73
Unveiling portrait (of past president of labor union). BED:89; BEDA:162
Welcoming the new club or organization president. DR: 103
See also Acceptance speeches-Nominations; Candidates; Educators; Executives; Inaugural addresses; Installation speeches; Nominations; Offices-Acceptance; Public officials; Testimonials; United States-President. Also subheads under this subject

---- PRESIDING
Address by a newly elected president of a young men's literary society. HAPR:151
Address of newly elected city official. AMEO 2:129
Address of president of board of education. AMEO 1:198
Appropriate remarks for presiding officer upon taking the chair. HILL:460
Banks, E. C.
Introducing a chairman of the day-two examples of. BRC:36, 38
Chairman's comments and his introduction of next speaker. HOA:370
Chairman's introduction of George Jessel at dinner in honor of Mannie Sack. JEYO:54
Chairman's or president's speech. PITT:100
Chairman's speeches - introductions and remarks after speeches. HOB:230
Club officer's refrain. NAT: 39
Depew, C. M.
Speech as president of the Pilgrims, January 2, 1924. LINM:393
Discussion of speeches presented in the performance of official duties. With examples of. GA:166
Good wishes to successor-examples of. BEC:127
"I have the honor to present" (suggestions for the pro gram chairman). BUT:84; BUTA:84; BUTB:84
Introducing committee chairman (at dedication of home for aged). BED:33; BEDA: 73
Introducing national representative (at charter presentation to labor union). BED:73
Introduction of speaker by presiding officer-eight examples of. STOC:125; STON:131-134
Mertz, P. A.
Opens a discussion meeting. PR:100

OFFICERS, PRESIDING (cont.)
Moran, E. B.
Chairman's remarks before introducing guests at speakers' table. PR:90
Offering chair to newly elected president. Speech by presiding officer. STOC:110
On being elected president of a society. BARB:145
Opening speech by temporary chairman (at charter presentation to labor union). BED:73
Opening speech (by temporary chairman at civic association). BED:14; BEDA:22
Organizing a Camera Club (opening speech by presiding officer). BEDA:17
Presenting newly-elected president (to a convention). BEDA:140
President's annual report. BEDA:137
Presiding officer's speeches-introductions, announcements, etc. HILL:460
Program chairman's remarks. FRIE:300
Role, purpose and function, etc. of the chairman. BRC: 13-32
Speech of presiding officer offering chair to newly elected president. STOC: 110
Speech of presiding officer, offering chair to newly elected president-two examples of. STON:116
Speech on taking the chair at a meeting. BARB:145
Suggestions for speeches of a presiding officer. With examples of. SOES:13
Suggestions on how to conduct a board meeting. BUT:151; BUTA:151; BUTB:151
Suggestions on how to preside over a meeting. With examples of. MO:486
Temporary chairman's remarks. BEDA:138
Tributes to installed official-six examples of. BEB:62-64
Villard, O.G.
Capitalism vs. Socialism (chairman's remarks). REEM sup 3:39
See also Closing speeches; Club speeches; Installation speeches; Opening addresses

---- RETIRING
Address to a retiring officer. HILL:467
Clapp, E.H.
Installation of officers: retiring speech. THOU 3:485
Compton, K.T.
Electron, its intellectual and social significance. SAR:363
Farewell address (by retiring secretary of labor union). BED:81; BEDA:154
Farewell to retiring worthy matron-examples of. MORA: 19
Greeting and welcome (at ceremony honoring retiring secretary of labor union). BED:80; BEDA:153
Houston, P.D.
Presents a gift of silver and a scroll of honor to retiring president of American Bankers Association, Robert M. Hanes. PR:106
Huston, H.L.
Presents gavel to a retiring president. PR:110
Introducing guest-of-honor (at ceremony honoring retiring secretary of labor union). BED:81; BEDA:154
Introducing speaker (at ceremony honoring retiring secretary of labor union). BED: 80; BEDA:153
Letter of resignation from a retiring officer. EDGS:413
McLain, H.O.
Accepting gift on retirement as club president. PR:103

Presentation of a gift to a retiring officer of a company. DR:23; LU:1128
Presentation of an emblem to a retiring officer of the lodge. Response of the officer. EDGS:371, 372
President's formal speech of retirement at annual meeting of a large club. WRA: 129
President's speech of retirement at annual meeting of any club. WRA:128
President's speech of retirement at annual meeting of Parent-Teacher Association. WRA:131
Resolution of thanks to retiring officer at end of his term. STOC:114
Resolution of thanks to retiring officer (at end of his term)-two examples of. STON:120
Response by retiring officer of the lodge on being presented an emblem. EDGS:372
Response by a retiring officer of the lodge on receiving an emblem. HE:119
Response by a retiring officer to presentation speech. EDGS:129
Retiring as president. FRIE: 66
Rotary club (retiring president expresses his appreciation). ED:121
Speech by retiring official-six examples of. BEB:103-105
Speech for retiring president of Kiwanis club. AMEO 2: 214
Speech of retiring officer at end of term. STOC:112
Speech of retiring presiding officer (at end of term)-three examples of. STON: 118
Suggestions for preparation of retirement speeches for club presidents. With examples of. WRA:126-132; WRB:182-186
Thomas, M. C.
Farewell to Bryn Mawr. GA:57
Tribute (to retiring secretary of labor union). BED:80; BEDA:154
Tribute to the outgoing club chairman. DR:97; LU:1165
Tributes to retiring officials. With examples of. BEB:64-67; BEC:132
Words of appreciation to retiring officers: examples of. BEC:126
Worthy matron's retiring addresses-examples of. MORA: 123-132
See also Retirement

OFFICES-ACCEPTANCE
Acceptance by president (of Speakers' Club). BED:19; BEDA:27
Acceptance of office. THOS: 162
Acceptance of office (at a convention). BEDA:141
Acceptance speech of mayor at his installation. BEDA:116
Accepting a chairmanship. BEB:13
Accepting a nomination for public office-seventeen model speeches. BEB:15-20
Accepting an office-various models of. BEC:30
Appreciation and thanks (at induction of a Judge). BEDA: 120
Blair, F. G.
Response to election as president of the National Education Association. BRAC:247
Brubacher, R. R.
Speech on election as president of Iowa Bankers Association. PR:127
Burke, E.
Speech to the electors of Bristol, November 3, 1774

OFFICES-ACCEPTANCE (cont.)
(on being elected to Parliament). BRTH:67; BRTHA: 67
Coolidge, C.
To the Senate on being elected its President. LINM:318
Douglass, S. C. H.
Address of acceptance of office in Knights of Pythias. THOU 3:137
Finch, F. M.
Office of the law (assuming chair of Presidency of New York State Bar Association). REEMA 2:496
Francis, S. C.
Response to election as president of American Nurses' Association. GA: 33
Green, W.
Acceptance of the presidency of the American Federation of Labor. LINM:61
Gregg, H. H.
Accepting the presidency of the American Pharmaceutical Association. SAB:217; SABA:299
Incoming addresses-three examples of. MORA:69-72
Incoming club officer submits his pledge of acceptance. DR:95; LU:1163
Incoming matron's address. MORA:67
Krantz, J., Jr.
Acceptance of club presidency. MCK:198
Meany, G.
Principles and program of AFL-CIO. BA 1955-56:78
Model and outline of acceptance speech. BAKS:149, 155
Mucklestone, Mrs. M.
Response to election as president of the American Auxiliary. GA:31
On accepting office-two examples of. STON:114
On being elected president of a club. BARB:146
On being elected president of a club. HE:117
On being elected president of a society. BARB:145
President's acceptance (at newly formed civic association). BED:15; BEDA:23
Rayburn, S.
Accepting the office of Speaker of the United States House of Representatives. SAB:219
Speech on being elected captain of a military company. BARB:147
Suggestions for preparation of reply to nomination for, or election to, an office. With examples of. YE:154
Three model speeches for accepting the presidency of an organization or lodge. BEB:19-20
Two speeches on accepting office. STOC:108
Wanamaker, P. A.
Accepting the presidency of National Education Association. YE:155
Words of appreciation by installed officers-various examples of. BEC:110
See also Inaugural addresses; Installation speeches; Oaths

---- REFUSAL
On declining office-three examples of. STON:115
Refusing office. FRIE:55
Speeches on declining office. STOC:109

---- RESIGNATIONS
Letter of resignation from a retiring officer. EDGS:413
Resignation of office. STOC: 111
Resignation of office-two examples of. STON:117

OFFICIALS See Educators; Executives; Inaugural addresses; Installation speeches; Law and lawyers; Nominations; Officers; Offices-Acceptance; Public officials; United States- Congress; United States-President; United States-Supreme Court
O'Flynn, Edward Francis
Savonarola-priest and patriot. SHUC:261
Ogburn, William F. See Hutchins, R. M., jt. auth.
Ogden, Robert C.
Vacation responsibilities. THOU 2:203
Oglesby, Richard
Royal corn. REEM 3:6; REEMA 3:6; REEMB 3:6
O'Hare, Edward
Men and tomorrow. BRP 8: 109; YR 9:31

OHIO
Hedges, J.E.
Ohio, the Presidency and Americanism. REEM 2:195; REEMB 2:197
Ohio society. SCHS:200
Pomerene, A.
Ohio. REEM 3:64; REEMB 3:65

OHIO STATE UNIVERSITY
Fullen, J.B.
Many happy returns of the day (75th anniversary of Ohio State University). YE: 303
O'Keefe, Larry
Introducing a music dealer
" a newspaper reporter
" an optometrist
" a railroad executive
" a realtor. BRC:218, 230, 231, 229, 206

OKLAHOMA, UNIVERSITY OF
Brooks, S.D.
Inaugural address as president of University of Oklahoma. WE 2:407

OLD AGE
Accepting building key (at dedication of home for aged). BED:34; BEDA:75
After 40-the best years. NAT: 2
Age-and youth. DR:291
Closing speech (at dedication of home for aged). BED: 36; BEDA:77
Dedicatory address (at dedication of home for aged). BED:33; BEDA:74
Drummond, R.
Emcee at a meeting of oldtimers. BRH:216
Farley, J.I.
Debt, not charity. BOA:417
Good old days. NATT:39
Greeting and welcome (at dedication of home for aged). BED:32; BEDA:73
Old in years, young in heart. NAT:49
Outline of a talk to old folks. BAKS:241
Presenting key (at dedication of home for aged). BED: 34; BEDA:75
Rettberg, M.
Indian summer. BRP 9:19
Seeking eternal youth. JA:163
Toast "Our oldest member"-to the oldest member of any club or group. WRA: 52
Weiner, M.
Best is yet to be. NOR 1947:83
You're never too old. JA:160
See also Age and employment; Aged-Medical care
Old Tassel, Indian chief
Plea for his home. BREW 7: 117
Olds, Lester
Introducing a meat dealer. BRC:201
O'Leary, John
Military mass of Spanish American war veterans in Boston.

O'Leary, John (cont.)
CATA 1:28

OLEOMARGARINE BILL See Dairying

Oliver, Robert T.
American foreign policy in the midst of the world revolution. BERS:122
Culture and communication. LINP:201

Olmsted, William C.
Virtue, mercy, and charity. THOU 3:377

Olney, Richard
Commerce and its relations to the law. BYRA:307; REEM 3:9; REEMB 3:9
John Marshall. REEM 5:318; REEMA 9:932; REEMB 9:358
Presents Woodrow Wilson. LY:202

Olson, William
Merry-go-round has stopped. INTW 1933:52; YR 5:263

O'Mahoney, Joseph C.
Industrial democracy. BOA:343
States rights or human rights. BOA:116

OMAR KHAYYAM
Hay, J.
Omar Khayyam. COP:679; COPB:706; HAZO 24:10211; MAS 24:10211; REEM 2:179; REEMA 2:598; REEMB 2:181

O'Meara, Thomas B.
Great adventure of Christopher Columbus. DU:150

Omile, Phoebe Fairgrave
Youth and aviation. GA:130

O'Neal, Barbara
Democracy is on trial. MOUG:238; MOUGA:238

Opdycke, John Baker
Relation of literature to advertising. REEM sup 2:261; REEMB 5:207

OPEN HOUSE
Huber, L. J.
Emcee at an open house. BRH:256

OPENING ADDRESSES
Addams, J.
Opening Fourth International Congress. GA:168
Address at opening of new Municipal building. AMEO 2:202
Allenby, E.
Opening the Hebrew University at Jerusalem. REEM sup 1:61; REEMB 7:33
Clark, B. P.
Opening conference on immigrant education. ONES:61
Four examples of addresses at opening ceremonies. BEB:45-46
Fourteen examples of opening addresses for miscellaneous occasions. BEB:42-45
Franklin, B.
Opening the assembly with prayer. REEM 10:8; REEMA 8:503; REEMB 11:8
Goheen, R. F.
Library and the chapel stand side by side (at opening exercises at Princeton University). BA 1964-65:113
Griswold, A.W.
Balancing moral responsibility and scientific progress-opening address at twentieth Annual Forum). BA 1951-52:147
Harrison, C. C.
Opening the ceremonies at the dedication of a new law building. ONES:64
Hawes, H. B.
Covered wagon. DOA:53
Hawkins, W. A.
Negro lawyer: his opportunity, his duty (at opening of Howard University Law School). DUNM:483

Hull, C.
Opening of the Pan American Conference. BA 1938-39:40
Morgenthau, H.
Opening the United Nations Monetary and Financial Conference at Bretton Woods, N.H. VO 1944-45:291
Opening a new railroad (speech at the driving of the last spike by the president). HILL:489
Opening address at a sales convention by the president of the company. WRA:80
Opening address at a sales convention by the sales manager. WRA:81
Opening address (at memorial service). BED:43; BEDA:84
Opening address (at mental health fund drive). BED:59; BEDA:104
Opening address for woman's literary club. AMEO 2:140
Opening for substitute speaker. FRIE:338
Opening of commemorative services (at Veterans' Day observance). BED:47; BEDA:92
Opening remarks by toastmaster. FRIT:33
Opening remarks-examples of. FRIE:293, 307
Opening speech at a convention. BEDA:134
Opening speech at Bill of Rights Day program. BEDA:172
Opening speech at birthday testimonial. BEDA:28
Opening speech (at cornerstone dedication of youth center). BED:40; BEDA:81
Opening speech at fifth anniversary of founding of Big Brother Athletic Association. BEDA:110
Opening speech at induction of a mayor. BEDA:114
Opening speech (at induction of members to labor union). BED:75; BEDA:147
Opening speech (at installation of officers of newly formed Speakers' Club). BED:16; BEDA:24
Opening speech (at installation of officials to labor union). BED:77; BEDA:149
Opening speech (at memorial service honoring deceased union member). BED:99; BEDA:176
Opening speech (at physician-of-the-year award). BED:50; BEDA:52
Opening speech at political meeting. BEDA:130
Opening speech at presentation of scientific award. BEDA:58
Opening speech (at testimonial dinner to journalist). BED:20; BEDA:34
Opening speech (at testimonial on retirement of public official). BED:27; BEDA:47
Opening speech at testimonial to a woman civic leader. BEDA:41
Opening speech (at testimonial to labor union official). BED:83; BEDA:156
Opening speech (at testimonial to philanthropist). BED:24; BEDA:45
Opening speech at Thanksgiving Day ceremonies. BEDA:88
Opening speech at United Nations anniversary ceremony. BEDA:122
Opening speech (at unveiling of plaque for Labor Temple). BED:86; BEDA:158
Opening speech by temporary chairman (at charter presentation to labor union). BED:73
Opening speech by temporary chairman (at civic association). BED:14; BEDA:22
Opening speech for Flag Day

OPENING ADDRESSES (cont.)
ceremonies. BEDA:95
Opening speech (on Labor Day by union official). BED:96; BEDA:168
Opening statement (at hospital fund drive and testimonial). BED:62; BEDA:98
Opening statement (on Human Rights Day). BED:68; BEDA:127
Organizing a Camera Club (opening speech by presiding officer). BEDA:17
Organizing a club (welcoming new chapter to Speakers' Club at opening meeting). BED:11; BEDA:15
Pusey, N. M.
Religion for now (opening convocation of Harvard Divinity School). BA 1953-54:193
Reuther, W. P.
Labor's principles and program. BA 1951-52:123
Speech at the opening of an eating house or hotel. Host's reply. BARB:140-1
Speech on opening a workingmen's club. BARB:144
Suggestions for openings using personal experiences. With examples of. BRM:177-190
Suggestions for openings when speaker finds himself in unusual situation. With examples of. BRM:213-228
Suggestions for unusual openings. With examples of. BRM:207-212
Suggestions for using a reference to a timely news event as an opening. With examples of. BRM:201-206
Suggestions on how to make a tactful opening. With examples of. BRM:191-200
Suggestions on how to make an effective general opening of a speech. With examples of. BRM:125-144
Suggestions on how to make dramatic openings. With examples of. BRM:165-174
Suggestions on how to make narrative openings. With examples of. BRM:145-164
Suggestions on how to open a speech with a quotation. With examples of. BRM:175-176
Westerdyk, J.
Place of the International Federation today. GA:171
See also Club speeches; Congratulations; Dedication addresses; Invocations; School, opening of; Welcoming addresses

OPERA
Cross, M.
Radio and opera. GLAD:291
Gilbert, W.S.
"Pinafore." COP:659; COPB:686; REEM 2:89; REEMA 2:524; REEMB 2:81
See also Metropolitan Opera Association; Music and musicians

OPINIONS See Public Opinion
Oppenheimer, J. Robert
Prospect in the arts and sciences (at Columbia University bicentennial anniversary celebration). COPB:642; HURG:319
Talk to undergraduates. BA 1957-58:146

OPPORTUNITY
Bain, M. E.
Possibilities. BOA:167; BOB:196
Compton, K. T.
Stuff of life; our talents and their care. SAR:13
Dearing, W. P.
Uplift and the undertow. SHU:103
Horton, J.
American opportunities. DO:13

Meisel, G. I.
Wanted: spunk, sense, and stamina. NOR 1941:11
Smith, F. M.
Around and around they go. BRP 7:60; YR 8:11
Spalding, J. L.
Opportunity (at opening of an educational institution). ONEM:512; REEM 6:379; REEMA 9:1076; REEMB 7:383; SHUM:312
You and your job. DR:32

OPTIMISM
Confidence plus optimism total success. NAT:9
Hyde, W. D.
Art of optimism. BLAA:94; BLAB:94; WERN 42:104
It might have been worse. NAT:38
Kaser, A. L.
Introducing an optimist. BRC:51
Let's be optimists. NAT:33
Munoz, J.
Optimism. BU:177
Purinton, E. E.
Efficient optimist. SHU:242

OPTOMETRISTS See Eyes

ORANGEMEN'S DAY
General declaration. THOU 1:506
Thoughts pertinent to Orangemen's Day. THOU 1:508
Why I am a Protestant. THOU 1:515

ORATORS
Cicero, M. T.
Great orators and their training. BEA:125
Meagher, T. F.
Orators of Ireland. HAZO 20:8477; MAS 20:8477

ORATORY See Public speaking

ORCHESTRA See Music and musicians

Order of the Eastern Star See Eastern Star, Order of
Order of King's Daughters and Sons See King's Daughters and Sons, Order of

ORDINATION
Prepared for every good work. JA:166

OREGON
Cobb, H.
"Fifty-four forty or fight." BREW 4:94
Stephens, A. H.
On the admission of Oregon. SOU 9:402

OREGON, UNIVERSITY OF
Hall, A.B.
Inaugural address as president of Oregon. WE 2:343

OREGON TRAIL
Hawes, H. B.
Covered wagon. DOA:53
O'Reilly, John Boyle
Moore, the Bard of Erin. REEM 3:13; REEMA 2:856; REEMB 3:13
O'Rell, Max See Blouet, Paul (Max O'Rell)
Orford, Horace Walpole, 4th Earl of. See Walpole, H.
Orford, Robert Walpole, 1st Earl of See Walpole, R.

ORGANIZED LABOR See Labor Unions

ORIENT
Dobson, J.
Our Pacific outlook. COUW:187
Emerson, J. G.
America and peace in the Orient. ASHF:308
Queer religion of the Orient. FRIE:236
Shearer, R.
Saxon versus Slav. COUW:157
Smith, R. L.

ORIENT (cont.)
Today's world in the Far East. BART 4:187
Warren, H.
New Orient. COUW:173
Wilbur, R. L.
Our destiny in the Pacific. COP:453; COPA:453
Yarnell, H. E.
Our stake in the Pacific. ON:78

ORIENTATION
Hopkins, E. M.
Orientation. ONEC:427
Mann, H.
Orient yourself. DICD:158; DICE:158
Origen.
Parable of the drag-net. LEEW 3:33

ORIGEN.
Gregory Thaumaturgus.
Panegyric on Origen. LEEW 3:45; PL:154
Orlando, V. E.
Speech at Peace Conference, 1919, Session January 25. REEM 11:323; REEMB 12:341
Speech at Peace Conference, 1919, Session February 15. REEM 11:341; REEMB 12:358
Oronhyatekha, W. F.
Foresters in Australia. THOU 3:262
Orphans See Bar Mitzvah speeches
O'Rourke, Arthur W.
Call of duty. SHUC:203
Orr, Alexander E.
Introducing M. Halstead to New York Chamber of Commerce, November 20, 1894. REEM 2:152
Orrok, George A.
Water-power costs versus steam-power costs. ONEC:281
Osborn, Frederick
United States, Russia, and the atomic bomb. HAR:211
Osborne, Charles S.
Northland to Dixieland. NESA:137
Osborne, James W.
Summation in support of the charges preferred by Senator Benn Conger. HICJ:604
Osburn, Henry Fairfield
John Burroughs. REEM 5:325; REEMB 9:366
Osgood, Charles Grosvenor
Proper study. NORR 3d ser:191
Osias, Camilo
Great commission. BOA:153; BOB:36
Osler, Sir William, Bart.
To the medical profession of the United States and Canada. KNAS:231; KNASA:231; ONEM:684; ONES:29; REEM sup 2:264; REEMB 6:285
Osmena, Sergio
First address to his cabinet. VO 1944-45:370
On the re-establishment of the Philippine government. HAN:350; VO 1945-46:93
Ostrander, Luther A.
Mightier than the sword. BOB:213
Ostroot, Patricia
Our living Constitution. DO:167
Otey, Peter J.
Tariff. SMI:223
Othello.
Negro slavery. WOON:14
Otho, Marcus Salvius
On becoming emperor. BRYW 2:245
To his soldiers before committing suicide. BRYW 2:251
To his soldiers in Rome. BRYW 2:248
Otis, Harrison Gray
Hamilton's influence on American institutions. BREW 8:248; CHAL 4:189; HAZO 9:3567; MAS 9:3567
Otis, James

Stamp Act, 1765. HELE:7
Writs of Assistance, February, 1761. ANG:62; BREW 8:262; BRYW 8:27; CHAL 2:333; CHEM 1:13; HARS: 7; HAZO 5:2031; HELE:2; JOHA 1 pt. 1:11; LAD:74; LEEW 8:23; MAS 5:2031; ORAMA 1:21; PE:114; PEA:114; PL:573; REEMA 14:1526; SAA:6
Ott, Edward A.
Sour grapes. IMMD:196

OTTOMAN EMPIRE
Winthrop, R. C.
Ottoman Empire. REEMA 3:1263
Oursler, Fulton and others (G. V. Denny, Jr.; I. Edman; and A. Pardue)
How can modern man find faith? HAR:480; MOA:484
Ousley, Clarence N.
Man's responsibility to the higher law. SHOU:191
Outerbridge, Eugene Harvey
Introducing Lord Cunliffe to Chamber of Commerce of New York. REEM 4:61; REEMB 4:144
Port of New York, December 13, 1921. REEM 3:16; REEMB 3:16
Port of New York, April 25, 1922. REEM 4:343; REEMB 5:210

OUTLINES (SPEECH) See Speeches-Outlines of
Overstreet, Harry L.
New problems, new philosophers. HAR:391
Owen, Robert L.
Currency Bill. BYRA:311; REEM 3:21; REEMB 3:21
Owen, Ruth Bryan
Modern Arabian Knights. EXEE:484
Modern politics. DOA:133
Unknown soldier. GA:87
Owens, Joseph T.
Intolerance. ASHF:166
Owsley, Alvin
America in 1940. BART 2:169
American Legion and the nation. REEM 7:303; REEMB 8:323
Respect for the flag. PROS: 33; REEMB 8:331
Owsley, Frank L.
Fundamental cause of the Civil War: egocentric sectionalism. TIN:77
Oxford and Asquith, Herbert Henry Asquith, 1st Earl of
Alfred Lyttelton. REEM 5:6; REEMB 9:35
At the first meeting of the Imperial Conference of 1911. KES 2:240
Call to arms. BRTH:334; BRTHA:334; SAA:228
Critical speech at Imperial Conference of 1911. KES 2: 301
Culture. BEA:331
England supports Belgium. HAY:328; REEM 11:51; REEMB 12:57
Government by competitive crime. BREW 1:169
House of Lords and financial measures, December 2, 1909 speech. EMS 1:165
House of Lords and financial measures, April 7, 1910 speech. EMS 1:181
Issues-true and false. CHAL 14:277
Loaded dice-the Lords against the Constitution. BREW 1: 170
Lord Kitchener. REEM 5:7; REEMB 9:36
Parliament Bill, 1911. EMS 1:188
Social fabric as the condition of values. BREW 1:178
Sovereign and the Ministry's right to dissolution of Parliament. EMS 1:53
Trade and the Empire. BRYW 5:201
Tribute to America. LEW:79

OXFORD AND ASQUITH, MARGOT (TENNANT) ASQUITH, COUNTESS OF
Gillilan, S.
Introducing Mrs. Asquith. REEM 2:95
Oxman, Stephen Alan
List. BU:154
Oxnam, G. Bromley
We intend to stay together. BA 1954-55:145
Pach, Walter
Stake of the arts in the democratic way of life. HAR: 398

PACIFIC See Orient; World War, 1939-1945-Campaigns-Pacific front

PACIFICISM
Blakely, R.
Modern primitivists. BRP 7:94; NOR 1936:34
Lash, J. P.
We won't fight. SAR:261
Salter, A. and others.
Pacificism-for and against. SAR:235

PACIFICO, DON
Palmerston, H. J. T.
On the case of Don Pacifico. ADR 4:125
Pacini, A. J.
Light and health. EXEE:578
Paciotti, Anthony F.
State! Keep your lawyers! YR 9:267

PACKING HOUSE INDUSTRY See Business men; Industry
Padererski, Ignace Jan
New Poland. REEM 7:313; REEMB 8:333
Padget, Fletcher, Jr.
Citizen's appreciation. BRP 10:7
Padilla, Ezequiel
At the Mexico City Conference. HAN:380
Page, Earle C.
Arrangements on this side. BERS:116
Page, Thomas Nelson
Old South. SMI:211
Torch of civilization. REEM 3:28; REEMA 3:861; REEMB 3:28
Page, Walter Hines
Closing educational conference. ONES:59
Fourth of July in London. REEM 11:231; REEMB 12: 248
Paget, Sir James, 1st Baronet
Scientific mind. HAY:261
Pailey.
For a Bar Mitzvah. ZEL:81
Paine, Ralph D., Jr.
Responds to an introduction. PRNE:62

PAINE, RALPH D., JR.
Stipp, J. E.
Introduces Ralph D. Paine, Jr., publisher of Fortune. PRNE:23
Paine, Thomas
American crisis. BRE:44; BREA:42; CROC:337; PO: 17
To the French National Convention. CHAL 3:74; HAZO 7:2642; MAS 7:2642; REEMA 14:1532

PAINE, THOMAS
Erskine, T.
Against Thomas Williams for the publication of Paine's Age of reason. ADR 2:273; BREW 6:12; GOOD: 761; ORBR 1:375; REEMA 13:949
Free speech and fundamental rights: defense of Tom Paine. BREW 6:43; BRTHA: 121; BRYW 4:71; PE:255; PEA:255

PAINTING See Art and artists
Painton, Edith Putnam
Class chronicles. WERN 54: 67
Parting hour (Valedictory).

WERN 54:99

PALESTINE
Bevin, E.
Statement on Palestine. VO 1945-46:710
Truman, H. S.
Statement on Palestine. VO 1945-46:713

Paley, William S.
Speech at Friars' Club dinner to Burns and Allen. JEYO: 90

PALEY, WILLIAM S.
Jessel, G.
Introducing William S. Paley at Friars' Club dinner to Burns and Allen. JEYO:89

PALM BEACH, FLORIDA
Ford, S.
Palm Beach. REEM 2:58; REEMB 2:58

Palmer, A. M.
Amending the Constitution. BOA:92

Palmer, George M.
Lawyer in politics. REEMA 3: 872

PALMER, JAMES
Griffin, C. E.
Presents James Palmer. LY:83

Palmer (Worthy Brother)
Invocation. THOU 3:468

Palmerston, Henry John Temple, 3d Viscount
Against war on Ireland. BREW 8:271
Arbitration. ORBR 2:119
House of Lords and financial measures. EMS 1:141
Illusions created by art. REEM 3:39; REEMA 3:876; REEMB 3:39
On affairs in Greece. BRYW 4:191; CHAL 5:348; HAZO 12:4819; MAS 12:4819
On the case of Don Pacifico. ADR 4:125
On the death of Cobden. BREW 8:268
Power to make war. EMS 1: 245
Protection of British subjects abroad. EMS 2:51
Sovereign advised to dismiss a Minister. EMS 1:26
Speech of February 12, 1858 (on India). KESI 1:319

PALMERSTON, HENRY JOHN TEMPLE, 3D VISCOUNT
Stanley, A. P.
Palmerston and the duty of England (funeral oration). BREW 9:274; ORBR 2:349

PAN AMERICAN CONFERENCE
See South America

PAN AMERICAN DAY
Hull, C.
Address before the Pan American Union, April 14, 1944. VO 1944-45:169

PAN AMERICAN UNION
Roosevelt, F. D.
Pan American Union. FIP: 203; SAA:281

PANAMA
Roosevelt, F.D.
Message to Congress, August 13, 1942. VO 1942-43: 438

PANAMA CANAL
Depew, C. M.
Panama Canal. HICF:340
Goethals, G. W.
Panama Canal completed. REEM 2:100; REEMB 2:92
Henry, R. L.
Texas and the Panama Canal. SHUO:217
Roosevelt, T.
"I took the Canal Zone." FIP:39
See also Goethals, George Washington

PANAMA-PACIFIC EXPOSITION
See Exhibitions

PANDIT, VIJAYA LAKSHMI (NEHRU)
Stevenson, A. E.
Presents Pandit Nehru. LY: 238

PANICS See Business cycles
Pankhurst, Christabel
Militant suffragette. BEA:337
Pankhurst, Mrs. Emmeline (Goulden)
Militant suffragists. COP:196; COPA:196; COPB:196; REEM 7:318; REEMB 7:324

PARALYSIS, INFANTILE See Medicine
Pardee, George Cooper
Address delivered in San Francisco at 250th anniversary of the settlement of the Jews in the United States. TWJ:172
Campaign speech. WAGN:414
Pardue, Austin See Oursler, F., jt. auth.

PARENT AND CHILD
Gregory, J. F.
Social bearing of the fifth commandment. DUNM:397
Parent psychology. NATM:13
Word to parents. NATS:11
See also Bar Mitzvah speeches; Family; Parents and Teachers Associations

PARENTS AND TEACHERS ASSOCIATIONS
By-products of teaching. JA: 169
Creations; a place, a plan, a pledge (a bank publicity speech for any business group, for a P.T.A. meeting, or for a student body). BAI:72
If I were the father I ought to be: for a Parent-Teacher banquet. CON:27
Kaser, A. L.
Introducing a P.T.A. president. BRC:193
Our P.T.A. NATM:41
Parent-Teacher association-cooperation between the school and home. DR:75; LU:1151
Parent and teacher association, by a parent. EDGS: 216
President's speech of retirement at annual meeting of Parent-Teacher association. WRA:131
Ramsey, H.
Introducing a speaker at a P.T.A. meeting. BRC:125
Steele, S.
Introducing a P.T.A. entertainment. BRH:65

PARIS
Cadman, S. P.
Lure of Paris. LINM:233
See also World war 1939-1945-France

PARIS TREATY, 1928
Kellogg, F. B.
To the American Society of International Law, April 28, 1928. KESB:398
Park, Edwards Amasa
Theology of the intellect and that of the feelings. BL: 624
Park, Marion Edwards
Introducing president Ada Louise Comstock. GA:14
Presentation of the M. Carey Thomas prize award. GA: 36
Welcome to Bryn Mawr's fiftieth anniversary. GA:22
Park, Rosemary
Inaugural address (as President of Barnard College). BA 1963-64:173
Parker, Alton B.
Our heritage. REEM 3:42; REEMB 3:43
Parker, Courtland

Parker, Courtland
Different motives of the settlers. THOU 1:222
Freedom of America the result of an open Bible. THOU 1:204
Parker, J.S.
New dynamics of corporate relations work. BAAGA:381
Parker, Junius
Introduction of Edwin P. Murrow. BRAC:236
Parker, Theodore
Children of the poor. ESEH: 189
Dangers from slavery. HAZO 16:6770; MAS 16:6770; RID:46
Discourse on the death of Daniel Webster. BREW 8: 274; PE:410; PEA:410; PL:669; SHAH:236
Philosophical idea of God and its relation to the scientific and religious wants of mankind now. BL:659
Reminiscence of Lexington. CLAY:139
State of the nation (1850). CHAL 8:108; CROC:345; HAZO 16:6732; MAS 16:6732
Parkhurst, Charles H.
Man of sorrows. THOU 2:80
On Garfield. CHAL 13:430; HAZO 24:10474; MAS 24: 10474
Piety and civic virtue. BLAA: 131; BLAB:131
Sermon to children. THOU 2: 164
Parkinson, C. Northcote
Responds to an introduction by Clinton Youle. PRC:22

PARKS See Dedication addresses -Parks

PARLIAMENTARY FORM OF GOVERNMENT See Great Britain-Parliament
Parmele, L.
Independence Day. REAC:79
Parnell, Charles Stewart
Against nonresident landlords. BREW 8:282; CHAL 14:31; HAZO 25:10572; MAS 25: 10572
At Ennis (boycotting defined and defended). KET:405
At Limerick-The land for the people. KET:402
Commission speech, 1888. KET:392
His first speech in America. BREW 8:280; PL:545
Meeting of Irish Parliamentary Party. KET:404
On a coercion bill in House of Commons. CHAL 14:35; HAZO 25:10576; KET:409; MAS 25:10576
On the forged letter printed in the London "Times." BRYW 6:224
On the Home Rule Bill. BRYW 6:230; COP:219; COPA: 219; COPB:219; PAUF 2: 159; PE:578; PEA:578
Parnell national tribute. KET: 406

PARNELL, CHARLES STEWART
Redmond, J.E.
One Parnell-15 years in the House of Commons. KET:429

PAROLE SYSTEM
Gardiner, C.H.
By the power invested. YR 8:249
Wines, F.H.
Indeterminate sentence, the parole, and the new criminology. PEAE:219
Parsons, Earl
Future of the American farmers. DOA:95
Parsons, Edward Lambe
Democracy and a prophetic idealism. NORR 1st ser:377

PARSONS, LOUELLA
Jessel, G.
Presenting Louella Parsons at dinner in her honor.

PARSONS, LOUELLA (cont.)
JEYO:141

PARTIES See Acceptance speeches-Parties Also Types of parties, e.g., Showers; Stag
Passfield, Baron See Webb, S.J., 1st Baron Passfield

PASSION
Saurin, J.
Effect of passion. BREW 9:141

PASSOVER
Passover greetings. BEC:152

PAST
Speech on the past. THOS:89
Spirit of the past. BOB:208
Pasteur, Louis
Depicts the spirit of science. PE:469; PEA:469
Pater, Walter
Raphael. REEMA 9:940

PATIENCE
Cyprian, Saint.
On the benefit of patience. HAZO 3:1114; MAS 3:1114
Tertullian, Q.S.F.
Beauty of patience. BREW 9:376
Paton, Andrew H.
Tamina's day. THOU 3:306
Patrick, Howard Allen
Challenge of chaos. YR 5:105
Patrick, Rembert W.
Mobile frontier. TIN:451

PATRICK, SAINT
Hall, J.
Doctrines held by St. Patrick. THOU 1:525
Ryan, M.J.
St. Patrick; his mission, his church, and social service. CATA 1:251
Slave boy who became a missionary. JAS:32
See also Saint Patrick's Day

PATRIOTISM
America-land of opportunity. LU:1225
Baruch, B.M.
Patriotism in industry. REEM 4:22; REEMB 4:62
Bell, E.I.
Not taps but reveille. BA 1944-45:307
Bolingbroke, H.S.-J.
Patriotism. BREW 2:147
Brousseau, G.H.
Defense of home and country. HICF:943
Bryan, W.J.
Essence of patriotism. BOA:80; BOB:112
Burrell, D.J.
Incentives to patriotism. SHU:160
Campbell, J.
Pseudo patriotism. YR 7:339
Can prayer save our nation? JA:175
Cannon, J.G.
Patriotism and partisanship. BREW 3:109
Chamberlain, J.
Patriotism. REEM 7:95; REEMA 7:161; REEMB 8:93
Clay, H.
Noblest public virtue. HAZO 10:4099; MAS 10:4099
Coolidge, C.
Toleration. REEM 1:208; REEMB 8:116
Ecklund, J.E., Jr.
Productive patriotism. YR 8:297
Everett, E.
On patriotism. CHAL 13:291; HAZO 24:10280; MAS 24:10280
Patriotic oration (50th anniversary of the independence of the United States of America). CHAL 6:92; HAZO 12:5148; MAS 12:5148
Folk, J.W.

Americans for America. BOA:204; BOB:173
Ford, J.F.
Catholicism and patriotism. CATA 1:187
Gibson, E.W.
Patriotism, the soul of a nation. BOA:75; BOB:116
Gilder, R.W.
New patriotism. BLAA:40; BLAB:40; BOB:120
Goldman, E.
Anarchy vs. patriotism. HURG:166
Grattan, H.
Unsurrendering fidelity to country. BREW 6:297; HAZO 7:2811; KET:140; MAS 7:2811
Hampden, J.
Patriot's duty defined: against own impeachment. BREW 6:349
Harrison, B.
Plea for patriotism (100th anniversary of Washington's inauguration). ESEH:199
Howell, C.
Man with his hat in his hand. BLAA:155; BLAB:155; SHUO:198
Incentives to patriotism. PROS:5
Ireland, J.
On patriotism. CHAL 13:204; HAZO 24:10192; MAS 24:10192
Jacobs, H.H.
Patriotism. TRUW:33
Jessel, G.
"I am an American" Day. JEYO:153
Kahn, O.H.
Prussianized Germany. SAA:274
King, T.S.
On the privilege and duties of patriotism. CHAL 10:395; HAZO 20:8748; MAS 20:8748
Kirby, J.H.
Patriotism. NESA:130
Lee, D.C.
Function for patriotism during the period of change. YR 5:243
McKinley, W.
American patriotism (at dedication of Cuyahoga County Soldiers' and Sailors' monument). BREW 8:35; CHAL 13:457; HAZO 24:10486; MAS 24:10486; REEM 7:264; REEMA 9:847
Map: a thought for changing a speech (for a patriotic speech, for Memorial Day, or a speech for peace). BAI:123
Miller, M.V.
Higher patriotism. BOA:63; BOB:109
My country-right or wrong. JA:172
Niebler, C.J.
Wanted-patriotism for American youth. YR 8:31
Norris, G.B.
Constructive patriotism. YR 9:205
Our great country. NAT:16
Patriotic speeches-examples of. MORA:99-104
Patriotic toasts-five examples of. STON:139-141
Patriotism and fraternity. THOS:15
Patriotism (plea for true patriotism). ED:53
Satterthwaite, J.B.
Fire and blood. YR 7:147
Schall, T.D.
Genius of patriotism. TRUW:157
Sheen, F.J.
Liberty and the Republic. BA 1938-39:245
Shelley, D.N.
Devotion to duty. BOB:192
Smith, C.E.
Patriotism. BLAA:185; BLAB:185
Thomas, G.
Pernicious virtue. YR 6:11
University and true patriotism.

PATRIOTISM (cont.)
DAVC:67
University of patriotism. AMEO 1:120
Walpole, R.
On patriots (at motion to dismiss him from Council). BREW 10:78; COP:151; COPA:151; COPB:151; PL:384
Whipple, E. P.
Patriotic oration. CHAL 9:398; HAZO 19:8022; MAS 19:8022
True glory of a nation. BOA:78; BOB:110
See also Citizenship; Fourth of July
Patsalidis, Andreas
Inaugural speech at Conference on the Problems of Economic Development. UAR:177
Speech at final session of Conference on the Problems of Economic Development. UAR:421
Patten, Bernard M.
Catholic citizen. CATA 1:226
Patterson, Grier D.
Greater man. BOB:32; HARSO:63
Patterson, James Willis
Relations of education to public questions. NORR 2d ser:185
Patterson, Malcolm R.
Sam Davis. HARSO:124
Patterson, R. M.
Communion sermon. THOU 2:421
Patterson, Richard C., Jr.
Sixth column. BA 1941-42:135; SAC:54
Patton, George S.
"Flanks are something for the enemy to worry about." HURG:274
Patton, James W.
Facets of the South in the 1850's. TIN:350
Paul, N.
Abolition of slavery. WOON:64
Paul, Saint
Paul to the Jews. BRIM:381; LAD:35
Paul's speech to Agrippa. BRIM:383; LAD:32; LEEW 3:27; PEAE:143; PL:151
To the men of Athens on Mars' Hill. BRIM:386; CORP:103; LA:166; LAD:38; PEAE:147; REEM 9:28; REEMB 10:29
Paull, George Alfred
Harvest thoughts. THOU 2:249
Paulson, Stanley
Spectrum of democracy. NOR 1942:71
Paxton, George M.
Scotch-Irishman's views of the Puritan. REEMA 3:880
Payne, George Henry
What shall we do with radio? SAR:107
Payne-Gaposchkin, Cecilia
New light on cosmic history. IOCP:85
Peabody, Andrew Preston
Connection between science and religion. NORR 1st ser:76
Peabody, Francis G.
Commercialism and idealism. SHU:257

PEACE
Adams, L. C.
Higher soldiery. BOB:179
Addams, J.
Closing the International Congress of Women. GA:175
Governmental efforts toward world peace. DOA:162
Opening Fourth International Congress. GA:168
Adolfson, L. H.
Ultimation of youth. YR 5:143
Allen, F. E.
Women and world peace. REEM sup 1:50; REEMB 6:1
Andocides.

On the peace with Sparta. MINA 1:498
Angell, J. B.
War and arbitration. FUL: 7, 9
Barrows, J. H.
National Peace Jubilee. FUL: 11, 14
Beaconsfield, B. D.
Peace with honor. BEA:25; COP:185; COPA:185; COPB:185; HAZO 14:6063; MAS 14:6063; REEM 9:303; REEMA 1:21; REEMB 10: 312
Beaubien, C. P.
Canada and peace. REEM sup 1:106; REEMB 8:36
Beaver, H. T.
Real problem of world peace. ASHF:294
Bragstad, R.
Child shall lead them. BRP 9:113
Bright, J.
Peace. KLEG:357; LEEW 7:291; PL:473
Peace and war. ORBR 2: 335
Bryan, W. J.
Against militarism. SHU: 164
Bryce, J. B.
Peace. REEM 1:180; REEMB 1:176
Burton, H. H.
America's road to lasting peace. BA 1943-44:106
Butler, N. M.
Will to peace. BRAC:325
Carnegie, A.
New century greeting. BLAA:261; BLAB:261
Carruth, W. H.
Heroisms of peace. NORR 2d ser:343
Chamberlain, N.
Returns in triumph from Munich. PE:765; PEA:765
Choate, J. H.
Peace between nations. REEM 1:256; REEMA 1:195; REEMB 1:257
Churchill, W. L. S.
Lights are going out. SAR: 289
Sinews of peace (speech at Fulton, Missouri). BA 1945-46:20; COPB:614; GRAC:144; HIB:298; PE: 803; PEA:803
Clémenceau, G.
Winning the right of peace. BREW 4:70
Clemes, W.
Sold! the temple of humanity. YR 10:77
Collins, F. C., Jr.
Bell tolls for thee. NOR 1946:53
Connally, T. T.
America and post-war cooperation. BA 1943-44:96
Corbett, A.
Achievement of peace. BLUE:34
Cox, G. V.
Challenge of war. ASHF: 339
Crisp, C. R.
Here's to peace. BOB:27
Daniels, B.
Peace. BRP 4:91
Demosthenes.
Oration on the peace. BREW 5:136; HAZO 2:481; MAS 2:481
Dern, G. H.
How to fight the war peril. SAR:254
Diaz, P.
Peace rooted in the hearts of all. CHAL 11:442; HAZO 22:9363; MAS 22:9363
Dulles, J. F.
"Not war, not peace." BA 1947-48:58
Eberts, H. W., Jr.
And there is no peace. AN: 13
Einstein, A.
Peace in the atomic era. BA 1949-50:63; COPB:635; HAR:58
Eisenhower, D. D.
Crusade for peace. BA

PEACE (cont.)
1952-53:92
Peace an absolute necessity. HIB:55
Peace and friendship, in freedom. BA 1959-60:25
Peace program. BA 1952-53:31
Price of peace: second inaugural address. BA 1956-57:19; BAAG:376; CHI:294; LOTI:263; USIN:263; USINA:263; WPRC:313
World peace: a balance sheet. BA 1949-50:51; YE:183

France, A.
Wanted-"Good Europeans." BREW 6:167

Funk, B.
Constitution; a guide to the world of tomorrow. DO:230

Gandhi, M.K.
Propounds his faith before an English judge. PE:727; PEA:727

Gannon, R.I.
Peace through business. GLAD:263

Garfield, J.A.
Revolution and the logic of coercion. BREW 6:198

George VI.
Christmas message of peace, 1939. SAA:288

Gideonse, H.
When to prepare for peace. ON:299

Gilkinson, B.A.
Old order changeth. ASHF:324

Goddard, J.L.
Way to lasting peace. BRP 1:71

Goldstein, M.W.
Builders of destiny. BRP 4:105; YR 6:93

Gray, S.E.
Influence of the teaching of history on world peace. ASHF:286

Gunnison, E.M.
Thumbs down. YR 7:257

Hardison, E.
Propaganda-a weapon of peace. YR 10:69

Harris, H.
America's peace responsibilities. DO:82

Hay, J.
America's love of peace. BOAM:63

Henderson, W.G.
What may man become? BRP 7:117

Herter, C.A.
Peaceful change. BA 1959-60:51

Hibben, J.G.
Comrades in peace. BOB:28

Hocking, W.E.
Crisis of our time. BA 1944-45:194

Hoffman, A.
Our Constitution and peace. DO:98

Holden, R.
Progress toward peace. BRP 3:29

Hootman, E.
Unfilled promise (possibilities of universal peace and ultimate attainment thru education). ASHF:347

Hoover, H.C.
Question of peace. BA 1940-41:196

Horton, E.
International understanding. BRP 2:87; YR 3:89

Howe, M.A.DeW.
New armor. BOB:31

Huckabee, B.
Rights to peace. DO:128

Hughes, C.E.
Pathway to peace. HICF:681

Hull, C.
Economic barriers to peace. SAR:276
Pillars of enduring peace. COP:558; COPB:550

Humphrey, C.J.
Crosspatch. BRP 8:23; YR 9:213

Imrie, N.A.

America and Britain: some problems in common. NESA: 154
Ireland, J.
Peace in the wake of victory. ORAMA 2:445
Isle, W.
Planting seeds of peace. BOB:33
Jones, L.
Breaking down barriers. YR 8:177
Kaltenborn, H.V. and others.
How can we secure peace in a hydrogen bomb world? BA 1949-50:101
Kaplan, A.
Half slave, half free. YR 9:195
Kennedy, J.F.
Peace through the United Nations. HIB:344
Step toward peace. BA 1963-64:20
Toward a strategy of peace. BA 1963-64:9
Ketcham, V.A.
Passing of war. SHUC:269
Kingsley, D.P.
Raise a standard. REEM 2:294; REEMB 2:298
Kirkpatrick, R.
Hope of peace. ONES:333
Krause, N.
We will not lay down arms. BA 1943-44:123
Lavelle, W.
Spirit of peace. YR 2:157
Lawson, R.
Furling the battle flags. YR 4:319
Leo I.
Blessedness of peacemaking. PL:190
Lie, T.
Road to peace. HAR:61
Littell, N.
Path to peace. ASHF:355
London, M.
International league to secure peace. HARSO:76
MacDonald, J.R.
Peace. COP:206; COPA: 206; COPB:206
McGenty, D.
Where peace abides. YR 2: 13
McLaughlin, J.J.
Peace in tomorrow's world. DO:119
Map: a thought for changing a speech (for a patriotic speech, for Memorial Day, or a speech for peace). BAI:123
Margulies, H.
No pot-luck peace. BRP 9: 91; NOR 1938:22
Miller, J.
Disarmament as the way to peace. HOD:108
Mirabeau, H.G.R.
Right of war and peace. CODS:75; CODSA:75; PE: 241; PEA:241
Moore, J.M.
Crisis. CORP:103
Mundt, K.E.
Peace-if we want it. BA 1944-45:93
Mussolini, B.
Absurdity of eternal peace. PL:816; SAR:268
Four-power Pact. BEA:323
Neff, P.M.
Battles of peace. BOA:185; BOB:167
Nelson, C.H.
Youth and lasting peace. AN:74
New peace. SHU:133
Niebuhr, R.
Crisis of our time. BA 1944-45:191
Osias, C.
Great commission. BOA: 153; BOB:36
Patterson, G.D.
Greater man. BOB:32; HARSO:63
Pearce, C.C.
Inglorious peace. TRUW: 245
Pennington, L.T.
Evolution of world peace. ASHF:270

PEACE (cont.)
Perdew, W. C.
Pitfalls of peace. ASHF: 332
Phillips, M. G.
Influence of the press on world peace. ASHF:316
Pittenger, W. A.
Patriots of peace. BRP 1:71
Pius XII.
Address in St. Peter's Square, Vatican City urging charitable peace. VO 1945-46:123
Appeal for peace. COP:525; COPA:525; COPB:503; VO 1941:167
Christmas eve broadcast to the world, 1943. VO 1943-44:585
To the College of Cardinals pleading for the safety of Rome and for peace. VO 1944-45:248
Povish, K.
Peacemakers. DO:108
Rabinowitz, D.
And the gentlemen cry peace. NOR 1948:133
Raschke, K.
It can be done. BRP 10:100
Reiman, A. C. E. W.
I am innocent of this blood (peace can only be achieved by education in the home, school, and church). ASHF: 302
Roosevelt, E. A.
Banquet address. GA:105
Roosevelt, F. D.
Message to Hitler and Mussolini, April 14, 1939. HAN:95
Quarantining the aggressors. ANG:477; BRE:357; BRYA: 539; FIP:233; HAN:91
Roosevelt, T.
America and international peace. SHU:231
Ryan, M. J.
Papacy and world peace. CATA 2:266
Schuman, F. L.
Peace without appeasement. HAR:40
Schurz, C.
Let us have peace. BLAA: 238; BLAB:238
Shively, T.
Bargain. BRP 5:76
Smuts, J. C.
Peace and Empire. COP: 391; COPA:391; COPB: 391; REEM 7:352; REEMB 8:387
Spellman, F. J.
One road to peace. BA 1940-41:187

Response at reception. BA 1945-46:203
Stallings, J.
America and brotherhood. DO:139
Stassen, H. E.
American world policy for peace and progress. BA 1944-45:56
Stearns, T.
Perishing with the sword. YR 8:199
Stewart, D. W.
Universal obligation. BOB: 39
Stoddard, A. J.
Education and the people's peace. BA 1944-45:272
Stubbs, C. W.
International peace. CHAL 14:15; HAZO 25:10545; MAS 25:10545
Swing, R. G.
Youth, war, and freedom. HAN:22
Thurston, J. M.
Humanity's cause triumphant. FUL:310
Truman, H. S.
Spirit of peace. GLAD:233
Vanocur, S.
State of mind. NOR 1949: 163
Vinson, C.
Path to peace. BOB:68
Wallace, H. A.
Before the Free World As-

sociation. PE:792; PEA: 792; VO 1942-43:270
Is American foreign policy leading to war? BA 1946-47:33
Webster, H.
Commerce and world peace. ASHF:278
Wheeler, B.K.
Against the resolution for collaboration for postwar peace. BA 1943-44:115
Whipper, W.
Non-resistance to offensive aggression. WOON:104
White, A.D.
Apostle of peace among the nations. CHAL 12:80; HAZO 22:9487; MAS 22:9487
Why peace is better than war. AMEO 2:107
Willkie, W.
Report to the nation on global war and peace. BOA: 17; HAN:194
Wilson, W.
Peace without victory. ANG: 428; BIR 4:20; COP:351; COPA:351; COPB:351; FIP:116; FKA:233; FO:287; HURG:173
Submitting the Peace Treaty to the Senate. BRAC:208
Wishard, G.P.
United States and universal peace. TRUW:216
See also Arbitration; Disarmament; Inter-American Conference on Problems of War and Peace; League of Nations; League to Enforce Peace; Pacificism; War; World War, 1939-1945-Peace and mediation

PEACE CONFERENCE, 1919
Clemenceau, G.
Opening address at Peace Conference, January 18, 1919. BREW 4:71; REEM 11:315; REEMB 12:332
Lloyd George, D.
Seconding the nomination of M.G. Clémenceau for President of the Peace Conference. REEM 11:313; REEMB 12:331
Poincaré, R.
Inaugural speech (Peace Conference, 1919). REEM 11:306; REEMB 12:323
Supreme judgment of history. BREW 8:361
What justice must banish. BREW 8:363
Sonnino, S.C.
Seconding the nomination of M.G. Clémenceau for President of the Peace Conference. REEM 11:314; REEMB 12:332
Wilson, W.
Nomination of M. Georges Clémenceau as President of the Conference. REEM 11: 312; REEMB 12:329

---- SESSION JANUARY 25
Bourgeois, L.
Peace Conference at Paris, Session January 25, 1919. REEM 11:324; REEMB 12: 342
Lloyd George, D.
Speech at January 25 Session Peace Conference, 1919. REEM 11:322; REEMB 12:340
Orlando, V.E.
Speech at Peace Conference, 1919 Session January 25. REEM 11:323; REEMB 12: 341
Wilson, W.
Speech at Peace Conference at Paris (Session January 25, 1919). COP:365; COPA: 365; COPB:365; FIP:130; HURG:185; REEM 11:318; REEMB 12:335

---- SESSION FEBRUARY 15
Barnes, G.N.
Speech at Peace Conference (Session of February 15, 1919). REEM 11:343;

PEACE CONFERENCE, 1919-
SESSION FEBRUARY 15
(cont.)
REEMB 12:360
Bourgeois, L.
Peace Conference at Paris, Session, February 15, 1919. REEM 11:333; REEMB 12: 351
Cecil of Chelwood, E.A.R.G. -C.
Speech at Peace Conference (Session of February 15, 1919). REEM 11:388; REEMB 12:355
Koo, W.
Speech at Peace Conference (Session on February 15, 1919). REEM 11:346; REEMB 12:364
Makino, N.
Speech at Peace Conference (Session February 15, 1919). REEM 11:342; REEMB 12: 360
Orlando, V.E.
Speech at Peace Conference, 1919 Session February 15. REEM 11:341; REEMB 12: 358
Venizelos, E.
Speech at Peace Conference (Session February 15, 1919). REEM 11:345; REEMB 12: 363
Wilson, W.
Speech at Peace Conference at Paris (Session February 15). REEM 11:327; REEMB 12:344

PEACE CORPS See United States- Peace Corps

PEACE TREATY, 1919
Wilson, W.
Presenting the treaty of Versailles for ratification, July 10, 1919. PO:129
Peale, Norman Vincent
How to have good relations with other people. BA 1954-55:153
Response to introduction. PR: 123

PEALE, NORMAN VINCENT
Lewe, J.C.
Presents Norman Vincent Peale. LY:165; PR:71
Pearce, Charles C.
Inglorious peace. TRUW:245

PEARL HARBOR See World War, 1939-1945-United States
Pearlman, Gilbert
Kingdom of fear. NOR 1950: 205
Pearlman, Rev.
Address to a Bar Mitzvah. ZEL:58
Pearson, Charles
Introducing a packing house executive. BRC:282
Pearson, Lester B.
Begins an address on "Canada-nation on the march." PRNE:57

PEARSON, LESTER B.
Davis, J.W.
Presents Lester B. Pearson. LY:208
McDonough, J.J.
Introducing Lester B. Pearson, Canadian statesman. PRNE:5
Peary, Robert Edwin
Farthest north. COP:683; COPB:710; REEM 3:48; REEMB 3:49
North Pole. REEM 3:47; REEMB 3:48
Pease, James
Comedy or tragedy. BOA:150; BRP 5:7; YR 6:131
Peck, George R.
Sovereignty follows the flag. BLAA:231; BLAB: 231; FUL:245, 247
Year of jubilee. FUL:243
Pecker, Edith L.
Consecration to humanity man's mission. WERN 54: 54

Peckham, Rufus William
Lochner v. New York, 1905: opinion for the Supreme Court. BIR 3:283
Pecora, Ferdinand
Should Mr. Roosevelt's plan for enlarging the Supreme Court be adopted? (affirmative) SAR:227

PECORA, FERDINAND
Introducing Ferdinand Pecora. NI:118; NIA:91
Pedley, Emmet A.
Hand of the living dead. BRP 3:89; YR 4:103
Pedrick, Willard
Tantalus. YR 8:113
Peel, Sir Robert, Bart.
Occasions for appeal to the people. EMS 1:84; PAUF 1:295
On the disabilities of the Jews. LEEW 7:181; PL:443; REEMA 14:1544
On the repeal of the Corn Laws. BREW 8:285; BRTH: 233; BRTHA:233; BRYW 4: 180; CHAL 5:409; HAZO 12:4886; MAS 12:4886; REEMA 14:1539
Papers exempt from liability to libel. EMS 1:224
Plea for higher education (installation speech as Lord Rector of University of Glasgow). BREW 8:290
Position of a Ministry not supported by the House of Commons, April 8, 1835 speech. EMS 1:62
Position of a Ministry not supported by the House of Commons, May 27, 1841 speech. EMS 1:66
Reform of the franchise. EMS 2:144
Resignation of Ministers, House of Commons, June 29, 1846.-Same as his Occasions for appeal to the people
Sovereign's responsibility for dismissal of Ministers. EMS 1:16

PELOPONNESIAN WAR
Pericles.
In favor of the Peloponnesian war. BRYW 1:9; HAZO 1:25; MAS 1:25
Peloubet, Maurice E.
Presents Robert C. Downie. LY:94
Peltier, Jean
Mackintosh, J.
In behalf of free speech: on the trial of Jean Peltier accused of libelling Napoleon Bonaparte. ADR 2:185; BREW 8:54; BRYW 4:84; CHAL 4:208; GOOD:827; HAZO 9:3585; LEEW 7:111; MAS 9:3585; PL:453

PEN AND SWORD
Ostrander, L. A.
Mightier than the sword. BOB:213
Pendelton, Edmund
Adoption of the Constitution. SMI:47
Liberty and government in America. BREW 3:293
On reconstruction. CHAL 10: 435; CHEM 4:247; HAZO 21:8790; JOHA 2 pt 2:141; MAS 21:8790

PENGUINS
Shackleton, E. H.
Penguins. REEM 3:201; REEMB 3:208
Penn, William
Golden rule against tyranny. BREW 8:299

PENN, WILLIAM
Ridge, J.
Respect for William Penn. SHE:43
Pennington, Gladys
Return, America. ONES:367
Pennington, Levi T.
Evolution of world peace. ASHF:270

PENNSYLVANIA
Scranton, W.W.
Inaugural address as Governor of Pennsylvania. BA 1962-63:173

PENNSYLVANIA, UNIVERSITY OF
Pepper, W.
Inaugural address as president of University of Pennsylvania. WE 1:95

PENSIONS
Curran, J. P.
Against pensions. BREW 4:314; KET:145

---- MILITARY
Chapman, V.
Saviors of civilization. BOB:65
Hergenroeder, P. J.
In the service of our country. NOR 1935:130
Hoover, H. C.
Bonus marchers: Press statement, March 29, 1932. FIP:189
Bonus marchers: Press statement, July 28, 1932. FIP:190
Bonus marchers: Press statement, September 14, 1932. FIP:191
McAdoo, W. G.
Soldiers' bonus. REEM 7:253; REEMB 8:273

PENTECOST
Francis de Sales, Saint
Sermon for the feast of Pentecost. LEEW 4:201
Recapturing Pentecost. JA:178
Secret of spiritual power. JA:181
What is the Church? JAS:54

PEP
Sadler, W. S.
Elements of pep. EXEE:36

PEP MEETINGS
Putting your project across (pep talk to be used at a sales meeting, to inspire a group of workers on a charity drive or any similar purpose). NAT:36
Sales meeting pep talk. NAT:41
Sifter: know your dough and you will grow (pep talk for bank personnel and business groups. Adaptable for club members, a war-veteran post member or any auxiliary member). BAI:31
Strikes: the striker and the strike-breaker (a changeable speech adaptable for Servicemen's posts, American War Mothers' or Gold Star Mothers' chapters, for a membership drive or a pep talk for cooperation). BAI:47
Voltage: the jolt of a volt (a changeable speech for many occasions, for a sales speech, a membership drive, or a pep talk). BAI:85
See also Sports
Pepper, Claude D.
Against aid to Greece and Turkey. BA 1946-47:67
All-out aid to Britain. BA 1940-41:49

PEPPER, CLAUDE D.
Blaine, J. B.
Introduces Claude Pepper. PR:49
Pepper, George Wharton
Greatest enterprise of Pittsburgh. LINM:483
Introducing Marshall Foch. LY:153; NESA:189
Presents Charles Evans Hughes. LY:137

PEPPER, GEORGE WHARTON
Mason, W. C.
Presents George Wharton Pepper. LY:141

Pepper, William
Inaugural address as President of University of Pennsylvania. WE 1:95
Perdew, William C.
Pitfalls of peace. ASHF:332
Pericles.
Against the demands of the Lacedaemonians.-Same as his In favor of the Pelopennesian war
Funeral orations.-Same as his On those who died in the war
In defense of himself. BRYW 1:27; HAZO 1:30; MAS 1:30
In favor of the Pelopennesian war. BRYW 1:9; HAZO 1:25; MAS 1:25
On the cause of Athenian greatness.-Same as his On those who died in the war
On those who died in the war. ARNS:216; BAAGA:404; BOU:205; BREW 8:306; BRYA:547; BRYW 1:16; CHAL 1:2; COP:3; COPA:3; COPB:3; CROC:358; HAZO 1:15; HIBS:484; LEEW 1:47; MAS 1:15; MEAR:107, PE:7; PEA:7; PL:26; REEM 9:2; REEMA 14:1563; REEMB 10:2
Perkins, Frances
Greetings from the United States. SAR:339
Perkins, George C.
Commercial future of United States. WAGN:349
Exclusion of the Chinese. REEMA 14:1572
Inaugural address as Governor of California. WAGN:348
Knights Templar address of welcome. WAGN:341
Perlman, Nathan A.
Making a new start (sermon marking Jewish New Year). BA 1955-56:159

PERMANENT COURT OF INTERNATIONAL JUSTICE
Harding, W. G.
World Court. FIP:149
Moore, J. B.
Permanent Court of International Justice. ONEC:241
Perrott, Russell See Forten, J., jt. auth.
Perry, Bliss
Amateur spirit. NORR 1st ser: 263
Perry, Charner M. See Appleby, P. H., jt. auth.
Perry, John Holliday
Newspaper law. BYRA:318; REEM sup 2:269; REEMB 6:290
Perry, Susan Teall
Children's day. THOU 2:182

PERSECUTION
Drama of the centuries. NIA:216
Persecuted triumph. NI:257; NIA:194
Savonarola, G.
Let me be persecuted (from Lenten sermons of 1497). CROC:396

PERSEVERANCE
Grosvenor, J. W.
Perseverance wins. THOU 3:539
Pershing, John J.
To the United States Senate. REEM 11:420; REEMB 12:442
To the unknown British warrier. REEM 11:433; REEMB 12:458

PERSHING, JOHN J.
Gifford, W. J.
Introducing General John J. Pershing. YE:125
Pershing. SCHS:202

PERSONALITY
Braasch, W. K.
Essentials of a pleasing personality. EXEE:356
Do you ring the bell? JAI:17
Hart, J. R.

PERSONALITY (cont.)
Positive and negative personalities. NESA:124
Power of projected personality. JA:202
Sandford, W. P.
Personality is yours for the taking. SAC:80
Spillman, H. C.
Cash value of personality. NESA:120
What do others see in you? JAI:11

PERSUASION
Power of persuasion. FRIE:162
PERSUASIVE SPEECHES
Anthony, S. B.
Are women persons? HIBS:451
Arpaia, A.
Matter of necessity. LINP:240
Black, Hugh L.
Bill of Rights. LINP:126
Brayman, H.
Formula for reform. MOUG:196; MOUGA:196
Churchill, W. L. S.
Address to Congress, January 17, 1952. BA 1951-52:30; MOUG:220; MOUGA:220
Save Europe by uniting Europe (May 14, 1947). HIBS:452
Crary, D. R.
Plague of people. LINP:211
Dean, V. M.
Anti-Westernism: cause and cure. BA 1959-60:116; LINP:234
Duesterbeck, R. M.
Man's other society. LINP:264
Eubanks, R. T.
Leadership and the "sane society." LINP:178
Fire prevention at home (outline of speech). MOA:315
Gebhart, D.
Why go to college? MOUGA:206
Geiman, C. K.
Are they really unteachable? LINP:122
Goss, B. C.
Trial outside the courtroom. LINP:250
Harlow, H. F.
Nature of love. LINP:84
Humphrey, G. M.
Businessmen must be active in politics. SABA:223
Jones, J. L.
Who is tampering with the soul of America? LINP:219
Jury is dismissed (outline of speech). MOA:338, 345
Kappel, F. R.
Business needs basic research. SABA:230
Kennedy, J. F.
Inaugural address. ARNS:256; BA 1960-61:35; BAAGA:398; BOU:3; CAP:231; CHI:301; FIP:374; HIB:283; LINP:161; LOTI:269; PEA:831; SOBP:335; USIN:267; USINA:267; WPRC:317
Intellectual and the politician. BA 1956-57:165; BARR:285; LINP:279
King, M. L.
"I have a dream." BA 1963-64:43; BOU:157; HIB:173; HILK:371; LINP:156; PEA:835
Kirk, G.
Responsibilities of the educated man (at centennial of University of Denver). LINP:165
Lacey, J. J.
Farmers need public understanding. SAB:143; SABA:236
Lilienthal, D. E.
My faith in democracy. HIBS:463; PE:808; PEA:807
Loomis, D. P.
Why not let competition go

to work in transporation? LINP:269
Lynch, G. J.
Pursuit of security (accepting an honorary degree by University of Dayton at graduation exercise). LINP: 186
MacArthur, D.
Defends his conduct of the war in Korea. ARNS:273; BA 1951-52:21; BOU:105; BRAP:61; CAP:206; COPB: 594; HAR:146; HIBS:465; HURG:293; MOUG:210; MOUGA:210 (outline p. 217); PE:816; PEA:816; YE:371
Farewell to the cadets (accepting Sylvanus Thayer award for service to his nation). HIB:58; LINP:150
McEntegart, B.
Totality of outlook. LINP: 175
Markel, L.
Future of the printed word. BRAP:143
Oliver, R. T.
Culture and communication. LINP:201
Our plenty is not so plentiful (outline of speech). MOA: 337, 338, 345
Plan outline of speech: Modern capitalism cannot meet needs of modern man. MOUGA:137
Roosevelt, F. D.
War address (December 8, 1941). BA 1941-42:17; BAAMP:265; BOU:99; BRAP:146; BRE:373; CAP: 200; COP:713; COPA:530; COPB:531; FIP:249; HAN: 174; HIBS:482; HURG:265; ON:179; PAR:507; PE: 790; PEA:790; VO 1941:553
Sevareid, E.
Vanishing family farm. BRAP:140
Stevenson, A. E.
"Let us work while it is yet day" (at University of California's 96th Charter Day). LINP:286
Straight, M.
Can modern capitalism meet the needs of modern man? MOUGA:141
Suggestions for preparation of persuasive speeches. BAAGA:281. With examples of. ANDS:141; BAAG:270; BARR:188; BRAP:138; MICS:173; MOUG:111; MOUGA:111; SABA:215; SOBP:209, 243
Thomas, N.
Can modern capitalism meet the needs of modern man? MOUG:138
Webster, D.
Reply to Hayne. BAAMP: 54; BIR 2:66; BRAO:185; BRE:153; BREA:137; BREW 10:112; BRYW 9:38; CAP:45; CHAL 5:171; CHEM 2:107; CLAW:117; CLAY:87, 122; CODS:348; CODSA:349; COP:270; COPA:270; COPB:270; FKA:17; FRY:24; FULB: 228; HARS:212; HARSO: 330; HAY:152; HAZO 10: 4303; HIBS:447; JOHA 1 pt. 1:248; KLEG:102; LEEW 9:177; MAS 10:4303; ONEM:211; ORAMA 2:5; PAR:179; PE:340; PEA: 340; PL:627; REEM 10:73; REEMA 15:2053; REEMB 11:74; SAA:144; SHAH:146
Webb, S.
On mousetraps. LINP:215
Wilkinsen, H. C.
How separate should government and God be? LINP: 112
Wilson, R. E.
Since King David's time. BAAG:374
Zimmerman, R.
Mingled blood. ARNS:99; LINP:197
See also Inspirational talks; Sales talks and salesman-

PERSUASIVE SPEECHES (cont.)
ship

PESSIMISM
Bliven, B.
Mid-century pessimists. NORR 3d ser:303
Petain, Henri Philippe
Address November 19, 1943. VO 1943-44:553
Address to the French people, August 12, 1941. VO 1941: 368
Broadcast April 4, 1943. VO 1943-44:154
"I need your confidence." COP:494; COPA:494; COPB:464
Petition for an armistice. HAN:128
Speech to French people, May 15, 1941. VO 1941:212
Peter, Damiani, Saint. See Damiani, Peter, Saint
Peters, Lauralee
What is totalitarianism? LINP: 69
Peterson, C. Donald
Then Hitler came. BRP 10:41; NOR 1939:34
Peterson, H. C. See Miller, C. R., jt. auth.
Peterson, Sigurd H.
Modern feudalism. TRUW:252

PETITION OF RIGHT, 1628
Eliot, J.
On the Petition of Right. ADR 1:13; BRYW 5:358; BRTH:21; BRTHA:21; BRYW 3:39; CHAL 2:23; GOOD:3; HAZO 4:1444; LEEW 6:37; MAS 4:1444; PL:362
LaFollette, R. M.
Petition to the U.S. Senate as candidate for President on the Progressive ticket, 1924. WHIP:305
Petition for charter. BEB:36
Petitions to a city council: a. For opening a street; b. Remonstrating against a nuisance; c. Against a policeman. HILL:421
Petitions to the State Legislature: a. Petition from farmers for the extermination of the Canada thistle; b. Petition from farmers relative to stock running at large; c. Petition to the Governor asking for pardon. HILL:421

PETROLEUM
Sanchez, J.
Our daily oil. BRAP:102
Pettee, Harold F., Jr.
Constitutional guarantees to all American citizens. YR 2:89

PETTINGER, SAMUEL B.
Haake, A. P.
Introduces Samuel B. Pettinger. PR:88
Pettit, George A.
Alma mater and the present. WERN 54:129
Petty, Ben
Taking care of your roads (outline). MO:398; MOA: 398
Petty, C. Wallace
Anatomy of character. EXEE: 255
Petty, J. A.
New frontiers. BOA:336
Petty, William, 1st Marquis of Lansdowne See Lansdowne, W. P. F., 1st Marquis of
Petty-Fitzmaurice, Henry Charles Keith, 5th Marquis Lansdowne. See Lansdowne, H. C. P. -F.
Peyton, Henry E.
Memorial address. SMI:204
Pfaf, Roger Alton
This diminishing world. BRP 2:67; YR 3:105
Pflum, James F.
Why I am glad I am an American. BOA:321

PHARMACY AND PHARMA-

CISTS
A druggist-speech at a service club meeting. WRA:240
Druggists (by an up-to-date pharmacist). ED:246
McGovern, S.
Introducing a druggist. BRC:202
See also American Pharmaceutical Society
Phelan, James D.
Goethe-Schiller memorial address. WAGN:356
Verdi memorial exercises address. WAGN:351
Phelps, Edward John
Farewell to England: to his friends in a foreign country. CHAL 10:186; HAZO 20:8407; MAS 20:8407; ONEM:681; ONES:25; REEM 3:55; REEMA 3:887; REEMB 3:56
Supreme Court and popular sovereignty (at centennial anniversary of organization of Supreme Court of the United States). REEMA 9:955
Phelps, Franklin
Emcee at an athletic banquet
" at a bachelors' club anniversary. BRH:315, 309
Introducing an animal trainer
" a harpist. BRH:62, 77
Phelps, William Lyon
Acceptance of American Education award. BA 1939-40:364
Art of living. BART 4:23
Commencement address. LINM:325
Literature as a revelation of life. KLEB:225
Owning books. COP:704; COPB:731; HURG:225
Presents André Chevrillon.
" Sir William Llewellyn. LY:63, 245

PHELPS, WILLIAM LYON
Graham, B.
Presenting the American Education award to W. L. Phelps. BA 1939-40:364
Phelps, William Walter
On sound currency. CHAL 13:276; HAZO 24:10257; MAS 24:10257

PHI BETA KAPPA
Shepardson, F.W.
Farewell to members at Sesquicentennial of Phi Beta Kappa. BRAC:275
Tolman, H.C.
Message of the key. NORR 2d ser:384
See also Greek letter societies.

PHILADELPHIA
Blankenburg, R.
Philadelphia. REEM 1:133; REEMB 1:130

PHILANTHROPY See Charities

PHILLIPPIDES.
Hypereides.
Against Philippides. MINA 2:410

PHILIPPINE ISLANDS
Baradi, M.
That America may know. BRP 2:49
Bashford, J.W.
Crisis. FUL:20
Philippines. FUL:18
Beveridge, A.J.
Philippine question. BAAMP:201; FUL:34; HARSO:219; SHAH:573; WERN 42:99
Bryan, W.J.
Annexation. FUL:39
Future of the Philippines. FUL:44
Dolliver, J.P.
American occupation of the Philippines. REEM 10:369; REEMA 13:919; REEMB 11:384
On Porto Rico and the Philippines. CHAL 14:374
Hoar, G.F.
Philippine question. BRIM:

PHILIPPINE ISLANDS (cont.)
339; FUL:148; LA:153; WERN 42:84
Subjugation of the Philippines iniquitous. BRYW 10:220; HICF:291; REEM 10:373; REEMA 13:194; REEMB 11:388
Kahn, J.
Civil government for the Philippine Islands. WAGN:405
Lodge, H. C.
Retain the Philippines (October 30, 1899). FUL:197, 201
Retention of the Philippines (March 7, 1900). COP:339; COPA:339; COPB:339
Long, J. D.
Our new problems. FUL:205; HAZO 24:10221; MAS 24:10221
MacArthur, D.
On the re-establishment of the Philippine government. HAN:349; VO 1945-46:92
McKinley, W.
Future of the Philippines. FUL:224, 226, 229; REEM 2:382; REEMA 2:818; REEMB 2:399
Instructions to the Philippine Commission. ANG:407
Osmena, S.
First address to his cabinet. VO 1944-45:370
On the re-establishment of the Philippine government. HAN:350; VO 1945-46:93
Quezon, M. L.
Broadcast to the Philippines. VO 1944-45:268
Reid, W.
General welfare. BLAA:209; BLAB:209; FUL:265
Roosevelt, F. D.
Address on the seventh anniversary of the government of the Commonwealth of the Philippines. VO 1942-43:670
Message to Congress on hastening Philippine independence. VO 1943-44:431
Message to the people of the Philippines. VO 1941:641
Radio address to the people of the Philippines, August 12, 1943. VO 1943-44:306
Statement on joint resolutions of Congress respecting the Philippines. VO 1944-45:284
Schurz, C.
"Americanizing" our new possessions. FUL:269, 272, 274, 277, 279, 281
Policy of imperialism. BRAS:242; CHAL 11:213; HAZO 21:9078; MAS 21:9078; REEM 10:364; REEMA 15:1834; REEMB 11:378
Smith, N.
Rushing to meet the sunrise. AN:1
Spooner, J. C.
On the government of the Philippines. REEMA 15:1913
Taft, W. H.
Philippines. RID:105
Teller, H. M.
Problem of the Philippines. BLAA:222; BLAB:222
See also United States-History-War of 1898; World War, 1939-1945-Philippine Islands
Philippus, Lucius
Against Lepidus. LEEW 2:68
Philips, J.
For a Bar Mitzah. ZEL:70
Philips, John F.
Old settler's home (at reunion of Tri-State Old Settlers Association, Keokuk, Iowa). SHUO:201
Philipson, David
Jew as a liberal force. TWJ:136
Phillips, C. Rose
On berth control. JUD:133
Phillips, Charles
Address to Catholics. BRYW 6:149

At a meeting of Roman Catholics at Cork. CHAL 5:361; HAZO 12:4832; MAS 12: 4832
Character of Napoleon. BRYW 6:157
Dinas Island speech on Washington. BREW 8:313; HAZO 12:4847; MAS 12:4847; REEMA 14:1583
Eulogium on Washington. THOU 1:164
Value of reputation. REAC: 138

Phillips, Harold C.
Religion-a prop for the weak. BA 1950-51:161

Phillips, J. S.
Our model Sabath school. THOU 2:205

Phillips, Lena Madesin
Today's challenge to women. GA:102

Phillips, Myron G.
Influence of the press on world peace. ASHF:316

Phillips, Nelson
San Jacinto address. PROS: 40
True American. SHU:83

Phillips, Wendell
Eulogy on Daniel O'Connell. BRAC:373; CLAY:129; ONEM:443; RINM:182; SHAH:359; SHU:252
Eulogy on Garrison. CHAL 8: 228; HARS:260; HAZO 16: 6959; KLEG:141; MAS 16: 6959
John Brown and the spirit of "59." BREW 8:318; FULB: 326; HAZO 16:6913; MAS 16:6913; REEM 10:182; REEMA 14:1588; REEMB 11:186
Leaps into the Abolitionist crusade. -Same as his Murder of Lovejoy
Lost arts. CHAL 8:200; HAZO 16:6931; MAS 16:6931; REEM 8:276; REEMA 6:831; REEMB 13:281
Murder of Lovejoy. BAAMP: 138; BOU:68; BRYW 8:222; CHAL 8:218; COP:281; COPA:281; COPB:281; FULB:323; HAZO 16:6949; HURG:74; JOHA 1 pt 2:102; KNAS:8; KNASA:8; MAS 16:6949; PE:371; PEA:371; PL:648; SHAH:348
On the philosophy of the Abolition movement. CHEM 3: 77; JOHA 1 pt 2:219
Plea for the Old South Church, Boston. CLAY:198
Puritan principle and John Brown. LEEW 10:179
Revolutions. SHU:188
Scholar in a Republic. BAAMP: 144; BAKF:253; BL:257; BOB:183; NORR 1st ser: 190; ONEM:795; PAR:333; SHUM:159
Toussaint L'Ouverture. BAKF: 156; CODS:291; CODSA: 291; FUL:330; PAR:311; REEM 8:291; REEMA 6: 846; REEMB 13:296; SHAH: 355
Under the flag. BRIM:230

PHILLIPS, WENDELL
Bestor, A. E.
Wendell Phillips the agitator. TRUW:117
Curtis, G. W.
Eulogy on Wendell Phillips. BREW 4:342; CHAL 10:346; HAZO 20:8699; KLEG:218; MAS 20:8699; SHU:169
Hubbard, W. R.
Wendell Phillips. COUW: 93
Long, J. D.
Eulogy on Wendell Phillips. CHAL 13:247; HAZO 24: 10216; MAS 24:10216

PHILOCLES.
Deinarchus.
Against Philocles. MINA 2: 290

PHILOSOPHY
Colden, C.

PHILOSOPHY (cont.)
Introduction to the study of phylosophy in America for the use of a young gentleman. BL:287
Conant, J.B.
National philosophy. BA 1948-49:165
Hull, W.J.
Philosophy reenthroned. YR 5:165
Overstreet, H.L.
New problems, new philosophers. HAR:391
Parker, T.
Philosophical idea of God and its relation to the scientific and religious wants of mankind now. BL:659
Porter, N.
Sciences of man versus the science of man. BL:455
Shulman, C.E.
Four philosophies of modern life. BA 1957-58:174

PHONOGRAPH
Barnes, W.H.L.
Spirit of the phonograph. WAGN:52

PHOTOGRAPHY
Amateur photographers, by an enthusiastic photographer. EDGS:196
Appealing for funds (for Camera Club). BEDA:18
Kaser, A.L.
Emcee at a camera fans' meeting. BRH:210
Organizing a Camera Club (opening speech by presiding officer). BEDA:17

PHYSICAL EDUCATION
Need of physical education. AMEO 1:47
See also Athletics; Sports

PHYSICIANS
Barker, L.F.
Wider influence of the physician. REEM 6:53; REEMB 6:19
Country doctors. AMEO 2:155
Dentists, by one of the profession. EDGS:182
Doctors (one of them tells a few secrets). ED:235
Draper, W.H.
Our medical advisers. REEM 1:412; REEMA 1:415; REEMB 1:418
Examples of introductions for doctors. BO:16-19
Farrand, L.
Work of a great physician. REEM 1:285; REEMB 6:123
Gilbert, E.J.
Introducing a dentist
" a doctor. BRC:190, 236
Holmes, O.W.
Leave no verbal message. CHAL 7:388; HAZO 15:6285; MAS 15:6285
Practical ethics of the physician. REEM 6:262; REEMA 8:677; REEMB 6:175
Huber, L.J.
Introducing a doctor. BRC:125
Kaser, A.L.
Introducing a baby specialist
" a dentist
" a doctor
" a doctor speaking on obesity
" a psychiatrist. BRC:114, 81, 143, 150, 87
Introducing an authority on diet. BRH:112
Keller, S.
Introducing a physician. BRC:68
Krantz, J.C., Jr.
On being a scientifically minded physician. MCK:169
McGovern, S.
Introducing a baby specialist-two examples. BRC:256, 260
Opening speech (at physician-of-the-year award). BED:

50; BEDA:52
Posner, G. A.
Introducing a psychiatrist. BRH:95
Presenting honorary membership card (at physician-of-the-year award). BED:52; BEDA:55
Ribicoff, A.
To tomorrow's doctors. ANGC:114
Skinner, C.O.
"Bottoms up" (toast to gynecologists). HURG:311
Smith, H.
Introducing a doctor. BRC: 161
To the physicians. CON:38
Tribute (at physician-of-the-year award). BED:50; BEDA:53
Tributes to scientists (at presentation of citation to physician). BEDA:59
Ward, S.B.
Medical profession. REEMA 3:1182
Winthrop, P.C.
Introducing a dentist. BRC: 66

PHYSIOLOGY
Haggard, H.W.
Physiology for the engineers. ON:19
Jones, H.I.
Study in self-management. EXEE:146
Rush, B.
Influence of physical causes on the moral faculty. BL: 312

PIANISTS See Music and musicians

PIANO
Piano dealer. SCHS:205
Pickell, C. Stacey
Fireside and iron bars. BRP 2:63; YR 3:73
Last line of defense. YR 2:119
Pickens, William
Kind of democracy the Negro race expects. WOON:654

PICTURES See Acceptances speeches-Pictures; Acceptance speeches-Portraits; Presentation speeches-Pictures; Presentation speeches-Portraits
Pieplow, Edwin E.
Greater increase. ACW:32
Pierce, Franklin
Inaugural address. CHI:110; LOTI:103; USIN:103; USINA:103
Pierce, Frederick
Releasing your latent power. EXEE:23
Pierson, Arthur T.
Pilgrims' Thanksgiving. THOU 2:308
Pierson, Lettie
Zazz age. YR 4:285

PIERSON, WARREN LEE
Stipp, J.E.
Introduces Warren Lee Pierson of Trans-World Airlines. PRNE:32

PILGRIM FATHERS
Adams, J.Q.
Oration at Plymouth (commemoration of the landing of the Pilgrims). BREW 1: 58; CHAL 4:273; HAZO 9: 3671; HURG:51; MAS 9: 3671; ORAMA 1:327
Bushnell, H.
Founders, great in their unconsciousness, 1849. BRAR 2:81
Choate, J.H.
America's golden age. REEMA 1:167
Depew, C.M.
Pilgrims in Holland. YE:324
Emerson, R.W.
Oration and response (250th anniversary of the landing of the Pilgrims). BRAR 2: 371
Evarts, W.M.

PILGRIM FATHERS (cont.)
Heritage of the Pilgrims, 1854. BRAR 2:235
Everett, E.
Achievements of the Pilgrims. CODS:482; CODSA: 482
Hale, E.E.
Ruling sentiment of the Pilgrims. THOU 1:334
Hall, J.P.
Discourse, 1847. BRAR 2: 1
Hillard, G.S.
Past and the future, 1851. BRAR 2:135
Holmes, O.W.
Oration, 1855. BRAR 2:267
Hopkins, M.
Central principle, 1853. BRAR 2:203
Humorous Yankee speech for the anniversary of the landing of the Pilgrims. BARB: 102
Knapp, S.L.
Address, 1829. BRAR 1:141
Kossuth, L.
At Plymouth. CHAL 7:35; HAZO 14:5824; MAS 14: 5824
Landing of the Pilgrims (patriotic tribute to our Puritan fathers). EDGS:42
Prentiss, S.S.
New England address. CHAL 7:349; HAZO 15:6306; MAS 15:6306
Robinson, D.C.
Their heritage to us (Pilgrims). THOU 1:354
'Rock' of the Pilgrims. JAI:86
Seward, W.H.
Pious pilgrimage. REEM 3:197; REEMA 3:1042; REEMB 3:204
Sumner, C.
Qualities that win. KLEG: 153; KLEM:71; REEM 3: 292; REEMA 3:1115; REEMB 3:309
Webster, D.
Landing at Plymouth. BRAR 1:354; KLEG:179
Plymouth oration. BREW 10: 184; CHAL 5:293; CLAY: 143; CODS:331; CODSA: 331; HAZO 11:4444; MAS 11:4444
Whelpley, P.M.
'Memory of the just is blessed," 1822. BRAR 1:101
Willis, F.B.
Virtues of the Pilgrims. SHU:124
Winthrop, R.C.
Address, 1839. BRAR 1:211
See also Forefathers' Day; Jews in the United States; Mayflower (ship); Puritans

PILGRIMS
Choate, J.H.
Pilgrim mothers. COP:643; REEM 1:253; REEMA 1:164; REEMB 1:254

Pinchback, Pinkney Benton Stewart
Address during Presidential campaign of 1880. DUNM: 151

Pinchot, Gifford
Theodore Roosevelt. BLAB: 325

Pinckney, Charles
Plan for a Federal Constitution. HAZO 8:3315; MAS 8: 3315; ORAMA 1:305

Pinero, Arthur Wing
Drama. REEM 3:59; REEMA 3:892; REEMB 3:60

Pinkerton, Alfred S.
Growth and conditions of I.O.O.F. THOU 3:94
Spirit of Odd-Fellowship. REEM 7:327; REEMA 9:964; REEMB 7:333

PINKLEY, VIRGIL
Ewald, H.T.
Presents Virgil Pinkley. LY:127

Pinkney, William
For relief of the slaves. BRYW 8:123; CHAL 4:181;

HAZO 9:3544; LAD:85; MAS 9:3544
Missouri question. BREW 8: 332; CHEM 3:13; HARS: 193; JOHA 1 pt 2:63; LEEW 9:117; REEMA 14:1603; SOU 9:226
Pinkstaff, Kathi
We are not ashamed. SOBP: 355
Pinney, N. Earl
Super-national mind. ONES: 304

PITKIN, WALTER B.
Gibbons, F.W.
Mr. Pitkin is interviewed. SAR:37
Pitt, William, 1st Earl of Chatham, 1708-1778
Address to the throne concerning affairs in America, November 18, 1777. ADR 1: 120; BRAO:75; BREW 3: 235; BRYW 3:211; CLAY: 18; CODS:99; CODSA:99; ESEH:204; FULB:8; GOOD: 134; HAZO 5:1856; LEEW 6:136; MAS 5:1856; ONEM: 189; PE:143; PEA:143; PL:303; REEM 9:97; REEMB 10:101
Against a motion for adjourning Parliament, December 11, 1777. GOOD:139
Against quartering of British soldiers on the inhabitants of Boston (May 27, 1774). GOOD:126; HAZO 5:1950; MAS 5:1950
Against search-warrants for seamen. CLAY:261; GOOD: 79
Against the Stamp Act. -Same as his On the right to tax America
Attempt to subjugate America. -Same as his Address to the throne concerning affairs in America
Chatham's last speech. BREW 3:254; CHAL 2:295; GOOD: 141; HAZO 5:1972; MAS 5: 1972
Debate in 1741 on wages of sailors. BREW 10:72, 77; BRYW 3:193; KLEG:129
Employment of native mercenaries. HAY:17
English Constitution. BREW 3: 245; FULB:15; GOOD:108; LEEW 6:119
On a motion for an address on the marriage of the Prince of Wales. GOOD:76
On American policy, January 20, 1775. BRTH:74; BRTHA: 74; CHAL 2:278; CROC: 365; GOOD:128; HAZO 5: 1955; MAS 5:1955
On motion for an address of thanks after the battle of Dettingen. GOOD:95
On putting a stop to hostilities in America (May 30, 1777 speech). CHAL 2:289; GOOD:132; HAZO 5:1966; MAS 5:1966
On removing troops from Boston. -Same as his On American policy, January 20, 1775
On the case of John Wilkes. -Same as his English Constitution
On the right to tax America. ADR 1:98; BOU:29; BRYW 3:197; CHAL 2:265; COP: 155; COPA:155; COPB:155; FULB:5; GOOD:103; HAZO 5:1902; HIB:118; MAS 5: 1902; ORBR 1:213; PAUF 1:57; PE:118; PEA:118; REEMA 12:563; SAA:13
On the Spanish Convention, March 8, 1739. GOOD:77
On the state of the nation (January 22, 1770). GOOD: 114; HAZO 5:1915; MAS 5: 1915
On the war in America. -Same as his Address to the throne concerning affairs in America, November 18, 1777
Reform of the franchise.

Pitt, William, 1st Earl of Chatham, 1708-1778 (cont.) EMS 2:111
Reply when attacked by Horatio Walpole, March 6, 1741. BEA:109; CHAL 2:263; GOOD:81; HAZO 5:1870; MAS 5:1870; PAUF 1:43
Second speech on Sir Robert Walpole, March 23, 1742. GOOD:89; HAZO 5:1891; MAS 5:1891
Speech in relation to the seizure of the Falkland Islands by Spain. GOOD:118; HAZO 5:1927; MAS 5:1927
Speech in support of Lord Limerick's second motion. PAUF 1:52
Speech on Sir Robert Walpole, March 9, 1742. GOOD:82; HAZO 5:1873; MAS 5:1873
Speech on Sir W. Yonge's motion respecting the Hanoverian troops. GOOD:93; PAUF 1:53
Taxation of colonies, December 17, 1765 speech. EMS 2:215
Would stop the war with the Colonies. -Same as his Address to the throne concerning affairs in America, November 18, 1777

Pitt, William, 1759-1806
Advises against accepting Bonaparte's overtures for peace. -Same as his On the refusal to negotiate with France
Against French Republicanism. BREW 8:339; BRTH:140; BRTHA:140; HAZO 8:3361; MAS 8:3361
Indicts the slave trade and foresees a liberated Africa. FULB:53; GOOD:579; HAY:80; HAZO 8:3369; MAS 8:3369; PAUF 1:125; PE:220; PEA:220; REEMA 14:1613
Misery of the American war. BRYW 4:3; CODS:462; CODSA:462
On an attempt to force his resignation. BRYW 4:5
On the deliverance of Europe, 1799. -Same as his Against French Republicanism.
On the refusal to negotiate with France, February 3, 1800. ADR 2:19; BRYW 4:7; CHAL 4:46; COP:169; COPA:169; COPB:169; GOOD:604; HAZO 8:3375; MAS 8:3375; ORBR 2:3; PE:282; PEA:282; PL:426; REEM 9:149; REEMB 10:156
On the rupture of negotiations with France. GOOD:595; LEEW 6:279
Position of a Ministry not supported by the House of Commons. EMS 1:59
Reform of the franchise, May 7, 1782 speech. EMS 2:125
Reform of the franchise, May 7, 1783 speech. EMS 2:129
Replies to a toast. HIBS:495; PE:318; PEA:318
Roman Catholic emancipation. BEA:345; PAUF 1:155

Pittenger, William A.
Patriots of peace. BRP 1:75

PITTSBURGH
Pepper, G.W.
Greatest enterprise of Pittsburgh. LINM:483

Pius XII (Eugenio Pacelli-Pope)
Address in St. Peter's Square, Vatican City, urging a charitable peace. VO 1945-46:123
Address to the College of Cardinals. VO 1945-46:249
Appeal for peace. COP:525; COPA:525; COPB:503; VO 1941:167
Christmas broadcast, December 24, 1944. VO 1944-45:625
Christmas eve broadcast to the world, 1943. VO 1943-44:585
Christmas message to the

world, 1942. VO 1942-43: 730
Easter message, 1941. -Same as his Appeal for peace
Plea for Rome. VO 1944-45: 132
Radio broadcast on war's end. VO 1945-46:202
To the College of Cardinals pleading for the safety of Rome and for peace. VO 1944-45:248

PLAGIARISM
Clemens, S. L.
Unconscious plagiarism. REEM 1:300; REEMA 1: 221; REEMB 1:301

PLANETS See Life on other planets

PLANNED ECONOMY See Price regulation; United States-Economic policy

PLAQUES See Acceptance speeches-Plaques; Presentation speeches-Plaques

PLATE
Thanksgiving silverware. LEHS:9
Platt, Horace G.
California. WAGN:212
John Marshall. WAGN:190
Speech at banquet to Chauncey Depew. WAGN:216

PLAY See Recreation
Playfair, Lord Lyon
Evolution of university extension. CHAL 9:413; HAZO 19:8045; MAS 19:8045

PLAYING CARDS See Cards
Pleasants, Aaron White
Reign of technicality. SHUC: 398

PLEDGES See Oaths
Plenty Coups, Crow chief
Farewell address. JON:122

Pliny the Younger
Panegyric on Trajan. CHAL 1: 360; HAZO 3:1106; LEEW 2:269; MAS 3:1106; PL: 140

PLUMBERS AND PLUMBING
Branen, J.
Emcee at a plumbers' convention. BRH:179
Hintz, A.
Introducing a plumber. BRC:154
Outline for a speech 'Do you avoid drips?" BARR:78
Plume, Charles Eagle
Indian's road to God. BART 4:159
Plummer, John M.
America's medieval empire. BRP 2:30; YR 3:65
Plunket, William Conyngham Plunket, 1st Baron
Denunciation of the Union with England. CHAL 4:178; HAZO 9:3541; MAS 9:3541
Incompetence of Irish Parliament to pass the Union. KET:285
On Catholic relief. BRYW 6: 162; PL:519
On the Irish Parliament and the Union. CHAL 4:175; HAZO 9:3538; MAS 9:3538
Prosecuting Robert Emmet. BREW 8:345; HAY:112
Plunkett, William B.
Introducing President McKinley to the Home Market Club, Boston, February 16, 1899. ONES:11; REEM 2: 382

PLYMOUTH COLONY See Forefathers' Day; Pilgrim Fathers; Pilgrims
Podgorny, Nikolai V.
Speech of October 18. RUS:36
Poe, Edgar Allan
Love for the beautiful in speech. BREW 8:350
Poetic principle. REEMA 6: 869

POE, EDGAR ALLAN
Mabie, H.W.
Poe's place in American literature (unveiling of bust of Edgar Allan Poe). REEMA 9:815

POETRY AND POETS
Bryant, W.C.
Poetry. REEMA 7:145
Eliot, S.A.
Source of song and story. REEMA 2:431
Farrar, F.W.
Poet and painter. REEMA 2:479
Hazlitt, W.
Living poets. REEMA 5:541
Holmes, O.W.
Lecture on religious poetry. CHAL 7:381; HAZO 15:6278; MAS 15:6278
Kaser, A.L.
Introducing a poet. BRC:173
Lowell, A.
Poetry and criticism. REEM 2:347; REEMB 2:360
Mottley, J.L.
Poet's corner. REEMA 2:842
Poe, E.A.
Love for the beautiful in speech. BREW 8:350
Poetic principle. REEMA 6:869
Pyre, J.F.A.
Poetry and freedom. TRUW:19
Robertson, F.W.
Highest form of expression. BREW 9:56
Rowland, D.
Influence of the poet (accepting bust of Irwin Russell). SHUO:83
See also Art and artists; Literature

Poincaré, Raymond
America supports our seizure of the Ruhr. CROC:373
Call to arms. BREW 8:353
Declaration of war by France. PL:740; REEM 11:38; REEMB 12:42
"Divine moment" of victory. BREW 8:356
Eulogy on services of Marshall Foch to his country and the Allies. BEA:353
France and world-empire. BREW 8:360
Inaugural speech (Peace Conference, Jan. 18, 1919). REEM 11:306; REEMB 12:323
Rouget de L'Isle and the Marseillaise. BREW 8:355
Supreme judgment of history. BREW 8:361
Verdun-"On ne passe pas!" BREW 8:363
What justice must banish. BREW 8:363

Polek, Bernard A.
You have to see it first. MIA:331

POLAND
Bismarck, O.
Mount the guards at the Warthe and the Vistula! CROC:21
Churchill, W.L.S.
Broadcast to the Polish people, May 3, 1941. VO 1941:190
Lamartine, A.M.L.
To a deputation of Poles, 1848. BRYW 7:187; CHAL 5:425; HAZO 12:4936; MAS 12:4936; PL:331
Mikolajczyk, S.
Broadcast to Poland. VO 1944-45:19
Nelson, S.P.
"Knight among the nations." COUW:241
Paderewski, I.J.
New Poland. REEM 7:313; REEMB 8:333
See also Berlin Conference, 1945; World War 1939-1945-Poland

POLAND-FOREIGN RELATIONS-

CZECHOSLOVAKIA
Fierlinger, Z.
Broadcast on Czech-Polish discussions in Moscow. VO 1945-46:373

---- ---- RUSSIA
Churchill, W. L. S.
Speech in Commons on the Soviet Polish frontier. VO 1944-45:611
Vyshinski, A. Y.
Statement on Soviet-Polish relations. VO 1943-44:195

---- ---- UNITED STATES
Stettinius, E. R., Jr.
Statement on Poland. VO 1944-45:618

POLAR REGIONS See Arctic Regions; North Pole

POLICE
Huber, L. J.
Introducing a policeman. BRC:305
Kaser, A. L.
Introducing a traffic officer. BRC:120
Keller, S.
Introducing a detective or policeman. BRC:104
Policemen (appropriate for occasions honoring the police force); EDGS:108
Steele, S.
Emcee at a policemens' ball. BRH:261
Winthrop, P. C.
Introducing a highway patrolman. BRC:105
See also International police (proposed); Secret service; Third degree
Poliomyelitis See Medicine

POLITICAL CONVENTIONS
Butler, N. M.
Events are temporal, principles eternal. SHU:74
Nominating candidate for political office at a convention. WRA:103
See also Acceptance speeches-Nominations; Candidates; Congresses and conventions; Democratic Party; Republican Party. Also subheads under this subject

---- DEMOCRATIC
Barkley, A. W.
People's crusade. BA 1952-53: 55
Bowers, C. S.
Keynote speech of Democratic convention. HICF: 781; ONEC:507
Bryan, W. J.
Cross of gold. BAAMP: 193; BIR 3:214; BOU:171; BRAS:182; BREW 2:294; BRIM:314; CAP:119; CHAL 14:415; COP:333; COPA: 333; COPB:333; CORP: 284; CROC:37; FO:225; FRY:45; HARS:169; HAZO 22:10935; HIB:155; HIBS: 461; HICF:179; HURG:147; MAS 25:10935; PAR:492; PE:637; PEA:637; PO: 103; REEM 10:326; REEMB 11:340; RID:75; SHAH:551; WERN 42:44
Opposing Parker for the temporary chairman, 1912. CORP:287
Cummings, H. S.
Keynote 1920 Democratic convention. ONEM:390
Roosevelt, E. A.
Address at Democratic National Convention, 1940. BUTA:211
Before the Democratic National Convention. BA 1956-57:109
Russell, W. E.
Address at the Democratic National Convention. BAKF: 398
Voorhees, D. W.
Speech in the Tilden convention. BREW 10:56; REEMA 15:2021

POLITICAL CONVENTIONS-REPUBLICAN
Cary, A. J.
Address to the Republican National Convention. HILK: 149
Curtis, G.W.
His sovereignty under his hat (1884). BREW 4:341; HAZO 20:8649; MAS 20: 8649; REEMA 12:780
Eastvold, D.
For seating Eisenhower delegates. BA 1952-53:49
Lodge, H. C.
At Republican convention, June 21, 1900. CHAL 14: 200; HAZO 25:10709; MAS 25:10709
Luce, C. B.
Address to the Republican National Convention. BUTA: 231
Roosevelt, T.
Armageddon speech. FRY: 58; SHAH:613

POLITICAL CORRUPTION See Corruption (in politics)

POLITICAL PARTIES
Dewey, T. E.
Party conflict and the modern dilemma. BA 1949-50: 110
Emerson, R.W.
Conservative. HAZO 14: 5973; MAS 14:5973; REEMA 4:377
See also Names of parties e. g. Democratic Party; Know Nothing Party; Progressive Party; Republican Party

POLITICAL SCIENCE
Alexander, R.
Religion as a force in government. BART 1:173
Baez, A. M.
Constitutional government. LEIO:126
Bancroft, G.
People in art, government, and religion. BL:94; BRYW 8:230; HAZO 13: 5630; LAD:96; MAS 13: 5630; REEM sup 1:88; REEMA 7:69; REEMB 7:55; WPRA:65
Business man's political obligations--response to a toast. DAVC:408
Cousin, V.
True politics. BREW 4:198; HAZO 12:5018; MAS 12: 5018
Dean of political writers. SCHS:97
Dix, J. A.
Christianity and politics. BREW 5:261
Donnelly, I.
Purpose of government. LA: 171
Ewert, W. F.
Individualism. COUW:63
Gokhale, G. K.
Students and politics. ZU: 12
Gormley, A. C.
Quo warranto? TRUW:1
Greiner, F. H., Jr.
Call to politics. BRP 9:72; NOR 1938:3
Humphrey, G. N.
Businessmen must be active in politics. SABA:223
Kennedy, J. F.
Intellectual and the politician. BA 1956-57:165; BARR:285; LINP:279
Religion in government (to Greater Houston Ministerial Association). HIB:178
LaFollette, R. M.
Which shall rule, manhood or money? COP:343; COPA:343; COPB:343; HURG:158; REEM 7:217; REEMA 13:1281; REEMB 7:252
Luther, Mrs. L.
Political implications of Mother Goose. BUT:182; BUTB:182

Owen, R. B.
Modern politics. DOA:133
Read, O.
Human nature and politics. EXEE:244
Root, E.
Business and politics. REEM 3:164; REEMB 3:167; WPRC:44
Invisible government: Short Ballot Amendment. BIR:4:12; HICF:444; ONEM:306
Roosevelt, F. D.
Philosophy of government. PO:163
Savanarola, G.
Sea of politics. CODS:57; CODSA:57
Schurz, C.
Public offices as private perquisites. BREW 9:154
Smith, A. E.
Religion and politics. COP:408; COPA:408; COPB:408; HICF:837; HURG:209
Tietgen, K. C.
Call to politics. YR 4:79
Wallace, H. A.
Statesmanship and religion. KLEB:153
White, A. D.
Evolution vs. revolution in politics. NORR 1st ser:233
Willkie, W. L.
Loyal opposition. COP:553; COPB:545; HURG:243
Wood, R.
Feet of clay. BRP 4:96
See also United States-Politics and government

POLITICS See also Campaign speeches, Candidates; Civil service; Corruption (in politics;) Political science; Politics, practical. Also Names of countries with subdivision Politics and government e. g. Great Britain-Politics and Government

---- PRACTICAL
Address of congratulation at the opening of a new political club. HAPR:125
Address on practical politics. BED:93; BEDA:131, 166
Bones: short and over can mean short of publicity and overlooking a patron (a speech to bank personnel, changeable for many occasions-business meeting or convention of sales personnel, at a graduation of nurses' group, for fund raising drives, to a telephone group, or by a political or labor speaker). BAI:94
Burnett, A. G.
Young men in politics. WAGN:256
Closing speech (at political rally urging citizens to vote). BED:95; BEDA:132, 167
Gilbert, E.J.
Introducing a politician. BRC:210
Livingston, H.
Fool's gold. BOA:354; YR 6:213
Opening speech at political meeting. BEDA:130
Opening speech (urging labor union members to take active interest in politics). BED:93; BEDA:165
Political stew. NATT:13
Posner, E. J.
Introducing a politician-two examples of. BRC:65, 242
Rotation in politics (for any business gathering). ED:93
Shepard, J.
Anvil chorus. YR 8:81
Speech after a political defeat (selected). PITT:99
Speech after a political victory (selected). PITT:99
Speech in a political canvass. PITT:97
To a meeting of young men interested in local politics. HAPR:104

POLITICS, PRACTICAL (cont.)
Young men in politics (advice to a group of young men). ED:103
Polk, James K.
First annual message. BIR 2:146
Inaugural address. CHI:94; LOTI:89; USIN:89; USINA:89
Pollard, William G.
Science as community. IOCP:49
Pollock, Channing
I am a reactionary. BART 1:239
Wake up, America! BART 2:27
What can we do for democracy? BART 4:219
Pollock, Earl
Great American myth. NOR 1948:127
Polyansky, Dmitri S.
Speech of October 23. RUS:62
Pomerene, Atlee
Ohio. REEM 3:64; REEMB 3:65
Pond, James Burton
Memories of the Lyceum. REEM 8:313; REEMA 6:893; REEMB 13:318
Ponomarev, Boris N.
Speech of October 24. RUS:83
Pontiac, Ottawa chief
Accuses Canadians as traitors to his cause. JON:44
Pool, Floyd
Restriction of immigration. COUW:219
Poole, Roy
Earth is the Lord's. AN:5

POOR See Poverty
Poore, B. P.
Capital and labor. THOU 1:427
Pope, A. B.
True thanksgiving. THOU 2:297

POPE, ALEXANDER
Lowell, J. R.
Pope and his times. BREW 7:392
Popović, Vladimir
Inaugural speech at Conference on the Problems of Economic Development. UAR:101
Speech at final session of Conference on the Problems of Economic Development. UAR:399

POPULATION
Crary, D. R.
Plague of people. LINP:211
Elder, A. L.
Chemist looks at the world population explosion. BA 1960-61:165
Fuller, F. L.
Our racial myopia. YR 2:55
Porter, Alex J., Jr.
Southern chivalry enemy number one. JUD:153

PORTER, HENRY L.
Moran, E. B.
Introduces Henry L. Porter. PR:99
Porter, Horace
Abraham Lincoln. REEMA 3:931
Assimilated Dutchman. REEMA 3:939
Citizen soldier. REEMA 3:924
Eulogy on Ulysses S. Grant. REEM 3:98; REEMA 3:944; REEMB 3:99; SHU:81; SHUM:259
France and the United States. REEM 3:104; REEMB 3:105
Friendliness of the French. REEM 3:89; REEMA 3:919; REEMB 3:90
How to avoid the subject. REEMA 3:904
In commemoration of William Tecumseh Sherman. CHAL 13:104; HAZO 23:10040; MAS 23:10040
Many sided Puritan. REEMA

3:928
Men of many inventions. CHAL 13:96; HAZO 23:10032; MAS 23:10032; REEM 3:72; REEMA 3:897; REEMB 3:73
"Our guests." CHAL 13:87; HAZO 23:10023; MAS 23:10023
Reverence for the flag. BLAA:92; BLAB:92
Sires and sons. REEM 3:94; REEMA 3:935; REEMB 3:95
Soldier's last salute. -Same as his Eulogy on Ulysses S. Grant
Trip abroad with Depew. REEM 3:79; REEMA 3:908; REEMB 3:80
Woman. ANDS:208; COP:651; COPB:678; KLEM:100; ONEM:653; REEM 3:84; REEMA 3:913; REEMB 3:85
Porter, Noah
Sciences of nature versus the science of man. BL:455
Teachings of science and religion. REEMA 3:950

PORTRAITS See Acceptance speeches-Portraits; Presentation speeches-Portraits

PORTUGAL
Canning, G.
On the policy of granting aid to Portugal. ADR 3:13; BRYW 4:115; CHAL 4:368; GOOD:875; HAZO 9:3837; LEEW 7:75; MAS 9:3837; ORBR 2:57; PL:447
Posey, Myrtle
America's contribution of constitutional government. LEIO:85
Posey, Walter B.
Protestant Episcopal Church: an American adaptation. TIN:377
Posner, George A.
Emcee at a baby shower
" at a bachelor dinner
Emcee at a birthday party
" at a bridal shower
" at a Christmas party
" at a father's day party
" at a housewarming
" at a ladies' day meeting (at the lodge, athletic club, social club or other meetings)
" at an office party or ceremony honoring a member leaving for army service
" at a retirement party (after thirty years of service in an office)
" at a surprise party. BRH: See Table of contents, section III for paging
Introducing a bathing beauty contest. BRH:187
Introducing an animal trainer or an animal act
" a children's act or a child entertainer
" a judge (or member of legal profession)
" a magician
" a musical act
" a psychiatrist BRH: See Table of contents, section II for paging
Introducting an artist
" a farmer
" a Hollywood actor
" a minister
" a politician-two examples of
" a professor. BRC:240, 296, 212, 248, 242, 84
Introductory remarks of an emcee to open a show. BRH:326
Pospelov, Petr N.
Speech of October 26, RUS:110
Post, Langdon
Taft-Ellender-Wagner Housing Bill. MO:460

POST WAR PLANNING See Reconstruction-World war 1939-1951; World war 1939-

POST WAR PLANNING (cont.)
1945-Peace and mediation

POSTAL SERVICE
Kaser, A. L.
Emcee at a letter carriers' club meeting. BRH:307
Postmaster, by a rural office holder. EDGS:116
Postle, Arthur S.
Introducing J.H. Ayres. MO:496

POSTS (VETERANS) See American Legion; Servicemen's posts
Potemkine, Vladimir
Efforts of conciliation, November 2, 1935 (on Ethiopian situation). KESK 2:83

POTSDAM CONFERENCE See Berlin Conference, 1945
Potter, Henry Codman
Church. REEMA 3:955
Eulogy on Phillips Brooks. CHAL 13:1; HAZO 23:9811; MAS 23:9811
Learn during Lent to say "No." THOU 2:86
Washington and American aristocracy (100th anniversary of Washington's first inauguration). BREW 8:365
Pound, Roscoe
Frame of mind. LINM:109
Renaissance of Masonry. THOU 3:41
Task of the American lawyer. BRYA:336; REEM sup 2:287; REEMB 6:308

POVERTY
George, H.
Crime of poverty. WPRA:244
Handicap of poverty and the value of thrift and cash in hand. AMEO 2:96
Parker, T.
Children of the poor. ESEH:189
Poverty and crime. AMEO 2:38
Povish, Kenneth
Peacemakers. DO:108
Powderly, Terence V.
Labor's greatest curse. WERN 42:187
New slavery. BOB:58
Powell, Adam Clayton, Jr.
For the Federal Fair Trade Employment Practices Act. BA 1949-50:154
Powell, John, Jr.
War of righteousness. ONES:378
Powell, Lawrence C.
Value of reading. ANGC:26

PRAISE
Give just credit. NATT:8
Old soft soap. NATM:46

PRAISE, SPEECHES OF See EULOGIES: TRIBUTES
Prasad, Rajindra
Independence day message. ZU:26
Prather, William L.
National unity and the state university. BLAA:214; BLAB:214
Pratt, Allan
Rivers of crime. YR 9:259
Pratt, Sir Charles See Camden, C. P., 1st Earl of

PRATT, E.J.
Lowe, J. A.
Presents E. J. Pratt. LY:58
Pratt, Paul A.
Introduces Frederick C. Crawford. PR:35
Pratt, Ruth
Seconding the nomination of President Hoover. GA:202

PRAYERS
Augustine, Saint.
On our Lord's prayer. BREW 1:187; BRYW 7:7; CHAL 1:368; HAZO 3:1187; MAS 3:1187; PL:180; REEM 9:51; REEMB 10:53

Benediction (at induction of a Judge). BEDA:122
Benediction (at memorial services honoring deceased union member). BED:99; BEDA:177
Can prayer save our nation? JA:175
Chaplain's prayer on Decoration Day. HILL:473
Closing benediction (at memorial services honoring deceased union member). BED:101; BEDA:179
Closing speech and benediction at a convention. BEDA:143
Closing speech and prayer (at cornerstone dedication of youth center). BED:42; BEDA:83, 84
Closing speech and prayer (at physician-of-the-year award). BED:54; BEDA:57
Consecration prayer (at dedication of home for aged). BED:35; BEDA:76
Dedication prayer and proclamation (at cornerstone dedication of youth center). BED:40; BEDA:82
Fénelon, F. de S. de la Mothe.
Sermon on prayer. LEEW 4:267
Four speeches of welcome to visitors in midweek prayer service. HNWS:25-26
Francis de Sales.
Divine love in prayer. PL:280
George VI.
Empire called to prayer. HAN:266
Knox, J.
Prayer. ORBR 1:29
McCracken, R.J.
When you pray, "Thy Kingdom come," what do you mean? BA 1955-56:167
Newman, J.H.
Communion with God. CHAL 6:446; HAZO 14:5682; MAS 14:5682
Prayer (at memorial service). BED:43; BEDA:84
Prayer (at Veterans Day observance). BED:47; BEDA:93
Prayer (for Bill of Rights Day program). BEDA:172
Roosevelt, F.D.
Invasion prayer to nation. BA 1943-44:46; HAN:265; VO 1944-45:261
Silverman, J.
Opening prayer at 250th anniversary of the settlement of the Jews in the United States. TWJ:5
Wycliffe, J.
Sermon on prayer. LEEW 4:35; PL:217

PREDESTINATION
Wesley, J.
Denounces the doctrine of predestination. PE:108; PEA:108

PREJUDICE See Discrimination
Preminger, Otto See Murrow, E.R., jt. auth.
Prentice, Russell
Three jewels. BRP 9:7
Prentice, William Kelley
Hellenic standards for the modern world. NORR 2d ser:296
Prentis, Henning Webb, Jr.
Competitive enterprise versus planned economy. BA 1944-45:217
Preserving the roots of liberty. BA 1941-42:201
Prentiss, Seargent Smith
Defalcations of the government. REEMA 14:1646
Lafayette. BRYW 8:218; KLEG:251; LAD:92; REEMA 9:971
Law of self-defense. LA:141
New England address. CHAL 7:349; HAZO 15:6306; MAS 15:6306
On New England's Forefathers' Day. BREW 8:372
To returned volunteers of the

Prentiss, Seargent Smith (cont.)
Mexican War (welcome home). LEEW 10:59
Wilkinson trial. SOU 9:390

PREPAREDNESS, MILITARY
See Names of countries or hemispheres with subdivision Defenses, e.g. United States-Defenses; Western hemisphere-Defenses
Prescott, Robert William
"Mercy that condemns." SHUC:392

PRESENT
Speech on the present. THOS: 90

PRESENTATION SPEECHES
Praise for the recipient-various models of. BEC:16
Preparation of a presentation speech. CORP:271
Presentation for an absent party. MORA:33
Suggestions for preparation of presentation speeches. BUT 99,101; LARW:109; MO: 527; PITT:57. With examples of. GA:34; YE:113
Suggestions for preparation of speeches of presentation. BARR:231; BRAB:496; MOUG:150; REAB:150 With examples of. HIBS: 278; SABA:282

---- ALTAR CLOTHS
Presentation of an altar cloth to church or lodge. EDGS: 375

---- AWARDS See Presentation speeches-Rewards (prizes)

---- BADGES
Presentation of a badge or jewel. THOS:108
Watts, F. O.
Presenting a badge. ONEM: 47

---- BOOKS
Bryan, W. J.
Presentation of Gray's Elegy. BRAC:258
Presentation of a book. WERN 54:75
Presentation of Bible to an initiate. MORA:34
Presenting a book to a teacher. HILL:465
Presenting a dictionary. BEB: 10; BEC:21
Spieker, E. H.
Presenting a book to Professor Basil L. Gildersleeve. ONES:44
Upon presenting a set of Dickens' novels to the best scholar of the school. HAPR:41

---- BUSTS
Morris, G. M.
Presenting the bust of Brandeis. ON:326

---- CANES
Presentation of a cane. WERN 54:75

---- CHAIRS
Baldwin, R.E.
Presenting a chair to a president of a normal college. WERN 54:72
Presentation address to a foreman by a workman. DAVC: 522

---- CHARTERS
Opening speech by temporary chairman (at charter presentation to labor union). BED:73
Presenting a charter. BEB:7; BEC:20
Presenting charter. BED:11; BEDA:15
Presenting charter (at labor union ceremony). BED:73

---- CITATIONS
Presenting a citation. BEB:7

Presenting the citation (at Camera Club meeting). BEDA:19
Presenting the citation (at testimonial to philanthropist). BED:24; BEDA:46
Stevenson, A.E.
World brotherhood in a space age. BA 1957-58:59
Tributes at a testimonial to a woman civic leader. BEDA:42
Tributes to scientist (at presentation of citation to a physician). BEDA:59

---- CLOTHING
Presentation of clothing to a (Masonic) brother who has been given office in Grand (or Provincial or District Grand) Lodge or has had London Grand Rank conferred upon him. EDW:67

---- CUPS
Choate, J.H.
Presenting a loving cup to George T. Wilson. REEM 3:412
Depew, C.M.
Presenting a loving cup to Admiral Dewey. ONES:42
Grimke, A.H.
On the occasion of the presentation of a loving cup to Hon. Joseph Benson Foraker, United States Senator. DUNM:337
Presenting gold cup (to retiring public official at testimonial dinner). BED:28; BEDA:48
See also Acceptance speeches-Cups; Presentation speeches-Rewards (prizes)

---- DEED TO A HOUSE
Speech in presenting the deed to a house. WERN 54:73

---- DEGREES, ACADEMIC
Collier, W.M.
Presenting Doctor of Laws degree to Sir Auckland Campbell Geddes. REEM 6:205; REEMB 7:176

---- DIPLOMAS
Address of superintendent of schools (granting diplomas). AMEO 1:11
Diploma presentation. FRIE:202
Diploma presentation. NATS:11
Presentation of diplomas: By a principal; Another in three parts: Address of principal, Address of president of Board of Education, Response of class president. PAIC:220-8

---- DONATIONS
Address to a minister of the gospel on presenting a donation. BARB:202

---- EMBLEMS
Presentation of an emblem to a retiring officer of the lodge. EDGS:371
Presentation of an emblem to a retiring officer of the lodge. HE:118

---- FLAGS
Couch, D.N.
Return of the flags. Presenting battle flags to the state. ONEM:708
Hill, B.H.
Stars and stripes. SOU 9:354
On presentation of flag to military organization. HAPR:11
On presenting a flag to a military company. BARB:11
On presenting a stand of colors to a regiment. BARB:13
Presentation of a banner to a temperance association. BARB:28
Presentation of flag. SOES:37

PRESENTATION SPEECHES-
FLAGS (cont.)
Presentation of a flag by a lady. HILL:464
Presentation of a flag to a lodge or patriotic organization. EDGS:373
Presentation of a flag to a military company by a patriotic citizen. EDGS:53
Presentation of a flag to a regiment departing for war. DAVC:520
Presentation of a flag to a school. WERN 54:75
Presentation of a flag to Boy Scouts. EDGS:246
Wallace, L.
Return of the flag (presenting battle flags to the state). ONEM:702; REEM 7:409; REEMA 9:1121; REEMB 8:424

---- FLOWERS
Presentation of a bouquet of yellow roses to a bride of fifty years ago. EDGS:282

---- GATEWAYS
Fisher, H. J.
Presenting the Cheney-Ives gateway to Yale University. KNAS:160; KNASA:160; ONEM:710; ONES:41

---- GAVELS
Bates, H.
Presenting gavel to George Meany, President of AFL-CIO. BA 1955-56:79
Condon, R. J.
Presentation of a gavel. BRAC:260
Huston, H. L.
Presents gavel to a retiring president. PR:110
Presenting a gavel. BEB:8; BEC:22
Presenting gavel (at induction of a judge). BEDA:118
Woodruff, C.
Presentation of a gavel. HOA:383

---- GIFTS
Gift presentation-examples of (in appreciation for good work as club officer). MORA:31-33
Gilbert, E. J.
Emcee at a testimonial for a long-term employee. BRH:191
Huber, L. J.
Emcee at a bridal shower. BRH:212
Emcee at a Christmas party for employees. BRH:275
Keyes, F. P.
Presenting a gift. GA:37
Posner, G. A.
Emcee at a retirement party (after thirty years service in an office.) BRH:200
Presentation by boys to teacher about to go abroad. HAPR:30
Presentation by player to the manager of a baseball club. HAPR:66
Presentation of gift to a departing clergyman by one of the congregation. EDGS:240
Presentation of a gift to a retiring official by an officer of the company. EDGS:128
Presentation of a gift to a retiring public official. EDGS:79
Presentation of a gift to principal of high school by a pupil. EDGS:219
Presentation of a gift to teacher of girls school by a pupil. EDGS:220
Presentation oration. AMEO 1:122
Presentation oration (humorous). DAVC:248
Presentation of a gift to a retiring officer of a company. DR:23; LU:1128

Presentation of a symbol of esteem. BEB:10
Presenting a gift. FRIT:44
Presenting a gift-three model speeches. BEB:9
Presenting a gift for successfully raising money. SOES: 18
Presenting a gift in appreciation of twenty-five years of service. BEB:9
Presenting a gift to a club leader. SOES:18
Presenting a gift to a fellow employee getting married. WRA:88
Presenting a gift to a member of a Conference Board. SOES:19
Presenting a gift to a retiring mailman. SOES:17
Procedure for presentation of gifts. CARP:10
Speeches on presenting a gift. STOC:151
Speeches on presenting a gift-seven examples of. STON: 157-160
Suggestions for preparation of speeches for presenting a gift BUT:98; BUTA:98, BUTB:98; MOUGA:150; RE:161; WRB:194 With examples of. GLAD:171; SOES:16; WRA:84
Suggestions for presenting a gift, an award, or a memorial. BRA:609; BRY:371; BRYA:403
Tendering the gift-various models of. BEC:18
Tribute (to retiring secretary of labor union). BED:80; BEDA:154
See also subheads under this subject by type of gift, e.g. Pins; Souvenirs; Token of Esteem

---- GOLDEN CHAIN LINKS
Golden chain link presentation address. AMEO 1:109

---- JEWELS
Presentation of a jewel for any Masonic occasion. THOS: 106

---- JUDICIAL ROBES
Presenting judicial robe (at induction of a judge). BEDA: 118
Two speeches presenting jewels to retiring officers. THOS:108,109

---- KEYS
Baker, G. F.
Presenting the keys of the George F. Baker Foundation to President Lowell. ONEC:50
Presentation of a key to a distinguished guest by a city official. EDGS:89
Presentation of the keys of a new school building by the architect. DAVC:543
Presenting key (at dedication of home for aged). BED:34; BEDA:75

---- LETTERS OF CREDENCE
Escobar, D. A. C.
Speech upon presentation of letters of credence as Ambassador of Argentina to the United States. VO 1944-45:91

---- MEDALS
Boyd, W. R., Jr.
Presentation of API gold medal to Charles F. Kettering. SAB:209; SABA:289
Finley, J. H.
Presenting a medal to Col. Lindbergh. ONEC:38
Jones, T. R.
Presentation of Gantt gold medal to Fowler McCormick. YE:114
Medallion presentation at fifth anniversary of founding of Big Brother Athletic Association. BEDA:112

PRESENTATION SPEECHES-MEDALS (cont.)
Mellon, A.W.
Presenting to Mr. Thomas A. Edison the medal bestowed upon him by Congress. ONEC:35
Presentation to the victor of an Inter-Academic baseball club. HAPR:34
Presenting a medal. BEB:10; BEC:23
Presenting a medal to outstanding citizen at annual meeting of Chamber of Commerce. WRA:89
Tribute (to labor union official at testimonial ceremony). BED:83; BEDA:156

---- MEMBERSHIPS
Presenting honorary membership card (at physician-of-the-year award). BED:52; BEDA:55

---- MEMORIALS
Presenting a memorial to a school. AMEO 1:136
Suggestions for presenting a gift, award, or memorial. BRA:509; BRY:371
Voorhees, O. M.
Presentation of a Phi Beta Kappa memorial hall. BRAC:262

---- MONEY
Presentation to the captain of a fishing schooner for an heroic rescue. HAPR:118
Presenting check (at hospital fund drive and testimonial). BED:63; BEDA:100

---- PICTURES
Address presenting a picture of President Harding to a high school. AMEO 1:230; same 2:185
Hand, L.
Presenting a portrait of Justice Holmes to the Harvard Law School. ONEC:43
Presentation of picture to publisher by authors. HAPR:179
Presenting a picture to the school. STOC:182
Presenting a picture to the school-two examples of. STON:186

---- PINS
Corlett, B. C.
Presents a past president's pin to the retiring president, Anderson Borthwick. PRC:8
Presentation of a diamond ring or breast pin to a popular politician. BARB:24
Presentation of 25 year pin. MORA:34
Presentation to a political leader. HAPR:53
Workman to foreman who is about to resign his position. HAPR:21

---- PLAQUES
Haire, A. J.
Presents Arthur Godfrey. LY:44
Presentation speech (at hospital fund drive and testimonial). BED:62; BEDA:99
Presenting plaque (at unveiling of plaque for Labor Temple). BED:86; BEDA:159

---- PLATE
Houston, P. D.
Presents a gift of silver and a scroll of honor to retiring president of American Bankers Association, Robert M. Hanes. PR:106
Maddox, R. F.
Presenting a silver service to the retiring president of the Bankers' Association. HOA:381; HOAP:271
Moses, G. H.
Presenting a silver tray to

Vice President Dawes. CORP:270
On presenting a service of plate to a public officer. BARB:20
Presentation speech at a silver wedding. HILL:464
Presenting a silver set to the chairman of the Entertainment committee. THOU 3:327
To a public official upon his retirment from office. HAPR:47

---- PORTRAITS
Greeting and welcome (at unveiling of portrait presented to Labor Temple). BED:89; BEDA:161
Presenting a portrait. BEB:11; BEC:23
Unveiling portrait (of past president of labor union). BED:89; BEDA:162

---- POTTERY
Presentation of some chinaware. WERN 54:74

---- REWARDS (PRIZES)
Birthday tribute and presentation of award. BEDA:29
Distribution of prizes to a school by a popular teacher. EDGS:214
Examples of introductions for prize winners. BO:28-29
Ford, K. L.
Presentation of award to Charles F. Kettering. YE:121
Graham, B.
Presenting the American Education award to W. L. Phelps. BA 1939-40:364
Guizot, F. P. G.
Address at the distribution of prizes at the University of Paris. CHAL 5:401; HAZO 12:4878; MAS 12:4878
Model and outline for presentation speech (scholarship prize). BAKS:118, 128
On distributing a collection of prizes among the successful marksmen of a target company. BARB:26
On presenting a prize to the winners of a rowing match. BARB:30
Park, M. E.
Presentation of the M. Carey Thomas prize award. GA:36
Presentation of a prize to the winners of a baseball match. BARB:43
Presentation of a silver cup or other prize to the winner of a sailing match. BARB:38
Presentation of prize to champion fisherman (humorous). HAPR:170
Presentation of prizes for target shooting, by a member of the club. EDGS:60
Presenting award to journalist at testimonial dinner. BED:20; BEDA:35
Reid, L.
Engineering of ideas (presenting Honor Awards to engineers). BRAB:545
Speech at a distribution of school prizes. BARB:44
Speech when presenting a prize. HILL:466
Suggestions for presentation of awards and prizes. RE:164
Suggestions for presentation of an award for service. RE:163
Suggestions for presenting a gift, an award, or a memorial. BRA:509; BRY:371. With examples of. GLAD:171
Taylor, D.
Presents Grace George. LY:38
Tendering the award-various models of. BEC:18
Upon presenting a prize for

PRESENTATION SPEECHES-REWARDS (PRIZES)
marksmanship. HAPR:26
See also Presentation speeches -Trophies

---- RINGS
Presentation of a diamond ring or breast pin to a popular politician. BARB:24
Presentation of a ring to a friend. WERN 54:74
Speech in presenting a diamond ring. WERN 54:73

---- SCROLLS
Houston, P.D.
Presents a gift of silver and a scroll of honor to retiring president of American Bankers Association, Robert M. Hanes. PR:106
Presentation of scroll (at testimonial to a musician). BEDA:39
Presenting a scroll. BEB:11; BEC:24
Presenting scroll (at presentation of Brotherhood award). BED:56; BEDA:64

---- SHEARS
Tighe, M.F.
Presenting a pair of golden shears to Secretary Hughes. ONEC:49

---- SILVERWARE See Presentation speeches-Plate

---- SOUVENIRS
Presentation of a souvenir by the pupils of a school to the principal. BARB:36
Presentation of a souvenir to a retiring public officer. BARB:40

---- STATUES
Appleton, D.F.
Presenting the Pilgrim statue to the New England Society. KNAS:153; KNASA: 153
Felton, C.C.
Delivering the statue of Daniel Webster to the Mayor of Boston. KNAS:156; KNASA:156
Woodford, S.L.
Presenting the statue to the city. KNAS:154; KNASA: 154; ONEM:709

---- SWORDS
Long, J.D.
Presentation of sword to Admiral Dewey. FUL:209; HAZO 24:10228; MAS 24: 10228
On presenting a sword to a military officer (2 speeches). BARB:16,18
Presentation of a sword to an army officer by a friend. EDGS:56
Presentation of sword and memorial. HAPR:16

---- TABLETS
Kingsley, D.P.
In honor of Charles M. Schwab. REEM 4:243; REEMB 5:62

---- TESTIMONIALS
On presenting a testimonial to a retiring president or superintendent of a railroad. BARB:33
Schultz, E.
David L. Gaskill. MO:536
Speech accompanying a testimonial of esteem. HILL: 467

---- THEATER
Purdue, I.P.
Presenting Chi Omega theater. GA:38

---- TOKEN OF ESTEEM
Presentation of a token of remembrance by the young lady pupils of a school to a favorite teacher. BARB:34

Presentation of token of esteem by fellow employee to co-worker who is leaving to accept promotion elsewhere with the same company. WRA:87
Presentation of token of esteem to a club member on his retirement from business. WRA:86
Presenting a token to a clergyman. THOS:111
Presenting a token to a police officer. THOS:110

--- TRIPS
Presenting a trip to Europe. WERN 54:73

---- TROPHIES
Presentation of a cue to the victor in a billiard tournament. BARB:41
Presentation of a golf trophy by a member of the trophy committee. EDGS:394
Presentation of a trophy. BURS:228
Presentation of trophy to the winner of a rowing match. EDGS:401
Presentation of trophy to the winner of a sailing race. EDGS:399
Presentation of trophy to the winner of a swimming contest. EDGS:397

---- TROWELS
Presenting trowel (at cornerstone dedication of youth center). BED:42; BEDA:83

---- WATCHES
Address to a retiring officer presenting a watch. HILL:467
Krantz, J. C., Jr.
Presentation speech (watch to retiring professor). MCK:120
On presenting a gold watch to a party leader. BARB:22
Presentation of a watch to a political leader. EDGS:75
Presentation of a watch to a young man (humorous). HAPR:113
Speech accompanying presentation of a watch to a clergyman. HILL:466

PRESERVING
Fruit preservers. SCHS:207

PRESIDENTS See Educators; Executives; Inaugural addresses; Installation speeches; Nominations; Officers; Offices-Acceptance; Public officials; Presidents-United States

---- UNITED STATES
Bayard, T. F.
Plea for conciliation in 1876. BREW 1:270
Gillilan, S.
Me and the President. REEM 2:93; REEMB 2:85
Hedges, J. E.
Ohio, the Presidency and Americanism. REEM 2:195; REEMB 2:197
Jackson, A.
Protest to the Senate, April 15, 1833. BIR 2:90
Kennedy, J.F. and others.
Conversation with the President. BA 1962-63:145
Role of the President. BA 1959-60:123
Taft, W. H.
President (November 16, 1912). ONEM:616; ONES:208
Thurman, A. G.
Tilden-Hayes election. BREW 9:403; REEMA 15:1986
Truman, H. S.
Broadcast to the armed forces of the United States upon his assumption of office. VO 1945-46:152
Powers of the President.

PRESIDENTS-UNITED STATES (cont.)
COPB:592; HURG:316
Speech to his neighbors in Independence, Mo. VO 1945-46:346
Speech at Chicago Library luncheon, July 10, 1956. BRAP:39
See also Inaugural addresses

---- ---- ELECTION
Kefauver, E.
Our Presidential election system. MO:464

---- ---- SUCCESSION
Doub, G.C.
Presidential inability; the Constitutional problem. BA 1959-60:131
Truman, H.S.
Message to Congress on Presidential succession. VO 1945-46:293
Tugwell, R.G.
For a third term. BA 1938-39:166

PRESIDING OFFICERS See Officers, presiding

PRESS
Ackerman, C.W.
Role of the press as a factor in public opinion and economic changes. BA 1937-38:198
Anderson, P.E.
Press despotism. YR 2:163
Barrie, J.M.
Literature and the press. COP:692; COPB:719; GLAD:181
Berryer, P.A.
Censorship of the press. BREW 2:48; HAZO 12:4943; MAS 12:4943
Brown, W.
Tomorrow's extra. YR 2:63
Bryant, W.C.
Press. REEMA 1:107
Campoamor Y Campoosorio, R.
Against the Press law. CHAL 9:205; HAZO 18:7751; MAS 18:7751
Dana, C.A.
Diplomacy and the Press. REEMA 1:318
DeYoung, R.
Women in the headlines. GA:149
Grant, U.S.
Characteristics of newspaper men. HOA:374; HOAP:261; REEMA 2:559
Hartger, H.V.
Skeleton of the press. YR 8:237
Hawley, J.R.
Press. HAZO 21:8964; MAS 21:8964; REEMA 2:593
Hay, J.
Power of the press. WERN 42:102
Irving, H.
Function of the newspaper. REEMA 2:681
Johnson, H.W.
Against intimidating the press. BREW 7:178
Lassalle, F.
Attacks the German press. PE:529; PEA:529
Lenroot, I.L.
Press and the government. LINM:39
Macomber, W.H.
News deal. BRP 4:82
Phillips, M.G.
Influence of the press on world peace. ASHF:316
Press, by a newspaper man. EDGS:189
Reid, W.
Press-right or wrong. REEMA 3:979
Response to the toast of "The Press." HILL:483
Roche, J.J.
Press. REEMA 3:988
Roosevelt, T.
Response to the National Press Fraternal Association, February 4, 1903.

THOU 3:19
Rosebery, A. P. P.
Power and responsibility of the press. BRTH:329; BRTHA:329
Royer-Collard, P. P.
Against press censorship. BREW 9:114; CHAL 4:172; HAZO 9:3535; MAS 9:3535; PL:329
Schottenfeld, A. C.
To read or not to read. BRP 8:62; NOR 1937:5
Smith, B.
Press of the South. REEMA 3:1057
Speeches at a dinner given to the religious press. PITT: 90
Stone, M. E.
Revolution of 1893 (Free press). REEM sup 3:120; REEMB 6:355
Swing, R. G.
Only one truth. SAR:34
Thompson, S.
Ethics of the Press. REEMA 3:1139
Walters, B. L.
Press-an unhidden persuader. SABA:205
Woolsey, J. M.
Opinion, December 6, 1933 (Ulysses Case-freedom of reading). ANG:468
See also Free speech; Journalism and Journalists; Liberty of the press; Publishers and publishing
Prettyman, J.
Odd Fellowship exemplified in Jesus only. THOU 3:124
Price, Byron
We must recapture valour. BA 1946-47:213
Price, Charles W.
Kansas and its governor. REEM 3:112; REEMB 3:113
Price, James Harry and others (G.V. Denny, Jr. and P. Weaver)
Is youth forgetting religion? HAR:489
Price, Joseph C.
Race problem stated. WOON: 488
Price, Julian
Presents Norman H. Davis. LY:250
Price, Richard
Hails the French Revolution. PE:236; PEA:236

PRICE REGULATION
Aldrich, E.W.
Free enterprise and "planned economy." COP: 434; COPA:434
Bowles, C.
Price control and inflation. BA 1945-46:144
Curtice, H.
Administered prices (before United States Senate). ARNS:208
DiSalle, M. and others.
How can we stop rising prices? HAR:285
Douglas, H. G.
Cost of living and inflation. BA 1947-48:118
Foster, W.T.
Government cannot control prices. ON:114
Henderson, L.
Equality of sacrifice. BA 1941-42:162
Hoffman, P. G.
Prices of things which farmers buy, including so-called management of prices by industry. HUS:255
Moulton, H. G.
Wartime price control. BA 1940-41:82
Reuther, W.
Administered prices (before United States Senate). ARNS: 199
Roosevelt, F. D.
Broadcast on the 9th anniversary of the National Farm Program. VO 1942-43:194
Message to Congress on price control. VO 1941:356

PRICE REGULATIONS (cont.)
Message to Congress, September 7, 1942. VO 1942-43:469
Swing, R. G.
Meaning of the home front. BA 1943-44:159
Taft, R. A.
Price control veto. BA 1945-46:154
---- and others.
American standard of living -how can it best be improved? BA 1947-48:103
Truman, H. S.
Broadcast on wages and prices. VO 1945-46:665
Message to Congress September 6, 1945. VO 1945-46:546
Williams, B. J.
Inflation can be controlled without price ceilings. SAB: 140

PRIESTS See Clergy
Prime, S. I.
Children and the church. THOU 2:174
Primrose, Archibald Philip, 5th Earl of Rosebery. See Rosebery, A. P. P.

PRINCETON UNIVERSITY
Goheen, R. F.
Library and the chapel stand side by side (at opening exercises at Princeton University). BA 1964-65:113
Wilson, W.
Equipment for service: inaugural address as president of Princeton University. BLAA:177; BLAB:177; BOA:159; BOB:168; WE 1: 63
Yale and Princeton - a response to a toast. DAVC: 390

PRINTING
Craig, A. H.
Toast to the printing press. EDGS:192
For a printer's banquet. BARB: 191
George V.
Priceless gift of printing. BREW 6:222
Speech at a printer's banquet. HILL:484

PRISONS
Duesterbeck, R. M.
Man's other society. LINP: 264
Willis, E. E.
Colleges for crooks. BRP 6:13; YR 7:189
See also Crime and criminals
Pritchard, Jeter C.
Prohibition in North Carolina. SHUO:298
Pritchett, Henry Smith
Modern culture and the human spirit. NORR 2d ser: 372
What is truth? BLAA:255; BLAB:255

PRIVATE SECRETARIES
Private secretaries. SCHS: 237

PRIZEFIGHTERS
Visk, A. G.
Fight announcer. BRH:336

PRIZES See Acceptance speeches-Rewards (prizes); Presentation speeches-Rewards (prizes)
Probst, Walter F., Jr.
Homeless America. BRP 5:17; YR 6:291
Prochnow, Herbert V.
Begins an address on "The International Situation." PRNE:65
Introduces Clarence B. Randall, Chairman of the Inland Steel Company. PRNE: 9

PROCLAMATIONS
Dedication prayer and proclamation (at cornerstone dedi-

cation of youth center). BED:40; BEDA:82
Harrison, B.
National holiday proclamations (Columbus Day). THOU 1:61
Victoria.
Proclamation to the princes, chief and people of India, November 1, 1858. KESI 1:382
Proctor, Redfield
Condition of Cuba. FUL:250, 253
Proctor, Samuel D.
Address (before United Negro College convocation). HILK:225
Prodicus.
Choice of Hercules. LEEW 1:35

PROFANITY
Johnson, B.
Lost art of profanity. EXEE:315

PROFESSIONAL ASSOCIATIONS
See Trade and professional associations

PROFESSIONS
Professions (for any professional gathering). ED:233

PROGRAM CHANGES, ANNOUNCEMENTS OF See Club speeches

PROGRESS
Brown, H. A.
One century's achievement (Valley Forge centennial). BREW 2:283
Butler, N. M.
Which way progress? BA 1937-38:138
Cameron, W. J.
Rock and flood. BA 1940-41:235
Cass, L.
American progress and foreign oppression. BREW 3:151
Chapin, E. H.
Source of modern progress. BREW 3:206
Clinton, D.
Achievements and responsibilities of the age. NORR 2d ser:9
Cortelyou, G. B.
Men of vision with their feet on the ground. REEM 1:342; REEMB 1:343
Durfee, J. L.
Influence of scientific discovery and invention on social and political progress. BL:381; NORR 1st ser:43
Goldstein, M. W.
Roar of the world and God. BRP 2:92; YR 3:167
Griswold, A. W.
Balancing moral responsibility and scientific progress. BA 1951-52:147
Henderson, W. G.
What may man become? BRP 7:117
Hill, B. H.
Education and progress. HARSO:48; SHUO:76
Howard, F. W.
Progress true and false. CATA 2:155
Jones, J. G.
Vision and purpose. REEM 4:228
Jones, L.
Breaking down barriers. YR 8:177
Jordan, T. W.
Penalties of progress (baccalaureate address). SHUO:86
Kaplan, A.
How many centuries of progress? BRP 6:31; YR 7:47
Leavitt, H. L.
Men of vision. COUW:203
Le Vander, H.
Date kernels. BRP 3:45; YR 4:151
Long, L. G.

PROGRESS (cont.)
Relation of modern-isms to progress. SHUC:42; TRUW:26
Lovald, S.D.
Unless they act. BRP 10:106
Manning, H.E.
On progress. ORBR 2:231
New frontiers. BOB:61
Pollock, C.
I am a reactionary. BART 1:239
Progress and prosperity. FRIE:170
Roosevelt, F.D.
Expanding frontiers of social progress. SAR:305
Ross, L.M.
Martyrs of progress. ASHF:174
Russell, J.R.
Science and literature as modes of progress. BREW 9:126
Smith, G.
Origin and causes of progress. BREW 9:239
Soltau, M.E.
Century of progress. INTW 1933:5; YR 5:345
Staley, H.
Chains or change? YR 5:187
Strandness, B.
Challenge to America. YR 8:141
Sumner, C.
Progress of humanity. NORR 2d ser:73; REAC:86
Van Dyke, V.
Second century of progress. BRP 4:22; INTW 1933:10
Walsh, G.
It hath not yet been shown what we shall be. YR 4:231
See also Civilization

PROGRESSIVE PARTY
LaFollette, R.M.
Official statement as Progressive candidate. WHIP:306
Petition to the U.S. Senate as candidate for President on the Progressive ticket-1924. WHIP:305
Wallace, H.A.
Progressive Party commitments. BA 1948-49:122

PROHIBITION
Borah, W.E.
Liquor problem. HICF:914
Cadman, S.P.
Is prohibition a failure? BLAB:300
Enstrom, R.
Lag. BRP 1:79
Evans, B.
Here stook an oak. YR 4:29
Grady, H.W.
Effects of prohibition in Atlanta, Georgia. THOU 1:568
Hasty, E.
For the Eighteenth Amendment. BLUE:63
Lee, J.
Lay the axe to the root of the evil. BLUE:94
Powderly, T.V.
Labor's greatest curse. WERN 42:187
Pritchard, J.C.
Prohibition in North Carolina. SHUO:298
Reed, J.A.
Prohibition. HICF:867
Sheppard, M.
Our dry United States. BOB:45
Smith, A.E.
Fight for repeal. BOB:43
Willebrandt, M.W.
Prohibition enters politics. HICF:827
Wooley, J.G.
Prohibition keynote. WERN 42:31
See also Temperance; Woman's Christian Temperance Union

PROLETARIAT See Labor and laboring classes

PROMISES See Behavior

PROMOTION See Sales talks and salesmanship

PROPAGANDA
Baird, A. C.
Propaganda. ON:244
Battle, G. G.
Propaganda in America. ON:44
Brenner, S. M.
Propaganda in a democracy. DO:48
Cartzdafner, J. P.
Puppets of propaganda. BRP 3:95; YR 4:295
Halifax, E. F. L. W.
Address to Association of Commerce, Baltimore. ON: 196
Hardison, E.
Propaganda-a weapon of peace. YR 10:69
Lehman, J. H.
Power of propaganda. YR 1:35
MacLeish, A.
Psychological front. HOC: 127
----and others.
Propaganda, good and bad. BA 1941-42:75
Margulies, N.
Modern "medicine men." BRP 8:92; NOR 1937:35
Miller, C. R. and others.
Propaganda. BA 1939-40: 191
Reed, E. H.
Facts or fallacies. YR 5: 301
Rowan, C. T.
Address delivered at Simpson College). HILK:108
Thompson, D.
Government by propaganda. GA:142
Stopping propaganda. BA 1938-39:87
See also Advertising

PROPERTY See Real estate

PROPHECIES
Brown, B. G.
Prophecy. BREW 2:275
Conant, J. B.
Skeptical chemist looks into the crystal ball. BA 1951-52:137
Horton, M. M.
Predictions for the unpredictable future. BRA:551
See also Commencement addresses-Class prophecies

PROSECUTION
Aeschines.
Against Ctesiphon. BREW 1:104; BRYW 1:186; LEEW 1:301; PL:60; REEM 9:14; REEMB 10:15
Andocides.
Against Alcidiades. MINA 1:542
Antiphon.
Against a step-mother, on a charge of poisoning. FRE: 86; MINA 1:14
First tetralogy; anonymous prosecution for murder (first and second speeches). MINA 1:52, 68
Second tetralogy; prosecution for accidental homicide (first and second speeches). MINA 1:88, 98
Third tetralogy: prosecution for murder of one who pleads that he was acting in self-defence (first and second speeches). MINA 1: 120, 130
Bingham, J. A.
Against assassins of President Lincoln. BREW 2:50
Borah, W. E.
Summation for the people in the Coeur D'Alene riot murder trial. HICJ:354
Brackett, E. T.
Summation for the managers in the Sulzer impeachment trial. HICJ:692
Burke, E.
Impeachment of Warren

PROSECUTION (cont.)
Hastings. BREW 2:337, 343; BRYW 6:50; CLAY:55; CODS:168; CODSA:180; COP:163; COPA:163; COPB:163; CROC:46; GOOD:362; HAZO 6:2193; KESI 1:114; MAS 6:2193; MEAR:118; PE:178; PEA: 178; REEM 9:126; REEMB 10:131
Cato, M. P.
Against the conspirators. HAZO 2:735; LEEW 2:47; MAS 2:735; PL:99
Cicero, M. T.
First oration against Catiline. BREW 3:333; BRYW 2:293; CHAL 1:278; COP: 36; COPA:36; COPB:36; HAZO 2:675; HIB:66; HIBS: 437; LEEW 2:174; MAS 2: 675; PE:27; PEA:27; PL: 119; REEM 9:30; REEMB 10:31
First oration against Mark Antony. BRYW 2:148; HAZO 3:911; MAS 3:911; PL:129
First oration against Verres. BRYW 2:51; HAZO 2:755; LA:129; MAS 2:755; PL: 108
Fourth book of the second pleading in the prosecution of Verres about the statutes. HAZO 2:781; MAS 2:781
Fourth oration against Cataline. HAZO 2:740; MAS 2: 740
Second oration against Cataline. BRYW 2:113; CHAL 1: 297; HAZO 2:694; MAS 2: 694
Third oration against Cataline. CHAL 1:313; HAZO 2: 710; MAS 2:710
Coke, E.
Prosecuting Sir Walter Raleigh. BREW 4:120; PL: 377
Speech on the gunpowder plot. HAZO 4:1401; MAS 4:1401
Conboy, M.
Summation for the Judiciary Committee in the investigation of the New York Socialists by the Assembly, Albany. HICJ:891
Crowe, R. E.
Closing argument for the prosecution in the Leopold-Loeb murder trial. HICJ: 1090
Curran, J. P.
Massey v. Headfort. GOOD: 814; KET:178
Deinarchus.
Against Aristogiton. CHAL 1:250; HAZO 2:649; MAS 2:649; MINA 2:264
Against Demosthenes. MINA 2:172
Against Philocles. MINA 2: 290
Demosthenes.
Assault and battery: quarrel in camp. FRE:114
Illegal union: against Neaera. FRE:191
Desmoulins, C.
Advocating the execution of Louis XVI. COP:70; COPA: 70; COPB:70; REEMA 13: 913
Dunne, P. F.
Summation for the Government in the San Francisco mint case. HICJ:434
Erskine, T.
Against Thomas Williams for the publication of Paine's Age of reason. ADR: 2:273; BREW 6:12; GOOD: 761; ORBR 1:375; REEMA 13:949
Garvan, F. P.
Opening address for the people in the Thaw murder trial. HICJ:488
Hypereides.
Against Athenogenes. CHAL 1:132; HAZO 1:214; MAS 1:214; MINA 2:430
Against Demosthenes.

MINA 2:500
Against Phillipides. MINA 2:410
Isaeus.
Menexenus and others against Dicaeogenes and Leochares. CHAL 1:104; HAZO 1:187; MAS 1:187
Ivins, W. M.
Opening address for the plaintiff in the Barnes-Roosevelt libel case. HICJ: 725
Lycurgus.
Against Leocrates. CHAL 1:119; HAZO 1:201; LEEW 1:175; MAS 1:201; MINA 2:14
Lysias.
Against Erathenes for murder (on the execution without trial of Polemarchus). BREW 7:428; BRYW 1:61; CHAL 1:78; FRE:54; HAZO 1:115; LEEW 1:81; MAS 1:115; PL:43
Against Pancleon (a claim to citizen's rights). FRE: 173
Embezzlement of trust funds; against a guardian. FRE:131
On the murder of Eratosthenes. FRE:43
Nottingham, H. F.
Opening the prosecution for regicide under Charles II (trial of T. Harrison). BREW 6:131
Osborne, J. W.
Summation in support of the charges preferred by Senator Benn Conger. HICJ: 604
Plunket, W.
Prosecuting Robert Emmet. BREW 8:345; HAY:112
Pym, J.
Against Strafford. CHAL 1: 472; HAZO 4:1416; MAS 4: 1416; REEM 9:66; REEMB 10:68
Romano, M. A.
Summation for the people in the O'Shea conspiracy case. HICJ:983
Scarlett, J.
Charge to the jury. CHAL 4:352; HAZO 9:3790; MAS 9:3790
Sheridan, R. B.
Against Warren Hastings. BREW 9:192; BRTH:106; BRTHA:106; BRYW 6:77; CHAL 3:393; CODS:265; COP:165; COPA:165; COPB:165; FULB:86; GOOD:407; HAY:53; HAZO 8:3069; LEEW 6:347; MAS 8:3069; ORBR 1:389; PAUF 1:212; PE:180; PEA:180; REEM 9:133; REEMA 15: 1872; REEMB 10:139
Proceedings against Mr. Hastings in Westminster Hall: second or Begum charge (speeches of June 3, 6, 13, 1788). KET:217, 226, 236
Webster, D.
Knapp White murder case. BAAMP:46; BREW 10:203; CHAL 5:304; HAZO 11: 4746; MAS 11:4746; ONEM: 3; PAR:122; SHAH:164; SHUM:65
Wellman, F. L.
Summation for the people in the Carlyle Harris murder trial. HICJ:261

PROSPERITY
Barss, R.
Great stampede. BOA:200; YR 6:55
Borden, R. L.
Cost of prosperity. BREW 2:156
DeBoer, R.
Nature's ice-pack. YR 7: 245
Finch, C. A.
Failure of success. BRP 1: 90; YR 2:169
Firestone, H. S.
Prosperity and better busi-

PROSPERITY (cont.)
ness methods. ONEC:274
Leacock, S. B.
Organization of prosperity. REEM 2:316; REEMB 2:320
McDonald, D. J.
Plan for prosperity. BA 1960-61:156
Nixon, R. M.
Prosperity and the economic health of the nation. BA 1956-57:74
Progress and prosperity. FRIE:170
Schamus, S. L.
Road to prosperity. YR 6:117
Prosser, W. A.
Beautiful and glorious banner. THOU 1:304
Free labor the basis of free America. THOU 1:421

PROTECTION See Free trade and protection

PROTESTANT DISSENTERS See Church

PROTESTANT EPISCOPAL CHURCH IN THE UNITED STATES
Posey, W. B.
Protestant Episcopal Church: an American adaptation. TIN:377
Prout, Mrs. Robert I. C.
Address (inaugural) as President of the General Federation of Women's Clubs. BUTB:243

PROVERBS
Morley of Blackburn, J. M.
Aphorisms. REEMA 5:809

PRUSSIA See Germany
Pryor, Roger Atkinson
Virginia's part in American history. REEMA 3:959

PSYCHIATRISTS See Physicians

PSYCHOLOGY
Right psychological approach. NAT:36
Seashore, C. E.
What is psychology? MO:513

---- SOCIAL
Jastrow, J.
Social traits and human nature. EXEE:97

PSYCHOTHERAPY
Rogers, C.
What we know about psychotherapy-objectively and subjectively. LINP:36

PUBLIC DEBTS See Debts, public

PUBLIC FINANCE See Finance

PUBLIC HEALTH
Truman, H. S.
Message to Congress on a national health program. VO 1945-46:724

PUBLIC LANDS
Marshall, T. R.
National power and the national peace policy (on public land sales, 1841). BREW 8:100

PUBLIC OFFICIALS
Acceptance speech of mayor at his installation. BEDA:116
Address of tribute (at testimonial dinner on retirement of public official). BED:29; BEDA:49
Brief inaugural of a mayor. HILL:469
Closing speech (at testimonial on retirement of public official). BED:31; BEDA:52
Examples of introductions for public officials. BO:24-27
Gilbert, E. J.

Introducing a governor. BRC:126
Grimm, P.
Introduces Thomas E. Dewey (Governor of the State of New York). PR:66
Installing mayor. BEDA:114
Introducing Mayor (at induction of a Mayor). BEDA:116
Introducing Mayor at Town Hall meeting. BEDA:71
Introducing public officials-seven examples of. BEB:50-51
Kaser, A. L.
Introducing the town mayor. BRC:139
Lewe, J.C.
Presents Thomas C. Clark (Attorney General of the United States). LY:149; PR:73
Marlow, F.
Introducing a state legislator. BRC:238
Mayor's address of welcome to Secretary of War. HILL:469
Miller, M. G.
Introduces Mayor Edward J. Jeffries. PR:61
Mitchell, J. P.
Mayor of New York. REEM 2:414; REEMB 2:430
Opening speech at induction of a mayor. BEDA:114
Opening speech (at testimonial on retirement of public official). BED:27; BEDA:47
Presenting gold cup (to retiring public official at testimonial dinner). BED:28; BEDA:48
Reed, P.D.
Introduces mayor of the convention city. PR:102
Response by guest-of-honor (at testimonial on retirement of public official). BED:30; BEDA:51
Roesch, C.E.
Inaugural address of the Mayor of Buffalo. ONEC:163
Speech of mayor at a volunteer firemen's review. HILL:469
Thanking speaker (at testimonial on retirement of public official). BED:30; BEDA:50
Tribute to a newly elected mayor (at his installation). BEDA:115
Walsh, J.J.
Introducing the mayor-elect of Boston. HOAP:264
Williams, H.
Introducing a high government official. BRC:63
See also Law and lawyers; United States-Congress

---- Introduction of - See Introductions

PUBLIC OPINION
Ackerman, C.W.
Role of the press as a factor in public opinion and economic changes. BA 1937-38:198
Baker, E.E.
Public opinion: its genesis, growth, and value, with an incidental discussion of fashion. WAGN:305
Frankfurter, F.
Public opinion and democratic government. BA 1946-47:145
Gallup, G.
Judgment of the common people. ON:200
Harris, E.
Thoughtlessness of American thought. AN:54
Highsaw, J. L., Jr.
Manufacture of consent. BOA:351; YR 6:23
Lee, G.C.
Strength of the people. SHUO:116
Lodge, H.C., Jr.
United Nations and world

PUBLIC OPINION (cont.)
opinion. BA 1954-55:43
Reed, F.N.
War and public opinion. SHUC:49; TRUW:209
What is your opinion? NAT: 26

PUBLIC RELATIONS
Kienzle, G.J.
Report of a research study in public relations. SABA: 197
Lindquist, R.
Beyond the dollar sign. MIA:375
Parker, J.S.
New dynamics of corporate relations work. BAAGA:381

PUBLIC SERVICE See Citizenship; Public Officials; Statesmanship

PUBLIC SPEAKING
Arnold, C.C.
Speech as a liberal study. ARNS:2
Bain, G.W.
Platform experiences. LINM:494
Bassett, L.E.
From dog house to doctorate. MOUG:244; MOUGA: 244
Beecher, H.V.
Squandering the voice. SHU: 245
Beveridge, A.J.
Public speaking. BYRA:13; REEM 1:XXXVII
Brigance, W.N.
Demagogues, "good" people, and teachers of speech. ARNS:13
Caird, J.
Art of eloquence. BREW 3: 34; HOB:18
Carleton, W.G.
Effective speech in a democracy. ARNS:5; BRAP:153
Compton, A.H.
Own method of speech training. BA 1945-46:109
Coolidge, C.
Address at International Oratorical Contest of 1925. LEIO:61
Address at the finals of the International Oratorical Contest. LEIO:56
Cousin, V.
Eloquence and the fine arts. BREW 4:186; CHAL 6:1; HAZO 12:5000; MAS 12: 5000
Crocker, L.
Leadership and the spoken word. BA 1941-42:100
Dawes, C.G.
Address at the finals of the International Oratorical Contest. LEIO:60
Eaton, C.
Professor talks to himself. ON:235
Emerson, C.E.
Oratory. WERN 42:131
For substitute speaker. NAT: 41
Halsey, D.P.
Oratory is not a lost art. SHUO:15
Hammond, J.H.
Address at International Oratorical Contest. LEIO: 66
Hewart, G.H.
Modern oratory. BEA:265
Hostettler, G.F.
Speech as a liberal art. BERS:207
Hunt, L.B.
Maiden speeches. JUD:43
"I ain't no public speaker." NAT:25
Jackson, R.H.
Own method of speech training. BA 1945-46:60
King, J.L.
Long live the orator. BLUE:98
Lee, E.
Special tips to the amateur radio broadcaster. BUT: 127

Lee, I. J.
Four ways of looking at a speech. ARNS:17
Maloney, M.
Speech at Rocky Mountain Speech Conference-original speech and dictaphone recording of the speech as actually presented. JUD: 330
Matthews, B.
Mark Twain as speechmaker and storyteller. DOA:288
Murray, G.
On public speaking. CHAL 11:380; HAZO 22:9301; MAS 22:9301
Nelson, B. G.
World's orator. TRUW:144
Nevin, A. P.
Speech for all occasions. MIA:416
Trick speech. LINM:65; SHUP:4
Opening for a substitute speaker. FRIE:338
Public speaking sensations. NATS:1
Public-speaking trials. FRIE: 319
Raether, H. C.
Speech of to-morrow. JUD: 99
Rahskopf, H. G.
Speech at mid-century. BA 1950-51:141
Reid, L.
Engineering of ideas (presenting Honor Awards to engineers). BRAB:545
Roosevelt, E. A.
Answers to questions at the opening of the 4th Public Speaking Class for Wives of Members of Congress. BUT: 107
Speech training for the youth. BUTA:223
Satterthwaite, J. B.
Plea for pebbles. YR 8:1
Scanlon, R.
Public address as a social force (dedicating new quarters for Speech Department at Queens College). BA 1961-62:159
Speak the speech. FRIE:325
Strong, W. A.
Address at International Oratorical contest. LEIO: 63
Substitute speaker. FRIE:333
Suggestions for openings and conclusions. With examples. of SOES:30-35.
Tittle, E. T.
Learning to speak. HUS: 284; MO:424; MOA:428
Watson, E. B.
Spoken word. SHUC:1
Weaver, A. T.
Toward understanding through speech. BERS:2
Wilson, M. E.
Stage fright. JUD:49
Wrage, E. J.
Antidote to anonymity. BA 1963-64:191
Yeager, W. H.
Art of speaking effectively to employees. SAB:150; SABA:248
See also Debates and debating; High school orations; Orators; Speeches-Outlines of. Also types of speeches, e. g. After-dinner speeches; Extemporaneous speeches; Introductions; Responses

PUBLIC UTILITIES
Cortelyou, G. B.
Men of vision with their feet on the ground. REEM 1:342; REEMB 1:343
Lee, I. L.
Publicity for public service corporations. REEM 4:288; REEMB 5:110
Untereiner, R. E.
Public interest in utility regulation. BA 1962-63:28
See also Electric railroads; Railroads

PUBLICITY
August, E. P.
Publicity programs and professional consciousness. GA:125
Creations: a place, a plan, a pledge (a bank publicity speech for any business group, for a P. T. A. meeting, or for a student body). BAI:72

PUBLISHERS AND PUBLISHING
Kaser, A. L.
Introducing a book publisher. BRC:165
Roberts, R.
Introducing a small town newspaper publisher. BRC:73
Puddicombe, T.
Broad of life. THOU 2:254
Puel, Maxime R.
French Constitution. LEIO:83

PUERTO RICO
Bailey, J.W.
Porto Rico tariff. REEMA 11:84
Dolliver, J. P.
On Porto Rico and the Philippines. CHAL 14:374
Littlefield, C.E.
Pearl of the Antilles. CHAL 14:227; HAZO 25:10755; MAS 25:10755
McCall, S.W.
Porto Rico tariff. HAZO 25:10736; MAS 25:10736
Roosevelt, F.D.
Message to Congress on Puerto Rico. VO 1943-44:97
Message to Congress on the need for amending the organic act of Puerto Rico. VO 1943-44:413
Teller, H. M.
On Porto Rico. CHAL 11:417; HAZO 22:9338; MAS 22:9338
Pulteney, William
Against standing armies. BREW 8:380
Army and the Parliament, 1746. BRTH:62; BRTHA:62
Information on foreign policy, March 3, 1738 speech. EMS 1:231
Information on foreign policy, February 6, 1739 speech. EMS 1:236
On a motion for reducing the army. CHAL 2:189; GOOD: 43; HAZO 4:1758; MAS 4: 1758
Secrecy of debates. EMS 1: 208
Pupin, Michael
In honor of Marconi. REEM 3: 116; REEMB 3:117
Purcell, J. Edward and others (C. Cassidy)
Greetings from Mexico. JUD: 107
Purdue, Ida Pace
Presenting Chi Omega Greek theater. GA:38
Purdy, Charles O.
Triumph of the individual. SHUC:190
Purinton, Edward Earle
Efficient optimist. SHU:242

PURITANS
Adams, W.
Address, 1852. BRAR 2:163
Bacon, L.
Address, 1838. BRAR 1:165
Beveridge, A. J.
Puritan spirit. BLAA:4; BLAB:4
Curtis, G.W.
Puritan principle: liberty under law. BAKF:430; BRY:468; BRYA:554; ONEM:573; PAR:359; REEM 1:355; REEMA 1: 290
Caldwell, H. C.
Blend of Cavalier and Puritan. REEM 1:201; REEMA 1:112; REEMB 1:202
Depew, C. M.
Unsolved problems. REEMA 1:361
Grady, H.W.

Lincoln as Cavalier and Puritan. THOU 1:477
Kelman, J.
Puritanism today. REEM 2:286; REEMB 2:290
McCabe, W. G.
Puritan and Cavalier. SHUO:21; SMI:229
Paxton, G. M.
Scotch-Irishman's views of the Puritan. REEMA 3:880
Porter, H.
Many-sided Puritan. REEMA 3:928
Puritan and the Dutchman-response to a toast at a banquet of the New England Society. DAVC:392
Storrs, R. S.
Puritan scheme of national growth, 1857. BRAR:2:327
Twichell, J. H.
Soldier stamp. REEMA 3:1153
Watterson, H.
Puritan and the Cavalier. BRAC:297; COP:675; COPB:702; ONEM:627; ONES:222; REEM 3:359; REEMA 3:1191; REEMB 3:375; SHUM:237
Weber, W. A
Puritan tradition. YR 2:39
Wilson, W.
Our ancestral responsibilities. REEMA 3:1248

Purvis, Robert
Appeal of forty thousand citizens threatened with disfranchisement to the people of Pennsylvania. WOON:96

Pusey, Edward Bouverie
Love of God for individual souls. HAZO 13:5614; MAS 13:5614

Pusey, Nathan M.
Religion for now. BA 1953-54:193
Responds to an introduction. PRNE:59

PUSEY, NATHAN M.
Stipp, J. E.
Introduces Nathan M. Pusey, President, Harvard University. PRNE:29

PUSHKIN, ALEKSANDER SERGIEVICH
Dostoevsky, F.
Celebrates the centenary of Pushkin's birth. PE:569; PEA:569

Pushmataha, Choctaw chief
Attention, my good red warriors! GRIS:38
To John C. Calhoun. BRYW 8:19
To Lafayette. BRYW 8:20; JON:69

Putnam, A. P.
Our flag. WERN 42:189

PUTNAM, AMELIA EARHART
See Earhart, Amelia

PUTNAM, HERBERT
Fess, S. D.
Putnam festival. CORP:266

Putnam, R. B.
National emblem. BOA:289; BOB:77

PYLE, ERNIE
Bradley, O. N.
Tribute to Ernie Pyle. SABA:285

Pyle, Howard
Begins an address before the Los Angeles Bar Association. PRNE:53

Pym, John
Against Strafford. CHAL 1:472; HAZO 4:1416; MAS 4:1416; REEM 9:66; REEMB 10:68
Law as the safeguard of liberty. BREW 8:389
On grievances in the reign of Charles I. ADR 1:37; BERS:18; BREW 8:388; BRYW 3:50; PL:368

Pyre, James F. A.
Poetry and freedom. TRUW:19

PYTHIAN SISTERS
  Purity, love, equality, and fidelity-motto of the Pythian Sisters. AMEO 2:54

QUAKERS See Friends, Society of

QUEBEC (PROVINCE)
  Maseres, F.
    Considerations on the expediency of procuring an act of Parliament for the settlement of the Province of Quebec. KES 1:12

QUEBEC CONFERENCE, 1943
  Churchill, W. L. S.
    Broadcast from Quebec, August 31, 1943. HAN:226; SAC:42; VO 1943-44:316
Quezon, Manuel L.
  Broadcast to the Philippines. VO 1944-45:268
Quincy, Josiah, 1744-1775
  Defence of British soldiers, 1770. CHAL 3:129; HAZO 7:2737; HELE:17; MAS 7:2737
  Lenity of the law to human infirmity (Weem et al: British soldiers arraigned for the Boston Massacre). BREW 8:399
Quincy, Josiah, 1772-1864
  Against the conquest of Canada. BREW 8:404
  At the second centennial of Boston. BREW 8:402
  Evils of the Embargo Act. PL:602
  Proposing a toast to Mrs. Charles Dickens. REEM 1:402
  On the admission of Louisiana. CHAL 4:411; HAZO 9:3879; JOHA 1 pt 1:180; MAS 9:3879; REEMA 14:1663
  Welcome to Dickens. REEM 3:122; REEMA 3:964; REEMB 3:123
Quintilian.
  Orator, physician, philosopher. LEEW 2:245
Quo, Tai-Chi Francis
  Restoration of the surplus Boxer indemnity to China by the United States. SHUC:305

R. F. C. See Reconstruction Finance Corporation
Rabanus Magnentius Maurus, Abp. of Mainz
  On Palm Sunday. HAZO 3:1239; MAS 3:1239
  Sermon for Sunday. LEEW 3:291
Rabinowitz, Deborah
  And the gentlemen cry peace. NOR 1949:133
Rabinowitz, H.
  For a Bar Mitzvah. ZEL:80

RACE IMPROVEMENT See Eugenics

RACE PREJUDICE See Brotherliness; Discrimination; International cooperation; Segregation

RACE PROBLEMS
  Barriers to racial brotherhood. JA:184
  Bowers, E. J.
    Negro problem. SHUO:258
  Bracken, H.
    Economic color line. BRP 10:62
  Branch, W. B.
    Strange fruit. NOR 1946:65
  Bunche, R. J.
    Barriers of race can be surmounted. YE:282
  Clark, F. H.
    Problem of the century. COUW:21
  Cobbs, J. A.
    Three score and ten. BRP 7:25; NOR 1934:97
  Coleman, H. F.
    Philosophy of the race problem. ASHF:158
  Davis, D. W.
    Sunday-school and church as

a solution of the Negro problem. DUNM:291
Dobson, J.
America's greatest problem. COUW:181; SHUC:103
Fleming, W.H.
Solution of the race problem. SHUO:269
Franklin, J.H.
America's window to the world: her race problem. HILK:201
Grady, H.W.
Race problem. BRAS:158; BREW 6:273; FULB:391; HARSO:258; HICF:139; IMMD:238; ONEM:585; REEM 2:115; REEMA 2:534; REEMB 2:107; SHAH:527; SHUM:214
Kanzell, H.N.
And the patient began to die. NOR 1947:95
McClain, W.
Scroll of destiny. BRP 5:54
Malcolm X.
Proclaims Muhammad as the man of the hour. HILK:304
Morgan, C., Jr.
Time to speak. BERS:87
Mossell, N.F.
Teachings of history considered in relation to race problems in America. DUNM:227
Moton, R.R.
Cooperation between races. SMI:273
Some elements necessary to race development. DUNM: 367
Nuetzman, D.
Steel spike. BRP 9:66
One family: five colors. JA: 187
Paulson, S.
Spectrum of democracy. NOR 1942:71
Price, J.C.
Race problem stated. WOON: 488
Proctor, S.D.
Address (before United Negro College convocation). HILK:225
Rainey, J.H.
Speech made in reply to an attack upon the colored state legislators of South Carolina by Representative Cox of New York. WOON: 378
Ripley, W.Z.
White man's burden. REEM sup 2:346; REEMB 5:248
Smuts, J.C.
Basis of trusteeship in African policy. CROC:400
Waldron, J.M.
Solution to the race problem. DUNM:389
See also Human relations; Immigration and emigration; Segregation

RACKETS AND RACKETEERING
See Crime and criminals; Munitions
Radack, Rev.
For a Bar Mitzvah. ZEL:38
Rader, William
Uncle Sam; or, The reign of the common people. WAGN: 170
Radhakrishnan, Sarvepalli
Real meaning of democracy. ZU:75

RADICALS AND RADICALISM
Gregory, J.R.
We call them radicals. BRP 4:101
Lee, D.C.
In defense of a perspective. YR 6:1

RADIO
Carty, J.J.
Wireless telephone. REEM 1:229; REEMB 1:230

---- BROADCASTING
Brown, A.
Children's hour. BRP 9:36
Bryson, L.
What should we do with the

RADIO BROADCASTING (cont.)
radio? BART 4:133
Chase, J.
Supreme Court of the ether. BRP 9:84; NOR 1938:15
Cross, M.
Radio and opera. GLAD: 291
Dalton, T.
Radio's raucous rattle. JUD: 139
Hart, R.
Introducing a radio station or television station manager. BRC:293
Kaser, A. L.
Introducing a radio actor. BRC:101
Lee, E.
Special tips to the amateur radio broadcaster. BUT: 127; BUTA:127
Marconi, G.
Progress of wireless telegraphy. REEM 6:321; REEMB 6:274
On the air. SCHS:7
Payne, G. H.
What shall we do with radio? SAR:107
Radio (for any organization interested in the radio). EDGS:168
Radio (its influence for good). ED:204
Reynolds, R. B.
Origin and character of the American Forum of the Air. BA 1939-40:86
Stegall, F.
Sport broadcast of a contest debate. JUD:71
Suggestions for preparation of radio and television speeches. GLAD:188; RE:224. With examples of. BUT:120; BUTA:120; GA:245; MO: 544; YE:389
Suggestion for radio speaking. BAAG:327; SOBP:289
Visk, A. G.
Fight announcer. BRH:336
See also Introductions; Sponsors

Radwan, Taher
Speech at final session of Conference on the Problems of Economic Development. UAR:385
Raether, Howard C.
Speech of to-morrow. JUD:99
Raffaelli, Jean François
Universality of art. REEMA 9:980

RAFFLES See Fairs

Rahl, James Andrew
Died at twenty: buried at seventy. BRP 9:103; NOR 1938:34
Rahskopf, Horace G.
Speech at mid-century. BA 1950-51:141

RAILROADS
Arkwright, P. S.
Don't hate your customers. SABA:267; SAC:29; YE: 305
Atterbury, W. W.
Public can secure the railroad service it wants. REEM 4:1; REEMB 4:12
Bell, J.
Trans-continental railroads. BREW 1:395
Clement, M. W.
Whither the railroads? YE: 260
Depew, C. M.
Half century with a railroad REEM 4:86; REEMB 4:171
Eastman, J. B.
How can we solve the railroad problem? BA 1938-39: 138
For a railroad directors' dinner. BARB:176
Huber, L. J.
Introducing a railroad executive. BRC:181
Knapp, M. A.
Necessity for adequate railway revenues. PEAE:107
Kruttschnitt, J.
Railroad situation. REEM 4:

263; REEMB 5:83
LaFollette, R. M.
Hours of service of railway employees. PEAE:111
Railroad Rate Bill. PEAE: 117
Leeson, J.
Introducing a railroad executive. BRC:299
Loomis, D. P.
Why not let competition go to work in transporation? LINP:269
Miller, S. F.
Wabash, St. Louis and Pacific Railroad Company v. Illinois, 1886: opinion for the Supreme Court. BIR 3: 150
O'Keefe, L.
Introducing a railroad executive. BRC:229
Opening a new railroad. HILL:489
Railroads (for meetings of railroad officials). EDGS: 164
Railroads (survey of the situation). ED:209
Rea, S.
American transportation. BYRA:354; REEM sup 2: 305; REEMB 5:216
Truman, H. S.
Railroad strike emergency. BA 1945-46:196
See also Berths; Electric railroads; International Brotherhood of Maintenance-Of-Way Employees

RAINBOW GIRLS, ORDER OF
Make your own rainbow. JA: 190
Three Rainbow girls. JA:193
Rainey, Joseph H.
Southern situation. WOON:300
Speech made in reply to an attack upon the colored state legislators of South Carolina by Representative Cox of New York. WOON:378
Speech on education. WOON: 380
Raish, Donald R.
Once in a lifetime. JUD:191
Raleigh, Sir Walter
Speech on the scaffold. BREW 9:19; BRYW 3:34

RALEIGH, SIR WALTER
Coke, E.
Prosecuting Sir Walter Raleigh. BREW 4:120; PL: 377

RALLIES
Suggestions for preparation of speeches for rallies and keynote speeches. MOUGA: 153
Ralls, Mary C.
We are glad to be here. GA: 30

RALLYING DAY
Ante-Rallying day thoughts. THOU 2:203
Bromfield, E. T.
Rallying Day and after. THOU 2:217
Rallying Day for the church. THOU 2:219
Fergusson, E. M.
Use of Rallying Day. THOU 2:211
Hallock, G. B. F.
Catch them young (Rallying Day address). THOU 2:214
Johnston, H. A.
Sabbath school kite strings. THOU 2:212
No finished task. JA:199
Ogden, R.
Vacation responsibilities. THOU 2:203
Phillips, J. S.
Our model Sabbath school. THOU 2:205
Reawakening. THOU 2:216
Voice of the silver trumpets. JA:196
Wanamaker, J.
Rallying Day. THOU 2:210
Worden, J. A.
How to make Rallying Day

RALLYING DAY (cont.)
a success. THOU 2:213
Rallying Day, the occasion and why. THOU 2:197
United movement for gathering in neglected children. THOU 2:206
Ramey, Frank M.
Abraham Lincoln. BRP 1:16
Ramsdell, Charles W.
Changing interpretation of the Civil War. TIN:23
Ramsey, David
Advantages of American independence. CHEM 1:95
Ramsey, Helen
Introducing a Boy Scout, speaker on
" a Father's day speaker
" a golden wedding anniversary, speaker at
" a parent at graduation banquet
" a P. T. A., meeting speaker at
" a public librarian
" a Sunday school banquet, speaker at
" a Y. M. C. A., speaker on
" a Y. W. C. A., speaker on. BRC: See Table of contents for paging
Randall, Clarence B.
Explaining what to whom. BA 1951-52:112
Our foreign economic policy. BA 1954-55:55

RANDALL, CLARENCE B.
Livingston, H. J.
Introduces Clarence B. Randall, Chairman of the Inland Steel Company. PRNE: 8
Prochnow, H. V.
Introduces Clarence B. Randall, Chairman of the Inland Steel Company. PRNE: 9
Randall, Jesse W.
Insurance side of highway safety. MO:518; MOA:524
Randall, John Herman, Jr.
Paradox of intellectual freedom. NORR 3d ser:86
Randall, Samuel Jackson
Tariff legislation. REEMA 14: 1671
Randolph, A. Philip
Labor and the struggle for a better tomorrow. HILK:175
Randolph, Edmund
Federal Constitution. CHEM 1: 161; LEEW 8:161; SMI:51
In defence of Aaron Burr, 1807. BREW 9:23; HELE: 146
In defence of the Union. REEMA 14:1678
Randolph, Edward H.
City of Shreveport (at laying of cornerstone of new City Hall). SHUO:226
Randolph, John
Against war with Great Britain. -Same as his Militia Bill
"Blifil and black George-Puritan and black-leg." BREW 9:31
British influence. -Same as his Militia Bill
Gregg Resolution. -Same as his On offensive war with England
Lays the ground for disunion. - Same as his On internal improvement
Militia Bill. CHEM 2:41; HARS:175; JOHA 1 pt 1:164; SHAH:82; SMI:97
On altering the Virginia Constitution. SMI:117
On foreign importations. -Same as his On offensive war with England
On internal improvements. PE:332; PEA:332
On offensive war with England. BRYW 8:186; CHAL 4:424; HAZO 9:3920; MAS 9:3920; ORAMA 1:351; SHAH:77
On the tariff (1824). REEMA 14:1697
Tariff and the Constitution (1816). PL:599

Rankin, Jeannette
War and world-control. BREW 9:39
Woman suffrage and war. BREW 9:37
Rankin, John E.
Naval supremacy or moral leadership. BRP 1:90
Ranney, Austin
All but inmost faith. NOR 1941:5
Ranney, Roger L.
Justice and the Negro. YR 1:85
Ransier, A.J.
Speech delivered at Charleston, South Carolina, March 9, 1871. WOON:411
Ranson, Reverdy C.
William Lloyd Garrison: a centennial oration. DUNM:305; WOON:531
Ranta, Esko
Spare our lives. YR 10:17
Rapen, J.H.
Educating temperance opinions. THOU 3:521

RAPHAEL SANZIO
Pater, W.
Raphael. REEMA 9:940
Rapier, James T.
Civil Rights Bill. WOON:338
Raschke, Kenneth
It can be done. BRP 10:100
Rashbaum, Phillips
Challenge of the unemployed. BRP 3:7; YR 3:161
Rathbun, James
Pick up the tools. NOR 1942:41

RATIONING
Henderson, L.
Equality of sacrifice. BA 1941-42:162
Ravely, Melville
New deal-a new day. BRP 5:48; YR 6:315

RAW MATERIALS
Roosevelt, F.D.
Statement on continuance of the combined British-Canadian-American production, raw materials and food boards. VO 1945-46:38
Rawson, Edward
Thanksgiving. HURG:20
Ray, Prafulla Chandra
Social reform for India. ZU:61
Rayburn, Samuel
Accepting the office of Speaker of the United States House of Representatives. SAB:219
---- and others (H. Donohue; H.G. Douglas; and J. Martin)
Repeal of the Taft-Hartley law. BA 1948-49:155

RAYBURN, SAMUEL
Dirksen, E.
At 44th anniversary of Congressional service of Speaker Sam Rayburn. BRAP:137
Gore, A.
At 44th anniversary of Congressional service of Speaker Sam Rayburn. BRAP:136
Johnson, L.B.
At 44th anniversary of Congressional service of Speaker Same Rayburn. BRAP:136
Mansfield, M.
At 44th anniversary of Congressional service of Speaker Sam Rayburn. BRAP:136
Martin, J.W.
Introducing Speaker Sam Rayburn. SAB:208; SABA:288
Raymond, Andrew V.V.
Dutch as enemies. REEMA 3:970
Dutch as neighbors. THOU 1:344

Raymond, Henry Jarvis
Administration theory. -Same as his On reconstruction
On reconstruction. CHAL 9:470; HAZO 19:8106; JOHA 2 pt 2:168; MAS 19:8106; WPRA:213
Rayner, Isador
Hero of Santiago. SHUO:252
Rea, Samuel
American transporation. BYRA:354; REEM sup 2:305; REEMB 5:216
Read, Herbert
In defense of abstract art. ARNS:57
Read, Opie
Human nature and politics. EXEE:244
Modern fiction. BLAA:194; BLAB:194; REAC:92; REEMA 3:976
Reading, Douglas K.
Puppets or patriots. BRP 6:99; NOR 1935:124
Reading, Rufus Daniel Isaacs, 1st Marquis of
Across the flood. REEM 3:127; REEMB 3:128

READING See Books and reading; Literature
Readlinger, Cleon
Dollars, doctors, and disease. BRP 6:78
Reagan, Nicholas
Faith, revelation, and the church. CATA 2:281
Reagan, Ronald
Speech at Friars' Club dinner to Burns and Allen. JEYO:85

REAL ESTATE
Coleridge, J. D. C.
On the value of clear views as to the enjoyment of property. CHAL 9:478; HAZO 19:8202; MAS 19:8202
Fourth estate and real estate. SCHS:136
Getman, A.
State and private rights to real property. ONEC:300
How to sell a house. MICS:138
O'Keefe, L.
Introducing a realtor. BRC:206
Real estate (for occasions when realtors convene). EDGS:153
Realtors. SCHS:215
Realtors (one of them sets forth his views). ED:217

REAL PROPERTY See Real Estate

REALITY
Wilson, H. A.
Challenge and the broad view. ANGC:130

REASON
Wesley, J.
Poverty of reason. BREW 10:212

RECHABITES
Harding, J.
Temperance in New Zealand. THOU 3:527

RECONSTRUCTION
Chase, S. P.
Mississippi v. Johnson, 1867: opinion for the Supreme Court. BIR 3:58
Texas v. White, 1869: opinion for the Supreme Court. BIR 3:84
Clark, T. D.
Country newspaper: a factor in Southern opinion, 1865-1930. TIN:211
Conkling, R.
Stalwart standpoint. BREW 4:141
Davis, D.
Ex parte Milligan, 1866: opinion for the Supreme Court. ANG:374; BIR 3:29
Davis, H. W.
Constitutional difficulties of

reconstruction. BREW 5: 32; CHAL 9:175; JOHA 2 pt 2:129
On reconstruction. HAZO 18:7721; MAS 18:7721
Donnelly, I.
On reconstruction. CHAL 12:31; HAZO 22:9423; MAS 22:9423
Galloway, C. B.
Reconstruction in the South; past and present (at dedication of Mississippi's new Capitol). SHUO:294
Garfield, J. A.
On the restoration of the South. REEMA 13:1054
Gibson, E.
Reconstruction acts. SMI: 196
Hill, B. H.
On the perils of the nation. CHAL 10:270; HAZO 20: 8557; MAS 20:8557
Stars and stripes. SOU 9: 354
Howell, C.
Our reunited country. FUL: 153, 155, 157; ONES:190; REEMA 2:647; REEMB 2: 342; WERN 42:64
Johnson, A.
Annual message to Congress, December 3, 1866. ANG: 387
Presidential plan of reconstruction. HARS:423
Veto of the first Reconstruction Act, 1867. BIR 3:41
Langston, J. M.
Other phase of reconstruction. WOON:417
Lee, F.
Flag of the Union forever. REEM 2:318; REEMA 2: 710; REEMB 2:322; SHUO: 241
Long, J. F.
Speech on disorders in the South. WOON:294
Lonn, E.
Reconciliation between the North and the South. TIN: 193
Meek, T. J.
John B. Gordon-the pacificator. TRUW:184
Moore, A. B.
One hundred years of reconstruction of the South. TIN:106
Morton, O. P.
On reconstruction. CHAL 10:224; HAZO 20:8501; MAS 20:8501
On the issues of 1868. HAZO 20:8486; MAS 20: 8486
Pendelton, G. H.
On reconstruction. CHAL 10:435; CHEM 4:247; HAZO 21:8790; JOHA 2 pt 2: 141; MAS 21:8790
Peyton, H. E.
Memorial address. SMI:204
Rainey, J. H.
Southern situation. WOON: 300
Raymond, H. J.
On reconstruction. CHAL 9: 470; HAZO 19:8106; JOHA 2 pt 2:168; MAS 19:8106; WPRA:213
Revels, H. R.
Speech on the Georgia Bill. WOON:286
Seward, W. H.
Reconciliation in 1865. BREW 9:178
Stevens, T.
On reconstruction. CHEM 4:269; JOHA 2 pt. 2:181; LEEW 10:285; WPRA:204
Radical view of reconstruction. BREW 9:292; HARS: 436; HAZO 12:5032; JOHA 2 pt 2: 181; MAS 12:5032
Stone, W. J.
Reconstruction in Missouri. SHUO:131
Williams, J. S.
Bridging the bloody chasm. HARSO:13

RECONSTRUCTION, 1914-1939
Bedford, A. C.

RECONSTRUCTION, 1914-1939 (cont.)
France in the reconstruction period. REEM 4:32; REEMB 4:72
Borden, R. L.
Walk, and not faint. REEM 7:41; REEMB 8:39
Evans, H. R.
House in order; to America lies the task of reconstruction. ASHF:377
Gary, E. H.
Reconstruction and readjustment. HICF:622
Hoover, H. C.
After war questions. REEM 4:212; REEMB 4:411
Recovering from destruction and inflation. BREW 7:71
Jenks, J. W.
America's role in Europe. LINM:288
Kock, K. H.
Whither world? YR 4:175
Nichols, W. H.
Chemist and reconstruction. REEM 4:334; REEMB 5:198
Patterson, G. D.
Greater man. BOB:32; HARSO:63
Wilson, W.
Mission of America. SHU:212
Wirth, J.
Via Dolorosa (to Reichstag). BREW 10:266

---- 1939-1951
Attlee, C. R.
Speech on the King's address. VO 1945-46:448
Blakely, R. J.
Greatest lack. BA 1945-46:241
Brigance, W. N.
Backwash of war. BA 1945-46:75
Brown, L.
Private agencies and public goals in the post war world. BA 1942-43:202; ON:76
Chiang Kai-Shek
Excerpts from victory message, September 3, 1945. VO 1945-46:533
Churchill, W. L. S.
Broadcast March 21, 1943 on the post war world. VO 1943-44:118
Broadcast on the war overseas and reconstruction at home. VO 1944-45:139
Save Europe by uniting Europe (May 14, 1947). HIBS:452
Speech in Commons on British policy in liberated countries. VO 1944-45:602
Clarke, L.
Day after V-day. NOR 1945:29
Conant, J. B.
Civil courage. BA 1945-46:223
DeJean, F. L.
Rehabilitation and reassimilation of fighting men and nations. AN:66
Denton, T. G.
Student responsibility. AN:38
George VI.
Address at opening of Parliament, August 15, 1945. VO 1945-46:438
Gideonse, H.
When to prepare for peace. ON:299
Hanna, E.
What part should the United States play in the economic recovery of Britain? HOD:102
Johnston, E. A.
Partners for peace. HOA:145
Steps toward a good world. HAN:374
Kovar, L.
All this, and for what? AN:78
Lampman, R. J.
Morgen die ganze welt. NOR 1942:65

Luce, C. B.
America in the post war air world. BA 1943-44:143; BOA:37
Marshall, G. C.
Address at Harvard University. ANG:525; GLAD:251; GRAC:152; HURG:283
Rodiger, W.
Outward bound. NOR 1944: 41
Schaeffer, J.
Back to the future. AN:30
Stassen, H. E.
American world policy for peace and progress. BA 1944-45:56
Stettinius, E. R., Jr.
Economic objective of United States foreign policy. HAN:403
Torreyson, V.
America's post war goals. HOD:103
Truman, H. S.
ERP:The Marshall Plan, December 19, 1947. FIP: 280
Message to Congress, September 6, 1945. VO 1945-46:546
Truman Doctrine. BRE: 384; FIP:275
Vandenberg, A. H.
European recovery program. BA 1947-48:24
Wallace, H. A.
Address at Cleveland, October 27, 1943. VO 1943-44: 469
Address at Detroit, July 25, 1943. VO 1943-44:280
Address before the Herald Tribune Forum. VO 1943-44:545
Address on Woodrow Wilson's birthday. HAN:367; VO 1942-43:744
America's part in world reconstruction. BA 1942-43: 93
Builders of to-morrow. ON: 74
Practical religion in the world of tomorrow. BA 1942-43:276
See also World War, 1939-1945-Peace and mediation

RECONSTRUCTION FINANCE CORPORATION
Hoover, H. C.
RFC:Press statement, January 22, 1932; FIP:182
RFC:Press statement, July 6, 1932: The Garner Wagner Relief Bill. FIP:183
RFC:Report of activities, March 25, 1932. FIP:183

RECREATION
Announcing entertainment. WRA:27
Chamber of Commerce president's speech dedicating a recreational park. WRA: 139
Closing speech (at dedication of recreation center). BED: 39; BEDA:80
Cornerstone laying address (at cornerstone dedication of youth center). BED:41; BEDA:82
Dedicatory address (at dedication of recreation center). BED:38; BEDA:79
Mabie, H. W.
Work and play. BLAA:58; BLAB:58
Need for recreation. DR:285
Opening speech (at cornerstone dedication of youth center). BED:40; BEDA:81
Recreational club-speech to establish a recreational club at an inner-office meeting. WRA:201
Taylor, P.
Party games. BRAP:122
Thanking speaker (at dedication of recreation center). BED:38; BEDA:80
Upton, T. D.
Re-creation through recreation. EXEE:392

RECRUITING
Kaser, A. L.
Introducing a recruting officer. BRC:172

RED CROSS
American Red Cross. DR:259
Appeal for funds for the Red Cross. BEB:23; BEC:43
Boardman, M. T.
Dedication of Delano Memorial. GA:65
Davison, H. P.
American Red Cross. REEM 11:296; REEMB 12:313
Eisenhower, D. D.
American Red Cross. BA 1948-49:74
Lincoln, H.
Introducing a Red Cross worker. BRC:42
Macdonald, C.
Lady of the lamp (Florence Nightingale). GA:78
Meyer, A. E.
Address to the Regional Conference of the American Red Cross. BUTA:246
Minnigerode, L.
Dedication of Delano Memorial. GA:67
Vaughan, E. R.
Accepting the Florence Nightingale medal. GA:45
Red Eagle, Creek chief
Surrender speech. JON:66
Red Jacket, Seneca chief
Defence of stiff-armed George. CHAL 3:383; HAZO 7:3041; MAS 7:3041
Missionary effort. BREW 7:119; BRYW 8:9; CHAL 3:388; COP:266; COPA:266; COPB:266; HAZO 7:3046; HURG:57; JON:55; MAS 7:3046; SHE:59
Reply to Mr. Cram. -Same as his Missionary effort
Reply to Samuel Dexter. CHAL 3:379; HAZO 7:3037; MAS 7:3037; ORAMA 1:181; REEM 10:55; REEMA 14:1726; REEMB 11:56
Speech at Fort Stanwix. -Same as his Reply to Samuel Dexter
Wyandot claim to supremacy. SHE:66

RED MEN, IMPROVED ORDER OF
Depew, C. M.
Example of Washington: centennial of his death. THOU 3:302
Green, G. E.
Patriotism of the order. THOU 3:287
Mitchell, S. L.
Tamina traditions. THOU 3:311
Paton, A. H.
Tamina's day. THOU 3:306
Rice, F. H.
Washington (memorial address at 100th anniversary of his death). THOU 3:298
Redding, J. Sanders
Sanctions of the American Negro's literary art. HILK:279
Redfield, Robert
Crisis of our time. BA 1944-45:197
---- See Hutchins, R. M., jt. auth.
Redfield, William C.
Facts and ideals. LINM:244; REEM 4:349; REEMB 5:229
First get the facts. REEM 6:362; REEMB 7:340
Three graces. REEM 3:134; REEMB 3:135
Redmond, John E.
English government in Ireland. KET:440
Exclusion of the Irish members. KET:435
Home rule as a dominant issue. BREW 9:41
Home rule Resolution. KET:441
Ireland and the Boer War. KET:430
Ireland and the coronation.

Redmond, John E. (cont.)
BRYW 6:255
Ireland and the war. BRTH: 350; KET:443; REEM 11: 29; REEMB 12:30
Irish freedom. BEA:359
Irish National Convention in Chicago, 1886. KET:427
Irish problem (1906). KET: 437
On Parnell-15 years in the House of Commons. KET: 429
Reed, Ernest H.
Facts and fallacies. YR 5:301
Reed, Frank N.
War and public opinion. SHUC: 49; TRUW:209
Reed, G. S. T. M.
Fifty years of Washington Masonry (semi-centennial address). THOU 3:66
Reed, George E.
Dedication of Embury Chapel, Brooklyn, THOU 2:461
Reed, James A.
Prohibition. HICF:867
Red line of corruption. BRAC:66
Tolerance. BYRA:367; REEM sup 2:318; REEMB 8:338
Reed, Philip D.
Introduces mayor of the convention city. PR:102
Reed, Thomas Brackett
At the dinner to Joseph H. Choate. REEM 3:136; REEMB 3:137
Closing the Wilson Tariff Bill debate. -Same as his Protection and prosperity
Immortality and good deeds (semi-centennial of Girard College). BLAA:33; BLAB: 33; BREW 9:44 REAC:103; SHUM:266
On national issues. CHAL 13: 316; HAZO 24:10305; MAS 24:10305
Protection and prosperity. BRYW 10:175; REEM 10: 311; REEMB 11:325
Reel, Frederick U.
Political paradox. NOR 1936: 22

REFORM
Emerson, R.W.
Man the reformer. BREW 5:378
Reform. THOS:146
Wilson, W.
Issues of reform. PEAE: 241
See also Great Britain-Politics and Government; Reform Act, 1867; Reform Bills (1831, 1832); Social problems

REFORM ACT (1867)
Beaconsfield, B. D.
Franchise and reform, 1867. BRTH:284; BRTHA: 284

REFORM BILLS (1831, 1832)
Brougham and Vaux, H. P. B.
Supports the Reform Bill. FULB:118; GOOD:915; HAY:164; PE:429; PEA: 429
Lytton, E. G. E. L. B.-L.
On the Reform Bill. LEEW 7:261
Macaulay, T. B.
Reform Bill. ADR 3:62; BRAO:252; BRTH:219; BRTHA:219; BRYW 4:126; CHAL 6:339; COP:177; COPA:177; COPB:177; HAZO 13:5545; MAS 13: 5545; PE:426; PEA:426 REEM 9:219; REEMB 10: 226
Peel, R.
Reform of the franchise. EMS 2:144
Russell, J. R.
Reform of the franchise. EMS 2:137
Smith, S.
Mrs. Partington in politics. BREW 9:247
Reform and stomach troubles. BREW 9:252
Wellington, A. M.

REFORM BILLS (1831, 1832) (cont.)
Reform of the franchise. EMS 2:148
See also Elections

REFORMATION
Froude, J. A.
Influence of the Reformation on Scottish character. HAZO 18:7806; MAS 18:7806

REFUGEES
Roosevelt, F.D.
Statement on war refugees. VO 1944-45:137
You are not alone (address to refugee students). NI:217; NIA:166
Regulus. See Kellogg, Elijah (accredited to).
Reicherson.
For a Bar-Mitzwa. ZEL:19
Reid, Helen M.R. See Reid, Mrs. Ogden
Reid, Ira De A.
Social changes, social relations, social work. HILK:165
Reid, Loren D.
Engineering of ideas (presenting Honor Awards to engineers). BRAB:545
How to improve classroom lectures fifty percent. BRAP:127
Reid, Mrs. Ogden
Introducing Matthew Woll to Ninth Annual Forum of the New York Herald Tribune. BA 1939-40:327
Presents Lillian Smith
" Walt Disney. LY:71, 42
Reid, Robert Threshie See Loreburn, R.T., 1st Earl of
Reid, Whitelaw
At the dinner in his honor. REEM 3:139; REEMB 3:140
Continental Union-Civil Service for the Islands. HICF:212
Fourth of July. REEM 3:144; REEMB 3:145
General welfare. BLAA:209; BLAB:209; FUL:265
Gladstone, England's greatest leader. REEMA 3:981
Introduces George Augustus Sala to Lotus Club. REEMA 3:1014
Introduces Wilkie Collins to Lotus Club. REEMA 1:261
Introduces William Gilbert and Sir Arthur Sullivan to Lotus Club. LY:41; REEM 2:89; REEMB 2:81
Path of duty. FUL:260
Press-right or wrong. REEMA 3:979
Purport of the treaty. FUL:256
Welcoming H.M. Stanley to the Lotus Club of New York, November 27, 1886. REEM 3:263; REEMB 3:281

REID, WHITELAW
Stedman, E.C.
Appreciating Whitelaw Reid. NESA:166
Reiman, Alfred C.E.W.
I am innocent of this blood (peace can only be achieved by education in the home, school, and church). ASHF:302

REINHARDT, MAX
Introducing Max Reinhardt. NI:128; NIA:97
Reith, Emma A.
Sunshine and moonshine, (class history). WERN 54:64

RELAXATION
Spencer, H.
Gospel of relaxation. KLEG:385; REEM 3:248; REEMA 3:1067; REEMB 3:265

RELIEF See Unemployed

RELIGION
Abbot, F.E.
Genius of Christianity and

religion. BL:680
Adler, F.
Nature and the religious mood. REEM 6:30; REEMB 7:30
Aelred, Saint.
Sermon after absence. BREW 1:100
Alexander, R.
Religion as a force in government. BART 1:173
Are you following the pattern? JAI:50
Are you still on the bottle? JAI:67
Augustine, Saint.
Sermon on the transfiguration. LEEW 3:238
Baker, E.E.
Religion and the nation. WAGN:318
Bancroft, G.
People in art, government, and religion. BL:94; BRYW 8:230; HAZO 13: 5630; LAD:96; MAS 13: 5630; REEM sup 1:88; REEMA 7:69; REEMB 7:55; WPRA:65
Baumner, F.L.
Religion and the sceptical tradition. NORR 3d ser:312
Baxter, R.
Unwillingness to improve. BREW 1:250
Bede.
On the nativity of St. Peter and St. Paul. CHAL 1:380; HAZO 3:1230; MAS 3:1230
Sermon for any day. BREW 1:348
Sermon on all Saints. BRYW 3:3; PL:198
Beecher, H.W.
On fellowship. HURG:118
Two revelations. BAAMP: 160
Beecher, L.
Faith once delivered to the Saints. WPRA:99
Bentley, W.
Sermon preached at the stone chapel in Boston. BL: 537
Better life. FRIE:260
Black, H.
Religion and commerce. REEM 1:129; REEMB 1:126
Blackwelder, O.F.
Contribution of the Christian faith. BA 1940-41:255
Blake, E.C.
Good faith. BA 1957-58:168
Boddy, W.H.
Life: a mirage or a fountain. SAR:436
Bonaventura, Saint.
Life of service. BREW 2: 149
Bonnell, J.S.
Glory and tragedy of man. BA 1946-47:239
Making life worth living. BA 1952-53:169
Bosley, H.
If anywhere, then everywhere. BA 1943-44:337
Bradley, P.
Business of religion and the religion of business. ONEC: 479
Bramble king. JAS:92
Brent, C.H.
Finding God among the Tommies. REEM 1:154; REEMB 1:151
Brooks, P.
Beauty of a life of service. CHAL 13:19; HAZO 23:9886; MAS 23:9886
Sermon of greeting. FULB: 369
True liberty. HAZO 23: 9945; MAS 23:9945
Bryan, W.J.
Moses vs. Darwin. WPRC: 107
Prince of peace. BLAB: 367; IMMD:165; PL:697; REEM 8:68; REEMB 13:70
Spoken word. REEM 8:89; REEMB 13:91
Bunyan, J.
Heavenly footman. BREW 2: 323; BRYW 3:149; HAZO 4: 1572; MAS 4:1572; ORBR 1:

RELIGION (cont.)
Burns, C.W.
Good will to men. ONEC: 471
Burrell, D.J.
Belief of an unbeliever. LAD:168
Bushnell, H.
Sermon on the outside saints. HAZO 14:5763; MAS 14:5763
Cahill, D.W.
Last judgment. BREW 3:30
Calhoun, R.L.
Christ-the hope of the world. BA 1954-55:161
Chalmers, T.
Fury not in God! HAZO 10: 4196; MAS 10:4196
Channing, W.E.
Likeness to God. BL:563
Chapin, E.H.
Nicodemus: the seeker after religion. HAZO 18:7460; MAS 18:7460
Cheever, G.B.
Elements of national greatness, 1842. BRAR 1:287
Chillingworth, W.
Sermon on making friends with the mammon of uprighteousness. HAZO 4:1493; MAS 4:1493
Christensen, D.E.
Slavery of man. AN:25
Christian mission. AMEO 2:75
Chrysostom, J.
Heroes of faith. BREW 3:307
Coffin, H.S.
God's mysterious educator. BA 1941-42:236
Compton, A.
Science and religion. BA 1939-40:421
Cook, J.
Certainties in religion. CHAL 13:173; HAZO 24: 10125; MAS 24:10125
Cotton, J.
God's promise to his plantations. CHAL 2:1; HAZO 4: 1422; MAS 4:1422
Cox, S.S.
Sermon on the mount. BREW 4:213
Cram (Moravian missionary)
Expounds his religious precepts to Red Jacket. JON:54
Culture of the imagination - an address before a Young Men's Christian Association. DAVC:484
Cyprian, Saint.
Unshackled living. BREW 4: 363
Dancy, J.C.
Future of the Negro church. DUNM:475
Delayed obedience. JAS:34
Dering, E.
For the encouragement of learning. BREW 5:181
Religious controversy in Parliament. BREW 5:184
Dollinger, J.J.
Founders of religions. REEMA 7:343
Door without a handle. JAI:70
Drummond, H.
"First!" (Speech to Boys Brigade). REEM 6:134; REEMA 7:371; REEMB 7: 116
Edwards, J.
God glorified in man's dependence. BL:517
Sinners in the hands of an angry God. BAAMP:15; BREW 5:355; CHAL 2:236; COP:227; COPA:227; COPB:227; HAZO 5:1811; HURG:21; MAS 5:1811; PAR:73; PL:566; REEM 9: 91; REEMB 10:94
Elson, E.L.R.
Nation under God. BA 1957-58:163
Finding time for God. JA:241
Follow the road signs. JAS:82
Fosdick, H.E.
Jesus' ethical message confronts the world. BA 1938-39:223
Shall Fundamentalists win? WPRC:97
Francis de Sales, Saint.

Sermon on meditation. HAZO 4:1412; MAS 4:1412
Sermon on perseverance in Holy Love. HAZO 4:1409; MAS 4:1409
Freeman, J. E.
Bishop's charge. REEM 1:348; REEMB 6:137
Fuller, T.
How far examples are to be followed. ORBR 1:89
Ill match well broken off. ORBR 1:97
Gannon, R.I.
Want of the world. BA 1948-49:229
Gates, E.D.
Time is running out. HAR:472
Gibbons, J.
To the Parliament of Religions. BREW 6:224; ORAMA 2:393
Truth and sincerity of character. SHUO:123
Gilkey, C.W.
Bridges into a better world. BA 1938-39:234
God's call and men's answers. JA:142
Graham, W. F.
National humility. HURG:339
Grains of sand. FRIE:223
Greene, T. M.
In praise of reflective commitment. NORR 3d ser:142
Gregory, J. F.
Social bearing of the fifth commandment. DUNM:397
Grossman, M. H.
Light that is darkness. YR 10:41
Growth - an address before a Christian Endeavor convention. DAVC:473
Gunsaulus, F.W.
Healthy heresies. BREW 6:317
Hall, C.N.
Christian victory. CHAL 9:114; HAZO 18:7638; MAS 18:7638
Haunted house. JAS:78
Herder, J. G. V.
Meaning of inspiration. BREW 7:37
Hidden lights. JAS:76
Hilary, Saint.
Homily on Psalm LIII. HAZO 3:1217; MAS 3:1217
Hillis, N.D.
Pulpit in modern life. REEM 6:249; REEMA 8:644; REEMB 6:162
Holmes, J. H.
Unknown soldier speaks. SAR:425
Inge, W.
Faith and reason. REEM 2:102; REEMB 6:213
Jones, S.
Thunder and lightning on sinner's head. SOU 9:500
Kalas, J. E.
Call to spiritual greatness. NOR 1950:199
Kennedy, G.
Awake the dawn. BA 1956-57:181
Kennedy, J. F.
Religion in government (to Greater Houston Ministerial Association). HIB:178
Kingdom in your heart. JAI:80
Kingsley, C.
Transfiguration. CHAL 9:248; HAZO 19:8060; MAS 19:8060
Knox, J.
Against tyrants. BREW 7:212; PL:235
LaFarge, J.
Religious philosophy and intergroup progress. HAR:506
Latimer, H.
On the pickings of officeholders. BREW 7:290
Sermon on the plow. BREW 7:285; ORBR 1:3; PL:231
Leo I.
Blessedness of peacemaking. PL:190
Homily on the Beatitudes.

RELIGION (cont.)
HAZO 3:1209; MAS 3:1209
On the feast of the Nativity. LEEW 3:274
Sermon on the community of goods. PL:188
Leo XIII.
Christian democracy. COP: 117; COPA:117; COPB:117; REEMA 14:1323
Let your light shine. JAS:26
Library without books. JAS:70
Liddon, H. P.
Adequacy of present opportunities. CHAL 11:232; HAZO 21:9097; MAS 21:9097
Living or a life. JA:121
Luther, M.
Sermon on the Good Shepherd. LEEW 4:69
Pith of Paul's chief doctrine. BREW 7:410
McArthur, H.K.
Truth and freedom. BA 1950-51:182
McConnell, F. J.
Giants and grasshoppers. REEM sup 2:197; REEMB 6:261
McCracken, R. J.
To have and not to hold. BA 1959-60:173
McEntegart, B.
Totality of outlook. LINP: 175
McGregor, A.
Charge to the people. THOU 2:473
Machen, J. G.
Christianity vs. modern liberalism. WPRC:120
McKeldin, T.
Relation of religion and morality to education. MCK: 209
McKelway, St. C.
Prayer and politics. REEM 2:378; REEMB 2:395
Malik, C.H.
Challenge to Communism. BA 1950-51:169
Man shortage in heaven. JA: 139
Mansfield, F.W.
Religious bigotry. CATA 2: 175
Marsh, G. P.
Address, 1844. BRAR 1: 371
Massilon, J. B.
Sermon on spirit of the Ministry. HAZO 4:1707; MAS 4:1707
Mather, C.
At the sound of the trumpet. BREW 8:120; PL:561
"Bostonian Ebenezer." CHAL 2:144; HAZO 4:1681; MAS 4:1681
Joyful sound of salvation. HIB:195
Melanchthon, P.
Safety of the virtuous. BREW 8:140; HAZO 4:1324; MAS 4:1324
Messages from the dead. JAI: 77
Miller, S.H.
Gospel of insecurity. BA 1964-65:138
Mirabeau, H. G. R.
Against the establishment of religion. BREW 8:164
Mitchell, O. M.
First view of the heavens. CLAY:103
Moses.
Ten commandments. PE:2; PEA:2
Mott, J. R.
Meditation. REEM 6:339; REEMB 7:289
Mullins, E. Y.
Christ's law of service. SOU 9:492
Newman, J. H.
Immortality of the soul. ORBR 2:177
Lecture on the use of private judgment. HAZO 14: 5693; MAS 14:5693
Niebuhr, R.
Adequate faith for the world crisis. BA 1947-48: 227
Christian life and an econ-

omy of abundance. BA 1956-57:191
Nikhilananda, S.
Need for a spiritual revival. HAR:495
Origen.
Parable of the drag-net. LEEW 3:33
Oursler, F. and others.
How can modern man find faith? HAR:480; MOA:484
Ousley, C. N.
Man's responsibility to the higher law. SHUO:191
Outline of a religious speech. BAKS:225
Oxnam, G. B.
We intend to stay together. BA 1954-55:145
Park, E. A.
Theology of the intellect and that of the feelings. BL:624
Peale, N. V.
How to have good relations with other people. BA 1954-55:153
Phillips, H. C.
Religion-a prop for the weak. BA 1950-51:161
Porter, N.
Teachings of science and religion. REEMA 3:950
Power of a song. JAS:28
Practice religion. FRIE:225
Price, J. H. and others.
Is youth forgetting religion? HAR:489
Pusey, N. M.
Religion for now. BA 1953-54:193
Queer religion of the Orient. FRIE:236
Rabanus Magnentius Maurus.
Sermon for Sunday. LEEW 3:291
Reagan, N.
Faith, revelation and the church. CATA 2:281
Ring, T. G.
Need of religion in modern life. CATA 2:255
Robbins, W. L.
Pulpit and the Bar. REEMA 3:985
Ryan, J. A.
Religion, the indispensable basis of democracy. BA 1939-40:408
Salvation. JAI:26
Samples that are convincing. JAI:60
Savonarola, G.
Do penance, penance, penance. HIB:187
On the degeneration of the Church. CHAL 1:393; HAZO 3:1280; MAS 3:1280; PL:221
Sermon on the Ascension. LEEW 4:45; PE:79; PEA:79
Seelye, J. H.
Relation of learning and religion; inaugural address as president of Amherst College. WE 1:163
Shadows of tomorrow. JA:247
Sheen, F. J.
Change of hearts. HURG:264
Cross and the double cross. COP:598; COPB:574
Judgment of nations. BA 1942-43:299
Liberty and the Republic. BA 1938-39:245
Signs of our times. BA 1946-47:246
Shepard, J. E.
Is the game worth the candle? DUNM:357
Should women keep silent? JA:244
Shulman, C. E.
Four philosophies of modern life. BA 1957-58:174
Shuster, G. N.
Doctrine for the time. ON:70
Smith, A. E.
Religion and politics. COP:408; COPA:408; COPB:408; HICF:837; HURG:209
Sockman, R. W.

RELIGION (cont.)
Comfort ye my people. BA 1950-51:191
Higher religion for higher education. BA 1948-49:216
Redeeming our regrets. BA 1946-47:271
This nation under God. BA 1942-43:267
Song of the Lord. JA:35
Souter, L.K.
Inevitable parallel. YR 1:165
Spring, G.
Remarks against the religion and morals of the people of Boston and its vicinity. BRAR 1:57
Spurgeon, C.H.
Everlasting oxydization. BREW 9:268
Stires, E.M.
Sincerity and sacrifice. LAD:153
Stockdale, A.A.
Making spiritual history. BART 1:13
Sunday, W.A.
Evangelism. HURG:170
Sunflower (short talk for any religious occasion). ED:305
Talmage, T.D.
Chant at the cornerstone. CHAL 12:44; HAZO 22:9448; MAS 22:9448
Tauler, J.
Sermon VI. LEEW 3:363
Taylor, J.
Foolish exchange. BREW 9:369
Teachers sent from God. JA:217
This side of heaven. JA:253
Thurman, H.
Good news for the underprivileged. HILK:258
Tillich, P.J.
Loneliness and solitude. BA 1957-58:185
"What is truth?" ARNS:182
Time to decide. JAS:38
Tittle, E.F.
Prince of Peace. BA 1943-44:329
To be kings among men-a chapel address by a college president. DAVC:478
Tucker, W.J.
Man's soul and his world (sermon at a Sunday evening service in college chapel). ONEM:775
Urban II.
Speech at the Council of Clermont. CROC:445; LEEW 3:323; PE:66; PEA:66
Wallace, H.A.
Practical religion in the world of tomorrow. BA 1942-43:276
Statesmanship and religion. KLEB:153
Walsh, E.A.
Religion and the modern mind. SAR:419
Weiss, J.
Task of religion. REEMA 9:1162
Wesley, J.
Free grace. ORBR 1:181
God's love to fallen man. BREW 3:173; CHAL 2:208; COP:153; COPA:153; COPB:153; HAZO 5:1783 HIB:199; MAS 5:1783; PL:486; REEM 9:85; REEMB 10:88
Sacra fames auri. BREW 10:215
What is your temperature? JAI:53
Whitefield, G.
On the method of grace. BRYW 3:181; CHAL 2:298; HAZO 5:1975; MAS 5:1975; PL:491
Whose side are you on? JAI:24
Wigmore, J.H.
Enlistment in the Christian ministry. REEM 6:421; REEMB 6:398
Winston, A.
There lies our frontier. BA 1952-53:175

Wycliffe, J.
Concerning a grain of corn. BREW 10:278
Good lore for simple folk. BREW 10:274
See also Church; Church and State; Clergy; Faith; God; Prayers; Sin; United States-Religious history

---- AND SCIENCE
Conant, J. B.
Science and spiritual values. ARNS:89
Hayes, P. J.
Faith and science. ONEC: 463
Parker, T.
Philosophical idea of God and its relation to the scientific and religious wants of mankind now. BL:659
Peabody, A. P.
Connection between science and religion. NORR 1st ser: 76
Pollard, W. G.
Science as community. IOCP:49
Wilson, R. E.
Since King David's time. BAAG:374

---- AND STATE See Church and state

RELIGIOUS EDUCATION
Bushnell, H. I.
Christian nurture. BL:605
Welcome to a new minister of religious education and family. HNWS:15

RELIGIOUS LIBERTY
Beecher, H. W.
Religious freedom (68th anniversary of New England Society). BEA:31; REEM 1:92; REEMA 1:41; REEMB 1:87
Bromley, I. H.
Connecticut's part in the business. REEMA 1:86
Bryan, W. J.
Religious liberty and the Ku Klux Klan. WHIP:290
Colby, B.
Religious liberty and the Ku Klux Klan. WHIP:298
Danton, G. J.
Freedom of worship. BREW 4:402; BRYW 7:132; CHAL 4:114; HAZO 8:3349; MAS 8:3349; PL:302
Fox, C. J.
Religious liberty, May 8, 1789 speech. EMS 2:6
Religious liberty, May 11, 1792 speech. EMS 2:12
Sheil, R. L.
Religious toleration. HAY: 138; KET:333
Walsh, D. I.
Religious tolerance. BOB: 67
Religious tolerance. BOA: 68; BOB:95
Williams, R.
Liberty of conscience or the sole means to obtain peace and truth. PL:558
Remond, Charles Lenox
Anti-slavery discourse. WOON: 237
Rights of colored citizens in traveling. WOON:144
Slavery and the Irish. WOON: 131
Slavery as it concerns the British. WOON:127
Speech before the New England Anti-Slavery Convention. WOON:229

REORGANIZATION ACT OF 1939 (UNITED STATES)
Coughlin, C. E.
Spirit of the Reorganization Bill. BA 1937-38:111

REPARATIONS-EUROPEAN WAR See European War, 1914-1918-Reparations

REPARTEE See Responses

REPENTANCE
Saurin, J.
Repentance of the unchaste woman. PL:285

REPORTS
Beard, G. G.
United Engineering and Foundry Company. SABA: 192
Benchley, R. C.
Treasurer's report. BOU: 198; HIBS:505; HURG:211
Kienzle, G. J.
Report of a research study in public relations. SABA: 197
Metzger, G. E.
Proposed grain marketing program. SAB:118
Myers, C. J.
Sources of our strength. MICS:158
Presenting a favorable report. FRIE:76
Presenting report. FRIE:67, 323
President's annual report. BEDA:137
Publicity committee report. BEDA:138
Report of the building committee of the----church. MICS: 155
Reports and how they sound. NAT:38
Suggestions for preparation of reports. BAAGA:244; BUT: 44; MO:19, 387, 633. With examples of. MICS:154; SAB:21, 99; SABA:165
Suggestions for preparation of reports on conventions. BUT:44; BUTA:44; BUTB: 44
Suggestions for the presentation of secretary's and treasurer's reports. REAB: 160
See also Club speeches; Congresses and conventions

REPUBLICAN PARTY
Barton, B.
One great issue. HOB:137; ON:253; SAR:132
Belin, D.W.
Party plight. NOR 1950:212
Burton, T. E.
Republican keynote speech, 1924. WHIP:155
Eisenhower, D. D.
Republican precinct day rally. BA 1954-55:71; LOMS:235; LOMSA:299
Fairfield, W.
Whom should the Republicans nominate for President? JUD:185
Frye, W. P.
Republican Party. REEMA 13:1031
Grant, U. S.
Why I am a Republican. BRYW 10:107; CHAL 10:182; HAZO 20:8403; MAS 20: 8403; REEM 10:284; REEMB 11:297; WERN 42:170
Hoover, H. C.
Road to freedom. SAR:128; WPRC:198
Hughes, C. E.
To a Republican club. KNAS:318; KNASA:318
Jackson, R. H. and others.
Essential differences between the Republican and Democratic parties. BA 1939-40:233
Lincoln, A.
Lincoln-Douglas joint debate at Alton, October 15, 1858. BAAMP:101; BIR 2: 226; CLAW:90
Lodge, H. C.
Party harmony and political friendship. BYRA:286; REEM 10:386; REEMB 11: 402
Nixon, R. M.
Republican cause in 1956. BA 1955-56:108
Vote Republican (1954). BA 1954-55:89
Vote Republican (1958). BA 1958-59:101

Political speech about the Republican Party. THOS:103
Republican Party (by a staunch supporter). ED:95
Republican speech. AMEO 2:122
Roosevelt, F.D.
Republican leadership and national defense. BA 1940-41:124
Smith, T.V.
Forward America. BA 1938-39:119
Stevenson, A.E.
Scoring the Republican record. BA 1955-56:120
Taft, R.A.
Forward America. BA 1938-39:130; BRYA:534
Vote Republican. BA 1950-51:117
Why I am a Republican. AMEO 2:117
Willkie, W.
Function of a political party. BA 1943-44:267
See also Campaign speeches; Political conventions-Republican

REPUBLICS See Democracy

REPUTATION
Philips, C.
Value of reputation. REAC:138

RESEARCH
Carty, J.J.
Twenty-five years of research. ONEC:114
Gladstone, W.E.
Age of research. KLEM:44; REEM 2:96; REEMA 2:530; REEMB 2:88
Huxley, T.H.
Method of scientific investigation. ARNS:260; BRY:455; BRYA:482
Kappel, F.R.
Business needs basic research. SABA:230
Smith, R.
Professor anonymous. BRP 4:33; INTW 1933:35; YR 5:93
See also Learning and scholarship

RESIGNATIONS
Acceptance of a resignation. STOC:113
Acceptance of resignation-three examples of. STON:119
Hammarskjold, D.
No right to resign. BOU:183
Resignation of membership. STOC:111
Resignation of membership-two examples of. STON:117
Resignation of office-two examples of. STON:117
Stubbs, W.
On resigning the Regius Professorship of History. KNAS:237; KNASA:237
See also Officers, retiring; Offices-Resignation

RESOLUTIONS
American Bar Association resolution adopted July 18, 1924. LEIO:129
Changed heart. JAS:124
Class resolutions. PAIC:335
Congratulatory letter to a club member who received honors. EDGS:412
Materials for use in composing resolutions. With examples of. BEC:46, 50
Resolution accepting resignation of a retiring officer by the officials of a company. EDGS:144
Resolutions complimenting a captain of a steamer on a successful voyage. HILL:418
Resolutions complimenting a public official upon retirement. HILL:418
Resolution endorsing political candidate-two examples of.

RESOLUTIONS (cont.)
BEB:33
Resolution for testimonial. BEB:35
Resolution for the passage of an interstate narcotic law. HE:112
Resolution of appreciation. BEB:31
Resolution of appreciation for hospitality (at a convention). BEDA:142
Resolution of praise-3 examples of. BEC:50
Resolution of praise (retiring clerk). BEB:34
Resolution of praise for raising funds. BEB:36
Resolution of praise on retirement-two examples. BEB: 105-106
Resolution of remonstrance against shooting and trapping of fur-bearing animals. HE:109
Resolution of remonstrance against the government restricting the employment of women. HE:109
Resolution of remonstrance by a spirited citizen. EDGS: 411
Resolution of thanks. BEC:53
Resolution of thanks. THOU 3: 500
Resolution of thanks for a benevolent action. EDGS: 415
Resolution of thanks for hospitality. BEC:52
Resolution of thanks (testimonial dinner). BEB:35
Resolution of thanks to retiring officer (at end of his term)-two examples of. STON:120
Resolution of tribute. BEC:53
Resolution on the cessstion of slavery and the slave trade. WOON:119
Resolution thanking press. BEB:34; BEC:52
Resolution to aid charity. BEB:32; BEC:51
Resolution to postpone any action to discontinue the South Side Bathing Beach. HE:111
Resolutions at a stockholder's meeting, in favor of a certain route. HILL:420
Resolutions at a temperance meeting. HILL:420
Resolutions complimenting a captain of a steamer on a successful voyage. BARB: 211
Resolutions complimenting a public official upon his retirement. BARB:213
Resolutions complimenting a retiring president of a club, society, or other institution. BARB:212
Resolutions complimenting a teacher. HILL:417
Resolutions congratulating a public officer on his appointment. BARB:210
Resolutions favorable to forming an association. HILL: 420
Resolution of thanks to retiring officer at end of his term. STOC:114
Resolution on the departure of a clergyman. HILL:420
Resolutions on the departure of a Sunday school teacher. HILL:420
Resolutions remonstrating against a nuisance. HILL: 420
Resolution thanking a conductor, and commending a railway. HILL:418
Scroll of appreciation. BEB: 31

---- MEMORIAL
Memorial resolution. HILL: 419
Memorial resolutions. STOC: 117-118
Memorial resolutions-two examples of. STON:123

On the death of a clergyman. HILL:418
On the death of a member of any society, club, or other association. HILL:418
Resolution of condolence on the death of a distinguished citizen. EDGS:416
Resolution of condolence on the death of a lodge member. EDGS:417
Resolution of condolence on the death of a member of a Civic Club. HE:108
Resolution of condolence on the death of a member of a women's club. HE:108
Resolution of sympathy (at memorial service). BED: 45; BEDA:86
Resolution on the death of a lodge member. HE:107
Resolution on the death of Queen Alexandra. YE:103
Resolutions of condolence to the family of a deceased clergyman. BARB:203
Resolutions of respect and condolence on the death of a Freemason. HILL:417
Resolutions on the death of a member of society, club, or other associations. BARB: 214
Six models of memorial resolutions. BEB:37-40
See also Condolences

RESPONSES
Chairman's responses to addresses by speakers-seven examples of. BEB:59-61
Emerson, R.W.
Oration and response (250th anniversary of the landing of the Pilgrims). BRAR 2: 371
Gideonse, H.D.
Reply to Nadine Miller's address "Is advertising responsible for our high standard of living?" MOA: 463
Repartee suggestions for speakers. With examples of. BRM:231-264
Some A B C directions for making speeches, toasts and responses. PITT:32-36
Suggestions for responding to Fourth of July speech. PITT:37
Suggestions for the preparation of the response. LARW: 112

---- TO CONGRATULATIONS
Bridegroom's acknowledgment to a tin wedding anniversary speech. BARB:74
Bridegroom's reply to a congratulation speech. BARB: 67
Bridegroom's reply to a tin wedding anniversary speech. BARB:71
Bridegroom's response to a crystal anniversary speech. BARB:78
Candidate's reply to speech of congratulation. HILL:468
Father's response to christening speeches for a girl or boy. BARB:82, 83
Husband's reply to a golden anniversary speech. BARB: 80
Husband's reply to an anniversary speech. BARB:69
Logan, J.A.
Response to Illinois Republican Association. HILL: 485
Reply of a candidate on being elected. BARB:90
Reply of a successful candidate to a speech in his honor. BARB:127
Reply of captain to congratulatory speech at end of voyage. BARB:149
Reply of young man on his 21st birthday to congratulatory speech. BARB:87
Response by the captain to congratulatory speech at

RESPONSES TO CONGRATULATIONS (cont.)
end of voyage. EDGS:350
Response of a college professor to a complimentary resolution. DAVC:602
Response of a fiance to engagement speech. EDGS: 254
Response of a new restaurant owner to congratulatory speech. EDGS:161
Response of a successful candidate to congratulatory speech. EDGS:66
Response of bridegroom to wedding speech. EDGS:258
Response of candidate to a congratulatory speech. EDGS:71
Response of host to house-warming speech. BARB:138
Response of husband to house-warming speech. EDGS:261
Response of husband to wedding anniversary speech. EDGS:266
Response to a birthday speech. BARB:85
Response to congratulations on twenty first birthday. EDGS: 284
Response to congratulatory speech on return from Europe. BARB:94
Responses of fathers to christening speech for a son and for a daughter. EDGS:292, 294
Responses of husbands to wooden, tin, crystal, silver, and golden wedding anniversary speeches. EDGS:270, 273, 276, 279, 281
Root, E.
Response on eightieth birthday. KLEB:139; LINM:259
See also Acceptance speeches

RESPONSES TO FAREWELL
Minister's response on departing for Europe. HAPR:97
Response of one going abroad to farewell dinner. EDGS: 330
Response to farewell speech on departure for Europe. BARB:92

---- TO INTRODUCTIONS
Acknowledging introduction-examples of. FRIE:310
Adenauer, K.
Responds to introduction by C.W.D. Hanson. PRC:27
Amory, H.
Addresses the American Chamber of Commerce in London. PRNE:55
Armstrong, R.H.
Opens his address after he has received a flowery introduction. PRNE:60
Response where toastmaster or chairman not only was flowery in his introduction, but gave him titles or offices to which he was not entitled. PRNE:61
Arnall, E.
Response to introduction. PR:120
Barkley, A.W.
Response to an introduction. PR:128
Barrington, J.
Responds to an introduction at an International Conference on Asian Problems. PRNE:52
Bates, K.L.
Response-America the beautiful. DOA:83
Bayar, C.
Begins an address before the American-Turkish Society. PRNE:73
Benson, E.T.
Responds to the introduction by Howard D. Murphy. PRC:31
Bradley, P.
Response to an introduction. PR:125
Byrd, R.E.
Response to introduction.

PR:121
Canham, E.D.
Responds to an introduction. PRNE:66
Carothers, N.
Response to introduction. PR:130
Caserio, M.J.
Responds to an introduction. PRC:10
Chase, I.
Responds to Clinton Youle's introduction. PRC:7
Childs, M.W.
Responds to an introduction. PRNE:63
Collins, T.
Response to an introduction. PR:118
Response to an introduction which included only his name and title. PR:126
Conick, H.C.
Begins an address on the occasion of the 88th annual meeting of National Fire Underwriters. PRNE:53
Cowles, G.
Responds to an introduction. PRNE:62
Davis, F.B., Jr.
Response to an introduction. PR:43
Depew, C.M.
Two responses to introductions. HOAP:34
Doe, R.W.
Response to an introduction. PR:121
Doolittle, J.H.
Response to an introduction. PR:134
Drown, H.J.
Responds to an introduction before the Rotary Club. PRNE:68
Drummond, R.
Response to an introduction. PR:119
Eisenhower, D.D.
Begins an address at the American Legion Convention. PRNE:73
Begins an address before the annual meeting of the Chamber of Commerce of the United States. PRNE:77
Responds to an introduction by the Prime Minister of Canada. PRNE:51
Examples of replies to introductions. BO:39-42
Five examples of responses to introductions. DR:15-16
Flack, G.
Responds to an introduction. PRNE:59
Foy, F.C.
Responds to an introduction by B. Stuart Weyforth, Jr. PRC:29
Frick, F.
Responds to introduction by Wilfrid Smith. PRC:18
Fulbright, J.W.
Response to an introduction. PR:122
Gillilan, S.W.
Response to a long-winded toastmaster. HOA:367
Gordon, D.
Responds to an introduction. PRC:9
Graff, J.V.
Response to an introduction. PR:132
Gruenther, A.M.
Responds to an introduction before the English-speaking Union of the Commonwealth. PRNE:56
Guernsey, S.K.
Response to introduction. PR:124
Hall, J.B.
Begins an address before the Women's Advertising Club. PRNE:56
Hanley, J.R.
Response to introduction. PR:119
Hendrickson, R.C.
Begins an address before the Secretary's Conference on Juvenile Delinquency.

RESPONSES TO INTRODUCTION (cont.)
PRNE:55
Hoey, C.R.
Response to introduction. PR:133
Hood, C.F.
Responds to an introduction. PRNE:69
Hoover, H.C.
Begins an address on the occasion of the State of Iowa's celebration of his eightieth birthday at his birthplace, West Branch, Iowa. PRNE:65
Jessel, G.
Response to introduction as Toastmaster General at dinner in honor of Mannie Sack, and introduction of principal speaker, David Sarnoff. JEYO:55
Jones, W.A.
Responds to an introduction. PRNE:76
Judd, W.H.
Responds to an introduction. PRNE:51
Kiekhofer, W.H.
Response to an introduction. PR:127
Kirk, G.
Responds to an introduction. PRNE:70
Leighty, G.E.
Responds to an introduction. PRC:9
Lewis, F., Jr.
Responds to an introduction. PRNE:62
Responds to an introduction. PRNE:70
Loomis, D.P.
Responds to introduction by Rudolph G. Rydin. PRC:12
Love, G.H.
Response to an introduction. PR:133
McCaffrey, J.L.
Begins address before the National Industrial Conference Board. PRNE:75
MacDonald, J.R.
Address to the House of Representatives. ONEC:10
McLain, H.O.
Two responses to introductions. PR:83, 131
McMillin, A.N.
Response to an introduction. PR:115
Malott, D.W.
Response to introduction. PR:120
Martin, J.W.
Begins an address at the Lions International Convention. PRNE:54
Modest acknowledgement of introduction. FRIE:338
Morrill, J.L.
Begins an address at the University of Minnesota. PRNE:78
Muskie, E.S.
Responds to an introduction. PRNE:58
Paine, R.D., Jr.
Responds to an introduction. PRNE:62
Parkinson, C.N.
Responds to an introduction by Clinton Youle. PRC:22
Peale, N.V.
Response to introduction. PR:123
Pearson, L.B.
Begins an address on "Canada-nation on the march." PRNE:57
Prochnow, H.V.
Begins an address on "The international situation." PRNE:65
Pusey, N.M.
Responds to an introduction. PRNE:59
Pyle, H.
Begins an address before the Los Angeles Bar Association. PRNE:53
Richberg, D.R.
Responds to an introduction at an annual meeting of the Industrial Research Insti-

tute. PRNE:51
Romney, G.
Responds to introduction by Howard D. Murphy. PRC: 24
Ross, W.O.
Begins an address at the annual Swing-In, Senior Class Program, Wayne University. PRNE:67
Schumann, M.M.
Responds to an introduction. PRNE:72
Sheen, F.J.
Responds to an introduction. PRNE:64
Short, D.
Response to introduction. PR:119
Sibley, C.
Response to introduction. PR:129
Snyder, F.B.
Response to an introduction. PR:128
Speckman, H.A.
Responds to an introduction. PRC:20
Stassen, H.E.
Two responses to introductions. PR:122,125
Suggestions for preparation of replies to introductions. With examples of. LU:1121; SUM:106; YE:166
Suggestions on how to counteract the long-winded introduction. With examples of. BRM:69-74
Suggestions on how to make humorous responses. With examples of. BRM:111-122
Suggestions on how to make successful responses to introductions. With examples of. BRM:12-26
Suggestions on how to reply to misinformation or exaggerated statements of chairman. With examples of. BRM:101-110
Suggestions on how to respond- for the speaker who arrives late. With examples of. BRM:91-94
Suggestions on how to respond when introduced without warning. With examples of. BRM:57-67
Suggestions on how to respond when speaker disagrees with chairman's point of view. With examples of. BRM:95-100
Suggestions on how to respond when the chairman flatters the speaker. With examples of. BRM:75-90
Taft, W.H.
Response to a lengthy introductory speech. HOA: 267; HOAP:251
Thompson, D.
Responds to an introduction at Executive's Club, where she was substituting for Clare Booth Luce. PRNE:74
Veeck, W.
Responds to introduction by Clinton Youle. PRC:26
Wagner, R.F.
Responds to introduction by Clinton Youle. PRC:13
Weber, W.
Remarks in response to introduction. PR:117
White, P.D.
Responds to the introduction by C.W.D. Hanson. PRC: 30
Wilson, R.E.
Begins an address before the Associated Colleges of Indiana dinner. PRNE:50
Wright, W.W.
Begins an address before the Sixth Annual Community Leader Oil Progress luncheon. PRNE:77
See also Responses to welcome

---- TO INVITATION TO SPEAK
See Extemporaneous speeches

RESPONSES TO PRESENTATION
See Acceptance speeches

RESPONSES TO SPEECHES OF BLAME See Defense, speeches of

RESPONSES TO TOASTS
Abstract of a response to a toast "Noblesse oblige." DAVC:623
Ayers, A.D.
In memory of a pal. NESA: 212
Barrie, J.M.
Barrie bumps Stevenson. REEMB 1:73
Literature and the press. COP:692; COPB:719; GLAD: 181
Braxton, A.C.
Fifteenth Amendment (response to toast). SHUO:266
Business man's political obligations. DAVC:408
Butler, B.F.
Humorous response to the toast "Our forefathers." PITT:50
Carpenter, M.H.
Replying to the Grand Duke Alexis (response to Duke's toast "To the President of the United States.") BREW 3:136
Chairman's reply to a toast to his health. BARB:55
Conant, J.B.
Response to toast "Forefather's day." HOC:30
Delmas, D.M.
Washington (response to toast "The character of Washington"). WAGN:259
Dickens, C.
English friendliness for America. COP:615; COPB: 655; REEMA 1:405
Everett, E.
Vegetable and mineral gold. LAD:137; REEMA 8:456
Foord, J.
Land o' cakes. REEMA 2: 500
Future of the nation. DAVC: 419
Host's reply to a toast of health. BARB:52
In reply to the toast "The Press." BARB:58
In response to the toast "Sweethearts and wives." BARB:135
Irving, H.
Looking forward. REEMA 2:676
Kernan, T.J.
Louisiana (response to toast). SHUO:224
Landlord's reply to speech at the opening of his eating house or hotel. BARB:141
Landsman's response to the toast of "The Navy." HILL: 482
Long, J.D.
Response to toast at National Druggists' Association. HOA:375; HOAP:262
Low, S.
Chamber of Commerce. REEM 4:298; REEMA 2: 731; REEMB 5:138
(Masonic) Master's reply to toast. EDW:43
Montague, W.F.
"Our guest;" reply to the toast. THOU 3:265
Outline of a response to the toast "Our country." PITT: 41
Outline of a speech in response to the toast "The day we celebrate." PITT: 39
Pitt, W., 1759-1806
Replies to a toast. HIBS: 495; PE:318; PEA:318
Plain people. DAVC:398
Puritan and the Dutchman-response to a toast at a banquet of New England Society. DAVC:392
Recollection, the strongest influence. DAVC:416
Reply for London Grand Rank

(Freemason). EDW:37
Reply of a distinguished guest to a speech in his honor. BARB:54
Reply of host to a toast in his honor. BARB:163
Reply of the Worshipful Master (Masonic) to the toast of a Lodge on its twenty-fifth anniversary meeting. EDW: 65
Reply to the toast "The bride" by the bridegroom. WRA: 65
Reply to the toast to the visitors at club meeting. WRA: 63
Reply to toast "Our host." BARB:51
Reply to toast "Our host and hostess." BARB:164
Reply to toast "Our host and hostess." HILL:483
Reply to toast "Prosperity to our sister societies." BARB:63
Response by chairman to a toast. EDGS:352
Response by host to a toast. EDGS:263
Response to a toast to "Our mothers" (at mother and daughter banquet). WRA: 64
Response to a toast to "The bridesmaids" by the best man. WRA:66
Response to captain of the winning team. EDGS:389
Response to the toast of "The Army." BARB:59
Response to the toast of "The Navy." HILL:482
Response to the toast of "The Navy." BARB:61
Response to the toast "Our dad" at father and son banquet. WRA:64
Response to toast "General Jackson: a diamond in the rough, but a diamond." PITT:93
Response to toast "The Navy: our country's best wall of defense." PITT:92
Response to the toast of "The Press." HILL:483
Response to the toast "The working man: may he have plenty of it, with good wages promptly paid." PITT:94
Responses to the toast "The ladies." BARB:47, 48, 50
Sketch of a speech in response to the toast "Our honored dead." PITT:43
Sovereignty of the United States. DAVC:411
Speech of a sentimentalist (in response to the toast "The ladies"). HILL:482
Suggestions for making responses to toasts and examples. WRA:62
Suggestions for responding to a toast. WRB:169
Thoughts for a speech in response to the toast "Washington: great as a soldier greater as a statesman, greatest as a pure patriot." PITT:49
Woman. DAVC:401
Yale and Princeton. DAVC: 390

---- TO TRIBUTES

Acceptance and thanks (by past president of labor union at unveiling of portrait). BED: 91; BEDA:164
Acceptance speech by woman civic leader. BEDA:44
Accepting honor and acknowledging tributes (at physician-of-the-year award). BED:53; BEDA:56
Acknowledging an honor. FRIE:337
Acknowledging appreciation (at hospital fund drive and testimonial). BED:66; BEDA: 102
Acknowledging ovation. NATM: 12

RESPONSES TO TRIBUTES (cont.)
Allen, G.
Response to tributes at Friars' Club dinner. JEYO: 111
Appreciation and acceptance (at presentation of Brotherhood award). BED:57; BEDA:66
Barkley, A.W.
Response to tribute by A.H. Vandenberg. BA 1948-49:98
Burns, G.
Response to tributes at Friars' Club dinner. JEYO:111, 113, 114
Cannon, J.G.
Response to tributes. HOA: 361
Eisenhower, D.D.
Unity won the war. HAN: 309; ON:330; PE:798; PEA:798
Farewell address (by retiring secretary of labor union). BED:81; BEDA:154
Guest-of-honor acknowledges praise and citation (at testimonial to philanthropist). BED:25; BEDA:47
Holmes, O.W., Jr.
"Live-I am coming:" response to birthday greetings. COP:377; COPA:377; COPB:377; HURG:215; YE:148
Hughes, C.E.
Response to a tribute. YE: 149
Jessel, G.
Acceptance speech at Friars' Club dinner, 1948. JEYO:125
Accepting the Humanitarian award at Friars' Club dinner, 1954. JEYO:118
Responding to tribute (by labor union official). BED:84; BEDA:157
Response by guest-of-honor (at testimonial on retirement of public official). BED:30; BEDA:51
Suggestions for preparation of replies to speeches of tribute. With examples of. YE:147
Thanks and appreciation (at birthday testimonial). BEDA: 32
Thanks and appreciation (by guest of honor at testimonial dinner to journalist). BED:22; BEDA:37
Two responses to birthday greetings. SOES:45, 46

---- TO WELCOME
Address in response to welcome. PITT:65
Anthony, K.V.
Response to address of welcome. YE:169
Bachelor's response to welcome on returning home from abroad. HAPR:62
Blaine, J.G.
Response to Chicago Board of Trade's welcome. HILL: 479
Bryan, W.J.
Response to a welcome address. HOAP:34
Cecil of Chelwood, E.A.R.G.
Speech of response to introduction by C. Depew at a Pilgrim dinner. COP: 690; COPB:717; LINM:398; REEM sup 1:179; REEMB 8:81
Coleridge, J.D.
In golden chains. REEMA 1:253
Collins, W.
American hospitality. REEMA 1:261
Colonel or Captain's reply to a welcome address to the regiment or company. BARB:114
Depew, C.M.
Response to welcome. BRAC:250
Eden, A.
Response to welcome at United Nations Conference.

MO:506; MOA:510
Eisenhower, D. D.
Response on being made honorary citizen of the City of New York. ON:327
Response to home town welcome. ON:259
Fraternity-response to welcome address. THOS:51
German, W. M.
Speech of response delivered before the members of the Metropolitan Insurance Company. LINM:492
Green, W.
Response to Toronto's welcome. ONEC:25
Humorous response to an address of welcome. THOS:55
Irving, W.
My native land. KNAS:185; KNASA:185; REEM 2:276; REEMA 8:736; REEMB 2:276
Jewell, B. R.
Response to address of welcome. THOU 3:488
Kooker, E. M.
Response to welcome of honor students. JUD:203
Kossuth, L.
On his welcome to New York. BRYW 7:249; CHAL 7:43; COP:106; COPA:106; COPB:106; HAZO 14:5832; MAS 14:5832; PE:465; PEA:465; PL:338
Response to the Governor of Pennsylvania. KNAS:221; KNASA:221; ONEM:691
Speech in Faneuil Hall. CHAL 7:20; HAZO 14:5809; MAS 14:5809; REEMA 13:1269
Lafayette, M. J. P. R. Y.
Response to Henry Clay's address of welcome. KNAS:218; KNASA:218
Lawson, R. C.
Response to welcome. GA:28
Leland, C. G.
Hans Breitman's return. REEMA 2:717
Lindbergh, C. A.
Response to New York's welcome. ONEC:21
Low, S.
Response to welcome. ONES:85
Lowell, J. R.
Return of the native (response to a welcome home). ONEM:697; REEM 2:363; REEMA 2:753; REEMB 2:376
MacDonald, J. R.
Response to the Honorable J. J. Walker. LINM:427
M'Nall, W.
Response to address of welcome by the mayor of the United Workmen. THOU 3:325
Matsuoka, Y.
Reply to Ribbentrop. VO 1941:144
Model and outline for speech of response to welcome address, BAKF:112, 117
Mussolini, B.
Response to Ambassador Child's speech. LINM:390
Our country: response to a welcome address. THOS:49
Parnell, C. S.
His first speech in America. BREW 8:280; PL:545
Phillips, C.
Dinas Island speech on Washington. BREW 8:313; HAZO 12:4847; MAS 12:4847; REEMA 14:1583
Ralls, M. C.
We are glad to be here. GA:30
Reply by foreman of a visiting fire company to a welcome speech. HILL:479
Reply by the president of a cricket club to reception address. BARB:120
Reply of a fire company foreman to a reception address. BARB:116
Reply of distinguished guest to

RESPONSES TO WELCOME (cont.)
welcome. HILL:462
Reply of president of a temperance association to welcome address. BARB:122
Reply of the president of a baseball club. BARB:115
Reply of traveler on his return from trip abroad. BARB:94
Reply to a boat club reception address. BARB:118
Reply to a speech of welcome. HILL:462
Reply to an address of welcome at a club meeting. WRA:74
Reply to the address of welcome at a formal meeting of a lodge or society. WRA:75
Response by a teacher to a welcome address delivered by the president of a teachers' association. AMEO 1:25
Response by a visitor to club welcome. EDGS:366
Response by the president of the Women's Club. SOES:26
Response of a member of the visiting baseball team to welcome speech. EDGS:391
Response of class president to address of president of board of education. AMEO 1:182
Response of traveler to welcome home address. EDGS:333
Response to address of welcome (Mystic Worker). THOU 3:465
Response to address of welcome to women social workers. AMEO 2:212
Response to an address of welcome. THOS:49
Response to an address of welcome at a lodge. THOS:52
Response to speech of welcome. HILL:470
Response to welcome address by the Eastern Star. THOS:57
Response to welcome by a former pastor. HNWS:55
Response to welcome by a guest evangelist. HNWS:57
Response to welcome by a guest speaker. HNWS:56
Response to welcome by a new pastor. HNWS:54
Response to welcome by one who has been absent for years. HAPR:75
Response to welcome of a guest denominational leader. HNWS:60
Response to welcome of a guest speaker at a father-son banquet. HNWS:58
Response to welcome of a guest speaker at a mother-daughter banquet. HNWS:58
Response to welcome of a guest speaker in men's brotherhood. HNWS:59
Response to welcome speech by a minister as a civic club speaker. HNWS:56
Responses to welcome-examples of. MORA:119-121
Roosevelt, T.
Response to formal greeting by citizens. ONES:93
Response to informal greeting by citizens. ONES:93
Response to the National Fraternal Press Association, February 4, 1903. THOU 3:19
Sala, G. A.
Friend and foe. REEMA 3:1014
Schurman, J. G.
Response to welcome. ONES:94
Senior response to welcome address at junior-senior banquet-theme: 'Robin Hood." AB:81
Spellman, F.

Response to welcome. BA 1945-46:203
Suggestions for preparation of a speech in response to a welcome address. BARR: 233; BRAB:495; REAB:157
Suggestions for preparation of responses to welcome. BRY:377; BRYA:408; RE: 169. With examples of. BRA:508; CON:7; GA:27; WRA:73; WRB:191; YE: 168
Two responses to welcome address. BURS:235, 241
Viviani, R. R.
To the House of Representatives. LEW:115
Wilson, W.
Speech in Boston on returning from the Peace Conference, February 25, 1919. HOAP:33
Winant, J. G.
Response to welcome. ON: 94

RESTAURANTS
Hotels and restaurants (dining-room a public benefactor). ED:179
Wade, A. C.
Introducing a restaurant or cafe manager. BRC:100

RESURRECTION See Easter

RETAIL TRADE See also Business; Business men

RETIREMENT
Acceptance speech by a retiring executive. SOES:20
Address of tribute (at testimonial dinner on retirment of public official). BED:29; BEDA:49
Andrew, J. A.
Valedictory to two branches of the legislature on retiring from office. CHAL 9: 313; HAZO 19:7897; MAS 19:7987
Banks, E. C.
Farewell to a district manager. BRC:325
Closing speech (at testimonial on retirement of public official). BED:31; BEDA:52
Corlett, B. C.
Presents a past president's pin to the retiring president, Anderson Borthwick. PRC: 8
Drummond, R.
Introducing a retired teacher. BRH:86
Evans, H. G.
Introduces and pays tribute to Eva Wirth, teacher on her retirement. PR:86
Farewell speech at complimentary dinner to retiring member of school board after twenty years' service. WRA:177
Huber, L. J.
Emcee at a retirement party. BRH:226
Kaser, A. L.
Introducing a retiring teacher. BRH:122
Lowell, J.
Humors of the Bench (retirement from Bench of the United States Circuit Court). BYRA:292; REEM 2:368; REEMA 2:766; REEMB 2: 381
Opening speech (at testimonial on retirement of public official). BED:27; BEDA:47
Posner, G. A.
Emcee at a retirement party (after thirty years service in an office). BRH: 200
Presentation speech to a club member on his retirement from business. WRA:86
Presenting a gift to a retiring mailman. SOES:17
Presenting gold cup (to retiring public official at testimonial dinner). BED:28; BEDA:48

RETIREMENT (cont.)
Public official's acceptance of a silver service upon his retirement. HAPR:50
Resolution of praise (retiring clerk). BEB:34
Resolution of praise on retirement-two examples. BEB: 105, 106
Resolution of thanks (testimonial dinner) for one retiring after ten years of service. BEB:35
Response by guest-of-honor (at testimonial on retirement of public official). BED:30; BEDA:51
Retirement addresses-6 examples of. BEC:128
Suggestions for preparation of speeches of retirment. With examples of. WRA:126
Suggestions for preparation of the farewell or retirement speech. BRAB:497
Thanking speaker (at testimonial on retirement of public official). BED:30; BEDA: 50
Toast to a retiring employee. FRIT:95
Toast to a retiring officer. FRIT:95
See also Officers, retiring; Presentation speeches; Testimonials

RETTBERG, MAIDA
Indian summer. BRP 9:19

REUNIONS
Address at a family reunion. AMEO 2:146
Artists' reunion. Response to the toast "Our Art and Artists." HILL:484
Drummond, R.
Emcee at a G.I. homecoming. BRH:299
Family reunion, by one of the family. EDGS:295
Family reunion speech. BURS: 242
For a dry goods merchants' reunion. BARB:183
For a reunion of artists. BARB:196
Harris, N.E.
Visions of the Civil War (at Confederate Veterans reunion, 1905). SHUO:26
Home-coming week, by a former resident. EDGS:107
Hoover, H.C.
Meaning of America (at home-coming in West Branch, Iowa). BA 1948-49:89; YE:286
Ingersoll, R.G.
Reunion address. BRAP: 104; REEM 10:269; REEMA 13:1241; REEMB 11:281
Its good to be back again. JA:88
Kaser, A.L.
Emcee at an army buddies' reunion. BRH:176
Emcee at a family reunion. BRH:216

Philips, J.F.
Old settler's home (at reunion of Tri-State Old Settler's Association, Keokuk, Iowa). SHUO:201
Schoenbrun, D.
An orange. HOA:402
Speech at a dry-goods-merchants reunion. HILL:482
Speech at Old Settlers' reunion. HILL:470
Visiting cousin adds a few remarks at the family reunion. DR:232; LU:1245
Who is your family? JA:91

---- CLASS
Abbott, W.R.
University of Virginia (before Alumni Association). SHUO:102
Address of welcome at an alumni dinner. DAVC:386
Address of welcome to a reunion banquet of class '14.

AMEO 1:104
Address of welcome to high school alumni. AMEO 1:63
Alma mater and the future. WERN 43:135
Alumni day-alumnus of ten years greets his class. DR: 71; LU:1149
Alumni dinner, by an alumnus. EDGS:224
Atkins, G. G.
Our university. YE:299
Choate, J. H.
Harvard University. REEM 1:262; REEMA 1:173; REEMB 1:263
Test examination. REEM 1: 245; REEMA 1:147; REEMB 1:246
Class reunion at West Point. SCHS:75
Cook, G. W.
Two seals. DUNM:370
Coudert, F. R.
Greeting from the alumni. ONES:76
Curtis, G. W.
Leadership of educated men. BAKF:282; ONEM:816; RINM:256
Noblesse oblige (at Harvard Alumni dinner). REEMA 1: 295
Davis, W. R.
Torch or shadows-which? WAGN:165
Depew, C. M.
Yale University. REEM 1: 391; REEMA 1:356; REEMB 1:392
Functions of an alumni organization. CON:45
Great teacher and some of his lessons: an address before college alumni. AMEO 1: 35
Holmes, O. W.
Welcome to alumni (1860). ONEM:674; WERN 54:127; REEMA 2:625
Welcome to alumni (1863). CHAL 7:403; HAZO 15: 6300; KLEM:52; MAS 15: 6300
Holmes, O. W., Jr.
Class of '61. REEMB 2: 232
Sons of Harvard who fell in battle. REEMA 2:630; REEMB 2:234
Kane, F. G.
Michigan Union. KNAS:272; KNASA:272
Long, J. D.
Class of 1857. KNAS:278; KNASA:278
Lowell, J. R.
Harvard alumni. REEMA 2: 737
Old grad discusses "The school spirit." DR:73
Pettit, G. A.
Alma mater and the present. WERN 54:129
Roosevelt, T.
Character and courage. WERN 54:137
Smith, H. L.
Culture afforded by scientific training (at Alumni reunion). SHUO:98
Titus-Werner, M. S.
Future of Athana. WERN 54:140
Toast to "Alma Mater." STOC:130; STON:136
Toast to an old graduate. STOC:132; STON:138
Toast to the alumni. STON: 137
Venable, F. P.
Duty of the educated man to his country (at Lafayette College Alumni Association). SHUO:90
Walsh, J. J.
Merry alumni dinner speech. WERN 54:128
Washington, B. T.
Address delivered at the Harvard Alumni dinner in 1896. BAKF:420; BOU:154; CHAL 14:318; COP:331; COPA:331; COPB:331; HAZO 25:10859; HILK:43; HURG:144; MAS 25:10859;

REUNIONS, CLASS (cont.)
REEM 7:421; REEMA 9: 1140; REEMB 8:437; WOON: 584
Reuther, Walter P.
Administered prices (before United States Senate). ARNS:199
Capital-labor problems (March 9, 1948). GLAD:287
Historical agreement. COPB: 646
Labor's principles and program. BA 1951-52:123
United Automobile Workers: aims and program. BA 1949-50:189
---- and others (G.V. Denny, Jr. and G.P. Romney)
Should industry grant labor's demand for a 30% wage increase? BA 1945-46: 165
See also DiSalle, M., jt. auth.; Taft, R.A., jt. auth.
Revels, Hiram R.
Speech on the Georgia Bill. WOON:286

REVIVALS See Church

REVOLUTION, AMERICAN See United States-History-Revolution

REVOLUTIONS
Barton, B.
What to do in a revolution. SAC:68
Phillips, W.
Revolutions. SHU:188
See also France-History-Revolution; Russia; United States-History-Revolution

REWARDS (PRIZES)
Greeting and welcome (at presentation of Brotherhood award). BED:55; BEDA:63
Opening speech (at physician-of-the-year award). BED: 50; BEDA:52
See also Acceptance speeches-Rewards (prizes); Presentation speeches-Rewards (prizes)
Reynaud, Paul
France will live again. COP: 493; COPA:493; COPB:463
Reynolds, George McClelland
Unleashing business for war. REEM 4:357; REEMB 5:237
Reynolds, Sir Joshua
Genius and imitation. BREW 9: 50
Reynolds, Lewis G.
Abraham Lincoln. DOA:22
Reynolds, Quentin
Campaign and men in uniform. BA 1944-45:123

REYNOLDS, QUENTIN
Introducing Quentin Reynolds. BA 1944-45:123

Reynolds, Robert R.
Origin and character of the American Forum of the Air. BA 1939-40:86
Suppression of crime. BOA: 281
See also Granik, T., jt. auth.
Rhees, Rush
Modernizing of liberal culture: inaugural address as president of University of Rochester. WE 1:215

RHEUMATISM See Medicine
Rhodes, Cecil
Crisis in South Africa. CHAL 14:292; HAZO 25:10833; MAS 25:10833; REEMA 14: 1730
Rhondda, Margaret Haig (Thomas) Mackworth, Viscountess
Against the leisured woman. REEM sup 3:79
Ribbentrop, Joachim, von
Greetings to Matsuoka, March 27, 1941. VO 1941:143
Statement on the Declaration of war on the Soviet Union, June 22, 1941. VO 1941: 301
Ribicoff, Abraham

To tomorrow's doctors. ANGC: 114
Ribot, Alexandre Felix Joseph
Greetings to America. LEW: 91
Rice, Frederick H.
Washington (memorial address at 100th anniversary of his death). THOU 3:298
Rice, George P., Jr.
Scholar and the twentieth century. BA 1949-50:220
Rice, John Holt
Virginia's deficiencies. SMI: 99
Rice, Merton S.
Value of great men. EXEE: 567
Rice, Walter Allen
Era of fraternalism. THOU 3: 361
Rice, William North
Scientific thought in the nineteenth century. REEMA 9: 984
Richard III, King of England
Oration to his army (from Shakespeare). HIB:212

RICHARDS, HARRY SANGER
Stevens, E.R.
Dean Richards-his service to the states. ONEC:137

RICHARDSON, ANNA STEESE
Introducing Anna Reese Richardson on her 75th birthday. SUM:80
Richardson, B.W.
Cures for drunkenness. THOU: 1:561
Richardson, Harry V.
Claflin yesterday, today and tomorrow (inaugural address as sixth President of Claflin University). HILK: 193
Richberg, Donald Randall
Current problems of industrial recovery. KLEB:107
Freedom and security under the N.R.A. BOB:17
How shall we deal with labor union monopolies? BA 1955-56:67
Responds to an introduction at an annual meeting of the Industrial Research Institute. PRNE:51

RICHELIEU, ARMAND JEAN DU PLESSIS DE, CARDINAL
Wishart, C.F.
Policy of Richelieu. SHUC: 247
Richter, Jean Paul
Greatness of the universe. DICD:152; DICE:152
Rickey, Branch
Greatest single thing a man can have. EXEE:268
Riddell, William Renwick
Canada. REEM sup 2:325; REEMB 8:345
Riddy, Donald Charles See Havighurst, R.J., jt. auth.
Ridenour, Louis N.
Science, technology and national security. HAR:312
Ridge, John (Cherokee Indian)
Respect for William Penn. SHE:43
Ridgway, Matthew B.
On assuming command of the 8th Army. HAR:138
Rieber, Paul
Them doll faces. BRP 6:25; YR 7:13

RIEL, LOUIS
Chapleau, J.A.
On the execution of Louis Riel. CHAL 13:365; HAZO 24:10346; MAS 24:10346
Riess, Oswald
Delightful marriage (50th anniversary). ACW:157
Rifkin, Harold
Racial intolerance. HOD:106
Riggenbach, J.C.
Seven words of Jesus on the cross. THOU 2:141

RIGHTEOUSNESS
Starnes, T.
Plea for righteousness.

RIGHTEOUSNESS (cont.)
YR 6:267

RIGHTS See Civil rights; Petition of Right, 1628; United States-Constitution

RILEY, JAMES WHITCOMB
Clemens, S. L.
Presents James Whitcomb Riley and Edgar Wilson Nye. LY:75
Riley, W. B.
Patriot's inheritance-its dangers. THOU 1:232
Rill, W. Albert
New blood. YR 5:17
Ring, Thomas G.
Need of religion in modern life. CATA 2:255
Ringe, Truston
Streamlined student. YR 10:1
Ripley, Robert K.
Freedom's destiny. DO:60
Ripley, William Z.
Control of corporations. BYRA: 374; REEM sup 2:342; REEMB 5:244
White man's burden. REEM sup 2:346; REEMB 5:248
Rising, Lloyd H.
Renaissance from war. ASHF: 370

RISKIN, ROBERT
Jessel, G.
Eulogy on Robert Riskin. JEYO:158
Ritchie, Albert C.
More business in government and less government in business. LINM:14
State responsibility. BLAB: 316
Which way America? SAR:139
Ritter, Claud D.
Friendship. BOA:177; BOB: 202
Ritzman, Carl H.
Eternal growth. YR 5:29
Rivers, Don
Bandwagon minds. NOR 1934: 104
Rivkin, Donald H.
People incarnate. NOR 1943: 29
Rivkin, William
Symbol of despotism. BRP 10: 23; NOR 1939:16

ROADS
Are good roads worth the cost? AMEO 2:144
Brosseau, A. J.
Highways and the tax payer. BRYA:49; REEM sup 1: 135; REEM 4:90
Petty, B.
Taking care of your roads (outline). MO 398; MOA: 398
Robbins, Sir Alfred Farthing
Freemasonry in England and America. REEM sup 2:348; REEMB 7:352
Robbins, Paul H.
Arlington-1935. YR 7:1
Robbins, W. L.
Pulpit and the Bar. REEMA 3:985
Roberts, Cecil
What Europe is thinking. EXEE:324
Roberts, Henry G.
Thinking on your feet. YE: 217
Roberts, John
House divided. BRP 9:59
Roberts, Owen J.
Trial procedure-past, present and future. ONEC:436
United States v. Butler et al, 1936: opinion for the Supreme Court. BIR 4:177
Roberts, Phyllis
Youth experiments. BRP 7: 106; YR 8:71
Roberts, Rome
Introducing an accountant
" a banker
" a Congressman
" a small town newspaper publisher. BRC:138, 112, 147, 73
Robertson, Frederick W.
Highest form of expression.

BREW 9:56
Loneliness of Christ. CHAL 9: 100; HAZO 18:7624; MAS 18:7624
Robertson, James
One idea. MO:245; MOA:245
Robertson, R. S.
Widespread influence of the flag. THOU 1:294
Robespierre, Maximilien
Against capital punishment. BREW 9:63; HAZO 8:3279; MAS 8:3279; REEM 9:202; REEMA 14:1746; REEMB 10:209
Against granting the King a trial. BRYW 7:136; CHAL 4:34; HAZO 8:3284; LEEW 5:99; MAS 8:3284; PL:310
Defense from the charge of tyranny. BREW 9:78; BRYW 7:145; CODS:459; CODSA:459; ESEH:214; HAZO 8:3310; MAS 8:3310; PE:275; PEA:275
Demanding the King's death. BREW 9:75; HAZO 8:3306; MAS 8:3306
Festival of the Supreme Being. BREW 9:77; COP:83; COPA:83; COPB:83; HAZO 8:3308; MAS 8:3308; REEM 9:211; REEMA 14:1750; REEMB 10:218
His defense of terrorism. BREW 9:68; HAZO 8:3296; MAS 8:3296; PE:272; PEA:272
"If God did not exist, it would be necessary to invent him." BREW 9:67; HAZO 8:3294; MAS 8:3294
In defiance of assassins. CROC:378
Last words. -Same as his Defense from the charge of tyranny
Moral ideas and Republican principles. BREW 9:71; HAZO 8:3300; MAS 8:3300
Universal suffrage. REEM 9: 205; REEMA 14:1756; REEMB 10:212

ROBESPIERRE, MAXIMILIEN
Gaudet, M. E.
Reply to Robespierre. BREW 6:216
Louvet, J. B.
Accusation of Robespierre. LEEW 5:75

ROBIN MOOR (SHIP)
Roosevelt, F. D.
Message to Congress on the sinking of the Robin Moor. VO 1941:289
Robinson, David C.
Their heritage to us (Pilgrims). THOU 1:354
Robinson, E. G.
Men: made, self-made, and unmade. BLAA:46; BLAB: 46; REAC:119
Robinson, Edgar Eugene
Can democracy survive the war? BA 1942-43:221
Man on the frontier. SHUC: 21; TRUW:238
Robinson, G. D.
Aim of the future. THOU 1: 498
Robinson, Hubert P.
Life's challenge to youth. BRP 4:54; INTW 1933:14
Robinson, Irwin J.
Must I die? NOR 1949:150
Robinson, Joseph Taylor
Jacob's voice but Easau's hands. WPRC:179
Robinson, Joseph T.
Women in industry. BOA:340
Robinson, Leroy T.
Edict of industry (present impossibility of war due to the inter-dependence of nations, industry, and capital). ASHF:262
Robinson, Maurise G.
Eleventh commandment. BLUE:19; BRAC:18

ROCHAMBEAU, JEAN BAPTISTE DONATIEN DE VIMEUR, COMTE DE
Lodge, H. C.

ROCHAMBEAU, JEAN BAPTISTE DONATIEN DE VIMEUR, COMTE DE (cont.)
France and Rochambeau. WERN 42:129
Roche, James Jeffrey
Press. REEMA 3:988
Roche, Josephine
Labor Day address. GA:81
Rockefeller, John Davison, Jr.
Character: the foundation of successful business. BYRA: 379; LINM:69; ONEC:220; REEM 4:364; REEMB 5:250
Christian church-what of its future? BA 1944-45:291
Our family creed. COP:708; COPB:735
Personal relation in industry. - Same as his Character: the foundation of successful business
Sign of the Blue Eagle. BOB: 12

Rockefeller, Laurence S.
Leisure: the new challenge. HIB:318
Rockefeller, Nelson A.
Inaugural address (as Governor of New York State). BA 1958-59:110
Jobs and prosperity. BA 1962-63:17

ROCKETS See World War 1939-1945-Aerial operations
Rockne, Knute
Athletics and leadership. EXEE:107

ROCKY MOUNTAIN SPEECH CONFERENCE See After dinner speeches
Rodee, H. A.
Our social crisis. COUW:85
Rodger, Margaret Elizabeth
Weapons versus wit. YR 8:187
Rodiger, William
Outward bound. NOR 1944:41
Rodriquez, Alfonso
Epilogue to freedom. BRP 9: 42
Roe, Anne
Psychology of the scientist. BAAGA:392
Roesch, Charles E.
Inaugural address of the Mayor of Buffalo. ONEC:163
Rogers, Carl
What we know about psychotherapy-objectively and subjectively. LINP:36
Rogers, Elmer E.
Lincoln's pluck and luck-what about ours? DICD:146; DICE:146
Rogers, J.T.
Fraternity and permanency. THOU 3:195
Rogers, Sherman
Spark plugs and live wires. EXEE:61
Rogers, Will
Ah, them was the days, lad! GRIS:59
Education and wealth. COP: 702; COPB:729; HURG: 200; REEM sup 2:361; REEMB 3:147
Nominating Calvin Coolidge. BARR:298
Presents Franklin Delano Roosevelt. LY:197
Settling the corset problem of this country. NESA:197
ROGERS, WILL
Lee, J.
Eulogy to Will Rogers. BOA:219
Rogness, Burnis M.
Minute men of a new era. BRP 5:60; YR 6:223
Walls of Jericho. YR 7:213
Rohde, Ruth Bryan Owen See Owen, Ruth Bryan
ROLL CALL
Roll call (at memorial services honoring deceased union member). BED:101; BEDA:179
Rolph, Alda
Plague uncovered. BRP 8:33; YR 9:155
Roman, Charles Victor
Knowledge of history conducive

to racial solidarity. WOON: 643

ROMAN CATHOLIC CHURCH
Catholicity. DAVC:150
Dowling, A.
Our critics. CATA 2:125
Relation of Catholics to civil government. CATA 1:129
Gibbons, J.
Supremacy of the Catholic religion. REEM 7:144; REEMA 8:505; REEMB 7: 183
Ireland, J.
Church and the age. ONEM: 719
Kenny, M.
Freemasonry and Catholicism in America. CATA 2: 194
Loughran, J. J.
Opposition to the church evidence of her divine origin and nature. CATA 2:185
Manning, H. E.
Triumph of the Church. CHAL 7:332; HAZO 15:6260; MAS 15:6260
Mulligan, B. J.
Mission of the Church; Fourth of July address. CATA 1:45
Newman, J. H.
Catholicism and the religions of the world. BRYW 4:216
Phillips, C.
Address to Catholics. BRYW 6:149
Plunket, W. C. P.
On Catholic relief. BRYW 6:162; PL:519
Potter, H. C.
Church. REEMA 3:955
Sheen, F. J.
Signs of our times. BA 1946-47:246
Smith, S.
Results of oppression. BREW 9:250
Supple, P. J.
Catholic Church, the salvation of society. CATA 2:167

ROMAN CATHOLICS IN GERMANY
Pius XII.
Address to the College of Cardinals. VO 1945-46:249

ROMAN CATHOLICS IN IRELAND
Gladstone, W. E.
On the disestablishment of the Irish Church. LEEW 7:311
Reply on the second reading of the Irish Church Bill, 1869. PAUF 2:175
Grattan, H.
Roman Catholic emancipation. BEA:225; PAUF 1:230
Magee, W. C.
Disestablishment of the Irish Church. PAUF 2:134
O'Connell, D.
Carries on the fight for Catholic emancipation. PE: 422; PEA:422
Catholic Association (June 16, 1815 speech). KET:302
Catholic rights in Ireland. BRTH:203; BRTHA:203; ORBR 2:79; REEMA 14: 1510
Struggle for Catholic emancipation. BEA:327
Phillips, C.
At a meeting of Roman Catholics at Cork. CHAL 5:361; HAZO 12:4832; MAS 12:4832
Pitt, W., 1759-1806
Roman Catholic emancipation. BEA:345; PAUF 1:155
Sheil, R. L.
In defense of Irish Catholics. BREW 9:189; CHAL 5: 436; HAZO 12:4946; MAS 12:4946; PL:536
Wellington, A. W.
On Catholic emancipation. CHAL 4:329; HAZO 9:3758; MAS 9:3758; REEMA 12: 2107

ROMAN CATHOLICS IN THE UNITED STATES
Catholics in American history, The. AMEO 2:79
Coyle, J. G.
Catholic American and the anti-Catholic crusade. CATA 1:202
Ford, J. F.
Catholicism and patriotism. CATA 1:187
Ireland, J.
Catholicism and Americanism. CATA 1:109
McCabe, F. X.
Can a Catholic be a citizen of the United States? CATA 1:231
O'Connell, W.
Position of Catholics. CATA 2:113
Patten, B. M.
Catholic citizen. CATA 1: 226

ROMANCE
Stubbins, T. A.
Spirit of romance. COUW: 45
Romano, Michael A.
Summation for the people in the O'Shea conspiracy case. HICJ:983

ROME
Alexander, H. R. L. G.
Broadcast to the people of Rome. VO 1944-45:256
Cavour, C. B., di
Rome and Italy. BREW 3: 174; BRYW 7:232; CHAL 8: 62; COP:103; COPA:103; COPB:103; HAZO 16:6678; MAS 16:6678; REEM 9:269; REEMA 12:530; REEMB 10: 277
Churchill, W. L. S.
Statement in Commons on the liberation of Rome and the landings in France. VO 1944-45: 264
Laurier, W.
British flag in Caesar's city. BREW 7:294
Manning, H. E.
Rome the eternal. BREW 8: 69; PL:500
Pius XII.
Plea for Rome. VO 1944-45:132
To the College of Cardinals pleading for the safety of Rome and for peace. VO 1944-45:248
Roosevelt, F. D.
Fall of Rome. BA 1943-44: 47; VO 1944-45:256
See also World War 1939-1945-Italy
Romeyn, John Broderick
Duty and reward of honouring God, 1821. BRAR 1:73
Romilly, Sir Samuel
Security against unlawful imprisonment. EMS 2:31
Sovereign's intervention in politics. EMS 1:5
Romney, George
Citizenship responsibility in education. BA 1959-60:159
Responds to introduction by Howard D. Murphy. PRC: 24
See Reuther, W. P., jt. auth.

ROMULO, CARLOS P.
Stone, H. L.
Introduces Gen. Carlos P. Romulo. PR:54
RONNAU, E. N.
Moran, E. B.
Introduces E. N. Ronnau. PR:53
Roosa, D. B. St. John
Introducing Theodore Roosevelt to Holland Society of New York, January 15, 1896. REEM 3:151; REEMB 3:154
Salt of the earth. REEM 3:146; REEMA 3:992; REEMB 3: 149
Roosevelt, Eleanor Anna
Address at Democratic National Convention, 1940. BUTA: 211

Answers to questions at the opening meeting of the 4th Public Speaking Class for Wives of Members of Congress. BUT:107
Banquet address. GA:105
Before the Democratic National Convention. BA 1956-57: 109
Civil liberties-the individual and the community. BA 1939-40:173
Speech training for the youth. BUTA:223
United Nations. HURG:297
United Nations as a bridge. COPB:640

ROOSEVELT, ELEANOR ANNA
Hancher, V. M.
Presents Eleanor Roosevelt. LY:240
Introducing Mrs. Franklin Delano Roosevelt. SUM:74
Stevenson, A. E.
Eulogy on Eleanor Roosevelt. BA 1962-63:178
Roosevelt, Franklin Delana
Acceptance of renomination for the Presidency, June 27, 1936. BIR 4:193
Acceptance speech on renomination for President July 20, 1944. VO 1944-45:309
Address at the annual gathering of the White House Correspondents' Association, February 12, 1943. VO 1943-44:52
Address in Ottawa, August 25, 1943. VO 1943-44:309
Address on his 60th birthday. VO 1942-43:128
Address on the seventh anniversary of the government of the Commonwealth of the Philippines. VO 1942-43:670
Address to the American Bankers' Association. KLEB: 3
Address to the closing session of the New York Herald Tribune Forum on Current Problems. VO 1942-43:677
Address to the Commonwealth Club, September 23, 1932. WPRC:146
Address to the delegates to the United Nations Food Conference. VO 1943-44: 228
Address to White House Correspondents' Association dinner, March 15, 1941. VO 1941:126
America accepts the challenge (December 9, 1941). ANG: 515; BA 1941-42:31; COP: 714; COPA:532; COPB: 532; HAN:176; VO 1941: 563; YE:357
America has not been disappointed. -Same as his Opening campaign speech at dinner of International Brotherhood of Teamsters
Announcing the opening of a second front in French North and West Africa. VO 1942-43:596
Annual message to Congress, January 6, 1942. -Same as his First war address before Congress
Appeal for neutrality, September 3, 1939. -Same as his This nation will remain neutral
Armistice Day address, 1941. VO 1941:503
Armistice Day, 1942. ON:343; VO 1942-43:649
Arsenal of democracy. -Same as his Preservation of American independence
At the dedication of the Thomas Jefferson Memorial, Washington, D.C. VO 1943-44:163
Atlantic Charter. -Same as his Eight common principles for a better world
Bill of Rights address. HAN: 104; VO 1941:622
Boston campaign speech, No-

Roosevelt, F.D. (cont.)
vember 4, 1944. VO 1944-45:541
Broadcast address, March 9, 1937 (proposal for the reform of the Federal Judiciary). BIR 4:199; FIP:224
Broadcast address to the coal miners. VO 1943-44:191
Broadcast at the Puget Sound Navy Yard on the war in the Pacific. VO 1944-45:373
Broadcast in connection with the opening of the Third War Loan Drive. VO 1943-44:336
Broadcast on Independence Day, 1941. ON:147; VO 1941:336
Broadcast on the community mobilization of human needs. VO 1941:451
Broadcast on the destroyer Greer. -Same as his Freedom of the seas
Broadcast on the 9th anniversary of the National Farm Program. VO 1942-43:194
Broadcast on Washington's birthday, 1942. BRAP:40; VO 1942-43:160
Broadcast to Canadians. VO 1942-43:149
Broadcast to International Student Assembly. VO 1942-43:463
Broadcast to the nation, April 28, 1942. VO 1942-43:249
Broadcast to the nation, September 7, 1942. VO 1942-43:479
Broadcast to the nation, October 12, 1942. VO 1942-43:545
Broadcast to the nation, July 28, 1943. ON:22; VO 1943-44:289
Broadcast to the nation on rubber. VO 1942-43:342
Broadcast to the nation on the setting up of UNRRA. FIP:252; VO 1943-44:536
Budget message, January 8, 1941. VO 1941:15
Budget message to Congress, January 13, 1944. VO 1944-45:29
Campaign address before the Foreign Policy Association in New York. VO 1944-45:492
Campaign address on progressive government. -Same as his Philosophy of government
Campaign broadcast from the White House, October 5, 1944. VO 1944-45:466
Campaign broadcast from the White House, November 2, 1944. VO 1944-45:538
Campaign for re-election, October 30, 1936. FIP:217
Campaign speech in Soldiers Field, Chicago. VO 1944-45:514
Canadian position of the United States. BA 1938-39:25; BIR 4:259
Challenge to youth. BOA:376
Christmas eve broadcast to the nation, 1943. VO 1943-44:579
Christmas message, December 24, 1942. VO 1942-43:729
Christmas message to the American people, December 24, 1944. VO 1944-45:624
"Date which will live in infamy" -Same as his War address (December 8, 1941)
Dedicatory address at the Naval Medical Center, Bethesda, Maryland. VO 1942-43:454
Democracy cannot survive in isolation (at birthplace of Woodrow Wilson). ON:146
Eight common principles for a better world. BA 1941-42:247; FIP:244; VO 1941:379
Expanding frontiers of social progress. SAR:305
Fall of Rome. BA 1943-44:47; VO 1944-45:256
Fear. -Same as his First in-

augural
Fireside chat: AAA and NRA, July 24, 1933. FIP:206
Fireside chat on the accomplishment of the New Deal. WPRC:162
Fireside chat on the outbreak of war. -Same as his This nation will remain neutral
First "fireside chat" on banking. DOA:146; MO:564; MOA:569; PE:751; PEA:751
First inaugural. BAAMP:260; BEA:365; BIR 4:95; BOA:210; BOB:205; BRE:338; BREA:318; CAP:189; CHI:259; COP:530; COPB:508; FO:363; FRY:114; HAY:370; HIB:274; HURG:219; LOTI:231; PAR:501; PE:745; PEA:745; PL:810; USIN:235; USINA:235; WPRC:157
First war address before Congress. COP:726; COPB:538; HURG:269; VO 1942-43:8
Flag Day address, June 13, 1942. VO 1942-43:344
For a declaration of war against Japan. -Same as his War address (December 8, 1941)
Four human freedoms. ANG:495; BA 1940-41:185; BOA:7; BRE:362; CROC:385; FIP:238; HAN:30; VO 1941:5
Fourth inaugural address. BA 1944-45:153; CHI:275; LOTI:247; USIN:248; USINA:248; VO 1945-46:40; WPRC:261
Freedom of the seas. COP:546; COPB:524; SAA:300; VO 1941:395
Good neighbor. -Same as his Pan American Union
Hemisphere defense for democracy. COP:534; COPB:512
In response to message from Prime Minister of Iceland. VO 1941:343
In the name of the people. -Same as his First inaugural
Independence Day statement, 1942. VO 1942-43:388
Informal remarks to members of the governing board of the Pan American Union. VO 1942-43:214
Invasion prayer to nation. BA 1943-44:46; HAN:265; VO 1944-45:261
Italy enters the war. BA 1939-40:76
Jackson Day address from the U.S.S. Potomac in the harbor of Ft. Lauderdale, Florida. VO 1941:144
Keeping political faith. -Same as his Opening campaign speech at dinner of International Brotherhood of Teamsters
Labor Day address (1941). VO 1941:392
Labor Day statement (1942). VO 1942-43:443
Lend lease, March 12, 1941. FIP:242
Liberty fleet day address. VO 1941:413
Message to Congress, June 1, 1934 (on public debts). KESK 1:247
Message to Congress; January 4, 1939. SAR:119
Message to Congress, April 27, 1942 (on inflation). VO 1942-43:242
Message to Congress, August 13, 1942, (on Panama). VO 1942-43:438
Message to Congress, September 7, 1942. VO 1942-43:469
Message to Congress, January 7, 1943. BA 1942-43:15; HAN:240; VO 1943-44:7
Message to Congress, September 17, 1943. HAN:251; VO 1943-44:364
Message to Congress, January

Roosevelt, F.D. (cont.)
11, 1944. BA 1943-44:15; VO 1944-45:21
Message to Congress asking for the recognition of a state of war with Germany and Italy. VO 1941:598
Message to Congress calling for the repeal of the Chinese exclusion laws. VO 1943-44:434
Message to Congress on Bretton Woods money and banking proposals. VO 1945-46: 57
Message to Congress on extension of selective service men. VO 1941:348
Message to Congress on hastening Philippine independence. VO 1943-44:431
Message to Congress on postwar education of service men and women. VO 1943-44:458
Message to Congress on price control. VO 1941:356
Message to Congress on Puerto Rico. VO 1943-44:97
Message to Congress on repeal of Embargo. BA 1939-40:26
Message to Congress on the food program. VO 1943-44: 482
Message to Congress on the Judiciary, February 5, 1937. FO:413
Message to Congress on the need for amending the organic act of Puerto Rico. VO 1943-44:413
Message to Congress on the servicemen's vote. VO 1944-45:54
Message to Congress on the Service men's Vote Bill. VO 1944-45:152
Message to Congress on the sinking of the Robin Moor. VO 1941:289
Message to Congress on the state of the nation, January 6, 1945. VO 1945-46:5
Message to Congress on the tariff, March 26, 1945. HAN:391
Message to Congress on U.S. occupation of Iceland. VO 1941:341
Message to Congress recommending appropriations for the work of the UNRRA. VO 1943-44:543
Message to Congress submitting two reports of the National Resources Planning Board. VO 1943-44:103
Message to Congress urging the arming of American flag ships engaged in foreign commerce. VO 1941: 455
Message to Congress vetoing the tax bill. VO 1944-45:106
Message to Hitler and Mussolini, April 14, 1939. HAN: 95
Message to the French, in French, November 8, 1942. VO 1942-43:598
Message to the French people, November 7, 1942. VO 1942-43:597
Message to the people of the Philippines. VO 1941:641
Mobilization of community needs. VO 1942-43:543
Modern education and the government. ONEC:183
National defense. BA 1939-40: 117; HIB:227
Navy Day address on the attack on the destroyer Kearney. HAN:160; VO 1941:462
Navy Day campaign speech in Shibe Park, Philadelphia. VO 1944-45:509
New deal must continue. BA 1938-39:97
Nomination of Alfred E. Smith. CORP:217; HICF:796; LINM:131; ONEC:497; YE:107
"One-third of a nation."- Same

as his Second inaugural
Opening campaign speech at dinner of International Brotherhood of Teamsters. BA 1944-45:134; BAAMP:267; MIA:356; ON:383; PAR:510; VO 1944-45:425
Opening the Fifth War Loan Drive. VO 1944-45:68
Our Constitution. BOA:103
Pan American Union. FIP:203; SAA:281
Philosophy of government. PO:163
Philosophy of social justice through social action (campaign speech in Detroit October 2, 1932). ARNS:129
Plea for neutrality. -Same as his This nation will remain neutral
Preservation of American independence. BA 1940-41:19; COP:539; COPB:517; HAN:99; HURG:246; WPRC:246
Quarantining the aggressors. ANG:477; BRE:357; BRYA:539; FIP:233; HAN:91
Radio address to the people of the Philippines, August 12, 1943. VO 1943-44:306
Rebuild and remodel. BOA:202; BOB:172
Remarks to the delegates to the Dumbarton Oaks Conference. VO 1944-45:387
Reorganization message to Congress (January 12, 1937). FO:405
Reply to Ambassador Escobar. VO 1944-45:93
Reply to President Camacho at Monterrey. VO 1943-44:171
Report to Congress on the Crimea Conference. -Same as his Yalta Conference
Republican leadership and national defense. BA 1940-41:124
Request for defense funds. -Same as his National defense
Right to security. BOA:411; FIP:212
Second inaugural address. BA 1937-38:11; CHI:265; FIP:221; FO:370; LOTI:237; USIN:240; USINA:240
Shoot on sight. -Same as his Navy Day address on the attack on the destroyer Kearney
Should Mr. Roosevelt's plan for enlarging the Supreme Court be adopted? (affirmative) SAR:214
Speech at Queen's University, Kingston, August 18, 1938. -Same as his Canadian position of the United States
Speech on site of the Jefferson Memorial. YE:204
State of emergency exists. BA 1940-41:57; VO 1941:219
Statement of war crimes. VO 1942-43:544
Statement on "Army Day." VO 1942-43:203
Statement on continuance of the combined British-Canadian-American production, raw materials and food boards. VO 1945-46:38
Statement on joint resolutions of Congress respecting the Philippines. VO 1944-45:284
Statement on punishment of war crimes. VO 1942-43:444
Statement on the anniversary of the signing of the Declaration by the United Nations. VO 1944-45:4
Statement on the use of poison gas. VO 1942-43:337
Statement on United States recognition of the French Committee of National Liberation. VO 1943-44:311
Statement on war refugees. VO 1944-45:137
Statement upon termination of diplomatic relations with the Vichy government. VO 1942-43:640

Roosevelt, F.D. (cont.)
Teamsters' Union speech. - Same as his Opening campaign speech at dinner of International Brotherhood of Teamsters
Third inaugural address. CHI: 271; LOTI:243; SAA:292; USIN:244; USINA:244; VO 1941:37
This nation will remain neutral. BA 1939-40:21; BRAS: 409; BIR 4:288; HAN:124; PL:839
To the delegates of the International Labor Organization. VO 1941:475
Truths that inspired Washington. BA 1942-43:217; VO 1943-44:83
Undelivered Jefferson Day address. CROC:392; VO 1945-46:147
United States policy toward the French Republic. VO 1941: 212
United States' policy toward war. BA 1938-39:35
Victory dinner address. BA 1937-38:101
War address (December 8, 1941). BA 1941-42:17; BAAMP:265; BOU:99; BRAP:146; BRE:373; CAP: 200; COP:713; COPA:530; COPB:531; FIP:249; HAN: 174; HIBS:482; HURG:265; ON:179; PAR:507; PE: 790; PEA:790; VO 1941:553
War and the plans for peace. - Same as his Broadcast to the nation July 28, 1943
We cannot save freedom with pitchforks. -Same as his Broadcast on Independence Day, 1941
We hold these truths. -Same as his Bill of Rights address
We must be the great arsenal of democracy. -Same as his Preservation of American independence
WPA, May 6, 1935. FIP:215
Yalta Conference. BA 1944-45: 19; FIP:269; VO 1945-46: 103

ROOSEVELT, FRANKLIN DELANO
Barkley, A.W.
Foreign policies of Roosevelt. BA 1938-39:53
Tribute to President Roosevelt. BA 1944-45:156
Baukhage, H.R.
Tribute to Roosevelt. BA 1944-45:167
Birthday of a great person-Franklin Delano Roosevelt. BEC:156
Churchill, W.L.S.
Humanity's loss. BA 1944-45:170; VO 1945-46:154
Douglas, H.G.
Address before the New York Herald Tribune Forum. BUTA:236
Douglas, W.O.
At the grave of Franklin Delano Roosevelt. MO:533; MOA:539
Earhart, A.
Speech for Roosevelt. GA: 154
Miller, E.G.
Seconding the nomination of President Roosevelt. GA: 203
Rogers, W.
Presents Franklin Delano Roosevelt. LY:197
Sheil, B.J.
Tribute to Roosevelt. BA 1944-45:165
Thompson, D.
Address, October 29, 1944. BUTA:239; ON:365
Tributes to Franklin Delano Roosevelt. BA 1944-45:156-57
Roosevelt, James
Welfare state. BA 1949-50:127
Roosevelt, Theodore
Accepting a horse and saddle. ONES:56
Accepting a soldiers' and sailors' monument. ONES:

49
Address at State Fair of Minnesota. BIR 3:253; CHAL 14:360; HAZO 25:10889; MAS 25:10889; REEM 10:398; REEMA 15:1759; REEMB 11:415
America and international peace. SHU:231
America greets France. ONES:70
American motherhood. BRYW 10:253; WERN 42:157
Americanism. BLAA:1; BLAB:1; PROS:88; REAC:84
Annual message, December 6, 1904. BIR 3:256
Armageddon speech. FRY:58; SHAH:163
"Big stick" speech. -Same as his Address at State Fair of Minnesota
Brownsville incident. FIP:54
Character and courage. WERN 54:137
Corollary to the Monroe Doctrine (from message to Congress, December 5, 1905). BRE:300; BREA:280; FIP:45; PO:122
Elemental citizenship virtues. SHU:14
First annual message to Congress. BIR 3:245; FO:252
Foundations of progress. RID:98
George Washington (birthday speech). ONES:156
Greatness in citizenship (dedication of Law School of University of Chicago). ONES:114
Greatness through strife. BOB:211
Hollander as an American. REEM 3:151; REEMA 3:998; REEMB 3:154
"I took the Canal Zone." FIP:39
Inaugural address (1905). BRYW 10:249; CHI:203; LA:122; LOTI:183; ONEM:485; USIN:183; USINA:183
Making of America: opening the Jamestown Exposition, April 26, 1907. BREW 9:85
Man with the muck-rake (at dedication Office Building of the House of Representatives). ARNS:102; BAAMP:211; BRAS:278; CAP:134; DOA:275; FIP:49; KNAS:133; KNASA:133; ONEM:530; PAR:482; SHAH:603 WERN 42:55
Nation of pioneers. -Same as his Address at State Fair of Minnesota
National duty and international ideals. REEM 11:99; REEMB 12:108
National expansion (St. Louis World's Fair). WERN 42:9
Need of an efficient navy. WERN 42:145
New nationalism (at dedication of John Brown Memorial Park, Osawatomic, Kansas). WPRC:27
On foreign affairs (from message to Congress, December 6, 1904). BRE:299; BREA:279; PO:117
On national issues. -Same as his Strenuous life
On reading the Bible. REEMA 15:1770
On trusts, August 25, 1902. FIP:35
Our responsibilities. PROS:103
Property rights and predatory wealth (H.W. Lawrence monument). BREW 9:94
Public domain: the people's heritage. FIP:62
Response to formal greeting by citizens. ONES:89
Response to informal greeting by citizens. ONES:93
Response to the National Fraternal Press Association, February 4, 1903. THOU 3:19
Right of the people to rule. HICF:396; REEM 10:408;

Roosevelt, Theodore (cont.)
REEMB 11:426
Seconding McKinley's nomination. CHAL 14:354; HAZO 25:10883; MAS 25:10883
Social and industrial injustice. SHU:214
Speech before the Ohio Constitutional Convention, 1912. BIR 3:298; FKA:114
Strenuous life. CHAL 14:341; COP:345; COPA:345; COPB:345; HAZO 25:10870; HURG:150; KLEG:351; MAS 25:10870; PE:655; PEA:655; PL:710; REEM 7:334; REEMA 9:995; REEMB 8:362; SAA:216
True Americanism and expansion. REEMA 3:1002
Trusts and tariff. REEMA 15:1776
Welcome to the Military Surgeons' Association. ONES:20
William McKinley (tribute). ONES:173

ROOSEVELT, THEODORE
Addams, J.
Seconding the nomination of Roosevelt for President. REEMB 8:1
Benschoten, W. H.
Opening address for the defendant in the Barnes-Roosevelt libel case. HICJ:742
Bowers, J. M.
Summation for the defendant in the Barnes-Roosevelt libel case. HICJ:762
Hart, A. S.
Theodore Roosevelt. BOA:231; BOB:142
Hickman, L. E.
Ideal American (Theodore Roosevelt). SHUP:225
Hogg, J. S.
President (Theodore) Roosevelt. SHUO:65
Ivins, W. M.
Opening address for the plaintiff in the Barnes-Roosevelt libel case. HICJ:725
Jusserand, J. J.
Tennis cabinet (on T. Roosevelt). BREW 7:187
Lodge, H. C.
Passing of 'Valiant for truth''(Theodore Roosevelt). BREW 7:380; REEM 5:280; REEMB 9:319
Morrow, E. P.
Theodore Roosevelt-American. NESA:193
Pinchot, G.
Theodore Roosevelt. BLAB:325
Roosa, D. B. St. J.
Introducing Theodore Roosevelt to Holland Society of New York, January 15, 1896. REEM 3:151; REEMB 3:154
Shurter, E. D.
Potency of Roosevelt's spirit. SHU:16
Straus, O. S.
Roosevelt pilgrimage. REEM 7:380; REEMB 8:401

ROOSEVELT, THEODORE, JR.
Introducing Theodore Roosevelt, Jr. NI:186; NIA:138
Root, Elihu
American ideals during the past half-century (birthday speech). ONEC:209; REEM sup 2:363; REEMB 8:373
At a luncheon given by General Brusiloff. REEM 3:162; REEMB 3:165
Boss rule. REEM 10:392; REEMB 11:408
Business and politics. REEM 3:164; REEMB 3:167; WPRC:44
Duties of the states. WERN 42:53
Every man's responsibility. BOA:197; BOB:170
Greetings to the Russia Republic. BREW 9:100
Home of the Oneidas. REEM 3

156; REEMB 3:159
How to preserve the local self-government of the states. FKA:48
Human freedom. REEM 3:159; REEMB 3:162
Internationalism as tyranny. BREW 9:100
Introducing and toasting Joseph B. Coghlan at the Union League Club, April 21, 1899. REEM 1:323; REEMB 1:324
Introducing H. Watterson to New England Society of New York. ANDS:198; LY:123; ONEM:669; ONES:4; REEM 3:359
Invisible government: Short Ballot Amendment. BIR 4: 12; HICF:444; ONEM:306
On receiving his degree of LL.D., 1907. KNAS:180; KNASA:180
Pan-American policy. SHU:233
Pan American spirit. BOAM: 83; KNAS:282; KNASA:282
Plea for the League of Nations. COP:374; COPA:374; COPB:374; REEM sup 2: 369; REEMB 3:177
Profit of the laborer and consumer. BLAA:105; BLAB: 105
Public service by the Bar. HICF:458
Response on eightieth birthday. KLEB:139; LINM:259
Rocking chairs and respect for the law. BREW 9:101; BYRA:391; REEM 3:172; REEMB 3:175
Seventy-fifth anniversary of the Century Club. REEM 6: 374; REEMB 7:365
Unveiling the statue of Lincoln in London, July 28, 1920. BOAM:93
War and discussion. REEM 11: 241; REEMB 12:256

ROPER, ELMO
Ford, H., II.
Presents Elmo Roper. LY: 96
Rose, George B.
Home brew. NESA:126
Rose, Joseph
Tomorrow should be the deadline. BRP 6:53
Rose, Uriah M.
Magna Charta. SHUO:318
Rosebery, Archibald Philip Primrose, 5th Earl of
At the Free Trade Hall, Manchester at the centenary of the Manchester Chamber of Commerce. BEA:369; PAUF 2:367
Duty of public service. ADR 4:318
England under socialism. BREW 9:103
Expansion and dum-dum bullets. BREW 9:105
Great Britain in panorama (welcome to Press Conference, June 6, 1919). BREW 9:109
Lord's veto. CHAL 14:73
Oration on Robert Burns (delivered before tomb at Dumfries, Scotland). ORBR 2:409
Penalizing poor but honest dukes. BREW 9:106
Portrait and landscape painting. REEM 3:176; REEMA 3: 1008; REEMB 3:182
Power and responsibility of the press. BRTH:329; BRTHA:329
Preparation for armageddon. BREW 9:110
Questions of Empire. REEMA 15:1785
Reform of the House of Lords. EMS 1:112
Robert Burns (delivered in St. Andrews Hall, Glasgow at Burns Centenary). BRYW 5: 174; LAD:212; REEM 5: 333; REEMA 9:1007; REEMB 9:375
Steaks from the living ox. BREW 9:108
True leverage of Empire.

Rosebery, Archibald Philip Primrose, 5th Earl of (cont.)
CHAL 14:59; HAZO 25: 10600; MAS 25:10600
Rosen, Abraham
For a Bar-Mitzwa. ZEL:27
To a Bar Mitzvah. ZEL:60
Rosen, Roman Romanovich, Baron
Russia. REEM 3:181; REEMB 3:188
Rosenberg, A.H.
Address for a Bar Mitzvah. ZEL:83

ROSENBERG, JULIUS AND ETHEL
Kaufman, I.J.
Sentencing atomic bomb spies. BA 1951-52:55

ROSENWALD, LESSING J.
Evans, L.H.
Presents Lessing J. Rosenwald. LY:66

ROSH HA SHANAH See New Year
Ross, Jonathan
Nation's relation to its island possession. CHAL 11:82; HAZO 21:8857; MAS 21: 8857
Ross, Leland M.
Martyrs of progress. ASHF: 174
Ross, W.O.
Begins an address at the annual Swing-In, Senior Class Program, Wayne University. PRNE:67
Rossnagel, W.T.
Abide with us (50th wedding anniversary). ACW:165

ROTARY CLUB
Message of appreciation before the local service club (Rotary, Kiwanis, Lions, etc.). DR:99; LU:1166
Power of projected personality. JA:202
Rotary. NATS:27
Rotary. SCHS:227
Rotary club (retiring president expresses his appreciation). ED:121
Short talk by a new member on admission to Ladies Rotary club. AMEO 2:67
War's alternative. JA:205
Rovere, Richard H.
Journalist critic's view of General MacArthur's speech to Congress. BRAP:155

ROWAN, ARCHIBALD HAMILTON
Curran, J.P.
England and English liberties in the case of Rowan. BREW 4:317; BRYW 6:99; CHAL 3:320; ESEH:201; GOOD:790; HAZO 7:2974; KET:147; MAS 7:2974; PL:516; REEMA 12:764
Second speech for Archibald Hamilton Rowan (February 4, 1795). KET:170
Rowan, Carl T.
Address delivered at Simpson College. HILK:108
Rowe, Mary Jane
Youth and the depression. JUD:241
Rowell, A.B.
Robert Burns. COUW:57
Rowland, Dunbar
Influence of the poet (accepting bust of Irwin Russell). SHUO:83
Roy, James C.
Twenty thousand leagues under the sea. YR 1:55

ROYAL ARCANUM
Avery, C.H.
Growth of fraternity. THOU 3:357
Broadhurst, W.A.
True fraternity. THOU 3: 368
Bronk, M.
Modern spirit of brotherhood. THOU 3:381
Burrows, A.S.
Royal Arcanum and Royal

law. THOU 3:382
Capen, J.S.
Installation address. THOU 3:394
Dow, E.E.
Danger of fraternity apathy. THOU 3:373
Eldridge, G.D.
Future of fraternalism. THOU 3:362
Farrier, E.
Law of protection. THOU 3:384
Fraternal spirit. THOU 3:367
Fraternity and business. THOU 3:370
Hall, F.
Address of welcome to the Grand Council of New York Royal Arcanum. THOU 3:398
Harris, H.R.
Decoration of graves-memorial address. THOU 3:415
Kenngott, G.F.
Church and fraternity. THOU 3:372
Langfitt, J.A.
Fraternal system. THOU 3:388
Twenty-fifth anniversary greeting. THOU 3:350
Lee, J.A.
Fraternity. THOU 3:354
Olmstead, W.C.
Virtue, mercy, and charity. THOU 3:377
Rice, W.A.
Era of fraternalism. THOU 3:361
Yeiser, N.E.
Fellowship. THOU 3:400

ROYAL TEMPLARS OF TEMPERANCE
Grosvenor, J.W.
Perseverance wins. THOU 3:539
Lessons from our history. THOU 3:533
Mills, C.
Instituting a new council. THOU 3:536

ROYALTY See Monarchy
Royce, Bob
Absent entertainer (to be used when an entertainer fails to appear). BRH:331
Emcee at a baseball fan club
" at a golden wedding celebration. BRH:199,306
Royce, Josiah
Duties of Americans in the present war. ONES:298
What is vital in Christianity? NORR 1st ser:404
Royer-Collard, Pierre Paul
Against press censorship. BREW 9:114; CHAL 4:172; HAZO 9:3535; MAS 9:3535; PL:329
"Sacrilege" in law. BREW 9:112; CHAL 4:169; HAZO 9:3532; MAS 9:3532

RUBBER
Knight, J.R.
Introduces H.E. Humphries, Jr., Chairman of the U.S. Rubber Company. PRNE:18
Roosevelt, F.D.
Broadcast to the nation on rubber. VO 1942-43:342
Rubber association. SCHS:230
Rucker, W.W. See Towner, H.T., jt. auth.
Rudolph, William C.
For democracy we fight. DO:125
Ruffin, George L.
Crispus Attucks (commemorative speech on Boston Massacre). DUNM:125
Ruffin, Josephine St. Pierre
Open letter to the Educational League of Georgia. DUNM:173

RUHR VALLEY-INVASION
Poincaré, R.
America supports our seizure of the Ruhr. CROC:373
Rumbold, Richard
Against booted and spurred privilege. BREW 9:119; BRYW 3:146; CHAL 2:89;

Rumbold, Richard (cont.)
HAZO 4:1555; MAS 4:1555
Speech from the scaffold. - Same as his Against booted and spurred privilege
Runciman, Walter Runciman, 1st Viscount
On Merchant Shipping (conveyance of munitions to Spain), Bill. KESK 2:187
Rupprecht, O. C.
Travelling together in light. ACW:39
Rural life
Huber, L. J.
Rural emcee. BRH:335

RURAL SCHOOLS See Schools, rural
Rush, Benjamin
Influence of physical causes on the moral faculty. BL:312
Rush, Marguerite
Forays into education. NOR 1945:23
Rusk, Dean
Address before the American Society of International Law. BA 1964-65:89
Chinese-American friendship. HAR:165
Underlying crisis: coercion vs. choice. BA 1961-62:19
Ruskin, John
Bemoans the degradation of modern life. PE:544; PEA:544
Iscariot in modern England. BREW 9:121
On the Greek myths. CHAL 9:345; HAZO 19:7929; MAS 19:7929
Reading for the thought. DICD:154; DICE:154
Work. REEM 8:334; REEMA 6:919; REEMB 13:339

RUSKIN, JOHN
Hillis, N. D.
John Ruskin. REEM 5:214; REEMA 5:579; REEMB 9:251
Russell, Bertrand
How to be free and happy. REEM sup 2:374; REEMB 7:370

RUSSELL, BERTRAND
Waller, H. H.
Presents Bertrand Russell. LY:108
Russell, C. E.
True tales of the secret service. EXEE:229
Russell, Horace
Introduction of Edward O. Wolcott to New England Society of New York, December 22, 1887. REEM 3:431
Russell, John Russell, 1st Earl of
Church of Ireland. ORBR 2:133
On the ballot. CHAL 6:36; HAZO 12:5065; MAS 12:5065
Position of a Ministry not supported by the House of Commons. EMS 1:78
Reform of the franchise. EMS 2:137
Rotten boroughs of England. PL:463
Science and literature as modes of progress. BREW 9:126
Sovereign advised to dismiss a Minister. EMS 1:20
Russell, W. E.
Address at the Democratic National Convention. BAKF:398
Russell, W. T.
Unveiling memorial in honor of Spanish war heroes. CATA 1:142
Russell, William F.
How to beat Communism. HOB:204
To bind up the wounds in the schools of all nations. BA 1943-44:287
Russell of Killowen, Charles Russell, Baron
American connection. KET:396
Boycotting. KET:394

Parnell Commission (October 1888 speech). KET:382
Two parties in Ireland. KET: 400

RUSSIA
Bakhmetieff, B.
New Russia. LEW:145
Howland, Henry E.
Russia. REEMA 2:657
Khrushchev, N. S.
Reveals some of the crimes of Stalin. PEA:826
Lenin, N.
Makes a world-shaking announcement, November 7, 1917. PEA:715
Speaks to a street crowd in Petrograd, Spring, 1917. PE:713; PEA:713
War, peace and revolutionary democracy. CROC:283
Lyndhurst, J. S. C.
Russia and the Crimean War. BREW 7:419; HAZO 9:3901; MAS 9:3901
Marshall, T. R.
Russian War Mission. REEM 2:392
Rosen, R. R.
Russia. REEM 3:181; REEMB 3:188
See also European War, 1914-1918; Russia (1923-) USSR; World War, 1939-1945-Campaigns-Russian front; World War, 1939-1945-Russia

---- NAVY
Dana, R. H.
Russia and the United States. REEMA 1:323

---- (1923-) USSR
Benson, S.
Soviet Russia. ONES:344
Browder, E.
Soviet Union. SAR:163
Johnston, E.
Mr. Perkins returns to the land of the Bolsheviks. BA 1956-57:40
McCann, W. R.
New Russia. YR 2:133
Molotov, V. M.
Report to the Supreme Soviet of the U. S. S. R. VO 1944-45:82
28th anniversary speech. VO 1945-46:676
Stalin, I.
May day order of the day (1945). VO 1945-46:183
Order of the day on the 24th anniversary of the Red Army. VO 1942-43:170
Order of the day on the 25th anniversary of the Red Army. VO 1943-44:85
Order of the day on the 27th anniversary of the Red Army and Navy. VO 1945-46:65
Position of Russia, November 6, 1941. HAN:164
Report on the 27th anniversary of the Revolution. VO 1944-45:546
Speech on Red Square on anniversary celebration, November 7, 1941. VO 1941: 480
27th anniversary order of the day. HAN:288; VO 1944-45:554
Wallace, H. A.
Address before Congress of American Soviet Friendship. VO 1942-43:605
See also Communist Party-Russia (22nd Congress)

---- ---- ARMED FORCES
Malinovsky, R. Y.
Speech of October 23. RUS: 59

---- ---- ECONOMIC CONDITIONS
Khrushchev, N. S.
Future of the Soviet economy (from his report on the Third Program of the Soviet Communist Party-delivered October 18). RUS:234
State of the Soviet economy

RUSSIA (1923-) USSR-ECONOMIC CONDITIONS (cont.)
(from his report for the Central Committee -delivered October 17). RUS: 184
Kosygin, A.N.
Speech of October 21. RUS: 216
Voronov, G.I.
Speech of October 19. RUS:227

---- ---- FOREIGN RELATIONS
Acheson, D.
United Nations and Soviet aggression. BA 1950-51:25
Churchill, W.L.S.
Sinews of peace (speech at Fulton, Missouri). BA 1945-46:20; COPB:614; GRAC:144; HIB:298; PE: 803; PEA:803

---- ---- ---- GREAT BRITAIN
Molotov, V.M.
Report on ratification of the Anglo-Soviet Treaty to the Supreme Soviet of the Union of Soviet Socialist Republics. VO 1942-43:349

---- ---- ---- HUNGARY
Dixon, P.
Against Soviet intervention in Hungary. BAAG:372
Lodge, H.C., Jr.
Hungary's struggle for freedom. BA 1956-57:36
Soviet suppression of Hungarian liberty. BA 1957-58:37

---- ---- ---- JAPAN See World war 1939-1945-Russia

---- ---- ---- POLAND
Churchill, W.L.S.
Speech in Commons on the Soviet Polish frontier. VO 1944-45:611
Vyshinski, A.Y.
Statement on Soviet-Polish relations. VO 1943-44:195
Russo, Ernesto
America as I find it. BART 1:41

RUTGERS UNIVERSITY
Clothier, R.C.
Inaugural address as president of University of New Jersey (Rutgers). WE 2:15

RUTHENBURG, LOUIS
Moran, E.B.
Introduces Louis Ruthenburg. PR:96
Rutherford, Ernest
Electrons and atomic explosions. BREW 9:135
Ruthven, Alexander G.
Victor Clarence Vaughan and the University (Michigan). ONEC:127
Rutledge, John
Speech in time of Revolution. BREW 9:138
To the General Assembly of South Carolina. CHAL 3: 83; HAZO 7:2651; LEEW 8: 281; MAS 7:2651
Ryan, John A.
Religion, the indispensable basis of democracy. BA 1939-40:408
Ryan, Michael J.
Papacy and the world peace. CATA 2:266
St. Patrick, his mission, his church, and social service. CATA 1:251
Ryan, Oswald
Abraham Lincoln. EXEE:347
Rydin, Rudolph G.
Introduces Daniel P. Loomis, President of the Association of American Railroads. PRC:11
Sabin, Florence R.
Acceptance of the M. Carey Thomas award. GA:49
Sabine, James E.
American youth and the Constitution. YR 2:111

Sacco, Nicola and Vanzetti, Bartolomeo
Proclaim their innocence. PE:741; PEA:741

SACHEVERELL, HENRY
Jekyll, J.
Resistance to unlawful authority (impeachment of H. Sacheverell). BREW 7:165

SACK, MANNIE
Jessel, G.
Response to introduction as Toastmaster General at dinner in honor of Mannie Sack, and introduction of principal speaker, David Sarnoff. JEYO:55
Sarnoff, D.
Speech at testimonial dinner in honor of Mannie Sack. JEYO:60
Sackett, Samuel
Justice and little boys. AN:50
Sackville, Edward See Dorset, E.S.

SACRIFICE
Stires, E.M.
Sincerity and sacrifice. LAD:153
Sadler, Frank P.
Mirabeau. TRUW:40
Sadler, William S.
Elements of pep. EXEE:36

SAFETY
Safety-a city-wide plea for careful drivers and cautious pedestrians. DR:42; LU:1137
Safety first. SCHS:232
Safety first on our highways-speech to establish a "safety first" committee at a convention. WRA:196
Spare our lives. YR 10:17
See also National Safety Congress; Traffic accidents
Saffi, Aurelio, Count
To the University of Edinburgh. KNAS:251; KNASA:251
Sagasta, Praxetes Mateo
In defense of the unity of Italy. CHAL 11:114; HAZO 21:8970; MAS 21:8970
Said, John
"Don't give up the ship." BRP 4:17
St. Albans, Francis Bacon, Viscount See Bacon, F.
St. John, Robert
Remarks preceding the reading over the radio of Chaplain Gittelsohn's address "That men might be free." BA 1945-46:16
Saint-Just, Louis Antoine Leon de
Invective against Danton. BRYW 7:156; CHAL 4:240; HAZO 9:3631; MAS 9:3631

SAINT LAWRENCE RIVER
Eisenhower, D.D.
Dedication of the Saint Lawrence Seaway. SABA:292

ST. LOUIS-WORLD'S FAIR
Odell, B.B., Jr.
Westward Ho! (St. Louis World's Fair). WERN 42:141

SAINT PATRICK'S DAY
Clifford, V.
Emcee at a St. Patrick's Day party. BRH:231
Culberson, C.A.
Tribute to Ireland (St. Patrick's Day address). SHUO:219
Hall, J.
Doctrine's of St. Patrick. THOU 1:525
McGlynn, E.
Lessons from St. Patrick's character and work. THOU 1:520
McKeldin, T.
St. Patrick's Day. MCK:136
Meagher, T.F.

SAINT PATRICK'S DAY (cont.)
Glory of Ireland (St. Patrick's Day speech). HAZO 20:8471; MAS 20:8471
Saint Patrick's Day (by a son of the Emerald Isle). EDGS: 13
Saint Patrick's Day-March 17. DR:133
Shortridge, S. M.
St. Patrick. WAGN:65
Speech for a St. Patrick's Day dinner. BARB:104

SAINT VALENTINE'S DAY See Valentine's Day
Sala, George Augustus
Friend and foe. REEMA 3:1014

SALA, GEORGE AUGUSTUS
Depew, C. M.
Our English visitors (welcoming George Augustus Sala). REEMA 1:338
Reid, W.
Introduces George Augustus Sala to Lotus Club. REEMA 3:1014

SALARIES See Hours of labor; Wages
Salas, Octaviano Campos
Inaugural speech at Conference on the Problems of Economic Development. UAR: 285
Sales, Francis de. See Francis de Sales, Saint

SALES TALKS AND SALESMANSHIP
Address of welcome at a sales convention by the president of the company. WRA:82
Alton, B.
Introducing an insurance salesman
" a shoe salesman (traveling). BRC:199,228
Barton, B.
Which knew not Joseph. BRAC:24; BRY:461; BRYA: 500; HUS:279; LINM:358; SABA:243
Bolden, J.
Introducing a salesmanager. BRC:264
Bones: short and over can mean short of publicity and overlooking a patron (a speech to bank personnel, changeable for many occasions-business meeting or convention of sales personnel, at a graduation of nurses' group, for fund raising drives, to a telephone group, or by a political or labor speaker). BAI:94
Characteristics and outline of a sales talk. BAKF:209
Collins, A.
Introducing an automobile salesman. BRC:280
Every salesman is a receptionist-speech by salesmanager at retail sales meeting to encourage improved retail selling. WRA:216
Ferris, E. E.
Art of personal contact. LINM:456
Forerunners of commerce. DU:154
Game of life or a top man is not a flop man (a changeable speech adaptable as an inspirational speech for sales people, student groups and for all workers, or for a sports dinner speaker). BAI:56
Gilbert, E. A.
Introducing a top salesman. BRC:196
Good will. FRIE:158
Haas, C. G.
I was a jockey. YR 9:249
Holler, W. E.
Automobile dealer. SAC:88
How to sell a house. MICS: 138
Hunt, L.
Introducing a house-to-house salesman. BRC:178

Iglehart, A. S.
Sale we've failed to make. SAB:169
Jeffries, H. A.
Salesman as a collector. LINM:47
Kaser, A. L.
Emcee at a salesmen's convention-two examples of. BRH:230, 295
Introducing an insurance salesman
" a top salesman. BRC: 82, 90
Knauth, O. W.
Fundamentals of merchandising. HOA:88
Ludlum, M. E.
Buy Reynolds' wrap. SAB: 160; SABA:258
McGovern, A. H.
Introducing a successful salesman
" a top salesman. BRC: 135, 121
Most important letter in a salesman's alphabet-speech by president or the salesmanager at a sales convention. WRA:213
Opening address at a sales convention by the salesmanager. WRA:81
Personality as a basic factor in selling. SPIM:183
Power of persuasion. FRIE: 162
Putting your project across (pep talk to be used at a sales meeting, to inspire a group of workers on a charity drive or any similar purpose). NAT:36
Right psychological approach. NAT:36
Sales convention report at company sales meeting. WRA:183
Sales meeting pep talk. NAT: 41
Sales meeting talk. FRIE:172
Salesmanship (advice to beginners). ED:223
Sandford, W. P.
Personality is yours for the taking. SAC:80
Suggestions for preparation of the sales talk. REAB:162
With examples of. MICS: 129; SABA:240
Value of a co-pilot in estate planning. MICS:130
Voltage: the jolt of a volt (a changeable speech for many occasions, for a sales speech, a membership drive, or a pep talk). BAI: 85
Wampler, W. N.
Why support the new bond issue? MICS:131
Woodbridge, C. K.
Salesmanship and advertising. BYRA:469; REEM sup 3:183; REEMB 5:396
Worsham, J. A.
Low pressure selling. SAB: 106; SABA:172
Yeager, W. H.
Art of speaking effectively to employees. SABA:248
See also Auctions
Salisbury, Robert Arthur Talbot Gascoyne-Cecil, 3d Marquis of
Abandonment of General Gordon. BRYW 5:109; CHAL 11:362; HAZO 22:9283; MAS 22:9283; REEM 9:313; REEMA 15:1808; REEMB 10:322
Burning question. CHAL 11: 360; HAZO 22:9281; MAS 22:9281
Egypt and the Soudan. BAKF: 333; CHAL 11:355
Egyptian question. CHAL 11: 355; HAZO 22:9276; MAS 22:9276
House of Lords as a check on legislation. EMS 1:146
Kitchener in Africa. REEM 3: 184; REEMA 3:1018; REEMB 3:191
Limehouse policy. BREW 3: 180

Salisbury, R. A. T. G. -C. (cont.)
One-man power. ORBR 2:361
Speech at Monmouthshire, October 8, 1885. PAUF 2:263
Tampering with the Constitution. CHAL 11:340; HAZO 22:9261; MAS 22:9261; REEMA 15:1821
Salmon, Lucy M.
Susan B. Anthony. KNAS:100; KNASA:100

SALONS See Societies
Salter, Alfred and others (W. Steed)
Pacificism-for and against. SAR:235
Salton, Melvin E.
Machine age. BOA:392

SALUTATORY ADDRESSES
Examples of greetings. BEC:149
Examples of various types of salutations. WRA:20
Greeting of the graduating class to the new seniors. STOC:179
Greeting of the graduating class to the new seniors-two examples of. STON:183-184
Latin salutatory. DAVC:10
Salutatory. DAVC:199
Salutatory for a college. REAC:30
Salutatory for a college or academy. PAIC:24
Salutatory for a college or university. AMEO 1:168
Salutatory for a first class of any school. PAIC:19
Salutatory for a grammar school. PAIC:15
Salutatory for a grammar school. REAC:22
Salutatory for a high school. AMEO 1:165
Salutatory for a high school. PAIC:22
Salutatory for a high school. REAC:25
Salutatory for a university. PAIC:29
Salutatory for either a grammar or high school. AMEO 1:163
Salutatory for either a grammar or high school. PAIC:16
Salutatory in parody form for a grammar school (from "As you like it"). PAIC:36
Salutatory in parody form for a high school (from "The Merchant of Venice"). PAIC:38
Salutatory in parody form for a high school (from "Thanatopsis"). PAIC:39
Salutatory in parody form for any grade (from "A Psalm of life"). PAIC:42
Salutatory in parody form for either a grammar school or high school (from "Hamlet"). PAIC:37
Salutatory- "Life." CRAI:420
Salutatory of novel form: Class declaration of independence. PAIC:43
Salutatory of novel form: Class diagnosis. PAIC:49
Salutatory of novel form: Class inventory. PAIC:52
Salutatory of novel form: Class lamentations (scriptural style). PAIC:47
Salutatory of novel form: The president's proclamation. PAIC:54
See also Opening addresses; Welcoming addresses

SALVATION ARMY
Karos, P. A.
Haven of the defeated. ARNS:160; NOR 1950:187
Sampson, Edith
Jane Addams' unfinished business (at Jane Addams centennial observance, Springfield, Illinois). HILK:294
Sampson, Martin Wright

Problems of American civilization. NORR 2d ser:278
Sampson, William Thomas
Victory in superior numbers. REEM 3:189; REEMA 3:1023; REEMB 3:196
Samuels, Maurice
Where the fruit is freedom. LINM:365

SAN FRANCISCO
Outline for a speech "By the Golden Gate." BARR:66

SAN FRANCISCO CONFERENCE, 1945 See United Nations Conference on International Organization, San Francisco, 1945
Sanchez, Joe
Our daily oil. BRAP:102
Sandburg, Carl
On Lincoln (at 150th anniversary of Lincoln's birth). HURG:347

SANDBURG, CARL
Gannett, L. S.
Carl Sandburg. SAR:371
Sanderson, J. Kent
Plan or perish. BRP 8:108; YR 9:69
Sandford, William P.
Membership meetings that click. SAB:66; SABA:88
Personality is yours for the taking. SAC:80

SANDWICH ISLANDS
Clemens, S. L.
Sandwich Islands. REEM 8:131; REEMA 4:253; REEMB 13:133
Saner, R. E. L.
Valley Forge. PROS:78
Sanger, Margaret
Is birth control legal? GA:273
Plea for birth-control legislation. GA:157

SANITARIUMS
Tribute by contrast. NI:277
Sarbin, Hershel
Let medicine wash its hands. NOR 1946:59
Sarnoff, David
Appeal for popular support of the Metropolitan Opera. MOA:312
Six thousand years. COP:429; COPA:429
Speech at testimonial dinner in honor of Mannie Sack. JEYO:60
Sarnoff, Robert W.
Television's role in the American democracy. BA 1962-63:136
Sassoonan, Delaware chief
Speaks at the Council held at the Courtho, of Philadia, Oct. 10th, 1728. SHE:70
Sastri, V. S. Srinivasa
Advice to students. ZU:9
Imperial Conference, 1921. KESB:62

SATAN
Devil's playground. JAI:71
No shadowboxer. JAI:32
Snake bites. THOT:81
Satank, Kiowa chief
Speech at Council. JON:107
Satterthwaite, James Buckley
Fire and blood. YR 7:147
Learned dust. YR 9:231
Plea for pebbles. YR 8:1

SATYAGRAHA (PHILOSOPHY) See India
Satyulov, Pavel A.
Speech of October 25. RUS:85
Saunders, Prince
People of Hayti and a plan of emigration. DUNM:13
Promoting the abolition of slavery, and improving the condition of the African race. WOON:56
Saurin, Jacques
Christian heroism. HAZO 4:1746; MAS 4:1746
Effect of passion. BREW 9:141
Repentance of the unchaste woman. PL:285
Sermon on the speech of Paul

Saurin, Jacques (cont.)
before Felix and Drusolla. LEEW 4:329

Savage, Howard P.
Address to the Legion dead. SHUP:216

Savage, Minot Judson
American wit and humor. REEMA 6:943
Education for life. BLAA:26; BLAB:26
What is Christianity? CHAL 13:408

SAVING AND THRIFT
Dollars and sense. NATT:25
Eyrich, G. F., Jr.
Thrift and citizenship. BYRA:148; REEM sup 1:282; REEMB 4:216
Fish, S.
Economy. REEM 4:128; REEMB 4:258
Handicap of poverty and the value of thrift and cash in hand. AMEO 2:96
Polek, B. A.
You have to see it first. MIA:331
Thrift from the banker's standpoint. AMEO 2:198

SAVINGS BONDS See Bonds, government

Savonarola, Girolamo
After his excommunication. BRYW 7:28
Do penance, penance, penance. HIB:187
Exhorts the people of Florence to repent. -Same as his Sermon on the Ascension
I bring you good news. BRYW 7:25; CODS:53; CODSA:53
Lazarus, come forth. CODS:55; CODSA:55
Let me be persecuted (from Lenten sermons of 1497). CROC:396
On the degeneration of the Church. CHAL 1:393; HAZO 3:1280; MAS 3:1280; PL:221
On the first epistle of St. John. CHAL 1:386; HAZO 3:1273; MAS 3:1273
On the love of Jesus Christ. CHAL 1:389; HAZO 3:1276; MAS 3:1276
Sea of politics. CODS:57; CODSA:57
Sermon on the Ascension. LEEW 4:45; PE:79; PEA:79

SAVONARLO, GIROLAMO
O'Flynn, E. F.
Savonarola-priest and patriot. SHUC:261

SAYLOR, LYNN
Hemery, J. L.
Introduces Lynn Saylor, advertiser. PR:90

Sayre, Francis B.
Challenge of international law. SAR:273
Corregidor. BA 1941-42:179
Major problems in the United States foreign policies. BA 1948-49:51

SAYRE, MORRIS
Hoffman, H. G.
Introduces Morris Sayre. PR:95

SCAFFOLD SPEECHES See Defense, speeches of

Scanlon, Ross
Public address as a social force (dedicating new quarters for Speech Department at Queens College). BA 1961-62:159

Scarborough, William Sanders
Party of freedom and the freedmen. DUNM:219

Scarlett, Sir James
Charge to the jury. CHAL 4:352; HAZO 9:3790; MAS 9:3790

Scarrooyady, Oneida chief
At a meeting of Commis-

sioners and Indians, at Carlisle, 1753. SHE:25
Schaeffer, Joan
Back to the future. AN:30
Schall, Thomas D.
Genius of patriotism. TRUW: 157
Schamus, Sanford Leonard
Road to prosperity. YR 6:117
Schary, David O.
Speech at Friars' Club dinner to Burns and Allen. JEYO: 72

SCHARY, DAVID O.
Jessel, G.
Remarks as toastmaster at Friars' Club to Burns and Allen. JEYO:71
Schelling, Felix Emanuel
Humanities, gone and to come. NORR 1st ser:286

SCHENCK, JOSEPH
Joseph Schenck-a eulogy. NIA: 135
Schenk, Noah Hunt
Truth and trade. REEMA 3: 1026
Scherer, Paul
Until he comes. BA 1955-56: 175
Scherer, Ruth M.
Blundering giant. BRP 7:31; YR 1:25
Schermerhorn, James
Soul of a city. NESA:149; SCHS:252
Schiff, Jacob H.
Introduction at the 250th anniversary of the settlement of the Jews in the United States. TWJ:8

SCHILLER, JOHANN CHRISTOPHER FRIEDRICH VON
Phelan, J. D.
Goethe-Schiller memorial address. WAGN:356
Schindler, John A.
How to live a hundred years happily. BERS:101; YE: 236
Schlegel, Karl Wilhelm F. Von
Philosophy of history. BREW 9:147; HAZO 10:3982; MAS 10:3982
Schlesinger, Arthur M., Jr.
Challenge of abundance. ARNS:221
Schley, Winfield Scott
Navy in peace and in war. REEMA 3:1031; SHUO:250
Schlicten, Erwin, von
International racketeers. BRP 8:11; YR 6:67
Schliemann, Heinrich
Beginnings of art. REEMA 3: 1034

SCHLIEMANN, HEINRICH
Scott, G.
Introduces Heinrich Schliemann to Royal Academy, London. REEMA 3:1034
Schmitt, William A.
Centennial oration (Druids). THOU 3:200
Schmitz, Howard E.
Old crank next door. BRY: 437; BRYA:488
Schnadig, Edgar L.
Presents Gerald Wendt. LY: 105; PR:93
Schneider, Abraham L.
Dilemma of democracy. BRP 10:35; NOR 1939:28
Schner, Charles
Fine white ashes. NOR 1950: 181

SCHNERING, OTTO
Taylor, H. J.
Integrity! a mighty force (tribute to Otto Schnering, head of Curtiss Candy Company). LARW:110
Schoenbrun, David
An orange. HOA:402

SCHOLARS See Learning and scholarship
Scholz, Arno C.
Prayer for mercy. ACW:21

SCHOOL BONDS See Education-Finance
SCHOOL BUILDINGS
My best piece of work-advising the construction of school buildings. AMEO 1:132
Why we need a new schoolhouse. AMEO 1:54

SCHOOL DISCIPLINE See Discipline

SCHOOL GRADES AND GRADING
Donnelly, M. C.
On scholastic despotism. BRP 9:118; YR 10:209

SCHOOL MANAGEMENT AND ORGANIZATION
Bergerot, P. A.
Personal and political interference with the administration of school affairs. WAGN:359
Booker, I. A.
American school board. DOA:184

SCHOOL, OPENING OF
Address at a school opening. AMEO 2:150
Address at the opening of a rural school. AMEO 1:27
Remarks by a teacher at the opening of school. HILL:462

SCHOOLS
Clifford, V.
Emcee at a school centennial. BRH:236
Congratulatory speech by mayor at opening of a new school. WRA:156
Farewell speech at complimentary dinner to retiring member of school board after twenty five years' service. WRA:177
An old grad discusses "The school spirit." DR:73
Our schools of today-improvement in half a century. AMEO 1:129
Wampler, W. N.
Why support the new bond issue? MICS:131
See also Dedication addresses-schools; Education; Sunday schools

---- FINANCIAL CONDITIONS
Holand, D.
Educational crisis. YR 6:277
Hunt, C.
Cotner College. BRP 5:42; YR 6:179
Pease, J.
Comedy or tragedy. BOA:150; BRP 5:7; YR 6:131

---- RURAL
Tate, W. K.
South Carolina's rural school problem. ONES:268

---- SUMMER
Advantage of teachers attending summer normals. AMEO 1:127
Schottenfeld, Alvin C.
To read or not to read. BRP 8:62; NOR 1937:5
Schrader, Dorothy
What will they believe? BRP 10:88

SCHRAM, EMIL
Wilson, P.
Introduces Emil Schram, president N. Y. Stock Exchange. PR:46
Schultz, A. L.
Creative education. ASHF:41
Schultz, Earle
David L. Gaskill. MO:536
Schuman, Frederick L.
Design for a people's peace. BA 1942-43:142
Peace without appeasement. HAR:40
Schumann, M. Maurice
Responds to an introduction.

PRNE:72
Schurman, Jacob Gould
Competition. BLAA:206; BLAB:206
Response to welcome. ONES: 94
Welcome to Cornell's 25th anniversary. ONES:23
Schurz, Carl
American tariffs. WERN 42: 179
"Americanizing" our new possessions. FUL:269, 272, 274, 277, 279, 281
Arraignment of Stephen A. Douglas. CHAL 11:193; HAZO 21:9048; MAS 21: 9048
Criminal aggression. FUL:284
General amnesty. BAKF:353; BRYW 10:27; HARS:469; ONEM:272; PAR:381; RINM:93
General Sherman. KLEM:147; ONES:164; REEM 5:344; REEMA 9:1026; REEMB 9: 386; RINM:93
Hill and Hillism. HICF:165
Imperialism hostile to liberty. FUL:287
International arbitration. SHUM:296
Let us have peace. BLAA: 238; BLAB:238
Necessity and progress of Civil Service reform. JOHA 2 pt 2:400
Old world and the new. COP: 656; COPB:683; HURG: 135; REEM 3:192; REEMA 3:1036; REEMB 3:199
Policy of imperialism. BRAS: 242; CHAL 11:213; HAZO 21:9078; MAS 21:9078; REEM 10:364; REEMA 15: 1834; REEMB 11:378
Public offices as private perquisites. BREW 9:154
True Americanism. BRE:236; BOAM:11; REEMA 9:1018
Schwab, Charles M.
Andrew Carnegie-his methods with men. REEM 5:247; REEMB 9:389
How to succeed. BYRA:394; HOA:385; KLEB:265; REEM 4:375; REEMB 5: 262
On being awarded a bronze tablet. REEM 4:387; REEMB 5:274
Stability in industry. ONEC: 257

SCHWAB, CHARLES M.
Kingsley, D. P.
In honor of Charles M. Schwab. REEM 4:243
Schwellenbach, Lewis B. See Granik, T., jt. auth.

SCIENCE AND RELIGION See Religion and science

SCIENCE AND SCIENTISTS
Acceptance of science award. BEDA:61
Ball, R.
Kinship of art and science. REEMA 1:16
Bondfield, M.
Science and the human factor. REEM sup 1:127; REEMB 4:74
Brown, H. S.
Science, technology and world development. ARNS: 84
Social responsibility of science. BA 1948-49:139; BARR:280
Commoner, B.
Scientific statesmanship. BA 1962-63:68
Compton, A. H.
Science and religion. BA 1939-40:421
Truth makes us free. BART 1:327
Compton, K. T.
State of science. HAR:294
Davis, W.
Creative and defensive science. ON:76
Dawson, S. E.
On the progress of science

SCIENCE AND SCIENTISTS (cont.)
in Canada. HAZO 19:8166; MAS 19:8166
Durfee, J.
Influence of scientific discovery and invention on social and political progress. BL:381; NORR 1st ser:43
Eisenhower, D. D.
Science and national security. BA 1957-58:20
Hesburgh, T. M.
Science and man. BA 1962-63:56
Huxley, T. H.
Method of scientific investigation. ARNS:260; BRY:455; BRYA:482
Science and art. COP:655; COPB:682; REEM 2:262; REEMA 2:670; REEMB 2:266
Kaplan, A.
How many centuries of progress? BRP 6:31; YR 7:47
Little, A. D.
Fifth estate. REEM sup 2:143; REEMB 6:244
Lodge, O. J.
Pure and applied science. REEM sup 2:160; REEMB 5:120
Miller, H.
Pledge science gives to hope. BREW 8:144
Millikan, R. A.
Science and spiritual values. ONEC:177
Science and the world tomorrow. BA 1938-39:187
Science leads us forward. BOA:145
Opening speech at presentation of scientific award. BEDA:58
Oppenheimer, J. R.
Prospect in the arts and sciences (at Columbia University bicentennial anniversary celebration). COPB:642; HURG:319
Paget, J.
Scientific mind. HAY:261
Pasteur, L.
Depicts the spirit of science. PE:469; PEA:469
Porter, N.
Sciences of nature versus the science of man. BL:455
Teachings of science and religion. REEMA 3:950
Rice, W. N.
Scientific thought in the nineteenth century. REEMA 9:984
Ridenour, L. N.
Science, technology, and national security. HAR:312
Roe, A.
Psychology of the scientist. BAAGA:392
Russell, J. R.
Science and literature as modes of progress. BREW 9:126
Sarnoff, D.
Six thousand years. COP:429
Scott, I. M.
Development of science (at dedication of Academy of Science, San Francisco). WAGN:234
Seaborg, G. T.
Scientific society-the beginnings: 29th John Wesley Powell lecture. BA 1961-62:110
Scientist as a human being (accepting Charles Lathrop Parsons Award). BA 1964-65:129
Sears, P. B.
Science, life, and landscape. BA 1961-62:187
Steady state: physical law and moral choice. NORR 3d ser:369
Shelby, J.
New frontiers for smart people. BART 3:277
Simon, S.
Vision of a scientist. BRP

6:47; NOR 1934:86
Smith, G.
Secret beyond science. BREW 9:244; BRYW 5:34
Smith, H. L.
Culture afforded by scientific training (at Alumni reunion). SHUO:98
Smyth, H. D.
Scientific manpower. HAR: 317
Snow, C. P.
Moral un-neutrality of science. BA 1960-61:41; BAAGA:423
Steele, R.
Introducing an atomic scientist. BRC:316
Stoddard, G. D.
Science and civilization. BA 1947-48:169
Thomson, J. J.
Energy and the explosion of the earth. BREW 9:402
Forces which move the world. BREW 9:401
Roentgen rays and other great discoveries. BREW 9:400
Toast to science by a layman. EDGS:186
Tributes to scientist (at presentation of citation to physician). BEDA:59
Tyndall, J.
Art and science. REEM 3: 345; REEMA 3:1160; REEMB 3:361
Urey, H. C.
Science and society (at 100th anniversary Academic convocation of Cooper Union for the advancement of science and art). ARNS: 79
Waterman, A. T.
Science in the sixties (accepting the William Proctor Prize of the Scientific Society of America). BA 1960-61:189
See also Atomic energy, Chemistry and chemists; Electrons
Scipio Africanus Major, Publius Cornelius
In his own defence. CHAL 1: 257; HAZO 2:654; MAS 2: 654
To his mutinous troops. BRYW 2:23
To his soldiers. BRYW 2:3; LEEW 2:101; PL:103

SCOTCH IN THE UNITED STATES
Carnegie, A.
Scotch-American. REEM 1: 215; REEMA 1:119; REEMB 1:216

SCOTLAND
Belhaven, J. H.
Plea for the national life of Scotland. BREW 1:376; BRTH:53; BRTHA:53; CHAL 2:127; GOOD:21; HAZO 4:1664; MAS 4:1664; ORBR 1:129
Carnegie, A.
Scotland and Holland. REEM 1:210; REEMB 1:211
Froude, J. A.
Influence of the Reformation on Scottish character. HAZO 18:7806; MAS 18: 7806
Scott, Charles
Women of the Confederacy. SHUO:34
Scott, Clifford
Profit and loss. YR 7:315

SCOTT, DRED See Dred Scott Decision
Scott, Emmett J.
Memorial address (on Booker T. Washington). WOON:607
Scott, Sir Gilbert
Introduces Heinrich Schliemann to Royal Academy, London. REEMA 3:1034
Introducing W. E. Gladstone to Royal Academy, May 5, 1877. REEM 2:96

Scott, Irving M.
Development of science (at dedication of Academy of Science, San Francisco). WAGN:234

SCOTT, SIR WALTER, BART.
Bryant, W.C.
Sir Walter Scott (unveiling statue in Central Park, New York). REEMA 7:155
Hay, J.
Sir Walter Scott (at unveiling of bust of Sir Walter Scott in Westminster Abbey). REEMA 8:614
Smith, G.
Lamps of fiction (at centenary of Sir Walter Scott). BREW 9:233; ONEM:541; REEMA 9:1068
Scott, Walter Francis, 5th Duke of Buccleuch
Introduces Lord Beaconsfield. REEM 9:303; REEMB 10:312
Scoville, D.C.
Truth and victory. SHU:196
Scranton, William W.
Inaugural address as Governor of Pennsylvania. BA 1962-63:173
Scribe, Michael
For a Bar Mitzvah. ZEL:23

SCROLLS
Materials for use in composing scrolls. BEC:46
See also Presentation speeches-Scrolls
Scullin, James Henry
Imperial Conference, 1930. KESB:208
Seabaugh, Rusby
Education for war. BLUE:100
Seaborg, Glenn T.
Scientific society-the beginnings: 29th John Wesley Powell lecture. BA 1961-62:110
Scientist as a human being (accepting Charles Lathrop Parsons Award). BA 1964-65:129
United States in the space age. ANGC:124
Seabury, David
How Jesus healed men's minds. BART 3:1
Social change and individual growth. BART 2:55

SEABURY, DAVID
McLain, H.O.
Presents David Seabury. LY:117; PR:105
Seamon, Sir Owen
Presents Stephen Leacock. LY:55
Searle, George M.
Are the planets habitable? REEMA 6:967
Sears, Paul B.
Science, life, and landscape. BA 1961-62:187
Steady state: physical law and moral choice. NORR 3d ser:369
Seashore, Carl E.
What is psychology? MO:513

SEASONS
Seasons. DR:310
Seattle, Dwamish chief
Speech to Isaac Stephens, Governor of Oregon Territory. JON:99
Seboldt, R.
Taking Jesus into marriage. ACW:79

SECESSION See Confederate States of America; State rights; United States-History-Civil War-Causes

SECRET SERVICE
Russell, C.E.
True tales of the secret service. EXEE:229

SECRET SOCIETIES
About fraternal orders. DICD:104
Avery, C.H.

Growth of fraternity. THOU 3:357
Broadhurst, W. A.
True fraternity. THOU 3:368
Charity, keynote of fraternalism. THOU 3:191
Comprehensive discourse. THOS:17
Davis, J. J.
Fraternalism. NESA:115
Dow, E. E.
Danger of fraternal apathy. THOU 3:373
Eldridge, G. D.
Future of fraternalism. THOU 3:362
Eliot, C. W.
Fraternalism. THOU 3:20
Fraternal fellowship. FRIE: 66
Fraternal insurance. THOU 3:189
Fraternal loyalty. THOU 3: 145
Fraternal spirit. THOU 3:367
Fraternal societies (brother asks a few questions). ED: 399
Fraternal toasts. DICD:121; DICE:121
Fraternalism. THOU 3:22
Fraternities. THOS:62
Fraternities, by a member. EDGS:367
Fraternity. THOU 3:127
Fraternity and business. DICD:108
Fraternity and business. THOU 3:370
Fraternity and Christianity. THOU 3:187
Fraternity as a moral farce. THOS:12
Fraternity song. EDGS:368
Functions of fraternalism. AMEO 2:44
General fraternity. THOS:38
Growth of fraternity. THOU 3:344
Haag, E. N.
Fraternity: speech to T. Roosevelt. THOU 3:17
Inherent strength of fraternalism. THOU 3:26
Hinds, C. G.
Fraternal greetings. THOU 3:318
Jessel, G.
Suggestions for speeches to fraternal organizations. With examples of. JEYO: 32
Kenngott, G. F.
Church and fraternity. THOU 3:372
Kline, B. J.
Fraternal societies, origin and history. THOU 3:185
Langfitt, J. A.
Fraternal system. THOU 3:388
Lee, J. A.
Fraternity. THOU 3:354
Lodges (visitor is asked to speak). ED:402
Matthew, M. A.
Fraternal life insurance. THOU 3:177
Morgan, W. L.
Don't forget those who gave us fraternity. THOU 3:181
National Fraternal Congress. THOU 3:161
Patriotism and fraternity. THOS:15
Rice, W. A.
Era of fraternalism. THOU 3:361
Rogers, J. T.
Fraternity and permanency. THOU 3:195
Secret order. THOS:142
Sentiment. THOS:14
Thayer, W.
Fraternity, the latest moral force. THOU 3:172
True fraternity. THOS:13
Western viewpoint. THOS:20
What is fraternity? THOU 3:21
Wholesale counsels. THOU 3: 164
Wooley, M. E.
Redefinition of secret societies. NORR 2d ser:312

SECRET SOCIETIES (cont.)
See also Brotherliness; Greek letter societies. Also Names of secret societies, e.g. Elks, Benevolent and Protective Order of; Freemasons; Kiwanis Club; Lions Club; Odd-fellows, Independent Order of

SECRETARIES, PRIVATE See Private secretaries

SECTIONAL PARTY See United States-Politics and Government

SECURITY See Insurance, social

SEDITION LAW, 1798. See Alien and sedition laws, 1798

Seelye, Julius Hawley
Relation of learning and religion: inaugural address as president of Amherst College. WE 1:163

Seelye, L. Clark
State versus anarchy. BLAA: 250; BLAB:250

SEGREGATION
Brady, T. P.
Segregation and the South. WPRC:333
Dawson, W. L.
Segregation in the armed forces. HAR:469
Example of a closing speech on joining a campaign against segregation. MICS: 174
McClain, W.
Our school of destiny. YR 6:81
Wilkins, R.
Deep South crisis. WPRC: 344
See also Discrimination; Negroes; Race problems; Segregation in education

SEGREGATION IN EDUCATION
Byrnes, J. F.
South respects the written Constitution. ARNS:144
Clement, R. E.
'How would you have us?" BA 1959-60:181
Davis, J.W.
For segregation in the schools. BA 1953-54:113
Fischer, J. H.
Educational problems of segregation and desegregation of public schools. BA 1962-63:111
Hill, O.W.
Case against segregated schools. ARNS:150
Hughes, C. E.
Opinion in the case of the Negro law student, Lloyd Gaines. ANG:486
Marshall, T.
Against segregation in the schools. BA 1953-54:118
See also Civil rights

SEGREGATION-RESISTANCE TO
King, M. L., Jr.
Love, law, and civil disobedience. HILK:345; LINP:52
Marshall, T.
Cry for freedom. HILK: 318
Mays, B. E.
Christian in race relations. HILK:120
Sampson, E.
Jane Addams's unfinished business (at Jan Addams centennial observance, Springfield, Illinois). HILK:294

SELF CULTURE
Channing, W. E.
Self-culture. REEMA 7:182
Le Vander, B.
Meet your friends. BRP 6: 19; YR 7:25
Self-made men. NATT:19
Williams, W.

Greatest battle ever won. BOA:170; BOB:197; PROS: 54; SHU:216

SELF DEFENSE See Defense, speeches of

SELF DISCIPLINE See Discipline

SELF GOVERNMENT (IN EDUCATION)
Holmes, J. H.
Honor system. PEAE:225

SELFISHNESS
Moore, D.
Depose king selfishness. BRP 3:66

SELFRIDGE, THOMAS
Dexter, S.
Argument in Selfridge's trial. CHAL 4:154; HAZO 8:3492; MAS 8:3492
Seligman, E. R. A.
Capitalism vs. Socialism: debate. REEM 3:42, 58, 69
Selikowitz, G.
Speech for a Bar Mitzvah: address of a Jewish boy when he becomes 13 years of age. ZEL:64
Speech for a Bar Mitzvah-3 speeches. ZEL:3, 5, 7

SELLING See Sales talks and salesmanship

SEMICENTENNIAL CELEBRATIONS. See Anniversaries

SEMINOLE WAR, 1st FLORIDA, 1817-1818
Clay, H.
On the Seminole War. BREW 4:26; CHAL 5:41; HAZO 10:4050; MAS 10: 4050; REEMA 12:672; SOU 9:193
Semmes, Thomas Jenkins
Personal characteristics of the Chief Justices (at centennial celebration of Supreme Court). REEMA 9: 1029
Seneca, Annaeus (Elder)
Suasoria VII. LEEW 2:123
Seneca, Lucius Annaeus
Address to Nero. BREW 9: 160; BRYW 2:242
Seneca George
At conference with Indians, Easton, 1761. SHE:33
Sener, William
Youth-today and tomorrow. YR 7:125

SEPTENNIAL BILL See Great Britain-Parliament

SERENADES
Defeated candidate's reply to a serenade. HILL:468
Speech in acknowledgement of a political serenade. BARB:90
Speech of a candidate when serenaded. HILL:467

SERMONS
Ball, J.
We have the pain and travail. CROC:1
Behold, a sower went forth to sow-address to a church congregation delivered by a layman. WRA:229
Savonarola, G.
Let me be persecuted (from Lenten sermons of 1497). CROC:396
Spurgeon, C. H.
Substance of sermons. ORBR 2:393
Suggestions for making and examples of sermons by the layman. WRA:227
Today-a layman's address at a church service. WRA: 232
Wycliffe, J.
Sixth Sunday gospel after Easter. CROC:485
See also Baccalaureate sermons; Church; Funeral

SERMONS (cont.)
sermons; Religion; also subjects of sermons, e.g. Faith

SERVICE See Citizenship; Social service

---- CLUBS
Address of welcome to new members at a service club meeting. WRA:70
Congratulatory address by international president of Acme Service Club at special meeting. WRA:161
A druggist-speech before a service club meeting. WRA:240
Grocer-speech before a club. WRA:238
International president's speech dedicating a home for underprivileged children-sponsored by the civic service club. WRA:41
Message of appreciation before the local service club (Rotary, Kiwanis, Lions, etc.) DR:99; LU:1166
Newly elected presiding officer's installation speech at annual meeting of any service club. WRA:119
President's installation address at service club. WRA:115
Response to invitation to speak by a member of an international service club visiting club for first time. WRA:248
Service club. FRIE:68
Service club. NATM:25
See also Names of clubs, e.g. Exchange Club; Kiwanis Club; Lions Club; Rotary Club

---- MEN See Army; Demobilization; Pensions, military; Recruiting; Soldiers; United States-Army; Veterans

SERVICE MEN, MILITARY See Soldiers

SERVICE MEN'S POSTS
Show-your-self (speech for the war veteran or auxiliary). BAI:144
Sifter: know your dough and you will grow (pep talk for bank personnel and business groups-adaptable for club members, a war-veteran post member or any auxiliary member). BAI:31
Strike: the striker and the strike-breaker (a changeable speech adaptable for Service men's posts, American War Mothers' or Gold Star Mothers' chapters, for a membership drive or a pep talk for co-operation). BAI:47
See also American legion

Serviss, Garrett Putnam
Napoléon Bonaparte. REEMA 6:983

SESQUICENTENNIAL CELEBRATIONS See Anniversaries

Sessions, Robert, Jr.
Constitution. LEIO:99; SHU:54

Sevareid, Eric
Vanishing family farm. BRAP:140
Western European attitudes, August, 1958. BA 1958-59:53

Seversky, Alexander P., de
Aviation vs isolationalism. ON:121
Will air power win this war? BA 1941-42:186

Seward, William Henry
Address to John Quincy Adams. KNAS:211; KNASA:211
Death of Napoleon. CODS:488; CODSA:488

Irrepressible conflict. BRAO: 298; BREW 9:164; BRYW 9:177; CHAL 6:458; COP: 295; COPA:295; COPB: 295; HARS:343; HAZO 14: 5709; HURG:99; JOHA 2 pt. 1:195; KLEG:331; MAS 14:5709; ORAMA 2:195; PL:656; REEM 10:161; REEMA 15:1849; REEMB 11:165
On secession. LEEW 10:203
On the admission of California to the Union. HICF: 1
Pious pilgrimage. REEM 3: 197; REEMA 3:1042; REEMB 3:204
Reconciliation in 1865. BREW 9:178
Speech on crisis of 1850. BIR 2:183
State of the country (1860). HAZO 14:5728; MAS 14: 5728
Tribute to John Quincy Adams. KNAS:85; KNASA:85

SEWING
Sew-it seams, a talk for the home economics group. DR: 305
SEX
Tierney, R.H.
Church and the sex problem. CATA 2:147

---- EDUCATION
Farish, E.
I knew Mary. YR 10:25

Seyle, Hans See Conn, J., jt. auth.
Shackelton, Sir Ernest Henry
Penguins. REEM 3:201; REEMB 3:208
Shaft, Harold D.
College man's creed. ASHF: 25
Shah, Manubhai
Inaugural speech at Conference on the Problems of Economic Development. UAR:187
Speech at final session of Conference on the Problems of Economic Development. UAR:369
Shahan, Louise
Through a child's eyes. AN: 42
Shairp, John Campbell
Literary theory of culture. REEMA 9:1052

SHAKESPEARE WILLIAM
Claretie, J. A. A.
Shakespeare and Moliere. REEMA 4:229
Davis, J.W.
Shakespeare's birthday memorial. REEM 1:369; REEMB 1:370
Ingersoll, R. G.
Shakespeare. BREW 7:133; HARSO:265; REEM 8:237; REEMA 5:627; REEMB 13: 241; SHU:136
Irving, H.
Character of Macbeth. REEMA 8:724
Müller, F. M.
Frankfort to Stratford-on-Avon (Shakespeare tercentenary). KNAS:261; KNASA: 261
Stubbs, C.W.
Shakespeare as a prophet. REEMA 9:1104
Thanksgiving for William Shakespeare (birthday sermon). HAZO 25:10559; MAS 25:10559

SHAME See Ethics
Shank, Clarence D.
Class day address. WERN 54: 45
Shapiro, Howard
In defense of youth. BRY:475
Shapley, Harlow
Design for fighting. BA 1944-45:245
See also Browne, L., jt. auth.
Shaw, Albert
Jefferson's doctrines under

Shaw, Albert (cont.)
new tests. NORR 1st ser: 298
Shaw, George Bernard
Menace of the leisured woman (introduction and summary of a debate). REEM sup 3: 74, 86
On his seventieth birthday. COP:208; COPA:208; COPB:208; REEM sup 2: 387; REEMB 3:212
Presents Major Barbara. LY: 60
So long, so long. SAR:263
Shaw, Henry Wheeler
Milk. REEM 8:358; REEMA 6:1011; REEMB 13:363
Shaw, Lemuel
Commonwealth v. Hunt. ANG: 257

SHAW, ROBERT GOULD
Washington, B. T.
Address delivered at dedication of the Robert Gould Shaw monument in Boston, May 31, 1897. CHAL 14: 320; DUNM:205; HAZO 25: 10861; MAS 25:10861; WOON:527
Shearer, Ralph
Saxon versus Slav. COUW: 157
Sheares, John
Address from dock. KET:275
Sheats, Paul H.
Salvage. BRP 1:44; YR 1:121
Sheehan, P. A.
Napoleon and O'Connell. WERN 42:38
Sheen, Fulton J., Bp.
Change of hearts. HURG:264
Cross and the double cross. COP:598; COPB:574
Judgment of nations. BA 1942-43:299
Liberty and the Republic. BA 1938-39:245
Responds to an introduction. PRNE:64
Signs of our times. BA 1946-47:246
SHEEN, FULTON J., Bp.
Nizer, L.
Presents Fulton John Sheen. LY:163; NI:111; NIA:85
Sheil, Bernard J.
Industrial democracy. ON: 149
Tribute to Roosevelt. BA 1944-45:165
Sheil, Richard Lalor
In defense of Irish Catholics. BREW 9:189; CHAL 5:436; HAZO 12:4946; MAS 12: 4946; PL:536
Ireland's part in English achievement. BREW 9:183; BRYW 6:173; REEMA 15: 1865
Irish aliens. -Same as his Ireland's part in English achievement
On the disabilities of the Jews. BRTH:251; BRTHA:251; BRYW 6:177; CHAL 5:438; HAZO 12:4948; MAS 12: 4948
Religious toleration. HAY: 138; KET:333
Shelburne, William Petty Fitzmaurice, Earl of
See Lansdowne, W. P. F., 1st Marquis
Shelby, James
New frontiers for smart people. BART 3:277
Sheldon, Verna
Boots for paving stones. WERN 54:56
Shelepin, Aleksandr N.
Speech of October 26. RUS: 96
Shelley, D. N.
Devotion to duty. BOB:192

SHELLEY, PERCY BYSSHE
McLean, C. M.
Poet Shelley. SHUC:144
Talfourd, T. N.
Queen against Moxon-Shelley as a blasphemer. BREW 9:345; HAZO 12: 5216; MAS 12:5216

Shepard, Edward Morse
Dishonor in American public life. NORR 2d ser:207
Shepard, James
Anvil chorus. YR 8:81
Shepard, James E.
Is the game worth the candle? DUNM:357
Shepardson, Francis W.
Farewell to members at Sesquicentennial of Phi Beta Kappa. BRAC:275
Shepherd, A. C.
Indian problem. COUW:29
Sheppard, Morris
Contributions of the Hebrew people to human advancement. SHUO:171
Eulogy on Washington. PROS: 30; SHU:246
Our dry United States. BOB: 45
Sheridan, Richard Brinsley
Against Warren Hastings. BREW 9:192; BRTH:106; BRTHA:106; BRYW 6:77; CHAL 3:393; CODS:265; COP:165; COPA:165; COPB:165; FULB:86; GOOD:407; HAY:53; HAZO 8:3069; LEEW 6:347; MAS 8:3069; ORBR 1:389; PAUF 1:212; PE:180; PEA:180; REEM 9:133; REEMA 15:1872; REEMB 10:139
Arraignment of Warren Hastings. PL:422
Desolation of Oude. CODSA: 265
Example of kings. BREW 9: 210
High crimes and misdemeanours. - Same as his Against Warren Hastings
Liberty of the press. EMS 2: 28
On the French Revolution. BREW 9:208
Patriotism and perquisites. BREW 9:209
Proceedings against Mr. Hastings in Westminster Hall; second or Begum charge (speeches of June 3, 6, 13, 1788). KET:217, 226, 236
Reply to Lord Mornington, 1794. PAUF 1:225
Robbery of the Princesses at Oude. KET:202
Sherman, Forrest P.
Navy of the future. YE:291
Sherman, John
Financial situation. CHAL 10: 202; HAZO 20:8441; MAS 20:8441; REEMA 15:1904
General financial policy of the government. BREW 9: 212
On silver coinage and treasury notes. HAZO 20:8429; JOHA 2 pt 2:329; MAS 20: 8429
On "The Crime of 1873." BRYW 10:198

SHERMAN, JOHN
Garfield, J. A.
John Sherman for President. BRYW 10:99; KNAS: 305; KNASA:305; LAD:104; REEM 10:261; REEMB 11: 273
Sherman, Stuart Pratt
Gaiety of Socrates. NORR 3rd ser:1
To business men only. REEM sup 2:398; REEMB 5:284
Sherman, William Tecumseh
Army and Navy (December 22, 1875 speech). CHAL 10:1; HAZO 19:8115; MAS 19: 8115
Army and the Navy (December 21, 1880 speech). REEM 3:206; REEMA 3:1046; REEMB 3:223
Reminiscence of the war. REEM 3:211; REEMA 3: 1051; REEMB 3:228
Speech of welcome at the reunion of the Army of the Tennessee. HILL:468

SHERMAN, WILLIAM TECUMSEH
Porter, H.

SHERMAN, WILLIAM TECUMSEH (cont.)
In commemoration of William Tecumseh Sherman. CHAL 13:104; HAZO 23:10040; MAS 23:10040
Schurz, C.
General Sherman. KLEM: 147; ONES:164; REEM 5:344; REEMA 9:1026; REEMB 9:386; RINM:93
Sherwood, Isaac R.
Tribute to Uncle Joe Cannon. HOA:359
Shhong, Sou
Inaugural speech at Conference on the Problems of Economic Development. UAR:243
Shigemitsu, Mamoru
Statement on Japan's observance of Potsdam Declaration. VO 1945-46:464
Shimada, Shigetaro
Speech to the Japanes Diet. VO 1943-44:452

SHIPPING
Cox, S. S.
On the revival of American shipping. CHAL 10:377; HAZO 20:8730; MAS 20:8730

SHIPWRECKS
Choate, J. H.
Argument in Admiralty for the 'Republic" (steamship). HICJ:183
Shively, Thornton
Bargain. BRP 5:76

SHIVERS, ALLAN
McDonough, J. J.
Introduces Allan Shivers, Governor of Texas. PRNE:7
Shoeler, Margaret
America's mother of men. YR 9:285

SHOES AND SHOE INDUSTRY
For a shoe trade entertainment. BARB:192
Shoe dealers. SCHS:240
Shoe manufacturers, by one of the leading shoe manufacturers. EDGS:139
See also Businessmen; Sales talks and salesmanship
Shorey, Paul
Can an American be an optimist? NORR 2d ser:496
Unity of the human spirit. NORR 1st ser:481
Short, Dewey
Response to introduction. PR:119
Short, Frank H.
Our untimely dead. WAGN:126

SHORT BALLOT. See Elections

SHORT PEOPLE See Man-Stature
Shortridge, Samuel M.
Abraham Lincoln. BOA:248; BOB:154
Eulogy on General Barnes. WAGN:84
Memorial Day address. WAGN:53
St. Patrick. WAGN:65
Washington: liberty under law. WAGN:88
Shoup, Paul
Necessity of moving on. ONEC:263

SHOWERS, BABY
Posner, G. A.
Emcee at a baby shower. BRH:268

---- BRIDAL
Huber, L. J.
Emcee at a bridal shower. BRH:212
Posner, G. A.
For an emcee at a bridal shower. BRH:193

SHREVEPORT, LOUISIANA
Randolph, E. H.
City of Shreveport (at lay-

ing of cornerstone of new City Hall). SHUO:226

SHRINES
Altars and fire. SCHS:12
Shuler, Bob, Jr.
Nation out of balance. YR 9: 89
Shulman, Charles E.
America at the crossroads. BART 3:75
Four philosophies of modern life. BA 1957-58:174
Shurter, Edwin Dubois
Influence of New England upon American institutions. SHU:27
Potency of Roosevelt's spirit. SHU:16
Shuster, George N.
Doctrine for the time. ON:70
Shvernik, Nikolai M.
Speech of October 24. RUS:78

SHYLOCKS See Industry
Sibley, Carroll
Response to introduction. PR:129

SICILY
Eden, A.
Address in the House of Commons, September 22, 1943. VO 1943-44:405
Hermocrates.
On the union of Sicily against invaders. BRYW 1: 55

SICK
Speeches calling attention to the illness or sickness of a member. STOC:114
Sidney, Algernon
Governments for the people and not the people for governments (scaffold speech). BREW 9:222; BRYW 3:142

SIDNEY, SIR PHILIP
Curtis, G.W.
Sir Philip Sidney. REEMA 4:357

Siegenthaler, Ray F.
New American tradition. YR 9:109

SIGHT See Eyes

SIGNS
Signs of the times. SCHS:249

---- ADVERTISING See Advertising
Sijaona, L. Nagwanda
Inaugural speech at Conference on the Problems of Economic Development. UAR:295
Speech at final session of Conference on the Problems of Economic Development. UAR:423
Sikkink, Don
Dollars and sense. NOR 1949: 175
Silbert, A.
To a Bar Mitzvah. ZEL:62
Silcox, Lucy Lee
Loneliness of genius. YR 3: 133
Silliman, Benjamin D.
Introducing and toasting R.B. Hayes to New England Society of Brooklyn, December 21, 1880. REEM 2:183
Introducing and toasting Rev. E.E. Hale. REEM 2:149
Introducing General Sherman to New England Society of Brooklyn, December 21, 1880. REEM 3:206
Silva, L.A. Rebello da
Eulogy on Abraham Lincoln. CHAL 10:84; HAZO 19: 8248; MAS 19:8248
Silver, James W.
Mississippi: the closed society. TIN:466

SILVER
Blaine, J.G.
On the remonetization of silver. CHAL 11:312; HAZO 21:9177; JOHA 2 pt 2:312; MAS 21:9177

SILVER (cont.)
Bland, R. P.
Free silver. REEMA 11: 273
Parting of the ways. BREW 2:132; BRYW 10:165
Bryan, W. J.
Cross of gold. BAAMP: 193; BIR 3:214; BOU:171; BRAS:182; BREW 2:294; BRIM:314; CAP:119; CHAL 14:415; COP:333; COPA: 333; COPB:333; CORP: 284; CROC:37; FO:225; FRY:45; HARS:169; HAZO 22:10935; HIB:155; HIBS: 461; HICF:179; HURG:147; MAS 25:10935; PAR:492; PE:637; PEA:637; PO:103; REEM 10:326; REEMB 11: 340; RID:75; SHAH:551; WERN 42:44
Gordon, J. B.
On silver coinage. CHAL 12:100
Jones, J. P.
On treasury notes and silver. JOHA 2 pt 2:347
Morrill, J. S.
On the remonetization of silver. JOHA 2 pt 2:296
Sherman, J.
On silver coinage and treasury notes. HAZO 20: 8429; JOHA 2 pt 2:329; MAS 20:8429
On "The crime of 1873." BRYW 10:198

SILVER WEDDING ANNIVERSARIES See Anniversaries-Wedding-Silver
Silverman, Joseph
Opening prayer at 250th anniversary of the settlement of the Jews in the United States. TWJ:5

SILVERWARE See Acceptance speeches-Plate; Plate; Presentation speeches-Plate
Simkins, Francis Butler
Tolerating the South's past. TIN:313
Simmons, David A.
Presents Walter S. Fenton. LY:143

SIMMONS, DAVID A.
Williams, E. K.
Presents David A. Simmons. LY:139
Simmons, Gladys
Cocktail hour. YR 8:39
Simon, Sir John Allesbrook
Address in House of Commons, April 30, 1934. KESK 2:10
General strike. BEA:381
Right of association. EMS 2: 82
Speech in House of Commons, November 27, 1922 (on establishment of Irish Free State). KESB:119
Toast to "His Excellency, the American Ambassador." REEM 3:216; REEMB 3: 233
Simon, Seymour
Vision of a scientist. BRP 6: 47; NOR 1934:86
Simons, Charles C.
John Brown. TRUW:96

SIMPLICITY
Fénelon, F.
True and false simplicity. BREW 6:109; BRYW 7:74; HAZO 4:1636; MAS 4:1636; PL:272; REEM 9:82; REEMB 10:85
Simpson, Alan See Biddle, F., jt. auth.
Simpson, Helen
Decline of the writer. GA: 116
Simpson, Matthew
On the resurrection of our Lord. CHAL 8:344; HAZO 17:7189; MAS 17:7189
Reflections on the New Year. THOU 2:41
Simpson, Wallis See Edward VIII, King of England (abdicated)

Sims, Hugo S., Jr.
Against the Federal Fair Trade Employment Practices Act. BA 1949-50:159
Sims, William Sowden
Criticism and preparedness (Washington birthday address). REEM 7:345; REEMB 8:380

SIN
Augustine, Saint
Sermon on the remission of sins. LEEW 3:231
Can we get rid of guilt? JAI: 22
Edwards, J.
Sinners in the hands of an angry God. BAAMP:15; BREW 5:355; CHAL 2:236; COP:227; COPA:227; COPB:227; HAZO 5:1811; HURG:21; MAS 5:1811; PAR:73; PL:566; REEM 9:91; REEMB 10:94
Wrath upon the wicked to the uttermost. BREW 5: 352; CHAL 2:222; HAZO 5: 1797; MAS 5:1797
Little sins. FRIE:227
Locke, D.R.
In search of the man of sin. REEMA 5:759
Vieyra, A.
Sermon on the great evil of sin. LEEW 4:355
Sinclair Sir Archibald
On Bilbao blockade. KESK 2: 221
Sinclair, John F.
Money, its uses and abuses. EXEE:436

SINGLE TAX See Taxation
Sinha, Sir Satyendra
Speech at Imperial War Conference, 1917. KES 2:401
Sitrick, Joseph
Vision for victory. NOR 1942: 53

SIXTH COLUMN
Patterson, R.C., Jr.
Sixth column. BA 1941-42: 135; SAC:54
Sizoo, Joseph Richard
Call to self-discipline. BA 1958-59:161

SKEPTICISM See Religion
Skeykill, Tom
Mussolini. EXEE:497

SKID ROW See Alcoholism; Housing; Salvation Army
Skinner, Charles R.
Age and growth of trees. THOU 1:46
Skinner, Cornelia Otis
"Bottoms up" (toast to gynecologists). HURG:311

SKY
Jeans, J.
Why the sky looks blue. BRY:432; BRYA:479

SLANDER See Gossip
Slattery, Francis E.
Church and liberty. CATA 2: 243

SLAVERY
Brougham and Vaux, H.P.B.
On emancipation for the Negro. BRYW 4:138; CHAL 5:88; HAZO 10: 4160; MAS 10:4160; PL: 457; REEMA 11:338
Brown, B.G.
On slavery in its national aspect as related to peace and war. CHAL 10:460; HAZO 21:8867; MAS 21: 8867
Castelar, E.
Abolition of slavery. REEMA 12:523
Danton, G.J.
On the abolition of slavery. CHAL 4:123; HAZO 8:3358; MAS 8:3358
Derby, E.G.V.S.
Emancipation of British Negroes. BREW 5:176; CHAL 6:330; HAZO 13:5526;

SLAVERY (cont.)
MAS 13:5526; REEMA 13: 908;
Mirabeau, H. G. R.
On the abolition of slavery in the French colonies. HAZO 7:2887; MAS 7:2887
Pitt, W., 1759-1806
Indicts the slave trade and foresees a liberated Africa. FULB:53; GOOD:579; HAY: 80; HAZO 8:3369; MAS 8: 3369; PAUF 1:125; PE: 220; PEA:220; REEMA 14: 1613
Randolph, A. P.
Labor and the struggle for a better tomorrow. HILK: 175
Wilberforce, W.
Appeal in behalf of Negro slaves in the West Indies. HAZO 8:3454; MAS 8:3454
Horrors of the British slave trade in the 18th century. BREW 10:299; BRYW 4:60; CHAL 4:96; HAZO 8:3443; MAS 8:3443; PE:212; PEA:212; PL: 437; REEMA 15:2120

---- IN THE UNITED STATES
Adams, J.
On the Constitutional war over slavery. REEMA 11: 17
Adams, J. Q.
On the Constitutional war power over slavery. JOHA 1 pt 2:115
Address to President Lincoln by the working men of Manchester, England, December 31, 1862. FO:199
Allen, G. T.
Washington and Lincoln's part in the Emancipation. THOU 1:261
Beecher, H. W.
Abolition of slavery. THOU 1:268
Nation's duty to slavery. CROC:3
Benjamin, J. P.
Slavery as established by law. BREW 1:408; CHAL 8:245; HAZO 16:6976; JOHA 2 pt 1:129; MAS 16: 6976
Bright, J.
On slavery in America. CHAL 8:188; HAZO 16: 6901; LAD:184; MAS 16: 6901
Calhoun, J. C.
On the slavery question. BAAMP:176; BIR 2:163; BOU:57; BRAO:271; BRAS: 44; BRE:164; BREA:148; BRYW 9:108; CHAL 5:310; CODS:472; CODSA:472; COP:286; COPA:286; COPB:286; FULB:246; HAZO 10:4276; HURG:77; JOHA 1 pt. 2:123; MAS 10: 4276; PE:397; PEA:397; PL:613; REEM 10:103; REEMA 12:457; REEMB 11:105
Slavery a positive good. HARS:249
Speech on Abolitionist petitions, 1839. BIR 2:139
Chase, S. P.
Three great eras. BREW 3:224
Clay, H.
Compromise of 1850 (February 5 & 6, 1850 speech). BAAMP:88; BRAO:271; BRAS, 7; BRE:162; BREA: 146; BREW 4:44; BRYW 9: 95; CODS:468; CODSA:468; COP:288; COP:288; COPA: 288; COPB:288; FULB:214; HARS:270; HAZO 10:4101; HURG:82; MAS 10:4101; PE: 392; PEA:392; SMI:162
Final speech. BIR 2:188
On the Compromise of 1850 (May 21, 1850 speech). CROC:88
On the Compromise of 1850 (July 22, 1850). JOHA 1 pt 2:202; REEM 10:125; REEMA 12:663; REEMB

11:128
Corwin, T.
Against the Compromise Bill. LEEW 9:371
Dayton, W. L.
Issues against slavery forced by the Mexican War. BREW 5:59
Douglas, S. A.
Fifth joint debate at Galesburgh, October 7, 1858. CLAW:83
Lincoln-Douglas joint debate, October 15, 1858. BAAMP:93
Opening speech of Lincoln-Douglas debate (Ottawa, August 21, 1858). BRYW 9:259; CHAL 8:421; CLAW: 55; HARSO:310; HAZO 17: 7401; MAS 17:7401; SHUM: 142
Reply to Lincoln, Freeport, August 27, 1858. BIR 2: 221; BREW 5:288; COP: 301; COPA:301; COPB: 301; HURG:94; JOHA 2 pt 1:184; ORAMA 2:285; REEM 10:171; REEMA 13: 833; REEMB 11:175
Douglass, F.
Nature of slavery (speech at Rochester, New York, December 1, 1850). CROC: 182
Reception speech-At Finsbury Chapel, Moorsfield, England, May 12, 1846. WOON:158
Slavery (July 4, 1854). PE:477; PEA:477
Slavery: speech at Rochester, July 5, 1852. PE: 477; WOON:197
Speech at Glasgow, Scotland, May 29, 1846. WOON: 170
Speech in Faneuil Hall, June 8, 1849. HILK:27; WOON:178
What to the slave is the Fourth of July? DUNM:41
Forten, J. and others.
Address to the humane and benevolent inhabitants of the city and county of Philadelphia. WOON:52
Garnet, H. H.
Address to the slaves of the United States of America. WOON:150
Memorial discourse. DUNM: 107
Garrison, W. L.
Address to the public, 1831. BIR 2:81
No compromise with slavery. WPRA:169
Speech in London, June 29, 1867. HAZO 15:6161; MAS 15:6161
Union and slavery. BREW 6:212; ORAMA 2:211
Giddings, J. R.
Denunciation of slavery. HAZO 13:5259; MAS 13: 5259
Slavery and the annexation of Cuba. BREW 6:234; CHAL 6:148
Hamlin, H.
On the Slavery Compromise Bill. CHAL 8:51; HAZO 16:6667; MAS 16:6667
Harper, F. E. W.
Address at the centennial anniversary of the Pennsylvania Society for promoting the abolition of slavery. DUNM:101
Houston, S.
Closes ominous debate on the repeal of the Missouri Compromise. PE:482; PEA:482
James, H., Sr.
Social significance of our institutions. BL:231
King, R.
On the Missouri Bill. JOHA 1 pt 2:33
Langston, C. H.
Should colored men be subject to the pains and penalties of the Fugitive Slave law? DUNM:49

SLAVERY IN THE U.S. (cont.)
Langston, J.M.
Address at the centennial of the Pennsylvania Society for promoting the abolition of slavery. DUNM:97
Lincoln, A.
Cooper Institute address. BRAS:137; BREW 7:351; CHAL 8:2; HAZO 16:6611; MAS 16:6611; ONEM:341; PAR:285; REEM 10:197; REEMA 14:1337; REEMB 11:208; SAA:156
Delivers first great speech, October 4, 1854 at Springfield. PE:485; PEA:485
First joint debate at Ottawa, August 21, 1858. BRYW 9:227; CLAW:63; FULB:291; HARS:323; HAZO 16:6586; MAS 16:6586
Lincoln-Douglas joint debate at Alton, October 15, 1858. BAAMP:101; BIR 2:226; CLAW:90
Reply to Douglas at Chicago. SHAH:389
Reply to the working men of Manchester, England, January 1963. FO:201
Second Joint debate at Freeport, August 27, 1858. BREW 7:345; REEM 10:224; REEMB 11:235
Speech at Peoria, October 16, 1854. BIR 2:196
Mann, H.
Institution of slavery. CHAL 6:223; HAZO 13:5334; MAS 13:5334
Martin, J.S.
Speech before the Paris Anti-slavery Conference, August 27, 1867. WOON:256
Morton, T.B.
Emancipation and its obligations. WAGN:330
Othello.
Negro slavery. WOON:14
Parker, T.
Dangers from slavery. HAZO 16:6770; MAS 16:6770; RID:46
Paul, N.
Abolition of slavery. WOON:64
Phillips, W.
On the philosophy of the Abolition movement. CHEM 3:77; JOHA 1 pt 2:219
Pinkney, W.
For relief of the slaves. BRYW 8:123; CHAL 4:181; HAZO 9:3544; LAD:85; MAS 9:3544
Missouri question. BREW 8:332; CHEM 3:13; HARS:193; JOHA 1 pt 2:63; LEEW 9:117; REEMA 14:1603; SOU 9:226
Remond, C.L.
Anti-slavery discourse. WOON:237
Slavery and the Irish. WOON:131
Slavery as it concerns the British. WOON:127
Speech before the New England Anti-Slavery convention. WOON:229
Resolution on the cessation of slavery and the slave trade. WOON:119
Saunders, P.
Promoting the abolition of slavery, and improving the condition of the African race. WOON:56
Seward, W.H.
Speech on crisis of 1850. BIR 2:183
Slavery by a free Negro. WOON:25
Smith, J.M.
Abolition of slavery and the slave trade in the French and British colonies. WOON:119
Stevens, T.
Against Webster and Northern compromisers. BREW 9:288; CHAL 6:14; HAZO 12:5022; MAS 12:

5022; REEMA 15:1943
Sumner, C.
On the repeal of the Fugitive Slave Law. JOHA 1 pt 2:268
Toombs, R.
Slavery in the United States; its consistency with Republican institutions, and its effect upon the slave and society. WPRA:158
Vance, Z. B.
Slavery question. CHAL 11:407; HAZO 22:9328; MAS 22:9328
Ward, S. R.
Speech on the Fugitive Slave Bill. WOON:193
Webster, D.
On the Clay Compromise. BAAMP:66; BIR 2:172; BOU:63; BRAR 2:121; BRAS:73; BRE:183; BREA:167; BRYW 9:64; HAZO 11:4568; MAS 11:4568; PE:401; PEA:401
Supporting the Compromise of 1850. BREW 10:206
Whipper, W.
Non-resistance to offensive aggression. WOON:104
Williams, P.
Oration on the abolition of the slave trade. WOON:32
Slavery and colonization. WOON:77
Wilson, H.
On the bill to confiscate the property and free the slaves of rebels. CHAL 8:377; HAZO 17:7222; MAS 17:7222
Wright, T. S.
Progress of the anti-slavery cause. WOON:86
See also Dred Scott Decision; Emancipation Day; Negroes; United States-History-Civil War

SLAVERY PARTY
Douglass, F.
Slavery Party. WOON:223

Slayden, James L.
Against the enlistment of Negro soldiers. SHUO:262
Sledge, Terrell
Warriors of the broken sword. SHU:51
Sloan, Alfred P., Jr.
Economic aspects of American defense. COP:438; COPA:438

SLOAT, JOHN D.
Bromley, G. T.
Sloat monument address. WAGN:339
Slocum, Walter
Wondersmith and the world (Edison). BRP 4:27; INTW 1933:57; YR 5:333
Slosson, Edwin E.
Creative chemistry. EXEE:187

SLUMS See Housing

SMALL PEOPLE See Man-Stature
Smart, Constance
Serpent in our midst. YR 7:37
Smart, Lowrie Jane
Vindication of a faith. BOA:284; BRP 5:66
Smathers, George
Put democracy on the offensive. MOA:461
Smith, A. Eleanor
Fashions in love. JUD:159
Smith, Albert P.
American Constitution. DO:207
Smith Alfred Emanuel
Business administration. REEM sup 2:408; REEMB 5:294
Come back to your father's house. WPRC:168
Cooing dove. BYRA:528
Fight for repeal. BOB:43
Government ownership. ONEC:536
Governorship of New York. REEM 3:220; REEMB 3:237

Smith, A. E. (cont.)
Religion and politics. COP: 408; COPA:408; COPB: 408; HICF:837; HURG:209

SMITH, ALFRED EMANUEL
Introducing Alfred E. Smith. NI:154; NIA:114
Robinson, J. T.
Jacob's voice but Esau's hands. WPRC:179
Roosevelt, F. D.
Nomination of Alfred E. Smith. CORP:217; HICF: 796; LINM:131; ONEC: 497; YE:107

Smith, Alonzo R.
Predatory rich. TRUW: 47
Smith, Ballard
Press of the South. REEMA 3:1057
Smith, Burl
American Constitution-for this we fight. DO:54
Smith, C. Alphonso
Literature and a lost cause. SHUO:19
Smith, Charles Emory
Introduces Charles A. Dana to New England Society. REEMA 1:321
Introducing and toasting Benjamin Harrison at New England Society of Pennsylvania, December 22, 1893. REEM 2:167
Ireland's struggle. REEMA 3: 1059
McKinley. WERN 42:135
Patriotism. BLAA:185; BLAB: 185
President's prelude. REEM 3: 227; REEMA 3:1062; REEMB 3:244
Republic's higher glory (at laying of cornerstone of new Federal Building at Chicago). FUL:294
War for humanity. FUL:290
Smith, Charles H.
Bill Arp's lecture. SOU 9:486
Smith, Charles Stewart
Introducing Horace Porter to Chamber of Commerce of New York, June 24, 1885. REEM 3:89
Introducing W. M. Evarts to Chamber of Commerce of New York, June 24, 1885. REEM 2:28
Smith, Ellison D.
States rights. BOA:111
Smith, Francis Hopkinson
Holland to-day. REEM 3:232; REEMB 3:249
Smith, Francis M.
Around and around they go. BRP 7:60; YR 8:11
Smith, Frederick Edwin, 1st Earl of Birkenhead See Birkenhead, F. E. S.
Smith, Gerrit
Liberty destroyed by national pride (Mexican Treaty and Monroe Doctrine). BREW 9:227
Smith, Goldwin
Evolution of the dominion. CHAL 10:249; HAZO 20: 8530; MAS 20:8530
Lamps of fiction (at centenary of Sir Walter Scott). BREW 9:233; ONEM:541; REEMA 9:1068
Origin and causes of progress. BREW 9:239
Secret beyond science. BREW 9:244; BRYW 5:34
Smith, Gretchen
English women's institutes receive official recognition. BUT:144; BUTA:144; BUTB:144
Smith, Henry Louis
Culture afforded by scientific training, (at Alumni reunion). SHUO:98
Smith, Horton
Introducing a Chamber of Commerce official
" a doctor
" a fat man
" a city fireman
" a game warden
" Supreme Court justice.
BRC:50, 161, 57, 64, 160, 302

Smith, Hugh
How backward is the front office? YE:51
Smith, J. Herbert See Browne, L., jt. auth.
Smith, James McCune
Abolition of slavery and the slave trade in the French and British colonies. WOON: 119
Toussaint L'Ouverture and the Haytian revolutions. DUNM:19
Smith, Jonathan
On the Federal Constitution. ARNS:266

SMITH, LILLIAN
Reid, Mrs. O.
Presents Lillian Smith. LY:71
Smith, Margaret Chase
Address to the United States Senate, September 21, 1961. BA 1961-62:27
Challenge to women. BUTB: 240
Impatience and generosity. BRAP:55
Political conscience. BA 1950-51:124; BUT:243
Smith, Nevitt
Rushing to meet the sunrise. AN:1
Smith, Richard
Professor anonymous. BRP 4: 33; INTW 1933:35; YR 5: 93
Smith, Robert A.
Address of welcome (United Workmen). THOU 3:323
Smith, Robert Vernon
Speech in House of Commons, February 16, 1858 (on India). KESI 1:355
Smith, Roy L.
Born rich. BRP 3:62
Greatest game in the world. BRP 2:20
Hardest thing in the world to be. BRP 5:27
Sane thinking in an insane world. BART 3:135
Today's world in the Far East. BART 4:187
What is right with youth? BRP 2:15
Smith, Samuel M.
Uses of a library (at dedication of Carnegie Library, Winthrop College, Rock Hill, South Carolina). SHUO:80
Smith, Sydney
Mrs. Partington in politics. BREW 9:247
Reform and stomach troubles. BREW 9:252
Results of oppression. BREW 9:250
"Wounds, shrieks, and tears" in government. BREW 9: 258
Smith, T.V.
Forward America. BA 1938-39:119
Smith, Walter Bedell
Opening of Colonial magazine and guardhouse. YE:201

SMITH, WALTER BEDELL
Lane, W. P., Jr.
Presents Walter Bedell Smith. LY:158
Stryker, H. M.
Introducing Lt. Gen. Walter Bedell Smith. YE:128
Smith, Wilfrid
Introduces Ford Frick, Commissioner of baseball. PRC:17
Smith, William Hawley
Other fellow. SHU:218

SMITH COLLEGE
Neilson, W. A.
Inaugural address as president of Smith College. WE 1:273

SMOKE PREVENTION
Kaber, W. C.
Value of district heating to the community. MO:458

SMOKING
Stolz, A. E.
Woman's choice. YR 4:331

SMOOT, REED
Bacon, A. O.
Case of Senator Reed Smoot. SHUO:129
Smuts, Jan Christian
Address before members of the two Houses of Parliament. HAN:204; VO 1942-43:560
At the final plenary session of the San Francisco Conference. HAN:440
Basis of trusteeship in Africa policy. CROC:400
British Commonwealth of Nations. ONEM:603; REEM 3:237; REEMB 3:254
Imperial Conference, 1921. KESB:43
Imperial relations, April 16, 1917 speech. EMS 2:269
Imperial relations, May 15, 1917 speech. EMS 2:273
Peace and Empire. COP:391; COPA:391; COPB:391; REEM 7:352; REEMB 8:387
Speech at Imperial War Conference, 1917. KES 2:392
Smyth, Henry D.
Scientific manpower. HAR:317
Snavely, Guy E.
Inaugural address as president of Birmingham-Southern College. WE 1:229
Sneed, Leonard
Wandering Jew. HARSO:288
Snell, Bertrand H.
Decision for youth. BOA:373
Snetman, Louis
Politics and a well-rounded nation. YR 9:135
Snow, Sir Charles Percy
Moral un-neutrality of science. BA 1960-61:41; BAAGA:423
Snowden, Philip, 1st Viscount of Iskornshaw
Attack on the Prime Minister Ramsay Macdonald. BEA:387
Reform of the franchise (Women's suffrage). EMS 2:195
Snyder, Franklyn Bliss
American youth in the present emergency. HUS:262
Another "shot heard round the world." BA 1941-42:142; HOC:35; ON:249; SAC:46
Introduces two debaters, Alfred P. Haake and Harold Laski. PR:84
My country. -Same as his Another "shot heard round the world."
Response to an introduction. PR:128

SNYDER, FRANKLYN BLISS
Hancher, V. M.
Presents Franklin Bliss Snyder. LY:119
Snyder, John I., Jr.
Total challenge of automation. BA 1963-64:154
Snyder, Ora
Woman employer. REEM sup 2:416; REEMB 5:302
Snyder, Rev.
Opening invocation of Rev. Snyder of the Mystic Workers. THOU 3:467

SOCIAL AND ECONOMIC SECURITY See Insurance, social

SOCIAL CHANGE
Reid, I. De A.
Social changes, social relations, social work. HILK:165
Seabury, D.
Social change and individual growth. BART 2:55
Smith, A. R.
Predatory rich. TRUW:47

SOCIAL PROBLEMS
Andrews, E. B.

Social plaint. NORR 1st ser: 216

Conant, J. B.
Social dynamite in our large cities: unemployed, out-of-school youth. HIB:324

Dinwoodie, S. D.
Inner city-our shame. ARNS:246

DuBois, W. E. B.
Training of Negroes for social reform. DUNM:491

Griggs, J. W.
Social discontent. BLAA: 146; BLAB:146; REEMA 2:564

Herron, G. D.
Message of Jesus to men of wealth. WPRA:276

Kaser, A. L.
Introducing a speaker on social reform. BRC:91

Literature on social problems. AMEO 2:171

Locke, D. R.
In search of the man of sin. REEMA 5:759

Locke, R. F.
Preservative element in American society. COUW: 51

Rodee, H. A.
Our social crisis. COUW: 85

Roosevelt, F. D.
Philosophy of social justice through social action (campaign speech in Detroit, October 2, 1932). ARNS: 129

Walton, J. A.
American problems. COUW:101

Williams, C. O.
Greetings to Forum on Current Problems. GA:24

See also Alcoholism; Child labor; Crime and criminals; Defective and delinquent classes; Immigration and emigration; Poverty; Race problems; Unemployed

SOCIAL PSYCHOLOGY See Psychology, social

SOCIAL SERVICE See Citizenship; Social work

SOCIAL WORK

Dunbar, A. M.
Life of social service as exemplified in David Livingstone (at centenary of his birth). DUNM:425

Gandhi, M. K.
Social service. ZU:71

Thomas, I.
Culture and service. SHUC: 380

SOCIALISM

Alexander, R.
Which way America? BA 1948-49:145

Bebel, A.
Socialism and assassination. REEM 9:349; REEMA 11:159; REEMB 10:360

Carson, R. M.
Scholar and the socialist. ONES:388

Clemenceau, G.
Democracy vs. Socialism (debate with J. Jaures). BRYW 7:214; PE:671; PEA:671; REEM 9:375; REEMB 10:386

Conboy, M.
Summation for the Judiciary Committee in the investigation of the New York Socialists by the Assembly, Albany. HICJ:891

Coyle, J. G.
Socialism from a Catholic viewpoint. CATA 2:77

Crispi, F.
Socialism and discontent. BREW 4:236

Flannery, E. A.
Is socialism a home destroyer? CATA 2:57

Free enterprise vs. socialism. FRIE:245

Hillquit, M.

SOCIALISM (cont.)
Summation for the Socialists in the investigation of the New York Socialists by the Assembly, Albany. HICJ:819
Jaures, J.
Program of Socialism (debate with G. Clemenceau). BRYW 7:208; PE:671; REEM 9:364; REEMB 10:375
Socialism and the war. REEM 11:6; REEMB 12:7
Kagawa, T.
New social order. PL:793
Lang, C. G.
Socialism in England. BREW 7:260
Morgan, F. E.
True Socialism. REAC:177
Nearing, S.
Capitalism vs. Socialism. REEM sup 3:51, 63, 71
Rosebery, A. P. P.
England under Socialism. BREW 9:103
Seligman, E. R. A.
Capitalism vs. Socialism. REEM 3:42, 58, 69
Thomas, N. M.
Is the New Deal Socialism? WPRC:188
Villard, O. G.
Capitalism vs. Socialism (chairman's remarks). REEM sup 3:39
See also Government ownership; Industry and state; Labor and laboring classes; Labor unions; National Socialism-Germany; Socialist Party

SOCIALIST PARTY
Thomas, N.
Choice before us. SAR:158

SOCIETIES
Howe, J. W.
Salon in America. REEMA 5:591
Sockman, Ralph W.
Comfort ye my people. BA 1950-51:191
Higher religion for higher education. BA 1948-49:216
Redeeming our regrets. BA 1946-47:271
This nation under God. BA 1942-43:267
Socrates.
Apology. CHAL 1:29; CROC:414; HAZO 1:66; MAS 1:66
In his own defense. BRYW 1:65
On being declared guilty. BREW 9:261; BRYW 1:77
On his condemnation to death. BOU:211; BRYW 1:82; COP:8; COPA:8; COPB:8; HIB:3; REEM 9:10; REEMB 10:10

SOIL BANK See Agricultural administration-United States
Sokolsky, George E.
American way of life. BART 1:269

SOLDIERS
Luce, C. B.
Address to the Republican National Convention. BUTA:231
Reynolds, Q.
Campaign and men in uniform. BA 1944-45:123
Toast to a man of service. FRIT:91
Truman, H. S.
Message to Congress, September 6, 1945. VO 1945-46:546
Welcome to visitors among military personnel. HNWS:28
See also Army; United States-Army; Veterans

SOLDIERS' BONUS See Pensions, military

SOLDIERS, DISCHARGED See Veterans

SOLDIERS-SUFFRAGE
Roosevelt, F.D.
Message to Congress on the Service men's Vote Bill. VO 1944-45:152
Message to Congress on the servicemen's vote. VO 1944-45:54

SOLICITATION OF FUNDS See Fund raising

SOLITUDE
Tillich, P.J.
Loneliness and solitude. BA 1957-58:185
Soltau, Melvin E.
Century of progress. INTW 1933:5; YR 5:345

SONGS See Music and musicians
Sonnino, Sidney Constantino, Baron
Seconding the nomination of M.G. Clémenceau for President of the Peace Conference. REEM 11:314; REEMB 12:332

SONS See Fathers and sons; Mothers and sons; Parent and child

SONS OF TEMPERANCE
Ames, O.
Address of greeting. THOU 3:493
Bradley, F.M.
Welcome to Washington. THOU 3:481
Clapp, E.H.
Annual address to the Sons of Temperance. THOU 3:500
Installation of officers: retiring speech. THOU 3:485
Cuyler, T.L.
Knock at the door of Christ's church. THOU 3:474
In memoriam. THOU 3:499
James A. Garfield, a tribute from the Sons of Temperance. THOU 3:495
Jewell, B.R.
Response to address of welcome. THOU 3:488
Littell, J.S.
Address of welcome (Sons of Temperance). THOU 3:486
Memorial tributes on the death of General Clinton B. Fisk by A.R. Temple, A. E. Ballard, E.H. Clapp, and General Rusling. THOU 3:495
Obituary reference on John B. Gough. THOU 3:498
Resolution of thanks. THOU 3:500
Temple, R.A.
Inaugural address at his installation as M.W.P. of Sons of Temperance. THOU 3:505
Responsive address on being presented a badge. THOU 3:486

SONS OF THE REVOLUTION
Wyman, W.
Sons of the Revolution. REEMA 3:1288
Soong, T.V. (Sung Tsu-Wen)
Address at first plenary session of San Francisco Conference. VO 1945-46:169

SORORITIES See Greek letter societies
Souter, Lex King
Inevitable parallel. YR 1:165
Our Constitution. BLUE:46; BRP 1:7

SOUTH AFRICAN WAR, 1899-1902
Balfour, A.J.

SOUTH AFRICAN WAR, 1899-1902 (cont.)
On the Boer War. REEMA 11:99
Davitt, M.
Against the South African War. KET:422
Laurier, W.
British policy in Africa. CHAL 13:394; HAZO 24:10459; MAS 24:10459
Redmond, J. E.
Ireland and the Boer War. KET:430
Wolseley, G. J.
Army in Transvaal. REEMA 3:1280

SOUTH AMERICA
Canning, G.
Recognition of the South American Republics. BEA:81; PAUF 1:257
Clay, H.
Emancipation of South American Republics. BREW 4:30; BRYW 9:76; CHAL 5:46; FKA:194; HAZO 10:4055; MAS 10:4055; PL:606; REEM 10:133; REEMA 12:676; REEMB 11:137
Hull, C.
Opening of the Pan American Conference. BA 1938-39: 40
Lansing, R.
Pan-Americanism. FKA:200
Root, E.
Pan-American policy. SHU:233
Pan-American spirit. BOAM:83; KNAS:282; KNASA:282
Tomlison, E.
New South America. EXEE:285
See also Inter-American Conference on Problems of War and Peace; Latin America; Pan-American Day; Western Hemisphere

SOUTH CAROLINA
Hoar, G. F.
South Carolina and Massachusetts. CHAL 11:2; HAZO 21:8888; MAS 21:8888; REEM 7:169; REEMA 8:659; REEMB 8:196
M'Cullough, J. A.
South Carolina and Civil War. SHUO:306

SOUTHERN ILLINOIS UNIVERSITY
Morris, D. W.
Inaugural address as 8th president of Southern Illinois University. SAB:188

SOUTHERN STATES
Abernathy, T. P.
Democracy and the Southern frontier. TIN:42
Binkley, W. C.
South and the West. TIN:255
Brady, T. P.
Segregation and the South. WPRC:333
Candler, E. S.
Development of the South. SHUO:276
Cappon, L. J.
Provincial South. TIN:239
Chase, H. W.
State University and the new South: inaugural address as president of University of North Carolina. WE 2:31
Clark, T. D.
Country newspaper: a factor in Southern opinion, 1865-1930. TIN:211
Cotterill, R. S.
Old South and the new. TIN:234
Coulter, E. M.
What the South has done about its history. TIN:3
Eaton, C.
Professor James Woodrow and the freedom of teach-

ing in the South. TIN:438
Fellows, J.R.
North and South. REEM 2:37; REEMA 2:482; REEMB 2:37
Freeman, J.
Solid South. SHUC:136
Galloway, C.B.
Reconstruction in the South; past and present (at dedication of Mississippi's new Capitol). SHUO:294
Grady, H.W.
Democracy and the South. HARSO:182; SHUO:288
New South. BAAMP:180; BOAM:41; BOU:80; BRAC:287; BRIM:301; BRYA:558; BRYW 10:141; CAP:96; CHAL 14:215; CLAW:159; CLAY:248; ESEH:226; FULB:385; HARS:490; HAZO 25:10724; IMMD:263; MAS 25:10724; ONEM:577; ORAMA 2:427; PAR:450; PE:628; PEA:628; PL:686; PROS:64; REEM 2:105; REEMA 8:579; REEMB 2:97; RINM:278; SAA:207; SHAH:496; SHU:45; SHUM:177; SOU 9:374; THOU 1:270, 273
Solid South. SHAH:511
South and her problems. SHAH:505
Green, F.M.
Democracy in the old South. TIN:177
Gregory, T.W.
Southern types. SHU:185
Hamer, P.M.
Records of Southern history. TIN:50
Hamilton, J.G. de R.
Three centuries of Southern records, 1607-1907. TIN:129
Hanna, K.A.
Roles of the South in the French intervention in Mexico. TIN:298
Henry, R.S.
West by South. TIN:366
Hill, B.H.
Work of universities in the South. REEMA 8:624
Hoover, H.C.
South, national problems, and the American home (158th anniversary of battle of King's Mountain). HICF:852
Houston, T.A.
Rise of the southern commons. SHUC:338
Humphreys, B.G.
Traditions of the South. BOB:100
Kendrick, B.B.
Colonial status of the South. TIN:90
Lamar, L.Q.C.
Charles Sumner. BRYW 10:61; CHAL 10:441; HAZO 21:8796; LA:134; LAD:93; MAS 21:8796; REEM 5:260; REEMA 8:767; REEMB 9:299; SHUO:230
Long, J.F.
Speech on disorders in the South. WOON:294
McClellan, G.B.
New York and the South. REEM 2:375; REEMB 2:388
McClure, H.
People of the South. BOB:99
Page, T.N.
Old South. SMI:211
Patton, J.W.
Facets of the South in the 1850's. TIN:350
Simkins, F.B.
Tolerating the South's past. TIN:313
Stephens, A.H.
Future of the South. ORAMA 2:263
South and the public domain. BREW 9:281; BRYW 9:137
Stephenson, W.H.
Half-century of Southern historical scholarship. TIN:155

SOUTHERN STATES (cont.)
Stires, E. M.
Southland. REEM 3:174; REEMB 3:291
Sydnor, C. S.
Southerner and the laws. TIN:62
Thomas, A.
South as a custodian. REEM 3:319; REEMB 3:336
Thornton, W. M.
Portrait of a lady. SMI: 234
Wilkins, R.
Deep South crisis. WPRC: 344
Woodward, C. V.
Irony of Southern history. TIN:284
Yancey, W. L.
South does not seek to aggrandize herself. SOU 9:337
Speech in protest in the Charleston Convention. BAAMP:118; BRYW 9:192; SOU 9:339
See also Confederate States of America; United States-History-Civil War

---- DESCRIPTION AND TRAVEL
Patrick, R.W.
Mobile frontier. TIN:451

SOUTHERN UNIVERSITY
Clark, F. O.
Founder's Day address (Southern University). HILK:73

SOUTHWEST, THE
Henry, R. S.
West by South. TIN:366

SOVIET SOCIALIST REPUBLICS, UNION OF See Russia (1923-) USSR

SPACE AGE See Astronautics and civilization

SPACE FLIGHT
Glenn, J. H.
Address before the Joint Meeting of Congress. BA 1961-62:202; HIB:98
Ley, W.
Conquest of space. BA 1960-61:115

SPAIN
Attlee, C. R.
Bilbao blockade (speech in House of Commons, April 14, 1937). KESK 2:214
Brougham and Vaux, H. P. B.
On the invasion of Spain by France. GOOD:904
Castelar, E.
Canditature of Amadeus. LEEW 5:267
Franco, F.
To Falangist Party Council praising German, Italian, and Spanish Fascism. VO 1942-43:725
Pitt, W., 1708-1778
Speech in relation to the seizure of the Falkland Islands by Spain. GOOD:118; HAZO 5:1927; MAS 5:1927
On the Spanish Convention, March 8, 1739. GOOD:77
Rodriquez, A.
Epilogue to freedom. BRP 9:42
Sinclair, A.
On Bilbao blockade. KESK 2:221

---- POLITICS AND GOVERNMENT
Castillo, A. C.
On Constitutional reform. CHAL 10:451; HAZO 21:8806; MAS 21:8806
Castelar, E.
Plea for Republican institutions. BREW 3:160; BRYW 7:255; CHAL 12:65; FRY:40; HAZO 22:9469; MAS 22:9469; PL:345; REEM 9:275; REEMA 12:517; REEMB 10:283
Spalding, John Lancaster

Opportunity (at opening of an educational institution). ONEM:512; REEM 6:379; REEMA 9:1076; REEMB 7: 383; SHUM:312

SPANISH AMERICA See Latin America

SPANISH AMERICAN WAR See United States-History-War of 1898

SPARKS, FRED
Hills, L.
Presents Fred Sparks. LY: 132

SPARTA
Andocides.
On the peace with Sparta. MINA 1:498

SPARTACUS. See Kellogg, Elijah (accredited to)
Spaulding, Asa T.
Wanted! More George Leigh-Mallorys. There are so many Mount Everests. HILK:231

SPEAKER, THANKING See Thanks

SPEAKING See Debates and debating; Extemporaneous speeches; Public speaking
Speckman, H. A.
Responds to an introduction. PRC:20

SPECULATION
Balmuth, S.
Man with a hat over his face. YR 6:45

SPEECH, FREEDOM OF See Free speech; Liberty of the Press

SPEECHES-OUTLINES OF
Depew, C. M.
Outline of speech on Decoration Day. PITT:47
Outline of address at dinner on the 70th birthday of John Jay. PITT:89
Outline of address at the centennial of capture of André. PITT:87
Outline of address at the reception to Henry M. Stanley by the Lotus Club. PITT:90
Fire prevention at home (outline of speech). MOA:315
General outline for all occasions. PITT:101
Jury is dismissed (outline of speech). MOA:338, 345
MacArthur, D.
Defends his conduct of the war in Korea. MOUGA:217
Our national park system (outline of speech). MOA:278, 280, 343
Our plenty is not so plentiful (outline of speech). MOA: 337, 338, 345
Outline for a narrative speech in chronological order "Out over Kicking Horse Pass." MICS:94
Outline for a speech "A house and a home." BARR:77
Outline for a speech "By the Golden Gate." BARR:66
Outline for a speech "Do you avoid drips?" BARR:78
Outline for a speech "Grand wagon" (station wagon). BARR:65
Outline for a speech "Let's face it: the guaranteed annual wage." MICS:93
Outline for a speech "Lingual logic." BARR:47
Outline for a speech "Love thyself in order to love thy neighbor." BARR:64
Outline for a speech "Man against man." BARR:97
Outline for a speech "Pigskin fans." BARR:99
Outline for a speech "Wanted: the right job." BARR:46

SPEECHES-OUTLINES OF (cont.)
Outline of a response to the toast "Our country." PITT: 41
Outline of a speech in response to the toast "The day we celebrate." PITT: 39
Outline of a spread-eagle speech in a foreign land. PITT:40
Outline of speech: Resolved that we should support a policy of further development of educational television. BAAGA:264
Outline of speech: Should we endorse the trend toward automation in American industry? BAAGA:307
Plan outline for speech: American business enterprise is not a malefactor but a benefactor to mankind. MOUGA:204
Plan outline of speech: Modern capitalism cannot meet needs of modern man. MOUGA:137
Price some paid for progress. SOBP:80
"Row-throw-go" (outline of a speech on how to rescue drowning persons). MOA: 317
Sample form for speech outline-informative, persuasive, or entertaining speeches. BUT:49: BUTA: 49
Sample form for speech outline-informative persuasive, or entertaining speeches. BUTB:49
Selected outline for a Thanksgiving speech. PITT:55
Sketch of a speech in response to the toast "Our honored dead." PITT:43
Suggestions for organization and outlining of speeches. With examples of. BAAGA: 67; SOBP:64
Suggestions for taking part in a discussion or conference, with outline for discussion on "What should be the role of the United States in the Middle East?" MICS:183
Traffic laws (outline of speech). MOA:242
What is democracy (outline of speech)? MOA:239

SPEED
Hutchings, R.
Toll of speed hysteria. BRP 2:59; YR 3:153
Speer, Emory
Last stand of Lee's veterans. SHUO:332
"One and inseparable." FUL: 297,300

SPELLING
Byars, W.V.
English spelling since Wyckliffe. BREW 2:11
Spellman, Francis J.
One road to peace. BA 1940-41:187
Response at reception. BA 1945-46:203
Spencer, Frank
Introduces James A. Farley. PR:77
Spencer, Henry R.
Introducing Anne O'Hare McCormick. YE:127
Spencer, Herbert
Gospel of relaxation. KLEG: 385; REEM 3:248; REEMA 3:1067; REEMB 3:265

SPENCER, HERBERT
Evarts, W.M.
Tribute to Herbert Spencer KLEM:113; REEMA 2:462
Spencer, Percival
Bombarding London. BREW 9: 299
Spencer, Robert Nelson
Native hue of resolution. NESA:134
Spencer, Selden P.

Lawyers and lawlessness. SHUO:61
Speyer, James
Introducing Robert L. Owen to the Economic Club of New York, November 10, 1913. REEM 3:21
Presents Talcott Williams. LY:124
Spieker, Edward H.
Presenting a book to Professor Basil L. Gildersleeve. ONES:44
Spillman, Harry Collins
Adjusting ourselves to a new era in business. BYRA: 407; REEM 7:359; REEMB 5:309
Aristocracy in thinking. ONEC: 452
Cash value of personality. NESA:120
Doing unto others. REEM 3: 254; REEMB 3:271

SPIRITUAL LIFE
Harper, F.
Gethsemane. YR 6:169

SPOILS SYSTEM See Corruption (in politics)

SPONSORS
Kaser, A. L.
Time out for the sponsor (a fill-in for the emcee). BRH:325
Spooner, John Coit
On the government of the Philippines. REEMA 10: 1913

SPORTS
Coleman, W.
Introducing a sporting goods manager. BRC:207
Follow the rules of the game. NAT:40
Game of life. JA:208
Game of life or a top man is not a flop man (a changeable speech adaptable as an inspirational speech for sales people, student groups or for all workers, or for a sports dinner speaker). BAI:56
Holm, W.
Introducing a track star. BRC:227
Home team welcomes its visiting opponents. DR:277; LU:1252
Kaser, A. L.
Emcee at a pre-game rally. BRH:317
McGovern, S.
Introducing a sportsman or where the speaker wants to use someone in the audience as the butt of his joke. BRC:262
On to victory-talk at the pre-game pep meeting. DR: 279; LU:1253
Outdoor sports (sportsman gives a toast). ED:415
Rickey, B.
Greatest single thing a man can have. EXEE:268
Smith, R. L.
Greatest game in the world. BRP 2:20
Speech for a sportsman's festival. BARB:168
Sportsmanship. CON:14
Sportsmen's club (for devotees of the rod and gun). EDGS:381
To the drill team. THOS:140
Victory toast to the winning team. DR:280; LU:1255
What field day means to me (for field day celebrations at schools or elsewhere). DR:282
See also Athletics; Physical education. Also Names of sports, e.g. Baseball; Football; Swimming. Also Names of Sport clubs, e.g. Boat club; Cricket club; Jockey club
Sprague, Charles
Life blood of the nation. BOB:207

Sprague, Charles (cont.)
Passing of the Indian. BOB: 124
Sprague, Leslie W.
Undiscovered America. BOA: 188; BOB:169; SHU:192
Spring, Gardiner
Remarks against the religion and morals of the people of Boston and its vicinity. BRAR 1:57
Tribute to New England, 1820. BRAR 1:9
Springer, John W.
Pioneers. SHU:183
Springer, William M.
Retrenchment, economy, and reform. REEMA 15:1924
Sproul, Robert Gordon
Inaugural address as president of University of California. WE 2:251
Spurgeon, Charles Haddon
Bible. BEA:391
Condescension of Christ. CHAL 12:385; HAZO 23: 9781; MAS 23:9781; PL: 503
Everlasting oxydization. BREW 9:268
First appearance of the risen Lord to the eleven. THOU 2:109
Jesus and the children. THOU 2:156
Men made rich by the poverty of Christ. BRYW 5:119
Soul satisfying bread. THOU 2:252
Substance of sermons. ORBR 2:393
Stafford, Wendell Phillips
College a training school for public service (college sesquicentennial). ONEM: 547; ONES:120
Liberty under law. SHU:240

STAG DINNERS
Huber, L. J.
Emcee at a stag dinner. BRH:222
Kaser, A. L.
Emcee at a stag dinner. BRH:218
Stag party, by one of the guests. EDGS:335
See also Bachelors

STAGE. See Actors and acting; Drama; Theatre
Stahr, Elvis J., Jr.
Challenge of the critical century. YE:196
Staley, Helen
Chains or change? YR 5:187
Stalin, Ioseph
"Defend every inch of Soviet soil." COP:517; COPA: 517; COPB:495; CROC: 429; ON:167; PE:785; PEA:785; VO 1941:330
Instructs his people ten days after the Nazi invasion.- Same as his "Defend every inch of Soviet soil"
Issues of the war. HAN:112
May Day order of the day (1945). VO 1945-46:183
Order of the day, November 7, 1942. VO 1942-43:593
Order of the day, May 1, 1943. VO 1943-44:187
Order of the day, May 1, 1944. 1944-45:198
Order of the day on "May Day," May 1, 1942. VO 1942-43:262
Order of the day on the 24th anniversary of the Red Army. VO 1942-43:170
Order of the day on the twenty-fifth anniversary of the Red Army. VO 1943-44:85
Order of the day on the 26th anniversary of the October revolution. VO 1943-44:518
Order of the day on the 26th anniversary of the Red Army. VO 1944-45:122
Order of the day on the 27th anniversary of the Red Army and Navy. VO 1945-46:65
Position of Russia, November

6, 1941. HAN:164
Radio address on the Japanese surrender. VO 1945-46:531
Report on international relations, November 6, 1942. VO 1942-43:582
Report on the 26th anniversary of the October revolution. HAN:232; VO 1943-44:509
Report on the 27th anniversary of the Revolution. VO 1944-45:546
Results of the past year, November 6, 1942. HAN:113
Review of the war. -Same as his Report on the 26th anniversary of the October revolution.
Russia presents its case. -Same as his 'Defend every inch of Soviet soil''
Speech on Red Square on anniversary celebration November 7, 1941. VO 1941:480
Statement extolling the Allied invasion of France. VO 1944-45:267
To the people of the Soviet Union, July 3, 1941. -Same as his 'Defend every inch of Soviet soil''
27th anniversary order of the day. HAN:288; VO 1944-45:554
Victory address. VO 1945-46:199

STALIN, IOSEPH
Henninger, L. L.
Man of steel. BLUE:74
Khrushchev, N. S.
Basic indictment (speech of October 17). RUS:17
Reveals some of the crimes of Stalin. PEA:826

Stallings, Jane
America and brotherhood. DO:139

STAMP ACT, 1765
Adams, J.
Stamp Act, 1765. HELE:11
Chauncy, C.
Good news from far country (repeal of Stamp Act). BREW 3:258; HAZO 5:1814; MAS 5:1814
Otis, J.
On the Stamp Act, 1765. HELE:7

STANFORD, LELAND
White, S. M.
Eulogy on Senator Stanford. WAGN:41

STANFORD UNIVERSITY
Jordan, D. S.
Inaugural address as president of Stanford University. WE 1:351
Sterling, J. E. W.
Lofty purpose ahead. BA 1950-51:150

Stanhope, Philip Dormer. See Chesterfield, Philip Dormer Stanhope, 4th Earl of

Stanley, A. O.
New despotism. BOA:358; BOB:49

Stanley, Albert Henry, 1st Baron Ashfield. See Ashfield, A. H. S.

Stanley, Arthur Penrhyn
America visited. REEM 3:259; REEMA 3:1073; REEMB 3:276
Jesus of Nazareth. CHAL 9:94; HAZO 18:7604; MAS 18:7604
Our common Christianity. HAZO 18:7609; MAS 18:7609
Palmerston and the duty of England (funeral oration). BREW 9:274

Stanley, Augustus O.
Lee and Appomatox. SHUO:153
Perils of paternalism. HARSO:119

Stanley, Edward George Villiers 17th Earl of Derby See Derby, E. G. V. S.

Stanley, Fred Veston
Optimism of Christianity. SHUC:5

Stanley, Sir Henry Morton
Rescue of Emin Pasha. REEMA 6:1047
Through the dark continent. COP:627; COPB:664; REEM 3:263; REEMA 3: 1077; REEMB 3:280
Through the great forest. REEM 8:372; REEMA 6: 1029; REEMB 13:377

STANLEY, SIR HENRY MORTON
Clemens, S. L.
Presents Henry M. Stanley. LY:252

STANS, MAURICE H.
Youle, C.
Introduces Maurice H. Stans, Director of the Bureau of Budget of the United States. PRC:14

Stansell, George
Constitution. LEIO:111

Stanton, Elizabeth Cady
Keynotes the first Woman's Rights Convention. BOU: 140; PE:388; PEA:388

Stanton, Frank
Benjamin Franklin lecture. BA 1961-62:78
Remarks on government regulation of broadcasting (accepting Printers' Ink Gold medal). ARNS:116

Staples, A. G.
Toast to the flag. PROS:43

Starnes, Trine
Plea for righteousness. YR 6: 267

Stassen, Harold Edward
American world policy for peace and progress. BA 1944-45:56
Two responses to introductions. PR:122, 125
Way to live as neighbors. ON:143
See also Dewey, T. E., jt. auth.

STASSEN, HAROLD EDWARD
Blume, C. E.
Introducing Harold E. Stassen. YE:127
Compton, K. T.
Presents Harold Edward Stassen. LY:104

STATE, THE
Baldwin, R. N.
Individual and the state. ONES:350
Channing, W. E.
Man above the state. BREW 3:200
Field, D. D.
Child and the state. BAKF: 310
Ritchie, A. C.
State responsibility. BLAB: 316
Seelye, L. C.
State versus anarchy. BLAA:250; BLAB:250
See also Church and state; Education and state; Industry and state

STATE GOVERNMENT
Cook, O. W. E.
City and the state. SHUC: 319
Root, E.
Duties of the states. WERN 42:53

STATE RIGHTS
Calhoun, J. C.
Force Bill. BREW 3:45; HAZO 10:4265; MAS 10: 4265; PE:350; PEA:350; REEMA 12:485; SHAH:183; WPRA:120
In support of State Rights. SHAH:184
Reply to Webster, February 26, 1833 (inserted in speech by Patrick Henry). CLAW:136 (See note in list of books indexed; FKA:27
Crowley, K. A.
States rights. BOA:120
Dinsmore, H. A.
South and the Constitution.

SHUO:109
Douglas, S. A.
Fifth joint debate at Galesburgh, October 7, 1858. CLAW:83
Opening speech of Lincoln-Douglas debate (Ottawa, August 21, 1858). BRYW 9:259; CHAL 8:421; CLAW:55; HARSO:310; HAZO 17:7401; MAS 17:7401; SHUM:142
Reply to Lincoln at Chicago, July 9, 1858. SHAH:387; WPRA:188
Ewing, T. C.
Ohio and the Northwest. REEMA 2:474
Hayne, R. Y.
On Foot's Resolution (January 19, 1830). CLAW:29
On Foot's Resolution (January 21, 1830). BREW 6:404; BRYW 9:3; CHAL 5:459; CLAW:104; CODS:475; CODSA:475; HAZO 12:4969; JOHA 1 pt. 1:233; LEEW 9:151; MAS 12:4969; ORAMA 2:97; REEMA 13:1170; SOU 9:342
Henry, P.
Against the Federal Constitution (June 5, 1788). BAAMP:32; BIR:1:136; BREW 7:28; BRYW 8:67; CHAL 3:46; CLAW:7; HARS:67; HAZO 6:2613; MAS 6:2613; ORAMA 1:63; WPRA:7
At the Virginia Convention (from speeches of June 5th and 7th, 1788). CLAW:133
Jackson, A.
Second inaugural address-"State rights and Federal sovereignty." BREW 7:145; BRYW 8:204; CHAL 4:294; CHI:63; COP:278; COPA:278; COPB:278; HAZO 9:3711; HURG:71; LOTI:61; MAS 9:3711; USIN:58; USINA:58
Madison, J.
Shall the states take precedence over the central government? CLAW:75
State sovereignty and federal supremacy. BAAMP:37; BREW 8:61; CHAL 3:366; CHEM 1:219; CLAW:19; COP:237; COPA:237; COPB:237; HAZO 7:3020; HURG:40; MAS 7:3020; SMI:55; WPRA:23
Marshall, J.
Barron v. Baltimore: opinion for the Supreme Court. BRE:158; BREA:142
O'Mahoney, J. C.
States rights or human rights. BOA:116
Reel, F. U.
Political paradox. NOR 1936:22
Root, E.
How to preserve the local self-government. FKA:48
Smith, E. D.
States rights. BOA:111
Webster, D.
Constitution not a compact between sovereign states. HAZO 11:4493; MAS 11:4493; WPRA:133
See also United States-History-Civil War-Causes

STATESMANSHIP
Frank, G.
Statesmanship of business and the business of statesmanship. EXEE:553
Larson, A.
Timocracy-why not? (education of statesmen). YR 1:155
World is calling for more statesmen. AMEO 2:210

See also Diplomacy

STATUES See Acceptance speeches-Statues; Dedication addresses-Statues; Presentation speeches-

STATUES (cont.)
Statues

STATURE See Man-Stature
Stearns, Trine
Perishing with the sword. YR 8:199
Stedman, Edmund C.
Appreciating Whitelaw Reid. NESA:166
To Parke Godwin (speech proposing a vote of thanks). KNAS:199; KNASA:199
Tribute to Richard Henry Stoddard. REEMA 3:1085
Work of Robert Louis Stevenson. REEMA 9:1098
Steed, Wickham See Salter, A., jt. auth.

STEEL
Bradford, L.
Vanadium steels. PEAE: 103

STEEL INDUSTRY AND TRADE See Industry
Steele, Raymond
Introducing an atomic scientist. BRC:316
Steele, Sidney
Emcee at a banquet
" at a beauty contest
" at a book-of-the-month club meeting
" at a Lincoln Day exercise
" at a policemen's ball. BRH:320, 318, 237, 312, 261
Introducing a contralto
" a high school symphony orchestra
" an impersonator
" a P.T.A. entertainment
" a pianist. BRH:87, 137, 51, 65, 89
Stefánsson, Vilhjálmur
Northward course of Empire. EXEE:518
Stegall, Frank
Sport broadcast of a contest debate. JUD:71
Stein, Louis
Accepting 1959 National Brotherhood award. SABA:301
Steinhoff, Lester
Equities in wealth. YR 8:123

STEINMETZ, CHARLES PROTEUS
Simon, S.
Vision of a scientist. BRP 6:47; NOR 1934:86
Stennis, John C.
For censure of Senator McCarthy. BA 1954-55:109
Stephan, Curtis C.
Lord is your shepherd. ACW:17
Stephan, Paul G.
Sharing life's burdens and blessings. ACW:12
Stephen, Leslie
Critic. REEM 3:271; REEMA 3:1091; REEMB 3:288
Stephens, Alexander Hamilton
At the unveiling of Carpenter's picture of Lincoln. LEEW 10:299
Cornerstone address.-Same as his On the Confederate Constitution
Future of the South. ORAMA 2:263
On the admission of Oregon. SOU 9:402
On the Confederate Constitution. BIR 2:234; BREW 9:283; CHAL 8:368; HARS: 383; HAZO 17:7213; JOHA 2 pt. 2:39; MAS 17:7213; REEMA 15:1936
Sanctity of the Union. LA:156
Secession. BAKF:401; CHAL 8:363; HAZO 17:7208; MAS 17:7208; REEM 10:192; REEMA 15:1932; REEMB 11:196
South and the public domain. BREW 9:281; BRYW 9:137
What is all this for? SOU 9:404

STEPHENS, ALEXANDER HAMILTON
Stewart, E.
Alexander Stephens. SHUC:

236
Stephenson, Wendell H.
Half-century of Southern historical scholarship. TIN: 155
Stepp, James M.
If I were a candidate for the Presidency. JUD:171
Sterling, John Edward Wallace
Lofty purpose shared. BA 1950-51:150
Stetson, Francis Lynde
Joseph Hodges Choate. REEM 5:355; REEMB 9:398
Stettinius, Edward R., Jr.
Address at final plenary session of United Nations Conference on International Organization. VO 1945-46: 304
Address at first plenary session of the San Francisco Conference. -Same as his United Nations Security Conference
Address at opening of San Francisco Conference. VO 1945-46:163
Before the Senate Foreign Relations Committee. VO 1945-46:378
Economic objective of United States foreign policy. HAN: 403
Radio report to the American people on the San Francisco Conference. VO 1945-46:222
Remarks at conclusion of the first phase of the Dumbarton Oaks conversations. VO 1944-45:456
Statement at conclusion of second phase of the Dumbarton Oaks conversations. VO 1944-45:470
Statement explaining policy of secrecy adopted for the Dumbarton Oaks Conference. VO 1944-45:395
Statement on British policy in Italy. VO 1944-45:595
Statement on Poland. VO 1944-45:618
Statement on representation in the assembly of the proposed United Nations Organization. VO 1945-46:137
United Nations Security Conference. BA 1944-45:68; VO 1945-46:165
Steuer, Max D.
Cross-examination, is it an art or an artifice? BYRA: 422; REEM sup 3:91; REEMB 6:326
Stevens, E. P.
League prayer meeting. THOU 2:506
Stevens, E. Ray
Dean Richards-his service to the state. ONEC:137
Stevens, Elmer T.
Introduces Paul G. Hoffman. PR:69
Stevens, J. Stanley
More stately mansions. BRP 3:77; YR 3:97
Stevens, James M.
Tomorrow we live. NOR 1943: 11
Stevens, Thaddeus
Against Webster and northern compromisers. BREW 9: 288; CHAL 6:14; HAZO 12: 5022; MAS 12:5022; REEMA 15:1943
Issue against Andrew Johnson. -Same as his Radical view of reconstruction
On reconstruction. CHEM 4: 269; JOHA 2 pt 2:181; LEEW 10:285; WPRA:204
Radical Republican theory. -Same as his On reconstruction
Radical view of reconstruction. BREW 9:292; HARS: 436; HAZO 12:5032; JOHA 2 pt 2:181; MAS 12:5032
Stevens, William B.
Divine strength and beauty of holy worship (dedication sermon at St. Thomas's Church, New York). THOU 2:449

Stevenson, Adlai E.
Address at the memorial service for Sir Winston Churchill. BA 1964-65:103
Agrees to run for President. BA 1952-53:66; BAAMP: 289; CAP:220; COPB:597; HURG:302; PE:821; PEA: 821
America's role. BA 1952-53: 83
City-a cause for statesmanship. ARNS:250
Commencement address. BA 1951-52:172
Cooper Union address. BA 1954-55:99
Educated citizen (commencement address at Princeton). BOU:18; BRYA:520
Eulogy on Eleanor Roosevelt. BA 1962-63:178
Four fears. BA 1953-54:65
"Let us work while it is yet day" (at University of California's 96th Charter Day). LINP:286
Madison Square Garden address, October 23, 1956. BA 1956-57:62
Political relevance of moral principle (A. Powell Davies memorial address). WPRC:355
Presents Pandit Nehru. LY: 238
Reply to Eisenhower's speech of October 8th, 1954. LOMS:244; LOMSA:309
Scoring the Republican record. BA 1955-56:120
Speech at Yale University, October 5, 1956. BRAP:59
Speech to the American Legion. BRY:471
There are no Gibraltors. WPRC:277
To the graduating class at Smith College. COPB:647
Tribute to John F. Kennedy at the General Assembly of the United Nations. BA 1963-64:31
United Nations: past and present. HIB:237
United States and the U.S.S.R. ANGC:184
United States Far Eastern policy. COPB:599
World brotherhood in a space age. BA 1957-58:59
See also Biddle, F., jt. auth.

STEVENSON, ADLAI E.
McCarthy, E.J.
Nomination of Adlai E. Stevenson. BA 1960-61:30
Stedman, E.C.
Work of Robert Louis Stevenson. REEMA 9:1098
Steward, Theophilus G.
Army as a trained force. DUNM:277
Stewart, Donald W.
Universal obligation. BOB:39
Stewart, Earl
Alexander Stephens. SHUC: 236
Stewart, James G.
Welcome to Cincinnati. YE: 134
Stewart, M.B.
Priest and soldier. NESA:183
Stewart, William H.
Eulogy on General Lee. SHUO:157
Stidger, William L.
Look ahead. BART 4:1
Stier, Bernice
Bulwark of democracy. YR 10:105
Stiles, Ezra
On the future glory of the United States. HAZO 5: 2041; MAS 5:2041
Washington. THOU 1:158
Stimson, Henry L.
Broadcast March 9, 1943. VO 1943-44:98
Grave situation. COP:586; COPB:565
Inaugural address of the Governor General of the Philippines. ONEC:157
London Naval Arms Conference. ONEC:233

Statement on the atomic bomb. VO 1945-46:407
Stinchfield, Frederick H.
Lawyer outside the court room. KLEB:201
Stipp, John E.
Introduces Dr. Will Durant, distinguished philosopher. PRNE:49
Introduces Edmund S. Muskie, Governor-elect of Maine. PRNE:31
Introduces Nathan M. Pusey, President, Harvard University. PRNE:29
Introduces Ralph D. Paine, Jr., publisher of Fortune. PRNE:23
Introduces Warren Lee Pierson of Trans-World Airlines. PRNE:32
Stires, Ernest M.
Sincerity and sacrifice. LAD: 153
Southland. REEM 3:274; REEMB 3:291

STOCK AND STOCK BREEDING
See Agriculture

STOCK EXCHANGE
Amos, M.B.
Crash (1929). BLUE:39
Kahn, O.H.
New York Stock Exchange and public opinion. BYRA: 251; REEM 4:230; REEMB 5:42
Stockdale, Allen A.
Making spiritual history. BART 1:13
Where do we go from here? BART 2:265

STOCKDALE, JOHN
Erskine, T.
Speech in behalf of John Stockdale. BRAO:141; BREW 6:24; CHAL 3:276; CODS:285; CODSA:285; FULB:69; GOOD:684; HAY: 73; HAZO 7:2918; MAS 7: 2918; PE:184; PEA:184

Stockdale, Thomas R.
Confederates are comin'. WERN 42:62

STOCKS AND BONDS
Huston, B.
Introducing a stock broker. BRC:303
See also Bonds, government
Stoddard, Alexander Jerry
Education and the people's peace. BA 1944-45:272
Stoddard, Charles A.
Another year of time. THOU 2:37
Stoddard, George D.
Fallacies and roadblocks. ANGC:150
Frontiers of youth. BA 1941-42:219
Science and civilization. BA 1947-48:169
See also Douglas, P.H., jt. auth.

STODDARD, RICHARD HENRY
Stedman, E.C.
Tribute to Richard Henry Stoddard. REEMA 3:1085
Stoke, Harold W.
University assembly. BA 1949-50:245
Stolz, Ardith E.
Woman's choice. YR 4:331
Stone, F.G.
Limiting bombardment by law. BREW 9:295
Stone, Harlan Fiske
Accepting bust of Brandeis. ON:327
Fifty years' of the United States Supreme Court. HICF:803
Training of lawyers. BYRA: 441; REEM sup 3:110; REEMB 6:345
United States v. Butler et al, 1936: dissenting opinion for the Supreme Court. BIR 4: 188
Stone, Harry L.
Introduces club members to

Stone, Harry L. (cont.)
compete with Quiz Kids
Introduces General Carlos P. Romulo
" James Conzelman, football coach. PR:79, 54, 38
Introductory remarks for a ladies' day meeting. PR: 99
Stone, Melville Elijah
Revolution of 1893 (Free press). REEM sup 3:120; REEMB 6:355
Stone, V.H.
Thoroughbred. LINM:304
Stone, William J.
Reconstruction in Missouri. SHUO:131
Stoner, Norman A.
Conceived in liberty. YR 8:49

STORES, RETAIL-LOCATION
Merrihue, W.V.
What a company looks for in seeking a new location. SABA:183
Storey, Carroll L.
Minister plenipotentiary. TRUW:137
Storrs, R.S.
Discontent of the times. THOU 1:453
Puritan scheme of national growth, 1857. BRAR 2:327
Rise of constitutional liberty (centennial oration at the Academy of Music, New York). CHAL 10:101; HAZO 19:8257; MAS 19: 8257
Victory at Yorktown. REEMA 3:1094
Story, Joseph
Appeal for liberty. CLAY:196
Characteristics of the age. - Same as his Intellectual achievement in America
Intellectual achievement in America. BREW 9:300; CHAL 5:115; HAZO 10: 4117; MAS 10:4117; NORR 2:37; ORAMA 1:379
Science and letters in our day. -Same as his Intellectual achievement in America.
Stout, John P.
Material wealth of Uncle Sam. REAC:191

STOWE, HARRIET BEECHER
Beecher, H.W.
Tribute to Harriet Beecher Stowe. REEMA 1:51
Strafford, Thomas Wentworth, 1st Earl of
Defense before the House of Lords. BREW 9:309; BRTH:27; BRTHA:27; BRYW 3:38; CHAL 2:33; GOOD:11; HAZO 4:1454; LEEW 6:51; MAS 4:1454; ORBR 1:53; REEM 9:63; REEMB 10:65
Speech in the Tower. HAZO 4:1466; MAS 4:1466
Speech on the scaffold. HAZO 4:1472; MAS 4:1472

STRAFFORD, THOMAS WENTWORTH, 1st EARL OF
Pym, J.
Against Strafford. CHAL 1:472; HAZO 4:1416; MAS 4: 1416; REEMB 10:68
Strahon, Mary
Public waits. BRP 8:56
Straight, Michael
Can modern capitalism meet the needs of modern man? MOUG:141
Two are alive. SAR:257
See also Canham, E.D., jt. auth.
Strandness, Bennie
Challenge to America. YR 8: 141
Stratton, William G.
Introduces Herbert Brownell, Jr., Attorney General of the United States. PRNE: 17
Straus, Gus
Introducing a furrier. BRC: 275
Straus, Nathan

End the slums. ON:250; SAR: 326

Straus, Oscar Solomon
Address delivered at Faneuil Hall on 250th anniversary of the settlement of the Jews in the United States. TWJ:69; REEM 7:374; REEMB 8:395

Growth of American prestige. REEM 3:279; REEMB 3: 296

Roosevelt pilgrimage. REEM 7:380; REEMB 8:401

Streeter, Frank S.
Introducing an educator (Frederick S. Jones). ONEM: 670; ONES:50

Streufert, Paul W.
God's children live in love. ACW:135

Stricker, Margery
Intellectual: his journey and his home (talk to secondary-school graduates who have won college scholarships). BRAB:533

STRIKES AND LOCKOUTS
Arpaia, A.
Matter of necessity. LINP: 240
Edgar, S.
Strikes in public utilities. BRAP:78
Filene, E. A.
Why men strike. BYRA: 151; REEM 4:115; REEMB 4:237
Hickman, A.
Case for the sit-down strike. BRP 8:68; NOR 1937:11
Johnston, E.
Warning to labor-and to management. BA 1943-44: 200
Lewis, J. L.
United Mine Workers demands. BA 1945-46:180
Murray, P.
Strikes, wages and industrial profits. BA 1946-47: 177
Simon, J. A.
General strikes. BEA:381
Strikes: the striker and the strike-breaker (a changeable speech adaptable for Service men's posts, American War Mothers' or Gold Star Mothers' chapters, for a membership drive or a pep talk for cooperation). BAI:47
Summers, H. W.
Internal solidarity. BA 1943-44:165
Taft, W. H.
Strikes, boycotts and injunctions (acceptance speech, July 28, 1908). BREW 9:340
Truman, H. S.
Railroad strike emergency. BA 1945-46:196
See also Injunctions

Strong, Walter A.
Address at International Oratorical Contest. LEIO:63

STRONG MEN See Actors and acting

Stryker, H. M.
Introducing Walter Bedell Smith. YE:128

Stryker, M. W.
Recognize the unions. BLAA: 197; BLAB:197

Stryker, William Scuddler
Dutch heroes of the new world. REEMA 3:1104

STUART, J. E. B.
Garnett, T. S.
Stuart, the Confederacy's Prince Rupert. SMI:190

Stubbins, T. A.
Spirit of romance. COUW:45

Stubbs, Charles William
International peace. CHAL 14: 15; HAZO 25:10545; MAS 25:10545
Shakespeare as a prophet. REEMA 9:1104

Stubbs, C.W. (cont.)
Thanksgiving for William Shakespeare (birthday sermon). HAZO 25:10559; MAS 25:10559
Stubbs, W.R.
Tree our oldest servant. DICD:159; DICE:159
Stubbs, William
On resigning the Regius Professorship of History. KNAS:237; KNASA:237
Stuck, Hudson
Alaska, fish and Indians. REEM 3:284; REEMB 3:301
Studebaker, John Ward
Democracy shall not be plowed under. BA 1939-40:375
Greetings to the Association of land-grant Colleges and Universities. YE:331
Morale building in our schools and colleges. BA 1941-42:120

STUDENT GOVERNMENT
MacCracken, H.N.
Student's share in college government. SAR:76

STUDENTS
Brodsky, J.C.
Student activities in undergraduate life. SHUC:359
Case, A.J.
Student's ups and downs. WERN 54:61
Creations: a place, a plan, a pledge (a bank publicity speech for any business group, for a P.T.A. meeting, or for a student body). BAI:72
Denton, T.G.
Student responsibility. AN:38
Dickens, C.
Volunteer student (on occasion of his inauguration as President of Birmingham and Midland Institute). REEMA 7:332
Eddy, E.D., Jr.
Our common denominator-the student. BA 1960-61:131
Foster, W.T.
Should students study? BRY:465; SAR:64
Game of life or a top man is not a flop man (a changeable speech adaptable as an inspirational speech for sales people, student groups and for all workers, or for a sports dinner speaker). BAI:56
Gokhale, G.K.
Students and politics. ZU:12
Gould, S.B.
Flavor for our daily bread. BA 1962-63:122
Harding, H.F.
College student as a critic. BRAP:152
Holth, I.
Youth aflame. YR 6:303
Huber, L.J.
Schoolboy emcee. BRH:341
Kildee, R.
Speech for honors day banquet. JUD:199
Oppenheimer, J.R.
Talk to undergraduates. BA 1957-58:146
Sastri, V.S.S.
Advice to students. ZU:9
Wert, R.J.
Restless generation and undergraduate education. BA 1964-65:145
You are not alone (address to refugee students). NI:217; NIA:166
See also Colleges and universities; Commencement addresses; Education, higher; Learning and scholarship; Student government; Youth

STUDY
Foster, W.T.

Should students study? BRY: 465; SAR:64
Satterthwaite, J. B.
Learned dust. YR 9:231
Stuenkel, Walter W.
God's assurance of his blessed presence. ACW:94

STUTTERING
Stuttering stanzas. FRIE:313

SUBSIDY See Taxation

SUBSTITUTE SPEAKERS See Extemporaneous speeches; Public speaking

SUBTREASURY BILL See Independent treasury

SUCCESS
Beck, J. M.
Successful life. SHU:23
Bell, C. H.
Worship of success. NORR 1st ser; 174
Bennett, W. R.
Man who can. EXEE:48
Bok, E. W.
Keys to success. BLAA: 172; BLAB:172; REEM 8: 19; REEMA 4:95; REEMB 13:20
Bower, H. F.
Price of success. BYRA: 136; REEM 4:34; REEMB 4:170
Bryson, L. and others.
Opportunities for success in the creative arts. SAR: 403
Burdette, R. J.
Advice to a young man. REAC:220
Buried gold. FRIE:253
Cameron, W. J.
Don't die on third. SAR: 43; SHU:42
Too soon to quit. SAR:41
Cleveland, G.
Education and the self-made man. BLAA:66; BLAB:66
Confidence plus optimism-total success. NAT:9
Discouragement does not mean defeat. FRIE:221
Don't be sidetracked. JAS:10
Ehninger, D.
Are we blind? BRP 7:82; NOR 1936:16
Fields, J. T.
Masters of the situation. REEMA 5:423
Foster, W. T.
Should students study? BRY:465; SAR:64
Garfield, J. A.
Success in life. REAC:95
Get up and go. NATT:46
Getting started. FRIE:257
Give to the world the best you have and the best will come back to you. AMEO 1:191
Greenewalt, C. H.
To reach high places. ANGC:18
How to begin. NATT:14
How to tell a big shot. NAT: 3
Lane, F. K.
Unconquerable soul. PROS: 37
Living a useful life. FRIE: 254
Love your work. FRIE:175
Mann, L. L.
Converting liabilities into assets. BA 1953-54:185; HIBS:499
Maury, M. F.
Rules of conduct-attributes of success. SMI:144
Meldrum, A. B.
Power and aim. REAC: 186
Nickerson, A. J.
Climbing the managerial ladder. BAAG:387
Opportunity everywhere. NATT:40
Pierce, F.
Releasing latent power. EXEE:23
Robinson, E. G.

SUCCESS (cont.)
Men: made, self-made and un-made. BLAA:46; BLAB:46; REAC:119
Rogers, S.
Spark plugs and live wires. EXEE:61
Schwab, C. M.
How to success. BYRA: 394; HOA:385; KLEB:265; REEM 4:375; REEMB 5: 262
Self-made man needs working parts. NAT:4
Sledge, T.
Warriors of the broken sword. SHU:51
Some thoughts on achieving success-speech of an older citizen at a young people's meeting. WRA:209
Spencer, R. N.
Native hue of resolution. NESA:134
Spirit of achievement. CON: 77
Stockdale, A. A.
Where do we go from here? BART 2:265
Stone, V. H.
Thoroughbred. LINM:304
Success. FRIE:251
Success in life. DAVC:571
Success talk for young people. NAT:42
Voss, L. C.
Success by overcoming obstacles. WERN 54:58
What constitutes success? THOS:155
What is success? AMEO 1:45
What is success? (An address delivered before the Syracuse, New York, Rotary Club). SPIM:213
Whipplc, F. L.
Personal goals. ANGC:11
Williams, W.
Greatest battle ever won. BOA:170; BOB:197; PROS: 54; SHU:216
Wilson, J. M.
Glow that comes from hunger. BAAG:385
Worth the try. NATT:5
You and your job. DR:32
See also Behavior; Fame; Inspirational talks; Victory

SUDAN See Egypt and Sudan Campaigns, 1882-1900
Sudow, Miriam
Masters of men. JUD:165

SUEZ CANAL
Eisenhower, D. D.
Agonized reappraisals: Hungary and Suez. FIP: 346

SUFFRAGE
Carpenter, M. H.
In favor of universal suffrage. BREW 3:140
Chamberlain, J.
Megaphone and manhood suffrage. BREW 3:196
Frelinghuysen, F. T.
In favor of universal suffrage. BREW 6:175
Hugo, V. M.
Against curtailing the right of suffrage. CLAY:149
Macaulay, T. B.
People's charter. REEMA 14:1377
Robespierre, M.
Universal suffrage. REEM 9:205; REEMA 14:1756; REEMB 10:212
See also Elections; Negroes-Politics and suffrage; Soldiers-Suffrage; Woman-suffrage
Sugarman, Norman A.
Assassin of youth. BRP 9:78; NOR 1938:9
Sullivan, A. M.
'Disesteem of the law" (from the dock at Dublin, 1868). HAZO 22:9233; MAS 22: 9233
On the Irish National demands. KET:372
On the Zulu war. BRYW 6: 217

Sullivan, Sir Arthur Seymour
Music. COP:662; COPB:689; REEM 3:290; REEMB 3: 307
Sullivan, Mark
What is liberalism? BART 1: 209
Sulzberger, Mayer
Oration at the 250th anniversary of the settlement of the Jews in the United States. TWJ:30

SULZER, WILLIAM
Brackett, E. T.
Summation for the managers in the Sulzer impeachment trial. HICJ:692
Hinman, H. D.
Opening address for the respondent in the Sulzer impeachment trial. HICJ: 660

SUMMER SCHOOLS See Schools, Summer
Summers, Hatton W.
Internal solidarity. BA 1943-44:165
Sumner, Charles
Claims on England. ORAMA 2:233
Crime against Kansas. BREW 9:323; BRYW 9:160; CHAL 8:262; CHEM 3:225; COP: 291; COPA:291; COPB: 291; HARS:294; HAZO 17: 6995; HURG:85; JOHA 2 pt. 1:88; MAS 17:6995; REEM 10:150; REEMA 15: 1952; REEMB 11:154; SHAH:314
Denouncing Douglas and Butler. -Same as his Crime against Kansas
Intercourse with China. REEMA 3:1110
On the repeal of the Fugitive Slave Law. JOHA 1 pt 2: 268
Progress of humanity. NORR 2d ser:73; REAC:86
Qualities that win. KLEG: 153; KLEM:71; REEM 3: 292; REEMA 3:1115; REEMB 3:309
True grandeur of nations. BREW 9:317; CHAL 8:284; CODS:487; CODS:487; HAZO 17:7017; LEEW 10: 113; MAS 17:7017; PL: 652; RID:36
War system of the Commonwealth of Nations. SHAH: 306

SUMNER, CHARLES
Brooks, P. S.
Assault on Sumner. BREW 2:254; BRYW 9:174; CHAL 9:453; HAZO 19:8085; JOHA 2 pt 1:121; MAS 19: 8085; REEMA 11:328
Burlingame, A.
Massachusetts and the Sumner assault. BREW 2: 420; CHAL 10:52; HAZO 19:8180; MAS 19:8180; REEMA 11:429
Conkling, R.
Against Senator Sumner. BREW 4:146
Elliott, R. B.
Eulogy of Charles Sumner. WOON:502
Lamar, L. Q. C.
Charles Sumner. BRYW 10: 61; CHAL 10:441; HAZO 21:8796; LA:134; LAD:93; MAS 21:8796; REEM 5:260; REEMA 8:767; REEMB 9: 299; SHUO:230
Sumner, G. Lynn
Presents Gertrude Lawrence. LY:47; SUM:70
Sumner, John Andrew Hamilton, 1st Viscount
Reform of the franchise. EMS 2:205
Sumner, William Graham
Forgotten man. WPRA:229
Sumrall, H. D.
On reporting the weather. BRAP:121
Sun, Yat Sen
National morale and world

Sun, Yat Sen (cont.)
tranquility. COP:399; COPA:399; COPB:399; CROC:436
Takes up the yellow man's burden. PE:664; PEA:664
Sunday, William A. (Billy Sunday)
Evangelism. HURG:170

SUNDAY SCHOOLS
Address to a Sunday school. SHUP:191
Bobby wild goose's ragged regiment. JAS:90
Johnston, H. A.
Sabbath school kite strings. THOU 2:212
Phillips, J. S.
Our model Sabbath school. THOU 2:205
Ramsey, H.
Introducing a speaker at a Sunday school banquet. BRC:79
Speech for a Sunday school picnic. BARB:109
Sunday school and the community. AMEO 2:179
Welcome to a guest speaker in Sunday school. HNWS: 41
Welcome to a new Sunday school superintendent (or other church official). HNWS:18
Welcome to visitors in a Sunday school. HNWS:22
See also Rallying day
Sunshine, Miriam
Procession. YR 6:339
Supple, Patrick J.
Catholic Church, the salvation of society. CATA 2:167

SUPREME COURT OF THE UNITED STATES See United States-Supreme Court

SURPRISE PARTIES
Huber, L. J.
Emcee at a surprise party. BRH:224
Posner, G. A.
Emcee at a surprise party. BRH:250
Suslov, Mikhail A.
Speech of October 21. RUS: 57

SUSSEX (STEAMSHIP)
Wilson, W.
Freedom of the seas: The "Sussex" affair. FIP:112
Sutherland, George
Adkins v. Children's Hospital, 1923: opinion for the Supreme Court. BIR 4:75
Private rights and government. REEM 7:383; REEMB 8: 404
Suzuki, Umetaro
Speech before the Japanese Imperial Diet. VO 1945-46: 285
Suzzallo, Henry
Inaugural address as president of University of Washington. WE 2:207
Swabb, Joel
Irresponsibles. BU:137
Swanson, Claude A.
Virginia. SMI:242
Sweet, Burton S.
Americanism. PROS:47

SWIFT, JONATHAN
Thackeray, W. M.
Swift. REEMA 6:1091

SWIMMING
Beavers. SCHS:33
Huber, L. J.
Introducing a swimming-diving act. BRH:132
Natant Leak of Nations. SCHS:191
Presentation of a trophy to the winner of a swimming contest. Response by the winner. EDGS:397, 399
Swing, David
Lincoln's birthday. THOU 1: 470
Novel in literature. REEMA

9:1114
Power of ideals. BOB:216
Man and his Thanksgiving. THOU 2:275
Washington and Lincoln. CHAL 11:473
Swing, Raymond Gram
Meaning of the home front. BA 1943-44:159
Only one truth. SAR:34
Wheel of judgment. BA 1940-41:163
Youth, war, and freedom. HAN:22
Swinton, John
Rights of the Negro. THOU 1:265

SWITZERLAND
Cheever, G. B.
Avalanches of the Jungfrau. CLAY:100

SWORDS See Acceptance speeches-Swords; Presentation speeches-Swords
Sydnor, Charles S.
Southerner and the laws. TIN:62
Sylla, Almamy
Inaugural speech at Conference on the Problems of Economic Development. UAR:143
Symington, W. Stuart
Freedom and military security. BA 1949-50:75
Our air force policy. YE:228
Time for action. BA 1957-58:32
Truth makes us free. BA 1952-53:42

SYRIA
Churchill, W. L. S.
Speech in Commons on Syria and Lebanon. VO 1945-46:257
DeGaulle, C.
Address before the French Consultative Assembly on the Levantine question. VO 1945-46:294
Press statement on Syria and Lebanon. VO 1945-46:247
Eden, A.
Statement on the Levant States. VO 1945-46:231

TABLETS See Acceptance speeches-Tablets; Presentation speeches-Tablets
Tacitus.
Calgacus to the Britons. LEEW 2:255
On the death of Agricola. LEEW 2:263
Taft, Lorado
Art and modern life. SAR:377
Taft, Robert A.
Against the appointment of Lilienthal. BA 1946-47:113
Basis of an American foreign policy. BA 1950-51:65
Failures of the Truman administration. BA 1951-52:100
Forward America. BA 1938-39:130; BRYA:534
North Atlantic Pact. BA 1949-50:15
Our misguided foreign policy. WPRC:285
Price control veto. BA 1945-46:154
Should the Taft-Hartley Labor Bill become law? BA 1946-47:196
Vote Republican. BA 1950-51:117
----and others (D. Cooke and W. P. Reuther)
American standard of living-how can it best be improved? BA 1947-48:103
---- and others (R. Blough and R. Weil)
Present crisis and the American economy. HAR:271

TAFT, ROBERT A.
Bricker, J. W.
Robert A. Taft. BA 1953-54:75
Kennedy, J. F.

TAFT, ROBERT A. (cont.)
Portraits of five senators in the Senate reception room. BA 1957-58:84
Watkins, F. C.
Introduces Robert A. Taft. PR:68
Taft, William Howard
Address at the unveiling of a monument to Chief Justice Salmon P. Chase. LINM: 144
America and England. REEM 3:299; REEMB 3:316
Antitrust: "Mere size is no sin." FIP:85
Canadian reciprocity: "They are coming to the parting of the ways." FIP:82
Catastrophe: The Ballinger affair. FIP:77
Delays and defects in the enforcement of law in this country. PEAE:211
Dollar diplomacy. FIP:89
Inaugural address. BREW 9: 332; CHI:207; LOTI: 189; USIN:187; USINA:187
Judiciary and progress. HICF:384
League of Nations. BRAS: 338; REEM 11:348; REEMB 12:366
Lincoln memorial. REEM 7: 398; REEMB 8:419
Our national dead. BLAB:305
Panic of 1907. FRY:51
Philippines. RID:105
President (November 16, 1912). ONEM:616; ONES: 208
Response to a lengthy introductory speech. HOA:367; HOAP:251
Strikes, boycotts, and injunctions (acceptance speech, July 28, 1908). BREW 9: 340
Tariff fiasco: the Winona address. FIP:72
Wealth and poverty in the courts. BREW 9:342

TAFT, WILLIAM HOWARD
Balfour, A. J. B.
Introducing Chief Justice Taft. REEM 1:69; REEMB 1:60
Cecil of Chelwood, E. A. R.
Great example (Taft). LINM:240
Taft-Ellender-Wagner Housing Bill See Housing

TAFT HARTLEY BILL See Labor laws and legislation-Taft-Hartley Law
Tagore, Rabindranath
Nationalism in India. COP: 393; COPA:393; COPB: 393

TAGORE, RABINDRANATH
Kabir, H.
Rabindranath Tagore. ZU: 66
Taiaeronk, Huron chief
Comforts nuns after burning of their chapel by the Iroquois. JON:34
Talbot, Philip
Introducing Sir Frederick James. MOA:501

TALENTS
Compton, K. T.
Stuff of life: our talents and their care. SAR:13
Talfourd, Thomas Noon
Queen against Moxon-Shelley as a blasphemer. BREW 9:345; HAZO 12:5216; MAS 12:5216
Talmage, Thomas Dewitt
Admiration for the Puritan character. -Same as his Behold the American.
Behold the American. COP: 646; KLEG:160; REEM 3: 307; REEMA 3:1122; REEMB 3:324; THOU 1: 339
Big blunders. BEA:397; ONEM:828; REEMA 6:1071
Capital and labor. PL:718
Chant at the cornerstone.

CHAL 12:44;HAZO 22: 9448; MAS 22:9448
God among the centuries.
Capital and labor. PL:718
Groups around the cross. THOU 2:72
Labor question. THOU 1:436
On Admiral Dewey and the American Navy. BREW 9: 364
Sleepers awakened. THOU 2: 132
Victory for God. WPRA:289
What I know about the Dutch. REEMA 3:1128
Tamanee, Indian chief See Indians of North America
Taminy Buck, Shawnee chief
At the court house at Lancaster, 1748. SHE:22
Taney, Roger Brooke
Charles River bridge v. Warren bridge, 1837 opinion for the Supreme Court. BIR 2:135
Dred Scott Case: opinion for the Supreme Court. BIR 2: 206; BRE:221; BREA:205
Opinion in the Merryman Case. ANG:310
Tang, Ching Ye
Cycle of civilization: China's need of Western civilization and a spirit of nationalism. ASHF:74
Tanner, Burton F.
Robert Burns. COUW:141

TANTALUS.
Pedrick, W.
Tantalus. YR 8:113
Tarhe, Wyandot chief
Speech at Council at Greenville. JON:75

TARIFF
Bailey, J.W.
Porto Rico tariff. REEMA 11:84
Bryan, W.J.
Tariff. CORP:284
Burges, T.
Rebuke to John Randolph. CHAL 4:392; HAZO 9: 3820; MAS 9:3820
Churchill, W.L.S.
Fiscal retaliation. BEA: 117
Clay, H.
American system. BREW 4:39; BURP:151; CHAL 5: 59; HAZO 10:4068; JOHA 2 pt 2:202; MAS 10:4068; REEMA 12:642
Cleveland, G.
On tariff revision. REEMA 12:687
Cockran, W.B.
Porto Rican tariff. FUL: 74, 77
Conn, R.H.
Tariff and the debenture clause. DOA:90
Crisp, C.F.
Tariff reform. BRYW 10: 186; REEM 10:318; REEMB 11:332
Dawes, H.L.
Tariff commission of 1880. BREW 5:52
Epes, S.P.
Tariff. SMI:225
Hurd, F.H.
Tariff for revenue only. JOHA 2 pt 2:238
McCall, S.W.
Porto Rico tariff. HAZO 25:10736; MAS 25:10736
McDuffie, G.
Tariff. SOU 9:287
Morrill, J.S.
Tariff and the public debt. CHAL 8:92; HAZO 16: 6708; MAS 16:6708
Otey, P.J.
Tariff. SMI:223
Randall, S.J.
Tariff legislation. REEMA 14:1671
Randolph, J.
On the tariff (1824). REEMA 14:1697
Tariff and the Constitution. (1816). PL:599
Roosevelt, F.D.
Message to Congress on

TARIFF (cont.)
the tariff, March 26, 1945. HAN:391
Roosevelt, T.
Trusts and tariff. REEMA 15:1776
Schurz, C.
American tariffs. WERN 42:179
Taft, W.H.
Tariff fiasco: the Winona address. FIP:72
Tupper, C.
In favor of a protective policy. CHAL 10:74; HAZO 19:8222; MAS 19:8222
Wilson, W.
First address to Congress. FIP:95
See also Commerce; Corn Laws; Free trade and protection
Tarkington, Booth
Indiana in literature and politics. REEM 3:314; REEMB 3:331
Where we come from. YE: 318

TARKINGTON, BOOTH
Garland, H.
In praise of Booth Tarkington. REEM 2:73; REEMB 2:74
McCutcheon, J.T.
Introducing Booth Tarkington. YE:132
Tarrant, John G.
John Marshall and the Constitution. LEIO:147
Tashrak.
For a Bar Mitzvah. ZEL:52
Tate, W.K.
South Carolina's rural school problem. ONES:268
Taulor, Johannes
God alone. PL:202
Sermon VI. LEEW 3:363
Tavenner, Clyde H.
Cause of labor. HARSO:23

TAXATION
Bacon, F.
Speech of the three subsidies. BRTH:16; BRTHA: 16
Balfour, A.J.B.
Dreadnoughts and dukes. BREW 1:218
Barkley, A.W.
Against Roosevelt's Tax Bill veto. BA 1943-44:188
Beaconsfield, B.D.
Reply in defence of his budget. PAUF 2:96
Bright, J.
Tax Bills: power of the House of Lords, House of Commons, July 6, 1860. PAUF 1:370
Brosseau, A.J.
Highways and tax payer. BYRA:49; REEM sup 1: 135; REEMB 4:90
Bryan, W.J.
On the income tax. REEMA 11:350
Burke, E.
On American taxation, April, 1774. CLAY:182; CODS:120; CODSA:120; EMS 2:221; GOOD:242; HARSO:353; KET:3
Camden, C.P.
Taxation of colonies. EMS 2:218
Chesterfield, P.D.S.
Against revenues from drunkeness and vice (1743). BREW 3:263; CHAL 2:194; GOOD:46; HAZO 5:1763; MAS 5:1763
Against the Gin Bill of the Ministry (1741). BRYW 3:165; ORBR 1:161; PL: 390
Cox, T.E.
Single tax. REAC:116
Danton, G.J.
Squeezing the sponge. BREW 4:402; BRYW 7:134; CHAL 4:115; HAZO 8:3350; MAS 8:3350; REEM 9:200; REEMA 12:802; REEMB 10: 207
Eisenhower, D.D.

New tax program (March 15, 1954 speech). MOA:573
Ellsworth, O.
Power of Congress to levy taxes. HAZO 7:2760; MAS 7:2760
Farr, N.C.
Introductory remarks on proposed Federal chain store tax. HOC:33
Fulkerson, R.
Inheritance tax. BRAC:407
Fuller, M.W.
Pollock v. Farmers' Loan and Trust Company, 1895: opinion for the Supreme Court. BIR 3:196
Harcourt, W. G. G. V. V.
Second reading of the Budget Bill, 1894. PAUF 2:286
Haroldson, W.
Tax racket. BRP 4:7; INTW 1933:40
Hughes, C.E.
United States v. Butler et al, 1936: dissenting opinion for the Supreme Court. BIR 4:188
Kaser, A. L.
Introducing a tax consultant. BRC:116
Kennedy, J. F.
Tax cut. FIP:393
Lansdowne, H. C. P. P. -F.
Predatory taxation and nationalizing land. BREW 7:265
Lloyd George, D.
The budget. HAY:305; PE:680; PEA:680; REEM 9:383; REEMB 10:395
Mansfield, W. M.
On the right to tax America. ADR 1:150; BRYW 3:230; CHAL 2:239; GOOD:148; HAZO 5:1832; MAS 5:1832; ORBR 1:199; PL:403; REEMA 14:1422
Massey, J. E.
Barbour Bill. SMI:201
Paying the piper. NAT:35
Pitt, W., 1708-1778
On the right to tax America. ADR 1:98; BOU:29; BRYW 3:197; CHAL 2:265; COP:155; COPA:155; COPB:155; FULB:5; GOOD:103; HAZO 5:1902; HIB:118; MAS 5:1902; ORBR 1:213; PAUF 1:57; PE:118; PEA:118; REEMA 12:563; SAA:13
Taxation of colonies, December 17, 1765. EMS 2:215
Pity the poor taxpayer. NAT:44
Roberts, O. J.
United States v. Butler et al, 1936: opinion for the Supreme Court. BIR 4:177
Roosevelt, F.D.
Message to Congress vetoing the tax bill. VO 1944-45:106
Rosebery, A. P. P.
Expansion and dumdum bullets. BREW 9:105
Penalizing poor but honest dukes. BREW 9:106
Taxes. FRIE:101
Truman, H. S.
Message to Congress, September 6, 1945. VO 1945-46:546
See also Tariff
Taylor, Bayard
Tribute to Goethe. REEMA 3:1136
Taylor, Deems
Presents Grace George. LY:38
University of music. BA 1940-41:238
See also Bryson, L., jt. auth.
Taylor, Doris Schwinn
Something of a man (in praise of John L. Lewis). MICS:166
Taylor, Harold
Ideals of American youth. HAR:462
Younger generation. BA 1947-48:179

Taylor, Henry J.
Integrity! a mighty force (tribute to Otto Schnering, head of Curtiss Candy Company). LARW:110

TAYLOR, HENRY J.
Miller, M. G.
Introduces Henry J. Taylor, radio commentator. PRNE: 35
Taylor, James Monroe
First and great commandment (baccalaureate sermon). WERN 54:25
Inaugural address as president of Vassar College. WE 1: 241
Taylor, Jeremy
Christ's advent to judgment. CHAL 2:83; HAZO 4:1533; MAS 4:1533
Foolish exchange. BREW 9: 369
Taylor, John W. See Havighurst, R. J., jt. auth.
Taylor, Laurette
Americans for America. BOA:313; BOB:91; PROS: 83
Taylor, Lawrence
Shrimps. JUD:117
Taylor, Maxwell D.
Some reflections on the subject of leadership. BRAP: 98
Taylor, Peggy
Party games. BRAP:122
Taylor, Robert L.
Address on Irish-American day. HARSO:155
Address to ex-Confederates. HARSO:8; PROS:92
Eulogy on Isham G. Harris. HARSO:84
Immortality. HARSO:72; SHU:63
Taylor, William L.
Civil rights and Federal responsibility. BA 1964-65: 21
Taylor, Zachary
Inaugural address. CHI:106; LOTI:99; SMI:158; USIN: 99; USINA:99

TAYLOR, ZACHARY
Winthrop, R. C.
Death of President Taylor. REEMA 9:1222

TAZEWELL, LITTLETON WALLER
Grigsby, H. B.
Littleton Waller Tazewell. SMI:152

TEACHERS
Address at a district teachers' association. AMEO 2:169
Barnhart, B.
Wherever diamonds. BRP 10:73
Beard, C. A.
Yes, we are ready. SAR: 101
Drummond, R.
Introducing a retired teacher. BRH:86
Examples of introductions for teachers. BO:20-23
Fells, S.
Teacher, the hope of America. BOA:147; BOB:186
How the supervision should help the teacher. AMEO 1:13
Huber, L. J.
Introducing a teacher. BRC:239
Influence of the great teacher. DAVC:598
Jones, O.
"Watchman, tell us of the night" (at 5th annual meeting of the Department of Superintendence of N. E. A.). BRAC:30
Kaser, A. L.
Introducing a retiring teacher. BRH:122
Ludlum, M. E.
My experiences as a teacher. YE:334
Reward of being a teacher.

JA:220
Teachers. SCHS:258
Teachers sent from God. JA: 217
Toast to a teacher. FRIT:90; STON:137
Toast to "Our faculty." STOC: 131; STON:137
Wagers, Z.
Formula for sugar. BRP 10:94
Wilford, H.C.
Introducing a teacher. BRC: 119
See also Education; Educators; Parents and teachers associations

TEACHING, FREEDOM OF
Eaton, C.
Professor James Woodrow and the freedom of teaching in the South. TIN:438
Eliot, C.W.
Academic freedom. NORR 1st ser:344
Heilbrin, L.H.
Look at academic freedom. ANGC:95
Ickes, H.L.
Academic freedom. BOA: 156
Kirk, H.H.
Academic freedom: are we ready for it? SAR:93
Lutz, R.H.
History of the concept of freedom. MIA:363
Narot, J.
Dare we discuss it? BRP 7:76; NOR 1936:10
Wright, Q.
Citizen's stake in academic freedom. HAR:369
Teague, Hilary
Liberia: its struggles and its promises. DUNM:33

TEAMS See Sports

TEAMWORK See Cooperation

TECHNOCRACY
Anderson, S.
Technocracy passes. BRP 4:59; INTW 1933:19; YR 5: 231

TECHNOLOGY
Brown, H.S.
Science, technology, and world development. ARNS: 84
Ridenour, L.N.
Science, technology, and national security. HAR:312
See also Atomic Energy
Tecumseh, Shawnee chief
Speech at Vincennes. BRYW 8:14; CHAL 4:362; COP: 268; COPA:268; COPB: 268; HAZO 9:3801; MAS 9:3801; ORAMA 1:345; REEM 10:52; REEMA 15: 1970; REEMB 11:53
Threatening speech. JON:85
To General Proctor. BREW 7:115; BRYW 8:14; CHAL 4:364; HAZO 9:3802; MAS 9:3802; ORAMA 1:347; REEM 10:53; REEMA 15: 1971; REEMB 11:54; SHE: 55
Teedyuscung, Delaware chief
At a conference, Philadelphia, 1758. SHE:27
At a conference with Indians held at Easton, October 20, 1758. SHE:45
Teehee, Houston B. (Cherokee Indian)
Dedicates marble statue of Sequoyah in Rotunda of Statuary Hall, Washington, D.C. JON:126
Tegner, Esaias
Before the University of Lund. CHAL 5:168; HAZO 10: 4262; MAS 10:4262

TELEGRAPH
Field, D.D.
Telegraph. REEM 2:48; REEMA 2:490; REEMB 2: 48
For a telegraphic banquet.

TELEGRAPH (cont.)
BARB:178
Marconi, G.
Conquest of the Atlantic. BREW 8:81
Telegraphy (toast to a group of telegraph operators). EDGS:170
See also Atlantic Cable

TELEPHONE
Bones: short and over can mean short of publicity and overlooking a patron (a speech to bank personnel, changeable for many occasions-business meeting or convention of sales personnel, at a graduation of nurses' group, for fund raising drives, to a telephone group, or by a political or labor speaker). BAI:94
Fisher, M.
Telomaniacs. JUD:147
Gifford, W.S.
Address before the Bond Club. YE:275
To Chicago Association of Commerce. SAC:101
Kaser, A. L.
Introducing a telephone executive. BRC:54
Telephony, by an official of the telephone company. EDGS:172
Thayer, H. B.
Some significant steps in the development of a national service. REEM sup 3:127; REEMB 5:324

TELEVISION BROADCASTING
Collins, L.
Speech to the directors of the National Association of Broadcasters. BA 1960-61: 178
Eisendrath, M. N.
Moral bankruptcy of television. ARNS:108
Gallup, G.
Mass information or mass entertainment? MOA:466
Hart, R.
Introducing a radio or television station manager. BRC:293
Kaser, A. L.
Introducing a television personality. BRH:152
Markel, L.
Future of the printed word. BRAP:143
Myers, N. J.
Moppet manipulation. ARNS:113
Nimow, N. N.
Television and the public interest. BA 1961-62:64
Sarnoff, R.W.
Television's role in the American democracy. BA 1962-63:136
Stanton, F.
Benjamin Franklin lecture. BA 1961-62:78
Remarks on government regulation of broadcasting (accepting Printers' Ink Gold medal). ARNS:116
Suggestions for adapting a speech to television. BRAB:459 With examples of. MOA:548
Suggestions for television speaking. BAAG:333; BAAGA:339; SOBP:289
Visk, A. G.
No butts about it: "a silly TV commercial." BRH:333
TELEVISION IN EDUCATION
Outline of speech: Resolved that we should support a policy of further development of educational television. BAAGA:264
Teller, Henry M.
On Porto Rico. CHAL 11:417; HAZO 22:9338; MAS 22: 9338
Problem of the Philippines. BLAA:222; BLAB:222
TELSTAR See Communication satellites

TEMPERAMENT
Fitzgerald, J. M.
Temperaments-the analysis of human talents. EXEE: 421
See also Character

TEMPERANCE
Address to a temperance meeting. HAPR:139
Borah, W. E.
Curse of liquor. BOB:45
Bryson, T. H.
Catholic total abstinence movement. CATA 2:89
Burrell, D. J.
Christian endeavors and the dram shop. THOU 1:566
Chenery, E.
Battle against alcohol. THOU 1:556
Cleary, J. M.
Saloon the giant curse. THOU 1:559
Cook, J.
Temperance. THOU 1:541
Cuyler, T. L.
Bad example of a stumbling block. THOU 1:574
Shot at the decanter. THOU 1:573
To the workingmen of Scotland. THOU 1:575
Dow, N.
Beer, a harmless drink? THOU 1:553

Churches and saloons. THOU 1:544
Effects of prohibition in Maine. THOU 1:571
Foster, E.
License system. THOU 1: 557
Fowler, C. H.
Impeachment of alcohol. THOU 1:574
Gains of temperance in Massachusetts. THOU 1:552
Gough, J. B.
Social responsibilities. REEM 8:192; REEMA 5: 495; REEMB 13:195
Temperance address, September 17, 1860. CHAL 9: 184; HAZO 18:7730; MAS 18:7730
Use only the best liquor! THOU 1:572
Grady, H. W.
Effects of prohibition in Atlanta. THOU 1:568
Harding, J.
Temperance in New Zealand. THOU 3:527
Ireland, J.
Total abstinence. THOU 1: 555
Murphy, T.
Gospel temperance reform. THOU 1:546
O'Callaghan, P. J.
Temperance. CATA 2:84
Pertinent facts and thoughts. THOU 1:576
Richardson, B. W.
Cures for drunkenness. THOU 1:561
Rotting quality of beer. THOU 1:554
Temperance address-The Nickel behind the bar. CRAI:444
Temperance Day. THOU 1: 538
Thompson, C.
"Christian liberty" not a license. THOU 1:543
Visit of a temperance association-address of welcome and reply by president. BARB:120-122
See also Alcoholism; Cadets of Temperance; Prohibition; Royal Templars of Temperance; Sons of Temperance; Woman's Christian Temperance Union
Temple, Genevieve
Beneath American roofs. BOA: 133; BOB:158; BRP 1:25
Temple, Henry John, 3d Viscount Palmerston. See Palmerston, H. J. T.
Temple, R. A.
Conclusion. THOU 3:506

Temple, R.A. (cont.)
Inaugural address at his installation as M.W.P. of Sons of Temperance. THOU 3:505
Responsive address on being presented a badge. THOU 3:486
Temple, William, Archbishop of York
Members one of another. BEA:9
Ten Bears, The Comanche
Do not ask us to give up the buffalo for the sheep. GRIS:44

TEN COMMANDMENTS
Ten commandments (for a young people's meeting). EDGS:237

TENNESSEE VALLEY AUTHORITY See Dams
Tenskwatawa, Tuscarora chief
Speech at Council. JON:82
Ter, Jacob
To a Bar Mitzvah: speech delivered by a pupil of a Talmud Torah. ZEL:29

TERMINIELLO, ARTHUR W.
Douglas, W.O. and others. Freedom of speech: Terminiello vs. City of Chicago. BA 1948-49:78
Terrell, Alexander
Tribute to James S. Hogg. SHUO:67

TERRITORIAL WATERS
Aiken, G.D.
Off-shore Oil Bill. BA 1953-54:60
Holland, S.L.
Tidelands oil. BA 1952-53:142
Lehman, H.H.
Tidelands oil. BA 1952-53:146
Tertullian, Quintus Septimius Florens
Beauty of patience. BREW 9:376
Prescription against heretics. LEEW 3:217
Shows. LEEW 3:225
Tessman, Abbott
Tomorrow, what? YR 4:217

TESTIMONIALS
Acknowledging appreciation (at hospital fund drive and testimonial). BED:66; BEDA:102
Address of tribute (at testimonial dinner on retirement of public official). BED:29; BEDA:49
Benny, J.
Remarks at Friars' Club dinner to Burns and Allen. JEYO:66, 68, 105, 108
Speech as toastmaster at Friars' Club dinner honoring George Jessel. JEYO:136
Cagney, J.
Speech at Friars' Club dinner to Burns and Allen. JEYO:81
Cantor, E.
Remarks at Friars' Club dinner to Burns and Allen. JEYO:77, 78
Cap: a testimonial speech. BAI:113
Closing speech (at hospital fund drive and testimonial). BED:66; BEDA:103
Closing speech (at testimonial dinner to journalist). BED:23; BEDA:38
Closing speech (at testimonial on retirement of public official). BED:31; BEDA:52
Closing speech at testimonial to a musician. BEDA:40
Closing speech (at testimonial to labor union official). BED:84; BEDA:157
Closing speech (at testimonial to philanthropist). BED:26
Flowers and auxiliaries: an

inspirational speech for auxiliary members or chapter members, changeable for a membership speech or a testimonial speech. BAI:131
Gilbert, E. J.
Emcee at a testimonial for a long-term employee. BRH:191
Goetz, W. E.
Speech at Friars' Club dinner to Burns and Allen. JEYO:75
Goldwyn, S.
Speech at Friars' Club dinner to Burns and Allen. JEYO:99
Greeting and welcome (at unveiling of portrait presented to Labor Temple). BED:89; BEDA:161
Guest-of-honor acknowledges praise and citation (at testimonial to philanthropist). BED:25; BEDA:47
Greetings to individuals and organizations on various anniversaries-seventeen examples of. BEB:83-89
Introducing guest of honor (at testimonial dinner to journalist). BED:22; BEDA:36
Introducing speaker (at testimonial ceremony honoring union official). BED:83; BEDA:156
Jessel, G.
Presenting Louella Parsons at dinner in her honor. JEYO:141
Speech at Roastmaster dinner in honor of Dean Martin and Jerry Lewis. JEYO:45
Toastmaster's speech at dinner honoring Jack Benny. JEYO:131
Kaye, D.
Speech at Friars' Club dinner to Burns and Allen. JEYO:102
Opening speech at birthday testimonial. BEDA:28
Opening speech (at testimonial dinner to journalist). BED:20; BEDA:34
Opening speech (at testimonial on retirement of public official). BED:27; BEDA:47
Opening speech at testimonial to a woman civic leader. BEDA:41
Opening speech (at testimonial to labor union official). BED:83; BEDA:156
Opening speech (at testimonial to philanthropist). BED:24; BEDA:45
Opening statement (at hospital fund drive and testimonial). BED:62; BEDA:98
Paley, W. S.
Speech at Friars' Club dinner to Burns and Allen. JEYO:90
Presentation speech (at hospital fund drive and testimonial). BED:62; BEDA:99
Presenting award (to journalist at testimonial dinner). BED:20; BEDA:35
Presenting check (at hospital fund drive and testimonial). BED:63; BEDA:100
Presenting gold cup (to retiring public official at testimonial dinner). BED:28; BEDA:48
Presenting the citation (at testimonial to philanthropist). BED:24; BEDA:46
Reagan, R.
Speech at Friars' Club dinner to Burns and Allen. JEYO:85
Resolution for testimonial. BED:35
Resolution of thanks (testimonial dinner). BEB:35
Response by guest-of-honor (at testimonial on retirement of public official). BED:30; BEDA:51

TESTIMONIALS (cont.)
Sarnoff, D.
Speech at testimonial dinner in honor of Mannie Sack. JEYO:60
Schary, D.O.
Speech at Friars' Club dinner to Burns and Allen. JEYO:72
Testimonial dinner toast. FRIT:94
Testimonials-7 models of. BEC:55
Thanking speaker (at testimonial on retirement of public official). BED:30; BEDA:50
Thanks and appreciation (by guest of honor at testimonial dinner to journalist). BED:22; BEDA:37
Thomas, D.
Speech at Friars' Club dinner to Burns and Allen. JEYO:93
Tribute to guest-of-honor and appeal for funds (at hospital fund drive and testimonial). BED:64; BEDA:101
Tribute (to labor union official at testimonial ceremony). BED:83; BEDA:156
Unveiling portrait (of past president of labor union). BED:89; BEDA:162
Welcoming address at testimonial to a musician. BEDA:38
See also Acceptance speeches-Testimonials; Anniversaries; Announcements; Eulogies; Presentation speeches-Testimonials; Tributes

Teves, Virgil W.
Three links of the I.O.O.F. THOU 3:102

TEXAS
Bailey, J.W.
Division of Texas. PROS:26; SHUO:221
Crozier, L.
Spirit of Texas. BOB:104
Henry, R.L.
Texas and the Panama Canal. SHUO:217
Phillips, N.
San Jacinto's address. PROS:40
Young, E.
Pioneer women of Texas. BOB:105

TEXAS, UNIVERSITY OF
Mezes, S.E.
Inaugural address as president of University of Texas. WE 2:387

Thackeray, William Makepeace
Authors and their patrons. BREW 9:383
George III. HAZO 17:7155; MAS 17:7155
Novelist's future labors. BREW 9:385
On charity and humor. BRYW 4:201; CHAL 8:325; HAZO 17:7136; MAS 17:7136
Reality of the novelist's creation. BREW 9:381
Swift. REEMA 6:1091

THANKS
Example of a thank you speech. FRIT:77
Examples of words of thanks. BO:61-63
Expression of appreciation and thanks-various models of. BEC:27
Four examples of speeches thanking a speaker at a club meeting. WRA:41-43
Guest gives thanks for courtesies extended. With examples of. STOC:157; STON:163-4
How do you say thank you? JAS:112
Lamont, T.W.
Thanking General Hugh Johnson for speaking. HOC:19
Malachowsky, H.
Thankfulness: address of

a poor boy speaking in the name of all pupils and expressing his thanks in public. ZEL:90
Resolution of thanks. THOU 3: 500
Resolution of thanks (testimonial dinner). BEB:35
Resolution of thanks to retiring officer (at end of his term)-two examples of. STON:120
Resolution thanking press. BEB:34
Response to speaker at presentation of scientific award. BEDA:60
Stedman, E. C.
To Parke Godwin (speech proposing a vote of thanks). KNAS:199; KNASA:199
Suggestions for and examples of speeches thanking a speaker. WRA:39; WRB: 161
Suggestion on how to thank the speaker publicly. BUT: 90; BUTA:90; BUTB:90
Thanking a speaker at a campaign canvassers' meeting. WRA:44
Thanking a speaker at a community center meeting. WRA:44
Thanking campaign workers. FRIE:85
Thanking committee (at United Nations anniversary ceremony). BEDA:126
Thanking Mayor at Town Hall meeting. BEDA:72
Thanking program chairman (at Garden Club meeting). BEDA:69
Thanking program chairman (of Labor union). BED:91; BEDA:164
Thanking speaker (at an annual Boy Scout drive). BEDA:109
Thanking speaker (at Camera Club). BEDA:20
Thanking speaker (at dedication of recreation center). BED:38; BEDA:80
Thanking speaker at Garden Club meeting. BEDA:69
Thanking speaker (at mental health fund drive). BED: 61; BEDA:106
Thanking speaker (at presentation of gold cup to retiring public official). BED: 28; BEDA:49
Thanking speaker (at testimonial on retirement of public official). BED:30; BEDA:50
Thanking speaker at Thanksgiving Day ceremony. BEDA:91
Thanking speaker-examples of. FRIE:304
Thanking speaker (on Human Rights Day address). BED: 70; BEDA:129
Thanking speaker (urging Labor union members to vote). BED:94; BEDA:167
Thanking the speaker-10 examples of. BEC:89
Thanking the speaker at a canvassers' dinner for an inspirational speech. WRA: 45
Thanks to speaker of evening. STOC:150
Toastmaster thanks entertainers. FRIT:45
Toastmaster thanks the speaker. FRIT:43
Toastmaster's compliments for those who arranged or served dinner. FRIT:15
Two model speeches expressing appreciation to members for understanding and support. BEB:20-21
See also Acceptance speeches; Responses to tributes

THANKSGIVING See Harvest festivals

THANKSGIVING DAY
Adams, W.

THANKSGIVING DAY (cont.)
Home gathering (Thanksgiving address). THOU 2:264
Thanksgiving: its memories and habits. THOU 2:286
Address for a Thanksgiving Day ceremony. BEDA:89
Bryan, W.J.
Thanksgiving address in London. CORP:286
Burrell, D.J.
Sursum corda: Thanksgiving address. THOU 2:289
Dana, O.
Historic Thanksgiving. THOU 2:305
Field, H.M.
Our feast of the tabernacles. THOU 2:294
First Thanksgiving. THOU 2:321
First Thanksgiving for the new world. THOU 2:261
Fisher, H.D.
Grace of thankfulness. THOU 2:291
Introducing a speaker on "The Thanksgiving holiday" at regular service club luncheon. WRA:37
Invocation for a Thanksgiving Day ceremony. BEDA:92
Invocation for Thanksgiving Day ceremony. BEDA:89
Lewis, L.
Thanksgiving manna. THOU 2:300
Miller, J.R.
Thanksgiving thoughts. THOU 2:282
New Englander as a citizen. DAVC:606
Old Colonial Thanksgiving. THOU 2:323
Opening speech at Thanksgiving Day ceremonies. BEDA:88
Owsley, A.
American Legion and the nation. REEM 7:303; REEMB 8:323
Pierson, A.T.
Pilgrim's Thanksgiving. THOU 2:308
Pope, A.B.
True Thanksgiving. THOU 2:297
Prepared table. LEHS:11
Rawson, E.
Thanksgiving. HURG:20
Selected outline for a Thanksgiving speech. PITT:55
Speech for a Thanksgiving banquet. BARB:98
Swing, D.
Man and his Thanksgiving. THOU 2:275
Thankful in all things. THOU 2:302
Thankless beggars. JA:226
Thanksgiving. NATS:22
Thanksgiving. PITT:53
Thanksgiving bouquet. LEHS:7
Thanksgiving Day. AMEO 2:27
Thanksgiving Day. NATM:38
Thanksgiving Day address. BURS:202
Thanksgiving Day address. THOS:32
Thanksgiving Day (for family and other reunions). EDGS:23
Thanksgiving Day (guest toasts our national birds). ED:40
Thanksgiving Day reverberates with gratitude. DR:172; LU:1204
Thanksgiving greetings. BEC:153
Thanksgiving in troublesome times. JA:223
Thanksgiving of the fathers. THOU 2:320
Thanksgiving silverware. LEHS:9
Thanksgiving speech. DAVC:603
Thoughts for a Thanksgiving speech. PITT:54
Toasts for a Thanksgiving festival. BARB:205
Toasts for Thanksgiving. PITT:54

Walker, J.B.
Grateful thanks. THOU 2: 293
Washington, G.
First Presidential Thanksgiving proclamation. THOU 2:262
Wheeler, B.I.
Address delivered in San Francisco at 250th anniversary of the settlement of the Jews in the United States. TWJ:180
Thayer, Harry Bates
Some significant steps in the development of the national service. REEM sup 3: 127; REEMB 5:324
Thayer, Wallace
Fraternity, the latest moral force. THOU 3:172

THEATER
Baker, E.D.
American theatre speech. WAGN:15
Belasco, D.
Forty years a theatrical producer. GLAD:168; REEM 1:110; REEMB 1: 105
Collyer, R.
Church and the stage. REEM 1:330; REEMA 1: 267; REEMB 1:331
Drummond, R.
Introducing an amateur theatrical. BRH:118
Habimah. NI:233; NIA:177
Hall, W.F.
Yarn of the manager bold. REEMA 2:581
Helburn, T.
Theater versus pictures. GA:109
Huber, L. J.
Introducing an amateur show. BRH:138
Lowell, J.R.
Stage. REEMA 2:745
Lytton, E. G. E. L. -B.
Macready and the English stage. REEMA 2:769
Macready, W.C.
Farewell to the stage. REEMA 2:791
Milliken, F.
Introducing a director of an amateur play. BRH:72
Posner, G. A.
Introductory remarks of an emcee to open a show. BRH:326
Purdue, I. P.
Presenting Chi Omega theater. GA:38
Theaters, by a member of a theatrical organization. EDGS:203
See also Actors and acting; Music and musicians; Opera

THEATER GUILD
Lippmann, W.
Theater Guild. REEM 2: 331; REEMB 2:335
Thiers, Louis Adolphe
At Arcachon. CHAL 6:238; HAZO 13:5385; MAS 13: 5385
Mexico and Louis Napoleon's policies. BREW 9:389; HAZO 13:5369; MAS 13: 5369; REEMA 15:1974
On the wastefulness of imperial France. PL:322
Thigpen, Walter
Death among the dailies. SOBP:338

THIRD DEGREE
Kitchen, J.M.
Arm of the law. BRP 3:18
Tholuck, A.
New Year's Day meditation. THOU 2:46
Thomas, Augustus
Gold medal for drama. REEM 6:387; REEMB 6: 362
Honoring Secretary Mellon. NESA:176
Individual liberty. REEM 3: 327; REEMB 3:344
South as a custodian. REEM

Thomas, Augustus (cont.)
3:319; REEMB 3:336
Thomas, Charles S.
Twentieth Amendment (negative). ONEC:321
Thomas, Clement
"Children of the gloom." COUW:235
Thomas, Danny
Speech at Friars' Club dinner to Burns and Allen. JEYO: 93

THOMAS, DANNY
Jessel, G.
Introducing Danny Thomas at Friars' Club dinner to Burns and Allen. JEYO:92
Thomas, Dylan
Visit to America. COPB:638
Thomas, Edwin Joel
High school commencement address. HAR:386
Thomas, Elbert D. See Granik, T., jt. auth.
Thomas, Gordon
Pernicious virtue. YR 6:11
Thomas, Isaac
Culture and service. SHUC: 380
Thomas, James Henry
Irish question. BEA:411
Thomas, James Shelby
We move in new directions. BART 4:255
Thomas, Jesse B.
Anno Domini (New Year sermon). THOU 2:20
Thomas, John M.
Man and the soil. SHU:181
Thomas, Lowell
Election of Truman. BA 1948-49:134
Thomas, M. Carey
Farewell to Bryn Mawr. GA: 57
Thomas, Norman
Acceptance speech. BA 1943-44:277
America and the war. COP: 595; COPB:582; HURG:261
America's duty in time of crisis. BA 1939-40:275
Can modern capitalism meet the needs of modern man? MOUG:138
Choice before us. SAR:158
Communism and Fascism; resemblances and differences. BART 2:93
How far shall we go? ON:82

Is the New Deal Socialism? WPRC:188
No democracy without civil liberty. BA 1937-38:45
Thomas, Percy E.
American infamy. TRUW:124
Thompson, Charles
"Christian liberty" not a license. THOU 1:543
Thompson, Dorothy
Address, October 29, 1944. BUTA:239; ON:365
Campaign as I see it. -Same as her Address October 29, 1944
Community chest campaign. YE:377
Freedom's back is against the wall. SAR:185
Government by propaganda. GA:142
Hitler's plans for Canada and the United States. COP: 601; COPB:577; HURG: 257
Let's face the facts. BA 1940-41:137
Responds to an introduction at Executive's Club, where she was substituting for Clare Booth Luce. PRNE: 74
Stopping propaganda. BA 1938-39:87
----and others (J. A. Danaher and G. V. Denny, Jr.)
Should the English-speaking democracies unite now? BA 1940-41:209
---- and others (G. P. Nye)
What does the European situation mean to us? BA 1937-38:52

THOMPSON, DOROTHY
Introducing Dorothy Thompson. NI:45; NIA:39
Meloney, Mrs. W. B.
Introducing Dorothy Thompson. GA:13; LY:125
Thompson, Sir John Sparrow
On the death of Alexander Mackenzie. CHAL 14:1; HAZO 24:10531; MAS 24:10531
Question of simple justice. CHAL 14:3; HAZO 24:10533; MAS 24:10533
Thompson, Slason
Ethics of the Press. REEMA 3:1139
Thompson, William, 1st Baron Kelvin. See Kelvin, W. T.
Thomson, John
Jay Treaty with Great Britain. SMI:88
Thomson, Sir Joseph John
Energy and the explosion of the earth. BREW 9:402
Forces which move the world. BREW 9:401
Roentgen rays and other great discoveries. BREW 9:400
Thonssen, Lester
Unrecorded legacy. BA 1958-59:133
Thorndike, Edward Lee
Education for initiative and originality. REEM 6:389; REEMB 7:391
Thorneycroft, Charles Mylton
Speech in British House of Commons, February 28, 1945. GRAC:139
Thornton, Henry Worth
Friendly nations. NESA:118
Over-reaching. REEM sup 3:142; REEMB 5:339
Thornton, William M.
Liberty and slavery in universities. NORR 2d ser:480
Portrait of a lady. SMI:234
Thorpe, Merle
Business of government. NESA:140

THOUGHT AND THINKING
Amidon, J.
Tragedy of incomplete thinking. BRP 6:95; YR 7:223
Arnold, R.
By rote contol. BRP 10:78
Hancher, V. M.
Art of contemplation. BA 1948-49:174; BAAGA:401
Harris, E.
Thoughtlessness of American thought. AN:54
Hill, B. H.
Hercules of the age. BOB:212
Holmes, O. W.
Mechanism in thought and morals. BL:415
Jepson, R. W.
Potted thinking. HOB:69; SAR:26
Ketcham, V. A.
Seven doors to the mind and how to open them. YE:266
Kline, R. E.
What do you think when you think? EXEE:218
Low-brows may be high-brows. FRIE:220
Mollenhoff, C. R.
Need for balanced thinking. ANGC:68
Rivers, D.
Bandwagon minds. NOR 1934:104
Spillman, H. C.
Aristocracy in thinking. ONEC:452
Thinking. CON:69
See also Intellect
Thrall, Harriet M.
Dignity and potency of language. WERN 54:57

THRIFT See Saving and thrift

THRONES See Monarchy
Thurlow, Edward, 1st Baron
Right to commit. EMS 1:211
Treaty-making power. EMS 1:239

Thurman, Allen G.
At the University of Virginia. CHAL 8:437; HAZO 17: 7418; MAS 17:7418
Tilden-Hayes election. BREW 9:403; REEMA 15:1956
Vested rights and the obligations of contracts. BREW 9:408
Thurman, Howard
Good news for the underprivileged. HILK:258
Thurston, John M.
Affairs in Cuba. BRIM:324; CHAL 14:98; CLAY:35; ESEH:221; HARS:244; HAZO 25:10615; LA:152; MAS 25:10615; SHUP:219
Humanity's cause triumphant. FUL:310
Lincoln, a man called of God. HARSO:213; WERN 42:154
Spain's heartless cruelty. FUL:304, 307
Union soldier. BLAA:42; BLAB:42; HARSO:280; REAC:72; WERN 42:112
Thwing, Charles F.
Value of judgment. BLAA:16; BLAB:16
Tibbetts, Roi B.
America's industrial crisis. COUW:211

TIDELANDS OIL See Territorial waters
Tierney, Richard H.
Church and the sex problem. CATA 2:147
Tietgen, Kenneth C.
Call to politics. YR 4:79
Tighe, Matthew F.
Presenting a pair of golden shears to Secretary Hughes. ONEC:49

TILAK, LOKMANYA BAL GANGADHAR
Kher, B. G.
Lokmanya Bal Gangadhar Tilak-a tribute. ZU:45
Tilden, Samuel Jones
Negro suffrage. REEM 10: 246; REEMA 15:1992; REEMB 11:258
On administrative reform. CHAL 8:469; HAZO 18: 7454; MAS 18:7454
Tillett, Charles W.
On the death of Senator Vance. SHUO:180
Tilley, Sir Samuel Leonard
On national policy. CHAL 9: 251; HAZO 18:7835; MAS 18:7835
Tillich, Paul J.
Loneliness and solitude. BA 1957-58:185
"What is truth?" ARNS:182
Tilton, Theodore
Woman. REEM 3:333; REEMA 3:1142; REEMB 3:350
Tinker, Ezra
Diligence and its reward. THOU 2:476

TIRE DEALERS See Business men

TITHES
Wedge of gold. JA:211
Will you be a beggar in heaven? JA:214
Tittle, Ernest Fremont
Learning to speak. HUS:284; MO:424; MOA:428
Prince of Peace. BA 1943-44: 329
Titus-Werner, M. S.
Future of Athana. WERN 54: 140

TOASTMASTERS
Benny, J.
Speech as toastmaster at Friars' Club dinner honoring George Jessel. JEYO: 136
Duties of the toastmaster. BAKS:188
Examples of toastmaster's closing remarks. FRIT: 32, 45
Examples of toastmaster's comment after speeches. FRIT:19, 24, 29, 31

Introduction of program chairman or toastmaster-five examples of. STOC:122; STON:128-131
Jessel, G.
Presenting Louella Parsons at dinner in her honor. JEYO:141
Remarks as toastmaster at Friars' Club dinner to Burns and Allen. JEYO:71
Response to introduction as Toastmaster General at dinner in honor of Mannie Sack, and introduction of principal speaker, David Sarnoff. JEYO:55
Toastmaster's speech at dinner honoring Jack Benny. JEYO:131
Lewis, J. H.
Response to presentation as toastmaster. BRAC:249
Opening remarks. FRIE:293
Opening remarks by toastmaster. FRIT:33
Origin of term "Toastmaster" and original functions of. BRH:23,21
Razz the toastmaster. NAT: 37
Speeches by the toastmaster at the 1936 Rocky Mountain Speech Conference. JUD: 318, 321, 322, 324, 325, 329
Suggestions for the amateur toastmaster. EDGS:XXVII
Suggestions for the M.C. LARW:108
Suggestions for toastmasters and six examples of introductions. MCK:96-100
Toastmaster. SCHS:262
Toastmaster explains purpose of meeting or type of entertainment. FRIT:16
Toastmaster's address at bankers' association. AMEO 2:101
Toastmaster's before and after talk by man who plays golf. FRIT:42
Toastmaster's closing remarks. NAT:45
Toastmaster's comment on limiting time of speeches. FRIT:35
Toastmaster's compliments for those who arranged or served dinner. FRIT:15
Toastmaster's greetings. NATM:34
Toastmaster's greetings. NATS:3
Toastmaster's remarks limiting speeches. FRIT:15
Toastmaster's reply to razz. FRIT:43
Toastmaster's request for keeping order. FRIT:20
Toastmaster's suggestion to speaker to avoid a subject. FRIT:36
Toastmaster's welcome remarks. NAT:19
Toastmistress' duties. BUT: 79; BUTA:79; BUTB:79
See also Announcements; Closing speeches; Emcees; Introductions; Officers, presiding; Opening addresses; Thanks; Welcoming addresses

TOASTMASTERS' CLUB
Toastmasters' Club. NATS: 28

TOASTS
Anniversary toast. FRIT:94
Appropriate toasts and speech thoughts for Christmas. PITT:51-52
At a party-prefacing the toast "Our host and hostess." HILL:483
Birthday toast. FRIT:94
Call of the wild (toast and welcome address to seniors). AB:55
Candland, H.
Toast to our school. JUD: 227
Class day toasts: Philosophy, Religion, Music, Art, Literature, History, Lan-

TOASTS (cont.)
guage, and Science. WERN 54:91
Examples of toasts-by vocation. FRIT:96-101
Examples of toasts for holidays. FRIT:102-103
Examples to toasts to members of family. FRIT:101-102
Examples of toasts to women. FRIT:89, 90, 92
Health of our chairman (for a reunion). EDGS:351
Lane, G.W.
Toast to the United States. REEM 2:139
Lawrence, E. G.
Our country. LA:176
The ladies. LA:172
Leighton of Stretton, F. L.
Toast "The health of Her Majesty's Ministers." REEM 3:175
MacDonald, J.R.
Mystic kinship. REEM sup 2:205; REEMB 2:391
Oh, mister moon-toast given at athletes' banquet. AB:15
Patriotic toasts-five examples of. STOC:133; STON:139-141
Quincy, J., Jr.
Proposing a toast to Mrs. Charles Dickens. REEM 1:402
Remarks on proposing the health of the host at a private party. BARB:51
Simon, J. A.
Toast to 'His Excellency, the American Ambassador." REEM 3:216; REEMB 3:233
Skinner, C. O.
"Bottoms up" (toast to gynecologists). HURG:311
Some A B C directions for making speeches, toasts and responses. PITT:32-36
Speech for a stag party-introducing a toast. BARB:139
Speech on proposing a toast "Our host and hostess" at a dinner party. BARB:163
Staples, A. G.
Toast to the flag. PROS:45
Suggestions for installing Master (Freemason). With example of toast of the initiate. EDW:45
Suggestions for proposing a toast. WRB:165. With examples of. WRA:47-61
Suggestions for proposing a toast for a Deputy of the Assistant Grand Master of a Provincial (Masonic Lodge). With example of. EDW:35
Suggestions for proposing a toast for a Provincial (or District Grand Master of a Masonic Lodge). With example of. EDW:33
Suggestions for proposing a toast of Masonic Charities. With example of. EDW:39
Suggestions for proposing a toast to a lecturer (at a Masonic meeting). With example of. EDW:73
Suggestions for proposing a toast to officers at a Masonic installation. With example of. EDW:57
Suggestions for proposing a toast to the Deputy Grand Master (of a Masonic Lodge). With example of. EDW:31
Suggestions for proposing a toast to "The Ladies" at a Masonic Ladies' Night. With example of. EDW:61
Suggestions for proposing a toast to visitors (to Masonic Lodge). With example of. EDW:51
Suggestions for proposing the (Masonic) Master's toast. With example of. EDW:42
Suggestions for toasts at high school athletic banquet. AB:20-25
Suggestion for toasts on a

Colonial theme for a junior-senior banquet. AB:34
Suggestion for toasts on a French theme for a junior-senior banquet. AB:49-50
Suggestions for toasts for a junior-senior banquet-theme: "Robin Hood." AB 80-84
Telegraphy (toast to a group of telegraph operators). EDGS:170
Testimonial dinner toast. FRIT:94
To the absent ones. NESA: 215
Toast by one leaving a city. THOS:159
Toast "The bride" - three examples of toasts to the bride by the officiating minister or a close friend of the family. WRA:57, 58
Toast "The bride's mother." WRA:59
Toast "The bridesmaids"-two typical toasts. WRA:60, 61
Toast "The health of our chairman." Chairman's reply. BARB:55
Toast "The Ladies." HILL:483
Toast "The Ladies"-at a ladies' night at a club meeting (mixed gathering). WRA: 48
Toast "The ladies"-at annual meeting of any men's club. WRA:49
Toast "The Ladies" -at annual meeting of mixed club (final meeting of any organization to mark close of season). WRA:50
Toast "The Ladies" at ladies' night. WRA:50
Toast "Our dads" at father and son banquet. WRA:56
Toast-"Our fraternity or sorority"-two examples of. STOC:129; STON:135-136
Toast "Our host and hostess." THOS:160
Toast "Our mothers:" Girl guide company entertaining mothers at a mother and daughter banquet. WRA:55
Toast "Our oldest member"-to the oldest member of any club or group. WRA: 52
Toast "Our visitors"-at regular meeting of almost any club. WRA:53
Toast "Prosperity to our sister societies." BARB:62
Toast to a bachelor. FRIT: 95
Toast to a beauty contest winner. FRIT:95
Toast to a champion. FRIT: 93
Toast to a club guest-two examples of. STOC:129; STON:135
Toast to a graduate. FRIT: 94
Toast to a graduating class. STOC:130
Toast to a man of service. FRIT:91
Toast "To a new member"-introduction of a new member to any club. WRA:53
Toast to a retiring employee. FRIT:95
Toast to a retiring officer. FRIT:95
Toast to a sportsman. FRIT: 94
Toast to a successful candidate. FRIT:90
Toast to a teacher. FRIT:90; STOC:131; STON:137
Toast to a team. FRIT:94
Toast to "Alma Mater." STOC: 130; STON:136
Toast to an old graduate. STOC:132; STON:138
Toast to charter member. FRIT:91
Toast to friendship. FRIT:93
Toast to our church. FRIT: 92
Toast to our city. FRIT:94
Toast to our city, by a loyal citizen. EDGS:93

TOASTS (cont.)
Toast to our country. FRIT: 92
Toast to "Our faculty." STOC: 131; STON:137
Toast to our guests-two examples of. FRIT:93
Toast to our host. FRIT:93
Toast to our host and hostess, by a guest, and reply by host. EDGS:262,263
Toast to science (by a layman). EDGS:186
Toast to the alumni. STOC: 131; STON:137
Toast to the "boss" by a faithful employee. EDGS:126
Toast to the bride. FRIT:88
Toast to the graduating class. STON:136
Toast to the ladies. NAT:45
Toast to the ladies. NATS:1
Toast to the "Ladies." THOS: 123,125
Toast to wife on wedding anniversary. FRIT:88
Toastmaster's introduction of the toast: "Dopey" and the toast. SOES:53
Toastmaster's introduction of the toast: "I've searched everywhere" and the toast. SOES:52
Toastmaster's introduction of toast: "Snow White" and the toast. SOES:55
Toastmaster's introduction of the toast: "Who is the fairest of them all," and the toast. SOES:51
Toasts for a Christmas dinner. BARB:205
Toasts for a Thanksgiving festival. BARB:205
Toasts for Thanksgiving. PITT:54
Toasts for the Fourth of July. BARB:206
Toasts for wedding anniversaries. BARB:207-209
Toasts to daughters by fathers. LEHS:53-54
Toasts to daughters by mothers. LEHS:51-53
Toasts to fathers by sons. LEHS:54-57
Toasts to mothers by daughters. LEHS:45-48
Toasts to sons by fathers. LEHS:58-60
Toasts to sons by mothers. LEHS:60
Victory toast to the winning team. DR:280; LU:1255
Walkley, A. B.
Toast to "Drama and Barrie." REEM 1:75; REEMB 1:66
"Wat?" In Dutch?"-toasts for a junior-senior banquet. AB:41
Wedding toast. NI:62; NIA: 197
See also After dinner speeches; Emcees; Introductions; Responses to toasts; Tributes

TOBACCO
For a tobacco trade banquet. BARB:198
See also Smoking
Tobias, Channing H.
Building for tomorrow's better living. HILK:159
Tocqueville, Alexis, de
Feels "A gale of revolution in the air." PE:454; PEA: 454

TODT, FRITZ
Hitler, A.
At the funeral of Reich Minister Dr. Fritz Todt. VO 1942-43:135
Togo, Hashimura
Baseball. WERN 54:170
Togo, Heihachiro, Count
Fallen heroes of Japan. WERN 42:50
Togo, Shigenori
To the Imperial Diet. VO 1941:515
Tojo, Hideki
At opening of 84th Diet. HAN 343; VO 1944-45:45

At opening of Imperial Diet. VO 1942-43:308
Broadcast on the consolidation of the Nation's total effort in the prosecution of the Greater East Asia war. VO 1942-43:410
Broadcast to Japan and the Empire, January 27, 1943. VO 1943-44:16
Broadcast to the Japanese Empire. VO 1942-43:423
Graduation address at Imperial University, Manchukuo. VO 1942-43:506
New Year's address, 1944. VO 1944-45:11
Radio address on the second anniversary of the Greater East Asia war. VO 1943-44:573
Remarks in cabinet meeting July 14, 1942. VO 1942-43:392
Report on war progress and plans. VO 1944-45:215
Speech as war minister to the Japanese Diet, October 26, 1943. VO 1943-44:448
Speech at closing of 84th Diet. VO 1944-45:138
Speech on Japan's total mobilization. VO 1943-44:409
Speech to the Japanese Diet, October 26, 1943. VO 1943-44:442

TOLERATION
Conwill, A.
Hitler wins. NOR 1943:17
Coolidge, C.
Toleration. REEM sup 1:208; REEMB 8:116
Feidler, E.
Intolerant still. YR 1:85
Johnston, E. A.
Intolerance. BA 1944-45:175
McCoy, F.
Shadow slaves. YR 1:105
Manak, J. F.
We sorely need tolerant minds. NOR 1942:47
Owens, J. T.
Intolerance. ASHF:166
Reed, J. B.
Tolerance. BYRA:367; REEM sup 2:318; REEMB 8:338
Tolerance. FRIE:230
Van Baarda, Mme. D.
Road toward international understanding. BUTB:245
Warren, E.
Charles Evans Hughes and the spirit of tolerance (dedication of hall in memory of Hughes). BA 1956-57:135
See also Discrimination; Religious liberty; Teaching, Freedom of

Toll, Henry W. See Gallagher, H., jt. auth.
Tolman, Herbert Cushing
Message of the key. NORR 2d ser:384
Tomlinson, Edward
New South America. EXEE:285
Tone, Theobold Wolfe
On being found guilty. BRYW 6:132; KET:279
Tonsor, Charles A.
Masonic retrospect. THOU 3:64
Tooke, John Horne
On the "Murders at Lexington and Concord." (at his trial for libel). BREW 9:415
Toombs, Robert
"Farewell to the Senate."-Same as his "Let us depart in peace"
"Let us depart in peace." BREW 9:428; BRYW 9:211; CHAL 8:143; CHEM 4:61; HAZO 16:6801; JOHA 2 pt 1:294; LEEW 10:217; MAS 16:6801; PL:661; REEMA 15:2003; SOU 9:312
On secession.-Same as his "Let us depart in peace"
Slavery in the United States; its consistency with Republican institutions, and its

Toombs, Robert (cont.)
effect upon the slave and society. WPRA:158
Territorial acquisition and Civil war. BREW 9:422
Torquatus, Titus Manlius
Against ransoming the prisoners. LEEW 2:116
Torreyson, Virginia
America's post war goals. HOD:103

TOTAL ABSTINENCE. See Temperance

TOTALITARIANISM
Holmes, J.H.
One supreme issue of this hour. BA 1939-40:391
Peters, L.
What is totalitarianism? LINP:69
See also Communism
Touchstone, W.W.
Introduces Dr. Francisco Villagran, Mexican Consul. PR:48

TOURNAMENTS See Debates and debating

TOUSSAINT L'OUVERTURE, PIERRE DOMINIQUE
Phillips, W.
Toussaint L'Ouverture. BAKF:156; CODS:490; CODSA:490; FULB:330; PAR:311; REEM 8:291; REEMA 6:846; REEMB 13:296; SHAH:355
Smith, J.M.
Toussaint L'Ouverture and the Haytian revolution. DUNM:19

TOWN HALL MEETINGS See Cities and towns
Towne, Charles E.
"Lest we forget." FUL:313, 316
Towner, H.J. and Rucker, W.W.
Nomination of opposing candidates for Speaker of the House of Representatives. BRAC:402
Toynbee, Arnold J.
Can we "live and let live?" MOA:457
Continuing effect of the American Revolution. BA 1961-62:95
Fulcrum of western civilization. HAR:77
Russian catfish and western herring. GLAD:279

TOYNBEE, ARNOLD J.
Brorby, M.
Introduces Arnold J. Toynbee, professor, author, and historian of Great Britain. PRNE:39
Tracy, Frederick P.
Pioneer celebration speech. WAGN:29

TRACK See Sports
Tracy, Sterling H.
America and Britain for civilization. ONES:338

TRADE See Business; Commerce

TRADE AND PROFESSIONAL ASSOCIATIONS
Address at a district teachers' association. AMEO 2:169
Humorous speeches for: Automobile Manufacturers p20; Credit Men's Association p90; Dairymen p95; Laundryowners p166; Lumbermen p175; Medical Association p177; Milk Dealers p185; Music Supervisors p188; Ohio Society p200; Piano Dealers p205; Realtors p215; Rubber Association p230; Shoe Dealers p240. SCHS
Naylor, E.H.
Trade Association. REEM 4:330; REEMB 5:193
Need of a Southern association of business college

teachers. AMEO 1:222
Response to invitation to speak by a visiting secretary of a trade association at regular meeting of a similar trade association. WRA: 250
Trade associations. AMEO 2: 181
See also Names of associations, e.g. National Education Association

TRADE UNIONS See Labor Unions

TRAFFIC ACCIDENTS
Hoff, M.C.
Jeepers creepers. BRP 10: 29; NOR 1939:22
Kunzmann, H.E., Jr.
Chance or a policy? BRAP: 85
Magnussen, J.W.
Enough of this. BRP 7:7; YR 8:261
Nason, J.T.
Some people learn the hard way. BRAP:31
Randall, J.W.
Insurance side of highway safety. MO:518; MOA:524
Yurk, C.
Lost: four friends. BERS: 13

TRAFFIC CLUB
Traffic Club. SCHS:265

TRAFFIC OFFICER See Police

TRAFFIC REGULATIONS
Traffic laws (outline of speech). MOA:242
Trail, Elsie
Keep it America. DO:74

TRAITORS See Treason; also Names of traitors, e.g. Arnold, Benedict

TRANSPORTATION See Aeronautics, commercial; Automobiles; Commerce; Communication; Electric railroads; Railroads; Roads; Traffic regulations

TRAVEL
Address to the captain at the end of an ocean voyage, by a passenger. Response by captain. EDGS:349,350
Address to the captain of a steamer at the conclusion of a voyage. Reply by the captain. BARB:148,149
Benton, T.H.
"There is East: there is India." BREW 2:34
Byrd, M.E.
Hobo hobbies. JUD:293
Drummond, R.
Introducing a "See America first" speaker. BRC:47
Erwin, D.
Introducing a hunter or extensive traveler. BRC:266
Hawes, H.B.
Covered wagon. DOA:53
Huber, L.J.
Introducing a traveler. BRC:170
Introducing a speaker on "planning a vacation." WRA: 36
Kaser, A.L.
Introducing a travel agent
" a world traveler. BRC:159,140
McGovern, S.
Introducing a world traveler. BRC:134
Our tourist trade-speech to encourage a new attitude toward the tourist trade at a meeting of Retail merchants' association or Board of trade. WRA:203
Travelogue. SCHS:267
A trip to the north-speech at a club meeting. WRA:186
Weston, P.
Introducing a world traveler. BRC:284
See also Aeronautics, com-

TRAVEL (cont.)
mercial; Automobiles; Berths; Presentation speeches-Trips; Railroads

TREASON
Doenitz, K.
Speech after attempt on Hitler's life. VO 1944-45: 313
Erskine, T.
In defense of Thomas Hardy. BREW 6:40; GOOD: 713
Goebbels, J.
Broadcast describing plot to assassinate Hitler. VO 1944-45:337
Goering, H.
Speech (after attempt on Hitler's life). VO 1944-45: 314
Hitler, A.
Radio speeches after attempt on his life. VO 1944-45:312
Kaufman, I. J.
Sentencing the atomic bomb spies. BA 1951-52:55
Noble, E.
Tito Melema. COUW:109
See also Names of traitors, e.g. Arnold, B.; Burr, A.

TREASURERS See Club speeches; Reports

TREATIES
Ames, F.
Jay Treaty. BREW 1:145; BRYW 8:155; CHAL 4:12; HARS:128; HAZO 8:3268; JOHA 1 pt 1:112; LAD:128; MAS 8:3264; ORAMA 1:269; PL:593; REEMA 11:43; SHAH:55
Barbour, J.
Treaties as supreme laws. BREW 1:220
Butler, H.
For the Bricker Amendment. BA 1953-54:122
Clayton, J. M.
Clayton-Bulwer Treaty and expansion. BREW 4:54
Fleming, D. F.
Irrepressible issue. BA 1943-44:138
Gallatin, A.
On the British Treaty. JOHA 1 pt 1:84
Speech on the British Peace Treaty (terminating War of 1812-1814). CHAL 4:138; HAZO 8:3476; MAS 8:3476
Gladstone, W. E.
Treaty-making power. EMS 1:248
Hennings, T. C., Jr.
Against the Bricker Amendment. BA 1953-54:128
Macdonald, J. A.
On the Treaty of Washington. BREW 8:29
Madison, J.
British Treaty (1796). ORAMA 1:161; REEMA 14: 1404
Thomson, J.
Jay Treaty with Great Britain. SMI:88
Thurlow, E.
Treaty-making power. EMS 1:239
Wilson, W.
Submitting the Peace Treaty to the Senate. BRAC:208
See also Arbitration; Berlin Conference, 1945; Berlin Congress and Treaty of; Indians of North America; Kellog Briand Pact, 1928; Lausanne, Treaty of; Locarno, Pact of, 1925; Moscow Conference of Foreign Ministers, 1945; North Atlantic Treaty Organization; Paris, Treaty of; World War, 1939-1945-Armistices

TREATY OF VERSAILLES, 1919
Knox, P. C.
Against the Treaty of

Paris. BREW 7:219

TREATY OF WASHINGTON See Canada

TREES
Barnes, W.H.L.
Redwoods. WAGN:50
Stubbs, W.R.
Tree our oldest servant. DICD:159; DICE:159
See also Arbor Day

Trester, Leonard M.
Better employee relations are needed. SAB:132

TRIAL BY JURY See Jury

TRIBUTES
Adams, J.Q.
Life and character of Lafayette. BREW 1:72; HAZO 9:3691; MAS 9:3691; PL: 641
Addams, J.
In memory of Henry Lloyd. REEM 5:1; REEMB 9:1
Address of tribute (at testimonial dinner on retirement of public official). BED:29; BEDA:49
Ade, G.
Tribute to Lipton. NESA: 180
Alseth, C.A.
Lion of the north (Gustavus Adolphus). COUW:195
Andrews, M.R.S.
Perfect tribute. PROS:80
Ayers, A.D.
In memory of a pal. NESA: 212
Bagstad, A.
Goethe. COUW:125
Baker, J.H.
Phillips Brooks. BLAA: 277; BLAB:277
Bancroft, G.
William Cullen Bryant. DOA:265; KNAS:96; KNASA: 96; REEM 1:72; REEMA 1:18; REEMB 1:63
Barkley, A.W.
Tribute to President Roosevelt. BA 1944-45:156
Barton, B.
Faith of Lincoln. BA 1939-40:161
Baruch, B.M.
Tribute to Gen. George C. Marshall. SAB:203
Baukhage, H.R.
Tribute to Roosevelt. BA 1944-45:167
Beecher, H.W.
Tribute to Harriet Beecher Stowe. REEMA 1:51
Tribute to Munkacsy. REEMA 1:62
Tribute to our honored dead. LA:173; REAC:78
Belmont, Mrs. A.
Tribute to Katharine Cornell. GA:94
Beveridge, A.J.
Tribute to Marcus A. Hanna. SHUM:274
Birrell, A.
Edmund Burke. BEA:43; BRYW 5:131; CHAL 14:151; HAZO 25:10660; MAS 25: 10660; REEM 5:10; REEMA 4:71; REEMB 9:39
Transmission of Dr. Johnson's personality. REEM 1:119; REEMA 7:87; REEMB 1:116
Birthday tribute. BEDA:31
Birthday tribute and presentation of award. BEDA:29
Bloom, S.
At the home of Mary Ball Washington. DOA:15
Bonaparte, C.J.
Chief Justice Marshall. SHUO:327
Bowers, C.G.
Sword bearer of democracy, (A. Jackson). BOA:243; BOB:150
Bradley, O.N.
Tribute to Ernie Pyle. SABA:285
Brooks, P.
Character of Abraham Lincoln. BREW 2:244;

TRIBUTES (cont.)
CHAL 13:38; HAZO 23: 9905; MAS 23:9905; REEM 5:37; REEMA 7:137; REEMB 9:67
Brown, M.V.
Confessional. YE:99
Buffington, J.
John Marshall, the foundation builder. BOA:245; BOB:153
Byrd, H. F.
80th anniversary of the birth of Senator Glass. YE: 102
Cadman, S. P.
Stonewall Jackson. REEM 5:49; REEMB 9:79
Candler, W. A.
Tribute to Lucious Q. C. Lamar. SHUO:234
Cannon, J. G.
Mark Twain. REEM 5:64; REEMB 9:94
Cap: a testimonial speech. BAI:113
Cecil of Chelwood, E. A. R.
Great example (Taft). LINM:240
Choate, J. H.
Tribute of Lord Houghton. REEMA 1:152
Tribute to General Miles. REEMA 1:193
Unveiling the statue of Rufus Choate. BLAA:262; BLAB:262; CHAL 12:56; HAZO 22:9461; KLEG:172; MAS 22:9461
Churchill, W. L. S.
Humanity's loss. BA 1944-45:170; VO 1945-46:154
Tribute to Neville Chamberlain. HIBS:290
Tribute to the late Duke of Kent. VO 1942-43:502
Clark, C.
Frank P. Blair. SHUO:208
Tribute to Uncle Joe Cannon. HOA:358
Collyer, R.
Tribute to Edwin Booth. REEM 1:329; REEMA 1: 266; REEMB 1:330
Cousins, R. G.
Tribute to the Maine victims. FUL:84
Cox, S. S.
Stephen A. Douglas and his place in history. BREW 4: 216
Crawford, F. M.
Pope Leo XIII. REEM 5: 85; REEMA 4:339; REEMB 9:115
Crowther, J. E.
Oliver Cromwell. COUW: 133
Curtis, G.W.
James Russell Lowell. REEM 5:93; REEMA 7:255; REEMB 9:124
Sir Philip Sidney. REEMA 4:357
Davis, J.W.
George Washington. REEM 1:363; REEMB 1:364
DeMorgenstierne, W. M.
Tribute to America. BOA: 309
Depew, C. M.
George Frisbie Hoar. ONES:176
To Premier Briand. REEM 1:396; REEMB 1:397
Washington and Lincoln. BOB:148
Dewey, O.
Genius of Demosthenes. BREW 5:198
Dickens, C.
Tribute to Washington Irving. REEMA 1:394
Dill, C. C.
Thomas Jefferson, the architect of Americanism. BOA:226; BOB:139
Dirksen, E.
At 44th anniversary of Congressional service of Speaker Sam Rayburn. BRAP:137
Dolliver, J. P.
Robert Emmet (114th anniversary of the birth of Robert Emmet). ONES:142;

REEM 5:140; REEMA 7: 363; REEMB 9:174
Douglas, P.H.
Five great Americans. BA 1951-52:85
Dumas, A.
Tribute to his father (on occasion of taking his seat in the French Academy). DUNM:95
Eaton, C. A.
Thomas A. Edison. BOA: 229; BOB:141
Emerson, R.W.
Memory of Burns. BEA: 179; COP:613; COPB:653; HAZO 14:5994; HURG:106; KNAS:104; KNASA:104; MAS 14:5994; ONEM:467; REEM 2:24; REEMA 2:439; REEMB 2:24
Evarts, W.M.
Tribute to Herbert Spencer. KLEM:113; REEMA 2:462
Farrar, F.W.
Phillip Brooks. KNAS:70; KNASA:70
Fess, S.D.
Putnam festival. CORP: 266
Foch, F.
To the French Academy (tribute to the French soldier). REEM 11:422; REEMB 12:445
Ford, S.
Me and Sir Henry. REEMA 2:505
Ford, T. L.
Tribute to William McKinley. WAGN:371
Fox, C.J.
Character of the Duke of Bedford. BREW 6:154
Gilbert, C.
Sir Christopher Wren. REEM sup 1:359; REEMB 6:148
Gildersleeve, B. L.
Daniel Coit Gilman. KNAS: 88; KNASA:88
Givens, W.E.
Tributes to James William Crabtree. YE:98
Goff, N.
Abraham Lincoln-the man of God. BOA:237; BOB: 145
Gore, A.
At 44th anniversary of Congressional service of Speaker Sam Rayburn. BRAP:136
Gorgias.
Encomium on Helen. CHAL 1:12; HAZO 1:49; MAS 1:49; PL:32
Greeting and welcome (at ceremony honoring retiring secretary of labor union). BED:80; BEDA:153
Grosvenor, G.
Byrd; the explorer and the man. DOA:72
Hall, G.S.
William McKinley. BLAB: 150
Harding, W.G.
At the grave of the unknown soldier. BLAB:321; BREW 6:368; PROS:7; SHU:36
Hart, A.S.
Theodore Roosevelt. BOA: 231; BOB:142
Hay, J.
Tribute to McKinley. BRYW 10:220; CHAL 13:223; ONEM:427; REEM 5:208; REEMA 13:1149; REEMB 9:244; WERN 42:164
Hickman, L.E.
Ideal American (Theodore Roosevelt). SHUP:225
Hoar, G.F.
Daniel Webster. BLAA:75; BLAB:75; KNAS:109; KNASA:109
Hock, H.
Lincoln. YE:104
Hogg, J.S.
President (Theodore) Roosevelt. SHUO:65
Holmes, O.W.
Dorothy Q. COP:662; COPB:662; HURG:139;

TRIBUTES (cont.)
REEM 2:220; REEMA 2: 627; REEMB 2:225
Longfellow. KNAS:58; KNASA:58
Tribute to Paul Morphy. CHAL 7:394; HAZO 15: 6291; MAS 15:6291
Holmes, O.W., Jr.
John Marshall. BLAA:110; BLAB:110
Honoring past matrons and past patrons: five examples of. MORA:50-51
Howe, J.W.
Tribute to Oliver Wendell Holmes. COP:618; COPB: 658; REEMA 2:645; REEMB 2:240
Hubbard, W.R.
Wendell Phillips. COUW:93
Hughes, C.E.
Speech of introduction at the celebration of the eightieth birthday of Elihu Root. KLEB:127; LINM:253
Hunt, F.
Story of ex-Justice Holmes. DOA:120
Story of Jane Addams. DOA: 112
Ingalls, J.J.
Tribute to the universal beneficence of grass. SHUP:155
Ingersoll, R.G.
At his brother's grave. BAAMP:177; BEA:285; BRAC:400; BREW 7:128; BRYW 10:81; CHAL 12:188; COP:324; COPA:324; COPB:324; HARSO:241; HAZO 22:9584; HOAP:269; HURG:156; IMMD:162; KLEG:384; LA:136; MAS 22:9584; ONEM:466; PE: 619; PEA:619; PL:689; REEM 10:282; REEMB 11: 294; SHAH:470
Shakespeare. BREW 7:133; HARSO:265; REEM 8:237; REEMA 5:627; REEMB 13: 241; SHU:136
Ishii, K.
Tribute to Washington. LEW:151
James A. Garfield, a tribute from the Sons of Temperance. THOU 3:495
Jessel, G.
To the Ladies of Hadassah. JEYO:146
Johnson, L.B.
At 44th anniversary of Congressional service of Speaker Sam Rayburn. BRAP:136
Remarks to a Joint Session of the Congress, November 27, 1963. BA 1963-64:37
Kahn, O.H.
Edward Henry Harriman. REEM 5:240; REEMB 9: 279
Kbir, H.
Rabindranath Tagore. ZU: 66
Keating, E.
Courage of Woodrow Wilson. HARSO:38
Kher, B.G.
Lokmanya Bal Gangadhar Tilak-a tribute. ZU:45
Laurier, W.
Character and work of Gladstone. BREW 7:296; ONES:167
On the death of Queen Victoria. BRYW 5:192; CHAL 13:381; HAZO 24:10446; LAD:197; MAS 24:10446; REEM 5:267; REEMB 9: 306
Lemieux, R.
Tribute to Laurier. NESA: 160; REEM 5:276; REEMB 9:315
Littleton, M.W.
Robert E. Lee (Hall of Fame, New York University). BLAB:290; BOA: 222; BOB:151; LINM:80
Longfellow, H.W.
Washington Irving. KNAS: 55; KNASA:55; REEMA 8: 786

Lord, J.
Oliver Cromwell. REEMA 5:787
Lowry, H. F.
"A Christmas Carol" at Wooster. YE:96
Ludlow, L.
Charles A. Lindbergh. BOA:224
Macaulay, T. B.
Tribute to the Jews. PE: 431
M'Clurg, M.
Tribute to President Mc-Kinley. SHUO:70
Macdonald, J. R.
Tribute to Queen Alexandra. YE:103
MacDonald, T.
Eagle of Golgotha (Billy Mitchell). AN:21
McFarland, W. H.
Benjamin Watkins Leigh. SMI:141
McKelway, St. C.
Tribute to Mark Twain. REEMA 2:811
McKinley, W.
Characteristics of Washington (at unveiling of Washington statue). KLEM:187; ONES:162; REEMA 9:845
MacLeish, A.
Tribute to Wendell Willkie. BA 1944-45:186
Mansfield, M.
At 44th anniversary of Congressional service for Speaker Sam Rayburn. BRAP:136
Mason, M. C. B.
Lincoln, the man of the hour. WOON:541
Memorial tributes on the death of General Clinton B. Fisk by A. R. Temple, A. E. Ballard, E. H. Clapp, and General Rusling. THOU 3:495
Miles, L. E.
Michael Angelo. COUW:149
Mill, J. S.
Tribute to Garrison. HAZO 15:6183; MAS 15:6183
Norvell, G.
Joan of Arc. COUW:165
Oxford and Asquith, H. H. A.
Alfred Lyttleton. REEM 5:6; REEMB 9:35
Lord Kitchener. REEM 5:7; REEMB 9:36
Parnell, C. S.
Parnell national tribute. KET:406
Past presidents' day. FRIE: 73
Pater, W.
Raphael. REEMA 9:940
Pershing. SCHS:202
Pinchot, G.
Theodore Roosevelt. BLAB: 325
Pupin, M.
In honor of Marconi. REEM 3:116; REEMB 3:117
Reed, T. B.
At the dinner to Joseph H. Choate. REEM 3:136; REEMB 3:137
Roosevelt, F. D.
Undelivered Jefferson Day address. CROC:392; VO 1945-46:147
Roosevelt, T.
William McKinley (tribute). ONES:173
Rosebery, A. P. P.
Oration on Robert Burns (delivered before tomb at Dumfries, Scotland). ORBR 2:409
Rowell, A. B.
Robert Burns. COUW:57
Salmon, L. M.
Susan B. Anthony. KNAS: 100; KNASA:100
Schultz, E.
David Gaskill. MO:536
Schurz, C.
General Sherman. KLEM: 147; ONES:164; REEM 5: 344; REEMA 9:1026; REEMB 9:386; RINM:93
Schwab, C. M.
Andrew Carnegie-his methods with men. REEM 5:

TRIBUTES (cont.)
247; REEMB 9:389
Serviss, G. P.
Napoleon Bonaparte. REEMA 6:983
Seward, W.H.
Tribute to John Quincy Adams. KNAS:85; KNASA: 85
Sheil, B.J.
Tribute to Roosevelt. BA 1944-45:165
Sherwood, I.R.
Tribute to Uncle Joe Cannon. HOA:359
Shoeler, M.
America' mother of men. YR 9:285
Shortridge, S.M.
Abraham Lincoln. BOA: 248; BOB:154
Shurter, E.D.
Potency of Roosevelt's spirit. SHU:16
Slocum, W.
Wondersmith and the world (Edison). BRP 4:27; INTW 1933:57; YR 5:333
Spring, G.
Tribute to New England, 1820. BRAR 1:9
Stanley, A. P.
Palmerston and the duty of England (funeral oration). BREW 9:274; ORBR 2:349
Stanley-Hall, G.
William McKinley. BLAA: 150; BLAB:150
Stedman, E.C.
Appreciating Whitelaw Reid. NESA:166
Tribute to Richard Henry Stoddard. REEMA 3:1085
Stevenson, A.E.
Tribute to John F. Kennedy at the General Assembly of the United Nations. BA 1963-64:31
Suggestions for preparation of speeches of tribute. With examples of. MO:526; MOA:532; MICS:165; SAB: 200,203; SABA:279; YE:89
Tanner, B. F.
Robert Burns. COUW:141
Taylor, B.
Tribute to Goethe. REEMA 3:1136
Taylor, H.J.
Integrity! a mighty force (tribute to Otto Schnering, head of Curtiss Candy Company). LARW:110
Terrell, A.
Tribute to James S. Hogg. SHUO:67
Thackeray, W.M.
Swift. REEMA 6:1091
Thomas, A.
Honoring Secretary Mellon. NESA:176
Tribute at a testimonial to a woman civic leader. BEDA: 42
Tribute (at physician-of-the-year award). BED:50; BEDA:53
Tribute by contrast. NI:277
Tribute by contrast (34th anniversary of a sanitarium). NIA:208
Tribute to a career woman. FRIT:89
Tribute to a humanitarian. FRIT:91
Tribute to guest of honor. NAT:46
Tribute (to labor union official at testimonial ceremony). BED:83; BEDA: 156
Tribute to newly elected mayor (at his installation). BEDA:115
Tribute to our air mail pilots. ED:160
Tribute to retiring official-examples of. BEB:64-67; BEC:132
Tribute (to retiring secretary of labor union). BED:80; BEDA:154
Tribute to the boss at the annual office banquet. DR:19; LU:1124

Tribute to the fine arts. ED: 276
Tribute to the ladies. NAT: 34
Tribute to the outgoing club chairman. DR:97; LU:1165
Tribute to women. FRIE:328
Tributes to Franklin Delano Roosevelt. BA 1944-45: 156-157
Tributes to installed officers. BEC:117
Tributes to installed official-six examples of. BEB:62-64
Tributes to scientist (at presentation of citation to scientist). BEDA:59
Tributes to "Uncle Joe" Cannon. HOAP:273
Trinkle, E.L.
Woodrow Wilson. BOA:240; BOB:147
Vandenberg, A.H.
Tribute to Senator Barkley. BA 1948-49:96
Vest, G.G.
Man's best friend-his dog. BOU:176; COP:650; COPB: 677; GRIS:21; HURG:161; SHU:201
Viviani, R.R.
Their monuments in our hearts. LEW:109
Tribute to Lincoln. LEW: 121
Walker, J.J.
Tribute to Robert E. Lee. SHU:107
Wallace, H.A.
Lincoln's Day address. VO 1944-45:90
Warren, E.
Charles Evans Hughes and the spirit of tolerance (dedication of hall in memory of Hughes). BA 1956-57:135
Tribute to John F. Kennedy delivered in the Rotunda of the Capitol. BA 1963-64: 33; HIB:21
White, T.
Life and character of Sir Wilfrid Laurier. KLEB:21
Whitfield, A.H.
Tribute to the women of the South (at dedication of Mississippi's new Capitol). SHUO:36
Wiley, A.
Brief remarks at conclusion of Senator Vandenberg's report on the United Nations Assembly. BA 1945-46:46
Wilkins, R.
Tribute to John F. Kennedy delivered at City Hall Plaza in New York City. BA 1963-64:34
Williams, J.S.
A giant among men (J. Davis). BOA:234
Winter, W.
Tribute to John Gilbert. REEM 3:418; REEMA 3: 1257; REEMB 3:425
Tribute to Lester Wallack. REEMA 3:1260
Wise, S.S.
Abraham Lincoln, man and American. COP:349; COPA: 349, COPB:349, HURG:109, LINM:87; REEM 5:409; REEMB 9:454
Woodrow Wilson. BLAB: 375
Woodrum, C.
Inserting the Baukhage tribute on Franklin Delano Roosevelt in the Congressional Record. BA 1944-45:165
See also Acceptance speeches; Comemorative addresses; Eulogies; Memorial speeches; Presentation speeches; Responses to tributes; Testimonials
Trine, Ralph Waldo
Man's true self. WERN 42: 190
Trinkle, E. Lee
Woodrow Wilson. BOA:240; BOB:147

Trinkle, E. L. (cont.)
Custodians of glory. LINM: 344

TRIPARTITE PACT
Matsuoka, Y.
Reply to Ribbentrop. VO 1941:144
Ribbentrop, J.
Greetings to Matsuoka. VO 1941:143

TRIPPE, JUAN T.
Presents Vannevar Bush. LY: 175
Troeger, Walter F.
Union made in Heaven. ACW: 62

TROPHIES See Acceptance speeches-Trophies; Presentation speeches-Trophies
Trotsky, Leon
To the Red Army. COP:140; COPA:140; COPB:140; PE:717; PEA:717; REEM 11:178; REEMB 12:192
Troup, C. V.
Two kinds of vision. HILK: 155
Trueblood, D. Elton
Herbert Clark Hoover. BA 1964-65:108
Truman, Harry S.
Address at final plenary session of United Nations Conference on International Organization. FIP:265; VO 1945-46:300
Address to Congress, April 16, 1945. BA 1944-45:156; HAN:320; VO 1945-46:148
Address to Congress on universal military training. VO 1945-46:652
Address to opening session of United Nations Conference on International Organization at San Francisco. HAN:433; VO 1945-46: 161
Aid to Greece and Turkey. BA 1946-47:43; GRAC:149
Announcement of Japanese acceptance of Potsdam Declaration. VO 1945-46:434
Announcement of the first use of the atomic bomb. FIP: 269; VO 1945-46:405
At dedication of Gilbertsville Dam. VO 1945-46:631
Broadcast on Japanese surrender. HAN:362; VO 1945-46:520
Broadcast on surrender of Germany. -Same as his VE day proclamation
Broadcast on wages and prices. VO 1945-46:665
Broadcast to the armed forces of the United States upon his assumption of office. VO 1945-46:152
Civil Rights, February 2, 1948. FIP:285
Democratic Party. BA 1949-50:117
"Doctor" Dewey and the Republican record. FIP:291
Emergency program for national preparedness. BA 1947-48:129
ERP: The Marshall Plan, December 19, 1947. FIP: 280
Fair Deal in retrospect, January 7, 1953. FIP:317
Farewell to the nation. BA 1952-53:101; WPRC:305
First address to nation. - Same as his Address to Congress, April 16, 1945
Hiroshima, August 6, 1945- Same as his Announcement of the first use of the atomic bomb
Inaugural address. BA 1948-49:27; CHI:277; COPB: 589; FIP:298; LOTI:251; USIN:251; USINA:251
Korea, July 19, 1950. FIP: 308
Korean crisis. -Same as his Preventing a new world war
MacArthur, April 11, 1951. -

Same as his Preventing a new war
McCarthyism, November 1, 1952. FIP:315
Madison Square Garden address. BA 1948-49:110
Message to Congress, September 6, 1945. VO 1945-46:546
Message to Congress asking emergency unemployment compensation legislation. VO 1945-46:219
Message to Congress on a national health program. VO 1945-46:724
Message to Congress on driving for victory against Japan. VO 1945-46:237
Message to Congress on labor legislation. VO 1945-46:756
Message to Congress on Presidential succession. VO 1945-46:293
Message to Congress on the atomic bomb. VO 1945-46:613
Message to Congress recommending Army-Navy merger. VO 1945-46:769
National emergency. BA 1950-51:94
Navy Day speech on foreign policy. VO 1945-46:659
Powers of the President. COPB:592; HURG:316
Presents Winston Churchill. LY:195
Preventing a new world war. BARR:291; FIP:311; HAR:140
Principles of the Democratic Party. BA 1958-59:105
Proclaims VJ day. -Same as his Broadcast on Japanese surrender
Railroad strike emergency. BA 1945-46:196
Ratify the charter. ON:139
"Red herrings." FIP:303
Report to the nation on the Potsdam Conference. VO 1945-46:424
Should the Taft-Hartley Labor Bill become law? BA 1946-47:190
Slandermongers and the Bill of Rights. BA 1951-52:65
Speech at American flag raising exercises in Berlin. VO 1945-46:388
Speech at Chicago Library luncheon, July 10, 1956. BRAP:39
Speech on world cooperation at Pemiscot county fair. VO 1945-46:625
Speech to his neighbors in Independence, Mo. VO 1945-46:346
Spirit of peace. GLAD:233
State of the Union (1950). BA 1949-50:28
State of the Union (1952). HAR:95
Statement and directive on displaced persons. VO 1945-46:777
Statement on labor policy. VO 1945-46:458
Statement on Palestine. VO 1945-46:713
Statement on U.S. policy toward China. VO 1945-46:767
Statement to Congress on reorganizing the government. VO 1945-46:217
Truman Doctrine. BRE:384; FIP:275
U.N.R.R.A. message to Congress. VO 1945-46:715
Valedictory. -Same as his Farewell to the nation
VE Day proclamation. BA 1944-45:37; HAN:308; VO 1945-46:191

TRUMAN, HARRY S.
Thomas, L.
Election of Truman. BA 1948-49:134
Webb, W. P.
Speech that was never made (introduction of Harry

TRUMAN, HARRY S. (cont.)
S. Truman intended for Mississippi Valley Historical Association meeting). GRIS:51

TRUMAN DOCTRINE See Reconstruction, 1939-1951
Trumbull, Lyman
Announcing the death of Douglas. BREW 9:436

TRUSTS, INDUSTRIAL
Battle, K.D.
Democracy and the trust. SHUC:254
Foraker, J.B.
Trusts. BLAA:19; BLAB:19
Goss, B.C.
Trial outside the courtroom. LINP:250
Harlan, J.M.
Northern Securities Company v. United States, 1904: Opinion for the Supreme Court. BIR 3:275
Knox, P.C.
Commerce clause of the Constitution and the trusts. BLAA:270; BLAB:270
Roosevelt, T.
First annual message to Congress. BIR 3:245; FO:252
On trusts, August 25, 1902. FIP:35
Trusts and tariff. REEMA 15:1776
Taft, W.H.
Antitrust: 'Mere size is no sin." FIP:85
White, E.D.
Standard Oil Company of New Jersey v. United States, 1911: opinion for the Supreme Court. BIR 3:295
See also Capitalism; Competition; Corporations; Monopolies

TRUTHFULNESS AND FALSEHOOD
Compton, A.H.
Truth makes us free. BART 1:327
Dod, A.B.
Value of truth. BREW 5:263
Hardin, M.
Truth about lies. JUD:307
Kaser, A.L.
Emcee at a liars' club meeting. BRH:300
Liars. NAT:22
McArthur, H.K.
Truth and freedom. BA 1950-51:182
Morley of Blackburn, J.M.
Golden art of truth telling. BREW 8:206
Pritchett, H.S.
What is truth? BLAA:255; BLAB:255
Scoville, D.C.
Truth and victory. SHU:196
Searching for the truth. NATT:16
Symington, W.S.
Truth makes us free. BA 1952-53:42
Tillich, P.J.
'What is truth?" ARNS:182
True or false. NATM:47
Watson, T.E.
Truth, in its relation to individuals, professions, laws and institutions. SOU 9:454
See also Honesty
Tsouderos, Emmanuel
Message to the Greeks, June 5, 1941. VO 1941:243
Tucker, Howard E.
Depression versus youth. JUD:235
Tucker, John Randolph
Virginia jurists. SMI:220
Tucker, William J.
Man's soul and his world (sermon at a Sunday evening service in college chapel). ONEM:775
New movement in humanity.

BLAA:23; BLAB:23
Welcome to "The Wheelock of succession." ONEM:678; ONES:18
Tufts, James Hayden
Present significance of scholarship. NORR 2d ser:265
Tugwell, Rexford Guy
For a third term. BA 1938-39:166

TULOSS, REES EDGAR
Weaver, C.I.
Introduces Dr. Rees Edgar Tuloss. PR:64

TUMBLING See Actors and acting

TUNISIA
De Gaulle, C.
Address in Tunis on the anniversary of the liberation of Tunisia. VO 1944-45:201

TUNNEY, GENE
Introducing Gene Tunney. SUM:99
Tupper, Sir Charles
In favor of a protective policy. CHAL 10:74; HAZO 19:8222; MAS 19:8222
National measure (in granting land to Canadian Pacific Railway). HAZO 19:8232; MAS 19:8232

TURENE, HENRI
Fléchier, E.
Death of Turene. BREW 6:146; HAZO 4:1629; LEEW 4:245; MAS 4:1629; PL:255

TURKEY
Kemal Atatürk, M.
Speech before the Republican Party. PL:788
Pepper, C.D.
Against aid to Greece and Turkey. BA 1946-47:67
Truman, H.S.
Aid to Greece and Turkey. BA 1946-47:43; GRAC:149
Vandenberg, A.H.
For aid to Greece and Turkey. BA 1946-47:51
Ward, H.F.
Turk must go. TRUW:75
Turner, Farron
What price war? BRP:1:67
Turner, Frederick Jackson
Contributions of the West to American democracy. FKA:72; SHU:88
Turner, Jack
Tragedy of ninety-eight cents. BRP 9:14; YR 10:217
Turner, Patricia Ann
Constitution-temple of liberty. BU:162
Turner, Robert G.
Young America on parade. BRP 8:38; YR 9:51
Turrill, Charles B.
Foundations of California. CATA 1:163
Memorial Day address at Calvary Cemetery, San Francisco. CATA 1:32

TUSKEGEE INSTITUTE
Franklin, J.H.
Booker T. Washington, the man and the education (Tuskegee Institute Founder's Day speech). HILK:212
Twain, Mark See Clemens, Samuel L.

TWENTIETH CENTURY
Barss, R.
Great stampede (1918-193?). BOA:200; YR 6:55
Browne, L. and others.
Has twentieth century civilization improved mankind? BA 1947-48:188
Churchill, W.L.S.
United we stand secure. BA 1948-49:35; HAR:3
Dangerous age. FRIE:243
Erdman, W.
True greatness of the

TWENTIETH CENTURY (cont.)
twentieth century. SHUC: 373
Houghton, Mrs. H. C.
Today's challenge. BUT: 250
Kaltenborn, H. V. and others.
How can we secure peace in a hydrogen bomb world? BA 1949-50:101
Mid-century. NATT:43
Rice, G. P.
Scholar and the twentieth century. BA 1949-50:220
Stahr, E. J., Jr.
Challenge of the critical century. YE:196
World today. NATT:29
Twentieth Century Club. SCHS:269

Twichell, Joseph Hopkins
Soldier stamp. REEMA 3:1153
Yankee notions. REEM 3:339; REEMA 3:1147; REEMB 3: 355

Tyler, Chaplin
Industry and you: the field for college graduates. SAR:397

Tyler, Don
Constitution. LEIO:116

Tyler, Frederick
Sovereign alchemist. NOR 1948:139

Tyler, John
Adams and Jefferson. SMI: 104
American liberty. SMI:129
Educational needs of Virginia. SMI:95

TYLER, JOHN
Clay, H.
Noblest public virtue. HAZO 10:4099; MAS 10: 4099
Gordon, A. C.
John Tyler. SMI:134

Tyndale, William
Use and abuse of images and relics. BREW 10:15

Tyndall, John
Art and science. REEM 3: 345; REEMA 3:1160; REEMB 3:361
Democracy and higher intellect. BREW 10:23
Origin of life. BREW 10:19

TYPEWRITER
Larger significance of the invention of the typewriter. SPIM:239
Under the red seal: speech delivered before Remington Typewriter managers. SPIM:127

TYRANNY
Fox, C. J.
On the East India Bill. BREW 6:164; BRYW 4:32; GOOD:462; PEA:171; PL: 418
Penn, W.
Golden rule against tyranny. BREW 8:299

U. N. N. R. R. A. See United Nations Relief and Rehabilitation Administration

Udall, Stewart L.
Conservation: physical and spiritual. ANGC:59

Udine, Prince of
To the House of Representatives. LEW:129

UKRAINE See Communism-Ukraine

Umbach, Herbert H.
Abiding peace. ACW:113

UNDERGROUND MOVEMENTS
Eisenhower, D. D.
Instructions to the underground resistance movements of Europe. VO 1944-45:219

UNDERTAKERS
Huber, L. J.
Undertaker emcee. BRH: 344

Underwood, Oscar W.
Liberty and freedom of in-

itiative. BREW 10:28
War finance corporation. BREW 10:27

UNEMPLOYED
Conant, J. B.
Social dynamite in our large cities: unemployed, out-of-school youth. HIB: 324
Greenwell, E.
Tramp! Tramp! Tramp! YR 9:41
Lee, J. B.
Technological unemployment and relief. BA 1938-39:108; ON:107,200
McCormick, J.
Human wreckage. YR 9:21
McDonald, D. J.
Plan for prosperity. BA 1960-61:156
Martin, M.
Character in the shadow. YR 7:93
Miller, C. A.
Man out of employment. WERN 42:42
O'Hare, E.
Men and tomorrow. BRP 8:109; YR 9:31
Rashbaum, P.
Challenge of the unemployed. BRP 3:7; YR 3:161
Rieber, P.
Them doll faces. BRP 6: 25; YR 7:13
Turner, R. G.
Young America on parade. BRP 8:38; YR 9:51
Willkie, W.
Why are you unemployed? BA 1939-40:306
Young, W. A.
Society and the pay roll. BRP 1:63; YR 2:141
See also Insurance, Unemployment

UNION CLUB
Choate, J. H.
Argument in equity for the plaintiff in the Union Club case. HICJ:1

UNIONS, TRADE See Labor unions

UNITARIANISM
Clarke, J. F.
Why am I a Unitarian? CHAL 8:70; HAZO 16:6686; MAS 16:6686

UNITED ANCIENT ORDER OF DRUIDS See Druids, United Ancient Order of

UNITED ENGINEERING AND FOUNDRY COMPANY
Beard, G. G.
United Engineering and Foundry Company. SABA: 192

UNITED NATIONS
Acheson, D.
United Nations and Soviet aggression. BA 1950-51: 25
Anderson, M.
Committee IV, on the report of the Trustee Council. HILK:222
Aranha, O.
New order through the United Nations. COPB:621
Attlee, C. R.
Speech in Commons on the United Nations charter. VO 1945-46:479
Austin, W. R.
Policies of the United Nations. BA 1946-47:13
United Nations and Korea. BA 1950-51:13
Byrnes, J. F.
Common interests of the United Nations. BA 1945-46:39
General Assembly a great forum. GLAD:173
Churchill, W. L. S.
Sinews of peace (speech at Fulton, Missouri). BA 1945-46:20; COPB:614;

UNITED NATIONS (cont.)
GRAC:144; HIB:298; PE: 803; PEA:803
Dedicating United Nations tree (at United Nations anniversary ceremony). BEDA 125
Eisenhower, D.D.
Address at the United Nations, September 22, 1960. BA 1960-61:55
Hammarskjold, D.
No right to resign. BOU: 183
Herter, C.A.
Peaceful change. BA 1959-60:51
Hoover, H.C.
United Nations. HURG:287
Introducing program chairman (at United Nations anniversary ceremony). BEDA:124
Jackson, H.M.
United States in the United Nations: an independent audit. BA 1961-62:55
Kennedy, J.F.
Addresses the General Assembly of the United Nations for the second and last time, September 22, 1963. PEA:840
Peace through the United Nations. HIB:344
Lie, T.
Road to peace. HAR:61
Lodge, H.C., Jr.
United Nations. HURG:344
United Nations and world opinion. BA 1954-55:43
What the United Nations means to the United States. MOA:517
Mendès-France, P.
Search for international cooperation. COPB:623
Opening speech at United Nations anniversary ceremony. BEDA:122
Roosevelt, E.A.
United Nations. HURG:297
United Nations as a bridge. COPB:640
Roosevelt, F.D.
Statement on the anniversary of the Declaration by the United Nations. VO 1944-45:4
Stettinius, E.R., Jr.
Before the Senate Foreign Relations Committee on the United Nations charter. VO 1945-46:378
Stevenson, A.E.
United Nations: past and present. HIB:237
Truman, H.S.
Ratify the charter. ON:139
Vandenberg, A.H.
United Nations Assembly: a report. BA 1945-46:45
See also Human Rights Day and Week

UNITED NATIONS CONFERENCE ON FOOD AND AGRICULTURE, 1943
Roosevelt, F.D.
Address to the delegates to the United Nations Food Conference. VO 1943-44: 228

UNITED NATIONS CONFERENCE ON INTERNATIONAL ORGANIZATION, SAN FRANCISCO, 1945
Connally, T.
Report to the Senate on the San Francisco Conference. VO 1945-46:348
Eden, A.
Job to be done. BA 1944-45: 76; VO 1945-46:174
Gromyko, A.A.
Address at final plenary session of United Nations Conference on International Organization. VO 1945-46:307
Halifax, E.F.L.W.
Address at final session of United Nations Conference on International Organization. VO 1945-46:306
Koo, V.K.W.

Address at final plenary session of United Nations Conference on International Organization. VO 1945-46: 305
Molotov, V.M.
Address at first plenary session of San Francisco Conference. HAN:437; VO 1945-46:170
Speech opposing admission of Argentina to the San Francisco Conference. VO 1945-46:185
Smuts, J.C.
At the final plenary session of the San Francisco Conference. HAN:440
Soong, T.V.
Address at first plenary session of San Francisco Conference. VO 1945-46: 169
Stettinius, E.R., Jr.
Address at final plenary session of United Nations Conference on International Organization. VO 1945-46:304
Address at opening of San Francisco Conference. VO 1945-46:163
Radio report to the American people on the San Francisco Conference. VO 1945-46:222
Statement on representation of the proposed United Nations Organization. VO 1945-46:137
United Nations Security Conference. BA 1944-45: 68; VO 1945-46:165
Truman, H.S.
Address at final plenary session of United Nations Conference on International Organization. FIP:265; VO 1945-46:300
Address to opening session of International Organization at San Francisco. HAN:433; VO 1945-46:161
Vandenberg, A.H.
Report to the Senate on the San Francisco Conference. ON:123; VO 1945-46:358

UNITED NATIONS MONETARY AND FINANCIAL CONFERENCE
Morgenthau, H.
Final address at the United Nations Monetary and Financial Conference at Bretton Woods. VO 1944-45:316
Opening the United Nations Monetary and Financial Conference at Bretton Woods, N.H. VO 1944-45: 291
Roosevelt, F.D.
Message to Congress on Bretton Woods money and banking proposals. VO 1945-46:57

UNITED NATIONS RELIEF AND REHABILITATION ADMINISTRATION
Lehman, H.
Speech as director general of NNRRA. HAN:382
Roosevelt, F.D.
Broadcast to the nation on the setting up of UNRRA. FIP:252; VO 1943-44:536
Message to Congress recommending appropriations for the work of the UNRRA. VO 1943-44:543
Truman, H.S.
UNRRA message to Congress. VO 1945-46:715
Welles, S.
Toward new horizons. HAN:370

UNITED ORDER OF AMERICANS
Address before the United Order of Americans. AMEO 2:56

UNITED STATES
Abbott, L.
Nation's greatness. BOB: 121
Abrams, M. M.
Guardians of the light. NOR 1940:21
Albert Honore Charles Grimaldi, Prince of Monaco
Two months in the United States. REEM 2:418; REEMB 2:434
Alexander, R.
Which way America? BA 1948-49:145
America and her future. AMEO 1:224
America-land of opportunity. DR:193; LU:1225
America-land of promise and fulfillment. DR:196
America, twenty years hence: a high school oration. AMEO 1:205
American leadership. DR:197; LU:1228
Anderson, F.
I discover America (by a Nazi). AN:45
Appleby, P. H. and others.
Complexity of America (Round Table discussion). MOA:627
Barksdale, L. S.
Meaning of America. BOA: 318
Berrien, J. M.
Effect of the Mexican conquest. BREW 2:44
Beveridge, A. J.
Republic that never retreats. CHAL 14:449; COP:336; COPA:336; COPB:336; FUL:31; HAZO 25:11002; MAS 25:11002; REEM 1:116; REEMA 1:70; REEMB 1:111
Blakely, R. J.
Greatest lack. BA 1945-46: 241
Bonaparte, C. J.
Our national dangers, real and unreal. HICF:196
Boutwell, G. S.
On the progress of American independence. CHAL 9:223; HAZO 18:7769; MAS 18:7769
Boynton, N.
Homeland. PROS:73; SHU: 209
Bradley, P.
Romance of life. BART 1: 63
Brownlow, W. G.
Value of the American union. BREW 2:290
Bryan, W. J.
America's mission. BOB: 209; FUL:48; ONEM:598; ONES:196; REEM 1:161; REEMA 1:94; REEMB 1: 158; SHUP:193
Bryce, J. B.
Changes of forty years in America. REEM 1:172; REEMB 1:168
Calhoun, J. C.
On internal improvement, 1817. HELE:174
Carpenter, M. H.
On the mission and future of the United States (dedication of Memorial Hall, Beloit College). CHAL 10: 414; HAZO 21:8767; MAS 21:8767
Chaplin, R.
Our responsibility to America. ON:51
Cheever, G. B.
Elements of national greatness, 1842. BRAR 1:287
Choate, R.
On American nationality (82nd anniversay of American independence). CHAL 6:318; HAZO 13:5493; MAS 13:5493
Clark, C.
National growth. REEM 1: 279; REEMB 1:280
Clay, C. M.
America as a moral force. BREW 3:387
Aspirations for the Union.

BREW 3:386
Clay, H.
In favor of a paternal policy of internal improvements. BREW 4:43; HAZO 10:4083; MAS 10:4083
Clayton, J. M.
Clayton-Bulwer Treaty and expansion. BREW 4:54
Cline, E. W.
Spirit of the past. BOA: 213
Cobb, I. S.
Our country. REEM 1:318; REEMB 1:319
Cobden, R.
Small states and great achievements. BREW 4:113
Columbus Day-America after 450 years. DR:167; LU: 1202
Conant, J. B.
America's fitness to survive. YE:253
National philosophy. BA 1948-49:165
Davis, E.
Are we worth saving? BA 1953-54:96
DeMorgenstierne, W. M.
Tribute to America. BOA: 309
Depew, C. M.
America's new era. FUL: 116
Our national safeguards. BLAA:143; BLAB:143
Devan, S. A.
Growth of the United States as a world-power. SHUC: 309
Dilke, C. W.
America. BREW 5:248
Dow, L., Jr.
Improvement in America. BREW 5:306
Drummond, R.
Introducing a "See America first" speaker. BRC:47
Drury, S. S.
My country. PROS:133
Durant, W.
Crisis in American civilization. BA 1939-40:208
Dyke, H. G.
Negative America. YR 2: 29
Edward VIII.
Recollections of America. REEM sup 1:18; REEMB 1:23
Elson, E. L. R.
Nation under God. BA 1957-58:163
Emerson, R. W.
Young American. PL:644
Evarts, W. M.
Republic and its outlook. REEMA 2:452
Farrar, F. W.
Farewell thoughts on America. REEMA 5:395
Fish, H.
Have faith in America. BOB:96
Flowers, M.
Have faith in America. EXEE:621
Friedrich, C. J.
What America means to me. HOC:103
Fulbright, J. W.
Present-day American life: its order of values, and its sense of direction. BA 1958-59:127
Future demands of American manhood. AMEO 2:111
Future of the nation-response to a toast. DAVC:419
Graves, J. T.
Second discovery of America. BART 2:191
Guérard, A. L.
Land where hatred expires. HARSO:93
Guggenheim, C.
Heart disease. NOR 1948: 115
Hadduck, C. B.
Elements of national greatness, 1841. BRAR 1:261
Halstead, M.
Our new country. REEM 2: 152; REEMA 2:584; REEMB 2:154

Handlin, I.
United we stand. DO:39
Harcourt, W.
Good will to America. HAZO 21:9034; KLEM:65; MAS 21:9034
Harding, W. G.
"It is our purpose to prosper America first." FIP: 143
United States-independent and sovereign. BREW 6: 366
Harrison, B.
Union of states. REEM 2: 167; REEMA 2:589; REEMB 2:169
Haskell, H. J.
What of America? BOA: 274; BOB:23
Hedges, J. E.
Last word. REEMB 2:205
Helm, W.
America I want to know. BART 1:295
Herbon, E., Jr.
America-upward and onward. DO:3
Hesseltine, W. B.
Four American traditions. TIN:413
Historical spots in the United States. AMEO 1:210
Hodge, F. S.
Is America safe? ASHF:58
Hoover, H. C.
Meaning of America (at homecoming in West Branch Iowa). BA 1948-49:89; YE:286
Hutchins, R. M. and others.
America and the atomic age. HAR:19
Ikeguchi, J.
Promised land. AN:58
Ingersoll, C. J.
Influence of America on the mind. BL:17
Ingersoll, R. G.
America's coming greatness. REAC:173
Ireland, J.
Just war is holy. FUL: 167, 170
Irving, W.
"My native land." KNAS: 185; KNASA:185; REEM 2:272; REEMA 8:736; REEMB 2:276
James, H., Sr.
Social significance of our institutions. BL:231
Jefferson, C. E.
Temptation from the mountain top. FUL:174, 178
Johnson, L. B.
State of the Union Message, January 8, 1964. FIP:409
Jones, J. L.
Who is tampering with the soul of America? LINP: 219
Kennan, G. F.
Liberal arts in contemporary American society. BA 1953-54:171
Kirk, G.
Historic perspective and current issues. BA 1952-53:151
United States and the world. ANGC:218
Knapp, F.
America first. BOA:66
Koch, R.
Between yesterday and tomorrow. NOR 1946:47
Lane, F. K.
American spirit incarnate. SHU:166

What is America? PROS: 118
Lewis, J. L.
Who are the Americans today? BA 1953-54:150
Lilienthal, D. E.
Bases of our nation's strength. HOA:159
Spirit of democracy. BA 1948-49:65
Lowell, J. R.
National growth of a century. REEM 2:354; REEMA 2:741; REEMB 2:367
Lumpkin, J. H.

Where to, America? YR 5: 323
MacArthur, D.
Our national goals. ANGC: 208
McCartney, C.E.
National apostasy. BOA: 61; BOB:88; HARSO:233; SHU:66; TRUW:130
McKeldin, T.
Have faith in America. MCK:228
McKinley, W.
Country reunited. WERN 42:133
Our country. REEMA 2: 815
MacVeagh, F.
Nation's heroism. FUL:232
Marshall, T.R.
National power and the national peace policy (on public land sales, 1841). BREW 8:100
Meaning of America. BOB: 114
Muehl, E.W.
Empires within. NOR 1940: 27
Mundt, K.E.
What's right with America? MIA:394
Murray, M.J.
America is worth fighting for. DO:133
My country 'tis of thee. NATS:15
Nixon, R.M.
Opening of the American National Exhibition in Moscow. SABA:209
Our country: response to a welcome address. THOS: 49
Outline of a response to the toast "Our country." PITT: 41
Owsley, A.
America in 1940. BART 2:169
Oxford and Asquith, H.H.A.
Tribute to America. LEW: 79
Parker, A.B.
Our heritage. REEM 3: 42; REEMB 3:43
Parker, T.
State of the nation (1850). CHAL 8:108; CROC:345; HAZO 16:6732; MAS 16: 6732
Pennington, G.
Return, America. ONES: 367
Pflum, J.F.
Why I am glad I am an American. BOA:321
Pollock, C.
I am a reactionary. BART 1:239
Wake up, America! BART 2:27
Pollock, E.
Great American myth. NOR 1948:127
Rader, W.
Uncle Sam: or, The reign of the common people. WAGN:170
Randolph, J.
On internal improvements. PE:332; PEA:332
Reed, T.B.
On national issues. CHAL 13:316; HAZO 24:10305; MAS 24:10305
Reid, W.
Continental Union-Civil Service for the islands. HICF:212
Ritchie, A.C.
Which way America? SAR: 139
Rodiger, W.
Outward bound. NOR 1944: 41
Roosevelt, T.
Foundations of progress. RID:98
Russo, E.
America as I find it. BART 1:41
Schoenbrun, D.
An orange. HOA:402
Schurz, C.
True Americanism.

UNITED STATES (cont.)
BOAM:11; BRE:236; REEMA 9:1018
Seaborg, G. T.
United States in the space age. ANGC:124
Shuler, B., Jr.
Nation out of balance. YR 9:89
Shulman, C. E.
America at the crossroads. BART 3:75
Smith, T. V.
Forward America. BA 1938-39:119
Sockman, R. W.
This nation under God. BA 1942-43:267
Sokolsky, G. E.
American way of life. BART 1:269
Soul of America-God. THOT: 114
Sovereignty of the United States (response to a toast). DAVC:411
Sprague, L. W.
Undiscovered America. BOA:188; BOB:169; SHU: 192
Stanley, A. P.
America visited. REEM 3: 259; REEMA 3:1073; REEMB 3:276
Stiles, E.
On the future glory of the United States. HAZO 5: 2041; MAS 5:2041
Storrs, R. S.
Puritan scheme of national growth, 1857. BRAR 2:327
Stout, J. P.
Material wealth of Uncle Sam. REAC:191
Straus, O. S.
Growth of American prestige. REEM 3:279; REEMB 3:296
Taft, R. A.
Forward America. BA 1938-39:130; BRYA:534
Talmage, T. D.
Behold the American. COP: 646; KLEG:160; REEMA 3:1122; REEMB 3:324; THOU 1:339
Taylor, L.
Americans for America. BOA:313; BOB:91; PROS: 83
Thomas, D.
Visit to America. COPB: 638
Thurman, A. G.
At the University of Virginia. CHAL 8:437; HAZO 17:7418; MAS 17:7418
Torreyson, V.
America's post war goals. HOD:103
Trail, E.
Keep it America. DO:74
Truman, H. S.
State of the Union (1950). BA 1949-50:28
State of the Union (1952). HAR:95
Upham, C. W.
Spirit of the day and its lessons, 1846. BRAR 1:417
Wallace, H. A.
Address at Detroit, July 25, 1943. VO 1943-44:280
Webster, D.
Our country. REAC:102
What America means to me. NATM:6
White, W. A.
Your young men shall see visions. SAR:1
Wilson, O. M.
United States and the changing world. ANGC:145
Wilson, W.
Mission of America. SHU: 212
"Too proud to fight" speech. BRAS:298; FIP: 106; FKA:178
Wise, S. S.
Conscience of the nation. REEM 3:423; REEMB 3: 430
Wishard, G. P.
United States and universal peace. TRUW:216

Zekaria, H.
Flight from Bagdad. BRP 8:98; YR 9:119
See also Liberty; New England; Northern states; Southern states; West; Western Hemisphere

---- AIR FORCE
Symington, W.S.
Our Air force policy. YE: 228
See also Aeronatucis; Aeronautics, military; World war 1939-1945-Aerial operations

---- ARMY
Bayard, T.F.
On the United States Army. CHAL 11:182; HAZO 21: 9037; MAS 21:9037; REEMA 11:134
Calhoun, J.C.
Increase of the Army. ORAMA 1:443
Cousins, R.G.
Regular Army. FUL:90
Dawson, W.L.
Segregation in the Armed forces. HAR:469
Eisenhower, D.D.
Quality of America's fighting men. BA 1944-45:114; HAN:312; VO 1945-46:288
Fleetwood, C.A.
Negro as a soldier. DUNM:187
Marshall, G.C.
National military strength. BA 1945-46:85
Roosevelt, F.D.
Statement on "Army Day." VO 1942-43:203
Roosevelt, T.
Brownsville incident. FIP: 54
Sherman, W.T.
Army and Navy (December 22, 1875 speech). CHAL 10: 1; HAZO 19:8115; MAS 19: 8115
Army and Navy (December 21, 1880 speech). REEM 3:206; REEMA 3:1046; REEMB 3:223
Slayden, J.L.
Against the enlistment of Negro soldiers. SHUO:262
Spirit of '76 and '77 (77th Division U.S. Army). NI: 222; NIA:170
Steward, T.G.
Army as a trained force. DUNM:277
Stimson, H.L.
Broadcast March 9, 1943. VO 1943-44:98
Truman, H.S.
Address to Congress on universal military training. VO 1945-46:652
Message to Congress recommending Army-Navy merger. VO 1945-46:769
Wheeler, J.
American soldier. SHUO: 243; REEM 3:375; REEMA 3:1220; REEMB 3:391
Woodruff, W.F.
Negroes in the United States Army. SHUC:109
See also Army; Conscription; Demobilization; Recruiting; Soldiers-Suffrage; Veterans

---- COMMISSION ON ORGANIZATION OF THE EXECUTIVE BRANCH OF THE GOVERNMENT
Knight, H.W.
Challenge of the Hoover report. MIA:411

---- CONGRESS
Eckert, R.W.
They are not mind readers. AN:17
Hughes, C.E.
150th anniversary of the First Congress. BA 1938-39:161; COP:431; COPA: 431; COPB:424; HURG: 237
Jepson, S.

UNITED STATES-CONGRESS (cont.)
Can our democracy survive our Congress? NOR 1943: 23
Kaser, A. L.
Introducing a Congressman. BRC:133
Kirsten, K.
Introducing a Senator or Congressman. BRC:156
Long, J. D.
Response to toast at National Druggists' Association. HOA:375; HOAP:262
McKelway, B. M.
Welcoming the members of Congress to Washington. SAB:210
Marshall, J.
Marbury v. Madison: opinion for the Supreme Court. BIR 1:259; BRE:116
Menard, J. W.
Negro's first speech in Congress: in defense of his election to Congress when his seat was contested and won by his political opponent. WOON:263
Roberts, R.
Introducing a Congressman. BRC:147
Roosevelt, F. D.
Budget message, January 8, 1941. VO 1941:15
Budget message to Congress, January 13, 1944. VO 1944-45:29
Expanding frontiers of social progress. SAR:305
Message to Congress, January 4, 1939. SAR:119
Message to Congress on the state of the nation, January 6, 1945. VO 1945-46:5
Smith, M. C.
Political conscience. BA 1950-51:124; BUT:243
Truman, H. S.
Address to Congress, April 16, 1945. BA 1944-45: 156; HAN:320; VO 1945-46:148
Message to Congress, September 6, 1945. VO 1945-46:546
Wilson, W.
"Little group of willful men." FIP:120
Yasinow, H. S.
Shield of irresponsibility. NOR 1950:193
For annual addresses of various Presidents see Names of Presidents e.g. Roosevelt, F. D.

---- ---- HOUSE OF REPRESENTATIVES
Hess, L. F.
Power of the Speaker of the House of Representatives. SHUC:242
Rayburn, S.
Accepting the office of Speaker of the United States House of Representatives. SAB:219

---- ---- SENATE
Bacon, A. O.
Case of Senator Reed Smoot. SHUO:129
Breckenridge, J. C.
Address preceding removal from Senate. CHAL 10:93; HAZO 19:8239; MAS 19: 8239; REEMA 11:296
Bruce, B. K.
Address delivered to the United States Senate in behalf of admitting P. B. S. Pinchback as Senator from the State of Louisiana. WOON:267
Depew, C. M.
Senatorial forecast. REEMA 1:380
Flanders, R. E.
Colossal innocence in the United States Senate. WPRC:301
Gallinger, J. H.
"Shell-shock" in the Senate.

BREW 6:187
Marshall, T. R.
Farewell to the United States Senate. BRAC:271; REEM 7:277; REEMB 8:290
Pershing, J. J.
To the United States Senate. REEM 11:420; REEMB 12:442
Webster, D.
Basis of the Senate. WPRA:54

---- CONSTITUTION
Adams, F. L.
Present significance of the Constitution. BOA:85; BOB:73
Adams, J. P.
Webster's defense of the Constitution. TRUW:7
Adams, J. Q.
Jubilee of the Constitution (50th). BREW 1:74; HAZO 9:3698; MAS 9:3698; REEM 10:68; REEMA 11:8; REEMB 11:69
Anthony, S. B.
For the Woman Suffrage Amendment. WPRA:318
Ashton, De W. C.
Citadel of freedom. BLUE:115
Bailey, J. W.
Constitutional convention. SHU:32
Republic of our fathers. SHU:146
Barkley, A. W.
Preserving the Constitution. BOA:99
Bearman, G. F.
Lincoln and the Constitution. LEIO:90
Black, H. L.
Bill of Rights. LINP:126
Blair, F. P.
On the 15th Amendment. BREW 2:121
Boone, L.
The Constitution-wherein lies its greatness. BOB:72
Braxton, A. C.
Fifteenth Amendment (response to toast). SHUO:266
Brown, E. K.
Marsh of the Constitution. TRUW:150
Brown, J. E.
Against the Woman Suffrage Amentment. WPRA:333
Burke, E. R.
How long will the American Republic last? HOC:28; SAR:200
Burton, L. J.
Rights we fight for. DO:145
Bylund, H.
Lincoln and the Constitution. LEIO:87
Byrnes, J. F.
South respects the written Constitution. ARNS:144
Carlson, D.
What the Constitution should mean to an American citizen. PROS:22
Casey, J. P.
Impending disaster. BRP 2:98
Christianson, T.
Our Constitution. BOA:96
Cleary, T. P.
Constitution. LEIO:97
Cockran, W. B.
Marshal and the Constitution. SHUM:280

Our Constitutional system. REEMA 1:232
Constitution in our every day life. DR:205
Corbin, F.
Answering Patrick Henry. BREW 4:166
Dallam, J. M.
Constitution. LEIO:122
Davis, R.
Youth and the Constitution. DO:224
Dawson, J.
Adoption of the Constitution. SMI:65

UNITED STATES-CONSTITUTION (cont.)
DeArmond, D. A.
For a Constitutional Convention. SHUO:254
DeLarge, R. C.
Speech on the enforcement of the Fourteenth Amendment. WOON:293
Dinsmore, H. A.
South and the Constitution. SHUO:109
Douglas, W. O.
John Peter Altgeld and the Bill of Rights. BA 1947-48: 207
Doyle, E. D.
Constitution. YR 2:127
Sacred trust. BRP 2:82
Draper, A. S.
March of the Constitution. BLAA:61; BLAB:61
Drum, T. B.
Constitution. LEIO:140
Dutter, P.
Is the Constitution ours? DO:217
Dyer, G. W.
Constitution and the present day problems. EXEE:531
Edmunds, G. F.
Constitution and the Electoral Commission. BREW 5:344
Ellsworth, O.
Union and coercion. BREW 5:365
Ferguson, D. F.
Upon this rock. DO:180
Franklin, B.
Dangers of a salaried bureaucracy. BREW 6:171; BRYW 8:56; CHAL 2:256; HAZO 5:1849; MAS 5:1849
Disapproving and accepting the Constitution. BOU:44; BREW 6:169; BRYW 8:53; CHAL 2:254; COP:236; COPA:236; COPB:236; HAZO 5:1847; HURG:34; MAS 5:1847; PE:194; PEA: 194; PL:580
Funk, B.
Constitution: a guide to the world of tomorrow. DO: 230
Gallatin, A.
Constitutional liberty and executive despotism. BREW 6:181
Glatfelter, P.
Abraham Lincoln and the Constitution. LEIO:114
Graham, A. V.
Constitution. LEIO:143
Granik, T.
Introductory remarks as radio moderator at celebration of 150th anniversary of Bill of Rights. BA 1941-42:96
Graper, E. E.
True defenders of liberty. BOA:125
Graves, A. L.
Constitution. LEIO:109
Gullion, E.
John Marshall and Federal supremacy. DOA:106
Hamilton, A.
Coercion of the delinquent states. BREW 6:325; FULB:189
On Section VIII of the Constitution. CHEM 1:261; CROC:225
On the Federal Constitution, June 20, 1788. CHEM 1:235; HARS:104; SHAH:34
On the Federal Constitution, June 24, 1788. BRYW 8:132; CHAL 4:2; CHEM 1:249; COP:242; COPB: 242; FULB:189; HAZO 8: 3254; HELE:85; HURG:35; JOHA 1 pt 1:39; LAD:81; LEEW 8:201; MAS 8:3254; ORAMA 1:253; PE:201; PEA:201; PL:586; REEM 10:21; REEMA 13:1117; REEMB 11:22
Hancock, J.
Moving the adoption of the Federal Constitution. BREW 6:353

Hardin, A.
Jefferson and the Constitution. LEIO:91
Henry, P.
Against the Federal Constitution (June 5, 1788). BAAMP:32; BIR 1:136; BREW 7:28; BRYW 8:67; CHAL 3:46; CLAW:7; HARS:67; HAZO 6:2613; MAS 6:2613; ORAMA 1:63; WPRA:7

Bill of Rights, June 14, 1788. BREW 7:24; CHAL 3:40; HAZO 6:2607; MAS 6:2607
Fears the strength of the proposed Constitution. PE:197; PEA:197
June 4 speech in the Virginia Ratifying Convention. BIR 1:133; CHEM 1:123; LEEW 8:121; ORAMA:61
June 24 speech in the Virginia Convention. BIR 1:148
A Nation-not a Federation, June 14, 1788 (on eighth section of Federal Constitution). BREW 7:20; CHAL 3:35; HAZO 6:2602; MAS 6:2602
'We, the people" or 'We, the states." BREW 7:18; CHAL 3:32; HAZO 6:2599; KLEG:132,344; MAS 6:2599; SMI:41; SOU 9:175
Henson, L.
Protectors of freedom. DO:172
Hoffman, A.
Our Constitution and peace. DO:98
Holmes, O.W., Jr.
Schenck v. United States: opinion for the Supreme Court. BRE:320; BREA:300
Hoover, H.C.
Bill of Rights. COP:419; COPA:419; COPB:421; HURG:229
Horton, J.
American opportunities. DO:13
Jensen, G.
For this we fight. DO:103
Kelly, T.F.
Lincoln and the Constitution. LEIO:137
King, R.
For federal government by the people. BREW 7:193
Knox, P.C.
Commerce clause of the Constitution and the trusts. BLAA:270; BLAB:270
Krasne, P.N.
Cornerstone of American liberty. LEIO:145
Kroloff, M.N.
Constitution. LEIO:104
Langston, J.M.
Equality before the law (anniversary of adoption of the Fifteenth Amendment). WOON:436
Lansing, A.
Answering Alexander Hamilton. BREW 7:271
Larson, A.
Constitution and American youth. BRP 2:35; YR 2:69
Lenarducci, D.
Guarantee of freedom. DO:197
Lilio, R.L.
American Constitution-for this we fight. DO:104
Lincoln, A.
First joint debate at Ottawa, August 21, 1858. BRYW 9:227; CLAW:63; FULB:291; HARS:323; HAZO 16:6586; MAS 16:6586
Livingston, R.R.
Wealth and poverty, aristocracy and Republicanism. BREW 7:361
Longnecker, F.M.
Constitution. LEIO:106
Lovejoy, O.R.
Twentieth Amendment (affirmative). ONEC:311,341

UNITED STATES-CONSTITUTION (cont.)
McBurney, J.H. and others.
Alexander Hamilton: his contribution to constitutional government. BA 1956-57:149
McElmeel, E.F.
John Marshall and the Constitution. LEIO:101
Madison, J.
On the expediency of adopting the Constitution. CHEM 1:199; HARS:89; JOHA 1 pt 1:53

Shall the states take precedence over the central government? CLAW:75
State sovereignty and federal supremacy. BAAMP: 37; BREW 8:61; CHAL 3: 366; CHEM 1:219; CLAW: 19; COP:237; COPA:237; COPB:237; HAZO 7:3020; HURG:40; MAS 7:3020; SMI:55; WPRA:23
Mangum, R.J.
Freedoms of the United States Constitution. DO: 212
Marshall, E.
Hamilton and the Constitution. TRUW:170
Marshall, J.
Barron v. Baltimore: opinion for the Supreme Court. BRE:158; BREA:142
Justice and the Federal Constitution. BREW 8:86; BRYW 8:143; CHAL 3:463; COP:240; COPA:240; COPB:240; HAZO 8:3222; MAS 8:3222; ORAMA 1:215; REEM 10:10; REEMA 14: 1440; REEMB 11:10; SMI: 58
McCulloch v. Maryland: opinion for the Supreme Court. BIR 2:2; BRE: 128; BREA:119
Martin, L.
Is the government federal or national? BREW 8:105
Portion of the report of the proceedings of the General Convention held at Philadelphia in 1787. SOU 9:179
Mason, G.
Adoption of the Constitution. SMI:44
Natural propensity of rulers to oppress. BREW 8:110
Meyer, E.
Constitution. LEIO:135
Miller, M.E.
Rights we defend. DO:114
Monroe, J.
Federal experiments in history. SMI:62
Moore, J.O.
Common man. DO:67
Morse, W.L.
Constitutional liberalism and the Democratic Party. BA 1956-57:93
Mullarky, J.A.
Constitution. LEIO:94
Mullens, C.J., Jr.
Living Constitution. DO: 202
Murphy, C.T.
Constitution. LEIO:131
Newburn, R.
Constitution of the United States. LEIO:119
Ostroot, P.
Our living Constitution. DO:167
Oxman, S.A.
List. BU:154
Padget, F., Jr.
Citizen's appreciation. BRP 10:7
Palmer, A.M.
Amending the Constitution. BOA:92
Pendelton, E.
Adoption of the Constitution. SMI:47
Liberty and government in America. BREW 8:293
Pettee, H.F., Jr.
Constitutional guarantees to all American citizens.

YR 2:95
Pinckney, C.
Plan for a Federal Constitution. HAZO 8:3315; MAS 8:3315; ORAMA 1:305
Posey, M.
America's contribution to constitutional government. LEIO:85
Randolph, E.
Federal Constitution. CHEM 1:161; LEEW 8:161; SMI:51
Randolph, J.
Tariff and the Constitution (1816). PL:599
Roosevelt, F.D.
Bill of Rights address. HAN:104; VO 1941:622
Message to Congress, January 11, 1944. BA 1943-44: 15; VO 1944-45:21
Our Constitution. BOA:103
Root, E.
Invisible government: Short Ballot Amendment. BIR: 4:12; HICF:444; ONEM: 306
Rudolph, W.C.
For democracy we fight. DO:125
Sabine, J.E.
American youth and the Constitution. YR 2:111
Sessions, R., Jr.
Constitution. LEIO:99; SHU:54
Smith, A.P.
American Constiution. DO: 207
Smith, B.
American Constitution-for this we fight. DO:54
Smith, J.
On the Federal Constitution. ARNS:266
Souter, L.K.
Our Constitution. BLUE: 46; BRP 1:7
Stansell, G.
Constitution. LEIO:111
Stier, B.
Bulwark of democracy. YR 10:105
Tarrant, J.G.
John Marshall and the Constitution. LEIO:147
Thomas, C.S.
Twentieth Amendment (negative). ONEC:321
Trail, E.
Keep it America. DO:74
Truman, H.S.
Slandermongers and the Bill of Rights. BA 1951-52: 65
Turner, P.A.
Constitution-temple of liberty. BU:162
Tyler, D.
Constitution. LEIO:116
Underwood, O.W.
Liberty and the freedom of initiative. BREW 10:28
Vandenberg, A.H.
Threatened Constitution. BOA:88
Walker, J.
Be loyal America-your Constitution lives. DO:192
Webster, D.
Constitution and the Union (December 23, 1850 speech). JOHA 1 pt 2:161; REEM 3: 365; REEMA 3:1210; REEMB 3:381
Constitution not a compact between sovereign states. HAZO 11:4493; MAS 11: 4493; WPRA:133
Wenig, H.E.
The Constitution. DOA:100; LEIO:67
Williams, M.H.
Constitution. BRP 1:34
Wilson, J.
For the Federal Constitution. HARS:54
Wright, D.J.
For this we die. DO:188
See also Bill of Rights Day; Prohibition; State rights
Also Names of Bills and Resolutions e.g. Foot's Resolution

UNITED STATES-DECLARATION OF INDEPENDENCE
Declaration of Independence. SCHS:99
Evarts, W.M.
What the age owes to America. CHAL 9:238; HAZO 18:7784; MAS 18: 7784; REEMA 13:962; REEMB 8:144; THOU 1:225
Graves, E.L.
Bible of democracy. SHU: 57
Hughes, C.E.
Maintaining the Declaration of Independence. SHU:120
Lincoln, A.
Independence Hall speech, February 2, 1861. CARP: 149; CHEM 4:157; SHUP: 156
Lippard, G.
Signing the Declaration. PROS:62
Signers of the Declaration. THOU 1:226
Unknown speaker. BOB:126
Wilson, W.
Meaning of the Declaration of Independence. BAKS: BOAM:109; ONEM:554; ONES:129
See also Fourth of July

---- DEFENSES
Acheson, D.
Deterring the aggressor. MIA:350
Baruch, B.
Full economic mobilization. BA 1950-51:83
Bradley, O.N.
Long range military policy. BA 1949-50:66
Bush, V.
Defense of the free world. HAR:54
Business in wartime. DR:34
Carmichael, J.H.
Air transporation-our second line of defense. SAB: 180
Clark, C.
Rearmament. BA 1938-39: 71
Clark, M.W.
Mobilizing and training a citizen army. HAR:265
Conant, J.B.
Present danger. HAR:256
Eisenhower, D.D.
Science and national security. BA 1957-58:20
State of the Union (January 9, 1958). BA 1957-58:65
Green, W.
Labor, freedom, and democracy. BA 1940-41:243
Harriman, W.A.
Mobilizing America's strength for world security. HAR:245
Hildebrand, J.H.
Are we educating for national strength? BA 1940-41:271
Hoover, H.C.
National defense. BA 1939-40:126
Johnson, F.L.
Battleship bubble. BRP 7: 13
Johnson, L.A.
National defense. BA 1949-50:85
Kennedy, J.F.
Address to the nation, October 22, 1962. BA 1962-63:7; FIP:388
Undelivered Dallas speech. FIP:402
Lanham, C.T.
Moral core of military strength. HAR:249
Lilienthal, D.E.
Bases of our nation's strength. HOA:159
Lindbergh, C.A.
Our air defense. BA 1940-41:75
Murray, P.
Equality in sacrifice. BA 1950-51:109
Nye, G.P., Jr.
For an adequate defense. BA 1938-39:65

Porter, H.
Citizen soldier. REEMA 3: 924
Ridenour, L. N.
Science, technology and national security. HAR:312
Roosevelt, F. D.
National defense. BA 1939-40:117; HIB:227
Republican leadership and national defense. BA 1940-41:124
State of emergency exists. BA 1940-41:57; VO 1941: 219
Sims, W. S.
Criticism and preparedness (Washington birthday address). REEM 7:345; REEMB 8:380
Sloan, A. P., Jr.
Economic aspects of American defense. COP:438; COPA:438
Smyth, H. D.
Scientific manpower. HAR: 317
Symington, W. S.
Freedom and military security. BA 1949-50:75
Our air force policy. YE: 228
Time for action. BA 1957-58:32
Thomas, N.
America's duty in time of crisis. BA 1939-40:275
Truman, H. S.
Emergency program for national preparedness. BA 1947-48:129
National emergency. BA 1950-51:94
Wilson, C. E.
Mobilizing for defense. HAR:281
Wilson, W.
Shadow lengthens: Preparedness. FIP:108
Wood, L.
National preparedness. REEM 7:427; REEMB 8: 440

---- ECONOMIC CONDITIONS
Ackerman, C. W.
Role of the press as a factor in public opinion and economic changes. BA 1937-38:198
Amos, M. B.
October. YR 3:29
Arlt, T.
Plea for action. YR 5:115
Berle, A. A., Jr.
Irrepressible issues of the 60s. ARNS:165
Bernard, W.
Crumbling pillars. YR 5: 129
Brown, L.
Private agencies and public goals in the post-war world. BA 1942-43:202
Chafee, Z., Jr.
Deluge is after us. NORR 3rd ser:28
Chester, C. M.
Management's new responsibility in our changing social economy. BA 1939-40: 293
Coleman, G.
Golden age lies onward. YR 5:81
Dalton, C.
Crisis in American economics. SHUC:220
Dewey, T. E.
Campaign speech in Buffalo. VO 1944-45:524
Opening campaign speech in Philadelphia. VO 1944-45:407
Disalle, M. and others.
How can we stop rising prices? HAR:285
Doran, H. J.
Eyes that see not. BRP 2: 54; YR 3:45
Douglas, H. G.
Cost of living and inflation. BA 1947-48:118
Douglas, P. H. and others.
Is America's economic frontier closed? HOB:262
Duncan, P.

UNITED STATES-ECONOMIC CONDITIONS (cont.)
Planners. BRP 3:39; YR 4:3
Earle, G. H.
New frontiers. BOA:415
Ellis, M.
Our goal. DO:18
Fairless, B.
What kind of America? BA 1953-54:131
Fay, C.
Way of life. BRP 6:42; NOR 1934:113
Griffin, L.
Walls of happiness. BRP 7:43
Harding, W. G.
Speech at Boston, May 14, 1920. BIR 4:53
Hoover, H. C.
Combating the depression. FRY:106
Hoven, A.
New lamps for old. BOA: 420; YR 5:41
Humes, B. A.
On trial. BRP 4:87
Johnson, H. S.
Depression and the President. COP:418; COPA:418
Kirby, J. H.
Re-Americanize America. BOA:397
LeVander, T.
Curse of plenty. YR 3:145
Linner, C.
Up from the balogney age. BRP 5:86
Maloney, H. S.
Prospects good. BRP 2:40; YR 3:81
Moore, D.
Depose king selfishness. BRP 3:66; YR 4:307
Morgan, N.
When men decay. YR 10: 175
Munsey, F. A.
Problems of the hour (1922). REEM 4:320; REEMB 5:178
Nixon, R. M.
Prosperity and the economic health of the nation. BA 1956-57:74
Olson, W.
Merry-go-round has stopped. INTW 1933:52; YR 5:263
Patrick, H. A.
Challenge of chaos. YR 5: 105
Peterson, C. D.
Then Hitler came. BRP 10:41; NOR 1939:34
Ravely, M.
New deal-a new day. BRP 5:48; YR 6:315
Richberg, D. R.
Current problems of industrial recovery. KLEB:107
Ritzman, C. H.
Eternal growth. YR 5:29
Rockefeller, N. A.
Jobs and prosperity. BA 1962-63:17
Roosevelt, F. D.
Address to the Commonwealth Club, September 23, 1932. WPRC:146
Broadcast to the nation, September 7, 1942. VO 1942-43:479
Campaign speech in Soldiers Field, Chicago. VO 1944-45:514
Fireside chat on the accomplishments of the New Deal. WPRC:162
Message to Congress, April 27, 1942. VO 1942-43: 242
New Deal must continue. BA 1938-39:97
Rebuild and remodel. BOA: 202; BOB:172
Sloan, A. P., Jr.
Economic aspects of American defense. COP:438; COPA:438
Smith, F. M.
Around and around they go. BRP 7:60; YR 8:11
Snell, B. H.
Decision for youth. BOA:

373
Strandness, B.
Challenge to America. YR 8:141
Taft, R.A.
Forward America. BA 1938-39:130; BRYA:534
----and others.
American standard of living-how can it best be improved? BA 1947-48:103
Present crisis and the American economy. HAR: 271
Thomas, N.M.
Is the New Deal Socialism? WPRC:188
Tough times. FRIE:256
Truman, H.S.
Fair Deal in retrospect, January 7, 1953. FIP:317
Tucker, H.E.
Depression versus youth. JUD:235
Walker, J.T.
Macbeth. YR 5:221
Wieferich, R.
Youth and the depression. JUD:247
Young, O.D.
Science of better living. BA 1937-38:190
Young, W.A.
Society and the pay roll. BRP 1:63; YR 2:141
See also Business cycles; Prosperity

---- ECONOMIC POLICY
Bingham, H.
American way. BOA:324
Brown, L.H.
Freedom or planned economy: there is no middle road. BA 1945-46:133
Conant, J.B.
Unique idea of American life. BA 1939-40:337
What are we arming to defend? COP:573; COPB: 558
Hart, M.K.
This American system: is it to be destroyed? SAR: 203
Houghton, Mrs. H.C.
Today's challenge. BUT: 250
Irwin, W.A.
American way. BA 1939-40:183
Prentis, H.W., Jr.
Competitive enterprise versus planned economy. BA 1944-45:217
Randall, C.B.
Our foreign economic policy. BA 1954-55:55
Wallace, H.A.
Charter for postwar prosperity. BA 1944-45:203
See also Laissez-faire; United States-Foreign relations

---- EXECUTIVE DEPARTMENTS See United States-Commission on Organization of the Executive Branch of the Government; United States-Politics and government
---- FOREIGN POLICY See United States-Foreign relations
---- FOREIGN RELATIONS
Acheson, D.
Deterring the aggressor. MIA:350
America first. BOB:94
Barkley, A.W.
Foreign policies of Roosevelt. BA 1938-39:53
Begg, J.T.
Our foreign relations and their effect on business. EXEE:449
Bell, J.
On non-intervention. CHAL 6:248; HAZO 13:5394; MAS 13:5394
Bennett, J.C.
Christian ethics and foreign policy. BA 1961-62: 132
Borah, W.E.

UNITED STATES-FOREIGN RELATIONS (cont.)
Being true to ourselves. BOA:316; BOB:92
Burns, R.W.
Freedom and war. ANGC:108
Cardon, P.V.
Some American agricultural policies and their impact on foreign relations. IOCP:115
Casey, V.
America-a leader or a hermit? YR 10:123
Churchill, W.L.S.
Broadcast to the world about the meeting with President Roosevelt, August 24, 1941. VO 1941:380
Clark, C.
Rearmament. BA 1938-39:71
Dean, V.M.
Anti-Westernism: cause and cure. BA 1959-60:116; LINP:234
United States and the Communist threat. ANGC:139
Dewey, T.E.
Minneapolis campaign speech. VO 1944-45:498
Douglas, P.H.
Foreign policy. BA 1950-51:72
Douglas, W.O.
World in revolution. HAR:169
Dulles, J.F.
Goal of our foreign policy. BA 1954-55:19
Modern foreign policy. HURG:324
Speech in New York, January 25, 1954. GRAC:167
United front against red aggression. BA 1950-51:54
Western European army. BA 1952-53:15
Eisenhower, D.D.
Address at the United Nations, September 22, 1960. BA 1960-61:55
Challenge of our times. BA 1951-52:14; HAR:529; MIA:337
European trip. BA 1959-60:7
Peace program. BA 1952-53:31
Price of peace: second inaugural address. BA 1956-57:19; BAAG:376; CHI:294; LOTI:263; USIN:263; USINA:263; WPRC:313
Faigan, Z.
United States obligation for feeding Europe's millions. HOD:106
Ford, B.
Moral basis for our leadership. MIA:388
Fox, C.J.
Foreign policy of Washington. BRYW 4:35
Fulbright, J.W.
America and internationalism. BA 1943-44:83
Foreign policy-old myths and new realities. BA 1963-64:91
Goldwater, B.
National objectives in American foreign policy. BA 1960-61:83
Hay, J.
American diplomacy. BLAB:10; REEM 2:173; REEMB 2:175
Hoffman, P.G.
Accepting the Robert Dollar award. SAB:221
Hogland, G.E.
Time for greatness. NOR 1946:35
Hoover, H.C.
Leadership for a free world. MO:568
Our national policies in this crisis. BA 1950-51:45; YE:363
Houghton, A.B.
Open diplomacy. BEA:277
Hull, C.
Broadcast on United States foreign policy. VO 1943-

44:357
Foreign policy of the United States (April 9, 1944 speech). BA 1943-44:67; GRAC:133; VO 1944-45:161
Opening of the Pan American Conference. BA 1938-39:40
Statement on U.S. foreign policy. VO 1944-45:135
Ireland, J.
America a world power. BLAA:202; BLAB:202; REAC:113
Kennan, G. F.
National interest of the United States. HAR:80
Kiltz, A. A.
America goes abroad (attack upon America's foreign policy in East and South). ASHF:246
Knox, P. C.
Internationalism and American independence. BREW 7:221
LaFollette, R. M., Jr.
America's foreign policy. BA 1937-38:69
Lippmann, W.
Philosophy and United States foreign policy. BA 1947-48:48
Lodge, H. C., Jr.
United Nations. HURG:344
Lord, Mrs. O. B.
World around us (commencement address at Temple University, Philadelphia). BUTB:236
Luce, C. B.
American morality and nuclear diplomacy. HIB:338
Lytton, H. B.
After-dinner speech. KLEG:150
MacArthur, D.
Defends his conduct of the war in Korea. ARNS:273; BA 1951-52:21; BOU:105; BRAP:61; CAP:206; COPB:594; HAR:146; HIBS:465; HURG:293; MOUG:210; MOUGA:210 (outline p. 217); PE:816; PEA:816; YE:371
Speech delivered to the Massachusetts legislature. MIA:342
McCarthy, J. R.
Great betrayal. WPRC:294
MacDonald, J. R.
Mystic kinship. REEM sup 2:205; REEMB 2:391
MacVeagh, F.
Our relations with the world. BLAA:218; BLAB:218
Malik, C. H.
Developing leadership in new countries. BA 1963-64:115
Morrow, W. W.
Foreign policy of the United States. WAGN:229
Oliver, R. T.
American foreign policy in the midst of the world revolution. BERS:122
Raschke, K.
It can be done. BRP 10:100
Roosevelt, F. D.
Campaign address before the Foreign Policy Association in New York. VO 1944-45:492
Message to Congress, January 4, 1939. SAR:119
Roosevelt, T.
Address at State Fair of Minnesota. BIR 3:253; CHAL 14:360; HAZO 25:10889; MAS 25:10889; REEM 10:398; REEMA 15:1759; REEMB 11:415
Annual message, December 6, 1904. BIR 3:256
On foreign affairs (from message to Congress, December 6, 1904). BRE:299; BREA:279; PO:117
Rusk, D.
Address before the American Society of International

UNITED STATES-FOREIGN POLICY (cont.)
Law. BA 1964-65:89
Sayre, F. B.
Major problems in the United States foreign policies. BA 1948-49:51
Schner, C.
Fine white ashes. NOR 1950:181
Schuman, F. L.
Peace without appeasement. HAR:40
Smathers, G.
Put democracy on the offensive. MOA:461
Stassen, H. E.
American world policy for peace and progress. BA 1944-45:56
Stettinius, E. R., Jr.
Economic objectives of United States foreign policy. HAN:403
Stevenson, A. E.
"Let us work while it is yet day" (at University of California's 96th Charter Day). LINP:286
Symington, W. S.
Truth makes us free. BA 1952-53:42
Taft, R. A.
Basis of an American foreign policy. BA 1950-51:65
Failures of the Truman administration. BA 1951-52:100
Our misguided foreign policy. WPRC:285
Taft, W. H.
Dollar diplomacy. FIP:89
Thompson, D. and others.
What does the European situation mean to us? BA 1937-38:52
Thornton, H. W.
Friendly nations. NESA:118
Toynbee, A.
Fulcrum of western civilization. HAR:77
Truman, H. S.
Navy Day speech on foreign policy. VO 1945-46:659
State of the Union (1952). HAR:95
Vandenberg, A. H.
American foreign policy. BA 1944-45:43; HAN:421; ON:182
Wallace, H. A.
Is American foreign policy leading to war? BA 1946-47:33
Welles, S.
America's foreign policy. BA 1943-44:53
Willkie, W. L.
World outlook needed for Americans. HOC:135
Yarnell, H. E.
Our stake in the Pacific. ON:78
See also Economic assistance, American; Monroe Doctrine; United States-Neutrality; Western hemisphere; World War, 1939-1945-United States-Aid to Great Britain

---- ---- CANADA
Bright, J.
Will the United States subjugate Canada? BREW 2:223
Falconer, R. A.
United States as a neighbor. REEM sup 1:285; REEMB 8:153
Harding, W. G.
Canadian-American relations. FIP:155
Laurier, W.
Canada, England and the United States in 1899. BREW 7:301; COP:381; COPA:381; COPB:381; FUL:181,183; PL:542; REEMA 13:1297
Roosevelt, F. D.
Address in Ottawa, August 25, 1943. VO 1943-44:309
Broadcast to Canadians. 1942-43:149

Canadian position of the United States. BA 1938-39: 25; BIR 4:259
Taft, W.H.
Canadian reciprocity: "They are coming to the parting of the ways." FIP: 82

---- ---- CHINA
Acheson, D. G.
Statement on liberation, January 15, 1953. GRAC: 164
Dulles, J. F.
Our policies toward Communism in China. BA 1957-58:48; GRAC:176
Rusk, D.
Chinese-American friendship. HAR:165
Truman, H.S.
Statement on U.S. policy toward China. VO 1945-46: 767
Wu, Hsiu-Chuan
Address to the Security Council of the United Nations. HAR:126
Wu Ting-Fang
China and the United States. REEMB 3:1284
Younger, K.
Critique of United States China policy, September, 1957. GRAC:181

---- ---- CUBA
Kennedy, J.F.
Address to the nation, October 22, 1962. BA 1962-63:7; FIP:388
Cuba I. FIP:385

---- ---- EAST (FAR EAST)
Acheson, D. G.
Speech in Washington, January 12, 1950. GRAC:159
United States policy toward Asia. HAR:154
Dulles, J. F.
Policy for the Far East. BA 1958-59:36
Stevenson, A.E.
United States Far Eastern policy. COPB:599

---- ---- EUROPE
Jenks, J.W.
America's role in Europe. LINM:288
Sevareid, E.
Western European attitudes, August, 1958. BA 1958-59: 53

---- ---- FRANCE
Estournelle de Constant, P. H. B.
France and the United States. BRYW 7:200
Evarts, W. M.
French alliance. REEMA 2:457
Hull, C.
On relation with the French Republic. VO 1941.245
Porter, H.
France and the United States. REEM 3:104; REEMB 3:105
Roosevelt, F.D.
Message to the French people, November 7, 1942. VO 1942-43:597
Statement on United States recognition of the French Committee of National Liberation. VO 1943-44:311
Statement upon the termination of diplomatic relations with the Vichy government. VO 1942-43:640
United States policy toward the French Republic. VO 1941:212
Welles, S.
Relations with the French government at Vichy. VO 1942-43:188
Status of French ships at Alexandria, Egypt. VO 1942-43:392

---- ---- GERMANY
Havighurst, R.J. and others.

UNITED STATES-FOREIGN RELATIONS-GERMANY (cont.)
What should America do now in Bizonia? MO:621

---- ---- GREAT BRITAIN
Butler, B. F.
Our debt to England. REEMA 1:110
Calhoun, J. C.
Oregon question. SOU 9:303
Chamberlain, A.
Anglo-American friendship. BEA:87
Churchill, W. L. S.
British-American cooperation. BA 1943-44:27; VO 1943-44:331
Depew, C. M.
England and America since the Spanish War. BREW 5:170; FUL:118; ORAMA 2:383
Dickens, C.
English friendship for America. COP:615; COPB:655; REEMA 1:405
Douglas, S. A.
"Expansion" and co-operation with England (Clayton-Bulwer Treaty). BREW 5:294
Geddes, A. C.
Cooperation between Great Britain and America. REEM 2:85; REEMB 2:77
Hanna, E.
What part should the United States play in the economic recovery of Britain? HOD:102
Hillard, G. S.
Influence of men of genius. REEMA 2:616
Imrie, N. A.
America and Britain: some problems in common. NESA:154
Johnston, E. A.
Steps toward a good world. HAN:374
Laurier, W.
Canada, England and the United States in 1899. BREW 7:301; COP:381; COPA:381; COPB:381; FUL:181,183; PL:542; REEMA 13:1297
MacDonald, J. R.
Mystic kinship. REEM sup 2:205; REEMB 2:391
Randolph, J.
On offensive war with England. BRYW 8:186; CHAL 4:424; HAZO 9:3920; MAS 9:3920; ORAMA 1:351; SHAH:77
Sumner, C.
Claims on England. ORAMA 2:233
Taft, W. H.
America and England. REEM 3:299; REEMB 3:316
Tracy, S. H.
America and Britain for civilization. ONES:338
See also Anglo-American Union (proposed); Great Britain-Foreign relations-United States; World War, 1939-1945-United States-Aid to Great Britain

---- ---- GREECE
Pepper, C. D.
Against aid to Greece and Turkey. BA 1946-47:67
Truman, H. S.
Aid to Greece and Turkey. BA 1946-47:43; GRAC:149
Vandenberg, H. A.
For aid to Greece and Turkey. BA 1946-47:51

---- ---- JAPAN
Ishii, K.
To the United States Senate. REEM 11:238; REEMB 12:253

---- ---- LATIN AMERICA
Donnelly, W. P.
Our responsibility to Latin America. ANGC:177

Hughes, C.E.
Latin-American relations. BLAB:293
Kennedy, J.F.
Alliance for progress. FIP:379
Wilson, W.
Address before the Southern Commercial Congress at Mobile on relations with Latin America. BIR 3:309; FO:276

---- ---- MEXICO
Reed, J.A.
Toleration (trouble with Mexico-1927). BYRA:367; REEM sup 2:318; REEMB 8:338
Roosevelt, F.D.
Reply to President Camacho at Monterrey. VO 1943-44:171
Wilson, W.
Pursuit of Villa. FIP:101
Tampico incident. FIP:99

---- ---- MIDDLE EAST
Douglas, P.H.
Speech in Senate on United States foreign policy in the Middle East. BRAP:129
Eisenhower, D.D.
Eisenhower Doctrine. FIP:351
Plan for peace in Lebanon. BA 1958-59:23
Suggestions for taking part in a discussion or conference, with outline for discussion on "What should be the role of the United States in the Middle East?" MICS:183

---- ---- NICARAGUA
Coolidge, C.
Neighbors and strangers; ways to peace. FIP:166

---- ---- ORIENT
Emerson, J.G.
America and peace in the Orient. ASHF:308

---- ---- PANAMA
Roosevelt, F.D.
Message to Congress, August 13, 1942. VO 1942-43:438

---- ---- POLAND
Stettinius, E.R., Jr.
Statement on Poland. VO 1944-45:618

---- ---- RUSSIA
Acheson, D.
Basis for Russian-American peace. BA 1949-50:38; HAR:85
Speech in Washington, April 22, 1950. GRAC:155
Dana, R.H.
Russia and the United States. REEMA 1:323
Dulles, J.F.
Berlin Conference. BA 1953-54:33
Freedom or despotism? BA 1956-57:25
Eisenhower, D.D.
U-2. FIP:362
Johnston, E.
Mr. Perkins returns to the land of the Bolsheviks. BA 1956-57:40
Knowland, W.F.
Coexistence and atomic stalemate. BA 1954-55:30
Lippmann, W.
Peace settlement with Russia. BA 1946-47:103
Lodge, H.C., Jr.
Stop being afraid: reply to attack on United States by Andrei Vyshinski. BA 1950-51:37; YE:171
Nixon, R.M.
Radio-television address from Moscow. ARNS:240; BA 1959-60:14
Rusk, D.
Underlying crisis: coercion vs. choice. BA 1961-62:19

UNITED STATES-FOREIGN RELATIONS-RUSSIA (cont.)
Stevenson, A.E.
United States and the U.S.S.R. ANGC:184
Symington, W.S.
Freedom and military security. BA 1949-50:75
Wallace, H.A.
Address before Congress of American Soviet Friendship. VO 1942-43:605
See also Berlin question 1945-

---- ---- SPAIN
Davis, C.K.
Our relations with Spain. FUL:101
See also Philippine Islands; United States-History-War of 1898

---- ---- TURKEY
Pepper, C.D.
Against aid to Greece and Turkey. BA 1946-47:67
Truman, H.S.
Aid to Greece and Turkey. BA 1946-47:43; GRAC:149
Vandenberg, H.A.
For aid to Greece and Turkey. BA 1946-47:51

---- ---- VIETNAM (REPUBLIC)
McGee, G.
Academic looks at Vietnam. BA 1964-65:73

---- GOVERNMENT See United States-Politics and government

---- HISTORY
Barré, I.
America's obligation to England. CHAL 2:341; HAZO 5:2039; MAS 5:2039
Bullock, A.H.
Intellectual leadership in American history. NORR 1st ser:128
Frankfurter, F.
Worth of our past. HOC: 111
Jones, E.D.
Adventures among great Americans. BART 1:115
MacArthur, R.S.
Present heroic era in American history. HARSO: 254; WERN 42:124
Pryor, R.A.
Virginia's part in American history. REEMA 3:959
Wilson, W.
Course of American history. REEM 6:423; REEMA 9:1199; REEMB 7:417
See also Names of historic events and acts, and wars, e.g. Foot's Resolution; Stamp Act, 1765; European War, 1914-1918; World War, 1939-1945-United States

---- ---- CONFEDERATION
Witherspoon, J.
Necessity of Confederation. HARS:41
Public credit under the Confederation. BREW 10: 269

---- ---- REVOLUTION
Adams, S.
American independence. BREW 1:83; BRYW 8:110; CHAL 2:312; CHEM 1:69; COP:234; COPA:234; COPB:234; HAZO 5:2010; HELE:67; HURG:31; JOHA 1 pt 1:24; LEEW 8:239; MAS 5:2010; ORAMA 1:3; PL:583; REEM 10:5; REEMA 11:21; REEMB 11: 5
Andrews, C.M.
Present-day thoughts on the American Revolution. NORR 2d ser:320
Burke, E.
Against coercing America. BREW 2:406
Conciliation with America.

ADR 1:182; BEA:65; BERS: 41; BOU:33; BRAO:3; BRYW 6:3; CHAL 2:344; COP:157; COPA:157; COPB:157; FULB:23; GOOD:266; HAZO 5:2114; HIB:124; KET:43; KLEG: 130; MAS 5:2114; ONEM: 139; ORBR 1:229; PAUF 1: 62; PE:131; PEA:131; PL:410; REEM 9:109; REEMA 11:368; REEMB 10:114; SAA:26; SHUM:11

Choate, J.H.
British evacuation of New York. REEMA 1:179

Dickinson, J.
Declaration of the Colonies on taking up arms. BREW 5:224; CHAL 2:435; HARS: 31; HAZO 6:2533; MAS 6: 2533

Drayton, W.H.
Charge to the Grand Jury. HAZO 7:2709; MAS 7:2709

Emerson, R.W.
Minute-man (at centennial celebration at Concord). HAZO 14:6000; MAS 14: 6000

Everett, E.
Issue in the Revolution. BRYW 8:196
Patriotic oration (50th anniversary of the independence of the United States of America). CHAL 6:92; HAZO 12:5148; MAS 12: 5148

Fox, C.J.
On the British defeat in America. BRYW 4:29; FULB:39

Grigsby, H.B.
American revolution. SMI: 69

Henry, P.
Liberty or death. BAAMP: 29; BOU:39; BRE:23; BREA:23; BREW 7:15; BRIM:209; BRYW 8:62; CAP:18; CHAL 3:28; CHEM 1:63; CLAY:5; CODS: 321; CODSA:321; COP: 232; COPA:232; COPB: 232; CROC:234; DICD: 156; DICE:156; DOA:327; ESEH:192; FKA:3; FRY: 7; FULB:168; HARS:26; HARSO:323; HAY:29; HAZO 6:2595; HELE:51; HIB:151; HIBS:443; HURG: 27; JOHA 1 pt. 1:18; LEEW 8:115; MAS 6:2595; ONEM:328; ORAMA 1:57; PAR:91; PE:139; PEA: 139; PL:569; PROS:130; REEM 10:1; REEMA 13: 1178; REEMB 11:1; RID: 8; SAA:95; SHAH:14; SOU 9:171

Higginson, T.W.
Battle of the cowpens. REEMA 8:618

Hurt, J.
To the Virginia brigands. SMI:38

Jay, J.
Protest against colonial government. BREW 7:149; CHAL 3:152; HAZO 7:2771; MAS 7:2771; ORAMA 1:149

Lawton, P.I.
Nineteenth of April. SHUC: 150

Lee, R.H.
Address to the people of England. BREW 7:312; CHAL 2:423; HAZO 6:2493; HELE:55; LEEW 8:221; MAS 6:2493; REEMA 14: 1313; SMI:32

Mansfield, W.M.
On the right to tax America. ADR 1:150; BRYW 3: 230; CHAL 2:239; GOOD: 148; HAZO 5:1832; MAS 5:1832; ORBR 1:199; PL: 403; REEMA 14:1422

Paine, T.
American crisis. BRE:44; BREA:42; CROC:337; PO: 17

Parker, T.
Reminiscence of Lexington. CLAY:139

UNITED STATES-HISTORY-REVOLUTION (cont.)
Pitt, W., 1708-1778
Address to the throne concerning affairs in America. ADR 1:120; BRAO:75; BREW 3:235; BRYW 3:211; CLAY:18; CODS:99; CODSA:99; ESEH:204; FULB:8; GOOD:134; HAZO 5:1856; LEEW 6:136; MAS 5:1856; ONEM:189; PE: 143; PEA:143; PL:393; REEM 9:97; REEMB 10: 101
Against quartering of British soldiers on the inhabitants of Boston (May 27, 1774). GOOD:126; HAZO 5:1950; MAS 5:1950
Employment of native mercenaries. HAY:17
On American policy, January 20, 1775. BRTH:74; BRTHA:74; CHAL 2:278; CROC:365; GOOD:128; HAZO 5:1955; MAS 5:1955
On putting a stop to hostilities in America (May 30, 1777 speech). CHAL 2:289; GOOD:132; HAZO 5:1966; MAS 5:1966
On the right to tax America. ADR 1:98; BOU:29; BRYW 3:197; CHAL 2:265; COP:155; COPA:155; COPB:155; FULB:5; GOOD:103; HAZO 5:1902; HIB:118; MAS 5:1902; ORBR 1:213; PAUF 1:57; PE:118; PEA:118; REEMA 12:563; SAA:13
Pitt, W., 1759-1806
Misery of the American War. BRYW 4:3; CODS: 462; CODSA:462
Toynbee, A. J.
Continuing effect of the American Revolution. BA 1961-62:95
Rutledge, J.
Speech in time of Revolution. BREW 9:138
To the General Assembly of South Carolina. CHAL 3:83; HAZO 7:2651; LEEW 8:281; MAS 7:2651
Saner, R. E. L.
Valley Forge. PROS:78
Storrs, R. S.
Victory at Yorktown. REEMA 3:1094
Warren, J.
Constitutional liberty and arbitrary power. BREW 10: 81; HELE:25
Wilkes, J.
Conquest of America. impossible (1777). BRYW 3: 246
On coercive measures in America. BRYW 3:243; SAA:20
Warning and a prophecy. BREW 10:239

Wilson, J.
In vindication of the colonies. CHEM 1:19; HAZO 7:2690; MAS 7:2690
Winthrop, R. C.
Centennial at Yorktown. HAZO 16:6646; MAS 16: 6646
Witherspoon, J.
Convention of Burgoyne. HAZO 5:2001; LEEW 8: 269; MAS 5:2001
See also Names of historic events, e.g. Boston Massacre, 1770; United States -Declaration of Independence

---- ---- 1783-1809
Bell, C. F.
Statesman and nation. SHUC:96

---- ---- WAR OF 1812
Brougham and Vaux, H. P. B.
Against Pitt and war with America. BREW 2:261; BRTH:214; BRTHA:214; HAZO 10:4142; MAS 10:

4142; REEMA 11:333
Clay, H.
Free trade and seamen's rights. CHAL 5:74; HAZO 10:4089; MAS 10:4089
On the War of 1812. CHEM 2:67; CLAY:47; FRY:15; JOHA 1 pt 1:205; ORAMA 1:415; SHAH:100
Gallatin, A.
Speech on the British Peace Treaty (terminating War of 1812-1814). CHAL 4:138; HAZO 8:3476; MAS 8:3476
Madison, J.
War message, 1812. BIR 1:273; PO:65
Quincy, J., Jr.
Against conquest of Canada. BREW 8:404
Randolph, J.
Militia Bill. CHEM 2:41; HARS:175; JOHA 1 pt 1:104; SHAH:82; SMI:97

---- ---- WAR WITH MEXICO
Corwin, T.
War with Mexico. BREW 4:172; BRYW 9:123; CHAL 6:113; HAZO 12:5184; MAS 12:5184; PE:378; PEA:378; PL:637; REEMA 12:724; SHAH:205
Dayton, W. L.
Arraigning President Polk. BREW 5:56
Douglas, S. A.
War with Mexico. HAZO 17:7356; MAS 17:7356
Kearny, S.W. and others.
Armijo is no longer your governor. GRIS:48
MacGregor, R. R.
Allegiance dominant! PROS: 95
Webster, D.
Objects of Mexican War. HAZO 11:4656; MAS 11: 4656

---- ---- CIVIL WAR
Adams, C. F., Jr.
Battle of Gettysburg. BREW 1:33
Adams, C. F.
States and the Union. BREW 1:29; CHAL 7:275; HAZO 15:6191; MAS 15: 6191
Address to Northern and Southern veterans. DAVC: 502
Allen, E.
Call to arms (1861). BREW 1:139
Baker, E.D.
On suppression of insurrection. BRYW 10:3; CHEM 4:161; JOHA 2 pt 2:51; SAA:173
Beecher, H.W.
Difficulties of Union (Edinburgh, October 14, 1863). FULB:350
Liverpool speech, October 16, 1863. BRAC:40; BRIM:250; BRYW 10:9; BURS:88; CHEM 4:201; CODS:429; CODSA:429; COP:317; COPA:317; COPB:317; FULB:354; HARS:395; HAZO 17:7254; JOHA 2 pt 2:93; LEEW 10: 259; MAS 17:7254; SAA: 188; SHAH:427
Moral conflict (London, October 20, 1863). FULB: 357
Principles of self-government (at Manchester, England, October 9, 1863). FULB:341
Raising the flag over Fort Sumter. BREW 1:352; CHAL 8:395; HAZO 17:7306; MAS 17:7306; ORAMA 2: 295; PL:672; REEM 10: 239; REEMA 11:180; REEMB 11:251; THOU 1: 305
Regulated liberty (at Glasgow October 13, 1863). FULB:345
Bell, J.
Against extremists, North

UNITED STATES-HISTORY-CIVIL WAR (cont.)
and South. BREW 1:389
Benjamin, J. P.
Farewell to the Union. BREW 1:401; HICF:94
Booth, N.
Debit and credit of the war. WAGN:38
Breckenridge, J. C.
On suppression of insurrection. CHEM 4:161; JOHA 2 pt 2:51; SAA:170
Breckenridge, W. C. P.
Who were the Confederate dead? SOU 9:418
Bright, J.
Against Mr. Roebuck's motion for recognition of the Southern Confederacy. HAZO 16:6846; MAS 16:6846
Brownlow, W. G.
Grape shot and hemp. BREW 2:290
Butler, B. F.
Character and results of the war. CHAL 9:264; HAZO 18:7848; MAS 18:7848; REEMA 12:445
Cannon, J. G.
Buchanan, and secession. BREW 3:111
Choate, R.
Preservation of the Union. COP:284; COPA:284; COPB:284; HURG:80; ORAMA 2:175; REEM 10:139; REEMA 12:575; REEMB 11:143
Colfax, S.
Confiscation of rebel property. BREW 4:133
Coyle, J. G.
Fredericksburg. CATA 1:181
Craven, A.
Price of union. TIN:269
Davis, H. W.
Reasons for refusing to part company with the South. BREW 5:27
Davis, J.
Against Clay and compromise. BREW 5:45
No divided flag. CHAL 7:298; HAZO 15:6217; MAS 15:6217
Decisive battle of the rebellion. DAVC:62
Dickinson, D. S.
At War Ratification meeting. CHAL 6:408; HAZO 13:5622; MAS 13:5622
Rebuking Senator Clemens of Alabama. BREW 5:220
Doolittle, J. R.
Attitude of the West in the Civil War. BREW 5:269
Dougherty, D.
On the perils of the Republic. HAZO 21:8947; MAS 21:8947
Douglas, S. A.
Issues of 1861. BREW 5:302
John Brown raid. BREW 5:299
Douglass, F.
'Men of color, to arms!" WOON:253
Union speech. HIB:165; WOON:247
Drake, C. D.
Against "Copperheads." BREW 5:309
Emerson, R. W.
War (commemoration of patriot heroes of Harvard College in Civil War). HAZO 14:5997; MAS 14:5997; REEMA 2:442
Garfield, J. A.
Revolution and the logic of coercion. BREW 6:198
Garrison, W. L.
At Charleston, South Carolina, 1865. BREW 6:213; RID:56
Beginning a revolution. BREW 6:209
Union and slavery. BREW 6:212; ORAMA 2:211
Harris, N. E.
Visions of the Civil War (at Confederate Veterans

reunion, 1905). SHUO:26
Hill, B.H.
Flag of our fathers. HARSO: 53

A little personal history. BREW 7:47
Howe, J.
At International Commercial Convention. CHAL 7: 211; HAZO 14:6095; MAS 14:6095
Hughes, T.
Cause of freedom. CHAL 10:287; HAZO 20:8568; MAS 20:8568
Ingraham, F.L.
Gettysburg. TRUW:68
Lincoln, A.
"A house divided against itself cannot stand." BIR 2: 217; BRE:232; BREA:216; BREW 7:337; BRYW 9: 222; COP:309; COPA:309; COPB:309; FO:156; HAZO 16:6562; HICF:49; HURG: 88; JOHA 2 pt 1:168; KLEG:323; LEEW 10:237; MAS 16:6562; ORAMA 2: 217; PE:490; PEA:490; REEM 10:216; REEMB 11: 227; SHAH:383; SHUM: 133; WPRA:180
Message to Congress, July 5, 1861. ANG:324
Lodge, H.C.
Blue and the Gray. REEMA 2:723
M'Cullough, J.A.
South Carolina and Civil War. SHUO:306
Mason, A.S.
Battle of Gettysburg. TRUW:1
Miller, H.R.
Second birth. REEM 7:298; REEMB 8:311
Phillips, W.
Under the flag. BRIM:230
Ramsdell, C.W.
Changing interpretation of the Civil War. TIN:23
Seward, W.H.
Irrepressible conflict. BRAO:298; BREW 9:164; BRYW 9:177; CHAL 6:458; COP:295; COPA:295; COPB:295; HARS:343; HAZO 14:5709; HURG:99; JOHA 2 pt 1:195; KLEG: 331; MAS 14:5709; ORAMA 2:195; PL:656; REEM 10: 161; REEMA 15:1849; REEMB 11:165
Sherman, W.T.
Reminiscence of the war. REEM 3:211; REEMA 3: 1051; REEMB 3:228
Stanley, A.O.
Lee and Appomatox. SHUO: 153
Stephens, A.H.
What is all this for? SOU 9:404
Stockdale, T.R.
Confederates are comin'. WERN 42:62
Storey, C.L.
Minister plenipotentiary. TRUW:137
Sumner, C.
Claims on England. ORAMA 2:233
Thurston, J.M.
Union soldier. BLAA:42; BLAB:42; HARSO:280; REAC:72; WERN 42:112
Toombs, R.
Territorial acquisition and Civil War. BREW 9:422
Vallandigham, C.L.
Centralization and the revolutionary power of federal patronage. BREW 10:31
On the war and its conduct. CHAL 10:24; HAZO 19: 8138; JOHA 2 pt 2:82; MAS 19:8138
Voorhees, D.W.
Opposition argument in 1862. BREW 10:59
Welfare of the nation. CHAL 11:140; HAZO 21: 8997; MAS 21:8997
Wallace, L.
Peacemakers of blessed

UNITED STATES-HISTORY-
CIVIL WAR (cont.)
memory. BLAA:169; BLAB:169
Watterson, H.
Blue and Gray. RID:71
Wiley, B.I.
Time of greatness. TIN: 325
Wilson, H.
On the bill to confiscate the property and free the slaves of rebels. CHAL 8: 377
See also Confederate States of America; Memorial Day; Reconstruction; Slavery in the United States

---- ---- ---- CAUSES
Andrew, J.A.
Eve of war. CHAL 9:295; HAZO 19:7879; MAS 19: 7879
Benjamin, J.P.
Right of secession. HICF: 57
Calhoun, J.C.
On nullification. JOHA 1 pt 1:303; LEEW 9:357
Chase, S.P.
Texas v. White, 1869: opinion for the Supreme Court. BIR 3:84
Cox, S.S.
On secession. CHEM 4: 103; JOHA 2 pt 1:312
Crittenden, J.J.
On the Crittenden Compromise. CHAL 5:376; HAZO 12:4853; JOHA 2 pt 1:275; MAS 12:4853
Davis, J.
Message to Congress, April 29, 1861.BIR 2:260
On withdrawing from the Union. BREW 5:36; BRYW 8:203; CHAL 7:287; COP: 305; COPA:305; COPB: 305; HARS:364; HAZO 15: 6206; HURG:109; JOHA 2 pt. 1:333; LEEW 10:225; MAS 15:6206; PE:503; PEA:503; PEAE:139; PL: 664; REEM 10:186; REEMA 12:815; REEMB 11:190; SOU 9:412
Hale, J.P.
On secession. CHAL 7:262; CHEM 4:13; HAZO 15:6175; JOHA 2 pt 1:230; MAS 15: 6175
Iverson, A.
On secession. CHAL 6: 282; HAZO 13:5436; JOHA 2 pt 1:235; MAS 13:5436
Jay, J.
America free-or America slave. CHAL 9:159; HAZO 18:7691; MAS 18:7691
Mann, H.
On the threatened dissolution of the Union. CHAL 6:215; HAZO 13:5326; MAS 13:5326
Owsley, F.L.
Fundamental cause of the Civil War: egocentric sectionalism. TIN:77
Seward, W.H.
On secession. LEEW 10: 203
State of the country (1860). HAZO 14:5728; MAS 14: 5728
Stephens, A.H.
Sanctity of the Union. LA: 156
Secession. BAKF:401; CHAL 8:363; HAZO 17: 7208; MAS 17:7208; REEM 10:192; REEMA 15: 1932; REEMB 11:196
Toombs, R.
"Let us depart in peace." BREW 9:428; BRYW 9:211; CHAL 8:143; CHEM 4:61; HAZO 16:6801; JOHA 2 pt 1:294; LEEW 10:217; MAS 16:6801; PL:661; REEMA 15:2003; SOU 9:312
Wade, B.
On secession, and the state of the Union. CHAL 6:372; CHEM 4:23; HAZO 13:5578; JOHA 2 pt 1:246; MAS 13:

5578

---- ---- WAR OF 1898

Angell, J. B.
War and arbitration. FUL: 7, 9
Barrows, J. H.
National Peace Jubilee. FUL:11, 14
Beveridge, A. J.
Takes up the white man's burden. FUL:24; PE:650; PEA:650
Clinton, D.
Against the military spirit. BREW 4:90
Coghlan, J. B.
Battle of Manila. REEM 1: 323; REEMA 1:239; REEMB 1:324
Cousins, R. G.
Causes and issues of the Spanish War. FUL:86
Heroes of the 'Maine disaster.'' DAVC:495; FUL: 84; REEMA 12:738
Davis, C. K.
Treaty of Paris. FUL:104, 108
Dolliver, J. P.
Stand by the government. FUL:128
Uphold the President. FUL: 122, 125
Graves, J. T.
Our country's birthday. FUL:131, 134, 137
Grow, G. A.
On Manila. CHAL 10:260; HAZO 20:8541; MAS 20: 8541
Howell, C.
No need of pessimism. FUL:160, 164
Howells, W. D.
Spanish prisoners of war. BLAA:78; BLAB:78
Ireland, J.
Peace in the wake of victory. ORAMA 2:445
Lindsay, W.
Law is with duty. FUL: 187, 191
Lodge, H. C.
Battle of Santiago. BLAA: 56; BLAB:56

Treaty of peace. FUL:194
McKinley, W.
Duty determines destiny. FUL:218
Nation indivisible forever. FUL:220, 222
Nation's duties and opportunities. HAZO 24:10497; MAS 24:10497
To the soldiers. WERN 42: 37
War message, April 11, 1898. BIR 3:230; FO:245
MacVeagh, F.
Anti-expansion bugbear. FUL:234, 237, 240
Miles, N. A.
Spanish-American War. REEMA 2:831
Peck, G. R.
Sovereignty follows the flag. BLAA:231; BLAB: 231; FUL:245, 247
Year of jubilee. FUL:243

Rayner, I.
Hero of Santiago. SHUO: 252
Reid, W.
Path of duty. FUL:260
Purport of the treaty. FUL: 256
Schurz, C.
Criminal aggression. FUL: 284
Imperialism hostile to liberty. FUL:287
Smith, C. E.
War for humanity. FUL: 290
Speer, E.
''One and inseparable.'' FUL:297, 300
Towne, C. E.
''Lest we forget.'' FUL:313, 316
Van Dyke, H.
American birthright and the Philippine pottage. FUL:

UNITED STATES-HISTORY-WAR OF 1898 (cont.)
319, 322, 326
Washington, B. T.
Negro in the late war. CHAL 14:325; FUL:333
Wolcott, E. O.
Treaty with Spain. FUL: 343
War inevitable. FUL:341

---- ---- EUROPEAN WAR, 1914-1918 See European War, 1914-1918

---- ---- WORLD WAR, 1939-1945 See World War, 1939-1945-United States

---- IMMIGRATION See Immigration and emigration

---- INFORMATION SERVICE
Larson, A.
United States Information Service. BRAP:80

---- NATIONAL CHARACTERISTICS See National characteristics, American

---- NATIONAL GUARD
Depew, C. M.
Our National Guard. FUL: 113

---- NAVY
Bayard, J. A.
Commerce and naval power. BREW 1:267
Carson, H. L.
Our Navy. REEMA 1:133
Cheves, L.
In favor of a stronger Navy. BREW 3:269
Clay, H.
On the increase of the Navy. LEEW 9:95
Cummings, A. J.
On the Naval Appropriation Bill. CHAL 13:419; HAZO 24:10431; MAS 24:10431
Hobson, R. P.
For a larger Navy. SHUO: 245
Johnson, F. L.
Battleship bubble. BRP 7: 13
King, E. J.
American postwar seapower and control of Pacific bases. BA 1944-45:83
Long, J. D.
American Navy. FUL:214; REEMA 2:727
Response to toast 'The Navy: our country's best wall of defense." PITT:92
Roosevelt, F. D.
Broadcast at the Puget Sound Navy Yard on the war in the Pacific. VO 1944-45:373
Freedom of the seas. COP: 546; COPB:524; SAA:300; VO 1941:395
Liberty fleet day address. VO 1941:413
Navy Day address on the attack of the destroyer Kearney. HAN:160; VO 1941:462
Navy Day campaign speech in Shibe Park, Philadelphia. VO 1944-45:509
Roosevelt, T.
Need of an efficient Navy. WERN 42:145
Sampson, W. T.
Victory in superior numbers. REEM 3:189; REEMA 3:1023; REEMB 3:196
Schley, W. S.
Navy in peace and in war. REEMA 3:1031; SHUO:250
Sherman, F. P.
Navy of the future. YE: 291
Sherman, W. T.
Army and Navy (December 22, 1875 speech). CHAL 10:1; HAZO 19:8115; MAS 19:8115
Army and Navy (December 21, 1880 speech). REEM 3: 206; REEMA 3:1046;

REEMB 3:223
Talmage, T. D.
On Admiral Dewey and the American Navy. BREW 9: 364
Truman, H. S.
Message to Congress recommending Army-Navy merger. VO 1945-46:769
Navy Day speech on foreign policy. VO 1945-46: 659
See also Navy; Recruiting

---- NEUTRALITY
Borah, W. E.
Against the repeal of Embargo. BA 1939-40:38
Broadcast address, February 22, 1936. BIR 4:172
Our imperative task: to mind our own business. SAR:279
Possible results of a European war. BA 1938-39:29
Bullitt, W. C.
America is in danger. COP:570
Butler, N. M.
Why war? BA 1938-39:13
Conant, J. B.
What are we arming to defend? COP:573; COPB: 558
Fosdick, H. E.
Ethical problems of neutrality. BA 1939-40:427
Hoeppner, C.
Moral neutrality. NOR 1945:17
Hutchins, R. M.
Drifing into suicide. ON: 300
Proposition is peace. COP: 592
Ickes, H. L.
What constitutes an American? COP:588; COPB: 567; HURG:260
Knox, F.
We must fight for our liberties. COP:606; COPB:571
Lindbergh, C. A.
Independent policy. COP: 576; COPB:576; HURG: 254
Millikan, R. A.
Isolationist fallacies. COP: 604
Moley, R.
Minding America's own business. BART 3:37
Nye, G. P., Jr.
Neutrality. BA 1939-40:53
Roosevelt, F. D.
Democracy cannot survive in isolation. ON:146
Message to Congress (on repeal of Embargo). BA 1939-40:26
Message to Congress urging the arming of American flag ships engaged in foreign commerce. VO 1941: 455
This nation will remain neutral. BA 1939-40:21; BIR 4:288; BRAS:409 HAN:124; PL:839
United States' policy toward war. BA 1938-39:35
Seversky, A. P., de
Aviation vs. isolationalism. ON:121
Sheen, J. J.
Cross and the double cross. COP:598; COPB:574
Stevenson, A. E.
There are no Gibraltors. WPRC:277
Stimson, H. L.
Grave situation. COP: 586; COPB:565
Straight, M.
Two are alive. SAR:257
Thomas, N.
America and the war. COP:595; COPB:582; HURG:261
America's duty in time of crisis. BA 1939-40:275
How far shall we go? ON: 82
Thompson, D.
Hitler's plans for Canada and the United States.

UNITED STATES-NEUTRALITY (cont.)
COP:601; COPB:577; HURG:257
Wallace, H. A.
America's second chance. COP:609; COPB:580
Waymack, W.W.
Challenge of America. BA 1939-40:155
Wheeler, B.K.
America's present emergency. WPRC:255
Keep this nation at peace. COP:580
Willkie, W. L.
Isolationism and the League of Nations. BA 1941-42:251
Wilson, W.
Neutrality message to the Senate, August 19, 1914. BIR 4:1; FIP:105
See also United States-Foreign relations

---- OFFICE OF PRICE ADMINISTRATION See Price regulation

---- PEACE CORPS
Kennedy, J. F.
Peace Corps. FIP:378

---- POLITICS AND GOVERNMENT
Baruch, B.
Government and the individual. ONEC:189
Benjamin, J. P.
Virtue the cornerstone of Republican government. LEEW 10:99
Bingham, J. A.
Sectional party. CHAL 9:77; HAZO 18:7567; MAS 18:7567
Blair, A.
Military government. BREW 2:109
Calhoun, J. C.
Self-government and civilization. BREW 3:77
Choate, R.
Necessity of compromise in American politics. BREW 3:295; HAZO 13:5458; MAS 13:5458
Clay, H.
Dictators in American politics. BREW 4:14; BRYW 9:87; CHAL 5:28; HAZO 10:4033; MAS 10:4033; REEMA 12:632
Clinton, DeW.
Federal power and local rights. BREW 4:87
Collins, D. E.
Government. WAGN:147
Compton, G. B.
Character and politics. SHUC:159
Conkling, R.
Stalwart standpoint. BREW 4:141
Dawes, C. G.
Business organization of the government. REEM 4:68; REEMB 4:150
Dew, T. R.
Influence of republican government on literature and character. SMI:123
Ditzen, L.
Evasive politics and a third party. YR 3:51
Eisenhower, D. D. and others.
Keeping the government house in order (television report to the nation). BA 1953-54:45
Farley, J. A.
Politics as a profession for businessmen. BA 1939-40:266
Fonville, D. R.
Public conscience. SHUC:166
Fulbright, J. W.
Moral revival in government. BA 1951-52:60
Gallagher, H. W. and others.
You and your government. SAR:174
Grady, H. W.
Against centralization. CLAY:41

Hand, L.
Preparation of citizens for their political duties. BA 1952-53:121
Hoffman, P. G.
Business, government, and education. HAR:429
Hoover, H. C.
Government by isms. BREW 7:72
Individual initiative. BOA: 401
Principles and ideals of the United States government. PO:143
Ingalls, J. J.
On the political situation (1891). CHAL 12:240; HAZO 22:9621; MAS 22: 9621; REEMA 13:1229
Jordan, D. S.
Nation's need of men. HARSO:238
Kennedy, J. F.
Education of an American politician. BRAP:123
Lehman, F. W.
Third house (commencement address). SHUO:312
Leigh, B. W.
Apportionment of representation. SMI:112
Lenroot, I. L.
Press and the government. LINM:39
Lincoln, A.
Central ideas of the Republic. REEM 2:321; REEMA 2:720; REEMB 2:325
Perpetuation of our political institutions (1837). HAY: 184; SHU:90
Livingston, R. R.
Oration before Cincinnati. CHAL 3:187; HAZO 7:2815; MAS 7:2815
Lodge, H. C.
Party harmony and political friendship. BYRA:286; REEM 10:386; REEMB 11: 402
Longworth, N.
Legislating for a Republic. REEM sup 2:168; REEMB 5:128
McBurney, J. H. and others.
Alexander Hamilton: his contribution to Constitutional government. BA 1956-57:149
Lippman, W.
Rise of personal government in the United States. BA 1937-38:122
McKelway, S. C.
Prayer and politics. REEM 2:378; REEMB 2:395
MacVeagh, W.
Ideals in American politics. CHAL 12:111; HAZO 22: 9507; MAS 22:9507
Marshall, T. R.
Golden rule of government (inaugural address to the Senate, March 4, 1917). BREW 8:103

Representative government. NESA:103
Mollenhoff, C. R.
Need for balanced thinking. ANGC:68
Mould, E. W. K.
Ethics in American public life. SHUC:154
Oberholzer, H. J.
American road. BLUE:4
Palmer, G. M.
Lawyer in politics. REEMA 3:872
Posey, M.
America's contribution of constitutional government. LEIO:85
Randolph, E.
In defence of the Union. REEMA 14:1678
Rill, W. A.
New blood. YR 5:17
Robinson, J. T.
Jacob's voice but Esau's hands. WPRC:179
Roosevelt, F. D.
Reorganization message to Congress (January 12, 1937). FO:405

UNITED STATES-POLITICS AND GOVERNMENT (cont.)
Right of the people to rule. HICF:396; REEM 10:408; REEMB 11:426
Root, E.
Every man's responsibility. BOA:197; BOB:170
Smith, A. E.
Come back to your father's house. WPRC:168
Smith, M. C.
Political conscience. BA 1950-51:124
Smith, T. V.
Forward America. BA 1938-39:119
Snetman, L.
Politics and a well-rounded nation. YR 9:135
Sprague, C.
Life blood of the nation. BOB:207
Springer, W. M.
Retrenchment, economy, and reform. REEMA 15: 1924
Stevenson, A. E.
Political relevance of moral principle (A. Powell Davies memorial address). WPRC:355
Sutherland, G.
Private rights and government. REEM 7:383; REEMB 8:404
Taft, R. A.
Forward America. BA 1938-39:130; BRYA:534
Tarkington, B.
Indiana in literature and politics. REEM 3:314; REEMB 3:331
Thomas, N. M.
Is the New Deal Socialism? WPRC:188
Thorpe, M.
Business of government. NESA:140
Tilden, S. J.
On administrative reform. CHAL 8:469; HAZO 18: 7454; MAS 18:7454
Truman, H. S.
Statement to Congress on reorganizing the government. VO 1945-46:217
Van Dyke, H.
People and their rulers. WERN 42:60
Webster, D.
American government unique. REEMA 9:1152
Whitehurst, Mrs. J. L.
Inaugural address (as president of General Federation of Women's Clubs). BUTA:224
See also Reorganization Act of 1939 (United States); Politics, practical

---- RELIGIOUS HISTORY
Jones, E. DeW.
Faith of our fathers. BA 1942-43:287

---- SOCIAL CONDITIONS
Dewey, J.
Education and new social ideals. WPRC:216
Hutchins, R. M.
Education and social improvement. WPRC:220

UNITED STATES STEEL CORPORATION
Blough, R. M.
Great expectations. MICS: 144

UNITED STATES-SUPREME COURT
Alessandroni, V.
Curbing the Supreme Court. YR 8:153
Beck, J. M.
Future of the Supreme Court. LINM:435
Burges, T.
Supreme Court. BREW 2: 329
Cardozo, B. N.
Helvering et al. v. Davis: opinion for the Supreme Court. BIR 4:249; BRE:353

Steward Machine Company v. Davis, 1937: opinion for the Supreme Court. BIR 4: 238
Chase, S. P.
Mississippi v. Johnson, 1867: opinion for the Supreme Court. BIR 3:58
Texas v. White, 1869: opinion for the Supreme Court. BIR 3:84
Davis, D.
Ex parte Milligan, 1866: opinion for the Supreme Court. BIR 3:29
Opinion in the Milligan Case. ANG:374
Fuller, M.W.
Pollock v. Farmers' Loan and Trust Company, 1895: opinion for the Supreme Court. BIR 3:196
Supreme Court. REEMA 2: 513
United States v. E. C. Knight Company, 1895: opinion for the Supreme Court. BIR 3:191
Glass, C.
Packing the Supreme Court. COP:422; COPA:422
Should Mr. Roosevelt's plan for enlarging the Supreme Court be adopted? (negative) SAR:224
Harlan, J. M.
Adair v. United States, 1908: opinion for the Supreme Court. BIR 3:292
Lottery case (Champion v. Ames), 1903: opinion for the Supreme Court. BIR 3: 262
Northern Securities Company v. United States, 1904: opinion for the Supreme Court. BIR 3:275
Holmes, J.H.
Should Mr. Roosevelt's plan for enlarging the Supreme Court be adopted? (negative). SAR:219
Holmes, O.W., Jr.
Dissenting opinion on Abrams vs. United States. ANG:458; FO:310
Lochner v. New York, 1905: dissenting opinion for the Supreme Court. BIR 3: 289
Schenck v. United States: opinion for the Supreme Court. BRE:320; BREA: 300
Hughes, C. E.
Judiciary. BA 1937-38:176
National Labor Relations Board v. Jones and Laughlin Steel Corporation, 1937: opinion for the Supreme Court. BIR 4:218
Near v. Minnesota: opinion for the Supreme Court. BRE:323; BREA:303
150th anniversary of the United States Supreme Court. ON:315
Opinion in the case of the Negro law student, Lloyd Gaines. ANG:486
Schechter Poultry Corporation v. United States, 1935: opinion for the Supreme Court. BIR 4:131
United States Supreme Court building. ON:301
West Coast Hotel Co. v. Parrish: opinion for the Supreme Court. BIR 4:231; BRE:344
Johnson, H. S.
Should Mr. Roosevelt's plan for enlarging the Supreme Court be adopted? (affirmative). SAR:221
Marshall, J.
Barron v. Baltimore: opinion for the Supreme Court. BRE:158; BREA:142
Cohens v. Virginia, 1821: opinion for the Supreme Court. BIR 2:34
Gibbons v. Ogden, 1824: opinion for the Supreme Court. BIR 2:53
McCulloch v. Maryland:

UNITED STATES-SUPREME COURT (cont.)
opinion for the Supreme Court. BIR 2:2; BRE:128; BREA:119
Marbury v. Madison: opinion for the Supreme Court. BIR 1:259; BRE:116
Trustees of Dartmouth College v. Woodward: opinion for the Supreme Court. BIR 2:19; BRE:140

Miller, S. F.
Slaughter house cases, 1875: opinion for the Supreme Court. BIR 3:102

Wabash, St. Louis and Pacific Railroad Company v. Illinois, 1886: opinion for the Supreme Court. BIR 3:150

Peckham, R. W.
Lochner v. New York, 1905: opinion for the Supreme Court. BIR 3:283

Pecora, F.
Should Mr. Roosevelt's plan for enlarging the Supreme Court be adopted? (affirmative) SAR:227

Phelps, E. J.
Supreme Court and popular sovereignty (at centennial anniversary of organization of Supreme Court of the United States). REEMA 9:955

Roberts, O. J.
United States v. Butler, et al, 1936: opinion for the Supreme Court. BIR 4:177

Roosevelt, F. D.
Broadcast address, March 9, 1937 (proposal for the reform of the Federal Judiciary). BIR 4:100; FIP:224
Judiciary, February 5, 1937. FO:413
Should Mr. Roosevelt's plan for enlarging the Supreme Court be adopted? (affirmative) SAR:214
Message to Congress on the

Semmes, T. J.
Personal characteristics of the Chief Justices (at centennial celebration of Supreme Court. REEMA 9:1029

Shaw, L.
Commonwealth v. Hunt. ANG:257

Smith, H.
Introducing a Supreme Court justice. BRC:302

Stone, H. F.
Fifty years' work of the United States Supreme Court. HICF:803
United States v. Butler et al, 1936: dissenting opinion for the Supreme Court. BIR 4:188

Sutherland, G.
Adkins v. Children's Hospital, 1923: opinion for the Supreme Court. BIR 4:75

Taft, W. H.
Judiciary and progress. HICF:384

Taney, R. B.
Charles River bridge v. Warren bridge: opinion for the Supreme Court. BIR 2:135
Dred Scott case: opinion for the Supreme Court. BIR 2:206; BRE:221; BREA:205
Opinion in the Merryman case. ANG:310

Waite, M. R.
Munn v. Illinois, 1876: opinion for the Supreme Court. BIR 3:117

Webster, D.
Dartmouth College case. BREW 10:190; HAZO 11:4696; MAS 11:4696; SHAH:129

Wheeler, B. K.
Should Mr. Roosevelt's plan for enlarging the Supreme Court be adopted?

(negative) SAR:229
White, E.D.
Standard Oil Company of New Jersey v. United States, 1911: opinion for the Supreme Court. BIR 3:295
Supreme Court. BYRA:451; REEM 3:380; REEMB 6:373
Woolsey, J.M.
Opinion December 6, 1933 (Ulysses case-freedom of reading). ANG:468
Wright, M.
Bulwark of safety. YR 9:127

---- TERRITORIAL EXPANSION
Berrien, J.M.
Conquest and territorial organization. BREW 2:41
Beveridge, A.J.
March of the flag. CHAL 14:426; FUL:27; HAZO 25:10979; HIB:43; HICF:188; LA:125; MAS 25:10979; PROS:58; REEM 10:358; REEMA 11:224; REEMB 11:372; WERN 42:89; WPRA:352
Star of Empire. BRAS:221
Caffery, D.
Acquisition of foreign territory. FUL:54, 57
Hoar, G.F.
Lust of empire. FUL:139, 141, 144
Roosevelt, T.
True Americanism and expansion. REEMA 3:1002
Ross, J.
Nation's relation to its island possession. CHAL 11:82; HAZO 21:8857; MAS 21:8857
Vest, G.G.
No colonies. SHUO:114
Watterson, H.
Expansion. BLAA:160; BLAB:160; REAC:136
Wild, R.
American jingo. TRUW:89

---- TREATIES See Treaties; World War 1939-1945-Armistices

UNITED WORKMAN, ANCIENT ORDER OF
Burial service, ode and ritual. THOU 3:328
Hinds, C.G.
Fraternal greetings. THOU 3:318
Honored dead. THOU 3:333
M'Nall, W.
Response to address of welcome. THOU 3:325
Our reserve fund. THOU 3:336
Smith, R.A.
Address of welcome (United Workmen). THOU 3:323
Wilson (Supreme Master)
Presentation address. THOU 3:327
Work of Father Upchurch. THOU 3:335

UNITY
Handlin, I.
United we stand. DO:39

UNIVERSAL DECLARATION OF HUMAN RIGHTS See Human Rights Day and Week

UNIVERSE
Richter, J.P.
Greatness of the universe. DICD:152; DICE:152
See also Creation

UNIVERSITIES AND COLLEGES
See Colleges and universities; Also Names of colleges and universities, e.g. Harvard University; Iowa State College; Yale University

UNIVERSITY EXTENSION
Playfair, L.
Evolution of university extension. CHAL 9:413; HAZO 19:8045; MAS 19:8045

UNIVERSITY OF VIRGINIA
Abbott, W.R.
University of Virginia (before Alumni Association). SHUO:102

UNKNOWN SOLDIER
Barton, B.
Unknown. BOB:38; BRP 2:7; PROS:1; SHU:111
Decoration of unknown graves and the address at the cemetery. HILL:473
Elyea, C.D., Jr.
Plea of the unknown soldier. DO:44
Harding, W.G.
At the grave of unknown soldier. BREW 6:368; BLAB:321; PROS:7; SHU:36
Holmes, J.H.
Unknown soldier speaks. SAR:425
O'Brien, F.M.
Armistice Day. SHU:207
Owen, R.B.
Unknown soldier. GA:87
Pershing, J.J.
To the unknown British warrior. REEM 11:433; REEMB 12:458
Robbins, P.H.
Arlington-1935. YR 7:1
Unknown soldier. DU:137

UNSELFISHNESS See Behavior
Untereiner, Ray E.
Public interest in utility regulation. BA 1962-63:28

UNVEILING SPEECHES See Dedication addresses; Presentation speeches

UPCHURCH, JOHN JORDAN
Work of Father Upchurch. THOU 3:335
Upham, Charles Wentworth
Spirit of the day and its lessons, 1846. BRAR 1:417
Upton, T. Dinsmore
Re-creation through recreation. EXEE:392
Urban II, Pope
Call for the crusade. -Same as his Speech at the Council of Clermont
Speech at the Council of Clermont. CROC:445; LEEW 3:323; PE:66; PEA:66
Urey, Harold C.
Atom bomb and war. BA 1945-46:95
Hydrogen bomb and international government. BA 1949-50:95
Science and society (at 100th anniversary Academic convocation of Cooper Union For The Advancement Of Science And Art). ARNS:79
See Biddle, F., jt. auth.

UTILITY
Hall, W.
Address before the Society of Phi Beta Kappa in Yale College. BL:205

UTOPIAS
Gallagher, B.G.
Preface to the study of Utopias (Founders Day lecture on the anniversary of Antioch College). BA 1960-61:201

V (Emblem)
Deutsch, M.E.
V emblem. HOC:34

V-E DAY
Churchill, W.L.S.
Germany surrenders. BA 1944-45:40; VO 1945-46:193
Speech to VE crowds in London. VO 1945-46:195
DeGaulle, C.
Before the French Consultative Assembly on the victory over Germany. VO 1945-46:208
VE Day broadcast to the

French people. VO 1945-46: 198
George VI.
VE Day address. VO 1945-46:195
Pius XII.
Radio broadcast on war's end. VO 1945-46:202
Stalin, I.
Victory address. VO 1945-46:199
Truman, H. S.
VE Day proclamation. BA 1944-45:37; HAN:308; VO 1945-46:191
See also World War 1939-45-Armistices; World War 1939-45-Germany-Surrender

V-J DAY
Chiang Kai-Shek
Excerpts from victory message September 3, 1945. VO 1945-46:533
Truman, H. S.
Broadcast on Japanese surrender. HAN:362; VO 1945-46:520
See also World War 1939-1945-Japan-Surrender

VACATIONS
Introducing a speaker on "Planning a vacation." WRA: 36
Take a vacation each year. NAT:48
See also Travel

VAGABONDS See Hoboes
Vail, Theodore Newton
Life and the farm. REEM 6: 401; REEMB 7:403

VALEDICTORY ADDRESSES
Andrew, J. A.
Valedictory to two branches of the legislature on retiring from office. CHAL 9: 313; HAZO 19:7897; MAS 19:7897
Brodsky, J. C.
Student activities in undergraduate life. SHUC:359
Bryan, W. J.
Valedictory at Illinois College. CORP:283
Conant, J. B.
Valedictory service address. BA 1942-43:257
Jessel, G.
Suggestions for preparation of valedictory address. With example of. JEYO:21
Kirby, J., Jr.
Labor and legislation (valedictory as President of National Association of Manufacturers). REEM 4:248; REEMB 5:67
Latin valedictory. DAVC:116
O'Neal, B.
Democracy is on trial. MOUG:238; MOUGA:238
Painton, E. P.
Parting hours (valedictory). WERN:54:99
Suggestions for preparation of valedictory addresses at graduating ceremony. With examples of. WRA:168, 171, 173
Valedictories to the class, faculty, president, trustees and undergraduates. DAVC: 156-160
Valedictory-two examples of. STOC:187; STON:191-196
Valedictory address. CRAI: 434
Valedictory address for a college. HILL:488
Valedictory address for a young lady in a Catholic school. AMEO 1:177
Valedictory "Catholicity." DAVC:150
Valedictory for a college. DAVC:127
Valedictory for a college. REAC:31
Valedictory for a college commencement. DAVC:136
Valedictory for a college or academy. PAIC:65
Valedictory for a college or

VALEDICTORY ADDRESSES (cont.)
university. AMEO 1:174
Valedictory for a dental college. DAVC:121
Valedictory for a grammar school. AMEO 1:170
Valedictory for a grammar school. PAIC:57
Valedictory for a grammar school. REAC:23
Valedictory for a high school. AMEO 1:172
Valedictory for a high school. PAIC:61
Valedictory for a high school. REAC:27
Valedictory for a school. DAVC:134
Valedictory for either a grammar or a high school. PAIC:59
Valedictory - "Good day." DAVC:141
Valedictory in parody form for a grammar school (after the rhythm of Tennyson). PAIC:72
Valedictory in parody form for a high school (from "Henry VIII"). PAIC:77
Valedictory in parody form for a high school (from "Macbeth"). PAIC:78
Valedictory in parody form for any class (after "Locksley Hall"). PAIC:79
Valedictory in parody form for either a grammar or a high school (from "Julius Caesar"). PAIC:73
Valedictory "Liberalism." DAVC:145
Valedictory of novel form: Class creed. PAIC:82
Valedictory of novel form: Class obituary. PAIC:87, 336
Valedictory of novel form: President's farewell message. PAIC:91
Valedictory - "Service." DAVC:119

Valentine, Alan
Mobilizing the mind. BA 1940-41:263

VALENTINE'S DAY
Saint Valentine's Day. BURS: 175
Saint Valentine's Day (a tribute to love's patron saint). EDGS:8
Story of St. Valentine. JAS: 24
Valentine's Day. DR:128

Valkenberg, J. Van
Biennial address of Knights of Pythias. THOU 3:133
Knights of Pythias eulogy. THOU 3:142

Vallandigham, Clement L.
Centralization and the revolutionary power of federal patronage. BREW 10:31
On the war and its conduct. CHAL 10:24; HAZO 19: 8138; JOHA 2 pt 2:82; MAS 19:8138

Van Baarda, Mme. D.
Road toward international understanding. BUTB:245

Van Buren, Martin
Inaugural address. CHI:67; LOTI:65; USIN:61; USINA: 61

Vance, J. Madison
In the wake of the coming ages. DUNM:177

Vance, Zebulon Baird
Scattered nation. REEM 8:390; REEMA 6:1115; REEMB 13:396; SHUO:175
Slavery question. CHAL 11: 407; HAZO 22:9328; MAS 22:9328

VANCE, ZEBULON BAIRD
Tillett, C.W.
On the death of Senator Vance. SHUO:180

Vandenberg, Arthur H.
American foreign policy. BA 1944-45:43; HAN:421; ON: 182
Charter, the hope of the

world. -Same as his Report to the Senate on the San Francisco Conference

European recovery program. BA 1947-48:24
For aid to Greece and Turkey. BA 1946-47:51
For the appointment of Lilienthal. BA 1946-47:122
Memorial Day address. BA 1937-38:39
Report to the Senate on the San Francisco Conference. ON:123; VO 1945-46:358
Threatened Constitution. BOA: 88
Tribute to Senator Barkley. BA 1948-49:96
United Nations Assembly: a report. BA 1945-46:45

VANDENBERG, ARTHUR H.
Wiley, A.
Brief remarks at conclusion of Senator Vandenberg's report on the United Nations Assembly. BA 1945-46:46

VANDERBILT UNIVERSITY
Kirkland, J. H.
Inaugural address as chancellor of Vanderbilt University. WE 1:327

Vandercook, John W.
Soul of France. BA 1942-43: 159

Vanderlip, Frank Arthur
Allied debt to United States. REEM 4:396; REEMB 5: 348

Vanderlip, Mrs. Frank R.
Hospitals-yesterday and today. GA:276

Vandervoort, Jocelyn
No man is an island. BRAP: 77

Van de Water, George Roe
Dutch traits. REEMA 3:1162

Van Dyke, Henry
Advantages of a mixed ancestry. THOU 1:329
American birthright and the Philippine pottage. FUL: 319, 322, 326
Aristocracy of service. BOA: 193; BOB:206
Books, literature, and the people. REEM 6:406; REEMA 7:391; REEMB 7: 408
Commerce. BLAA:140; BLAB: 140
Democratic aristocracy (Sesquicentennial of Phi Beta Kappa). BRAC:315; NORR 2d ser:528
Home as a nation builder. BOA:140; BOB:164
Introducing John Morley. NESA:162
Of fame. LINM:219
People and their rulers. WERN 42:60
Salt. BRYA: 505; ONEM:732; REEMA 7:380; SHUM:326
Sign of the muck-rake. BOA: 363; BOB:51
Typical Dutchman. DOA:301; ONEM:641; ONES:232; REEM 3:347; REEMA 1: 418; REEMB 3:363
William Dean Howells. REEM 5:370; REEMB 9:414

Van Dyke, Vernon
Second century of progress. BRP 4:22; INTW 1933:10

Vane, Sir Henry
Against Richard Cromwell. BREW 10:38; BRYW 3:137; LEEW 6:87
At his trial for high treason. BREW 10:39; BRYW 3:139; CHAL 2:71; HAZO 4:1511; MAS 4:1511
On the petition and advice. LEEW 6:75

Van Hise, Charles Richard
Government regulation. REEM 7:403; REEMB 5:362
Inaugural address as president of University of Wisconsin. WE 2:161

VAN LOON, HENDRIK
Introducing Henry Van Loon-2 examples of; 1st and 2nd visits to Advertising Club. SUM:102,104
Vanocur, Sander
State of mind. NOR 1949:163
See also Kennedy, J. F., jt. auth.
Vanzetti, Bartolomeo See Sacco, Nicola and Vanzetti, Bartolomeo
Vargas, Antonio Seleme
Inaugural speech at Conference on the Problems of Economic Development. UAR:303
Speech at final session of Conference on the Problems of Economic Development. UAR:391
Varney, G.R.
Jew. COUW:9

VASSAR COLLEGE
Taylor, J. M.
Inaugural address as president of Vassar College. WE 1:241
Vaughan, Elsbeth R.
Accepting the Florence Nightingale medal. GA:45

VAUGHAN, VICTOR CLARENCE
Ruthven, A. G.
Victor Clarence Vaughan and the University (Michigan). ONEC:127
Vaughan, W. R.
Druidism. THOU 3:237
Veeck, William
Responds to an introduction by Clinton Youle. PRC:26

VEECK, WILLIAM
Youle, C.
Introduces William Veeck, President of the Chicago White Sox. PRC:25
Velde, Harold H. See Fischer, L., jt. auth.
Venable, Francis P.
Duty of the educated man to his country (at Lafayette College Alumni Association). SHUO:90

VENEREAL DISEASES
Ahrendts, H.
Illinois disease. YR 9:145
Berolsheimer, H.
Clean hands. BLUE:27
Holmes, G. H.
Eleventh plague. BRP 8:80
Keesey, R.
Aristocracy of the unfit. BRP 8:44; YR 9:165
Rolph, A.
Plague uncovered. BRP 8:33; YR 9:155
Woodard, B.
Yellow silence. YR 9:177

VENEZUELA
Bolivar, S.
I will act as trustee of the Supreme Authority. CROC:29
Venizelos, Eleutherios
Greece enters the war. REEM 11:138; REEMB 12:150
On the League of Nations. BREW 10:43
Speech at Peace Conference (Session February 15, 1919). REEM 11:345; REEMB 12:363

VENTRILOQUIST See Actors and acting
Verdery, Marion J.
Introducing Augustus Thomas to Southern Society of New York, December 14, 1906. REEM 3:319
South in Wall Street. REEMA 3:1168

VERDI, GIUSEPPE
Phelan, J. D.
Verdi memorial exercise address. WAGN:351
Vergil. See Virgil
Vergniaud, Pierre Victurnien
Reply to Robespierre. BREW 10:48; HAZO 8:3168; MAS

8:3168; PE:266; PEA:266
Situation in France. BRYW 7: 117; CHAL 3:428; HAZO 8: 3174; LEEW 5:45; MAS 8: 3174; PE:246; PEA:246; PL:303
To the camp. BREW 10:46; HAZO 8:3165; MAS 8:3165
Verhage, William
Meaning of Americanism. ASHF:1
Vernon, William T.
"Plea for a suspension of judgment." WOON:618
Verplanck, Gulian C.
Advantages and dangers of the American scholar. BL:115

VERRES, GAIUS
Cicero, M.T.
First oration against Verres. BRYW 2:51; HAZO 2: 755; LA:129; MAS 2:755; PL:108
Fourth book of the second pleading in the prosecution of Verres about the statutes. HAZO 2:781; MAS 2: 781
Ver Steeg, Clarence See McBurney, J.H., jt. auth.
Vest, George Graham
Man's best friend-his dog. BOU:176; COP:650; COPB: 677; GRIS:21; HURG:161; SHU:201
No colonies. SHUO:114
On Indian schools. CHAL 11: 463; HAZO 22:9384; MAS 22:9384; REEMA 15:2013

VETERANS
Address before United Spanish War Veterans. AMEO 2: 52
Address to Northern and Southern veterans. DAVC: 502
Brigance, W.N.
Backwash of war. BA 1945-46:75
Clarke, L.
Day after V-Day. NOR 1945:29
Kovar, L.
All this, and for what? AN: 78
Membership talk on the Society of Foreign Wars of the United States. AMEO 2: 109
See also American Legion; Pensions, military; Veterans' Day

---- EDUCATION
Roosevelt, F.D.
Message to Congress on post-war education of service men and women. VO 1943-44:458

VETERANS' DAY
Armistice Day. CON:107
Armistice Day. SCHS:18
Armistice Day address. AMEO 2:31
Armistice Day (in memory of our soldier and sailor dead). EDGS:40
Armistice Day-November 11. DR:170
Closing speech (at Veterans' Day observance). BED:49; BEDA:94
Coolidge, C.
Armistice Day. BEA:145
Statesmanship of peace (Liberty Memorial, Kansas City, November 11, 1926). HICF:762
Lang, C.G.
Lest you forget. BEA:5
Littleton, M.W.
Armistice Day, 1921. REEM 7:230; REEMB 8:250
McAdoo, W.G.
Soldiers' bonus. REEM 7: 253; REEMB 8:273
Memorial address (at Veterans' Day observance). BED:47; BEDA:93
Mucklestone, Mrs. M.
Armistice Day address. GA:77
Opening of commemorative

VETERANS' DAY (cont.)
services (at Veterans' Day observance). BED:47; BEDA:92
Pittenger, W. A.
Patriots of peace. BRP 1:75
Prayer (at Veterans' Day observance). BED:47; BEDA:93
Roosevelt, F. D.
Armistice Day, 1941. VO 1941:503
Armistice Day, 1942. ON:343; VO 1942-43:649
Savage, H. P.
Address to the Legion dead. SHUP:216
Veterans' Day. FRIE:113
Warren, E.
Charles Evans Hughes and the spirit of tolerance (dedication of hall in memory of Hughes). BA 1956-57:135
Willkie, W. L.
Loyal opposition. COP:553; COPB:545; HURG:243
Wilson, W.
Signing of the Armistice. LINM:308

VETERANS OF FOREIGN WARS
Veterans of Foreign Wars. NATS:30
Victoria, Queen of Great Britain
Proclamation to the princes, chiefs, and people of India, November 1, 1858. KESI 1:382

VICTORIA, QUEEN OF GREAT BRITAIN
Celebration of Queen Victoria's birthday in America. HILL:489
Laurier, W.
On the death of Queen Victoria. BRYW 5:192; CHAL 13:381; HAZO 24:10446; LAD:197; MAS 24:10446; REEM 5:267; REEMB 9:306
Queen's diamond jubilee. CHAL 13:379; HAZO 24:10444; MAS 24:10444

VICTORY
Celebration of a political victory (congratulatory address by an influential party member). EDGS:72
Humorous speech at the celebration of a political victory. BARB:128
On to victory-talk at the pregame pep meeting. DR:279; LU:1253
Roosevelt, F. D.
Victory dinner address. BA 1937-38:101
Scoville, D. C.
Truth and victory. SHU:196
Sitrick, J.
Vision for victory. NOR 1942:53
Speech after a political victory (selected). PITT:99
Speeches after a victory-three examples of. STOC:141; STON:147-149
Victor of Marengo. SHU:223
Victory toast to the winning team. DR:280; LU:1255
Winning team, by one of the college or towns-people. Response by captain. EDGS:388, 389
See also V (Emblem); V-E Day; V-J Day; World war 1939-1945-Germany-surrender; World war 1939-1945-Japan-surrender

VIETNAM See United States-Foreign relations-Vietnam (Republic); Vietnamese War 1957-

VIETNAMESE WAR, 1957-
Morse, W. L.
To what purpose war in Asia? BA 1964-65:62
Vieuzac, Bertrand Barère, de. See Barère de Vieuzac,

Bertrand
Vieyra, Antonio
Sermon on the great evil of sin. LEEW 4:355
Vigil, Bantista See Kearny, S.W., jt. auth.

VILLAGRAN, FRANCISCO
Touchstone, W.W.
Introduces Dr. Francisco Villagran, Mexican Consul. PR:48
Villard, Oswald Garrison
Capitalism vs. Socialism (chairman's remarks). REEM sup 3:39
Vincent, George Edgar
Doctor and the changing order. REEM sup 3:151; REEMB 6:364
Inaugural address as President of University of Minnesota. PEAE:197
Washington's birthday. REEM 3:352; REEMB 3:368
Vincent, John H.
Perfect life. WERN 54:21
Vincent, Norris Brooks
Men like war. YR 9:221

VINCI, LEONARDO DA
Hubbard, E.
Masterpiece of God (Mona Lisa). SHU:259
Vinson, Carl
Path to peace. BOB:68

VIRGIL.
Eliot, T.S.
What is a classic? ARNS: 47
Florus.
Was Virgil an orator or a poet? LEEW 2:307
Virgin Mary. See Mary, Virgin

VIRGINIA
Alderman, E.A.
Virginia. REEM 1:23; REEMB 1:26
Marshall, J.
Cohens v. Virginia, 1821: opinion for the Supreme Court. BIR 2:34
Pryor, R.A.
Virginia's part in American history. REEMA 3:959
Randolph, J.
On altering the Virginia Constitution. SMI:117
Rice, J.H.
Virginia's deficiencies. SMI:99
Swanson, C.A.
Virginia. SMI:242
Tucker, J.R.
Virginia jurists. SMI:220
Tyler, J.
Educational needs of Virginia. SMI:95

VIRGINIA, UNIVERSITY OF
Alderman, E.A.
University of Virginia in the life of the nation: inaugural address as president of University of Virginia. WE 2:73

VIRTUE
Olmsted, W.C.
Virtue, mercy and charity. THOU 3:377

VISITORS See Guests, - Welcoming addresses
Visk, A. Guy
Emcee at a silver wedding anniversary. BRH:313
Fight announcer. BRH:336
Introducing a backwoods pianist
" a comedian
" a juggler. BRH:83, 124, 120
No butts about it: "a silly TV commercial." BRH:333
Twisted news (to be delivered by an emcee at bachelor parties, bridal parties, or wedding receptions). BRH: 328
Viviani, René Raphael
Addresses in America (at Mount Vernon and Auditorium, Chicago). REEM

Viviani, R.R. (cont.)
11:208,210; REEMB 12: 223,225
Declaration of war by France. REEM 11:40; REEMB 12: 45
It has been sworn. BREW 10: 53
Our heritage of liberty. LEW: 103
Peace made possible by justice. BREW 10:55
Spirit of France. COP:129; COPA:129; COPB:129; REEM 11:82; REEMB 12:91
Their monuments in our hearts. LEW:109
To the House of Representatives. LEW:115
Tribute to Lincoln. LEW:121

VOCATIONAL EDUCATION
Vocational training. AMEO 2: 161
See also Manual training

VOCATIONAL GUIDANCE
Getting a job-speech by well-known business man at closing exercises of a school. WRA:224
Gould, S.B.
Flavor for our daily bread. BA 1962-63:122
Introducing a speaker on "vocational guidance." WRA:35
Krause, N.L.
Man's reach. NOR 1940:34
Outline for a speech "Wanted: the right job. BARR:46
Vocational guidance. DR:85
See also Occupations, choice of

VOCATIONS
Finding your place. JAI:94
Lindley, E.H.
University and the vocations of man: inaugural address as president of University of Kansas. WE 2: 217
See also Occupations, choice of

VOLCANOES
Griggs, R.F.
Our friend-the volcano. MOUG:184; MOUGA:184

VOLTAIRE, FRANCOIS MARIE AROUET DE
Hugo, V.M.
On the centennial of Voltaire's death. BREW 7:98; CHAL 7:1; COP:91; COPA:91; COPB:91; HAZO 14:5776; MAS 14: 5776; REEM 5:277; REEMA 8:710; REEMB 9: 265
Voorhees, Daniel W.
In defence of John E. Cook. CHAL 11:125; HAZO 21: 8982; MAS 21:8982
Opposition argument in 1862. BREW 10:59
Speech in the Tilden convention. BREW 10:56; REEMA 15:2021
Welfare of the nation. CHAL 11:140; HAZO 21:8997; MAS 21:8997
Voorhees, Oscar M.
Presentation of a Phi Beta Kappa memorial hall. BRAC:262
Voorsanger, Jacob
Influence of Americanism upon the Jew. TWJ:183
Voronov, Gennadi I.
Speech of October 19. RUS: 227
Voroshilov, Kliment Y.
Statement to the Congress (October 26). RUS:116
Voss, Lewis C.
Success by overcoming obstacles. WERN 54:58

VOTING See Elections; Soldiers-Suffrage; Woman suffrage
Vyshinsky, Andrei Y.
On negotiations with Finland for an armistice. VO 1944-45:185

Statement on Soviet-Polish relations. VO 1943-44:195
W. P. A. See Works Progress Administration
Wade, Anton C.
Introducing a filling station manager
" a restaurant or cafe manager. BRC:99,100
Wade, Benjamin Franklin
On secession and the state of the Union. CHAL 6:372; CHEM 4:23; HAZO 13:5578; MAS 13:5578
Wade, Martin J.
Highest achievement of civilization. SHU:93
Wager, Ralph
Agassiz, a great teacher. WERN 54:59
Wagers, Zella
Formula for sugar. BRP 10:94

WAGES
Black, H. L.
Wages and Hours Bill. ON:173
Hughes, C. E.
West Coast Hotel Co. v. Parrish: opinion for the Supreme Court. BIR 4:231; BRE:344
Lewis, J. L.
United Mine Workers demands. BA 1945-46:180
Murray, P.
Strikes, wages, and industrial profits. BA 1946-47:177
Wages and prices in the steel industry. GLAD:305
Outline for a speech "Let's face it; the guaranteed annual wage." MICS:93
Reuther, W. P. and others.
Should industry grant labor's demands for a thirty percent wage increase? BA 1945-46:165
Sutherland, G.
Adkins v. Children's Hospital, 1923: opinion for the Supreme Court. BIR 4:75
Truman, H. S.
Broadcast on wages and prices. VO 1945-46:665
Message to Congress, September 6, 1945. VO 1945-46:546
Railroad strike emergency. BA 1945-46:196
Statement on labor policy. VO 1945-46:458
Wagner, B. K.
Address. THOU 3:450

WAGNER, RICHARD
Ingersoll, R. G.
Music of Wagner. REEM 2:264; REEMA 2:672; REEMB 2:268
Wagner, Robert F.
Emancipation of childhood. BOA:379

WAGNER, ROBERT F.
Introducing Robert F. Wagner. NI:134; NIS:101
Youle, C.
Introduces Robert F. Wagner, Mayor of New York City. PRC:12
Wagner, Robert F., Jr.
Responds to the introduction by Clinton Youle. PRC:13
Welcomes the convention of Lions International. PRNE:71
Waite, Morrison Remick
Munn v. Illinois, 1876: opinion for the Supreme Court. BIR 3:117
Wakefield, J. C.
Introduces Robert A. Walsh, pharmacist. PR:94
Waldron, J. Milton
Solution to the race problem. DUNM:389
Wales, Edward Albert, prince of. See Edward VIII, King of England (abdicated)

WALES
Birkenhead, F. E. S.
Welsh disestablishment.

WALES (cont.)
BEA:35
Walker, Baxter
Introducing a coroner
" a department store buyer
" a jeweler. BRC:205,235, 222
Walker, Harry Judson
Intensive and extensive development. SHUC:118
Walker, J.B.
Grateful thanks. THOU 2:293
Walker, James
Be loyal America-your Constitution lives. DO:192
Tribute to Robert E. Lee. SHU:107
Walker, James J.
Welcome to the Right Honorable J. Ramsay Macdonald. LINM:425; YE:138
Welcoming Colonel Charles A. Lindberg. ONEC:11; PROS: 112
WALKER JAMES J.
Introducing James J. Walker. NI:142; NIA:107
Walker, John Turnley
Macbeth. YR 5:221
Walkley, A.B.
Toast to "Drama and Barrie." REEM 1:75; REEMB 1:66
Wallace, Henry Agard
Address at Chicago, September 11, 1943. VO 1943-44:351
Address at Cleveland, October 27: 1943. VO 1943-44:469
Address at Detroit, July 25, 1943. VO 1943-44:280
Address before Congress of American Soviet Friendship. VO 1942-43:605
Address before the Herald-Tribune Forum. VO 1943-44:545
Address on Woodrow Wilson's birthday. HAN:367; VO 1942-43:744
America's part in world reconstruction. BA 1942-43:93
America's second chance. COP:609; COPB:580
Before the Free World Association. PE:792; PEA:792; VO 1942-43:270
Broadcast from Seattle, Washington. VO 1944-45:300
Builders of tomorrow. ON:74
Century of the common man. - Same as his Price of free world victory
Charter for postwar prosperity. BA 1944-45:203
Community of interest between labor, capital, and agriculture. BA 1937-38:146
"I shall run in 1948." BA 1947-48:137
Introducing Winston Churchill. ON:338
Is American foreign policy leading to war? BA 1946-47: 33
Jackson Day dinner address. VO 1944-45:53
Lincoln's Day address. VO 1944-45:90
Practical religion in the world of tomorrow. BA 1942-43: 276
Price of free world victory. BA 1941-42:46; BOA:26; HOC:151
Progressive Party commitments. BA 1948-49:122
Proposals for a free world. - Same as his Address on Woodrow Wilson's birthday
Rebirth of liberalism. ON:201
Statesmanship and religion. KLEB:153
Tenant farming and its evils. SAR:332
Wallace, Hugh C.
Southerner in the West. REEMA 3:1178
Wallace, Karl R.
Ethical basis of communication. BERS:181
Wallace, Lew
Peacemakers of blessed memory. BLAA:169; BLAB:169
Return of the flag (presenting battle flags to the state). ONEM:702; REEM 7:409; REEMA 9:1121; REEMB 8:

424
Wallace, Robert Minor
Stephen F. Austin and Sam Houston (at acceptance of their statues in Capitol). SHUO:211

WALLACK, LESTER
Winter, W.
Tribute to Lester Wallack. REEMA 3:1260
Waller, Edmund
Tyrant's plea, necessity (impeaching Justice Crawley). BREW 10:63
Waller, Helen H.
Presents Bertrand Russell. LY:108
Presents Estes Kefauver. LY: 221
Walpole, Horace, 4th Earl of Orford
Debate in 1741 on wages of sailors. BREW 10:75
Debate in 1741 on wages of sailors. BREW 10:71, 73
Defense of Walpole. -Same as his On patriots
Frequency of general elections. EMS 2:105
House of Lords Bill, 1719. EMS 1:105
Information on foreign policy. EMS 1:233
On his proposed removal from office. BRYW 3:154; CHAL 2:171; GOOD:35; HAZO 4: 1728; MAS 4:1728; ORBR 1:143; REEMA 15:2025
On patriots (at motion to dismiss him from Council). BREW 10:78; COP:151; COPA:151; COPB:151; PL: 384
On the Septennial Bill. LEEW 6:103; GOOD:32
Peerage Bill. BEA:421; PAUF 1:33

WALPOLE, SIR ROBERT, 1ST EARL OF ORFORD
Pitt, W., 1708-1778
Second speech on Sir Robert Walpole, March 23, 1742. GOOD:89; HAZO 5: 1891; MAS 5:1891
Speech on Sir Robert Walpole, March 9, 1742. GOOD:82; HAZO 5:1873; MAS 5:1873
Wyndham, W.
Attack on Sir Robert Walpole, March 13, 1734. BREW 10:279; GOOD:31
Walsh, David I.
Religious tolerance. BOB:67
Religious tolerance. BOA:68; BOB:95
Walsh, Edmund
Religion and the modern mind. SAR:419
Walsh, Grace
It hath not yet been shown what we shall be. YR 4: 231
Walsh, James J.
Merry alumni dinner speech. WERN 54:128
Religious hospital as the need of our times. CATA 2:221
Walsh, John J.
Introducing the mayor-elect of Boston. HOAP:264
Walters, Alexander
Abraham Lincoln and fifty years of freedom. DUNM: 325; WOON:554
Walters, Basil L.
Press-an unhidden persuader. SABA:205

WALTHALL, EDWARD C.
Williams, J. S.
Southern gentleman (commemorating Edward C. Walthall). SHUO:45
Walton, Clayton
Our courts, a challenge. BRP 5:106
Walton, James A.
American problems. COUW: 101
Wampler, W. Norman
Why support the new bond issue? MICS:131

Wanacek, Earl M.
Introduces Charles A. Eaton. PR:72
Wanamaker, John
Rallying day. THOU 2:210
Wanamaker, Pearl A.
Accepting the presidency of National Education Association. YE:155
Wangerin, W.M.
King's prayer for your home. ACW:8

WAR
Addams, J.
Women and war. HICF:439
Allen, J.G., Jr.
Shall we make a rendezvous with death? YR 7:281
Barton, B.
Unknown. BOB:38; BRP 2:7; PROS:1; SHU:111
Bearman, A.
Gilded curtain. BRP 7:37; YR 2:48
Beckwith, D.E.
Weapons for a cold war. NOR 1949:169
Bingham, J.B.
Enlightened materialism. YR 6:151
Bismarck, O. von
War and armaments in Europe. COP:121; COPA:121; COPB:121; PL:733; REEM 9:336; REEMA 11:244; REEMB 10:346
Bliven, B.
Mid-century pessimists. NORR 3d ser:303
Borah, W.E.
How to end war. LINM:74
Briand, A.
On the anti-war treaty. PL:770
Brigance, W.N.
Backwash of war. BA 1945-46:75
Bryce, J.
War and despotism. BREW 2:307
War spirit and the God of battles. BREW 2:309
Burns, R.W.
Freedom and war. ANGC:108
Butler, N.M.
How long must the war go on? BOB:30
Why war? BA 1938-39:13
Carlisle, Von A.
Mankind's quarrel with war. YR 3:139
Carty, W.
Big parade. BRP 5:11; YR 6:235
Case, F.
Modern paradox. COUW:257
Catt, C.C.
Call to action. REEM 7:91; REEMB 8:77
Chalmers, T.
War and truth. BOU:117; BREW 3:189; PL:498
Chamberlain, N.
Renunciation of appeasement. HAN:88
Churchill, W.L.S.
Causes of war. KLEB:43
Shall we commit suicide? REEM sup 1:191; REEMB 8:103
Civilian faces the prospect of war. DR:209
Conzelman, J.G.
Young man's physical and mental approach to war. SAC:60
Cox, G.V.
Challenge of war. ASHF:339
Crittenden, J.J.
Against warring on the weak. BREW 4:244
Cross of war: delivered in the Congress of the United States. DAVC:489
Dallinger, C.
They that take the sword. BRP 5:36; YR 6:191
Deiss, J.
Undergraduate looks at war. YR 4:187
Drama of the centuries. NI:288

Dreiling, N.R.
This paradox called war. AN:62
Dulles, J.F.
"Not war, not peace." BA 1947-48:58
Dunbar, E.M.
Supreme menace (denunciation of cause and effects of war). ASHF:256
Eliot, C.W.
Arming of the nations. REEM 2:8; REEMB 2:8
Enstrom, R.
"Lilliputians." BRP 2:25
Finch, C.A.
War prayer. BRP 1:49
Fleming, D.F.
Irrepressible issue. BA 1943-44:138
Fortino, A.
Insidious germ. YR 9:185
Fosdick, H.E.
Christian conscience about war. BAAMP:274; BRAC: 222; HICF:731; PL:776; REEM sup 1:333; REEMB 6:126
Freeman, S.
Enemy of peace. BRP 4: 49
Gladstone, W.E.
Power to make war. EMS 1:242
Gordon, S.
Is war inevitable under capitalism? YR 7:327
Gowacke, J.C.
Hickory stumps. BRP 1:53
Hahn, H.L.
Merchants of war. YR 7: 201
Higdon, H.
Desirability of war. JUD: 281
Humphrey, C.J.
Crosspatch. BRP 8:23; YR 9:213
Inge, W.R.
Causes of war. BEA:281
Ingersoll, R.G.
Vision of war, 1876 speech. BREW 7:130; DICD:136; DICE:136; REEM 10:266; REEMA 13:1238; REEMB 11:278; RID:59; SHAH:473
Vision of war (Decoration Day address, 1888). BAAMP:169; CODS:420; CODSA:420
Ireland, J.
Just war is holy. FUL:167, 170
Jordan, D.S.
Pyramids of skulls. BREW 7:180
Kaplan, A.
Half slave, half free. YR 9:195
Kuizenga, H.B.
Significance of the insignificant. YR 7:269
Larson, A.
Indian medicine. BRP 1:38
Larson, D.
Battle of baloney. BRP 5: 22
Lawson, L.
Must war be? BRP 7:19; NOR 1935:143
Lee, J.B.
Drafting of wealth in time of war. BA 1938-39:60
LeVander, H.
Date kernels. BRP 3:45; YR 4:151
MacArthur, D.
Seventy-fifth birthday address. BA 1954-55:34
MacBride, D.
Brass checks. YR 10:49
McCreight, W.E.
Through the eyes of youth. YR 7:67
Mara, E.
If we break faith. BRP 1: 84
Margulies, N.
Age of anxiety. MO:453
Maxim, H.
Airships and high explosives in war (1909). BREW 8:126
Mirabeau, H.G.R.
Right of war and peace. CODS:75; CODSA:75; PE: 241; PEA:241

WAR (cont.)
Moore, C.E.
Profit in loss. BRP 6:7; YR 7:155
Outline for a speech 'Man against man." BARR:97
Palmerston, H.J.T.
Power to make war. EMS 1:245
Rankin, J.
Woman suffrage and war. BREW 9:37
Ranney, A.
All but inmost faith. NOR 1941:5
Reading, D.K.
Puppets or patriots. BRP 6:99; NOR 1935:124
Reed, F.N.
War and public opinion. SHUC:49; TRUW:209
Rising, L.H.
Renaissance from war. ASHF:370
Robinson, I.J.
Must I die? NOR 1949:150
Robinson, L.T.
Edict of industry (present impossibility of war due to the interdependence of nations, industry, and capital). ASHF:262
Rodger, M.E.
Weapon versus wit. YR 8:187
Rogness, B.M.
Walls of Jericho. YR 7:213
Roosevelt, F.D.
Message to Hitler and Mussolini, April 14, 1939. HAN:95
Quarantining the aggressors. ANG:477; BRE:357; BRYA:539; HAN:91; FIP:233
United States' policy toward war. BA 1938-39:35
Rosebery, A.P.P.
Preparation for Armageddon. BREW 9:110
Scott, C.
Profit and loss. YR 7:315
Seabaugh, R.
Education for war. BLUE:100
Shaw, G.B.
So long, so long. SAR:263
Straight, M.
Two are alive. SAR:257
Sumner, C.
War system of the Commonwealth of Nations. SHAH:306
This ugly world. NATM:11
Turner, F.
What price war? BRP 1:67
Urey, H.C.
Atom bomb and war. BA 1945-46:95
Vincent, N.B.
Men like war. YR 9:221
Wallace, H.A.
Is American foreign policy leading to war? BA 1946-47:33
War. SHU:235
War's alternative. JA:205
Why peace is better than war. AMEO 2:107
William II.
Mailed fist. BEA:431
See also Army; Chemical warfare; Disarmament; Inter-American Conference on War and Peace; Navy; Peace; United States-Neutrality; War and education; Also Names of wars, e.g. European war, 1914-1918; World war, 1939-1945

WAR, OUTLAWRY OF See World war, 1939-1945-Peace and mediation

WAR AND EDUCATION
Barr, S.
How can our schools meet the war emergency? BA 1941-42:231
Conant, J.B.
Valedictory service address. BA 1942-43:257
Deutsch, M.E.
Preservation of the university. BA 1942-43:248
Gannon, R.I.

Wisdom before information. BA 1941-42:192
Hancher, V. M.
Postwar planning-for what? BA 1943-44:319
Harding, H. F.
Can the liberal arts tradition survive? BA 1943-44: 306
Hutchins, R. M.
University in war and peace. BA 1942-43:235
Prentis, H.W., Jr.
Preserving the roots of liberty. BA 1941-42:201
Russell, W. F.
To bind up the wounds in the schools of all nations. BA 1943-44:287
Shapley, H.
Design for fighting. BA 1944-45:245
Stoddard, A. J.
Education and the people's peace. BA 1944-45:272
Frontiers of youth. BA 1941-42:219
Studebaker, J.W.
Morale building in our schools and colleges. BA 1941-42:120
Weaver, A. T.
Challenge of the crisis. BA 1944-45:229
See also Veterans-Education

WAR BONDS See Bonds, government

WAR CRIMINALS See World war, 1939-1945-War criminals

WAR DEBTS See Debts, public

WAR LOANS See Bonds, government

WAR OF 1812 See United States-History-War of 1812

WAR TRIALS See World war, 1939-1945-War Criminals

WAR VETERANS See American Legion, Pensions, military; Veterans; Veterans' Day
Warburg, Paul Moritz
Inflation as a world problem and our relations thereto. REEM 4:410; REEMB 5: 368

WARBURG, PAUL FELIX
Introducing Paul Felix Warburg. NI:189; NIA:140
Warcaziwin, Sioux Indian
Indian in American history. JON:116
Ward, Artemus, pseud. See Browne, Charles Farrar
Ward, Asa
Faces in the crowd. EXEE: 118
Ward, Frederick A.
Introducing Thomas N. Page to the New England Society of Brooklyn, December 21, 1899. REEM 3:28; REEMA 3:861; REEMB 3: 28
Ward, Harry F.
Turk must go. TRUW:75
Ward, Sir Joseph
Speech at the Imperial Conference of 1911. KES 2:247

WARD, MATT FLOURNOY
Marshall, T.
Matt Ward case. SOU 9: 398
Ward, Samuel Baldwin
Medical profession. REEMA 3:1182
Ward, Samuel R.
Speech on the Fugitive Slave Bill. WOON:193
Warner, Charles Dudley
George William Curtis, litterateur. REEMA 9:1130
Pursuit of happiness. BLAA: 187; BLAB:187; REAC:88; WERN 42:127
Rise of the "Atlantic." REEMA 3:1186

WARNER, JACK
Jessel, G.
Introducing Jack Warner. JEYO:49
Warren, Earl
Address at the Louis Marshall Award dinner. BA 1962-63:97
California welcomes the United Nations. MO:505; MOA:509
Charles Evans Hughes and the spirit of tolerance (dedication of hall in memory of Hughes). BA 1956-57:135
Free investigation and faithful experiment. BA 1953-54:87
Home for American jurisprudence (dedication of American Bar Center in Chicago). COPB:611
Tribute to John F. Kennedy delivered in the Rotunda of the Capitol. BA 1963-64: 33; HIB:21
Warren, Howard
New Orient. COUW:173
Warren, Joseph
Boston Massacre. CHAL 3: 107; CHEM 1:43; HAZO 7: 2675; LEEW 8:93; MAS 7: 2675
Constitutional liberty and arbitrary power. BREW 10:81; HELE:25
Warren, Lindsay C.
Dedicating national shrine at Kitty Hawk. CORP:189
Warren, Shields
Biology in the atomic age. IOCP:71
Warren, Winslow
Spirit of the Revolution. THOU 1:493
Spirit of true American. THOU 1:500
Washburne, Emory
College as an element of the state. NORR 2d ser:162
Washington, Booker T.
Abraham Lincoln. HICF:359; KLEG:213
Address at the opening of the Atlanta Exposition. BAAMP: 189; BAKF:210; BLAA:113; BLAB:113; BRAG:8; BRY: 479; BRYA:566; CAP:110 CHAL 14:312; DOA:333; DUNM:181; HARS:503; HAZO 25:10583; HILK:38; MAS 25:10583; ONEM:509; ONES:102; PAR:461; PE: 633; PEA:633; PL:707; REEM 7:417; REEMA 9: 1136; REEMB 8:433; SMI: 206; WOON:580
Address delivered at dedication of the Robert Gould Shaw monument in Boston, May 31, 1897. CHAL 14: 320; DUNM:205; HAZO 25: 10861; MAS 25:10861; WOON:527
Address delivered at the Harvard Alumni dinner in 1896. BAKF:420; BOU:154; CHAL 14:318; COP:331; COPA: 331; COPB:331; HAZO 25: 10859; HILK:43; HURG: 144; MAS 25:10859; REEM 7:421; REEMA 9:1140; REEMB 8:437; WOON:584
American standard. -Same as his Address delivered at the Harvard Alumni dinner in 1896.
Better part. -Same as his Test of the American Negro
Negro in the late war. CHAL 14:325; FUL:333
Plea for the Negro race. - Same as his Address at the opening of the Atlanta Exposition
Progress of the American Negro. Same as his Address at the opening of the Atlanta Exposition
Teamwork. HILK:45
Test of the American Negro. FUL:330; WERN 42:34
Uplifting the Negro race. - Same as his Address at the opening of the Atlantic Exposition
WASHINGTON, BOOKER T.
Franklin, J. H.

Booker T. Washington, the man and the education (Tuskegee Institute Founder's Day speech). HILK:212

Lewis, W. H.
Booker T. Washington-a lover of his fellow-men. WOON:596

Moton, R. R.
Life of achievement (at memorial meeting in honor of Booker T. Washington). WOON:602

Scott, E. J.
Memorial address (on Booker T. Washington). WOON:607

Washington, George
Acceptance of military commission. BRAC:267; BRYW 8:77
Address to the American troops before the battle of Long Island. ESEH:212; THOU 1:156
Farewell address. ANG:194; BIR 1:219; BRE:101; BREA:99; BREW 10:94; BRYW 8:85; CAP:25; CARP:151; CHAL 2:468; CHEM 2:13; COP:248; COPA:248; COPB:248; CROC:447; DOA:228; FKA:185; FO:108; FOS:23; FRY:10; HARS:152; HAZO 6:2511; HIB:247; HURG:44; LEEW 8:293; MAS 6:2511; ORAMA 1:31; PO:29; REEM 10:29; REEMA 15:2036; REEMB 11:30; RID:12; SAA:103; SMI:79
First inaugural address. ANG:184; BEA:427; BOU:48; BRE:97; BREA:95; BREW 10:91; BRYW 8:79; CHAL 2:463; CHI:1; COP:245; COPA:245; COPB:245; HAZO 6:2506; HELE:98; KLEG:195; LOTI:3; MAS 6:2506; ORAMA 1:27; PL:576; REEMA 15:2032; SMI:77; USIN:1; USINA:1
First Presidential Thanksgiving proclamation. THOU 2:262
Second inaugural address. CHI:5; LOTI:7; USIN:5; USINA:5

WASHINGTON, GEORGE

Addams, J.
Washington's birthday. COP:346; COPA:346; COPB:346; GA:73; HURG:163; REEM 1:16; REEMB 1:16

Ames, F.
Eulogy on Washington, 1800. HELE:113; LEEW 9:41; THOU 1:161

Bloom, S.
At the home of Mary Ball Washington. DOA:15

Brief speech for Washington's birthday. BARB:106

Chase, H. W.
Spirit of Washington. HICF:935

Choate, R.
Birthday of Washington. REAC:70

Clay, C. M.
Address at Yale College (centennial birthday of Washington. CHAL 8:134; HAZO 10:6792, MAS 10:6792

Coyle, J. G.
Army of democracy: Washington birthday speech. ONEM:570; ONES:137

Daniel, J. W.
Dedication of the Washington monument. BREW 4:383; PROS:107; REEM 5:112; REEMA 7:295; SMI:215

Davis, J. W.
George Washington. REEM 1:363; REEMB 1:364

Davis, T.
Washington and the cause of '76. THOU 1:156

Delmas, D. M.
Washington (response to toast, "The character of Washington"). WAGN:259

WASHINGTON, GEORGE (cont.)
Depew, C. M.
Example of Washington: centennial of his death. THOU 3:302
One hundredth anniversary of Washington's inauguration. HAZO 23:9713; KLEG:169; MAS 23:9713; RINM:220
Washington and Lincoln. BOB:148
Everett, E.
Character of Washington. FULB:275
Farley, J. M.
George Washington. CATA 1:10
Faunce, W. H. P.
George Washington. BLAB: 296
Fox, C. J.
Foreign policy of Washington. BRYW 4:35
Washington as President. THOU 1:159
George Washington-a man of peace. DR:130; LU:1179
George Washington's birthday. BURS:179
Gunning, J.
First in agriculture. YR 10:159
Gunsaulus, F. W.
Washington's genius. HARSO: 292; WERN 42:142
Harrison, B.
Plea for patriotism (100th anniversary of Washington's inauguration). ESEH:199
Hillis, N. D.
Washington: the ideal American. HARSO:296; WERN 42:26
Hunter, R. M. T.
Oration (dedication of equestrian statue of Washington). SMI:148
Ishii, K.
Tribute to Washington. LEW:151
Jones, E. D.
Adventures among great Americans. BART 1:115
Lee, H.
Funeral oration on Washington. BREW 7:304; CHAL 3:474; HAZO 8:3242; HELE:103; LEEW 8:323; MAS 8:3242; ORAMA 1:243; REEM 5:274; REEMA 13: 1304; REEMB 9:313; RID: 26; SMI:86
Littleton, M. W.
Washington and Lincoln. KLEM:181
Lowell, G.
Our literature (100th anniversary of Washington's inauguration). BAKF:423; REEMA 2:758
McKinley, W.
Characteristics of Washington (at unveiling of Washington statue). KLEM:187; ONES:162; REEMA 9:845
Washington, a Masonic eulogy. THOU 3:80
Mason, J. M.
Eulogy on Washington. HAZO 9:3805; MAS 9:3805
Montague, A. J.
George Washington. SMI: 269
Moore, J. R.
Washington, nation builder. YR 4:117
Obligations of wealth-a Washington's birthday address. DAVC:498
Phillips, C.
Dinas Island speech on Washington. BREW 8:313; HAZO 12:4847; MAS 12: 4847; REEMA 14:1583
Eulogium on Washington. THOU 1:164
Potter, H. C.
Washington and American aristocracy (100th anniversary of Washington's first inauguration). BREW 8:365
Rice F. H.
Washington (memorial address at 100th anniversary of his death). THOU 3:298

Roosevelt, F.D.
Broadcast on Washington's birthday, 1942. BRAP:40; VO 1942-43:160
Truths that inspired Washington. BA 1942-43:217; VO 1943-44:83
Roosevelt, T.
George Washington (birthday speech). ONES:156
Sheppard, M.
Eulogy on Washington. SHU: 246
Shortridge, S.M.
Washington: liberty under law. WAGN:88
Sims, W.S.
Criticism and preparedness (Washington birthday address). REEM 7:345; REEMB 8:380
Stiles, Dr.
Washington. THOU 1:158
Swing, D.
Washington and Lincoln. CHAL 11:473
Thoughts for a speech in response to the toast "Washington: great as a soldier, greater as a statesman, greatest as a pure patriot." PITT:49
Vincent, G.E.
Washington's birthday. REEM 3:352; REEMB 3:368
Viviani, R.R.
Their monuments in our hearts. LEW:109
Washington birthday address. CRAI:407
Washington birthday address. THOS:21
Washington's birthday. DAVC: 457
Washington's birthday. FRIE: 111
Washington's birthday. NATS: 20
Washington's birthday address. DAVC:455
Washington's birthday (honoring our first President). EDGS:10
Washington's birthday (human side of our first President). ED:28
Washington's birthday oration. DAVC:241
Washington's birthday speech. HILL:488
Webster, D.
Character of Washington (at centennial anniversary of Washington's birthday). HAZO 10:4400; MAS 10: 4400
Whipple, E.P.
Genius of Washington. THOU 1:160
Wilson, W.
Mount Vernon's message to mankind. SMI:255
Wirt, W.
Washington as a model for formation of character. THOU 1:166

WASHINGTON, MARY BALL
Bloom, S.
At the home of Mary Ball Washington. DOA:15

WASHINGTON, D.C.
Grady, H.W.
Home and the Republic. SHU:155

WASHINGTON, UNIVERSITY OF
Suzzallo, H.
Inaugural address as president of University of Washington. WE 2:207
Waste, William H.
Mother's influence. ONEC:119

WATCHES See Acceptance speeches-Watches; Presentation speeches-Watches
Waterman, Alan T.
Science in the sixties (accepting the William Procter Prize of the Scientific Society of America). BA 1960-61:189
Waters, Robert
After dinner speaking. WERN

Waters, Robert (cont.)
54:145
Watkins, Ann
Introducing Rachel Crothers. ON:339
Watkins, Ferre C.
Introduces Robert A. Taft. PR:68
Watson, Ernest B.
Spoken word. SHUC:1
Watson, John
Scottish traits. BEA:299; REEM 8:416; REEMA 6:1143; REEMB 13:423
Watson, Thomas E.
Truth, in its relation to individuals, professions, laws and institutions. SOU 9:454

WATSON, THOMAS J.
Essence of civilization. COP:451; COPA:451
Watson, Thomas J., Jr.
Self protection: individualism (commencement address at Brown University). HIB:331

WATT, JAMES
Wertenbaker, T.J.
James Watt, inventor and pioneer. SAR:369
Watterson, Henry
Abraham Lincoln. HARSO:262; PROS:52; REAC:68; REEM 5:376; REEMA 6:1159; REEMB 9:420; SHUO:161
Birth of greatness. -Same as his Memorial Day
Blue and Gray. RID:71
Expansion. BLAA:160; BLAB:160; REAC:136
Francis Scott Key (at dedication of monument). REEMA 9:1143
Heroes in homespun. PROS:75; SHU:39
Memorial Day. FUL:337; WERN 42:82
Negro question. WERN 42:97
New Americanism. ESEH:207
Once a Kentuckian, always a Kentuckian. SOU 9:472
Our wives. REEM 3:357; REEMA 3:1189; REEMB 3:373
Puritan and the Cavalier. BRAC:297; COP:675; COPB:702; ONEM:627; ONES:222; REEM 3:359; REEMA 3:1191; REEMB 3:375; SHUM:237
Star-spangled banner. HARSO:269; PROS:24

WATTERSON, HENRY
Root, E.
Introducing H. Watterson to New England Society of New York. ANDS:198; LY:123; ONEM:669; ONES:4; REEM 3:359
Watts, F.O.
Presenting a badge. ONES:47
Wavell, Archibald Percival, 1st Viscount
At joint session of Legislative Assembly and Council of State of India. HAN:340; VO 1944-45:94
Wayland, Francis
Philosophy of analogy. BL:344
Wayland, H. L.
Causes of unpopularity. REEMA 3:1201
Force of ideas. REEMA 3:1197
Introduces Chauncey M. Depew to New England Society. REEMA 1:349
Our New England forefathers. THOU 1:321
Waymack, William Wesley
Challenge of America. BA 1939-40:155
King of energies. BA 1947-48:80
Wayne, Anthony
Reply to Little Turtle. JON. 78

WEALTH
Buried gold. FRIE:253

Bushnell, H.
True wealth or weal of nations. NORR 1st ser:1
Chase, E. A.
Pursuit of wealth. COUW: 15
Dewey, O.
Lust of riches. BREW 5: 201
Farkas, E.
How much land does a man need? BRP 4:76; YR 5:289
Fulkerson, R.
Dollar chasing. LINM:374
James, N. S.
New frontier (distribution of wealth and labor conditions). ASHF:81
Million dollars worth of assets. THOT:24
Mills, T. A.
Fiddles and fortunes. EXEE:11
Mr. new rich. FRIE:263
Money and wealth. NATT:7
Newman, J. H.
Property as a disadvantage. BREW 8:230; PL:496
Obligations of wealth-a Washington's birthday address. DAVC:498
Rogers, W.
Education and wealth. COP: 702; COPB:729; HURG: 200; REEM sup 2:361; REEMB 3:147
Smith, A. R.
Predatory rich. TRUW:47
Steinhoff, L.
Equities in wealth. YR 8: 123
Wealth and progress. DAVC: 532
See also Money

WEALTH, CONSCRIPTION OF
Lee, J. B.
Drafting of wealth in time of war. BA 1938-39:60

WEATHER
Clemens, S. L.
New England weather. BOU: 193; CHAL 12:447; COP: 666; COPB:693; DOA:296; HAZO 23:9871; HIB:94; HURG:128; LOMSA:295; MAS 23:9871; REEM 1:288; REEMA 1:210; REEMB 1: 290
Grant, U. S.
Remarkable climate. COP: 665; COPB:692; REEM 2: 137; REEMA 2:557; REEMB 2:129
Malone, T.
Out of the storm. YE:390
Sumrall, H. D.
On reporting the weather. BRAP:121
Weatherford, William, Creek chief
To General Jackson. BREW 7: 118
Weaver, Andrew Thomas
Challenge of the crisis. BA 1944-45:229
Charles Henry Woolbert. ONEC:129
Toward understanding through speech. BERS:2
Weaver, Chancey I.
Introduces Dr. Rees Edgar Tuloss. PR:64
Weaver, Paul See Price, J. H., jt. auth.
Weaver, Robert C.
Negro as an American. BA 1963-64:58
Webb, Col., Head Mingo of the Choctaws
Reply to the agent of the United States. SHE:13
Webb, Sally
On mousetraps. LINP:215
Webb, Sidney James, 1st Baron Passfield
Statute of Westminster. EMS 2:295
Webb, Walter Prescott
Speech that was never made (introduction of Harry S. Truman intended for Mississippi Valley Historical Association meeting). GRIS: 51

Weber, E. P.
Fulfill our joy. ACW:103
Weber, Wallace A.
Puritan tradition. YR 2:39
Weber, Wally
Remarks in response to introduction. PR:117
Webster, Daniel
American citizenship. PROS: 126
American government unique. REEMA 9:1152
American idea. -Same as his Bunker Hill monument
At laying of the cornerstone of addition to Capitol. HAZO 11:4621; MAS 11:4621
Basis of the Senate. WPRA:54
Bunker Hill monument. BREW 10:166; BRYW 9:24; CHAL 5:268; CLAY:73; CODS: 341; CODSA:341; CROC: 463; DOA:239; ESEH:186; FOS:75; HAZO 11:4419; HURG:62; LEEW 9:303; MAS 11:4419; ONEM:492; PAR:102; PL:621; REEM 10:101; REEMA 15:2090; REEMB 11:103; SAA:127; THOU 1:234
Celebrates the American heritage. -Same as his Eulogy on Adams and Jefferson
Character of Washington (at centennial anniversary of Washington's birthday). HAZO 10:4400; MAS 10: 4400
Constitution and the Union (March 7, 1850). -Same as his On the Clay Compromise
Constitution and the Union (December 23, 1850 speech). JOHA 1 pt 2:161; REEM 3: 365; REEMA 3:1210; REEMB 3:381
Constitution not a compact between sovereign states. HAZO 11:4493; MAS 11: 4493; WPRA:133
Dartmouth College case. BREW 10:198; HAZO 11: 4696; MAS 11:4696; SHAH: 129
Defence of the Kennistons. CLAY:216
Eulogy on Adams and Jefferson. BREW 10:186; CHAL 5:296; CLAY:10; FKA:9; HARSO:348; HAZO 11:4447; KLEG:135; MAS 11:4447; PE:327; PEA:327; PROS: 139; REEMA 15:2082; SHAH:134,138
Knapp White murder case. BAAMP:46; BREW 10:203; CHAL 5:304; HAZO 11: 4746; MAS 11:4746; ONEM:3; PAR:122; SHAH: 164; SHUM:65
Landing at Plymouth. BRAR 1: 354; KLEG:179
Liberty and Union. -Same as his Reply to Hayne
Objects of Mexican War. HAZO 11:4656; MAS 11: 4656
On being defeated for the candidacy of the Presidency, 1852. HILL:468
On Foot's Resolution (January 20, 1830). CLAW:41
On the Clay Compromise. BAAMP:66; BIR 2:172; BOU:63; BRAR 2:121; BRAS:73; BRE:183; BREA: 167; BRYW 9:64; HAZO 11: 4568; MAS 11:4568; PE: 401; PEA:401
Our country. REAC:102
Plymouth oration. BREW 10: 184; CHAL 5:293; CLAY: 143; CODS:331; CODSA: 331; HAZO 11:4444; MAS 11:4444
Progress of mechanic arts. BREW 10:194
Reply to Hayne. BAAMP:54; BIR 2:66; BRAO:185; BRE:153; BREA:137; BREW 10:112; BRYW 9:38; CAP:45; CHAL 5:171; CHEM 2:107; CLAW:117; CLAY:87,122; CODS:348; CODSA:349; COP:270;

COPA:270; COPB:270; FKA:17; FRY:24; FULB: 228; HARS:212; HARSO: 330; HAY:152; HAZO 10: 4303; HIBS:447; JOHA 1 pt 1:248; KLEG:102; LEEW 9: 177; MAS 10:4303; ONEM: 211; ORAMA 2:5; PAR:179; PE:340; PEA:340; PL:627; REEM 10:73; REEMA 15: 2053; REEMB 11:74; SAA: 144; SHAH:146
Seventh of March speech. - Same as his On the Clay Compromise
Supporting the Compromise of 1850. BREW 10:206
To the Royal Agricultural Society. KNAS:290; KNASA: 290
United States of America. - Same as his Reply to Hayne

WEBSTER, DANIEL
Adams, J. P.
Webster's defense of the Constitution. TRUW:7
Choate, R.
Death of Webster (October 28, 1852 speech). HAY:218; LEEW 10:73; REEM 5:69; REEMA 7:210; REEMB 9:99
On the death of Daniel Webster (Speech at Dartmouth, July 27, 1853). BRYW 9: 149; CHAL 6:294; HAZO 13: 5469; KLEG:236; MAS 13: 5469; PL:633; SHAH:258
Felton, C. C.
Delivering the statue of Daniel Webster to the Mayor of Boston. KNAS:156; KNASA:156
Hoar, G. F.
Daniel Webster. BLAA:75; BLAB:75; KNAS:109; KNASA:109
Jones, E. D.
Adventures among great Americans. BART 1:115
Kennedy, J. F.
Portraits of five senators in the Senate reception room. BA 1957-58:84
Lodge, H. C.
On Daniel Webster (at unveiling of statue in Washington). CHAL 14:179; HAZO 25:10688; MAS 25:10688
Webster as an orator. SHU:76
Parker, T.
Discourse on the death of Daniel Webster. BREW 8: 274; PE:410; PEA:410; PL:669; SHAH:236
Yancey, W. L.
On Mr. C. J. Ingersoll's Resolution of inquiry into the conduct of Daniel Webster, in expending the Contingent Fund while Secretary of State. SOU 9:329

Webster, Hugh
Commerce and world peace. ASHF:278

Webster, Pauline
From behind closed doors. YR 5:209

WEDDING SPEECHES
Biel, K. W.
Jesus-the savior of the home. ACW:84
Brueggemann, G. R.
Keep yourselves in the love of God. ACW:140
Bruening, W. F.
Dual obligation of marriage. ACW:127
Dobelstein, E. G.
God's order for a more abundant life. ACW:57
Eifert, W. H.
Invitation to Jesus and his disciples. ACW:76
Engelbrecht, H. H.
Follow after peace. ACW: 91
Essig, E. H.
Give thanks to God. ACW: 98
Felicitating a bridegroom. Also his response to the congratulatory speech. BARB: 66, 67

WEDDING SPEECHES (cont.)
Geiseman, O. A.
Blessings of a Christian marriage. ACW:48
Gruell, E. F.
Put on charity. ACW:118
Harman, C. H.
Promise of Christ's abiding presence. ACW:66
Huber, L. J.
Bridegroom emcee. BRH: 350
Kleiner, H. G.
Voice of God and the verdict of experience. ACW: 52
Klemp, O. C.
Commit your way unto the Lord. ACW:25
Koehneke, M. L.
Two heirs of God on an adventure in faith. ACW:131
Kramer, H. G.
Home blessed with peace. ACW:71
Lindemann, H.
Preservation for life's paths. ACW:45
Loeber, A. H. A.
Wilt thou go with this man? ACW:1
Nerger, E. A.
To remain in perfect love. ACW:87
Pieplow, E. E.
Greater increase. ACW:32
Presenting a gift to a fellow employee getting married. WRA:88
Reply to the toast "The bride" by the bridegroom. WRA: 65
Response to a toast to "The bridesmaids" by the best man. WRA:66
Rupprecht, O. C.
Travelling together in light. ACW:30
Scholz, A. C.
Prayer for mercy. ACW:21
Seboldt, R.
Taking Jesus into marriage. ACW:79
Speeding the would-be groom to his matrimonial doom at the bachelor's dinner. DR: 185
Stephan, C. C.
Lord is your shepherd. ACW:17
Stephan, P. G.
Sharing life's burdens and blessings. ACW:12
Streufert, P. W.
God's children live in love. ACW:135
Stuenkel, W. W.
God's assurance of his blessed presence. ACW:94
Three wedding speeches, by guest, bride's father, and groom. BURS:213, 218, 221
Troeger, W. F.
Union made in heaven. ACW:62
Two wedding speeches, by guests, and response by bridegroom. EDGS:255, 257, 258
Umbach, H. H.
Abiding peace. ACW:113
Visk, A. G.
Twisted news (to be delivered by an emcee at bachelor parties, bridal parties, or wedding receptions). BRH:328
Wangerin, W. M.
King's prayer for your home. ACW:8
Weber, E. P.
Fulfill our joy. ACW:103
Wedding. MORA:91
Weddings (guest is requested to say a few words). ED: 339
Weinhold, T. A.
God's prescription for a happy marriage. ACW:108
Wiederaenders, R.
Ship of matrimony. ACW: 28
Threefold promise. ACW:4
Word to the bride and groom on their wedding day. DR: 188; LU:1214

Zschoche, M. J.
Blessed triangle of a Christian marriage. ACW:122
See also Anniversaries, wedding; Bachelors; Engagements; Marriages; Showers, bridal

WEDDING TOASTS See Toasts
Weil, Richard See Taft, R. A., jt. auth.
Weinberg, Alvin M.
Nuclear energy development and military technology. HAR:321
Weiner, Milton
Best is yet to be. NOR 1947: 83
Weinhold, T. A.
God's prescription for a happy marriage. ACW:108
Weinstock, Harris
Jesus the Jew. WAGN:395
Weiss, John
Task of religion. REEMA 9: 1162

WELCOMING ADDRESSES
Address of welcome at a convention. BEDA:135
Address of welcome at a sales convention by the president of the company. WRA:02
Address of welcome at an alumni dinner. DAVC:386
Address of welcome by the president of the Rotary Club. SOES:25
Address of welcome to a convention. SOES:24
Address of welcome to a personage. BURS:233
Address of welcome to a reunion banquet of Class of '14. AMEO 1:104
Address of welcome to graduates of Hamilton High School by association president. WRA:71
Address of welcome to high school alumni. AMEO 1:63
Address of welcome to new members at a service club meeting. WRA:70
Address of welcome to new superintendent of schools. AMEO 1:75
Address of welcome to Patriotic Order Sons of America. AMEO 2:86
Admiral Byrd: welcome home address. SCHS:56
Ainslie, G.
Welcome to Richmond. ONES:22
Alderman, E. A.
Greetings to Johns Hopkins. ONES:82
Ames, O.
Address of greeting. THOU 3:493
Apeland, C.
Welcome to new citizens. PRNE:219
Argyll, C. D. C.
Welcome to Garrison. HAZO 20:8423; MAS 20: 8423
At a dinner in honor of an old friend after years of absence. HAPR:73
At the opening of a meeting of physicians. HAPR:77
Atkinson, J.
Welcome to the Society of Certified Public Accountants. LINM:382
Aulish, F. J.
Welcome to new citizens. SABA:290
Beaconsfield, B. D.
To the King of the Belgians. KNAS:208; KNASA:208; REEMA 1:30
Birkenhead, F. E. S.
Welcome to the American Ambassador. REEMB 1:114
Bowman, J. B.
Welcome to American nurses. GA:18
Bradley, F.M.
Welcome to Washington. THOU 3:481
Bruisloff, A.
Welcoming Elihu Root, June 27, 1917. REEM 3:162

WELCOMING ADDRESSES (cont.)
Burnham, H. L. W. L.
Welcome to the Associated Advertising Clubs of the world. LINM:28
Bush, I. T.
In honor of Secretary Hughes. REEM sup 1:145; REEMB 1:183
Butler, N. M.
Welcoming Briand. REEM 1:187; REEMB 1:188
Byrnes, J. F.
General Assembly a great forum. GLAD:173
Call of the wild (toast and welcome address to seniors). AB:55
Churchill, W. L. S.
Address to the Pilgrims, March 18, 1941 (welcoming Ambassador Winant). ON: 313; VO 1941:137
Class greeting. WERN 54:35
Clay, H.
To Lafayette. CHAL 5:84; HAZO 10:4114; HELE:180; KNAS:216; KNASA:216; MAS 10:4114; REEM 5:83; REEMA 7:247; REEMB 9: 113
Conant, J. B.
Address of welcome: tercentenary conference at Harvard University. ON:39; SAR:111
Coolidge, C.
Welcome to Charles A. Lindbergh. BRAC:240; SHU: 7; SHUP:163
Covell, W. E. R.
Welcome to Educational group. BRAC:243
Dawes, C. G.
Welcoming the Jewish Welfare Board. ONEC:13
Delayed welcome by toastmaster. FRIT:31
Depew, C. M.
Our English visitors (welcoming George Augustus Sala). REEMA 1:338
Welcome to Mayor Cooper. REEMA 1:330
Eastern Star welcome address. THOS:47
Eliot, C. W.
Speech of welcome to Prince Henry of Prussia. BAKF:221; ONEM:676; ONES:15
Elliott, D.
Class day greeting. WERN 54:35
Elliott, E. B.
Welcome to the National Education Association. ON: 321
Elmhurst club president's welcoming address to members of visiting club. WRA:69
Examples of welcoming remarks by toastmaster; Sincerity; Nothing spared; Ladies' day; Enjoy yourselves; Recipe for fun; Room for one more. FRIT: 46-47
Examples of words of welcome. BO:51-54
Fennell, D. L.
Welcoming National Safety Congress. ON:320
Four speeches of welcome to visitors in midweek prayer service. HNWS:25-26
Frank, G.
Welcome to freshmen. REEM sup 1:344; REEMB 7:158
General fraternity: an address of welcome. THOS:38
Greeting and welcome (at ceremony honoring retiring secretary of labor union). BED:80; BEDA:153
Greeting and welcome (at dedication of home for aged). BED:32; BEDA:73
Greeting and welcome (at dedication of recreation center). BED:37; BEDA:78
Greeting and welcome (at presentation of Brotherhood award). BED:55; BEDA:63

Greeting and welcome (at unveiling of portrait presented to Labor Temple). BED: 89; BEDA:161
Greeting ladies. NATT:23
Greeting to the club guest. STOC:129
Greetings to forum. BEC:161
Greetings to ladies. FRIT:35
Hadley, A. T.
To the Brotherhood of Yale, 1901. KNAS:205; KNASA:205; ONEM:672; ONES:13
Hall, F.
Address of welcome to the Grand Council of New York Royal Arcanum. THOU 3: 398
Hancher, V.
Introducing Joseph F. Newton at a combined honors convocation and baccalaureate service at the State University of Iowa. BA 1945-46:214
Harding, W. G.
Welcome to the Daughters of the American Revolution. LINM:140
Hinds, C. G.
Fraternal greetings. THOU 3:318
Hodgkinson, H. D.
Welcome to the Conference on Distribution. YE:133
Holmes, O.W.
Welcome to alumni (1860). ONEM:674; REEMA 2:625; WERN 54:127
Welcome to alumni (1863). CHAL 7:403; HAZO 15: 6300; KLEM:52; MAS 15: 6300
Holt, G. N.
Address of welcome to Mystic Workers. THOU 3: 403
Home team welcomes its visiting opponents. DR:277; LU:1252
Hughes, C. E.
In honor of Lord Reading. REEM 2:256; REEMB 2: 260
Humorous address of welcome. THOS:43
Iverson, S.
Address of welcome to United Workmen. THOU 3: 323
Jessel, G.
To welcome a newly born-a model speech. JEYO:13
King, W. L. M.
To Marshall Foch. REEM 7:202; REEMB 8:229
Knights of Pythias: an address of welcome. THOS: 39
Krantz, J. C., Jr.
Welcome to Baltimore. MCK:178
Welcome to Maryland. MCK:179
Lamont, T. W.
American bankers' responsibilities. BYRA:265; HOA: 371; HOAP:257; REEM 4: 272; REEMB 5:93
Lansing, R.
Pan-Americanism. FKA: 200
Larson, C.
Address of welcome (at Kappa Kappa Gamma initiation banquet). MOUG:242; MOUGA:242
Lehman, H.
Welcome to National Education of the United States. ON:316
Lewis, I. J.
Welcome to National Education Association. GA:20
Littell, J. S.
Address of welcome (Sons of Temperance). THOU 3: 486
Lord, C. S.
Welcoming Mary Garden to Lotus Club, New York, January 29, 1922. REEM 2:61
Loveless, H. C.
Welcome address at Iowa State College centennial.

WELCOMING ADDRESSES (cont.)
IOCP:13
Lucas, S.W.
Welcoming President Eduard Benes. BA 1942-43:56
Lyon, J.H.
Right hand of fellowship (welcoming one into the Pilgrim Church of Providence, R.I.). THOU 2:471
MacDonald, J.R.
Address to the House of Representatives. ONEC:10
Address to the Senate. LINM:431; ONEC:7
McKelway, B.M.
Welcoming the members of Congress to Washington. SAB:210
MacLean, A.W.
Welcoming aviators to Kitty Hawk. CORP:260
McMaster, S.J.
Welcoming the American Federation of Labor. ONEC:15
Mao Tse-tung
C C P greetings. RUS:34
Marshall, T.R.
Russian War Mission. REEM 2:392; REEMB 2:409
To the Belgian War Misson. REEM 2:391; REEMB 2:408
Welcome to the Italian Commission. BRAC:245
Masonic address of welcome. THOS:41
Mayor of Tuscon welcomes Arizona Bankers Association. PR:112
Mayor's address of welcome at a business convention. WRA:68
Mayor's address of welcome to Convention of Knights Templar. AMEO 2:58
Mayor's address of welcome to Secretary of War. HILL:468
Model and outline of a welcome speech (welcome to city). BAKS:105,110
Moore, H.E.
Welcome to secondary school principals. YE:135
My father. Fathers' Day address of welcome by a son. EDGS:318
Nobles of the Mystic Shrine: an address of welcome. THOS:39
Opening address at a sales convention by president of company. WRA:80
Opening address at Town Hall meeting. BEDA:70
Organizing a club (welcoming new chapter to Speakers' Club at opening meeting). BED:11; BEDA:15
Osborne, C.S.
Northland to Dixieland. NESA:137
Park, M.E.
Welcome to Bryn Mawr's fiftieth anniversary. GA:22
Perkins, G.C.
Knights Templar address of welcome. WAGN:341
Philosophical address of welcome. THOS:44
Prentiss, S.S.
To returned volunteers of the Mexican War (welcome home). LEEW 10:59
Preparation of a welcome address. CORP:264
Quincy, J., Jr.
Welcome to Dickens. REEM 3:122; REEMA 3:964; REEMB 3:123
Reception of a baseball club-speech of welcome, and reply of president of club. BARB:114
Reception of a visiting fire company. HILL:479
Reid, W.
Welcoming H.M. Stanley to Lotus Club, November 27, 1886. REEM 3:263; REEMB 3:280
Roosevelt, T.
America greets France. ONES:70
Welcome to the Military

Surgeons' Association. ONES:20
Root, E.
Greetings to the Russian Republic. BREW 9:100
Rosebery, A. P. P.
Great Britain in panorama (welcome to Press Conference, June 6, 1919). BREW 9:109
Schurman, J. G.
Welcome to Cornell's 25th anniversary. ONES:23
Senior class address of welcome. AMEO 2:124
Seward, W.H.
Address to John Quincy Adams. KNAS:211; KNASA: 211
Sherman, W. T.
Speech of welcome at reunion of the Army of the Tennessee. HILL:468
Small town welcomes its favorite son. DR:47; LU:1145
Smith, R. A.
Address of welcome (United Workmen). THOU 3:323
Speech to the Hay Fever Association of America by the Mayor of Duluth, Minnesota. LARW:113
Stewart, J. G.
Welcome to Cincinnati. YE: 134
Suggestions for preparation of speeches of welcome. BARR:233; BRA:507; BRAS:494; MOUG:150; MOUGA:150; RE:168; REAB:156. With examples of. BEB:46; BEC:75; CON: 7; GA:16; GLAD:172; LARW:113; MCK:177; MO: 500; MORA:113-118; PITT: 63-64; SABA:282; SOES: 23; WRA:67, 77; WRB: 187; YE:132
Suggestions for welcoming an individual or a group. BRY:375; BRYA:406
To the drill team. THOS:140
Toastmaster's welcome remarks. NAT:19
Toastmaster's welcome to the seniors. SOES:49
Toastmaster's welcoming remarks. FRIT:13
Tucker, W. J.
Welcome to "The Wheellock Succession." To his successor in office. ONEM: 678; ONES:18
Two speeches welcoming a guest soloist. HNWS:35-36
Two speeches welcoming a guest speaker at a stewardship banquet. HNWS:39-40
Two speeches welcoming visitors in a worship service. HNWS:21
Two welcome speeches to new Christians. HNWS:31-32
Upon tendering a dinner to a popular young bachelor just returned from abroad. HAPR:60
Visit of a boat club-reception address. BARB:119
Visit of a cricket club-reception address, and reply by president of club. BARB: 119
Visit of a fire company-reception speech to the foreman. Reply by foreman. BARB:115
Visit of a military regiment or company reception address. BARB:113
Visit of a temperance association-address of welcome, and reply by the president. BARB:120
Wagner, R. F., Jr.
Welcomes the convention of Lions International. PRNE: 71
Walker, J. J.
Welcome to the Right Honorable J. Ramsay MacDonald. LINM:425; YE:138
Welcoming Colonel Charles A. Lindberg. ONEC:11; PROS:112
Warren, E.

WELCOMING ADDRESSES (cont.)
California welcomes the United Nations. MO:505; MOA:509
Watterson, H.
Once a Kentuckian, always a Kentuckian. SOU 9:472
Wayland, H. L.
Force of ideas. REEMA 3:1197
Welcome address at a Garden Club meeting. BEDA:67
Welcome address to a distinguished guest. HILL:462
Welcome remarks. NAT:49
Welcome to a delegation of boy or girl scouts (or other youth groups). HNWS:50
Welcome to a delegation of laymen. HNWS:52
Welcome to a delegation of pastors. HNWS:51
Welcome to a denominational leader. HNWS:45
Welcome to a distinguished visitor by a prominent citizen. EDGS:334
Welcome to a district or state church convention. HNWS:47
Welcome to a foreign guest by a citizen on the welcoming committee. EDGS:327
Welcome to a former pastor by present pastor. HNWS:13
Welcome to a former pastor's wife. HNWS:14
Welcome to a general delegation (4H, Future Homemakers, etc.). HNWS:52
Welcome to a group. CON:9
Welcome to a guest evangelist. HNWS:34
Welcome to a guest minister. HNWS:34
Welcome to a guest missionary. HNWS:37
Welcome to a guest speaker at a father-son banquet. HNWS:38
Welcome to a guest speaker in Sunday school. HNWS:41
Welcome to a guest speaker in Woman's Missionary Society. HNWS:41
Welcome to a minister as civic club speaker. HNWS:17
Welcome to a minister of another denomination. HNWS:43
Welcome to a minister of another nationality. HNWS:44
Welcome to a minister of another race. HNWS:44
Welcome to a national convention. HNWS:48
Welcome to a new associate pastor and family. HNWS:19
Welcome to a new minister of music and family. HNWS:16
Welcome to a new minister of religious education and family. HNWS:15
Welcome to a new pastor and family. HNWS:11
Welcome to a new Sunday school superintendent (or other church official). HNWS:18
Welcome to a newly-ordained minister. HNWS:20
Welcome to a returned traveler by a friend who remained at home. EDGS:331
Welcome to a visiting baseball team. EDGS:390
Welcome to an evangelist singer. HNWS:36
Welcome to an individual. CON:8
Welcome to annual Boy Scout drive. BEDA:107
Welcome to dignitaries. THOS:46
Welcome to Grand Officers. THOS:138
Welcome to guests. NATS:1
Welcome to new church members (transfers from another church). HNWS:30
Welcome to new Americans. SOES:36

Welcome to new neighbors. DR:234
Welcome to one returning. BURS:237
Welcome to visiting club members. FRIT:34
Welcome to visitors among military personnel. HNWS: 28
Welcome to visitors at general church dinner. HNWS:27
Welcome to visitors in a Sunday school. HNWS:22
Welcome to visitors in Men's Brotherhood. HNWS:25
Welcome to visitors in midweek church dinner. HNWS: 26
Welcome to visitors in revival service. HNWS:29
Welcome to visitors in the Baptist Training Union. HNWS:23
Welcome to visitors in the Woman's Missionary Society. HNWS:24
Welcome to wife of a new pastor. HNWS:12
Welcoming address at testimonial to a musician. BEDA:38
Welcoming addresses and toasts for a junior-senior banquet-theme: "Last round up." AB:73-77
Welcoming friends. FRIE:336
Welcoming new member. NATM:31
Welcoming the new club or organization president. DR: 103
Welcoming visitors. NATM: 37
Weygant, C.V.
Welcoming Judge Kingsley A. Taft to Ohio Supreme Court. YE:138
Williams, C.O.
Greetings to Forum on Current Problems. GA:24
See also Emcees; Introductions; Opening addresses; Responses to welcome; Reunions; Toastmasters; Toasts
Welday, Wheeler J.
Danger signal-foreign immigration. SHUC:281
Welles, Orson See Bryson, L., jt. auth.
Welles, Sumner
America's foreign policy. BA 1943-44:53
At third meeting of Ministers of Foreign Affairs of the American Republics. VO 1942-43:35
Memorial Day address at the Arlington National amphitheater. VO 1942-43:321
On the German Reich's attack on the Soviet Union. VO 1941:325
Post-war leadership. BA 1941-42:270
Relations with the French government at Vichy. VO 1942-43:188
Status of French ships at Alexandria, Egypt. VO 1942-43:392
Toward new horizons. HAN:370
Wellington, Arthur Wellesley, 1st Duke of
Reform of the franchise. EMS 2:148
On Catholic emancipation. CHAL 4:329; HAZO 9:3758; MAS 9:3758; REEMA 15: 2107
Wellman, Francis L.
Summation for the people in the Carlyle Harris murder trial. HICJ:261
Wendell, Barrett
Mystery of education. NORR 1st ser:442
WENDT, GERALD
Schnadig, E. L.
Presents Gerald Wendt. LY:185; PR:93
Wenig, Hebert Edward
The Constitution. DOA:100; LEIO:67
Wentworth, Peter
In behalf of the liberties of

Wentworth, Peter (cont.)
Parliament.-Same as his Liberty of the Commons
Liberty of the Commons. BRTH:6; BRTHA:6; CHAL 1:457; HAZO 4:1386; MAS 4:1386
Wentworth, Thomas, 1st Earl of Strafford. See Strafford, T.W.
Wenzel, Richard E.
German-American. SHUC:365
Werner, Eloise M.
Others. BRP 8:7
Werner, James
Sleeping giant. MIA:333
Wert, Robert J.
Restless generation and undergraduate education. BA 1964-65:145
Wertenbacker, Thomas Jefferson
James Watt, inventor and pioneer. SAR:369
Wesley, Charles H.
Education for citizenship in a democracy. HILK:55
Wesley, John
Denounces the doctrine of predestination. PE:108; PEA:108
Free grace. ORBR 1:181
God's love to fallen man. BREW 3:173; CHAL 2:208; COP:153; COPA:153; COPB:153; HAZO 5:1783; HIB:199; MAS 5:1783; PL:486; REEM 9:85; REEMB 10:88
On dressing for display. BREW 10:218
Poverty of reason. BREW 10:212
Sacra fames auri. BREW 10:215

WEST, THE
Binkley, W.C.
South and the West. TIN:255
Morris, M.H.
Conquering West. BUT:180; BUTB:180
Robinson, E.E.
Man on the frontier. SHUC:21; TRUW:238
To the West. THOS:97
Turner, F.J.
Contributions of the West to American democracy. FKA:72; SHU:88
Wallace, H.C.
Southerner in the West. REEMA 3:1178
Wolcott, E.O.
Bright land to westward. REEM 3:431; REEMA 3:1273; REEMB 3:438

WEST POINT
MacArthur, D.
Farewell to the cadets (accepting Sylvanus Thayer award for service to his nation). HIB:58; LINP:150
Westcott, John W.
Destiny of democracy. SHU:238
Westerdyk, Johanna
Place of the International Federation today. GA:171

WESTERN HEMISPHERE
Berle, A.A., Jr.
Relations between the two Americas. SAR:292
Bonsal, P.W.
Inter-American relationship. HOC:144
Hull, C.
Address before the Pan American Union, April 14, 1943. VO 1943-44:164
MacLean, D.A.
Americas in the world crisis. HOC:121

---- DEFENSES
Bru, F.L.
United Hemisphere defense. COP:567; COPB:471
Granik, T. and others.
America's policy toward insular possessions of other countries. BA 1939-40:86
Hull, C.
Pillars of enduring peace.

COP:558; COPB:550
Roosevelt, F.D.
Freedom of the seas. COP: 546; COPB:524; SAA:300; VO 1941:395
Hemisphere defense for democracy. COP:534; COPB:512
Message to Congress on U.S. occupation of Iceland. VO 1941:341
Pan American Union. SAA: 281

WESTMINSTER, STATUTE OF (1931)
Bennett, R.B.
Statute of Westminster (June 30, 1931 speech). KESB:255
Buckmaster, S.O.
Statute of Westminster, 1931. EMS 2:293
Churchill, W.L.S.
Statute of Westminster, November 20, 1931 speech. KESB:274
Cripps, S.
Statute of Westminster, November 20, 1931 speech. KESB:297
Inskip, T.
Statute of Westminster, November 20, 1931 speech. KESB:284
Lapointe, E.
Statute of Westminster (June 30, 1931 speech). KESB: 260
Latham, J.G.
Statute of Westminster (July 17, 1931 speech). KESB: 263
Lemass, S.
Statute of Westminster (July 19, 1931 speech). KESB: 242
McGilligan, P.
Statute of Westminster (speeches of July 16, 17, 23, 1931). KESB:231, 245, 251
Webb, S.J.
Statute of Westminster. EMS 2:295

WESTMINSTER ABBEY
Kingsley, C.
Westminster Abbey. REEMA 5:691
Weston, Paul
Introducing a humorist
" a world traveler. BRC: 309, 284
Weyforth, B. Stuart, Jr.
Introduces Fred C. Foy, Chairman of the Board and President of Koppers Company. PRC:28
Introduces Rear Admiral George J. Dufek. PRC:16
Weygant, Carl V.
Welcoming Judge Kingsley A. Taft to Ohio Supreme Court. YE:138

WHALEN, GROVER A.
Introducing Grover Whalen. SUM:72
Nizer, L.
Presents Grover A. Whalen. LY:81; NI:179; NIA:132
Whalen, Robert S.
"Give us a break." JUD:255
Wheatley, John
Right of association. EMS 2: 87
Wheeler, Alfred
Labor question. THOU 1:404
Wheeler, Benjamin Ide
Address delivered in San Francisco at 250th anniversary of the settlement of the Jews in the United States. TWJ:180
Christianity and life. SHU: 249
Effective living. SHU:86
Introductory address to students of the University of California. WAGN:428
Things human. NORR 1st ser: 276
Wheeler, Burton K.
Against the resolution for collaboration for postwar peace. BA 1943-44:115

Wheeler, Burton K. (cont.)
America's present emergency. WPRC:255
Keep this nation at peace. COP:580
On Indian affairs. DOA:211
Should Mr. Roosevelt's plan for enlarging the Supreme Court be adopted? (negative) SAR:229
United Mine Workers' convention. BA 1939-40:316

Wheeler, Joseph
American soldier. REEM 3:375; REEMA 3:1220; REEMB 3:391; SHUO:243

Whelpley, Philip Melancthon
"Memory of the just is blessed," 1822. BRAR 1:101

WHIG AND TORY
Meagher, T. F.
Indictment of the Whigs. HAZO 20:8463; MAS 20:8463

Whipper, William
Non-resistance to offensive aggression. WOON:104

Whipple, E. P.
China emerging from her isolation. REEMA 3:1225
Genius of Washington. THOU 1:160
Patriotic oration. CHAL 9:398; HAZO 19:8022; MAS 19:8022
Sphere of woman. REEMA 3:1229
True glory of a nation. BOA:78; BOB:110
Wit and humor. REEMA 6:1189

Whipple, Fred L.
Personal goals. ANGC:11

WHIPPLE, GEORGE H.
Merriam, J. C.
Presents George H. Whipple. LY:190

White, Andrew Dickson
Apostle of peace among the nations. CHAL 12:80; HAZO 22:9487; MAS 22:9487
Commerce and diplomacy. REEMA 3:1232
Evolution vs. revolution in politics. NORR 1st ser:233
Field of historical study. REEMA 9:1177
Inaugural address as president of Cornell University. WE 1:245

White, Edward Douglas
Standard Oil Company of New Jersey v. United States, 1911: opinion for the Supreme Court. BIR 3:295
Supreme Court. BYRA:451; REEM 3:380; REEMB 6:373

White, Frank Edson
New ideas for an old industry (meat packing). REEM sup 3:160; REEMB 5:382

White, George H.
Defense of the Negro race. DUNM:233; WOON:403

White, John H.
Odd Fellowship and Masonry. THOU 3:126

White, Paul Dudley
Responds to the introduction by C. W. D. Hanson. PRC:30

WHITE, PAUL DUDLEY
Hanson, C. W. D.
Introduces Dr. Paul Dudley White, distinguished physician and cardiac specialist. PRC:29

White, Stephen M.
Eulogy of Senator Stanford. WAGN:41

White, Sir Thomas
Life and character of Sir Wilfrid Laurier. KLEB:21

White, Thomas, Jr.
Twenty years of Liberal-Conservative administration in Canada. CHAL 11:324; HAZO 22:9207; MAS 22:9207

White, William Allen
Country newspaper. REEM 6:412; REEMB 6:381

Education of a democracy. BOB:188; SHU:128
Speaking for the consumer. COP:427; COPA:427; COPB:417; HURG:234
Your young men shall see visions. SAR:1
White Eyes, Delaware chief
Speaks at Friends meeting, New Comerstown, 1773. SHE:18

WHITE HOUSE CONFERENCE ON CHILD HEALTH AND PROTECTION See Children
Whitefield, George
Kingdom of God. BREW 10:223
On the method of grace. BRYW 3:181; CHAL 2:290; HAZO 5:1975; MAS 5:1975; PL:491
Whitehurst, Mrs. John L.
Inaugural address (as President of General Federation of Women's Clubs). BUTA:224
Whitfield, Albert H.
Tribute to the women of the South (at dedication of Mississippi's new Capitol). SHUO:36
Whitlock, Brand
Lafayette, apostle of liberty. REEM 11:224; REEMB 12:239

WHITMAN, WALT
Ingersoll, R. G.
Eulogy on Walt Whitman. HARSO:196; WERN 42:87
Whitney, John Hay
Challenges and exellences (accepting degree). BA 1964-65:120

WHITTIER, JOHN GREENLEAF
Norton, C.E.
Castles in Spain. REEMA 2:850

WHITTINGTON CLUB
Jerrold, D.W.
Whittington Club. REEMA 8:739
Wickersham, George Woodward
American Law Institute. BYRA:459; REEM sup 3:163; REEMB 6:390
Wideraenders, R.
Ship of matrimony. ACW:28
Threefold promise. ACW:4
Wieferich, Robert
Youth and the depression. JUD:247
Wiers, Charles R.
Swarm of bees (business advice). REEM sup 3:171; REEMB 5:386
Wiggen, Evelyn
American home. BUT:246
Wiggin, Kate Douglas
Sov'ran woman. REEM 3:388; REEMB 3:395
Speech in rhyme. REEM 3:391; REEMB 3:398
Wigmore, John Henry
Enlistment in the Christian ministry. REEM 6:421; REEMB 6:398
My creed for the nation. REEM 3:394; REEMB 3:401
Wilber, Laura Ann
Without a word. BRAP:74
Wilberforce, William
Appeal in behalf of Negro slaves in the West Indies. HAZO 8:3454; MAS 8:3454
Horrors of the British slave trade in the 18th century. BREW 10:299; BRYW 4:60; CHAL 4:96; HAZO 8:3443; MAS 8:3443; PE:212; PEA:212; PL:437; REEMA 15:2120
Wilbur, Ray Lyman
Our destiny in the Pacific. COP:453; COPA:453

WILBUR, RAY LYMAN
Merriam, J.C.
Presents Ray Lyman Wilbur. LY:189
Wilcox, Dwight
Introducing a symphony or-

Wilcox, Dwight (cont.)
chestra conductor. BRC: 286
Wild, Robert
American jingo. TRUW:89
Wilde, Oscar
Home decoration. ARNS:72
Wiley, Alexander
Brief remarks at conclusion of Senator Vandenberg's report on the United Nations Assembly. BA 1945-46:46

WILEY, ALEXANDER
Day, J.E.
Introduces United States Senator, Alexander Wiley. PRNE:36
Wiley, Bell Irvin
Time of greatness. TIN:325

WILEY, CALVIN HENDERSON
Joyner, J.Y.
Tribute to Calvin Henderson Wiley (at unveiling of monument). SHUO:284
Wiley, Harvey Washington
Ideal woman. REEM 3:404; REEMA 3:1240; REEMB 3: 411
Wilford, Howard C.
Introducing a barber
" a baseball player
" a teacher. BRC:148,110, 119
Wilhelmina, Queen of the Netherlands.
Address to Congress. VO 1942-43:427
Wilkes, John
Commons and its rights, 1776. BRTH:81; BRTHA: 81
Conquest of America impossible (1777). BRYW 3:246
Denies the right of the House of Commons to reject duly elected members. PE:126; PEA:126
On coercive measures in America. BRYW 3:243; SAA:20
Warning and a prophecy. BREW 10:239

WILKES, JOHN
Mansfield, W.M.
In the case of John Wilkes. BREW 8:75; GOOD:154
Wilkins, Roy
Deep South crisis. WPRC:344
Tribute to John F. Kennedy delivered at City Hall Plaza in New York City. BA 1963-64:34

WILKINSON, EDWARD C.
Prentiss, S.S.
Wilkinson trial. SOU 9:390
Wilkinson, Howard C.
How separate should government and God be? LINP: 112
Willard, Frances E.
Work done for humanity (1890). BRYW 10:162; PL: 694; REEM 7:424; REEMB 7:414; WERN 42:162
Willcox, William R.
Introducing G.W. Goethals to the Economic Club of New York, March 5, 1914. LY: 182; REEM 2:100

Willebrandt, Mabel Walker
Prohibition enters politics. HICF:827

WILLIAM I (THE CONQUEROR OF ENGLAND)
Guizot, F.P.G.
At the unveiling of the statue of William the Conqueror. CHAL 5:404; HAZO 12:4881; MAS 12:4881
William II, German Emperor
Address to the German people. COP:127; COPA:127; COPB:127; PL:738; REEM 11:6; REEMB 12:6
German youth. WERN 42:24
Is outraged and adamant (speeches on July 2, 27, August 2, 1900). PE:660-

663; PEA:660-663
Mailed fist. BEA:431
Moses and Amalek. REEM 11: 1; REEMA 15:2129; REEMB 12:1
William, Duke of Normandy
Rage of battle; address to his army before the battle of Hastings, 1066. BRTH:2; BRTHA:2

WILLIAM AND MARY COLLEGE
Chandler, J.C.C.
Inaugural address as president of William and Mary College. SMI:261
Williams, Ben J.
Inflation can be controlled without price ceilings. SAB: 140
Williams, Charl Ormond
Greetings to Forum on Current Problems. GA:24
Women must work. GA:265
Williams, Clyde C. (Slim)
Blazing an international trail by motorcycle. BART 2:231
Williams, Esten K.
Presents David A. Simmons. LY:139
Williams, George
Fifty years old (Y.M.C.A. talk). THOU 2:493
Williams, Hillery
Introducing a certified public accountant
" a high government official. BRC:62,63
Williams, Homer D.
Introducing George W. Pepper to the Citizens' Committee, University of Pittsburgh. LINM:481
Williams, J. Harvie See McBurney, J.H., jt. auth.
Williams, Jesse Feiring
Evolution of conscience. SHUC: 182; TRUW:230
Williams, John Sharp
Bridging the bloody chasm. HARSO:13
Farewell to his friends. BRAC:274
Jefferson Davis: giant among men. BOA:234; HICF:431; PROS:49
Southern gentleman (commemorating Edward C. Walthall). SHUO:45
Thomas Jefferson. REEM 5: 405; REEMB 9:449
Who will haul down that flag? BRAC:206
Williams, Milton H.
Constitution. BRP 1:34
Williams, Peter
Oration on the abolition of the slave trade. WOON:32
Slavery and colonization. WOON:77
Williams, Robert Gray
Robert Edward Lee. SMI:299
Williams, Roger
Liberty of conscience or the sole means to obtain peace and truth. PL:558
Williams, T. Harry
Gentleman from Louisiana: demagogue or Democrat? TIN:398

WILLIAMS, TALCOTT
Speyer, J.
Presents Talcott Williams. LY:124
Williams, Vernon
Inner light. YR 9:275
Williams, Ward
Men wanted. YR 4:241
Williams, Wilson
Greatest battle ever won. BOA:170; BOB:197; PROS: 54; SHU:216

WILLIAMSBURG, VIRGINIA
Smith, W.B.
Opening of Colonial magazine and guardhouse. YE: 201
Williamson, E.E.
Results achieved by the soldiers and sailors. THOU 1: 264
Willis, Edgar E.
Colleges for cabbages. JUD: 111

Willis, Edgar E. (cont.)
Colleges for crooks. BRP 6:13; YR 7:189
Willis, Frank B.
Virtues of the Pilgrims. SHU:124
Willis, H. Parker
Changing status of American scholarship. ONEC:194
Willkie, Wendell L.
Acceptance speech. BA 1940-41:93
American liberty. COP:555; COPB:547
Economic freedom of the world. BA 1942-43:105
Function of a political party. BA 1943-44:267
Isolationism and the League of Nations. BA 1941-42:251
Lidice. BA 1942-43:163
Loyal opposition. COP:553; COPB:545; HURG:243
Our reservoir of world respect and hope. -Same as his Report to the nation on global war and peace
Report to the nation on global war and peace. BOA:17; HAN:194
We cannot win with quick dramatics or momentary heroics. HAN:107
Why are you unemployed? BA 1939-40:306
World outlook needed for Americans. HOC:135

WILLKIE, WENDELL
Lewis, J. L.
In support of Willkie. BA 1940-41:113
MacLeish, A.
Tribute to Wendell Willkie. BA 1944-45:186
Wilson, Charles Erwin
Five years of industrial peace. YE:221
Mobilizing for defense. HAR:281
Wilson, Dorothy Jean
Eighty million suckers. BRP 8:28
WILSON, EDITH (BOLLING) (MRS. WOODROW WILSON)
New war. BOB:18
Wilson, George Grafton
Monroe Doctrine and the program of the League to Enforce Peace. FKA:224
Wilson, George T.
On receiving a loving cup. REEM 3:412; REEMB 3:419
Wilson, Henry
On the bill to confiscate the property and free the slaves of rebels. CHAL 8:377; HAZO 17:7222; MAS 17:7222
Wilson, Herbert A.
Challenge and the broad view. ANGC:130
Wilson, Homer T.
America's uncrowned queen. HARSO:162; REEMA 6:1213
Wilson, James
For the Federal Constitution. HARS:54
In vindication of the colonies. CHEM 1:19; HAZO 7:2690; MAS 7:2690
Wilson, John Laird
Arbor Day, the children's holiday. THOU 1:41
Wilson, John M.
Glow that comes from hunger. BAAG:385

WILSON, MARY ELLEN
Stage fright. JUD:49
Wilson, O. Meredith
United States and the changing world. ANGC:145
Wilson, Percy
Introduces Emil Schram, President N.Y. Stock Exchange. PR:46
Wilson, Peter, Indian chief
On the Empire state. BRYW 8.25
Wilson, Robert E.
Begins an address before the Associated Colleges of Indiana dinner. PRNE:50
Since King David's time.

BAAG:374

WILSON, ROBERT E.
Miller, M.G.
Introduces Dr. Robert E. Wilson, Chairman, Standard Oil Company of Indiana. PRNE:22
Wilson, Russell
Introduction of George White. BRAC:238
Wilson, W.H.
Americanism. BOA:305
Wilson, Willard
Willard Wilson. BRP 7:54; YR 8:59
Wilson, William
Discovery and conquest of America. THOU 1:65
Wilson, Woodrow
Abraham Lincoln (dedicating Lincoln's birthplace). ONEM:537; ONES:98; SHU:18
Address at Gettysburg. REEM 10:421; REEMB 11:438
Address before the Southern Commercial Congress at Mobile on relations with Latin America. BIR 3:309; FO:276
Address to the Senate, January 22, 1917. -Same as his Peace without victory
American college. ONEM:612; ONES:202
Americanism and the foreign-born. -Same as his "Too proud to fight" speech
At Lotus Club dinner, 1906. NESA:169
Be not conformed to this world (baccalaureate sermon). WERN 54:18
Bible and progress. PEAE:163
Conscription Proclamation. FKA:175
Constitution of the League of Nations (Paris, February 14, 1919). BREW 10:252
Course of American history. REEM 6:423; REEMA 9:1199; REEMB 7:417
Declaration of war. -Same as his War message to Congress, April 2, 1917
Education and trade. SHU:153
Equipment for service: inaugural address as president of Princeton University. BLAA:177; BLAB:177; BOA:159; BOB:168; WE 1:63
Essence of the flag. BOA:297; BOB:81
"Eyes of the people opened" (extract from address to Congress, December 4, 1917). BREW 10:258
First address to Congress. FIP:95
First inaugural address. ANG:417; BAAMP:220; BIR 3:302; BRAC:361; BRIM:398; CHI:220; FO:272; LOTI:199; ONEM:488; PAR:466; USIN:199; USINA:199; WPRC:40
First political address (accepting the nomination for governor of New Jersey). PE:684; PEA:684
Flag Day address. LEW:39; REEM 11:217; REEMB 12:232; SAA:263; SMI:258
For the League of Nations (Des Moines, Iowa speech). BAAMP:232; CAP:171
Force to the utmost. REEM 11:280; REEMB 12:297
Fourteen points (January 8, 1918). BIR 4:38; BRE:316; BREA:296; BREW 10:243; CAP:161; COP:360; COPA:360; COPB:360; CROC:477; FIP:126; FO:303; HICF:541; HURG:180; KESK 1:1; PL:758; REEM 11:264; REEMB 12:280
Freedom of the seas: The "Sussex" affair. FIP:112
Goes to the people in behalf of the League of Nations (Pueblo, Colorado speech). BOU:119; FIP:133; PE:724; PEA:724; WPRC:76

Wilson, Woodrow (cont.)
Heroes of Vera Cruz. BRAC: 343
Issues against autocracy. BREW 10:251
Issues of reform. PEAE:241
Jackson Day dinner (Washington, January 8, 1912). PEAE:227
Keeping the faith. -Same as his Goes to the people in behalf of the League of Nations (Pueblo, Colorado speech)
League of Nations. -Same as his Peace Conference at Paris: Session, January 25, 1919
League of Nations (Kansas City, September 6, 1919). SHAH:656
"Little group of willful men." FIP:120
Mission of America. SHU:212
Meaning of the Declaration of Independence. BAKS:166; BOAM:109; ONEM:554; ONES:129
Memorial Day address, 1917. LEW:33
Message to the Pope. LEW: 155
Mount Vernon's message to mankind. SMI:255
Neutrality message to the Senate, August 19, 1914. BIR 4:1; FIP:105
New call to duty. BRAC:3
Nomination of M. Georges Clémenceau as President of the Conference. REEM 11:312; REEMB 12:329
Our ancestral responsibilities. REEMA 3:1248
Patriotic speech. DOA:288
Peace Conference at Paris: Session, January 25, 1919. COP:365; COPA:365; COPB:365; FIP:130; HURG: 185; REEM 11:318; REEMB 12:335
Peace without victory. ANG: 428; BIR 4:20; COP:351; COPA:351; COPB:351; FIP:116; FKA:233; FO: 287; HURG:173
Presenting the treaty of Versailles for ratification, July 10, 1919. PO:129
Pursuit of Villa. FIP:101
Reason for war. -Same as his War message to Congress, April 2, 1917
Second inaugural address. CHI:226; LEW:3; LOTI: 203, USIN:203; USINA:203
Shadow lengthens: Preparedness. FIP:108
Signing of the Armistice. LINM:308
Speech at Peace Conference at Paris (Session February 15, 1919). REEM 11:327; REEMB 12:344
Speech in Boston on returning from the Peace Conference, February 25, 1919. HOAP: 33
Spirit of learning. NORR 1st ser:466
Submitting the Peace Treaty to the Senate. BRAC:208
Tampico incident. FIP:99
To make the world "safe for democracy."-Same as his War message to Congress, April 2, 1917
"Too proud to fight" speech. BRAS:298; FIP:106; FKA: 178
Training the intellect. BAAGA: 431; KLEG:203; ONEM: 844; ONES:261
War message to Congress, April 2, 1917. ANG:442; BAAMP:224; BIR 4:27; BRAS:301; BRE:302; BREA: 282; BREW 10,249,250; CAP 147; COP:353; COPA: 353; COPB:353; FIP:122; FKA:242; FO:294; FRY:82; HAY:345; HICF:478; HURG: 177; LEW:13; PAR:472; PE:706; PEA:706; PROS: 122; REEM 11:190; REEMB 12:205; SAA:242; SHAH:642;

SMI:251
World safe for democracy. - Same as his War message to Congress, April 2, 1917

WILSON, WOODROW
Alderman, E. A.
Woodrow Wilson. HICF: 702; LINM:186; REEM sup 1:21; REEMB 9:6
Baruch, B.
Woodrow Wilson (commemorating centennial anniversary of birth of Wilson). BA 1956-57:141
Keating, E.
Courage of Woodrow Wilson. HARSO:38
Mathews, S.
Introducing Woodrow Wilson. ONEM:671; ONES:6
Miller, D. H.
Woodrow Wilson. HICF:696
Olney, R.
Presents Woodrow Wilson. LY:202
Roosevelt, F. D.
Democracy cannot survive in isolation. ON:146
Trinkle, E. L.
Woodrow Wilson. BOA:240; BOB:147
Wallace, H. A.
Address on Woodrow Wilson's birthday. HAN:367; VO 1942-43:744
Wise, S. S.
Woodrow Wilson. BLAB: 375
Woodrow Wilson's epitaph. SCHS:277
Zueblin, C.
Did Woodrow Wilson fail? LINM:276
Winant, John G.
Response to welcome. ON:94
Security for a people: a creative lift of the spirit. SAR: 328

WINCHELL, WALTER
Introducing Walter Winchell. NI:106; NIA:82
Windham, William
On the peace of Amiens. HAZO 7:2963; MAS 7:2963
Windolph, F. Lyman
Religio advocati. NORR 3d ser: 101

WINE See Liquors
Wines, Frederick Howard
Indeterminate sentence, the parole, and the new criminology. PEAE:219
Wingate, Harry S.
Beyond the ranges: conflict between tradition and progressive spirit and its application to America. ASHF:237
Winston, Alexander
There lies our frontier. BA 1952-53:175
Winter, William
Tribute to John Gilbert. REEM 3:418; REEMA 3: 1257; REEMB 3:425
Tribute to Lester Wallack. REEMA 3:1260
Winthrop, John
Little speech on liberty. CHAL 2:18; HAZO 4:1439; HURG: 17; MAS 4:1439; PL:555
Winthrop, Paul C.
Introducing a business man (head of firm)
" a dentist
" a highway patrolman. BRC:98, 66, 105
Winthrop, Robert C.
Address, 1839. BRAR 1:211
Centennial at Yorktown. HAZO 16:6646; MAS 16:6646
Death of John C. Calhoun. REEMA 9:1219
Death of President Taylor. REEMA 9:1222
Eulogy on Edward Everett. CHAL 8:41; HAZO 16:6637; MAS 16:6637
Men of 1776. THOU 1:213
Ottoman Empire. REEMA 3: 1263
Our American age. THOU 1: 205

Winthrop, Robert C. (cont.)
Pioneers of American independence. THOU 1:69
Trust to succeeding generations. THOU 1:208

WIRELESS TELEGRAPH AND TELEPHONE See Radio
Wirick, Rebecca
When disaster strikes. YR 2:149
Wirt, William
Burr and Blennerhasset (at trial of Burr). BREW 10:262; CHAL 4:457; HAZO 10:3955; LEEW 9:83; MAS 10:3955; REEMA 15:2135; SOU 9:386
Death of Jefferson and Adams. BREW 10:259
Genius as the capacity of work. BREW 10:264
Trial of Aaron Burr. -Same as his Burr and Blennerhasset
Washington as a model for the formation of character. THOU 1:166
Wirth, Fred A.
Four-minute man. ONES:295; REEM sup 3:181; REEMB 6:400
Wirth, Joseph
Via Dolorosa (to Reichstag). BREW 10:266

WISCONSIN, UNIVERSITY OF
Van Hise, C.R.
Inaugural address as president of University of Wisconsin. WE 2:161
Wise, Henry A.
Free schools for the farmer's children. SMI:139
Know-Nothingism. REEMA 15:2141
Wise, John Sergeant
Cadets at New Market. SMI:184

Legal profession. BYRA:467; REEM 3:421; REEMA 3:1271; REEMB 3:428
Wise, Stephen Samuel
Abraham Lincoln, man and American. COP:349; COPA:349; COPB:349; HURG:169; LINM:87; REEM 5:409; REEMB 9:454
Conscience of the nation. REEM 3:423; REEMB 3:430
Fifty years of Zionism. BA 1946-47:262
Woodrow Wilson. BLAB:375

WISE, STEPHEN SAMUEL
Introducing Stephen S. Wise and Julian W. Mack. NI:113; NIA:87
Wise, Theodore
Home, the seminary of the nation. BOA:138
Wishard, Glenn P.
United States and universal peace. TRUW:216
Wishard, S. E.
Rights of laboring men. THOU 1:450
Unconverted children. THOU 2:179
Wishart, Charles F.
Policy of Richelieu. SHUC:247

WIT AND HUMOR
Hazlitt, W.
On wit and humor. BREW 6:412
Savage, M. J.
American wit and humor. REEMA 6:943
Thackeray, W. M.
On charity and humor. BRYW 4:201; CHAL 8:325; HAZO 17:7136; MAS 17:7136
Whipple, E. P.
Wit and humor. REEMA 6:1189
See also dinner speeches; Humorists
Witherspoon, John
Convention of Burgoyne. HAZO 5:2001; LEEW 8:269; MAS 5:2001
Necessity of Confederation. HARS:41
Public credit under the Con-

federation. BREW 10:269

WIVES See Women
Woelfle, Janice
What freedom means to me. BU:181
Wolcott, Edward Oliver
Bright land to westward. REEM 3:431; REEMA 3:1273; REEMB 3:438

Treaty with Spain. FUL:343
War inevitable. FUL:341
Wolfe, James
To his army before Quebec. BRYW 3:191
Wolfe, Paul A.
Challenge to America. ASHF:17
Woll, Matthew
Labor's contribution to American democracy. BA 1939-40:327
Limitation of labor injunctions (affirmative). ONEC:355
Organized labor and current international developments. HAR:410
Wolseley, Lord Garnet Joseph
Army in Transvaal. REEMA 3:1280
Wolsey, Thomas, Cardinal
Foresees his fall (from Shakespeare). HIB:213

WOMAN
Addams, J.
Closing the International Congress of Women. GA:175
Women and war. HICF:439
Allen, F.E.
Women and world peace. REEM sup 1:50; REEMB 6:1
Anthony, S.B.
Are women persons? HIBS:451
Barton, B.
How long should a wife live? ONEC:255
Beard, M.R.
Status of woman and the modern state. GA:282
Blouet, P.
Monsieur and Madame. REEMA 1:79
Buck, P.
Women's place in a democracy. BUTA:212
Carmack, E.W.
Builders of men. BOA:262; BOB:134
Chesterton, G.K. BOA:
For the leisured woman. REEM sup 3:83
Clemens, S.L.
"The Ladies." NESA:105
Woman, God bless her. COP:671; COPB:698; REEM 1:304; REEMA 1:225; REEMB 1:305
Cope, N.G.
They tip their hats. BRP 9:48
Coulter, T.H.
Introduces Dr. Will Durant, author and philosopher on Ladies' day at Executive Club of Chicago. PRNE:43
Crummel, A.
Black woman of the South: her neglects and her needs. DUNM:159
Curzon, G.N.
Women's work. BEA:161
Depew, C.M.
Woman. COP:639; COPB:673; HURG:125; KLEG:147; REEM 1:389; REEMA 1:327; REEMB 1:389
DeYoung, R.
Women in the headlines. GA:149
Dickinson, Mrs. L.
Citadels of peace, arsenals of power (inaugural address as President of General Federation of Women's Clubs). BUTA:229
Elizabeth, Consort of George VI.
Broadcast to the women of the Empire. BUTA:227
Examples of introductions for women. BO:30-34

WOMAN (cont.)
Examples of toasts to women. FRIT:89, 90, 92
Greeting ladies. NATT:23
Greetings to ladies. FRIT:35
Gunnison, E. M.
Thumbs down. YR 7:257
Hardin, B. L.
Mother Eve. SOU 9:480
Hawkins, E.
Bride of the State. BRP 10: 11; NOR 1939:3
Home and wife (satisfied husband speaks). ED:323
Huber, L. J.
Introducing a housewife. BRH:105
Hurley, P. J.
Pioneer woman (dedicating statue of the Pioneer woman in Ponca, Oklahoma). BOA:256; BOB:131; GRIS: 62
Jessel, G.
To the Ladies of Hadassah. JEYO:146
Jordan, D. S.
Higher education of women. REEM 6:295; REEMA 8: 745; REEMB 7:244
Just a housewife (the homemaker's forum). DR:3-7
Kottemann, D.
Sleeping beauties. NOR 1944:35
Ladies. SCHS:163
The ladies, by one of the opposite sex. EDGS:342
Ladies' night. FRIE:52
Ladies' night address. NAT: 20
Lawrence, E. G.
Ladies. LA:172
McGhee, G. C.
American women and the goal of world community. ANGC:159
M'Iver, C. D.
Education of women. SHUO: 95
Maloney, P. R.
Hard way. NOR 1944:53
Mason, M.
College woman and the 20th century home. ONES: 383
Melish, W. B.
The ladies. REEM 2:404; REEMA 2:825; REEMB 2: 421
Opening speech at testimonial to a woman civic leader. BEDA:41
Our wives. NATT:48
Phillips, L. M.
Today's challenge to women. GA:102
Porter, H.
Woman. ANDS:208; COP: 651; COPB:678; KLEM: 100; ONEM:653; REEM 3: 84; REEMA 3:913; REEMB 3:85
Posner, G. A.
Emcee at a ladies' day meeting (at the lodge, athletic club, social club, or other meetings). BRH:302
Rhondda, M. H.
Against the leisured woman. REEM sup 3:79
Scott, C.
Women of the Confederacy. SHUO:34
Second after dinner speech. FRIT:21
Shaw, G. B.
Menace of the leisured woman (introduction and summary of a debate). REEM sup 3:74, 86
Should women keep silent? JA:244
Smith, G.
English women's institutions receive official recognition. BUT:144; BUTA: 144; BUTB:144
Smith, M. C.
Challenge to women. BUTB: 240
Speech of a sentimentalist in response to the toast "The ladies." HILL:482
Sudow, M.
Masters of men. JUD:165

Suggestions for proposing a toast to "The Ladies" at a Masonic Ladies' Night. With examples of. EDW:61
Thornton, W. M.
Portrait of a lady. SMI: 234
Tilton, T.
Woman. REEM 3:333; REEMA 3:1142; REEMB 3: 350
To the ladies: a tribute. THOS:120, 122
To the ladies: speech for the men's banquet. CON: 35
Toast-The ladies. HILL:483
Toast "The ladies"-at a ladies' night at a club meeting (mixed gathering). WRA:48
Toast "The ladies"-at annual meeting of any men's club. WRA:49
Toast "The ladies"-at annual meeting of mixed club (final meeting of any organization to mark close of season). WRA:50
Toast "The ladies"-at ladies' night. WRA:50
Toast to the ladies. NAT:45
Toast to the ladies. NATS:1
Toastmaster's welcoming remarks on Ladies' day. FRIT:46
Tribute to a career woman. FRIT:89
Tribute to the ladies. NAT:34
Tribute to women. FRIE:328
Tributes at testimonial to a woman civic leader. BEDA: 42
War against women. NI:205; NIA:214
Watterson, H.
Our wives. REEM 3:357; REEMA 3:1189; REEMB 3: 373
Welcome to visitors in the Woman's Missionary Society. HNWS:24
Westerdyk, J.
Place of the International Federation today. GA:171
Whipple, E. P.
Sphere of woman. REEMA 3:1229
Whitfield, A. H.
Tribute to the women of the South (at dedication of Mississippi's new Capitol). SHUO:36
Wiggin, K. D.
Sov'ran woman. REEM 3: 388; REEMB 3:395
Wiley, H. W.
Ideal woman. REEM 3:404; REEMA 3:1240; REEMB 3: 411
Wilson, H. T.
America's uncrowned queen. HARSO:162; REEMA 6:1213
Wives are that way. NATS:4
Woman-response to a toast. DAVC:401
Woman's day. DR:301
Word to the wives. NAT:10
Young, E.
Pioneer women of Texas. BOB:105

---- SUFFRAGE
Anthony, S. B.
Enfranchisement of women. BOU:136; BRYW 10:50; COP:321; COPA:321; COPB:321; HICF:104; HURG:123; PL:691

For the Woman Suffrage Amendment. WPRA:318
Astor, N. W. L.
Reform of the franchise (Women's suffrage). EMS 2: 199
Baldwin, S. B.
Reform of the franchise (Women's suffrage). EMS 2:202
Birkenhead, F. E. S.
Reform of the franchise (Women's suffrage). EMS 2: 209
Blake, E.
Suffrage for woman. CHAL

Woman Suffrage (cont.)
12:230; HAZO 22:9611; MAS 22:9611
Brown, J. E.
Against the Woman Suffrage Amendment. WPRA:333
Catt, C. C.
World movement for woman suffrage. HICF:368
Dowling, A.
Church and the woman. CATA 1:281
Higginson, T. W.
For self-respect and self-protection. CHAL 10:309; HAZO 20:8610; MAS 20: 8610
Jacobi, M. P.
Woman suffrage. WERN 42:17
Mill, J. S.
Reform of the franchise (Women's suffrage). EMS 2: 182
Pankhurst, C.
Militant suffragette. BEA: 337
Militant suffragists. COP: 196; COPA:196; COPB:196; REEM 7:318; REEMB 7:324
Rankin, J.
Woman suffrage and war. BREW 9:37
Snowden, P.
Reform of the franchise (Women's suffrage). EMS 2: 195
Stanton, E. C.
Keynotes the first Woman's Rights Convention. BOU: 140; PE:388; PEA:388
Zearing, J. H.
Issue of justice: equal suffrage for women. SHUC: 35
See also Women in politics

WOMAN'S CHRISTIAN TEMPERANCE UNION
Chaperone in the heart. JA: 238

WOMEN IN BUSINESS
Anderson, M.
Peculiar problems of women workers. GA:133
Bowman, G. M.
Address of the president. GA:179
Careers for women (address to a class of girls). EDGS: 225
Ferguson, M.
Women in business. REEM sup 1:311; REEMB 4:219
For such a time as this. JA: 32
Martin, M.
Character in the shadow. YR 7:93
Robinson, J. T.
Women in industry. BOA: 340
Snyder, O.
Woman employer. REEM sup 2:416; REEMB 5:302
Williams, C. O.
Women must work. GA:265
Greetings to Forum on Current Problems. GA:24
Women in business. SCHS:279
Women in the modern business world. AMEO 2:113
You can't turn back the clock. JA:29
See also Occupations, choice of

WOMEN IN POLITICS
Astor, N. W.
Women in politics. COP: 207; COPA:207; COPB:207; REEM 7:36; REEMB 6:14
Catt, C. C.
Political parties and women voters. REEM 7:84; REEMB 8:70
Smith, M. C.
Challenge to women. BUTB:240
See also Woman-suffrage

WOMEN IN SCIENCE
Sabin, F. R.
Acceptance of the M. Carey Thomas award. GA: 48

WOMEN'S CLUBS See Club speeches

WONDERS OF THE WORLD
Old wonders made new. THOS: 152
Wood, Sir Charles
Speech in House of Commons, June 6, 1861 (on India). KESI 2:3
Wood, Leonard
National preparedness. REEM 7:427; REEMB 8:440
Wood, Ruth
Feet of clay. BRP 4:96
Woodard, Barbara
Yellow silence. YR 9:177
Woodbridge, C. K.
Salesmanship and advertising. BYRA:469; REEM sup 3: 183; REEMB 5:396
Woodburn, James Albert
Nationalism and humanity. NORR 2d ser: 423
Woodford, Stewart L.
Greeting from the founders (Cornell University 25th anniversary). ONES:81
Introduces Frederick René Coudert to New England Society of New York. REEMA 1:277
Presenting the statue to the city. KNAS:154; KNASA: 154; ONEM:709

WOODMEN OF THE WORLD
Fraternal Woodmen memorial. THOS:70
Modern Woodmen: at the unveiling of a monument. THOS:72
Modern Woodmen-friendship ties. THOS:78
Woodmen circle. THOS:65
Woodmen of the world-in memoriam. THOS:85

Woodrow, James
Evolution. BL:517
WOODROW, JAMES
Eaton, C.
Professor James Woodrow and the freedom of teaching in the South. TIN:438
Woodruff, Caroline S.
Presentation of a gavel. HOA: 383
Woodruff, Timothy L.
Lincoln and McKinley. WERN 42:95
Woodruff, William Francis
Negroes in the United States Army. SHUC:109
Woodrum, Clifton
Inserting the Baukhage tribute on Franklin Delano Roosevelt in the Congressional Record. BA 1944-45:165
Woodward, C. Vann.
Irony of Southern history. TIN:284
WOOLBERT, CHARLES HENRY
Weaver, A. T.
Charles Henry Woolbert. ONEC:129
Wooldridge, Charles W.
Introducing Carl Bolte by stating qualities exactly opposite to his. PR:47
Wooley, John G.
Prohibition keynote. WERN 42: 31
Wooley, Mary E.
Introducing Mrs. Franklin D. Roosevelt. GA:12
Redefinition of fraternity. NORR 2d ser:312

WOOLMAN, John
Douglas, P. H.
Five great Americans. BA 1951-52:85
Woolsey, John M.
Opinion December 6, 1933 (Ulysses case-freedom of reading). ANG:468
Worden, James A.
How to make Rallying day a success. THOU 2:213
Rallying day, the occasion and

Worden, James A. (cont.)
why. THOU 2:197
United movement for gathering in the neglected children. THOU 2:206
Wordsworth, William
On laying the cornerstone of the new grammar school at Bowness. KNAS:121; KNASA:121

WORDSWORTH, WILLIAM
Arnold, M.
To the Wordsworth Society. KNAS:43; KNASA:43

WORK
Beveridge, A. J.
Work and habits. KLEG: 187
Do your own work. NAT:30
Experience pays but who collects? NAT:13
Get out and work. FRIE:60
Help! Help! FRIE:163
Hibben, J. G.
Day's work. BLAB:343
Love your work. FRIE:175
Mabie, H. W.
Work and play. BLAA:58; BLAB:58
Norris, L. W.
On mixing ethics with business. BRAB:539
Ruskin, J.
Work. REEM 8:334; REEMA 6:919; REEMB 13: 339
Speech for a workingman's banquet. BARB:174
Wirt, W.
Genius as the capacity of work. BREW 10:264
You and your job. DR:32
See also Age and employment; Labor and laboring classes; Occupations, choice of; Success; Vocational guidance; Women in business

WORKS PROGRESS ADMINISTRATION
Dewey, T. E.
Calendar of unpunished crimes. BA 1939-40:257
Lee, J. B.
Technological unemployment and relief. BA 1938-39:108; ON:107, 200
Roosevelt, F. D.
WPA: May 6, 1935. FIP: 215

WORLD COURT See Permanent Court of International Justice

WORLD FELLOWSHIP See International cooperation

WORLD WAR, 1939-1945
Barton, B.
What to do in a revolution. SAC:68
Bevin, E.
Labor and the war against Nazism. COP:481; COPA: 481
Binder, C.
World in the news. BART 4:103
Chamberlain, N.
Munich Agreement. COP: 457; COPA:457; COPB: 429; ON:90
Chiang Kai-Shek
New Year's message to the Chinese people, 1944. HAN: 336; VO 1944-45:7
Christensen, G.
Darkness and the dawn. NOR 1945:5
Churchill, W. L. S.
Address to Congress, December 26, 1941. BA 1941-42:20; BERS:91; COP:720; COPB:451; HAN:183; HOC: 31; VO 1941:630; YE:167, 350
Address to Congress, May 19, 1943. BA 1942-43:30; VO 1943-44:205
Broadcast, February 15, 1942. VO 1942-43:142
Broadcast from Quebec, August 31, 1943. HAN:226;

SAC:42; VO 1943-44:316
Broadcast to the world about the meeting with President Roosevelt, August 24, 1941. VO 1941:380
Speech to the Allied delegates, June 12, 1941. VO 1941:278
Deutsch, M.E.
V emblem. HOC:34
Doyle, D.C.
Will this war end Christianity? BART 4:83
Durant, W.
World conflict. BART 3:221
Eberts, H.W., Jr.
And there is no peace. AN:13
Eisenhower, D.D.
Unity won the war. HAN:309; ON:330; PE:798; PEA:798
Fogel, S.
We, You, and I. NOR 1945:11
Helman, B.
Nationalism. AN:9
Hull, C.
Broadcast to the world, July 23, 1942. HAN:188; VO 1942-43:394
We shall not fail. COP:566
MacLeish, A.
Psychological front. HOC:127
Pius XII.
Appeal for peace. COP:525; COPA:525; COPB:503; VO 1941:167
Poole, R.
Earth is the Lord's. AN:5
Roosevelt, F.D.
Address in Ottawa, August 25, 1943. VO 1943-44:309
Christmas eve broadcast to the nation, 1943. VO 1943-44:579
Shahan, L.
Through a child's eyes. AN:42
Sheen, F.J.
Judgment of nations. BA 1942-43:299
Smith, R.L.
Sane thinking in an insane world. BART 3:135
Stevens, J.M.
Tomorrow we live. NOR 1943:11
Swing, R.G.
Youth, war, and freedom. HAN:22
Thompson, D.
Let's face the facts. BA 1940-41:137
Willkie, W.
Report to the nation on global war and peace. BOA:17; HAN:194
Winant, J.G.
Response to welcome. ON:94

---- AERIAL OPERATIONS
Arnold, H.H.
Our air power. HAN:245
Churchill, W.L.S.
Debate in the House of Commons on Libyan operations and bombing of Germany. VO 1942-43:332
Speech in Commons on robot bomb attacks. VO 1944-45:294
Speech in Commons on the military and political scene. VO 1944-45:108
Statement in Commons on the German use of V-2 long range rockets. VO 1944-45:559
To the British public on the bombings. HAN:146
Fisher, G.J.B.
Demolition bombs. ON:233
Murrow, E.R.
Orchestrated Hell. BA 1943-44:37; BAAG:361

---- AFRICA
Churchill, W.L.S.
Broadcast, November 29, 1942. VO 1942-43:695
DeGaulle, C.
Address in Tunis on the anniversary of the libera-

WORLD WAR, 1939-1945-AFRICA (cont.)
tion of Tunisia. VO 1944-45:201
Declaration, January 2, 1943. VO 1943-44:5
On the political problem of North Africa. VO 1943-44: 37
Speech at the Brazzaville Conference. VO 1944-45:71
See also World War-Campaigns-African front

---- ALLIED MILITARY GOVERNMENT See Allied Military Government

---- ARMISTICES
Dulles, J. F.
Japanese Peace Treaty. BA 1951-52:41; HAR:175
Petain, H. P.
Petition for an armistice. HAN:128
Vyshinsky, A. Y.
On negotiations with Finland for an armistice. VO 1944-45:185
See also V-E Day; V-J Day; World War 1939-1945-Germany-Surrender; World War, 1939-1945-Italy; World War 1939-45-Japan-Surrender

---- ATROCITIES
Grew, J. C.
Radio broadcast from Washington, August 30, 1942. VO 1942-43:447
Novar, L. F.
Price for pity. AN:34
Roosevelt, F. D.
Statement of war crimes. VO 1942-43:544
Statement on punishment of war crimes. VO 1942-43: 444
See also World war, 1939-1945-War criminals

---- AUSTRALIA
Curtin, J.
Broadcast to Britain May 7, 1944. VO 1944-45:204
Speech from the Melbourne Herald. VO 1941:638

---- BELGIUM
Eisenhower, D.
Order of the day on the German counteroffensive in Belgium and Luxembourg. VO 1944-45:623
Kaltenborn, H. V.
Germany invades Holland and Belgium. BA 1939-40: 68

---- CAMPAIGNS-AFRICAN FRONT
Churchill, W. L. S.
Debate in House of Commons, November 11, 1942. VO 1942-43:651
Debate in the House of Commons on Libyan operations and bombing of Germany. VO 1942-43:332
North Africa campaign. HAN:218
Report to Parliament on the war situation, February 11, 1943. VO 1943-44: 40
Speech at the Mansion House, November 10, 1942. VO 1942-43:640
Speech in the House of Commons on the war situation, June 8, 1943. VO 1943-44:234
Eisenhower, D. D.
Proclamation to the French, November 7, 1942. VO 1942-43:599
DeGaulle, C.
Broadcast to North Africa. HAN:222
Giraud, H. H.
Appeal to the French forces in North Africa, November 8, 1942. VO 1942-43:600
Roosevelt, F. D.

Announcing the opening of a second front in French North and West Africa. VO 1942-43:596
Message to the French people, November 7, 1942. VO 1942-43:597

---- ---- ITALIAN FRONT
Churchill, W. L. S.
Speech in Commons on the military and political scene. VO 1944-45:108
Eisenhower, D. D.
Broadcast to the Italian people, July 29, 1943. VO 1943-44:295
See also World War, 1939-1945-Italy

---- ---- MEDITERRANEAN FRONT
Churchill, W. L. S.
Debate in the House of Commons, July 2, 1942. VO 1942-43:364
Eisenhower, D. D.
Plea to the French people upon the Allied invasion of Sicily. VO 1943-44:267
See also World War, 1939-1945-Greece

---- ---- PACIFIC FRONT
Greenslade, J. W.
Our war in the Pacific. HAN:331
Osmena, S.
First address to his cabinet. VO 1944-45:370
Roosevelt, F. D.
Broadcast at Puget Sound Navy Yard on the war in the Pacific. VO 1944-45:373
See also World War, 1939-1945-Philippine Islands

---- ---- RUSSIAN FRONT
Churchill, W. L. S.
War on Russia. COP:475; COPA:475; COPB:439; HAN:156; VO 1941:320
Hitler, A.
Broadcast to the German people, October 3, 1941. VO 1941:439
Stalin, I.
"Defend every inch of Soviet soil." COP:517; COPA:517; COPB:495; CROC:429; ON:167; PE:785; PEA:785; VO 1941:330
Report on international relations, November 6, 1942. VO 1942-43:582
Report on the 26th anniversary of the October revolution. HAN:232; VO 1943-44:509

---- ---- SICILY See Sicily

---- ---- WESTERN FRONT
Churchill, W. L. S.
Speech in Commons on the military and political scene. VO 1944-45:108
Statement in Commons on the liberation of Rome and the landings in France. VO 1944-45:264
DeGaulle, C.
Broadcast to the French people on the liberation. VO 1944-45:303
Invasion message to France. VO 1944-45:263
Speech on the liberation of Paris, delivered at the Hotel de Ville in Paris. VO 1944-45:389
Eisenhower, D. D.
Army hour broadcast from Paris on the need for ammunition. VO 1944-45:568
Broadcast to the peoples of Western Europe. HAN:272; VO 1944-45:262
Instructions to organized cells of foreign workers in Germany. VO 1944-45:432
Instructions to the underground resistance movements of Europe. VO 1944-45:219

WORLD WAR, 1939-1945-CAMPAIGNS-WESTERN FRONT (cont.)

Message to Allied invasion troops in France. VO 1944-45:267

Order of the day on the German counteroffensive in Belgium and Luxembourg. VO 1944-45:623

Order of the day to the Allied armies in France, August 13, 1944. VO 1944-45:380

Order of the day to the Allied troops invading France. HIB:54; VO 1944-45:260

Warning to the people of Rhineland and the Ruhr. VO 1944-45:415

Hicks, G.

Invasion starts. HAN:268

Montgomery, B. L.

Message to his invasion troops. VO 1944-45:260

Patton, G. S.

"Flanks are something for the enemy to worry about." HURG:274

Roosevelt, F.D.

Invasion prayer to nation. BA 1943-44:46; HAN:265; VO 1944-45:261

Stalin, I.

Statement extolling the Allied invasion of France. VO 1944-45:267

---- CANADA

Churchill, W. L. S.

Speech to the Canadian Parliament, December 30, 1941. VO 1941:642

King, W. L. M.

Address to both Houses of Parliament, at Westminster, on Canada's war effort and the Commonwealth. VO 1944-45:207

Canada and the war. COP: 488; COPA:488; COPB: 458

---- CAUSES

Hitler, A.

Address at Berlin Sports Palace, January 30, 1941. VO 1941:51

---- CHINA

Chiang Kai-Shek

Message to friendly nations, July 7, 1941. VO 1941:337

Message to friendly powers, July 7, 1939. HAN:67

Message to the Indian people, February 21, 1942. VO 1942-43:158

Statement on the occasion of the sixth anniversary of the outbreak of war with Japan. VO 1943-44:263

War between justice and force. COP:523; COPA: 523; COPB:501

Chiang, Mei-Ling

Address at the citizen's mass meeting at Hollywood Bowl. VO 1943-44:147

Fighting for the common cause. BA 1942-43:81; ON: 83

Japan is first U. S. foe. BA 1942-43:85; HAN:201; VO 1943-44:60

King-Chau Mui

China and the international situation. HAN:327

Lim-Yuen, P.

Pacific Charter. NOR 1942:59

---- CIVILIAN ACTIVITIES

Johnston, E.

Crisis on the home front. SAC:114

Nelson, D. M.

MacArthur day celebration speech. BA 1941-42:152

Patterson, R. C., Jr.

Sixth column. BA 1941-42: 135; SAC:54

Roosevelt, F. D.

Message to Congress, January 7, 1943. BA 1942-43:

15; HAN:240; VO 1943-44: 7
Summers, H.W.
Internal solidarity. BA 1943-44:165
Swing, R. G.
Meaning of the home front. BA 1943-44:159

---- CZECHOSLOVAKIA
Benes, E.
What are we fighting for? BA 1942-43:56
Kaltenborn, H.V.
Czechoslovakia capitulates. BA 1938-39:18
Willkie, W.L.
Lidice. BA 1942-43:163

---- DISPLACED PERSONS See Displaced persons; Jews

---- ENGLAND See World War, 1939-1945-Great Britain; World War, 1939-1945-United States-AID TO GREAT BRITAIN

---- FINLAND
Davis, E.
Finland surrenders. BA 1939-40:63

---- FOOD QUESTION See Food; Rationing

---- FRANCE
Churchill, W.L.S.
To the French people (October 21, 1940). BRAP:65
Daladier, E.
Broadcast on declaration of war on Germany. HAN:121
France cannot stand by. PL:832
Darlan, J.F.
Address to all French at home and abroad. VO 1942-43:680
Broadcast to the French people, May 23, 1941. VO 1941:217
Speech to the French people, June 10, 1941. VO 1941:253
DeGaulle, C.
Appeal to Frenchmen, June 18, 1940. CROC:153; HAN:130; PE:782; PEA:782
Before the French Consultative Assembly on the victory over Germany. VO 1945-46:208
Broadcast on French policy in war and peace. VO 1945-46:54
Broadcast to North Africa. HAN:222
Broadcast to the French people on liberation. VO 1944-45:393
Speech on the liberation of Paris delivered at the Hotel de Ville in Paris. VO 1944-45:389
Statement after Giraud's address, March 15, 1943. VO 1943-44:118
Eisenhower, D.D.
Plea to the French people upon the Allied invasion of Sicily. VO 1943-44:267
Proclamation to the French, November 7, 1942. VO 1942-43:599
Giraud, H.H.
Appeal to the French forces in North Africa, November 8, 1942. VO 1942-43:600
To the Alsace-Lorraine Society. VO 1943-44:114
---- and others.
General Charles De Gaulle's and General Henri Giraud's appeal to France, June 4, 1943. VO 1943-44:226
Henry-Haye, G.
Statement at Washington, June 6, 1941. VO 1941:247
Hitler, A.
Appeal to the French on the entry of German troops into unoccupied France. VO 1942-43:644
Hull, C.
Statement on Franco-Ger-

WORLD WAR, 1939-1945-FRANCE (cont.)
man collaboration, June 13, 1941. VO 1941:282
Petain, H. P.
Petition for an armistice. HAN:128
Roosevelt, F.D.
Message to Marshal Henri Petain. VO 1942-43:602
Vandercook, J.W.
Soul of France. BA 1942-43:159
Welles, S.
Status of French ships at Alexandria, Egypt. VO 1942-43:392
See also World War, 1939-1945-Campaigns-Western Front

---- GERMANY
Daladier, E.
Nazis' aim is slavery. COP:491; COPA:491; COPB:461
Doenitz, K.
Announcement of Hitler's death. VO 1945-46:182
Eisenhower, D. D.
Statement covering activities of the Allied Military Government in Germany. VO 1944-45:430
Goebbels, P. J.
Broadcast, February 18, 1943. VO 1943-44:63
Broadcast describing plot to assassinate Hitler. VO 1944-45:337
New Year's speech, December 31, 1943. VO 1943-44: 599
Plea for clothing for troops on the Russian front. VO 1941:624
Presenting Hitler's proclamation, January 30, 1943. VO 1943-44:19
Speech at harvest Thanksgiving festival in Berlin. VO 1943-44:421
Goering, H.
Broadcast October 4, 1942. VO 1942-43:538
Order of the day, December 31, 1943. VO 1943-44: 598
Speech, May 20, 1942. VO 1942-43:290
Hitler, A.
Address at Berlin Sports Palace, January 30, 1941. VO 1941:51
Address at opening of the winter relief campaign, September 30, 1942. VO 1942-43:507
Address to the Reichstag, April 26, 1942. VO 1942-43:217
Appeal to the French on the entry of German troops into unoccupied France. VO 1942-43:644
Before the Old Guard of his party, November 8, 1941. VO 1941:482
Broadcast plea for winter aid, August 30, 1942. VO 1942-43:453
Broadcast to the German people, October 3, 1941. VO 1941:439
Broadcast to the world, March 21, 1943 (celebrating Heroes' Memorial Day). VO 1943-44:129
German conquests. COP: 506; COPA:506; COPB: 484; VO 1941:192
Germany could no longer remain idle. PL:819
Germany's claims. BERS: 142; COP:496; COPA:496; COPB:474
Memorial address, 1941. VO 1941:133
New Year Proclamation, December 31, 1943. VO 1943-44:607
New Year's broadcast to the German people, December 31, 1944. HAN:291; VO 1944-45:637
New Year's order of the

day to the German Armed Forces, December 31, 1940. VO 1941:4
No more territorial demands. COP:502; COPA: 502; COPB:480
Order for a last stand in the East. VO 1945-46:152
Order of the day, December 31, 1943. VO 1943-44: 604
Order of the day calling for invasion of Yugoslavia and Greece, April 6, 1941. VO 1941:152
Order of the day to the German troops on the Eastern front, October 2, 1941. VO 1941:437
Order to his Western armies concerning guerilla warfare. VO 1945-46:160
Proclamation on war with Soviet Union, June 22, 1941. VO 1941:292
Speech at Berlin Sports Palace, January 30, 1942. VO 1942-43:101
Speech commemorating the twentieth birthday of the Nazi Party. CROC:238; VO 1943-44:520
Speech delivered at Munich, Germany, February 24, 1941. VO 1941:95
Speech on the surrender of Italy. VO 1943-44:339
Threat to destroy the British Empire. HAN:143
To Reichstag on the declaration of war against the United States. VO 1941:572

Lochner, L. P.
Inside Germany. BA 1942-43:168

Molotov, V. M.
Nazi war on Russia. COP: 515; COPA:515; COPB: 493; VO 1941:318

Ribbentrop, J.
Statement on the declaration of war on the Soviet Union. VO 1941:301

Welles, S.
On the German Reich's attack on the Soviet Union. VO 1941:325

Wyman, E.
Can these be the enemy? NOR 1944:47

See also World War, 1939-1945-Campaigns-Western front

---- ---- SURRENDER

Churchill, W. L. S.
Germany surrenders. BA 1944-45:40; VO 1945-46: 193

Doenitz, K.
Broadcast informing the German people of their unconditional surrender. VO 1945-46:190

Eisenhower, D. D.
Instructions to German troops and to foreign workers in preparation for defeat of Germany. VO 1945-46:130
Victory order of the day, and his proclamation on Germany's defeat. VO 1945-46:197

Krosigk, L. S.
Broadcast to the German people. VO 1945-46:188

Truman, H. S.
Speech at American flag raising in Berlin. VO 1945-46:388
V E day proclamation. BA 1944-45:37; HAN:308; VO 1945-46:191

See also Allied Military Government; V E Day

---- GREAT BRITAIN

Chamberlain, N.
Britain must go to war. PL:826

Churchill, W. L. S.
Address at the Lord Mayor's luncheon, November 9, 1943. VO 1943-44:532
Address at the Lord Mayor

WORLD WAR, 1939-1945-GREAT BRITAIN (cont.)
of London's luncheon, November 9, 1944. VO 1944-45:556
Address in Commons on relations among Britain, the U.S., and the U.S.S.R. VO 1945-46:19
Address in the House of Commons, September 21, 1943. VO 1943-44:380
Address on receiving the freedom of the City of London. VO 1943-44:251
Address to the Pilgrims, March 18, 1941. ON:313; VO 1941:137
Addressed the House of Commons in a review of the war, September 8, 1942. VO 1942-43:487
"Blood, sweat and tears." BOA:3; BOU:102; BRTHA:350; COP:459; COPA:459; COPB:431; CROC:76; HAN:132; HIB:280; PE:772; PEA:772
Britain stands alone in the breach. HAN:140
Broadcast on "five years of war." VO 1945-46:203
Broadcast on the war overseas and reconstruction at home. VO 1944-45:139
Broadcast on war with Japan. VO 1941:555
Broadcast report on war, May 10, 1942. VO 1942-43:280
Debate in House of Commons, June 10, 1941. (Defense of Crete). VO 1941:255
Debate in the House of Commons, January 27, 1942. VO 1942-43:66
Debate in the House of Commons, February 24, 1942. VO 1942-43:179
Debate in the House of Commons, July 2, 1942. VO 1942-43:364
Debate in the House of Commons, November 11, 1942. VO 1942-43:651
Debate in the House of Commons, on Libyan operations and bombing of Germany. VO 1942-43:332
Debate with Anthony Eden on withdrawal of Forces from Greece, April 30, 1941. VO 1941:184
Dunkirk. BRTHA:352; COP:461; COPA:461; COPB:433; HAN:133; PE:774; PEA:774
Freeman of Edinburgh. HOC:202
"Give us the tools, and we'll finish the job." ON:88; VO 1941:77
Never in the field of human conflict. BRTHA:364
Report on the war, April 27, 1941. VO 1941:175
Report to Parliament on the war situation, February 11, 1943. VO 1943-44:40
Report to the House of Commons on the war, February 17, 1942. VO 1942-43:150
Review of the war in the House of Commons, November 12, 1941. VO 1941:506
Review of the war to the House of Commons, September 30, 1941. VO 1941:416
Review of the war to the House of Commons, December 11, 1941. VO 1941:600
Review of war before the House of Commons, April 9, 1941. VO 1941:155
Speech at Bradford Town Hall. VO 1942-43:723
Speech at Edinburgh, Scotland, October 12, 1942. VO 1942-43:553
Speech at Mansion House, November 10, 1941. VO 1941:498
Speech at the Mansion House, November 10, 1942.

VO 1942-43:640
Speech following the King's speech from the throne, November 29, 1944. VO 1944-45-575
Speech in Commons on the military and political scene. VO 1944-45:108
Speech in Commons on the war, September 28, 1944. HAN:282; VO 1944-45:438
Speech in Commons on the war, October 27, 1944. VO 1944-45:503
Speech in Commons on the war situation, August 2, 1945. HAN:278; HIB:232; VO 1944-45:351
Speech in the House of Commons, January 29, 1942. VO 1942-43:90
Speech in the House of Commons, July 27, 1943. VO 1943-44:285
Speech in the House of Commons on the war situation, June 8, 1943. VO 1943-44:234
"Their finest hour." BRTHA: 359; COP:467; COPA:467; COPB:439; CROC:78; HAN: 138; PE:781; PEA:781
To the British public on the bombings. HAN:146
To the Central Council of the Conservative Party. VO 1942-43:204

Eden, A.
Debate with Winston Churchill on withdrawal of Forces from Greece, April 30, 1941. VO 1941:185
Firm policy. COP:455; COPA:455; COPB:427

Elizabeth, Consort of George VI.
Broadcast to the women of the Empire. BUTA:227

George VI.
At opening of the House of Lords and the House of Commons, November 12, 1941. VO 1941:505
Christmas message of peace, 1939. SAA:288
Empire called to prayer. HAN:266
King's broadcast on declaration of war on Germany. HAN:122
Speech delivered at the opening of Parliament, November 23, 1943. VO 1943-44:535
Speech from the throne to both Houses of Parliament, January 29, 1944. VO 1944-45:573
Speech to Parliament, November 10, 1942. VO 1942-43:635
To the British public, September 23, 1940. HAN:148

Halifax, E. F. L. W.
All Britain is united. COP: 479; COPA:479

Hitler, A.
Threat to destroy the British Empire. HAN:143

Lloyd George, D.
Gives some advice to Prime Minister Chamberlain. PE: 768; PEA:768

Murrow, E. R.
Spring comes to England. BA 1940-41:157

Smuts, J. C.
Address before members of the two Houses of Parliament. HAN:204; VO 1942-43:560

---- GREECE

Churchill, W. L. S.
Debate in House of Commons, June 10, 1941 (Defense of Crete). VO 1941: 255
Debate with Anthony Eden on withdrawal of Forces from Greece, April 30, 1941. VO 1941:184
Review of the war in the House of Commons, April 9, 1941. VO 1941:155

Eden, A.

WORLD WAR, 1939-1945-
GREECE (cont.)
Debate with Winston Churchill on withdrawal of Forces from Greece, April 30, 1941. VO 1941:184
George II.
Address to U. S. Congress June 15, 1942. VO 1942-43:347
Hitler, A.
Order of the day calling for invasion of Yugoslavia and Greece. VO 1941:152
Tsouderos, E.
Message to the Greeks, June 5, 1941. VO 1941:243

---- INDIA
Chiang Kai Shek
Message to the Indian people, February 21, 1942. VO 1942-43:158

---- ITALY
Churchill, W. L. S.
Speech in the House of Commons, July 27, 1943. VO 1943-44:285
Eisenhower, D. D.
Test of the proclamation broadcast on the surrender of Italy. VO 1943-44:335
Hitler, A.
Speech on the surrender of Italy. VO 1943-44:339
Mussolini, B.
Address delivered at Rome, Italy, February 23, 1941. VO 1941:87
Anniversary of Italy's entry in the war. COP:511; COPA:511; COPB:489
Calling to Italians to resume fighting against the Allies. VO 1943-44:377
Hour of irrevocable decision has come! CROC:331; HIB:225
Speech before Chamber of Fasces and Corporations, June 10, 1941. VO 1941: 249
Speech to the Chamber of Fasci and Corporations, December 2, 1942. VO 1942-43:705
War statement, December 11, 1941. VO 1941:597
Roosevelt, F. D.
Fall of Rome. BA 1943-44: 47; VO 1944-45:256
Italy enters the war. BA 1939-40:76
See also Rome; World War, 1939-1945-Campaigns-Italian front

---- JAPAN
Chiang- Mei-Ling
Japan is first U. S. foe. BA 1942-43:85; HAN:201; VO 1943-44:60
Churchill, W. L. S.
Broadcast on war with Japan. VO 1941:555
Grew, J. C.
Menace of Japan. BA 1942-43:72
Radio broadcast from Washington, August 30, 1942. VO 1942-43:447
Koiso, K.
Broadcast to the Japanese people. HAN:346; VO 1944-45:368
New Year's address, 1945. VO 1945-46:4
Konoye, F.
Triple alliance. COP:522; COPA:522; COPB:500
Kurusu, S.
Broadcast November 26, 1942. VO 1942-43:681
Shimada, S.
Speech to the Japanese Diet. VO 1943-44:452
Tojo, H.
At opening of the 84th Diet. HAN:343; VO 1944-45:45
Broadcast on the consolidation of the Nations total effort in the prosecution of the Greater East Asia war. VO 1942-43:410
Broadcast to Japan and the

Empire, January 27, 1943. VO 1943-44:16
New Year's address, 1944. VO 1944-45:11
Radio address on the second anniversary of the Greater East Asia war. VO 1943-44:573
Report on war progress and plans. VO 1944-45:215
Speech as war minister to the Japanese Diet, October 26, 1943. VO 1943-44:448
Speech at closing of 84th Diet. VO 1944-45:138
Speech on Japan's total mobilization. VO 1943-44: 409
Speech to the Japanese Diet, October 26, 1943. VO 1943-44:442

---- ---- OCCUPATION See Japan-History-Allied occupation

---- ---- SURRENDER
Attlee, C. R.
Broadcast on Japan's surrender. VO 1945-46:437
Chiang Kai-Shek
Victory message, August 15, 1945. VO 1945-46:446
George VI.
Address at opening of Parliament, August 15, 1945. VO 1945-46:438
Higashi-Kuni, N.
Address before Diet on reasons for defeat. VO 1945-46:540
Hirohito.
Broadcast to the Japanese people on surrender. HAN: 357; VO 1945-46:436
Rescript read before the Japanese Diet. VO 1945-46: 540
Surrender rescript to Japanese troops. VO 1945-46: 460
MacArthur, D.
Remarks and final speech at Japanese surrender. BA 1945-46:13; HAN:360; VO 1945-46:528, 529
Statement at the conclusion of Manila Conference with Japanese surrender envoys. VO 1945-46:467
Nimitz, C.W.
Remarks at Japanese surrender. VO 1945-46:531
Stalin, I.
Radio address on the Japanese surrender. VO 1945-46:531
Truman, H. S.
Announcement of Japanese acceptance of Potsdam Declaration. VO 1945-46: 434
Broadcast on Japanese surrender. HAN:362; VO 1945-46:520
See also Berlin Conference, 1945; Japan-History-Allied occupation; V-J Day; World War, 1939-1945-Armistices

---- LATIN AMERICA
Alfaro, R.
What will Latin America do? BART 4:281

---- LUXEMBOURG
Eisenhower, D.D.
Order of the day on the German counteroffensive in Belgium and Luxembourg. VO 1944-45:623

---- MEXICO
Camacho, M. A.
War message to the extraordinary session of the Mexican Congress, May 28, 1942. VO 1942-43:314

---- NAVAL OPERATIONS
King, E. J.
American postwar seapower and control of Pacific bases. BA 1944-45:83
Roosevelt, F.D.
Freedom of the seas. COP: 546; COPB:524; SAA:300;

WORLD WAR, 1939-1945-NAVAL OPERATIONS (cont.)
VO 1941:395
Message to Congress on the sinking of the Robin Moor. VO 1941:289
Navy day address on the attack of the destroyer Kearney. HAN:160; VO 1941:462

---- NETHERLANDS
Kaltenborn, H. V.
Germany invades Holland and Belgium. BA 1939-40: 68.
Wilhelmina.
Address to Congress. VO 1942-43:427

---- PEACE AND MEDIATION
Arnold, T. W.
Full production after the war. HOC:166
Burton, H. H.
America's road to lasting peace. BA 1943-44:106
Butler, N. M.
American plan to prevent war. BA 1941-42:259
Connally, T. T.
America and post-war cooperation. BA 1943-44:96
Eden, A.
America and Great Britain in the post war world. BA 1942-43:131
Speech on power and responsibility. VO 1944-45: 147
Fleming, D. F.
Who says it can't be done? BA 1941-42:265
Krause, N.
We will not lay down arms. BA 1943-44:123
Lodge, H. C., Jr.
Fruitful approach to a prolonged peace. BA 1942-43: 116
Pius XII.
Address in St. Peter's Square, Vatican City, urging a charitable peace. VO 1945-46:123
Roosevelt, F. D.
Eight common principles for a better world. BA 1941-42:247; FIP:244; VO 1941:379
Schuman, F. L.
Design for a people's peace. BA 1942-43:142
Welles, S.
Post war leadership. BA 1941-42:270
Wheeler, B. K.
Against the resolution for collaboration for postwar peace. BA 1943-44:115
Willkie, W. L.
Economic freedom of the world. BA 1942-43:105
Isolationism and the League of Nations. BA 1941-42:251
See also Berlin Conference, 1945; Council of Foreign Ministers, 1945; Crimea Conference, 1945; Moscow Conference of Foreign Ministers, 1945; United Nations Conference on International Organization, San Francisco, 1945; V-E day; V-J day

---- PHILIPPINE ISLANDS
Fleming, D.
Reminiscence on starvation. AN:82
Osmena, S.
First address to his cabinet. VO 1944-45:370
Roosevelt, F. D.
Radio address to the people of the Philippines, August 12, 1943. VO 1943-44:306
See also World War, 1939-1945-Campaigns-Pacific front

---- POLAND
Churchill, W. L. S.
Broadcast to Polish people. VO 1941:190
Vyshinsky, A. Y.

Statement on Soviet-Polish relations. VO 1943-44:195
See also Berlin Conference, 1945; Poland

---- PORTUGAL
Churchill, W. L. S.
Statement in the House of Commons, on British occupation of the Azores. VO 1943-44:435

---- REFUGEES See Refugees

---- RUSSIA
Beaverbrook, W. M. A.
Russia must be sustained. COP:482; COPA:482
Byrnes, J. F.
Statement on the Soviet declaration of war on Japan. VO 1945-46:416
Churchill, W. L. S.
War on Russia. COP:475; COPA:475; COPB:439; HAN:156; VO 1941:320
Gottschalk, L. and others.
Soviet Russia at war (radio discussion). BA 1940-41: 168
Harriman, W. A.
Speech at final meeting at the Conference of U. S., Great Britain, and the U. S. S. R. VO 1941:430
Hitler, A.
Proclamation on war with Soviet Union, June 22, 1941. VO 1941:292
Hunt, F.
Those incredible Russians. BA 1942-43:185
Kalinin, M.
New Year's address. VO 1944-45:5
Molotov, V. M.
Nazi war on Russia. COP: 515; COPA:515; COPB: 515; VO 1941:318
Ribbentrop, J.
Statement on the declaration of war on the Soviet Union. VO 1941:301
Stalin, I.
"Defend every inch of Soviet soil." COP:517; COPA: 517; COPB:495; CROC: 429; ON:167; PE:785; PEA:785; VO 1941:330
Issues of the war. HAN: 112
May Day order of the day (1945). VO 1945-46:183
Order of the day, November 7, 1942. VO 1942-43: 593
Order of the day, May 1, 1943. VO 1943-44:187
Order of the day, May 1, 1944. VO 1944-45:198
Order of the day on "May Day," May 1, 1942. VO 1942-43:262
Order of the day on the 26th anniversary of the October revolution. VO 1943-44:518
Order of the day on the 26th anniversary of the Red Army. VO 1944-45:122
Order of the day on the 27th anniversary of the Red Army and Navy. VO 1945-46:65
Position of Russia, November 6, 1941. HAN:164
Report on international relations, November 6, 1942. VO 1942-43:582
Report on the 26th anniversary of the October revolution. HAN:232; VO 1943-44: 509
Report on the 27th anniversary of the Revolution. VO 1944-45:546
Results of past year, November 6, 1942. HAN:113
27th anniversary order of the day. HAN:288; VO 1944-45:554
See also World War, 1939-1945-Campaigns-Russian front

WORLD WAR, 1939-1945-
SECOND FRONT (cont.)
Churchill, W. L. S.
Debate in House of Commons, November 11, 1942. VO 1942-43:651
Roosevelt, F. D.
Announcing the opening of a second front in French North and West Africa. VO 1942-43:596
Stalin, I.
Report on international relations, November 6, 1942. VO 1942-43:582

---- SOUTH AMERICA
Roosevelt, F. D.
Informal remarks to members of the governing board of the Pan American Union. VO 1942-43:214
Welles, S.
At third meeting of Ministers of Foreign Affairs of the American Republic. VO 1942-43:35

---- UNDERGROUND ORGANIZATIONS See Underground movements

---- UNITED STATES
Arnold, H. H.
Our air power. HAN:245
Barber, P.
Wake up, America. DO:23
Bisel, D.
For what do we fight? DO:93
Brenner, S. M.
Propaganda in a democracy. DO:48
Burton, H. C.
What price freedom? DO:7
Burton, L. J.
Rights we fight for. DO:145
Chapman, V.
On the war resolution against Japan. BA 1941-42:40
Chiang, Mei-Ling
Japan is first U. S. foe. BA 1942-43:85; HAN:201; VO 1943-44:60
Davis, A.
Challenge of the war to American youth. DO:87
Dutter, P.
Is the Constitution ours? DO:217
Eisenhower, D. D.
Army hour broadcast from Paris on the need for ammunition. VO 1944-45:568
Quality of America's fighting men. BA 1944-45:114; HAN:312; VO 1945-46:288
Eliot, G. F.
How safe are we from attack? BART 3:115
Ellis, M.
Our goal. DO:18
Elyea, C. D., Jr.
Plea of the unknown soldier. DO:44
Ford, N. A.
What are you Negroes fighting for? ON:194
Handlin, I.
United we stand. DO:39
Harris, H.
America's peace responsibilities. DO:82
Herbon, E., Jr.
America-upward and onward. DO:3
Jensen, G.
For this we fight. DO:103
Kuroki, B.
War isn't over at home. BA 1945-46:208
Lilio, R. L.
American Constitution-for this we fight. DO:184
MacLean, D. A.
Americas in the world crisis. HOC:121
Marshall, G. C.
We are ready to carry the war to the enemy. HAN: 258
McNutt, P. V.
Labor and the war. BA 1941-42:170
Maxtel, S.

Are you a little bored with war? HAN:273
Miller, M.E.
Rights we defend. DO:114
Moore, J.O.
Common man. DO:67
Murray, M.J.
America is worth fighting for. DO:133
Myer, C.R.
Remember Pearl Harbor. DO:34
Ockerlander, D.
Building stairways. DO:29
Our greatest wartime blunder (by a Nisei student). LOMS: 228; LOMSA:287
Rathbun, J.
Pick up the tools. NOR 1942:41
Reynolds, Q.
Campaign and men in uniform. BA 1944-45:123
Ripley, R.K.
Freedom's destiny. DO:60
Roosevelt, F.D.
Address at the annual gathering of the White House Correspondents' Association, February 12, 1943. VO 1943-44:52
Address to the closing session of the New York Herald Tribune Forum on Current Problems. VO 1942-43:677
America accepts the challenge (December 9, 1941). ANG:515; BA 1941-42:31; COP:714; COPA:532; COPB:532; HAN:176; VO 1941:563; YE:357
Broadcast at the Puget Sound Navy Yard on the war in the Pacific. VO 1944-45:373
Broadcast on Washington's birthday, 1942. BRAP:40; VO 1942-43:160
Broadcast to International Student Assembly. VO 1942-43:463
Broadcast to the nation, April 28, 1942. VO 1942-43:249
Broadcast to the nation, September 7, 1942. VO 1942-43:479
Broadcast to the nation, October 12, 1942. VO 1942-43:545
Broadcast to the nation, July 28, 1943. ON:22; VO 1943-44:289
Budget message to Congress, January 13, 1944. VO 1944-45:29
Campaign broadcast from the White House, November 2, 1944. VO 1944-45: 538
First war address before Congress. COP:726; COPB: 538; HURG:269; VO 1942-43:8
Freedom of the seas. COP: 546; COPB:524; SAA:300; VO 1941:395
In response to message from Prime Minister of Iceland. VO 1941:343
Message to Congress, January 7, 1943. BA 1942-43: 15; HAN:240; VO 1943-44: 7
Message to Congress, September 17, 1943. HAN: 351; VO 1943-44:364
Message to Congress, January 11, 1944. BA 1943-44: 15; VO 1944-45:21
Message to Congress asking for the recognition of a state of war with Germany and Italy. VO 1941:598
Message to Congress on the sinking of the Robin Moor. VO 1941:289
Message to Congress on the state of the nation, January 6, 1945. VO 1945-46:5
Navy Day address on the attack of the destroyer Kearney. HAN:160; VO 1941: 462
Navy Day campaign speech

WORLD WAR, 1939-1945-
UNITED STATES (cont.)
in Shibe Park, Philadelphia. VO 1944-45:509
Opening campaign speech at dinner of International Brotherhood of Teamsters. BA 1944-45:134; BAAMP: 267; MIA:356; ON:383; PAR:510; VO 1944-45:425
Statement on the use of poison gas. VO 1942-43: 337
This nation will remain neutral. BA 1939-40:21; BIR 4:288; BRAS:409; HAN:124; PL:839
War address (December 8, 1941). BA 1941-42:17; BAAMP:265; BOU:99; BRAP:146; BRE:373; CAP: 200; COP:713; COPA:530; COPB:531; FIP:249; HAN: 174; HIBS:482; HURG: 265; ON:179; PAR:507; PE:790; PEA:790; VO 1941:553

Rudolph, W. C.
For democracy we fight. DO:125

Sayre, F. B.
Corregidor. BA 1941-42: 179

Sitrick, J.
Vision for victory. NOR 1942:53

Smith, B.
American Constitution-for this we fight. DO:54

Summers, H. W.
Internal solidarity. BA 1943-44:165

Thomas, J. S.
We move in new directions. BART 4:255

Trail, E.
Keep it America. DO:74

Truman, H. S.
Address to Congress, April 16, 1945. BA 1944-45: 156; HAN:302; VO 1945-46:148
Message to Congress on driving for victory against Japan. VO 1945-46:237

Vandenberg, A. H.
American foreign policy. BA 1944-45:43; HAN:421; ON:182

Willkie, W.
We cannot win with quick or momentary heroics. HAN:107

Wright, D. J.
For this we die. DO:189

See also Iceland; United States-Defenses; United States-Foreign relations; United States-Neutrality; World War, 1939-1945-Civilian activities

---- ---- AID TO GREAT BRITAIN

Conant, J. B.
Aid to Allies. HAN:150

Donovan, W. J. and others.
Shall we do whatever is necessary to insure a British victory? BA 1940-41: 33

Pepper, C. D.
All-out aid to Britain. BA 1940-41:49

Roosevelt, F. D.
Address to White House Correspondents' Association dinner, March 15, 1941. VO 1941:126
Preservation of American independence. BA 1940-41: 19; COP:539; COPB:517; HAN:99; HURG:246; WPRC: 246

---- VICTORY See V-E Day; V-J Day; World War 1939-1945-Armistices

---- WAR AIMS

Benes, E.
What are we fighting for? BA 1942-43:56

Berle, A. A., Jr.
Warfare of free souls. BA 1941-42:57

Chiang, Mei-Ling
Fighting for the common cause. BA 1942-43:81; ON: 83
Japan is first U.S. foe. BA 1942-43:85; HAN:201; VO 1943-44:60
Eden, A.
British war aims, May 29, 1941. VO 1941:232
Fleming, D. F.
What is it that we fight? BA 1942-43:67
Hayes, C. J. H.
American war aims. BA 1942-43:47
Grew, J. C.
Menace of Japan. BA 1942-43:72
Howell, W. S.
Democratic issue. BA 1941-42:64
Wallace, H. A.
Price of free world victory. BA 1941-42:46; BOA:26; HOC:151

---- WAR CRIMINALS
Jackson, R. H.
Opening address before Nurenberg International Military Tribunal. BA 1945-46:60; VO 1945-46:734
Statement on War Trials Agreement. VO 1945-46: 432
Roosevelt, F. D.
Statement on punishment of war criminals. VO 1942-43:444

---- YUGOSLAVIA
Churchill, W. L. S.
Message to the Yugoslav people, April 13, 1941. VO 1941:166
Review of the war in the House of Commons, April 9, 1941. VO 1941:155
Hitler, A.
Order of the day calling for invasion of Yugoslavia. VO 1941:152

WORLD'S ECONOMIC CONFERENCE
George V.
Inauguration of the World's Economic Conference. BEA:1
Worsham, James A.
Low pressure selling. SAB: 106; SABA:172

WORSHIP
Tyndale, W.
Use and absue of images and relics. BREW 9:15
See also Prayers
Wrage, Ernest J.
Antidote to anonymity. BA 1963-64:191

WREN, SIR CHRISTOPHER
Gilbert, C.
Sir Christopher Wren. REEM sup 1:359; REEMB 6:148
Krantz, J., Jr.
Architect designed a needle (hypodermic). MCK:237
Wright, Donna Jeanne
For this we die. DO:188
Wright, Frances
Fourth of July oration. PE: 359; PEA:359
Wright, Frank Lloyd
On architecture. COPB:633; HURG:241
Wright, Mary
Bulwark of safety. YR 9:127
Wright, Quincy
Citizen's stake in academic freedom. HAR:309
Wright, Stephen J.
Price of excellence. HILK:321
Wright, Theodore S.
Prejudice against the colored man. WOON:92
Progress of the anti-slavery cause. WOON:86
Wright, Willard W.
Begins an address before the Sixth Annual Community Leader Oil Progress luncheon. PRNE:77

Wright, Wilson B.
"Dr. Jekyll or Mr. Hyde?" YR 4:165

Wriston, Henry Merritt
Free enterprise. BA 1943-44: 230
Introductory remarks on individualism. HOC:34
Validity of the educational process. BA 1961-62:171

WRITS OF ASSISTANCE
Otis, J.
Writs of Assistance, February, 1761. ANG:62; BREW 8:262; BRYW 8:27; CHAL 2:333; CHEM 1:13; HARS:7; HAZO 5:2031; HELE:2; JOHA 1 pt. 1:11; LAD:74; LEEW 8:23; MAS 5:2031; ORAMA 1:21; PE: 114; PEA:114; PL:573; REEMA 14:1526; SAA:6
Wu, Hsiu-Chuan
Address to the Security Council of the United Nations. HAR:126
Wu Ting-Fang
China and the United States. REEMB 3:1284
Grant. WERN 42:48
Teachings of Confucius. REEM 8:429; REEMA 6: 1225; REEMB 13:437

WULFF, LEE
Coulter, T.H.
Presents Lee Wulff. LY: 255
Miller, M.G.
Introduces Lee Wulff, lecturer with films. PRNE:47
Wycliffe, John
Concerning a grain of corn. BREW 10:278
Good lore for simple folk. BREW 10:274
Mercy to damned men in Hell. BREW 10:276
Rule for decent living. BREW 10:272; BRYW 3:8
Sermon on prayer. LEEW 4: 35; PL:217
Sixth Sunday gospel after Easter. CROC:485
Wylie, Andrew
Inaugural address as president of Indiana University. WE 2:97
Wyman, Eugene
Can these be the enemy? NOR 1944:47
Wyman, Walter
Sons of the Revolution. REEMA 3:1288
Wyndham, Sir William, Bart
Attack on Sir Robert Walpole, March 13, 1734. BREW 10: 279; GOOD:31
Royal prerogative delegated from the people (Army Bill, 1734). BREW 10:281
Secrecy of debates. EMS 1: 205

WYNNE, SHIRLEY
Introducing Shirley Wynne. NI:182; NIA:134
Xenophon.
Defence against false accusation. HAZO 1:180; MAS 1: 180
In council of war. CHAL 1: 96; HAZO 1:172; MAS 1: 172

YACHT CLUB See Boat club

YALE UNIVERSITY
Depew, C.M.
Yale University. REEM 1: 391; REEMA 1:356; REEMB 1:392
Eliot, C.W.
Harvard and Yale. CHAL 12:302; COP:673; COPB: 700; HAZO 23:9683; HURG: 130; MAS 23:9683; REEM 2:4; REEMA 2:427; REEMB 2:4
Fisher, H.J.
Presenting the Cheney-Ives gateway to Yale University. KNAS:160; KNASA:160; ONEM:710; ONES:41

Hadley, A. T.
Acceptance of the Cheney-Ives gateway. KNAS:161; KNASA:161; ONEM:713; ONES:48
Inaugural address as president of Yale University. WE 1:43
Opening the ceremonies held on observance of a university centennial (Yale Medical School). ONES:67
To the Brotherhood of Yale. KNAS:205; KNASA:205; ONEM:672; ONES:13
Heckscher, A.
Paramount duty. YR 8:273
Yale's conservatism. YR 7:137
Yale and Princeton-a response to a toast. DAVC:390

YALTA CONFERENCE See Crimea Conference, 1945
Yancey, William Lowndes
Alabama platform. -Same as his Speech of protest in the Charleston Convention
For Southern rights. -Same as his Speech in protest in the Charleston Convention
On Mr. C. J. Ingersoll's Resolution of inquiry into the conduct of Daniel Webster, in expending the Contingent Fund while Secretary of State. SOU 9:329
South does not seek to aggrandize herself. SOU 9:337
Speech in protest in the Charleston Convention. BAAMP:118; BRYW 9:192; SOU 9:339

YANKEES See National characteristics, American
Yarnell, Harry E.
Our stake in the Pacific. ON:78
Yasinow, Harvey S.
Shield of irresponsibility. NOR 1950:193

Yeager, Willard Hayes
Art of speaking effectively to employees. SAB:150; SABA:248

YEAR, CLOSING See Closing year addresses
Yeiser, N. E.
Fellowship. THOU 3:400
Yonge, Sir William
Constituents and members. EMS 2:108
Yorke, Peter C.
Watchman, what of the night? WAGN:419
Youle, Clinton
Introduces Ilka Chase. PRC:6
Introduces Maurice H. Stans, Director of the Bureau of Budget of the United States. PRC:14
Introduces Professor C. Northcote Parkinson. PRC:21
Introduces Robert F. Wagner, Mayor of New York City. PRC:12
Introduces William Veeck, President of the Chicago White Sox. PRC:25
Youman, Thomas
Plea for India. YR 4:355
Young, Dailey and others (H. C. Ahrend; N. M. Butler; J. E. Denning; J. T. Hickerton; R. W. P. Kay-Schuttleworth; L. A. Larson)
Shall we have government monopoly on armaments? SAR:246
Young, Bennett H.
Tribute to Winnie Davis. SHUO:145
Young, Clifford S.
Introduces William McChesney Martin, Chairman of the Board of Governors of the Federal Reserve System. PRNE:10
Young, Empress
Pioneer women of Texas. BOB:105

Young, Owen D.
Courage for the future. HOC: 29; SAR:9
Culture. -Same as his How we meet ourselves
Dawes plan. BYRA:478; REEM sup 3:192; REEMB 5:405
Dedicating the George F. Baker Foundation. ONEC: 79
How we meet ourselves (semicentennial of Hendrix College). COP:706; COPB: 733; HURG:227
St. Lawrence University summer school commencement address. GLAD:255
Science of better living. BA 1937-38:190
Use of knowledge. -Same as his How we meet ourselves
World of to-day. SHUP:200
Young, Robert R.
Marriage of business and education. BA 1952-53:135
Young, Towne
Triumph of individualism. SHUC:196
Young, William A.
Society and the pay roll. BRP 1:63; YR 2:141

YOUNG MEN'S CHRISTIAN ASSOCIATION
On the anniversary of a Young Men's Christian Association. BARB:143
Ramsey, H.
Introducing a speaker on the Y. M. C. A. BRC:129
Tinker, E.
Diligence and its reward. THOU 2:493
Williams, G.
Fifty years old (Y. M. C. A. talk). THOU 2:493
Young Men's Christian Association, by one of the leaders. EDGS:243

YOUNG PEOPLE'S SOCIETY OF CHRISTIAN ENDEAVOR
Cook, J.
Watchwords for the 20th century. THOU 2:502

YOUNG WOMEN'S CHRISTIAN ASSOCIATION
Address at a girl's high "Y" banquet. AMEO 2:157
Ramsey, H.
Introducing a speaker on the Y. W. C. A. BRC:241
Young Women's Christian Association, by a member of the organization. EDGS: 244
Younger, Kenneth
Critique of United States China policy, September, 1957. GRAC:181

YOUTH
Address at fifth anniversary of founding of Big Brother Athletic Association. BEDA:111
Advice to youth. FRIE:203
Age-and youth. DR:291
Anderson, L. R.
Prisoner at the bar. YR 1: 113
Axson, S.
World and the new generation. REEM 6:33; REEMB 7:34
Brown, R.W.
Crime against youth. SAR: 81
Burroughs, J.
Integrity of youth. YR 7:115
Butler, N. M.
De Juventute. ON:33
Cameron, W. J.
Liberal youth. SAR:46
What shall we tell the young men of to-day? SAR:41
Challenge for youth. NATT:34
Conant, J. B.
Social dynamite in our large cities: unemployed, out-of-school youth. HIB: 324
Conzelman, J. C.
Young man's physical and

mental approach to war.
SAC:60
Cutten, G.B.
Arise, let us go hence.
BA 1938-39:210
Davis, A.
Challenge of the war to
American youth. DO:87
Davis, R.
Youth and the Constitution.
DO:224
Dearing, W.P.
Uplift and the undertow.
SHU:103
Emerson, R.W.
Young American. PL:644
Ferris, W.N.
Give American youth a
chance. EXEE:459
Gantz, G.
Doors without keys. YR 6:
203
Greenwell, E.
Tramp! Tramp! Tramp!
YR 9:41
Grunwald, E.
Toward saner values. BRP
4:64; INTW 1933:46; YR
5:311
Harvest time of life. NATT:
37
Holth, I.
Youth aflame. YR 6:303
Hunter, W.
New birth of freedom.
BRP 6:88
Informal chat with members
of a youth organization about
their and other similar
groups. DR:116; LU:1220
Irwin, R.
Banners and bluebirds. BRP
7:70; NOR 1936:3
Juliana, Queen of the Nether-
lands
Students of Paris. BUT:
242; BUTB:235
Larson, A.
Constitution and American
youth. BRP 2:35; YR 2:69
Lazar, W.T.
Reveille of the dead. NOR
1941:35
Lindquist, C.
Liquor problem and youth.
BRP 10:68
McCreight, W.E.
Through the eys of youth.
YR 7:67
Maloney, M.J.
Call us dissenters. YR 8:
21
Nelson, C.H.
Youth and lasting peace.
AN:74
Nichols, E.R., Jr.
Everyman. BRP 7:112; YR:
8:103
Niebler, C.J.
Wanted-patriotism for
American youth. YR 8:31
Nuesse, C.
Bourne of youth. YR 4:251
Opening speech at fifth anni-
versary of founding of Big
Brother Athletic Associa-
tion. BEDA:110
Price, J.H. and others.
Is youth forgetting religion?
HAR:489
Problems that puzzle youth.
JA:85
Rathbun, J.
Pick up the tools. NOR
1942:41
Reverence due from the old to
the young. DAVC:85
Roberts, P.
Youth experiments. BRP 7:
106; YR 8:71
Robinson, H.P.
Life's challenge to youth.
BRP 4:54; INTW 1933:14
Roosevelt, E.A.
Speech training for the
youth. BUTA:223
Roosevelt, F.D.
Challenge to youth. BOA:
376
Rowe, M.J.
Youth and the depression.
JUD:241
Sener, W.
Youth to-day and to-mor-
row. YR 7:125
Shadows of tomorrow. JA:247

YOUTH (cont.)
Shapiro, H.
In defense of youth. BRY: 475
Smith, F.M.
Around and around they go. BRP 7:60; YR 8:11
Smith, R.L.
What is right with youth? BRP 2:15
Snell, B.H.
Decision for youth. BOA: 373
Snyder, F.B.
American youth in the present emergency. HUS: 262
Stoddard, G.D.
Frontiers of youth. BA 1941-42:219
Success talk for young people. NAT:42
Swing, R.G.
Youth, war, and freedom. HAN:22
Talk to young people. NATT: 31
Taylor, H.
Ideals of American youth. HAR:462
Younger generation. BA 1947-48:179
This side of heaven. JA:253
Tucker, H.E.
Depression versus youth. JUD:235
Turner, R.G.
Young America on parade. BRP 8:38; YR 9:51
Wallace, H.A.
Builders of to-morrow. ON:74
Welcome to a delegation of boy or girl scouts (or other youth groups). HNWS:50
White, W.A.
Your young men shall see visions. SAR:1
Who wants to stay young? JAI:55
Wieferich, R.
Youth and the depression. JUD:247
William II.
German youth. WERN 42: 24
Wilson, W.
Willard Wilson. BRP 7:54; YR 8:59
Youth aflame. JAS:18
Youth yesterday and today. SCHS:282
See also Boys; Children; DeMolays, Order of; Girls; Students

YOUTH CENTERS See Recreation

YU, TSUNE-CHI
Presents H.H. Kung. LY:200; ON:338

YUGOSLAVIA See World War, 1939-1945-Yugoslavia
Yurk, Clarence
Lost: four friends. BERS:13
Zacharias, Milton
New freedom. YR 7:57
Zearing, Joseph Hazen
Issue of justice: equal suffrage for women. SHUC:35
Zeff, Joseph
Our children: address at a Bar-Mitzvah. ZEL:49
Zekaria, Harold
Flight from Bagdad. BRP 8: 98; YR 9:119
Ziebarth, E.W.
First class man: introducing Commissioner Robert E. Lee of Federal Communications Commission. BRC:39
Ziffren, Paul
Creative citizen. BRP 6:65; NOR 1935:118
Zimmerman, C.H.
Labor organizations. THOU 1: 411
Zimmerman, Ralph
Mingled blood. ARNS:99; LINP:197

ZINC
Zinc. SCHS:284
Zinsser, Hans

Scientist's view of the Medical Center. REEM sup 3: 204; REEMB 6:402

ZIONISM
Wise, S. S.
Fifty years of Zionism. BA 1946-47:262
Zola, Emile
Appeal for Dreyfus. BREW 10: 285; CHAL 13:355; COP: 112; COPA:112; COPB: 112; CROC:489; HAZO 24: 10330; HIB:80; MAS 24: 10330; PE:594; PEA:594; REEM 7:436; REEMA 9: 1226; REEMB 7:437
Zschoche, Martin J.
Blessed triangle of a Christian marriage. ACW:122
Zueblin, Charles
Did Woodrow Wilson fail? LINM:276

ZULU WAR, 1879
Sullivan, A. M.
On the Zulu War. BRYW 6:207
Zwingli, Huldreich
Evils of foreign military service. BRYW 7:30; CHAL 1:412; HAZO 3:1309; MAS 3:1309; PL:238
Sermon on Mary, the pure mother of God. LEEW 4:93

Selected List of Titles
Explanation

Titles listed in the Selected List of Titles can be located by referring back to the Speech Index proper under the name of the author, or the subject which follows each title.

Included in this list are the titles which the compiler thought would be difficult for the user to locate if he does not know the name of the author, and if the meaning in the title bears no resemblance to the topic discussed, or there are no key words in the title to guide him to the proper subject entry. Examples of titles in this category are: "Acres of diamonds," "Which knew not Joseph," and "Sun-beams may be extracted from cucumbers, but the process is tedious."

This list does not include titles which obviously can be located readily by subject or type of speech. "Necessity for Courage" can be found under COURAGE; "Sinews of peace" under PEACE; "Principles and program of AFL-CIO" under LABOR UNIONS; and "Good faith" under RELIGION by checking the cross reference from FAITH to RELIGION.

Many titles of war speeches delivered by warriors or by civilians are included in this list because the entry is usually under the name of a specific war rather than WAR in general.

By excluding the numerous titles under types of speeches as INTRODUCTIONS, RESPONSES, INAUGURAL ADDRESSES, ACCEPTANCE SPEECHES, PRESENTATION SPEECHES, etc. much repitition was avoided, and the list kept simple enough to be quickly scanned for vaguely remembered titles, variant titles, and titles of speeches where the author is not known.

The compiler sincerely hopes the users of the Speech Index will find this feature helpful.

Selected List of Titles

A B C of racketeering - Dewey, T. E.
Abandonment of Candahar - Lytton, E. R. B. -L.
Abide with us - Rossnagel, W. T.
Abiding peace - Umbach, H. H.
Accuses Canadians as traitors to his cause - Pontiac.
Achievements and responsibilities of the age - Clinton, D.
Acquisition of foreign territory - Caffery, D.
Acres of diamonds - Conwell, R. H.
Acrobat - Cobb, I. S.
Across the flood - Reading, R. D. I.
Act of faith - MacLeish, A.
Adar v. United States - Harlan, J. M.
Address at the grave of Ole Bull - Björnson, B.
Address in honor of Eduard Benes - Lucas, S. W.
Address to his army at the beginning of the Italian campaign - Napoléon I.
Address to his soldiers - Hannibal.
Address to Nero - Seneca, L. A.
Address to the humane and benevolent inhabitants of the city and county of Philadelphia - Forten, J.
Address to the people of England - Lee, R. H.
Address to the throne concerning affairs in America - Pitt, W., 1708-1778
Address to troops - Nicias.
Adequacy of present opportunities - Liddon, H. P.
Administration theory - Raymond, H. J.
Admiration for the Puritan character - Talmage, T. D.
Admonition to a fallen virgin - Basil the Great.
Adopted citizen - Grant, U. S.
Advantages of a mixed ancestry - Van Dyke, H.
Advantages of American independence - Ramsey, D.
Adventures among great Americans - Jones, E. DeW.
Advice to a young man - Bernard, Saint; Burdette, R. J.
After war questions - Hoover, H. C.
Again we turned fate away - Hitler, A.
Against a step-mother, on a charge of poisoning - Antiphon.
Against booted and spurred privilege - Rumbold, R.
Against centralization - Grady, H.
Against coercing America - Burke, E.
Against conquest of Canada - Quincy, J.
Against "Copperheads" - Drake, C. D.
Against Ctesiphon - Aeschines.
Against English imperialism - Grattan, H.
Against enlistment of Negro soldiers - Slayden, J. L.
Against extremists, North and South - Bell, J.
Against Lepidus - Philippus, L.
Against liberalism: a Prussian royalist confession of faith - Bismarck, O.
Against militarism - Bryan, W. J.
Against nonresident landlords - Parnell, C. S.
Against Pancleon - Lysias.
Against Pitt and war with America - Brougham and Vaux, H. P. B.

Against ransoming the prisoners-
Torquatus, T. M.
Against revenues from drunkenness and vice - Chesterfield, P. D. S.
Against search-warrants for seamen - Pitt, W., 1708-1778
Against standing armies - Pulteney, W.
Against Sulla - Lepidus, M. A.
Against the accomplices of Catiline - Cato, M. P. (Uticensis)
Against the charge of treason - Mirabeau, H. G. R.
Against the Compromise Bill - Corwin, T.
Against the conspirators - Cato, M. P. (The Censor)
Against the demands of the Lacedaemonians - Pericles.
Against the Gin Bill of the Ministry - Chesterfield, P. D. S.
Against the humiliation of the Southern Army - Garibaldi, G.
Against the military spirit - Clinton, D.
Against the power of nobility - Memmius, C.
Against the Sicilian expedition - Nicias.
Against the Stamp Act - Pitt, W., 1708-1778
Against the Tribunes - Claudius, A.
Against tyrants - Knox, J.
Against the Union - Grattan, H.
Against war with Germany - LaFollette, R. M.
Against warring on the weak - Crittenden, J. J.
Against Webster and northern compromisers - Stevens, T.
Age and growth of trees - Skinner, C. R.
Age of action - Churchill, R. H. S.
Age of anxiety - Margulies, N. L.
Age of erudition - Jameson, J. F.
Agonized reappraisals: Hungary and Suez - Eisenhower, D. D.
Agrees to run for President - Stevenson, A. E.
Ah, them was the days, lad - Rogers, W.
Ahab and Micaish - Maclaren, A.
Aim of the future - Robinson, G. D.
Air - Jouett, J. H.
Air-borne traveling man - Lentz, H. J.
Alabama platform - Yancey, W. L.
Alchemy of influence - Drummond, H.
Alive - Evans, L. H.
Alive in God - Arnold, T.
All but inmost faith - Ranney, A.
All this and for what - Kovar, L.
Allegiance dominant - MacGregor, R. R.
Alliance for progress - Kennedy, J. F.
Allied war gains - Churchill, W. L. S.
All's well - Davis, W. R.
Aloha Ke Akua - Akaka, A. K.
America a world power - Ireland, J.
America accepts the challenge - Roosevelt, F. D.
America and Britain for civilization - Tracy, S. H.
America and brotherhood - Stallings, J.
America and Great Britain in the post war world - Eden, A.
America and the Allies - Beck, J. M.
America and the war - Thomas, N.
America as I find it - Russo, E.
America beware - Ames, K.
America first - Knapp, F.
America free or America slave - Jay, J.
America goes abroad - Kiltz, A. A.
America has not been disappointed - Roosevelt, F. D.
America I want to know - Helm, W.

America in 1940 - Owsley, A.
America in the post-war air world - Luce, C.B.
America is worth fighting for - Murray, M.J.
America-its national and individual ideals - Haygood, S.C.
America only - Beveridge, A.J.
America-upward and onward - Herbon, E., Jr.
American birthright and the Philippine pottage - Van Dyke, H.
American college - Wilson, W.
American connection - Russell of Killowen, C.R.
American crisis - Paine, T.
American gratitude to France - Jusserand, J.J.
American Hall of Fame - Depew, C.M.
American hospitality - Collins, W.
American idea - Webster, D.
American independence - Adams, J.Q.; Adams, S.
American infamy - Thomas, P.E.
American invasion of England - Kipling, R.
American jingo - Wild, R.
American morality and nuclear diplomacy - Luce, C.B.
American opportunities - Horton, J.
American pioneer - Lane, F.K.
American plan to prevent war - Butler, N.M.
American problems - Walton, J.A.
American road - Oberholzer, H.J.
American scholar - Emerson, R.W.
American soldier - Wheeler, J.
American spirit incarnate - Lane, F.K.
American standard - Washington, B.T.
American standard of living - Taft, R.A. and others
American Swastika - Bagwell, P.D.
American system - Clay, H.
American transportation - Rea, S.
American war aims - Hayes, C.J.H.
American way - Bingham, H.; Irwin, W.A.
American way of life - Sokolsky, G.E.
Americanism - Borah, W.E.
Americanism and the foreign-born - Wilson, W.
"Americanizing" our new possessions - Schurz, C.
Americans for America - Folk, J.W.
America's answer to Japan's challenge - Roosevelt, F.D.
America's biggest business - Bennet, L.L.
America's coming greatness - Ingersoll, R.G.
America's domineering tradition - Levy, N.
America's duty in time of crisis - Thomas, N.
America's golden age - Choate, J.H.
America's greatest problem - Dobson, J.
Americas in the world crisis - MacLean, D.A.
America's medieval empire - Plummer, J.M.
America's mission - Bryan, W J.
America's mother of men - Shoeler, M.
America's obligation to England - Barré, I.
America's policy toward insular possessions of other countries - Granik, T.
America's post war goals - Torreyson, V.
America's present emergency - Wheeler, B.K.
America's role - Stevenson, A.E.
America's role in Europe - Jenks, J.W.
America's second chance - Wallace, H.A.

America's uncrowned queen - Wilson, H. T.
America's window to the world - Franklin, J. H.
And the patient began to die - Kanzell, H. N.
Angel's song - Henson, P. S.
Annexation - Bryan, W. J.
Anno Domini - Thomas, J. B.
Another "shot heard round the world" - Snyder, F. B.
Another year of time - Stoddard, C. A.
Answer to William J. Bryan - Cockran, W. R.
Answering Alexander Hamilton - Lansing, J.
Anticipates the battle of Britain-Churchill, W. L. S.
Antidote to anonymity - Wrage, E. J.
Anti-expansion bugbear - MacVeagh, F.
Antitrust: "Mere size is no sin" - Taft, W. H.
Anti-Westernism: cause and cure - Dean, V. M.
Anvil chorus - Shepard, J.
Apologia - Nixon, R. M.
Apology - Socrates.
Appeal of forty thousand citizens threatened with disfranchisement to the people of Pennsylvania - Purvis, R.
Appeal of Horatius - Livius, (P.) Titus
Appeal of the Independent Democrats - Douglas, S. A.
Appeal to his soldiers - Korniloff, L. G.
Appeal to our brothers in white - Gaines, W. J.
Appeal to the American people on the seizure of his nation-Benes, E.
Appeal to the nation - Lloyd George, D.
Appeal to the people - Desmoulins, C.
Apportionment of representation - Leigh, B. W.
Architect designed a needle - Krantz, J. C., Jr.
Are they really unteachable - Geiman, C. K.
Are we blind - Ehninger, D.
Are you a little bored with war - Maxted, S.
Are you following the pattern - RELIGION
Are you still on the bottle - RELIGION
Areopagiticus - Isocrates.
Argument for graduated deterrence - Buchan, A.
Arise, let us go hence - Cutten, G. B.
Aristocracy of brains - Hopkins, E. M.
Aristocracy of the unfit - Keesey, R.
Arlington-1935 - Robbins, P. H.
Arm of the law - Kitchen, J. M.
Armageddon speech - Roosevelt, T.
Arming of the nations - Eliot, C.
Army in Transvaal - Wolseley, G. J.
Army of democracy - Coyle, J. G.
Around and around they go - Smith, F. M.
Arraigning President Polk - Dayton, W. L.
Arrangements on this side - Page, E. C.
Arsenal of democracy - Roosevelt, F. D.
Art of contemplation - Hancher, V. M.
Art of eloquence - Caird, J.
Art of living - Phelps, W. L.
Art of personal contact - Ferris, E. E.
As a literary guest of America - Dickens, C.
Aspirations for the Union - Clay, C. M.
Ass laden with gold - Bryce, J. B.
Assault and battery: quarrel in camp-Demosthenes.
Assassin of youth - Gilbertson, A.; Locks, E. S.; Sugarman, N. A.
At a child's grave - Ingersoll,

R. G.
At his brother's grave - Ingersoll, R. G.
At the Bar of the House of Lords - Butt, I.
At the Concord centennial celebration - Curtis, G.W.
At the Congress of Angostura - Bolivar, S.
At the sign of the dollar - Hamm, H.
At the sound of the trumpet - Mather, C.
At the tomb of Napoléon - Ingersoll, R. G.
"Atlantic" and its contributors - Howells, W.D.
Atoms for peace - Eisenhower, D.D.
Attempt to subjugate America - Pitt, W., 1708-1778
Attention, my good red warriors - Pushmataha.
Authentic revolution - Canham, E.D.
Authors and their patrons - Thackeray, W.M.
Avarice and usury - Chrysostom, J.
Awake the dawn - Kennedy, G.

Babies - Clemens, S. L.
Bad example of a stumbling block - Cuyler, T. L.
Bald head and a mustache - Makar, J.
Bandwagon minds - Rivers, D.
Banners and bluebirds - Irwin, R.
Banning nuclear tests - Humphrey, H. H., Jr.
Barbour Bill - Massey, J. E.
Bargain - Shively, T.
Bargains in sweat - Gunnison, E.M.
Barrie bumps Stevenson - Barrie, J.M.
Barron v. Baltimore - Marshall, J.
Bases of our nation's strength - Lilienthal, D.E.
Basic indictment - Khrushchev, N.S.
Battle of baloney - Larson, D.
Battle of Santiago - Lodge, H.C.
Battle of the cowpens - Higginson, T.W.
Battleship bubble - Johnson, F. L.
Be a "somebody" - FAME
Be not conformed to this world - Wilson, W.
Beautiful and glorious banner - Prosser, W.A.
Beauty of a life of service - Brooks, P.
Beer, a harmless drink - Dow, N.
Before the Corps Législatif - Favre, J.
Before the Diet of Worms - Luther, M.
Beggars of the sea - Depew, C.M.
Begin now - Crowder, E.H.
Beginning a revolution - Garrison, W.L.
Beginning of constitutionality - Greenhalge, F.T.
Beginning of government - Adams, B.
Behind the scenes in Hollywood - Hays, W.H., Jr.
Behold, a sower went forth to sow - SERMONS
Behold the American - Talmage, T.D.
Being civilized to death - Fosdick, H.E.
Being one's self - Bush, D.
Being true to ourselves - Borah, W.E.
Belgium ready - Albert I.
Belief of an unbeliever - Burrell, D.J.
Believe it or not - Humphrey, C.J.
Bell tolls for thee - Collins, F.C., Jr.
Bemoans the degradation of modern life - Ruskin, J.
Bench and Bar - Choate, J.H.
Beneath American roofs - Temple, G.
Benjamin Franklin lecture - Stanton, F.

Best gift - IMMORTALITY
Best is yet to be - Heyler, W.B.; Weiner, M.
Better part - Washington, B.T.
Between yesterday and tomorrow - Koch, R.
Beware of poison - LIFE
Beyond the dollar sign - Lindquist, R.
Beyond the ranges - Wingate, H.S.
Bible of democracy - Graves, E.L.
Big blunders - Talmage, T.D.
Big parade - Carty, W.
"Big stick" speech - Roosevelt, T.
Bill Arp's lecture - Smith, C.H.
Birmingham - Kennedy, J.F.
Birth of greatness - Watterson, H.
Bishop's charge - Freeman, J.E.
Black horse and his ride - Lippard, G.
Blazing an international trail by motorcycle - Williams, C.C.
Blazing bulwarks - Fergen, G.
Blessed triangle of a Christian marriage - Zschocle, M.J.
"Blifil and black George-Puritan and blackleg" - Randolph, J.
Blood, sweat and tears - Churchill, W.L.S.
Blue and the Gray - Bradley, W.O.; Lodge, H.C., Watterson, H.
Blundering giant - Scherer, R.M.
Boards for life's buildings - Clement, G.C.
Bobby wild goose's ragged regiment - SUNDAY SCHOOLS
Bold go toward their time - Lang, W.C.
Bombarding London - Spencer, P.
Bondmen and freemen - Ball, J.
Bonds of national sympathy - Houghton, R.M.M.
Bonus marchers - Hoover, H.C.
Booms and depressions - Lawrence, D.
Boots for paving stones - Sheldon, V.
Born rich - Smith, R.L.
Boss rule - Root, E.
Bostonian Ebenezer - Mather, C.
"Bottoms up" - Skinner, C.O.
Boy who changed his name - GUTENBERG, J.
Bramble king - RELIGION
Brass checks - MacBride, D.
Bread of life - Puddicombe, T.
Breaking down barriers - Jones, L.
Bremen flyers - AERONAUTICS
Bride of the state - Hawkins, E.
Bridging the bloody chasm - Williams, J.S.
Bright land to westward - Wolcott, E.O.
British influence - Randolph, J.
British flag in Caesar's city - Laurier, W.
British Lion and the American Eagle - Choate, J.H.
British war aims - Lloyd George, D.
Broadcast plea for winter aid - Hitler, A.
Broaden our horizons for correctional service - Gray, W.H., Jr.
Broken bulwark - Langdon, H.
Brownsville Incident - Roosevelt, T.
Brutality as an imperial method - Morley of Blackburn, J.M.
Buford case - Breckenridge, J.C.
Builders of destiny - Goldstein, M.W.
Builders of empire - Michaels, M.G.
Builders of men - Carmack, E.W.
Builders of to-morrow - Wallace, H.A.
Building for tomorrow's better living - Tobias, C.H.
Building stairways - Ockerlander, D.
Bully will be torn from his seat - Lloyd George, D.

Bulwark of democracy - Stier, B.
Bulwark of safety - Wright, M.
Bunker Hill monument - Webster, D.
Buried gold - SUCCESS
Burning question - Salisbury, R. A. T. G. -C.
Business of government - Thorpe, M.
"But for the grace of God" - Morse, J.
Buy Reynolds' wrap - Ludlum, L. E.
By rote control - Arnold, R.
By the power invested - Gardiner, C. H.

Cadets at New Market - Wise, J. S.
Calendar of unpunished crimes - Dewey, T. E.
Calgacus to the Britons - Tacitus.
Call for the crusade - Urban II.
Call to action - Catt, C. C.
Call to arms - Allen, E.; Henry, P.; Mussolini, B.; Oxford and Asquith, H. H. A.; Poincaré, R.
Call to spiritual greatness - Kalas, J. E.
Call us dissenters - Maloney, M. J.
Called or commanded - CLERGY
Calls for aid to downtrodden Hungary - Kossuth, L.
Can an American be an optimist-Shorey, P.
Can every man be bought - BEHAVIOR
Can minds be changed - Gossage, N.
Can our democracy survive our Congress - Jepson, S.
Can the liberal arts tradition survive - Harding, H. F.
Can these be the enemy - Wyman, E.
Can we "live and let live" - Toynbee, A. J.
Can you keep a secret - BEHAVIOR
Can you quit - HABIT
Canadian lesson for the United States - Hill, J. J.
Canadian reciprocity: "They are coming to the parting of the ways" - Taft, W. H.
Candidature of Amadeus - Castelar, E.
Candles of understanding - Edgerton, J. E.
Cape Cod folk - Lincoln, J.
Case of Allan Evans - Mansfield, W. R.
Case of Mr. James Crow - Bailey, L.
Casossa speech - Bismarck, O.
Castle in Spain - Norton, C. E.
Catastrophe: The Ballinger affair - Taft, W. H.
Catch them young - Hallock, G. B. F.
Catiline's departure - Cicero, M. T.
Cato and the Stoics - Cicero, M. T.
Cause of freedom - Hughes, T.
Cause of Gracchi - Craven, A. J.
Causes of unpopularity - Wayland, H. L.
Celebrates the American heritage - Webster, D.
Centennial at Yorktown - Winthrop, R. C.
Central ideas of the Republic - Lincoln, A.
Central principle, 1853 - Hopkins, M.
Centralization and the revolutionary power of federal patronage - Vallandigham, C. L.
Century of isolation - Gallagher, R. M.
Century of protection - Blaine, J. G.
Century of the comman man - Wallace, H. A.
Certified conditions - Aiken, D. D.
Chains or change - Staley, H.
Challenge and the broad view - Wilson, H. A.
Challenge of abundance - Schlesinger, A. M., Jr.
Challenge of America - Baker,

N.D.; Waymack, W.W.
Challenge of chaos - Patrick, H.A.
Challenge of our times - Eisenhower, D.D.
Challenge of the crisis - Weaver, A.T.
Challenge of the critical century - Stahr, E.J., Jr.
Challenge of the Hoover report - Knight, H.W.
Challenge of ugliness - Heckscher, A.
Challenge to America - Strandness, B.; Wolfe, P.
Challenges and excellences - Whitney, J.H.
Chance or a policy - Kunzmann, H.E., Jr.
Change is the essence of progress - Brown, L.H.
Change of hearts - Sheen, F.J.
Changed heart - RESOLUTIONS
Chant at the corner-stone - Talmage, T.D.
Character and results of the war - Butler, B.F.
Character in the shadow - Martin, M.
Character of Macbeth - Irving, H.
Character of the Duke of Bedford - Fox, C.J.
Characteristics of the age - Story, J.
Charge to Justice Hutton - Bacon, F.
Charge to the Grand Jury - Drayton, W.H.
Charge to the jury - Medina, H.R.; Scarlett, J.
Charge to the people - McGregor, A.
Charles River bridge v. Warren bridge, 1837 - Taney, R.B.
Charms of Kildare - O'Connell, D.
Charter for postwar prosperity - Wallace, H.A.
Charter, the hope of the world - Vandenberg, A.H.
Checker speech - Nixon, R.M.
Chicago and New York Gold speech - Ingersoll, R.G.
Chief - Maxwell, W.
Child conversion - Judson, E.
Child shall lead them - Bragstad, R.
Children in court - Hatfield, M.
Children of toil - Altgeld, J.P.
Children's hour - Brown, A.
Choice before us - Thomas, N.
Choice of books - Avebury, J.L.; Harrison, F.
Choice of Hercules - Prodicus.
Christian endeavors and the dramshops - Burrell, D.J.
"Christian liberty" not a license - Thompson, C.
Christian life and an economy of abundance - Niebuhr, R.
Christian victory - Hall, C.N.
"Christmas carol" at Wooster - Lowry, H.F.
Christ's law of service - Mullins, E.Y.
Cincinnatus from Indiana - Ade, G.
Citadel of freedom - Ashton, D.C.
Citadels of peace, arsenals of power - Dickinson, L.
Citizen - Dwyer, J.F.
Citizen soldier - Porter, H.
Citizens of the world - Depew, C.M.
Civilized interiors - John, V.S.
Claims on England - Sumner, C.
Clean hands - Berolsheimer, H.
Clean out the attic - NEW YEAR
Climbing the managerial ladder - Nickerson, A.J.
Cocktail hour - Simmons, G.
Coercion and repression as imperial policies - Lansdowne, H.C.K.P.
Coercion of delinquent states - Hamilton, A.
Coexistence and atomic stalemate - Knowland, W.F.
Cohens v. Virginia, 1821 - Marshall, J.
Collective responsibility of the Ministry - Baldwin, S.
College fetish - Adams, C.F., Jr.

College graduate's debt to society and the state - Craven, L.
College man's creed - Shaft, H.D.
Colleges for crooks - Willis, E.E.
Columbian oration - Depew, C. M.
Combating the depression - Hoover, H.C.
Come back to your father's house - Smith, A.E.
Come near, ye nations, to hear - Isaiah.
Comedy or tragedy - Pease, J.
Comfort and fun: morality in a nice society - Lerner, D.
Comfort ye my people - Sockman, R.W.
Comforts nuns after burning of their chapel by the Iroquois - Taiaeronk.
Coming through the Wry - Hendricks, T.V.
Commercial politics - Barnave, A.P.J.M.
Commit your way unto the Lord - Klemp, O.C.
Common confusions - Davidson, C.
Common ground of humility - Brebner, J.B.
Common people - McKissick, J.R.
Commonwealth v. Hunt - Shaw, L.
Communion with God - Newman, J.H.
Compact theory on the Constitution - Calhoun, J.C.
Competition - Bailey, J.W.
Competitive enterprise versus planned economy - Prentis, H.W., Jr.
Complexity of America - Appleby, P.H.
Comrades of the mist - Beatty, D.
Concerning a grain of corn - Wycliffe, J.
Conciliation with America - Burke, E.
Confederates are comin' - Stockdale, T.R.
Confessional - Brown, M.V.
Confiscation of rebel property - Colfax, S.
Conflict of ideas in America - Garfield, J.A.
Conquerors - MacLaughlin, C.
Conquers London - Eisenhower, D.D.
Conquest of America impossible (1777) - Wilkes, J.
Conquest of the Atlantic - Marble, S.
Conscience of the nation - Wise, S.S.
Consciousness of innocence - Lomasney, W.F.
Consecration to humanity man's mission - Pecker, E.L.
Consent or force in government - Macaulay, T.B.
Constant crusades - Blakely, R.J.
Constituents and members - Fox, C.J.; Yonge, W.
Constitutional liberty and arbitrary power - Warren, J.
Continental Union - Civil service for the islands - Reid, W.
Convention of Burgoyne - Witherspoon, J.
Converting liabilities into assets - Mann, L.L.
Cooing dove - Smith, A.E.
Cooper Institute address - Lincoln, A.
Cooper Union address - Stevenson, A.E.
Corner-stone of American liberty - Krasne, P.N.
Coronation Day sermon - Mercier, D.F.F.J.
Cost of "Blood and iron" - Field, D.D.
Cost of heritage - Morrow, E.P.
Cost of the Revolution - FOURTH OF JULY
Costly heritage - FOURTH OF JULY
Cotner College - Hunt, C.
Country reunited - McKinley, W.
Courage for the future - Young, O.D.

Covered wagon - Hawes, H.B.
Crash (1929) - Amos, M.B.
Credo - Lilienthal, D.E.
Criminal aggression - Schurz, C.
Crisis - Bashford, J.W.; Moore, J.M.

Crisis of 1938 - McIlvenna, E.A.
Crisis of our time - Hocking, W.E.; Hutchins, R.M.; Niebuhr, R.; Redfield, R.
Crisis of 1793 - Cambon, P.J.
Criticism and preparedness - Simms, W.S.
Cross and the double cross - Sheen, F.J.
Cross-examination, is it an art or an artifice - Steuer, M.D.
Cross of gold - Bryan, W.J.
Crosspatch - Humphrey, C.J.
Crucifixion of Cavius - Cicero, M.T.
Crumbling pillars - Bernard, W.
Crusade and the war - King, W.L.M.
Cry baby - Johnson, M.
Cry for freedom - Marshall, T.
Cuba I. - Kennedy, J. F.
Cuba II. - Kennedy, J. F.
Culture - Young, O.D.
Curse of a malignant tongue - Massillon, J.B.
Curse of plenty - LeVander, T.
Curtain speech - Arliss, G.
Custodians of glory - Trinkle, E.L.
Cynic critic - JUDGMENT

Damage to a farm - Demosthenes.
Dancing daughters - McBride, L.
Dangerous age - TWENTIETH CENTURY
Dangers of a salaried bureaucracy - Franklin, B.
Dangers of the present - Brown, H.A.
Dare we discuss it - Narot, J.
Darkness and the dawn - Christensen, G.
Darkness into dawn - Canham, E.D.
Dartmouth College case - Webster, D.
Date kernels - LeVander, H.
Date which will live in infamy - Roosevelt, F.D.
"Daughter nations," not satellites - Laurier, W.
Davy Crockett's tongue-tied admirers - Gunderson, R.G.
Day after V-day - Clarke, L.
Day we celebrate - Evarts, W.M.
Days which the Lord hath made - Hecht, H.L.
Dead upon the field of honor - Higginson, T.W.
Death among the dailies - Thigpen, W.
Death penalty - Hugo, V.M.
Debate on question of allotments - Arch, J.
Debating whether or not to become King of England - Cromwell, O.
Debit and credit of the war - Booth, N.
Debt, not charity - Farley, J.I.
Debt we owe to the Dutch - Gregg, D.
Declaration of the Colonies on taking up arms - Dickinson, J.
Declaration of the Labor Party - Kerensky, A.
Declaration of war - Wilson, W.
Declaration of war by France - Poincaré, R.; Viviani, R.R.
Declining the election at Bristol, September 9, 1780 - Burke, E.
Dedicated to a proposition - Kennedy, G.
Defalcations of the government - Prentiss, S.S.
Defence of stiff-armed George - Red Jacket.
"Defend every inch of Soviet soil" - Stalin, I.
Defense and protection - Foster, G.E.
Defense of home and country - Brousseau, G.H.
Defiance of Hitler - Churchill,

W. L. S.
efying the French aristocracy- Mirabeau, H. G. R.
e Juventute - Butler, N. M.
elayed obedience - LIFE
elirium of conquest - Hoar, G. F.
eliverance of Europe, 1799 - Pitt, W., 1759-1806
eliverance of the Holy Land - Bernard, Saint
eluge is after us - Chafee, Z.
emagogues, "good" people, and teachers of speech - Brigance, W. N.
emands of the hour - Buckley, J. M.
emocratic aristocracy - Van Dyke, H.
emolition bombs - Fisher, G. J. B.
en of youth - Dailey, B.
enouncing Douglas and Butler - Sumner, C.
enunciation of the Union with England - Plunket, W. C.
eo et Caesari fidelis - Montalembert, C. F. R.
epartment of good works - Ludlow, L.
epression and the President - Johnson, H. S.
Der tag" - Jusserand, J. J.
esign for a people's peace - Schuman, F. L.
esign for fighting - Shapley, H.
esolation of Oude - Sheridan, R. B.
estiny and individual aspirations - Gladstone, W. E.
eterring the aggressor - Acheson, D. G.
etour ahead - Fairless, B. F.
eveloping leadership in new countries - Malik, C. H.
evotion to freedom - Montalembert, C. F. R.
iamonds in the rough - LIFE
ictators in American politics - Clay, H.
ied at twenty: buried at seventy - Rahl, J. A.
Different motives of the settlers - Parker, C.
Dilemma of democracy - Schneider, A. L.
Diligence and its reward - Tinker, E.
Discontent of the times - Storrs, R. S.
Discouragement does not mean defeat - SUCCESS
Discovery and conquest of America - Wilson, W.
"Discretion" as despotism - Hyde, E.
Disesteem of the law - Sullivan, A. M.
Dishonor in American public life - Shepard, E. M.
Dismantling of the era of terror - Murray, T. E.
Dissent in the case of the Russian aliens - Holmes, O. W., Jr.
Dissenting opinion on Abram vs. United States - Holmes, O. W., Jr.
Disunion and war inseparable - Clay, H.
Diversions of a Marquis - Curran, J. P.
"Divine moment" of victory - Poincaré, R.
Divine strength and beauty of holy worship - Stevens, W. B.
Divine tragedy - Abelard, P.
Divinity school address - Emerson, R. W.
Do not ask us to give up the buffalo for the sheep - Ten Bears.
Do penance, penance, penance - Savonarola, G.
Do you have a weak spot - CHARACTER
Do you ring the bell - PERSONALITY
Do you want to commit suicide - Deever, L.
Do your part - Green, W.
Doctor and the changing order - Vincent, G. E.
"Dr. Jekyll or Mr. Hyde" -

Wright, W.B.
Doctor, the world is sick - INTERNATIONAL RELATIONS
Doctrine for the time - Shuster, G.N.
Doctrine of good fellowship - CHURCH
Does the individual count for nothing - Brewer, D.J.
Doing unto others - Spillman, H.C.
Dollar chasing - Fulkerson, R.
Dollar diplomacy - Taft, W.H.
Dollars and sense - Sikkink, D.
Don't be a dead bug - LIFE
Don't be sidetracked - SUCCESS
Don't be tricked - LIFE
Don't die on third - Cameron, W.J.
"Don't give up the ship" - Said, J.
Don't hate your customers - Arkwright, P.S.
"Don't join the book burners" - Eisenhower, D.D.
Door without a handle - RELIGION
Doors without keys - Gantz, G.
Dorothy Q. - Holmes, O.W.
Down with the Pope - Cahill, M.
Drama of the centuries - PERSECUTION
Dreadnoughts and dukes - Balfour, A.J.B.
Dream come true - Dwyer, J.F.
Dream true - Hunter, E.
Dreams and realities - Bunche, R.J.
Drifting into suicide. Hutchins, R.M.
DROOPING WINGS - BEHAVIOR
Dropping down explosives - Capper, J.E.
Dry humor in Latin - Balfour, A.J.B.
Durable satisfactions of life - Eliot, C.W.
Dutch as enemies - Raymond, A.V.V.
Dutch as neighbors - Raymond, A.V.V.
Duties and respect of judges - Latimer, H.
Duties of Americans in the pre[sent] war - Royce, J.
Duty determines destiny - McKinley, W.
Duty of Christian freemen to elect Christian leaders - Ely, E.S.
Duty of the educated man to his country - Veneable, F.P.
Dying year - Hubbert, J.M.; Leech, S.V.

Eagle comes to earth - Doyle, J.E.
Eagle of Golgotha - MacDonald, T.
Earth is the Lord's - Poole, F
Eastern question - Argyll, D.C. C.; Gladstone, W.E.
Eating and drinking unworthily Deems, C.F.
Economic freedom of the world Willkie, W.L.
Economy - Fish, S.
Educated citizen - Stevenson, A.E.
Educated English public opinion in the cause of the north - Bright, J.
Educating for temperance opinions - Rapen, J.H.
Education for manhood - Miller K.
Education in the obvious - Holmes, O.W., Jr.
Education is non-sectarian - Eliot, C.W.
Educational crisis - Holand, D.
Effect of the Mexican conquest Berrien, J.M.
Effect of the resurrection upon the character of Peter - Judson, E.
Effective living - Wheeler, B.I.
Effective speech in a democracy Carleton, W.G.
Effects of conciliation - Hoare,
Efficiency - Cortelyou, G.B.
Efforts on conciliation - Laval, P.; Potemkine, V.
Eight common principles for a better world - Roosevelt, F.
Eighty million suckers - Wilson

D. J.
Election speech in Midlothian - Gladstone, W.E.
Elements of national greatness, 1842 - Cheever, G.B.
Eleventh commandment - Robinson, M.G.
Eleventh plague - Holmes, G.H.
Eloquence - Emerson, R.W.
Embezzlement of trust funds - Lysias.
Emergency program for national preparedness - Truman, H.S.
Empire and alien domination - Balfour, A.J.B.
Empire called to prayer - George V.
Empire Day - MacDonald, J.R.
Empires within - Muehl, E.W.
Employment of native mercenaries - Pitt, W., 1708-1778
End of peace - Grey of Fallodon, E.G.
End of slums - Straus, N.
Enemy of peace - Freeman, S.
Energy and the explosion of the earth - Thomson, J.J.
Enfranchisement of women - Anthony, S.B.
England supports Belgium - Oxford and Asquith, H.H.A.
England's position- Grey of Fallodon, E.G.
English and French experiment - Evarts, W.M.
English friendship for America - Dickens, C.
Englishmen and Americans - Cecil of Chelwood, E.A.R.G.C.
Enlistment in the Christian ministry - Wigmore, J.H.
Enough of this - Magnussen, J.W.
Enthusiasm - Norton, C.D.
Epilogue to freedom - Rodriquez, A.
Equality before the law - Langston, J.M.
Equality of nations - Gladstone, W.E.
Equality of rights for all citizens, black and white, alike - Grimke, F.J.
Equality of sacrifice - Henderson, L.; Murray, P.
Equipment for service - Wilson, W.
ERP: The Marshall Plan - Truman, H.S.
Estate of Ciron - Isaeus.
Eternal growth - Ritzman, C.H.
Eternal vigilance - Lowden, F.O.
Eulogium on South Carolina - Hayne, R.Y.
European trip - Eisenhower, D. D.
Evangelism - Sunday, W.A.
Eve of war - Andrew, J.A.
Events are temporal, principles eternal - Butler, N.M.
Everlasting oxydization - Spurgeon, C.H.
Everlasting pyramids - Barnes, G.O.
Everyman - Nichols, E.R., Jr.
Everyman's responsibility - Root, E.
Evolution of the dominion - Smith, G.
Examination before the House of Commons - Franklin, B.
Example of our Lord - Colenso, J.W.
Exhorts his soldiers before Harfleur - Henry V.
Exordium of the speech for the Rhodians - Cato, M.P. (The Censor)
Expanding frontiers of social progress - Roosevelt, F.D.
Expansion - Watterson, H.
Expansion and dum-dum bullets - Rosebery, A.P.P.
Expense fund speech - Nixon, R.M.
Explaining what to whom - Randall, C.
Explosives from balloons - Baden-Powell, B.F.S.
Eyeless in Gaza - Dupee, G.G.
"Eyes of the people opened" - Wilson, W.
Eyes that see not - Doran, H.J.

Face the world unafraid - BEHAVIOR

Facts and fallacies - Reed, E. H.
Facts and ideals - Redfield, W. C.
Failure of success - Finch, C. A.
Failures of the Truman administration - Taft, R. A.
Fair Deal in retrospect - Truman, H. S.
Faith and courage - Duffield, H.
Faith and reason - Inge, W. R.
Faith in mankind - Hadley, A. T.
Faith of our fathers - Jones, E. DeW.
Faith, revelation, and the Church - Reagan, N.
Fallacies and roadblock - Stoddard, G. D.
False faces - HYPOCRISY
False pretenses - Chillingsworth, W.
False security - Churchill, W. L. S.
Fanfare for Prometheus - Hand, L.
Farewell to the Senate - Toombs, R.
Farthest north - Peary, R. E.
Fear - Roosevelt, F. D.
Federal Court orders must be upheld - Eisenhower, D. D.
Federal experiments in history - Monroe, J.
Federal judiciary - Bayard, J. A.
Federalist No. X - Madison, J.
Feels "A gale of revolution in the air" - Tocqueville, A., de
Feet of clay - Wood, R.
Festival of the Supreme Being - Robespierre, M.
Fiddles and fortunes - Mills, T. A.
Fifth estate - Little, A. D.
Fifth horseman - Kelley, G. V.
Fifth Philippic - Cicero, M. T.
Fifty-four forty or fight - Cobb, H.
Fight for repeal - Smith, A. E.
Fighting for the common cause - Chiang, Mei-Ling
Filtering our industrial waste - Brown, H.
Final test - Livingston, E. M.
Finding your place - VOCATIONS
Fine white ashes - Schner, C.
Fire always makes room for itself - Cowley, W. H.
Fire and blood - Satterthwaite, J. B.
Fireside and iron bars - Pickell, C. S.
Firm policy - Eden, A.
"First" (speech to Boys' Brigade) - Drummond, H.
First and great commandment - Taylor, J. M.
First class man - Ziebarth, E. W.
First get the facts - Redfield, W. C.
First Olynthiac oration - Demosthenes.
First oration against Catiline - Cicero, M. T.
First oration against Verres - Cicero, M. T.
First oration on the crown - Aeschines.
First Philippic - Cicero, M. T.; Demosthenes.
First tetralogy - Antiphon.
First view of the heavens - Mitchell, O. M.
Fiscal retaliation - Churchill, W. L. S.
Five great Americans - Douglas, P. H.
Five nations - McKeldin, T. R.
"Flanks are something for the enemy to worry about" - Patton, G. S.
Flavor of our daily bread - Gould, S. B.
Flight from Bagdad - Zekaria, H.
Flood-gate flung wide - Blake, E. H.
Foes of the humanities - Deutsch, M. E.
Follow after peace - Engelbrecht, H. H.
Follow the leader - Johnson, H. S.
Follow the road signs - RELIGION
Follow the rules of the game - BEHAVIOR

ood control - a war measure - Hoover, H.C.
'oods for the homeland - Foster, G.E.
'oolish exchange - Taylor, J.
'oolish rich man - Landis, J.C.
'ool's gold - Livingston, H.
'or a mess of pottage - Campbell, G.R.
'or bimetalism - Hill, D.B.
'or Euphiletos - Isaeus.
'or federal government by the people - King, R.
'or Mantitheus - Lysias.
'or seating Eisenhower delegates - Eastvold, D.
'or self-respect and self-protection - Higginson, T.W.
'or Southern rights - Yancey, W.L.
'or the encouragement of learning - Dering, E.
'or the Old South Meeting-house - Lowell, J.R.
'or the poet Archias - Cicero, M.T.
'or this we die - Wright, D.J.
'or this we fight - Jenson, G.
'or those yet to be - Forsythe, C.
'or what do we fight - Bisel, D.
'orce Bill - Calhoun, J.C.
'orce of ideas - Wayland, H.L.
'orce to the utmost - Wilson, W.
'orces which move the world - Thomson, J.J.
'ords with balloon tires - Bloomstein, M.
'orgiveness of injuries - Cranmer, T.
'orgotten men - Sumner, W.G.
'ormula for reform - Brayman, H.
'ormula for sugar - Wagers, Z.
'orward America - Smith, T.V.; Taft, R.A.
'oundations of progress- Roosevelt, T.
'ounders, great in their unconsciousness, 1849 - Bushnell, H.
'our American traditions - Hesseltine, W.B.
Four human freedoms - Roosevelt, F.D.
Four-minute man -Wirth, F.A.
Four power pact - Mussolini, B.
Four ways of looking at a speech - Lee, I.J.
Fourteen points - Wilson, W.
Fourteenth Philippic - Cicero, M.T.
Fourth cross - JESUS CHRIST
Fourth Philippic - Cicero, M.T.; Demosthenes.
Frame of mind - Pound, R.
France cannot stand by - Daladier, E.
Frank and candid light - Limb, B.C.
Free enterprise and "planned economy" - Aldrich, W.W.
Free grace - Wesley, J.
Free investigation and faithful experiment - Warren, E.
Free society - Harris, R.C.
Free world can't trade on a one way street - Ford, H., II.
Freedom of America the result of an open Bible - Parker, C.
Freedom of the seas - Roosevelt, F.D.
Freedom of the seas: The "Sussex" affair - Wilson, W.
Freedom or despotism - Dulles, J.F.
Freedom or planned economy, there is no middle road - Brown, L.H.
Freedom through education - Bruce, R.C.
Freedom's back is against the wall - Thompson, D.
Freedom's destiny - Ripley, R.K.
Freedom's holy light - Nodel, J.J.
Freedom's natal day - Lawson, J.
Freeman of Edinburgh - Churchill, W.L.S.
Friend and foe - Sala, G.A.
Friendly nations - Thornton, H.W.
Friends across the sea - Dickens, C.

From a coronation sermon - Flavel, J.
From behind closed doors - Webster, P.
From dog house to doctorate - Bassett, L.E.
From fame to infamy - Hardy, C.D.; Marble, S.
From klansman's robe to justice's gown - Atkinson, M.E.
From where the sun now stands- Joseph, Chief
Fruitful approach to prolonged peace - Lodge, H.C., Jr.
Frustration of our time - Lippmann, W.
Fulcrum of western civilization - Toynbee, A.
Fulfil our joy - Weber, E.P.
Full economic mobilization - Baruch, B.M.
Full production after the war - Arnold, T.
Fundamentals of merchandising - Knauth, O.W.
Furling the battle flags - Lawson, R.
Fury not in God - Chalmers, T.
Future of Athana - Titus-Werner, M.S.
Future of the printed word - Markel, L.
Future seen "Through the blood red mists" - Clemenceau, G.

Gaiety of Socrates - Sherman, S.P.
Gather inspiration from the past - Albertson, C.C.
General Assembly a great forum - Byrnes, J.F.
General Sherman - Schurz, C.
General welfare - Reid, W.
Gentleman from Louisiana: demagogue or Democrat - Williams, T.H.
German conquests - Hitler, A.
German peace proposal - Briand, A.
Germany begins the war - Bethman-Hollweg, T.
Germany could no longer remain idle - Hitler, A.
Germany will never capitulate - Hitler, A.
Germany's claims - Hitler, A.
Get off the ball - BEHAVIOR
Get up and go - SUCCESS
Gethsemane - Harper, F.
Getting started - SUCCESS
Giants and grasshoppers - McConnell, F.J.
Gibbons v. Ogden, 1824 - Marshall, J.
Give and take - Imrie, N.A.
Give just credit - BEHAVIOR
Give one day - Bowles, C.
Give thanks to God - Essig, E.H.
"Give us a break" - Whalen, R.
Give us the tools and we'll finish the job - Churchill, W.L.S.
Glorious dead - Meighen, A.
Glory - Hughes, L.
Glory and tragedy of man - Bonnell, J.S.
Glory has departed - Nehru, J.
Glow that comes from hunger - Wilson, J.M.
God among the centuries - Talmage, T.D.
God and history will remember your judgment - Haile Selassie I.
God's assurance of his blessed presence - Stuenkel, W.W.
God's children live in love - Streufert, P.W.
God's faithfulness vindicated by our experience - Noble, F.
God's love of fallen men - Wesley, J.
God's mysterious educator - Coffin, H.S.
God's power for a more abundant life - Dobelstein, E.G.
God's power over that of Kings Knox, J.
God's promise to his plantation Cotton, J.
God's vengeance against public robbers - Cobbett, W.
Gold in the clay jars (Dead Sea Scrolls) - Bowman, J.
Golden age lies onward - Coleman, G.

Good lore for simple folk - Wycliffe, J.
Good neighbor - Roosevelt, F.D.
Good news for the underprivileged - Thurman, H.
Good news from a far country - Chauncy, C.
Golden rule in government - Marshall, T.R.
Golden speech - Elizabeth I.
Good will to America - Harcourt, W. G. G. V. V.
Good will to men - Burns, C.W.
Gospel of insecurity - Miller, S. H.
Government and the individual - Baruch, B.M.
Government by competitive crime - Oxford and Asquith, H. H. A.
Government of the tongue - Butler, J.
Governmental conduct of business - Hoover, H. C.
Governmental integrity - Dewey, T. E.
Governments for the people and not people for governments - Sidney, A.
Grains of sand - BEHAVIOR
Grand mission of America - Bacon, L.
Grape shot and hemp - Brownlow, W. G.
Grateful thanks - Walker, J. B.
Grave situation - Stimson, H. L.
Great American myth - Pollock, E.
Great betrayal - McCarthy, J.R.
Great Britain in panorama - Rosebery, A. P. P.
Great commission - Osias, C.
Great example - Cecil of Chelwood, E. A. R. G. C.
Great expectations - Blough, R. M.
Great future - Mowrer, J. M.
Great stampede - Barss, R.
Greater increase - Pieplow, E. E.
Greater man - Patterson, G. D.
Greatest battle ever won - Williams, W.
Greatest game in the world - Smith, R. L.
Greatest lack - Blakely, R. J.
Greatest single thing a man can have - Rickey, B.
Greatest thing in the world - Drummond, H.
Greatness of a plain American - Emerson, R. W.
Greatness through strife - Roosevelt, T.
Greece enters the war - Venizelos, E.
Greetings from Belgium - Moncheur, B. L.
Greetings to America - Ribot, A. F. J.
Greetings to Matsuoka - Ribbentrop, J.
Greetings to the Association of land-grant colleges and universities - Studebaker, J. W.
Gregg Resolution - Randolph, J.
Grievances in the reign of Charles I. - Pym, J.
Growing confidence - Borden, R. L.
Growth of American prestige - Straus, O. S.
Guarantee of freedom - Lenarducci, D.
Guardians of light - Abrams, M. M.
Guilded curtain - Bearman, A.
Guillotine - Hugo, H. M.
Guilty until proven innocent - Halle, R.

Half slave, half free - Kaplan, A.
Hallowed ground - Harding, W. G.
Halt! Who goes there - IMMIGRATION AND EMIGRATION
Hand of the living dead - Pedley, E. A.
Hans Breitman's return - Leland, C. G.
Happy is the nation - FOURTH OF JULY
Happy mean - Hull, C.
Hard way - Maloney, P. R.
Hardest thing in the world to be - Smith, R. L.

Harvest of justice - Dechanal, P.
Harvest time of life - YOUTH
Has one government the right to intervene in the internal affairs of another - Chateaubriand, F. A. R.
Has the last word been said - DeGaulle, C.
Haunted house - RELIGION
Have faith in America - Flowers, M.; McKeldin, T. R.
Haven of the defeated - Karos, P. A.
Haywood trial - Darrow, C.
He died in rawhide - Knickerbocker, W. H.
He who loves silver - LIFE
Healthier than healthy - Menninger, K.
Healthy heresies - Gunsaulus, F. W.
Hear the word of the Lord, O King of Judah - Jeremiah.
Heart disease - Guggenheim, C.
Heart statistics - CHARITIES
Heavenly footman - Bunyan, J.
Held in bondage - Berquist, G.
Hellenic standards for the modern world - Prentice, W. K.
Help! Help! - WORK
Help in times past - Brustat, A. W.
Help today for health tomorrow - Eaton, L. J., Jr.
Hercules of the age - Hill, B. H.
Here stood an oak - Evans, B.
Hero of Santiago - Rayner, I.
Heroes of the Civil War - Eliot, C. W.
Heroes of the faith - Chrysostom, J.
Heroes of Vera Cruz - Wilson, W.
Hexaemeron-Basil the Great
Hickory stumps - Gowacke, J. C.
Hidden lights - RELIGION
Hidden worlds - IMMORTALITY
Hideous doctrine of Prussianism - Borah, W. E.
Hideous outrages of subjugation - Davidson, R. T.
High cost of bigotry - Johnston, E.
High crimes and misdemeanours - Sheridan, R. B.
High obligations - McKinley, W.
Higher soldiery - Adams, L. C.
Highest form of expression - Robertson, F. W.
Hill and Hillism - Schurz, C.
Hines policy - numbers case - Dewey, T. E.
Hiroshima, August 6, 1945 - Truman, H. S.
His defense of terrorism - Robespierre, M.
His sovereignty under his hat - Curtis, G. W.
Historical agreement - Reuther, W. P.
Historical perspective and current issues - Kirk, G.
History of the concept of freedom - Lutz, R. H.
Hitler wins - Conwill, A.
Hitler's plans for Canada and the United States - Thompson, D.
Hold that tiger - BEHAVIOR
Holy crusade for liberty - Hoover, H. C.
Home brew - Rose, G. B.
Home for American jurisprudence - Warren, E.
Home gathering - Adams, W.
Home of the Oneidas - Root, E.
Homeland - Boynton, N.
Homily of Caesarea - Basil, The Great
Homily on Isaiah XXVI, 13-21 - Knox, J.
Homily on Psalm LIII - Hilary, Saint
Homily of the Beatitudes - Leo I.
Honor system - Holmes, J. H.
Honor the flag - O'Donnell, T. J.
Honor to the patriotic spy - Hale, E. E.
Honor vindicated - Canning, G.
Honoring a great American day - Kazmark, L. A.
Hour of irrevocable decision has come - Mussolini, B.
House divided - Roberts, J.
House divided against itself cannot stand - Lincoln, A.
House in order, to America lies

the task of reconstruction - Evans, H. R.
House of Lords and financial measures - Balfour, A. J. B.; Chelmsford, F. J. N. T.; Curzon of Kedleston, G. N. C.; Oxford of Asquith, H. H. A.; Palmerston, H. J. T.
House of Lords as a check on legislation - Campbell-Bannerman, H.; Lyndhurst, J. S. V.; Salisbury, R. A. T. G.
House of Lords Bill - Walpole, R.
House which never was finished - DEATH
How are the mighty fallen - Nott, E.
How backward is the front office - Smith, H.
How brave are you - BEHAVIOR
How different types of institutions are planning for the future - Kiewiet, C. W.
How far examples are to be followed - Fuller, T.
How far shall we go - Thomas, N.
How long should a wife live - Barton, B.
How long will the American Republic last - Burke, E. R.
How much land does a man need - Farkas, E.
How safe are we from attack - Eliot, G. F.
How to avoid the subject - Porter, H.
How to begin - SUCCESS
How to face temptation - BEHAVIOR
How to fight the war peril - Dern, G. H.
How to get along in a free world without being subpoenaed - Crosby, J.
How to have good relations with other people - Peale, N. V.
How to improve classroom lectures fifty per cent - Reid, L. D.
How to keep out of trouble - BEHAVIOR
How to tell a big shot - SUCCESS
How we meet ourselves - Young, O. D.
How would you have us - Clement, R. E.
Human factor in the balance sheet - Ecker, F. H.
Human soot - Kingsley, C.
Human values - Lyda, H.
Human wreckage - McCormick, J.
Humanities: mirror of genius - Klausner, N. W.
Humanity's cause triumphant - Thurston, J. M.
Humanity's loss - Churchill, W. L. S.
Humpty dumpty - Cox, R.

I am a reactionary - Pollock, C.
"I am a Roman citizen" - Cicero, M. T.
"I am an American" - Liebermann, E.
"I am an American Day" - Jessel, G.
I am innocent of this blood Reiman, A. C. E. W.
I am somebody - Hill, R. L.
I bring you good news - Savonarola, G.
I, Christian nurture - Bushnell, H.
"I have a dream" - King, M. L.
I knew Mary - Farish, E.
I need your confidence - Petain, H. P.
"I took the Canal Zone" - Roosevelt, T.
Ideal American (Theodore Roosevelt) - Hickman, L. E.
Ideal of the Christian state - Bismarck, O.
Ideologies and their dynamics and their excesses - MacCracken, H. N.
If anywhere, then everywhere - Bosley, H.
If I had your chance - Garrett, P.
If we break faith - Mara, E.
If we cancel - Lawson, R.
If we're good enough, we can

take it - Davis, E.
Ill match well broken off - Fuller, T.
Ill-used men - Dawson, G.
Illegal union - Demosthenes.
Illinois disease - Ahrendts, H.
Imaginary invalid - Jerome, J. K.
Immortal statesman - Brougham and Vaux, H. P. B.
Immortality and good deeds - Reed, T. B.
Impassable barrier between brutes and man - Müller, F. M.
Impatience and generosity - Smith, M. C.
Impeachment of alcohol - Fowler, C. H.
Impending disaster - Carey, J. P.
Imperial relations - Balfour, A. J. B.; Borden, R. L.; Smuts, J. C.
Imperial rescript opening the 87th Diet - Hirohito.
Imperialism, democracy, and peace - Briand, A.
Imperialism hostile to liberty - Schurz, C.
Imponderable move the world - Butler, N. M.
Importance of being an individual - Dodds, H. W.
In behalf of the Kaghlir pledges - Jackson, J.
In council of war - Xenophon.
In defense of a perspective - Lee, D. C.
In favor of a paternal policy of internal improvements - Clay, H.
In defense of the Union - Randolph, E.
In defiance of assassins - Robespierre, M.
In favor of re-union -Doolittle, J. R.
In favor of slitting Prynne's nose - Dorset, E. S.
In favor of a protective policy - Tupper, C.
In golden chains - Coleridge, J. D.
In honor of Lord Reading - Hughes, C. E.
In honor of patriot heroes - Andrew, J. A.
In Lucem gentium - Birge, E. A.
In memory of a pal - Ayers, A. D.
In opposition to a new Agrarian Law - Cicero, M. T.
In praise of reflective commitment - Greene, T. M.
In reply to General Crary - Corwin, T.
In support of the Athenian expedition to Sicily - Alcibiades.
In support of the Oppian law - Cato, M. P. (The Censor)
In the camp Santo of Pisa - Castelar, E.
In the case for Zenger - Hamilton, A.
In the case of McCardle - necessity as an excuse for tyranny - Field, D. D.
In the case of the Dean of St. Asaph - Mansfield, W. M.
In the name of ten million dead - Lloyd George, D.
In the service of our country - Hergenroeder, P. J.
In the shadows of the mountains - Gerry, M. B.
In the suit against Dicaegenes and Leochardes - Isaeus.
In the wake of the coming ages - Vance, J. M.
In vindication of his political party - Gracchus, G.
In vindication of the colonies - Wilson, J.
Independence day - Nehru, J.; Prasad, R.
Independent in politics - Morse, W.
Independent policy - Lindbergh, C. A.
Indian medicine - Larson, A.
Indictment of millions - Martin, J.
Individual and the democratic adventure - Dykstra, C. A.
Individual and the state - Baldwin, R. N.

ndividual initiative - Hoover, H. C.
ndividual liberty - Butler, N. M.
ndustrial democracy - O'Mahoney, J. C.; Sheil, B. J.
nevitable parallel - Souter, L. K.
nfluence of America on the mind - Ingersoll, C. J.
nfluence of men of genius - Hillard, G. S.
nfluence of physical causes on the moral faculty - Rush, B.
Information on foreign policy - Pulteney, W.; Walpole, R.
Inner light - Williams, V.
Inoffensive gentlemen on a magic island - Barrie, J. M.
Inside Germany - Lochner, L. P.
Inside story of a racket- Dewey, T. E.
Insidious germ - Fortino, A.
Inspiration and the highest education - Kelvin, W. T.
Instituting a new council - Mills, C.
Insurance side of highway safety - Randall, J. W
Integrity - Taylor, H. J.
Intellectual achievement in America - Story, J.
Intellectual and the politician - Kennedy, J. F.
Intellectual; his journey and his home - Stricker, M.
Intensive and extensive development - Walker, H. J.
Inter-American relationship - Bonsal, P. W.
Internal security - Douglas, P. H.
Internal solidarity - Summers, H. W.
International Brotherhood - Abbott, L.
International conciliation - Butler, N. M.
International racketeer - Jones, C.; Schlicten, E.
International situation in 1937 - Eden, A.
International understanding - Horton, A.
Internationalism and American independence - Knox, P. C.
Invasion prayer - Roosevelt, F. D.
Invasion starts - Hicks, G.
Invective against Danton - Saint-Just, L. A. L.
Invictive against Corry - Grattan, H.
Invisible government - Root, E.
Invitation to Jesus and his disciples - Eifert, W. H.
Invocation to the Saviour - Anselm, Saint.
Iron curtain has descended - Churchill, W. L. S.
Irrepressible conflict - Seward, W. H.
Irrepressible issue - Fleming, D. F.
Irrepressible issues of the 60's - Berle, A. A., Jr.
Irresponsibles - Swabb, J.
Is America safe - Hodge, F. S.
Is it I - Brooks, P.
Is outraged and adamant - William II.
Is the game worth the candle - Shepard, J. E.
Is the government federal or national - Martin, L.
Iscariot in modern England - Ruskin, J.
Issue - Debs, E.
Issue of justice - Zearing, J. H.
Issues against autocracy - Wilson, W.
Issues of the war - Stalin, I.
Issues-true and false - Oxford and Asquith, H. H. A.
It can be done - Raschke, K.
It has been sworn - Viviani, R. R.
It has not yet been shown what we shall be - Walsh, G.
"It is our purpose to prosper America first" - Harding, W. G.
It is time to speak up for America - Nixon, R. M.
It might happen to you - Abbott, M.
Its the human thing to do - BEHAVIOR

Ivy oration - Heater, L. A.

Jacob's voice but Esau's hands - Robinson, J. T.
Jeepers creepers - Hoff, C.
Jerusalem, Jerusalem - JESUS CHRIST
Job to be done - Eden, A.
Jobs and prosperity - Rockefeller, N. A.
John Brown raid - Douglas, S. A.
José Maria Martinez! Stand up! - Benedict, K.
Joyful sound of salvation - Mather, C.
Joys of the trail - Garland, H.
Judgment in Campbell v. Hall, 1774 - Mansfield, W. M.
Judgment of nations - Sheen, F. J.
Judiciary - Hughes, C. E.; Morris, G.
Judiciary and progress - Taft, W. H.
Just as one friend to another - Insull, S.
Just give credit - PRAISE
Justice and little boys - Sackett, S.

Keep it America - Trail, E.
Keep the home fires burning - McIntosh, G.
Keep this nation at peace - Wheeler, B. K.
Keep yourselves in the love of God - Bruggeman, G. R.
Keeping political faith - Roosevelt, F. D.
Keeping the faith - Wilson, W.
"King can do no wrong" - Ehrensperger, R.
King of energies - Waymack, W. W.
King v. Robinson for bigamy - Burrowes, P.
King v. Edward Sheridan, M. D. - Burrowes, P.
Kingdom in your heart - RELIGION
King's prayer for your home - Wangerin, W. M.
Knapp-White murder case - Webster, D.
Knight among the nations - Nelson, S. P.
Knowledge of history conducive to racial solidarity - Roman, C. V.

Labor and the war against Naziism - Bevin, E.
Labor's attitude - Gompers, S.
Labor's greatest curse - Powderly, T. V.
Lady of the lamp - MacDonald, C.; Malone, T.
Lag - Enstrom, R.
Lamps of fiction - Smith, G.
Land and labor - Leach, C.
Land o' cakes - Foord, J.
"Land we live in" - McGee, T.
Land where hatred expires - Guérard, A. L.
Landing at Plymouth - Webster, D.
Last entry into Jerusalem - Abelard, P.
Last judgment - Cahill, D. W.
Last line of defense - Pickell, C. S.
Last stand of Lee's veterans - Speer, E.
Late bill before the Senate of Pennsylvania - Forten, J.
Law is with duty - Lindsay, W.
Law of protection - Farrier, E.
Law of service - Abbott, L.
Lay the axe to the root of the evil - Lee, J.
Lazarus, come forth - Savonarola, G.
Leaders of public spirit - Alderman, E. A.
Leadership for a free world - Hoover, H. C.
League prayer meeting - Steven E. P.
Learn during Lent to say "No" - Potter, H. C.
Learned dust - Satterthwaite, J. B.
Learning to speak - Tittle, E. F
Leave no verbal message - Holmes, O. W.
Lecture on private use of judg-

ment - Newman, J.H.
Legality of arrest - Meany, S.J.
Legislating for a republic - Longworth, N.
Lenity of the law to human infirmity - Quincy, J.
Lessening of international tension - Bulganin, N.A.
"Lest we forget" - Jordan, D.S.; Towne, C.E.
Lest you forget - Lang, C.G.
Let France be free - Danton, G.J.
Let them in - IMMIGRATION AND EMIGRATION
Let there be light - Burroughs, J.
"Let us call a truce to terror" - Kennedy, J.F.
"Let us depart in peace" - Toombs, R.
Let us look at the doughnut - Cooper, R.C.
Let us make peace - Dulles, J.F.
"Let us work while it is yet day" - Stevenson, A.E.
Let your light shine - LIFE
Let's face the facts - Thompson, D.
Lewis contempt case - Goldsborough, T.A.
Liberal arts in contemporary American society - Kennan, G.F.
Liberties of the indolent - Curran, J.P.
Liberty and freedom of initiative - Underwood, O.W.
Liberty and government in America - Pendleton, E.
Liberty and the New Atlantis - Hecker, F.K.F.
Liberty and Union - Webster, D.
Liberty as an inalienable right - Grattan, H.
Liberty fleet day address - Roosevelt, F.D.
Liberty of conscience or the sole means to obtain peace and truth - Williams, R.
Liberty or empire - Henry, P.
Liberty tree in Paris - Hugo, V.M.
Liberty we need now - Loose, J.W.
Library and the chapel stand side by side - Goheen, R.F.
Library without books - RELIGION
License system - Foster, E.
Life blood of the nation - Sprague, C.
Life of achievement - Moton, R.R.
Life of service - Bonaventure, Saint
Life university - BACCALAUREATE ADDRESSES
Lifestream of the nation - Oberg, W.
Lift up your hearts - FOURTH OF JULY
Light that is darkness - Grossman, M.H.
Lights are going out - Churchill, W.L.S.
"Lilliputians" - Enstrom, R.
Limehouse policy - Salisbury, R.A.T.G.-C.
Limiting bombardment by law - Stone, F.G.
Link or barrier - CHURCH
Lions of the North - Alseth, C.A.
List - Oxman, S.A.
Little group of willful men - Wilson, W.
Little personal history - Hill, B.H.
Little Rock, Eisenhower, D.D.
Live free or die - Desmoulins, C.
"Live -I am coming" - Holmes, O.W., Jr.
Liverpool speech - Beecher, H.W.
Living a useful life - SUCCESS
Living or a life - RELIGION
Living witness of the resurrection - Hendrix, E.R.
Loaded dice-the Lords against the Constitution - Oxford and Asquith, H.H.A.
Lochner v. New York - Holmes, O.W., Jr.; Pecker, R.W.

Lofty purpose shared - Sterling, J. E. W.
Logic of blood and iron - Clemenceau, G.
Loneliness and solitude - Tillich, P. J.
Long range military policy - Bradley, O. N.
Look ahead - Stidger, W. L.
Looking back over forty years - Edison, T. A.
Looking forward - Irving, H.
Lost: four friends - Yurk, C.
Lost star - CHRISTMAS
Lottery case - Harlan, J. M.
Louisiana Returning Board - Carpenter, M. H.
Love for the beautiful in speech - Poe, E. A.
Love, law, and civil disobedience - King, M. L.
Loyal crusaders - Bradley, O. M.
Loyal opposition - Willkie, W.
Loyalty to the nation - Dibble, H. C.
Lust of empire - Hoar, G. F.
Lust of empire as the cause of catastrophe - Balfour, A. J. B.
Luxuries a Christian cannot afford - BEHAVIOR

Macbeth - Walker, J. T.
McCulloch v. Maryland - Marshall, J.
Mad men in a world - McGahey, W.
Maiden speeches - Hunt, L. B.
Mailed fist - William II.
Making a new start - Perlman, N. A.
Making life worth living - Bonnell, J. S.
Making of a national spirit - Alderman, E. A.
Making of America - Roosevelt, T.
Making spiritual history - Stockdale, A. A.
Man and monkeys - Agassiz, L. J. R.
Man and the soil - Thomas, J. M.
Man of all peoples - Lloyd George, D.
Man of sorrows - Parkhurst, C. H.
Man of steel - Henninger, L. L.
Man on the frontier - Robinson, E. E.
Man on the tower - Cobbett, W.
Man shortage in heaven - RELIGION
Man thinking - Griswold, A. W.
Man who can - Bennett, W. R.
Man who walks alone - Lowther, J. B.
Man with a hat in his hand - Howell, C.
Man with a hat over his face - Balmuth, S.
Man with the muck-rake - Roosevelt, T.
Man without a country - Hale, E. E.
Manifesto to Europe - Lamartine, A. M. L.
Man's best friend - Vest, G. G.
Man's development and attainment - Dickinson, H.
Man's other society - Duesterbeck, R. M.
Man's reach - Krause, N. L.
Man's responsibility to the higher law - Ousley, C. N.
Man's soul and his world - Tucker, W. J.
Man's true self - Trine, R. W.
Manufacture of consent - Highsaw, J. L., Jr.
Marbury v. Madison - Marshall, J.
March of the flag - Beveridge, A. J.
Marks of an educated man - Kahn, B. M.
Martyrs of Cosenza - Mazzini, G.
Mass information or mass entertainment - Gallup, G.
Masses against classes - George H.
Master or victim - Bean, F. A.
Masterpiece of God - Hubbard, E.
Masters of men - Sudow, M.
Masters of the situation - Fields J. T.

Mastery of mind - Blakesley, R.H.
Matchless story of American history - O'Bryne, J.
Material wealth of Uncle Sam - Stout, J.P.
Materialistic idealism - Dunham, W.H.
Matter of necessity - Arpaia, A.
Me and Sir Henry - Ford, S.
Meaning of America - Barksdale, L.S.; Hoover, H.C.
Meaning of America's entrance into the war - Lloyd George, D.
Meaning of inspiration - Herder, J.G.
Meaning of the Lord's Supper - Baker, S.
Meaning of the times - Beveridge, A.J.
Mechanism in thought and morals - Holmes, O.W.
Mediocrity triumphant - Magidson, A.B.
Meet your friends - LeVander, B.
Members one to another - Temple, W.
Membership meetings that click - Sanford, W.P.
Memories of my father - Grosvenor, E.B.
"Memory of the just is blessed" - Whelpley, P.M.
Men and tomorrow - O'Hare, E.
Men and women with antennae - Brown, K.I.
Men: made, self-made, and unmade - Robinson, E.G.
Men must be taken as they are - Gracchus, G.
Men of destiny - Mussen, M.
Men of low estate - Conwell, R.H.
Men of 1776 - Winthrop, R.C.
Men of vision - Leavitt, H.L.
Men of vision with their feet on the ground - Cortelyou, G.B.
Men to match our mountains - Bruntz, G.G.
Men wanted - Williams, W.
Menace of Japan - Grew, J.C.
Menexemus and others against Dicaeogenes - Isaeus.
Mental wealth of Uncle San - Donelan, C.
Mere words - Dana, J.C.
Merely players - Adelman, A.
Merry-go-round has stopped - Olson, W.
Message of Flanders Fields - Aurner, R.R.
Message of the key - Tolman, H.C.
Message of the West - Lane, F.K.
Message to Garcia - Hubbard, E.
Message to Hitler and Mussolini - Roosevelt, F.D.
Message to the Pope - Wilson, W.
Messages from the dead - RELIGION
Mid-century - TWENTIETH CENTURY
Middletown and the way out - Fosdick, R.B.
Mightier than the sword - Ostrander, L.A.
Military mass of Spanish American war veterans in Boston - O'Leary, J.
Military spirit in America - Depew, C.M.
"Millennium," "Pandemonium," and "Pons Asinorium" - Morley of Blackburn, J.M.
Milligan case - Davis, D.; Field, D.D.
Million dollars worth of assets - WEALTH
Mind cultivation man's noblest object - Danforth, E.
Mind the master force - Campbell, A.
Minding America's own business - Moley, R.
Mingled blood - Zimmerman, R.
Minister plenipotentiary - Storey, C.L.
Minute-man - Emerson, R.W.
Minute men of a new era - Rogness, B.M.
Mirage - Hibbs, H.L.
Misery of the American war -

Pitt, W., 1759-1806
Misery of war - Bright, J.
Misfortune and exile - Bolingbroke, H. S. J.
Missing part - CHARACTER
Mission of America - Beveridge, A. J.; Boudinot, E.; Wilson, W.
Missionary effort - Red Jacket.
Missouri question - Pinkney, W.
Mistaken identity - Clemens, S. L.
Mr. Perkins returns to the land of the Bolsheviks - Johnston, E.
Mrs. Partington in politics - Smith, S.
Mobile frontier - Patrick, R. W.
Mobilizing America's strength for world security - Harriman, W. A.
Mobilizing for defense - Wilson, C. E.
Mobilizing the mind - Valentine, A.
Mobilization of community needs - Roosevelt, F. D.
Modern Arabian Knights - Owen, R. B.
Modern harpies - Elliott, A. R.
Modern issues in ancient Welsh - Lloyd George, D.
Modern "medicine men" - Margulies, N.
Modern paradox - Case, F.
Modern primitivists - Blakely, R.
Modern Shylocks - Buhler, I.
Molten gold - Driftmier, F.
Moppet manipulation - Myers, N. J.
Moral basis for our leadership - Ford, B.
Moral code of military strength - Lanham, C. T.
Moral force in world politics - Hugo, V. M.
Moral forces which make American progress - Everett, E.
Moral ideas and Republican principles - Robespierre, M.
Moral neutrality - Hoeppner, C.
Moral rearmament - BEHAVIOR
Moral revival in government - Fulbright, J. W.
Moral wealth of Uncle Sam - Bowlus, N.
Morality and military greatness - Bright, J.
Moratorium - Hoover, H. C.
More kindling - Enstrom, R.
More men - Kitchener of Khastoum, H. H. K.
More stately mansions - Stevens J. S.
Morgen die ganze welt - Lampman, R. J.
Moses and Amalek - William II.
Moses vs. Darwin - Bryan, W. J
Most valuable British asset - Curzon of Kedleston, G. N. C.
Mother Eve - Hardin, B. L.
Mount Vernon's message to mankind - Wilson, W.
Munn v. Illinois, 1876- Waite, M. R.
Murder of Lovejoy - Phillips, W.
"Music goes round and round" - Barrett, M.
Must I die - Robinson, I. J.
Mutations of time - Depew, C. M
My brother's keeper - Cox, G. V
My country - Drury, S. S.; Snyder, F. B.
My country! My Mother! My God - M'Teer, J. P.
My father, do not rest - Naidu, S.
My native land - Irving, W.
My ode to the "Orioles" - BASEBALL
My problem and yours - Cobbs, J. A.
Mystic kinship - MacDonald, J. R.

Naboth's vineyard - Bryan, W. J.
Nation indivisible forever - McKinley, W.
Nation-not a Federation - Henry, P.
Nation of pioneers - Roosevelt, T.
Nation out of balance - Shuler, B., Jr.

Nation under God - Elson, E.L. R.
National apostasy - McCartney, C.E.
National emblem - Putnam, R.B.
National emergency - Truman, H.S.
National expansion - Roosevelt, T.
National growth - Clark, C.
National growth of a century - Lowell, J.R.
National interest of the United States - Kennan, G.F.
National issues - Ford, T.L.; Reed, T.B.; Roosevelt, T.
National measures - Tupper, C.
National military strength - Marshall, G.
National morale and world tranquility - Sun, Yat Sen
National morality - Angell, J.R.
National power and the national peace policy - Marshall, T.R.
National problem - Barrington, J.W.
National sentiments - Hayes, R.B.
Nation's duties and opportunities - McKinley, W.
Nation's greatness - Abbott, L.
Nation's heroism - MacVeagh, F.
Nation's need of men - Jordan, D.S.
Nation's relations to its island possession - Ross, J.
Native gentlemen at home and abroad - Curzon of Kedleston, G.N.C.
Native hue of resolution - Spencer, R.N.
Natural propensity of rulers to oppress - Mason, G.
Nature's ice-pack - DeBoer, R.
Naval supremacy and moral leadership - Rankin, J.E.
Nazi aim is slavery - Daladier, E.
Near v. Minnesota - Hughes, C.E.
Necessity of moving on - Shoup, P.
Negro and southern restoration - Grady, H.
Negro as a soldier - Fleetwood, C.A.
Negroes and the national war effort - Douglass, F.
Neighbors and strangers: ways to peace - Coolidge, C.
Never again - Milner, A.M.
Never in the field of human conflict - Churchill, W.L.S.
New American tradition - Siegenthaler, R.F.
New armor - Howe, M.A.deW.
New birth - Caldwell, J.T.
New blood - Rill, W.A.
New bodies for a new world - EASTER
New call to duty - Wilson, W.
New century greeting - Carnegie, A.
New day - Garrison, W.L.
New despotism - Stanley, A.O.
New dynamics of corporate relations work - Parker, J.S.
New England address - Prentiss, S.S.
New England and the South - Alderman, E.A.
New Englanders - Grant, U.S.
New freedom - Zacharias, M.
New frontier - James, N.S.; Kennedy, J.F.; Petty, J.A.
New frontiers - Earle, G.H.
New frontiers for smart people - Shelby, J.
New lamps for old - Hoven, A.
New light on cosmic history - Payne-Gaposchkin, C.
New look at the old ticker - Klumpp, T.G.
New movement in humanity - Tucker, W.J.
New opportunities in a new age - Mathews, S.
New perspectives on American security - McGovern, G.
New revolution - O'Brien, Q.
New slavery - Powderly, T.V.
New steel world - Longden, Mrs. J.
New war - Wilson, E.B.
News deal - Macomber, W.H.
Next step in our economic de-

velopment - Chapman, L. F.
1946-year of decision - Brigance, W. N.
Nineteenth of April - Lawton, P. I.
No butts about it - Visk, A. G.
No colonies - Vest, G. G.
No divided flag - Davis, J.
No man is an island - Vandervoort, J.
No man is worth his salt without pepper - BUSINESS
No more territorial demands - Hitler, A.
No need of pessimism - Howell, C.
Noblesse oblige - Curtis, G. W.
Noblest public virtue - Clay, H.
Non-cooperation - Gandhi, M. K.
Non resistance to offensive aggression - Whipper, W.
North to adventure - Montague, S. R.
Northern Securities Company v. United States - Harlan, J. M.
Northland to Dixieland - Osborne, C. S.
Northward course of Empire - Stefansson, V.
Not taps but reveille - Bell, B. I.
Novelist's future labors - Thackeray, W. M.
Numbers; or the majority and the remnant - Arnold, M.

Occasions for appeal to the people - Beaconsfield, B.; Cavendish, S. C.; Devonshire, S. C. C.; Gladstone, W. E.; Peel, R.
October - Amos, M. B.
Ohio and the Northwest - Ewing, T. C.
Old crank next door - Schmitz, H. E.
Old faith - Borah, W. E.
Old order - Davis, J. W.
Old order changeth - Gilkinson, B. A.
Old settler's home - Phillips, J. F.
Old soft soap - PRAISE
Old soldiers never die - MacArthur, D.
Old traditions - Humphreys, B. G.
Old world and the new - Schurz, C.
Oldest free assemblies - Balfour, A. J. B.
Olympiac oration - Lysias.
Omphalism - Dilke, C. W.
On a motion for an address on the marriage of the Prince of Wales - Pitt, W., 1708-1778
On a piece of chalk - Huxley, T. H.
On a recreant nun - Basil the Great.
On abhorring the sword - Meagher, T. F.
On administrative reform - Tilden, S. J.
On American nationality - Choate, R.
On American policy- Pitt, W., 1708-1778
On appeal from the caucas - Davis, D.
On becoming emperor - Otho, M. S.
On beginning the Russian campaign - Napoleon I.
On being accused of low origin - Marius, C.
On being declared guilty - Socrates; Tone, T. W.
On coercive measure in America - Wilkes, J.
On colonial possessions - Caprivi de Caprera de Montecuccoli, G. L.
On Constitutional reform - Castillo, A. C.
On domestic and foreign affairs - Gladstone, W. E.
On dressing for display - Wesley, J.
On fellowship - Beecher, H. W.
On foreign importations - Randolph, J.
On his condemnation to death - Socrates.
On his return - Andocides.
On internal improvements -

Calhoun, J.C.
On Job - Gregory I.
On Liberal aims - Chamberlain, J.
On maintaining the Constitution - Gaudet, M.E.
On Manila - Grow, G.A.
On manliness - Aelred, Saint
On merchant shipping - Runciman, W.R.
On motion for an address of thanks after the battle of Dettingen - Pitt, W., 1708-1778
On mousetraps - Webb, S.
On national policy - Tilley, S.L.
On Necker's project - "And yet you are deliberate" - Mirabeau, H.G.R.
On non-intervention - Bell, J.
On offensive war with England - Randolph, J.
On Palm Sunday - Rabanus Magnentius Maurus.
On patriots - Walpole, R.
On presenting the estimates for the Ministry of Foreign Affairs - Azeglio, M.T.
On punishing the conspirators - Caesar, C.J.
On putting a stop to hostilities in America - Pitt, W., 1708-1778
On ransoming the prisoners - Junius, M.
On receiving sentence - Debs, E.
On repeal of the Union - O'Connell, D.
On scholastic despotism - Donnelly, M.C.
On seas of ink - Crocker, L.
On secret influence - Fox, C.J.
On some lessons of antiquity - Müller, F.M.
On submission - Legare, H.S.
On suffering persecution - Calvin, J.
On suppression of insurrection - Baker, E.D.; Breckenridge, J.C.
On the Agrarian law - Cicero, M.T.
On the beginning of the Russian campaign - Napoleon I.
On the Canticles - Bernard, Saint
On the cause of the Athenian greatness - Pericles.
On the Chersoneus - Demosthenes.
On the Choreutes - Antiphon.
On the conspiracy of Catiline - Caesar, C.J.
On the cost of the crown - Dilke, C.W.
On the creation of an Imperial squadron - Churchill, W.L.S.
On "The crimes of 1873" - Sherman, J.
On the Crittenden Compromise - Crittenden, J.J.
On the crown - Demosthenes.
On the degeneration of the Church - Savonarola, G.
On the disestablishment of the Irish Church - Gladstone, W.E.
On the dissolution of the Chamber of Deputies - Constant, B.
On the Eastern crisis and the danger of war, 1878- Bright, J.
On the Empire state - Wilson, P.
On the evacuation of Candahar - Beaconsfield, B.D.
On the Feast of the nativity - Leo I.
On the firing line - Dooling, M.T.
On the German Reich's attack on the Soviet Union - Welles, S.
On the method of Grace - Whitefield, G.
On the grievances of church and commonwealth - Colepepper, J.
On the Halonneus - Hegesippus.
On the issues of 1868 - Morton, O.P.
On the maker of heaven and earth - Cyril, Saint
On the murder of Eratosthenes - Lysias.
On the murder of his family - Logan, J.
On the 'Murders at Lexington

and Concord" - Tooke, J.H.
On the mysteries - Andocides.
On the Nabob of Arcot's debts - Burke, E.
On the nativity of St. Peter and Paul - Bede.
On the Navy Boards - Demosthenes.
On the occupation of the Scinde - Napier, C.
On the peace with France - Fox, C.J.
On the people's democratic dictatorship - Mao Tse-tung
On the perils of the nation - Hill, B.H.
On the perils of the Republic - Dougherty, D.
On the petition and advice - Vane, H.
On the picking of office holders - Latimer, H.
On the place of the intellectual in America - Dodds, H.W.
On the political situation - Beaconsfield, B.D.
On the progress of American independence - Boutwell, G.S.
On the property doctrine - Benjamin, J.P.
On the punishment of the Mytileneans - Cleon.
On the punishments - Cicero, M.T.
On the quartering of British troops in Boston - Pitt, W., 1708-1778
On the recognition of South American republics - Canning, G.
On the refusal to negotiate with France - Pitt, W., 1759-1806
On the rejection of Napoleon's overtures - Fox, C.J.
On the removal of troops around Paris - Mirabeau, H.G.R.
On the restoration of the South - Garfield, J.A.
On the revenue - Gracchus, G.
On the right to tax America - Pitt, W., 1708-1778
On the sale of public lands - Hayne, R.Y.
On the spirit of the age - Cass, L.
On the Spoils system - Curtis, G.W.
On the statues - Chrysostom, J.
On the suppression of Sati - Bentinck, W.
On the threatened dissolution of the Union - Mann, H.
On the Transvaal Constitution - Churchill, W.L.S.
On the twelve years - Demades.
On the undertakers - Bacon, F.
On the Westminster scrutiny - Fox, C.J.
On those who died in the war - Pericles.
On treating with the Samnites - Lentulus, L.
On trial - Humes, B.A.
On the war and its conduct - Vallandigham, C.L.
On withdrawing from the Union - Davis, J.
Once in a lifetime - Raish, D.R.
One aim: victory - Clemenceau, G.
"One and inseparable" - Speer, E.
One conspicuous failure of our government - Field, L.
One great issue - Barton, B.
One man in his time - Carmichael, C.W.
One-man power - Salisbury, R.A.T.G.-C.
One supreme issue of this hour - Holmes, J.H.
One-third of a nation - Roosevelt, F.D.
Only one truth - Swing, R.G.
Open diplomacy - Houghton, A.B.
Open skies at the Summit - Eisenhower, D.D.
Opening of Colonial magazine and guardhouse - Smith, W.B.
Operation crossroad - Burnstein, J.
Opinion in the case of the Negro law student - Hughes, C.E.
Opinion in the Merryman case - Taney, R.B.

Opportunity everywhere - SUCCESS
Opposition argument in 1862 - Voorhees, D.W.
Orange - Schoenbrun, D.
Oration for the crown - Barnave, A. P. J. M.
Oration for the Megalopolitans - Demosthenes.
Oration on Halonnesus - Demosthenes.
Oration on liberal studies - Brownson, O. A.
Oration on the arrival of the Egyptians - Gregory of Nazianzus, Saint
Oration on the duties of the state - Demosthenes.
Oration on the embassy - Demosthenes.
Oration on the letter - Demosthenes.
Oration on the liberty of the Rhodians - Demosthenes.
Oration on the treaty with Alexander - Demosthenes.
Orator, physician, philosopher - Quintilian.
Orchestrated Hell - Murrow, E.R.
Oregon question - Calhoun, J. C.
Other fellow - Smith, W.H.
Others - Werner, E. M.
Ottawa Conference - Hailsham, D. M. H.
Our absent brothers - Dooling, M. T.
Our American age - Winthrop, R. C.
Our ancestors and ourselves - Howland, H. E.
Our ancestral responsibilities - Wilson, W.
Our brethren overseas - Davis, J. W.
Our clients - Coudert, F.R.
Our commission - Lloyd George, D.
Our country - Lawrence, E. G.; McKinley, W.; Webster, D.
Our country's birthday - Graves, J. T.
Our critics - Dowling, A.
Our daily oil - Sanchez, J.
Our class colors - Adams, M.D.
Our destiny in the Pacific - Wilbur, R. L.
Our dry United States - Sheppard, M.
Our English visitors - Depew, C. M.
Our feast of Tabernacles - Field, H. M.
Our forefathers - Lodge, H. C.
Our goal - Ellis, M.
Our government - Hughes, C. E.
Our guests - Porter, H.
Our heritage - Parker, A. B.
Our heritage, how gained-our duty - Bacon, L.
Our imperative task: to mind our business - Borah, W. E.
Our kin across the sea - Depew, C. M.
Our last chance - Barsness, J.
Our Lord walking on the sea - Anselm, Saint
Our Merchant Marine - Blaine, J. B.
Our national dangers, real and unreal - Bonaparte, C. J.
Our national dead - Taft, W.H.
Our national emblem - Beecher, H.W.
Our national goals - MacArthur, D.
Our national influence - Armitage, T.
Our national objects and aims - Grant, G. M.
Our national policies in this crisis - Hoover, H. C.
Our national position - Harcourt, W. V.
Our national safeguards - Depew, C. M.
Our new country - Halstead, M.
Our new problems - Long, J.D.
Our Pacific outlook - Dobson, J.
Our problem and yours - Massey, V.
Our racial myopia - Fuller, F. L.
Our relations with the world - MacVeagh, F.
Our representatives in Congress - Long, J. D.
Our reservoir of world respect

and hope - Willkie, W. L.
Our responsibilities - Roosevelt, T.
Our reunited country - Howell, C.
Our school of destiny - McClain, W.
Our stake in the Pacific - Yarnell, H.E.
Our task - BEHAVIOR
Our too liberal arts - Keefe, D.F.
Our untimely dead - Short, F.H.
Our wives - Watterson, H.
Out of the storm - Malone, T.
Outlook - Gaynor, W.J.
Outward bound - Rodiger, W.
Over-reaching - Thornton, H.W.
Owning books - Phelps, W. L.

Pacific charter - Lim-Yuen, P.
Panegyric - Isocrates.
Panegyric on Origen - Gregory Thaumaturgus
Panegyric on Trajan - Pliny the Younger
Papers exempt from liability to libel - Peel, R.
Parable of the drag-net - Origen.
Paramount duty - Heckscher, A.
Participation of the Dominions in future Hague conventions - Grey of Fallodon, E. G.
Parting of ways - Bland, R. P.
Partners of peace - Johnston, E.
Party games - Taylor, P.
Party of freedom and the freedmen - Scarborough, W.S.
Party plight - Belin, D.W.
Passing of "Valiant-for-truth" - Lodge, H. C.
Passing of war - Ketcham, V. A.
Past and the future, 1851 - Hillard, G. S.
Path of duty - Reid, W.
Pathetic prophecy - Oconostota.
Patriotism and perquisites - Sheridan, R.B.
Patriot's inheritance - Riley, W.B.
Paul Revere's ride - Curtis, G.W.
Peace made possible by justice - Viviani, R.R.
Peace settlement with Russia - Lippmann, W.
Peacemakers of blessed memory - Wallace, L.
Pearl of the Antilles - Littlefield, C. E.
Pearl, or, seven rhythms on the faith - Ephraem, S.
Peasants - Lenin, N.
Penalizing poor but honest dukes - Rosebery, A. P. P.
Pennsylvania idea - Dallas, G. M.
Penny wise and pound foolish - Estes, J.W., Jr.
People and the Fatherland - Fichte, J. G.
People and their rulers - Van Dyke, H.
People are like apples - LIFE
People emancipated by defeat - Grady, H.
People incarnate - Rivkin, D.H.
People's charter - Macaulay, T.B.
People's crusade - Barkley, A. W.
People's heritage squandered - Curtin, A. G.
People's rights above privilege - Gracchus, G.
Perfect manhood - Beecher, H. W.
Perils of paternalism - Stanley, A. O.
Period of exclusiveness is past - McKinley, W.
Perishing with the sword - Stearns, T.
Pernicious virtue - Thomas, G.
Personal goals - Whipple, F. L.
Phi Beta Kappa oration - Everett, E.
Physiology of Atelectasis - Henderson, Y.
Pick up the tools - Rathbun, J.
Piety and civic virtue - Parkhurst, C.H.
"Pinafore" - Gilbert, W.S.
Pioneer woman - Hurley, P.J.
Pioneers of American independ-

ence - Winthrop, R. C.
Pith of Paul's chief doctrine - Luther, M.
Pious pilgrimage - Seward, W. H.
Place and price of excellence - Barzun, J.
Peace of Amiens - Windham, W.
Place of the International Federation today - Westerdyk, J.
Plague of people - Crary, D. R.
Plague uncovered - Rolph, A.
Plain people - RESPONSES TO TOASTS
Planners - Duncan, P.
Platform experiences - Bain, G. W.
Playing "old men" parts - Gilbert, J.
"Plea for a suspension of judgment" - Vernon, W. T.
Plea for action - Arlt, C. T.
Plea for clothing for troops on the Russian front - Goebbels, P. J.
Plea for conciliation in 1876 - Bayard, T. F.
Plea for his home - Old Tassel.
Plea for imperial armament - Bismarck, O.
Plea for industrial opportunity - Coppin, F. J.
Plea for mercy - Darrow, C.
Plea for my people - Gilman, R.
Plea for pebbles - Satterthwaite, J. B.
Plea for Republican institutions - Castelar, E.
Plea for the Negro race - Washington, B. T.
Plea for the man in the ranks - Hall, E. K.

Pleasures of reading - Balfour, A. J. B.
Plumed knight - Ingersoll, R. G.
Plurality of worlds - Lardner, D.
Plymouth oration - Webster, D.
Poetical and practical in America - Lowell, J. R.
Poetic effusion - AFTER DINNER SPEECHES
Policy of conciliation - McGee, T. D.
Political conscience - Smith, M. C.
Political destinies of the globe - Bryce, J. B.
Political outlook, 1814 - O'Connell, D.
Political paradox - Reel, F. U.
Political relevance of moral principle - Stevenson, A. E.
Political testament - Gokhale, G. K.
Politics and a well-rounded nation - Snetman, L.
Pollock v. Farmers' Loan and Trust Company, 1895 - Fuller, M. W.
Pomp and circumstance - Hartman, W. R.
Poor Dukes and piratical tatterdemalions - Denman, T. D.
Popular sovereignty - Douglas, S. A.
Portrait of a lady - Thornton, W. M.
Portraits of five senators in the Senate reception room - Kennedy, J. F.
Position of a Ministry not supported by the House of Commons - Macaulay, T. B.; Peel, R.; Pitt, W., 1759-1806; Russell, J. R.
Possible results of a European war - Borah, W. E.
Possibilities - Baine, M. E.
Post-war leadership - Welles, S.
Postwar planning-for what - Hancher, V. M.
Power and aim - Meldrum, A. B.
Power of a song - LIFE
Power to lay taxes - Madison, J.
Prayer for mercy - Scholz, A. C.
Praying mantis - Fisher, Mrs. J. W.
Predatory rich - Smith, A. R.
Predictions for the unpredictable future - Horton, M. M.
Preoration on the murder of Herodes - Antiphon.

Preparation for armageddon - Rosebery, A. P. P.
Preparation for learning - Drummond, H.
Prepayment plans - Hawley, P. R.
Prerogative and public right - Macdonald, J. A.
Prescription against heretics - Tertullian, Q. S. F.
Present danger - Conant, J. B.
Present-day American life: its order of values, and its sense of direction - Fulbright, J. W.
Preservation for life's paths - Lindemann, H.
Preservation of American independence - Roosevelt, F. D.
Preservation of free enterprise the common objective of capital and labor - Green, W.
Preservation of the Union - Choate, R.
Preservation of the university - Deutsch, M. E.
Preservative element in American society - Locke, R. P.
President's prelude - Smith, C. E.
Preventing a new world war - Truman, H. S.
Price and the public interest - Blough, R. M.
Price for pity - Novar, L. F.
Price of excellence - Wright, S. J.
Price of free world victory - Wallace, H. A.
Priest and soldier - Stewart, M. B.
Primacy of Athens - Isocrates.
Price of union - Craven, A.
Prince of peace - Bryan, W. J.; Tittle, E. F.
Prisoner at the bar - Anderson, L. R.
Private agencies and public goals in the post-war world - Brown, L. H.
Private rights and government - Sutherland, G.
Privilegitis Americanus - DeBoer, R.
Problem of the age - Macon, A. R.
Problem of the century - Clark, F. H.
Problems - Bede, J. A.
Problems of the hour, 1922 - Munsey, F. A.
Procession - Sunshine, M.
Proclamation to his army - Napoleon I.
Professor anonymous - Smith, R.
Professor talks to himself - Eaton, C.
Profit and loss - Scott, C.
Profit in loss - Moore, C. E.
Progress and prosperity - BUSINESS
Progress of mechanic arts - Webster, D.
Progress of the American Negro - Washington, B. T.
Progress of the divine ordinance of government - Evarts, W. M.
Progress of the franchise - Beecher, H. W.
Projecting canker worms and caterpillars - Grimston, H.
Promise of aid to Russia - Churchill, W. L. S.
Promise of Christ's abiding presence - Harman, C. H.
Promised land - Ikeguchi, J.
Proper study - Osgood, C. G.
Property as a disadvantage - Newman, J. H.
Property rights and predatory wealth - Roosevelt, T.
Proposals for a free world - Wallace, H. S.
Proposition is peace - Hutchins, R. M.
Propounds his faith before an English judge - Gandhi, M. K.
Prose writers of Canada - Dawson, S. E.
Prospect of imperial disintegration - Gladstone, W. E.
Prospects - Kandt, W.
Prospects good - Maloney, H. S.
Protection and prosperity - Reed, T. B.
Protection of British subjects

abroad - Palmerston, H. J. T.
Protest against colonial government - Jay, J.
Protector and Parliament - Cromwell, O.
Protectors of freedom - Henson, L.
Protest against sentence as a traitor - Emmet, R.
Protest to the Senate - Jackson, A.
Protests against withdrawal of sanctions against Italy - DeWater, C.
Prudent compromise - Foster, G. E.
Psychological front - MacLeish, A.
Public domain: the people's heritage - Roosevelt, T.
Public offices as private perquisites - Schurz, C.
Public waits - Strahon, M.
Pulpit in modern life - Hillis, N. D.
Puppets - Link, E. P.
Puppets or patriots - Reading, D. K.
Purport of the treaty - Reid, W.
Purpose of Loomis Institute - Batchelder, N. H.
Pursuit of excellence - Dwight, T.
Pursuit of security - Lynch, G. J.
Pursuit of truth - Ashmore, H. L.
Pursuit of Villa - Wilson, W.
Put on charity - Gruell, E. F.
Pyramids of skulls - Jordan, D. S.

Qualities that win - Sumner, C.
Quality of America's fighting men - Eisenhower, D. D.
Quarantining the aggressors - Roosevelt, F. D.
Queen and the royal succession - Elizabeth I.
Queen takes a king - Atkinson, M. L.
Queen's diamond jubilee - Laurier, W.
Question of Constitutional rights - Hoar, G. F.
Quo warranto - Gormley, A. C.

Raccoon in the bag - Crittenden, J. J.
Radical Republican theory - Stevens, T.
Radio speech after attempt on his life - Hitler, A.
Rage of battle - William, Duke of Normandy
Rainbows in the storm - LIFE
Raising the flag over Fort Sumter - Beecher, H. W.
Rains came - a review - Kyburg, E. E.
Raise a standard - Kingsley, D. P.
Raising potatoes - Lee, R.
Rallies her army during the Armada peril - Elizabeth I.
Ratify the charter - Truman, H. S.
Ready, aye, ready - Laurier, W.
Real cause of the war - MacArthur, A. S.
Realism versus romanticism - Garland, H.
Reality of the novelist's creation - Thackeray, W. M.
Reality of the unseen - FREEMASONS
Realization of a dream - Crookes, W.
Reallocation of world responsibilities - Ball, G. W.
Re-Americanize America - Kirby, J. H.
Reason for war - Wilson, W.
Reason immutable and sovereign - Mirabeau, H. G. R.
Reasons for refusing to part company with the South - Davis, H. W.
Rebecca at the well - Hildebert of Lavardin.
Rebuild and remodel - Roosevelt, F. D.
Rebuke to John Randolph - Burges, T.
Recalls when Job Hedges unearthed a speech for all occasions - Davis, R. H.

Recollection, the strongest influence - RESPONSES TO TOASTS
Recommends the values of blood and iron - Bismarck, O.
Reconciliation between the North and the South - Lonn, E.
Reconciliation in 1865 - Seward, W.H.
Recovering from destruction and inflation - Hoover, H.C.
Rectitude higher than morality - Chapin, E.H.
"Red herrings" - Truman, H.S.
Redeeming our regrets - Sockman, R.W.
Redwoods - Barnes, W.H.L.
Refuses to bow to French demands - Grangula.
Refuses to support French interests - Dekanisora.
Regulus to the Carthagenians - Kellogg, E.
Regulus to the Romas Senate - Kellogg, E.
Rehabilitation and reassimilation of fighting men and nations - DeJean, F.L.
Reign of technicality - Pleasants, A.W.
Reign of the common people - Beecher, H.W.
Rejoiner to debate - Khrushchev, N.S.
Relations between the two Americas - Berle, A.A., Jr.
Release us unto Barabbas - Beyer, L.
Releasing your latent power - Pierce, F.
Relief of Khartum - Kitchener of Khartoum, H.H.K.
Relief of Protestant dissenters - Fox, C.J.
Religio advocati - Windolph, F.L.
Religious repose and future of our country - Lee, J.
Reminiscence of Lexington - Parker, T.
Reminiscence of the war - Sherman, W.T.
Reminiscence on starvation - Fleming, D.
Removing troops from Boston - Pitt, W., 1708-1778
Rendezvous with despair - Dewey, T.E.
Renunciation speech - Flood, H.
Reply to club delegates - Larmartine, A.M.L.
Reply to Douglas - Lincoln, A.
Reply to Eisenhower's speech of October 8th, 1954 - Stevenson, A.E.
Reply to Flood - Grattan, H.
Reply to Hayne - Webster, D.
Reply to Horace Walpole - Pitt, W., 1708-1778
Reply to John Randolph - Clay, H.
Reply to Lincoln - Douglas, S.A.
Reply to Little Turtle - Wayne, A.
Reply to Mr. Cram - Red Jacket.
Reply to Robespierre - Gaudet, M.R.; Vergniaud, P.V.
Reply to Samuel Dexter - Red Jacket.
Reply to the agent of the United States - Webb, Col.
Reply to the working men of Manchester England - Lincoln, A.
Reply to Webster - Calhoun, J.C.
Replying to Henry Clay - Calhoun, J.C.
Report on the "Vengeur" - Barere de Vieuzac, B.
Representative government - Marshall, T.R.
Republic and its outlook - Evarts, W.M.
Republic of our fathers - Bailey, J.W.
Republic that never retreats - Beveridge, A.J.
Republic's higher glory - Smith, C.E.
Resistance to unlawful authority - Jekyll, J.
Responsibilities of Empire - Gladstone, W.E.
Responsibility of the Imperial Chancellor - Bismarck, O.
Responsibility of youth - Butler,

N. M.
Restful occasion - AFTER-DINNER SPEECHES
Restless generation and undergraduate education - Wert, R. J.
Restoration of the surplus Boxer indemnity to China by the United States - Quo, Tai-Chi Francis
Results achieved by the soldiers and sailors - Williamson, E. E.
Retort instant - AFTER-DINNER SPEECHES
Results of oppression - Smith, S.
Resurrection of Lazarus - Abelard, P.
Retort to Inglass - Blackburn, J. C. S.
Retrenchment, economy, and reform - Springer, W. M.
Return, America - Pennington, G.
Return of the native - Lowell, J. R.
Returns in triumph from Munich - Chamberlain, N.
Reveille of the dead - Lazar, W. T.
Revolution and the logic of coercion - Garfield, J. A.
Revolution of 1893 - Stone, M. E.
Rhapsody - Clay, C. M.
Right hand of fellowship - Lyon, J. H.
Right of association - Haldane, R. B.; Halisbury, H. S. G.; Loreburn, R. T.; Simon, J.; Wheatley, J.
Right of possession - Cullom, S.
Right of public meeting - Bradlaugh, C.; Bright, J.; Canning, G.; Fox, C. J.; Loreburn, R. T.
Right of the people to rule - Roosevelt, T.
Right or wrong - BEHAVIOR
Right to commit - Ashburton, J. D.; Barré, I.; Fox, C. J.; Thurlow, E.
Righteousness - Hibben, J. G.
Righteousness of revolt - Burke, T. F.
Rights of manhood - Hughes, C. E.
Rights of men - Northcott, W. A.
Rights we defend - Miller, M. E.
Rights we fought for - Burton, L. J.
Rise and fall of the mustache - Burdette, R. J.
Rivers did not forget - Atkinson, M. E.
Road back - McBurney, G. W.
Road to freedom - Hoover, H. C.
Road toward international understanding - Van Baarda, D.
Robbery of the Princesses at Oude - Sheridan, R. B.
Rock and flood - Cameron, W. J.
Roentgen rays and other great discoveries - Thomson, J. J.
Romance of the West - Baldwin, S.
Room for all - Kohler, K.
Ropes - Clinton, S.
Rose of the Southern commons - Houston, T. A.
Rotten boroughs of England - Russell, J. R.
Rouget de L'Isle and the Marseillaise - Poincaré, R.
Rough riders - Fosdick, H. E.
Rough road ahead - Baldwin, R. N.
Royal prerogative delegated from the people - Wyndham, W.
Royal road - Daugherty, L. A.
Rule for decent living - Wycliffe, J.
Rule that works - GOLDEN RULE
Rushing to meet the sunrise - Smith, N.
Russia enters the war - Nicholas II.
Russia must be sustained - Beaverbrook, W. H.
Russian catfish and western herring - Toynbee, A.
Russian War Mission - Marshall, T. R.

Sabbath school kite strings - Johnston, H. A.
Sacra fames auri - Wesley, J.
Sacred cause of the human race - Lacordaire, J. B. H.
Sacred trust - Doyle, E. D.
Sacrifice that failed - Bumby, J. H.
Safety of the virtuous - Melanchthon, P.
Saint Andrew and Saint Mark - Clemens, S. L.
Sales representation of John Bull and Co. - Howard of Penrith, E. W. H.
Salon in America - Howe, J. W.
Salt - Van Dyke, H.
Salt of the earth - Roosa, D. B. St. J.
Salvage - Sheats, P. H.
SALVATION - RELIGION
Samples that are convincing - RELIGION
Samson and the pillars - Hulbert, H. B.
Sanctity of the Union - Stephens, A. H.
Sandwich-grabber - Elliott, A. R.
Sane thinking in an insane world - Smith, R. L.
Saviors of civilization - Chapman, V.
Saxon versus Slav - Shearer, R.
Scarlet letter - Grossman, H.
Scattered nation - Vance, Z. B.
Schechter Poultry Corporation v. United States - Hughes, C. E.
Schenck v. United States - Holmes, O. W., Jr.
Scholar in a Republic - Phillips, W.
Science and letters in our day - Story, J.
Science of better living - Young, O. D.
Scrap of paper - Lloyd George, D.
Scroll of destiny - McClain, W.
Sea of life - Anselm, Saint
Second birth - Miller, H. R.
Second discovery of America - Graves, J. T., II.
Second Olynthiac - Demosthenes.
Second oration against Catiline - Cicero, M. T.
Second Philippic - Cicero, M. T.; Demosthenes.
Second reading of the Budget Bill, 1894 - Harcourt, W. G. G. V. V.
Second sermon on the card - Latimer, H.
Second tetralogy - Antiphon.
Sectionalism and nationality - Alderman, E. A.
Security against unlawful imprisonment - Romilly, S.
Security for a people - Winant, J. G.
Seeking the abundant life - BACCALAUREATE ADDRESSES
Self government and civilization - Clay, J. C.
Self protection: individualism - Watson, T. J., Jr.
Senior charge - Heater, L. A.
Sense of destiny - BACCALAUREATE ADDRESSES
Sentencing atomic bomb spies - Kaufman, I. J.
Sepulcher in the garden - Beecher, H. W.
Sermon against Auxentius. - Ambrose, Saint
Sermon on foolishness of the cross conquering - Chrysostom, J.
Serpent in our midst - Smart, C.
Service the genius of progress - Briggs, G. W.
Services of a patriotic militia - Cartwright, R. J.
Serving your country - Goethals, G. W.
Settling the corset problem of this country - Rogers, W.
Seven doors to the mind and how to open them - Ketcham, V. A.
Seventh of March speech - Webster, D.
Shadow lengthens: Preparedness - Wilson, W.
Shadow of the Swastika - Benz, L. L.

Shadow slaves - McCoy, F.
Shadows - Aggert, O., Jr.
Shadows of tomorrow - RELIGION
Shall the states take precedence over the central government - Madison, J.
Shall we commit suicide - Churchill, W. L. S.
Shall we make a rendezvous with death - Allen, J. G., Jr.
Shame of a nation - Leary, F. W.
Shame of America - Grimke, A. H.
Sharing life's burdens and blessings - Stephan, P. G.
Shield of irresponsibility - Yasinow, H. S.
Ship-money-impeaching Lord Keeper Finch - Falkland, L. C.
Shoot on sight - Roosevelt, F. D.
Shoot to kill - Fossey, L.
Shot at the decanter - Cuyler, T. L.
Should the English-speaking democracies unite now - Thompson, D. and others.
Shovel leaners - Cameron, W. J.
Shows - Tertullian, Q. S. F.
Shrimps - Taylor, L.
Sign of the Blue Eagle - Rockefeller, J. D., Jr.
Significance of the insignificant - Kuizenga, H. B.
Sign of the muck-rake - Van Dyke, H.
Sign of the times - Sheil, B. J.
Simple fools - Howells, P. K.
Simplicity to wonder - Krantz, J. C., Jr.
Since King David's time - Wilson, R. E.
Sinews of peace - Churchill, W. L. S.
Sinister shadows - Goldman, D.
Situation in France - Vergniaud, P. V.
Sixth Philippic - Cicero, M. T.
Six thousand years - Sarnoff, D.
Sixth Sunday gospel after Easter - Wycliffe, J.
Sixty years of sectionalism - Clay, H.
Slander - Barrow, I.
Slandermongers and the Bill of Rights - Truman, H. S.
Slaughter house cases - Miller, S. F.
Slave boy who became a missionary - PATRICK, SAINT
Slavery of man - Christensen, D. E.
Sleepers awakened - Talmage, T. D.
Sleeping beauties - Kottemann, D.
Sleeping giant - Werner, J.
Small number of the Elect - Massillon, J. B.
Small states and great achievements - Cobden, R.
Smashed crockery - McKelway, St. C.
Smith and so forth - Cox, S. S.
Snake bites - BEHAVIOR
So long, so long - Shaw, G. B.
Social and industrial injustice - Roosevelt, T.
Social bearings of the fifth commandment - Gregory, J. F.
Social fabric as the condition of values - Oxford and Asquith, H. H. A.
Social morality - Lewis, C. S.
Social plaint - Andrews, E. B.
Social responsibilities - Gough, J. B.
Social significance of our institutions - James, H., Sr.
Social traits and human nature - Jastrow, J.
Society and the pay roll - Young, W. A.
Sold! The temple of humanity - Clemes, W.
Soldier boy - Long, J. D.
Soldier stamp - Twichell, J. H.
Soldier's last salute - Porter, H.
Some people learn the hard way - Nason, J. T.
Some significant results of the Emancipation - Douglass, J. H.
Some significant steps in the development of the national service - Thayer, H. B.

Some telling facts and figures - Bromfield, E. T.
Something lost - Ensor, W.
Something of a man - Taylor, D. S.
Son of Phaeton - Keane, S.
Sons of Harvard who fell in battle - Holmes, O.W., Jr.
Sorcerer's responses - Choate, J. H.
Soul aflame - Beard, S. C., Jr.
Soul of France - Vandercook, J. W.
Soul satisfying bread - Spurgeon, C. H.
Sound currency - Phelps, W. W.
Sour grapes - Ott, E. A.
Source of song and story - Eliot, S. A.
Source of strength - CHURCH
Sources of our strength - Myers, C. J.
South Carolina Doctrine - Hayne, R. Y.
Southern gentleman - Williams, J. S.
Southern situation - Rainey, J. H.
Sovereign advised to dismiss a minister - Palmerston, H. J. T.; Russell, J. R.
Sovereign alchemist - Tyler, F.
Sovereign and the Constitution - Beaconsfield, B. D.
Sovereign and the Ministry's right to dissolution of Parliament - Oxford and Asquith, H. H. A.
Sovereign's intervention in politics - Erskine, T.; Lansdowne, W. P. F.; Romilly, S.
Sovereign's responsibility for dismissal of Ministers - Peel, R.
Spain's heartless cruelty - Thurston, J. M.
Spanish prisoners of war - Howells, W. D.
Spare our lives - Ranta, E.
Spark plugs and live wires - Rogers, S.
Spartacus to the gladiators - Kellogg, E.
Spartacus to the Roman envoys - Kellogg, E.
Speaking for the consumer - White, W. A.
Speech as a liberal art - Hostetler, G. F.
Speech as a liberal study - Arnold, C. C.
Speech at Council - Big Mouth; Satank; Tenskwatawa.
Speech at Council at Greenville - Tarhe.
Speech at the stake - Cranmer, T.
Speech before signing treaty to swear allegiance to King of England - Little Carpenter.
Speech for honors day banquet - Kildee, R.
Speech in Council - Little Turtle.
Speech in protest in the Charleston Convention - Yancey, W. L.
Speech in rhyme - Wiggin, K. D.
Speech in the Tilden convention - Voorhees, D. W.
Speech in the tower - Strafford, T. W.
Speech of Phoinix - Homer.
Speech of the three subsidies - Bacon, F.
Speech on Abolitionist petitions - Calhoun, J. C.
Speech on crisis of 1850 - Seward, W. H.
Speech on Home Rule - Butt, I.
Speech on power and responsibility - Eden, A.
Speech on selling writing - Hughes, L.
Speech on the enforcement of the Fourteenth Amendment - DeLarge, R. C.
Speech on the Georgia Bill - Revels, H. R.
Speech on the King's address - Attlee, C. R.
Speech on the scaffold - Harrison, T.
Speech to Agrippa - Paul, Saint
Speech to the electors of Bristol - Burke, E.
Speech to the French, November, 1753 - Half King, T.
Speech on the gunpowder plot -

Coke, E.
Speech to 166th Ohio Regiment - Lincoln, A.
Spirit of achievement - SUCCESS
Spirit of devotion - Hadley, A.T.
Spirit of France - Viviani, R.R.
Spirit of learning - Wilson, W.
Spirit of Locarno - Butler, N.M.
Spirit of '76 and the barbarian culture - Jones, L.W.
Spirit of the day and its lessons, 1846 - Upham, C.W.
Spirit of the past - Cline, E.W.
Spirit of the Revolution - Warren, W.
Spirit of true American - Warren, T.
Spirit that should animate - CHRISTIANITY
Splendid isolation - Chamberlain, J.
Spoken word - Bryan, W.J.; Watson, E.B.
Squandering the voice - Beecher, H.W.
Squeezing the sponge - Danton, G.J.
Stage fright - Wilson, M.E.
Stalwart standpoint - Conkling, R.
Stand by the government - Dolliver, J.P.
Standard Oil Company of New Jersey v. United States, 1911 - White, E.D.
Star of empire - Beveridge, A.J.
Star of the wise men - Blencowe, E.
Star-spangled banner - Watterson, H.
Star, the cross, and the cloud - JESUS CHRIST
Stars and stripes - Hill, B.H.
State of emergency exists - Roosevelt, F.D.
State of mind - Vanocur, S.
State of the country - Seward, W.H.
States and the Union - Adams, C.F.
Statesman and nation - Bell, C.F.
Statesmanship of peace - Coolidge, C.
Steady state; physical law and moral choice - Sears, P.B.
Steaks from the living ox - Rosebery, A.P.P.
Steel spike - Nuetzman, D.
Steps toward a good world - Johnston, E.
Stewardship fantasy - CHURCH
Stop being afraid - Lodge, H.C., Jr.
Strange drama - Griffin, R.S.
Strange fruit - Branch, W.B.
Streamlined student - Ringe, T.
Strength of being clean - Jordan, D.S.
Strength of the people - Lee, G.C.
Strenuous life - Roosevelt, T.
Students of Paris - Juliana.
Study in ghosts - Dunbar, P.
Study in self management - Jones, H.I.
Suasoria VII - Seneca, A.
Substance and show - King, T.S.
Summing up in the Haddock court-martial - Conklin, R.
Sun-beams may be extracted from cucumbers, but the process is tedious - Daggett, D.
Sunflower - RELIGION
Sunny slopes of forty - Nicholson, M.
Sunshine and moonshine - Reith, E.A.
Super-national mind - Pinney, N.E.
Supremacy and its conditions - Guild, C., Jr.
Supremacy of the people - Campbell-Bannerman, H.
Supreme Court of the ether - Chase, J.
Supreme judgment of history - Poincaré, R.
Supreme menace - Dunbar, E.M.
Surrender speech - Red Eagle.
Survey of four centuries - Macaulay, T.B.
Suspension of the Habeas Corpus Act - Bright, J.
Swarm of bees - Wiers, C.R.

Sweet sixteen - Jessel, G.
Sweetmeats on gilded trays - Ditzen, L.
Sword bearer of democracy - Bowers, C. G.
"Sword shall pierce thy heart" - Franzen, F. M.
Symbol of despotism - Rivkin, W.
System of slavery - Beecher, H. W.

Take along a bit of honey - AFTER-DINNER SPEECHES
Takes up the white man's burden - Beveridge, A. J.
Takes up the yellow man's burden - Sun, Yat Sen
Taking stock - Churchill, W. L. S.
Tales from distant lands - MISSIONS AND MISSIONARIES
Talk to undergraduates - Oppenheimer, J. R.
Tamina traditions - Mitchell, S. L.
Tamina's day - Paton, A. H.
Tampering with the Constitution - Salisbury, R. A. T. G. -C.
Tampico incident - Wilson, W.
Tantalus - Pedrick, W.
Target practice - Applegate, A. W.
Taxing under Cyrenius - Burrell, D. J.
Teacher to his pupils - Gildersleeve, B. L.
Teamsters' Union speech - Roosevelt, F. D.
Teamwork - Hays, W.; Washington, B. T.
Telesis - Jones, G.
Tell her to go in peace - Houston, T.
Tell me how to belong - Klein, A.
Temptation from the mountain top - Jefferson, C. E.
Ten years naval holiday - Hughes, C. E.
Tennis cabinet - Jusserand, J. J.
Tenth Philippic - Cicero, M. T.
Testifying - Morley of Blackburn, J. M.
That America may know - Baradi, M.
That men might be free - Gittelsohn, R. B.
Their finest hour - Churchill, W. L. S.
Their heritage to us - Robinson, D. C.
Their ideal of education - Low, S.
Their monuments in our hearts - Viviani, R. R.
Them doll faces - Rieber, P.
Then Hitler came - Peterson, C. D.
There are no Gibraltors - Stevenson, A. E.
"There is East, there is India" - Benton, T. H.
There lies our frontier - Winston, A.
"Theses" that shook the world - LUTHER, M.
They are not mindreaders - Eckert, R. W.
They that take the sword - Dallinger, C.
They tip their hats - Cope, N. G.
They were exploitable - Hill, F.
Things human - Wheeler, B. I.
Things that are Caesar's - Dean, J. J.
Thinking on your feet - Roberts, H. G.
Third discourse against the Arians - Athanasius, Saint.
Third house - Lehman, F. W.
Third Olynthiac - Demosthenes.
Third Philippic - Cicero, M. T.
Third tetralogy - Antiphon.
Thirtieth man - Finley, J. H.
This American system: is it to be destroyed - Hart, M. K.
This cause is our cause - MacLeish, A.
This diminishing world - Pfaf, R. A.
This I believe - Carey, J. B.; Lehman, H. H.
This is a good place to start - McKeldin, T. R.
This nation under God - Sockman, R. W.

This nation will remain neutral - Roosevelt, F.D.
This tournament - Howie, R.
This trash must go - Beard, R. S.
Thoroughbred - Stone, V. H.
Those incredible Russians - Hunt, F.
Thou shalt not steal - Bryan, W. J.
Threat to destroy the British Empire - Hitler, A.
Three graces - Redfield, W. C.
Three great eras - Chase, S. P.
Three jewels - Prentice, R.
Three parts of morality - Lewis, C. S.
Three score and ten - Cobbs, J. A.
Threefold promise - Wiederaenders, R.
Through the dark continent - Stanley, H. M.
Through the great forest - Stanley, H. M.
Thumbs down - Gunnison, E. M.
Thunder and lightning on sinner's heads - Jones, S.
Thunders for unity - Danton, G. J.
Thy speech betrayeth thee - BEHAVIOR
Ties of kinship and common speech - Arnold, E.
Tilden-Hayes election - Thurman, A. G.
Time for action - Symington, W. S.
Time for greatness - Hogland, G. E.
Time is running out - Gates, E. D.
Time of day - Lloyd, A. H.
Time of greatness - Wiley, B. I.
Time to decide - RELIGION
Time to speak - Morgan, C., Jr.
Timocracy-why not - Larson, A.
Tithes - Grattan, H.
Title 28, number 426 - Nye, L. E.
Tito Melema - Noble, E.
To a gathering of friends - Lysias.
To American comrades in arms - Lloyd George, D.
To bind up the wounds in schools of all nations - Russell, W. F.
To dare again, ever to dare - Danton, G. J.
To have and not to hold - McCracken, R. J.
To his army before Quebec - Wolfe, J.
To his army at the beginning of the Italian campaign - Napoleon I.
To his army in Scotland - Agricola.
To his generals before invading Silesia - Frederick II.
To his generals before the battle of Leuthen - Frederick II.
To his mutinous troops - Germanicus.
To his soldiers - Catiline; Garibaldi, G.; Napoleon I.; Otho, M. S.; Scipio Africanus Major, P. C.
To make the world "safe for democracy" - Wilson, W.
To reach high places - Greenwalt, C. H.
To read or not to read - Schottenfeld, A. C.
To remain in perfect love - Nerger, E. A.
To returned volunteers of the Mexican war - Prentiss, S. S.
To the conspirators - Catiline.
To the French people - Churchill, W. L. S.
To the great counsellors of the 13 fires - Cornplanter.
To the King of the Belgians - Beaconsfield, B. D.
To the men of Athens on Mars' Hill - Paul, Saint
To the officers of the Piave - Annunzio, G.
To the Red Army - Trotsky, L.
To the soldiers - McKinley, W.
To the soldiers on entering Milan - Napoleon I.
To the Spartans - Alcibiades.
To the tribunals - Danton, G. J.
To the Virginia brigands - Hurt, J.

To the young men of Italy - Mazzini, G.
To workingmen and soldiers - Kerensky, A.
Today's challenge - Houghton, H.C.
Tomb with a broken seal - EASTER
Tomorrow should be the deadline - Rose, J.
Tomorrow we live - Stevens, J.M.
Tomorrow, what - Tessman, A.
Tomorrow's extra - Brown, W.
"Too proud to fight" speech - Wilson, W.
Too soon to quit - Cameron, W.J.
Torch or shadow-which - Davis, W.R.
Tory principles - Beaconsfield, B.D.
Tory Squires and servant girls' dollars - Dillon, J.
Total abstinence - Ireland, J.
Totality of outlook - McEntegart, B.
Toward new horizons - Welles, S.
Toward saner values - Grunwald, E.
Toward understanding through speech - Weaver, A.T.
Trade and the Empire - Oxford and Asquith, H.H.A.
Tragedies of this tournament - Harlan, R.E.
Tragedy of ninety-eight cents - Turner, J.
Tramp, Tramp, Tramp - Greenwell, E.
Transfiguration - Kingsley, C.
Travelling together in light - Rupprecht, O.C.
Treason to democracy - Langdon, W.H.
Treasurer's report - Benchley, R.C.
Treaty of Paris - Davis, C.K.
Treaty of peace - Lodge, H.C.
Treaty of peace with Germany - Lodge, H.C.
Treaty with Spain - Wolcott, E.O.
Trent affair - Bright, J.
Trial outside the courtroom - Goss, B.C.
Trial procedure-past, present and future - Roberts, O.J.
Triple alliance - Konoye, F.
Triumph of Irish independence - Grattan, H.
Triumph of the Church - Manning, H.E.
Trojan horse in America - Dies, M.
True American - Phillips, N.
True Americanism - Brandeis, L.D.
True conquerors - Brougham and Vaux, H.P.B.
True glory of a nation - Whipple, E.P.
True grandeur of nations - Sumner, C.
True greatness - King, T.S.
True leverage of empire - Rosebery, A.P.P.
True patriotism - Bolton, H.W.
Trust to succeeding generations - Winthrop, R.C.
Trustees of Dartmouth College v. Woodward - Marshall, J.
Truth and light - Eliot, C.W.
Trumpets of the dawn - Kiefer, A.F.
Trusteeship of literature - Iles, G.
Truth and trade - Schenk, N.H.
Truth makes us free - Compton, A.H.
Turk must go - Ward, H.F.
Twenty thousand leagues under the sea - Roy, J.C.
Twisted news - Visk, A.G.
Two are alive - Straight, M.
Two heirs of God on an adventure in faith - Koehneke, M.L.
Two kinds of vision - Troup, C.V.
Two seals - Cook, G.W.
Two revelations - Beecher, H.W.
Typical American - Grady, H.
Tyrant's plea, necessity - Waller, E.

U-2 - Eisenhower, D.D.
Ultimation of youth - Adolfson, L.H.
Unchanging challenge-lest we forget - Morrill, J.L.
Uncle Sam - his character - Grant, W.
Uncle Sam: or, The reign of the common people - Rader, W.
Uncle Sam's responsibility for his children - Hall, S.B.
Unconquerable soul - Lane, F.K.
Uncrowned queen - Beck, J.M.
Under the flag - Phillips, W.
Under which flag - Daniel, J.W.
Underlying crisis - Rusk, D.
Underworld on top - Fiske, A.W.
Undiscovered country - Ingalls, J.J.
Unfilled promise - Hootman, E.
Union and coercion - Ellsworth, O.
Union made in heaven - Troeger, W.F.
Union of states - Harrison, B.
Union soldier - Thurston, J.M.
Union speech - Douglass, F.
Unique ideal of American life - Conant, J.B.
United Mine Workers' convention - Wheeler, B.K.
United States in Pan-American trade - Martin, W.B.
United States obligation for feeding Europe's millions - Faigan, Z.
United States v. Butler et al - Roberts, O.J.; Stone, H.F.
United States v. E.C. Knight Company, 1895 - Fuller, M.W.
United we stand secure - Churchill, W.L.S.
Unity of the human spirit - Shorey, P.
Unity won the war - Eisenhower, D.D.
Universal obligation - Stewart, D.W.
University in war and peace - Hutchins, R.M.
Unknown - Barton, B.
Unknown quantities - Frisbie, M.T.
Unless they act - Lovald, S.D.
Unrecorded legacy - Thonssen, L.
Unshackled living - Cyprian, Saint
Unsolved problems - Depew, C.M.
Until he comes - Scherer, P.
Unwillingness to improve - Baxter, R.
Unwritten alliance - Laurier, W.
Up from the balogney age - Linner, C.
Uphold the President - Dolliver, J.P.
Upholding the American standard of motherhood - Norton, M.T.
Uplift and the undertow - Dearing, W.P.
Uplifting the Negro race - Washington, B.T.
Upon this rock - Ferguson, D.F.
Use and abuse of images and relics - Tyndale, W.
Use only the best liquor - Gough, J.B.
Use of knowledge - Young, O.D.
Uses of great men - Emerson, R.W.

Vacation responsibilities - Ogden, R.C.
Valley Forge - Saner, R.E.L.
Value of great men - Rice, M.S.
Value of universal study - Hazeltine, M.W.
Values in a crazy world - Ise, J.
Vanishing American - Dilley, J.
Vegetable and mineral gold - Everett, E.
Verdun - Ginisty, M-A.C.
Verdun-"On ne passe pas" - Poincaré, R.
Vested rights and the obligations of contracts - Thurman, A.G.
Via Dolorosa (to Reichstag) - Wirth, J.
Victory at Yorktown - Storrs, R.S.
Victory for God - Talmage, T.D.
Victory for man - Ingersoll, R.G.

Victory for the Allies and the United States a ground of rejoicing, of thanksgiving - Grimke, F.J.
Victory in superior numbers - Sampson, W.T.
Victory or defeat: no half-way house - Lloyd George, D.
Villany of landlords - Lloyd George, D.
Vindication of faith - Smart, L.J.
Vindication of the Volunteers - Flood, H.
Virtue the cornerstone of Republican government- Benjamin, J.P.
Vision of the people - Lloyd George, D.
Vision of unity - Manning, W.T.
Visit to America - Thomas, D.
Voice of God and the verdict of experience - Kleiner, H.G.
Voice of the Empire - Borden, R.L.

Wabash, St. Louis and Pacific Railroad Company v. Illinois, 1886 - Miller, S.F.
Wake up, America - Barber, P.; Pollock, C.
Walk, and not faint - Borden, R.L.
Walls of happiness - Griffin, L.
Walls of Jericho - Rogness, B.M.
Want of the world - Gannon, R.I.
Wanted: a Marshall Plan for the arts in America-Lynch, R.
Wanted-"Good Europeans" - France, A.
Wanted! More George Leigh-Mallorys. There are so many Mount Everests - Spaulding, A.T.
Wanted: spunk, sense, and stamina - Meisel, G.I.
Wanted: 10,000 new martin homes - Lloyd, L.
War - Emerson, R.W.
War address - Roosevelt, F.D.
War and arbitration - Angell, J.B.
War and discussion - Root, E.
War and human freedom - Hull, C.
War and peace - Fox, C.J.
War and world-control - Rankin, J.
War between justice and force - Chiang Kai-Shek
War cry to America - Annunzio, G.
War finance corporation - Underwood, O.W.
War for freedom - Choate, J.H.
War for humanity - Smith, C.E.
War inevitable - Wolcott, E.O.
War isn't over at home - Kuroki, B.
War on righteousness - Powell, J., Jr.
War on Russia - Churchill, W.L.S.
War, peace and revolutionary democracy - Lenin, N.
War with Russia - Cobden, R.
Warfare of free souls - Berle, A.A., Jr.
Warning and a prophecy - Wilkes, J.
Warning, flying rocks - BEHAVIOR
Warnings of history - Higley, W.
Warns the nobility and clergy of Provence of the impending storm - Mirabeau, H.G.R.
Warriors of the broken sword - Bentley, A.; CHARACTER; Sledge, T.
Waste-a problem of distribution - Hoover, H.C.
Watch your patches - LIFE
Watchdogs - Gordon, T.H.
"Watchman, tell us of the night" - Jones, O.
Watchman, what of the night - Yorke, P.C.
Watchwords of the 20th century - Cook, J.
Water-power costs versus steam-power costs- Orook, G.A.
Way in the sea and a path in the mighty waters - Cohen, S.S.
Way to honor our patriotic dead - Gregg, D.
Way to live as neighbors -

Stassen, H.E.
We are not ashamed - Pinkstaff, K.
We are ready to carry the war to the enemy - Marshall, G.C.
We cannot save freedom with pitchforks - Roosevelt, F.D.
We cannot win with quick dramatics or momentary heroics - Willkie, W.L.
We have the pain and travail - Ball, J.
We hold these truths - Roosevelt, F.D.
We intend to stay together - Oxnam, G.B.
We move in new directions - Thomas, J.S.
We must be the great arsenal of democracy - Roosevelt, F.D.
We must fight for our liberties - Knox, F.
We must recapture valour - Price, B.
We shall not fail - Hull, C.
"We, the people" or "We, the states" - Henry, P.
We will not lay down arms - Krause, N.
We won't fight - Lash, J.P.
We, You, and I - Fogel, S.
Weakest spot in the American system - Evarts, W.M.
Wealth and poverty, aristocracy and Republicanism - Livingston, R.R.
Wealth and poverty in the courts - Taft, W.H.
Weapons for a cold war - Beckwith, D.E.
Weapons versus wit - Rodger, M.E.
Weaving our destiny - Hoover, H.C.
Weighed in balance - McKay, H.W.
Weighted scales - Corbett, F.E.
Welfare of the nation - Voorhees, D.W.
Welfare state - Roosevelt, J.
West Coast Hotel Co. v. Parrish - Hughes, C.E.
Western European army - Dulles, J.F.
Western European attitudes - Sevareid, E.
Westward, Ho - Odell, G.B., Jr.
What a company looks for in seeking a new location - Merrihue, W.V.
What America means to me - Friedrich, C.J.
What are we arming to defend - Conant, J.B.
What are we fighting for - Benes, E.
What are you worth - LIFE
What constitutes an American - Ickes, H.L.
What do others see in you - PERSONALITY
What does atonement mean - JESUS CHRIST
What every Yale freshman should know - Morgan, E.S.
What freedom means to me - Woelfe, J.
What have we gained in the year - Harris, J.L.
What I believe about people - BEHAVIOR
What I know about the Dutch - Talmage, T.D.
What is a classic - Eliot, T.S.
What is a free society - Blakely, R.J.
What is all this for - Stephens, A.H.
What is America - Lane, F.K.
What is it we fight - Fleming, D.F.
What is the American people - Hale, E.E.
What is your temperature - RELIGION
What justice must banish - Poincaré, R.
What kind of America- Fairless, B.F.
What may man become - Henderson, W.G.
What of America - Baskell, H.J.
What price freedom - Hutchins, R.M.
What price speed - Lane, J.R.

What should America do now in Bizonia - Havighurst, R. J.
What the black men wants - Douglass, F.
What this age owes to America - Evarts, W. M.
What will he do with it - Hale, E. E.
What will they believe - Schrader, D.
What's right with America - Mundt, K. E.
What's wrong with the world - Kennedy, J. B.
Whatsoever things are true- Croessmann, D.
When color is forgotten - DISCRIMINATION
When men decay - Morgan, N.
Whence and whither - Carter, R. A.
Where are we to look for survival - Haile Selassie I.
Where do we go from here - Stockdale, A. A.
Where the fruit is freedom - Samuels, M.
Where to, America - Lumpkin, J. H.
Where we come from - Tarkington, B.
Wherever diamonds - Barnhart, B.
Which knew not Joseph - Barton, B.
Which shall rule, manhood or money - Lafollette, R. M.
Which way America - Alexander, R.; Ritchie, A. C.
White man's burden - Ripley, W. Z.
White peril - Johnson, R. D.
Whither midst falling due - Harrison, H. T.
Whither world - Kock, K. H.
Who are the Americans today - Lewis, J. L.
Who is tampering with the soul of America - Jones, J. L.
Who says it can't be done - Fleming, D. F.
Whose side are you on - RELIGION
Why do we fight Germany - Lane, F. K.
Why I am glad I am an American - Pflum, J. F.
Why not 'Do this in remembrance of Christ" - MacLeod, N.
Will a million members be enough - Mast, C. L., Jr.
Wilt thou go with this man - Loeber, A. H. A.
Wisdom before information - Gannon, R. I.
With brains, Sir - Hole, S. R.
Withering influence of provincial subjection - Meagher, T. F.
Without a word - Wilber, L. A.
Woman's choice - Stolz, A. E.
Wondersmith and the world - Slocum, W.
Words of encouragement to the oppressed - Garrison, W. L.
Work among the young - Bradley, F. M.
Work done for humanity (1890) - Willard, F. E.
Working people in the next twenty years - Larson, A.
World a whispering gallery - Hillis, N. D.
World and the new generation - Axson, S.
World around us - Lord, Mrs. O. B.
World at 91 - Depew, C. M.
World brotherhood in a space age - Stevenson, A. E.
World conflict - Durant, W.
World Court - Harding, W. G.
World in revolution - Douglas, W. O.
World in the news - Binder, C.
World of today - Young, O. D.
World outlook needed for Americans - Willkie, W. L.
World safe for democracy - Wilson, W.
World state of emergency, On the - Matsuoka, Y.
World today - AFTER-DINNER SPEECHES
World's great things - AFTER-DINNER SPEECHES
Worth of our past - Frankfurter, F.

Wounding with intent to kill - Lysias.
"Wounds, shrieks, and tears" in government - Smith, S.
Wrath upon the wicked to the utmost - Edwards, J.
Wyandot claim to supremacy - Red Jacket.

Yankee - Bachellor, I.
Yankee notions - Twichell, J. H.
Yarn of the manager bold - Hall, W. F.
Ye olde time forensics - Gaw, J. G.
Year of jubilee - Peck, G. R.
Yellow peril - Ginn, G.
Yes, we are ready - Beard, C. A.
YOU are not alone - REFUGEES
You have to see it first - Polek, B. A.
"You pay too damn much" - AFTER-DINNER SPEECHES
Young America on parade - Turner, R. G.
Young American - Emerson, R. W.
Young men, to the front - Greener, R. T.
Your brother's keeper - BEHAVIOR
Your speech and ours - Houghton, R. M. M.
Your young men shall see visions - White, W. A.
Youth and opportunity - Hoover, H. C.